Constant-Growth Dividend Discount Model

If the initial dividend is $1 (paid in 1 year), and if the dividend grows thereafter at a constant rate of g, the present value of the dividend stream is $P_0 = \dfrac{\text{DIV}_1}{r - g}$ (page 176)

Capital Budgeting

Break-Even Point

The sales revenue necessary for the firm to break even (in terms of accounting profits) is

$$\text{Break-even revenue} = \frac{\text{fixed costs including depreciation}}{\text{additional profit from each additional dollar of sales}} \quad \text{(page 282)}$$

Operating Leverage

The degree of operating leverage, DOL, is the sensitivity of profits to changes in sales:

$$\text{DOL} = \frac{\text{percentage change in profits}}{\text{percentage change in sales}} = 1 + \frac{\text{fixed costs}}{\text{profits}} \quad \text{(pages 287–88)}$$

Risk and Return

Measures of Risk and Return

Mean or expected return = probability-weighted average of possible outcomes   (page 315)

Variance = σ^2 = probability-weighted average of squared deviations around the expected return   (page 316)

Standard deviation = $\sigma = \sqrt{\text{Variance}}$ (page 316)

Variance of a sample of observations = sum of the square deviations around the average return, divided by the number of observations minus 1   (page 317)

Standard deviation of a sample = $\sqrt{\text{sample variance}}$ (page 317)

Beta = Expected increase in stock return for an extra 1 percent increase in the return on the market index = $\dfrac{\text{cov}(r_j,\, r_m)}{\sigma_m^2}$ (pages 339–41)

Capital Asset Pricing Model

The expected rate of return on a risky security equals the rate of return on risk-free assets plus a risk premium that depends on the security beta:

$$r = r_f + \beta(r_m - r_f) \quad \text{(page 347)}$$

Capital Structure

Weighted-Average Cost of Capital

$$\text{WACC} = \frac{D}{V} \times r_{\text{debt}}(1 - T_c) + \frac{E}{V} \times r_{\text{equity}}$$

where T_c is the corporate tax rate, D is debt, E is equity, and $V = D + E$ (page 372)

Return on Assets

Return on assets equals the weighted average of the returns of the firm's outstanding securities:

$$r_{\text{assets}} = r_{\text{debt}} \frac{D}{V} + r_{\text{equity}} \frac{E}{V}$$

(pages 371 and 473)

(continued on inside back cover)

www.mcgrawhill.ca/edumarketinsight

Check out your textbook's Web site for details on how this special offer enhances the value of your purchase!

Welcome to the Educational Version of Market Insight!

1. To get started, use your Web browser to go to **www.mcgrawhill.ca/edumarketinsight**

2. Enter your site ID exactly as it appears below.

3. You may be prompted to enter the site ID for future use—please keep this card

1203

Your site ID is:
oa17a231

If you purchased a used book, this site ID may have expired. For new password purchase, please go to **www.mcgrawhill.ca/edumarketinsight**. Password activation is good for a 6-month duration.

third canadian edition

Fundamentals of Corporate Finance

Richard A. Brealey
London School of Business

Stewart C. Myers
Sloan School of Management,
Massachusetts Institute of Technology

Alan J. Marcus
Wallace E. Carroll School of Management,
Boston College

Elizabeth M. Maynes
Schulich School of Business, York University

Devashis Mitra
University of New Brunswick

 McGraw-Hill
Ryerson

Toronto Montréal Boston Burr Ridge, IL Dubuque, IA Madison, WI New York
San Francisco St. Louis Bangkok Bogotá Caracas Kuala Lumpur Lisbon London
Madrid Mexico City Milan New Delhi Santiago Seoul Singapore Sydney Taipei

Fundamentals of Corporate Finance
Third Canadian Edition

ISBN: 0-07-094651-5

1 2 3 4 5 6 7 8 9 10 QPD 0 9 8 7 6

Printed and bound in the U.S.A.

Publisher: Lynn Fisher
Senior Marketing Manager: Kelly Smyth
Developmental Editor: Daphne Scriabin
Production Coordinator: Paula Brown
Supervising Editor: Anne Nellis
Copy Editor: Karen Rolfe
Editorial Associate: Stephanie Hess
Cover Design: Greg Devitt
Cover Credits: Gettyone/Mike Brinson
Interior Designer: Greg Devitt
Composition: Greg Devitt
Printer: Quebecor Printing Dubuque

Library and Archives Canada Cataloguing in Publication

Fundamentals of corporate finance / Richard A. Brealey ... [et al.]. — 3rd Canadian ed.

Includes bibliographical references and index.
ISBN 0-07-094651-5

1. Corporations—Finance—Textbooks. I. Brealey, Richard A.

HG4026.F85 2006   658.15   C2005-903556-0

E.M.M.   *To Bruce and David*
D.M.   *To Koumari*

Richard A. Brealey

Professor of Finance at the London Business School. He is the former president of the European Finance Association and a former director of the American Finance Association. He is a Fellow of the British Academy and has served as a special advisor to the Governor of the Bank of England and director of a number of financial institutions. Professor Brealey is also the author (with Professor Myers) of this book's sister text, *Principles of Corporate Finance*.

Stewart C. Myers

Gordon Y. Billard is Professor of Finance at MIT's Sloan School of Management. Dr. Myers is past President of the American Finance Association and a Research Associate of the National Bureau of Economic Research. His research has focused on financing decisions, valuation methods, the cost of capital, and financial aspects of government regulation of business. Dr. Myers is a Director of The Brattle Group, Inc., and is active as a financial consultant. He is also author (with Professor Brealey of this book's sister text, *Principles of Corporate Finance*.

Alan J. Marcus

Professor of Finance in the Wallace E. Carroll School of Management at Boston College. His main research interests are in derivatives and securities markets. He is co-author (with Alex Kane and Zvi Bodie) of the texts *Investments* and *Essentials of Investments*. Professor Marcus has recently been a Visiting Professor at MIT's Sloan School of Management and has served as a Research Fellow at the National Bureau of Economic Research. Professor Marcus spent two years at Freddie Mac, where he helped to develop mortgage pricing and credit risk models. He currently serves on the Research Foundation Advisory Board of the Association for Investment Management and Research (AIMR).

Elizabeth M. Maynes

Associate Professor of Finance at the Schulich School of Business, York University, Toronto. Her current research interests are in experimental economics and finance, where theories are tested with human subjects. Through this research, she has examined peoples' decisions whether to evade tax, whether to tender shares in a takeover bid, and how much to contribute towards a public good. In addition, Professor Maynes conducts research on the role and value of voting rights of shareholders, initial public offerings, and takeovers. Her research has been funded by the Social Sciences and Humanities Research Council of Canada and the Financial Research Foundation. Professor Maynes has extensive experience teaching introductory and corporate finance to undergraduate, MBA and EMBA students, and to managers.

Devashis Mitra

Associate Dean (International) and Professor of Finance at the Faculty of Business Administration, University of New Brunswick, Fredericton. He has extensive experience teaching introductory and advanced courses to undergraduate and MBA students. His teaching interests are in Corporate Finance, Entrepreneurial Finance, and International Finance. Professor Mitra has conducted research in areas such as dividend policy, working capital, international capital budgeting, financial markets, and venture capital. Professor Mitra's research projects have been funded by the Social Sciences and Humanities Research Council of Canada and the Shastri Indo-Canadian Institute. He has served as a past Division Chair, Academic Reviewer, and Program Chair at conferences of the Administrative Sciences Association of Canada.

PREFACE xiii

PREFACE

This book is about corporate finance. It focuses on how companies invest in real assets and how they raise the money to pay for these investments.

Financial management is important, interesting, and challenging. It is important because today's capital investment decisions may determine the businesses in which the firm is involved in 10, 20, or more years. Also, a firm's success or failure depends in large part on its ability to find the capital it needs.

Finance is *interesting* for several reasons. Financial decisions often involve huge sums of money; large investment projects or acquisitions may involve billions of dollars. Also, the financial community is international and fast moving with colourful heroes and a sprinkling of unpleasant villains.

Finance is *challenging*. Financial decisions are rarely cut and dried, and the financial markets in which companies operate change rapidly. Good managers can cope with routine problems, but only the best managers can respond to change. To handle new problems, managers need more than rules of thumb; they need to understand why companies and financial markets behave as they do and when common practice may not be best practice. With a consistent framework for making financial decisions, complex problems become more manageable.

This book provides the framework for making financial decisions. It is not an encyclopedia of finance; it focuses instead on setting out the basic principles of financial management and applying them to the main decisions faced by the financial manager. It explains why the firm's owners would like the manager to increase firm value, and it shows how managers value investments that may pay off at different points of time or have different degrees of risk. It also describes the main features of financial markets and discusses why companies may prefer a particular source of finance.

Some texts shy away from modern finance, sticking instead to more traditional, procedural, or institutional approaches, which are supposed to be easier or more practical. We disagree emphatically. The concepts of modern finance, properly explained, make the subject simpler, not more difficult. They are also more practical. The tools of financial management are easier to grasp and can be used effectively when presented in a consistent conceptual framework. Modern finance provides that framework.

Modern financial management is not "rocket science." It is a set of ideas that can be made clear by words, graphs, and numerical examples. The ideas provide the "why" behind the tools that good financial managers use to make investment and financing decisions.

WHY USE THIS BOOK

We wrote this book to make financial management clear, useful, interesting, and fun for the beginning student. We set out to show that modern finance and good financial practice go together—even for the financial novice. The key to this is a thorough understanding of the principles and mechanics of the time value of money. This material underlies almost all of this text, and we spend a lengthy Chapter 4 providing extensive practice with this key concept.

The second component of our approach is the extensive use of numerical examples. Each chapter presents detailed numerical examples to help the reader become familiar and comfortable with the material. We have peppered the book with real-life illustrations of the chapters' topics. Some of these are excerpts from the financial press found in Finance in Action boxes; others are built into the text as examples. By connecting concepts with practice, we strive to give students a working ability to make financial decisions.

We have streamlined the treatment of most topics to avoid getting bogged down in unnecessary detail that can overwhelm a beginner. We don't assume users will have a lot of background knowledge.

We have written the book in a relaxed and informal writing style. We use mathematical notation only where necessary. Even when we present an equation, we usually write it in words before using symbols. This approach has two advantages: it is less intimidating, and it focuses attention on the underlying concept rather than the formula.

CHANGES IN THE THIRD CANADIAN EDITION

This third Canadian edition of *Fundamentals* includes many changes. We have enhanced the analytical tools used with the book: there are more spreadsheet boxes integrated into the chapters; most chapters now contain end-of-chapter student exercises using the Educational Version of Standard & Poor's Market Insight; and end-of-chapter problems include exercises that ask students to use a variety of Internet resources to solve financial problems.

In addition, we have rewritten, rearranged, and added new material to improve readability and update coverage across chapters. New problem material has been added in many chapters, including a number of comprehensive and integrative problems. Here are some examples of the changes that we have made.

Chapter 1 (The Firm and the Financial Manager) has been updated and rearranged, focusing on the organization of the firm, the role of the financial manager and financial markets, and the goals of a corporation. The chapter contains expanded discussion of ethical issues and the importance of aligning management objectives with the firm's goals.

Chapter 2 (The Financial Environment) is a new chapter that introduces students to the financial environment. It shows how financial managers interact with financial markets and institutions, and illustrates how markets may provide managers with information about the opportunity cost of funds used.

Chapter 3 (Accounting and Finance) includes a discussion of recent accounting scandals. The discussion of cash flow has been reorganized to clarify the links between the statement of cash flow, cash flow from assets, and financing flow.

Chapter 4 (The Time Value of Money) has been updated and rearranged to improve logical flow. Several spreadsheet applications have been incorporated. The section on effective annual interest rates has been extended to more fully explain the conversion of effective annual rates into annual percentage rates and back.

Chapter 5 (Valuing Bonds) has been updated and includes a spreadsheet box illustrating special bond valuation functions. New material on callable bonds, including calculation of the yield to call, the Canada (Doomsday) call, and the Canada yield price have been included. The discussion of the level and shape of the yield curve has been extended in a new section and includes the expectations and liquidity preference theories. Two new, optional appendices, one covering forward rates and yield curve theories in more detail and the other discussing duration, have been added.

Chapter 6 (Valuing Stocks) now contains much of the material previously found in a separate chapter on market efficiency. New material on insider trading also has been added, including a recent case of illegal trading by a company's insiders. The discussion includes a new section on the dot.com bubble and behavioural finance. The placement of market efficiency with stock valuation enhances the discussion of each topic. Also, the chapter now includes the valuation of preferred shares using information from the stock listing.

Chapter 7 (Net Present Value and Other Investment Criteria) has been streamlined and reorganized. It also contains a new concluding section summarizing and organizing the salient features of each criterion discussed in the chapter.

Chapter 8 (Using Discounted Cash Flow Analysis to Make Investment Decisions) works through a realistic comprehensive example of capital budgeting analysis and includes updated information on capital cost allowance (CCA). An appendix showing how the CCA tax shield is derived is available to the reader at the Online Learning Centre at **www.mcgrawhill.ca/college/brealey**.

We have integrated economic value added (EVA®) into **Chapter 9** (Project Analysis). We show how EVA can be used to evaluate projects, emphasizing the opportunity cost of the capital employed in the project. We also have added an introduction to real options to this chapter. The chapter concludes with an expanded and updated discussion of capital budgeting practices in corporate Canada and the United States.

The material on risk and return in Part Three has been revised. The data in **Chapter 10** has been updated and new material on covariance and correlation has been added. The Excel functions VAR, STDEV, COVAR, and CORREL have been incorporated into the chapters. In **Chapter 12** (The Cost of Capital), unlevered and levered equity betas have been added, allowing for a more detailed discussion of the impact of capital structure changes on equity risk. Examples of unlevering and relevering equity betas in both the no-tax and corporate tax cases have been added, extending the discussion of project cost of capital.

Part Four has also been comprehensively revised. **Chapter 13** (An Overview of Corporate Financing) has been extensively updated. An appendix to the chapter contains expanded discussion of a firm's bond refunding decision that is now examined separately for straight bond issues as well as bonds with the Canada (Doomsday) call feature. A new spreadsheet model is included to enhance the analysis.

Extensive updates have also been made in **Chapter 14** (How Corporations Issue Securities). An appendix to the chapter discussing the financing of new and small enterprises has been rewritten to reflect changes in the venture capital industry and other sources of small business financing in Canada. The appendix now includes new discussion on venture capital exits.

Chapter 15 (The Capital Structure Decision) has been updated with Canadian examples and statistics in the discussions on costs of financial distress and explaining financing choices. A new appendix describes income trusts, including their organizational structure. The appendix also discusses the capital structure implications of income trusts and examines reasons for their popularity as financing vehicles in Canada.

Parts Six and Seven contain a significant amount of new material. **Chapter 17** (Financial Statement Analysis) has been updated and has new material on the calculation and interpretation of EVA. **Chapter 18** (Financial Planning) has a new introduction that provides context for the role of financial planning models.

Chapter 19 (Working Capital Management and Short-Term Planning) includes an expanded discussion of commitment fees, syndicated loans, and term loans. New numerical examples have been added to facilitate the discussion on commitment fees and to illustrate the costs of commercial paper.

Chapter 20 (Cash and Inventory Management) has additional treatment of just-in-time policy and also includes an expanded discussion together with a numerical illustration of the Miller-Orr approach to managing uncertain cash balances.

Chapter 21 (Credit Management and Collection) has new coverage, with additional numerical illustration, of the credit decision and now includes discussion pertaining to the evaluation of a credit policy switch.

Part Eight has been updated. **Chapter 23** (Mergers, Acquisitions, and Corporate Control) contains many new Canadian examples and added discussion of synergies (and failed synergies) in mergers. **Chapter 24** (International Financial Management) has expanded discussion on hedging.

In addition to the appendix on the Black-Scholes option valuation model, **Chapter 25** (Options) now has a Black-Scholes spreadsheet, allowing for the valuation of European call options.

LEARNING SOLUTIONS

To provide guidance and insights throughout the text, we include a number of proven pedagogical aids including:

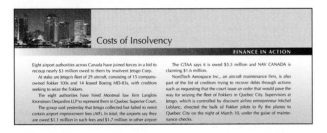

Chapter Opening

Each chapter begins with an overview relating the material to be covered in the chapter to the real world. Learning goals are contained in this section, which are referred to again in the Summary that closes each chapter.

Examples

Separated numbered and titled examples are extensively integrated into the chapters to provide detailed applications and illustrations of the text material.

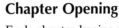

Finance in Action Boxes

Almost every chapter includes at least one Finance in Action box. These are excerpts, usually from the financial press, providing real-life illustrations of the chapter's topics, such as ethical choices in finance, new views about stock valuation, Internet IPOs, or corporate takeover battles abroad.

International Icon

An international icon appears where the authors discuss global issues.

Key Formulas

Called out in the text, key formulas are identified by a number. A summary of key formulas can be found at the Online Learning Centre at **www.mcgrawhill.ca/college/brealey**.

Key Points

Located every few pages throughout the text, these points underscore and summarize the importance of the immediately preceding material, at the same time helping students to focus on the most relevant topics critical to their understanding.

> To summarize, the corporation is a distinct, permanent legal entity. Its advantages are limited liability and the ease with which ownership and management can be separated. These advantages are especially important for large firms. The disadvantage of corporate organization is double taxation.

Check Point Questions

Check Point questions are provided within each chapter and enable students to check their understanding as they read. Both conceptual and calculation-type questions have been included in this edition. Answers are provided at the end of the chapter.

Calculator Boxes and Exercises

In a continued effort to help students grasp the critical concept of time value of money, many pedagogical tools have been added throughout the first section of the text. Financial Calculator boxes provide examples of solving a variety of problems with directions for the three most popular financial calculators.

Excel Spreadsheets

Excel Spreadsheet boxes are integrated into several chapters and provide the student with detailed examples of how to use spreadsheets when applying financial concepts. They give students a valuable introduction to financial modelling. We show how spreadsheets can be used in time value of money and security valuation problems as well as in long- and short-term planning applications.

END OF CHAPTER

A variety of end-of-chapter features are offered to support the concepts presented throughout each chapter and include a Summary, Related Web Links, Key Terms, Questions and Problems, Solutions to Check Points, and Minicases.

The Questions and Problems now incorporate Internet questions, S&P questions, questions with guided steps, integrative questions, qualitative/conceptual questions, and questions that require the use of Excel or an equivalent spreadsheet to solve. Each question is labelled with a level of difficulty and answers to selected questions (identified by an asterisk) are provided in Appendix B.

19. **Integrative.** Big Door Company has 10 million shares outstanding, which are currently trading for about $15 per share and have an equity beta of 1.2. Big Door has 20,000 outstanding bonds, with a 6 percent coupon rate, payable semi-annually and due in 10 years. The bonds are rated BBB. Currently the credit spread for BBB is 95 basis points over equivalent-maturity Government of Canada debt. The current yield on 10-year Canada bonds is 4 percent, compounded semi-annually. The risk-free interest rate is 2.5 percent, and the market risk premium is 6.5 percent. The company has a 35 percent tax rate.
a. Calculate Big Door's WACC.

20. **Comprehensive.** Two ambitious business graduates, Boris and Isabelle, are considering purchasing Premier Pizza, a frozen pizza manufacturer. Forecasted annual sales for the coming year are $10 million, with operating costs equal to 75 percent of sales, including taxes, and required annual investment in new equipment of 5 percent of sales. Sales and costs are expected to grow 4 percent in perpetuity. Based on their analysis of the industry, Boris and Isabelle anticipate financing their company with 30 percent debt. The required rate of return on the debt will be 6 percent and the required rate of return on the equity will be 15 percent. Premier Pizza's corporate tax rate is 35 percent. The risk-free interest rate is 3 percent and the market risk premium is 7 percent.

New S&P Questions

Analytical and decision-oriented questions are now included in the end-of-chapter Questions and Problems. The questions directly incorporate the Educational Version of Market Insight, a service based on Standard & Poor's renowned Computstat database.

22. **Standard & Poor's.** Go to www.mcgrawhill.ca/edumarketinsight. Compare the leverage ratios of two retailers for the past 10 years: Abercrombie & Fitch (ANF) and Wal-Mart (WMT). On the Company page, enter each stock ticker, hit "Go" and then click on "Excel Analytics." The annual ratio reports are found at "Ann. Ratio Rpt." Can you guess which company relies more heavily on operating leases? See if you are right by examining the most recent annual report for each company, found on their Web sites. Look carefully in the notes to the financial statements. Why are operating leases relatively more important to one of the companies?

Internet Problems

Students are presented with problems to solve using the wealth of material available on the Internet.

Excel Questions

Excel questions are incorporated into the end-of-chapter Questions and Problems and are identified by the icon in the margin. These templates are available for download on the text's Online Learning Centre.

MINICASE

Zoe Ashtropova, CEO and sole shareholder of Dog Delights, pored over the brochure showing the fully automated baking system capable of producing 1,000 dog biscuits an hour. "Wow!" she thought, "If we had that equipment, we could double our annual production. Just think of all the dog biscuits we could make!" Then reality returned. The equipment cost $1.2 million and would be completely worn out in 10 years.

impact of the equipment purchase on the company's financial performance? She would prepare annual pro forma financial statements, ending December 31, 2009, and use them to consider different scenarios.

Considering first the sales forecast, Zoe decided she would have to hire a new salesperson and increase the advertising budget. She estimated that sales would increase 20 percent in

MiniCase

Integrative minicases end most chapters and allow students to apply their knowledge to relatively complex, practical situations.

ROUTES THROUGH THE BOOK

There are about as many effective ways to organize a course in corporate finance as there are teachers. For this reason, we have ensured that the text is modular, so that topics can be introduced in different sequences.

We discuss the principles of valuation before plunging into detailed financial statement analysis or issues of financial planning. Nevertheless, we recognize that many instructors will prefer to move directly from Chapter 3 (Accounting and Finance) to Chapter 17 (Financial Statement Analysis) in order to provide a gentler transition from the typical prerequisite accounting course. We have made sure that Part Six (Financial Planning) can easily follow Part One (Introduction).

Similarly, we discuss working capital after the student is familiarized with the basic principles of valuation and financing, but we recognize that many instructors prefer to reverse our order. There should be no difficulty in using Part Seven (Short-Term Financial Decisions) out of order.

When we discuss project valuation in Part Two (Value), we stress that the opportunity cost of capital depends on project risk. But we do not discuss how to measure risk or how return and risk are linked until Part Three (Risk). This ordering can easily be modified. For example, the chapters on risk and return can be introduced before, after, or midway through the material on project valuation.

COMPREHENSIVE TEACHING AND LEARNING PACKAGE
New for this Edition

Lyrx Assessment for Finance [LAFIN]

Based on *Fundamentals of Corporate Finance*, by Brealey, Myers, Marcus, Maynes, and Mitra, Lyrx Assessment for Finance is a leading-edge online assessment system, designed to support both students and instructors. The assessment takes the form of a homework assignment called a Lab. The assessments are algorithmically generated and automatically graded so that students get instant grades and feedback. New Labs are randomly generated each time, providing the student with unlimited opportunities to try a type of question. After they submit a Lab for marking, students receive extensive feedback on their work, thus promoting their learning experience.

For the Instructor: The goal of **LAFIN** is for instructors to use these Labs for course marks instead of creating and marking their own assignments, saving instructors and teaching assistants valuable time to instead help students directly. After registering their courses with Lyrx, instructors can create Labs of their choice by selecting problems from our bank of questions, and set a deadline for each one of these Labs. The content, marking, and feedback of the problems has been developed and implemented

with the help of experienced instructors in finance. Instructors have access to all their students' marks and can view their best Labs. At any time, the instructors can download the class grades for their own programs.

For the Student: **LAFIN** offers algorithmically generated and automatically graded assignments. Students get instant grades and instant feedback—no need to wait until the next class to find out how well they did! Grades are instantly recorded in a grade book that the student can view.

Students are motivated to do their Labs for two reasons: first because it can be tied to assessment, and second, because they can try the Lab as many times as they wish prior to the due date with only their best grade being recorded.

Instructors know from experience that if students are doing their finance homework, they will be successful in the course. Recent research regarding the use of Lyrx has shown that when Labs are tied to assessment, even if worth only a small percentage of the total grade for the course, students WILL do their homework—and MORE THAN ONCE!!

Please contact your *i*Learning Sales Specialist for additional information on the Lyrx Assessment Finance system.

Visit http://lyrx.com

For the Student:

The Online Learning Centre (www.mcgrawhill.ca/ college/brealey)

The OLC, updated by William Lim, York University, includes the following online study material: quiz questions, annotated Web links, Internet questions, Excel templates, video clips, key terms and searchable glossary, a link to the Standard & Poor's Educational Version of Market Insight©, Finance Around the World, Study to Go, and newsfeeds from *The Globe and Mail*.

Study Guide—Now Available Online & Interactive

Prepared by Keith Cheung, University of Windsor, the online interactive Study Guide is a valuable resource that provides students with an overview and additional review problems for each chapter. The online Study Guide contains a thorough list of activities for the student, including the introduction to the chapter, sources of business information, chapter outlines, key concepts and terms, multiple-choice questions, completion questions, and problems with accompanying solutions. Please contact your *i*Learning Sales Specialist for details on how to make access to this online learning resource available for your students.

Educational Version of Standard & Poor's Market Insight

STANDARD &POOR'S

McGraw-Hill Ryerson and the Institutional Market Services division of Standard & Poor's is pleased to announce an exclusive partnership that, with each new textbook, offers instructors and students *free* access to the Educational Version of Standard & Poor's Market Insight©. This rich online resource provides six years of fundamental financial data for over 1,000 Canadian, U.S., and international companies in the database. S&P–specific problems can be found in the end-of-chapter Questions and Problems. For more details, please see the bound-in card inside the front cover of the text or visit **www.mcgrawhill.ca/edumarketinsight**.

For the Instructor:

Instructor Online Learning Centre (www.mcgrawhill.ca/ college/brealey)

The Online Learning Centre includes a password-protected Web site for instructors. The site contains downloadable instructor supplements and PageOut, the McGraw-Hill Ryerson course Web site development centre.

Instructor's CD-ROM including:

Instructor's Manual
Updated and enhanced by the authors, this supplement includes a descriptive preface containing alternative course formats and case teaching methods, a chapter overview and outline, key terms, and concepts. The second section of the Instructor's Manual includes complete solutions to all end–of-chapter problems.

Microsoft® PowerPoint® Presentation Software
Prepared by Sujata Madan, McGill University, these visually stimulating slides have been fully updated with graphs, charts, and lists. These slides can be edited or manipulated to fit the needs of a particular course.

Computerized Test Bank
Andrea Chance, George Brown College, has adapted the test questions which consist of true/false, multiple-choice, and discussion questions and problems. Questions are identified by level of difficulty and complete answers are provided for all questions and problems, along with a reference to their location in the text.

eInstruction's Classroom Performance System (CPS)

Bring interactivity into the classroom or lecture hall
CPS is a student response system using wireless connectivity. It gives instructors and students immediate feedback from the entire class. The response pads are remotes that are easy to use and engage students.

- **CPS** helps you to increase **student preparation, interactivity, and active learning** so you can receive immediate feedback and know what students understand.
- **CPS** allows you to administer quizzes and tests, and provide **immediate grading**.
- With **CPS** you can create lecture questions that can be multiple-choice, true/false, and subjective. You can even create questions on the fly, as well as conduct group activities.
- **CPS** not only allows you to **evaluate classroom attendance, activity, and grading** for your course as a whole, but also allows you to provide students with an immediate study guide. All results and scores can easily be imported into Excel and can be used with various classroom management systems.

CPS-ready content is available for use with this text. Please contact your *i*Learning Sales Specialist for more information on how you can integrate CPS into your finance classroom.

Mobile Learning

Study To Go
The businesses and companies of today want their new employees to be adept in all aspects of the changing business environment. They are quick to tell us they want graduates with the skills of tomorrow—today. From laptops to cell phones to PDAs, the new medium is mobility.

As a leader in technology and innovation, McGraw-Hill Ryerson has developed material providing students with optimum flexibility for use anytime, anywhere they need to study—whether with a laptop, PDA, or tablet. These innovations provide instructors with a number of exciting ways to integrate technology into the learning process.

With **Study To Go** we have introduced wireless activities as a part of our Online Learning Centre. Now, whether you are waiting in line, riding on transit, or just filling some spare time, homework and practice are just a click away.

PowerWeb

Keeping your course current can be a job in itself, and now McGraw-Hill Ryerson can do it for you.

PowerWeb extends the learning experience beyond the core text by offering all the latest news and developments pertinent to your course via the Internet, without all the clutter and dead links of a typical online search.

PowerWeb offers current articles related to investments, weekly updates with assessment tools, informative and timely world news culled by a finance expert, refereed Web links, and more. In addition, PowerWeb provides an array of helpful learning aids, including self-grading quizzes and interactive glossaries and exercises. Students may also access study tips, conduct online research, and learn about different career paths. Visit the PowerWeb site at **http://dushkin.com/powerweb** and see firsthand what PowerWeb can mean to your course.

PowerWeb To Go is a new McGraw-Hill content offering designed specifically for use on handheld devices. PowerWeb To Go content consists of current news stories, weekly updates, and magazine articles developed specifically for the study of investments. It is revised daily, giving you the most up-to-date, course-specific information available, and is easily loaded onto your Pocket PC or Palm OS handheld device. Visit the PowerWeb To Go site at **www.powerwebtogo.com** for information on how you can sign up today.

Course Management

McGraw-Hill Ryerson's course management system, **PageOut**, is the easiest way to create a Web site for your finance course. There is no need for HTML coding, graphing design, or a thick how-to book. Just fill in a series of boxes in plain English and click on one of our professional designs. In no time, your course is online!

For the integrated instructor, we offer *finance* content for complete online courses. Whatever your needs, you can customize the *Fundamentals of Corporate Finance* Online Learning Centre content and author your own online course materials. It is entirely up to you. You can offer online discussion and message boards that will complement your office hours and reduce the lines outside your door.

Content cartridges are also available for course management systems, such as **WebCT** and **Blackboard**. Ask your *i*Learning Sales Specialist for details.

SUPERIOR SERVICE

Service takes on a whole new meaning with McGraw-Hill Ryerson and finance. More than just bringing you the text, we have consistently raised the bar in terms of innovation and educational research—both in finance and in education in general. These investments in learning and the education community have helped us understand the needs of students and educators across the country and allowed us to foster the growth of truly innovative, integrated learning.

Integrated Learning

Your Integrated *i*Learning Sales Specialist is a McGraw-Hill Ryerson representative who has the experience, product knowledge, training, and support to help you assess and integrate any of our products, technology, and services into your course for optimum teaching and learning performance. Whether it is using our test bank software, helping your students improve their grades, or putting your entire course online, your *i*Learning Sales Specialist is there to help you do it. Contact your *i*Learning Sales Specialist today to learn how to maximize all of McGraw-Hill Ryerson's resources!

*i*Learning Services

McGraw-Hill Ryerson offers a unique *i*Services package designed for Canadian faculty. Our mission is to equip providers of higher education with superior tools and resources required for excellence in teaching. For additional information, visit www.mcgrawhill.ca/highereducation/iservices.

Teaching, Technology & Learning Conference Series

The educational environment has changed tremendously in recent years, and McGraw-Hill Ryerson continues to be committed to helping you acquire the skills you need to succeed in this new milieu. Our innovative Teaching, Technology & Learning Conference Series brings faculty together from across Canada with 3M Teaching Excellence award winners to share teaching and learning best practices in a collaborative and stimulating environment. Pre-conference workshops on general topics, such as teaching large classes and technology integration, will also be offered. We will also work with you at your own institution to customize workshops that best suit the needs of your faculty.

ACKNOWLEDGEMENTS

We take this opportunity to thank all of those individuals who helped us prepare this Third Edition. We want to express our appreciation to those instructors whose insightful comments and suggestions were invaluable to us during this revision.

Margaret Beresford, Kwantlen University College
Bram Cadsby, University of Guelph
Keith Cheung, University of Windsor
Craig Dunbar, University of Western Ontario
David Kennedy, Lethbridge Community College
Marie Madill-Payne, George Brown College
Bonnie Martel, Niagara College
Michael McIntyre, Carleton University
Douglas Nakano, College of the Rockies
David Peters, University of Western Ontario
Clifton Philpott, Kwantlen University College
Aziz Rajwani, Langara College
M. Rashid, University of New Brunswick
Francis Tapon, University of Guelph
Joan Wallwork, Kwantlen University College
Eric Wang, Athabasca University
Eric Wickham, Centennial College

We owe much to our colleagues at the University of New Brunswick and the Schulich School of Business, York University. Special thanks to Professor Tom Beechy, York University, for his willingness to share his accounting expertise, and Professors Isaac Otchere and Gopalan Srinivasan, University of New Brunswick, for many useful suggestions. Thanks also to the Faculty of Business Administration, University of New Brunswick, for some research support on this project.

In addition, we would like to thank our supplement authors Andrea Chance, Keith Cheung, Sujata Madan, and William Lim. Their efforts will help students and instructors alike.

We would like to thank Vishaal Baulkaran, University of New Brunswick, for research and computational assistance, and Marilyn Davis and Angela Larlee, University of New Brunswick for secretarial assistance. As well, we would like to thank Nancy Bower, University of Guelph, for her excellent technical review of the text, and Helen Prankie, of the Canadian Securities Institute, for her technical review of the solutions contained in the Instructor's Manual.

We are also grateful to the talented staff at McGraw-Hill Ryerson, especially Lynn Fisher, Publisher; Daphne Scriabin, Developmental Editor; Kelly Dickson, Manager, Editorial Services; and Anne Nellis, Supervising Editor. We want to thank copy editor Karen Rolfe for her energetic attention to the details.

Finally, we cannot overstate the thanks due to our spouses, Bruce Rhodes and Koumari Mitra, and to David Rhodes, Elizabeth's son. They supported us and forgave us when we were very absorbed in the project.

E.M.M.
D.M.

PART ONE
Introduction

THE FIRM AND THE FINANCIAL MANAGER

This book is an introduction to corporate finance and the profession of financial management. In this chapter we begin by summarizing the decisions that a financial manager is required to make.

To survive and prosper, a business must satisfy its customers. It must also produce and sell its products and services at a profit. To do all this, a business requires assets—plant, equipment, offices, computers and software, trademarks, patents or licences, laboratories for research and development, and so on. The financial manager has to help the business decide which assets to buy and how to pay for them. In other words, the financial manager has to guide both *investment decisions* and *financing decisions*.

We begin this chapter by explaining the differences between a corporation and a sole proprietorship or partnership. We note the pros and cons of these three ways of organizing a business. Then we offer an overview of the role of the corporate financial manager and describe several career paths in finance.

Next, we turn to the financial goals of the corporation and ask what makes for a good financial decision. Should it maximize value, or is it enough to survive and avoid bankruptcy? Should the organization strive to be a good corporate citizen? To maximize value to the firm's stockholders? We also consider the conflicts of interest that arise in large corporations and review the mechanisms that align the interests of the firm's managers with the interests of stockholders. Finally, we look ahead to the rest of this book and look back to some entertaining snippets of financial history.

After studying this chapter you should be able to
- Explain the advantages and disadvantages of corporations, sole proprietorships, and partnerships.
- Cite the major decisions that financial managers make, and explain the special roles of the chief financial officer (CFO), treasurer, and controller.
- Give examples of career paths in finance.

- Explain why maximizing market value is the logical financial goal of the corporation.
- Understand why conflicts of interest arise in large corporations.
- Explain how corporations provide incentives for everyone to work toward a common end.

1.1

ORGANIZING A BUSINESS

SOLE PROPRIETORSHIPS

In 1934, Roy Thomson acquired his first newspaper, the Timmins Press, in Timmins, Ontario. Today, with 39,000 employees worldwide, the Thomson Corporation is a leading global e-information and solutions company, with sales revenues of over $10.5 billion in 2004. Thomson Corporation's income was recently ranked number 12 on *The Globe and Mail*'s list of Canada's largest profitable corporations. If, like Roy Thomson, you start a business on your own, with no partners or share-holders, you are said to be a **sole proprietor**. You bear all of the costs and keep all of the profits after Canada Revenue Agency (CRA) has taken its cut. The advantages of a proprietorship are the ease with which it can be established and the lack of regulations governing it. This makes it well suited for a small company with an informal business structure.

As a sole proprietor, you are responsible for all the business's debts and other liabilities. If the business borrows from the bank and subsequently cannot repay the loan, the bank has a claim against your personal belongings. It could force you into personal bankruptcy if the business debts are big enough. Thus as sole proprietor you have *unlimited liability*.

sole proprietor Sole owner of a business that has no partners and no shareholders. The proprietor is personally liable for all the firm's obligations.

PARTNERSHIPS

Instead of starting on your own, you may wish to pool money and expertise with friends or business associates. If so, a sole proprietorship is obviously inappropriate. Instead, you can form a **partnership**. Your *partnership agreement* will set out how management decisions are to be made and the proportion of the profits to which each partner is entitled. The partners then pay personal income tax on their share of these profits.

Partners, like sole proprietors, have the disadvantage of unlimited liability. If the business runs into financial difficulties, each partner has unlimited liability for *all* the business's debts, not just his share. The moral is clear and simple: "Know thy partner."

Many professional businesses are organized as partnerships. They include the large accounting, legal, and management consulting firms. Several large Canadian investment dealers, such as BMO Nesbitt Burns, Scotia Capital, and CIBC World Markets, have their origins in partnerships, as do most large investment banks in the United States, such as Morgan Stanley, Salomon, Smith Barney, Merrill Lynch, and Goldman Sachs.[1] A number of large and growing Canadian companies, such as Saputo Inc. and the Jean Coutu Group, and international companies, such as Microsoft and Apple Computer, also started life as partnerships. But eventually these companies and their financing requirements grew too large for them to continue as partnerships.

partnership Business owned by two or more people who are personally responsible for all its liabilities.

CORPORATIONS

As your firm grows, you may decide to form a **corporation**. You may *incorporate* your firm federally, under the *Canadian Business Corporation Act*, or provincially, under the relevant provincial laws. A provincially incorporated firm may conduct its business in that province but may need additional permissions to do business elsewhere. The incorporation documents are called *articles of incorporation* in most provinces.[2] When approved by the relevant government agency, these documents provide the charter to the firm to conduct its business as a corporation. Unlike

corporation Business owned by shareholders who are not personally liable for the business's liabilities.

---

[1] Investment dealers assist investors in buying and selling securities for a fee. They also assist firms in issuing new securities.

[2] They are also called *letters patent* or *memorandum of association* in some provinces.

a proprietorship or partnership, a corporation is legally distinct from its owners. As such, it is treated like a human being for many legal purposes and given rights and responsibilities. For example, it can borrow or lend money, and it can sue or be sued. It pays its own taxes—but it cannot vote!

The corporation is owned by its shareholders, and they get to vote on important matters. Unlike proprietorships or partnerships, corporations have **limited liability**, which means that the shareholders cannot be held personally responsible for the obligations of the firm. When Air Canada filed for bankruptcy in 2003, no one could demand that its shareholders put up more money to pay off the debts. The most a shareholder can lose is the amount invested in the stock.

limited liability The owners of the corporation are not personally responsible for its obligations.

While the shareholders of a corporation own the firm, they do not usually manage it. Instead, they elect a *board of directors*, which in turn appoints the top managers. The board is the representative of shareholders and is supposed to ensure that management is acting in their best interests.

This *separation of ownership and management* is one distinctive feature of corporations. In other forms of business organization, such as proprietorships and partnerships, the owners are the managers.

The separation between management and ownership gives a corporation more flexibility and permanence than a partnership. Even if managers of a corporation quit or are dismissed and replaced by others, the corporation can survive. Similarly, today's shareholders may sell all their shares to new investors without affecting the business. In contrast, ownership of a proprietorship cannot be transferred without selling out to another owner-manager.

By organizing as a corporation, a business may be able to attract a wide variety of investors. The shareholders may include individuals who hold only a single share worth a few dollars, receive only a single vote, and are entitled to only a tiny proportion of the profits. Shareholders may also include giant pension funds and insurance companies, the investment of which may run into the millions of shares and which are entitled to a correspondingly large number of votes and proportion of the profits.

Given these advantages, you might be wondering why all businesses are not organized as corporations. One reason is the time and cost required to manage a corporation's legal machinery. There can also be an important tax reason. Because the corporation is a separate legal entity, it is taxed separately. So corporations pay tax on their profits, and, in addition, shareholders pay tax on any dividends that they receive from the company.[3] By contrast, income received by partners and sole proprietors is taxed only once as personal income.

When you first establish a corporation, the shares may all be held by a small group, perhaps the company's managers and a small number of backers who believe the business will grow into a profitable investment. Your shares are not publicly traded and your company is *closely held*. Eventually, when the firm grows and new shares are issued to raise additional capital, the shares will be widely traded. Such corporations are known as public companies. Most well-known corporations are public companies.[4]

> To summarize, the corporation is a distinct, permanent legal entity. Its advantages are limited liability and the ease with which ownership and management can be separated. These advantages are especially important for large firms. The disadvantage of corporate organization is double taxation.

---

[3] To avoid taxing the same income twice, Canada's tax system, like that of several other countries, allows shareholders some credit for the taxes their company has already paid. Although this feature of Canadian tax law reduces the "double taxation" of dividend income, it does not usually eliminate it completely. We will discuss the dividend tax credit in more detail in Chapter 3.

[4] For example, when Microsoft was initially established as a corporation, its shares were closely held by a small number of employees and backers. Microsoft shares were issued to the public in 1986. In contrast, McCain Foods is still closely held despite being one of Canada's largest multinational food manufacturers.

The financial managers of a corporation are responsible, by way of top management and the board of directors, to the corporation's shareholders. Financial managers are supposed to make financial decisions that serve shareholders' interests. Table 1.1 presents the distinctive features of the major forms of business organization.

HYBRID FORMS OF BUSINESS ORGANIZATION

Businesses do not always fit into these neat categories. Some are hybrids of the three basic types: proprietorships, partnerships, and corporations.

For example, businesses can be set up as *limited partnerships*. In this case, partners are classified as general or limited. General partners manage the business and have unlimited personal liability for the business's debts. Limited partners, however, are liable only for the money they contribute to the business. They can lose everything they put in, but not more.

Limited partners usually have a restricted role and cannot take part in the day-to-day management of the partnership, but they have the right to share in partnership profits and to have their contributions returned if the business is dissolved. Forming a limited partnership requires that a written agreement be registered provincially that details the capital contributions of the limited partners and identifies the general partners.

Now firms can also be set up as *limited liability partnerships (LLP)*, which are relatively new in Canada and are often designed to meet the liability concerns of professionals such as accountants or lawyers.[5] Individual partners in an LLP continue to have unlimited liability for their own professional negligence or malpractice, as in an ordinary partnership, but they are not liable for the negligence or malpractice of their other partners. The firm retains overall liability and so its assets and any insurance policies it owns can be used to meet losses. Provincial laws determine whether members of individual professions are allowed to form LLPs. Limited liability partnerships combine the tax advantage of a partnership with the limited liability advantage of incorporation.

Professionals such as engineers or accountants may also incorporate using *limited liability corporations (LLC)* provided they are specifically permitted to do so by the laws governing the particular profession in that province.[6] Typically incorporation does not protect the professional from personal liability for negligence. Another variation on the theme is the *professional corporation (PC)*, which is commonly used by doctors, lawyers, and accountants. In this case, the

TABLE 1.1
Characteristics of business organizations

	Sole Proprietorship	Partnership	Corporation
Who owns the business?	The manager	Partners	Shareholders
Are manager(s) and owner(s) separate?	No	No	Usually
What is the owner's liability?	Unlimited	Unlimited	Limited
Are the owner and business taxed separately?	No	No	Yes

[5] *Limited Liability Partnerships*, Report 77 (Edmonton: The Alberta Law Reform Institute, 1999) p. 5. The report also recommends that LLPs in Canada should be available to enterprises generally as is the case in many states in the United States.

[6] For further discussion, see D. Duplessis, S. Enman, S. Gunz, and S. O'Byrne, *Canadian Business Law* (Scarborough, Ontario: Nelson Thomson Learning, 2001) pp. 530–532.

business has limited liability but the professional can still be sued personally for malpractice, even if the malpractice occurs in the role of corporation employee. Despite their advantages, these forms of business organization still do not suit the largest firms for which widespread share ownership and separation of ownership and management are essential.

Check Point 1.1

Which form of business organization might best suit the following?
a. A consulting firm with several senior consultants and support staff.
b. A house painting company owned and operated by a university student who hires some friends for occasional help.
c. A paper goods company with sales of $100 million and 2,000 employees.

1.2   THE ROLE OF THE FINANCIAL MANAGER

real assets Assets used to produce goods and services.

financial assets Claims to the income generated by real assets. Also called securities.

To carry on business, companies need an almost endless variety of **real assets**. Many of these assets are tangible, such as machinery, factories, and offices; others are intangible, such as technical expertise, trademarks, and patents. All must be paid for.

To obtain the necessary money, the company sells **financial assets**, or *securities*.[7] These pieces of paper have value because they are claims on the firm's real assets and the cash that those assets will produce. Let's take two examples:

- Macronics is a public corporation with shares trading on the Toronto Stock Exchange. It sells 500,000 new shares to individual investors for $40 per share. It thereby raises $20 million, which it invests in research and development (R&D). The real asset is the knowledge and technology generated by the R&D program. The financial assets are the new shares, which have value because the new shareholders now own part of the company.
- Mycronics borrows $10 million from a bank to buy land for a new factory. The real asset is the land. The financial asset is the bank loan. From the bank's point of view, the loan is an investment in Mycronics. The investment has value because Mycronics has promised to repay the loan with interest.

In each case cash is raised from outside investors and put to use in the firm. Notice that the investors may be individuals participating in *financial markets*, such as the Toronto Stock Exchange, or a *financial institution*, such as a bank. We will say more about financial markets and institutions in the next chapter.

Financial managers stand between the firm's operations and outside investors. The financial manager's role is shown in Figure 1.1, which traces how money flows from investors to the firm and back to investors again. The flow starts when financial assets are sold to raise cash (arrow 1 in the figure). The cash is employed to purchase the real assets used in the firm's operations (arrow 2). Later, if the firm does well, the real assets generate enough cash inflow to more than repay the initial investment (arrow 3). Finally, the cash is either reinvested (arrow 4a) or returned to the investors who contributed the money in the first place (arrow 4b). Of course the choice between arrows 4a and 4b is not a completely free one. For example, if a bank lends the firm money at stage 1, the bank has to be repaid this money plus interest at stage 4b.

capital budgeting decision Decision as to which real assets the firm should acquire.

This flow chart suggests that the financial manager faces two basic problems. First, how much money should the firm invest, and what specific assets should the firm invest in? This is the firm's *investment*, or **capital budgeting**, **decision**. Second, how should the cash required for an investment

---

[7] For present purposes we are using *financial assets* and *securities* interchangeably, though securities usually refers to financial assets that are widely held, like the shares of Nortel Networks. An IOU ("I owe you") from your brother-in-law, which you might have trouble selling outside the family, is also a financial asset, but most people would not think of it as a security.

FIGURE 1.1
Flow of cash between investors and the firm's operations. Key: (1) Cash raised by selling financial assets to investors; (2) cash invested in the firm's operations; (3) cash generated by the firm's operations; (4a) cash reinvested; (4b) cash returned to investors

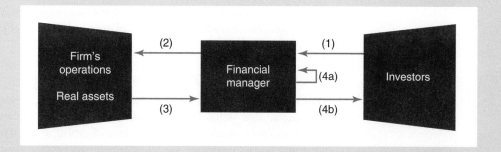

financing decision Decision as to how to raise the money to pay for investments in real assets.

be raised? This is the **financing decision**. We have already seen two examples of a financing decision. Macronics raised money by issuing new shares. Mycronics took out a bank loan.

THE CAPITAL BUDGETING DECISION

Capital budgeting decisions are central to the company's success or failure. Consider Boeing's decision to "bet the company" by developing the 757 and 767 jets. Boeing's investment in these planes was $3 billion, more than double the total value of stockholders' investment as shown in the company's accounts at the time. By 2002, estimated cumulative profits from this investment were approaching $10 billion, and the planes were still selling.

Not all capital investments succeed, of course. The Iridium communications satellite system, which offered its users instant telephone connections worldwide, soaked up a $5 billion investment before it started operations in 1998. It needed 400,000 subscribers to break even, but attracted only a small fraction of that number. Iridium defaulted on its debt and filed for bankruptcy in August 1999. The Iridium system was sold a year later for just $25 million.

Consider also the case of Canada's Bombardier, which decided to diversify into aerospace in 1986, and within a few years, invested over $5 billion to acquire, develop, and market product lines of small regional and business aircraft that the larger aircraft manufacturers such as Boeing do not produce. The company's bet on this niche market for 20- to 90-seat aircraft appeared to have paid off until 2001. The company had a large and growing number of orders for its Dash 8 turboprops, CRJ regional jets, and the Canadair and Learjet business jets. Since then, with a general slump in the airline industry, this sector of Bombardier's business has not performed well.

Iridium's decision to invest in its satellite system or Boeing's and Bombardier's decisions to invest in a new generation of airliners are both examples of capital budgeting decisions. The success of such decisions is usually judged in terms of value. Good investment projects are worth more than they cost. Adopting such projects increases the value of the firm and therefore the wealth of its shareholders. For example, Boeing's investment produced a stream of cash flows that were worth much more than its $3 billion outlay.

Not all capital investments are for tangible assets. For example, Gillette spent around $300 million to advertise the launch of its Mach3 razor. This was an investment in an intangible asset—brand recognition and acceptance. Moreover, traditional manufacturing firms are not the only ones that make important capital budgeting decisions. For example, Nortel Networks' R&D expenditures in 2002 were more than $2.1 billion. This investment in future products and product improvement will be crucial to the company's ability to retain its existing customers and attract new ones.

Today's investments provide benefits in the future. Thus the financial manager is concerned not solely with the size of the benefits but also with how long the firm must wait for them. The sooner the profits come in, the better. In addition, these benefits are rarely certain; a new project may be a great success—but then again it could be a dismal failure. The financial manager needs a way to place a value on these uncertain future benefits.

We will spend considerable time in later chapters on project evaluation. While no one can guarantee that you will avoid disasters like Iridium or that you will be blessed with successes like the 757 and 767, a disciplined, analytical approach to project proposals will weight the odds in your favour.

THE FINANCING DECISION

The financial manager's second responsibility is to raise the money to pay for the investment in real assets. This is the financing decision. When a company needs financing, it can invite investors to put up cash in return for a share of profits or it can promise investors a series of fixed payments. In the first case, the investor receives newly issued shares of stock and becomes a shareholder, a part-owner of the firm. In the second, the investor becomes a lender who must one day be repaid. The choice of the long-term financing mix is often called the **capital structure** decision, since *capital* refers to the firm's sources of long-term financing.

capital structure   A firm's mix of long-term financing.

Suppose the company decides to borrow. Should it go to capital markets for long-term debt financing, or should it borrow from a bank? Should it borrow in Paris, receiving and promising to repay euros, or should it borrow Canadian dollars in Toronto? Should it demand the right to pay off the debt early if future interest rates fall? We will look at these and other choices in later chapters.

The decision to invest in a new factory or to issue new shares of stock has long-term consequences. But the financial manager is also involved in some important short-term decisions. For example, she needs to make sure that the company has enough cash on hand to pay next week's bills and that any spare cash is put to work to earn interest. Such short-term financial decisions involve both investment (how to invest spare cash) and financing (how to raise cash to meet a short-term need).

Businesses are inherently risky, but the financial manager needs to ensure that risks are managed. For example, the manager will want to be certain that the firm cannot be wiped out by a sudden rise in oil prices or a fall in the value of the dollar. In later chapters, we will look at the techniques that managers use to explore the future and some of the ways that the firm can be protected against nasty surprises.

Check Point 1.2

Are the following capital budgeting or financing decisions?
a. Ballard Power decides to spend $500 million to develop a new fuel cell.
b. Volkswagen decides to raise 350 million euros through a bank loan.
c. Nova Corporation constructs a pipeline to transport natural gas to Chile's remote southern Magallanes region.
d. Royal Caribbean Cruises sells $300 million (US) of new debt to upgrade its cruise liners.
e. Biochem Pharma buys a licence to produce and sell a new drug developed by a biotech firm.
f. Loblaw issues new shares to help finance the acquisition of Provigo, a retail grocery company.

Check Point 1.3

Do you understand the following distinctions? Briefly explain in each case.
a. real versus financial assets
b. investment versus financing decisions
c. capital budgeting versus capital structure decisions

1.3   WHO IS THE FINANCIAL MANAGER?

In this book we will use the term *financial manager* to refer to anyone responsible for a significant corporate investment or financing decision. But except in the smallest firms, no *single* person is responsible for all the decisions discussed in this book. Responsibility is dispersed throughout the firm. Top management is, of course, constantly involved in financial decisions. But the engineer who designs a new production facility is also involved: the design determines the kind of asset in which the firm will invest. Likewise, the marketing manager who undertakes a major advertising campaign is making an investment decision: the campaign is an investment in an intangible asset that will pay off in future sales and earnings.

Nevertheless, there are managers who specialize in finance, and their functions are summarized in Figure 1.2. The **treasurer** is usually the person most directly responsible for looking after the firm's cash, raising new capital, and maintaining relationships with banks and other investors who hold the firm's securities.

For small firms, the treasurer is likely to be the only financial executive. Larger corporations usually also have a **controller**, who prepares the financial statements, manages the firm's internal accounting, and looks after its tax affairs. You can see that the treasurer and controller have different roles: the treasurer's main function is to obtain and manage the firm's capital, whereas the controller ensures that the money is used efficiently.

The largest firms usually appoint a **chief financial officer (CFO)** to oversee both the treasurer's and the controller's work. The CFO is deeply involved in financial policy making and corporate planning. Often he will have general responsibilities beyond strictly financial issues.

Usually the treasurer, controller, or CFO is responsible for organizing and supervising the capital budgeting process. However, major capital investment projects are so closely tied to plans for product development, production, and marketing that managers from these other areas are inevitably drawn into planning and analyzing the projects. If the firm has staff members specializing in corporate planning, they are naturally involved in capital budgeting too.

Because of the importance of many financial issues, ultimate decisions often rest by law or by custom with the board of directors.[8] For example, only the board has the legal power to declare a dividend or to sanction a public issue of securities. Boards usually delegate decision-making authority for small- or medium-sized investment outlays, but the authority to approve large investments is almost never delegated.

CAREERS IN FINANCE

In Canada, well over half a million people work in financial services, and many others work in the finance departments of corporations. We can't tell you what each person does all day, but we can give you some idea of the variety of careers in finance. The nearby Finance in Action box summarizes the experience of a small sample of recent (fictitious) graduates.

treasurer   Manager responsible for financing, cash management, and relationships with financial markets and institutions.

controller   Officer responsible for budgeting, accounting, and auditing.

chief financial officer (CFO)   Officer who oversees the treasurer and controller and sets overall financial strategy.

SEE BOX P. 10

FIGURE 1.2
The financial managers in large corporations

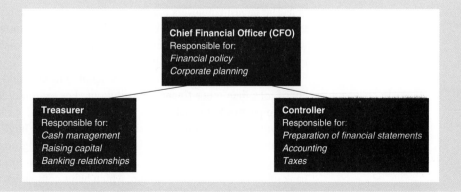

---

[8] Often the firm's chief financial officer is also a member of its board of directors.

Working in Finance

Susan Webb, Research Analyst,
Mutual Fund Group

After majoring in biochemistry, I joined the research department of a large mutual fund group. Because of my background, I was assigned to work with the senior pharmaceuticals analyst. I start the day by reading the business sections of *The Globe and Mail* and *Financial Post* and reviewing the analyses that come in each day from stockbroking firms. I also read about market activity and news worldwide from the Bloomberg Web site on my computer. Sometimes we need to revise our earnings forecasts and meet with the portfolio managers to discuss possible trades. The remainder of my day is spent mainly in analyzing companies and developing forecasts of revenues and earnings. I meet frequently with pharmaceutical analysts in stockbroking firms, and we regularly visit company management. In the evenings I study for the Chartered Financial Analyst exam. Since I did not study finance at college, this is quite challenging. I hope eventually to move from a research role to become a portfolio manager.

Richard Gradley, Project Finance,
Large Energy Company

After leaving university, I joined the finance department of a large engineering and construction company. I spent my first year helping to analyze capital investment proposals. I then moved to the project finance group, which is responsible for analyzing engineering infrastructure and construction projects around the world. Recently, I have been involved in a turnkey contract proposal to set up a large sulphuric acid plant in Europe. We built a spreadsheet model of the project to ensure that it was viable and we had to check that the contracts with the builders, operators, suppliers, and so on were all in place before we could arrange bank financing for the project.

Albert Rodriguez, Emerging Markets Group,
Major Toronto Bank

I joined the bank after majoring in finance. I spent the first six months in the bank's training program, rotating between departments. I was assigned to the Latin America team just before the 1998 Brazilian crisis when interest rates jumped to nearly 50 percent and the currency fell by 40 percent. There was a lot of activity, with everyone trying to figure out what was likely to happen next and how it would affect our business. My job is largely concerned with analyzing economies and assessing the prospects for bank business. There are plenty of opportunities to work abroad, and I hope to spend some time in one of our Latin American offices, such as Argentina or Brazil.

Emma Kuletsky, Customer Service Representative,
Regional Bank

My job is to help look after customers in a large branch. They seem to expect me to know about everything. I help them with financial planning and with their applications for loans. In a typical day, I may have to interview a new customer who wants to open an account with the bank and calm an old one who thinks she has been overcharged for a wire transfer. I like dealing with people, and one day I hope to be manager of a branch like this one.

We explained earlier that corporations face two principal financial decisions: the investment decision and the financing decision. Therefore, as a newly recruited financial analyst, you may help to analyze a major new investment project. Or you may instead help raise the money to pay for it, perhaps by a new issue of debt or by arranging to lease the plant and equipment. Other financial analysts work on short-term financial issues, such as collecting and investing the company's cash or checking whether customers are likely to pay their bills. Financial analysts are also involved in monitoring and controlling risk. For example, they may help to arrange insurance for the firm's plant and equipment, or they may assist with the purchase and sale of options, futures, and other tools for managing risk.

Instead of working in the finance department of a corporation, you may join a financial institution. The largest employers are the commercial banks. Banks collect deposits and re-lend the cash to corporations and individuals. If you join a bank, at some point you may well work in a branch, where individuals and small businesses come to deposit cash or to seek a loan. Alternatively, you may be employed in the head office, helping to analyze a $100 million loan to a large corporation.

Banks do many things in addition to lending money, and they probably provide a greater variety of jobs than other financial institutions. For example, individuals and businesses use banks to make payments to each other. So if you work in the cash management department of a large bank, you may help companies electronically transfer huge sums of money as wages, taxes, and payments to suppliers. Banks also buy and sell foreign exchange, so you could find yourself working in front of one of those computer screens in a foreign exchange dealing room. Another bank job is in the derivatives group, which helps companies manage their risk by buying and selling options, futures, and so on. This is where the mathematicians and the computer buffs thrive.

Investment dealers such as Scotia Capital or CIBC World Markets help companies sell their securities to investors. They also have large corporate finance departments, which assist firms in major reorganizations such as takeovers. When firms issue securities or try to take over another firm, a lot of money is at stake and the firms may need to move quickly. Thus working for an investment bank can be a high-pressure activity with long hours. It can also pay very well.

The distinction between commercial banks and investment dealers is narrowing. The same company may own both investment dealers and commercial banks; for example, RBC Dominion Securities (an investment dealer and brokerage house) and the Royal Bank of Canada (a commercial bank) are both owned by Royal Bank Financial Group.

The insurance industry is another large employer. Much of the insurance industry is involved in designing and selling insurance policies on people's lives and property, but businesses are also major customers. So if you work for an insurance company or a large insurance broker, you could find yourself arranging insurance on a Learjet 60 in Canada or a pipeline in Chile.

A mutual fund collects money from individuals and invests in a portfolio of stocks or bonds. A financial analyst for a mutual fund analyzes the prospects for the securities and works with the investment manager to decide which ones should be bought and sold. Many other financial institutions also contain investment management departments. For example, you might work as a financial analyst in the investment department of an insurance company and help invest the premiums. Or you could be a financial analyst in the trust department of a bank that manages money for retirement funds, universities, and charitable bodies.

Stockbroking firms and bond dealers help investment management companies and private individuals invest in securities. They employ sales staff and dealers who make the trades. They also employ financial analysts to analyze the securities and help customers decide which ones to buy or sell. Many stockbroking firms are owned by chartered banks, such as Bank of Montreal.

The big commercial banks, investment dealers, insurance companies, and stockbroking firms are mostly headquartered in and around Toronto. Of course, large financial institutions have their headquarters in other cities as well. For instance, National Bank of Canada, Caisse de dépôt et placement du Québec and Desjardins-Laurentian Financial Corporation are headquartered in Montreal while Great-West Life Assurance and Investors Group are headquartered in Winnipeg. Many financial institutions have significant business interests outside Canada. Finance is a global business, so you may spend some time working in an overseas branch or travel occasionally to one of the major international financial centres, such as New York, London, Frankfurt, Hong Kong, or Singapore.

Finance professionals tend to be well paid. Starting salaries for new graduates are in the region of \$40,000, rather more in a major Toronto investment bank and somewhat less in a small regional bank. But let us look ahead a little: Table 1.2 gives you an idea of the compensation that you can look forward to when you become a senior financial manager. Table 1.3 directs you to some Internet sites that provide useful information about careers in finance.

Check Point 1.4

Sal and Sally went to business school together 10 years ago. They have just been hired by a midsized corporation that wants to bring in new financial managers. Sal studied finance, with an emphasis on financial markets and institutions. Sally majored in accounting and became a chartered accountant (CA) five years ago. Who is more suited to be treasurer? Controller? Briefly explain.

1.4   GOALS OF THE CORPORATION

SHAREHOLDERS WANT MANAGERS TO MAXIMIZE MARKET VALUE

For small firms, shareholders and management may be one and the same. But for large companies, separation of ownership and management is a practical necessity. For example, BCE has over 900 million outstanding shares, which are owned by some large institutional investors and thousands of small shareholders. There is no way that these shareholders can be actively involved in management; it would be like trying to run the City of Toronto by town meetings. Authority has to be delegated.

TABLE 1.2
Representative salaries for senior jobs in finance

Career	Annual Salary
Banking, large-size chartered bank[a]	
Chief executive officer	$1,080,874 + bonus
President	646,923 + bonus
Vice president, wealth management	375,000 + bonus
Corporate Finance, large-size company[b]	
Chief financial officer	$239,000
Vice president, finance	195,000
Corporate controller	144,750
Assistant controller	110,000
Investment banking	
Chief executive officer[a]	$302,000 + bonus
Managing director, finance[a]	260,000 + bonus
Financial analyst, manager[b]	88,750
Money management[a]	
Chief financial officer	$306,250 + bonus
Senior vice president, funds division	225,000 + bonus
Insurance[a]	
Chief investment officer	$330,000 + bonus
Chief financial officer	300,000 + bonus

Sources: a. Management proxy information circulars from **www.sedar.com**.
    b. *Robert Half Finance and Accounting/Accountemps Salary Guide 2004*, pp. 12–13. (The amounts represent maximums reported.)

TABLE 1.3
Internet sites for careers in finance

Site	URL	Comment
Canadian Careers	www.canadiancareers.com	This site provides a collection of resources by occupation, occupational profiles, and Canadian career planning and occupational links. Information on Canadian labour market trends is also provided.
Canada WorkinfoNET	www.workinfonet.ca	This is a good source of career, education, and labour market information for Canadians. Links to provincial and regional information resources are also provided.
Human Resources and Skills Development Canada (HRSDC)	www.hrsdc.gc.ca/en/home.shtml	This federal government site provides occupation descriptions, salary and wage information, employment prospects, and access to related publications. You can access the HRSDC site by province by clicking on the province's name under the category titled "Services Where You Live."
The Career Organization	www.careers.org	This site provides exhaustive links to employment and university resources available in the United States and Canada. This site also gives a detailed list of financial services and organizations in the United States and Canada, and offers links to financial company sites.
University of British Columbia Library	http://toby.library.ubc.ca/subjects/subjpage2.cfm?id=31	This site provides a collection of Web links to various compensation, salary, and wage information resources.
University of Waterloo	www.adm.uwaterloo.ca/infocecs	This Web site provides comprehensive student and employer manuals under the co-operative and career-related services program of the university.

How can shareholders decide how to delegate decision making when they all have different tastes, wealth, time horizons, and personal opportunities? Delegation can work only if the shareholders have a common objective. Fortunately there is a natural financial objective on which almost all shareholders can agree: this is to maximize the current value of their investment.

A smart and effective financial manager makes decisions that increase the current value of the company's shares and the wealth of its shareholders. That increased wealth can then be put to whatever purposes the shareholders want. They can give their money to charity or spend it in glitzy nightclubs; they can save it or spend it now. Whatever their personal tastes or objectives, they can all do more when their shares are worth more.

Sometimes you hear managers speak as if the corporation has other goals. For example, they may say that their job is to "maximize profits." That sounds reasonable. After all, don't shareholders want their company to be profitable? But taken literally, profit maximization is not a well-defined corporate objective. Here are three reasons:

1. "Maximizing profits" leaves open the question of "which year's profits?" The company may be able to increase current profits by cutting back on maintenance or staff training, but shareholders may not welcome this if profits are damaged in future years.
2. A company may be able to increase future profits by cutting this year's dividend and investing the freed-up cash in the firm. That is not in the shareholders' best interests if the company earns only a very low rate of return on the extra investment.
3. Different accountants may calculate profits in different ways. So a decision that improves profits using one set of accounting rules may reduce them using another.

In a free economy a firm is unlikely to survive if it pursues goals that reduce the firm's value. Suppose, for example, that a firm's only goal is to increase its market share. It aggressively reduces prices to capture new customers, even when the price discounts cause continuing losses. What would happen to such a firm? As losses mount, it will find it more and more difficult to borrow money, and it may not even have sufficient profits to repay existing debts. Sooner or later, however, outside investors would see an opportunity for easy money. They could offer to buy the firm from its current shareholders and, once they have tossed out existing management, increase the firm's value by changing its policies. They would profit by the difference between the price paid for the firm and the higher value it would have under new management. Managers who pursue goals that destroy value often land in early retirement.

> The natural financial objective of the corporation is to maximize current market value. Managers who consistently ignore this objective are likely to be replaced.

ETHICS AND MANAGEMENT OBJECTIVES

Crime Does Not Pay

For a public company, maximizing current market value means maximizing today's stock price. (The firm's market value is the total amount that investors are willing to pay for all of its shares.) Does that objective justify pumping up stock price by fraud or deception? Of course not. But there will be occasional bad apples in the barrel, companies that attempt to increase market value in unethical ways.

The years since 2001 have revealed an unusual number of bad apples. For example, telecom giant WorldCom admitted that it failed to report $3.8 billion (US) of operating expenses. (The expenses were classified as investments, contrary to the rules of accounting.) Thus WorldCom's income was overstated by $3.8 million (US). In the meantime, WorldCom had run up $41 billion (US) of debt. When the company's true profitability was discovered, it was bankrupt within a month—the largest U.S. bankruptcy ever.

The second-largest bankruptcy was Enron, the energy trading and investment company. In late 2001 it announced over $1.7 billion (US) in losses that had previously been concealed in "special purpose entities" (SPEs). We need not delve into SPEs here, except to say that the company broke basic rules of accounting and that one of Enron's top financial executives allegedly used SPEs to pocket millions at the expense of Enron and its shareholders. The bad news came out all at once in October and November 2001, and Enron was bankrupt by year-end.

In 2003, Italian food giant Parmalat filed for bankruptcy protection after it was revealed that the company had manipulated its financial statements to conceal a deficit of 10 billion euros (about $16.4 billion). Canadian corporations were not immune from this problem either. Nortel Networks, once hailed as an icon of high technology, released revised financial statements in early 2005 that effectively reduced its 2003 profit from $732 million (US) to $434 million (US). Executives of the company, who had received bonuses based on the faulty accounting of higher profits, would now have to repay $8.6 million (US).

We suspect that WorldCom, Enron, and Parmalat's accounting misdeeds were in part a desperate attempt to stave off bankruptcy. In the end these misdeeds were the proximate cause of bankruptcy. Crime, fraud, and deceit do not pay.

The Ethics of Maximizing Value

Let us shift the focus back to the great majority of financial managers, who are honest and conscientious. Some idealists say that these managers should not be obliged to act in the selfish interests of their stockholders. Some realists argue that, regardless of what managers ought to do, they in fact look after themselves rather than their shareholders.

Let us respond to the idealists first. Does maximizing value mean that managers must act as greedy mercenaries riding roughshod over the weak and helpless? No, in most instances there is little conflict between doing well (maximizing value) and doing good.

The first step in doing well is doing good by your customers. Here is how Adam Smith put the case in 1776:

> It is not from the benevolence of the butcher, the brewer, or the baker, that we expect our dinner, but from their regard to their own interest. We address ourselves, not to their humanity but to their self-love, and never talk to them of our own necessities but of their advantages.[9]

By striving to enrich themselves and their shareholders, businesspeople have to provide their customers with the products and services they truly desire.

Of course, ethical issues do arise in business as in other walks of life. When the stakes are high, competition is intense, and a deadline is looming, it's easy for financial managers to blunder, and not to inquire as deeply as they should about the legality or morality of their actions.

Written rules and laws can help only so much. In business, as in other day-to-day affairs, there are also unwritten rules of behaviour. These work because everyone knows that such rules are in the general interest. But they are reinforced because good managers know that their firm's reputation is one of its most important assets and therefore playing fair and keeping one's word are simply good business practices. Thus huge financial deals are regularly completed on a handshake and each side knows that the other will not renege later if things turn sour. For example, the motto of the London Stock Exchange is "My word is my bond."

Reputation is particularly important in financial management. If you buy a well-known brand in a store, you can be fairly sure what you are getting. But in financial transactions the other party may have more information than you and it is less easy to be sure of the quality of what you are buying. The reaction of honest financial firms is to build long-term relationships with their customers and establish a name for fair dealing and financial integrity. Major banks and securities firms protect their reputations by emphasizing their long history and their responsible behaviour when seeking new customers. When something happens to undermine that reputation the costs can be enormous.

---

[9] Adam Smith, *An Inquiry into the Nature and Causes of the Wealth of Nations* (New York: Random House, 1937; first published 1776), p. 14.

Consider the scandal that engulfed Canadian Imperial Bank of Commerce (CIBC) after the U.S. Securities and Exchange Commission (SEC) began investigating the bank's complex financial dealings with Enron corporation. The bank was recently hit by the SEC with a $80 million (US) penalty for enabling Enron to mislead investors by hiding its borrowings as asset sales. These "disguised loans" enabled Enron to increase its reported earnings by $1 billion and avoid disclosing more than $2.6 billion in debt. Two former CIBC executives also agreed to pay the SEC $623,000 (US) in penalties. The bank avoided prosecution by agreeing to demands by U.S. and Canadian financial regulators to discontinue the types of structured finance transactions it had engaged in with Enron, and to submit to more scrutiny. Before long, the bank became embroiled in another scandal involving illegal trading of mutual funds in the United States when one of its employees was indicted by a U.S. grand jury. Although the bank has since launched a rigorous review of its corporate governance procedures and practices, its reputation has been damaged. The bank's credit rating has been downgraded, and a number of shareholder lawsuits have been filed against it. The bank is seeking to maintain its reputation and credibility with investors by taking strict steps to prevent unethical behaviour by its employees in the future.

A more dramatic and much more costly case is the Salomon Brothers 1991 bidding scandal in the United States.[10] A Salomon trader tried to evade rules limiting its participation in auctions of U.S. Treasury bonds by submitting bids in the names of the company's customers without the customers' knowledge. When this was discovered, Salomon settled the case by paying almost $200 million (US) in fines and establishing a $100 million (US) fund for payments of claims from civil lawsuits. Yet the value of Salomon Brothers stock fell by far more than $300 million. In fact, the price dropped by about a third, representing a $1.5 billion (US) decline in market value.

Why did the value of Salomon drop so dramatically? Largely because investors were worried that the firm would lose business from customers who now distrusted the company. In these examples, the damage to CIBC's and Salomon's reputations was far greater than the explicit costs of the scandals, and hundreds or thousands of times as costly as the potential gains the firms could have reaped from the illegal trades.

SEE BOX P. 16 ▶

It is not always easy to know what is ethical behaviour, and there can be many grey areas. For example, should the firm be prepared to do business with a corrupt or repressive government? Should it employ child labour in countries where that is the norm? The nearby Finance in Action box presents several simple situations that call for an ethically based decision, along with survey responses to the proper course of action in each circumstance. Compare your decisions with those of the general public.

✓ **Check Point 1.5**

Without knowing anything about the personal ethics of the owners, which company would you trust more to keep its word in a business deal?

a. Harry's Hardware has been in business for 50 years. Harry's grandchildren, now almost adults, plan to take over and operate the business. Hardware stores require considerable investment in customer relations to become established.

b. Victor's Videos just opened for business. It rents a storefront in a strip mall and has financed its inventory with a bank loan. Victor has little of his own money invested in the business. Video shops usually command little customer loyalty.

DO MANAGERS REALLY MAXIMIZE FIRM VALUE?

Owner-managers have no conflicts of interest in their management of the business. They work for themselves, reaping the rewards of good work and suffering the penalties of bad work. Their *personal* well-being is tied to the value of the firm.

---

[10] This discussion is based on Clifford W. Smith, Jr., "Economics and Ethics: The Case of Salomon Brothers," *Journal of Applied Corporate Finance*, 5 (Summer 1992), pp. 23–28.

What constitutes *fair* behaviour by companies? One survey asked a number of individuals to state whether they regarded a particular action as acceptable or unfair. Before we tell you how they responded, think how you would rate each of the following actions:

1a. A small photocopying shop has one employee who has worked in the shop for 6 months and earns $9 per hour. Business continues to be satisfactory, but a factory in the area has closed and unemployment has increased. Other small shops in the area have now hired reliable workers at $7 an hour to perform jobs similar to those done by the photocopying shop employee. The owner of the photocopying shop reduces the employee's wage to $7.

1b. Now suppose that the shop does not reduce the employee's wage but she leaves. The owner decides to pay a replacement $7 an hour.

2. A house painter employs two assistants and pays them $9 per hour. The painter decides to quit house painting and go into the business of providing landscape services, where the going wage is lower. He reduces the workers' wages to $7 per hour for the landscaping work.

3a. A small company employs several workers and has been paying them average wages. There is severe unemployment in the area and the company could easily replace its current employees with good workers at a lower wage. The company has been making money. The owners reduce the current workers' wages by 5 percent.

3b. Now suppose instead that the company has been losing money and the owners reduce wages by 5 percent.

4. A grocery store has several months' supply of peanut butter in stock on shelves in the storeroom. The owner hears that the wholesale price of peanut butter has increased and immediately raises the price on the current stock of peanut butter.

5. A hardware store has been selling snow shovels for $15. The morning after a large snowstorm, the store raises the price to $20.

6. A store has been sold out of popular Beanie Baby dolls for a month. A week before Christmas a single doll is discovered in a storeroom. The managers know that many customers would like to buy the doll. They announce over the store's public address system that the doll will be sold by auction to the customer who offers to pay the most.

Now compare your responses with the responses of a random sample of individuals:

	Percent Rating the Action As	
Action	**Acceptable**	**Unfair**
1a	17	83
1b	73	27
2	63	37
3a	23	77
3b	68	32
4	21	79
5	18	82
6	26	74

Source: Adapted from D. Kahneman, J. L. Knetsch, and R. Thaler, "Fairness as a Constraint on Profit Seeking: Entitlements in the Market," *American Economic Review* 76 (September 1986), pp. 728–741. Reprinted by permission of American Economic Association and the authors.

In most large companies the managers are not the owners and they might be tempted to act in ways that are not in the best interests of the owners. For example, they might buy luxurious corporate jets for their travel, or overindulge in expense-account dinners. They might shy away from attractive but risky projects because they are worried more about the safety of their jobs than the potential for superior profits. They might engage in empire building, adding unnecessary capacity or employees. Such problems can arise because the managers of the firm, who are hired as agents of the owners, may have their own axes to grind. Therefore these conflicts are called **agency problems**.

agency problems   Conflict of interest between the firm's owners and managers.

Think of the company's net revenue as a pie that is divided among a number of claimants. These include the management and the work force as well as the lenders and shareholders who put up the money to establish and maintain the business. The government is a claimant, too, since it gets to tax the profits of the enterprise. It is common to hear these claimants called **stakeholders** in the firm. Each has a stake in the firm and their interests may not coincide.

stakeholder   Anyone with a financial interest in the firm.

All these stakeholders are bound together in a complex web of contracts and understandings. For example, when banks lend money to the firm, they insist on a formal contract stating the rate of interest and repayment dates, perhaps placing restrictions on dividends or additional borrowing. Similarly, large companies have carefully worked out personnel policies that establish employees' rights and responsibilities. But you can't devise written rules to cover every possible future event. So the written contracts are supplemented by understandings. For example, managers understand that in return for a fat salary they are expected to work hard and not spend the firm's money on unwarranted personal luxuries.

What enforces these understandings? Is it realistic to expect managers always to act on behalf of the shareholders? The shareholders can't spend their lives watching through binoculars to check that managers are not shirking or dissipating company funds on the latest executive jet. Companies do act on allegations of impropriety by senior managers. Recently, Chicago-based Hollinger International filed a $1.25 billion lawsuit against Conrad Black, its former chairman and CEO, and David Radler, former chief operating officer. The lawsuit alleges that Lord Black and others used Hollinger "as a cash cow to be milked of every possible drop of cash" and improperly took millions of dollars in management fees, non-competition payments, and bonuses. According to the lawsuit, the company paid $90,000 to refurbish a Rolls-Royce limousine and $4.7 million to $6.5 million a year for two corporate jets, which were often used for personal purposes by the senior executives.[11]

A closer look reveals several arrangements that help to ensure that the shareholders and managers are working toward common goals.

Compensation Plans

Managers are spurred on by incentive schemes that provide big returns if shareholders gain but are valueless if they do not. For example, when Michael Eisner was hired as CEO by the Walt Disney Company, his compensation package had three main components: a base annual salary of $750,000 (US); an annual bonus of 2 percent of Disney's net income above a threshold of "normal" profitability; and a 10-year option that allowed him to purchase 2 million shares of stock for $14 (US) per share, which was about the price of Disney stock at the time. Those options would be worthless if Disney's shares were selling for below $14 but highly valuable if the shares were worth more. This gave Eisner a huge personal stake in the success of the firm.

As it turned out, by the end of Eisner's six-year contract the value of Disney shares had increased by $12 billion, more than sixfold. Eisner's compensation over the period was $190 million (US).[12] Was he overpaid? We don't know (and we suspect nobody else knows) how much Disney's success was due to Michael Eisner or how hard Eisner would have worked with a different compensation scheme.

SEE BOX P. 18 ▶

SEE BOX P. 19 ▶

Of course, as the nearby Finance in Action box shows, a CEO can appear to be overpaid if the company is not performing as well as it used to and its share price is down. While stock option plans have recently been criticized for being too favourable to managers (see nearby Finance in Action box), they are still used widely by companies in order to provide managers with a strong financial incentive to increase firm value. Table 1.4 lists some of Canada's top-earning CEOs and their company's performance in 2002. Notice the importance of short-term bonuses as well as long-term incentives, including stock options, in the total compensation package. Notice that if a company and the stock markets generally have not done well in a particular year, the CEO may not have any earnings from stock options. This appears to have been the case for J.R. Shaw of Shaw Communications.

Of course, if employee compensation plans are not designed properly, they can create incentives for errant behaviour by management. In 2004, Nortel Networks admitted that accounting mistakes would halve its reported profits for 2003 and would lead to a second restatement of the company's earnings since 2001. It was later revealed that the company's controversial "return to profitability" bonus plan, which allowed many employees to receive large payouts based on results of one fiscal quarter, may have given senior management an incentive to manipulate profits. Millions of dollars were paid out to executives under this bonus program including over $2 million to its CEO. The company's board of directors sought to take corrective action by firing its CEO and two other top officials. As we shall see next, corporate boards often do act to replace managers who are perceived not to have acted in the best interest of shareholders.

---

[11] See, for instance, Richard Blackwell, "Hollinger Paid Expenses: Lawsuit," *The Globe and Mail*, May 11, 2004.

[12] This discussion is based on Stephen F. O'Byrne, "What Pay for Performance Looks Like: The Case of Michael Eisner," *Journal of Applied Corporate Finance* 5 (Summer 1992), pp. 135–136.

Are CEOs of These Companies Overpaid?

Bombardier Inc.

Lost $615 million in fiscal 2003, ended Jan. 31, 2003.

Chairman Laurent Beaudoin took home $25 million in fiscal 2003. Although Bombardier posted the largest loss of any S&P/TSX firm in fiscal 2003—and saw its share price fall 65 percent during the fiscal year—Mr. Beaudoin cashed out stock options for a gain of $23.8 million. Bombardier said the options would have expired in 2003 if Mr. Beaudoin had not exercised them.

BCE Emergis Inc.

Lost $96.8 million in 2003.

CEO Tony Gaffney received a bonus of $143,174.

In a year when profits climbed more than 107 percent on average for S&P/TSX companies, BCE Emergis posted a loss of $96.8 million and saw its share price fall 26 percent. The company said Mr. Gaffney, who became CEO last May, received a bonus because the company met its profit target and exceeded the customer satisfaction target.

Potash Corp. of Saskatchewan

Lost $126 million (U.S.) in 2003.

CEO William Doyle took home $5.4 million (Cdn).

Although Potash Corp. plunged into red ink in 2003, Mr. Doyle saw his annual bonus climb 12 percent in 2002. He also made $3.4 million from exercising stock options. The company said its top managers, including Mr. Doyle, agreed to cut their salaries by 10 percent as of July 1, 2003, as part of cost-savings measures undertaken throughout the company. But with a higher bonus and stock option gains, Mr. Doyle's belt-tightening couldn't have hurt too much.

Royal Group Technologies Ltd.

Lost $58.2 million in fiscal 2003, ended Sept. 30.

CEO Douglas Dunsmuir received a bonus of $780,250.

Royal Group executives agreed to cut their whopping multimillion-dollar bonuses after shareholders protested their huge 2002 compensation. On the other hand, executives still received large bonuses—and got huge boosts to their base salaries—even though their company posted a $58 million loss for 2003 and its share price fell 12 percent. Chairman Vic De Zen and Mr. Dunsmuir both received bonuses of $780,250 for the year, on top of base salaries of $900,000.

Empire Co. Ltd.

Earned $154 million in fiscal 2003, ended April 30.

CEO Paul Sobey earned $1.2 million.

The holding company, which controls grocery chain Sobeys Inc., saw its profit dip 21 percent in 2003, while its share price fell 17 percent. Mr. Sobey's base salary climbed 3.6 percent and he was paid a bonus of $340,261, down from $500,000 in 2002. The company said he earned his bonus by exceeding established targets. Meanwhile, Sobeys' CEO Bill McEwan took home a total of $2.2 million last year, including an extra one-time incentive bonus paid to all executive officers of Sobeys for meeting earnings per share growth targets. Sobeys saw profit fall 15 percent in fiscal 2003, while its share price slid 17 percent.

Source: Excerpt from *The Globe and Mail*, "Are They Worth It?" April 30, 2004. http://theglobeandmail.com. Reprinted with permission from *The Globe and Mail*.

The Board of Directors

Boards of directors are sometimes portrayed as passive supporters of top management. But when company performance starts to slide, and managers don't offer a credible recovery plan, boards do act. In recent years, the chief executives of Hollinger International, Nortel Networks, Lucent, Sunbeam, Ford, and Apple Computer all were forced out. The nearby Finance in Action box points out that boards in Europe recently have become more aggressive in their willingness to replace underperforming managers.

SEE BOX P. 20

If shareholders believe that the corporation is underperforming and that the board of directors is not sufficiently aggressive in holding the managers to task, they can try to replace the board in the next election. The dissident shareholders will attempt to convince other shareholders to vote for their slate of candidates to the board. If they succeed, a new board will be elected, and it can replace the current management team.

Conrad Black had to leave his position as CEO of Hollinger International following revelations of the payment of millions of dollars in so-called "non-compete" fees to related companies and executives allegedly made without the approval of the board of directors. A shareholder had requested the company's board to take action on such fees.

Takeovers

Poorly performing companies are also more likely to be taken over by another firm. After the takeover, the old management team may find itself out on the street. In recent years, the CEOs of Canadian Airlines and Chapters were replaced following such takeovers. Recently, when the

Pay CEOs with Stock Options or Stocks?

Pay for performance at many companies means doling out stock options on the principle that the interests of executives will then be aligned with shareholders.

Critics argue that rather than align the interests of CEOs with shareholders, stock options tend to have the opposite effect. Richard Rooney, president of Toronto-based Burgundy Asset Management Ltd., argues, "The worst thing about it is the behavioural aspects stock options encourage. Those differences in behaviour make you too interested in short-term stock price performance rather than corporate performance."

Executives face few of the risks their shareholders do. Suppose a CEO's options are worthless at the end of the grant period due to a steady decline in the share price over a number of years. The CEO

has still earned an annual salary and bonus, but moreover, the CEO has suffered no loss in net worth. The same can't be said for the shareholders who have suffered a real decline in their portfolios.

Options don't cost anything to the bottom line so companies have little to lose in the short term by handing them out like candy.

In the long term, the more stock options are exercised, the further total shareholdings are diluted—lowering such measures as earnings per share and stock prices. Rooney suggests the only way for CEOs to truly have their interests tied to those of shareholders is for them to own shares, not options.

Source: Excerpted from *Financial Post*, "Shareholders No Longer Whisper about CEO's Pay," May 22, 2001, C5.

share price of beleaguered Nortel Networks plummeted after the company admitted to accounting mistakes and fired its CEO, investment bankers reportedly tried to put together a hostile takeover bid for the company. We discuss takeovers in Chapter 23.

Specialist Monitoring

Finally, managers are subject to the scrutiny of specialists. Their actions are monitored by the security analysts who advise investors to buy, hold, or sell the company's shares. Managers are also reviewed by banks, which keep an eagle eye on the progress of firms receiving their loans.

TABLE 1.4

Earnings[1] of Top Executives and Company Performance in 2002

Executive & Company	Base Salary[a]	Bonus[a]	Long-Term Incentives[2a]	Total Direct Compensation[a]	Revenue in Millions[b]	Earnings per Share[b]
Frank Stronach, Chair, Magna International Inc.	$314	0	$51,823	$52,137	(US) $13,044	(US) 5.83
Travis Engen, Pres. & CEO, Alcan Inc.	$1,924	$2,520	$13,011	$17,456	(US) $12,553	(US) 1.15
Paul Tellier, Pres. & CEO, Canadian National Railway Co.	$1,727	$629	$9,904	$12,261	$6,173	2.87
Gwyn Morgan, Pres.& CEO, EnCana Corp.	$1,182	$2,500	$8,403	$12,085	$11,031	2.92
Jean Monty, Former Chair & CEO, BCE Inc.	$692	$1,336	$9,770	$11,798	$19,809	3.96
Dominic D'Alessandro, Pres. & CEO, Manulife Financial Corp.	$1,200	$2,400	$6,708	$10,308	$16,532	2.90
Peter Godsoe, Pres. & CEO, Bank of Nova Scotia	$1,350	$1,350	$7,384	$10,084	$18,310	3.36
Richard Harrington, Pres. & CEO, Thomson Corp.	$1,932	$2,659	$4,256	$8,846		
Donald Stewart, Chair & CEO, Sun Life Financial Services	$850	$1,500	$5,107	$7,457	$23,101	1.84
JR Shaw, Exec. Chair, Shaw Communications	$900	$6,327	0	$7,227	$1,906	−1.43
Rick George, Pres. & CEO, Suncor Energy Inc.	$810	$850	$5,543	$7,202	$4,913	1.64
Frank Dunn, Pres. & CEO, Nortel Networks Corp.	$1,296	0	$4,751	$6,047	(US) 10,621	(US) −0.93

1 The amounts for base salary, bonus, long-term incentives, and total direct compensation are in thousands of dollars (rounded off).
2 The value of long-term incentives includes the estimated value of stock options as well as the present value of other long-term awards granted during the period.
Sources: a. "50 Top-Paid Executives." Canada's Power Book: Special 20th Annual Issue, Report on Business, *The Globe and Mail* (July 2003), p. 147.
     b. "Ranking by Profits." Canada's Power Book: Special 20th Annual Issue, Report on Business, *The Globe and Mail* (July 2003), pp. 80–109.
Reprinted with permission from *The Globe and Mail*.

Corporate Goodbyes in Europe

The European corporate chief—long protected by cozy politicians, boardroom cronies and compliant shareholders—is suddenly an endangered species.

The ouster this week of Ron Sommer as the chief executive of Deutsche Telekom is the strongest evidence yet that the web of ties that once shielded European bosses from the wrath of the market is fraying.

From Percy N. Barnevik, the patrician former chairman of ABB Ltd., to Jean-Marie Messier, the flashy would-be mogul of Vivendi Universal, the heads of European companies are being ushered out of their jobs at a rate, and for reasons, that would have been unthinkable a few years ago.

"The Europeans are, for good or ill, moving faster to remove people," said Jeffrey Sonnenfeld, an associate dean of the Yale School of Management and an expert on the role of the chief executive.

Mr. Sommer, the charismatic, Israeli-born salesman, [was] appointed by the former German chancellor, Helmut Kohl, in 1966 to transform Deutsche Telekom from a sheltered state monopoly into a publicly traded company with shareholders around the world.

Mr. Sommer enjoyed the support of Mr. Kohl's successor, Gerhard Schröder, even while piling up $67 million in debt and presiding over the decimation of the company's stock, the most widely held in Germany.

Then, two weeks ago, Deutsche Telekom's shrinking share price became a political issue in Germany's coming federal elections, when Mr. Schröder's conservative opponent, Edmund Stoiber, seized on it to illustrate what he sees as the chancellor's shaky economic policies.

With a swiftness that Jacques A. Nasser, late of Ford Motor, or Richard A. McGinn, former chief of Lucent Technologies, could appreciate, Mr. Sommer's support withered, and he was forced to step down.

"People said, 'Mr. Chancellor, you must do something because the decline in Telekom's share price is hurting the small investor in Germany,'" said Boris Beohm, a fund manager at Nordinvest, an asset management firm in Hamburg that owns 1.3 million shares in the company.

Nearly 13 million Germans, or about 20 percent of the population, now own stocks. That compares with 13 percent in 1999 and only 9 percent in 1997. Though Germany trails the United States, where about half of all adults own stock, shareholders have become a powerful constituency.

With the rise of shareholders has come the rise of shareholder activists, big and small, who think nothing of filing motions against chief executives or publicly scolding them for laggard results.

Shareholders also played an important, if more behind-the-scenes, role in ousting Mr. Messier at Vivendi, the transatlantic entertainment company. The Bronfman family, the largest single shareholder in Vivendi, tried to mobilize opposition to Mr. Messier on the board, which is dominated by French executives.

Initially, the French directors seemed determined to protect their countryman. But then a respected French industrialist, Claude Bébéar, chairman of the giant insurer AXA, publicly criticized Mr. Messier and lobbied against him with French directors. Within days of surviving a no-confidence vote by the board, Mr. Messier was negotiating the details of his severance package.

Source: Condensed from M. Lander, "Politics Hastens the Corporate Goodbye in Europe," *New York Times*, July 18, 2002, pp. W1, W7.

We do not want to leave the impression that corporate life is a series of squabbles and endless micromanagement. It isn't, because practical corporate finance has evolved to reconcile personal and corporate interests—to keep everyone working together to increase the value of the whole pie, not merely the size of each person's slice.

> The agency problem is mitigated in practice through several devices: compensation plans that tie the fortune of the manager to the fortunes of the firm; monitoring by lenders, stock market analysts, and investors; and ultimately, the threat that poor performance will result in the removal of the manager.

Check Point 1.6 Corporations are now required to publish the amount and form of compensation (e.g., stock options versus salary versus performance bonuses) received by their top executives. Of what use would that information be to a potential investor in the firm?

Check Point 1.7 What is an agency problem? Give two or three examples of decisions by managers that lead to agency costs.

1.5   TOPICS COVERED IN THIS BOOK

This book covers investment decisions first, then financing decisions, and then a variety of planning issues that require understanding of both investments and financing. But first there are two further introductory chapters that should be helpful to readers making a first aquaintance with financial management. Chapter 2 is an overview of financial markets and institutions. Chapter 3 reviews the basic concepts of accounting.

In Parts Two and Three we look at different aspects of the investment decision. The first is the problem of how to value assets, and the second is the link between risk and value. Our discussion of these topics occupies Chapters 4 through 12.

Nine chapters devoted to the simple problem of finding real assets that are worth more than they cost may seem excessive, but that problem is not so simple in practice. We will require a theory of how long-lived, risky assets are valued, and that requirement will lead us to basic questions about capital markets. For example:

- How are corporate bonds and stocks valued in capital markets?
- What risks are borne by investors in corporate securities? How can these risks be measured?
- What compensation do investors demand for bearing risk?
- What rate of return can investors in common stocks reasonably expect to receive?
- Do stock prices accurately reflect the underlying value of the firm?

Intelligent capital budgeting and financing decisions require answers to these and other questions about how capital markets work.

Financing decisions occupy Parts Four and Five. The two chapters in Part Four describe the kinds of securities corporations use to raise money and explain how and when they are issued. These chapters also describe the sources of financing of new and small business ventures.

Part Five continues the analysis of the financing decision, covering dividend policy and debt policy. We will also describe what happens when firms find themselves in financial distress because of poor operating performance, excessive borrowing, or both.

Part Six covers financial planning. Decisions about investment, dividend policy, debt policy, and other financial issues cannot be reached independently. They have to add up to a sensible overall financial plan for the firm, one that increases the value of the shareholders' investment yet still retains enough flexibility for the firm to avoid financial distress and pursue unexpected new opportunities.

Part Seven is devoted to decisions about the firm's short-term assets and liabilities. We discuss channels for short-term borrowing or investment, management of liquid assets (cash and marketable securities), and management of accounts receivable (money lent by the firm to its customers) and inventories.

Part Eight covers four important problems that require decisions about both investment and financing. First, we discuss the concept of leasing and the analysis of leasing decisions. Next, we look at mergers and acquisitions. Then we consider international financial management. All the financial problems of doing business at home are present overseas, but the international financial manager faces the additional complications created by multiple currencies, different tax systems, and special regulations imposed by foreign institutions and governments. Finally, we look at risk management and the specialized securities, including futures and options, that managers can use to hedge or lay off risks.

SNIPPETS OF HISTORY

SEE BOX PP. 23–24

Now let's lighten up a little. In this book we will describe how financial decisions are made today. But financial markets also have an interesting history. Look at the nearby Finance in Action box, which lays out bits of this history, starting in prehistoric times, when the growth of bacteria anticipated the mathematics of compound interest, and continuing nearly to the present. We have keyed each of these episodes to the chapter of the book that discusses it.

1.6   SUMMARY

1. What are the advantages and disadvantages of the most common forms of business organization? Which forms are most suitable to different types of businesses?

Businesses may be organized as **sole proprietorships**, **partnerships**, or **corporations**. A corporation is legally distinct from its owners. Therefore, the shareholders who own a corporation enjoy **limited liability** for its obligations. Ownership and management of corporations are usually separate, which means that the firm's operations need not be disrupted by changes in ownership. On the other hand, corporations are subject to double taxation. Large public companies are always corporations.

2. What are the two major decisions made by financial managers?

Financial management can be broken down into (1) the investment, or **capital budgeting**, **decision** and (2) the **financing decision**. The firm has to decide (1) how much to invest and which real assets to invest in and (2) how to raise the necessary cash.

3. What does "real asset" mean? What is a "financial asset"?

Real assets include all assets used in the production or sale of the firms' products or services. Real assets can be tangible (plant and equipment, for example) or intangible (patents or trademarks, for example). Financial assets are securities (such as shares) sold by the firm to raise money, and represent claims on the firm's real assets and the cash generated by those assets.

4. Who is the financial manager?

Almost all managers are involved to some degree in investment decisions, but some managers specialize in finance, for example, the treasurer, controller, and CFO.

5. Why does it make sense for corporations to maximize their market value?

Value maximization is the natural financial goal of the firm. Maximizing value maximizes the wealth of the firm's owners, its shareholders. Shareholders can invest or consume that wealth as they wish.

6. Is value maximization ethical?

Modern finance does not condone attempts to pump up stock price by unethical means. But there need be no conflict between ethics and value maximization. The surest route to maximum value starts with products and services that satisfy customers. A good reputation with customers, employees, and other stakeholders is also important for the firms' long-term profitability and value.

7. How do corporations ensure that managers' and stockholders' interests coincide?

Conflicts of interest between managers and stockholders can lead to agency problems. These problems are kept in check by compensation plans that link the well-being of employees to that of the firm; by monitoring of management by the board of directors, security holders, and creditors; and by the threat of takeover.

Related Web Links

www.careers-in-finance.com Career information

www.wageweb.com Career information and salary data

www.corpgov.net

www.thecorporatelibrary.com Discussion of recent issues regarding the role of directors and management.

www.financewise.com A search engine for finance-related sites

www.forbes.com News about financial management

www.corpmon.com/index.htm The corporate monitoring project dedicated to inducing firms to make good decisions

www.bombardier.com Bombardier

www.nortelnetworks.com Nortel Networks

www.ontarioteachers.com Ontario Teachers' Pension Plan information from Armquest investment counsellors and portfolio managers

www.alcan.com Alcan

www.tsx.ca Toronto Stock Exchange

www.bmo.com Bank of Montreal

www.bankofcanada.ca Bank of Canada

www.theglobeandmail.com

Finance through the Ages

Date unknown *Compound Growth.* Bacteria start to propagate by subdividing. They thereby demonstrate the power of compound growth. (*Chapter 4*)

c. 1800 b.c. *Interest Rates.* In Babylonia, Hammurabi's Code established maximum interest rates on loans. Borrowers often mortgaged their property and sometimes their spouses, but in these cases the lender was obliged to return the spouse in good condition within three years. (*Chapter 4*)

c. 1000 b.c. *Options.* One of the earliest recorded options is described by Aristotle. The philosopher Thales knew by the stars that there would be a great olive harvest, so having a little money, he bought options for the use of olive presses. When the harvest came Thales was able to rent the presses at great profit. Today financial managers need to be able to evaluate options to buy or sell a wide variety of assets. (*Chapter 25*)

15th century *International Banking.* Modern international banking has its origins in the great Florentine banking houses. But the entire European network of the Medici empire employed only 57 people in eight offices. Today the RBC Financial Group has over 60,000 employees and an international network of 99 offices in over 30 countries. (*Chapter 13*)

1650 *Futures.* Futures markets allow companies to protect themselves against fluctuations in commodity prices. During the Tokugawa era in Japan, feudal lords collected rents in the form of rice but often they wished to trade their future rice deliveries. In Canada, the Winnipeg Commodity Exchange started operating in 1887 and established futures markets in wheat, oats, and flaxseed in 1904. (*Chapter 26*)

17th century *Joint Stock Corporations.* Although for a long time investors have combined to be joint owners of an enterprise, the modern corporation with a large number of shareholders originates with the formation in England of the great trading firms like the East India Company (est. 1599). Another early trading firm, Hudson's Bay (est. 1670), still survives and is one of Canada's largest companies. (*Chapter 14*)

17th century *Money.* Through the 17th century until well into the 19th, coins from many countries, such as England, France, Portugal, and Spain, circulated freely in the French and British colonies in North America. Different colonies rated coins differently, sometimes deliberately overrating (overvaluing) or underrating (undervaluing) them relative to others, based on their weight in gold or silver, in order to encourage or discourage their use. In such circumstances, overrated coins drove underrated coins from circulation—an application of Gresham's Law,

"bad money drives out good." A chronic coin shortage encouraged the introduction of paper money. For instance, in 1685, card money was introduced in New France, which initially consisted of playing cards cut to different sizes according to denomination and signed by colonial officials. The first bank notes in Canada denominated in dollars were issued by the Montreal Bank in 1817. A distinctive Canadian currency came into being when the Province of Canada revised the *Currency Act* in 1857, requiring all provincial accounts to be kept in dollars. Silver and bronze coins bearing "Canada" were issued for the first time. Private bank notes were gradually phased out when the Bank of Canada started operations in 1935 and was given the sole right to issue bank notes.[13] (*Chapter 20*)

1720 *New Issue Speculation.* From time to time investors have been tempted by speculative new issues. During the South Sea Bubble in England, one company was launched to develop perpetual motion. Another enterprising individual announced a company "for carrying on an undertaking of great advantage but nobody to know what it is." Within 5 hours he had raised £2000; within 6 hours he was on his way out of the country. (*Chapter 14*)

1792 *Formation of Stock Exchanges.* In North America the New York Stock Exchange (NYSE) was founded in 1792 when a group of brokers met under a buttonwood tree and arranged to trade shares with one another at agreed rates of commission. Today the NYSE is the largest stock exchange in the world, trading on average about a billion shares a day. The Toronto Stock Exchange was established in 1852. Today the Toronto Stock Exchange (TSX) belongs to the TSX Group and, Canada's largest stock exchange. In April 2005, the TSE traded an average of 212 million shares valued at about $3.6 billion each day. (*Chapter 6*)

1929 *Stock Market Crashes.* Common stocks are risky investments. In September 1929, stock prices in the United States reached an all-time high and the economist Irving Fisher forecast that they were at "a permanently high plateau." Some three years later stock prices were almost 90 percent lower and it was to be a quarter of a century before the prices of September 1929 were seen again. Contrary to popular impression, no Wall Street broker jumped out the window. (*Chapter 10*)

1960s *Eurodollar Market.* In the 1950s, the Soviet Union transferred its dollar holdings from the United States to a Russian-owned bank in Paris. This bank was best known by its telex address, EUROBANK, and consequently dollars held outside the United States came to be known as eurodollars. In the 1960s, U.S. taxes and regulation made it much cheaper to borrow and

---

[13] Information for this excerpt was compiled from J. Powell, "A History of the Canadian Dollar" at the Bank of Canada Web site, **www.bankofcanada.ca/en/dollar_book.index**

lend dollars in Europe rather than in the United States and a huge market in eurodollars arose. (*Chapter 13*)

1972 *Financial Futures.* Financial futures allow companies to protect themselves against fluctuations in interest rates, exchange rates, and so on. It is said that they originated from a remark by the economist Milton Friedman that he was unable to profit from his view that sterling was overpriced. The Chicago Mercantile Exchange founded the first financial futures market. Today futures exchanges in the United States trade 200 million contracts a year of financial futures. In Canada, a new market for futures contracts on treasury coupons and long-term government bonds was created in 1979. Canadian financial futures are traded on the Montreal Exchange. (*Chapter 26*)

1986 *Capital Investment Decisions.* The largest investment project undertaken by private companies was the construction of the tunnel under the English Channel. It started in 1986 and was completed in 1994 at a total cost of $15 billion (US). (*Chapter 7*)

1988 *Mergers.* The 1980s saw a wave of takeovers culminating in the $25 billion (US) takeover of RJR Nabisco. Over a period of six weeks, three groups battled for control of the company. As one of the contestants put it, "We were charging through the rice paddies, not stopping for anything and taking no prisoners." The takeover was the largest in history and generated almost $1 billion in fees for the banks and advisers. (*Chapter 23*)

1993 *Inflation.* Financial managers need to recognize the effect of inflation on interest rates and on the profitability of the firm's investments. In the United States inflation has been relatively modest, but some countries have suffered from hyperinflation. In Hungary after World War II the government issued banknotes worth 1000 trillion pengoes. In Yugoslavia in October 1993 prices rose by nearly 2,000 percent and a dollar bought 105 million dinars. (*Chapter 4*)

1780 and 1997 *Inflation-Indexed Debt.* In 1780, Massachusetts paid Revolutionary War soldiers with interest-bearing notes rather than its rapidly eroding currency. Interest and principal payments on the notes were tied to the rate of subsequent inflation. After a 217-year hiatus, the United States Treasury issued 10-year inflation-indexed notes. Many other countries, including Britain and Israel, had done so previously. (*Chapter 4*)

1993 *Controlling Risk.* When a company fails to keep close tabs on the risks being taken by its employees, it can get into serious trouble. This was the fate of Barings, a 220-year-old British bank that counted the queen among its clients. In 1993 it discovered that Nick Leeson, a trader in its Singapore office, had hidden losses of $1.3 billion (US) (£869 million) from unauthorized bets on the Japanese equity market. The losses wiped out Barings and landed Leeson in jail with a six-year sentence. (*Chapter 26*)

1999 *The Euro.* Large corporations do business in many currencies. In 1999 a new currency came into existence when 11 European countries adopted the euro in place of their separate currencies. This was not the first time that different countries have agreed on a common currency. In 1865, France, Belgium, Switzerland, and Italy came together in the Latin Monetary Union, and they were joined by Greece and Romania the following year. Members of the European Monetary Union (EMU) hope the euro will be a longer-lasting success than earlier experiments. (*Chapter 24*)

2002 *The Euro (An Update).* In early 2001, Greece became the 12th country to adopt the euro and join the euro zone. By January 2002, euro notes and coins were in circulation in the 12 countries. More than 90 percent of cash payments in these countries are now carried out in euros. Consumers can still use the respective national currencies, although they are being phased out. (*Chapter 24*).[14]

---

[14] For more information about the euro, you can visit the Web site of the Financial Times at **http://specials.ft.com/euro**

Key Terms

sole proprietor	3	financial assets	6	controller	9
partnership	3	capital budgeting decision	6	chief financial officer	
corporation	3	financing decision	7	(CFO)	9
limited liability	4	capital structure	8	agency problems	16
real assets	6	treasurer	9	stakeholder	16

Questions and Problems

*Answers in Appendix B

BASIC

*1. **Financial Decisions.** Fit each of the following terms into the most appropriate space: *financing, real, stock, investment, executive airplanes, financial, capital budgeting, brand names.*

Companies usually buy ___ assets. These include both tangible assets such as ___ and intangible assets such as ___. In order to pay for these assets, they sell ___ assets such as ___. The decision regarding which assets to buy is usually termed the ___ or ___ decision. The decision regarding how to raise the money is usually termed the ___ decision.

2. **Value Maximization.** Give an example of an action that might increase profits but at the same time reduce stock price.

3. **Corporate Organization.** You may own shares of IBM, but you still can't enter corporate headquarters whenever you feel like it. In what sense then are you an owner of the firm?

4. **Corporate Organization.** What are the advantages and disadvantages of organizing a firm as a proprietorship, partnership, or corporation? In what sense are LLPs or professional corporations *hybrid* forms of business organization?

5. **Corporate Organization.** What do we mean when we say that corporate income is subject to *double taxation*?

6. **Financial Managers.** Which of the following statements more accurately describes the treasurer than the controller?
   a. Likely to be the only financial executive in small firms
   b. Monitors capital expenditures to ensure that they are not misappropriated
   c. Responsible for investing the firm's spare cash
   d. Responsible for arranging any issue of common stock
   e. Responsible for the company's tax affairs

7. **Internet.** Go to Thomson corporation's Web site at **www.thomson.com**. When you click on the caption "About Us," you will be able to get to the pages describing the company's history. Notice that the company's origins were in a sole proprietorship. Can you browse the web and find a large Canadian corporation that had its origins in a partnership?

8. **Standard & Poors.** If you bought this book in Canada or the United States, the text provides you with access to a very powerful database of company information, called Standard & Poor's Market Insight. You have access via the following link (a password is provided in your book cover) to six years of data for 355 companies. The site provides 14 different Excel Analytics Reports including financial statements, ratios (6 years of ratios, actual and charted, with comparisons to the firm's industry), stock performance reports, and much more. Industry information (companies and profile) and company business activity are also reported.

www.mcgrawhill.ca/edumarketinsight

Enter the above link and review the introductions page. Proceed by clicking on the "Continue" icon, then enter your "ID" number, and you are in! Carefully review the "News and Notes" Table of Contents to the right and the profile presented for each area. Take a look at the 355 companies in the database by clicking the "Company" icon at the top of the page, then "Population." Select one company of interest to review. Click on the highlighted link and review the contents available from Market Insight. Look over the reports via the Table of Contents on the right. Throughout the coming chapters we will ask you to review or analyze Market Insight reports.

The "Company Profile" contains recent market valuation information and a link to the company's Web site. The "Financial Highlights" provides current-quarter information on sales, market data, ratios, etc. Click the linked terms, for example, "Employees," and you will be provided a definition of the term, a very useful feature when getting started.

PRACTICE

9. **Real versus Financial Assets.** Which of the following are real assets and which ones are financial?

   *a.　A share of stock
   b.　A personal IOU
   c.　A trademark
   *d.　A truck

   e.　Undeveloped land
   *f.　The balance in the firm's chequing account
   *g.　An experienced and hardworking sales force
   h.　A bank loan agreement

10. **The Financial Manager.** Give two examples of capital budgeting decisions and financing decisions.

11. **Goals of the Firm.** You may have heard big business criticized for focusing on short-term performance at the expense of long-term results. Explain why a firm that strives to maximize stock price should be less subject to an overemphasis on short-term results than one that maximizes profits.

12. **Goals of the Firm.** We claim that the goal of the firm is to maximize stock price. Are the following actions necessarily consistent with that goal?
    a.　The firm donates $3 million to the local art museum.
    b.　The firm reduces its dividend payment, choosing to reinvest more of earnings in the business.
    c.　The firm buys a corporate jet for its executives.

13. **Goals of the Firm.** Explain why each of the following may not be appropriate corporate goals:
    a.　Increase market share
    b.　Minimize costs
    c.　Underprice any competitors
    d.　Expand profits

*14. **Agency Issues.** Sometimes lawyers work on a contingency basis. They collect a percentage of their client's settlement instead of receiving a fixed fee. Why might clients prefer this arrangement? Would this sort of arrangement be more appropriate for clients who use lawyers regularly or infrequently?

15. **Reputation.** As you drive down a deserted highway you are overcome with a sudden desire for a hamburger. Fortunately, just ahead are two hamburger outlets; one is owned by a national brand, the other appears to be owned by "Joe." Which outlet has the greater incentive to serve you cat meat? Why?

*16. **Agency Problems.** If agency problems can be mitigated by tying the manager's compensation to the fortunes of the firm, why don't firms compensate managers *exclusively* with shares in the firm?

*17. **Agency Problems.** Many firms have devised defences that make it much more costly or difficult for other firms to take them over. How might such takeover defences affect the firm's agency problems? Are managers of firms with formidable takeover defences more or less likely to act in the firm's interests rather than their own?

18. **Agency Issues.** One of the "Finance through the Ages" episodes that we cite on pages 23–24 is the 1993 collapse of Barings Bank when one of its traders lost $1.3 billion (US). Traders are compensated in large part according to their trading profits. How might this practice have contributed to an agency problem?

19. **Agency Issues.** Discuss which of the following forms of compensation is most likely to align the interests of managers and shareholders:

    a.   A fixed salary

    b.   A salary linked to company profits

    c.   A salary that is paid partly in the form of the company's shares

    d.   An option to buy the company's shares at an attractive price

20. **Agency Issues.** When a company's stock is widely held, it may not pay an individual shareholder to spend time monitoring the manager's performance and trying to replace poor management. Explain why. Do you think that a bank that has made a large loan to the company is in a different position?

21. **Ethics.** In some countries, such as Japan and Germany, corporations develop close long-term relationships with one bank and rely on that bank for a large part of their financing needs. In the United States or Canada companies are more likely to shop around for the best deal. Do you think that this practice is more or less likely to encourage ethical behaviour on the part of the corporation?

22. **Ethics.** Is there a conflict between "doing well" and "doing good"? In other words, are policies that increase the value of the firm (doing well) necessarily at odds with socially responsible policies (doing good)? When there are conflicts, how might government regulations or laws tilt the firm toward doing good? For example, how do taxes or fees charged on pollutants affect the firm's decision to pollute? Can you cite other examples of "incentives" used by governments to align private interests with public ones?

23. **Ethics.** The following report appeared in the *Financial Times* (October 28, 1999, p. 1): "Coca-Cola is testing a vending machine that automatically raises the price of the world's favourite soft drink when the temperature increases . . . [T]he new machine, believed to have been tested in Japan, may well create controversy by using hot weather to charge extra. One rival said the idea of charging more when temperatures rose was 'incredible.'" Discuss.

24. **Internet.** Go to the Government of Canada Web site for Canada Business Service Centre Canada at **www.cbsc.org**. Follow the links and arrive at the page that provides information on sole proprietorships, partnerships, and corporations. Check out the rules for forming sole proprietorships, partnerships, or corporations in different provinces across Canada. Are the regulations very different across provinces?

25. **Internet.** If you would like to learn about careers in finance, log on to **www.careers-in-finance.com**. This site describes jobs in commercial banking, corporate finance, financial planning, insurance, investment banking, money management, and real estate. For each area the site describes the types of jobs available, the skills and talents needed, salary ranges, and so on. Corporate finance is the focus of this text, so we suggest you start there. Which jobs in corporate finance do you think would best suit you? Now compare the skills needed for these jobs. How do you match up? How will you match up when your education is completed?

    The Web site also provides links to the job pages of major U.S. financial institutions. Investigate some of these sites and some Canadian sites and compare their descriptions of the different functions. Are these descriptions consistent with those at **www.careers-in-finance.com**?

    We have listed several other useful job Web sites earlier in this chapter in Table 1.3.

26. **Internet.** Go to *The Globe and Mail* Web site at **www.theglobeandmail.com**. Follow the links until you get to the Report on Business section. See if you can find the results of a recent comprehensive survey of CEO compensation. How much was the highest overall compensation for 2003? How much was the highest compensation in terms of stock options for 2003? If you are unable to get the numbers for 2003, see if you can get them for the last reported year.

Solutions to Check Points

1.1 a. The consulting firm is most suited to a partnership. Each senior consultant might be a partner, with partial responsibility for managing the firm and its clients.

 b. The university student would set up the business as a sole proprietorship. She is the only manager and has little need for partners to contribute capital.

 c. The large firm would be set up as a corporation. It requires great amounts of capital, and with the budgetary, payroll, and management issues that arise with such a large number of employees, it probably needs a professional management team.

1.2 a. The development of a fuel cell is a capital budgeting decision. The investment of $500 million will purchase a real asset, the fuel cell.

 b. The bank loan is a financing decision. This is how Volkswagen will raise money for its investment.

 c. Capital budgeting.

 d. Financing.

 e. Capital budgeting. Though intangible, the licence is a real asset that is expected to produce future sales and profits.

 f. Financing.

1.3 a. Real assets support the operations of the business. They are necessary to produce future profits and cash inflows. Financial assets or securities are claims on the profits and cash inflows generated by the firm's real assets and operations.

 b. A company *invests* in real assets to support its operations. It *finances* the investment by raising money from banks, shareholders, or other investors.

 c. Capital budgeting deals with investment decisions. Capital structure is the composition of the company's sources of financing.

1.4 Sal would more likely be the treasurer and Sally the controller. The treasurer raises money from the credit and financial markets and requires background in financial institutions. The controller is more of an overseer who requires background in accounting.

1.5 Harry's has a far bigger stake in the reputation of the business than Victor's. The former has been in business for a long time. The owners have spent years establishing customer loyalty. In contrast, Victor's has just been established. The owner has little of his own money tied up in the firm, and so has little to lose if the business fails. In addition, the nature of the business results in little customer loyalty. Harry's is probably more reliable.

1.6 An investor would like top management to be compensated according to the fortunes of the firm. If management is willing to bet its own compensation on the success of the firm, that is good news; first, because it shows management has confidence in the firm, and second, because it gives managers greater incentives to work hard to make the firm succeed.

1.7 Agency problems arise when managers and shareholders have different objectives. Managers may empire build with excessive investment and growth. Managers may be unduly risk averse, or they may try to take excessive salaries or perquisites.

THE FINANCIAL ENVIRONMENT

If a corporation needs to issue more shares of stock, then its financial manager must understand how the stock market works. If the corporation wants to take out a bank loan, the financial manager must understand how banks and other financial institutions work. That much is obvious. But the capital investment decision also requires a broader understanding of financial markets. We have said that a successful investment is one that increases the market value of the firm. How do investors value the firm? What level of profitability do investors require from the firm's capital investments? To answer these questions, we will need to think clearly about the cost of the capital that the firm raises from outside investors.

Financial markets and institutions are the firm's financial environment. You don't have to understand everything about that environment to begin the study of financial management, but a general understanding provides useful context for the work ahead. For example, that context will help you to understand why you are calculating the yield to maturity of a bond in Chapter 5, the net present value of a capital investment in Chapter 8, or the weighted-average cost of capital for a company in Chapter 12.

This chapter does two things. First, it surveys financial markets and institutions. We will cover the stock and bond markets, mutual and pension funds, and banks and insurance companies. Second, we will set out the functions of financial markets and institutions. What do they do for corporations and for the economy?

After studying this chapter you should be able to
- Understand how financial markets and institutions channel savings to corporate investment.
- Understand the basic structure of mutual funds, pension funds, banks, and insurance companies.
- Enumerate the functions of financial markets and institutions.
- Understand why the cost of capital for corporate investment is determined by investment opportunities in financial markets.

THE FLOW OF SAVINGS TO CORPORATIONS

The money that corporations invest in real assets comes ultimately from savings by investors. But there can be many stops on the road between savings and corporate investment. The road can pass through financial markets, financial intermediaries, or both.

Let's start with the simplest case of a small, closely held corporation. We'll suppose that it owns timberland, harvests logs, and runs a small sawmill. Its shares are closely held by local investors. If the company decides to expand, it may be able to pay for the expansion with cash generated from its operations. If that source of cash is insufficient, it can ask local investors to put more of their savings in the firm. If the investors agree, they will stop by the company's office and hand over cheques in exchange for stock certificates.

The gold arrows in Figure 2.1 show the flow of savings to investment in this simple case. There are two possible paths: The firm can sell new shares (arrow 1) or it can reinvest cash back into the firm's operations (arrow 4a). Reinvestment means additional savings by existing shareholders. The reinvested cash could have been paid out to those shareholders (arrow 4b) and spent by them on personal consumption. By not taking and spending the cash, shareholders have reinvested their savings in the corporation.

> Cash retained and reinvested in the firm's operations is cash saved and invested on behalf of the firm's shareholders.

Of course this small corporation has other financing choices. It could take out a bank loan, for example. The bank in turn may have raised money by attracting savings accounts. In this case investors' savings flow through the bank to the firm.

Now consider a large, public forest-products firm, such as Domtar Inc. or Abitibi-Consolidated. What is different? Scale, for one thing: Those corporations invest hundreds of millions per year in land, sawmills, plywood mills, paper-making machinery, distribution centres, computer systems, and so on. Financing requirements are correspondingly large, and the linkages between investors and the corporation are much more diverse.

The flow of savings to large public corporations is shown in Figure 2.2. Notice two key differences from Figure 2.1. First, public corporations can draw savings from investors worldwide. Second, the savings flow through financial markets, financial intermediaries, or both. Suppose, for example, that Bank of Montreal raises $300 million by a new issue of shares. An Italian investor buys 1,000 of the new shares for $60 per share. Now Bank of Montreal takes that $60,000, along with money raised by the rest of the issue, and makes a $300 million loan to Domtar. The Italian investor's savings end up flowing through financial markets (the stock market), to a financial intermediary (Bank of Montreal), and finally to Domtar.

FIGURE 2.1

Flow of savings to corporate investment (gold arrows). In this example, a closely held corporation invests in timberland. Investors purchase shares with personal savings (1), which are invested (2). Timber harvests generate cash (3), which is reinvested (4a) or paid out to shareholders (4b). Reinvestment (4a) represents additional saving on behalf of shareholders.

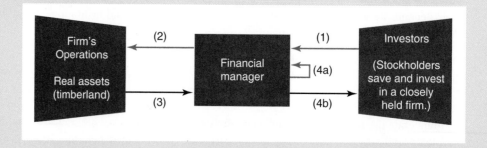

FIGURE 2.2

Flow of savings to a large public corporation (gold arrows), in this example a paper and forest products company. Savings, which can come from investors worldwide, may flow through financial markets or financial intermediaries. Savings may also flow into financial intermediaries through financial markets or into financial markets through financial intermediaries.

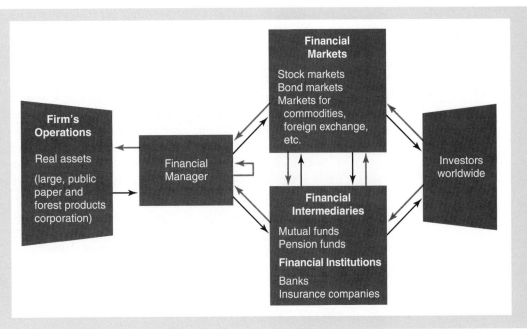

Of course, our Italian friend's $60,000 doesn't literally arrive at Domtar in an envelope marked "From L. DaVinci." Investments by the purchasers of Bank of Montreal's stock issue are pooled, not segregated. Sr. DaVinci would own a share of all of Bank of Montreal's assets, not just one loan to Domtar. Nevertheless, investors' savings flow through the financial markets and the bank to finance Domtar's capital investments.

THE STOCK MARKET

> **financial market** Market where securities are issued and traded.

A **financial market** is a market where securities are issued and traded. A security is just a traded financial asset, such as a share of stock. For a corporation, the stock market is probably the most important financial market.

As corporations grow, their requirements for outside capital can expand dramatically. At some point the firm will decide to "go public" by issuing shares on an organized exchange such as the Toronto Stock Exchange (TSX) in Canada or the New York Stock Exchange (NYSE) in the United States; that first issue is called an *initial public offering* or IPO. The sale of the securities is usually managed by a group of investment dealers such as CIBC World Markets or RBC Dominion Securities. The buyers of the IPO are helping to finance the firm's investment in real assets. In return, the buyers become part-owners of the firm and share in its future success or failure. (Most investors in the Internet IPOs of 1999 and 2000 are by now sorely disappointed, but many IPOs pay off handsomely. If only we had bought Microsoft shares on their IPO day in 1986. …) Of course, a corporation's IPO is not its last chance to issue shares. For example, Bank America went public in the 1930s, but it could make a new issue of shares tomorrow.

An IPO is not the only occasion on which newly issued stock is sold to the public. Established firms also issue new shares from time to time. For example, suppose Alcan needs to raise funds to renovate an aluminum smelting plant. It might hire an investment banking firm to sell $500 million of Alcan stock to investors. Some of this stock may be bought by individuals; the remainder will be bought by financial institutions such as pension funds and insurance companies.

> **primary market** Market for the sale of new securities by corporations.

A new issue of securities increases both the amount of cash held by the company and the amount of stocks or bonds held by the public. Such an issue is known as a *primary issue* and it is sold in the **primary market**. But in addition to helping companies raise new cash, financial markets also allow investors to trade stocks or bonds between themselves. For example, Voth might decide to raise some cash by selling her BCE stock at the same time that Schloo invests his spare cash in BCE. The result is simply a transfer of ownership from Voth to Schloo, which has no effect on the company itself. Such purchases and sales of existing securities are known as *secondary transactions,* and they take place in the **secondary market**.

secondary market   Market in which already issued securities are traded among investors.

Some financial assets have no secondary market. For example, when a small company borrows money from the bank, it gives the bank an IOU promising to repay the money with interest. The bank will keep the IOU and will not sell it to another bank. Other financial assets are regularly traded. Thus when a large public company raises cash by selling new shares to investors, it knows that many of these investors will subsequently decide to sell their shares to others.

Stock markets are also called *equity markets*, since stockholders are said to own the common equity of the firm. You will hear financial managers refer to the capital structure decision as "the choice between debt and equity financing."

Most trading in the shares of large Canadian corporations takes place on stock exchanges such as the Toronto Stock Exchange (TSX), now part of the TSX Group. As of April 2004, the TSX had 1,389 companies listed with a daily average value of shares traded of about $3.5 billion. Trading in the shares of smaller and emerging companies is done through the TSX Venture Exchange (TSX-V), which in April 2004 listed about 1,993 companies. The TSX Venture Exchange, like the TSX, belongs to the TSX Group. Trading in shares can also be done in *over-the-counter* (OTC) markets, which do not have a centralized physical location like the TSX but consist of a network of security dealers who trade with each other over the phone and, increasingly nowadays, over electronic networks. In Canada, the volume of OTC equity trading has traditionally been quite small and until recently was conducted through a large network linking dealers across Canada called the Canadian Dealing Network (CDN). The most actively traded stocks on the CDN moved to the TSX Venture Exchange. In November 2000, a new electronic entrant, Nasdaq Canada, launched operations in Montreal for the purpose of trading shares listed on the Nasdaq stock market. Based in the United States, this stock market consists of a network of security dealers who use an electronic system known as NASDAQ[1] to quote prices at which they will buy and sell shares. In this respect, it is a large *over-the-counter* (OTC) market and lists a wide range of stocks, from small, upcoming companies to giants such as Microsoft and Intel. When Nasdaq Canada was started, 146 of the approximately 5,000 NASDAQ-listed companies were Canadian. As of April 2004, the number of Nasdaq-listed companies is approximately 3,300.

Now may be a good point to stress that the financial manager plays on a global stage and needs to be familiar with markets around the world. For example, larger Canadian companies having sizable global operations, such as Alcan or Canadian Imperial Bank of Commerce, tend to be *cross-listed* on the TSX as well as other large international exchanges such as the New York Stock Exchange (NYSE). In 2003, 176 Canadian firms had their stocks inter-listed in this manner on U.S. stock exchanges.

We return to trading and pricing of shares in Chapter 6.

OTHER FINANCIAL MARKETS

Debt securities are also traded in financial markets. For example, Alcan has issued long-term bonds to investors. The bonds are securities representing Alcan's promise to make regular interest payments and to repay investors' money on a specified future date.

A few corporate debt securities are traded on the Toronto or New York stock exchanges, but most corporate debt securities are traded over-the-counter, not on NASDAQ, but on a network of banks and securities dealers. Government debt is also traded over-the-counter.

A bond is a more complex security than a share of stock. A share is just a proportional ownership claim on the firm, with no definite maturity. Bonds and other debt securities can vary in maturity, the degree of protection or collateral offered by the issuer, and the level and timing

---

[1] National Association of Security Dealers Automated Quotation system.

of interest payments. Some bonds make "floating" interest payments tied to the future level of interest rates. Many can be "called" (repurchased and retired) by the issuing company before the bonds' stated maturity date. Some bonds can be converted into other securities, usually the stock of the issuing company. You don't need to master these distinctions now; just be aware that the debt or **fixed-income market** is a complicated and challenging place. A corporation must not only decide between debt and equity finance but also consider the *design* of debt. We return to the trading and pricing of debt securities in Chapter 5.

fixed-income market Market for debt securities.

The markets for long-term debt and equity are called **capital markets**. A firm's *capital* is its long-term financing. Short-term securities are traded in the **money markets**. "Short term" means less than one year. For example, large, creditworthy corporations raise short-term financing by issues of *commercial paper*, which are debt issues with maturities of at most one year. Commercial paper is issued in the money market.

capital market Market for long-term financing.

money market Market for short-term financing (less than one year).

Check Point 2.1

Do you understand the following distinctions? Briefly explain in each case.
a. Primary versus secondary market.
b. Trading on the TSX or NYSE versus over-the-counter trading on NASDAQ.
c. Capital market versus money market.
d. Stock market versus fixed-income market.

The financial manager regularly encounters other financial markets. Here are three examples, with references to the chapters where they are discussed:

- *Foreign-Exchange Markets* (Chapter 24). Any corporation engaged in international trade must be able to transfer money from dollars to other currencies, or vice versa. Foreign exchange is traded over-the-counter through a network of the largest international banks.
- *Commodities Markets* (Chapter 26). Dozens of commodities are traded on organized exchanges, such as the New York Mercantile Exchange or the Chicago Board of Trade in the United States or the Winnipeg Commodity Exchange in Canada. You can buy or sell corn, wheat, cotton, fuel oil, natural gas, copper, silver, platinum, and so on.
- *Markets for Options and Other Derivatives* (Chapters 25 and 26). Derivatives are securities whose payoffs depend on the prices of other securities or commodities. For example, you can buy an option to purchase Nortel Networks shares at a fixed price on a fixed future date. The option's payoff depends on the price of Nortel's shares on that date. Commodities can be traded by a different kind of derivative security called a futures contract.

Commodity and derivative markets are not sources of financing, but markets where the financial manager can adjust the firm's exposure to various business risks. For example, an electric generating company may wish to "lock in" the future price of natural gas or fuel oil by trading in commodity markets, thus eliminating the risk of a sudden jump in the price of its raw materials.

FINANCIAL INTERMEDIARIES

A **financial intermediary** is an organization that raises money from investors and provides financing for individuals, companies, and other organizations. For corporations, intermediaries are important sources of financing. Intermediaries are a stop on the road between savings and real investment. We will start with two important classes of intermediaries, mutual funds and pension funds.

financial intermediary An organization that raises money from investors and provides financing for individuals, corporations, or other organizations.

Mutual funds raise money by selling shares to investors. The investors' money is pooled and invested in a portfolio of securities. The AIM Canadian Premier Fund, for example, had about $746 million in total assets in March 2004. It held a portfolio of more than 90, mostly Canadian, stocks with a total market value of $17 billion. You could buy additional shares in the fund with an initial investment of as little as $500. By doing so, you would contribute $500 more to the portfolio

mutual fund A mutual fund pools the savings of many investors and invests in a portfolio of securities.

and gain a tiny percentage of the portfolio's subsequent dividends and price appreciation.[2] You could also sell your shares back to the fund if you decide to cash out of your investment.[3]

The advantages of a mutual fund should be clear: Unless you are very wealthy, you cannot buy and manage a 160-stock portfolio on your own, at least not efficiently.

> Mutual funds offer investors low-cost diversification and professional management. For most investors, it's more efficient to buy a mutual fund than to assemble a diversified portfolio of stocks and bonds.

Mutual fund managers also try their best to "beat the market," that is, to generate superior performance by finding the stocks with better-than-average returns. Whether they can pick winners consistently is another question, which we will address in later chapters.

In exchange for their services, the fund's managers take out a management fee. There are also the expenses of running the fund. For AIM Canadian Premier, the management expense ratio (MER), which measures the total costs of operating the fund as a percentage of average total assets, is 2.54 percent. The MER differs across funds and fund managers. For instance, the Altamira Growth and Income Portfolio fund does not have any MER whereas the Acuity Pooled Canadian Small Cap fund has an MER of just 0.3 percent. In some cases fees and expenses add up to over 3 percent per year. That's a big bite out of your investment return.

Mutual funds are a stop on the road from savings to corporate investment. Suppose Canadian Premier purchases part of the new issue of shares by Bank of Montreal, which lends to Domtar. Again we show the flow of savings to investment by gold arrows:

Over 1,900 mutual funds operate in Canada. In fact there are more mutual funds than public companies listed on the Toronto Stock Exchange! The funds pursue a wide variety of investment strategies. Some funds specialize in safe stocks with generous dividend payouts. Some specialize in high-tech growth stocks. Some "balanced" funds offer mixtures of stocks and bonds. Some specialize in particular countries or regions. For example, the Fidelity Investments mutual fund group sponsors funds for Canada, Japan, China, Europe, Latin America, and so on. Table 2.1 provides details on five top mutual funds in Canada.

There are other ways of pooling and investing savings. Consider a **pension fund** set up by a corporation or other organization on behalf of its employees. There are several types of pension

pension fund Investment plan set up by an employer to provide for employees' retirement.

TABLE 2.1
Top Mutual Fund Assets
($000s)

Company	April 2004 Asset Values
1 RBC Asset Management Inc.	43,812,070
2 Investors Group	42,281,503
3 CIBC Asset Management	40,747,197
4 AIM Trimark Investments	40,414,918
5 C.I. Mutual Funds Inc.	40,144,829

Source: The Investment Funds Institute of Canada Web site at **www.ific.ca**.

---

[2] Mutual funds are not corporations, but investment companies. They pay no tax, providing that all income from dividends and price appreciation is passed on to the funds' shareholders. The shareholders pay personal tax on this income.

[3] AIM Canadian Premier, like most mutual funds, is an open-end fund. It stands ready to issue new shares to new investors in the fund and to buy back existing shares when its shareholders decide to cash out. The purchase and sale prices depend on the fund's net asset value (NAV) on the day of purchase or redemption. *Closed-end* funds have a fixed number of shares traded on an exchange. If you want to invest in a closed-end fund, you must buy shares from another stockholder in the fund.

plan. Here is just one example. In a *defined contribution plan*,[4] a percentage of the employee's monthly paycheque is contributed to a pension fund. (The employer and employee may each contribute 5 percent, for example.) Contributions from all participating employees are pooled and invested in securities or mutual funds. (Usually the employees can choose from a menu of funds with different investment strategies.) Each employee's balance in the plan grows over the years as contributions continue and investment income accumulates. When retirement age arrives, the balance in the plan can be used to finance living expenses.

Pension funds are designed for long-term investment. They provide professional management and diversification. They also have an important tax advantage: Contributions are tax-deductible, and investment returns inside the plan are not taxed until cash is finally withdrawn.[5]

Pension plans are among the most important vehicles for savings. Some pension plans, such as Caisse de dépôt et placement du Québec or the Ontario Teachers' Plan are among the largest and most influential investors in the country. For instance, the Ontario Teachers' Plan held over $75 billion in net assets, that is, assets minus liabilities, in December 2003. A significant proportion of the plan's assets comprised equity and bond securities.

private equity Equity capital that is not publicly traded.

In recent years, another category of financial intermediaries, namely, **private equity** firms, have become increasingly prominent. Generally speaking, private equity refers to equity investments in enterprises where the equity is not publicly traded on a stock market. Often, private equity firms provide financing and help nurture growing or troubled companies toward stable long-term growth. Some important categories of private equity investments include venture capital, angel investing, and leveraged buyouts. We will discuss venture capital and angel investing in more detail in Chapter 14. Leveraged buyouts are discussed further in Chapter 23. Large established companies that have received private equity funding include Polaroid, Universal Studios, and Houghton Mifflin.

Private equity firms may be organized as sole proprietorships, partnerships, or closely held corporations. In many instances, they are organized as limited partnerships, wherein general partners make investment decisions and manage funds on behalf of the limited partners. Some well-known and powerful international private equity firms include the Carlyle Group and the Blackstone Group.

✓ Check Point 2.2   Individual investors can buy bonds and stocks directly, or they can put their money in a mutual fund or a defined-contribution pension fund. What are the advantages of the second strategy?

FINANCIAL INSTITUTIONS

financial institution A bank, insurance company, or similar financial intermediary.

Banks and insurance companies are **financial institutions**.[6] A financial institution is an intermediary that does more than just pool and invest savings. Institutions raise financing in special ways; for example, by accepting deposits or selling insurance policies, and they provide additional financial services. Unlike a mutual fund, they not only invest in securities but also loan money directly to individuals, businesses, or other organizations.

---

[4] In a defined contribution plan, each employee owns a portion of the pension fund and accumulates an investment balance to pay for retirement. The amount available for retirement depends on the accumulated contributions and on the rate of return earned on the invested contributions. In a *defined benefit* plan, the employer promises a certain level of retirement benefits (set by a formula) and the *employer* invests in the pension plan. The plan's accumulated investment value has to be large enough to cover the promised benefits. If not, the employer must put in more money.

[5] Defined benefit pension plans share these same advantages, except that the employer invests rather than the employees. In a defined benefit plan, the advantage of tax deferral on investment income accrues to the employer. This deferral reduces the cost of funding the plan.

[6] We may be drawing too fine a distinction between financial intermediaries and institutions. A mutual fund could be considered a financial institution. But "financial institution" usually suggests a more complicated intermediary, such as a bank.

Banks lend money to corporations. (In the United States, they are generally not allowed to make equity investments in corporations, although banks in most other countries can do so.) Suppose that our local forest products company negotiates a short-term bank loan for $2.5 million. The flow of savings is

The bank provides a service. To cover the costs of this service, it charges borrowers a higher interest rate than it pays its depositors.

At present, Canadian residents are served by 70 banks that operate in different parts of the country and manage over $1.8 trillion in assets. Of these, 19 are domestic banks, while the remaining 51 are foreign bank subsidiaries and branches. All banks operating in Canada fall under the purview of federal regulations contained in the *Bank Act* and are categorized under Schedules I, II, and III. The shares of banks classified as Schedule I tend to be widely held. The Big Six domestic chartered banks, which are perhaps the country's most familiar financial intermediaries, are all Schedule I banks. They account for about 90 percent of the country's bank industry assets and over 50 percent of the total domestic assets held by the financial sector.[7] Shares of some Canadian banks are closely held, perhaps by large foreign banks or other financial institutions. These banks are classified as Schedule II under Canada's *Bank Act*. Examples of such banks include Citibank Canada and HSBC Bank Canada. Branches of foreign banks operating in Canada are regulated under Schedule III; these include ABN Amro Bank, NV, and Deutsche Bank AG. Banks are, however, only one group of financial intermediaries operating in Canada. There are many others such as caisses populaires, credit unions, insurance companies, pension funds, and trust companies. Let us describe these financial intermediaries in a little more detail.

Like banks, trust companies, credit unions, and caisses populaires accept deposits and make loans. In addition, trust companies engage in fiduciary services such as managing assets, like registered retirement savings plans, for estates or pension plans. Some major trust companies experienced difficulties following the collapse of the real estate market in the early 1990s and, over the years, they have been consolidated with the chartered banks. Of course, not all trust companies experienced financial difficulties at the time of consolidation. An example is the assimilation of Canada Trust with Toronto Dominion Bank.

Credit unions and caisses populaires are typically run as cooperatives and are an important source of financing for residential mortgages as well as small and medium enterprises. Caisses populaires are mainly located in Québec although a number operate in Manitoba, Ontario, and the Maritime provinces; for example, there are over 45 caisses populaires acadiennes in New Brunswick. Credit unions can be found across Canada but are particularly active in British Columbia and Saskatchewan. Some of Canada's caisses populaires and credit unions are very large. Québec-based Mouvement Desjardins is a conglomerate involved in a wide array of activities and ranks among the top eight financial institutions in the country based on assets. Mouvement des caisses Desjardins includes a network of 671 caisses populaires in Québec and over 65 caisses populaires outside Québec.

Insurance companies include health, life, property, and casualty insurance companies. They are massive investors in corporate stocks and bonds and they often make long-term loans directly to corporations. For instance, life insurance companies make loans from funds received from the sale of life insurance policies and products such as registered retirement savings plans (RRSP) and registered retirement income funds (RRIF).

In Canada, large pension funds and insurance companies, particularly life and health insurance firms, invest more in the *long-term financing* of business than banks. They are massive investors in corporate stocks and bonds and occasionally make long-term loans directly to corporations.

[7] In 2004, the largest chartered banks, in order of assets, were Royal Bank of Canada, Scotiabank, the Toronto Dominion Bank, CIBC, Bank of Montreal, Desjardins Group, and National Bank of Canada. Shares in these banks are widely held by a large number of shareholders. For more information and statistics about Canada's banking industry, you can visit the Web site of the Canadian Bankers Association at **www.cba.ca**.

Suppose a company needs a loan for nine years, not nine months. It could issue a bond directly to investors, or it could negotiate a nine-year loan with an insurance company:

The money to make the loan comes mainly from the sale of insurance policies. Say you buy a fire insurance policy on your home. You pay cash to the insurance company and get a financial asset (the policy) in exchange. You receive no interest payments on this financial asset, but if a fire does strike, the company is obliged to cover the damages up to the policy limit. This is the return on your investment.

The company will issue not just one policy, but thousands. Normally the incidence of fires "averages out," leaving the company with a predictable obligation to its policyholders as a group. Of course, the insurance company must charge enough for its policies to cover selling and administrative costs, pay policyholders' claims, and generate a profit for its shareholders.

Why is a financial intermediary different from a manufacturing corporation? First, it may raise money differently; for example, by taking deposits or selling insurance policies. Second, it invests that money in *financial* assets; for example, in stocks, bonds, or loans to businesses or individuals. The manufacturing company's main investments are in plant, equipment, and other *real* assets.

Check Point 2.3   What are the key differences between a mutual fund and a bank or an insurance company?

TOTAL FINANCING OF CANADIAN CORPORATIONS

The pie chart in Figure 2.3 shows the investors in Canadian corporate bonds and debentures. Notice the importance of non-residents and institutional investors such as insurance companies, trusteed pension plans and, to a lesser extent, Canadian banks and mutual funds. Individual investors and unincorporated businesses hold only a small slice of the debt pie.

FIGURE 2.3
Holdings of Canadian corporate bonds and debentures, 2003

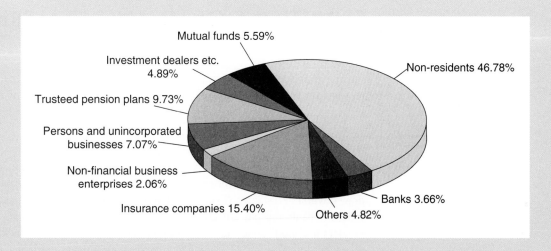

Source: Adapted from Statistics Canada CANSIM database http://cansim2.statcan.ca Table 378-0004.
Notes:
1. The category "Other Canadian Bonds" comprises mainly bonds and debentures issued by Canadian corporations.
2. Investment dealers include investment dealers; issuers of asset-backed securities; and sales, finance, and consumer loan companies.
3. Insurance companies include life, accidental, and property and casualty insurance companies.
4. Banks include chartered banks and near banks, which comprise Quebec saving banks, credit unions and caisses populaires, trust companies, and mortgage loan companies.
5. Non-financial business enterprises include non-financial private corporations and non-financial government business enterprises.

FIGURE 2.4
Holdings of Canadian corporate equities, 2003

Source: Adapted from Statistics Canada CANSIM database http://cansim2.statcan.ca Table 378-0004.

Notes:
1. The category "Shares" includes common and preferred shares in addition to some other items such as contributed surplus and mutual fund shares.
2. Investment dealers include investment dealers; issuers of asset-backed securities; and sales, finance, and consumer loan companies.
3. Insurance companies include life, accidental, and property and casualty insurance companies.
4. Banks include chartered banks and near banks, which comprise Quebec saving banks, credit unions and caisses populaires, trust companies, and mortgage loan companies.
5. Non-financial business enterprises include non-financial private corporations and non-financial government business enterprises.

The pie chart in Figure 2.4 shows holdings of shares issued by Canadian corporations. Here, individual investors and unincorporated businesses make a much stronger showing, about 49 percent of the total. Insurance companies, trusteed pension funds, mutual funds, and banks add up to about 36 percent of the total. The "Others" slice is about 7 percent.

The aggregate amounts represented in these figures are enormous. There is $0.46 trillion of debt behind Figure 2.3 and $1.25 trillion of equity behind Figure 2.4, $1,259,144,000,000, to be more exact. Chapter 14 reviews corporate financing patterns in more detail.

2.2   FUNCTIONS OF FINANCIAL MARKETS AND INTERMEDIARIES

Financial markets and intermediaries provide financing for business. They channel savings to real investment. That much should be clear from the first section of this chapter. But there are other functions that may not be quite so obvious and we'll enumerate them.

TRANSPORTING CASH ACROSS TIME

Individuals need to transport expenditures in time. If you have money now that you wish to save for a rainy day, you can (for example) put the money in a savings account at a bank and withdraw it with interest later. If you don't have money today, say to buy a car, you can borrow money from the bank and pay off the loan later. Modern finance provides a kind of time machine. Lenders transport money forward in time, borrowers transport it back. Both are happier than if they were forced to spend income as it arrives. Of course, individuals are not alone in needing to raise cash from time to time. Firms with good investment opportunities, but a shortage of internally generated cash, raise cash by borrowing or selling new shares. Many governments run deficits and finance current outlays by issuing debt.

Young people saving for retirement may transport their current earnings 30 or 40 years into the future by means of a pension fund. They may even transport income to their heirs by purchase of a life insurance policy.

In principle, individuals or firms with cash surpluses could take out newspaper advertisements or surf the Net looking for counterparties with cash shortages. But it is usually cheaper and more convenient to use financial markets and intermediaries. It is not just a matter of avoiding the cost of searching for the right counterparty. Follow-up is needed. For example, banks don't just loan money and walk away. They monitor the borrower to make sure that the loan is used for its intended purpose and that the borrower's credit stays solid.

LIQUIDITY

liquidity The ability to sell or exchange an asset for cash on short notice.

Markets and intermediaries also provide **liquidity**, that is, the ability to turn an investment back into cash when needed. Suppose you deposit $5,000 in a savings bank on February 1. During that month, the bank uses your deposit and other new deposits to make a six-month construction loan to a real estate developer. On March 1, you realize that you need your $5,000 back. The bank can give it to you. Because the bank has thousands of depositors, and other sources of financing if necessary, it can make illiquid loans financed by liquid deposits. If you lend out your money for six months directly to the real estate developer, you will have a hard time retrieving it one month later.

The shares of public companies are liquid because they are traded more or less continuously in the stock market. An Italian investor who puts $60,000 into Royal Bank of Canada shares can recover that money on short notice. (A $60,000 sell order is a drop in the bucket, compared with the normal trading volume of Royal Bank of Canada shares.) Mutual funds can redeem their shares for cash on short notice because the funds invest in traded securities, which can be sold as necessary.

Of course, liquidity is a matter of degree. Foreign-exchange markets for major currencies are exceptionally liquid. Royal Bank of Canada or Deutsche Bank could buy $200 million worth of yen or euros in the blink of an eye, with hardly any affect on foreign exchange rates. Treasury securities are also very liquid, and the shares of the largest companies on the major international stock exchanges only slightly less so.

Liquidity is most important when you're in a hurry. If you try to sell $500,000 worth of the shares of a small, thinly traded public company all at once, you will probably knock down the price to some extent. If you're patient and don't surprise other investors with a large, sudden sell order, you may be able to unload your shares on better terms. It's the same problem you will face in selling real estate. A house or condominium is not a liquid asset in a panic sale. If you're determined to sell in an afternoon, you won't get full value.

THE PAYMENT MECHANISM

Think how inconvenient life would be if you had to pay for every purchase in cash or if General Motors of Canada had to ship truckloads of hundred-dollar bills round the country to pay its suppliers. Chequing accounts, credit cards, and electronic transfers allow individuals and firms to send and receive payments quickly and safely over long distances. Banks are the obvious providers of payment services, but they are not alone. For example, if you buy shares in a money-market mutual fund, your money is pooled with that of other investors and used to buy safe, short-term securities. You can then write cheques on this mutual fund investment, just as if you had a bank deposit.

REDUCING RISK

Financial markets and intermediaries allow investors and businesses to reduce and reallocate risk. Insurance companies are an obvious example. When you buy homeowner's insurance, you greatly reduce the risk of loss from fire, theft, or accidents. But your policy is not a risky bet for the insurance company. It diversifies by issuing thousands of policies, and it expects losses to average out over the policies.[8] The insurance company allows you to pool risk with thousands of other homeowners.

---

[8] Unfortunately for insurance companies, the losses don't always average out. Hurricanes and earthquakes can damage thousands of homes at once. The potential losses are so great that property insurance companies buy *reinsurance* against such catastrophes.

Investors should diversify too. For example, you can buy shares in a mutual fund that holds hundreds of stocks. In fact, you can buy *index funds* that invest in all the stocks in the popular market indexes.[9] For example, in the United States, the Vanguard Index 500 fund holds the stocks in the Standard & Poor's Composite stock market index. (The "S&P 500" tracks the performance of the largest U.S. stocks. It is the index most used by professional investors.) Similarly, the CIBC Canadian Index Fund seeks to approximate the performance of the S&P/TSX Composite Index. This index includes the largest and most liquid companies listed on the TSX. If you buy such index funds, you are insulated from the company-specific risks of the companies in the respective indices. These risks are averaged out by diversification. Of course, you are still left with the risk that the level of the stock market as a whole will fall. In fact, we will see in Chapter 10 that investors are mostly concerned with *market risk*, not the specific risks of individual companies.

Financial markets provide other mechanisms for sharing risks. For example, a wheat farmer and a baking company are each exposed to fluctuations in the price of wheat after the harvest. The farmer worries about low prices, the baker about high prices. They can both rest easier if the baker can agree with the farmer to buy wheat in the future at a fixed price. The farmer and baker would not negotiate the trade face to face, however. They would each trade in commodity markets, the farmer as a seller and the baker as a buyer.

INFORMATION PROVIDED BY FINANCIAL MARKETS

In well-functioning financial markets, you can see what securities and commodities are worth, and you can see—or at least estimate—the rates of return that investors can expect on their savings. The information provided by financial markets is often essential to a financial manager's job. Here are three examples of how this information can be used.

Commodity Prices

Catalytic converters are used in the exhaust systems of cars and light trucks to reduce pollution. The catalysts include platinum, which is traded on the New York Mercantile Exchange.

In August a manufacturer of catalytic converters is planning production for October. How much per ounce should the company budget for purchases of platinum in that month? Easy: The company's CFO looks up the market price of platinum on the New York Mercantile Exchange—$517 per ounce for delivery in October. (This was the closing price for platinum on August 1, 2002, for delivery in October.) The CFO can lock in that price if she wishes. The details of such a trade are covered in Chapter 25.

Interest Rates

The CFO of Catalytic Concepts has to raise $400 million in new financing. She considers an issue of 10-year bonds. What will the interest rate on the bonds be? To find out, the CFO looks up interest rates on existing bonds traded in financial markets.

The results are shown in Table 2.2. Notice how the interest rate climbs as credit quality deteriorates: the largest, safest companies, which are rated AAA ("triple-A"), can borrow for 10 years at a 6.25 percent interest rate. The interest rates for AA, A, and BBB climb to 6.37, 6.69, and 7.53 percent, respectively. Triple-B companies are still regarded as *investment grade*, that is, good quality, but the next step down takes the investor into *junk bond* territory. The interest rate for double-B companies climbs to 9.97 percent. Single-B companies are riskier still, so investors demand 11.35 percent.

There will be more on bond ratings and interest rates in Chapter 5. But you can see how a financial manager can use information from fixed-income markets to forecast the interest rate on new debt financing. For example, if Catalytic Concepts can qualify as a BBB-rated company, and interest rates are as shown in Table 2.2, it should be able to raise new debt financing for approximately 7.5 percent.

---

[9] Index funds don't always own every stock in the index, but most of them—enough that the performance of the fund tracks the index almost perfectly.

TABLE 2.2
Interest rates on 10-year corporate bonds, May 2002. The interest rate is lowest for top-quality (AAA) issuers. The rate rises as credit quality declines.

Credit Rating	Interest Rate
AAA	6.25%
AA	6.37
A	6.69
BBB	7.53
BB	9.97
B	11.35

Source: Standard & Poor's Statistical Service, June 2002, p. 27.

TABLE 2.3
Calculating the total market values of Wi-LAN Inc. and other companies. Stock prices are as of May 27, 2004. Shares and market values in millions.

Company	Stock Price ×	Number of Shares =	Market Value
Wi-LAN	$3.13	38.894	$121.74
Air Canada	$1.13	79.076	$89.36
Maple Leaf Foods	$12.21	91.199	$1,113.54
Aliant	$27.00	133.087	$3,593.35
Loblaw	$63.04	274.697	$17,316.90
Nortel Networks	$5.24	4,173.153	$21,867.32

Source: *Financial Post* FP Analyzer. Retrieved May 27, 2004, from **www.fpinfomart.ca**.

Company Values

How much was Wi-LAN Inc. worth on May 27, 2004? How about Air Canada, Maple Leaf Foods, Aliant, Loblaw, or Nortel Networks? Table 2.3 shows the answers. We simply multiply the number of shares outstanding by the price per share in the stock market. Investors valued Wi-LAN Inc. at about $121 million, Nortel Networks at roughly $22 billion.

Stock prices and company values summarize investors' collective assessment of how well a company is doing, both its current performance and its future prospects. Thus an increase in stock price sends a positive signal from investors to managers.[10] That is why top management's compensation is linked to stock prices. A manager who owns shares in his company will be motivated to increase the company's market value. This reduces agency costs by aligning the interests of managers and stockholders.

This is one important advantage of going public. A private company can't use its stock price as a measure of performance. It can still compensate managers with shares, but the shares will not be valued in a financial market.

Check Point 2.4

Which of the functions described in this section require financial markets? Explain briefly.

THE OPPORTUNITY COST OF CAPITAL

cost of capital Minimum acceptable rate of return on capital investment.

Financial managers look to financial markets to measure, or at least estimate, the cost of capital. The **cost of capital** is the minimum acceptable rate of return for capital investments. Investment projects offering rates of return higher than the cost of capital add value to the firm. Projects offering rates of return less than the cost of capital are not worthwhile financially.

We can start with a simple example. Catalytic Concepts has $1 million earmarked for purchase of a new defenestrator. This investment will generate $100,000 per year in additional income, a 10 percent return on the $1 million investment (100,000/1,000,000 = .10, or 10%). Is the project worthwhile? Is $100,000 per year enough to justify the investment?

---

[10] We can't claim that investors' assessments of value are always correct. Finance can be a risky and dangerous business—dangerous for your wealth, that is. With hindsight we see horrible mistakes by investors, most recently the gross overvaluation of Internet and telecom companies. On average, however, it appears that financial markets collect and assess information quickly and accurately. We'll discuss this issue again in Chapter 6.

Let's ask that question in a different way. You're a Catalytic Concepts stockholder. That $1 million is in part your money. Are you happy if the company invests your money at a 10 percent return? Your answer will depend on the return you could earn in financial markets if the $1 million were returned to you and your fellow shareholders.

Suppose that the defenestrator's return is safe, that is, absolutely predictable. In that case you would compare the returns from the project to returns on safe investments like the top-quality corporate bonds at the top of Table 2.2. These offer only 6 to 7 percent rates of return, so you are happy for Catalytic Concepts to invest at 10 percent on your behalf. But if the defenestrator had offered only a 5 percent return, you would vote against the project. There is no point in the firm investing at 5 percent when 6 to 7 percent can be earned in financial markets.

But the returns to capital investments are usually risky, not safe. The future returns on the project are just forecasts, not certainties. Suppose investing in defenestrators is just as risky as investing in the overall stock market. You estimate the expected rate of return on the stock market at 10 percent. In this case the defenestrator project is, from the investors' point of view, just breakeven. You get the same expected return (and risk) if the firm invests or if you invest in the stock market.

If the project's return were 15 percent, you would endorse it enthusiastically. But at 5 percent, you would vote no and hope that Catalytic Concepts pays out the cash to you and other shareholders for investment in the stock market at 10 percent.

Figure 2.5 summarizes this trade-off. The firm can invest, or it can pay out cash to shareholders. Shareholders can invest for themselves in financial markets. Capital investments by the firm should therefore offer rates of return at least as high as those available in financial markets at the same level of risk. If they do not, the firm should not invest.

> The cost of capital for corporate investment is set by the rates of return on investment opportunities in financial markets.

You can see why financial managers refer to the *opportunity cost* of capital. When the firm invests, shareholders lose the opportunity to invest in financial markets.

For safe investments, you can observe the opportunity cost of capital by looking up current interest rates on safe debt securities. For risky investments, the opportunity cost of capital has to be estimated. That is one of the harder tasks in financial management. We will return to this task in Chapter 5 and in several later chapters.

Notice that the opportunity cost of capital is generally not the interest rate that the firm pays on a loan from a bank or insurance company. If the company is making a risky investment, the opportunity cost is the expected return that investors can achieve in financial markets at the same level of risk. The expected return on risky securities will normally be well above the interest rate on corporate borrowing.

FIGURE 2.5

The firm can either keep and reinvest cash or return it to investors. (Arrows represent possible cash flows or transfers.) If cash is reinvested, the opportunity cost is the expected rate of return that shareholders could have obtained by investing in financial assets.

Check Point 2.5   Investing $100,000 in additional raw materials today—mostly in palladium—should allow Cryogenic Concepts to increase production and earn an additional $112,000 next year. This payoff would cover the investment today, plus a 12 percent return. Palladium is traded in commodity markets. The CFO has studied the history of returns on investments in palladium and believes that investors in that precious metal can reasonably expect a 15 percent return. Is Cryogenic's investment in palladium a good idea? Why or why not?

2.3   SUMMARY

1. **Where does the financing for corporations come from?**

   The ultimate source of financing is individuals' savings. The savings flow through **financial markets** and **intermediaries**. The intermediaries include mutual funds, pension funds, and financial institutions, such as banks and insurance companies.

2. **What if a corporation finances investment by retaining and reinvesting cash generated from its operations?**

   In that case the corporation is saving on behalf of its shareholders. Although shareholders will receive smaller dividends now, reinvestment of their funds may help generate more wealth and provide higher future returns.

3. **What are the key advantages of mutual funds and pension funds?**

   Mutual and **pension funds** allow investors to diversify in professionally managed portfolios. Pension funds offer an additional tax advantage, because the returns on pension investments are not taxed until withdrawn from the plan.

4. **What are the functions of financial markets?**

   Financial markets help channel savings to corporate investment, and they help match up borrowers and lenders. They provide **liquidity** and diversification opportunities for investors. Trading in financial markets provides a wealth of useful information for the financial manager.

5. **Do financial institutions have different functions?**

   Financial institutions carry out a number of similar functions but in different ways. They channel savings to corporate investment, and they serve as intermediaries between borrowers and lenders. Banks also provide liquidity for depositors and, of course, play a special role in the economy's payments systems. Insurance companies allow policyholders to pool risks.

6. **How does the financial manager identify the cost of the capital raised by a corporation?**

   The **cost of capital** is the minimum acceptable rate of return on capital investment. It's an opportunity cost, that is, a rate of return that investors could earn in financial markets. For a safe capital investment, the opportunity cost is the interest rate on safe debt securities, such as high-grade corporate bonds. For riskier capital investments, the opportunity cost is the expected rate of return on risky securities, investments in the stock market, for example.

Related Web Links

www.tsx.com The TSX Group, which includes the Toronto Stock Exchange and the TSX Venture Exchange

www.cba.ca The Canadian Bankers' Association; contains good information on Canada's banking industry

www.ific.ca The Investment Funds Institute of Canada; contains good information on Canada's mutual fund industry

www.ida.ca Investment Dealers' Association

www.insurance-canada.ca Provides consumers and industry professionals with information on insurance in Canada

www.desjardins.com Web site of Desjardins Group, a large Canadian co-operative financial institution with 5 million member-owners

www.standardandpoors.com Web site of Standard and Poor's, a leading international provider of independent credit ratings and indices, risk evaluation, investment research, data, and valuations

www.dbrs.com Dominion Bond Rating Service

www.otpp.com Web site of Ontario Teachers' Pension Plan, which invests and administers the pensions of Ontario teachers

www.cdp.ca Web site of Caisse de dépôt et placement du Québec, a leading institutional and pension fund manager

www.nyse.com The New York Stock Exchange

www.nasdaq.com The Nasdaq over-the-counter stock market

www.123world.com/stockexchanges Links to exchanges

www.ici.org The Investment Company Institute; contains good information on the mutual fund industry

http://finance.yahoo.com General information, including very good mutual fund data

www.morningstar.com Information on mutual funds, including performance data

www.americanbanker.com and

www.us-banker.com Banking journals with links to related sites

Key Terms

financial market	31	money market	33	financial institution	35
primary market	31	financial intermediary	33	liquidity	39
secondary market	32	mutual fund	33	cost of capital	41
fixed-income market	33	pension fund	34		
capital market	33	private equity	35		

Questions and Problems

*Answers in Appendix B

BASIC

1. **Corporate Financing.** Is it possible for an individual to save and invest in a corporation without lending money to it or purchasing additional shares? Explain.

2. **Financial Markets.** What is meant by over-the-counter trading? Is this trading mechanism used for stocks, bonds, or both?

*3. **Financial Markets.** The stock and bond markets are not the only financial markets. Give two or three additional examples.

*4. **Financial Intermediaries.** You are a beginning investor with only $5,000 in savings. How can you achieve a widely diversified portfolio at reasonable cost?

5. **Financial Intermediaries.** What are the key advantages of a defined contribution pension plan as a vehicle for retirement savings?

6. **Financial Intermediaries.** Is an insurance company also a financial intermediary? How does the insurance company channel savings to corporate investment?

7. **Corporate Financing.** What are the largest institutional investors in bonds? In shares?

*8. **Financial Markets.** You discover a 6-ounce gold nugget. A friend offers to pay you $1,500 for it. How do you check whether this is a fair price?

9. **Financial Markets.** What kinds of useful information can a financial manager obtain from financial markets? Give examples.

10. **Cost of Capital.** Why do financial managers refer to the opportunity cost of capital? How would you find the *opportunity cost* of capital for a safe investment?

PRACTICE

11. **True or false?**
    a. Financing for public corporations must flow through financial markets.
    b. Financing for private corporations must flow through financial intermediaries.
    c. The sale of policies is a source of financing for insurance companies.
    d. Almost all foreign-exchange trading occurs on the floors of the FOREX exchanges in New York and London.
    e. The opportunity cost of capital is the capital outlay required to undertake a real investment opportunity.
    f. The cost of capital is the interest rate paid on borrowing from a bank or other financial institution.

12. **Liquidity.** Securities traded in active financial markets are liquid assets. Explain why liquidity is important to individual investors and to mutual funds.

13. **Liquidity.** Bank deposits are liquid; you can withdraw money on demand. How can the bank provide this liquidity and at the same time make illiquid loans to businesses?

14. **Corporate Financing.** Financial markets and intermediaries channel savings from investors to corporate investment. The savings make this journey by many different routes. Give a specific example for each of the following routes:
    a. Investor to financial intermediary, to financial markets, and to the corporation.
    b. Investor to financial markets, to a financial intermediary, and to the corporation.
    c. Investor to financial markets, to a financial intermediary, back to financial markets, and to the corporation.

15. **Mutual Funds.** Why are mutual funds called financial intermediaries? Why does it make sense for an individual to invest her savings in a mutual fund rather than directly in financial markets?

16. **Cost of Capital.** In a stroke of good luck, your company has uncovered an opportunity to invest for 1 year at a guaranteed 5 percent rate of return. What is the opportunity cost of capital? Assume interest rates as in Table 2.2.

*17. **Cost of Capital.** Pollution Busters, Inc., is considering purchase of 10 additional carbon sequesters for $100,000 apiece. The sequesters last for only one year until saturated. Then the carbon is sold to the government.
    a. Suppose the government guarantees the price of carbon. At this price, the payoff after 1 year is guaranteed to be $115,000. How would you determine the opportunity cost of capital for this investment?
    b. Suppose instead that the sequestered carbon has to be sold on the London Carbon Exchange. Carbon prices have been extremely volatile, but Pollution Busters' CFO learns that average rates of return from investment on that exchange have been about 20 percent. She thinks this is a reasonable forecast for the future. What is the opportunity cost of capital in this case? Is purchase of additional sequesters a worthwhile capital investment?

18. **Financial Markets.** What is meant by over-the-counter trading? Is this trading mechanism used for stocks, bonds, or both?

19. **Financial Institutions.** We gave banks and insurance companies as two examples of financial institutions. What other types of financial institutions can you identify?

20. **Internet.** Most mutual funds in Canada belong to The Investment Funds Institute of Canada. Log in to its Web site at **www.ific.ca**. You will find some essential information about mutual funds and a useful fact book titled "Mutual Fund Investing." Ensure that you know the basic types of fund. For example, can you explain the difference between a bond fund and a money market mutual fund? Look on the Web site for the amount of assets managed by mutual funds. Have mutual fund assets been increasing or decreasing over the years? What are the advantages and also some of the risks associated with investing through a mutual fund?

21. **Internet.** Here are the Web sites for three of the largest mutual fund companies in Canada:
    a. RBC Asset Management: **www.rbcam.com**
    b. Investors' Group: **www.investorsgroup.com**
    c. AIM Trimark Investments: **www.aimtrimark.com**

    Pick three or four funds from one of these sites and compare their investment objectives, risks, past returns, fund fees, and so on. Read the prospectuses for each of these funds; they are usually clear and informative. Who do you think should, or should not, invest in each fund? Which one would be most appropriate for a young financial executive saving for retirement?

22. **Internet.** We mentioned in Chapter 1 that large banks have their fingers in many pies. The Web sites of the very largest banks are equally massive. The Royal Bank of Canada (**www.royalbank.com**) and Scotiabank (**www.scotiabank.com**) are examples of two of Canada's largest banks with relatively straightforward Web sites. Use these Web sites and the bank's annual reports to find what services banks provide to individuals, small businesses, and large corporations.

CHALLENGE

23. **Internet.** The Globefund section of GlobeandMail.com provides data on mutual fund performance. Log in to **www.globefunddb.theglobeandmail.com/gishome/plsql/gis.analyser**. This gives recent returns by category of fund. Similarly, if you go to **www.globefund.com/review**, you will find performance tables for different categories of mutual funds over 1, 5, and 10 years. Select any two or three categories; for instance, you could select Canadian Equity, Canadian Short-Term Bond, or Labour-Sponsored Venture Capital funds. From the performance data, can you discern whether a particular mutual fund has performed unusually well or badly at certain times? Can you provide any explanations for such performance? Now go to the "tools" sidebar and click on "fund filter." By selecting the above mutual funds can you state how these funds have performed over the last 30 days? Are these funds investing in small rather than large company stock, growth rather than value stocks, or specializing in a particular industry, such as precious metals or real estate?

24. **Financial Markets.** In most years, new issues of stock are a tiny fraction of total stock market trading. In other words, secondary market volume is much greater than primary market volume. Does the fact that firms only occasionally sell new shares mean that the stock market is largely irrelevant to the financial manager? Hint: How is the price of the firm's stock determined, and why is it important to the financial manager?

Solutions to Check Points

2.1 a. Corporations sell securities in the primary market. The securities are later traded in the secondary market.

b. The TSX or NYSE are formal exchanges that centralize all trades. NASDAQ is an electronic network of traders.

c. The capital market is for long-term financing, the money market for short-term financing.

d. The market for stocks versus the market for bonds and other debt securities.

2.2 Efficient diversification and professional management. Pension funds offer an additional advantage, because investment returns are not taxed until withdrawn from the fund.

2.3 Mutual funds are financial intermediaries that pool and invest money raised from investors in portfolios of securities. Banks and insurance companies are financial institutions that do more than just pool and invest savings. These financial institutions raise money in special ways; for example, by accepting deposits or selling insurance policies. They not only invest in securities but also lend directly to businesses. They provide various other financial services.

2.4 Liquidity, risk reduction by investment in diversified portfolios of securities (through a mutual fund, for example), information provided by trading.

2.5 It is not a good investment if the opportunity cost of capital is 15 percent. The investment offers only a 12 percent return.

ACCOUNTING AND FINANCE

In Chapter 1 we pointed out that a large corporation is a team effort. All the players—the shareholders, lenders, directors, management, and employees—have a stake in the company's success and all therefore need to monitor its progress. For this reason the company prepares regular financial accounts and arranges for an independent firm of auditors to certify that these accounts present a "true and fair view."

Until the mid-19th century most businesses were owner-managed and seldom required outside capital beyond personal loans to the proprietor. When businesses were small and there were few outside stakeholders in the firm, accounting could be less formal. But with the industrial revolution and the creation of large railroad and canal companies, shareholders and bankers demanded information that would help them gauge a firm's financial strength. That was when the accounting profession began to come of age.

We don't want to discuss the details of accounting practice. But because we will be referring to financial statements throughout this book, it may be useful to review their main features briefly. In this chapter we introduce the major financial statements: the balance sheet, the income statement, and the statement of cash flows. We discuss the important differences between income and cash flow and between book values and market values. We also discuss the Canadian tax system.

After studying this chapter you should be able to
- Interpret the information contained in the balance sheet, income statement, and statement of cash flows.
- Distinguish between market and book value.
- Explain why income differs from cash flow.
- Understand the essential features of the taxation of corporate and personal income.

THE BALANCE SHEET

balance sheet Financial statement that shows the value of the firm's assets and liabilities at a particular time.

The company we have chosen to look at is Maple Leaf Foods Inc., a major Canadian food processor whose brands include Maple Leaf, Schneiders, and Dempster's Bread. To see its 2004 annual report, go to **www.mapleleaf.com** and select "Investor Relations," then "Annual Reports." Table 3.1 shows Maple Leaf's consolidated **balance sheet** as of December 31, 2004, and 2003.[1]

The balance sheet presents a snapshot of the firm's assets and the source of the money that was used to buy those assets. The assets are listed on the left-hand side of the balance sheet. Some assets can be turned more easily into cash than others; these are known as *liquid assets*. The accountant puts the most liquid assets at the top of the list and works down to the least liquid.

Look at the left-hand column of Table 3.1. You can see that Maple Leaf had $111.8 million of cash and marketable securities. In addition it had sold goods worth $292.5 million but had not yet received payment. These payments are due soon and therefore the balance sheet shows the unpaid bills, or *accounts receivable* (or simply *receivables*), as an asset. The next asset consists of inventories. These may be (1) raw materials and ingredients that the firm bought from suppliers, (2) work in process, and (3) finished products waiting to be shipped from the warehouse. Of course there are always some items that don't fit into neat categories. So the current assets category includes a fourth entry, *other current assets*.

Up to this point all the assets in Maple Leaf's balance sheet are likely to be used or turned into cash in the near future. They are therefore described as *current assets*. The second part of

TABLE 3.1
Consolidated balance sheet for Maple Leaf Foods Inc.

Consolidated Balance Sheet for Maple Leaf Foods Inc., as of December 31 ($ millions)					
Assets	**2004**	**2003**	**Liabilities and Shareholders' Equity**	**2004**	**2003**
Current assets			Current liabilities		
Cash and equivalents	111.8	38.9	Accounts payable and accruals	621.6	502
Accounts receivable	292.5	242.3	Other current liabilities	27.7	12.2
Inventories	385.1	259.8	Current portion of		
Other current assets	19.9	14.2	long-term debt	105.9	5.0
Total current assets	809.3	555.2	Total current liabilities	755.2	519.2
Fixed assets					
Property and equipment, gross	1,889.1	1,537	Long-term debt	1,059.5	826.7
Less accumulated depreciation	915.4	734.2	Other long-term liabilities	234.7	85.7
Net property and equipment	973.7	802.3	Minority interest	74.1	70.1
Investments in associated companies	82.3	58.2	Total liabilities	2,123.5	1,501.7
Goodwill and other intangibles	899.2	531.9	Shareholders' equity		
Other assets	257.2	201.1	Share capital	731.3	565
Total assets	3,021.7	2,148.7	Retained earnings	159.1	75
			Other shareholders' equity	7.8	7
			Total shareholders' equity	898.2	647.0
			Total liabilities and shareholders' equity	3,021.7	2,148.7

Source: Maple Leaf Foods Inc.

[1] "Consolidated" means that the balance sheet shows the position of Maple Leaf and any companies it owns. In Maple Leaf's case, this includes its 87 percent interest in Canada Bread. We have somewhat simplified Maple Leaf's financial statements by removing some of the detail.

the balance sheet includes long-term assets not likely to be turned into cash soon. The first group of long-term assets is known as *tangible capital assets* or *fixed assets* such as buildings, equipment, and vehicles. The second entry, *investments in associated companies*, shows Maple Leaf's ownership interest in some other businesses.

The balance sheet shows that the gross value of Maple Leaf's fixed assets is $1,889.1 million. This is what the assets originally cost. But they are unlikely to be worth that now. For example, suppose the company bought a delivery van two years ago; that van may be worth far less now than Maple Leaf paid for it. It might in principle be possible for the accountant to estimate separately the value today of the van, but this would be costly and somewhat subjective. Accountants rely instead on rules of thumb to estimate the depreciation in the value of assets and with rare exceptions they stick to these rules. For example, in the case of that delivery van the accountant may deduct a third of the original cost each year to reflect its declining value. So if Maple Leaf bought the van two years ago for $15,000, the balance sheet would show that accumulated depreciation is $2 \times \$5,000 = \$10,000$. Net of depreciation the value is only $5,000. Table 3.1 shows that Maple Leaf's total accumulated depreciation on fixed assets is $915.4 million. So while the assets cost $1,889.1 million, their net value in the accounts is only $1,889.1 – $915.4 = $973.7 million.

The fixed assets in Maple Leaf's balance sheet are all tangible assets. But Maple Leaf also has valuable intangible assets, such as its brand name, skilled management, and a well-trained labour force. Accountants are generally reluctant to record these intangible assets in the balance sheet unless they can be readily identified and valued.

There is, however, one important exception. When Maple Leaf has acquired other businesses in the past, it has paid more for these assets than the value shown in the other firms' accounts. This difference is shown in Maple Leaf's balance sheet as *goodwill and other intangibles*. The final assets listed, *other assets*, are long-term assets that do not fit elsewhere.

Now look at the right-hand portion of Maple Leaf's balance sheet, which shows where the money to buy the assets came from. The accountant starts by looking at the company's liabilities—that is, the money owed by the company. First come those liabilities that are likely to be paid off most rapidly. *Bank debt* is often the first current liability listed; it indicates the amount of money the company must pay its bankers within the next year. Maple Leaf did not show any bank debt. It owes its suppliers $621.6 million for goods that have been delivered but not yet paid for. These unpaid bills are shown as *accounts payable* (or *payables*). The *current portion of long-term debt* shows the amount of long-term debt due to be repaid in the coming year. In 2005 Maple Leaf will have to pay its long-term lenders $105.9 million. Both the borrowings and the payables are debts that Maple Leaf must repay within the year. They are therefore classified as current liabilities.

Maple Leaf's current assets total $809.3 million; its current liabilities amount to $755.2 million. Therefore the difference between the value of Maple Leaf's current assets and its current liabilities is $809.3 – $755.2 = $54.1 million. This figure is known as Maple Leaf's *net current assets* or *net working capital*. It roughly measures the company's potential reservoir of cash.

Below the current liabilities Maple Leaf's accountants have listed the firm's long-term liabilities—that is, debts that come due after the end of a year. You can see that banks and other investors have made long-term loans to Maple Leaf of $1,059.5 million. Also listed are other long-term liabilities. This is a collection of liabilities that arise from the accounting system used, such as future income taxes and pension benefits.

Maple Leaf's liabilities are financial obligations to various parties. For example, when Maple Leaf buys goods from its suppliers, it has a liability to pay for them; when it borrows from the bank, it has a liability to repay the loan. Thus the suppliers and the bank have first claim on the firm's assets. What is left over after the liabilities have been paid off belongs to the shareholders. This figure is known as the *shareholders' equity*. For Maple Leaf the total value of shareholders' equity amounts to $898.2 million. Part of this sum ($731.3 million) has resulted from the sale of shares to investors. The bulk of the remainder ($159.1 million) has come from earnings that Maple Leaf has retained and invested on shareholders' behalf with the rest from *other shareholders' equity*.

Finally, what is the minority interest entry, just above the shareholders' equity section? Since Maple Leaf's accountants are required to prepare a consolidated statement, all of the assets and

FIGURE 3.1
The main balance
sheet items

THE MAIN BALANCE SHEET ITEMS

Current assets } = { Current liabilities
  Cash & securities   Payables
  Receivables   Short-term debt
  Inventories
      +   +
Long-term assets   Long-term liabilities
  Tangible assets   +
  Intangible assets   Shareholders' equity

liabilities of Canada Bread are included in the balance sheet, as if Maple Leaf were the 100 percent owner of the bakery. However, Maple Leaf owns only 87 percent of Canada Bread's equity. The minority interest entry represents the book value of the 13 percent of Canada Bread's equity not owned by Maple Leaf.

Figure 3.1 shows how the separate items in the balance sheet link together. There are two classes of assets—current assets, which will soon be used or turned into cash, and long-term assets, which may be either tangible or intangible.[2] There are also two classes of liability—current liabilities, which are due for payment shortly, and long-term liabilities.

The difference between the assets and the liabilities represents the amount of the shareholders' equity. This is the basic balance sheet identity. Shareholders are sometimes call "residual claimants" on the firm. We mean by this that shareholders' equity is what is left over when the liabilities of the firm are subtracted from its assets:

$$\text{Shareholders' equity} = \text{Total assets} - \text{Total liabilities}$$

By the way, it is easy to obtain the financial statement of almost any publicly traded Canadian company. For example, the Web site **www.sedar.com** allows you to access all Canadian public securities filings, including annual reports. For U.S. companies, check out **www.reportgallery.com**. In addition, the Market Insight Web site that comes with this text provides Excel spreadsheets containing annual financial statements for U.S., Canadian, and other international firms for several years. See **www.mcgrawhill.ca/edumarketinsight**.

✓ Check Point 3.1

Suppose that Maple Leaf borrows $500 million by issuing new long-term bonds. It places $100 million of the proceeds in the bank and uses $400 million to buy new machinery. What items of the balance sheet would change? Would shareholders' equity change?

BOOK VALUES AND MARKET VALUES

Throughout this book we will frequently make a distinction between the book values of the assets shown in the balance sheet and their market values.

generally accepted accounting principles (GAAP) Procedures for preparing financial statements.

Items in the balance sheet are valued according to **generally accepted accounting principles**, commonly called **GAAP**. These state that assets must be shown in the balance sheet at their *historical cost* adjusted for depreciation. These **book values** are therefore "backward-looking" measures of value. They are based on the past cost of the asset, not its current market price or value to the firm. For example, suppose that a printing press cost McGraw-Hill Ryerson $1 million two years ago, but

book value Net worth of the firm according to the balance sheet.

---

[2] Sometimes long-term assets are called *fixed assets.* However, the term *fixed assets* is best used to describe tangible long-term assets, such as property, plant, and equipment.

in today's market such presses sell for $1.3 million. The book value of the press would be less than its market value and the balance sheet would understate the value of McGraw-Hill Ryerson's assets.

Or consider a specialized plant that Intel develops for producing special-purpose computer chips at a cost of $800 million. The book value of the plant is $800 million less depreciation. But suppose that shortly after the plant is constructed, a new chip makes the existing one obsolete. The market value of Intel's new plant could fall by 50 percent. In this case market value would be less than book value.

The difference between book value and market value is greater for some assets than for others. It is zero in the case of cash but potentially very large for fixed assets where the accountant starts with the initial cost of the fixed assets and then depreciates that figure according to a pre-specified schedule. The purpose of depreciation is to allocate the original cost of the asset over its life, and the rules governing the depreciation of asset values do not reflect actual loss of market value. As a result, the book value of fixed assets is often much higher than the market value, although often it is less.

The same goes for the right-hand side of the balance sheet. In the case of liabilities the accountant simply records the amount of money that you have promised to pay. For short-term liabilities this figure is generally close to the market value of that promise. For example, if you owe the bank $1 million tomorrow, the accounts show a book liability of $1 million. As long as you are not bankrupt, that $1 million is also roughly the value to the bank of your promise. But now suppose that $1 million is not due to be repaid for several years. The accounts still show a liability of $1 million, but how much your debt is worth depends on what happens to interest rates. If interest rates rise after you have issued the debt, lenders may not be prepared to pay as much as $1 million for your debt; if interest rates fall, they may be prepared to pay more than $1 million.[3] Thus the market value of a long-term liability may be higher or lower than the book value.

> The market values of assets and liabilities do not generally equal their book values. Book values are based on historical or original values. Market values measure current values of assets and liabilities.

The difference between book value and market value is likely to be greatest for shareholders' equity. The book value of equity measures the cash that shareholders have contributed in the past plus the cash that the company has retained and reinvested in the business on their behalf. But this often bears little resemblance to the total market value that investors place on the shares.

This is the case for Maple Leaf. At year-end, December 31, 2004, the market value of Maple Leaf's outstanding common equity was $1,873.9 million, based on a closing stock price of $14.97, but the book value of equity was only $898.2 million.

If the market price of the firm's shares falls through the floor, don't try telling the shareholders that the book value is satisfactory—they won't want to hear it. Shareholders are concerned with the market value of their shares; market value, not book value, is the price at which they can sell their shares. Managers who wish to keep their shareholders happy will focus on market values.

We will often find it useful to think about the firm in terms of a *market-value balance sheet*. Like a conventional balance sheet, a market-value balance sheet lists the firm's assets, but it records each asset at its current market value rather than at historical cost less depreciation. Similarly, each liability is shown at its market value.

> The difference between the market values of assets and liabilities is the market value of the shareholders' equity claim. The stock price is simply the market value of shareholders' equity divided by the number of outstanding shares.

---

[3] We will show you how changing interest rates affect the market value of debt in Chapter 5.

| EXAMPLE 3.1 | **MARKET- VERSUS BOOK-VALUE BALANCE SHEETS** |

Jupiter has developed a revolutionary auto production process that enables it to produce cars 20 percent more efficiently than any rival. It has invested $10 billion in building its new plant. To finance the investment, Jupiter borrowed $4 billion and raised the remaining funds by selling new shares of stock in the firm. There are currently 100 million shares of stock outstanding. Investors are very excited about Jupiter's prospects. They believe that the flow of profits from the new plant justifies a stock price of $75.

If these are Jupiter's only assets, the book-value balance sheet immediately after it has made the investment is as follows:

BOOK-VALUE BALANCE SHEET FOR JUPITER MOTORS
($ billions)

Assets		Liabilities and Shareholders' Equity	
Auto plant	$10	Debt	$4
		Shareholders' equity	6

Investors are placing a market value on Jupiter's equity of $7.5 billion ($75 per share × 100 million shares). We assume that the debt outstanding is worth $4 billion.[4] Therefore, if you owned all Jupiter's shares and all its debt, the value of your investment would be 7.5 + 4 = $11.5 billion. In this case you would own the company lock, stock, and barrel and would be entitled to all its cash flows. Because you can buy the entire company for $11.5 billion, the total value of Jupiter's assets must also be $11.5 billion. In other words, the market value of the assets must be equal to the market value of the liabilities plus the market value of the shareholders' equity.

We can now draw up the market-value balance sheet as follows:

MARKET-VALUE BALANCE SHEET FOR JUPITER MOTORS
($ billions)

Assets		Liabilities and Shareholders' Equity	
Auto plant	$11.5	Debt	$4
		Shareholders' equity	7.5

Notice that the market value of Jupiter's plant is $1.5 billion more than the plant cost to build. The difference is due to the superior profits that investors expect the plant to earn. Thus in contrast to the balance sheet shown in the company's books, the market-value balance sheet is forward looking. It depends on the benefits that investors expect the assets to provide.

Is it surprising that market value exceeds book value? It shouldn't be. Firms find it attractive to raise money to invest in various projects because they believe the projects will be worth more than they cost. Otherwise why bother? You will usually find that shares of stock sell for more than the value shown in the company's books.

Check Point 3.2

a. What would be Jupiter's price per share if the auto plant had a market value of $14 billion?
b. How would you reassess the value of the auto plant if the value of outstanding stock were $8 billion?

---

[4] Jupiter has borrowed $4 billion to finance its investment, but if the interest rate has changed in the meantime, the debt could be worth more or less than $4 billion.

3.2

THE INCOME STATEMENT

income statement Financial statement that shows the revenues, expenses, and net income of a firm over a period of time.

If Maple Leaf's balance sheet resembles a snapshot of the firm at a particular time, its **income statement** is like a video. It shows how profitable the firm has been during the past year.

Look at the summary income statement in Table 3.2. You can see that during 2004 Maple Leaf sold goods worth $6,365 million. The total expenses of producing and selling goods were $5.985 million. Included in these expenses are the costs of raw materials, labour, advertising and other marketing expenses, and head office costs. Maple Leaf's earnings before interest, taxes, depreciation, and amortization (EBITDA) were $380 million.

In addition to these out-of-pocket expenses, Maple Leaf also made a deduction for the value of the plant and equipment used up in producing the goods. In 2004 this charge for depreciation and amortization was $125.5 million. Thus Maple Leaf's total *earnings before interest and taxes (EBIT)* were

$$\text{EBIT} = \text{sales} - \text{operating expenses} - \text{depreciation and amortization}$$
$$= \$6,365 - \$5,985 \qquad - \$125.5$$
$$= \$254.5 \text{ million}$$

The remainder of the income statement shows where these earnings went. As we saw earlier, Maple Leaf has partly financed its investment in property and equipment by borrowing. In 2004 it paid $83.5 million of interest on this borrowing. A further slice of the profit went to the government in the form of taxes. This amounted to $58.9 million in 2004. The final slice was the minority interest entry of $9.9 million. Following the principles of consolidation, Maple Leaf's accountants included all of the revenues and expenses of Canada Bread as if Maple Leaf was the 100 percent owner. However, the earnings of the minority shareholders of Canada Bread must be subtracted to determine the earnings of the Maple Leaf shareholders. The net earnings of $102.2 million belonged to the Maple Leaf shareholders. Of this sum, Maple Leaf paid out $18.1 million in dividends and the remaining $84.1 million was reinvested in the business. Presumably, these invested funds made the company more valuable.

PROFITS VERSUS CASH FLOW

It is important to distinguish between Maple Leaf's profits and the cash that the company generates. Here are three reasons profits and cash are not the same:

TABLE 3.2
Consolidated Income Statement for Maple Leaf Foods Inc., 2004

Consolidated Income Statement for Maple Leaf Foods Inc., 2004 ($ millions)	
Sales	6,365.0
Total operating expenses	5,985.0
Earnings before interest, taxes, depreciation, and amortization (EBITDA)	380.0
Depreciation and amortization	125.5
Earnings before interest and taxes (EBIT)	254.5
Net interest expense	83.5
Taxable income	171.0
Taxes	58.9
Earnings before minority interest	112.1
Minority interest	9.9
Net Earnings	102.2
Allocation of net earnings	
Dividends	18.1
Addition to retained earnings	84.1

Source: Maple Leaf Foods Inc.

1. When Maple Leaf's accountants prepare the income statement, they do not simply count the cash coming in and the cash going out. Instead the accountants start with the cash payments but then divide these payments into two groups—current expenditures (such as wages) and capital expenditures (such as the purchase of new machinery). Current expenditures are deducted from current revenues. However, rather than deducting the cost of machinery in the year it is purchased, the accountants make an annual charge for depreciation. Thus the cost of machinery is spread over its forecast life.

   When calculating profits, the accountants *do not* deduct the expenditure on new equipment that year, even though cash is paid out. However, the accountants *do* deduct depreciation on assets previously purchased, even though no cash is currently paid out.

   For example, suppose a $100,000 investment is depreciated by $10,000 a year.[5] This depreciation is treated as an annual expense, although the cash actually went out of the door when the asset was first purchased. For this reason, the deduction for depreciation is classified as a *non-cash* expense.

   > To calculate the cash produced by the business it is necessary to add back the depreciation charge (which is not a cash payment) and to subtract the expenditure on new capital equipment (which is a cash payment).

2. Consider the following stages in a manufacturing business. In period 1 the firm produces the goods; it sells them in period 2 for $100; and it gets paid for them in period 3. The general rule is to recognize revenue at the time of the sale rather than when the cash is actually received. Therefore, although the cash does not arrive until period 3, the sale is included in the income statement for period 2. However, the accountant does not ignore the fact that the bills have not been paid. When the sale is made in period 2, the figure for accounts receivable in the balance sheet is adjusted to show that the company's customers owe an extra $100 in unpaid bills. Next period, when the customers pay their bills, the firm receives cash and receivables decline by $100. This payment has no impact on profits in that period.

   > The cash that the company receives is equal to the sales shown in the income statement less the increase in unpaid bills:

Period:	2	3
Sales	100	0
− Change in receivables	100	(100)
= Cash received	0	+100

3. The accountant also tries to match the costs of producing the goods with the revenues from the sale. For example, suppose that it costs $60 in period 1 to produce the goods that are then sold in period 2 for $100. It would be misleading to say that the business had a loss in period 1 (when it produced the goods) and was very profitable in period 2 (when it sold them). Therefore, to provide a fairer measure of the firm's profitability, the income statement will not show the $60 as an expense of producing the goods until they are sold in period 2. This practice is known as accrual accounting. The accountant gathers all expenses that are associated with a sale and deducts them from the revenues to calculate profit, even though the expenses may have occurred in an earlier period.

   Of course the accountant cannot ignore the fact that the firm spent money on producing the goods in period 1. So the expenditure will be shown in period 1 as an *investment* in inventories. Subsequently in period 2, when the goods are sold, the inventories will decline again.

---

[5] We discuss depreciation rules in Chapter 8.

In our example, the cash is paid out when the goods are manufactured in period 1 but this expense is not recognized until period 2 when the goods are sold.

The cash *outflow* is equal to the cost of goods sold, which is shown in the income statement, plus the change in inventories:

Period:	2	3
Costs of goods sold	0	60
− Change in inventories	60	(60)
= Cash paid out	+60	+0

Check Point 3.3

A firm pays $100 in period 1 to produce some goods. It sells those goods for $150 in period 2 but does not collect payment from its customers until period 3. Calculate the cash flows to the firm in each period by completing the following table. Do the resulting values for net cash flow in each period make sense?

Period:	1	2	3
Sales			
Change in accounts receivable			
Cost of goods sold			
Change in inventories			
Net cash flow			

3.3   THE STATEMENT OF CASH FLOWS

The firm requires *cash* when it buys new plant and machinery or when it pays interest to the bank and dividends to the shareholders. Therefore, the financial manager needs to keep track of the cash that is coming in and going out.

We have seen that the firm's cash flow can be quite different from its net income. These differences can arise for at least two reasons:

1. The income statement does not recognize capital expenditures as expenses in the year that the capital goods are paid for. Instead, it spreads those expenses over time in the form of an annual deduction for depreciation.
2. The income statement uses the accrual method of accounting, which means that revenues and expenses are recognized as they are incurred rather than when the cash is received or paid out.

statement of cash flows
Financial statement that shows the firm's cash receipts and cash payments over a period of time.

A simple way to measure how much cash a company generated is to calculate the change in its cash balances. From the balance sheet in Table 3.1, we see that Maple Leaf's cash and equivalents[6] increased by $72.9 million, from $38.9 million in 2003 to $111.8 million in 2004. Where did this cash come from? The **statement of cash flows** shows the firm's cash inflows and outflows from operations as well as from its investment and financing activities. Table 3.3 is the cash flow statement for Maple Leaf Foods. Look at the last line of Maple Leaf's cash flow statement. It shows that Maple Leaf's cash and equivalents increased $72.9 million, exactly matching the change in cash calculated from the balance sheet. By studying the statement of cash flow, you will learn where the cash came from.

The statement of cash flow contains three sections. The first shows the cash generated from Maple Leaf's operating activities, such as the production and sale of meat and bakery products.

---

[6] Marketable securities, such as commercial paper and government treasury bills, are typically considered as good as cash in the bank as these investments are easily sold.

TABLE 3.3
Consolidated Statement of
cash flows for Maple Leaf
Foods Inc.

Consolidated Statement of Cash Flows for Maple Leaf Foods Inc., 2004 ($ millions)	
Operating Activities	
Net earnings	102.2
Depreciation and amortization of property and equipment	125.5
Other adjustments	(29.5)
Cash provided by (used in) non-cash operating working capital	41.0
Cash provided by (used in) operating activities	239.2
Investing Activities	
Net additions to property and equipment	(144.2)
Purchase of Canada Bread shares	(18.9)
Purchase of net assets of businesses	(382.7)
Other	2.6
Cash provided by (used in) investing activities	(543.2)
Financing Activities	
Increase in long-term debt	1,023.0
Decrease in long-term debt	(772.1)
Increase in share capital	166.2
Cash dividends	(18.1)
Other	(22.1)
Cash provided by (used in) financing activities	376.9
Increase in cash and equivalents	72.9

Source: Maple Leaf Foods Inc. **Annual Report** 2004.

Next comes the cash that Maple Leaf has invested in plant and equipment or in the acquisition of new businesses. The final section reports cash flows from financing activities such as the sale of new debt or shares. We will look at these sections in turn.

The first section, operating activities, starts with net earnings (or net income) and then adjusts that figure for those parts of the income statement that do not involve cash coming in or going out. Therefore, the allowances for depreciation and amortization are added back because these are not cash flows even though they are treated as expenses in the income statement. Adjustments for any other non-cash items, such as future taxes and accounting gains or losses on the sale of fixed assets, are also made in this section of the cash flow statement. In Maple Leaf's case, additional net (non-cash) items of $29.5 million were subtracted.

Any additions to current assets, excluding cash and equivalents, need to be subtracted from net earnings, since these earnings absorb cash but do not show up in the income statement. Conversely, any additions to current liabilities need to be added to net income because these release cash.

In 2004, Maple Leaf reported that $41 million in cash was generated from changes in working capital, increasing Maple Leaf's cash flow. Cash flow from Maple Leaf's 2004 operating activities[7] was

Cash flow provided by operating activities (3.1)

$$= \text{Net earnings} + \text{depreciation and amortization}$$
$$+ \text{cash from (used in) other income statement adjustments}$$
$$+ \text{cash from (used in) non-cash working capital}$$
$$= \$102.2 \text{ million} + \$125.5 \text{ million} - \$29.5 \text{ million} + \$41 \text{ million}$$
$$= \$239.2 \text{ million}$$

---

[7] An equivalent way to calculate operating cash flow is: Sales – operating expenses, excluding depreciation and all other non-cash items – taxes + cash from (used in) working capital. Sales less operating expenses, excluding depreciation is also called EBITDA (earnings before interest, taxes, depreciation, and amortization), giving another expression for operating cash flow: EBITDA – taxes + cash from (used in) working capital. Done properly, all of these formulas give the identical value for operating cash flow.

We have pointed out that depreciation is not a cash payment; it is simply the accountant's allocation to the current year of the original cost of the capital equipment. However, cash does go out the door when the firm actually buys and pays for new capital equipment. Therefore, these capital expenditures are set out in the second section of the cash flow statement. You can see that Maple Leaf spent $144.2 million on new capital equipment, $18.9 million to purchase additional Canada Bread shares, and $382.7 million to acquire new businesses. Total cash used for investments was $543.2 million.[8]

In 2004, Maple Leaf generated $239.2 million in cash from its operating activities and spent $543.2 million in cash on its investing activities. Therefore, its **cash flow from assets** was $239.2 − $543.2, or −$304 million:

cash flow from assets Cash flow generated by the firm's operations, after investment in working capital and fixed assets. Also called free cash flow.

Cash flow from assets   = cash flow provided by operating activities   (3.2)
**   + cash flow from (used in) investments**
**   = $239.2 million − $543.2 million = −$304 million**

In 2004, Maple Leaf spent more cash on its investments than was generated through its operations. Where did the cash come from to cover the shortfall? Companies raise cash from investors by selling bonds and stocks and also by using their surplus cash in the bank.

The third section of the cash flow statement shows the details of the financing activities during the year. In 2004, Maple Leaf raised $1,023 million in cash by selling new long-term debt but also spent $772.1 million to retire other long-term debt, resulting in a net increase in cash of $250.9 million. Maple Leaf raised $166.2 million by selling additional common shares through a public offering and also paid $18.1 million in dividends. With an additional $22.1 million spent on other financing activities, the total cash flow raised from financing activities was $376.9 million.

Maple Leaf raised more cash from investors than it needed to cover the negative cash flow from assets. Extra cash raised from investors was added to Maple Leaf's bank account:

Increase (decrease) in cash in the bank   (3.3)
**   = Cash flow from assets + Cash flow from (used in) financing activities**
**   = −$304 million + $376.9 million = $72.9 million**

The last line of Maple Leaf's cash flow statement shows the $72.9 million increase in cash.

Check Point 3.4

Would the following activities increase or decrease the firm's cash balances?
a. Inventories are increased.
b. The firm reduces its accounts payable.
c. The firm issues additional common stock.
d. The firm buys new equipment.

3.4

CASH FLOW FROM ASSETS, FINANCING FLOW, AND FREE CASH FLOW

A company's cash flow from assets is the cash it generates through its operating activities, net of its investments in working capital and fixed assets. In addition, a company engages in financing activities, raising cash by issuing stocks and bonds, and paying out cash to its investors. Finally, it can add to or use cash in its bank account.   The *fundamental cash flow identity* states that cash flow from

---

[8] If you have only the balance sheet and income statement for a company, you can calculate net capital expenditures for a year as the change in net fixed assets plus depreciation: net capital expenditures = closing net fixed assets − closing net fixed asset from previous year + depreciation.

assets must be equal to cash flow to its bondholders and shareholders plus any change in cash in the bank. By rearranging Equation 3.3 we can show the fundamental cash flow identity:[9]

Cash flow from assets = Cash flow used in (from) financing activities   (3.4)
+ Increase (decrease) in cash in the bank

free cash flow Another term for cash flow from assets.

Often, cash flow from assets is called **free cash flow**. It is *free* because the cash flow from assets is the cash available to pay out to its bondholders and shareholders. We must warn you that there is no standard definition of free cash flow. If you see free cash flow reported, it is always wise to check how it has been measured. The sum of cash flows to bondholders, shareholders, and the change in cash balances is also called the company's **financing flow**. The fundamental cash flow identity says that a company's free cash flow must equal its financing flow.

financing flow Cash flow to bondholders and shareholders plus increase in cash balances; also equals cash flow to assets.

In Maple Leaf's case, cash flow from assets or free cash flow was –$304 million. Its cash flow used in financing activities was –$376.9 million and the bank balance increased $72.9 million, giving a financing flow of $-$376.9 million + $72.9 million, or $-$304 million.

You may have noticed that one important category of payment to bondholders is not listed in the financial activities section of the statement of cash flows: interest payments. When creating the cash flow statement, accountants treat interest as an operating expense, not as a financing activity. However, to measure cash flow from assets, independently of how the firm chooses to finance itself, interest expense should be classified as a financing activity. To do this, add back the interest expense to cash flow from assets and also add interest as a financing flow.[10]

Maple Leaf spent $83.5 million on interest. Its cash flow from assets, adjusted to remove the interest expense is

Cash flow from assets (adjusted) = Cash flow from assets + interest expense   (3.5)
= $-$304 million + $83.5 million = $-$220.5

As you would expect, treating interest as a financing flow increases Maple Leaf's cash flow from assets. Likewise the cash flow to bondholders and shareholders now includes interest paid, increasing financing flows to $-$220.5 million.

✓ **Check Point 3.5**   A firm's net earnings for the year were $7.3 million and its depreciation expense was $1.9 million. Working capital increased $2.6 million and $3.5 million was spent on new equipment. The company borrowed $1.5 million, raised no new equity, paid $.6 million in interest and $2 million in dividends. What was cash flow from assets for the year, treating interest as a financing flow? Show that cash balances must have increased $2.6 million. What was financing flow for the year?

Why is understanding a company's cash flow from assets and financing flow important? Financial managers care about the cash flow from assets and financing flow because it is their job to manage the company's inflows and outflows of cash. For a company with positive cash flow from assets, managers must decide how much of that cash to pay out to shareholders, either as dividends or through share repurchases, whether to pay off their debt, or to stockpile the surplus cash in the bank. As we saw with Maple Leaf, cash flow from assets can also be negative. In this case, managers must decide whether to either raise new financing by borrowing or issuing shares, or draw down cash reserves. Financing decisions and dividend policy decisions are at the very heart of financial management, and we will look at them in depth in later chapters.

---

[9] When rearranging Equation 3.3, the cash flow from financing activities is subtracted to move it to the other side of the equal sign. To incorporate the negative sign, we use cash flow *used in* financing activities rather than *from*. The number is same, just the sign changes.

[10] To be really precise, we should be using the *after-tax* interest expense. In Section 3.5 you will learn that interest expense is tax-deductible for a corporation. Thus the actual *cash* spent on interest is the after-tax amount, interest expense $\times$ (1 $-$ tax rate).   This adjustment is necessary for some methods of business valuation.

Investors are also interested in understanding a company's free cash flow. For example, if free cash flow is negative, can the firm survive? Negative free cash flow is quite common for new and growing firms, with greater investment expenditures than cash flow from operations. However, this is not sustainable in the long run. Investors will refuse to pour money into the business if they have no hope of receiving any return of cash flow. If the company's cash flow from assets is continuously negative, the financial managers may fail in their attempts to raise the needed financing to keep the company going and the company may fall into bankruptcy.

Free cash flow is also an important component used in the valuation of the company's assets. As we shall see in Chapter 4, the value of an asset depends on the cash flows you expect to receive. The value of a company's assets will depend on the cash flow those assets generate—its cash flow from assets. In Chapter 8 we will show you how to evaluate a firm's investment projects by measuring the project's cash flows. Those cash flows are the same as the firm's cash flow from assets.

3.5 ACCOUNTING PRACTICE AND ACCOUNTING MALPRACTICE

While generally accepted accounting principles (GAAP) go a long way to standardize accounting practice in Canada, accountants still have significant leeway in how they measure earnings and book values. Managers who are under pressure to perform can be tempted to take this leeway to present their financial statements in the best possible light. There are many ways that this can be done. Here are just two examples:

1. *Allowance for Bad Debts.* Most firms sell goods on credit and must make an allowance for the fact that some customers will not pay. But it can sometimes be tempting to take a rosy view of the proportion of bills that will go unpaid.
2. *Revenue Recognition.* As we saw above, firms record a sale when it is made, not when the customer actually pays. But there are occasions when it can be hard to know when the sale occurs. An extreme (and potentially fraudulent) version of this problem is know as "channel stuffing." The firm "sells" large quantities of goods to customers but gives them the right to later refuse delivery or return the product. The revenue from the "sale" is booked immediately, but the likely returns are not recognized until they occur in a future accounting period. Channel stuffing hit the headlines in 1997 when the head of Sunbeam Corporation, "Chainsaw" Al Dunlap, allegedly moved millions of dollars of appliances to distributors and retailers to produce record earnings.

Investors worry that some companies may be particularly tempted to inflate their earnings in such ways. They refer to such companies as having "low-quality" earnings, and they place a correspondingly lower value on the firms' stock.

Firms that aggressively exploit any latitude in the accounting rules are liable to find that it is only a small step further to produce fraudulent accounts. Enron broke accounting rules to hide its debt and overstate earnings in 2001. It subsequently went bankrupt. A few months later WorldCom admitted to inflating its profits by booking nearly $4 billion of expenses as capital expenditures. Accounting fraud is not just an American problem. In 2003, Parmalat, an Italian multinational dairy producer, went bankrupt after it was discovered the company had falsified its financial statements, including overstating its cash and sales. In 2004, Nortel Networks, one of Canada's largest companies, came under scrutiny for accounting problems that led to over-stated profits. The Nortel board of directors fired the CEO, the CFO, and controller and initiated an investigation to assess who was responsible for the accounting manipulations. In each case, the stock price of the company plummeted on the news of the frauds, and the negative effects spilled over to other companies as investors lost faith in many firms' financial statements.

Accounting practices can vary greatly from one country to another. For example, in Canada and the United States firms generally maintain one set of accounts that is sent to investors and a different set of accounts that is used to calculate their tax bill.[11] That would not be allowed in most countries. On the other hand, Canadian and U.S. standards are more stringent in most other regards. For example, German firms have far greater leeway to tuck money away in hidden reserve accounts. When Daimler-Benz AG, producer of the Mercedes-Benz automobile, decided to list its shares on the New York Stock Exchange in 1993, it was required to revise its accounting practices to conform to U.S. standards. While it reported a modest profit in the first half of 1993 using German accounting rules, it reported a *loss* of 1 billion marks ($592 million US) under the much more revealing U.S. rules, primarily because of differences in the treatment of reserves.

Such differences in international accounting standards pose a problem for financial analysts who attempt to compare firms using data from their financial statements. This is why foreign firms must restate their financial results using the generally accepted accounting principles (GAAP) of Canada before their shares can be listed on a Canadian stock exchange. Likewise, the United States requires foreign companies wishing to list on a U.S. stock exchange to restate their financial results using U.S. GAAP. However, some larger Canadian companies wishing to list shares and sell debt to Americans enjoy special access to the U.S. market through the multijurisdictional disclosure system (MJDS), which allows them less extensive disclosure requirements than other foreign issuers. Many foreign firms do make the accounting accommodations required to be able to access the large U.S. financial market. However, many firms have been reluctant to do this and list their shares elsewhere.

Currently, some countries allow firms to list on their stock exchange if the financial statements are prepared according to the International Accounting Standards (IAS), an alternative to GAAP rules. Why not have one set of accounting rules for all companies, regardless of country, to make it easier for investors to understand the financial health of companies and reduce the paperwork of companies? Although the negotiations are tricky, many countries are working toward this goal. The nearby Finance in Action box reports on the continued efforts to converge to one worldwide financial accounting system.

SEE BOX P. 62 ▶

3.6

TAXES

Taxes often have a major effect on financial decisions. Therefore, we should explain how corporations and investors are taxed.

CORPORATE TAX

Companies pay both federal and provincial tax on their income. The federal corporate tax rate is 22.12 percent. To assist small businesses, the federal tax rate is only 13.12 percent on the first $250,000 of the taxable income of Canadian-controlled private corporations. The appropriate provincial corporate tax rate is added to the federal rate to give the overall tax rate.[12] For example, a small business operating in New Brunswick pays 13.12 percent federal tax plus 2.75 percent provincial tax, giving a 15.87 percent total tax rate. Table 3.4 summarizes the main federal and provincial rates for 2004.[13] However, at the time of writing, future cuts to federal and provincial corporate tax rates had been announced. For example, the small business income limit is scheduled to increase to $300,000 in 2005. Visit PricewaterhouseCoopers' tax Web site, **www.ca.taxnews.com**, or the Canadian Tax Foundation Web site, **www.ctf.ca**, for current rates.

---

[11] For example, in their published financial statements most firms in Canada use straight-line depreciation. In other words, they make the same deduction for depreciation in each year of the asset's life. However, when they calculate taxable income, the same companies calculate their capital cost allowance, a form of accelerated depreciation—that is, they make larger deductions for depreciation in the early years of the asset's life and smaller deductions in the later years.

[12] Not all corporate income is subject to provincial taxation; for instance, income earned outside Canada. In this case, 10 percentage points are added to the federal rate, giving a basic federal rate of 32.12 percent.

[13] We have not included any federal or provincial surtaxes.

Closing the GAAP

International standards are ready to fly. But will convergence between the United States and the world cause delays?

After years of planning, the world is heading toward convergence of accounting standards, with most industrialized countries already pledged to commit by 2007 at the latest.

If standards convergence sounds like a yawn, it isn't. The benefits for stakeholders are enormous, ranging from the obvious (not having to pay to produce two or more sets of numbers; for instance, Swiss pharmaceutical giant Roche Group, which operates in more than 100 countries, once estimated it could save about $100 million annually if it produced just one set of books) to some much more substantial, such as enabling investors to make apples-to-apples financial comparisons of companies regardless of where they are based.

Just how close are international standards to becoming a reality? Very. "Already there's a whole body of international standards; these are very real," says Tricia O'Malley, a board member of the London-based International Accounting Standards Board (IASB), which started up in April 2001 and is charged with spearheading international accounting standard-setting efforts.

The more interesting question, says O'Malley, is: how close are we to converged international standards? "The answer is we're more so than many people would have believed possible only a year or two ago. Recent accounting scandals have reminded investors of how important transparent financial reporting really is to strong capital markets. In turn, investor demands have galvanized standard setters worldwide: we're getting into initiatives that otherwise might have taken years to launch."

According to GAAP Convergence 2002, a report produced by the world's six largest accounting firms, of the 59 countries surveyed, 95 percent say that they have adopted international standards or expect to; of those, 39 percent have a formal plan to adopt or to converge — including Canada. Just as important, both the Financial Accounting Standards Board (FASB) and the IASB say that the convergence of US GAAP and of international standards is a primary objective of both boards.

With the adoption of international standards, "investors and other stakeholders will be able to compare like with like," notes Frits Bolkestein, European commissioner and directorate general for the Internal Market. "It will help European firms to compete on equal terms when raising capital on world markets." Others see the same kind of benefits. "By drawing on the best of US GAAP, international and other national standards, the world's capital markets will have a set of global accounting standards that investors can trust," says IASB chair Sir David Tweedie.

The bottom line: accounting standard setters realize the world simply cannot afford the inefficiencies of even two significantly different standard-setting systems, particularly if those variances impede the flow of capital worldwide, slow or kill investment decisions, help mask accounting irregularities or impede the release of accurate financial information. "If you can reduce the cost of capital worldwide by even a few basis points, that's an enormous amount of money," says IASB board member Tony Cope.

So why not break out the convergence champagne and celebrate a new international standard-setting organization brought about with remarkably little rancor for a major multilateral effort? There are plenty of reasons. The IASB is still in its infancy, little more than two years old. Currently there are some completed international standards on its books that don't need major improvements or changes before more accounting professionals worldwide buy into them; these improvement efforts are ongoing. Standards that will cover some of the most important yet contentious global accounting concerns (those regarding business combinations, for instance, and financial instruments, stock options, and performance reporting) are in the developmental, writing, or rewriting stages, while others such as leases and extractive industries are just getting on the radar screen. Many of them are a year or two away from being finalized.

Adapted from Lawrence Richter Quinn, "Closing the GAAP," *CAmagazine* 126 (August 2003), pp. 16–22. Reproduced by permission–from *CAmagazine*, published by the Canadian Institute of Chartered Accountants, Toronto, Canada.

When firms calculate taxable income they are allowed to deduct expenses such as labour and material costs, marketing and selling costs, and administration expenditures. However, the costs of equipment, new factories, and other fixed assets cannot be deducted all at once, but instead, are deducted over time, depreciating the value of the assets. The allowable depreciation for tax purposes is determined by the *Income Tax Act* and is called the *capital cost allowance* (CCA).[14] Although the capital cost allowance is similar in concept to the GAAP depreciation charge reported in financial statements, the two systems are sufficiently different that taxes paid to Canada Revenue Agency (CRA) may be very different from the tax expense reported in the income statement.[15]

---

[14] We will tell you more about these allowances in Chapter 8.

[15] The capital cost allowance is a type of accelerated depreciation, allowing bigger deductions at the beginning of the life of an asset. This reduces taxable income and taxes relative to what they would be according to the GAAP straight-line depreciation used in the income statement. Future taxes, a liability account on the balance sheet, is an adjustment needed to reconcile the tax expense on the income statement with the actual taxes paid to CRA.

TABLE 3.4
Federal and provincial
corporate tax rates, 2004

	GENERAL RATE (%)		SMALL BUSINESS RATE (%), INCOME UP TO $250,000	
Federal	22.12		13.12	
	Prov.	Fed + Prov.	Prov.	Fed + Prov.
British Columbia	13.5	35.62	4.5	17.62
Alberta	11.75	33.87	3.25	16.37
Saskatchewan	17	39.12	5.5	18.62
Manitoba	15.5	37.62	5	18.12
Ontario	14	36.12	5.5	18.62
Quebec	8.9	31.02	8.9	22.02
New Brunswick	13	35.12	2.75	15.87
Nova Scotia	16	38.12	5	18.12
Prince Edward Island	16	38.12	7.5	20.62
Newfoundland and Labrador	14	36.12	5	18.12
Northwest Territories	14	36.12	4	17.12
Nunavut	12	34.12	4	17.12
Yukon	15	37.12	6	19.12
Average Rate	13.9	36.0	5.1	18.3

Source: PricewaterhouseCoopers, *Tax Figures for Individuals and Corporations,* Canada 2004.

The company is also allowed to deduct interest paid to debtholders when calculating its taxable income, but dividends paid to shareholders are not deductible. These dividends are therefore paid out of after-tax income. Table 3.5 provides an example of how interest payments reduce corporate taxes. Although both companies have earnings before interest and taxes of $100, Firm A pays only $21 in tax, leaving it with $100 – $21, or $79, to pay to bondholders and shareholders. Firm B has only $100 – $35, or $65, to distribute.

The bad news about taxes is that each extra dollar of revenues increases taxable income by $1 and results in 35 cents of extra taxes. The good news is that each extra dollar of expense reduces taxable income by $1 and therefore reduces taxes by 35 cents. For example, if the firm borrows money, every dollar of interest it pays on the loan reduces taxes by 35 cents. Therefore, after-tax income is reduced by only 65 cents.

Check Point 3.6

Recalculate the figures in Table 3.5 assuming that Firm A now has to make interest payments of $60 million. What happens to taxes paid? Does net income fall by the additional $20 million interest payment compared with the case considered in Table 3.5, where interest expense was only $40 million?

TABLE 3.5
Firms A and B both have
earnings before interest and
taxes (EBIT) of $100 million,
but A pays out part of its
profits as debt interest. This
reduces the corporate tax
paid by A.

	FIRM A	FIRM B
	($ millions)	
EBIT	$100	$100
Interest	40	0
Pretax income	60	100
Tax (35% of pretax income)	21	35
Net income	39	65

When firms make profits, they pay 35 percent of the profits to CRA. But the process doesn't work in reverse; if the firm takes an operating loss, CRA does not send it a cheque for 35 percent of the loss. However, the firm can carry the losses back, deduct them from taxable income in earlier years, and claim a refund of past taxes. Losses can also be carried forward and deducted from taxable income in the future. Currently, operating losses can be carried back a maximum of three years and carried forward for up to seven years.

PERSONAL TAX

Table 3.6 shows the 2004 federal and provincial personal tax rates for employment income, interest income, and unincorporated business income. Dividends and capital gains are taxed at special rates, and we discuss them later in the section.

marginal tax rate Additional taxes owed per dollar of additional income.

The tax rates presented in Table 3.6 are **marginal tax rates** and they apply to various income tax brackets. The marginal tax rate is the tax the individual pays on each extra dollar of income. As a federal taxpayer, you would pay 16 cents for each extra dollar of income you earn when your income is below $35,001, but you would pay 22 cents of tax on each dollar of income in excess of $35,001 and up to $70,000. As outlined in Table 3.6, the federal personal tax system has four income brackets and marginal tax rates. This is a progressive tax system—the higher the income, the higher the tax rate. Almost all provincial and territorial systems are progressive. Alberta is the exception, where a flat tax rate of 10 percent is charged on all income.

For example, suppose you live in Saskatchewan and your taxable income is $50,000. Your federal tax is 16 percent of the first $35,000 and 22 percent on the remaining $15,000:

$$\text{Federal tax} = (.16 \times \$35,000) + (.22 \times \$15,000) = \$8,900$$

From Table 3.6 we see that the Saskatchewan provincial tax rate is 11 percent on the first $36,155 of taxable income and 13 percent on income in excess of $36,155. Your provincial tax is

$$\text{Provincial tax} = (.11 \times \$36,155) + (.13 \times \$13,845) = \$5,776.9$$

As you can see, taxpayers end up calculating their taxes twice: once for the federal government and once for their provincial government. It's no wonder that computerized tax preparation software is popular!

average tax rate Total taxes owed divided by total income.

What is your tax rate? The **average tax rate** is simply the total tax bill divided by total income. In this example, total tax is $8,900 + $5,776.9, or $14,676.9, giving an average tax rate of $14,676.9/$50,000 = .294, or 29.4 percent. At the margin, however, an extra dollar of income is taxed at 22 percent federally and 13 percent provincially, making a combined marginal tax rate of 22 percent plus 13 percent, or 35 percent. The marginal tax rate is usually the most important for making financial decisions because different types of income are taxed at different marginal rates, as we will discuss next.

Financial managers need to know about personal tax rates because dividends and interest payments that companies make to individuals are both subject to tax. If these payments are heavily taxed, individuals will be more reluctant to buy the company's shares or bonds. Remember that each dollar of income that the company earns is taxed at the corporate rate. If the company then pays a dividend out of this after-tax income, the shareholder also pays personal income tax on that dividend. Thus the income that is paid out as a dividend is taxed twice, once in the hands of the firm and once in the hands of the shareholder. Suppose instead that the company earns a dollar that is then paid out as interest. This dollar escapes corporate tax, but an individual who received the interest must pay personal tax.

The personal tax rates in Table 3.6 apply to interest income but not to dividend income. In Canada, dividends paid by Canadian companies to individuals are taxed at a lower rate, giving credit for some of the corporate tax already paid.

The calculation of personal tax on dividends is a bit messy but not tough. Suppose you receive $50 of dividends and your marginal federal tax rate is 26 percent. To calculate your federal tax,

TABLE 3.6
Federal and provincial personal income tax rates, 2004

TAX RATES AND BRACKETS					
Federal	16.0	0–35,000	Nova Scotia	8.79	0–29,590
	22.0	35,001–70,000		14.95	29,591–59,180
	26.0	70,001–113,804		16.67	59,181–93,000
	29.0	113,805 and over		17.5	93,001 and over
British Columbia	6.05	0–32,476	Prince Edward	9.8	0–30,754
	9.15	32,477–64,954	Island	13.80	30,755–61,509
	11.7	64,955–74,575		16.70	61,510 and over
	13.7	74,576–90,555			
	14.7	90,556 and over	Newfoundland	10.57	0–29,590
			and Labrador	16.16	29,591–59,180
Alberta	10.0	All income		18.02	59,181 and over
Saskatchewan	11.0	0–36,155	Northwest	7.20	0–33,245
	13.0	36,156–103,300	Territories	9.90	33,246–66,492
	15.0	103,301 and over		11.95	66,493–108,101
				13.55	108,102 and over
Manitoba	10.9	0–30,544			
	14	30,545–65,000	Nunavut	4.00	0–35,000
	17.4	65,001 and over		7.00	35,001–70,000
				9.00	70,001–113,804
Ontario	6.05	0–33,375		11.5	113,805 and over
	9.15	33,376–66,752			
	11.16	66,753 and over	Yukon	7.04	0–35,000
				9.68	35,001–70,000
Quebec	16.00	0–27,635		11.44	70,001–113,804
	20.00	27,636–55,280		12.76	113,805 and over
	24.00	55,281 and over			
New Brunswick	9.68	0–32,183			
	14.82	32,184–64,368			
	16.52	64,369–104,648			
	17.84	104,649 and over			

Note: All surtaxes have been ignored.
Source: Based on data from Canada Revenue Agency, http://www.cra-arc.gc.ca/tax/individuals/faq/2004_rate-e.html.

first "gross up" your dividends to 125 percent of the actual dividends received, to get *grossed-up* or *taxable* dividends:

$$\text{Grossed-up dividends} = \text{gross-up factor} \times \text{dividends}$$
$$= 1.25 \times \$50, \text{ or } \$62.50$$

The gross federal tax on the grossed-up dividends is

$$\text{Gross federal tax} = \text{federal tax rate} \times \text{grossed-up dividends}$$
$$= .26 \times \$62.50, \text{ or } \$16.25$$

However, you don't pay this amount! Subtract the federal dividend tax credit of 13.33 percent of the grossed-up dividend (or 16.66 percent of the actual dividend paid):

$$\text{Federal dividend tax credit} = \text{federal dividend tax credit rate} \times \text{grossed-up dividends}$$
$$= .1333 \times \$62.50, \text{ or } \$8.33.$$

Your net federal dividend tax is gross federal tax less the dividend tax credit:

$$\text{Federal dividend tax} = \text{gross federal dividend tax} - \text{federal dividend tax credit}$$
$$= \$16.25 - \$8.33 = \$7.92$$

To calculate the provincial tax on the $50 dividend, repeat the steps using the appropriate provincial tax rate and provincial dividend tax credit. The B.C. dividend tax credit is 5.1 percent of grossed-up dividends, Alberta's is 6.4 percent, Manitoba's is 5 percent, Ontario's is 5.13 percent,

Quebec's is 10.83 percent, New Brunswick's is 3.7%, Nova Scotia's is 7.7 percent, PEI's is 7.7 percent, Newfoundland and Labrador's is 5 percent, Northwest Territories's is 6 percent, Nunavut's is 4 percent, and Yukon's is 5.87 percent.

EXAMPLE 3.2

CALCULATING THE TAX ON DIVIDENDS

You live in Ontario and receive $50 in dividends in 2004. Your federal marginal tax rate is 26 percent and your provincial marginal tax rate is 11.16 percent. The federal dividend tax is $7.92, as calculated above. Your Ontario dividend tax is

$$\text{Ontario dividend tax} = \text{gross Ontario dividend tax} - \text{Ontario dividend tax credit}$$
$$= .1116 \times \$62.50 - .0513 \times \$62.50 = \$3.77$$

Total dividend tax is $7.92 + $3.77, or $11.69.

In Example 3.2, the after-tax dividend income is the $50 dividend less the $11.69 in taxes, or $38.31. The effective tax rate on dividend income equals the dividend tax divided by dividends received, $11.69/$50, or 23.4 percent. This is substantially less than the combined federal-provincial marginal tax rate on salary and interest income of 26 percent + 11.16 percent, or 37.16 percent.

In addition to salary, interest, and dividend income, individuals can also earn capital gains income. A capital gain occurs when an asset is sold for more than its original purchase price. If you sell the asset for less than the original purchase price, you have a capital loss. Currently, 50 percent of capital gains are taxable; in other words, capital gains are taxed at one-half of the regular or full personal tax rate. Capital losses can be used to reduce your capital gains. If you don't have a capital gain in the current year to offset capital loss, you can carry the loss back up to three years or carry it forward indefinitely to reduce capital gains from another year. Capital gains and losses are *realized* only when you sell the asset. If you don't sell, you pay no tax.

EXAMPLE 3.3

DETERMINING CAPITAL GAINS TAX

You bought shares in Bio-technics stock when it was selling for 10 cents a share. Its market price is now $1 a share. As long as you hold on to the stock, there is no tax to pay on your gain. But if you sell for $1, you realize a capital gain of 90 cents and must pay tax. If your combined marginal federal and provincial tax rate is 40 percent, the capital gains tax rate is 20 percent, and the capital gains tax is .2 × $0.90, or $0.18. Your after-tax capital gain is $0.90 – $0.18, or $0.72 per share sold.

✔ **Check Point 3.7**

Suppose in 2004 you lived in British Columbia and earned interest income of $1,000 and dividend income of $1,000, and realized a capital gain of $1,000. Calculate the tax, the after-tax income, and the tax rate for each of the different types of income assuming you are in the lowest tax bracket. Redo the calculations assuming you are in the highest tax bracket. Rank high and low income taxpayers' tax rates on the different types of income.

The tax rates in Table 3.6 apply to individuals. But financial institutions are major investors in shares and bonds. These institutions often have special rates of tax. For example, pension funds, which hold huge numbers of shares, are not taxed on either dividend income or capital gains.

The financial policies of companies affect the taxes paid by both the company and its investors, the bondholders and shareholders. By selecting financial policies that minimize investors' taxes, financial managers can increase the wealth of their investors. We will return to the important issue of investor taxation when we examine financing and dividend payout decisions of companies in Chapters 15 and 16.

3.7   SUMMARY

1. What information is contained in the balance sheet, income statement, and statement of cash flows?

Investors and other stakeholders in the firm need regular financial information to help them monitor the firm's progress. Accountants summarize this information in a balance sheet, income statement, and statement of cash flows.

The **balance sheet** provides a snapshot of the firm's assets and liabilities. The assets consist of current assets that can be rapidly turned into cash and long-term assets, which may be fixed assets such as plant and machinery. The liabilities consist of current liabilities that are due for payment shortly and long-term debts. The difference between the assets and the liabilities represents the amount of the shareholders' equity.

The **income statement** measures the profitability of the company during the year. It shows the difference between revenues and expenses.

The **statement of cash flows** measures the sources and uses of cash during the year. The change in the company's cash balance is the difference between the sources and uses.

2. What is the difference between market and book value?

It is important to distinguish between the book values that are shown in the company accounts and the market values of the assets and liabilities. **Book values** are historical measures based on the original cost of an asset. For example, the assets in the balance sheet are shown at their historical cost less an allowance for depreciation. Similarly, the figure for shareholders' equity measures the cash that shareholders have contributed in the past or that the company has contributed on their behalf.

3. Why does accounting income differ from cash flow?

Income is not the same as cash flow. There are two reasons for this: (1) investment in fixed assets is not deducted immediately from income but is instead spread over the expected life of the equipment, and (2) the accountant records revenues when a sale is made rather than when the customer actually pays the bill, and at the same time, deducts the production costs even though those costs may have been incurred earlier.

4. What are a firm's cash flows?

Cash flow from assets measures the cash generated through operating activities and after making necessary investments in net working capital and fixed assets. This cash flow is either distributed to the firm's investors, creditors, and shareholders, or held in reserve by the firm as cash and marketable securities. We call this the **financing flow** of the firm. Cash flow from assets must equal the financial flows.

5. What are the essential features of the taxation of corporate and personal income?

For large companies the marginal rate of tax on income is around 36 percent and around 18 percent for small businesses. In calculating taxable income the company deducts an allowance for depreciation and interest payments. It cannot deduct dividend payments to the shareholders.

Individuals are also taxed on their income, which includes dividends and interest on their investments. Dividends are taxed at lower rates than interest and employment income. Capital gains are taxed at one-half the personal tax rate, but only when the investment is sold and the gain realized.

Related Web Links

www.sedar.com Annual reports and other documents of Canadian public companies

www.reportgallery.com Useful links to financial statements and other documents of mainly U.S. public companies

www.ibm.com/investor/financialguide Guide to understanding financial data in an annual report, from IBM

http://philanthropy.ml.com/ipo/resources/pdf/understandingfinancial.pdf The Merrill Lynch Guide to Understanding Financial Reports

http://www.icaew.co.uk/library/index.cfm?AUB=TB2I_25631 Links to accounting standard setters around the world

www.ca.taxnews.com PricewaterhouseCoopers tax site; click on "News and Views" and then on "Tax Facts and Figures" for current tax rates

Key Terms

Questions and Problems

*Answers in Appendix B

BASIC

*1. **Balance Sheet.** Construct a balance sheet for Sophie's Sofas given the following data. What is shareholders' equity?

Cash balances = $10,000
Inventory of sofas = $200,000
Store and property, net = $100,000
Accounts receivable = $22,000
Accounts payable = $17,000
Long-term debt = $170,000

2. **Financial Statements.** Earlier in the chapter, we characterized the balance sheet as providing a snapshot of the firm at one point in time and the income statement as providing a video. What did we mean by this? Is the statement of cash flows more like a snapshot or a video?

3. **Income versus Cash Flow.** Explain why accounting revenue generally differs from a firm's cash inflows.

4. **Working Capital.** QuickGrow is in an expanding market, and its sales are increasing by 25 percent annually. Would you expect its net working capital to be increasing or decreasing? Explain.

5. **Tax Rates.** Using Table 3.6, calculate the combined federal and provincial marginal and average tax rates for both an Albertan and Newfoundlander with the following incomes:
   a. $20,000
   *b. $60,000
   c. $100,000
   d. $3,000,000

6. **Tax Rates.** What would be the marginal and average tax rates for a Manitoban corporation with an income level of $100,000?

*7. **Taxes.** John Flynn lives in Nova Scotia. In 2004 he earned $1,500 in interest income and $3,000 in dividend income, and realized a $2,000 capital gain. Calculate his after-tax income and tax rate for each type of income, assuming that his marginal federal tax rate was 26 percent, his marginal provincial tax rate was 17.5 percent, the dividend gross-up factor is 125 percent, the federal dividend tax credit is 13.33 percent of grossed-up dividends, and the provincial dividend tax credit is 7.7 percent of grossed-up dividends.

8. **Cash Flows.** What impact will the following actions have on the firm's cash balance?
   a. The firm sells some goods from inventory.
   b. The firm sells some machinery to a bank and leases it back for a period of 20 years.
   c. The firm buys back 1 million shares from existing shareholders.

PRACTICE

*9. **Balance Sheet/Income Statement.** The year-end 2005 balance sheet of Brandex Inc. lists common stock at $1,100,000 and retained earnings at $3,400,000. The next year, retained earnings were listed at $3,700,000. The firm's net income in 2006 was $900,000. There were no stock repurchases during the year. What were dividends paid by the firm in 2006?

10. **Taxes.** You set up your tax preparation firm as an incorporated business in Nova Scotia. You took $70,000 from the firm as your salary. The firm's taxable income for the year (net of your salary) was $30,000. How much tax must be paid, including both your personal taxes and the firm's taxes? By how much will you reduce the total tax bill by reducing

your salary to $50,000, thereby leaving the firm with taxable income of $50,000? Use the tax rates presented in Tables 3.4 and 3.6.

11. **Market versus Book Values.** The founder of Alchemy Products, Inc. discovered a way to turn lead into gold and patented this new technology. He then formed a corporation and invested $200,000 in setting up a production plant. He believes that he could sell his patent for $50 million.

   *a.   What are the book value and market value of the firm?

   *b.   If there are 2 million shares of stock in the new corporation, what would be the price per share and the book value per share?

   c.   Why are the price per share and book value per share so different?

*12. **Income Statement.** Sheryl's Shingles had sales of $10,000 in 2004. The cost of goods sold was $6,500, general and administrative expenses were $1,000, interest expenses were $500, and depreciation was $1,000. Working capital increased $200 and capital expenditures were $900. The firm's tax rate is 35 percent.

   a.   What is earnings before interest and taxes?

   b.   What is net income?

   c.   What is cash flow from operating activities?

   d.   What is cash flow from assets?

13. **Cash Flow.** Can cash flow from operating activities be positive if net income is negative? Can operating cash flow be negative if net income is positive? Give examples.

EXCEL

14. **Cash Flows.** Ponzi Products produced 100 chain letter kits this quarter, resulting in a total cash outlay of $10 per unit. It will sell 50 of the kits next quarter at a price of $11, and the other 50 kits in two quarters at a price of $12. It takes a full quarter for it to collect its bills from its customers. (Ignore possible sales in earlier or later quarters.)

   a.   Prepare an income statement for Ponzi for today and for each of the next three quarters. Ignore taxes.

   b.   What are the cash flows for the company today and in each of the next three quarters?

   c.   What is Ponzi's net working capital in each quarter?

15. **Profits versus Cash Flow.** During the last year of operations, accounts receivable increased by $10,000, accounts payable increased by $5,000, and inventories decreased by $2,000. What is the total impact of these changes on the difference between profits and cash flow?

EXCEL

16. **Income Statement.** A firm's income statement includes the following data. The firm's average tax rate was 20 percent.

Cost of goods sold	$8,000
Income taxes paid	2,000
Administrative expenses	3,000
Interest expense	1,000
Depreciation	1,000

   a.   What was the firm's net income?

   b.   What must have been the firm's revenues?

   c.   What was EBIT?

17. **Profits versus Cash Flow.** Butterfly Tractors had $14 million in sales last year. Cost of goods sold was $8 million, depreciation expense was $2 million, interest payment on outstanding debt was $1 million, capital expenditures were $1 million, and the firm's tax rate was 35 percent.

   a.   What were the firm's net income, cash flows from operations, and cash flow from assets?

   b.   What would happen to net income and cash flows if depreciation were increased by $1 million? How do you explain the differing impact of depreciation on income versus cash flow?

c. Would you expect the change in income and cash flows from the change in depreciation to have a positive or negative impact on the firm's stock price?

d. Now consider the impact on net income and cash flow if the firm's interest expense were $1 million higher. Why is this case different from part (b)?

18. **Cash Flow.** Candy Canes, Inc. spends $100,000 to buy sugar and peppermint in April. It produces its candy and sells it to distributors in May for $150,000, but it does not receive payment until June. For each month, find the firm's sales, net income, and operating cash flow.

19. **Financing Flows.** Interest expense for Rhodes Manufacturing was $500,000 in 2005. During 2005, $3.7 million in old debt was repaid and $2.0 million was raised through new borrowing. Dividends of $425,000 were paid and $1.75 million was raised through new share sales.

a. Calculate the cash flow to bondholders. Treat interest as a financing flow.

b. Calculate the cash flow to shareholders.

c. If cash and marketable securities increased $300,000 in 2005, what were the 2005 financing flow and cash flow from assets? Treat interest as a financing flow.

*20. **Financial Statements.** Here are the 2004 and 2005 (incomplete) balance sheets for Nobel Oil Corp.

NOBEL OIL CORP. BALANCE SHEET, AS OF END OF YEAR

Assets	2005	2004	Liabilities and Shareholders' Equity	2005	2004
Current assets	$ 420	$ 310	Current liabilities	$240	$210
Net fixed assets	1,420	1,200	Long-term debt	920	830

a. What was owners' equity at the end of 2004 and 2005?

b. If Nobel paid dividends of $100 in 2005, what must have been net income during the year? Assume no shares were issued or retired.

c. If Nobel purchased $300 in fixed assets during the year, what must have been the depreciation charge on the income statement? See footnote 8, page 58.

d. What was the change in net working capital between 2004 and 2005?

e. If Nobel issued $200 of new long-term debt, how much debt must have been paid off during the year?

f. What were the 2005 cash flow from operations and cash flow from assets?

g. What were the 2005 cash flow to bondholders, cash flow to shareholders, and the financing flow?

21. **Financial Statements.** South Sea Baubles has the following (incomplete) balance sheet and income statement.

SOUTH SEA BAUBLES BALANCE SHEET, AS OF END OF YEAR
($ millions)

Assets	2005	2004	Liabilities and Shareholders' Equity	2005	2004
Current assets	$140	$ 90	Current liabilities	$ 60	$ 50
Net fixed assets	900	800	Long-term debt	750	600

INCOME STATEMENT, 2005
($ millions)

Revenue	$1,950
Cost of goods sold	1,030
Depreciation	350
Interest expense	240

a. What is shareholders' equity in 2004 and 2005?

b. What is net working capital in 2004 and 2005?

c. What is taxable income and taxes paid in 2005? Assume the firm pays taxes equal to 35 percent of taxable income.

d. What is cash flow provided by operations during 2005? Pay attention to changes in net working capital.

e. Net fixed assets increased from $800 million to $900 million during 2005. What must have been South Sea's gross investment in fixed assets (capital expenditures) during 2005? See footnote 8, page 58.

f. If South Sea reduced its outstanding accounts payable by $35 million during 2005, what must have happened to its other current liabilities?

g. What are the 2005 cash flow from assets, and cash flow to bondholders and shareholders?

CHALLENGE

Here are some data on Fincorp, Inc., that you should use for problems 22 to 30. The balance sheet items correspond to values at year-end of 2004 and 2005, while the income statement items correspond to revenues or expenses during the year ending in either 2004 or 2005. All values are in thousands of dollars.

	2004	2005
Accounts payable	350	300
Revenue	$4,100	$4,000
Depreciation	520	500
Inventories	350	300
Long-term debt	2,400	2,000
Administrative expenses	550	500
Federal and provincial taxes[a]	420	400
Accounts receivable	450	400
Interest expense	150	150
Net fixed assets[b]	5,800	5,000
Notes payable	600	1,000
Dividends paid	410	410
Cost of goods sold	1,700	1,600
Cash and marketable securities	300	800

a Taxes are paid in their entirety in the year that the tax obligation is incurred.
b Net fixed assets are fixed assets net of accumulated depreciation since the asset was installed.

22. **Balance Sheet.** Construct a balance sheet for Fincorp for 2004 and 2005. What is shareholders' equity?

*23. **Working Capital.** What happened to net working capital during the year? What about non-cash net working capital?

EXCEL

24. **Income Statement.** Construct an income statement for Fincorp for 2004 and 2005. What was the addition to retained earnings for 2005? How does that compare with the increase in shareholders' equity between the two years?

*25. **Earnings per Share.** Suppose that Fincorp has 500,000 shares outstanding. What were earnings per share?

26. **Taxes.** What was the firm's average tax bracket for each year? Do you have enough information to determine the marginal tax bracket?

27. **Balance Sheet.** Examine the values for depreciation in 2005 and net fixed assets in 2004 and 2005. What was Fincorp's gross investment in plant and equipment during 2005?

28. **Cash Flows.** Construct a statement of cash flows for Fincorp for 2005 using Table 3.3 as a guide. Treat interest as an operating expense.

29. **Operating Cash Flow.** Calculate Fincorp's operating cash flow two ways: start with net income and then start with revenues. See footnote 7. Treat interest as a financing flow.

30. **Free Cash Flows.**
    a. Using the data for Fincorp, determine the cash flow from assets, cash flow to bondholders, cash flow to shareholders, and financing flows. Treat interest as a financing flow.
    b. Assuming that Fincorp's tax rate is 32 percent, calculate its after-tax interest expense. Why is it appropriate to convert the interest expense to its after-tax cost but not appropriate to adjust dividends?
    c. Using the after-tax interest expense, recalculate cash flow from assets and financing flow. Compare with your answers in problem (a). In what ways are the values different?

EXCEL

*31. **Book versus Market Value.** Now suppose that the *market value* (in thousands of dollars) of Fincorp's fixed assets in 2005 is $6,000, and that the value of its long-term debt is only $2,400. In addition, the consensus among investors is that Fincorp's past investments in developing the skills of its employees are worth $2,900. This investment of course does not show up on the balance sheet. What will be the price per share of Fincorp stock?

32. **Cash Flow from Assets and Financing Flow.** Using the financial statements for Small Time Products, calculate cash flow from assets and financing flow in 2006. Treat interest as a financing flow.

2006 INCOME STATEMENT

Revenues	$1,301
Cost of goods sold	1,031
Depreciation	140
Interest expense	38
Taxes	29
Net income	63

SMALL TIME PRODUCTS BALANCE SHEET
FOR 2005 AND 2006, AS OF YEAR-END

	2006	2005		2006	2005
Cash	$ 41	42	Bank loan	40	40
Accounts receivable	70	86	Accounts payable	108	120
Inventory	12	14	Current liabilities	148	160
Current assets	123	142	Long-term debt	420	464
Net property and equipment	886	974	Capital stock	100	110
			Retained earnings	341	382
Total assets	1,009	1,116	Total liabilities and shareholders' equity	1,009	1,116

33. **Taxes.** Reconsider the data in problem 10. What are the total personal and corporate taxes if you pay yourself a salary of $50,000 and a dividend of $20,000?

34. **Internet.** Go to **www.sedar.com**, the Web site where public Canadian companies must post their annual reports and other corporate documents. Click on "Search Database," then "Public Company." Select document type "Annual Report" then "Search" and you

will get a list of recent annual reports. Pick one and read it. What do you learn about the nature of the business and of the company's successes and failures? What type of assets and liabilities are listed on the balance sheet? Using the cash flow statement, calculate the cash flow from assets and the financing flow. Treat interest as a financing flow.

35. **Standard & Poor's.** Find Microsoft (MSFT) and Rogers Communication (RG) on Market Insight (**www.mcgrawhill.ca/edumarketinsight**), and briefly describe their main business activities. Examine the financial statements of each. Which firm uses more debt finance? Which firm has higher cash as percentage of total assets? Which has higher profits per dollar of total assets? Which has higher profits per dollar of shareholders' equity? How have these ratios varied over time?

36. **Standard & Poor's.** Continue with Microsoft and Rogers Communications in the previous problem. For each, use the statement of cash flows to calculate cash flow from assets and financing flow for each year. Treat interest as a financing flow, not as an operating flow. Get the interest expense from the income statement. Describe the cash flows of each company.

Solutions to Check Points

3.1 Cash and equivalents would increase by $100 million. Property and equipment would increase by $400 million. Long-term debt would increase by $500 million. Shareholders' equity would not increase: assets and liabilities have increased equally, leaving shareholders' equity unchanged.

3.2 a. If the auto plant were worth $14 billion, the equity in the firm would be worth $14 billion – $4 billion = $10 billion. With 100 million shares outstanding, each share would be worth $100.

   b. If the outstanding stock were worth $8 billion, we would infer that the market values the auto plant at $8 billion + $4 billion = $12 billion.

3.3

Period:	1	2	3
Sales	0	150	0
– Change in accounts receivable	0	150	(150)
– Cost of goods sold	0	100	0
– Change in inventories	100	(100)	0
Net cash flow	–100	0	+150

The net cash flow pattern does make sense. The firm expends $100 in period 1 to produce the product, but it is not paid its $150 sales price until period 3. In period 2 no cash is exchanged.

3.4 a. An increase in inventories uses cash, reducing the firm's net cash balance.

   b. A reduction in accounts payable uses cash, reducing the firm's net cash balance.

   c. An issue of common stock is a source of cash.

   d. The purchase of new equipment is a use of cash, and it reduces the firm's net cash balance.

3.5   **Cash flow from Assets ($ millions):**

Net income	$7.3
Plus: depreciation	1.9
Plus: interest expense	0.6
Less: increase in working capital	(2.6)
Operating cash flow (adjusted)	7.2
Less: capital expenditures	(3.5)
Cash flow from assets	$3.7

Cash flow to Bondholders and Shareholders ($ millions):

Interest expense	$0.6
New borrowing	(1.5)
Dividends	2.0
Cash flow to bondholders and shareholders	1.1

Increase in cash in the bank = Cash flow from assets − cash flow to bondholders
− cash flow to shareholders

= $3.7 million − $1.1 million = $2.6 million

Financing flow = cash flow to bondholders + cash flow to shareholders
+ increase in cash in the bank

= $1.1 million + $2.6 million = $3.7 million

3.6

	Firm A	Firm B
	($ millions)	
EBIT	100	100
Interest	60	0
Pretax income	40	100
Tax (35% of pre-tax income)	14	35
Net income	26	65

Taxes owed by Firm A fall from $21 million to $14 million. The reduction in taxes is 35 percent of the extra $20 million of interest income. Net income does not fall by the full $20 million of extra interest expense. It instead falls by interest expense less the reduction in taxes, or $20 million − $7 million = $13 million.

3.7		**Lowest Tax Bracket**	**Highest Tax Bracket**
	Federal tax rate	16%	29%
	B.C. tax rate	6.05%	14.7%
	Combined tax rate	22.05%	43.7%
1.	Interest income	$1,000	$1,000
	Tax on interest income	.2205 × $1,000 = $220.5	.437 × $1,000 = $437
	After-tax interest income	$1,000 − $220.5 =$779.5	$1,000 − $437= $563
	Interest income tax rate	$220.5/$1,000 = 22.05%	$437/$1,000 = 43.7%
2.	Dividend income	$1,000	$1,000
	Grossed-up dividend	1.25 × $1,000 = $1,250	1.25 × $1,000 = $1,250
	Gross federal tax	.16 × $1,250 = $200	.29 × $1,250 = $362.5
	Less: Federal dividend tax credit	.1333 × $1,250 = $166.63	.1333 × $1,250 = $166.63
	Net federal dividend tax	$200 − $166.63 = $33.37	$362.5 − $166.63 = $195.88
	Gross provincial tax	.0605 × $1,250 = $75.625	.147 × $1,250 = $183.75
	Less: Provincial dividend tax credit	.051 × $1,250 = $63.75	.051 × $1,250 = $63.75
	Net provincial dividend tax	$75.625 − 63.75 = $11.875	$183.75 − $63.75 = $120
	Net tax on dividend income	$33.37 + $11.875 = $45.245	$195.88 + $120 = $315.88
	After-tax dividend income	$1,000 − $45.245 = $954.755	$1,000 − $315.88 = $684.12
	Dividend tax rate	$45.245/$1,000 = 4.52 %	$315.88/$1,000 = 31.59%
3.	Capital gains income	$1,000	$1,000
	Tax on capital gains	.2205 × .5 × $1,000 =$110.25	.437 × .5 × $1,000 = $218.5
	After-tax capital gains	$1,000 − $110.25 = $889.75	$1,000 − $218.5 = $781.5
	Capital gains tax rate	$110.25/$1,000 = 11.03%	$218.5/$1,000 = 21.85%

For the low-income investor, dividends are taxed the least (4.52%), then capital gains (11.03%), and finally interest (22.05%). For the high-income investor, capital gains are taxed the least (21.85%), followed by dividends (31.59%) and finally interest income (43.7%).

PART TWO
Value

THE TIME VALUE OF MONEY

Companies invest in lots of things. Some are tangible assets—that is, assets you can kick, like factories, machinery, and offices. Others are intangible assets, such as patents or trademarks. In each case the company lays out some money to start in the hopes of receiving even more money later. Individuals also make investments. For example, your university or college tuition may cost you $6,000 per year. That is an investment you hope will pay off in the form of a higher salary later in life. You are sowing now and expecting to reap later.

Companies pay for their investments by raising money and in the process assume liabilities. For example, they may borrow money from a bank and promise to repay it with interest later. You may also have financed your investment in higher education by borrowing money that you plan to pay back out of that fat salary.

All these financial decisions require comparisons of cash payments at different dates. Will your future salary be sufficient to justify the current expenditure on university or college tuition? How much will you have to repay the bank if you borrow to finance your education?

In this chapter we take the first steps toward understanding the relationship between the value of the dollar today and in the future. We start by looking at how funds invested at a specific interest rate will grow over time. We next ask how much you would need to invest today to produce a specified sum of money in the future, and we describe some shortcuts for working out the value of a series of cash payments. Then we consider how inflation affects these financial calculations.

After studying this chapter you should be able to
- Calculate the future value to which money invested at a given interest rate will grow.
- Calculate the present value of a future payment.
- Calculate present and future values of streams of cash payments.
- Find the interest rate implied by the present or future value.
- Understand the difference between real and nominal cash flows and between real and nominal interest rates.
- Compare interest rates quoted over different time intervals—for example, monthly versus annual rates.

There is nothing complicated about these calculations, but if they are to become second nature, you should read the chapter thoroughly, work carefully through the examples (we have provided plenty), and make sure you tackle the Check Point questions. We are asking you to make an investment now in return for a payoff later.

4.1   FUTURE VALUES AND COMPOUND INTEREST

You have $100 invested in a bank account. Suppose banks are currently paying an interest rate of 6 percent per year on deposits. So after a year, your account will earn interest of $6:

$$\text{Interest} = \text{interest rate} \times \text{initial investment}$$
$$= .06 \times \$100 = \$6$$

You start the year with $100 and you earn interest of $6, so the value of your investment will grow to $106 by the end of the year:

$$\text{Value of investment after 1 year} = \$100 + \$6 = \$106$$

Notice that the $100 invested grows by the factor $(1 + .06) = 1.06$. In general, for any interest rate, r, the value of the investment at the end of 1 year is $(1 + r)$ times the initial investment:

$$\text{Value after 1 year} = \text{initial investment} \times (1 + r)$$
$$= \$100 \times (1.06) = \$106$$

What if you leave this money in the bank for a second year? Your balance, now $106, will continue to earn interest of 6 percent. So

$$\text{Interest in Year 2} = .06 \times \$106 = \$6.36$$

You start the second year with $106 on which you earn interest of $6.36. So by the end of the year the value of your account will grow to $106 + $6.36 = $112.36.

In the first year your investment of $100 increases by a factor of 1.06 to $106; in the second year the $106 again increases by a factor of 1.06 to $112.36. Thus the initial $100 investment grows twice by a factor of 1.06:

$$\text{Value of account after 2 years} = \$100 \times 1.06 \times 1.06$$
$$= \$100 \times (1.06)^2 = \$112.36$$

If you keep your money invested for a third year, your investment multiplies by 1.06 each year for three years. By the end of the third year, it will total $100 \times (1.06)^3 = $119.10, scarcely enough to put you in the millionaire class, but even millionaires have to start somewhere.

Clearly for an investment horizon of t years, the original $100 investment will grow to $100 \times (1.06)^t$. For an interest rate of r and a horizon of t years, the **future value** of your investment will be

future value (FV) Amount to which an investment will grow after earning interest.

$$\textbf{Future value of \$100} = \textbf{\$100} \times \textbf{(1 + r)}^t$$

Notice in our example that your interest income in the first year is $6 (6 percent of $100), and in the second year it is $6.36 (6 percent of $106). Your income in the second year is higher because you now earn interest on *both* the original $100 investment and the $6 of interest earned in the previous year. Earning interest on interest is called *compounding* or **compound interest**. In contrast, if the bank calculated the interest only on your original investment, you would be paid **simple interest**. With simple interest your bank balance is only $112 after two years, $100 + 2 \times $6.

compound interest Interest earned on interest.

simple interest Interest earned only on the original investment; no interest is earned on interest.

Table 4.1 and Figure 4.1 illustrate the mechanics of compound interest. Table 4.1 shows that in each year, you start with a greater balance in your account—your savings have been increased by the previous year's interest. As a result, your interest income also is higher.

TABLE 4.1
Mechanics of compound
interest—interest is earned
on previous years' interest

Year	Balance at Start of Year	Interest Earned During Year	Balance at End of Year
1	$100.00	.06 × $100.00 = $6.00	$106.00
2	$106.00	.06 × $106.00 = $6.36	$112.36
3	$112.36	.06 × $112.36 = $6.74	$119.10
4	$119.10	.06 × $119.10 = $7.15	$126.25
5	$126.25	.06 × $126.25 = $7.57	$133.82

Obviously, the higher the rate of interest, the faster your savings will grow. Figure 4.2 shows that a few percentage points added to the (compound) interest rate can dramatically affect the future balance of your savings account. For example, after 10 years $100 invested at 10 percent will grow to $100 $\times$ $(1.10)^{10}$ = $259.37. If invested at 5 percent, it will grow to only $100 $\times$ $(1.05)^{10}$ = $162.89.

The future value, FV, of any investment can be calculated with the future value formula. The formula for the future value of I dollars at r percent interest per period for t periods is

$$\text{FV of } \$I \text{ investment} = I \times (1 + r)^t \tag{4.1}$$

Calculating future values is easy using almost any calculator. If you have patience, you can multiply your initial investment by $1 + r$ once for each period of your investment. A simpler procedure is to use the power key (the y^x key) on your calculator. For example, with a 6 percent interest rate and a 10-year investment, you want to compute $(1.06)^{10}$. Enter 1.06, press the y^x key, enter 10, press = and discover that the answer is 1.7908. (Try this!)

If you don't have a calculator, you can use a table of future values such as Table 4.2. It shows the future value of a $1 investment for various interest rates and investment periods. We call the future value of a $1 investment at r percent per period for t periods the **future value interest factor** (or just **future value factor**) and write it as FVIF(r,t):

$$\text{Future value factor, FVIF}(r,t) = (1 + r)^t \tag{4.2}$$

future value interest factor
Future value of a current cash
flow of $1.

FIGURE 4.1
Compound interest.
Future value of $100
invested at 6 percent in
each of the 5 years

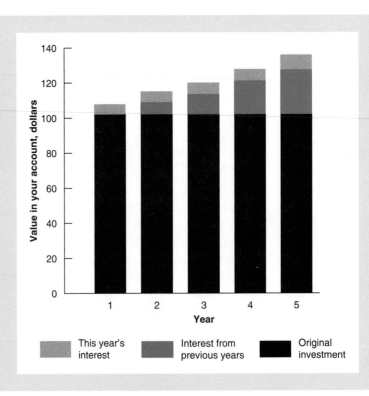

FIGURE 4.2

Future values of $100 invested at various interest rates, with compound interest

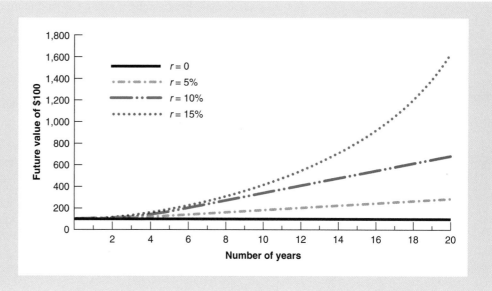

You can see that the future value of an investment can be calculated by multiplying the invested amount by the future value factor of a $1 investment for the same time period and interest rate:

$$\text{FV} = I \times \text{future value factor} = I \times \text{FVIF}(r,t) = I \times (1 + r)^t \qquad (4.3)$$

Check that you can use Table 4.2 to work out the future value of a 10-year investment of $1 at 6 percent. First find the row corresponding to 10 periods. Now work along that row until you reach the column for a 6 percent interest rate. The entry shows that $1 invested for 10 periods at 6 percent grows to $1.7908. Suppose you invested $20, instead of $1? Multiply the same future value factor by $20 to get its future value of $35.816 (= $20 × 1.7908).

Now try one more example. If you invest $1 for 20 years at 10 percent and do not withdraw any money, what will you have at the end? Your answer should be $6.7275.

Suppose you invest $50? Multiply the future value factor for 10 percent and 20 years by $50 and you end up with $336.375 (= $50 × 6.7275).

Table 4.2 gives future values for only a small selection of years and interest rates. Table A.1 in Appendix A (please see the Online Learning Centre at www.mcgrawhill.ca/college/brealey) is a bigger version of Table 4.2. It presents the future value of a $1 investment for a wide range of time periods and interest rates.

Future value tables are tedious, and as Table 4.2 demonstrates, they show future values only for a limited set of interest rates and time periods. For example, suppose that you want to calculate future values using an interest rate of 7.835 percent. The power key on your calculator will be faster and easier than future value tables. A third alternative is to use a financial calculator or a spreadsheet. We show you how to do this in several boxes later in the chapter.

TABLE 4.2

Future value factors—future values of $1, invested at various interest rates for different periods

Number of Periods	Interest Rate per Period					
	5%	6%	7%	8%	9%	10%
1	1.0500	1.0600	1.0700	1.0800	1.0900	1.1000
2	1.1025	1.1236	1.1449	1.1664	1.1881	1.2100
3	1.1576	1.1910	1.2250	1.2597	1.2950	1.3310
4	1.2155	1.2625	1.3108	1.3605	1.4116	1.4641
5	1.2763	1.3382	1.4026	1.4693	1.5386	1.6105
10	1.6289	1.7908	1.9672	2.1589	2.3674	2.5937
20	2.6533	3.2071	3.8697	4.6610	5.6044	6.7275
30	4.3219	5.7435	7.6123	10.0627	13.2677	17.4494

How do you calculate future value if interest is paid more often than annually, say monthly? As long as you know the interest per period and the number of periods, the procedure is the same. For example, suppose Money Bank is paying 1 percent per month on deposits. If you invest $500 for 20 months, the future value of your investment is

$$FV = \$500 \times FVIF(.01, 20) = \$500 \times (1.01)^{20} = \$500 \times 1.2202 = \$610.10$$

Later in the chapter, we will show you how to compare interest rates when they are quoted for different periods, such as weekly or semi-annually.

EXAMPLE 4.1   **MANHATTAN ISLAND**

An interesting example of the power of compound interest is the sale of Manhattan Island for $24 in 1626 to Peter Minuit. Based on New York real estate prices today, it seems that Minuit got a great deal. But consider the future value of that $24 if it had been invested for 380 years (2006 minus 1626) at an interest rate of 8 percent per year:

$$\$24 \times FVIF(.08, 380) = \$24 \times (1.08)^{380} = \$120,569,700,000,000$$
$$= \$120.5697 \text{ trillion}$$

Perhaps the deal wasn't as good as it appeared. The total value of land in Manhattan today is only a fraction of $121 trillion.

Though entertaining, this analysis is actually somewhat misleading. First, the 8 percent interest rate we've used to compute future values is quite high by historical standards. At a 3.5 percent interest rate, which is more consistent with historical experience, the future value of the $24 would be *dramatically* lower, only $24 \times (1.035)^{380} = \$11,416,794$! Second, we have understated the returns to Mr. Minuit and his successors: We have ignored the rental income that the island's land has generated over the last three or four centuries.

All things considered, if we had been around in 1626, we would have gladly paid $24 for the island.

The power of compounding is not restricted to money. Foresters try to forecast the compound growth rate of trees, demographers the compound growth rate of population. An American social commentator once observed that the number of lawyers in the United States is increasing at a higher compound rate than the population as a whole (3.6 versus .9 percent in the 1980s), and calculated that in about two centuries there will be more lawyers than people! In all these cases, the principle is the same:

> Compound growth means that value increases each period by the factor (1 + growth rate). The value after t periods will equal the initial value times (1 + growth rate)^t. When money is invested at compound interest, the growth rate is the interest rate.

Check Point 4.1

Suppose that Peter Minuit did not become the first real estate tycoon in New York, but instead had invested his $24 at a 5 percent interest rate in New Amsterdam Savings Bank. What would have been the balance in his account after five years? 50 years?

Check Point 4.2

Start-up Enterprises had sales last year of only $0.5 million. However, a stock market analyst is bullish on the company and predicts that sales will double each year for four years. What are projected sales at the end of this period?

PRESENT VALUES

Money can be invested to earn interest. If you are offered the choice between $100,000 now and $100,000 at the end of the year, you naturally take the money now to get a year's interest. Financial managers make the same point when they say that money in hand today has a time value or perhaps when they quote the most basic financial principle:

> A dollar today is worth more than a dollar tomorrow.

present value (PV)   Value today of a future cash flow.

We have seen that $100 invested for 1 year at 6 percent will grow to a future value of $100 \times 1.06 = \$106$. Let's turn this around: How much do we need to invest now in order to produce $106 at the end of the year? Financial managers refer to this as the **present value (PV)** of the $106 payoff.

Future value is calculated by multiplying the present investment by one plus the interest rate, .06, or 1.06. To calculate present value, we simply reverse the process and divide the future value by 1.06:

$$\text{Present value} = PV = \frac{\text{future value}}{1.06} = \frac{\$106}{1.06} = \$100$$

What is the present value of, say, $112.36 to be received 2 years from now? Again we ask, how much would we need to invest now to produce $112.36 after 2 years? The answer is obviously $100; we've already calculated that at 6 percent $100 grows to $112.36:

$$\$100 \times (1.06)^2 = \$112.36$$

However, if we don't know, or forgot the answer, we just divide future value by $(1.06)^2$:

$$\text{Present value} = PV = \frac{\$112.36}{(1.06)^2} = \$100$$

In general, for a future value or payment t periods away, the present value formula is

$$\text{Present value} = \frac{\text{future value after } t \text{ periods}}{(1 + r)^t} \tag{4.4}$$

discount rate   Interest rate used to compute present values of future cash flows.

In this context the interest rate r is known as the **discount rate**, and the present value is often called the *discounted value* of the future payment. To calculate present value, we discounted the future value at the interest r.

EXAMPLE 4.2

SAVING TO BUY A NEW COMPUTER

Suppose you need $3,000 next year to buy a new computer. The interest rate is 8 percent per year. How much money should you set aside now in order to pay for the purchase? Just calculate the present value at an 8 percent interest rate of a $3,000 payment at the end of 1 year. This value is

$$PV = \frac{\$3,000}{1.08} = \$2,778$$

Notice that $2,778 invested for 1 year at 8 percent will provide just enough to buy your computer:

$$\text{Future value} = \$2,778 \times 1.08 = \$3,000$$

The longer the period before you must make a payment, the less you need to invest today. For example, suppose that you can postpone buying that computer until the end of two years. In this case we calculate the present value of the future payment by dividing $3,000 by $(1.08)^2$:

$$PV = \frac{\$3,000}{(1.08)^2} = \$2,572$$

Thus you need to invest $2,778 today to provide $3,000 in 1 year but only $2,572 to provide the same $3,000 in 2 years.

We repeat the basic procedure:

> To work out how much you will have in the future if you invest for t periods at an interest rate r, multiply the initial investment by $(1 + r)^t$. To find the present value of a future payment, run the process in reverse and divide by $(1 + r)^t$.

Present values are always calculated using compound interest. Whereas the ascending lines in Figure 4.2 show the future value of $100 invested with compound interest, when we calculate present values we move back along the lines from future to present.

Thus present values decline, other things being equal, when future cash payments are delayed. The longer you have to wait for money, the less it's worth today, as we see in Figure 4.3. Notice how very small variations in the interest rate can have a powerful effect on the value of distant cash flows. At an interest rate of 10 percent, a payment of $100 in Year 20 is worth $14.86 today. If the interest rate increases to 15 percent, the value of the future payment falls by about 60 percent to $6.11.

The present value formula is sometimes written differently. Instead of dividing the future payment by $(1 + r)^t$, we could just as easily multiply it by $1/(1 + r)^t$:

$$PV = \frac{\textbf{future payment}}{(1 + r)^t}$$

$$= \textbf{future payment} \times \frac{1}{(1 + r)^t} \qquad (4.5)$$

discount factor or present value interest factor   Present value of a $1 future payment.

The expression $1/(1+r)^t$ is called the **discount factor** or the **present value interest factor**, PVIF(r, t). It measures the present value of $1 to be received in t years from today at a discount rate of r percent. The present value of a future payment of I dollars at r percent per period for t periods can be written as

$$PV = I \times \textbf{discount factor} = I \times \textbf{PVIF}(r,t) = I \times \frac{1}{(1 + r)^t} \qquad (4.6)$$

The simplest way to find the discount factor is to use a calculator, but financial managers sometimes find it convenient to use tables of discount factors. For example, Table 4.3 shows discount factors for a small range of years and interest rates. Table A.2 in Appendix A provides a set of discount factors for a wide range of years and interest rates.

FIGURE 4.3
Present value of a future cash flow of $100, using various interest rates. Notice that the longer you have to wait for your money, the less it is worth today.

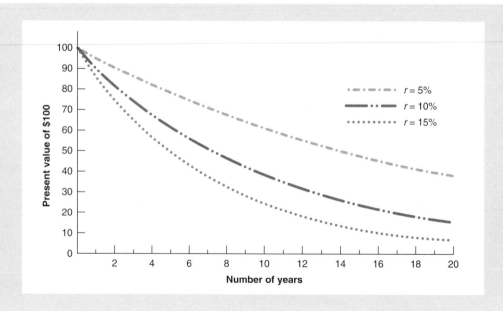

TABLE 4.3
Discount factors—present value of $1 for various interest rates and different periods

Number of Periods	Interest Rate per Period					
	5%	6%	7%	8%	9%	10%
1	0.9524	0.9434	0.9346	0.9259	0.9174	0.9091
2	0.9070	0.8900	0.8734	0.8573	0.8417	0.8264
3	0.8638	0.8396	0.8163	0.7938	0.7722	0.7513
4	0.8227	0.7921	0.7629	0.7350	0.7084	0.6830
5	0.7835	0.7473	0.7130	0.6806	0.6499	0.6209
10	0.6139	0.5584	0.5083	0.4632	0.4224	0.3855
20	0.3769	0.3118	0.2584	0.2145	0.1784	0.1486
30	0.2314	0.1741	0.1314	0.0994	0.0754	0.0573

Try using Table 4.3 to figure out how much to put aside for that $3,000 computer purchase. If the interest rate is 8 percent, the present value of $1 paid at the end of 1 year is $.9259. So the present value of $3,000 is

$$PV = \$3,000 \times PVIF\,(.08,1) = \$3,000 \times \frac{1}{1.08} = \$3,000 \times .9259 = \$2,778$$

which matches the value we obtained in Example 4.2.

What if the computer purchase is postponed until the end of two years? Table 4.3 shows that the present value of $1 paid at the end of 2 years is .8573. So the present value of $3,000 is

$$PV = \$3,000 \times PVIF\,(.08,2) = \$3,000 \times \frac{1}{(1.08)^2} = \$3,000 \times .8573 = \$2,572$$

as we found in Example 4.2.

Notice that as you move along the rows in Table 4.3, moving to higher interest rates, present values decline. As you move down the columns, moving to longer discounting periods, present values again decline. Why does this make sense?

EXAMPLE 4.3   **COCA-COLA ENTERPRISES BORROWS SOME CASH**

In 1995 Coca-Cola Enterprises needed to borrow about a quarter of a billion dollars for 25 years. It did so by selling IOUs, each of which simply promised to pay the holder $1,000 at the end of 25 years.[1] The market interest rate at the time was 8.53 percent. How much would you have been prepared to pay for one of the company's IOUs?

To calculate present value we multiply the $1,000 future payment by the 25-year discount factor:

$$PV = \$1,000 \times PVIF\,(.0853,25) = \$1,000 \times \frac{1}{(1.0853)^{25}}$$
$$= \$1,000 \times .1292 = \$129.20$$

Instead of using a calculator to find the discount factor, we could use Table A.2 in Appendix A. You can see that the 25-year discount factor is .1460 if the interest rate is 8 percent and .1160 if the rate is 9 percent. For an interest rate of 8.5 percent, the discount factor is roughly halfway between at .131, a shade higher than the exact figure.

---

[1] "IOU" means "I owe you." Coca-Cola's IOUs are called bonds. Usually bond investors receive a regular *interest* or *coupon* payment. The Coca-Cola Enterprises bond will make only a single payment at the end of Year 25. It was therefore known as a *zero-coupon* bond. More on this in the next chapter.

Check Point 4.3

Suppose that Coca-Cola had promised to pay $1,000 at the end of 10 years. If the market interest rate was 8.53 percent, how much would you have been prepared to pay for a 10-year IOU of $1,000?

EXAMPLE 4.4   **FINDING THE VALUE OF FREE CREDIT**

Kangaroo Autos is offering free credit on a $10,000 car. You pay $4,000 down and then the balance at the end of 2 years. Turtle Motors next door does not offer free credit but will give you $500 off the list price. If the interest rate is 10 percent, which company is offering the better deal?

Notice that you pay more in total by buying through Kangaroo, but since part of the payment is postponed, you can keep this money in the bank where it will continue to earn interest. To compare the two offers, you need to calculate the present value of the payments to Kangaroo. The *time line* in Figure 4.4 shows the cash payments to Kangaroo. The first payment, $4,000, takes place today. The second payment, $6,000, takes place at the end of 2 years. To find its present value, we need to multiply by the two-year discount factor. The total present value of the payments to Kangaroo is therefore

$$PV = \$4,000 + \$6,000 \times PVIF\,(.10,2) = \$4,000 + \$6,000 \times \frac{1}{(1.10)^2}$$

$$= \$4,000 + \$4,958.68 = \$8,958.68$$

Suppose you start with $8,958.68. You make a down payment of $4,000 to Kangaroo Autos and invest the balance of $4,958.68. At an interest rate of 10 percent, this will grow over 2 years to $4,958.68 × 1.10² = $6,000, just enough to make the final payment on your automobile. The total cost of $8,958.68 is a better deal than the $9,500 charged by Turtle Motors.

These calculations illustrate how important it is to use present values when comparing alternative patterns of cash payment.

> You should *never* compare cash flows occurring at different times without first discounting them to a common date. By calculating present values, we see how much cash must be set aside today to pay future bills.

Check Point 4.4

You have won a contest and now must decide which prize you want. With Prize A, you receive $5,000 today and another $5,500 in one year. Prize B gives you $1,000 today and another $10,000 in one year. The interest rate is 4 percent. Prove to yourself that it does not matter the point in time at which you compare the prizes' cash flows: the better prize has both the bigger present value and future value.

FIGURE 4.4
Present value of the cash flows to Kangaroo Autos. Drawing a time line can help with the calculation of the present value of cash flow.

From Here to Eternity

FINANCE IN ACTION

Politicians, you may be aware, are fond of urging people to invest in the future. It would appear that some investors are taking them a bit too literally of late. The latest fad among emerging-market bond investors, eager to get a piece of the action, is to queue up for bonds with 100-year maturities, such as those issued by the Chinese government and Tenaga Nasional, a Malaysian electrical utility.

Not to be outdone by these century bonds, Eurotunnel, the beleaguered company that operates the railway beneath the English Channel, is trying to tempt investors with a millennium's worth of profits. Last week, in a bid to sweeten the pot for its shareholders and creditors, who must agree on an unpalatable financial restructuring, it asked the British and French governments to extend its operating franchise from a mere 65 years to 999 years. By offering investors some windfall profits, the firm hopes they will be more likely to ratify its plan. Has the distant future become the latest place to make a financial killing?

Alas, the future is not all that it is cracked up to be. Although at first glance, 999 years of profits would seem far better than 65 years, those last nine centuries are really nothing to get excited about. The reason is that a dollar spent today (human nature being what it is) is worth more to people than a dollar spent tomorrow. So when comparing profits in the future with those in the present, the future profits must be "discounted" by a suitable interest rate.

Under the relentless pressures of compound interest, the value of future profits is ground to nothing as the years go by. Suppose, for example, that you had a choice between making the following two gifts to a university: You could write a cheque for $10,000 today or give $1,000 a year for the next century. The latter donation might seem the more generous one, but at a 10% interest rate, they are worth the same amount. By the time compound discounting had finished with it, that final $1,000 payment would be worth only $.07 today (see diagram).

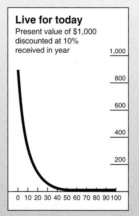

Live for today
Present value of $1,000 discounted at 10% received in year

What does this mean for Eurotunnel's investors? Extending its franchise by 934 years should increase its value to today's investors by only 10–15%, after discounting. If they are feeling generous, perhaps the British and French governments should toss in another year and make the franchise an even 1,000.

Source: © 1997 The Economist Newspaper Group Inc. Reprinted with permission. Further reproduction prohibited. **www.economist.com**.

SEE BOX ABOVE ▶

The importance of discounting is highlighted in the Finance in Action box above, which examines the value of an extension of Eurotunnel's operating franchise from 65 to 999 years. While such an extension sounds as if it would be extremely valuable, the article (and its accompanying diagram) points out that profits 65 years or more from now have negligible present value.

FINDING THE INTEREST RATE

When we looked at Coca-Cola's IOUs in Example 4.3, we used the interest rate to compute a fair market price for each IOU. Sometimes you are given the price and have to calculate the interest rate that is being offered.

For example, when Coca-Cola borrowed money, it did not announce an interest rate. It simply offered to sell each IOU for $129. Thus we know that

$$PV = \$1,000 \times \frac{1}{(1 + r)^{25}} = \$129.20$$

What is the interest rate?

There are several ways to approach this. First, you might calculate the discount factor in the equation:

$$\text{Discount factor, PVIF } (r, 25) = \frac{\$129.2}{\$1,000} = .1292$$

Use a table of discount factors to find the interest rate for which the 25-year discount factor equals .1292. Look at Table A.2 in Appendix A and run your finger along the row corresponding to 25 years. You can see that an interest rate of 8 percent gives too high a discount factor and a rate of 9 percent gives too low a discount factor. The interest rate on the Coca-Cola loan is about halfway between at 8.5 percent.

Using Financial Calculators to Find NPV and IRR

Financial calculators are designed with present value and future value formulas already programmed. Therefore, you can readily solve many problems simply by entering the inputs for the problem and punching a key for the solution.

The basic financial calculator uses five keys that correspond to the inputs for common problems involving the time value of money.

Each key represents the following input:

- n is the number of periods. (We have been using t to denote the length of time, or number of periods. Most calculators use n for the same concept.)
- i is the interest rate per period, expressed as a percentage (not a decimal). For example, if the interest rate is 8 percent, you would enter 8, not .08. On some calculators this key is written I/Y or I/YR. (We have been using r to denote the interest rate or discount rate.)
- PV is the present value.
- FV is the future value.
- PMT is the amount of any recurring payment (called an annuity). In single cash-flow problems such as those we have considered so far, PMT is zero.

Given any four of these inputs, the calculator will solve the fifth. We will illustrate with several examples.

Future Values

Recall Example 4.1, where we calculated the future value of Peter Minuit's $24 investment. Enter 24 into the PV register. (You enter the value by typing 24 and then pushing the PV key.) We assumed an interest rate of 8 percent, so enter 8 into the i register. Because the $24 had 380 years to compound, enter 380 into the n register. Enter 0 into the PMT register because there is no recurring payment involved in the calculation. Now ask the calculator to compute FV. On some calculators you simply press the FV key. On others you need to first press the "compute" key (which may be labelled $COMP$ or CPT), and then press FV. The exact sequence of keystrokes for three popular financial calculators are as follows:[1]

Hewlett-Packard HP-10B	Sharpe EL-733A	Texas Instruments BA II Plus
24 $\boxed{PV}$	24 $\boxed{PV}$	24 $\boxed{PV}$
380 $\boxed{N}$	380 $\boxed{n}$	380 $\boxed{N}$
8 $\boxed{I/YR}$	8 $\boxed{i}$	8 $\boxed{I/Y}$
0 $\boxed{PMT}$	0 $\boxed{PMT}$	0 $\boxed{PMT}$
$\boxed{FV}$	$\boxed{COMP}$ $\boxed{FV}$	$\boxed{CPT}$ $\boxed{FV}$

You should find after hitting the FV key that your calculator shows a value of –120.5697 trillion, which, except for the minus sign, is the future value of the $24.

Why does the minus sign appear? Most calculators treat cash flows as either inflows (shown as positive numbers) or outflows (negative

Second, you can rearrange the equation and use your calculator to solve for r:

$$\$129.20 \times (1 + r)^{25} = \$1,000$$

$$(1 + r)^{25} = \frac{\$1,000}{\$129.20} = 7.74$$

$$(1 + r) = (7.74)^{1/25} = 1.0853$$

$$r = .0853, \text{ or } 8.53\%$$

SEE BOXES ABOVE AND ON P. 90 In general this is more accurate. You can also use a financial calculator (see the Financial Calculator box above) or a spreadsheet (see Excel Spreadsheet box on page 90).

EXAMPLE 4.5 **DOUBLE YOUR MONEY**

How many times have you heard of an investment adviser who promises to double your money? Is this really an amazing feat? That depends on how long it will take for your money to double. With enough patience, your funds eventually will double even if they earn only a very modest interest rate. Suppose your investment adviser promises to double your money in eight years? What interest rate is implicitly being promised?

numbers). For example, if you borrow $100 today at an interest rate of 12 percent, you receive money now (a *positive* cash flow), but you will have to pay back $112 in a year, a negative cash flow at that time. Therefore, the calculator displays FV as a negative number. The following time line of cash flows shows the reasoning employed. The final negative cash flow of $112 has the same present value as the $100 borrowed today.

$PV = \$100$

Year: 0 ——————————————— 1

$FV = \$112$

If, instead of borrowing, you were to *invest* $100 today to reap a future benefit, you would enter PV as a negative number (first press 100, then press the +/– key to make the value negative, and finally press PV to enter the value into the PV register). In this case, FV would appear as a positive number, indicating that you will reap a cash inflow when your investment comes to fruition.

Present Values

Suppose your savings goal is to accumulate $10,000 by the end of 30 years. If the interest rate is 8 percent, how much would you need to invest today to achieve your goal? Again, there is no recurring payment involved, so PMT is zero. We therefore enter the following: $n = 30$; $i = 8$; $FV = 10,000$; $PMT = 0$. Now compute PV, and you should get

an answer of –993.77. The answer is displayed as a negative number because you need to make a cash outflow (an investment) of $993.77 now in order to enjoy a cash inflow of $10,000 in 30 years.

Finding the Interest Rate

The 25-year IOU from Coca-Cola Enterprises in Example 4.3 sold at $129 and promised a final payment of $1,000. We may obtain the market interest rate by entering $n = 25$, $FV = 1,000$, $PV = -129$, and $PMT = 0$. Compute i and you will find that the interest rate is 8.53 percent. This is the value we computed directly (but with more work) in the example.

How Long an Investment?

In Example 4.5, we consider how long it would take for an investment to double in value. This sort of problem is easily solved using a calculator. If the investment is to double, we enter $FV = 2$ and $PV = -1$. If the interest rate is 9 percent, enter $i = 9$ and $PMT = 0$. Compute n and you will find that $n = 8.04$ years. If the interest rate is 9.05 percent, the doubling period falls to 8 years, as we found in the example.

[1] The BA II Plus calculator requires a little extra work to initialize. When you buy the calculator, it is set to automatically interpret each period as a year and assumes that interest compounds monthly. In our experience, it is best to change the compounding frequency to once per period. To do so, press 2nd {P/Y} 1 ENTER , then press ↓ 1 ENTER and finally press 2nd {QUIT} to return to standard calculator mode. You should need to do this only once, even if the calculator is turned off.

The adviser is promising a future value of $2 for every $1 invested today. Therefore, we find the interest rate by solving for *r* as follows:

$$\text{Future value} = PV \times (1 + r)^t$$
$$\$2 = \$1 \times (1 + r)^8$$
$$1 + r = 2^{1/8} = 1.0905$$
$$r = .0905, \text{ or } 9.05\%$$

By the way, there is a convenient rule of thumb that one can use to approximate the answer to this problem. The *Rule of 72* states that the time it will take for an investment to double in value equals approximately $72/r$, where *r* is expressed as a percentage. Therefore, if the doubling period is 8 years, the Rule of 72 implies an (approximate) interest rate of 9 percent (since $72/9 = 8$ years). This is quite close to the exact solution of 9.05 percent.

Check Point 4.5

The Rule of 72 works best with relatively low interest rates. Suppose the time it will take for an investment to double in value is 12 years. Find the interest rate. What is the approximate rate implied by the Rule of 72? Now suppose that the doubling period is only two years. Is the approximation better or worse in this case?

Interest-Rate Functions

	A	B	C	D	E	F	G
1	**Finding the future value of $24 using a spreadsheet**						
2							
3	Present value (*pv*)	24					
4	Interest rate (*rate*)	0.08					
5	Payment (*pmt*)	0					
6	Periods (*nper*)	380					
7							
8	Future value	$120,569,740,656,495					
9							
10							
11	The formula in cell B8 is = FV (B4,B6,B5–B3). Notice that we enter the present value						
12	as the negative of the value in cell B3, since the "purchase price" is a cash outflow.						
13							
14	You can confirm for yourself that changing the entry in cell B4 to .035 will reduce						
15	the value to $11,416,794.						

Just as financial calculators largely replaced interest rate tables in the 1980s, these calculators are today giving way to spreadsheets. Like financial calculators, spreadsheets provide built-in functions that solve the equations linking the five variables in a time-value-of-money problem: the number of periods, the interest rate per period, the present value, the future value, and any recurring payment (the annuity). For single cash flow problems such as the ones we've encountered so far, the recurring payment is zero. We will illustrate the use of these spreadsheets by using Microsoft Excel™.

The four Excel functions relevant for single cash-flow problems are

Future value = FV (*rate, nper, pmt, pv*)
Present value = PV (*rate, nper, pmt, fv*)
Interest rate = RATE (*nper, pmt, pv, fv*)
Number of periods = NPER (*rate, pmt, pv, fv*)

As you can see, each spreadsheet formula requires four inputs—just as financial calculators require four inputs—and provides the solution for the fifth variable. Also like most calculators, the spreadsheet functions interpret cash inflows as positive values and cash outflows as negative values. Unlike financial calculators, however, most spreadsheets require that interest rates be input as decimals rather than whole numbers (e.g., .06 rather than 6 percent). Note also the use of = signs in front of the formulas to alert Excel to the fact that these are predefined formulas. In the Financial Calculator box, we saw how to use calculators to solve several problems. Let's see how we would use spreadsheets to solve the same problems.

Future Values

The box above shows a spreadsheet that solves Example 4.1 on the future value of the $24 spent to acquire Manhattan Island. The interest rate is entered as a decimal in cell B4. The formula for future value in cell B8 takes as its last input the negative of cell B3, because the $24 purchase price is treated as cash outflow. Note how the spreadsheet shows more digits for future value than the calculator. You can use the Excel ROUND function to ROUND the spreadsheet future value to the calculator value.

Present Values

We next considered an individual who wishes to accumulate a future value of $10,000 by the end of 30 years. If the interest rate is 8 percent, and there is no recurring payment involved, you can find the necessary investment today (the present value) by entering the formula =PV (.08,30,0,10000). If you try this, you will see that the solution is reported as a negative value: the positive future payoff of $10,000 requires an initial payment (cash outflow) of 993.77. (Notice also that we don't use commas when entering the $10,000 future value. The spreadsheet would think that the comma was being used to separate two inputs to the function.)

Finding the Interest Rate

We showed how to use a calculator to find the interest rate on a 25-year $1,000 IOU sold today for $129.20. In Excel, we can compute =RATE (25,0,–129.20,1000) to confirm again that the interest rate is 8.53 percent.

How Long an Investment?

Example 4.5 asks how long it would take an investment to double if it earned interest at a rate of 9 percent. We treat the present value as a $1 investment (cash outflow) and the future value as a $2 cash payback. Therefore, enter =NPER(.09,0,–1,2) to find that the doubling period is 8.04 years.

FINDING THE INVESTMENT PERIOD

In Example 4.2, we looked at how much money to set aside to pay for a new computer in one year. Suppose instead you have $1,890 but need $3,000 to buy the computer. How long will it take for you to have enough money if the interest rate is 8 percent? We know that

$$PV = \$3,000 \times \frac{1}{(1.08)^t} = \$1,890$$

What is the number of periods?

Just as was the case for finding the interest rate, the solution can be found several ways. First, calculate discount factor by rearranging the above equation:

$$PV(.08,\ t) = \frac{1}{(1.08)^t} = \frac{\$1,890}{\$3,000} = .6300$$

Go to Table A.2 in Appendix A and look at the column corresponding to 8 percent. You will see that the discount factor for 6 years is .6303, indicating that it will take about 6 years for your savings to grow big enough to buy the computer.

You can also rearrange the present value formula and solve[2] for t or use a financial calculator or a spreadsheet. Both of the nearby Financial Calculator and Excel Spreadsheet boxes show you how to solve for the length of an investment.

**SEE BOXES,
PP. 88–90**

4.3

MULTIPLE CASH FLOWS

So far, we have considered problems involving only a single cash flow. This is obviously limiting. Most real-world investments, after all, will involve many cash flows over time. When there are many payments, you'll hear businesspeople refer to a *stream of cash flows*.

FUTURE VALUE OF MULTIPLE CASH FLOWS

Recall the computer you hope to purchase in two years (see Example 4.2). Now suppose that instead of putting aside a lump sum in the bank to finance the purchase, you plan to save a bit of money each year. You might be able to put $1,200 in the bank now, and another $1,400 in 1 year. If you earn an 8 percent rate of interest, how much will you be able to spend on a computer in 2 years?

The time line in Figure 4.5 shows how your savings grow. There are two cash inflows into the savings plan. The first cash flow will have 2 years to earn interest and, therefore, will grow to $1,200 \times (1.08)^2 = \$1,399.68$ while the second deposit, which comes a year later, will be invested for only 1 year and will grow to $1,400 \times (1.08) = \$1,512$. Therefore after 2 years, your total savings will be the sum of these two amounts, or $2,911.68.

FIGURE 4.5
Drawing a time line can help to calculate the future value of your savings

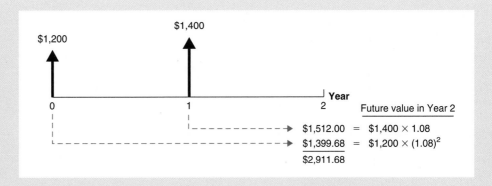

---

[2] To solve for t, rewrite the discount factor as $(1.08)^{-t}$
   $(1.08)^{-t} = .6300$
   $\log (1.08)^{-t} = \log .6300$
   $-t \log 1.08 = \log .6300$
   $t = -\log .6300/\log 1.08 = 6.003$
   Most calculators have log function key, often labeled as LN or LOG.

EXAMPLE 4.6	**EVEN MORE SAVINGS**

Suppose that the computer purchase can be put off for an additional year and that you can make a third deposit of $1,000 at the end of the second year. How much will be available to spend three years from now?

Again we organize our inputs using a time line as in Figure 4.6. The total cash available will be the sum of the future values of all three deposits. Notice that when we save for three years, the first two deposits each have an extra year for interest to compound:

$$\$1,200 \times (1.08)^3 = \$1,511.65$$
$$\$1,400 \times (1.08)^2 = \quad 1,632.96$$
$$\$1,000 \times \ 1.08 \ \ = \quad \underline{1,080.00}$$
$$\text{Total future value} = \$4,224.61$$

Check Point 4.6

Suppose you are planning a one-month European vacation when you graduate two years from now. The cost of the trip will be $3,500. Right now you have $1,500 and will put it into a bank account that pays 6 percent interest. How much more money will you need to deposit one year from now to have enough money for the trip two years from now?

We conclude that problems involving multiple cash flows are simple extensions of single cash flow analysis.

> To find the value at some future date of a stream of cash flows, calculate what each cash flow will be worth at that future date, and then add up these future values.

As we will now see, a similar adding-up principle works for present value calculations.

PRESENT VALUE OF MULTIPLE CASH FLOWS

When we calculate the present value of a future cash flow, we are asking how much that cash flow would be worth today. If there is more than one future cash flow, we simply need to work out what each flow would be worth today and then add these present values.

FIGURE 4.6
To find the future value of a stream of cash flows, calculate the future value of each flow and then add them

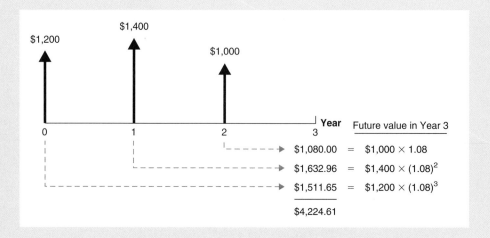

| EXAMPLE 4.7 | **CASH UP FRONT VERSUS AN INSTALMENT PLAN** |

Suppose that your auto dealer gives you a choice between paying $15,500 for a new car or entering into an instalment plan where you pay $8,000 down today and make payments of $4,000 in each of the next 2 years. Which is the better deal? Before reading this chapter, you might have compared the total payments under the two plans: $15,500 versus $16,000 in the instalment plan. Now, however, you know that this comparison is wrong, because it ignores the time value of money. For example, the last instalment of $4,000 is less costly to you than paying out $4,000 now. The true cost of that last payment is the present value of $4,000.

Assume that the interest rate you can earn on safe investments is 8 percent. Suppose you choose the instalment plan. As the time line in Figure 4.7 illustrates, the present value of the plan's three cash flows is

		Present Value	
Immediate payment	$8,000	=	$8,000.00
Second payment	$4,000/1.08	=	3,703.70
Third payment	$4,000/(1.08)²	=	3,429.36
Total present value		=	$15,133.06

Because the present value of the three payments is less than $15,500, the instalment plan is in fact the cheaper alternative.

The instalment plan's present value equals the amount that you would need to invest now to cover the three future payments. Let's check.

Here is how your bank balance would change as you make each payment:

Year	Initial Balance	−	Payment	=	Remaining Balance	+	Interest Earned	=	Balance at Year-End
0	$15,133.06		$8,000		$7,133.06		$570.64		$7,703.70
1	7,703.70		4,000		3,703.70		296.30		4,000.00
2	4,000.00		4,000		0		0		0

If you start with the present value of $15,133.06 in the bank, you could make the first $8,000 payment and be left with $7,133.06. After 1 year, your savings account would receive an interest payment of $7,133.06 × .08 = $570.64, bringing your account to $7,703.70. Similarly, you would make the second $4,000 payment and be left with $3,703.70. This sum left in the bank would grow with interest to $4,000, just enough to make the last payment.

FIGURE 4.7
To find the present value of a stream of cash flows, calculate the present value of each flow and then add them

Multiple Cash Flows

	A	B	C	D	E	F	G	H
1	Finding the present value of multiple cash flows by using a spreadsheet							
2								
3	**Time until CF**	**Cash flow**	**Present value**	**Formula in Column C**				
4	0	8000	$8,000.00	= PV(B10,A4,0,-B4)				
5	1	4000	$3,703.70	= PV(B10,A5,0,-B5)				
6	2	4000	$3,429.36	= PV(B10,A6,0,-B6)				
7								
8	SUM:		$15,133.06	= SUM(C4:C6)				
9								
10	**Discount rate:**	0.08						
11								
12	Notice that the time until each payment (*nper*) is found in column A.							
13	Once we enter the formula for present value in cell C4, we can copy it to cells C5 and C6.							
14	The present value for other interest rates can be found by changing the entry in cell B10.							

While uneven cash flow problems are conceptually straightforward, they rapidly become tedious and prone to errors from "typos," even if you use a financial calculator. It really helps to use spreadsheets. The following figure is a spreadsheet solution of Example 4.7.

The spreadsheet uses the present value formula, PV (*rate, nper, pmt, fv*), to calculate the present value of each cash flow. The discount rate (*rate*) is in cell B10. The number of periods until each payment (*nper*) is in column A. With no recurring payment, the value of pmt is 0. The values for the cash flow in each future period (*fv*) are entered as negative numbers in the PV formula. The present values (column C) therefore appear as positive numbers.

The present value of a stream of future cash flows is the amount you would have to invest today to generate that stream.

Check Point 4.7

In order to avoid estate taxes, your rich aunt Frederica will pay you $10,000 per year for 4 years, starting 1 year from now. What is the present value of your benefactor's planned gifts? The interest rate is 7 percent. How much will you have 4 years from now if you invest each gift at 7 percent?

4.4

LEVEL CASH FLOWS: PERPETUITIES AND ANNUITIES

Frequently, you may need to value a stream of equal cash flows. For example, a home mortgage might require the homeowner to make equal monthly payments for the life of the loan. For a 25-year loan, this would result in 300 equal payments. A 4-year car loan might require 48 equal monthly payments. Any such sequence of equally spaced, level cash flows is called an **annuity**. If the payment stream lasts forever, it is called a **perpetuity**.

annuity Equally spaced and level stream of cash flows.

HOW TO VALUE PERPETUITIES

perpetuity Stream of level cash payments that never ends.

Some time ago the British government borrowed by issuing perpetuities. Instead of repaying these loans, the British government pays the investors holding these securities a fixed annual payment in perpetuity.

How might we value such a security? Suppose that you could invest $100 at an interest rate of 10 percent. You would earn annual interest of $.1 \times \$100 = \$10$ per year and could withdraw this amount from your investment account each year without ever running down your balance. In other words, a $100 investment could provide a perpetuity of $10 per year. In general:

$$\text{cash payment from perpetuity} = \text{interest rate} \times \text{present value}$$
$$C = r \times \text{PV}$$

We can rearrange this relationship to derive the present value of a perpetuity, given the interest rate r and the cash payment C:

$$\textbf{PV of perpetuity} = \frac{C}{r} = \frac{\textbf{cash payment}}{\textbf{interest rate}} \tag{4.7}$$

Suppose some worthy person wishes to endow a chair in finance at your university. If the rate of interest is 10 percent, and the aim is to provide $100,000 a year forever, the amount that must be set aside today is

$$\text{Present value of perpetuity} = \frac{C}{r} = \frac{\$100,000}{.10} = \$1,000,000$$

Two warnings about the perpetuity formula. First, at a quick glance you can easily confuse the formula with the present value of a single cash payment. A payment of $1 at the end of 1 year has a present value $1/(1 + r)$. The perpetuity has a value of $1/r$. These are quite different.

Second, the perpetuity formula tells us the value of a regular stream of payments starting one period from now. Thus an endowment of $1 million would provide the university with its first payment of $100,000 1 year hence. If the worthy donor wants to provide the university with an additional payment of $100,000 up front, he or she would need to put aside $1,100,000.

Sometimes you may need to calculate the value of a perpetuity that does not start to make payments for several years. For example, suppose that our philanthropist decides to provide $100,000 a year with the first payment 4 years from now. As the time line in Figure 4.8 shows, we know that in Year 3 this endowment will be an ordinary perpetuity with payments starting at the end of 1 year. So our perpetuity formula tells us that in Year 3 the endowment will be worth $100,000/r$. But it is not worth that much now. To find today's value we need to multiply by the three-year discount factor. Thus, the "delayed" perpetuity is worth

$$\$100,000 \times \frac{1}{r} \times \frac{1}{(1 + r)^3} = \$1,000,000 \times \frac{1}{(1.10)^3} = \$751,315$$

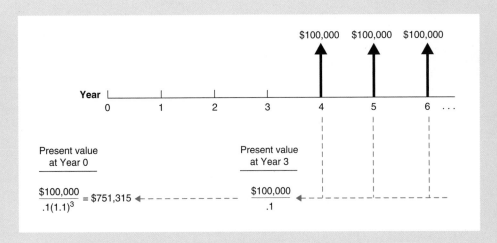

FIGURE 4.8
Time line for a delayed perpetuity—$100,000 per year forever, to start in 4 years

Check Point 4.8   A British government perpetuity pays £4 a year forever and is selling for £48. What is the interest rate?

HOW TO VALUE ANNUITIES

There are two ways to value an annuity, that is, a limited number of cash flows. The slow way is to value each cash flow separately and add up the present values. The quick way is to take advantage of the following simplification. Figure 4.9 shows the cash payments and values of three investments.

Row 1. The investment shown in the first row provides a perpetual stream of $1 payments starting in Year 1. We have already seen that this perpetuity has a present value of $1/r$.

Row 2. Now look at the investment shown in the second row of Figure 4.9. It also provides a perpetual stream of $1 payments, but these payments don't start until Year 4. This stream of payments is identical to the delayed perpetuity that we just valued. In Year 3, the investment will be an ordinary perpetuity with payments starting in 1 year and will therefore be worth $1/r$ in Year 3. To find the value today, we simply multiply this figure by the three-year discount factor. Thus

$$PV = \frac{1}{r} \times \frac{1}{(1+r)^3} = \frac{1}{r(1+r)^3}$$

Row 3. Finally, look at the investment shown in the third row of Figure 4.9. This provides a level payment of $1 a year for 3 years. In other words, it is a three-year annuity. You can also see that, taken together, the investments in rows 2 and 3 provide exactly the same cash payments as the investment in row 1. Thus the value of our annuity (row 3) must be equal to the value of the row 1 perpetuity minus the value of the delayed row 2 perpetuity:

$$\text{Present value of a 3-year \$1 annuity} = \frac{1}{r} - \frac{1}{r(1+r)^3}$$

The general formula for the value of an annuity that pays C dollars a year for each of t years is

$$\textbf{Present value of } t\textbf{-year annuity} = C \times \left[\frac{1}{r} - \frac{1}{r(1+r)^t} \right] \qquad (4.8)$$

annuity factor   Present value of a $1 annuity.

The expression in square brackets shows the present value of a t-year annuity of $1 a year. It is generally known as the t-year **annuity factor** and can be written as PVA (r,t). Therefore, another way to write the value of an annuity is

$$\textbf{Present value of } t\textbf{-year annuity} = \textbf{payment} \times \textbf{annuity factor} = C \times \textbf{PVA } (r,t) \qquad (4.9)$$

FIGURE 4.9
Valuing an annuity as the difference between an immediate perpetuity (A) and a delayed perpetuity (B)

| | Present value (Year 0) | \multicolumn{6}{c}{Cash flow each year} |
		1	2	3	4	5	6 ...
1. Perpetuity A	$\frac{1}{r}$	$1	$1	$1	$1	$1	$1...
2. Perpetuity B	$\frac{1}{r(1+r)^3}$	0	0	0	$1	$1	$1...
3. Three-year annuity	$\frac{1}{r} - \frac{1}{r(1+r)^3}$	$1	$1	$1			

FIGURE 4.10
Time line for Kangaroo Autos' "Easy Payment" scheme of $4,000 a year for 3 years, Example 4.8. To find the present value of the annuity; calculate the present value of each cash flow. It is usually quicker to use the annuity formula.

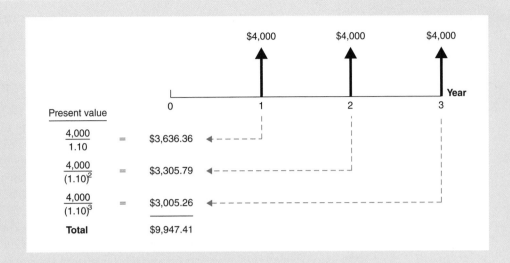

Remembering formulas is about as difficult as remembering other people's birthdays. But as long as you bear in mind that an annuity is equivalent to the difference between an immediate and a delayed perpetuity, you shouldn't have any difficulty.

| EXAMPLE 4.8 | **BACK TO KANGAROO AUTOS** |

Let us return to Kangaroo Autos for, almost, the last time. Most instalment plans call for level streams of payments. So let us suppose that this time Kangaroo offers an "easy payment" scheme of $4,000 a year at the end of each of the next 3 years. First let's do the calculations the slow way; to show that if the interest rate is 10 percent, the present value of the three payments is $9,947.41. The time line in Figure 4.10 shows these calculations. The present value of each cash flow is calculated and then the three present values are summed. The annuity formula, however, is much quicker:

$$\text{Present value} = \$4,000 \times \text{PVA} (.10,3) = \$4,000 \times \left[\frac{1}{.10} - \frac{1}{.10(1.10)^3} \right]$$
$$= \$4,000 \times 2.48685 = \$9,947.41$$

You can use a calculator to work out annuity factors or you can use a set of annuity tables. Table 4.4 is an abridged annuity table (an extended version is shown in Table A.3 in Appendix A). Check that you can find the 3-year annuity factor for an interest rate of 10 percent.

69.78.   72.358
72.2

TABLE 4.4
Annuity factors—present value of a $1 received each of t periods, at various interest rates

Number of Periods	Interest Rate per Period					
	5%	6%	7%	8%	9%	10%
1	0.9524	0.9434	0.9346	0.9259	0.9174	0.9091
2	1.8594	1.8334	1.8080	1.7833	1.7591	1.7355
3	2.7232	2.6730	2.6243	2.5771	2.5313	2.4869
4	3.5460	3.4651	3.3872	3.3121	3.2397	3.1699
5	4.3295	4.2124	4.1002	3.9927	3.8897	3.7908
10	7.7217	7.3601	7.0236	6.7101	6.4177	6.1446
20	12.4622	11.4699	10.5940	9.8181	9.1285	8.5136
30	15.3725	13.7648	12.4090	11.2578	10.2737	9.4269

Check Point 4.9

If the interest rate is 8 percent, what is the 4-year discount factor? What is the 4-year annuity factor? What is the relationship between these two numbers? Explain.

EXAMPLE 4.9

WINNING BIG AT A SLOT MACHINE

In January 2001, a 37-year-old Ontario flight attendant put $15 in a Las Vegas slot machine and walked away with $9.37 million. We suspect she received unsolicited congratulations, good wishes, and requests for money from dozens of more or less worthy charities, relatives, and newly devoted friends. In response she could fairly point out that her prize wasn't really worth $9.37 million. That sum was to be paid in 25 annual instalments of $374,800 each. What is the present value of the jackpot? The interest rate at the time was about 5 percent.

The present value of these payments is simply the sum of the present values of each payment. But rather than valuing each payment separately, it is much easier to treat the cash payments as a 25-year annuity. To value this annuity we simply multiply $374,800 by the 25-year annuity factor:

$$PV = \$374,800 \times PVA\,(.05,25)$$

At an interest rate of 5 percent, the annuity factor is

$$PVA\,(.05,25) = \left[\frac{1}{.05} - \frac{1}{.05(1.05)^{25}} \right] = 14.0939$$

(We also could look up the annuity factor in Table A.3.) The present value of the $374,800 annuity is $374,800 × 14.0939 = $5,282,394. That $9.37 million prize has a true value of about $5.3 million.

This present value is the price that investors would be prepared to offer for the series of cash flows. For example, the gambling casino might arrange for an insurance company to actually make the payments to the lucky winner. In this case, the company would charge a bit less than $5.3 million to take over the obligation. With this amount in hand today, it could generate enough interest income to make the 25 payments before running its "account" down to zero. (In case you are wondering, most Canadian casinos and lotteries pay out the stated prize amount as a lump sum.)

EXAMPLE 4.10

HOW MUCH LUXURY AND EXCITEMENT CAN $54 BILLION BUY?

Bill Gates is reputedly the world's richest person, with wealth estimated at $46.6 billion in 2004. We haven't yet met Mr. Gates, so we cannot fill you in on his plans for allocating the $46.6 billion between his charitable works and the cost of his life of luxury and excitement (L&E). So to keep things simple, we will just ask the following, entirely hypothetical, question: How much could Mr. Gates spend yearly on 40 more years of L&E if he were to devote the entire $46.6 billion to those purposes? Assume that his money is invested at 9 percent interest.

The 40-year 9 percent annuity factor is 10.757. Thus

$$\text{Present value} = \text{annual spending} \times PVA\,(.09,40)$$
$$\$46,600,000,000 = \text{annual spending} \times 10.757$$
$$\text{Annual spending} = \$4,332,062,843$$

Warning to Mr. Gates: We haven't considered inflation. The cost of buying L&E will increase, so $4.3 billion won't buy as much L&E in 40 years as it will today. More on that later.

Check Point 4.10

Suppose you retire at age 70. You expect to live 20 more years and to spend $55,000 per year during your retirement. How much money do you need to save by age 70 to support this consumption plan? Assume an interest rate of 7 percent.

EXAMPLE 4.11

HOME MORTGAGES

Sometimes you may need to find the series of cash payments that would provide a given value today. For example, home purchasers typically borrow the bulk of the house price from a lender. The most common loan arrangement is a 25-year loan that is repaid in equal monthly instalments. Suppose that a house costs $150,000, and that the buyer puts down 25 percent of the purchase price, or $37,500, in cash, borrowing the remaining $112,500 from a mortgage lender such as a bank. What is the appropriate monthly mortgage payment?

The borrower repays the loan by making monthly payments over the next 25 years (300 months). The bank needs to set these monthly payments so that they have a present value of $112,500. Thus

$$\text{Present value} = \text{mortgage payment} \times \text{300-month annuity factor}$$
$$= \$112,500$$
$$\text{Mortgage payment} = \frac{\$112,500}{\text{300-month annuity factor}}$$

Suppose that the interest rate is 1% a month. Then

$$\text{Mortgage payment} = \frac{\$112,500}{\left[\dfrac{1}{.01} - \dfrac{1}{.01(1.01)^{300}}\right]} = \frac{\$112,500}{94.9466} = \$1,184.88$$

The mortgage loan in Example 4.11 is an example of an *amortizing loan.* "Amortizing" means that part of the monthly payment is used to pay interest on the loan and part is used to reduce the amount of the loan. Table 4.5 illustrates a 4-year amortizing loan of $1,000 with an interest rate of 10 percent and annual payments starting in 1 year. The annual payment (annuity) that would repay the loan is $315.47. (Confirm this for yourself.) At the end of the first year, the interest payment is 10 percent of $1,000, or $100. So $100 of your first payment is used to pay interest, and the remaining $215.47 is used to reduce (or "amortize") the loan balance to $784.53.

Next year, the outstanding balance is lower, so the interest charge is only $78.45. Therefore, $315.47 − $78.45 = $237.02 can be applied to amortization. Amortization in the second year is higher than in the first, because the amount of the loan has declined and therefore less of the

FIGURE 4.11

Mortgage amortization. This figure shows the breakdown of mortgage payments between interest and amortization. Monthly payments within each year are summed, so the figure shows the annual payment on the mortgage.

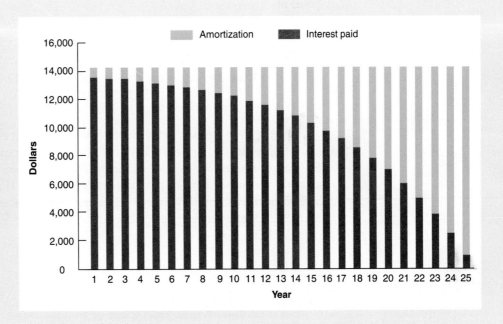

TABLE 4.5
An example of an amortizing loan. If you borrow $1,000 at an interest rate of 10 percent, you would need to make an annual payment of $315.47 over 4 years to repay the loan with interest.

Year	Beginning-of-Year Balance	Year-End Interest Due on Balance	Year-End Payment	Amortization of Loan	End-of-Year Balance
1	$1,000.00	$100.00	$315.47	$215.47	$784.53
2	$784.53	$78.45	$315.47	$237.02	$547.51
3	$547.51	$54.75	$315.47	$260.72	$286.79
4	$286.79	$28.68	$315.47	$286.79	$0

payment is taken up in interest. This procedure continues until the last year, when the amortization is just enough to reduce the outstanding balance on the loan to zero.

Because the loan is progressively paid off, the fraction of each payment devoted to interest steadily falls over time, while the fraction used to reduce the loan (the amortization) steadily increases. Figure 4.11 illustrates the amortization of the mortgage loan in Example 4.11. In the early years, almost all of the mortgage payment is for interest. Even after 15 years, the bulk of the monthly payment is interest.

Check Point 4.11

What will be the monthly payment if you take out a $100,000 15-year mortgage at an interest rate of 1 percent per month? How much of the first payment is interest and how much is amortization?

ANNUITIES DUE

The perpetuity and annuity formulas assume that the first payment occurs at the end of the period. They tell you the value of a stream of cash payments starting one period hence.

However, streams of cash payments often start immediately. For example, Kangaroo Autos in Example 4.8 might have required three annual payments of $4,000 starting immediately. A level stream of payments starting immediately is known as an **annuity due**.

annuity due Level stream of cash flows starting immediately.

If Kangaroo's loan was paid as an annuity due, you could think of the three payments as equivalent to an immediate payment of $4,000, plus an ordinary annuity of $4,000 for the remaining 2 years. This is made clear in Figure 4.12, which compares the cash flow stream of the Kangaroo Autos loan, treating the three payments as an annuity (panel a) and as an annuity due (panel b).

In general, the present value of an annuity due of t payments of $1 per period is the same as $1 plus the present value of an ordinary annuity providing the remaining $t - 1$ payments. The present value of an annuity due of $1 for t periods, PVAD (r,t) is therefore

PV annuity due = 1 + PV ordinary annuity of $t - 1$ payments

$$= 1 + \left[\frac{1}{r} - \frac{1}{r(1+r)^{t-1}} \right] \qquad (4.10)$$

By comparing the two panels in Figure 4.12, you can see that each of the three cash flows in the annuity due comes one period earlier than the corresponding cash flow of the ordinary annuity. This gives us another way to value an annuity due. The present value of an annuity due is $(1 + r)$ times the present value of an equivalent ordinary annuity.[3] Figure 4.12 shows that bringing the Kangaroo loan payments forward by 1 year increases their value from $9,947.41 (as an annuity) to $10,942.15 (as an annuity due). Notice that $10,942.15 = $9,947.41 \times 1.10$.

---

[3] Your financial calculator is equipped to handle annuities due. You simply need to put the calculator in "begin" mode, and the stream of cash flows will be interpreted as starting immediately. The begin key is labelled *BGN* or *BEG/END*. Each time you press the key, the calculator will toggle between ORDINARY ANNUITY versus ANNUITY DUE mode.

FIGURE 4.12
Annuity versus annuity due:
(a) 3-year ordinary annuity
(b) 3-year annuity due

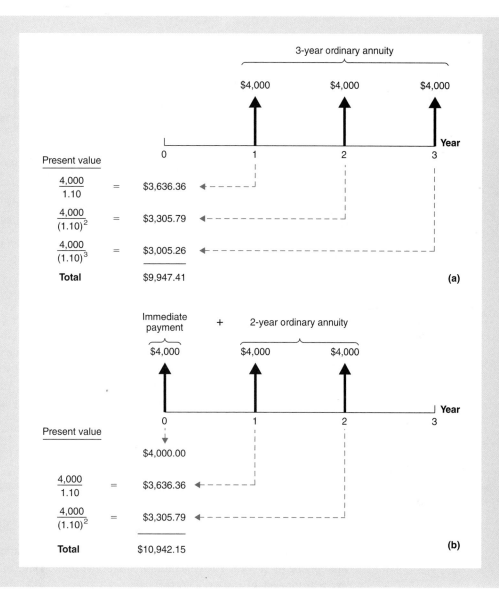

Check Point 4.12

When calculating the value of the slot machine winnings in Example 4.9, we assumed that the first of the 25 payments occurs at the end of 1 year. However, the first payment was probably made immediately, with the remaining payments spread over the following 24 years. What is the present value of the $9.37 million prize?

FUTURE VALUE OF AN ANNUITY

You are back in savings mode again. This time you are setting aside $3,000 at the end of every year in order to buy a car. If your savings earn interest of 8 percent per year, how much will they be worth at the end of 4 years? We can answer this question with the help of the time line in Figure 4.13. Your first year's savings will earn interest for 3 years, the second will earn interest for 2 years, the third will earn interest for 1 year, and the final savings in Year 4 will earn no interest. The sum of the future values of the four payments is

$$(\$3,000 \times 1.08^3) + (\$3,000 \times 1.08^2) + (\$3,000 \times 1.08) + \$3,000 = \$13,518$$

FIGURE 4.13

Future value of a 4-year, $3,000 per year annuity invested at 8 percent

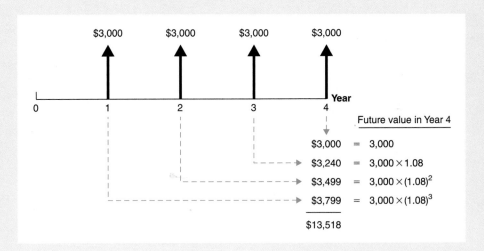

But wait a minute! We are looking here at a level stream of cash flows—an annuity. We have seen that there is a shortcut formula to calculate the *present* value of an annuity. So there ought to be a similar formula for calculating the *future* value of a level stream of cash flows.

Think first how much your stream of savings is worth today. You are setting aside $3,000 in each of the next 4 years. The *present* value of this 4-year annuity is therefore equal to

$$PV = \$3,000 \times \text{4-year annuity factor}$$

$$= \$3,000 \times \left[\frac{1}{.08} - \frac{1}{.08(1.08)^4} \right] = \$9,936$$

Now think how much you would have after 4 years if you invested $9,936 today. Simple! Just multiply by $(1.08)^4$:

$$\text{Value at end of Year 4} = \$9,936 \times 1.08^4 = \$13,518$$

We calculated the future value of the annuity by first calculating the present value and then multiplying by $(1 + r)^t$. The general formula for the future value of a stream of cash flows of $1 per year for each of t years, FVA (r,t), is

Future value of annuity of $1 per year, FVA (r,t) = **present value of annuity of $1 per year** $\times$ $(1 + r)^t$

$$\text{FVA } (r,t) = \left[\frac{1}{r} - \frac{1}{r(1 + r)^t} \right] \times (1 + r)^t$$

$$\text{FVA } (r,t) = \frac{(1 + r)^t - 1}{r}$$

(4.11)

If you need to find the future value of just four cash flows, as in our example, it is a toss-up whether it is quicker to calculate the future value of each cash flow separately (as we did in Figure 4.13) or to use the annuity formula. If you are faced with a stream of 10 or 20 cash flows, there is no contest.

You can find a table of the future value of an annuity in Table 4.6, or use the more extensive Table A.4 in Appendix A. You can see that in the row corresponding to $t = 4$ and the column corresponding to $r = 8\%$, the future value of an annuity of $1 a year is $4.5061. Therefore, the future value of the $3,000 annuity is $3,000 $\times$ 4.5061 = $13,518.

EXAMPLE 4.12   **SAVING FOR RETIREMENT**

In only 45 more years, you will retire. Have you started saving yet? Suppose you believe you will need to accumulate $500,000 by your retirement date in order to support your desired standard of living. How much must you save each year between now and your retirement to meet that future goal? Let's say that the interest rate is 10 percent per year. You need to find how large the annuity in the following figure must be to provide a future value of $500,000:

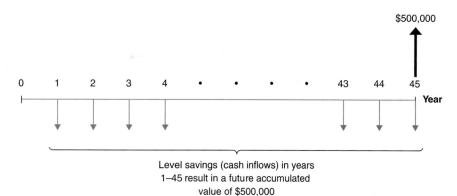

Level savings (cash inflows) in years
1–45 result in a future accumulated
value of $500,000

We know that if you were to save $1 each year your funds would accumulate to

$$\text{Future value of annuity of \$1 a year} = \frac{(1 + r)^t - 1}{r} = \frac{(1.10)^{45} - 1}{.10}$$

$$= \$718.905$$

**SEE BOXES,
PP. 105, 106**

(Rather than compute the future value formula directly, you could look up the future value annuity factor in Table 4.6 or Table A.4. Alternatively, you can use a financial calculator or spreadsheet as we describe in the nearby Financial Calculator and Spreadsheet Solutions boxes.) Therefore, if we save an amount of $C each year, we will accumulate $C × 718.905.

We need to choose C to ensure that $C × 718.905 = $500,000. Thus C = $500,000/718.905 = $695.50. This appears to be surprisingly good news. Saving $695.50 a year does not seem to be an extremely demanding savings program. Don't celebrate yet, however. The news will get worse when we consider the impact of inflation.

Check Point 4.13

What is the required savings level if the interest rate is only 5 percent? Why has the amount increased?

TABLE 4.6
Future value factors—future value of a $1 annuity invested at various interest rates for different periods

Number of Periods	Interest Rate per Period					
	5%	6%	7%	8%	9%	10%
1	1.0000	1.0000	1.0000	1.0000	1.0000	1.0000
2	2.0500	2.0600	2.0700	2.0800	2.0900	2.1000
3	3.1525	3.1836	3.2149	3.2464	3.2781	3.3100
4	4.3101	4.3746	4.4399	4.5061	4.5731	4.6410
5	5.5256	5.6371	5.7507	5.8666	5.9847	6.1051
10	12.5779	13.1808	13.8164	14.4866	15.1929	15.9374
20	33.0660	36.7856	40.9955	45.7620	51.1601	57.2750
30	66.4388	79.0582	94.4608	113.2832	136.3075	164.4940

Remember that our ordinary annuity formulas assume that the first cash flow does not occur until the end of the first period. If the first cash flow comes immediately, the future value of the cash flow stream is greater, since each flow has an extra year to earn interest. For example, at an interest rate of 8 percent, the future value of an annuity due would be exactly 8 percent greater than the future value of an ordinary annuity. More generally,

Future value of annuity due = future value of ordinary annuity $\times$ (1 + r)

EXAMPLE 4.13	**FUTURE VALUE OF ANNUITIES VERSUS ANNUITIES DUE**

In Example 4.12, we showed that an annual savings stream of $695.50 invested for 45 years at 10 percent would satisfy a savings goal of $500,000. What savings stream would be necessary if we invested our money at the beginning rather than the end of each year?

We know from Example 4.12 that the future value of a $1 ordinary 45-year annuity at an interest rate of 10 percent is $718.905. Therefore,

$$\text{FV of \$1 annuity due} = \text{FV of \$1 ordinary annuity} \times (1 + r)$$
$$= \$718.905 \times 1.10 = \$790.80$$

We need to choose C to ensure that $C \times 790.80 = \$500,000$. Thus $C = \$632.27$. Notice that $632.27 equals the (ordinary) annuity we found in Example 4.12 divided by 1.10.

CASH FLOWS GROWING AT A CONSTANT RATE—VARIATIONS ON PERPETUITIES AND ANNUITIES

The perpetuity and annuity formulas make valuing streams of equal cash flows easy. Unfortunately, many streams of cash flows are not equal. If, however, the cash flow stream grows at a constant rate, convenient valuation formulas are available. The present value of a perpetual stream of payments growing at a constant rate is

Present value of a perpetual stream of payments growing at a constant rate $= \dfrac{C_1}{r - g}$ **(4.12)**

where C_1 is the payment to occur at the end of the first period, r is the discount rate and g is the growth rate of the payments. If the growth rate, g, is zero, the formula becomes the familiar perpetuity formula, C/r. A perpetual stream of cash flows growing at a constant rate is sometimes called a **growing perpetuity**.

growing perpetuity An infinite stream of cash flows growing at a constant rate.

EXAMPLE 4.14	**VALUING A CONDO**

You are considering purchasing a condominium as an investment. Currently, the type of condo you want generates $12,000 in cash flow (rent minus expenses) annually. If the cash flow grows 3 percent per year, the building lasts forever, and the interest rate is 8 percent, what is the present value of the condo's cash flows?

$$\text{Present value} = \frac{\$12,000}{.08 - .03} = \$240,000$$

The formulas for both the present value and future value of an annuity are also built into your financial calculator. Again, we can input all but one of the five financial keys, and let the calculator solve for the remaining variable. In these applications, the *PMT* key is used to either enter or solve for the value of an annuity.

Solving for an Annuity

In Example 4.12, we determined the savings stream that would provide a retirement goal of $500,000 after 45 years of saving at an interest rate of 10 percent. To find the required savings each year, enter *n* = 45, *i* = 10, *FV* = 500,000, and *PV* = 0 (because your "savings account" is currently empty). Compute *PMT* and find that it is –$695.50. Again, your calculator is likely to display the solution as –695.50, since the positive $500,000 cash value in 45 years will require 45 cash payments (outflows) of $695.50.

The sequence of key strokes necessary to solve this problem on three popular calculators are as follows:

Hewlett-Packard HP-10B	Sharpe EL-733A	Texas Instruments BA II Plus
0 [PV]	0 [PV]	0 [PV]
45 [n]	45 [n]	45 [n]
10 [I/YR]	10 [i]	10 [I/Y]
500,000 [FV]	500,000 [FV]	500,000 [FV]
[PMT]	[COMP] [PMT]	[CPT] [PMT]

Your calculator displays a negative number, as the 45 cash-outflows of $695.50 are necessary to provide for the $500,000 cash value at retirement.

Present Value of an Annuity

In Example 4.11 we considered a 25-year mortgage with monthly payments of $1,184.88 and an interest rate of 1 percent per month. Suppose we didn't know the amount of the mortgage loan. Enter *n* = 300 (months), *i* = 1, *PMT* = –1,184.88 (we enter the annuity level paid by the borrower to the lender as a negative number since it is a cash outflow), and *FV* = 0 (the mortgage is paid off after 25 years; there are no final future payments beyond the normal monthly payment). Compute *PV* to find that the value of the loan is $112,500.

What about the balance left on the mortgage after seven years have passed? This is easy: The monthly payment is still *PMT* = –1,184.88,

and we continue to use *i* = 1 and *FV* = 0. The only change is that the number of monthly payments remaining has fallen from 300 to 216 (18 years are left on the loan). So enter *n* = 216 and compute *PV* as 104,675.97. This is the balance remaining on the mortgage.

Future Value of an Annuity

In Figure 4.13, we showed that a 4-year annuity of $3,000 invested at 8 percent would accumulate to a future value of $13,518. To solve this on your calculator, enter *n* = 4, *i* = 8, *PMT* = –3,000 (we enter the annuity paid by the investor to her savings account as a negative number since it is a cash outflow), and *PV* = 0 (the account starts with no funds). Compute *FV* to find that the future value of the savings account after 3 years is $13,518.

Calculator Self-Test Review (answers below)

1. Turn back to Kangaroo Autos in Example 4.8. Can you now solve for the present value of the three instalment payments using your financial calculator? What key strokes must you use?
2. Now use your calculator to solve for the present value of the three instalment payments if the first payment comes immediately, that is, as an annuity due.
3. Find the annual spending available to Bill Gates using the data in Example 4.10 and your financial calculator.

Solutions to Calculator Self-Test Review Questions

1. Inputs are *n* = 3, *i* = 10, *FV* = 0, and *PMT* = 4,000. Compute *PV* to find the present value of the cash flows as $9,947.41.
2. If you put your calculator in "begin" mode and recalculate *PV* using the same inputs, you will find that *PV* has increased by 10 percent to $10,942.15. Alternatively, as depicted in Figure 4.12, you can calculate the value of the $4,000 immediate payment plus the value of a 2-year annuity of $4,000. Inputs for the 2-year annuity are *n* = 2, *i* = 10, *FV* = 0, and *PMT* = 4,000. Compute *PV* to find the present value of the cash flows as $6,942.15. This amount plus the immediate $4,000 payment results in the same total present value: $10,942.15.
3. Inputs are *n* = 40, *i* = 9, *FV* = 0, *PV* = –46,600 million. Compute *PMT* to find that the 40-year annuity with present value of $46.6 billion is $4,331.9 million. Slight differnce is due to rounding.

Another useful present value formula can be used if the cash flows grow at a constant rate for a limited or finite period. The present value of a finite stream of cash flows growing at a constant rate is

$$\text{Present value of a finite stream of payments growing at a constant rate} = \frac{C_1}{r-g}\left(1 - \left[\frac{1+g}{1+r}\right]^t\right) \tag{4.13}$$

where C_1 is the payment to occur at the end of the first period, r is the discount rate, t is the number of payments, and g is the growth rate of the payments. If the growth rate, g, is zero, after a bit of jiggling, the formula becomes the familiar present value of an annuity formula. A finite stream of cash flows growing at a constant rate is some times referred to as a **growing annuity**.

growing annuity A finite stream of cash flows growing at a constant rate.

Annuities

By now it should be no surprise that the *pmt* variable in Excel's time-value-of-money functions denotes the level of an annuity. In addition, Excel provides another function to solve for annuity levels given the values of the other variables: PMT (*rate, nper, pv, fv*). Thus in Example 4.12, we can find the savings stream providing a future retirement goal of $500,000 after 45 years by entering =PMT(.10,45,0,500000), which results in an answer of –$695.50. Notice that we enter 0 for *pv* because our savings account starts with no funds.

Present Value of an Annuity

Example 4.11 examines a 25-year mortgage loan with 300 monthly payments of $1,184.88 each when the interest rate is 1 percent per month. The present value of this annuity =PV(.01,300,1184.88,0), which (except for trivial rounding error) is $112,500. We can also find the balance on the loan after 10 years, when there are 180 remaining payments, as =PV(.01,180,1184.88,0) = $98,726.17.

Future Value of an Annuity

We confirmed on our calculators in the Financial Calculator box that a 4-year annuity of $3,000 invested at 8 percent has a future

value of $13,518 (see Figure 4.13). You can also confirm this value on your spreadsheet by entering =FV(.08,4,3000,0).

Annuities Due

Excel will calculate the value of an annuity due rather than an ordinary annuity if you add an extra 1 at the end of the function. For example, we just calculated the present value of 300 monthly mortgage payments. Now assume the first payment comes immediately rather than after one month. In other words, the payments are an annuity due. Then the present value is found as =PV(.01,300,1184.88,0,1), which equals $113,625, exactly 1 percent more than the value of the payments as an ordinary annuity. Similarly, the future value of the 4-year, $3,000 annuity that we just looked at also is higher if the first payment is made immediately. As an annuity due, the future value is =FV (.08,4,3000,0,1) = $14,600, which is 8 percent higher than the future value of the ordinary annuity.

Spreadsheet Self-Test Review

In the previous box, we gave you three self-test review questions for your calculator. Now solve these problems using a spreadsheet program.

EXAMPLE 4.15   **ANOTHER LOOK AT THE VALUE OF A CONDO**

Upon reflection, the condo in Example 4.13 will not likely be around forever. If the building is torn down in 20 years, what is the present value of the cash flows if the first cash flow is $12,000, the growth rate 3 percent, and the interest rate 8 percent?

$$\text{Present value} = \frac{\$12,000}{.08 - .03}\left(1 - \left[\frac{1.03}{1.08}\right]^{20}\right) = \$147,000.50$$

4.5   INFLATION AND THE TIME VALUE OF MONEY

When a bank offers to pay 6 percent on a savings account, it promises to pay interest of $60 for every $1,000 you deposit. The bank fixes the number of dollars that it pays, but it doesn't provide any assurance of how much those dollars will buy. If the value of your investment increases by 6 percent, while the prices of goods and services increase by 10 percent, you actually lose ground in terms of the goods you can buy.

REAL VERSUS NOMINAL CASH FLOWS

inflation Rate at which prices as a whole are increasing.

Prices of goods and services continually change. Textbooks may become more expensive (sorry!) while computers become cheaper. An overall rise in prices is known as **inflation**. If the inflation rate is 5 percent per year, then goods that cost $1 a year ago typically cost $1.05 this year. The increase in the general level of prices means that the purchasing power of money has eroded. If a dollar bill bought a loaf of bread last year, the same dollar this year buys only part of a loaf.

Economists track the general level of prices using several different price indexes. The best known of these is the *consumer price index*, or CPI. This measures the number of dollars that it

FIGURE 4.14
Consumer Price Index,
1950–2004

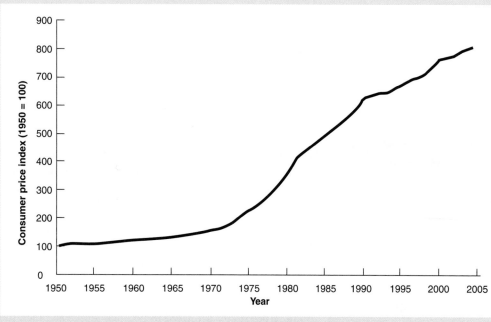

Source: Author's calculations, based on annual CPI, CANSIM II Series V737344.

takes to buy a specified basket of goods and services, which is supposed to represent the typical family's purchases.[4] Thus the percentage increase in the CPI from one year to the next measures the rate of inflation.

Figure 4.14 graphs the CPI from 1950 to 2004. We have set the index for the end of 1950 to 100, so the graph shows the price level in each year as a percentage of 1950 prices. For example, the index in 1951 was 110. This means that on average $110 in 1951 would have bought the same quantity of goods and services as $100 in 1950. The inflation rate between 1950 and 1951 was therefore 10 percent. By mid-2003, the index was 821, meaning that prices were 8.21 times as high as 1950 prices.[5]

In 2003 the consumer price index was 821 and in 1970 the index was 162. The index had increased 5.07 (821/162) times between 1970 and 2003. A dollar in 2003 would buy only 12 percent of the goods it could buy in 1950 (1/8.21 = .12). In this case, we would say that the **real value of $1** declined by 100 – 12 = 88 percent from 1950 to 2003.

real value of $1
Purchasing power-adjusted value of a dollar.

As we write this in the summer of 2005, inflation is less than 2 percent per year and a few countries are even experiencing falling prices, or deflation. This has led some economists to argue that inflation is dead; others are less sure. In Canada, the Bank of Canada is responsible for setting monetary policy to control inflation. Visit **www.bankofcanada.ca** to learn more about its efforts to manage inflation.

| EXAMPLE 4.16 | **TALK IS CHEAP** |

Suppose that in 1970 a telephone call to your Aunt Hilda in London cost $10, while the price to air-mail a letter was $.50. By 2003 the price of the phone call had fallen to $3, while that of the air-mail letter had risen to $1. What was the change in the real cost of communicating with your aunt?

---

[4] Don't ask how you buy a "basket" of services.

[5] The choice of 100 for the index in 1950 is arbitrary. For example, we could have set the index at 50 in 1950. In this case, the index in 1951 would have been 10 percent higher at 55 (that is, $50 in 1950 and $55 in 1951 would have bought the same basket of goods).

In 2003 the consumer price index was 5.07 (=821/162) times its level in 1970. If the price of telephone calls had risen in line with inflation, they would have cost 5.07 × $10 = $50.70 in 2003. That was the cost of a phone call measured in terms of 2003 dollars rather than 1970 dollars. Thus over the 33 years the real cost of an international phone call declined from $50.7 to $3, a fall of over 94 percent.

What about the cost of sending a letter? If the price of an airmail letter had kept pace with inflation, it would have been 5.07 × $.50 = $2.54 in 2003. The actual price was only $1. So the real cost of letter writing has also declined.

Check Point 4.14

Consider a telephone call to London that currently costs $5. If the real price of telephone calls does not change in the future, how much will it cost you to make a call to London in 50 years, if the inflation rate is 5 percent (roughly its average over the past 33 years)? What if inflation is 10 percent?

Economists sometimes talk about *current* or *nominal dollars* versus *constant* or *real dollars*. Current or nominal dollars refer to the actual number of dollars of the day; constant or real dollars refer to the amount of purchasing power.

Some expenditures are fixed in nominal terms, and therefore *decline* in real terms. Suppose you took out a 25-year house mortgage in 1990. The monthly payment was $800. It was still $800 in 2003, even though the CPI increased by a factor of 1.31 (=821/626) over those years.

What's the monthly payment for 2003 expressed in real 1990 dollars? The answer is $800/1.31, or $610.69 per month. The real burden of paying the mortgage was less in 2003 than in 1990.

Check Point 4.15

The price index in 1980 was 352. If a family spent $250 a week on their typical purchases in 1950, how much would those purchases cost in 1980? If your salary in 1980 was $30,000 a year, what would be the real value of that salary in terms of 1950 dollars?

INFLATION AND INTEREST RATES

Whenever anyone quotes an interest rate, you can be fairly sure that it is a nominal rate, not a real rate. It sets the actual number of dollars you will be paid with no offset for future inflation.

nominal interest rate Rate at which money invested grows.

If you deposit $1,000 in the bank at a **nominal interest rate** of 6 percent, you will have $1,060 at the end of the year. But this does not mean you are 6 percent better off. Suppose that the inflation rate during the year is also 6 percent. Then the goods that cost $1,000 last year will now cost $1,000 × 1.06 = $1,060, so you've gained nothing:

$$\text{Real future value of investment} = \frac{\$1,000 \times (1 + \text{nominal interest rate})}{(1 + \text{inflation rate})}$$

$$= \frac{\$1,000 \times 1.06}{1.06} = \$1,000$$

real interest rate Rate at which the purchasing power of an investment increases.

In this example, the nominal rate of interest is 6 percent, but the **real interest rate** is zero. The real rate of interest is calculated by

$$1 + \textbf{real interest rate} = \frac{1 + \textbf{nominal interest rate}}{1 + \textbf{inflation rate}} \tag{4.14}$$

In our example, both the nominal interest rate and the inflation rate were 6 percent. So

$$1 + \text{real interest rate} = \frac{1.06}{1.06} = 1$$

$$\text{real interest rate} = 0$$

What if the nominal interest rate is 6 percent but the inflation rate is only 2 percent? In that case the real interest rate is $1.06/1.02 - 1 = .039$, or 3.9 percent. Imagine that the price of a loaf of bread is \$1, so that \$1,000 would buy 1,000 loaves today. If you invest that \$1,000 at a nominal interest rate of 6 percent, you will have \$1,060 at the end of the year. However, if the price of bread has risen in the meantime to \$1.02, then your money will buy you only $1,060/1.02 = 1,039$ loaves. The real rate of interest is 3.9 percent.

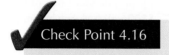

Check Point 4.16

a. Suppose that you invest your funds at an interest rate of 8 percent. What will be your real rate of interest if the inflation rate is zero? What if it is 5 percent?

b. Suppose that you demand a real rate of interest of 3 percent on your investments. What nominal interest rate do you need to earn if the inflation rate is zero? If it is 5 percent?

Here is a useful approximation. The real rate approximately equals the difference between the nominal rate and the inflation rate:[6]

$$\text{Real interest rate} \approx \text{nominal interest rate} - \text{inflation rate} \qquad (4.15)$$

Our example used a nominal interest rate of 6 percent, an inflation rate of 2 percent, and a real rate of 3.9 percent. If we round to 4 percent, the approximation gives the same answer:

$$\text{Real interest rate} \approx \text{nominal interest rate} - \text{inflation rate}$$
$$\approx 6 - 2 = 4\%$$

The approximation works best when both the inflation rate and the real rate are small.[7] When they are not small, throw the approximation away and do it properly.

EXAMPLE 4.17   **REAL AND NOMINAL RATES**

In Canada in 2004, the interest rate on 1-year government borrowing was about 2.6 percent. The inflation rate was 1.5 percent. Therefore, the real rate can be found by computing

$$1 + \text{real interest rate} = \frac{1 + \text{nominal interest rate}}{1 + \text{inflation rate}}$$
$$= \frac{1.026}{1.015} = 1.0108$$
$$\text{real interest rate} = .0108, \text{ or } 1.08\%$$

The approximation rule gives a similar value of $2.6 - 1.5 = 1.1$ percent. But the approximation would not have worked in the German hyperinflation of 1922/1923, when the inflation rate was well over 100 percent per month (at one point you needed one million marks to mail a letter), or in Peru in 1990, when prices increased by nearly 7,500 percent.

VALUING REAL CASH PAYMENTS

Think again about how to value future cash payments. Earlier in the chapter you learned how to value payments in current dollars by discounting at the nominal interest rate. For example, suppose

---

[6] The squiggle ($\approx$) means "approximately equal to."

[7] When the interest and inflation rates are expressed as decimals (rather than percentages), the approximation error equals the product (real interest rate $\times$ inflation rate).

that the nominal interest rate is 10 percent. How much do you need to invest now to produce $100 in a year's time? Easy! Calculate the present value of $100 by discounting by 10 percent:

$$PV = \frac{\$100}{1.10} = \$90.91$$

You get exactly the same result if you discount the *real* payment by the *real interest rate*. For example, assume that you expect inflation of 7 percent over the next year. The real value of that $100 is therefore only $100/1.07 = $93.46. In one year's time your $100 will buy only as much as $93.46 today. Also with a 7 percent inflation rate, the real rate of interest is only about 3 percent. We can calculate it exactly from the formula:

$$(1 + \text{real interest rate}) = \frac{1 + \text{nominal interest rate}}{1 + \text{inflation rate}}$$

$$= \frac{1.10}{1.07} = 1.028$$

$$\text{real interest rate} = .028, \text{ or } 2.8\%$$

If we now discount the $93.46 real payment by the 2.8 percent real interest rate, we have a present value of $90.91, just as before:

$$PV = \frac{\$93.46}{1.028} = \$90.91$$

The two methods should always give the same answer.[8] Remember,

> Current dollar cash flows must be discounted by the nominal interest rate; real cash flows must be discounted by the real interest rate.

Mixing up nominal cash flows and real discount rates (or real rates and nominal flows) is an unforgivable sin. It is surprising how many sinners one finds.

Check Point 4.17   You are owed $5,000 by a relative who will pay you back in 1 year. The nominal interest rate is 8 percent and the inflation rate is 5 percent. What is the present value of your relative's IOU? Show that you get the same answer (a) discounting the nominal payment at the nominal rate, and (b) discounting the real payment at the real rate.

EXAMPLE 4.18   **HOW INFLATION MIGHT AFFECT BILL GATES**

We showed earlier (Example 4.10) that at an interest rate of 9 percent, Bill Gates could, if he wished, turn his $46.6 billion (US) wealth into a 40-year annuity of $4.3 billion per year of luxury and excitement (L&E). Unfortunately L&E expenses inflate just like gasoline and groceries. Thus Mr. Gates would find the purchasing power of that $4.3 billion steadily declining. If he wants the same luxuries in 2044

---

[8] If they don't equal there must be an error in your calculations. All we have done in the second calculation is to divide both the numerator (the cash payment) and the denominator (1 plus the nominal interest rate) by the same number (1 plus the inflation rate):

$$PV = \frac{\text{payment in current dollars}}{1 + \text{nominal interest rate}}$$

$$= \frac{(\text{payment in current dollars})/(1 + \text{inflation rate})}{(1 + \text{nominal interest rate})/(1 + \text{inflation rate})}$$

$$= \frac{\text{payment in constant dollars}}{1 + \text{real interest rate}}$$

as in 2004, he'll have to spend less in 2004, and then increase expenditures in line with inflation. How much should he spend in 2004? Assume the long-run inflation rate is 5 percent.

Mr. Gates needs to calculate a 40-year real annuity. The real interest rate is a little less than 4 percent:

$$1 + \text{real interest rate} = \frac{1 + \text{nominal interest rate}}{1 + \text{inflation rate}}$$
$$= \frac{1.09}{1.05} = 1.038$$

so the real rate is 3.8 percent. The 40-year annuity factor at 3.8 percent is 20.396. Therefore, annual spending (in 2004 dollars) should be chosen so that

$$\$46,600,000,000 = \text{annual spending} \times 20.396$$
$$\text{annual spending} = \$2,284,762$$

Mr. Gates could spend that amount on L&E in 2004 and 5 percent more (in line with inflation) in each subsequent year. This is only about half the value we calculated when we ignored inflation. Life has many disappointments, even for tycoons.

Check Point 4.18   You have reached age 60 with a modest fortune of $3 million and are considering early retirement. How much can you spend each year for the next 30 years? Assume that your spending is stable in real terms. The nominal interest rate is 10 percent and the inflation rate is 5 percent.

REAL OR NOMINAL?

Any present value calculation done in nominal terms can also be done in real terms, and vice versa. Most financial analysts forecast in nominal terms and discount at nominal rates. However, in some cases real cash flows are easier to deal with. In our example of Bill Gates, the *real* expenditures were fixed. In this case, it was easiest to use real quantities. On the other hand, if the cash flow stream is fixed in nominal terms (for example, the payments on a loan), it is easiest to use all nominal quantities.

4.6

EFFECTIVE ANNUAL INTEREST RATES

Thus far in this chapter we have used *annual* interest rates to value a series of *annual* cash flows. But interest rates may be quoted for days, months, years, or any convenient interval. How should we compare rates when they are quoted for different periods, such as monthly versus annually?

Consider your credit card. Suppose you have to pay interest on any unpaid balances at the rate of 1 percent *per month*. What is it going to cost you if you neglect to pay off your unpaid balance for a year?

Don't be put off because the interest rate is quoted per month rather than per year. The important thing is to maintain consistency between the interest rate and the number of periods. If the interest rate is quoted as a percent per month, then we must define the number of periods in our future value calculation as number of months. So if you borrow $100 from the credit card company at 1 percent per month for 12 months, you will need to repay $100 \times (1.01)^{12} = \$112.68$. Thus your debt grows after 1 year to $112.68. Therefore, we can say that the interest rate of 1 percent a month is equivalent to an **effective annual interest rate (EAR)**, or *annually compounded rate*, of 12.68 percent.

effective annual interest rate (EAR)   Interest rate that is annualized using compound interest.

In general, the effective annual interest rate is defined as the annual growth rate allowing for the effect of compounding. Therefore, the effective annual equivalent to a monthly rate of interest is

$$1 + \text{effective annual rate} = (1 + \text{monthly rate})^{12} \qquad (4.16)$$

When comparing interest rates, it is best to use effective annual rates. This compares interest paid or received over a common period (one year) and allows for possible compounding during the period. Unfortunately, short-term rates are sometimes annualized by multiplying the rate per period by the number of periods in a year. In fact, truth in lending laws in Canada *require* that rates be annualized in this manner. Such rates are called **annual percentage rates (APRs)**.[9] The interest rate on your credit card loan was 1 percent per month. Since there are 12 months in a year, the APR on the loan is $12 \times 1\% = 12\%$.

annual percentage rate (APR)   Interest rate that is annualized using simple interest.

If the credit card company quotes an APR of 12 percent, how can you find the effective annual interest rate? The solution is simple:

Step 1. Take the quoted *APR* and divide by the number of compounding periods in a year to recover the rate per period actually charged. In our example, the interest was calculated monthly. So we divide the *APR* by 12 to obtain the interest rate per month

$$\text{Monthly interest rate} = \frac{APR}{12} = \frac{12\%}{12} = 1\%, \text{ or } .01$$

Step 2. Now convert to an annually compounded interest rate:

$$1 + \text{effective annual rate} = (1 + \text{monthly rate})^{12} = (1 + .01)^{12} = 1.1268$$

The annual interest rate is .1268, or 12.68 percent.

Putting Steps 1 and 2 together gives the formula for converting any *APR* with *m* compounding periods in the year into its effective annual equivalent rate:

$$1 + \text{effective annual rate} = \left(1 + \frac{APR}{m}\right)^{m} \qquad (4.17)$$

In other words, if you invest at the effective annual rate, the payoff in one year will be the same as investing at the per period rate, APR/*m*, compounded for the number of periods in the year. For example, a bank loan requiring monthly interest and carrying an APR of 20 percent has an effective annual interest rate of $(1 + .20/12)^{12} - 1 = .2194$, or 21.94 percent. To summarize,

> The effective annual rate is the rate at which invested funds will grow over the course of a year. It equals the rate of interest per period compounded for the number of periods in a year.

How do you calculate a per period rate that is equivalent to an annual rate? Rearrange the effective annual equivalent equation to solve for *APR*/*m*, which is the per period rate

$$\text{Per period interest rate} = \frac{APR}{m} = (1 + \text{effective annual rate})^{1/m} - 1 \qquad (4.18)$$

Let's try an example. What is the monthly interest rate equivalent to 8 percent per annum?

$$\text{Monthly interest rate} = \frac{APR}{m} = (1.08)^{1/12} - 1 = .00643$$

Earning interest of .643 percent per month is the same as earning 8 percent, paid annually. To convert the monthly rate to its APR, multiply by 12, the number of compounding periods in the year: $APR = 12 \times .643\% = 7.716\%$.

---

[9] Although the APR must be disclosed in the loan document, financial institutions typically (though not always) advertise effective rates when marketing their products. APRs are not commonly used or quoted for securities used in the big leagues of finance.

Check Point 4.19

Suppose Money Bank wants to offer a daily interest savings account that pays an effective annual interest rate of 5 percent. What daily interest rate should it pay? What will be the quoted APR for the account?

$\dfrac{r\%}{12} = 12$

How can you tell if a rate is an APR or an EAR if it's not specifically stated? It can be difficult but sometimes clues are provided. Generally, if the frequency of payment is mentioned, the rate is likely an APR. For example, if the bank is charging 10 percent interest, payable semi-annually, you should suspect that this is an APR. Interest of 5 percent is charged every 6 months and the EAR is $(1.05)^2 - 1 = .1025$ or 10.25 percent.

Does the frequency of payments matter? Yes, because if interest is paid more frequently, you earn interest on your interest sooner and it builds up over time. Table 4.7 shows how the effective annual rate increases as interest is paid more frequently, even though in each case the APR is 6 percent.

In the limit, interest can be paid in a continuous stream rather than in fixed intervals. With one year's *continuous compounding*, \$1 grows to e^{APR}, where $e = 2.718$ (a figure that may be familiar to you as the base for natural logarithms). Thus if you deposited \$1 in a bank that offered a continuously compounded rate of 6 percent, your investment would grow by the end of the year to $(2.718)^{.06} = \$1.061837$, just a hair's breadth more than if interest were compounded daily.

Check Point 4.20

A car loan requiring quarterly payments carries an APR of 8 percent. What is the quarterly interest rate? What is the effective annual rate of interest?

EXAMPLE 4.19

FIGURING OUT CANADIAN MORTGAGE INTEREST RATES

In Example 4.11 we showed you how to calculate monthly payments on a mortgage when the interest rate was 1 percent per month. However, before you apply for a job at a bank, you need to know more about Canadian mortgage interest rates. For reasons unclear to us, although mortgage payments are typically made monthly, the mortgage interest rates are APRs quoted with semi-annual compounding. For example, if the posted mortgage interest rate is 7.75 percent, this means 7.75 percent, *compounded semi-annually*. In other words, the six-month interest rate is 7.75/2 or 3.875 percent. To get the appropriate discount rate for a mortgage with monthly payments, we need to figure out the equivalent monthly interest rate.

TABLE 4.7
Compounding frequency and effective annual interest rate (APR = 6%)

Compounding Period	Periods per Year (*m*)	Per-Period Interest Rate	Growth Factor of Invested Funds	Effective Annual Rate
1 year	1	6%	1.06	6.0000%
Semi-annually	2	3	$1.03^2 = 1.0609$	6.0900
Quarterly	4	1.5	$1.015^4 = 1.061364$	6.1364
Monthly	12	.5	$1.005^{12} = 1.061678$	6.1678
Weekly	52	.11538	$1.0011538^{52} = 1.061800$	6.1800
Daily	365	.01644	$1.0001644^{365} = 1.061831$	6.1831
Continuous			$e^{.06} = 1.061837$	6.1837

First, convert the quoted APR rate to its effective annual equivalent using Equation 4.17:

$$\text{Effective annual rate} = \left(1 + \frac{APR}{m}\right)^m - 1 = \left(1 + \frac{.0775}{2}\right)^2 - 1 = 0.079, \text{ or } 7.9\%$$

Now convert the effective annual rate to its monthly equivalent rate using Equation 4.18.

$$\text{Per period interest rate} = (1 + \text{effective annual rate})^{1/m} - 1$$
$$= (1.079)^{1/12} - 1 = 0.00635646163, \text{ or about } 0.636\%$$

One final point about Canadian mortgages. Typically, the mortgage payment is calculated over an amortization period much longer than the term of the mortgage. For example, a bank commits to lend the money at an APR of 7.75 percent for a term of 5 years but calculates the mortgage payment as if the mortgage will last 25 years. This mortgage has a *term* of 5 years and an *amortization period* of 25 years.

Check Point 4.21   Suppose you arrange a $200,000 mortgage with a 25-year amortization period at the posted mortgage interest rate of 6 percent. What will be your monthly mortgage payment? Check the answer with a mortgage calculator available at any Canadian bank Web site. We went to **www.royalbank.com/mortgage** and clicked on "Mortgage Calculator." Keep in mind that bankers calculate to 10 decimal places.

4.7   SUMMARY

1. If you invest money at a given interest rate, what will be the future value of your investment?

An investment of $1 earning an interest rate of r will increase in value each period by the factor $(1 + r)$. After t periods its value will grow to $\$(1 + r)^t$. This is the **future value** of the $1 investment with compound interest.

2. What is the present value of a cash flow to be received in the future?

The **present value** of a future cash payment is the amount that you would need to invest today to match that future payment. To calculate present value, we divide the cash payment by $(1 + r)^t$ or, equivalently, multiply by the **discount factor** $1/(1 + r)^t$. The discount factor measures the value today of $1 received in period t.

3. How can we calculate present and future values of streams of cash payments?

A level stream of cash payments that continues indefinitely is known as a **perpetuity**; one that continues for a limited number of years is called an **annuity**. The present value of a stream of cash flows is simply the sum of the present value of each cash flow. Similarly, the future value of an annuity is the sum of the future value of each individual cash flow. Shortcut formulas make the calculations for perpetuities and annuities easy. Variations of these formulas make it easy to calculate the present value of cash flows growing at a constant rate.

4. What is the difference between real and nominal cash flows and real and nominal interest rates?

A dollar is a dollar but the amount of goods that a dollar can buy is eroded by **inflation**. If prices double, the **real value of a dollar** halves. Financial managers and economists often find it helpful to re-express future cash flows in terms of real dollars—that is, dollars of constant purchasing power.

Be careful to distinguish the **nominal interest rate** and the **real interest rate**—that is, the rate at which the real value of the investment grows. Discount nominal cash flows (that is, cash flows measured in current dollars) at nominal interest rates. Discount real cash flows (cash flows measured in constant dollars) at real interest rates. *Never* mix and match nominal and real.

5. How should we compare interest rates quoted over different time intervals—for example, monthly versus annual rates?

Interest rates for short time periods are often quoted as annual rates by multiplying the per-period rate by the number of periods in a year. These **annual percentage rates** (APRs) do not recognize the effect of compound interest, that is, they annualize, assuming simple interest. The **effective annual rate** (EAR) annualizes using compound interest. It equals the rate of interest per period compounded for the number of periods in a year.

Related Web Links

www.bankrate.com/can Canadian interest rates for a variety of purposes, some calculators, links to U.S. interest rates

www.financenter.com Calculators for evaluating financial decisions of all kinds

www.bankofcanada.ca Canadian interest rates and Canadian monetary policy

www.royalbank.com/mortgage Mortgage information and calculator

www.hsbc.ca Mortgage calculator and other financial calculators

www.tdcanadatrust.com/mortgages/index.jsp Mortgage calculator

Key Terms

future value (FV)	79	annuity	94	real value of $1	107
compound interest	79	perpetuity	94	nominal interest rate	108
simple interest	79	annuity factor	96	real interest rate	108
future value interest factor	80	annuity due	100	effective annual interest	
present value (PV)	83	growing perpetuity	104	rate (EAR)	111
discount rate	83	growing annuity	105	annual percentage rate	
discount factor	84	inflation	106	(APR)	112

Questions and Problems

*Answers in Appendix B

BASIC

1. **Present Values.** Compute the present value of a $100 cash flow for the following combinations of discount rates and times:
   *a. $r = 8$ percent, $t = 10$ years
   b. $r = 8$ percent, $t = 20$ years
   c. $r = 4$ percent, $t = 10$ years
   d. $r = 4$ percent, $t = 20$ years

*2. **Future Values.** Compute the future value of a $100 cash flow for the same combinations of rates and times as in problem 1.

3. **Future Values.** You deposit $1,000 into your bank account. If the bank pays 4 percent simple interest, how much will you accumulate in your account after 10 years? If the bank pays compound interest, how much of your earnings will be interest on interest?

*4. **Present Values.** You will require $700 in 5 years. If you earn 5 percent interest on your funds, how much will you need to invest today in order to reach your savings goal?

*5. **Calculating Interest Rate.** Find the interest rate implied by the following combinations of present and future values:

Present Value	Years	Future Value
$400	11	$684
$183	4	$249
$300	7	$300

6. **Present Values.** Would you rather receive $1,000 per year for 10 years or $800 per year for 15 years if
   a. the interest rate is 5 percent?
   b. the interest rate is 20 percent?

   Why do your answers to parts (a) and (b) differ?

Unless otherwise stated, assume all cash flows occur at the *end* of each period.

*7. **Present Values.** What is the present value of the following cash flow stream if the interest rate is 5 percent?

Year	Cash Flow
1	$200
2	$400
3	$300

EXCEL

8. **Number of Periods.** How long will it take for $400 to grow to $1,000 at the interest rate specified?
   * *a.   4 percent
   b.   8 percent
   c.   16 percent

*9. **Present Value of Annuities.** Compute the present value of a $100 annual annuity for the same combination of rates and time periods as in problem 1.

*10. **Future Value of Annuities.** Compute the future value of a $100 annual annuity for the same combination of rates and time periods as in problem 1.

EXCEL

*11. **Calculating Interest Rate.** Find the effective annual interest rate for each case:

APR	Compounding Period
12%	1 month
8%	3 months
10%	6 months

*12. **Calculating Interest Rate.** Find the per period rate and the APR (the stated interest rate) for each case:

Effective Annual Interest Rate	Compounding Period
10.00%	1 month
6.09%	6 months
8.24%	3 months

*13. **Growth of Funds.** If you earn 8 percent per year on your bank account, how long will it take an account with $100 to double to $200?

14. **Comparing Interest Rates.** Suppose you can borrow money at 8.5 percent per year (APR), compounded semi-annually or 8.4 percent per year (APR) compounded monthly. Which is the better deal?

*15. **Calculating Interest Rate.** Lenny Loanshark charges "one point" per week (that is, 1 percent per week) on his loans. What APR must he report to consumers? Assume there are exactly 52 weeks in a year. What is the effective annual rate?

EXCEL

16. **Compound Interest.** Investments in the stock market have increased at an average compound rate of about 5 percent per year since 1900.
    a.   If you invested $1,000 in the stock market in 1900, how much would that investment be worth in 2005?
    b.   If your investment in 1900 has grown to $1 million in 2005, how much did you invest in 1900?

17. **Compound Interest.** Old Time Savings Bank pays 5 percent interest on its savings accounts. If you deposit $1,000 in the bank and leave it there, how much interest will you earn in the first year? The second year? The 10th year?

Unless otherwise stated, assume all cash flows occur at the *end* of each period.

18. **Compound Interest.** New Savings Bank pays 4 percent interest on its deposits. If you deposit $1,000 in the bank and leave it there, will it take more or less than 25 years for your money to double? You should be able to answer this without a calculator or interest rate tables.

19. **Calculating Interest Rate.** A zero-coupon bond that will pay $1,000 in 10 years is selling today for $422.41. What interest rate does the bond offer?

PRACTICE

20. **Loan Payments.** If you take out a 4-year $8,000 car loan that calls for monthly payments at an APR of 10 percent, compounded monthly, what is your monthly payment? What is the effective annual interest rate on the loan?

21. **Annuity Values.**
    a. What is the present value of a 3-year annuity of $100 if the discount rate is 6 percent?
    b. What is the present value of the annuity in part (a) if you have to wait two years instead of one year for the payment stream to start?

EXCEL

*22. **Annuities and Interest Rates.** Professor's Annuity Corp. offers a lifetime annuity to retiring professors. For a payment of $80,000 at age 65, the firm will pay the retiring professor $600 a month until death.
    a. If the professor's remaining life expectancy is 20 years, what is the monthly rate on this annuity? What is the effective annual rate? What is the APR?
    b. If the monthly interest rate is .5 percent, what monthly annuity payment can the firm offer to the retiring professor?

23. **Calculating Interest Rate.** In a discount interest loan, you pay the interest payment up front. For example, if a 1-year loan is stated as $10,000 and the interest rate is 10 percent, the borrower "pays" .10 × $10,000 = $1,000 immediately, thereby receiving net funds of $9,000 and repaying $10,000 in a year.
    *a. What is the effective interest rate on this loan?
    *b. If you call the discount d (for example, $d = 10\%$ using our numbers), express the effective annual rate on the loan as a function of d.
    c. Why is the effective annual rate always greater than the stated rate d?

24. **Annuity Due.** Recall that an annuity due is like an ordinary annuity except that the first payment is made immediately instead of at the end of the first period.
    a. Why is the present value of an annuity due equal to $(1 + r)$ times the present value of an ordinary annuity?
    b. Why is the future value of an annuity due equal to $(1 + r)$ times the future value of an ordinary annuity?

25. **Comprehensive.** You need a $10,000 car loan and are talking to two different banks.
    a. Big Bank offers you a $10,000 auto loan requiring 48 monthly payments of $275, paid at the end of each month. What is the APR of the loan? What is the effective annual rate?
    b. Little Bank's loan has four annual year-end instalments, each equal to 12 times the Big Bank monthly loan payments. Should you accept Little Bank's loan?
    c. What annual payment would make the Little Bank loan equivalent to the Big Bank loan? Why is it not simply 12 times the Big Bank monthly payment?

26. **Annuity Value.** Your landscaping company can lease a truck for $8,000 a year (paid at year-end) for 6 years. It can buy the truck for $40,000. The truck will be valueless after six years.
    a. If the interest rate your company can earn on its funds is 7 percent, is it cheaper to buy or lease?
    b. If the lease payments are an annuity due, is it cheaper to buy or lease?

Unless otherwise stated, assume all cash flows occur at the *end* of each period.

27. **Annuity Due.** A store offers two payment plans. Under the instalment plan, you pay 25 percent down and 25 percent of the purchase price in each of the next 3 years. If you pay the entire bill immediately, you can take a 10 percent discount from the purchase price.
   a. If you can borrow or lend funds at a 6 percent interest rate, which is the better deal?
   b. If the payments on the 4-year instalment plan do not start for a full year, which plan is a better deal?

*28. **Annuity and Annuity Due Payments.**
   a. If you borrow $1,000 and agree to repay the loan in five equal annual payments at an interest rate of 12 percent, what will your payment be?
   b. If you make the first payment on the loan immediately instead of at the end of the first year, what is your payment?

*29. **Valuing Delayed Annuities.** Suppose that you will receive annual payments of $10,000 for a period of 10 years. The first payment will be made four years from now. If the interest rate is 6 percent, what is the present value of this stream of payments?

EXCEL

*30. **Mortgage.** You take out a $175,000 mortgage with a 25-year amortization period, a 5-year term, and a 6 percent posted mortgage interest rate. What is your monthly mortgage payment? When the mortgage expires in five years, what is the unpaid balance?

31. **Mortgage.** You are arranging a $350,000 mortgage with a 25-year amortization period and a 7 percent posted interest rate. What is the monthly mortgage payment? Suppose the bank offers you the opportunity to pay your monthly payments in two equal instalments (pay one-half of the monthly payment every two weeks). How much faster will you pay off your mortgage this way?

32. **Amortizing Loan.** Consider a four-year amortizing loan. You borrow $1,000 initially, and repay it in four equal annual year-end payments.
   a. If the interest rate is 8 percent, show that the annual payment is $301.92.
   b. Fill in the following table, which shows how much of each payment comprises interest versus principal repayment (that is, amortization) and the outstanding balance on the loan at each date.
   c. Show that the loan balance after 1 year is equal to the year-end payment of $301.92 times the 3-year annuity factor.

Time	Loan Balance	Year-End Interest Due on Balance	Year-End Payment	Amortization of Loan
0	$1,000	$80	$301.92	$221.92
1	———	———	301.92	———
2	———	———	301.92	———
3	———	———	301.92	———
4	0	0	—	—

33. **Annuity Value.** You've borrowed $4,248.68 and agreed to pay back the loan with monthly payments of $200. If the interest rate is 12 percent stated as an APR, how long will it take you to pay back the loan? What is the effective annual rate on the loan?

34. **Annuity Value.** The $40 million lottery payment that you just won actually pays $2 million per year for 20 years. If the discount rate is 8 percent, and the first payment comes in 1 year, what is the present value of the winnings? What if the first payment comes immediately?

*35. **Real Annuities.** A retiree wants level consumption in real terms over a 30-year retirement. If the inflation rate equals the interest rate she earns on her $450,000 of savings, how much can she spend in real terms each year over the rest of her life?

Unless otherwise stated, assume all cash flows occur at the *end* of each period.

36. **EAR versus APR.** You invest $1,000 at 6 percent compounded monthly. How much will you have in one year? In 1.5 years?

37. **Annuity Value.** You just borrowed $100,000 to buy a condo. You will repay the mortgage in equal monthly payments of $804.62 over the next 30 years. What monthly interest rate are you paying on the mortgage? What is the effective annual rate on that mortgage? What rate is the lender more likely to quote on the mortgage?

38. **EAR.** If a bank pays 4 percent interest with continuous compounding, what is the effective annual rate?

39. **Annuity Values.** You can buy a car that is advertised for $12,000 on the following terms: (a) pay $12,000 and receive a $1,000 rebate from the manufacturer, or (b) pay $250 a month for 4 years, for total payments of $12,000, implying zero percent financing. Which is the better deal if the interest rate is 1 percent per month?

40. **Continuous Compounding.** How much will $100 grow to if invested at a continuously compounded interest rate of 10 percent for 6 years? What if it is invested for 10 years at 6 percent?

*41. **Future Values.** I now have $20,000 in the bank earning interest of .5 percent per month. I need $30,000 to make a down payment on a house. I can save an additional $100 per month. How long will it take me to accumulate the $30,000?

*42. **Perpetuities.** A bank advertises the following deal: "Pay us $100 a year for 10 years and then we will pay you (or your beneficiaries) $100 a year forever." Is this a good deal if the interest rate available on other deposits is 8 percent?

43. **Perpetuities.** A bank will pay you $100 a year for your lifetime if you deposit $2,500 in the bank today. If you plan to live forever, what interest rate is the bank paying?

44. **Perpetuities.** A property will provide $10,000 a year forever. If its value is $125,000, what must be the discount rate?

45. **Calculating Interest Rate.** A store will give you a 3 percent discount on the cost of your purchase if you pay cash today. Otherwise, you will be billed the full price with payment due in one month. What is the implicit effective annual borrowing rate being paid by customers who choose to defer payment for the month?

46. **Quoting Rates.** Banks sometimes quote interest rates in the form of "add-on interest." In this case, if a 1-year loan is quoted with a 20 percent interest rate and you borrow $1,000, then you pay back $1,200. But you make these payments in monthly instalments of $100 each. What are the true APR and effective annual rate on this loan? Why should you have known that the true rates must be greater than 20 percent even before doing any calculations?

47. **Compound Interest.** Suppose you take out a $1,000, 3-year loan using add-on interest (see previous problem) with a quoted interest rate of 20 percent per year. What will your monthly payments be? (Total payments are $1,000 + $1,000 × .20 × 3 = $1,600.) What are the true APR and effective annual rate on this loan? Are they the same as in the previous problem?

48. **Calculating Interest Rate.** What is the effective annual rate on a 1-year loan with an interest rate quoted on a discount basis (see problem 23) of 20 percent?

49. **Effective Rates.** First National Bank pays 6.2 percent interest compounded semi-annually. Second National Bank pays 6 percent interest, compounded monthly. Which bank offers the higher effective annual rate?

50. **Calculating Interest Rate.** You borrow $1,000 from the bank and agree to repay the loan over the next year in 12 equal monthly payments of $90. However, the bank also charges

Unless otherwise stated, assume all cash flows occur at the *end* of each period.

you a loan-initiation fee of $20, which is taken out of the initial proceeds of the loan. Taking into account the impact of the initiation fee, what is the effective annual interest rate on the loan?

51. **Applying Time Value.** A top-ranked quarterback just signed a 5-year contract, providing $3 million per year, payable at the end of each month. A hockey superstar accepts a 5-year contract, with a $4 million signing bonus, payable immediately and $2.1 million per year, payable at the end of each month. The quarterback brags that his contract is better because he is getting $15 million and the hockey player is getting only $14.5 million. Is the quarterback right? The interest rate is 8 percent, EAR.

52. **Applying Time Value.** Bill needs a new car and can afford monthly car payments of $400. The interest rate on new car loans is 7 percent, APR and payments are made at month-end. Bill wonders whether to arrange a 48- or 60-month loan. With either loan, Bill will borrow the maximum amount and buy the most expensive car possible. The average annual rate of depreciation of a car's value is 18 percent. Bill can invest his spare cash in a mutual fund expected to pay 5 percent, compounded monthly.
   a. What is the maximum he can spend on a car if he arranges a 48-month loan? What if he arranges a 60-month loan?
   b. Compare Bill's wealth (the value of his car plus his investments) after 5 years if he arranges a 48-month loan to his wealth if he arranges a 60-month loan.

53. **Applying Time Value.** You can buy property today for $3 million and sell it in 5 years for $4 million. (You earn no rental income on the property.)
   a. If the interest rate is 8 percent, what is the present value of the selling price?
   b. Is the property investment attractive to you? Why or why not?
   c. Would your answer to part (b) change if you also could earn $200,000 per year rent on the property?

54. **Applying Time Value.** A factory costs $400,000. You forecast that it will produce cash inflows of $120,000 in Year 1, $180,000 in Year 2, and $300,000 in Year 3. The discount rate is 12 percent. Is the factory a good investment? Explain.

*55. **Applying Time Value.** You invest $1,000 today and expect to sell your investment for $2,000 in 10 years.
   a. Is this a good deal if the discount rate is 5 percent?
   b. What if the discount rate is 10 percent?

EXCEL

56. **Applying Time Value.** You believe you will need to save $500,000 by the time you retire in 40 years, in order to live comfortably. If the interest rate is 5 percent per year, how much must you save each year to meet your retirement goal?

57. **Applying Time Value.** How much would you need in the previous problem if you believe that you will inherit $100,000 in 10 years?

*58. **Applying Time Value.** You believe you will spend $40,000 per year for 20 years once you retire in 40 years. If the interest rate is 5 percent per year, how much must you save each year until retirement to meet your retirement goal?

*59. **Applying Time Value.** A couple thinking about retirement decide to put aside $3,000 each year in a savings plan that earns 8 percent interest. In 5 years they will receive a gift of $10,000, which can also be invested.
   a. How much money will they have accumulated 30 years from now?
   b. If their goal is to retire with $800,000 of savings, how much extra do they need to save every year?

Unless otherwise stated, assume all cash flows occur at the *end* of each period.

60. **Applying Time Value.** A couple will retire in 50 years; they plan to spend about $30,000 per year in retirement, which should last about 25 years. They believe that they can earn 8 percent interest on retirement savings.

   a.   If they make annual payments into a savings plan, how much will they need to save each year? Assume the first payment is made in one year.

   b.   How would the answer to part (a) change if the couple also realize that in 20 years they will need to spend $60,000 on their child's university or college education?

61. **Integrative.** Acme needs a new $20,000 copier machine and must decide whether to lease or buy it. If the company buys the copier, they expect to sell it for $5,000 in 5 years. The bank has offered a 5-year amortizing loan of $20,000 at 8 percent, compounded monthly. Loan payments will be due at the end of each month. If Acme leases the copier, monthly lease payments will be paid at the beginning of each month and the copier returned to the lessor at the end of five years. Calculate the monthly lease payment that would make the lease equivalent to the loan.

62. **Real versus Nominal Dollars.** An engineer in 1950 was earning $6,000 a year. Today, in 2006, she earns $60,000 a year. However, on average, goods today cost 8.2 times what they did in 1950.

   a.   What is her real income today in terms of constant 1950 dollars?

   b.   Calculate her salary's annual inflation rate and the cost of goods annual inflation rate.

*63. **Real versus Nominal Rates.** If investors are to earn a real interest rate at 4 percent, what nominal interest rate must they earn if the inflation rate is

   a.   zero

   b.   4 percent

   c.   6 percent

64. **Real Rates.** If investors receive an 8 percent interest rate on their bank deposits, what real interest rate will they earn if the inflation rate over the year is

   a.   zero

   b.   3 percent

   c.   6 percent

EXCEL

*65. **Real versus Nominal Rates.** You will receive $100 from a savings bond in 3 years. The nominal interest rate is 8 percent.

   a.   What is the present value of the proceeds from the bond?

   b.   If the inflation rate over the next few years is expected to be 3 percent, what will the real value of the $100 payoff be in terms of today's dollars?

   c.   What is the real interest rate?

   d.   Show that the real payoff from the bond in part (b), discounted at the real interest rate in part (c) gives the same present value for the bond as you found in part (a).

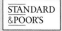

STANDARD
&POOR'S

66. **Standard and Poor's.** Go to Market Insight (**www.mcgrawhill.ca/edumarketinsight**) and look up Thomson Corp. (TOC). Briefly describe its main business activities. Using its annual income statement, calculate the compound annual growth rate over the past five years for sales, net income, and dividends. Convert these results into real growth rates using the U.S. inflation rate, since Thomson reports in US dollars. Calculate the compound average annual U.S. inflation rate for the past five years by using the "Inflation Calculator" at **www.bls.gov/cpi#news**.

67. **Internet.** Using the Bank of Canada inflation calculator, **www.bankofcanada.ca/en/ inflation_calc.htm**, answer the following questions:

   a.   What annual salary in 2004 was equivalent to $5,000 a year in 1940?

   b.   Find the average annual inflation rate from 1914 to the current year.

Unless otherwise stated, assume all cash flows occur at the *end* of each period.

Now access the investment calculator by either clicking the button at the bottom of the page or going to **www.bankofcanada.ca/en/rates/investment.htm** and answer these questions:

  c. With the calculator, determine the future value of a five-year investment. Use the average inflation from part (b) and look up the current five-year GIC rate at **www.bankofcanada.ca/en/interest-look.htm**. Verify the calculations made by the calculator. Be sure that you can replicate them all.

  d. Explain the second part of the calculation. Why is it important that the future value entered be the amount of money you want to have in today's dollars (after the effects of inflation have been calculated.)? Hint: What interest rate is used by the calculator?

68. **Real versus Nominal Dollars.** Your consulting firm will produce cash flows of $100,000 this year, and you expect cash flow to keep pace with any increase in the general level of prices. The interest rate currently is 8 percent, and you anticipate inflation of about 2 percent.

  a. What is the present value of your firm's cash flows for years 1 through 5?

  b. How would your answer to part (a) change if you anticipated no growth in cash flow?

*69. **Real versus Nominal Annuities.** Good news: You will almost certainly be a millionaire by the time you retire in 45 years. Bad news: The inflation rate over your lifetime will average about 3 percent.

  a. What will be the real value of $1 million by the time you retire, in terms of today's dollars?

  b. What real annuity (in today's dollars) will $1 million support if the real interest rate at retirement is 2 percent and the annuity must last for 20 years?

*70. **Rule of 72.** Use the Rule of 72 to figure out how long it will take for your money to quadruple in value if the interest rate is 8 percent per year.

*71. **Inflation.** Inflation in Brazil in 1992 averaged about 23 percent per month. What was the annual inflation rate?

72. **Perpetuities.** British government perpetuities at 4 percent pay £4 interest each year forever. Another bond, 2.5 percent perpetuities, pays £2.50 per year forever. What is the value of 4 percent perpetuities if the long-term interest rate is 6 percent? What is the value of 2.5 percent perpetuities?

CHALLENGE

73. **Comprehensive.**

  a. You plan to retire in 30 years and want to accumulate enough by then to have $30,000 per year for 15 years. If the interest rate is 10 percent, how much must you accumulate by the time you retire?

  b. How much must you save each year until retirement in order to finance your retirement consumption?

  c. You remember that the expected annual inflation rate is 4 percent. If a loaf of bread costs $1 today, what will it cost by the time you retire?

  d. You really want to consume $30,000 a year in real dollars during retirement and wish to save an equal real amount each year until then. What is the real amount of savings that you need to accumulate by the time you retire?

  e. Calculate the required preretirement real annual savings necessary to meet your consumption goals. Compare your answer to part (b). Why is there a difference?

  f. What is the nominal value of the amount you need to save during the first year? (Assume the savings are put aside at the end of each year.) The 30th year?

74. **Integrative.** In 1880, five Aboriginal trackers were each promised $1 Australian for helping to capture the notorious outlaw Ned Kelley. In 1993, the granddaughters of two of the trackers claimed that this reward had not been paid. The Australian prime minister stated that if this were the case, the government would be happy to pay them each $1. The grand-

---

Unless otherwise stated, assume all cash flows occur at the *end* of each period.

daughters did not think that $1 was sufficient. As their financial adviser, prepare a counterproposal for the granddaughters to send to the prime minister. You may use the following data for 1880–1993: average annual inflation rate—3 percent; average annual nominal interest rate paid on savings accounts at Australian commercial banks—3.2 percent; average annual nominal rate of return on Australian stocks—9.5 percent.

75. **Annuity Value.** What is the value of a perpetuity that pays $100 every 3 months forever? The discount rate quoted on an APR basis is 12 percent.

*76. **Changing Interest Rates.** If the interest rate this year is 8 percent and the interest rate next year will be 10 percent, what is the future value of $1 after 2 years? What is the present value of a payment of $1 to be received in 2 years?

EXCEL

77. **Changing Interest Rates.** Your wealthy uncle established a $1,000 bank account for you when you were born. For the first 8 years of your life, the interest rate earned on the account was 8 percent. Since then, rates have been only 6 percent. Now you are 21 years old and ready to cash in. How much is in your account?

78. **Applying Time Value.** You would like to travel around the world in a sailboat for two years, leaving five years from now. One year before you leave, you will purchase the sailboat at an expected cost of $150,000. During the pretrip year, you will learn how to sail the boat. Once the trip is underway, you forecast that your monthly expenses will be $2,200, payable at the start of the month. In addition, you would like to have an emergency fund of $45,000 available on the day you depart. How much do you need to save every month-end for the next five years if you can earn an effective annual interest of 6 percent?

79. **Applying Time Value.** You are thinking of buying a used car for $4,000 for driving to school. Your parents are willing to lend you the $4,000 and charge only 2.4 percent APR. They want the loan repaid equally in 48 monthly payments, with the first payment due at the end of the month in which you buy the car. You estimate that the monthly cost of operating the car, including gas, insurance, maintenance, and licence fees, will be $200 and payable at the start of each month. The cost of a monthly bus pass is $80. You expect that the car will be totally worn out in four years, with zero resale value, when you are finished school. Your discount rate is 6 percent, compounded annually.

    a. If you have three roommates who also need transportation to and from school, how much do you need to charge each of them a month in order to cover all your costs? (You all plan to go to summer school, so you can assume 12 payments a year.)

    b. Does it make financial sense to buy the car? Explain your answer.

80. **Applying Time Value.** You and your friend are avid snowboarders and bike racers. Nearly every other weekend you travel to a race in a rented van. Now that both of you have full-time jobs, your friend is pressuring you to purchase a van.

    Here's how the conversation goes:

    Friend: "Just think of how much we will save on rentals. The rented van costs us $100 a weekend, plus $.50 per kilometre. Most trips are 100 km, one way. With our own van, we will only have to pay for fuel, about $.08 per km; and maintenance, about $.25 per km. A used van will only cost about $20,000. Think of the convenience!"

    You: "What about insurance? What about depreciation?"

    Friend: "Insurance will be only $1,200 per year. The salesperson says the van will depreciate slowly, only 10 percent per year. If we retire from the race circuit in 5 years, the van will still have value. Shouldn't we at least think about it?"

    You: "I guess. I think a nominal discount rate of 9 percent is about right."

Unless otherwise stated, assume all cash flows occur at the *end* of each period.

a. Do you think you should buy the van? Be sure to state your assumptions.

b. What if all costs are subject to a 3 percent annual inflation? Do you change your mind?

81. **Applying Time Value.** You are working as a financial planner. A couple has asked you to put together an investment plan for the education of their daughter. She is a bright 7-year-old (her birthday is today), and everyone hopes she will go to university or college after high school in 10 years, on her 17th birthday. You estimate that today the cost of a year of university is $10,000, including the cost of tuition, books, accommodation, food, and clothing. You forecast that the annual inflation rate will be 4 percent. You may assume that these costs are incurred at the start of each university year. A typical university program lasts four years. The effective annual interest rate is 6 percent and is nominal.

a. Suppose the couple invests money on her birthday, starting today and ending one year before she starts college. How much must they invest each year to have money to send their daughter to college?

b. If the couple waits one year, until their daughter's 8th birthday, how much more do they need to invest annually?

82. **Applying Time Value.** A cottage is for sale for $580,000. Currently it generates annual cash flows, net of all expenses and taxes, of $35,000. If the cottage lasts forever, what rate of growth of the annual cash flows will be necessary for you to earn an 8 percent annual rate of return on your investment?

83. **Applying Time Value.** A real estate appraiser is assessing the value of a piece of land in Vancouver. Currently the land is unoccupied but is zoned for commercial use. Plans have been approved to build a five-story office building. Construction is expected to start in 1 year and will take 2 years to complete, at a total cost of $3 million. For simplicity, assume that the costs are paid in equal amounts at the start of each construction year.

a. Suppose a constant annual cash flow of $400,000, net of all taxes and operating costs, is expected at the end of each year of operation, and the building lasts for 50 years. What is the maximum you would be willing to pay for the land if the discount rate is 8 percent? Explain your answer.

b. If the cash flow from the tenants grows at 1.5 percent per year, after the first year of occupancy, recalculate the price you would be willing to pay for the land.

84. **Integrative.** The Smiths are planning to retire in 35 years. They want an annual real income of $45,000, paid at the end of each month of their expected 20-year retirement and to bequeath $500,000, in real dollars, to their son at the end of their retirement. In addition, their son's 4-year university education, to begin in 8 years, is expected to cost $10,000 real dollars per year, due at the start of each year. They recently purchased a house for $250,000, with $50,000 cash and a $200,000, 20-year mortgage, carrying a 7 percent interest rate, compounded monthly and paid monthly. Over the next 55 years, the nominal house value is expected to grow 4 percent annually. The Smiths plan to live in their house for the rest of their lives, and the house will be sold on their demise. The expected annual inflation rate is 3 percent. The Smiths expect to earn 6 percent nominal effective annual interest rate on their retirement savings.

a. How much do they need to save in real dollars at the end of each month, for the next 35 years, on top of their monthly mortgage payment, to meet their financial goals? Clearly state any assumptions you make.

b. What will be the total real and nominal mortgage payment plus savings in the last month of the mortgage?

c. How much do they need to save in real and nominal terms in the last month before retirement?

Unless otherwise stated, assume all cash flows occur at the *end* of each period.

85. **RESP Calculator.** The Canadian government is encouraging saving for post-secondary education through registered education savings plans (RESPs) and the Canada Education Savings Grant. Under current rules, a maximum of $4,000 may be saved each year, with a total lifetime maximum of $42,000. The Canada Education Savings Grant, paid annually by the federal government, is 20 percent of the contribution to a maximum of $400 per year, to a maximum of $7,200. Although the contributions are not tax-deductible, they grow tax-free, and then are taxed at the student's, presumably lower, tax rate when he or she attends university or college.

Go to **www.mackenziefinancial.com/en/pub/tools/calculators/index.shtml** and click on "RESP calculator." Look at the impact of different interest rates and inflation assumptions on required savings. Create a hypothetical family with a one-year-old child. Prepare a report for the parents outlining how much they should be saving to cover the cost of the child's education. In your report, show them the impact on the needed annual savings of waiting two years before starting the RESP, rather than starting immediately. Be sure to clearly lay out your assumptions, including different inflation and interest rate scenarios.

86. **Internet.** Many banks provide loan and mortgage calculators.
   a. For example, go to the HSBC Bank of Canada Web site at **www.hsbc.ca**, and select "Calculators." A list of different calculators will appear. Select "Mortgage and Credit Calculators" and then "Loan Payments Calculator." Check that your answer to problem 20 is correct.
   b. At the same Web site, select the "Mortgage and Credit Calculators," then select "Mortgage Payments Calculator." For a $200,000 mortgage, at annual interest of 6 percent and 25-year amortization, compare the payments if you pay monthly, semimonthly, bi-weekly, or weekly. Can you figure out how the numbers are calculated? Do your own calculations.
   c. Go to **www.tdcanadatrust.com** and find another mortgage calculator for the same mortgage as you used in (b); get the bi-weekly payments. Compare them to HSBC's. Are they the same? What does that tell you about the importance of assumptions in the time value of money calculations and the need to be careful using Internet calculators?
   d. U.S. mortgage rates are quoted as the APR of the *monthly* rate. If the mortgage rate is 6 percent, the appropriate monthly rate is 6/12 or 0.5 percent. Go to **www.smartmoney.com**, click on "Personal Finance" and go to "Real Estate." Use the mortgage calculator to figure out the U.S. monthly mortgage payment for the mortgage in part(b). Verify that you can calculate the monthly payment yourself.

Solutions to Check Points

4.1 Value after 5 years would have been $24 \times (1.05)^5 = \$30.63$; after 50 years, $24 \times (1.05)^{50} = \$275.22$.

4.2 When an amount doubles, it increases by 100 percent of itself, giving a growth rate of 100 percent. The future value factor for doubling in 1 year is $(1 + 100\%)$, or $(1 + 1)$, which of course is 2. So at the end of the first year, sales will be $.5 million $\times$ 2, or $1 million. With 4 years of doubling each year, the future value factor is $(2)^4 = 16$, and projected sales after 4 years are $.5 \times 16 = \$8$ million.

4.3 Multiply the $1,000 payment by the 10-year discount factor:

$$PV = \$1,000 \times \frac{1}{(1.0853)^{10}} = \$441.06$$

4.4 The present value of Prize A is $5,000 + $5,500/1.04 = $10,288.46. The present value of Prize B is $1,000 + $10,000/1.04 = $10,615.38. Prize B has the highest present value. The future value of Prize A is $5,000 \times 1.04 + $5,500 = $10,700. The future value of Prize B

Unless otherwise stated, assume all cash flows occur at the *end* of each period.

is $1,000 \times 1.04 + $10,000 = $11,040. Prize B has the highest future value. It does not matter at which point in time you compare the prizes' value.

4.5   If the doubling time is 12 years, then $(1 + r)^{12} = 2$, which implies that $1 + r = 2^{1/12} = 1.0595$, or $r = 5.95$ percent. The Rule of 72 would imply that a doubling time of 12 years is consistent with an interest rate of 6 percent: $72/6 = 12$. Thus the Rule of 72 works quite well in this case. If the doubling period is only 2 years, then the interest rate is determined by $(1 + r)^2 = 2$, which implies that $1 + r = 2^{1/2} = 1.414$, or $r = 41.4$ percent. The Rule of 72 would imply that a doubling time of 2 years is consistent with an interest rate of 36 percent: $72/36 = 2$. Thus the Rule of 72 is quite inaccurate when the interest rate is high (or the time to double is short).

4.6   Let D be the unknown deposit to be made in 1 year. The future value of that deposit in 2 years is $D \times 1.06$. It will have only 1 year to grow at 6 percent. We also know that the future value in 2 years of the $1,500 you have right now will be $1,500 \times (1.06)^2$. The time line below summarizes all of the information:

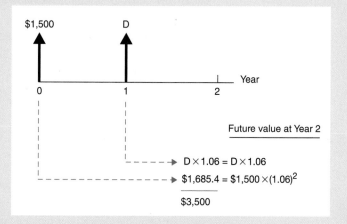

Since the future value of the two deposits must add up to the needed $3,500, you can rearrange to see that $D \times 1.06 = $3,500 − $1,685.4$. Solving for D gives

$$D = $1,814.6/(1.06) = $1,711.89$$

You will need to deposit about $1,712 in 1 year to have enough. Perhaps you better start lobbying your family for a large cash present in one year!

4.7

Gift at Year	Present Value	
1	$10,000/(1.07)$	= $ 9,345.79
2	$10,000/(1.07)^2$	= 8,734.39
3	$10,000/(1.07)^3$	= 8,162.98
4	$10,000/(1.07)^4$	= 7,628.95
		$33,872.11

Gift at Year	Future Value at Year 4	
1	$10,000 \times (1.07)^3$	= $12,250.43
2	$10,000 \times (1.07)^2$	= 11,449
3	$10,000 \times (1.07)$	= 10,700
4	10,000	= 10,000
		$44,399.43

4.8   The rate is $4/48 = .0833$, about 8.3 percent.

4.9   The 4-year discount factor is $1/(1.08)^4 = .735$. The 4-year annuity factor is $[1/.08 - 1/(.08 \times 1.08^4)] = 3.312$. This is the difference between the present value of a \$1 perpetuity starting next year and the present value of a \$1 perpetuity starting in Year 5:

$$\text{PV (perpetuity starting next year)} = \frac{1}{.08} = 12.50$$

$$- \text{PV (perpetuity starting in Year 5)} = \frac{1}{.08} \times \frac{1}{(1.08)^4} = 12.50 \times .735 = 9.188$$

$$= \text{PV (4-year annuity)} \qquad\qquad = 12.50 - 9.188 = 3.312$$

4.10 You will need the present value at 7 percent of a 20-year annuity of \$55,000:

$$\text{Present value} = \text{annual spending} \times \text{annuity factor}$$

The annuity factor is $[1/.07 - 1/(.07 \times 1.07^{20})] = 10.594$.
Thus you need $55,000 \times 10.594 = \$582,670$.

4.11 Fifteen years means 180 months. Then

$$\text{Mortgage payment} = \frac{100,000}{\text{180-month annuity factor}}$$

$$= \frac{100,000}{83.32}$$

$$= \$1,200.17 \text{ per month}$$

\$1,000 of the payment is interest. The remainder, \$200.17, is amortization.

4.12 Calculate the value of a 24-year annuity, then add the immediate \$374,800 payment:

$$\text{24-year annuity factor} = \frac{1}{r} - \frac{1}{r(1 + r)^{24}}$$

$$= \frac{1}{.05} - \frac{1}{.05(1.05)^{24}}$$

$$= 13.7986$$

$$\text{PV} = \$374,800 \times 13.7956 = \$5,171,731$$

$$\text{Total value} = \$5,171,731 + \$374,800$$

$$= \$5,546,531$$

Starting the 25-year cash flow stream immediately, rather than waiting 1 year, increases value by nearly \$264,137.

4.13 If the interest rate is 5 percent, the future value of a 45-year, \$1 annuity will be

$$\frac{(1.05)^{45} - 1}{.05} = 159.70$$

Therefore, we need to choose the cash flow, C, so that $C \times 159.70 = \$500,000$. This requires that $C = \$500,000/159.70 = \$3,130.87$. This required savings level is much higher than we found in Example 4.12. At a 5 percent interest rate, current savings do not grow as rapidly as when the interest rate was 10 percent; with less of a boost from compound interest, we need to set aside greater amounts in order to reach the target of \$500,000.

4.14 The cost in dollars will increase by 5 percent each year to a value of $\$5 \times (1.05)^{50} = \$57.34$. If the inflation rate is 10 percent, the cost will be $\$5 \times (1.10)^{50} = \$586.95$.

4.15 The weekly cost in 1980 is $\$250 \times (352/100) = \$880$. The real value of a 1980 salary of \$30,000 expressed in real 1950 dollars is $\$30,000 \times (100/352) = \$8,523$.

4.16 a. If there's no inflation, real and nominal rates are equal at 8 percent. With 5 percent inflation, the real rate is $(1.08/1.05) - 1 = .02857$, a bit less than 3 percent.

b. If you want a 3 percent *real* interest rate, you need a 3 percent nominal rate if inflation is zero and an 8.15 percent rate if inflation is 5 percent. Note $1.03 \times 1.05 = 1.0815$.

4.17 The present value is

$$PV = \frac{\$5,000}{1.08} = \$4,629.63$$

The real interest rate is 2.857 percent (see Check Point 4.16a). The real cash payment is $5,000/(1.05) = $4,761.90. Thus

$$PV = \frac{\$4,761.90}{1.02857} = \$4,629.63$$

4.18 Calculate the real annuity. The real interest rate is $1.10/1.05 - 1 = .0476$. We'll round to 4.8 percent. The real annuity is

$$\text{Annual payment} = \frac{\$3,000,000}{\text{30-year annuity factor}}$$

$$= \frac{\$3,000,000}{\dfrac{1}{.048} - \dfrac{1}{.048(1.048)^{30}}}$$

$$= \frac{\$3,000,000}{15.73} = \$190,728$$

You can spend this much each year in dollars of constant purchasing power. The purchasing power of each dollar will decline at 5 percent per year, so you'll need to spend more in nominal dollars: $190,728 \times 1.05 = $200,264 in the second year, $190,728 \times 1.05^2 = $210,278 in the third year, and so on.

4.19 Use equation 4.18 to calculate the daily rate of interest.

$$\text{Per period rate} = (1 + \text{effective annual rate})^{1/m} - 1$$

$$= (1.05)^{1/365} - 1 = .0001337, \text{ or } 0.01337 \text{ percent}$$

The annual percentage rate equivalent to 0.01337 percent per day is

$$APR = m \times \text{per period rate}$$

$$= 365 \times .0001337 = .0488, \text{ or } 4.88 \text{ percent, compounded daily.}$$

4.20 The quarterly rate is $8/4 = 2$ percent. The effective annual rate is $(1.02)^4 - 1 = .0824$, or 8.24 percent.

4.21 The posted rate is 6 percent, compounded semi-annually, or 3 percent every 6 months. The effective annual equivalent rate of this is $(1.03)^2 - 1 = .0609$ or 6.09 percent. Now convert this to its equivalent monthly rate:

$$\text{Monthly interest rate} = (1.0609)^{1/12} - 1 = .004938622, \text{ or } .4938622 \text{ percent}$$

The 300-month, 0.4938622 percent annuity factor is 156.297225, and your payments will be

$$\text{Monthly mortgage payment} = \frac{\text{mortgage amount}}{\text{annuity factor}}$$

$$= \frac{\$200,000}{156.297225} = \$1,279.61$$

With a calculator, the inputs are $n = 300$, $i = 0.4938622$, $PV = -200,000$. Compute PMT to find the monthly mortgage payment is $1,279.61.

MINICASE

Alfred Road has reached his 70th birthday and is ready to retire. Mr. Road has no formal training in finance but has saved his money and invested carefully.

Mr. Road owns his home—the mortgage is paid off—and does not want to move. He is a widower, and he wants to bequeath the house and any remaining assets to his daughter.

He has accumulated savings of $180,000, conservatively invested. The investments are yielding 9 percent interest. Mr. Road also has $12,000 in a savings account at 5 percent interest. He wants to keep the savings account intact for unexpected expenses or emergencies.

Mr. Road's basic living expenses now average about $1,500 per month, and he plans to spend $500 per month on travel and hobbies. To maintain this planned standard of living, he will have to rely on his investment portfolio. The interest from the portfolio is $16,200 per year (9 percent of $180,000), or $1,350 per month.

Mr. Road will also receive $750 per month in Canada Pension and Old Age Security payments for the rest of his life. These payments are indexed for inflation. That is, they will be automatically increased in proportion to changes in the consumer price index.

Mr. Road's main concern is with inflation. The inflation rate has been below 3 percent recently, but a 3 percent rate is unusually low by historical standards. His pension payments will increase with inflation, but the interest on his investment portfolio will not.

What advice do you have for Mr. Road? Can he safely spend all the interest from his investment portfolio? How much could he withdraw at year-end from that portfolio if he wants to keep its real value intact?

Suppose Mr. Road will live for 20 more years and is willing to use up all of his investment portfolio over that period. He also wants his monthly spending to increase along with inflation over that period. In other words, he wants his monthly spending to stay the same in real terms. How much can he afford to spend per month?

Assume that the investment portfolio continues to yield a 9 percent rate of return and that the inflation rate is 4 percent.

VALUING BONDS

Investment in a new plant and equipment requires money—often a lot of money. Sometimes firms may be able to save enough out of previous earnings to cover the cost of investments, but often they need to raise cash from investors. In broad terms, we can think of two ways to raise new money from investors: borrow the cash or sell additional shares of common stock.

If companies need the money for only a short while, they may borrow it from a bank; if they need it to make long-term investments, they generally issue bonds, which are simply long-term loans. When companies issue bonds, they promise to make a series of fixed interest payments and then to repay the debt. As long as the company generates sufficient cash, the payments on a bond are certain. In this case, bond valuation involves straightforward time value of money computations. But there is some chance that even the most blue-chip company will fall on hard times and will not be able to repay its debts. Investors take this default risk into account when they price the bonds and demand a higher interest rate to compensate.

In the first part of this chapter we sidestep the issue of default risk and we focus on Government of Canada bonds. We show how bond prices are determined by market interest rates and how those prices respond to changes in rates. We also consider the yield to maturity and discuss why a bond's yield may vary with its time to maturity.

Later in the chapter we look at corporate bonds where there is also a possibility of default. We will see how bond ratings provide a guide to the default risk and how low-grade bonds offer higher promised yields.

In Chapter 13 we will look in more detail at the securities that companies issue, and we will see that there are many variations on bond design. But for now, we'll keep our focus on garden-variety bonds and general principles of bond valuation.

After studying this chapter you should be able to
- Distinguish among the bond's coupon rate, current yield, and yield to maturity.
- Find the market price of a bond given its yield to maturity, find a bond's yield given its price, and demonstrate why prices and yields vary inversely.
- Explain what a yield curve is and why expected short-term interest rates affect its shape.
- Show why bonds exhibit interest rate risk and how interest rate risk affects the shape of the yield curve.
- Understand why investors pay attention to bond ratings and demand a higher interest rate for bonds with low ratings.

BOND CHARACTERISTICS

bond Security that obligates the issuer to make specified payments to the bondholder.

Governments and corporations borrow money by selling **bonds** to investors. The money they collect when the bond is issued, or sold to the public, is the amount of the loan. In return, they agree to make specified payments to the bondholders, who are the lenders. When you own a bond, you generally receive a fixed interest payment each year until the bond matures. This payment is known as the **coupon** because most bonds used to have coupons that the investors clipped off and mailed to the bond issuer to claim the interest payment. At maturity, the debt is repaid: The borrower pays the bondholder the bond's **face value** (equivalently, its *par value*, *maturity value*, or *principal*).

coupon The interest payments paid to the bondholder.

How do bonds work? Several years ago, the federal government raised money by selling 7.25 percent coupon, June 1, 2007 maturity, Government of Canada bonds. Each bond has a face value of $1,000. Because the **coupon rate** is 7.25 percent, the government makes coupon payments of 7.25 percent of $1,000, or $72.50 each year.[1] When the bond matures on June 1, 2007, the government must pay the face value of the bond, $1,000, in addition to the final coupon payment.

face value Payment at the maturity of the bond. Also called par value, maturity value, or principal.

Suppose that in 2004 you decided to buy the 7.25s of 2007, that is, the 7.25 percent coupon bonds maturing in 2007. If you planned to hold the bond until maturity, you would then have looked forward to the cash flows depicted in Figure 5.1. The initial cash flow is negative and equal to the price you have to pay for the bond. Thereafter, the cash flows equal the annual coupon payment until the maturity date in 2007, when you receive the face value of the bond, $1,000, in addition to the final coupon payment.

coupon rate Annual interest payment as a percentage of face value.

READING THE FINANCIAL PAGES

Bond prices are reported in the financial press and are always for the previous day's trading activity. Figure 5.2 is an excerpt from the bond quotations for June 1, 2004, reported in *The Globe and Mail*, on June 2, 2004. The entry for the 7.25 percent Canada bonds maturing in June 2007 that we just looked at is highlighted. The prices reported in this newspaper were provided by CBID Markets Inc., a Canadian electronic bond market.

The prices quoted are the closing prices as of 4 p.m. The *bid* price is the price you receive if you *sell* the bond to a bond dealer. Prices are quoted as percentage of face value. Thus for the

FIGURE 5.1
Cash flows to an investor in the 7.25% coupon bond, maturing in the year 2007

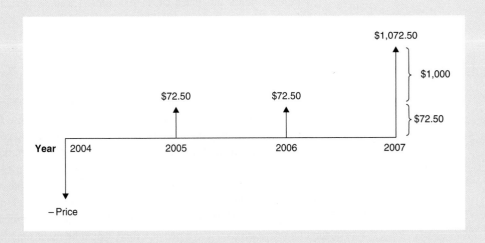

---

[1] In Canada, these coupon payments typically would come in two semi-annual instalments of $36.25 each. To keep things simple for now, we will assume one coupon payment per year.

FIGURE 5.2
Government of Canada bond quotes for June 1, 2004

CANADIAN BONDS

Bond quotations supplied by CBID Markets Inc. Closing prices and yields as of 4:00 p.m. yesterday. Most active based on volume traded. Yields are semi-annual compound to maturity. "Yield Chg" is the change in ask yield from the previous close.

Issue	Coupon	Maturity Date	Bid Price	Ask Price	Bid Yld.	Ask Yld.	Yield Chg	Issue	Coupon	Maturity Date	Bid Price	Ask Price	Bid Yld.	Ask Yld.	Yield Chg
Government of Canada Benchmarks								CMHC	5.500	2012-Jun-01	104.28	104.38	4.85	4.83	+0.059
2 Year	3.000	2006-Jun-01	99.76	99.76	3.12	3.12	+0.055	Canada	5.000	2004-Sep-01	100.69	100.74	2.07	1.87	+0.018
5 year	4.250	2008-Sep-01	100.95	101.00	4.00	3.99	+0.038	Canada	10.500	2004-Oct-01		102.78		1.92	+0.014
10 Year	5.250	2013-Jun-01	103.23	103.32	4.80	4.79	+0.028	Canada	4.250	2004-Dec-01	101.01	101.04	2.17	2.12	+0.046
20 Year	8.000	2023-Jun-01	132.65	132.80	5.26	5.25	+0.024	Canada	9.000	2004-Dec-01	103.34	103.38	2.16	2.08	+0.036
30 Year	5.750	2029-Jun-01	105.80	105.95	5.33	5.32	+0.023	Canada	3.500	2005-Jun-01	100.93	100.98	2.54	2.50	+0.041
								Canada	12.250	2005-Sep-01		111.60		2.70	+0.034
Active Provincials and Agencies								Canada	6.000	2005-Sep-01	103.94	104.01	2.75	2.70	+0.034
Ontario	5.000	2014-Mar-08	98.02	98.12	5.26	5.25	+0.032	Canada	8.750	2005-Dec-01	108.51	108.56	2.89	2.86	+0.043
Ontario	4.750	2013-Jun-02	97.10	97.18	5.16	5.15	+0.032	Canada	5.750	2006-Sep-01	105.34	105.35	3.26	3.25	+0.064
Ontario	5.850	2033-Mar-08	100.42	100.59	5.82	5.81	+0.029	Canada	7.000	2006-Dec-01	108.62	108.62	3.37	3.37	+0.045
BC	6.000	2008-Jun-09	107.04	107.09	4.08	4.07	+0.028	Canada	7.250	2007-Jun-01	110.38	110.40	3.56	3.56	+0.044
Quebec	6.000	2029-Oct-01	101.78	101.92	5.86	5.85	+0.038	Canada	4.500	2007-Sep-01	102.50	102.54	3.67	3.66	+0.042
								Canada	6.000	2008-Jun-01	107.62	107.67	3.92	3.91	+0.035
Active Corporates								Canada	4.250	2008-Sep-01	100.95	101.00	4.00	3.99	+0.038
Bombard Cap	6.600	2004-Nov-29	100.52	101.12	5.44	4.20	+0.048	Canada	5.500	2009-Jun-01	105.78	105.84	4.21	4.19	+0.038
Bell CDA	6.150	2009-Jun-15	106.54	106.76	4.67	4.63	+0.024	Canada	5.500	2010-Jun-01	105.60	105.66	4.43	4.41	+0.035
BNS	4.295	2008-Aug-22	99.97	100.08	4.30	4.27	+0.033	Canada	6.000	2011-Jun-01	108.37	108.45	4.59	4.57	+0.030
Telus Corp.	7.500	2006-Jun-01	106.50	106.75	4.07	3.94	+0.044	Canada	5.250	2012-Jun-01	103.54	103.61	4.71	4.70	+0.030
Loblaw CoLtd	5.400	2013-Nov-20	99.60	100.12	5.45	5.38	+0.030	Canada	5.250	2013-Jun-01	103.23	103.32	4.80	4.79	+0.028
								Canada	5.000	2014-Jun-01	100.95	101.05	4.88	4.87	+0.034
Active Strips (Coupons and Residuals)								Canada	11.250	2015-Jun-01		154.74		4.79	+0.030
Ontario	0.000	2007-Dec-02	87.08	87.34	4.00	3.91	+0.033	Canada	8.000	2023-Jun-01	132.65	132.80	5.26	5.25	+0.024
Ontario	0.000	2009-Dec-02		77.82		4.62	+0.033	Canada	8.000	2027-Jun-01	135.08	135.23	5.33	5.33	+0.023
Ontario	0.000	2009-Jun-02	79.70	80.16	4.59	4.48	+0.033	Canada	5.750	2029-Jun-01	105.80	105.95	5.33	5.32	+0.023
Canada	0.000	2005-Jun-01	97.10	97.55	3.02	2.53	+0.018	Canada	5.750	2033-Jun-01	106.69	106.83	5.30	5.29	+0.028
Canada	0.000	2008-Dec-01	82.67	83.11	4.28	4.16	+0.030								
								Real Return Bonds							
Government of Canada and Agencies								Canada	4.250	2021-Dec-01		129.10		2.23	+0.024
BusDevBk Cda	5.650	2005-Aug-17	103.39	103.46	2.76	2.71	+0.034	Canada	4.250	2026-Dec-01		134.76		2.27	+0.016
CMHC	5.750	2004-Dec-01	101.76	101.84	2.15	1.99	-0.006	Canada	4.000	2031-Dec-01		134.60		2.30	+0.016
CMHC	5.300	2007-Dec-03	104.73	104.76	3.84	3.83	+0.029	Canada	3.000	2036-Dec-01		115.86		2.30	+0.019

Source: *The Globe and Mail*, June 2, 2004, p. B25. Reprinted with permission of *The Globe and Mail*.

7.25 percent bond, the price of 110.38 means 110.38 percent of the $1,000 face value, or $1,103.80. If you want to *buy* the bond, you pay the *asked* price of $1,104.00. Just as used car dealers earn their living by reselling cars at higher prices than they paid for them, so the bond dealer needs to charge a *spread* between the bid and asked prices.

The next two columns, "Bid Yld" and "Ask Yld," stand for *bid yield to maturity* and *ask yield to maturity*. The Ask Yld measures the return that investors will receive if they buy the bond at the asked price and hold it to maturity in 2007. The final column, "Yield Chg," is the change in ask yield from the previous day's close. We will explain shortly how these figures were calculated.

If you wanted to buy the Canada 7.25s of 2007, you would contact a bond dealer. Dealers hold inventories of bonds and are typically part of financial institutions such as banks and brokerage houses. For example, TD Waterhouse offers bonds to retail investors through its online brokerage service (**www.TDWaterhouse.ca**). At TD Waterhouse's Web site on June 1, 2004, you could sell the 7.25 percent bond for $1,099 (bid price) and buy it for $1,108.9 (ask price). The spread between the bid and ask prices is $1,108.9 – $1,099 = $9.9, or about 1 percent of the bond's value. The spread for a large investor, such as a pension fund, would be much smaller, closer to the spread reported in the newspaper for that day, $1,104.0 – $1,103.8 = $.2, or about .02 percent of the bond's value.

Traditionally, bonds have been traded in an *over-the-counter market*, where securities are not traded in one central place but traded over the telephone. However, the development of electronic markets for bond trading, such as CBID (**www.CBID.ca**) and CanDeal (**www.CanDeal.ca**), are changing the structure of the bond market. See the nearby Finance in Action box for a discussion of these changes and their expected impact on bond bid-ask spreads.

SEE BOX P. 133

Trading Bonds

Why is it so hard to trade a bond? If you don't believe me, call your bank, broker, or financial planner, and tell them that your auntie died and left you a corporate bond, say a Loblaw Cos. Ltd. bond due in 2028, with an interest coupon of 6.45%, and you want to sell it and need a price—now! Assuming you get past several "don't bothers," someone just might give you a firm price.

When it comes to stocks, newspapers and the Internet are stuffed with prices, and reams of other data. Commissions on trades are transparent as well. So what gives for bonds? For the individual investor, there is no central public market, no quoted bid and ask prices, and no other detailed stats.

Last year, according to the Investment Dealers Association of Canada, $4.4 trillion worth of Government of Canada bonds changed hands, or more than $140,000 worth for every man, woman and screaming baby in Canada. But where?

Bond traders still use phones for an estimated 95% of trades. In recent years, dealers have only toyed with internal electronic trading systems. They strongly prefer that investors not trade bonds directly with one another. For one thing, the margins would just get too thin. Also, remember that banks have debt-based instruments like GICs and bond funds to sell you at a markup. Letting you trade bonds directly would make those products less attractive.

By the way, if you're still on the phone waiting for a price on your Loblaw bond, ask a buddy to call another dealer to say he'd like to buy the same bond. Compare the spread between the price one dealer is willing to pay and the price at which the other dealer is willing to sell. In this case, the spread could be up to 2.5%. Most of that is dealer commission, which is much higher than it would be for an equivalent stock transaction. To buy and sell 1,000 shares of Loblaw stock (worth about $60,000) would cost roughly $150, including commission and a narrow price spread. For bonds, that round trip (a buy and sale) could cost $1,500.

Bond transactions don't have to be reported publicly, ever. And the fact that the dealer's profit is embedded in the price makes it impossible to figure out if you got a good deal.

Dealers do have a fiduciary responsibility to get you the best price possible when you buy something from them—except bonds. They aren't required to scour the market for the best price; they only check with their own trading desks. Who makes the rules? The Investment Dealers Association of Canada, the dealers' self-regulatory organization.

Things are changing. The Ontario Securities Commission is starting to see the future, and is considering new rules for bond traders. Electronic markets are springing up: In the United States, ValuBond offers the best execution on bond traders for several large dealers. In Canada, CanDeal and CBID Markets (in which my fund has an investment) are quickly catching the attention of market participants.

These markets have also caught the eye of TD, CIBC, Laurentian, JP Morgan, Merrill Lynch and HSBC; they realize that electronic markets help them trade. *The Globe* now publishes daily bond prices from CBID. Smallers dealers such as E*TRADE Canada have signed up as well.

Extract from: Doug Steiner, "Bonds vs. Psychics," *Report on Business Magazine*, June 2004, p. 25.

Check Point 5.1 Find the 5.5 percent June 1, 2010, Canada bond in Figure 5.2.
    a.   If you already own this bond, at what price can you sell it?
    b.   If you want to buy the bond, what price will you pay?
    c.   Why is the selling price different than the purchase price?
    d.   What annual interest payment does the bond make?
    e.   What is the bond's ask yield to maturity?

5.2   BOND PRICES AND YIELDS

In Figure 5.1 we set out the cash flows received by an investor in 7.25 percent Canada bonds. How much would you have been willing to pay for these cash flows? The value of a security is the present value of the cash flows it will pay to its owners. To find this value, we need to discount each future payment by the interest rate that investors expect to earn on their bonds.

The 7.25s were not the only Canada bond that matured in 2007. Almost identical bonds maturing at the same time offered an interest rate of about 3.6 percent. So, if the 7.25s had offered a lower return than 3.6 percent, no one would have been willing to hold them. Equally, if they had offered a higher return, everyone would have rushed to sell their other bonds and buy the 7.25s. In other words, if investors were on their toes, the 7.25s had to offer the same 3.6 percent rate of interest as similar Canada bonds. You might recognize 3.6 percent as the opportunity cost of funds invested in the bond, as we discussed in Chapter 2. This is the rate of return that investors could earn by placing their funds in similar securities rather than in this bond.

We can now calculate the present value of 7.25s of 2007 by discounting the cash flows at 3.6 percent:

$$PV = \frac{\$72.50}{(1 + r)} + \frac{\$72.50}{(1 + r)^2} + \frac{\$1,072.50}{(1 + r)^3}$$

$$= \frac{\$72.50}{(1.036)} + \frac{\$72.50}{(1.036)^2} + \frac{\$1,072.50}{(1.036)^3} = \$1,102.06$$

Bond prices are usually expressed as a percentage of their face value. Thus we can say that our 7.25 percent Canada bond is worth 110.206 percent of face value, and its price would usually be quoted as 110.206. (The price of the bond shown in Figure 5.2 is $1,104.0, which is slightly higher than our calculation. This is largely due to rounding error in the interest rate we used to discount the bond's cash flows.)

Did you notice that the coupon payments on the bond are an annuity? In other words, the holder of our 7.25 percent Canada bond receives a level stream of coupon payments of $72.50 per year for each of the 3 years. At maturity the bondholder gets an additional payment of $1,000. Therefore, you can use the annuity formula to value the coupon payments and then add on the present value of the final payment of face value:

PV (bond) = PV (coupons) + PV (face value)
= (coupon × annuity factor) + (face value × discount factor)   (5.1)

$$= \$72.50 \times \left[\frac{1}{.036} - \frac{1}{.036(1.036)^3} \right] + 1,000 \times \frac{1}{1.036^3}$$

= $202.73 + $899.33 = $1,102.06

If you need to value a bond with many years to run before maturity, it is usually easiest to value the coupon payments as an annuity and then add on the present value of the final payment.

Check Point 5.2

Calculate the present value of a 6-year bond with a 9 percent coupon. The interest rate is 12 percent.

EXAMPLE 5.1

BOND PRICES AND SEMI-ANNUAL COUPON PAYMENTS

Thus far we've assumed that interest payments occur annually. This is the case for bonds in many European countries, but in Canada most bonds make coupon payments *semi-annually*. So when you hear that a bond in Canada has a coupon rate of 7.25 percent, you can generally assume that the bond makes a payment of $72.50/2 = $36.25 every 6 months. Similarly, when investors in Canada refer to the bond's interest rate, they usually mean the semi-annually compounded interest rate. Thus an interest rate quoted at 3.6 percent really means that the 6-month rate is 3.6/2 = 1.8 percent.[2]

---

[2] You may have noticed that the interest rate compounded semi-annually on the bond is also the bond's *APR*, although this term is generally not used by bond investors. To find the effective rate, we can use a formula that we used in Section 4.6:

$$\text{Effective annual rate} = \left(1 + \frac{APR}{m}\right)^m - 1$$

where m is the number of payments each year. In the case of our Canada bond,

$$\text{Effective annual rate} = \left(1 + \frac{.036}{2}\right)^2 - 1 = (1.018)^2 - 1 = .0363, \text{ or } 3.63\%$$

FIGURE 5.3

Cash flows to an investor in the 7.25 percent coupon bond, maturing in 2007. The bond pays semi-annual coupons, so there are two payments of $36.25 each year.

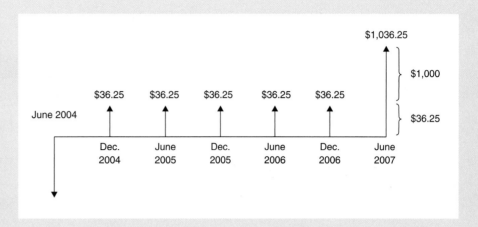

The actual cash flows on the Canada bond are illustrated in Figure 5.3. To value the bond a bit more precisely, we should have discounted the series of semi-annual payments by the semi-annual rate of interest as follows:

$$PV = \frac{\$36.25}{(1.018)} + \frac{\$36.25}{(1.018)^2} + \frac{\$36.25}{(1.018)^3} + \frac{\$36.25}{(1.018)^4} + \frac{\$36.25}{(1.018)^5} + \frac{\$1,036.25}{(1.018)^6}$$
$$= \$1,102.92$$

which is slightly more than the value of $1,102.06 that we obtained when we treated the coupon payments as annual rather than semi-annual.[3] Since semi-annual coupon payments just add to the arithmetic, we will often stick to our simplification and assume annual interest payments.

HOW BOND PRICES VARY WITH INTEREST RATES

As interest rates change, so do bond prices. For example, suppose that investors demanded an interest rate of 7.25 percent on 3-year government bonds. What would be the price of the Canada 7.25s of 2007? Just repeat the last calculation with a discount rate of $r = .0725$:

$$PV \text{ at } 7.25\% = \frac{\$72.5}{(1.0725)} + \frac{\$72.5}{(1.0725)^2} + \frac{\$1,072.5}{(1.0725)^3} = \$1,000.00$$

Thus when the interest rate is the same as the coupon rate (7.25 percent in our example), the bond sells for its face value.

We first valued the Canada bond with an interest rate of 3.6 percent, which is lower than the coupon rate. In that case the price of the bond was higher than its face value. We then valued it using an interest rate that is equal to the coupon rate and found that bond price equalled face value. You have probably already guessed that when the cash flows are discounted at a rate that is higher than the bond's coupon rate, the bond is worth less than its face value. The following example confirms that this is the case.

---

[3] Why is the present value a bit higher in this case? Because now we recognize that half the annual coupon payment is received only six months into the year, rather than at year-end. Because part of the coupon income is received earlier, its present value is higher. To match the price reported in Figure 5.2, calculate the bond's value with semi-annual payments and a 6-month rate of 3.56%/2 = 1.78 percent. You should get the bond's value to be $1,104.1.

| EXAMPLE 5.2 | **BOND PRICES AND INTEREST RATES** |

Investors will pay $1,000 for a 7.25 percent, 3-year Canada bond, when the interest rate is 7.25 percent. Suppose that the interest rate is higher than the coupon rate at, say, 15 percent. Now what is the value of the bond? Simple! We just repeat our initial calculation but with $r = .15$:

$$PV \text{ at } 15\% = \frac{\$72.5}{(1.15)} + \frac{\$72.5}{(1.15)^2} + \frac{\$1,072.5}{(1.15)^3} = \$823.05$$

The bond sells for 82.31 percent of face value.

> We conclude that when the market interest rate exceeds the coupon rate, bonds sell for less than face value. When the market interest rate is below the coupon rate, bonds sell for more than face value.

YIELD TO MATURITY VERSUS CURRENT YIELD

Suppose you are considering the purchase of a 3-year bond with a coupon rate of 10 percent. Your investment adviser quotes a price for the bond. How do you calculate the rate of return the bond offers?

For bonds priced at face value the answer is easy. The rate of return is the coupon rate. We can check this by setting out the cash flows on your investment:

	Cash Paid to You in Year			
You Pay	**1**	**2**	**3**	**Rate of Return**
$1,000	$100	$100	$1,100	10%

Notice that in each year you earn 10 percent on your money ($100/$1,000). In the final year you also get back your original investment of $1,000. Therefore, your total return is 10 percent, the same as the coupon rate.

Now suppose that the market price of the 3-year bond is $1,136.16. Your cash flows are as follows:

	Cash Paid to You in Year			
You Pay	**1**	**2**	**3**	**Rate of Return**
$1,136.16	$100	$100	$1,100	?

current yield Annual coupon payment divided by bond price.

What's the rate of return now? Notice that you are paying out $1,136.16 and receiving an annual income of $100. So your income as a proportion of the initial outlay is $100/$1,136.16 = .088, or 8.8 percent. This is sometimes called the bond's **current yield**.

However, total return depends on both interest income and any capital gains or losses. A current yield of 8.8 percent may sound attractive, only until you realize that the bond's price must fall. The price today is $1,136.16, but when the bond matures 3 years from now, the bond will sell for its face value, or $1,000. A price decline (i.e., a *capital loss*) of $136.16 is guaranteed, so the overall return over the next 3 years must be less than the 8.8 percent current yield.

Let us generalize. A bond that is priced above its face value is said to sell at a *premium*. Investors who buy a bond at a premium face a capital loss over the life of the bond, so the return on these bonds is always less than the bond's current yield. A bond priced below face value sells at a *discount*. Investors in discount bonds face a capital gain over the life of the bond; the return on these bonds is *greater* than the current yield:

> Because it focuses only on current income and ignores prospective price increases or decreases, the current yield mismeasures the bond's total rate of return. It overstates the return of premium bonds and understates that of discount bonds.

yield to maturity   Interest rate for which the present value of the bond's payments equals the price.

We need a measure of return that takes account of both current yield and the change in a bond's value over its life. The standard measure is called **yield to maturity**. The yield to maturity is the answer to the following question: At what interest rate would the bond be correctly priced?

> The yield to maturity is defined as the discount rate that makes the present value of the bond's payments equal to its price.

If you can buy the 3-year bond at face value, the yield to maturity is the coupon rate, 10 percent. We can confirm this by noting that when we discount the cash flows at 10 percent, the present value of the bond is equal to its $1,000 face value:

$$\text{PV at } 10\% = \frac{\$100}{(1.10)} + \frac{\$100}{(1.10)^2} + \frac{\$1,100}{(1.10)^3} = \$1,000.00$$

But if you have to buy the 3-year bond for $1,136.16, the yield to maturity is only 5 percent. At that discount rate, the bond's present value equals its actual market price, $1,136.16:

$$\text{PV at } 5\% = \frac{\$100}{(1.05)} + \frac{\$100}{(1.05)^2} + \frac{\$1,100}{(1.05)^3} = \$1,136.16$$

EXAMPLE 5.3   **CALCULATING YIELD TO MATURITY FOR THE CANADA BOND**

We found the value of the 7.25 percent coupon Canada bond by discounting at a 3.6 percent interest rate. We could have phrased the question the other way around: If the price of the bond is $1,102.06, what return do investors expect? We need to find the yield to maturity, in other words, the discount rate r that solves the following equation:

$$\text{Price} = \frac{\$72.5}{(1 + r)} + \frac{\$72.5}{(1 + r)^2} + \frac{\$1,072.5}{(1 + r)^3} = \$1,102.06$$

To find the yield to maturity, most people use a financial calculator or a spreadsheet. For our Government of Canada bond you would enter a PV of $1,102.06.[4] The bond provides a regular payment of $72.5, entered as $PMT = 72.5$. The bond has a future value of $1,000, so $FV = 1,000$. The bond life is 3 years, so $n = 3$. Now compute the interest rate, and you will find that the yield to maturity is 3.6 percent. The nearby Financial Calculator and Excel Spreadsheet boxes review the use of the financial calculator and spreadsheets in bond valuation problems.

SEE BOXES
PP. 138 AND 140 ▶

The yield to maturity is a measure of a bond's total return, including both coupon income and capital gain. If an investor buys the bond today and holds it to maturity, his return will be the yield to maturity. Bond investors often refer loosely to a bond's "yield." It's a safe bet that they are talking about its yield to maturity rather than its current yield.

The only *general* procedure for calculating yield to maturity is trial and error. You guess at an interest rate and calculate the present value of the bond's payments.[5] If the present value is greater than the actual price, your discount rate must have been too low, so try a higher interest rate (since a higher rate results in a lower PV). Conversely, if PV is less than price, you must reduce the interest rate. In practice, investors use a financial calculator or a computer spreadsheet to do the trial and error for them. The nearby boxes provide examples.

---

[4] Actually on most calculators you would enter 1,102.06 as a negative number, (−1,102.06), because the purchase of the bond represents a cash *outflow*.

[5] This approximation formula will give you a good first guess. Check the estimate and fine-tune it using the trial-and-error method to be confident of its accuracy.

$$\text{YTM} = \frac{\text{annual coupon payment} + (\text{face value} - \text{current price})/\text{years to maturity}}{(\text{face value} + \text{current price})/2}$$

In Chapter 4 we saw that financial calculators can compute the present values of level annuities as well as the present values of one-time future cash flows. Coupon bonds present both of these characteristics: The coupon payments are level annuities and the final payment of par value is an additional one-time payment. Thus for the coupon bond we looked at in Example 5.3, you would treat the periodic payment as $PMT = \$72.5$, the final or future one-time payment as $FV = \$1,000$, the number of periods as $n = 3$ years, and the interest rate as the yield to maturity of the bond, $i = 3.6$ percent. You would thus compute the value of the bond using the following sequence of key strokes. By the way, the order in which the various inputs for the bond valuation problem are entered does not matter.

Hewlett-Packard HP-10B		Sharp EL-733A		Texas Instruments BA II Plus	
72.5	PMT	72.5	PMT	72.5	PMT
1000	FV	1000	FV	1000	FV
3	N	3	n	3	N
3.6	I/YR	3.6	i	3.6	I/Y
PV		COMP	PV	CPT	PV

Your calculator should now display a value of –1,102.06. The minus sign reminds us that the initial cash flow is negative: You have to pay to buy the bond.

You can also use the calculator to find the yield to maturity of a bond. For example, if you buy this bond for $1,102.06, you should find that its yield to maturity is 3.6 percent. Let's check that this is so. You enter the PV as –1,102.06 because you buy the bond for this price. Thus to solve for the interest rate, use the following key strokes:

Hewlett-Packard HP-10B		Sharp EL-733A		Texas Instruments BA II Plus	
72.5	PMT	72.5	PMT	72.5	PMT
1000	FV	1000	FV	1000	FV
3	N	3	n	3	N
–1102.06	PV	–1102.06	PV	–1102.06	PV
I/YR		COMP	i	CPT	I/Y

Your calculator should now display 3.6 percent, the yield to maturity of the bond.

EXAMPLE 5.4   YIELD TO MATURITY WITH SEMI-ANNUAL COUPON PAYMENTS

Let's redo Example 5.3, but this time assume the coupons are paid semi-annually. Instead of three annual coupons of $72.50, the bond makes six semi-annual payments of $36.25. We can find the *semi-annual* yield to maturity on our calculators by using these inputs: $n = 6$ (semi-annual) periods, $PV = -1,102.06$, $FV = 1,000$, $PMT = 36.25$. We then compute the interest rate to find that it is 1.814 percent. This of course is a six-month, not an annual, rate. Bond dealers typically annualize the semi-annual rate by doubling it, so the yield to maturity would be quoted as $1.814 \times 2 = 3.628$ percent. In Excel (see nearby Excel Spreadsheet box), you can confirm that =YIELD(DATE(2004,6,1), DATE(2007,6,1),.0725,110.206,100,2) = .0363. A better way to annualize would be to account for compound interest. A dollar invested at 1.814 percent for two 6-month periods would grow to $1 \times (1.01814)^2 = \$1.0366$. The *effective* annual yield is therefore 3.66 percent.

SEE BOX P. 140 ▷

✔ **Check Point 5.3**

A 4-year maturity bond with a 14 percent coupon rate can be bought for $1,200. What is the yield to maturity if the coupon is paid annually? What if it is paid semi-annually? You will need a spreadsheet or a financial calculator to answer this question.

Figure 5.4 is a graphical view of yield to maturity. It shows the present value of the 7.25 percent Canada bond for different interest rates. The actual bond price, $1,102.06, is marked on the vertical axis. A line is drawn from this price over to the present value curve and then down to the interest rate, 3.6 percent. If we picked a higher or lower figure for the interest rate, then we would not obtain a bond price of $1,102.06. Thus we know that the yield to maturity on the bond must be 3.6 percent.

FIGURE 5.4
The value of the 7.25 percent bond is lower at higher discount rates. The yield to maturity is the discount rate at which price equals present value of cash flows.

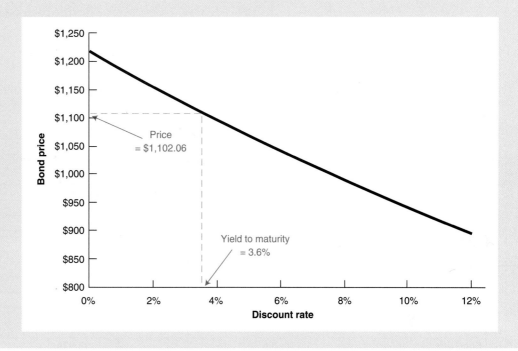

Figure 5.4 also illustrates a fundamental relationship between interest rates and bond prices:

> When the interest rate rises, the present value of the payments to be received by the bondholder falls, and bond prices fall. Conversely, declines in the interest rate increase the present value of those payments and result in higher prices.

A warning! People sometimes confuse the interest, or coupon, *payment* on the bond with the *interest rate*—that is, the return that investors require. The $72.5 coupon payments on our Canada bond are fixed when the bond is issued. The coupon rate, 7.25 percent, measures the coupon payment ($72.5) as a percentage of the bond's face value ($1,000) and is therefore also fixed. However, the interest rate changes from day to day. These changes affect the *present value* of the coupon payments but not the payments themselves.

RATE OF RETURN

When you invest in a bond, you receive a regular coupon payment. As bond prices change, you may also make a capital gain or loss. For example, suppose you buy the 7.25 percent Canada bond today for a price of $1,102.06 and sell it next year at a price of $1,112.46. The return on your investment is the $72.5 coupon payment plus the price change of ($1,112.46 – $ 1,102.06) = $10.40. The **rate of return** on your investment of $1,102.06 is

rate of return   Total income per period per dollar invested.

$$\text{Rate of return} = \frac{\text{coupon income} + \text{price change}}{\text{investment}} \tag{5.2}$$

$$= \frac{\$72.5 + \$10.40}{\$1,102.06} = .0752, \text{ or } 7.52\%$$

Because bond prices fall when market interest rates rise and rise when market rates fall, the rate of return that you earn on a bond will also fluctuate with market interest rates. This is why we say bonds are subject to interest rate risk.

Do not confuse the bond's rate of return over a particular investment period with its yield to maturity. The yield to maturity is defined as the discount rate that equates the bond's price to the

Bond Valuation

Excel and most other spreadsheet programs provide built-in functions to compute bond values and yields. They typically ask you to input both the date you buy the bond (called the settlement date) and the maturity date of the bond.

The Excel function for bond value is

=PRICE(*settlement date, maturity date, annual coupon rate, yield to maturity, final payment, number of coupon payments per year*).

	A	B	C	D	E	F	G	H
1								
2		**Valuing bonds using a spreadsheet**						
3								
4		**7.25% coupon**			**6% coupon**			
5		**maturing June 2007**			**10-year maturity**			
6								
7	Settlement date	6/01/04			1/1/00			
8	Maturity date	6/01/07			1/1/10			
9	Annual coupon rate	.0725			0.06			
10	Yield to maturity	.036			0.07			
11	Final payment (% of face value)	100			100			
12	Coupon payments per year	1			1			
13								
14	**Bond price (% of par)**	**110.206**			**92.976**			
15								
16								
17		The formula entered here is: =PRICE(B7,B8,B9,B10,B11,B12)						

For our 7.25 percent coupon bond, we would enter the values in column B of the spreadsheet above. Alternatively, we could simply enter the following function in Excel:

=PRICE(DATE(2004,06,01),DATE(2007,06,01),.0725,.036,100,1).

The DATE function in Excel, which we use for both the settlement and maturity date, uses the format DATE(year,month,day).

Notice that the coupon rate and yield to maturity are expressed as decimals, not percentages. In most cases, final payment will be 100 (i.e., 100 percent of face value), and the resulting price will be expressed as a percentage of face value. Occasionally, however, you may encounter bonds that pay off at a premium or discount to face value. One example would be callable bonds, discussed at the end of the chapter.

The value of the bond assuming annual coupon payments is 110.206 percent of face value, or $1,102.06. If we wanted to assume semi-annual coupon payments, we would simply change the entry in cell B12 to 2, and the bond value would change to 110.292 percent of face value, as we found in Example 5.1. To see this, express the bond value from Example 5.1 as a percentage of its face value:

$$100 \times (\$1,102.92/\$1,000) = 110.292$$

present value of all its promised cash flows. It is a measure of the average rate of return you will earn over the bond's life if you hold it to maturity. In contrast, the rate of return can be calculated for any particular holding period and is based on the actual income and the capital gain or loss on the bond over that period. The difference between yield to maturity and rate of return for a particular period is emphasized in the following example.

EXAMPLE 5.5　　**RATE OF RETURN VERSUS YIELD TO MATURITY**

Our 7.25 percent coupon bond with maturity in 2007 currently has 3 years left until maturity and sells today for $1,102.06. Its yield to maturity is 3.6 percent. Suppose that by the end of the year, interest rates have fallen and the bond's yield to maturity is now only 1.5 percent. What will be the bond's one-year rate of return?

In this example, we assume that the first coupon payment comes in exactly one period (either a year or a half-year). In other words, the settlement date is precisely at the beginning of the period. However, the PRICE function will make the necessary adjustments for intraperiod purchase dates.

	A	B	C	D	E	F	G	H
1								
2		**Finding yield to maturity using a spreadsheet**						
3		**June 2007 maturity bond, coupon rate = 7.25%, maturity = 3 years**						
4								
5		**Annual coupons**			**Semi-annual coupons**			
6								
7	Settlement date	6/01/04			6/01/04			
8	Maturity date	6/01/07			6/01/07			
9	Annual coupon rate	.0725			.0725			
10	Bond price	110.206			110.206			
11	Final payment (% of face value)	100			100			
12	Coupon payments per year	1			2			
13								
14	**Yield to maturity (decimal)**	**.036**			**.0366**			
15								
16								
17		The formula entered here is: =YIELD(B7,B8,B9,B10,B11,B12)						

Suppose now that you wish to find the price of a 10-year maturity bond with a coupon rate of 6 percent (paid annually), selling at a yield to maturity of 7 percent. You are not given a specific settlement or maturity date. You can still use the PRICE function to value the bond. Simply choose an arbitrary settlement date (January 1, 2000 is convenient) and let the maturity date be 10 years hence. The appropriate inputs appear in column E of the spreadsheet on the previous page, with the resulting price, 92.976 percent of face value, appearing in cell E14. You can confirm this value on your calculator using the inputs: $n = 10$, $i = 7$, $FV = 1000$, $PMT = 60$.

Excel also provides a function for yield to maturity. It is

=YIELD(settlement date, maturity date, annual coupon rate, bond price, final payment as percentage of face value, number of coupon payments per year).

For example, to find the yield to maturity in Example 5.3, we would use column B of the above spreadsheet. If the coupons were paid semi-annually, as in Example 5.4, we would change the entry for payments per year to 2 (see cell E12), and the yield would increase to 3.66 percent.

At the end of the year, the bond will have only two years to maturity. If investors then demand an interest rate of 1.5 percent, the value of the bond will be

$$PV \text{ at } 1.5\% = \frac{\$72.5}{(1.015)} + \frac{\$1,072.5}{(1.015)^2} = \$1,112.46$$

You invested $1,102.06. At the end of the year you receive a coupon payment of $72.5 and have a bond worth $1,112.46. Your rate of return is therefore

$$\text{Rate of return} = \frac{\$72.5 + (\$1,112.46 - \$1,102.06)}{\$1,102.06} = .0752, \text{ or } 7.52\%$$

The yield to maturity at the start of the year was 3.6 percent. However, because interest rates fell during the year, the bond price rose, and this increased the rate of return.

Check Point 5.4

Suppose that the bond's yield to maturity had risen to 5 percent during the year. Show that its rate of return would have been less than the yield to maturity.

Is there *any* connection between yield to maturity and the rate of return during a particular period? Yes: If the bond's yield to maturity remains unchanged during an investment period, its rate of return will equal that yield. We can check this by assuming that the yield on 7.25 percent Canada bonds stays at 3.6 percent. If investors still demand an interest rate of 3.6 percent at the end of the year, the value of the bond will be

$$PV = \frac{\$72.5}{(1.036)} + \frac{\$1,072.5}{(1.036)^2} = \$1,069.24$$

At the end of the year you receive a coupon payment of $72.5 and have a bond worth $1,069.24, somewhat less than you paid for it. Your total profit is $72.5 + ($1,069.24 − $1,102.06) = $39.68. The return on your investment is therefore $39.68/$1,102.06 = .036, or 3.6 percent, just equal to the yield to maturity.

> When interest rates do not change, the bond price changes with time so that the total return on the bond is equal to the yield to maturity. If the bond's yield to maturity increases, the rate of return during the period will be less than that yield. If the yield decreases, the rate of return will be greater than the yield.

Check Point 5.5

Suppose you buy the bond next year for $1,069.24, and hold it for yet another year, so that at the end of that time it has only 1 year to maturity. Show that if the bond's yield to maturity is still 3.6 percent, your rate of return also will be 3.6 percent and the bond price will be $1,035.23.

The solid curve in Figure 5.5 plots the price of a 30-year maturity, 7.25 percent Canada bond over time assuming that its yield to maturity remains at 3.6 percent. The price declines gradually until the maturity date, when it finally reaches face value. In each period, the price decline offsets the coupon income by just enough to reduce total return to 3.6 percent. The dotted curve in

FIGURE 5.5
Bond prices over time, assuming an unchanged yield to maturity. Prices of both premium and discount bonds approach face value as their maturity date approaches.

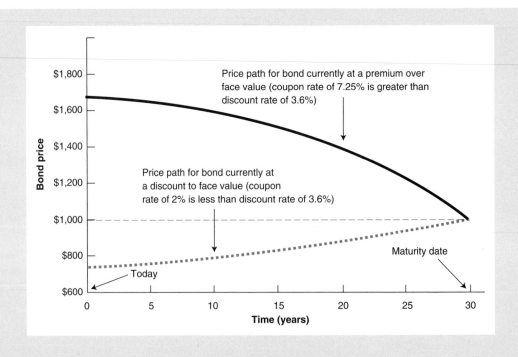

Figure 5.5 shows the corresponding price path for a 30-year maturity, 2 percent coupon Canada bond, also assuming its yield to maturity remains at 3.6 percent. This low-coupon bond currently sells at a discount to face value. The coupon income provides less than a competitive rate of return, so the bond sells below par. Its price gradually approaches face value, however, and the price gain each year brings its total return up to the market interest rate of 3.6 percent.

TAXES AND RATES OF RETURN

Taxes reduce the rate of return on an investment. Let's go back to Example 5.5. You bought a bond for $1,102.06 and sold it 1 year later for $1,112.46 and received one coupon payment of $72.50. The *before-tax* rate of return on your 1-year investment was 7.52 percent. However, as we discussed in Chapter 3, interest income is fully taxable, and 50 percent of capital gains are taxable. To figure out the after-tax rate of return on the investment, convert the cash flows to their after-tax values by subtracting the relevant taxes. If your personal tax rate is 35 percent, the tax on the coupon payment of $72.50 is

$$\text{Tax on coupon income} = \text{personal tax rate} \times \text{coupon income}$$
$$= .35 \times \$72.50 = \$25.375$$

After taxes, the coupon income is

$$\text{After-tax coupon income} = \text{coupon income} - \text{tax on coupon income}$$
$$= \$72.5 - \$25.375 = \$47.125$$

Likewise, the tax on the capital gain is

$$\text{Tax on capital gain} = \text{personal tax rate} \times .5 \times \text{capital gain}$$
$$= .35 \times .5 \times (\$1,112.46 - \$1,102.06) = \$1.82$$

and the after-tax capital gain is

$$\text{After-tax capital gain} = \text{capital gain} - \text{tax on capital gain}$$
$$= (\$1,112.46 - \$1,102.06) - \$1.82 = \$8.58$$

Your after-tax rate of return is therefore

$$\text{After-tax rate of return} = \frac{\text{after-tax coupon income} + \text{after-tax capital gain}}{\text{investment}}$$
$$= \frac{\$47.125 + \$8.58}{\$1,102.06} = .0505, \text{ or } 5.05\%$$

As you can see, taxes have a material effect on the rate of return on your investment! Here, the 7.52 percent before-tax rate of return is only 5.05 percent once you consider the taxes you must pay on your investment income.

> ✓ Check Point 5.6   Suppose you bought an 8 percent coupon bond for $1,200 and sold it 1 year later for $1,215. Calculate the before-tax and after-tax rate of return on your investment, if your personal tax rate is 40 percent.

In our examples we have considered only one-year investments. How do you calculate the rate of return if the investment lasts longer than one year? Suppose you buy the 7.25 percent coupon bond for $1,102.06 and sell it in 2 years for $1,066.4. You receive cash flows at two different points in time: a $72.50 coupon payment after one year, and then another $72.50 coupon plus the cash from selling the bond after 2 years. If you ignore the fact that you received the first $72.50 early, you can add up all the coupon payments and calculate the rate of return like we did above. This method understates your rate of return—you ignored the value of investing the first coupon during the time of the bond investment. The standard approach to calculating the rate of return is to assume that the first coupon is reinvested for the remaining life of the investment. In other words, calculate the future value of that first coupon payment at the end of the second year.

Suppose when you received the first coupon payment you immediately invested at 4 percent for 1 year. That coupon payment will be worth 72.5×1.04, or $75.4, 1 year later. At the end of the 2 years, the total value of coupon income received is $75.4 + $72.5, or $147.9. The price change on the bond is a capital loss: $1,066.4 − $1,102.06, or −$35.66. Using Equation 5.2, the rate of return on the investment is

$$\text{Rate of return} = \frac{\text{coupon income} + \text{price change}}{\text{investment}}$$
$$= \frac{\$147.9 - \$35.66}{\$1,102.06} = .1018, \text{ or } 10.18\%$$

Did you notice that this is a *two-year* rate of return? The effective annual equivalent is $(1.1018)^{1/2} - 1$, or 4.97 percent.

How do you know the rate at which the intermediate coupon payments are invested? You can use the actual rates available at the time you received the coupons. Another approach is to use a variation on the yield-to-maturity calculation. Using this method, your rate of return is the discount rate that equates the purchase price to the present value of the coupons and the price you receive when you sell the bond. This assumes that all of the coupons are invested at that discount rate for the remaining time you own the bond. You can use this approach to calculate the after-tax rate of return too—just use the after-tax cash flows. We will see this approach to calculating rates of return again in Chapter 7, but there we will call it the *internal rate of return*.

EXAMPLE 5.6	**CALCULATING THE RATE OF RETURN ON A TWO-YEAR BOND INVESTMENT**

You buy a 7.25 percent bond for $1,102.06 and sell it for $1,066.4 2 years later. What is the rate of return on your investment if you use the yield-to-maturity approach? Using a calculator, enter $PV = -\$1,102.06$, $PMT = \$72.5$, $FV = \$1,066.4$, and $n = 2$. Now compute the interest rate, which is your rate of return. You should get 5 percent.

5.3   DETERMINANTS OF BOND YIELDS

Look back for a moment to Figure 5.2. The Canada bonds are arranged in order of their maturity. Notice that the longer the maturity, the higher the yield. This is usually the case, though sometimes long-term bonds offer *lower* yields.

Figure 5.6 plots the relationship between bond yields and maturities. This is known as the **yield curve** or the **term structure of interest rates**. Each yield curve in Figure 5.6 is a snapshot of yields for Canada bonds of different maturities on a specific date. Take a look at the yield curve for July 31, 2004, the lowest line on Figure 5.6. It shows that bonds with 3 months to maturity offered a yield of 2 percent; those with more than 10 years of maturity offered 4.8 percent. Compare that curve to the yield curve for 4 years earlier, July 31, 2000, when 3-month treasury bills were yielding 5.6 percent and long-term bonds were yielding 5.9 percent. The yield curve for July 31, 1990, is much higher than other two and downward sloping, with yields on short-term maturities higher than for long-term bonds. At that time, the 3-month T-bill yield was 13.4 percent and the 10-year Canada bond yield was 10.7 percent.

Figure 5.6 reveals two important characteristics of interest rates. First, the yields on bonds that differ only in their maturities are not the same. For example, on July 31, 2004, the 10-year bond was earning an extra 2.8 percentage points over the 3-month T-bill. Why? Second, the general level of interest rates changes over time. The July 31, 2004, 3-month T-bill yield was 3.6 percentage points lower than in 2000 and over 11 percentage points lower than in 1990. Why?

yield curve or term structure of interest rates   Graph of the relationship between time to maturity and yield to maturity, for bonds that differ only in their maturity dates.

FIGURE 5.6

The yield curve. A plot of yield to maturity as a function of time to maturity for Government of Canada bills and bonds on various dates

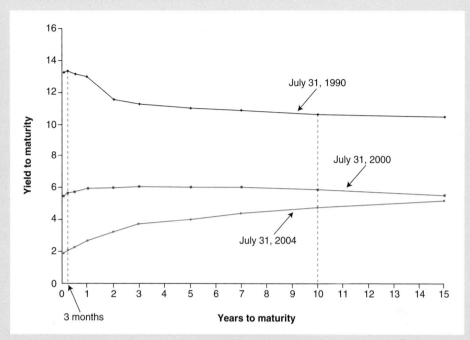

Source: Adapted from the Statistics Canada CANSIM database (http://cansim2.statcan.ca) series B14059, B14060, B14061, B14062, B14067, B14068, B14069, B14070, B14071, and B14072.

Economists have long sought answers to these questions and will continue seeking for years to come. For now, we can give you some general answers. We will first consider why the general level of interest rates changes over time, affecting the *level* of the yield curve, and then look at factors affecting the *shape* of the yield curve.

NOMINAL AND REAL RATES OF INTEREST

In Chapter 4 we drew a distinction between nominal and real rates of interest. The cash flows on the 7.25 percent Canada bonds are fixed in nominal terms. Investors are sure to receive an interest payment of $72.50 each year, but they do not know what that money will buy them. The *real* interest rate on the bonds depends on the rate of inflation. For example, if the nominal rate of interest is 3.6 percent and the inflation rate is 1.5 percent, then the real interest rate is calculated as follows:

$$(1 + \text{real interest rate}) = \frac{1 + \text{nominal interest rate}}{1 + \text{inflation rate}} = \frac{1.036}{1.015} = 1.0207$$

$$\text{Real interest rate} = .0207, \text{ or } 2.07\%$$

Since the inflation rate is uncertain, so is the real rate of interest on the bonds.

real return bond Bond with variable nominal coupon payments, determined by a fixed real coupon payment and the inflation rate.

You *can* nail down a real rate of interest by buying an indexed or **real return bond**, whose payments are linked to inflation. The Government of Canada began issuing inflation-indexed or real return bonds, RRBs, in 1991. The real cash flows are fixed, but the nominal cash flows (coupon payments and principal) are increased as the consumer price index increases. For example, the 4.25 percent RRB due December 1, 2021, pays annual real coupons of $42.50. In Figure 5.2, prices and yields of the four issues of Government of Canada real return bonds are seen at the bottom of the second column.

To see how the nominal coupon is calculated, suppose the Government of Canada issues a 3 percent, 2-year real return bond. The real cash flows are fixed but the nominal cash flows will depend on the increase in the consumer price index. Suppose inflation turns out to be 5 percent in Year 1 and a further 4 percent in Year 2. The real and nominal cash flows of the bonds would be

	Year 1	Year 2
Real cash flows	$30	$1,030
Nominal cash flows	$30 × 1.05 = $31.50	$1,030 × 1.05 × 1.04 = $1,124.76

For the 4.25 percent RRB, the nominal value of each coupon is calculated when the coupon payment is due and reflects the inflation that has occurred since the issue of the bond. We won't know the nominal value of the principal until just before the bond matures in 2021.

Currently, all real return bond issues of the Government of Canada have maturities of at least 17 years. From Figure 5.2 we can see that the yield to maturity on the Canada RRBs was about 2.3 percent in June 2004. This yield is a real interest rate. It measures the amount of extra goods your investment will allow you to buy. Figure 5.2 also shows that the yield to maturity on the Canada bonds with similar term to maturity was 5.3 percent. An estimate of the expected annual inflation rate used by market participants when discounting future cash flows can be found by rearranging the formula for the real interest rate:

$$(1 + \text{inflation rate}) = \frac{1 + \text{nominal interest rate}}{1 + \text{real interest rate}} = \frac{1.053}{1.023} = 1.0293$$
$$\text{Inflation rate} = .0293, \text{ or } 2.93\%$$

If the annual inflation rate proves to be higher than 2.93 percent, you will earn a higher nominal return by holding RRBs; if the inflation rate is lower than 2.93 percent, the reverse will be true.

Inflation-indexed bonds have been issued by other governments and corporations. The United Kingdom has issued indexed bonds since 1982. The United States Treasury began to issue Treasury Inflation-Protected Securities, or TIPs, in 1997 and structured them similarly to the Government of Canada Real Return Bonds. In 2000, 407 International Inc., owner of the largest electronic toll highway in Canada, just north of Toronto, sold real return bonds with a 5.29 percent real coupon rate, maturing in 2039.

What determines the real rate of interest demanded by investors? The classical economist Irving Fisher's answer is that real interest rates depend on the supply of savings and the demand for new investment.[6] As this supply-demand balance changes, real interest rates change. But they do so gradually.

According to Fisher, the nominal interest rate reflects both the real interest rate and the expected inflation. In other words, the nominal interest rate is determined by real rate of interest and the expected inflation. This is known as the Fisher effect. More formally, the **Fisher effect** is

Fisher effect The nominal interest rate is determined by the real interest rate and the expected rate of inflation.

1 + nominal interest rate = (1 + real interest rate) × (1 + expected inflation rate)   (5.3)

When inflation and the real interest rate are not high, a reasonable approximation to Equation (5.3) is

Nominal interest rate = real interest rate + expected inflation rate   (5.4)

Suppose that investors upwardly revise their forecast of inflation by 1 percent. How will this affect interest rates? According to Fisher, if investors are concerned about the purchasing power of their money, the changed forecast should not affect the real rate of interest. The nominal interest rate must therefore rise by 1 percent to compensate investors for the higher inflation prospects.

How well does Fisher's theory of interest rates work? The gold line in Figure 5.7 shows that the real interest rate on the Government of Canada Real Return bonds has fluctuated within a

---

[6] See Irving Fisher's great book: *The Theory of Interest: As Determined by Impatience to Spend Income and Opportunity to Invest It*, August M. Kelley, New York, 1965; originally published in 1930.

FIGURE 5.7
The bottom line shows the real yield on long-term Canada Real Return bonds. The top line shows the yield on long-term Canada nominal bonds. Notice that the real yield has been much more stable than the nominal yield.

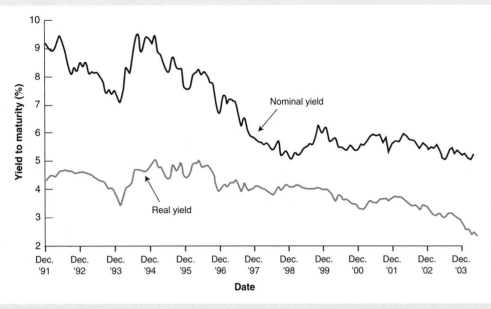

Source: Bank of Canada. Series B14072 and B14081 retrieved August 6, 2004 from www. bankofcanada.ca/en/rates/bond-look.htm

relatively narrow range, between 2.3 percent and 5 percent since 1991. The blue line shows the nominal interest rate on ordinary long-term Government of Canada bonds. The nominal rate is more variable than the real rate, ranging between 5 percent and 9.5 percent since 1991.

Some economists disagree with Fisher's theory that inflation does not affect the real rate of interest. For example, if inflation causes companies to change their investment activities, the real interest rate will change. Looking at Figure 5.7 you can clearly see the impact on the steady decline in inflation during most of the 1990s, causing nominal yields to fall. The figure suggests that the real rate also fell too, but less dramatically. Unfortunately, no one has yet sorted out the complex relationship between inflation and interest rates. However, a financial manager can use the Fisher effect as a valuable rule of thumb. If the expected inflation rate changes, it is a good bet that there will be a corresponding change in the nominal interest rate.

Check Point 5.7   Go back to Figure 5.6. Do you think the inflation rate in 1990 was higher or lower than the 2004 inflation rate? Explain your thinking.

TERM STRUCTURE OF INTEREST RATE

We have seen that the general level of interest rates is largely determined by the real interest rate and the expected rate of inflation. But why do long-term bonds offer different yields than short-term bonds? Generally the yield curve is upward sloping. However sometimes it is the other way around, with short rates higher than long rates. As seen in Figure 5.6, the yield curve was downward sloping in 1990. The yield curve can be flat, as it nearly was in 2000, or humped, with rising short-term yields followed by lower long-term yields.

EXPECTATIONS THEORY

A major factor determining the shape of the yield curve is expected inflation. To see why, consider the following example. Suppose you want to invest your money for two years. You could buy a one-year bond now. A year from now when the bond matures, you reinvest the proceeds in another one-year bond and enjoy whatever rate the bond market offers then. Alternatively, you could buy a two-year bond today. According to the expectations theory of interest rates, interest rates will adjust such that you don't care whether you invest in a two-year loan or in two successive one-year loans. This means an upward-sloping yield curve tells you that investors expect short-term interest rates to rise. Likewise, a downward-sloping yield curve means that investors expect short-term rates to fall.

Why would future short-term interest rates be expected to be higher than today's current short-term rate? As we saw above, expected inflation is a key component of nominal interest rates. So, if investors expect inflation to increase, they will demand higher short-term rates in the future, which tends to result in an upward-sloping yield curve. Expected decreases in future inflation will tend to lead to a downward-sloping yield curve.

INTEREST RATE RISK AND THE LIQUIDITY PREMIUM

The expectations theory cannot provide a complete explanation of the yield curve because it does not consider risk.

interest rate risk The risk in bond prices due to fluctuations in interest rates.

We have seen that bond prices fluctuate as interest rates change. In other words, bonds exhibit **interest rate risk**. Bond investors cross their fingers that market interest rates will fall, so that the price of their bond will rise. If they are unlucky and the market interest rate rises, the value of their investment falls.

But all bonds are not equally affected by changing interest rates. Compare the two curves in Figure 5.8. The gold line shows how the value of the 3-year, 7.25 percent coupon bond varies with the level of the interest rate. The blue line shows how the price of a 30-year, 7.25 percent bond varies with the level of interest rates. You can see that the 30-year bond is more sensitive to interest rate fluctuations than the 3-year bond. This should not surprise you. If you buy a 3-year bond when the interest rate is 3.6 percent, and rates then rise, you will be stuck with a bad deal—you have just loaned your money at a lower interest rate than if you had waited. However, think how much worse it would be if the loan had been for 30 years, rather than 3 years. The longer the period of the loan, the more income you have lost by accepting what turns out to be a low coupon rate. This shows that the price of the longer-term bond had a greater decline. Of course, there is a flip side to this effect, which you can also see from Figure 5.8. When interest rates fall, the longer-term bond responds with a greater increase in price.

Check Point 5.8   Suppose that the interest rate rises overnight from 3.6 percent to 10 percent. Calculate the present values of the 7.25 percent, 3-year bond and of the 7.25 percent, 30-year bond both before and after this change in interest rates. Confirm that your answers correspond with Figure 5.8. Use your financial calculator or a spreadsheet.

We saw in Figure 5.8 that a longer-term bond has greater interest risk than a short-term bond with the same coupon rate. If two bonds have the same maturity but unequal coupons, the bond with the lower coupon will have the greater interest rate risk. In Appendix 5.A, we examine why coupon rates affect bonds' interest rate risk and introduce the important concept of *duration*, a method of measuring a bond's life. We show that bonds with longer duration also have greater interest rate risk.

If investors don't like price fluctuations, they invest their funds in short-term bonds unless they receive a higher yield to maturity on long-term bonds. This extra return has various names including a liquidity premium, a maturity risk premium, and an interest rate risk premium. According to this theory, known as the liquidity preference theory, the yield curve will tend to upward sloping because of the liquidity premium needed to induce investors to buy the riskier longer bonds.

The expectations theory and the liquidity preference theory together predict that the yield curve will tend to be upward sloping both because of increases in future inflation and the

FIGURE 5.8
Plots of bond prices as a function of the interest rate. Long-term bond prices are more sensitive to the interest rate than prices of short-term bonds.

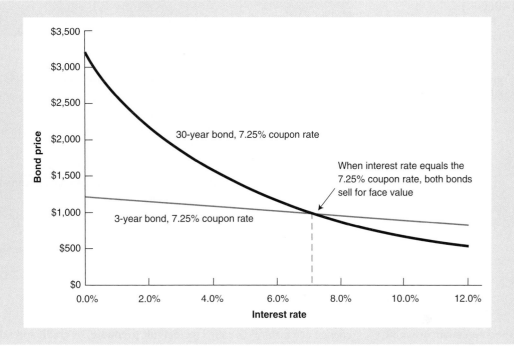

DEFAULT RISK

Our focus so far has been on Government of Canada bonds. But the federal government is not the only issuer of bonds. Provincial and municipal governments borrow by selling bonds. So do corporations. Canadian governments and corporations also borrow in the United States and in other countries. The bonds may be denominated in Canadian dollars, U.S. dollars, and sometimes in another currency, such as the British pound or Japanese yen.

There is an important distinction between bonds issued by corporations and those issued by the Government of Canada. National governments don't go bankrupt—they just print more money.[7] So investors do not worry that the Canadian government will *default* on its bonds. However, there is some chance that corporations may get into financial difficulties and may default on their bonds. Thus the payments promised to corporate bondholders represent a best-case scenario: The firm will never pay more than the promised cash flows, but in hard times it may pay less.

default (or credit) risk The risk that a bond issuer may default on its bonds.

The risk that a bond issuer may default on its obligations is called **default risk** (or **credit risk**). It should be no surprise to find that to compensate for this default risk companies need to promise a higher rate of interest than the Canadian government when borrowing money. The difference between the promised yield on a corporate bond and the yield on a Canada bond with the same

---

[7] But they can't print money of other countries. Therefore, when a government borrows in a foreign currency, investors worry that in some future crisis the government may not be able to come up with enough of the foreign currency to repay the debt. This worry shows up in the yield that investors demand on such debt. For example, in the summer of 2002, concerns about a possible Brazilian default caused yields on the U.S. dollar bonds issued by the Brazilian government to rise to 13 percentage points above the yields on comparable U.S. Treasury issues.

TABLE 5.1
Key to Dominion Bond Rating Service (DBRS), Standard & Poor's (S&P,) and Moody's bond ratings. The highest quality bonds are rated triple A, then come double A bonds, and so on.

DBRS/S&P	Moody's	Safety
AAA	Aaa	The strongest rating; ability to repay interest and principal is very strong.
AA	Aa	Very strong likelihood that interest and principal will be repaid.
A	A	Strong ability to repay, but some vulnerability to change in circumstances.
BBB	Baa	Adequate capacity to repay; more vulnerability to changes in economic circumstances.
BB	Ba	Considerable uncertainty about ability to repay.
B	B	Likelihood of interest and principal payments over sustained periods is questionable.
CCC CC	Caa Ca	Bonds in the CCC and CC classes may already be in default or in danger of imminent default.
C	C	Little prospect for interest or principal on the debt ever to be repaid.
D	D	Debt payments have been missed; debt is in default.

default premium or credit spread The additional yield on a bond that investors require for bearing credit risk.

coupon and maturity is called the **default premium**, or **credit spread**. The greater the chance that the company will get into trouble, the higher the default premium demanded by investors.

The safety of most corporate bonds can be judged from bond ratings provided by the Dominion Bond Rating Service (DBRS), Moody's, Standard & Poor's (S&P), or other bond-rating firms. Table 5.1 lists the possible bond ratings in declining order of quality. For example, the bonds that receive the highest rating are known as AAA, or "triple A" bonds. Then come AA, or "double A," A bonds, BBB bonds, and so on. Bonds rated BBB and above are called **investment grade**, while those with a rating of BB or below are referred to as *speculative grade*, *high-yield*, or **junk bonds**.

investment grade Bond rated Baa or above by Moody's, or BBB or above by Standard and Poor's or DBRS.

junk bond Bond with a rating below Baa or BBB.

It is rare for highly rated bonds to default. For example, since 1971 fewer than one in a thousand triple A bonds have defaulted within 10 years of issue. However, when an investment-grade bond does default, the shock waves can be considerable. For example, in May 2001 WorldCom sold $11.8 billion of bonds with an investment-grade rating. Within little more than a year WorldCom filed for bankruptcy and its bondholders had lost more than 80 percent of their investment. For low-grade issues, defaults are less rare. For example, almost half of the bonds that were rated CCC by Standard & Poor's at issue have defaulted within 10 years.

Of course, bonds rarely fall suddenly from grace. As time passes and the company becomes progressively more shaky, the agencies revise the bond's rating downward to reflect the increasing probability of default. Consider the case of Air Canada's senior unsecured debt. Originally rated BB by DBRS in 1997, it was downgraded to BB (low) in February 2001, in response to Air Canada's large debt load, rising costs, and increased competition. With the terrorist attacks of September 11, 2001, and the worsening economic slowdown, DBRS dropped the rating to B in September 2001. As Air Canada's financial situation worsened, it filed for bankruptcy protection in April 2003, prompting DBRS to lower the rating to C. By April 2004, the debt rating was cut to D. Air Canada negotiated a debt-for-equity swap with its debtholders, who agreed to exchange their debt for shares worth about one-tenth of the amount owed. In September 2004, the company emerged from bankruptcy protection with a substantially reduced debt load, carrying a B rating and a new name, ACE Aviation Holdings.

As you would expect, the yield on corporate bonds varies with the bond rating. Figure 5.9 presents the yields to maturity on default-free, long-term Government of Canada bonds, AAA and AA-rated corporate bonds, A-rated bonds, and BBB-rated bonds on December 31 since 1976. You can see that yields on the four groups of bonds track each other closely over time. However, at any point in time, the promised yield is higher as bond safety gets lower.

FIGURE 5.9
Canadian yields on long-term bonds. Bonds with greater credit risk promise higher yields to maturity.

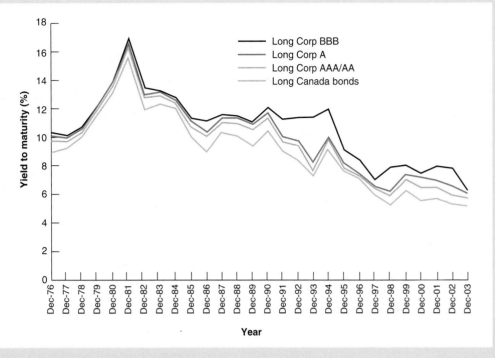

Source: PC Bond Index Team. Scotia Capital Inc.

EXAMPLE 5.7	**PROMISED VERSUS EXPECTED YIELD TO MATURITY**

Bad Bet Inc. issued bonds several years ago with a coupon rate (paid annually) of 10 percent and face value of $1,000. The bonds are due to mature in six years. However, the firm is currently in bankruptcy proceedings, the firm has ceased to pay interest, and the bonds sell for only $200. Based on *promised* cash flow, the yield to maturity on the bond is 63.9 percent. (On your calculator, set $PV = -200$, $FV = 1,000$, $PMT = 100$, $n = 6$, and compute i.) But this calculation is based on the very unlikely possibility that the firm will resume paying interest and come out of bankruptcy. Suppose that the most likely outcome is that after 3 years of litigation, during which no interest will be paid, debtholders will receive $.27 on the dollar—that is, they will receive $270 for each bond with $1,000 face value. In this case the expected return on the bond is 10.5 percent. (On your calculator, set $PV = -200$, $FV = 270$, $PMT = 0$, $n = 3$, and compute i.) When default is a real possibility, the promised yield can depart considerably from the expected return. In this example, the default premium is greater than 50 percent.

VARIATIONS IN CORPORATE BONDS

Most corporate bonds are similar to the 7.25 percent Canada bonds that we examined earlier in the chapter. In other words, they promise to make a fixed nominal coupon payment for each year until maturity, at which point they also promise to repay the face value. However, you will find that there is greater variety in the design of corporate bonds. We will return to this issue in Chapter 13, but here are a few types of corporate bonds that you may encounter.

Zero-Coupon Bonds.   Corporations sometimes issue zero-coupon bonds. In this case, investors receive $1,000 face value at the maturity date but do not receive a regular coupon payment. In other words, the bond has a coupon rate of zero. You learned how to value such bonds in Chapter 4. These bonds are issued at prices considerably below face value, and the investor's return comes from the difference between the purchase price and the payment of face value at maturity.

Stripped (or Strip) Bonds.   Even if companies don't issue zero-coupon bonds, investment dealers can create them by taking conventional bonds and selling the coupons and principal ("residuals") separately. For example, a 5-year Canada bond with a 5 percent coupon rate becomes 11 separate zero-coupon bonds. Ten of the bonds are the $25 semi-annual coupon payments and the last is the $1,000 principal payment. Figure 5.2 shows prices of actively traded strips of Ontario Government and Canada bonds. Notice how each bond has zero coupons and sells at a discount to its maturity value.

Floating-Rate Bonds.   Sometimes the coupon rate can change over time. For example, floating-rate bonds make coupon payments that are tied to some measure of current market rates. The rate might be reset once a year to the current T-bill rate plus 2 percent. So if the T-bill rate at the start of the year is 6 percent, the bond's coupon rate over the next year would be set at 8 percent. This arrangement means that the bond's coupon rate always approximates current market interest rates.

Convertible Bonds.   If you buy a convertible bond, you can choose later to exchange it for a specified number of shares of common stock. For example, a convertible bond that is issued at par value of $1,000 may be convertible into 50 shares of the firm's stock. Because convertible bonds offer the opportunity to participate in any price appreciation of the company's stock, investors will accept lower interest rates on convertible bonds.

Callable Bonds.   Suppose that a company issues a 6.5 percent, 30-year bond at a price of $1,000. Five years later interest rates have fallen to 4 percent and the bond price has risen dramatically. If you were the company's treasurer, wouldn't you like to be able to retire the bond issue and issue some new bonds at the lower interest rate? Well, with some bonds, known as *callable bonds,* the company does have the option to buy them back early for the *call price.* Of course, holders of callable bonds will know that the company will be tempted to buy back the bond if interest rates fall and therefore the price of the bond will not rise above the call price.

Figure 5.10 shows the risk of a call to the bondholder. The blue line is the value of a 30-year, 6.5 percent coupon "straight," that is, non-callable bond; the gold line is the value of a bond with

FIGURE 5.10
Prices of callable versus straight debt. When interest rates fall, bond prices rise. But the price of the callable bond (gold line) is limited by the call price.

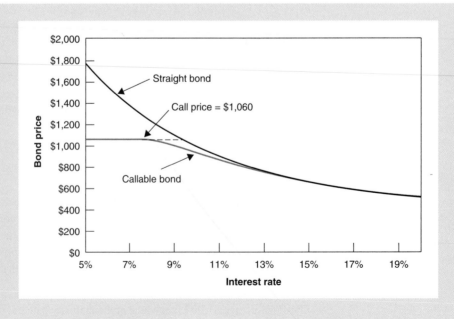

the same coupon rate and maturity, but callable at $1,060 (i.e., 106 percent of face value). At very high interest rates, the risk of call is negligible, and the values of the bonds are nearly identical. As rates fall, the non-callable bond steadily increases in value, but because call becomes more likely in this region, the value of the callable bond is limited by its call price.

Recognizing this pattern, bond investors calculate yield to call rather than yield to maturity for bonds at high risk of being called. The yield to call is calculated like yield to maturity with time until call replacing time until maturity, and the call price replacing face value.

EXAMPLE 5.8   YIELD TO CALL

Suppose a 8.5% coupon, 30-year maturity bond (making annual coupon payments) sells for $1,040 and is callable in 10 years at a call price of $1,060. We would calculate its yield to maturity and yield to call on our calculators as follows:

	Calculator Input	Yield to Call	Yield to Maturity
Coupon payment	PMT	85	85
Number of periods	n	10	30
Final payment	FV	1,060	1,000
Price	PV	–1,040	–1,040
ANSWER:	Compute i	8.30%	8.14%

In Excel, we could solve for these rates as: yield to call =YIELD(DATE(2000,1,1), DATE(2010,1,1),.085,104,106,1) and yield to maturity =YIELD(DATE(2000,1,1), DATE(2030,1,1),.085,104,100,1). The yield to call is higher because the firm has to pay a premium to call the bonds.

Check Point 5.9   Find the yield to call and yield to maturity of the bond in Example 5.8 if it pays its coupons semi-annually.

Most callable Canadian corporate bonds have a special call feature known as the Canada call or the Doomsday call. With a Canada call, the call price is not set in advance but is determined at the time of the call. The call price is calculated to generate a specific yield, with par value as the minimum price. A typical Canada call provision states that the call price, referred to as the Canada yield price, must offer an equivalent yield of a Government of Canada bond of the same maturity plus an additional prestated amount, for default risk.

With the Canada call, the call price increases as interest rates fall, making it less attractive to call the bond. By contrast, the call price for a conventional call provision is fixed and if interest rates fall enough, it becomes profitable for the issuer to call the bond. You won't be surprised to learn that bonds with a Canada call are rarely called.

EXAMPLE 5.9   CALCULATING THE CANADA YIELD PRICE

A Loblaw 6.5% bond due January 19, 2011, is callable (redeemable) at any time on minimum 30 and maximum 60 days notice at the greater of Canada Yield Price (Canada Yield plus 0.25%) and par. The Canada Yield is the yield to maturity for a Government of Canada bond with the same maturity date as the Loblaw bond. To determine the call price, the remaining cash flows of the Loblaw bond are discounted at the Canada yield plus .25 percent.

What was the call price on July 19, 2004? The bond was selling for $1,092 and had a yield to maturity of 4.82 percent. Equivalent-maturity Canada bonds were yielding 4.37 percent. The call price, set using a yield to maturity of .0437 + .0025, or 4.62 percent, was $1,104.5. (The Loblaw bond is 6.5 years to maturity, with 13 coupon payments of $32.50 remaining to be paid. On your calculator, set $FV = 1,000$, $PMT = 65/2 = 32.5$, $n = 13$, $i = 4.62/2 = 2.31$, and compute PV.) Even though the Loblaw bond's coupon rate is greater than its current yield to maturity, the bond won't be called. The call price of $1,104.5 is greater than its current market price. If interest rates fall further, to say 3 percent, the call price rises higher, to $1,205.

5.4   SUMMARY

1. What are the differences between the bond's coupon rate, current yield, and yield to maturity?

A bond is a long-term debt of a government or corporation. When you own a bond, you receive a fixed interest payment each year until the bond matures. This payment is known as the coupon. The **coupon rate** is the annual coupon payment expressed as a fraction of the bond's **face value**. At maturity the bond's **face value** is repaid. In Canada most bonds have a face value of $1,000. The **current yield** is the annual coupon payment expressed as a fraction of the bond's price. The **yield to maturity** measures the average rate of return to an investor who purchases the bond and holds it until maturity, accounting for coupon income as well as the difference between purchase price and face value.

2. How can one find the market price of a bond given its yield to maturity and find a bond's yield given its price? Why do prices and yields vary inversely?

Bonds are valued by discounting the coupon payments and the final repayment by the yield to maturity on comparable bonds. The bond payments discounted at the bond's yield to maturity equal the bond price. You may also start with the bond price and ask what interest rate the bond offers. This interest rate that equates the present value of bond payments to the bond price is the yield to maturity. Because present values are lower when discount rates are higher, price and yield to maturity vary inversely.

3. Why do interest rates change over time?

The general level of interest rates varies over time with changes in the real rate of interest and expected inflation.

The **Fisher effect** says that the nominal interest rate equals the real rate of interest plus expected inflation.

4. What determines the difference between yields on long-term and short-term bonds?

The **yield curve** is a snapshot of yields on bonds of different maturities at a point in time. Typically, it is upward sloping but can also be downward sloping or humped. According to the *expectations theory*, bonds are priced so that the expected return over any period is independent of the maturity of the bonds held. Consequently, a higher yield on a longer-term bond implies that investors expect future short-term interest rates to rise. However, the expectations theory ignores **interest rate risk**, which arises from the fact that bond prices rise when market interests fall, and fall when market rates rise. Long-term bonds exhibit greater interest rate risk than short-term bonds. According to the *liquidity-preference theory*, long-term bonds earn extra return to compensate for interest rate risk, resulting in higher yields on long-term bonds and a tendency for the yield curve to be upward sloping.

5. Why do investors pay attention to bond ratings and demand a higher interest rate for bonds with low ratings?

Investors demand higher promised yields if there is a high probability that the borrower will run into trouble and default. **Credit risk** implies that the promised yield to maturity on the bond is higher than the expected yield. The additional yield investors require for bearing credit risk is called the **default premium**. Bond ratings measure the bond's credit risk.

Related Web Links

www.finpipe.com The Financial Pipeline is an Internet site dedicated to financial education; see the page on bonds, ignore the out-of-date Canadian bond market commentary

www.investopedia.com/university.advancedbond Good explanation of term structure and duration

www.bondmarkets.com/publications Various bond books, many free as pdf

www.dbrs.com Web site for Dominion Bond Rating Service

www.standardpoor.com Standard & Poor's provides information on how it rates securities

www.bankofcanada.ca For yield-to-maturity data

www.bondsonline.com Good U.S. bond data

Key Terms

bond	131	rate of return	139	default (or credit) risk	149
coupon	131	yield curve or term structure		default premium or	
face value	131	of interest rates	144	credit spread	150
coupon rate	131	real return bond	145	investment grade	150
current yield	136	Fisher effect	146	junk bond	150
yield to maturity	137	interest rate risk	148		

Questions and Problems

*Answers in Appendix B

BASIC

*1. **Bond Yields.** A 30-year Canada bond is issued with par value of $1,000, paying interest of $60 per year. If market yields increase shortly after the bond is issued, what happens to the bond's
   a. coupon rate
   b. price
   c. yield to maturity
   d. current yield

2. **Bond Yields.** If a bond with par value of $1,000 and a coupon rate of 8 percent is selling at a price of $970, is the bond's yield to maturity more or less than 8 percent? What about the current yield?

*3. **Bond Yields.** A bond with par value $1,000 has a current yield of 7.5 percent and a coupon rate of 8 percent. What is the bond's price if it pays interest annually?

*4. **Bond Pricing.** A 6-year Circular File bond pays interest of $80 annually and sells for $950. What is its coupon rate, current yield, and yield to maturity?

5. **Bond Pricing.** If Circular File (see previous problem) wants to issue a new six-year bond at face value, what coupon rate must the bond offer?

6. **Bond Yields.** A BCE bond has 10 years until maturity and a coupon rate of 8 percent payable annually, and sells for $1,050.
   a. What is the current yield on the bond?
   b. What is the yield to maturity?

7. **Coupon Rate.** General Matter's outstanding bond issue has a coupon rate of 10 percent and a current yield of 9.6 percent, and it sells at a yield to maturity of 9.25 percent. The firm wishes to issue additional bonds to the public at par value. What coupon rate must the new bonds offer in order to sell at par?

8. **Financial Pages.** Turn back to Figure 5.2. What is the current bid yield of the Canada 5.5 percent, June 1, 2010 maturity? What price would you have had to pay to buy the bond that day?

*9. **Rate of Return.** You bought a 10-year, 5 percent coupon bond for $1,000 and sold it 1 year later for $1,100. What is the rate of return on your investment if the bond pays interest annually?

*10. **After-Tax Rate of Return.** Refer to problem 9. If your marginal tax rate is 30 percent, what is the after-tax rate of return on your bond investment?

PRACTICE

*11. **Bond Prices and Returns.** One bond has a coupon rate of 8 percent, another a coupon rate of 12 percent. Both bonds have 10-year maturities and sell at a yield to maturity of 10 percent. If their yields to maturity next year are still 10 percent, what is the rate of return on each bond? Does the higher coupon bond give a higher rate of return? Assume the bonds pay annual interest.

EXCEL

*12. **Bond Returns.**
   a. If the BCE bond in problem 6 has a yield to maturity of 8 percent 1 year from now, what will its price be?
   b. What will be your rate of return if you buy it today and sell it in one year?
   c. If the inflation rate during the year is 3 percent, what is the real rate of return on the bond?

EXCEL

13. **Bond Pricing.** A Stelco bond carries a coupon rate of 8 percent, payable semi-annually, has 9 years until maturity, and sells at a yield to maturity of 9 percent.
   a. What interest payments do bondholders receive each year?
  *b. At what price does the bond sell?
   c. What will happen to the bond price if the yield to maturity falls to 7 percent?

14. **Bond Pricing.** A 30-year maturity bond with $1,000 face value makes annual coupon payments and has a coupon rate of 8 percent. What is the bond's yield to maturity if the bond is selling for
   a. $900
   b. $1,000
  *c. $1,100

15. **Bond Pricing.** Repeat the previous problem if the bond makes semi-annual coupon payments.

EXCEL

16. **Bond Pricing.** Fill in the table below for the following zero-coupon bonds. The face value of each bond is $1,000.

Price	Maturity (Years)	Yield to Maturity
$300	30	—
$300	—	8%
—	10	10%

17. **Consol Bonds.** Perpetual Life Corp. has issued consol bonds with coupon payments of $60. (Consols pay interest forever and never mature. They are perpetuities.) If the required rate of return on these bonds at the time they were issued was 6 percent, at what price were they sold to the public? If the required return today is 10 percent, at what price do the consols sell?

EXCEL

*18. **Bond Pricing.** Sure Tea Co. has issued 9 percent annual coupon bonds, which are now selling at a yield to maturity of 10 percent and current yield of 9.8375 percent. What is the remaining maturity of these bonds?

19. **Bond Pricing.** Large Industries bonds sell for $1,065.95. The bond life is 9 years, and the yield to maturity is 7 percent. What must be the coupon rate on the bonds? Coupons are paid semi-annually.

*20. **Bond Prices and Yields.**
   a. Several years ago, Castles in the Sand, Inc., issued bonds at face value at a yield to maturity of 8 percent. Now, with 8 years left until the maturity of the bonds, the company has run into hard times, and the yield to maturity on the bonds has increased to 14 percent. What has happened to the price of the bond? Coupons are paid semi-annually.

b.   Suppose that investors believe that Castles can make good on the promised coupon payments, but that the company will go bankrupt when the bond matures and the principal comes due. The expectation is that investors will receive only 80 percent of face value at maturity. If they buy the bond today, what yield to maturity do they expect to receive?

*21.   **Bond Returns.** You buy an 8 percent coupon, paid annually, 10-year maturity bond for $980. A year later, the bond price is $1,050.

a.   What is the yield to maturity on the bond today? What is it in one year?

b.   What is your rate of return over the year?

EXCEL

22.   **Bond Returns.** You buy an 8 percent coupon, 10-year maturity bond when its yield to maturity is 9 percent. A year later, the yield to maturity is 10 percent. What is your rate of return over the year?

23.   **Rate of Return.** A 2-year maturity bond with $1,000 face value makes annual coupon payments of $80 and is selling at face value. What will be the rate of return on the bond if its yield to maturity at the end of the year is

a.   6 percent

b.   8 percent

c.   10 percent

24.   **Rate of Return.** A bond that pays coupons annually is issued with a coupon rate of 4 percent, maturity of 30 years, and a yield to maturity of 8 percent. What rate of return will be earned by an investor who purchases the bond and holds it for 1 year if the bond's yield to maturity at the end of the year is 9 percent?

*25.   **Rate of Return.** Five years ago you purchased an 8 percent coupon bond for $975. Today you sold the bond for $1,000. What is your rate of return on the bond in each of the following situations:

a.   All coupons were immediately spent when received.

b.   All coupons were reinvested in your bank account, which pays 1 percent interest until the bond is sold.

c.   All coupons were reinvested at 8.64 percent until the bond is sold.

*26.   **Rate of Return.** Looking back at the previous question, use the yield-to-maturity method to compute the rate of return on your bond investment.

27.   **Bond Pricing.** Are the following statements true or false? Provide simple examples to support your assessment.

a.   If interest rates rise, bond prices rise.

b.   If the bond's yield to maturity is greater than its coupon rate, the price is greater than the bond's face value.

c.   High-coupon bonds of a given maturity sell for lower prices than otherwise identical low-coupon bonds.

d.   If interest rates change, the price of a high-coupon bond changes proportionately more than the price of a low-coupon bond of the same maturity and default risk.

e.   A investor who owns a 10 percent, 5-year Canada bond is wealthier if interest rates rise from 4 percent to 5 percent.

28.   **Internet.** Use historical yield-to-maturity data from the Bank of Canada Web site at **www.bankofcanada.ca** to look at bonds of different types. Go to **www.bankofcanada.ca/en/rates/bond-look.htm** and follow the instructions. Download 60 months of yield-to-maturity data for long-term corporate bonds (series V122518), long-term provincial bonds (V122517), and long-term Canada bonds (series V122544), and put the data into a spreadsheet. Calculate the average spreads of the corporate and provincial bonds over the Canada bonds. Graph the yields to maturity over time. What do you see? Does it make sense?

29. **Yield Curve.** The following table shows the prices of strips of Canada bonds in December 2004. Each strip makes a single payment of $100 at maturity.

Maturity	Price ($)
June 2006	94.81
June 2008	86.58
June 2012	69.56
June 2017	52.61
June 2022	38.92

   a. Calculate the annually compounded, yield to maturity (spot interest rate) for each bond.

   b. Is the term structure upward or downward sloping?

30. **Bond Pricing.** Diamond Corporation is planning a bond issue with an escalating coupon rate. The annual coupon rate will be 4 percent for the first 3 years, 5 percent for the subsequent 3 years, and 6 percent for the final 3 years. If bonds of this risk are yielding 5 percent, estimate the bond's current price.

31. **Interest Rate Risk.** Consider three bonds with 8 percent coupon rates, all selling at face value. The short-term bond has a maturity of 4 years, the intermediate-term bond has maturity of 8 years, and the long-term bond has maturity of 30 years.

   a. What will happen to the price of each bond if their yields increase to 9 percent?

   b. What will happen to the price of each bond if their yields decrease to 7 percent?

   c. What do you conclude about the relationship between time to maturity and the sensitivity of bond prices to interest rates?

*32. **Bond Risk.** A bond's credit rating provides a guide to its risk. Long-term bonds rated AA currently offer yields to maturity of 8.5 percent EAR. A-rated bonds sell at yields of 8.8 percent EAR. If a 10-year bond with a coupon rate of 8 percent, paid semi-annually, is downgraded by DBRS from AA to A rating, calculate the likely effect on the bond price.

33. **Internet.** It is difficult to get on-line yield-to-maturity and credit spread data for Canadian corporate bonds with different debt ratings. However, U.S. data is available. Go to **www.bondsonline.com/asp/corp/spreadbank.html**. You will see a table showing current extra yields to maturity (credit spreads) of corporate bonds of different risk over comparable-term U.S. government bonds. Spreads are provided for different industries. Select "Industrials" (at the bottom of the page). Using the data in the table, estimate the required rate of return on a 10-year debt issue by a U.S. company with A1 or A-rated debt. What if its debt had a B1 or B rating? The current yield to maturity on U.S. government bonds is at **www.bondsonline.com/asp/news/composites.html**.

34. **Internet.** From either *The Globe and Mail* or the *National Post*, find five different corporate bonds. Look up their ratings at either **www.dbrs.com** or **www.standardpoor.com**. Compare the bonds' yields to maturity to comparable-term Government of Canada bonds. Do the yields make sense relative to their bond ratings?

35. **Real Rate of Interest.** You have been told that the yield to maturity on 3-month Treasury bills is 4 percent and the current inflation rate is 2 percent. Estimate the real rate of interest.

36. **Real Returns.** Suppose that you buy a 1-year maturity bond for $1,000 that will pay you $1,000 plus a coupon payment of $60 at the end of the year. What real rate of return will you earn if the inflation rate is

   *a. 2 percent

   b. 4 percent

   c. 6 percent

   d. 8 percent

EXCEL

37. **Real Returns.** Now suppose that the bond in the previous problem is a real return bond with a coupon rate of 4 percent. What will the cash flow provided by the bond be for each of the four inflation rates? What will be the real and nominal rates of return on the bond in each scenario?

38. **Real Returns.** Now suppose the real return bond in the previous problem is a two-year maturity bond. What will be the bondholder's cash flows in each year in each of the inflation scenarios?

39. **Yield to Call.** A 6.25 percent 15-year bond, paying interest annually, can be called at 110 percent of par value in 10 years. The bond currently sells for $1,048.
    a. What is the yield to maturity?
    b. What is the yield to call?

40. **Canada Call Price.** A 7 percent corporate bond with 6 years to maturity has a Canada call. The bond's yield to maturity is 4.8 percent. The call price must offer an equivalent yield to a Canada bond plus .35 percent. Currently, six-year Government of Canada bonds are yielding 4 percent. Assume coupons are paid annually.
    a. What is the current bond price?
    b. What is the current call price?

41. **Canada Call.** When ABC Company originally issued its callable 5.5 percent, 10-year bond, it was rated AA and priced to sell at par. The bond is callable at the price that offers an equivalent yield to a Canada bond plus .15 percent. At that time, the credit spread over 10-year Canada bonds was .25 percent. The bond pays interest annually.
    a. What was the call price at issue?

    Now, 5 years later, the bond rating agencies have raised the bond rating to AAA and the bond's yield to maturity is 5 percent. Equivalent-maturity Canada bonds are yielding 4.9 percent.

    b. What is the current call price?
    c. Would ABC Company consider calling the bond now?

CHALLENGE

42. **Interest Rate Risk.** Suppose interest rates increase from 8 percent to 9 percent. Which bond will suffer the greater percentage decline in price: a 30-year bond paying annual coupons of 8 percent, or a 30-year zero coupon bond? Can you explain intuitively why the zero exhibits greater interest rate risk even though it has the same maturity as the coupon bond?

43. **After-Tax Rate of Return.** Using the information in problem 25, calculate your after-tax rate of return on your bond investment assuming that your marginal tax rate is 35 percent. You pay tax on the interest when it is received.

44. **Bond Prices and Yields.** Big Time Company is planning to raise $15 million by selling 10-year bonds. The bond rating agency has advised the company that the bonds will have an A rating. Currently, the difference between the yield to maturity of A-rated corporate bonds over similar-maturity Government of Canada bonds is 150 basis points (1 basis point equals .01 percentage points). If 10-year Canada bonds are currently priced to yield 5 percent, what coupon rate should Big Time select if the new issue is to sell at par value.

STANDARD &POOR'S

45. **Standard & Poor's.** Go to Market Insight (**www.mcgrawhill.ca/edumarketinsight**) and find the bond rating of BCE (BCE) and Agrium (AGU) in the "Financial Highlights" section. Which has the higher bond rating (i.e., S&P Issuer Credit Rating)? What are the main business activities of each of these companies? Compare their ability to pay their interest obligations by calculating the ratio of EBIT to interest payments. The higher this "times interest earned" ratio, the greater a company's ability to make its interest payments. Also,

calculate both companies' indebtedness, as measured by the ratio of debt to equity. The higher the times interest earned and the lower the indebtedness, the more likely a company will be able to make its debt payments. Are the debt ratings consistent with the calculated ratios?

Solutions to Check Points

5.1 a. The bid price, your selling price, is 105.6 percent of face value, or $1,056.
     b. The ask price, your purchase price, is $105.66 percent of face value, or $1,056.6.
     c. The dealer sets a spread to cover her costs of holding inventory of bonds. She buys the bond from you at a lower price (the bid) than she is willing to sell to you (the ask).
     d. The annual coupon is 5.5 percent of face value, or $55, paid in two semi-annual instalments.
     e. The yield to maturity, based on the ask price, is 4.41 percent.

5.2 The coupon is 9 percent of $1,000, or $90, a year. First value the six-year annuity of coupons:

$$PV \text{ (coupon)} = \$90 \times \text{(6-year annuity factor)}$$

$$= \$90 \times \left[\frac{1}{.12} - \frac{1}{.12(1.12)^6} \right]$$

$$= \$90 \times 4.11 = \$370.03$$

Then value the final payment and add up:

$$PV \text{ (face value)} = \frac{\$1,000}{(1.12)^6} = \$506.63$$

$$PV \text{ (bond)} = \$370.03 + \$506.63 = \$876.66$$

5.3 The yield to maturity assuming annual coupons is about 8 percent, because the present value of the bond's cash returns is $1,199 when discounted at 8 percent:

$$PV \text{ (bond)} = PV \text{ (coupons)} + PV \text{ (face value)}$$

$$= \text{(coupon} \times \text{annuity factor)} + \text{(face value} \times \text{discount factor)}$$

$$= \$140 \times \left[\frac{1}{.08} - \frac{1}{.08(1.08)^4} \right] + \$1,000 \times \frac{1}{1.08^4}$$

$$= \$463.70 + \$735.03 = \$1,199$$

To obtain a more precise solution on your calculator, these would be your inputs:

	Annual Payments	Semi-Annual Payments
n	4	8
PV	−1,200	−1,200
FV	1,000	1,000
PMT	140	70

Compute i to find yield to maturity (annual payments) = 7.97%. Yield to maturity (semi-annual payments) = 4.026% per 6 months, which would be reported in the financial press as 8.05% annual yield.

5.4 The 7.25 percent coupon bond with maturity in 2007 starts with 3 years left until maturity and sells for $1,102.06. At the end of the year, the bond has only 2 years to maturity and investors demand an interest rate of 5 percent. Therefore, the value of the bond becomes

$$PV \text{ (bond) at } 5\% = \frac{\$72.5}{(1.05)} + \frac{\$1,072.5}{(1.05)^2} = \$1,041.84$$

You invested $1,102.06. At the end of the year you receive a coupon payment of $72.5 and have a bond worth $1,041.84. Your rate of return is therefore

$$\text{Rate of return} = \frac{\$72.5 + (\$1,041.84 - \$1,102.06)}{\$1,102.06} = .0111, \text{ or } 1.11\%$$

The yield to maturity at the start of the year was 3.6 percent. However, because interest rates rose during the year, the bond price fell and the rate of return was below the yield to maturity.

5.5   By the end of this year, the bond will have only one year left until maturity. It will make only one more payment of coupon plus face value, so its price will be $1,072.5/1.036 = $1,035.23. The rate of return is therefore

$$\frac{\$72.5 + (\$1,035.23 - \$1,069.24)}{\$1,069.24} = .036, \text{ or } 3.6\%$$

5.6   The coupon payment is .08 × $1,000, or $80, before tax. The tax on the coupon interest is .4 × $80, or $32. A capital gain of $1,215 − $1,200 = $15 is made. The capital gains tax is .5 × .4 × $15, or $3. The before-tax rate of return is

$$\frac{\$80 + (\$1,215 - \$1,200)}{\$1,200} = .0792, \text{ or } 7.92\%$$

The after-tax rate of return is

$$\frac{\$80 - \$32 + (\$1,215 - \$1,200) - \$3}{\$1,200} = .05 \text{ or } 5.0\%$$

5.7   The general level of (nominal) interest rates in July 1990 was much higher than in 2004. This suggests that investors were expecting much higher inflation in 1990 than in 2004. The inflation rate in 1990 was about 5 percent and was about 2 percent in 2004.

5.8   At an interest rate of 3.6 percent, the 3-year bond sells for $1,102.06. If the interest rate jumps to 10 percent, the bond price falls to $931.61, a decline of 15.5 percent. The 30-year bond sells for $1,662.98 when the interest rate is 3.6 percent, but its price falls to $740.76 at an interest rate of 10 percent, a much larger percentage decline of 55.5 percent.

5.9   The semi-annual coupon is $42.50. The number of payments will be 20 if the bond is called after 10 years, or 60 if it is held until maturity. Therefore, use these inputs:

	Yield to Call	Yield to Maturity
Coupon payment (*PMT*)	42.50	42.50
Number of periods (*n*)	20	60
Final payment (*FV*)	1,060	1,000
Price (*PV*)	−1,040	−1,040

The yield to call is 4.15% semi-annual, or 8.30% annualized. The yield to maturity is 4.07% semi-annual, or 8.14% annualized. These yields are actually slightly higher than those calculated by using annual payments but are the same to two decimal places.

Appendix 5.B

A MORE DETAILED LOOK AT THE YIELD CURVE

In the summer of 2004 you could invest in a one-year Government of Canada stripped bond yielding about 2.5 percent.[9] A two-year Canada strip had a yield of about 3.4 percent. These are *spot rates*, interest rates available today on investments today. If you invested in the 1-year strip, by the summer of 2005, every dollar invested would have grown to $1 \times (1.025) = \$1.025$. If instead you invested in the two-year strip, by the end of two years, the summer of 2006, every dollar invested would grow to $1 \times (1.034)^2 = \$1.069156$. By keeping your money invested for the extra year, your savings grow from \$1.025 to \$1.069156, an increase of 4.3 percent ($=1.069156/1.025 - 1$). This extra 4.3 percent that you earn by investing for two years, rather than one, is called the *forward interest rate*.

The forward interest rate is an interest rate calculated using spot rates. Let r_1 be the current one-year spot rate and r_2 be the current two-year spot rate. Invest for one year, each dollar grows to $(1 + r_1)$. Invest for two years in the two-year bond, your investment grows to $(1 + r_2)^2$. The extra rate of return that you earn in the second year is the forward rate, f_2. In our example,

$$f_2 = \frac{(1 + r_2)^2}{(1 + r_1)} - 1 = \frac{(1.069156)}{1.025} - 1 = .043, \text{ or } 4.3\% \tag{5A.1}$$

Twist this equation around and you get an expression for the two-year spot rate, r_2, in terms of the one-year spot rate, r_1, and the forward rate, f_2:

$$(1 + r_2)^2 = (1 + r_1) \times (1 + f_2) \tag{5A.2}$$

In other words, you can think of the two-year investment as earning the one-year spot rate for the first year and the extra return, or forward rate, for the second year.

Forward rates can be calculated for other years, provided that you have the appropriate spot rates. For example, if the 5-year spot rate, r_5, is 6% and the 6-year spot rate, r_6, is 6.5 percent, the forward rate for the 6th year, f_6, must satisfy this equation:

$$(1 + r_6)^6 = (1 + r_5)^5 \times (1 + f_6) \tag{5A.3}$$

In other words, the Year 6 forward rate is the extra return for investing for the 6th year. In this case, $f_6 = (1.065)^6/(1.06)^5 - 1$, or 9 percent. Generally, the forward rate for the nth year, f_n, must satisfy the following equation:

$$(1 + r_n)^n = (1 + r_{n-1})^{n-1} \times (1 + f_n) \tag{5A.4}$$

The Expectations Theory

How attractive is the extra 4.3 percent return for investing for two years rather than one in the summer of 2004? It depends on how you expect interest rates to change over the coming year. Suppose, for example, you expected interest rates to rise, so that by the summer of 2005 the one-year rate would be 6 percent. In that case, rather than investing in a two-year bond and earning the extra 4.3 percent, you would do better if you invested in the one-year bond and, when that matured, reinvested the money for a further year at 6 percent. If all investors thought like you, no one would want to buy the two-year bond. Its price would fall. The price would continue to fall until the extra return on the two-year bond equaled the expected future one-year rate. We use the symbol $_1r_2$ to represent the expected future one-year spot rate on a loan maturing at the end of Year 2.

According the expectations theory, in equilibrium the forward rate, f_2, equals the expected one-year spot rate, $_1r_2$. The expectations theory implies that the *only* reason for an upward-sloping yield curve is that investors expect short-term interest rates to rise. Likewise, the *only* reason for a downward-sloping yield curve is that investors expect short-term rates to fall.

If the expectations theory is correct, you can use the current spot rates to calculate investors' expected future spot rates. For example, suppose the current one-year spot rate is 3 percent and the current two-year spot rate is 6 percent. What is the expected one-year spot rate for Year 2? According to the expectations theory,

$$_1r_2 = f_2 = \frac{(1 + r_2)^2}{(1 + r_1)} - 1 = \frac{(1.06)^2}{1.03} - 1 = .0909, \text{ or } 9.09\%$$

---

[9] A stripped bond, or strip, is a bond that makes only one payment at maturity. Stripped bonds are also called zero-coupon bonds.

If short-term rates are much lower than long-term rates, it may be tempting to borrow short term. However, the expectations theory tells us to not be fooled. Long-term rates are connected to short-term rates. If long-term rates are higher, it must be the case that the market is expecting interest rates to rise.

The Liquidity-Preference Theory

The expectations theory implies that investing in a series of one-year bonds earns the same expected return as investing in long-term bonds. However, as we pointed out in Section 5.3, investing in long-term bonds is riskier than short-term bonds because long-term bond prices are more variable than short-term bond prices. To compensate for the extra risk of lending long, investors demand a liquidity risk premium. With this liquidity premium added to the bond yield, it is no longer the case that the forward rate must equal the expected future spot rate. In fact, the forward rate must be higher than the expected future spot rate to compensate investors for the liquidity risk.

Together, the expectations and liquidity-preference theories can partially explain the shape of yield curves. The yield on a longer-term bond reflects both expectations of future short-term interest rates and the liquidity risk premium. Other theories exist but are beyond the scope of this book.

Questions and Problems

5A.1 Calculating Forward Rates. The following are the yields to maturity on Canada strip bonds with various years to maturity.

Years to Maturity	Yield to Maturity (%)
1	5.0
2	5.4
3	5.7
4	5.9
5	6.0

a. Calculate the forward rate for each period.

b. Calculate the price today of the following Canada bonds:
   i. 5 percent, 2-year bond.
  ii. 5 percent, 5-year bond.
  iii. 10 percent, 5-year bond.

c. Calculate the yields to maturity on each of the bonds in part (b).

d. Why is the yield to maturity on the 10 percent bond less than the yield on 5 percent, 5-year bond?

5A.2 Term Structure Theories. Refer back to question 5A.1.

a. If the expectations theory of the term structure is correct, what do the forward rates calculated in (a) tell you about expected future short-term interest rates?

b. If the liquidity-preference theory is added, what can you conclude about expected future short-term rates?

5A.3 Calculating Forward Rates. Suppose in June 2007, the Canada June 2008 strip was selling for $970.87, the Canada June 2009 strip was selling for $924.56, and the Canada June 2010 strip was selling for $863.84.

a. Calculate the yield to maturity for each bond.

b. Calculate annually compounded, one-year forward rate of interest at June 2008, June 2009, and June 2010.

c. Using the available information, estimate the June 2007 price of a 5 percent, Canada bond maturing June 2010. Explain your assumptions.

5A.4 Understanding the Yield Curve. Assume that the term structure is upward sloping. How would you respond to the following statement? "Given the current yield curve, a company should borrow short term rather than long term. It will be cheaper."

VALUING STOCKS

Instead of borrowing cash to pay for its investments, a firm can sell new shares of common stock to investors. Whereas bond issues commit the firm to make a series of specified interest payments to the lenders, stock issues are more like taking on new partners. The shareholders all share in the fortunes of the firm according to the number of shares they hold. In this chapter, we will take a first look at stocks, the stock market, and principles of stock valuation.

We start by looking at how stocks are bought and sold. Then we look at what determines stock prices and how stock valuation formulas can be used to infer the rate of return that investors are expecting. We will see how the firm's investment opportunities are reflected in the stock price and why stock market analysts focus so much attention on the price earnings, or P/E ratio, of the company.

Why should you care how stocks are valued? After all, if you want to know the value of a firm's stock, you can look up the stock price in a business newspaper or with its on-line services, such as *The Globe and Mail's* **www.globeandmail.com** or other on-line service such as **ca.finance. yahoo.com**. But you need to know what determines prices for at least two reasons. First, you may wish to check that any shares that you own are fairly priced to gauge your beliefs against the rest of the market. Second, corporations need to have some understanding of how the market values firms in order to make decisions about good capital budgeting. A project is attractive if it increases shareholder wealth. But you can't judge that unless you know how shares are valued.

There may be a third reason you would like to know how stocks are valued. You may be hoping that the knowledge will allow you to make a killing in the stock market. It's a pleasant thought, but we will see that even professional investors find it difficult to outsmart the competition and earn consistently superior returns.

After studying this chapter you should be able to
- Understand the stock trading reports in the financial pages of newspapers.
- Calculate the present value of a stock given forecasts of future dividends and future stock price.
- Use stock valuation formulas to infer the expected rate of return on a common stock.
- Interpret price-earnings ratios.
- Understand what professionals mean when they say that there are no free lunches on Wall Street or Bay Street.

6.1

common stock Ownership shares in a publicly held corporation.

STOCKS AND THE STOCK MARKET

A shareholder of the **common stock** of a firm, as part-owner of a firm, is entitled to the firm's residual cash flow, the remaining cash flow after all other suppliers, lenders, and the government have been paid. Common shareholders are also entitled to elect the board of directors and to cast one vote per share owned at shareholders' meetings. Some firms in Canada, the United States, and many European countries also issue shares that are entitled to the residual cash flow, but do not have full voting rights. For example, Canadian Tire has two classes of equity, Class A non-voting shares and common shares. Although the Class A shares do not usually vote at shareholders' meetings, they do elect three members of the board of directors.[1] The common shareholders have one vote per share. There were 77.7 million Class A shares outstanding on January 1, 2005, but only 3.4 million common shares. The Class A shares are entitled to $.01 of dividends each year before the common shares are paid the same amount. However, both classes share equally in any further dividends paid. Recently both shares have received the same dividends of $.58 per share.

Firms issue shares of common stock to the public when they need to raise money.[2] They typically engage investment dealers such as RBC Capital Markets or BMO Nesbitt Burns to help them market these shares. Sales of new stock by the firm are said to occur in the **primary market**. There are two types of primary market issues. In an **initial public offering**, or **IPO**, a company that has been privately owned sells stock to the public for the first time. Some IPOs have proved very popular with investors. For example, a star performer in 2000 was 724 Solutions. Its shares were sold to investors at $37.31 each, and by the end of the first day, they had reached $103.50, a gain of over 277 percent. Within one month, the 724 stock price reached over $330!

Established firms that already have issued stock to the public also may decide to raise money from time to time by issuing additional shares. Sales of new shares by such firms are also primary market issues and are called *seasoned offerings*. When a firm issues new shares to the public, the previous owners share their ownership of the company with additional shareholders. In this sense, issuing new shares is like having new partners buy into the firm.

Shares of stock can be risky investments. For example, by 2003 those shares of 724 Solutions had fallen below $1. The company decided to exchange 10 old shares for 1 new share, reducing the number of shares outstanding. By June 2004, the reported share price was about $4.20 or $0.42 per original share. If you had bought a share at the end of the first day of trading in 2000, you had lost over 99 percent of your original investment. You can understand why investors would be unhappy if forced to tie the knot with a particular company forever. So large companies usually arrange for their stocks to be listed on a stock exchange, which allows investors to trade existing stocks among themselves. Exchanges are really markets for secondhand stocks, but they prefer to describe themselves as **secondary markets**.

The major stock exchange in Canada is the Toronto Stock Exchange, TSX, **www.tsx.ca**, listing shares of established, large companies. The TSX Venture Exchange, TSX-V, lists new, smaller companies, including those active in natural resource exploration, manufacturing, and technology. The TSX-V is a wholly owned subsidiary of the TSX. The common ownership of the two stock exchanges makes it easier for successful TSX-V companies to move up to the larger TSX. All Canadian markets are electronic *auction markets*. Each stock exchange maintains an electronic order book, showing offers to buy and sell, with shares sold to the highest bidder.

The two major exchanges in the United States are the New York Stock Exchange (NYSE) and the Nasdaq market. The NYSE is also an auction market. By contrast, Nasdaq operates a

primary market Market for the sale of new securities by corporations.

initial public offering (IPO) First offering of stock to the general public.

secondary market Market in which already-issued securities are traded among investors.

---

[1] Having the right to elect board members is not typical of Canadian non-voting shares. Most companies' non-voting shareholders are not entitled to vote on typical corporate matters, such as changes to the compensation of senior officers or electing members of the board. However, in special circumstances, such as the decision to wind up the company, non-voting shareholders are entitled to vote.

[2] We use the terms "shares," "stock," and "common stock" interchangeably, as we do "shareholders" and "stockholders."

dealer market, in which dealers use computer links to quote prices for shares they are willing to buy and sell. A broker must survey the prices quoted by different dealers to get a sense of where the best price can be had.

An important development in recent years has been the advent of electronic communication networks, or ECNs, which have captured ever-larger shares of trading volume. These are electronic auction houses that match investors' orders to buy and sell shares. For example, TD Waterhouse offers after-hours trading of Nasdaq and selected TSX– and NYSE–listed securities to its clients through an ECN owned by a group of U.S. brokerage firms.

Of course, there are stock exchanges in many other countries. The major exchanges in cities such as London, Tokyo, and Frankfurt trade vast numbers of shares. But there are also literally hundreds of smaller exchanges throughout the world. For example, the Eastern Caribbean Securities Market was established in 2001 and has grown from two to seven traded stocks.

READING THE STOCK MARKET LISTINGS

When you read the stock market pages in the newspaper, you are looking at the secondary market. Figure 6.1 is an excerpt from *The Globe and Mail* of TSX trading on April 14, 2005. The highlighted bar in the figure emphasizes the listing for Canadian Tire Corp. Class A non-voting shares, CTR.NV. Listed stocks are organized by company name and identified by their ticker symbol. The TSX requires the letters "NV" after the company ticker to indicate that this is a non-voting class.[3] The two numbers to the left of the company's name are the stock's highest and lowest prices in the last 12 months, $60 and $42.37, respectively. That's a reminder of just how much stock prices can fluctuate.

FIGURE 6.1
TSX stock market listings from *The Globe and Mail*, April 15, 2005

TORONTO

High (365-day)	Low	Stock	Sym	Div	High	Low	Close	Chg	Vol (100s)	Yield	P/E ratio
7.65	2.10	Call-net	FON.NV.B		7.43	7.25	7.25	-0.20	950		
7.69	2.13	Call-net	FON		7.58	7.30	7.31	-0.02	73		
4.17	2.15	Cambior	CBJ		2.49	2.29	2.36	-0.02	13397		
60.87	19.81	Cameco	CCO	0.24	48.27	45.05	45.25	-2.25	22850	0.5	27.8
15.75	9.15	CanWest	CGS.SV		14.66	14.25	14.40	-0.18	2789		14.1
15.68	9.05	CanWest	CGS.NV		14.35	14.35	14.35	-0.09	7		14.1
11.10	7.96	Canacord	CCI	0.15	10.26	10.10	10.10	-0.35	233	1.5	6.6
60.25	25.30	Cda Bread	CBY	0.24	59.70	58.32	58.32	-0.53	50	0.4	22.3
28.50	25.40	CdaLif	CL.PR.B	1.562	26.96	26.69	26.71	-0.14	26	5.8	
11.00	5.10	Cda Sthrn	CSW		7.75	7.60	7.60	-0.28	2		33.0
18.55	12.10	Cdn Gnrl	CGI	0.84	16.69	16.11	16.25	-0.37	434	5.2	3.0
12.60	6.30	Cdn Gn	CGI.WT		11.40	11.40	11.40		14		
1.14	0.43	Cdn Gold	CGH		0.78	0.72	0.72	-0.08	1060		
4.55	2.40	Cdn Hydro	KHD		4.11	4.00	4.01	-0.14	105		66.8
74.74	61.10	CIBC	CM	2.60	74.70	73.95	74.35	+0.34	4749	3.5	12.4
28.55	26.50	CIBC	CM.PR.A	1.325	27.24	27.05	27.23	+0.08	46	4.9	
27.76	25.11	CIBC	CM.PR.B	1.50	26.44	26.32	26.32	-0.10	72	5.7	
27.68	25.06	CIBC	CM.PR.C	1.50	26.40	26.24	26.35	-0.03	114	5.7	
27.25	24.75	CIBC	CM.PR.D	1.437	26.33	26.23	26.26	+0.01	1028	5.5	
27.39	24.70	CIBC	CM.PR.E	1.40	26.15	26.05	26.06	+0.11	33	5.4	
27.03	24.87	CIBC	CM.PR.G	1.35	25.75	25.40	25.54	-0.46	340	5.3	
24.15	23.81	CIBC	CM.PR.H		24.10	23.95	24.05	+0.14	170		
27.10	24.07	CIBC	CM.PR.P	1.375	25.80	25.75	25.80	+0.02	43	5.3	
78.50	50.20	CN Rail	CNR	1.00	74.15	71.51	72.60	-1.75	12556	1.4	16.0
74.75	35.08	Cdn Naturl	CNO	0.45	66.45	64.42	64.66	-0.89	16557	0.7	12.3
46.52	29.36	CP Railway	CP	0.53	44.74	42.22	43.00	-1.55	10976	1.2	16.5
25.18	14.48	CP Ships	TEU	.198	17.45	17.18	17.26	-0.06	2770	1.1	17.6
2.28	1.20	Cdn Roylt	CZZ		1.73	1.66	1.70		159		
2.85	1.32	Cdn Superi	SNG		1.96	1.92	1.94	-0.02	322		
104.00	53.05	Cdn Tire	CTR	0.58	101.00	97.00	97.50	-0.90	22	0.6	27.4
60.00	42.37	Cdn Tire	CTR.NV	0.58	59.88	58.85	59.05	-0.35	923	1.0	16.6
64.27	51.40	Cdn Util	CU.X	2.20	63.45	63.45	63.45	+1.15	6	3.5	13.0
64.92	51.42	Cdn Util	CU.NV	2.20	63.75	61.75	62.84	+0.59	147	3.5	12.9
28.25	24.90	Cdn Utili	CU.PR.B	1.50	26.35	26.15	26.15	-0.20	40	5.7	
25.90	24.20	Cdn Util	CU.PR.V	1.325	25.15	24.92	25.15	+0.25	215	5.3	

Source: *The Globe and Mail*, April 15, 2005, p. B14. Reprinted with permission from *The Globe and Mail*.

---

[3] An "MV" or "SV" following a ticker indicates that the stock is either *multiple voting* or *subordinate voting*, respectively. If it is multiple voting, each stock has more than one vote per share. If it is subordinate voting, it has a vote but there exists another class of equity with more votes per shares.

In the columns "high," "low," and "close" are prices for April 14. The Class A Non-voting shares hit a high of $59.88, a low of $58.85 and closed the day at $59.05. The stock closed $.35 lower than the previous day's close, seen in the "chg" column.

dividend Periodic cash distribution from the firm to its shareholders.

The 0.58 value to the right of CTR.NV is the annual **dividend** per share to be paid by the company.[4] In other words, investors in Canadian Tire shares currently receive an annual income of $.58 on each share. Of course, Canadian Tire is not bound to keep that level of dividend in the future. Shareholders hope earnings and dividends will rise, but it's possible that profits will slump and Canadian Tire will cut its dividend.

The dividend yield, under the heading Yield, tells you how much dividend income you receive for each $100 that you invest in the stock. For CTR.NV, the yield is $.58/$59.05 = .01, or 1.0 percent. Therefore, for every $100 invested in the stock, you would receive annual dividend income of $1.00. The dividend yield on the stock is like the current yield on a bond. Both look at the current income as a percentage of price. Both ignore prospective capital gains or losses and therefore do not correspond to total rates of return.

If you scan Figure 6.1, you will see that dividend yields vary widely across companies. Some of the shares are not receiving dividends and therefore have zero yields. While Canadian Utilities non-voting shares (CU.NV) have a relatively high yield of 3.5 percent, Canadian Gold Hunter Corporation common shares (CGH) don't receive any dividend and therefore have a zero yield. Investors are content with a low or zero current yield as long as they can look to higher future dividends and rising share prices.

price-earnings (P/E) multiple Ratio of stock price to earnings per share.

The **price-earnings (P/E) multiple** for CTR.NV is reported as 16.6. This is the ratio of the share price to earnings per share. The P/E ratio is a key tool of stock market analysts. For example, low P/E stocks are sometimes touted as good buys for investors. We will have more to say about P/E later in the chapter.

The column headed "Vol 100s" shows that the trading volume in CTR.NV was 923 round lots. Each round lot is 100 shares, so 92,300 shares traded on this day. A trade of less than 100 shares is an *odd lot*.

Canadian Tire's common shares (CTR) are also listed for trading on the TSX and closed at $97.50, substantially more than the non-voting shares. The common shares are traded less heavily—with only 2,200 shares traded on April 14, 2005; on some days no shares are traded.

preferred stock Stock that takes priority over common stock in regards to dividends.

Figure 6.1 shows prices for **preferred stock**, seen with "PR" in their ticker symbol. Preferred stock typically have fixed dividends that must be paid before the common shareholders receive any dividends. Figure 6.1 lists eight different preferred shares for CIBC. For example, the last CIBC preferred share, CM.PR.P, promises to pay an annual dividend of $1.375. Preferred shares can have many different features. We discuss these in more detail in Chapter 13.

Check Point 6.1   Explain the entries for Canadian Pacific Railways (CP) in Figure 6.1.

6.2

BOOK VALUES, LIQUIDATION VALUES, AND MARKET VALUES

Why are Canadian Tire shares selling at $59.05 per share when the stock of CIBC (CM) is priced at $74.35? And why does it cost $16.60 to buy one dollar of Canadian Tire earnings, while CIBC is selling at 12.4 times earnings? Do these numbers imply that one stock is a better buy than the other?

Finding the value of Canadian Tire stock may sound like a simple problem. Each year Canadian Tire publishes a balance sheet that shows the value of the firm's assets and liabilities. The simplified balance sheet in Table 6.1 shows that the book value of all Canadian Tire's assets—stores and warehouses, inventories of materials, cash in the bank, and so on—was

---

[4] Actually, it's the most recent quarterly dividend multiplied by 4.

TABLE 6.1
Balance sheet

BALANCE SHEET FOR CANADIAN TIRE CORP., JANUARY 1, 2005 ($ millions)			
Assets		**Liabilities and Shareholders' Equity**	
Plant, equipment, and other assets	5,218.6	Liabilities	2,967.4
		Equity	2,251.2

book value   Net worth of the firm according to the balance sheet.

$5,218.6 million on January 1, 2005. Canadian Tire's liabilities—money that it owes the banks, taxes that are due to be paid, and the like—amounted to $2,967.4 million. The difference between the value of the assets and the liabilities was $2,251.2 million. This was the **book value** of the firm's equity.[5] Book value records all the money that Canadian Tire has raised from its shareholders plus all the earnings that have been plowed back on its behalf.

Book value is a reassuringly definite number. In Canadian Tire's Annual Report, 2004 (p. 83), Deloitte & Touche, one of Canada's largest accounting firms, tells us

> In our opinion, these consolidated financial statements present fairly, in all material respects, the financial position of the company [Canadian Tire Corporation] as at January 1, 2005 and January 3, 2004 and the results of its operations and its cash flows for the years then ended in accordance with Canadian generally accepted accounting principles.

But does the stock price equal book value? Let's see. Canadian Tire has issued 81.1 million common and non-voting shares, so the balance sheet suggests that each share was worth $2,251.2/81.1 = $27.75.

But Canadian Tire Class A non-voting shares were actually selling at $56.21 on January 3, 2005, almost double their book value. This and the other cases shown in Table 6.2 tell us that investors in the stock market do not just buy and sell at book value per share.

Investors know that accountants don't even try to estimate market values. The value of the assets reported on the firm's balance sheet is equal to their original (or "historical") cost less an allowance for depreciation. But that may not be a good guide to what the firm would need to pay to buy the same assets today. For example, in 1970, United Airlines bought four new Boeing 747s for $128 million each. By the end of 1986 they had been fully depreciated and were carried in the company accounts at a residual book value of $200,000 each. But actual secondhand aircraft prices have often *appreciated*, not depreciated.[6] In fact, the planes could have been sold for upward of $20 million each.

liquidation value   Net proceeds that would be realized by selling the firm's assets and paying off its creditors.

Well, maybe stock price equals **liquidation value** per share, that is, the amount of cash per share a company could raise if it sold off all its assets in secondhand markets and paid off all its debts. Wrong again. A successful company ought to be worth more than liquidation value. That's the goal of bringing all those assets together in the first place.

TABLE 6.2
Market versus book values based on stock price for April 18, 2005

Firm	Stock Price ($)	Book Value per Share ($)	Ratio: Price/Book Value
Aliant	27.35	10.86	2.52
BCE	29.87	13.35	2.24
Biomira	2.43	0.32	7.60
Call-Net Enterprises	6.83	4.96	1.38
Canada Bread	58.90	18.75	3.14
Shaw Communications	24.15	7.63	3.17
Sun-Rype Products	11.15	3.55	3.14
Westjet Airlines	10.19	4.69	2.17

Source: Stock prices and book values from FP Analyzer, **www.FPinfomart.ca**.

---

[5] "Equity" is yet another word for stock. Thus shareholders are often referred to as "equity investors."

[6] This is partly due to inflation. Book values for Canadian and U.S. corporations are not inflation-adjusted. Also, when the accountants set up the original depreciation schedule, nobody anticipated how long these aircraft would remain in service.

The difference between a company's actual value and its book or liquidation value is often attributed to *going-concern value*, which refers to three factors:

1. *Extra earning power*. A company may have the ability to earn more than an adequate rate of return on assets. For example, if United can make better use of its planes than its competitors make of theirs, it will earn a higher rate of return. In this case the value of the planes to United will be higher than their book value or secondhand value.

2. *Intangible assets*. There are many assets that accountants don't put on the balance sheet. Some of these assets are extremely valuable to the companies owning or using them but would be difficult to sell intact to other firms. Take Biomira, a biotechnology company developing drugs for treating cancer. As you can see from Table 6.2, it sells for about 7.6 times book value. Where did all that extra value come from? Largely, it resulted from the expected success of its extensive research and development (R&D) program. Canadian accountants don't recognize R&D as an investment and don't put it on the company's balance sheet. Successful R&D and the expectation of successful R&D do show up in stock prices, however.

3. *Value of future investments*. If investors believe a company will have the opportunity to make exceedingly profitable investments in the future, they will pay more for the company's stock today. When 360networks, Inc., a provider of fibre-optic communications products and services first sold its stock to investors on April 20, 2000, the book value of shareholders' equity was about $1.58 per share; yet, investors paid $21 per share in the IPO. Within a month, the shares were trading at $330—far exceeding the book value. 360networks, Inc., was a *growth company*. In large part, the high market value reflected the value of future investments in fibre-optic networks and the accompanying revenues to be collected from companies using the networks.

> Market price need not, and generally does not, equal either book value or liquidation value. Unlike market value, neither book value nor liquidation value treats the firm as a going concern.

It is not surprising that stocks virtually never sell at book or liquidation values. Investors buy shares based on present and *future* earning power. Two key features determine the profits the firm will be able to produce: first, the earnings that can be generated by the firm's current tangible and intangible assets, and second, the opportunities the firm has to invest in lucrative projects that will increase future earnings.

EXAMPLE 6.1   **PACIFIC NORTHERN GAS AND RESEARCH IN MOTION**

Pacific Northern Gas, a gas pipeline servicing northern British Columbia, is not a growth company; its market is limited to the geographic area it services. More importantly, it is a regulated utility so its profits on present and future investment are limited. In April 2005, its price-to-book ratio was only .9.

Contrast this with Research in Motion (RIM), the Canadian designer and manufacturer of the wireless BlackBerry handheld communication device. In March 2000, RIM's stock price reached $227, putting the market value of RIM's equity at more than $16 billion. Yet RIM had only miniscule earnings. The value of the stock came from the company's wildly successfully BlackBerry technology and the promise of new, related products that presumably would lead to future earnings. RIM was a growth firm, because its market value depended substantially on intangible assets and the profitability of new investments. While Pacific Northern Gas stock has typically sold for less than book value, RIM at its peak sold for 33 times book value.

Future investment opportunities are great sources of market value but vunerable to rapid loss when expectations of the future change. In contrast, earnings from current assets are much more stable. Companies with significant value from growth, such as RIM, experience wider price swings than those with less value from growth, such as Pacific Northern Gas.

TABLE 6.3
Market-value balance sheet

A MARKET-VALUE BALANCE SHEET	
Assets	**Liabilities and Shareholders' Equity**
Assets in place	Market value of debt and other obligations
Investment opportunities	Market value of shareholders' equity

market-value balance sheet
Financial statement that uses the market value of all assets and liabilities.

Financial executives are not bound by generally accepted accounting principles, and they sometimes construct a firm's **market-value balance sheet**. Such a balance sheet helps them to think about and evaluate the sources of firm value. Take a look at Table 6.3. A market-value balance sheet contains two classes of assets: (1) assets already in place, both tangible and intangible, and (2) opportunities to invest in attractive future ventures. Pacific Northern Gas's stock market value is dominated by tangible assets in place; RIM's by the value of future investment opportunities.

Other firms, like Microsoft, have it all. Microsoft earns plenty from its current products. These earnings are part of what makes the stock attractive to investors. In addition, investors are willing to pay for the company's ability to invest profitably in new ventures that will increase future earnings.

Let's summarize. Remember:

- *Book value* records what a company has paid for its assets with a simple and often unrealistic deduction for depreciation and no adjustment for inflation. It does not capture the true value of a business.
- *Liquidation value* is what the company could net by selling its assets and repaying its debts. It does not capture the value of a successful "going concern."
- *Market value* is the amount that investors are willing to pay for the shares of the firm. This depends on the earning power of today's assets and the expected profitability of future investments.

The next question is: What determines market value?

Check Point 6.2

In the 1970s, the computer industry was dominated by IBM and was growing rapidly. In the 1980s, many new competitors entered the market, and computer prices fell. Computer makers in the last decade, including IBM, struggled with thinning profit margins and intense competition. How has IBM's market-value balance sheet changed over time? Have assets in place become proportionately more or less important? Do you think this progression is unique to the computer industry? Think about RIM.

6.3   VALUING COMMON STOCKS

TODAY'S PRICE AND TOMORROW'S PRICE

The cash payoff to owners of common stocks comes in two forms: (1) cash dividends, and (2) capital gains or losses. Usually investors expect to get some of each. Suppose that the current price of a share is P_0, that the expected price a year from now is P_1, and that the expected dividend per share is DIV_1. The subscript on P_0 denotes "time zero," which is today; the subscript on P_1 denotes "time 1," which is 1 year hence. We simplify by assuming that dividends are paid only once a year and that the next dividend will come in one year. The rate of return that investors expect from this share over the next year is the expected dividend per share DIV_1 plus the expected increase in price $P_1 - P_0$, all divided by the price at the start of the year P_0:

$$\text{Expected return} = r = \frac{DIV_1 + P_1 - P_0}{P_0} \tag{6.1}$$

Let us now look at how our formula works. Suppose Blue Skies' stock is selling for $75 a share ($P_0 = \$75$). Investors expect a $3 cash dividend over the next year ($DIV_1 = \$3$). They also expect the stock to sell for $81 a year hence ($P_1 = \$81$). Then the expected return to shareholders is 12 percent:

$$r = \frac{\$3 + \$81 - \$75}{\$75} = .12, \text{ or } 12 \text{ percent}$$

Notice that this expected return comes in two parts, the dividend and capital gain:

$$\text{Expected rate of return} = \text{expected dividend yield} + \text{expected capital gain}$$

$$= \frac{DIV_1}{P_0} + \frac{P_1 - P_0}{P_0}$$

$$= \frac{\$3}{\$75} + \frac{\$81 - \$75}{\$75}$$

$$= .04 + .08 = .12, \text{ or } 12 \text{ percent}$$

Of course, the *actual* return for Blue Skies may turn out to be more or less than investors expect. For example, the Canadian Tire Class A non-voting (CTR.NV) share price on April 14, 2004 was \$44.25. One year later, it was \$59.05. During the year, dividends of \$0.50 were paid,[7] providing a rate of return of (\$0.50 + \$59.05 − \$44.25)/\$44.25 = .346 , or 34.6 percent!

Canadian Tire's stock's rate of return is almost certainly above investor expectations. At the other extreme, the price of Bombardier subordinate voting shares (BBD.SV) fell from \$6.30 on April 14, 2004, to \$2.38 a year later. During the 12 months, dividends of \$0.0916 were paid. Investors earned an actual rate of return of (\$.0916 + \$2.38 − \$6.30)/\$6.30 = − .61, or negative 61 percent! Who would buy the shares expecting to lose money? Never confuse the actual outcomes with the expected outcome.

For many investors, both dividends and capital gains are taxable. Consequently, the investor's *after-tax* rate of return is the best measure of the actual earnings on a stock. To calculate the after-tax rate of return on a stock investment, first determine the taxes on dividends and capital gains and use the after-tax cash flows in the return calculation:

$$\textbf{After-tax rate of return} = \frac{\textbf{Div}_1 - \textbf{dividend tax}}{\textbf{\textit{P}}_0} + \frac{\textbf{Capital gain} - \textbf{capital gains tax}}{\textbf{\textit{P}}_0} \qquad \textbf{(6.2)}$$

EXAMPLE 6.2   **TAXES AND RATE OF RETURN**

You purchased shares of Big Time Toys for \$15 a share and sold them a year later for \$17 each. During the year, you received dividends per share of \$1. Before considering taxes, the rate of return on your investment was (\$1 + \$17 − \$15)/\$15 = .2, or 20 percent. However, your tax rate for dividend income is 20 percent and for capital gains is 16 percent.[8] Thus the dividend tax is \$0.20 (= .2 × \$1) and the capital gains tax is \$0.32 (= .16 × (\$17 − \$15)). The after-tax rate of return is

$$\text{After-tax rate of return} = \frac{\$1 - \$.2}{\$15} + \frac{\$2 - \$.32}{\$15} = \frac{\$2.48}{\$15} = .1653, \text{ or } 16.53 \text{ percent}$$

We saw how to work out the expected return on Blue Skies stock given today's stock price and forecasts of next year's stock price and dividends. You can also explain the market value of the stock in terms of investors' forecasts of dividends and price, and the expected return offered by other equally risky stocks. This is just the present value of the cash flows the stock will provide to its owner:

$$\text{Price today} = P_0 = \frac{DIV_1 + P_1}{1 + r}$$

---

[7] Canadian Tire increased its annual dividend from \$.50 to \$.58, effective April 27, 2005. Thus, *The Globe and Mail* stock listing in Figure 6.1 shows the *promised* dividend of \$.58. When calculating the stock's actual rate of return, use the dividends paid.

[8] Go back to Chapter 3 for details on the taxation of dividends and capital gains.

For Blue Skies $DIV_1 = \$3$ and $P_1 = \$81$. If stocks of similar risk offer an expected return of $r = 12$ percent, then today's price for Blue Skies should be $75:

$$P_0 = \frac{\$3 + \$81}{1.12} = \$75$$

How do we know that $75 is the right price? Because no other price could survive in competitive markets. What if P_0 were above $75? Then the expected rate of return on Blue Skies stock would be lower than on other securities of equivalent risk. Investors would bail out of Blue Skies stock and substitute the other securities. In the process they would force down the price of Blue Skies stock. If P_0 were less than $75, Blue Skies stock would offer a *higher* expected rate of return than equivalent-risk securities. Everyone would rush to buy, forcing the price up to $75. When the stock is priced correctly (that is, price equals present value), the *expected* rate of return on Blue Skies stock is also the rate of return that investors *require* to hold the stock.

> At each point in time all securities of the same risk are priced to offer the same expected rate of return. This is a fundamental characteristic of prices in well-functioning markets. It is also common sense.

Check Point 6.3

Androscoggin Copper is increasing next year's dividend to $5 per share. The forecast stock price next year is $105. Equally risky stocks of other companies offer expected rates of return of 10 percent. What should Androscoggin common stock sell for?

THE DIVIDEND DISCOUNT MODEL

We have managed to explain today's stock price P_0 in terms of the dividend DIV_1 and the expected stock price next year P_1. But future stock prices are not easy to forecast directly, though you may encounter individuals who claim to be able to do so. A formula that requires tomorrow's stock price to explain today's stock price is not generally helpful.

As it turns out, we can express a stock's value as the present value of all the forecast future dividends paid by the company to its shareholders without referring to the future stock price. This is the **dividend discount model**:

dividend discount model
Discounted cash flow model of today's stock price that states that share value equals the present value of all expected future dividends.

$$P_0 = \text{present value of } (DIV_1, DIV_2, DIV_3, \ldots, DIV_t, \ldots)$$
$$= \frac{DIV_1}{1+r} + \frac{DIV_2}{(1+r)^2} + \frac{DIV_3}{(1+r)^3} + \ldots + \frac{DIV_t}{(1+r)^t} + \ldots$$

How far out in the future could we look? In principle, 40, 60, or 100 years or more—corporations are potentially immortal. However, far-distant dividends will not have significant present values. For example, the present value of $1 received in 30 years using a 10 percent discount rate is only $.057. Most of the value of established companies comes from dividends to be paid within a person's working lifetime.

How do we get from the one-period formula $P_0 = (DIV_1 + P_1)/(1 + r)$ to the dividend discount model? We look at increasingly long investment horizons.

Let's consider investors with different investment horizons. Each investor will value the share of stock as the present value of the dividends that she expects to receive plus the present value of the price at which the stock is eventually sold. Unlike bonds, however, the final horizon date for stocks is not specified—stocks do not "mature." Moreover, both dividends and final sales price can be only estimated. But the general valuation approach is the same. For a one-period investor, the valuation formula looks like this:

$$P_0 = \frac{DIV_1 + P_1}{1+r}$$

A 2-year investor would value the stock as

$$P_0 = \frac{\text{DIV}_1}{1+r} + \frac{\text{DIV}_2 + P_2}{(1+r)^2}$$

and a 3-year investor would use the formula

$$P_0 = \frac{\text{DIV}_1}{1+r} + \frac{\text{DIV}_2}{(1+r)^2} + \frac{\text{DIV}_3 + P_3}{(1+r)^3}$$

In fact we can look as far out into the future as we like. Suppose we call our horizon date H. Then the stock valuation formula would be

$$P_0 = \frac{\text{DIV}_1}{1+r} + \frac{\text{DIV}_2}{(1+r)^2} + \ldots + \frac{\text{DIV}_H + P_H}{(1+r)^H} \qquad (6.3)$$

> In words, the value of a stock is the present value of the dividends it will pay over the investor's horizon plus the present value of the expected stock price at the end of that horizon.

Does this mean that investors of different horizons will all come to different conclusions about the value of the stock? No! Regardless of the investment horizon, the stock value will be the same. This is because the stock price at the horizon date is determined by expectations of dividends from that date forward. Therefore, as long as the investors are consistent in their assessment of the prospects of the firm, they will arrive at the same present value. Let's confirm this with an example.

EXAMPLE 6.3

VALUING BLUE SKIES STOCK

Take Blue Skies. The firm is growing steadily and investors expect both the stock price and the dividend to increase at 8 percent per year. Now consider three investors: Erste, Zweiter, and Dritter. Erste plans to hold Blue Skies for 1 year, Zweiter for 2, and Dritter for 3. Compare their payoffs:

	Year 1	Year 2	Year 3
Erste	$\text{DIV}_1 = 3$ $P_1 = 81$		
Zweiter	$\text{DIV}_1 = 3$	$\text{DIV}_2 = 3.24$ $P_2 = 87.48$	
Dritter	$\text{DIV}_1 = 3$	$\text{DIV}_2 = 3.24$	$\text{DIV}_3 = 3.50$ $P_3 = 94.48$

Remember, we assumed that dividends and stock prices for Blue Skies are expected to grow at a steady 8 percent. Thus $\text{DIV}_2 = \$3 \times 1.08 = \$3.24$, $\text{DIV}_3 = \$3.24 \times 1.08 = \$3.50$, and so on.

Erste, Zweiter, and Dritter all require the same 12 percent expected return. So we can calculate present value over Erste's one-year horizon:

$$PV = \frac{\text{DIV}_1 + P_1}{1+r} = \frac{\$3 + \$81}{1.12} = \$75$$

or Zweiter's two-year horizon:

$$PV = \frac{\text{DIV}_1}{1+r} + \frac{\text{DIV}_2 + P_2}{(1+r)^2}$$
$$= \frac{\$3.00}{1.12} + \frac{\$3.24 + \$87.48}{(1.12)^2}$$
$$= \$2.68 + \$72.32 = \$75$$

or Dritter's three-year horizon:

$$PV = \frac{DIV_1}{1 + r} + \frac{DIV_2}{(1 + r)^2} + \frac{DIV_3 + P_3}{(1 + r)^3}$$

$$= \frac{\$3}{1.12} + \frac{\$3.24}{(1.12)^2} + \frac{\$3.50 + \$94.48}{(1.12)^3}$$

$$= \$2.68 + \$2.58 + \$69.74 = \$75$$

All agree the stock is worth $75 per share. This illustrates our basic principle: The value of a common stock equals the present value of dividends received out to the investment horizon plus the present value of the forecast stock price at the horizon. Moreover, when you move the horizon date, the stock's present value should not change. The principle holds for horizons of 1, 3, 10, 20, and 50 years or more.

Check Point 6.4   Refer to Check Point 6.3. Assume that Androscoggin Copper's dividend and share price are expected to grow at a constant 5 percent rate per year. Calculate the current value of Androscoggin stock with the dividend discount model using a three-year horizon. You should get the same answer as in Check Point 6.3.

Look at Table 6.4, which continues the Blue Skies example for various time horizons, still assuming that the dividends are expected to increase at a steady 8 percent compound rate. The expected price increases at the same 8 percent rate. Each row in the table represents a present value calculation for a different horizon year. Note that present value does not depend on the investment horizon. Figure 6.2 presents the same data in a graph. Each column shows the present

TABLE 6.4
Value of Blue Skies' stock for various time horizons, given 8 percent growth of dividends

Horizon, Years	PV (Dividends)	+	PV (Terminal Price)	=	Value per Share
1	$ 2.68		$72.32		$75.00
2	5.26		69.74		75.00
3	7.75		67.25		75.00
10	22.87		52.13		75.00
20	38.76		36.24		75.00
30	49.81		25.19		75.00
50	62.83		12.17		75.00
100	73.02		1.98		75.00

FIGURE 6.2
Value of Blue Skies for different horizons

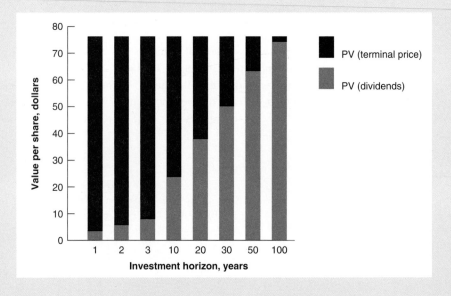

value of the dividends up to the horizon and the present value of the price at the horizon. As the horizon recedes, the dividend stream accounts for an increasing proportion of present value, but the *total* present value of dividends plus terminal price always equals $75.

If the horizon is infinitely far away, then we can forget about the final horizon price—it has almost no present value—and simply say

Stock price = PV (all future dividends per share)   (6.4)

This is the dividend discount model.

6.4   SIMPLIFYING THE DIVIDEND DISCOUNT MODEL

THE DIVIDEND DISCOUNT MODEL WITH NO GROWTH

Consider a company that pays out all its earnings to its common shareholders. Such a company could not grow because it could not reinvest.[9] Stockholders might enjoy a generous immediate dividend, but they could forecast no increase in future dividends. The company's stock would offer a perpetual stream of equal cash payments, $DIV_1 = DIV_2 = \ldots = DIV_t = \ldots$.

The dividend discount model says that these no-growth shares should sell for the present value of a constant, perpetual stream of dividends. We learned how to do that calculation when we valued perpetuities in Chapter 4. Just divide the annual cash payment by the discount rate. The discount rate is the rate of return demanded by investors in other stocks of the same risk:

$$P_0 = \frac{DIV_1}{r} \qquad (6.5)$$

Since our company pays out all its earnings as dividends, dividends and earnings are the same, and we could just as well calculate stock value by

$$\text{Value of a no-growth stock} = P_0 = \frac{EPS_1}{r}$$

where EPS_1 represents next year's earnings per share of stock. Thus some people loosely say, "Stock price is the present value of future earnings," and calculate value by this formula. Be careful—this is a special case. We'll return to the formula later in this chapter.

EXAMPLE 6.4   **PREFERRED SHARES: SHARES WITH NON-GROWING DIVIDENDS**

A preferred share is an example of a share with constant, non-growing dividend. Look back to Figure 6.1 at CIBC's preferred share, CM.PR.P, with a promised annual dividend of $1.375. The price of this preferred share can be calculated with the no-growth dividend formula, Equation 6.5. Assume that rate of return demanded by investors in preferred shares of this risk is 5.33 percent. Given its constant dividend, DIV, of $1.375, the price of CM.PR.P is

$$P_0 = \frac{DIV}{r} = \frac{\$1.375}{.0533} = \$25.80$$

Where did the discount rate in Example 6.4 come from? We calculated the expected rate of return by rearranging the no-growth formula as

$$r = \frac{DIV}{P_0} = \frac{\$1.375}{\$25.80} = .0533, \text{ or } 5.33 \text{ percent}$$

You should not be surprised that the price calculated in Example 6.4 equals the price of the preferred share reported in Figure 6.1!

---

[9] Assuming it does not raise money by issuing new shares.

Moonshine Industries has produced a barrel per week for the past 20 years but cannot grow because of certain legal hazards. It earns $25 per share per year and pays it all out to shareholders. The shareholders have alternative, equivalent-risk ventures yielding 20 percent per year on average. How much is one share of Moonshine worth? Assume the company can keep going indefinitely.

THE CONSTANT-GROWTH DIVIDEND DISCOUNT MODEL

The dividend discount model requires a forecast of dividends for every year into the future, which poses a bit of a problem for stocks with lives that are potentially infinite. Unless we want to spend a lifetime forecasting dividends, we must use simplifying assumptions to reduce the number of estimates. The easiest simplification assumes a no-growth perpetuity that works for no-growth common shares and most preferred shares.

Here's another simplification that finds a good deal of practical use: Suppose forecast dividends grow at a constant rate into the indefinite future. If dividends grow at a steady rate, then instead of forecasting an infinite number of dividends, we need to forecast only the next dividend and the dividend growth rate.

Recall Blue Skies. It will pay a $3 dividend in 1 year. If the dividend grows at a constant rate of $g = .08$ (8 percent) thereafter, then dividends in future years will be

$$
\begin{aligned}
\text{DIV}_1 &= \$3 && = \$3.00 \\
\text{DIV}_2 &= \$3 \times (1 + g) = \$3 \times 1.08 && = \$3.24 \\
\text{DIV}_3 &= \$3 \times (1 + g)^2 = \$3 \times 1.08^2 && = \$3.50
\end{aligned}
$$

Plug these forecasts of future dividends into the dividend discount model:

$$
\begin{aligned}
P_0 &= \frac{\text{DIV}_1}{1 + r} + \frac{\text{DIV}_1(1 + g)}{(1 + r)^2} + \frac{\text{DIV}_1(1 + g)^2}{(1 + r)^3} + \frac{\text{DIV}_1(1 + g)^3}{(1 + r)^4} + \cdots \\
&= \frac{\$3}{1.12} + \frac{\$3.24}{1.12^2} + \frac{\$3.50}{1.12^3} + \frac{\$3.78}{1.12^4} + \cdots \\
&= \$2.68 + \$2.58 + \$2.49 + \$2.40 + \cdots
\end{aligned}
$$

Although there is an infinite number of terms, each term is proportionately smaller than the preceding one as long as the dividend growth rate g is less than the discount rate r. Because the present value of far-distant dividends will always get closer to zero, the sum of all of these terms is finite despite the fact that an infinite number of dividends will be paid. The sum can be shown to equal

$$
P_0 = \frac{\text{DIV}_1}{r - g} \tag{6.6}
$$

constant-growth dividend discount model Version of the dividend discount model in which dividends grow at a constant rate.

This equation is called the **constant-growth dividend discount model**, or the *Gordon growth model*, after Myron Gordon, who popularized it.[10]

---

[10] Notice that the first dividend is assumed to come at the *end* of the first period and is discounted for a full period. If the stock has just paid its dividend, then next year's dividend will be $(1 + g)$ times the dividend just paid. So another way to write the valuation formula is

$$
P_0 = \frac{\text{DIV}_1}{r - g} = \frac{\text{DIV}_0 \times (1 + g)}{r - g}
$$

EXAMPLE 6.5	**BLUE SKIES VALUED BY THE CONSTANT-GROWTH MODEL**

Let's apply the constant-growth model to Blue Skies. Assume a dividend has just been paid. The next dividend, to be paid in a year, is forecast at $DIV_1 = \$3$, the growth rate of dividends is $g = 8$ percent, and the discount rate is $r = 12$ percent. Therefore, we solve for the stock value as

$$P_0 = \frac{DIV_1}{r - g} = \frac{\$3}{.12 - .08} = \$75$$

The constant-growth formula is close to the formula for the present value of a perpetuity. Suppose you forecast no growth in dividends ($g = 0$). Then the dividend stream is a simple perpetuity, and the valuation formula is $P_0 = DIV_1/r$. This is precisely the formula you used in Check Point 6.5 to value Moonshine, a no-growth common stock.

The constant-growth model generalizes the perpetuity formula to allow for constant growth in dividends. Notice that as g increases, the stock price also rises. However, the constant-growth formula is valid only when g is less than r. If someone forecasts perpetual dividend growth at a rate greater than investors' required return r, then two things happen:

1. The formula explodes. It gives nutty answers. (Try a numerical example.)
2. You know the forecast is wrong because far-distant dividends would have incredibly high present values. (Again, try a numerical example. Calculate the present value of a dividend paid after 100 years, assuming $DIV_1 = \$3$, $r = .12$, but $g = .20$.)

ESTIMATING EXPECTED RATES OF RETURN

We argued earlier in Section 6.3 that in competitive markets common stocks with the same risk are priced to offer the same expected rate of return. But how do you figure out what that expected rate of return is?

It's not easy. Consensus estimates of future dividends, stock prices, or overall rates of return are not published in *The Globe and Mail* or reported by TV newscasters. Economists argue about which statistical models give the best estimates. There are nevertheless some useful rules of thumb that can give sensible numbers.

One rule of thumb is based on the constant-growth dividend discount model. Remember that it forecasts a constant growth rate g in both future dividends and stock prices. That means forecast capital gains equal g per year.

We can calculate the expected rate of return by rearranging the constant-growth formula as

$$r = \frac{\mathbf{DIV_1}}{\mathbf{P_0}} + \mathbf{g} \tag{6.7}$$
$$= \textbf{dividend yield} + \textbf{growth rate}$$

For Blue Skies, the expected first-year dividend is $3 and the growth rate 8 percent. With an initial stock price of $75, the expected rate of return is

$$r = \frac{DIV_1}{P_0} + g$$
$$= \frac{\$3}{\$75} + .08 = .04 + .08 = .12, \text{ or 12 percent}$$

Suppose we found another stock with the same risk as Blue Skies. It ought to offer the same expected rate of return even if its immediate dividend or expected growth rate is very different. The required rate of return is not the unique property of Blue Skies or any other company; it is set in the worldwide market for common stocks. Blue Skies cannot change its value of r by paying higher or lower dividends, or by growing faster or slower, unless these changes also affect the risk of the stock. When we use the rule of thumb formula, $r = \text{DIV}_1/P_0 + g$, we are not saying that r, the expected rate of return, is *determined* by DIV_1 or g. It is determined by the rate of return offered by other equally risky stocks. That return determines how much investors are willing to pay for Blue Skies' forecast future dividends:

$$\underbrace{\frac{\text{DIV}_1}{P_0} + g}_{\substack{\text{Given DIV}_1 \text{ and} \\ g, \text{ investors set} \\ \text{the stock price}}} = r = \underbrace{\substack{\text{expected rate of return offered} \\ \text{by other, equally risky stocks}}}_{\substack{\text{so that Blue Skies offers an} \\ \text{adequate expected rate of return, } r}}$$

EXAMPLE 6.6   **BLUE SKIES GETS A WINDFALL**

Blue Skies has won a lawsuit against its archrival, Nasty Manufacturing; the lawsuit forces Nasty Manufacturing to withdraw as a competitor in a key market. As a result Blue Skies is able to generate 9 percent per year future growth without sacrificing immediate dividends. Will that increase r, the expected rate of return?

This is very good news for Blue Skies shareholders. The stock price will jump to

$$P_0 = \frac{\text{DIV}_1}{r - g} = \frac{\$3}{.12 - .09} = \$100$$

But at the new price Blue Skies will offer the same 12 percent expected return:

$$r = \frac{\text{DIV}_1}{P_0} + g$$

$$= \frac{\$3}{\$100} + .09 = .12, \text{ or } 12 \text{ percent}$$

Blue Skies' good news is reflected in a higher stock price today, not in a higher expected rate of return in the future. The unchanged expected rate of return corresponds to Blue Skies' unchanged risk.

Check Point 6.6   Androscoggin Copper can grow at 5 percent per year indefinitely. It's selling at $100, and next year's dividend is $5. What is the expected rate of return from investing in Carrabasset Mining common stock? Carrabasset and Androscoggin shares are equally risky.

Few real companies are expected to grow in such a regular and convenient way as Blue Skies or Androscoggin Copper. Nevertheless, in some mature industries, growth is reasonably stable and the constant-growth model approximately valid. In such cases the model can be turned around to infer the rate of return expected by investors.

NON-CONSTANT GROWTH

Many companies grow at rapid or irregular rates for several years before finally settling down. Obviously we can't use the constant-growth dividend discount model in such cases. However, we have already looked at an alternative approach. Set the investment horizon (Year H) at the future year by which you expect the company's growth to settle down. Calculate the present value of dividends from now to the horizon year. Forecast the stock price in that year and discount it also to present value. Then add it up to get the total present value of dividends plus the ending stock price. The formula is

$$P_0 = \frac{DIV_1}{1+r} + \frac{DIV_2}{(1+r)^2} + \cdots + \underbrace{\frac{DIV_H}{(1+r)^H}}_{\substack{\text{PV of dividends from} \\ \text{Year 1 to horizon}}} + \underbrace{\frac{P_H}{(1+r)^H}}_{\substack{\text{PV of stock price} \\ \text{at horizon}}} \qquad (6.8)$$

The stock price in the horizon year is often called *terminal value*.

EXAMPLE 6.7   **ESTIMATING THE VALUE OF UNITED BIRD SEED'S STOCK**

Ms. Dawn Chorus, founder and president of United Bird Seed, is wondering whether the company should make its first public sale of common stock and, if so, at what price.

The company's financial plan envisages rapid growth over the next three years but only moderate growth afterward. Forecast earnings and dividends are as follows:

Year	1	2	3	4	5	6	7	8
Earnings per share	$2.45	3.11	3.78	5% growth thereafter				
Dividends per share	$1.00	1.20	1.44	5% growth thereafter				

Thus you have a forecast of the dividend stream for the next three years. The tricky part is to estimate the price in the Year 3 horizon. Ms. Chorus could look at stock prices for mature pet food companies whose scale, risk, and growth prospects today roughly match those projected for United Bird Seed in Year 3. Suppose further that these companies tend to sell at price-earnings ratios of about 8. Then you could reasonably guess that the P/E ratio of United will likewise be 8. That implies

$$P_3 = 8 \times \$3.78 = \$30.24$$

You are now in a position to determine the value of shares in United. If investors demand a return of $r = 10$ percent, then the price today should be

$$P_0 = \text{PV (dividends from Years 1 to 3)} + \text{PV (forecast stock price in Year 3)}$$

$$\text{PV (dividends from Years 1 to 3)} = \frac{\$1.00}{1.10} + \frac{\$1.20}{1.10^2} + \frac{\$1.44}{1.10^3} = \$2.98$$

$$\text{PV}(P_H) = \frac{\$30.24}{(1.10)^3} = \$22.72$$

$$P_0 = \$2.98 + \$22.72 = \$25.70$$

Thus, the price today should be about $25.70 per share.

United Bird Seed is looking forward to several years of very rapid growth, so you could not use the constant-growth formula to value United's stock today. But the formula may help you check your estimate of the terminal price in Year 3, when the company has settled down to a steady rate of growth. From then on dividends are forecast to grow at a constant rate of $g = .05$, or 5 percent. Thus the expected dividend in Year 4 is

$$DIV_4 = 1.05 \times DIV_3 = 1.05 \times \$1.44 = \$1.512$$

and the expected terminal price in Year 3 is

$$P_3 = \frac{DIV_4}{r-g} = \frac{\$1.512}{.10 - .05} = \$30.24$$

the same value we found when we used the P/E ratio to predict P_3. In this case our two approaches give the same estimate of P_3, though you shouldn't bet on that always being the case in practice.

✔ Check Point 6.7   Suppose that another stock market analyst predicts that United Bird Seed will not settle down to a constant 5 percent growth rate in dividends until after Year 4, and that dividends in Year 4 will be $1.73 per share. What is the fair price for the stock according to this analyst?

6.5   GROWTH STOCKS AND INCOME STOCKS

We often hear investors speak of *growth stocks* and *income stocks*. They seem to buy growth stocks primarily in the expectation of capital gains, and they are interested in the future growth of earnings rather than in next year's dividends. On the other hand, they buy income stocks principally for the cash dividends. Let us see whether these distinctions make sense.

Think back once more to Blue Skies. It is expected to pay a dividend next year of $3 ($DIV_1 = 3$), and this dividend is expected to grow at a steady rate of 8 percent a year ($g = .08$). If investors require a return of 12 percent ($r = .12$), then the price of Blue Skies should be $DIV_1/(r - g) = \$3/(.12 - .08) = \$75$.

Suppose that Blue Skies' existing assets generate earnings per share of $5. It pays out 60 percent of these earnings as a dividend. This **payout ratio** results in a dividend of $.60 \times \$5 = \$3$. The remaining 40 percent of earnings, the **plowback ratio**, is retained by the firm and "plowed back" into a new plant and new equipment. (The plowback ratio is also called the earnings *retention ratio*.) On this new equity investment Blue Skies earns a return of 20 percent.

payout ratio   Fraction of earnings paid out as dividends.

plowback ratio   Fraction of earnings retained by the firm. Also called *retention ratio*.

If all of these earnings were plowed back into the firm, Blue Skies would grow at 20 percent per year. Because a portion of earnings is not reinvested in the firm, the growth rate will be less than 20 percent. The higher the fraction of earnings plowed back into the company, the higher the growth rate. So assets, earnings, and dividends all grow by

$$g = \text{return on equity} \times \text{plowback ratio}$$
$$= .20 \times .40 = .08, \text{ or 8 percent} \tag{6.9}$$

What if Blue Skies did not plow back any of its earnings into a new plant and new equipment? In that case it would pay out all its earnings as dividends but would forgo any growth in dividends. So we could recalculate value with $DIV_1 = \$5$ and $g = 0$:

$$P_0 = \frac{\$5.00}{.12 - 0} = \$41.67$$

Thus if Blue Skies did not reinvest any of its earnings, its stock price would not be $75 but $41.67. The $41.67 represents the value of earnings from the assets that are already in place. The rest of the stock price ($75 − $41.67 = $33.33) is the net present value of the future investments that Blue Skies is expected to make. This is reflected in the market-value balance sheet, Table 6.5.

What if Blue Skies kept to its policy of reinvesting 40 percent of its profits, but the forecast return on this new investment was only 12 percent? In that case the expected growth in dividends would also be lower:

$$g = \text{return on equity} \times \text{plowback ratio}$$
$$= .12 \times .40 = .048, \text{ or 4.8 percent}$$

If we plug this new value for g into our valuation formula, again we come up with a value of $41.67 for Blue Skies stock:

$$P_0 = \frac{DIV_1}{r - g} = \frac{\$3.00}{.12 - .048} = \$41.67$$

TABLE 6.5
Market-value balance sheet for Blue Skies

MARKET-VALUE BALANCE SHEET FOR BLUE SKIES (all quantities on a per-share basis)			
Assets		**Liabilities and Shareholders' Equity**	
Assets in place	$41.67	Shareholders' equity	$75
Investment opportunities	33.33	Debt*	0

*We assume the firm is all-equity financed.

Plowing earnings back into new investments may result in growth in earnings and dividends, but it does not add to the current stock price if that money is expected to earn only the return that investors require. Plowing earnings back does add to value if investors believe that the reinvested earnings will earn a higher rate of return than investors require.

To repeat, if Blue Skies did not plow back earnings or if it earned only the return that investors required on the new investment, its stock price would be $41.67. The total value of Blue Skies stock is $75. Of the $75, $41.67 is the value of the assets already in place, and the remaining $33.33 is the present value of the superior returns on assets to be acquired in the future. The latter is called the **present value of growth opportunities**, or **PVGO**. (Remember that investors expected Blue Skies to earn 20 percent on its new investments, well above the 12 percent expected return necessary to attract investors.)

By the way, growth rates calculated as

$$g = \text{return on equity} \times \text{plowback ratio}$$

are often referred to as **sustainable growth rates**.

present value of growth opportunities (PVGO) Net present value of a firm's future investments.

sustainable growth rate Steady rate at which a firm can grow; return on equity times plowback ratio.

Check Point 6.8

Suppose that instead of plowing money back into lucrative ventures, Blue Skies' management is investing at an expected return on equity of 10 percent, which is below the return of 12 percent that investors could expect to get from comparable securities.

a. Find the sustainable growth rate of dividends and earnings in the above circumstances. Assume a 60 percent payout ratio.

b. Find the new value of its investment opportunities. Explain why this value is negative despite the positive growth rate of earnings and dividends.

c. If you were a corporate raider, would Blue Skies be a good candidate for an attempted takeover?

THE PRICE-EARNINGS RATIO

The superior prospects of Blue Skies are reflected in its price-earnings ratio. With a stock price of $75 and earnings of $5, the P/E ratio is $75/$5 = 15. If Blue Skies had no growth opportunities, its stock price would be only $41.67 and its P/E would be $41.67/$5 = 8.33. The P/E ratio is, therefore, an indicator of Blue Skies' rosy prospects.

Does this mean that the financial manager should celebrate if the firm's stock sells at a high P/E? The answer is usually yes. The high P/E suggests that investors think that the firm has good growth opportunities. However, firms can have high P/E ratios not because the price is high but because earnings are temporarily depressed. A firm that earns *nothing* in a particular period will have an *infinite* P/E.

VALUING ENTIRE BUSINESSES

Investors routinely buy and sell shares of common stock. Companies frequently buy and sell entire businesses. So it is natural to ask whether the formulas that we have presented in this chapter can also be used to value these businesses.

Sure! Take the case of Blue Skies. Suppose that it has 2 million shares outstanding. It plans to pay a dividend of $DIV_1 = \$3$ a share. So the *total* dividend payment is 2 million × $3 = $6 million. Investors expect a steady dividend growth of 8 percent a year and require a return of 12 percent. So the total value of Blue Skies is

$$PV = \frac{\$6 \text{ million}}{.12 - .08} = \$150 \text{ million}$$

Company valuation is not a precise science. When two companies dispute the price that one should pay for the other, a battle between their investment bankers can be guaranteed.

AT&T bought McCaw Cellular in 1994. As a result it acquired McCaw's 52 percent stake in the shares of a cellular communications company, LIN Broadcasting, and assumed an obligation to buy the remaining 48 percent of the shares at their fair value. The process for determining fair value was laid down when McCaw acquired its initial stake in LIN. AT&T and LIN had 30 days to come up with an initial valuation of the shares and then a further 15 days to consider their final numbers. If the two companies' valuations were less than 10 percent apart, AT&T would be obliged to buy at the average of the two prices. If they were more than 10 percent apart, an independent arbitrator would be appointed. If the arbitrator decided that the true value was about midway between the two companies' valuations, then the arbitrator's valuation would be used. If it was close to AT&T's valuation, then the arbitrator's price and AT&T's price would be averaged, and LIN's valuation would be ignored. Conversely, if it was close to LIN's figure, then the arbitrator's price would be averaged in with LIN's valuation and AT&T's figure would be ignored.

Each company appointed an investment bank to prepare and argue its case. AT&T's case was presented by Morgan Stanley while LIN's case was prepared by Bear Stearns and Lehman Brothers. Each side faced a quandary. AT&T's advisers were tempted to go for a low figure, while LIN's advisers were tempted to come up with a high figure. But if the dispute went to arbitration, then an extreme valuation was more likely to be out of line with the arbitrator's figure, and therefore was more likely to be ignored. It seemed to make sense to take an extreme position only if each could be sure that the other side would do so also. Conversely, a more middle-of-the-road posture made sense if each could be confident that the other would provide a middle-of-the-road valuation.

When the two parties met at Morgan Stanley's offices to examine each other's valuations, there was a stunned silence, and then Bear Stearns' team began to laugh. Morgan Stanley's valuation was $100 a share, while Lehman Brothers and Bear Stearns came up with a figure of $162 a share. Since AT&T was proposing to buy 25 million LIN shares, the disagreement amounted to a thumping $1.6 billion.

Fifteen days later the two sides met again to exchange their final valuations. There was an air of shock in the room; despite hearing the other side's arguments, the difference in their valuations had barely narrowed. It seemed that an independent arbitrator was required, and so another investment bank, Wasserstein Perella, was called in to provide an independent valuation.

Some weeks later a herd of about 50 investment bankers and lawyers crowded into the offices of Wasserstein Perella to defend their estimates of the value of LIN. Comparisons were made with the value of other cellular communications companies. Each side presented projections of LIN's future profits and dividends. There were also arguments about the rate at which these future dividends should be discounted. For example, each side argued that the other had failed to properly measure the risk of the stock.

The final upshot: After hearing the arguments from both sides, Wasserstein Perella placed a value of $127.50 on each share of LIN. This meant that the total cost of the shares to AT&T was about $3.3 billion.

Source: The story of the valuation of LIN Broadcasting is set out in S. Neish, "Wrong Number," *Global M&A* (Summer 1995).

Alternatively, we could say that the total value of the company is the number of shares times the value per share:

$$PV = 2 \text{ million} \times \$75 = \$150 \text{ million}$$

SEE BOX ABOVE Of course things are always harder in practice than in principle. Forecasting cash flows and settling on an appropriate discount rate require skill and judgment. As the above Finance in Action box shows, there can be plenty of room for disagreement.

6.6 THERE ARE NO FREE LUNCHES ON WALL STREET OR BAY STREET

We have explained how common stocks are valued. Does that mean that we have just given the game away and told you how to make an instant fortune on the stock market? We are sorry to disappoint you. It is not so easy to beat the market, and even highly paid pros find it very difficult to do so with any consistency.

Look, for example, at Figure 6.3, which shows the average performance of general equity mutual funds over three decades compared to that of the Standard & Poor's 500 Index. You can see that in some years these mutual funds did beat the market, but as often as not, it was the other way around. Of course, it would be surprising if some of the managers were not smarter than others and

FIGURE 6.3
Annual returns on S&P
500 Index versus general
equity mutual funds

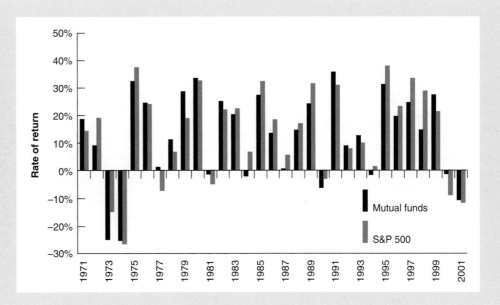

were able to earn superior returns. But it seems hard to spot the smart ones, and the top-performing managers one year have about an average chance of falling on their face the next year.

EXAMPLE 6.8 PERFORMANCE OF MONEY MANAGERS

Forbes Magazine, a widely read investment magazine, publishes annually an honour roll of the most consistently successful mutual funds. Suppose that every year starting in 1975, you invested an equal sum in each of these successful funds when *Forbes* announced its honour roll. You would have outperformed the market in only 5 of the following 16 years and your average annual return would have been more than 1 percent below the return on the market.[11]

Confronted with this evidence, many large investors have given up the search for superior investment returns, and instead they simply buy and hold the market. Corporate pension funds now invest over a quarter of their equity holdings in the market index.

Why is it so difficult to beat the market consistently? Let's look at two possible ways that you might attempt to do so.

METHOD 1: TECHNICAL ANALYSIS

technical analysts Investors who attempt to identify undervalued stocks by searching for patterns in past stock prices.

Some investors try to achieve superior returns by spotting and exploiting patterns in stock prices. These investors are known as **technical analysts**.

Technical analysis sounds plausible. For example, you might hope to beat the market by buying stocks when they are on their way up and by selling them on their way down. Unfortunately, it turns out that such simple rules don't work. A large price rise in one period may be followed by a further rise in the next period, but it is just as likely to be followed by a fall.

Look, for example, at Figure 6.4. The horizontal axis shows the return on the TSX Composite's index in one week, while the vertical axis shows the return in the following week.

---

[11] See B. G. Malkiel, "Returns from Investing in Equity Mutual Funds 1971 to 1991," *Journal of Finance* 50 (June 1995), pp. 549–72.

FIGURE 6.4

Each dot shows the returns on the TSX Composite Index on two successive weeks between January 1977 and July 2004. The circled dot shows a weekly return of +6.9%, followed by –6.3% in the next week. The scatter diagram shows no significant relationship between returns on successive weeks.

Each point in the chart represents a different week between January 1977 and July 2004. If a market rise one week tended to be followed by a rise the next week, the points in the chart would plot along an upward sloping line. But you can see that there was no such tendency; the points are scattered randomly across the chart. Statisticians sometimes measure the relationship between these changes by the coefficient of correlation. In our example, the correlation between the market movements in successive weeks is .05—in other words, effectively zero.

Financial economists and statisticians who have studied stock price movements have concluded that you won't get rich looking for consistent patterns in price changes. This seems to be so regardless of whether you look at the market as a whole (as we did in Figure 6.4) or at individual stocks. Prices appear to wander randomly, virtually equally likely to offer a high or low return on any particular day, *regardless of what has occurred on previous days*. In other words, prices seem to follow a **random walk**.

random walk Security prices change randomly, with no predictable trends or patterns.

If you are not sure what we mean by "random walk," consider the following example. You are given $100 to play a game. At the end of each week a coin is tossed. If it comes up heads, you win 3 percent of your investment; if it is tails, you lose 2.5 percent. Therefore, your payoff at the end of the first week is either $103.00 or $97.50. At the end of the second week the coin is tossed again. Now the possible outcomes are as follows:

This process is a random walk because successive changes in the value of your stake are independent. That is, the odds of making money each week are the same, regardless of the value at the start of the week or the pattern of heads or tails in the previous weeks.

FIGURE 6.5
One of these charts shows the TSX Composite's Index for a five-year period. The other shows the results of playing our coin-toss game for five years. Can you tell which is which? (The answer is given in footnote 12.)

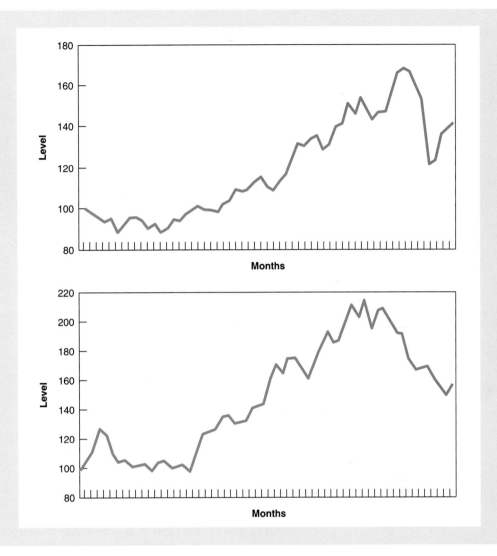

If a stock's price follows a random walk, the odds of an increase or decrease during any day, month, or year do not depend at all on the stock's previous price moves. The historical path of prices gives no useful information about the future—just as a long series of recorded heads and tails gives no information about the next toss.

If you find it difficult to believe that stock prices could behave like our coin-tossing game, then look at the two charts in Figure 6.5. One of these charts shows the outcome from playing our game for five years; the other shows the actual performance of the TSX Composite's Index for a five-year period. Can you tell which one is which?[12]

Does it surprise you that stocks seem to follow a random walk? If so, imagine that it were not the case and that changes in stock prices were expected to persist for several months. Figure 6.6 provides a hypothetical example of such a predictable cycle. You can see that an upswing in the market started last month when the index was 1,100 and is expected to carry the price to 1,300 next month. What will happen when investors perceive this bonanza? Since stocks are a bargain at their current level, investors will rush to buy. They will stop buying only when stocks are fairly priced. Thus, as soon as a cycle becomes apparent to investors, they immediately eliminate it by their trading.

---

[12] The top chart in Figure 6.5 shows the real TSX Composite's Index for the years 1994 through 1998. The bottom chart was generated by a series of random numbers. You may be among the 50 percent of our readers who guess right, but we bet it was just a guess.

FIGURE 6.6
Cycles self-destruct as soon as they are recognized by investors. The stock price instantaneously jumps to the present value of the expected future price.

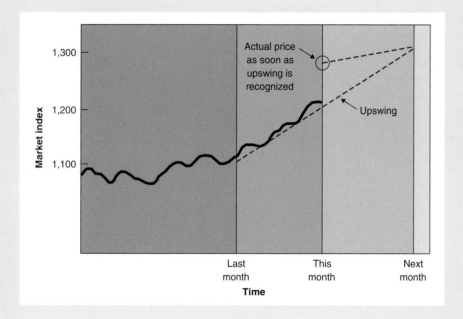

METHOD 2: FUNDAMENTAL ANALYSIS

You may not be able to earn superior returns just by studying past stock prices, but what about other types of information? After all, most investors don't just look at past stock prices. Instead they try to gauge a firm's business prospects by studying the financial and trade press, the company's financial accounts, the president's annual statements, and other items of news. These investors are called **fundamental analysts**, in contrast to technical analysts, who focus on past stock price movements.

fundamental analysts Investors who attempt to find mispriced securities by analyzing fundamental information, such as accounting data and business prospects.

Suppose that you study the financial press carefully and buy a stock when the news about the company is good. Figure 6.7 illustrates why this strategy is unlikely to work. It shows how stock prices react to one particular item of news—the announcement of a takeover. In most takeovers the acquiring company is willing to pay a hefty premium to induce the shareholders of the target company to give up their shares. You can see from Figure 6.7 that the stock price of the target company typically jumps up on the day that the public becomes aware of a takeover attempt (day 0 in the graph). However, this adjustment in the stock price is immediate; thereafter there is no further drift in the stock price, either upward or downward. By the time that the acquisition has been made public, it is too late to buy.

Researchers have looked at the stock price reaction to many other types of news, such as earnings and dividend announcements, and plans to issue additional stock or repurchase existing stock. All this information seems to be rapidly and accurately reflected in the price of the stock, so that it is impossible to make superior returns by buying or selling after the announcement.

inside information Relevant information about a company known by its board of directors, management and/or employees and other insiders but not by the public.

insiders Members of the board of directors, management, employees and others with close relationship to a company, including lawyers, financial advisors, and accountants.

What if you get the news about the corporate event *before* it is released to the market? You might be able to act on it before other market participants figure out what is going on. However, if that information is **inside information**, information about a company from an **insider** and not

FIGURE 6.7

The performance of the stocks of target companies compared with that of the market. The prices of target stocks jump up on the announcement day, but from then on, there are no unusual price movements. The announcement of the takeover attempt seems to be fully reflected in the stock price on the announcement day.

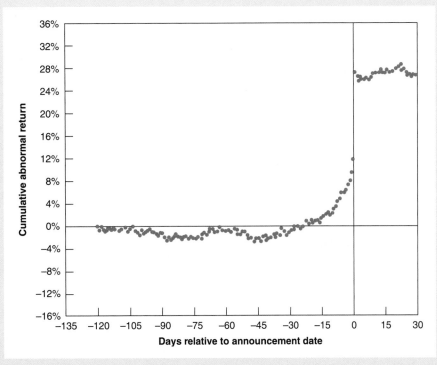

Source: A. Keown and J. Pinkerton, "Merger Announcements and Insider Trading Activity," *Journal of Finance* 36 (September 1981), pp. 855–69.

insider trading Illegal trading of securities, including stocks, bonds, and options, by insiders or those who are tipped by insiders, on the basis of inside information.

yet publicly announced, it is illegal to use. Insiders include members of the board, management, employees, and those with a close relationship with the company, such as lawyers, financial advisers, and accountants. If you receive information from an insider, you are a *tippee* and also not allowed to trade on the information. Investors guilty of illegal **insider trading** face heavy financial penalties and possible jail time. It can be difficult to catch insider traders but it does happen.

EXAMPLE 6.9

THE PERILS OF TRADING ON INSIDE INFORMATION

In April 2005, Joanne Chang, the former head of investor relations at ATI Technologies Inc. and her husband, David Stone, agreed to pay nearly $1.5 million to settle insider trading charges brought by the Ontario Securities Commission. Chang was also banned from trading in the market for 20 years and Stone was banned for life. Both of the accused sold shares just before ATI released unexpected news about poor financial performance. The news caused ATI's stock price to fall 53 percent in two days. The chairman of the OSC panel was quoted as saying, "You have both admitted your conduct in this matter was wrong and illegal. It's an activity that erodes public confidence in the market. This, I'm sure, has been a severe lesson for both of you."[13]

A THEORY TO FIT THE FACTS

efficient market Market in which prices reflect all available information.

Economists often refer to the stock market as an **efficient market**. By this they mean that the competition to find misvalued stocks is intense. So, when new information comes out, investors rush to take advantage of it and thereby eliminate any profit opportunities. Professional investors express the same idea when they say that there are no free lunches on Wall Street or Bay Street.

---

[13] Simon Avery, "ATI Insider, Husband to Pay $1.5-million; Cease-Trading Order, Directorship Ban Also Part of Settling OSC Charges," *The Globe and Mail*, April 12, 2005, B2.

weak-form efficiency
Market prices rapidly reflect all information contained in the history of past prices.

semi-strong form efficiency
Market prices rapidly reflect all publicly available information.

strong-form efficiency
Market prices rapidly reflect all information that could in principle be used to determine true value.

It is useful to distinguish three types of information and three degrees of efficiency. The term **weak-form efficiency** describes a market in which prices already reflect all the information contained in past prices. In such a market, share price changes are random and technical analysis that searches for patterns in past returns is valueless. Figure 6.4, which looked at successive weekly and monthly changes in the market index, is evidence in favour of weak-form efficiency.

Semi-strong form efficiency describes a market in which prices reflect not just the information contained in past prices but all publicly available information. In such a market it is impossible to earn consistently superior returns simply by reading the financial press, studying the company's financial statements, and so on. Figure 6.7, which looked at the market reaction to merger announcements, was just one piece of evidence in favour of semi-strong efficiency.

Finally, **strong-form efficiency** refers to a market where prices impound all available information. In such a market no investor, no matter how hard working, could expect to earn superior profits. Figure 6.3, which showed the performance of mutual funds, was consistent with strong-form efficiency.

Check Point 6.10   Technical analysts and fundamental analysts all try to earn superior returns in the stock market. Explain how their efforts help keep the market efficient.

SOME PUZZLES AND ANOMALIES

Few simple economic theories are as well supported by the evidence as the efficient market theory. However, no theory this simple can be universally true; there are always some puzzles or apparent exceptions. Let us look at two examples.

The Earnings Announcement Puzzle

In an efficient stock market, a company's stock price should react instantly at the announcement of unexpectedly good or bad earnings. But Bernard and Thomas found that the stocks with the best earnings news outperformed the stocks with the worst earnings news by more than 4 percent during the 2 months following the earnings announcements.[14] Apparently stock prices did not reflect all available information at the ends of the earnings-announcement days. It seems instead that investors underreacted to the earnings announcement and became aware of the full significance only as further information arrived.

The New-Issue Puzzle

When firms issue stock to the public, investors typically rush to buy. On average, those lucky enough to receive stock receive an immediate capital gain. However, researchers have found that these early gains often turn into losses. For example, suppose that you bought stock immediately following each initial public offering and then held that stock for five years. Over the period 1970 to 1998 your average annual return would have been 33 percent less than the return on a portfolio of similar-sized stocks.

The jury is still out on these studies of longer-term anomalies. We can't be sure whether they are important exceptions to the efficient market theory or a coincidence that stems from the efforts of many researchers to find interesting patterns in the data. There may also be other explanations. Take, for example, the new-issue puzzle. Most new issues during the past 30 years have involved growth stocks with high market values and limited book assets. Perhaps the stocks performed badly not because they had just been issued but because all growth stock happened to perform badly during this period. Of course, if that is true, we need to address another question: Why have growth stocks performed poorly over such a long period of time? We will come back to this question in Chapter 11.

---

[14] See V. L. Bernard and J. K. Thomas, "Post-Earnings-Announcement Drift: Delayed Price Response or Risk Premium?" *Journal of Accounting Research* 27 (Supplement 1989), pp. 1–36.

6.7   BEHAVIOURAL FINANCE AND THE RISE AND FALL OF THE DOT.COMS

Investors in technology stocks in the 1990s saw an extraordinary run-up in the value of their holdings. The Nasdaq market index, which is heavily weighted toward high-tech stocks, rose 580 percent from the start of 1995 to March 2000. But then even more rapidly than it began, the boom ended. By October 2002 the Nasdaq index had fallen 78 percent.

Some of the largest price gains and losses were experienced by the new "dot.com stocks." For example, Yahoo shares, which began trading in April 1996, appreciated by 1,400 percent in just 4 years. At this point Yahoo stock was valued at $124 billion, more than that of General Motors, Heinz, and Boeing combined. It was not, however, to last; just over a year later Yahoo's market capitalization was little more than $6 billion.

A tech stock high-flyer was Nortel Networks, a Canadian multinational telecommunications equipment manufacturer. At its peak of $123.10 in July 2000, Nortel accounted for 40 percent of the TSX Composite Index. However, by the fall of 2002, Nortel's stock was worth less than $1.

What caused the boom in high-tech stocks? Had there been a sharp improvement in the prospects for dividend growth? Or had investors decided that they did not need such high returns from common stocks? Neither explanation seemed capable of explaining the prices that investors were prepared to pay. Could it be that the theory of efficient markets was another casualty of the rise and fall of the dot.coms?

Some believe that the answers to these questions lie in behavioural psychology. People are not 100 percent rational 100 percent of the time. This shows up in two broad areas—their attitudes to risk and the way that they assess probabilities.

1. *Attitudes toward risk.* Psychologists have observed that, when making risky decisions, people are particularly loath to incur losses, even if those losses are small. Losers are liable to regret their actions and kick themselves for having been so foolish. To avoid this unpleasant possibility, individuals will tend to avoid those actions that may result in loss.

   The pain of a loss seems to depend on whether it comes on the heels of earlier losses. Once investors have suffered a loss, they may be even more cautious not to risk a further loss. Conversely, just as gamblers are known to be more willing to take large bets when they are ahead, so investors may be more prepared to run the risk of a stock market dip after they have experienced a period of substantial gains. If they do then suffer a small loss, they at least have the consolation of being up on the year.

   You can see how this sort of behaviour could lead to a stock-price "bubble." The early investors in Yahoo, Amazon.com, and other dot.coms were big winners. They may have stopped worrying about the risk of loss. They may have thrown caution to the winds and piled even more investment into these companies, driving stock prices far above fundamental values. The day of reckoning came when investors woke up and realized how far above fundamental value prices had soared.

2. *Beliefs about probabilities.* Most investors do not have a Ph.D. in probability theory and may make common errors in assessing the probability of uncertain outcomes. Psychologists have found that, when judging the possible future outcomes, individuals commonly look back to what has happened in recent periods and then assume that this is representative of what may occur in the future. The temptation is to project recent experience into the future and to forget the lessons learned from the more distant past. For example, an investor who places too much weight on recent events may judge that glamorous growth companies are very likely to continue to grow rapidly, even though very high rates of growth cannot persist indefinitely.

   A second common bias is that of overconfidence. Most of us believe that we are better-than-average drivers, and most investors think that they are better-than-average stockpickers. We know that two speculators who trade with one another cannot both make money from the deal; for every winner there must be a loser. But presumably investors are prepared to continue trading because each is confident that it is the other one who is the patsy.

You can see how such behaviour may have reinforced the dot.com boom. As the bull market developed, it generated "irrational exuberance" about the future[15] and stimulated demand for shares. The more that investors racked up profits on their stocks, the more confident they became in their views and the more willing they became to bear the risk that the next month might not be so good.

It is too early to say how far behavioural finance scholars can help to sort out some of the puzzles and explain events like the dot.com boom. One thing, however, seems clear: It is relatively easy for statisticians to spot anomalies with the benefit of hindsight and for psychologists to provide an explanation for them. It is much more difficult for investment managers who are at the sharp end to spot and invest in mispriced securities. And that is the basic message of the efficient market theory.

6.8   SUMMARY

1. What information about company stocks is regularly reported in the financial pages of newspapers and on-line financial services?

Firms that wish to raise new capital may either borrow money or bring new "partners" into the business by selling shares of **common stock**. Large companies usually arrange for their stocks to be traded on a stock exchange. The stock listings report the stock's dividend yield, price, and trading volume.

2. How can one calculate the present value of a stock given forecasts of future dividends and future stock price?

Shareholders generally expect to receive (1) cash **dividends**, and (2) capital gains or losses. The rate of return that they expect over the next year is defined as the expected dividend per share DIV_1 plus the expected increase in price $P_1 - P_0$, all divided by the price at the start of the year P_0.

Unlike the fixed interest payments that the firm promises to bondholders, the dividends that are paid to shareholders depend on the fortunes of the firm. That's why a company's common stock is riskier than its debt. The return that investors expect on any one stock is also the return that they demand on all stocks subject to the same degree of risk. The present value of a stock equals the present value of the forecast future dividends and future stock price, using that expected return as the discount rate.

3. How can stock valuation formulas be used to infer the expected rate of return on a common stock?

The present value of a share is equal to the stream of expected dividends per share up to some horizon date plus the expected price at this date, all discounted at the return that investors require. If the horizon date is far away, we simply say that stock price equals the present value of all future dividends per share. This is the **dividend discount model**.

If dividends are expected to grow forever at a constant rate g, then the expected return on the stock is equal to the dividend yield (DIV_1/P_0) plus the expected rate of dividend growth. The value of the stock according to this constant-growth dividend discount model is $P_0 = DIV_1/(r - g)$.

4. How should investors interpret price-earnings ratios?

You can think of a share's value as the sum of two parts— the value of the assets in place and the **present value of growth opportunities**, that is, of future opportunities for the firm to invest in high-return projects. The price-earnings (P/E) ratio reflects the market's assessment of the firm's growth opportunities.

---

[15] The term "irrational exuberance" was coined by Alan Greenspan, chairman of the Federal Reserve Board, to describe the dot.com boom. It was also the title of a book by Robert Shiller that examined the boom. See R. Shiller, *Irrational Exuberance* (Broadway Books, 2001). For another view of the dot.com boom check out John Cassidy's book, *Dot.con: How America Lost Its Mind and Money in the Internet Era* (Perennial Currents, 2003).

5. How does competition among investors lead to efficient markets?

Competition between investors will tend to produce an **efficient market**—that is, a market in which prices rapidly reflect new information, and investors have difficulty making consistently superior returns. Of course, we all hope to beat the market, but, if the market is efficient, all we can rationally expect is a return that is sufficient on average to compensate for the time value of money and for the risks we bear.

The efficient market theory comes in three flavours. The **weak form** states that prices reflect all the information contained in the past series of stock prices. In this case it is impossible to earn superior profits simply by looking for past patterns in stock prices. The **semi-strong form** of the theory states that prices reflect all published information, so that it is impossible to make consistently superior returns just by reading the newspaper, looking at the company's annual accounts, and so on. The **strong form** states that stock prices effectively impound all available information. This form tells us that private information is hard to come by, because in pursuing it you are in competition with thousands—perhaps millions—of active and intelligent investors. The best you can do in this case is to assume that securities are fairly priced.

The evidence for market efficiency is voluminous and there is little doubt that skilled professional investors find it difficult to win consistently. Nevertheless, there remain some puzzling instances where markets do not seem to be efficient. Some financial economists attribute these apparent anomalies to behavioural foibles.

Related Web Links

www.tsx.com Information about stocks trading on the Toronto Stock Exchange and the TSX Venture Exchange

www.nasdaq.com Web site of Nasdaq stock market

www.nyse.com Web site of the New York Stock Exchange

www.123world.com/stockexchanges Links to exchanges

www.fibv.com Web site of World Federation of Exchanges

www.globeinvestor.com Information about companies and their share prices

ca.finance.yahoo.com Useful company and market information

www.fool.com/School/HowtoValueStocks.htm How investors value firms

www.dividenddiscountmodel.com Calculator for estimating stock values

www.valuepro.net More elaborate software for estimating stock values

Key Terms

common stock	165	market-value balance sheet	170	random walk	184
primary market	165	dividend discount model	172	fundamental analysts	186
initial public offering (IPO)	165	constant-growth dividend		inside information	186
secondary market	165	discount model	176	insiders	186
dividend	167	payout ratio	180	insider trading	187
price-earnings (P/E)		plowback ratio	180	efficient market	187
multiple	167	present value of growth		weak-form efficiency	188
preferred stock	167	opportunities (PVGO)	181	semi-strong form	
book value	168	sustainable growth rate	181	efficiency	188
liquidation value	168	technical analysts	183	strong-form efficiency	188

Questions and Problems

BASIC

1. **Dividend Discount Model.** Rogers Wireless Communications has never paid a dividend, but in July 2004 its share price was $39.25 and the market value of its stock is $5,605 million. Does this invalidate the dividend discount model?

2. **Dividend Yield.** Favoured stock will pay a dividend this year of $2.40 per share. Its dividend yield is 8 percent. At what price is the stock selling?

*3. **Preferred Stock.** Preferred Products has issued preferred stock with a $7 annual dividend that will be paid in perpetuity.
   a. If the discount rate is 12 percent, at what price should the preferred sell?
   b. At what price should the stock sell one year from now?
   c. What is the dividend yield, the capital gains yield, and the expected rate of return of the stock?

4. **Constant-Growth Model.** Waterworks has a dividend yield of 8 percent. If its dividend is expected to grow at a constant rate of 5 percent, what must be the expected rate of return on the company's stock?

5. **Dividend Discount Model.** How can we say that price equals the present value of all future dividends when many investors may be seeking capital gains and planning to hold their shares for only a year or two? Explain.

*6. **Rate of Return.** Steady As She Goes, Inc. will pay a year-end dividend of $2.50 per share. Investors expect the dividend to grow at a rate of 4 percent indefinitely.
   a. If the stock currently sells for $25 per share, what is the expected rate of return on the stock?
   b. If the expected rate of return on the stock is 16.5 percent, what is the stock price?

7. **Dividend Yield.** BMM Industries pays a dividend of $2 per quarter. The dividend yield on its stock is reported at 4.8 percent. What price is the stock selling at?

*8. **Forms of Efficient Markets.** Supply the missing words from the following list: *fundamental, semi-strong, strong, technical, weak.*

   There are three forms of the efficient market theory. Tests that have found there are no patterns in share price changes provide evidence for the _____ form of the theory. Evidence for the _____ form of the theory is provided by tests that look at how rapidly markets respond to new public information, and evidence for the _____ form of the theory is provided by tests that look at the performance of professionally managed portfolios. Market efficiency results from competition between investors. Many investors search for information about the company's business that would help them to value the stock more accurately. This is known as _____ analysis. Such research helps to ensure that prices reflect all available information. Other investors study past stock prices for recurrent patterns that would allow them to make superior profits. This is known as _____ analysis. Such research helps to eliminate any patterns.

9. **Information and Efficient Markets.** "It's competition for information that makes securities markets efficient." Is this statement correct? Explain.

PRACTICE

EXCEL

*10. **Stock Values.** Integrated Potato Chips paid a $1 per share dividend *yesterday*. You expect the dividend to grow steadily at a rate of 4 percent per year.
   a. What is the expected dividend in each of the next three years?
   b. If the discount rate for the stock is 12 percent, at what price will the stock sell?
   c. What is the expected stock price three years from now?
   d. If you buy the stock and plan to hold it for three years, what payments will you receive? What is the present value of those payments? Compare your answer to part (b).

11. **Constant-Growth Model.** A stock sells for $40. The next dividend will be $4 per share. If the rate of return earned on reinvested funds is 15 percent and the company reinvests 40 percent of earnings in the firm, what must be the discount rate?

*12.   **Constant-Growth Model.** Gentleman Gym just paid its annual dividend of $2 per share, and it is widely expected that the dividend will increase by 5 percent per year indefinitely.
    a.   What price should the stock sell at? The discount rate is 15 percent.
    b.   How would your answer change if the discount rate were only 12 percent? Why does the answer change?

13.   **Constant-Growth Model.** Arts and Crafts, Inc. will pay a dividend of $5 per share in 1 year. It sells at $50 a share, and firms in the same industry provide an expected rate of return of 14 percent. What must be the expected growth rate of the company's dividends?

EXCEL

*14.   **Constant-Growth Model.** Eastern Electric currently pays a dividend of about $1.64 per share and sells for $27 a share.
    a.   If investors believe the growth rate of dividends is 3 percent per year, what rate of return do they expect to earn on the stock?
    b.   If investors' required rate of return is 10 percent, what must be the growth rate they expect of the firm?
    c.   If the sustainable growth rate is 5 percent and the plowback ratio is .4, what must be the rate of return earned by the firm on its new investments?

15.   **Constant-Growth Model.** You believe that the Non-Stick Gum Factory will pay a dividend of $2 on its common stock next year. Thereafter, you expect dividends to grow at a rate of 6 percent a year in perpetuity. If you require a return of 12 percent on your investment, how much should you be prepared to pay for the stock?

16.   **Negative Growth.** Horse and Buggy Inc. is in a declining industry. Sales, earnings, and dividends are all shrinking at a rate of 10 percent per year.
    a.   If $r = 15$ percent and $DIV_1 = \$3$, what is the value of a share?
    b.   What price do you forecast for the stock next year?
    c.   What is the expected rate of return on the stock?
    d.   Can you distinguish between "bad stocks" and "bad companies"? Does the fact that the industry is declining mean that the stock is a bad buy?

*17.   **Constant-Growth Model.** Metatrend's stock will generate earnings of $5 per share this year. The discount rate for the stock is 15 percent and the rate of return on reinvested earnings is also 15 percent.
    a.   Find both the growth rate of dividends and the price of the stock if the company reinvests the following fraction of its earnings in the firm: (1) 0 percent, (2) 40 percent, (3) 60 percent.
    b.   Redo part (a) now assuming that the rate of return on reinvested earnings is 20 percent. What is the present value of growth opportunities for each reinvestment rate?
    c.   Considering your answers to parts (a) and (b), can you briefly state the difference between companies experiencing growth versus companies with growth opportunities?

18.   **Internet.** The major stock exchanges are members of the World Federation of Exchanges, found at **www.fibv.com**. Click on "Members," and select a region and stock exchange. Click on the exchange's symbol to go to the stock exchange's Web site. You can also find links to stock exchanges at **www.123world.com/stockexchanges**. Visit the Web sites of three stock exchanges from different continents. Describe their differences and similarities and compare them to the Toronto Stock Exchange, **www.tsx.com**.

19.   **Internet.** Do you think that all stock exchanges trade stocks? Check out the Hollywood Stock exchange on **www.hsx.com**. Buy shares in your favourite actors, movies, and music artists and watch their values rise or fall based on the success of their careers and personal life. Join and play for free. It's 90 percent fun but it will also get you used to some stock market jargon. Real stock values are established with "votes," just like on the HSX, but the votes cost real money.

*20. **Non-Constant Growth.** You expect a share of stock to pay dividends of $1, $1.25, and $1.50 in each of the next 3 years. You believe the stock will sell for $20 at the end of the third year.
   a.   What is the stock price if the discount rate for the stock is 10 percent?
   b.   What is the dividend yield?

21. **Constant-Growth Model.** Here are recent data on two stocks, both of which have discount rates of 15 percent:

	Stock A	Stock B
Return on equity	15%	10%
Earnings per share	$2.00	$1.50
Dividends per share	$1.00	$1.00

   a.   What are the dividend payout ratios for each firm?
   b.   What are the expected dividend growth rates for each firm?
   c.   What is the proper stock price for each firm?

*22. **P/E Ratios.** Web Cites Research projects a rate of return of 20 percent on new projects. Management plans to plow back 30 percent of all earnings into the firm. Earnings this year will be $2 per share, and investors expect a 12 percent rate of return on the stock.
   a.   What is the sustainable growth rate?
   b.   What is the stock price?
   c.   What is the present value of growth opportunities?
   d.   What is the P/E ratio?
   e.   What would the price and P/E ratio be if the firm paid out all earnings as dividends?
   f.   What do you conclude about the relationship between growth opportunities and P/E ratios?

23. **Constant-Growth Model.** Fincorp will pay a year-end dividend of $4.80 per share, which is expected to grow at a 4 percent rate indefinitely. The discount rate is 12 percent.
   a.   What is the stock selling for?
   b.   If earnings are $6.20 a share, what is the implied value of the firm's growth opportunities?

*24. **P/E Ratios.** No-Growth Industries pays out all of its earnings as dividends. It will pay its next $4 per share dividend in a year. The discount rate is 12 percent.
   a.   What is the price-earnings ratio of the company?
   b.   What would the P/E ratio be if the discount rate were 10 percent?

25. **Growth Opportunities.** Stormy Weather has no attractive investment opportunities. Its return on equity equals the discount rate, which is 10 percent. Its expected earnings this year are $3 per share. Find the stock price, P/E ratio, and growth rate of dividends for plowback ratios of
   a.   zero
   b.   .40
   c.   .80

*26. **Growth Opportunities.** Trend-line Inc. has been growing at a rate of 6 percent per year and is expected to continue to do so indefinitely. The next dividend is expected to be $5 per share.
   a.   If the market expects a 10 percent rate of return on Trend-line, at what price must it be selling?
   b.   If Trend-line's earnings per share will be $8, what part of Trend-line's value is due to assets in place, and what part to growth opportunities?

27. **P/E Ratios.** Castles in the Sand generates a rate of return of 20 percent on its investments and maintains a plowback ratio of .30. Its earnings this year will be $2 per share. Investors expect a 12 percent rate of return on the stock.
   a. Find the price and P/E ratio of the firm.
   b. What happens to the P/E ratio if the plowback ratio is reduced to .20? Why?
   c. Show that if plowback equals zero, the earnings-price ratio, E/P, falls to the expected rate of return on the stock.

28. **Dividend Growth.** Grandiose Growth has a dividend growth rate of 20 percent. The discount rate is 10 percent. The end-of-year dividend will be $2 per share.
   a. What is the present value of the dividend to be paid in Year 1? Year 2? Year 3?
   b. Could anyone rationally expect this growth rate to continue indefinitely?

EXCEL

*29. **Stock Valuation.** Start-up Industries is a new firm, which has raised $100 million by selling shares of stock. Management plans to earn a 24 percent rate of return on equity, which is more than the 15 percent rate of return available on comparable-risk investments. Half of all earnings will be reinvested in the firm.
   a. What will be Start-up's ratio of market value to book value?
   b. How would that ratio change if the firm can earn only a 10 percent rate of return on its investments?

30. **Non-Constant Growth.** Planned Obsolescence has a product that will be in vogue for three years, at which point the firm will close up shop and liquidate the assets. As a result, forecast dividends are $DIV_1 = \$2$, $DIV_2 = \$2.50$, and $DIV_3 = \$18$. What is the stock price if the discount rate is 12 percent?

31. **Non-Constant Growth.** Tattletale News Corp. has been growing at a rate of 20 percent per year, and you expect this growth rate in earnings and dividends to continue for another 3 years.
   a. If the last dividend paid was $2, what will the next dividend be?
   b. If the discount rate is 15 percent and the steady growth rate after 3 years is 4 percent, what should the stock price be today?
   c. What is your prediction for the stock price in one year?
   d. Show that the expected rate of return equals the discount rate.

32. **Non-Constant Growth.** ToyTime's common stock's annual dividend for the next three years is expected to be $0.50. Thereafter, the dividend is expected to grow 4 percent per year. Stocks of ToyTime's risk are expected to earn 11 percent per annum.
   a. Calculate the share price today and at the beginning of each of the next four years.
   b. Calculate the dividend yield and capital gains yield for each year. Does the dividend yield plus the capital gains yield equal the expected return each year?

33. **Non-Constant Growth.** Earnings per common share of ABC Industries for the current year are expected to be $3 and to grow 10 percent per year over the next 4 years. At the end of the five years, earnings growth rate is expected to fall to 5 percent and continue at that rate for the foreseeable future. ABC's dividend payout ratio is 40 percent. If the expected return on ABC's common shares is 15 percent, calculate the current share price.

34. **Internet.**
   a. Create a list of preferred shares traded on the TSX using the Filter button at **www.globeinvestor.com**. Select "Preferred" from the "Security" menu. Find BCE's Series A preferred shares, which pays an annual dividend of $1.3625. Use the current share price to calculate the expected rate of return on the share.
   b. Go to **http://www.cibc.com/ca/investor-relations/share-info/preferred-shares.html**. Using Globeinvestor, see if you can match the listed preferred shares of CIBC with their trading prices. Using the dividend discount model, calculate the discount rate for each preferred share.

35. **Internet.** Go to **www.globeinvestor.com/static/hubs/quotes.html**, enter ATY-T, and click "Go." Click on "Company Snapshot" and find out what the company does and visit its Web site. What type of information is provided to its investors? Repeat for SRF-T. Compare and contrast the information provided to shareholders.

36. **Internet.** Canadian corporate insiders are now required to post their trades at **www.sedi.ca**. Visit the site and look up the trading activity of Gerald Schwartz, Frank Stronach and Kenneth Thomson, three wealthy Canadian businessmen. Look at the other sorts of information provided at the site. Do you think this information might be of value to you as an investor? Explain.

*37. **After-Tax Rate of Return.** One year ago you purchased 100 shares of Dog Bites common stock for $25. You received dividends of $.70 per share and just sold the shares for $26.25 each. What are your before- and after-tax rates of return? Your marginal personal tax rate is 40 percent, your dividend tax rate is 30 percent, and capital gains are taxed at 50 percent of your personal rate.

38. **Interpreting the Efficient Market Theory.** How would you respond to the following comments?
   a. "Efficient market, my eye! I know lots of investors who do crazy things."
   b. "Efficient market? Balderdash! I know at least a dozen people who have made a bundle in the stock market."
   c. "The trouble with the efficient market theory is that it ignores investors' psychology."

39. **Investment Performance.** It seems that every month we read an article in *The Globe and Mail* or *National Post* about a stockpicker with a marvellous track record. Do these examples mean that financial markets are not efficient?

*40. **Implications of Efficient Markets.** The president of Good Fortunes, Inc., states at a press conference that the company has a 30-year history of ever-increasing dividend payments. Good Fortunes is widely regarded as one of the best-run firms in its industry. Does this make the firm's stock a good buy? Explain.

41. **Implications of Efficient Markets.** "Long-term interest rates are at record highs. Most companies, therefore, find it cheaper to finance with common stock or relatively inexpensive short-term bank loans." Discuss.

42. **Expectations and Efficient Markets.** Geothermal Corp. just announced good news: its earnings have increased by 20 percent. Most investors had anticipated an increase of 25 percent. Will Geothermal's stock price increase or decrease when the announcement is made?

CHALLENGE

43. **Sustainable Growth.** Computer Corp. reinvests 60 percent of its earnings in the firm. The stock sells for $50, and the next dividend will be $2.50 per share. The discount rate is 15 percent. What is the rate of return on the company's reinvested funds?

44. **Non-Constant Growth.** A company will pay a $1 per share dividend in 1 year. The dividend in 2 years will be $2 per share, and it is expected that dividends will grow at 5 percent per year thereafter. The expected rate of return on the stock is 12 percent.
   a. What is the current price of the stock?
   b. What is the expected price of the stock in a year?
   c. Show that the expected return, 12 percent, equals dividend yield plus capital appreciation.

45. **Non-Constant Growth.** Phoenix Industries has pulled off a miraculous recovery. Four years ago it was near bankruptcy. Today, it announced a $1 per share dividend to be paid a year from now, the first dividend since the crisis. Analysts expect dividends to increase by $1 a year for another 2 years. After the third year (in which dividends are $3 per share),

dividend growth is expected to settle down to a more moderate long-term growth rate of 6 percent. If the firm's investors expect to earn a return of 14 percent on this stock, what must be its price?

46. **Non-Constant Growth.** Compost Science, Inc. (CSI) is in the business of converting Calgary's sewage sludge into fertilizer. The business is not in itself very profitable. However, to induce CSI to remain in business, the Metropolitan District Commission (MDC) has agreed to pay whatever amount is necessary to yield CSI a 10 percent return on investment. At the end of the year, CSI is expected to pay a $4 dividend. It has been reinvesting 40 percent of earnings and growing at 4 percent a year.

   a. Suppose CSI continues on this growth trend. What is the expected rate of return from purchasing the stock at $100?

   b. What part of the $100 price is attributable to the present value of growth opportunities?

   c. Now the MDC announces a plan for CSI to treat Edmonton sewage. CSI's plant will therefore be expanded gradually over five years. This means that CSI will have to reinvest 80 percent of its earnings for 5 years. Starting in Year 6, however, it will again be able to pay out 60 percent of earnings. What will be CSI's stock price once this announcement is made and its consequences for CSI are known?

EXCEL

47. **Non-Constant Growth.** Better Mousetraps has come out with an improved product, and the world is beating a path to its door. As a result, the firm projects growth of 20 percent per year for 4 years. By then, other firms will have copycat technology, competition will drive down profit margins, and the sustainable growth rate will fall to 5 percent. The most recent annual dividend was $DIV_0 = \$1.00$ per share.

   a. What are the expected values of DIV_1, DIV_2, DIV_3, and DIV_4?

   b. What is the expected stock price four years from now? The discount rate is 10 percent.

   c. What is the stock price today?

   d. Find the dividend yield, DIV_1/P_0.

   e. What will next year's stock price, P_1, be?

   f. What is the expected rate of return to an investor who buys the stock now and sells it in one year?

48. **After-Tax Rate of Return.** You live in B.C. and your marginal federal tax rate is 22 percent, your marginal provincial tax rate is 11.9 percent, the dividend gross-up factor is 125 percent, the federal dividend tax credit is 13.33 percent of grossed-up dividends, and the provincial dividend tax credit is 6.6 percent of grossed-up dividends. If you bought shares of Mighty Mixer for $50, received dividends of $2, and sold the shares for $53 one year after you bought them, what are your before- and after-tax rates of return?

49. **After-Tax Rate of Return.** Refer back to problem 48. Suppose you bought the shares of Mighty Mixer for $50, received annual dividends of $2, and sold the shares for $55 three years after you bought them. What are your before- and after-tax rates of return on your investment? *Hint:* You will need to make an assumption about what happens to the $2 dividends received in Year 1 and Year 2.

50. **After-Tax Rate of Return.** You have $10,000 to invest and are considering either a consol (a perpetual bond) or preferred shares of Canada Leasing. The consol has a $1,000 par value, an annual coupon rate of 4 percent, and never matures. The preferred share pays fixed dividends of $6 and is expected to continue indefinitely. Currently, the consol is selling for $800 and the preferred share for $120.

   a. What is the before-tax expected rate of return on each of the investments?

   b. If your personal tax rate is 35 percent, your dividend tax rate is 29 percent, and capital gains are taxed at 50 percent of the personal tax rate, what is the after-tax expected rate of return on each investment?

c. What is the expected rate of return on each investment to a Canadian corporation with a corporate tax rate of 35 percent?

d. Why do you think that many of the preferred shares sold by Canadian corporations are purchased by other Canadian corporations?

51. **Non-Constant Growth.** Skyward Ideas currently pays no dividends but invests all of its earnings into the company. Analysts expect that 3 years from today, the company will pay its first annual dividend of $.50 and dividends will grow at 6 percent thereafter. If the discount rate is 10 percent, at what price should the stock sell today?

52. **Non-Constant Growth.** City Garden Suppliers paid a $1 dividend yesterday. It is expected that the dividend will grow at 10 percent per year for 4 years, 8 percent per year for 10 years, and then at 5 percent per year thereafter. If the investors' expected rate of return is 12 percent, what is the stock worth today? *Hint:* Use the present value formula for a growing annuity from Chapter 4.

53. **Non-Constant Growth.** Golddigger, a gold exploration and development company, currently pays no dividends. Using the company's assay reports, analysts have determined the following possible outcomes of Goldigger's exploration efforts in one year:

Event	Probability	Annual Dividend per Share
High-quality gold vein	40%	$8
Medium-quality gold vein	50	2
No gold	10	0

If gold is found, the mine is expected to operate for 20 years and then be exhausted. If investors expect to earn 9 percent on gold mining stocks, what will be the price of the stock today?

54. **Non-Constant Growth.** ABC Manufacturing pays dividends annually. Today is May 1, 2006. Its next dividend, to be paid one year from today, will be $1.20 per share. The company is involved in a research and development (R&D) program to develop a new widget. The results are expected in one year. The discount rate is 10 percent.

a. It is May 1, 2007. The new widget is a great success, and ABC pays its previously announced $1.20 dividend and announces the 2008 dividend will be $2.50 per share. What will be the stock price on May 1, 2007, if dividends beyond 2008 are expected to grow at 6 percent in perpetuity?

b. Suppose, instead, it is May 1, 2007, and the company announces that the widget program has ended and that the next annual dividend will be $1.248, 4 percent larger than the dividend it just paid. What is the stock price May 1, 2007?

c. If the probability of success of the R&D is 30 percent, what price would you expect the stock to be today?

d. Suppose you bought the stock for the price you calculated in part (c) and the research and development program is successful; what will be the one-year rate of return on your investment? What will be the one-year rate of return on your investment if the R&D is not successful? What is the expected rate of return?

55. **Yield Curve and EMH.** If the yield curve is downward sloping, meaning that long-term interest rates are lower than current short-term rates, what might investors believe about *future* short-term interest rates?

56. **Implications of EMH.** Suppose that a company *splits* its stock two-for-one, meaning that it doubles the number of shares outstanding. Each shareholder is given a new share for

each one previously held, so that the number of shares held doubles. The split is not associated with any change in the firm's investment policy.

a. Has the firm acquired any new assets as a result of the split?

b. Has anything happened to the value of the firm's real assets (its projects)?

c. What will happen to earnings per share?

d. What should happen to the firm's stock price?

e. What should happen to the dollar value of the shareholder's stock? Has investor wealth changed?

57. **Internet.** An on-line dividend growth model is available at **www.dividenddiscountmodel .com**. The "simple model" is the constant dividend growth model and calculates the stock price as $DIV_1/(r - g)$, where DIV_1 is "current dividend," r is "discount rate," and g is the dividend growth rate and is assumed to equal the "projected EPS growth." The projected EPS growth rate provided is based on analysts' forecasts for the next five years. Although stocks listed on U.S. stock exchanges are included in the database, not all have a forecasted EPS growth rate. Try out the model for Heinz (HNZ). Value the stock using the simple model, assuming that the discount rate is equal to the expected return shown in the table. Apart from rounding error, the estimated value should be the same as the current stock price. Calculate the stock price if investors decided that they required a one-percentage-point higher return from the stock. Change the current dividend to $1, projected EPS growth rate to 5 percent, and use 10 percent discount rate to verify that calculator is working properly.

58. **Standard & Poor's.** Go to **www.mcgrawhill.ca/edumarketinsight**. Select companies from five different industry subgroups. For each company calculate the market value per share, the book value per share, and the ratio of price to book, as we did in Table 6.2. Also, get the industry average for each company, found in "Financial Highlights." Which companies and industries have the highest price-to-book ratios? Which have the lowest? Try to explain any patterns that you see.

59. **Standard & Poor's.** From the Company Profile and Financial Highlights reports for H.J. Heinz (HNZ) and BCE (BCE) at **www.mcgrawhill.ca/edumarketinsight**, find their current dividends, the five-year dividend growth rates and the current share prices. Forecast each stock's next year's dividend with this information. Estimate each stock's current required rates of return using the constant dividend growth stock valuation model.

60. **Integrative.** At Green Construction, earnings before interest and taxes (EBIT) for the year just ended were $70 million and are not expected to grow. The company pays $10 million in interest each year on its perpetual bonds. The expected rate of return on its bonds is 5 percent and on its stocks is 11 percent. Last year, interest rates were higher and the bond's expected rate of return was 6 percent. Green's corporate tax rate is 30 percent. Green's dividend payout ratio is 100 percent. Green has 15 million shares outstanding and 150,000 bonds with $1,000 par value. Calculate Green's current share price and its current bond price.

Solutions to Check Points

6.1 CP's high and low prices over the past 52 weeks have been $46.52 and $29.36 per share. Its annual dividend is $0.53 per share. The highest price at which the shares traded during the day was $44.74, the lowest was $42.22, and the closing price was $43.00, which was $1.55 lower than the previous day's close. Trading volume was 1,097,600 shares. The ratio of stock price to earnings per share, the P/E ratio was 16.5, and dividend yield was 1.2 percent.

6.2 IBM's forecast future profitability has fallen. Thus the value of future investment opportunities has fallen relative to the value of assets in place. This happens in all growth industries sooner or later, as competition increases and profitable new investment opportunities shrink. RIM has experienced a similar shift, its assets in place increasing relative to its growth opportunities. By July 2005, RIM's price-to-book ratio had fallen to 6.7.

6.3 $P_0 = \dfrac{DIV_1 + P_1}{1 + r} = \dfrac{\$5 + \$105}{1.10} = \$100$

6.4   Since dividends and share price grow at 5 percent,

$$DIV_2 = \$5 \times 1.05 = \$5.25, \ \ DIV_3 = \$5 \times 1.05^2 = \$5.51$$

$$P_3 = \$100 \times 1.05^3 = \$115.76$$

$$P_0 = \dfrac{DIV_1}{1 + r} + \dfrac{DIV_2}{(1 + r)^2} + \dfrac{DIV_3 + P_3}{(1 + r)^3}$$

$$= \dfrac{\$5.00}{1.10} + \dfrac{\$5.25}{1.10^2} + \dfrac{\$5.51 + \$115.76}{1.10^3} = \$100$$

6.5 $P_0 = \dfrac{DIV}{r} = \dfrac{\$25}{.20} = \$125$

6.6   The two firms have equal risk, so we can use the data for Androscoggin to find the expected return on either stock:

$$r = \dfrac{DIV_1}{P_0} + g = \dfrac{\$5}{\$100} + .05 = .10, \text{ or } 10 \text{ percent}$$

6.7   We've already calculated the present value of dividends through Year 3 as $2.98. We can also forecast stock price in Year 4 as

$$P_4 = \dfrac{\$1.73 \times 1.05}{.10 - .05} = \$36.33$$

$$P_0 = PV \text{ (dividends through Year 3)} + PV(DIV_4) + PV(P_4)$$

$$= \$2.98 + \dfrac{\$1.73}{1.10^4} + \dfrac{\$36.33}{1.10^4}$$

$$= \$2.98 + \$1.18 + \$24.81 = \$28.97$$

6.8   a. The sustainable growth rate is

$$g = \text{return on equity} \times \text{plowback ratio}$$
$$= .10 \times .40 = .04, \text{ or } 4 \text{ percent}$$

b. First value the company. At a 60 percent payout ratio, $DIV_1 = \$3.00$ as before. Using the constant-growth model,

$$P_0 = \dfrac{\$3}{.12 - .04} = \$37.50$$

which is $4.17 per share less than the company's no-growth value of $41.67. In this example Blue Skies is throwing away $4.17 of potential value by investing in projects with unattractive rates of return.

c. Sure. A raider could take over the company and generate a profit of $4.17 per share just by halting all investments offering less than the 12 percent rate of return demanded by investors. This assumes the raider could buy the shares for $37.50.

6.9   a. False. The *levels* of successive stock prices are related. If a stock is selling for $100 per share today, the best guess of its price tomorrow is $100.

b. True. *Changes* in stock prices are unrelated. Whether a stock price increases or decreases today has no bearing on whether it will do so tomorrow.

c. False. There is no such thing as a "normal" price. If there were, you could make easy profits by buying shares selling below their normal prices (which would tend to be rising back toward those normal levels) and selling shares currently selling above their normal prices. Under a random walk, prices are equally likely to rise or fall.

d. True. Under a random walk, prices are equally likely to rise or fall regardless of their past history.

6.10 Fundamental analysts ensure that stock prices reflect all publicly available information about the underlying value of the firm. If share prices deviate from their fundamental values, such analysts will generate buying or selling pressure that will return prices to their proper levels. Similarly, technical analysts ensure that if there is useful information in stock price history, it will be reflected in current share prices.

MINICASE

Terence Breezeway, the CEO of Prairie Home Stores, wondered what retirement would be like. It was almost 20 years to the day since his uncle Jacob Breezeway, Prairie Home's founder, had asked him to take responsibility for managing the company. Now it was time to spend more time riding and fishing on the old Lazy Beta Ranch.

Under Mr. Breezeway's leadership Prairie Home had grown slowly but steadily and was solidly profitable. (Table 6.6 shows earnings, dividends, and book asset values for the last five years.) Most of the company's supermarkets had been modernized and its brand name was well known.

Mr. Breezeway was proud of this record, although he wished that Prairie Home could have grown more rapidly. He had passed up several opportunities to build new stores in adjacent counties. Prairie Home was still just a family company. Its common stock was distributed among 15 grandchildren and nephews of Jacob Breezeway, most of whom had come to depend on generous regular dividends. The commitment to high-dividend payout[16] had reduced the earnings available for reinvestment and thereby constrained growth.

Mr. Breezeway believed the time had come to take Prairie Home public. Once its shares were traded in the public market, the Breezeway descendants who needed (or just wanted) more cash to spend could sell off part of their holdings. Others with more interest in the business could hold on to their shares and be rewarded by higher future earnings and stock prices.

But if Prairie Home did go public, what should its shares sell for? Mr. Breezeway worried that shares would be sold, either by Breezeway family members or by the company itself, at too low a price. One relative was about to accept a private offer for $200, the current book value per share, but Mr. Breezeway had intervened and convinced the would-be seller to wait.

Prairie Home's value did not just depend on its current book value or earnings, but on its future prospects, which were good. One financial projection (shown in the top panel of Table 6.7) called for growth in earnings of over 100 percent by 2015. Unfortunately this plan would require reinvestment of all Prairie Home's earnings from 2010 to 2015. After that the company could resume its normal dividend payout and growth rate. Mr. Breezeway believed this plan was feasible.

He was determined to step aside for the next generation of top management. But before retiring he had to decide whether to recommend that Prairie Home Stores "go public"—and before that decision, he had to know what the company was worth.

The next morning he rode to work thoughtfully. He left his horse at the south corral and ambled down the dusty street to Mike Gordon's Saloon, where Francine Firewater, the company's CFO, was having her usual steak-and-beans breakfast. He asked Ms. Firewater to prepare a formal report to Prairie Home shareholders, valuing the company on the assumption that its shares were publicly traded.

Ms. Firewater asked two questions immediately: First, what should she assume about investment and growth? Mr. Breezeway suggested two valuations: one assuming more rapid expansion (as in the top panel of Table 6.7) and another just projecting past growth (as in the bottom panel of Table 6.7).

Second, what rate of return should she use? Mr. Breezeway said that 15 percent, Prairie Home's usual return on book equity, sounded right to him, but he referred her to an article in the *Journal of Finance* indicating that investors in rural supermarket chains, with risks similar to Prairie Home Stores, expected to earn about 11 percent on average.

TABLE 6.6
Financial data for Prairie Home Stores, 2005–2009 ($ millions)

	2005	2006	2007	2008	2009
Book value, start of year	$62.7	66.1	69.0	73.9	76.5
Earnings	$9.7	9.5	11.8	10.0	11.2
Dividends	$6.3	6.6	6.9	7.4	7.7
Addition to retained earnings	$3.4	2.9	4.9	2.6	3.5
Book value, end of year	$66.1	69.0	73.9	76.5	80.0

Notes:
1. Prairie Home Stores has 400,000 common shares.
2. The company's policy is to pay cash dividends equal to 10 percent of start-of-year book value.

[16] The company traditionally paid out cash dividends equal to 10 percent of start-of-period book value. See Table 6.6.

TABLE 6.7
Financial projections for
Prairie Home Stores,
2010–2015 ($ millions)

	2010	2011	2012	2013	2014	2015
Rapid-Growth Scenario						
Book value, start of year	80	92	105.8	121.7	140.0	147.0
Earnings	12	13.8	15.9	18.3	21.0	22.0
Dividends	0	0	0	0	14	14.7
Addition to retained earnings	12	13.8	15.9	18.3	7.0	7.3
Book value, end of year	92	105.8	121.7	140.0	147.0	154.3
Constant-Growth Scenario						
Book value, start of year	80	84	88.2	92.6	97.2	102.1
Earnings	12	12.6	13.2	13.9	14.6	15.3
Dividends	8	8.4	8.8	9.3	9.7	10.2
Addition to retained earnings	4	4.2	4.4	4.6	4.9	5.1
Book value, end of year	84	88.2	92.6	97.2	102.1	107.2

Notes:

1. Both panels assume earnings equal to 15 percent of start-of-year book value. This profitability rate is constant.

2. The top panel assumes all earnings are reinvested from the start of 2010 to the end of 2014. At the end of 2015 and later years, two-thirds of earnings are paid out as dividends and one-third reinvested.

3. The bottom panel assumes two-thirds of earnings are paid out as dividends in all years.

CHAPTER 7

NET PRESENT VALUE AND OTHER INVESTMENT CRITERIA

The investment decision, also known as *capital budgeting*, is central to the success of the company. We have already seen that capital investments sometimes absorb substantial amounts of cash; they also have very long-term consequences. The assets you buy today may determine the business you are in many years hence.

For some investment projects "substantial" is an understatement. Consider the following examples:

- Construction of the Channel Tunnel linking England and France cost about $15 billion (US) from 1986 to 1994.
- Capital spending by Canadian Oil Sands Trust on Oil Sands projects in 2004 alone totalled $942 million.
- Ford, GM, and DaimlerChrysler have been spending more than $500 million (US) annually since the mid-1990s to develop a hybrid electric automobile.
- ExxonMobil's plans to develop the Sakhalin Island oil and gas field in eastern Russia involve a likely outlay of $12 billion (US).
- Production and merchandising costs for Sony's *Spider-Man* movie were around $150 million (US).
- The cost of bringing one new prescription drug to market was estimated to be at least $800 million (US).
- Production and merchandising costs for three new *Star Wars* movies are estimated at about $3 billion (US).
- The cost of developing the world's largest airliner, Airbus Industries' A380 Superjumbo is reportedly in excess of $12 billion (US)
- The 13-kilometre-long Confederation Bridge linking New Brunswick and Prince Edward Island cost $1 billion.

- The Sable Island Offshore Energy Project, which will bring natural gas to the Atlantic Provinces and northeastern United States through hundreds of kilometres of pipelines, is estimated to have cost over $2 billion (US) in its first phase.

Notice from these examples of big capital projects that many projects require heavy investment in intangible assets. The costs of drug development are almost all research and testing, for example, and much of the development of the hybrid auto is for design and testing. Any expenditure made in the hope of generating more cash later can be called a *capital investment project*, regardless of whether the cash outlay goes to tangible or intangible assets.

A company's shareholders prefer to be rich rather than poor. Therefore, they want the firm to invest in every project that is worth more than it costs. The difference between a project's value and its cost is termed the net present value. Companies can best help their shareholders by investing in projects with a positive net present value.

We start this chapter by showing how to calculate the net present value of a simple investment project. We also examine other criteria that companies sometimes consider when evaluating investments, such as the project's payback period or book rate of return. We will see that these are little better than rules of thumb. Although there is a place for rules of thumb in this world, an engineer needs something more accurate when designing a 100-story building, and a financial manager needs more than a rule of thumb when making a substantial capital investment decision.

Instead of calculating a project's net present value, companies sometimes compare the expected rate of return from investing in a project with the return that shareholders could earn on equivalent-risk investments in the capital market. Companies accept only those projects that provide a higher return than shareholders could earn for themselves. This rate of return rule generally gives the same answers as the net present value rule, but as we shall see, it has some pitfalls.

We then turn to more complex issues such as project interactions. These occur when a company is obliged to *choose* between two or more competing proposals; if it accepts one proposal, it cannot take the other. For example, a company may need to choose between buying an expensive, durable machine or a cheap and short-lived one. We will show how the net present value criterion can be used to make such choices.

Sometimes the firm may be forced to make choices because it does not have enough money to take on every project that it would like. We will explain how to maximize shareholder wealth when capital is rationed. It turns out that the solution is to pick the projects that have the highest net present value per dollar invested. This measure is known as the *profitability index*.

After studying this chapter you should be able to
- Calculate the net present value of an investment.
- Calculate the internal rate of return of a project and know what to look out for when using the internal rate of return rule.
- Explain why the payback and discounted payback rules and book rate of return rule *don't* always make shareholders better off.
- Use the net present value rule to analyze three common problems that involve competing projects: (a) when to postpone an investment expenditure, (b) how to choose between projects with equal lives, and (c) when to replace equipment.
- Calculate the profitability index and use it to choose between projects when funds are limited.

7.1   NET PRESENT VALUE

In Chapter 4 you learned how to discount future cash payments to find their present value. We now apply these ideas to evaluate a simple investment proposal.

Suppose that you are in the real estate business. You are considering construction of an office block. The land would cost $50,000 and construction would cost a further $300,000. You foresee a shortage of office space and predict that a year from now you will be able to sell the building for $400,000. Thus you would be investing $350,000 now in the expectation of realizing

$400,000 at the end of the year. You should go ahead if the present value of the $400,000 payoff is greater than the investment of $350,000.

Assume for the moment that the $400,000 payoff is a sure thing. The office building is not the only way to obtain $400,000 a year from now; you could invest in a one-year Treasury bill. Suppose the T-bill offers interest of 7 percent. How much would you have to invest in it in order to receive $400,000 at the end of the year? That's easy: you would have to invest

$$\$400,000 \times \frac{1}{1.07} = \$400,000 \times .935 = \$373,832$$

Therefore, at an interest rate of 7 percent, the present value of the $400,000 payoff from the office building is $373,832.

Let's assume that as soon as you have purchased the land and laid out the money for construction, you decide to cash in on your project. How much could you sell it for? Since the property will be worth $400,000 in a year, investors would be willing to pay at most $373,832 for it now. That's all it would cost them to get the same $400,000 payoff by investing in a government security. Of course, you could always sell your property for less, but why sell for less than the market will bear?

The $373,832 present value is the only price that satisfies both buyer and seller. In general, the present value is the only feasible price, and the present value of the property is also its *market price* or *market value*.

opportunity cost of capital
Expected rate of return given up by investing in a project.

To calculate present value, we discounted the expected future payoff by the rate of return offered by comparable investment alternatives. The discount rate—7 percent in our example—is often known as the **opportunity cost of capital**. It is called the opportunity cost because it is the return that is being given up by investing in the project.

net present value (NPV)
Present value of cash flows minus initial investment.

The building is worth $373,832, but this does not mean that you are $373,832 better off. You committed $350,000, and therefore your **net present value (NPV)** is $23,832. Net present value is found by subtracting the required initial investment from the present value of the project cash flows:

$$\textbf{NPV = PV − required investment} \qquad (7.1)$$
$$= \$373,832 - \$350,000 = \$23,832$$

In other words, your office development is worth more than it costs—it makes a net contribution to value.

> The net present value rule states that managers increase shareholders' wealth by accepting all projects that are worth more than they cost. Therefore, they should accept all projects with a positive net present value.

A COMMENT ON RISK AND PRESENT VALUE

In our discussion of the office development we assumed we knew the value of the completed project. Of course, you will never be certain about the future values of office buildings. The $400,000 represents the best *forecast*, but it is not a sure thing.

Therefore, our initial conclusion about how much investors would pay for the building is wrong. Since they could achieve $400,000 risk-free by investing in $373,832 worth of T-bills, they would not buy your building for that amount. You would have to cut your asking price to attract investors' interest.

Here we can invoke a basic financial principle:

> A risky dollar is worth less than a safe one.

Most investors avoid risk when they can do so without sacrificing return. However, the concepts of present value and the opportunity cost of capital still apply to risky investments. It is still proper to discount the payoff by the rate of return offered by a comparable investment. But we have to think of *expected* payoffs and the *expected* rates of return on other investments.

Not all investments are equally risky. The office development is riskier than a T-bill, but is probably less risky than investing in a start-up biotech company. Suppose you believe the office development is as risky as an investment in the stock market and that you forecast a 12 percent rate of return for stock market investments. Then 12 percent would be the appropriate opportunity cost of capital. That is what you are giving up by not investing in comparable securities. You can now recompute NPV:

$$PV = \$400,000 \times \frac{1}{1.12} = \$400,000 \times .893 = \$357,143$$
$$NPV = PV - \$350,000 = \$7,143$$

If other investors agree with your forecast of a \$400,000 payoff and with your assessment of a 12 percent opportunity cost of capital, then the property ought to be worth \$357,143 once construction is underway. If you tried to sell for more than that, there would be no takers because the property would then offer a lower expected rate of return than the 12 percent available in the stock market. The office building still makes a net contribution to value, but it is much smaller than our earlier calculations indicated.

Check Point 7.1

What is the office development's NPV if construction costs increase to \$355,000? Assume the opportunity cost of capital is 12 percent. Is the development still a worthwhile investment? How high can development costs be before the project is no longer attractive? Now suppose that the opportunity cost of capital is 20 percent with construction costs of \$355,000. Why is the office development no longer an attractive investment?

VALUING LONG-LIVED PROJECTS

The net present value rule works for projects of any length. For example, suppose that you have identified a possible tenant who would be prepared to rent your office block for 3 years at a fixed annual rent of \$16,000. You forecast that after you have collected the third year's rent the building could be sold for \$450,000. Thus the cash flow in the first year is $C_1 = \$16,000$, in the second year it is $C_2 = \$16,000$, and in the third year it is $C_3 = \$466,000$. For simplicity, we will again assume that these cash flows are certain and that the opportunity cost of capital is $r = 7$ percent.

Figure 7.1 shows a time line of these cash flows and their present values. To find the present values, we discount the future cash flows at the 7 percent opportunity cost of capital:

$$PV = \frac{C_1}{1+r} + \frac{C_2}{(1+r)^2} + \frac{C_3}{(1+r)^3}$$

$$= \frac{\$16,000}{1.07} + \frac{\$16,000}{(1.07)^2} + \frac{\$466,000}{(1.07)^3} = \$409,323$$

The net present value of the revised project is NPV = \$409,323 − \$350,000 = \$59,323. Constructing the office block and renting it for three years makes a greater addition to your wealth than selling the office block at the end of the first year.

Of course, rather than subtracting the initial investment from the project's present value, you could calculate NPV directly, as in the following equation, where C_0 denotes the initial cash outflow required to build the office block. (Notice that C_0 is negative, reflecting the fact that it is a cash outflow.)

$$NPV = C_0 + \frac{C_1}{1+r} + \frac{C_2}{(1+r)^2} + \frac{C_3}{(1+r)^3}$$

$$= -\$350,000 + \frac{\$16,000}{1.07} + \frac{\$16,000}{(1.07)^2} + \frac{\$466,000}{(1.07)^3} = \$59,323$$

FIGURE 7.1
Cash flows and their present values for the office block project. Final cash flow of $466,000 is the sum of the rental income in Year 3 plus the forecast sales price for the building

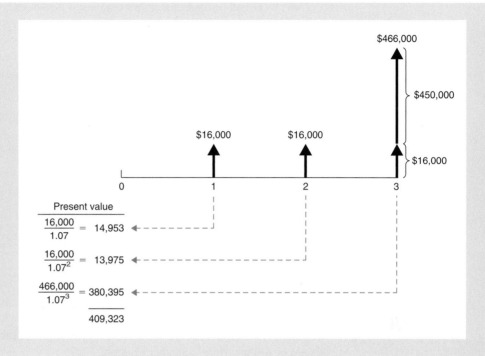

Let's check that the owners of this project really are better off. Suppose you put up $350,000 of your own money, commit to build the office building, and sign a lease that will bring in $16,000 a year for 3 years. Now you can cash in by selling the project to someone else.

Suppose you sell 1,000 shares in the project. Each share represents a claim to 1/1,000 of the future cash flows. Since the cash flows are sure things, and the interest rate offered by other sure things is 7 percent, investors will value the shares for

$$\text{Price per share} = P = \frac{\$16}{1.07} + \frac{\$16}{(1.07)^2} + \frac{\$466}{(1.07)^3} = \$409.30$$

Thus you can sell the project to outside investors for 1,000 × $409.30 = $409,300, which, save for rounding, is exactly the present value we calculated earlier. Your net gain is

$$\text{Net gain} = \$409,300 - \$350,000 = \$59,300$$

which is the project's NPV. This equivalence should be no surprise, since the present value calculation is designed to calculate the value of future cash flows to investors in the capital markets.

Notice that in principle there could be a different opportunity cost of capital for each period's cash flow. In that case, we would discount C_1 by r_1, the discount rate for one-year cash flows; C_2 would be discounted by r_2; and so on. Here we assume that the cost of capital is the same regardless of the date of the cash flow. We do this for one reason only—simplicity. But we are in good company: with only rare exceptions, firms decide on an appropriate discount rate and then use it to discount all project cash flows.

EXAMPLE 7.1

VALUING A NEW COMPUTER SYSTEM

Obsolete Technologies is considering the purchase of a new computer system to help handle its warehouse inventories. The system costs $50,000, is expected to last 4 years, and should reduce the cost of managing inventories by $22,000 a year. The opportunity cost of capital is 10 percent. Should Obsolete proceed?

Don't be put off by the fact that the computer system does not generate any sales. If the expected cost savings are realized, the company's cash flows will be $22,000 a year higher as a result of buying the computer. Thus we can say that the computer increases cash flows by $22,000 a year for each of 4 years. To calculate present value, you can discount each of these cash flows by 10 percent. However, it is smarter to recognize that the cash flows are level and therefore you can use the annuity formula to calculate the present value:

$$\text{PV} = \text{cash flow} \times \text{annuity factor} = \$22{,}000 \times \left[\frac{1}{.10} - \frac{1}{.10(1.10)^4} \right]$$

$$= \$22{,}000 \times 3.170 = \$69{,}740$$

The net present value is

$$\text{NPV} = -\$50{,}000 + \$69{,}740 = \$19{,}740$$

The project has a positive NPV of $19,740. Undertaking it would increase the value of the firm by that amount.

The first two steps in calculating NPVs—forecasting the cash flows and estimating the opportunity cost of capital—are tricky, and we will have a lot more to say about them in later chapters. But once you have assembled the data, the calculation of present value and net present value should be routine. Here is another example.

EXAMPLE 7.2	**CALCULATING EUROTUNNEL'S NPV**

One of the world's largest commercial investment projects was construction of the Channel Tunnel by the Anglo-French company Eurotunnel. Here is a chance to put yourself in the shoes of Eurotunnel's financial manager and find out whether the project looked like a good deal for shareholders. The figures in the column headed "cash flow" in Table 7.1 are based on the forecasts of construction costs and revenues that the company provided to investors in 1986.

The Channel Tunnel project was not a safe investment. Indeed the prospectus to the Channel Tunnel share issue cautioned investors that the project "involves significant risk and should be regarded at this stage as speculative. If for any reason the Project is abandoned or Eurotunnel is unable to raise the necessary finance, it is likely that equity investors will lose some or all of their money."

To induce them to invest in the project, investors needed a higher prospective rate of return than they could get on safe government bonds. Suppose investors expected a return of 13 percent from investments in the capital market that had a degree of risk similar to that of the Channel Tunnel. That was what investors were giving up when they provided the capital for the tunnel. To find the project's NPV, we therefore discount the cash flows in Table 7.1 at 13 percent.

Since the tunnel was expected to take about seven years to build, there are seven years of negative cash flows in Table 7.1. To calculate NPV you just discount all the cash flows, positive and negative, at 13 percent and sum the results. Call 1986 Year 0, 1987 Year 1, and so on. Then

$$\text{NPV} = C_0 + \frac{C_1}{1+r} + \frac{C_2}{(1+r)^2} + \ldots + \frac{C_{24}}{(1+r)^{24}}$$

$$= -\pounds457 + \frac{-\pounds476}{1.13} + \frac{-\pounds497}{(1.13)^2} + \ldots + \frac{\pounds17{,}781}{(1.13)^{24}} = \pounds251 \text{ million}$$

Net present value of the forecast cash flows is £251 million, making the tunnel a worthwhile project, though not by a wide margin, considering the planned investment of nearly £4 billion.

TABLE 7.1
Forecast cash flows and present values in 1986 for the Channel Tunnel. The investment apparently had a small positive NPV of £251 million (figures in £ millions).

Year	Cash Flow	PV at 13 Percent
1986	−£457	−£457
1987	−476	−421
1988	−497	−389
1989	−522	−362
1990	−551	−338
1991	−584	−317
1992	−619	−297
1993	211	90
1994	489	184
1995	455	152
1996	502	148
1997	530	138
1998	544	126
1999	636	130
2000	594	107
2001	689	110
2002	729	103
2003	796	100
2004	859	95
2005	923	90
2006	983	86
2007	1,050	81
2008	1,113	76
2009	1,177	71
2010	17,781	946
Total		+£251
	NPV = total = £251 million	

Note: Cash flow for 2010 includes the value in 2010 of forecast cash flows in all subsequent years.

Source: Eurotunnel Equity II Prospectus, October 1986. Used by permission. Some of these figures involve guesswork because the prospectus reported accumulated construction costs including interest expenses.

Of course, NPV calculations are only as good as the underlying cash flow forecasts. The well-known Pentagon Law of Large Projects states that anything big takes longer and costs more than you were originally led to believe. As the law predicted, the tunnel proved much more expensive to build than anticipated in 1986, and the opening was delayed by more than a year. Revenues also have been below forecast, and Eurotunnel has not even generated enough profits to pay the interest on its debt. Thus, with hindsight, the tunnel was a negative-NPV venture. The Excel spreadsheet box nearby illustrates the Eurotunnel problem.

SEE BOX P. 210

7.2   OTHER INVESTMENT CRITERIA

Use of the net present value rule as a criterion for accepting or rejecting investment projects will maximize the value of the firm's shares. However, other criteria are sometimes also considered by firms when evaluating investment opportunities. Some of these rules are liable to give wrong answers; others simply need to be used with care. In this section, we introduce four of these alternative investment criteria: payback and discounted payback periods, internal rate of return, and book rate of return.

PAYBACK

These days almost all large companies use discounted cash flow in some form, but sometimes they use it in combination with other theoretically inappropriate measures of performance. We next examine three of these measures: the payback period, the discounted payback period, and the book rate of return.

We suspect that you have often heard conversations that go something like this: "A washing machine costs about $400. But we are currently spending $3 a week, or around $150 a year, at

	A	B	C	D	E
1	**Year**	**Time**	**Cash Flow**	**PV at 13%**	**Formula in column D**
2	1986	0	-457	-457	=C2/1.13^B2
3	1987	1	-476	-421	=C3/1.13^B3
4	1988	2	-497	-389	=C4/1.13^B4
5	1989	3	-522	-362	=C5/1.13^B5
6	1990	4	-551	-338	=C6/1.13^B6
7	1991	5	-584	-317	=C7/1.13^B7
8	1992	6	-619	-297	=C8/1.13^B8
9	1993	7	211	90	=C9/1.13^B9
10	1994	8	489	184	=C10/1.13^B10
11	1995	9	455	151	=C11/1.13^B11
12	1996	10	502	148	=C12/1.13^B12
13	1997	11	530	138	=C13/1.13^B13
14	1998	12	544	126	=C14/1.13^B14
15	1999	13	636	130	=C15/1.13^B15
16	2000	14	594	107	=C16/1.13^B16
17	2001	15	689	110	=C17/1.13^B17
18	2002	16	729	103	=C18/1.13^B18
19	2003	17	796	100	=C19/1.13^B19
20	2004	18	859	95	=C20/1.13^B20
21	2005	19	923	91	=C21/1.13^B21
22	2006	20	983	85	=C22/1.13^B22
23	2007	21	1,050	81	=C23/1.13^B23
24	2008	22	1,113	76	=C24/1.13^B24
25	2009	23	1,177	71	=C25/1.13^B25
26	2010	24	17,781	946	=C26/1.13^B26
27	**Sum:**			250	=SUM(D2:D26)
28					
29	Instead, use Excel's NPV function:			250	=NPV(0.13,C3:C26) + C2

Computer spreadsheets are tailor-made to calculate the present value of a series of cash flows. For example, the spreadsheet above sets up the Eurotunnel problem as an Excel spreadsheet. Cells D2 to D26 calculate the present value of each year's cash flows and D27 shows the sum of these separate present values.

Excel also provides a built-in function to calculate net present values. The formula is =NPV(rate,list of cash flows). So, instead of computing the present value of each cash flow separately and then summing, we could have used the NPV function in cell D29. The first entry in the function is the discount rate expressed as a decimal, in this case .13. That is followed by a list of the cash flows that appear in column C.

Why is the first entry in the cash flow list cell C3 rather than C2, which contains the immediate cash flow, –457? It turns out that Excel always assumes the first cash flow comes after one period, the next after two periods, and so on. If the first cash flow actually comes immediately, as in our example, we do not want it discounted, nor do we want the other cash flows discounted for an extra period. Therefore, we don't include the immediate cash flow in the NPV function, instead adding it undiscounted to the present value of the other cash flows (see cells D29 and E29).

the laundromat. So the washing machine should pay for itself in less than 3 years." You have just encountered the payback rule.

payback period Time until cash flows recover the initial investment of the project.

A project's **payback period** is the length of time before you recover your initial investment. For the washing machine the payback period was just under three years.

> The payback rule states that a project should be accepted if its payback period is less than a specified cutoff period.

For example, if the cutoff period is four years, the washing machine makes the grade; if the cutoff is two years, it doesn't.

As a rough rule of thumb the payback rule may be adequate, but it is easy to see that it can lead to nonsensical decisions. For example, compare projects A and B. Project A has a two-year payback and a large positive NPV. Project B also has a two-year payback but a negative NPV. Project A is clearly superior but the payback rule ranks both equally. This is because payback does not consider any cash flows that arrive after the payback period. A firm that uses the payback criterion with a cutoff of two or more years would accept both A and B despite the fact that only A would increase shareholder wealth.

| Project | Cash Flows, $ | | | | Payback Period, Years | NPV at 10% |
	C_0	C_1	C_2	C_3		
A	−2,000	+1,000	+1,000	+10,000	2	$7,249
B	−2,000	+1,000	+1,000	0	2	−264
C	−2,000	0	+2,000	0	2	−347

A second problem with payback is that it gives equal weight to all cash flows arriving *before* the cutoff period despite the fact that the more distant flows are less valuable. For example, look at Project C. It also has a payback period of 2 years but it has an even lower NPV than Project B. Why? Because its cash flows arrive later within the payback period.

To use the payback rule a firm has to decide on an appropriate cutoff period. If it uses the same cutoff regardless of project life, it will tend to accept too many short-lived projects and reject too many long-lived ones. The payback rule will bias the firm against accepting long-term projects because cash flows that arrive after the payback period are ignored.

Earlier in the chapter we evaluated the Channel Tunnel project. Large construction projects of this kind inevitably have long payback periods. The cash flows that we presented in Table 7.1 implied a payback period of just over 14 years. But most firms that employ the payback rule use a much shorter cutoff period than this. If they used the payback rule mechanically, long-lived projects like the Channel Tunnel wouldn't have a chance.

In our example, the payback works out to be exactly two years for all three projects. Suppose the numbers don't work out exactly, as in Project D below:

| Year | Project D Cash Flow, $ | | | | Payback Period, Years |
	0	1	2	3	
Cash Flow	−2,000	+1,000	+500	+1,000	
Cumulative Cash Flow	−2,000	−1,000	−500	+500	2.5

We see that the initial investment is $2,000, whereas the cash inflows over years 1 to 3 are $2,500. The cumulative cash flows are negative until Year 2 but they become positive by Year 3. This means that the project pays back sometime in the third year. If we assume that cash inflows occur uniformly across time, we can figure out the fractional year. We see that out of the total cash flow of $1,000 in Year 3, the first $500 comes in by $500/1,000 = 0.5$ years. The payback is therefore 2.5 years.

The primary attraction of the payback criterion is its simplicity. But remember that the hard part of project evaluation is forecasting the cash flows, not doing the arithmetic. Today's spreadsheets make discounting a trivial exercise. Therefore, the payback rule saves you only the easy part of the analysis.

We have had little good to say about payback. So why do many large companies continue to use it? Senior managers don't truly believe that all cash flows after the payback period are irrelevant. It seems more likely (and more charitable to those managers) that payback survives because the deficiencies are relatively unimportant or because there are some offsetting benefits. Thus managers may point out that payback is the simplest way to *communicate* an idea of project desirability. Investment decisions require discussion and negotiation between people from all parts of the firm, and it is important to have a measure that everyone can understand. Perhaps, also, managers favour quick payback projects even when they have lower NPVs, because they believe that quicker profits mean quicker promotion. That takes us back to Chapter 1 where we discussed the need to align the objectives of managers with those of the shareholders.

In practice, payback is most commonly used when the capital investment is small or when the merits of the project are so obvious that more formal analysis is unnecessary. For example, if a project is expected to produce constant cash flows for 10 years and the payback period is only 2 years, the project in all likelihood has a positive NPV.

DISCOUNTED PAYBACK

discounted payback period
The time until discounted cash flows recover the initial investment in the project.

Sometimes managers calculate the **discounted payback period**. This is the number of periods before the present value of prospective cash flows equals or exceeds the initial investment.

> The discounted payback rule asks: How long must the project last in order to offer a positive net present value?

This surmounts the objection that equal weight is given to all cash flows before the cutoff date. However, the discounted payback rule still takes no account of cash flows after the cutoff date.

Project A

Year	Cash Flows, $	Discounted Cash Flows at 10%, $	Cumulative Discounted Cash Flows, $
0	−2,000	−2,000	−2,000
1	+1,000	909	−1,091
2	+1,000	827	−264
3	+10,000	7,513	+7,249
		NPV = 7,249	

To show how this would work suppose we look at the cash flows for Project A once again. These cash flows are discounted at 10 percent; the total discounted cash flows represent the project's NPV of $7249. The cumulative discounted cash flows are negative until Year 2 but sizably positive by Year 3. This means the project pays back sometime in the third year. Once again, assuming uniform cash inflows across time, we can figure out the fractional year. We see that out of the total discounted cash flow of $7,513 in Year 3, the first $264 comes in by 264/7,513 = 0.04 years. The discounted payback is therefore 2.04 years.

The discounted payback does offer one important advantage over the normal payback criterion. If a project meets a discounted payback cutoff, it must have a positive NPV because the cash flows that accrue up to the discounted payback period are (by definition) just sufficient to provide a present value equal to the initial investment. Any cash flows after that date tip the balance and ensure positive NPV.

Despite this advantage, the discounted payback rule has little to recommend it. It still ignores all cash flows occurring after the arbitrary cutoff date and, therefore, will incorrectly reject some positive NPV opportunities. It is no easier to use than the NPV rule because both project cash flows and an appropriate discount rate must be determined. The best that can be said is it is a better criterion than the (even more unsatisfactory) payback rule. See the Excel spreadsheet nearby.

SEE BOX P. 213

Check Point 7.2

A project costs $3,000 and will generate annual cash flows of $660 for 7 years. What is the payback period? If the interest rate is 6 percent, what is (a) the discounted payback period, and (b) the project NPV? Should the project be accepted?

Discounted Payback Period

	A	B	C	D	E	F
1	Year	Time	Cash Flow	PV at 13%	Cumulative PV	Formula for column E
2	1986	0	-457	-457	-457	=D2
3	1987	1	-476	-421	-878	=E2+D3
4	1988	2	-497	-389	-1267	=E3+D4
5	1989	3	-522	-362	-1629	=E4+D5
6	1990	4	-551	-338	-1967	=E5+D6
7	1991	5	-584	-317	-2284	=E6+D7
8	1992	6	-619	-297	-2581	=E7+D8
9	1993	7	211	90	-2492	=E8+D9
10	1994	8	489	184	-2308	=E9+D10
11	1995	9	455	151	-2156	=E10+D11
12	1996	10	502	148	-2008	=E11+D12
13	1997	11	530	138	-1870	=E12+D13
14	1998	12	544	126	-1745	=E13+D14
15	1999	13	636	130	-1615	=E14+D15
16	2000	14	594	107	-1508	=E15+D16
17	2001	15	689	110	-1397	=E16+D17
18	2002	16	729	103	-1294	=E17+D18
19	2003	17	796	100	-1195	=E18+D19
20	2004	18	859	95	-1099	=E19+D20
21	2005	19	923	91	-1009	=E20+D21
22	2006	20	983	85	-924	=E21+D22
23	2007	21	1,050	81	-843	=E22+D23
24	2008	22	1,113	76	-767	=E23+D24
25	2009	23	1,177	71	-697	=E24+D25
26	2010	24	17,781	946	250	=E25+D26
27	SUM:			250		
28						
29				**23.7360** = Discounted Payback { = 23 +(-E25/D26) }		

Once we have the cumulative present values in place, calculating the discounted payback period is quite easy on Excel. The discounted payback period for the Channel Tunnel project is provided in cell E29. The period is returned as a decimal.

INTERNAL RATE OF RETURN

Instead of calculating a project's net present value, companies often prefer to ask whether the project's return is higher or lower than the opportunity cost of capital. For example, think back to the original proposal to build the office block. You planned to invest $350,000 to get back a cash flow of C1 = $400,000 in 1 year. Therefore, you forecast a profit on the venture of $400,000 − $350,000 = $50,000, and a rate of return of

$$\text{Rate of return} = \frac{\text{profit}}{\text{investment}} = \frac{C_1 - \text{investment}}{\text{investment}} = \frac{\$400,000 - \$350,000}{\$350,000}$$

$$= .1429, \text{ or about } 14.3\%$$

The alternative of investing in a T-bill would provide a return of only 7 percent. Thus the return on your office building is higher than the opportunity cost of capital.[1]

---

[1] Recall that we are assuming the profit on the office building is risk-free. Therefore, the opportunity cost of capital is the rate of return on other risk-free investments.

This suggests two rules for deciding whether to proceed with an investment project:

1. *The NPV rule.* Invest in any project that has a positive NPV when its cash flows are discounted at the opportunity cost of capital.
2. *The rate of return rule.* Invest in any project offering a rate of return that is higher than the opportunity cost of capital.

Both rules set the same cutoff point. An investment that is on the knife edge with an NPV of zero will also have a rate of return that is just equal to the cost of capital.

Suppose that the rate of interest on T-bills is not 7 percent but 14.3 percent. Since your office project also offers a return of 14.3 percent, the rate of return rule suggests that there is now nothing to choose between taking the project and leaving your money in T-bills.

The NPV rule also tells you that if the interest rate is 14.3 percent, the project is evenly balanced with an NPV of zero:[2]

$$\text{NPV} = C_0 + \frac{C_1}{1 + r} = \frac{-\$350{,}000 + \$400{,}000}{1.143} = 0$$

The project would make you neither richer nor poorer; it is worth what it costs. Thus the NPV rule and the rate of return rule both give the same decision on accepting the project.

A CLOSER LOOK AT THE RATE OF RETURN RULE

We know that if the office project's cash flows are discounted at a rate of 7 percent the project has a net present value of $23,832. If they are discounted at a rate of 14.3 percent, it has an NPV of zero. In Figure 7.2 the project's NPV for a variety of discount rates is plotted. This is often called the *NPV profile* of the project. Notice two important things about Figure 7.2:

1. The project rate of return (in our example, 14.3 percent) is also the discount rate that would give the project a zero NPV. This gives us a useful definition: *the rate of return is the discount rate at which NPV equals zero.*[3]

FIGURE 7.2
The value of the office project is lower when the discount rate is higher. The project has positive NPV if the discount rate is less than 14.3 percent.

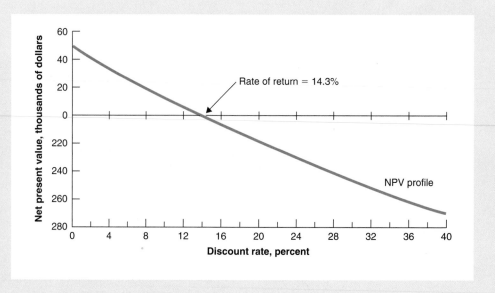

---

[2] Notice that the initial cash flow C_0 is negative. The *investment* in the project is therefore $-C_0 = -(-\$350{,}000)$, or $350,000.

[3] Check it for yourself. If NPV $= C_0 + C_1/(1 + r) = 0$, then rate of return $= (C_1 + C_0)/-C_0 = r$.

2. If the opportunity cost of capital is less than the project rate of return, then the NPV of your project is positive. If the cost of capital is greater than the project rate of return, then NPV is negative. Thus the rate of return rule and the NPV rule are equivalent.

CALCULATING THE RATE OF RETURN FOR LONG-LIVED PROJECTS

There is no ambiguity in calculating the rate of return for an investment that generates a single payoff after one period. Remember that C_0, the time 0 cash flow corresponding to the initial investment, is negative. Thus

$$\text{Rate of return} = \frac{\text{profit}}{\text{investment}} = \frac{C_1 - \text{investment}}{\text{investment}} = \frac{C_1 + C_0}{-C_0}$$

internal rate of return (IRR)
Discount rate at which project NPV = 0.

But how do we calculate return when the project generates cash flows in several periods? Go back to the definition that we just introduced—*the project rate of return is also the discount rate that gives the project a zero NPV*. Managers usually refer to this figure as the project's **internal rate of return**, or **IRR**.[4] It is also known as the *discounted cash flow (DCF) rate of return*.

Let's calculate the IRR for the revised office project. If you rent out the office block for three years, the cash flows are as follows:

Year	0	1	2	3
Cash flows	−$350,000	+16,000	+16,000	+466,000

The IRR is the discount rate at which these cash flows would have zero NPV. Thus

$$\text{NPV} = -\$350,000 + \frac{\$16,000}{1 + \text{IRR}} + \frac{\$16,000}{(1 + \text{IRR})^2} + \frac{\$466,000}{(1 + \text{IRR})^3} = 0$$

There is no simple general method for solving this equation. You have to rely on a little trial and error. Let us arbitrarily try a zero discount rate. This gives an NPV of $148,000:

$$\text{NPV} = -\$350,000 + \frac{\$16,000}{1.0} + \frac{\$16,000}{(1.0)^2} + \frac{\$466,000}{(1.0)^3} = \$148,000$$

With a zero discount rate the NPV is positive. So the IRR must be greater than zero.
The next step might be to try a discount rate of 50 percent. In this case NPV is −$194,000:

$$\text{NPV} = -\$350,000 + \frac{\$16,000}{1.50} + \frac{\$16,000}{(1.50)^2} + \frac{\$466,000}{(1.50)^3} = -\$194,000$$

NPV is now negative. So the IRR must lie somewhere between zero and 50 percent. In Figure 7.3 we have plotted the net present values for a range of discount rates. You can see that a discount rate of 12.96 percent gives an NPV of zero. Therefore, the IRR is 12.96 percent.[5] You can always find the IRR by plotting an NPV profile, as in Figure 7.3, but it is quicker and more accurate to let a computer or specially programmed financial calculator do the trial and error for you. The nearby Financial Calculator and Excel spreadsheet boxes illustrate how to do so.

SEE BOXES PP. 216, 217

> The rate of return rule tells you to accept a project if the rate of return exceeds the opportunity cost of capital.

---

[4] In Chapter 5 you learned how to calculate the yield to maturity on a bond. A bond's yield to maturity is just its internal rate of return.

[5] You can find an appropriate answer for IRR by trial and error and interpolation. By interpolating, after a few trials, one can usually arrive at a reasonably close answer, See end-of-chapter problem 46 if you wish to try out the interpolation technique for solving for IRR.

Using Financial Calculators to Find NPV and IRR

We saw in Chapter 4 that the formulas for the present and future values of level annuities and one-time cash flows are built into financial calculators. However, as the example of the office block illustrates, most investment projects entail multiple cash flows that cannot be expected to remain level over time. Fortunately, many calculators are equipped to handle problems involving a sequence of uneven cash flows. In general, the procedure is quite simple. You enter the cash flows one by one into the calculator, and then you press the IRR key to find the project's internal rate of return. The first cash flow you enter is interpreted as coming immediately, the next cash flow is interpreted as coming at the end of one period, and so on. We can illustrate using the office block as an example. To find the project IRR, you would use the following sequence of keystrokes:

Hewlett-Packard HP-10B		Sharpe EL-733A		Texas Instruments BA II Plus	
−350,000	CFj	−350,000	CFi	CF	
16,000	CFj	16,000	CFi	2nd {CLR Work}	
16,000	CFj	16,000	CFi	−350,000	ENTER ↓
466,000	CFj	466,000	CFi	16,000	ENTER ↓
				16,000	ENTER ↓
				466,000	ENTER ↓
☐ {IRR/YR}		IRR		IRR	
				CPT	

The calculator should display the value 12.96, the project's internal rate of return.

To calculate project NPV, the procedure is similar. You need to enter the discount rate in addition to the project cash flows, and then simply press the NPV key. Here is the specific sequence of keystrokes, assuming that the opportunity cost of capital is 7 percent:

Hewlett-Packard HP-10B		Sharpe EL-733A		Texas Instruments BA II Plus	
−350,000	CFj	−350,000	CFi	CF	
16,000	CFj	16,000	CFi	2nd {CLR Work}	
16,000	CFj	16,000	CFi	−350,000	ENTER ↓
466,000	CFj	466,000	CFi	16,000	ENTER ↓
7	I/YR	7	i	16,000	ENTER ↓
				466,000	ENTER ↓
☐ {NPV}		NPV		NPV	
				7	ENTER
				↓	CPT

The calculator should display the value 59,323, the project's NPV when the discount rate is 7 percent.

By the way, you can check the accuracy of our earlier calculations using your calculator. Enter 50 percent for the discount rate (press 50, then press i) and then press the NPV key to find that NPV = −194,148. Enter 12.96 (the project's IRR) as the discount rate and you will find that NPV is just about zero (it is not exactly zero, because we are rounding off the IRR to only two decimal places).

You can see from Figure 7.3 why this makes sense. Because the NPV profile is downward sloping, the project has a positive NPV as long as the opportunity cost of capital is less than the project's 12.96 percent IRR. If the opportunity cost of capital is higher than the 12.96 percent IRR, NPV is negative. Therefore, when we compare the project IRR with the opportunity cost of

FIGURE 7.3
The internal rate of return is the discount rate for which NPV equals zero.

Internal Rate of Return

	A	B	C	D	E	F
1		Calculating IRR by using a spreadsheet				
2						
3	Year	Cash Flow				Formula
4	0	-350,000		IRR =	0.1296	=IRR(B4:B7)
5	1	16,000				
6	2	16,000				
7	3	466,000				

Calculating internal rate of return in Excel is as easy as listing the project cash flows. For example, to calculate the IRR of the office-block project, you could simply type in its cash flows as in the spreadsheet (left), and then calculate IRR as we do in cell E4. As always, the interest rate is returned as a decimal.

capital, we are effectively asking whether the project has a positive NPV. This was true for our one-period office project. It is also true for our three-period office project. We conclude that

> The rate of return rule will give the same answer as the NPV rule *as long as the NPV of a project declines smoothly as the discount rate increases*.

The usual agreement between the net present value and internal rate of return rules should not be a surprise. Both are *discounted cash flow* methods of choosing between projects. Both are concerned with identifying those projects that make shareholders better off and both recognize that companies always have a choice: they can invest in a project or, if the project is not sufficiently attractive, they can give the money back to shareholders and let them invest it for themselves in the capital market.

Check Point 7.3

Suppose the cash flow in Year 3 is only $416,000. Redraw Figure 7.3. How would the IRR change?

A WORD OF CAUTION

Some people confuse the internal rate of return on a project with the opportunity cost of capital. Remember that the project IRR measures the profitability of the project. It is an *internal rate* of return in the sense that it depends only on the project's own cash flows. The opportunity cost of capital is the standard for deciding whether to accept the project. It is equal to the return offered by equivalent-risk investments in the capital market.

SOME PITFALLS OF THE IRR RULE

Many firms use the internal rate of return rule instead of net present value. We think that this is a pity. When used properly, the two rules head to the same decision, but the rate of return rule has several pitfalls that can trap the unwary. Here are a couple of examples.

Pitfall 1: Lending or Borrowing? Remember our condition for the IRR rule to work: the project's NPV must fall as the discount rate increases. Now consider the following projects:

	Cash Flows, $			
Project	C_0	C_1	IRR, %	NPV at 10%
J	−100	+150	+50	+$36.4
K	+100	−150	+50	−$36.4

Each project has an IRR of 50 percent. In other words, if you discount the cash flows at 50 percent, both of them would have zero NPV.

Does this mean that the two projects are equally attractive? Clearly not. In the case of J we are paying out $100 now and getting $150 back at the end of the year. That is better than any bank account. But what about K? Here we are getting paid $100 now but we have to pay out $150 at the end of the year. That is equivalent to borrowing money at 50 percent.

If someone asked you whether 50 percent was a good rate of interest, you could not answer unless you also knew whether that person was proposing to lend or borrow at that rate. Lending money at 50 percent is great (as long as the borrower does not flee the country), but borrowing at 50 percent is not usually a good deal (unless of course you plan to flee the country). When you lend money, you want a *high* rate of return; when you borrow, you want a *low* rate of return.

If you plot a graph like Figure 7.2 for Project K, you will find the NPV increases as the discount rate increases. (Try it!) Obviously, the rate of return rule will not work in this case.

Project K is a fairly obvious trap, but if you want to make sure you don't fall into it, calculate the project's NPV. For example, suppose that the cost of capital is 10 percent. Then the NPV of Project J is +$36.4 and the NPV of Project K is –$36.4. The NPV rule correctly warns us away from a project that is equivalent to borrowing money at 50 percent.

When NPV rises as the interest rate rises, the rate of return rule is reversed:

> When NPV is higher as the discount rate increases, a project is acceptable only if its internal rate of return is less than the opportunity cost of capital.

Pitfall 2: Multiple Rates of Return.   Here is a trickier problem. King Coal Corporation is considering a project to strip-mine coal. The project requires an investment of $22 million and is expected to produce a cash inflow of $15 million in each of years 1 through 4. However, the company is obliged in Year 5 to reclaim the land at a cost of $40 million. At a 10 percent opportunity cost of capital the project has an NPV of $.7 million.

To find the IRR, we have calculated the NPV for various discount rates and plotted the results in Figure 7.4. You can see that there are two discount rates at which NPV = 0. That is, *each* of the following statements holds:

$$NPV = -22 + \frac{15}{1.06} + \frac{15}{1.06^2} + \frac{15}{1.06^3} + \frac{15}{1.06^4} - \frac{40}{1.06^5} = 0$$

and

$$NPV = -22 + \frac{15}{1.28} + \frac{15}{1.28^2} + \frac{15}{1.28^3} + \frac{15}{1.28^4} - \frac{40}{1.28^5} = 0$$

FIGURE 7.4
King Coal's project has two internal rates of return. NPV = 0 when the discount rate is either 6 percent or 28 percent

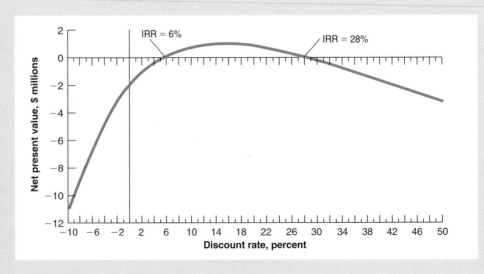

In other words, the investment has an IRR of both 6 and 28 percent. The reason for this is the double change in the sign of the cash flows. There can be as many different internal rates of return as there are changes in the sign of the cash flow stream.[6]

Is the coal mine worth developing? The simple IRR rule—accept if the IRR is greater than the cost of capital—won't help. For example, you can see from Figure 7.4 that with a low cost of capital (less than 6 percent) the project has a negative NPV. It has a positive NPV only if the cost of capital is between 6 percent and 28 percent.[7]

> When there are multiple changes in the sign of the cash flows, the IRR rule does not work, but the NPV rule always does.

BOOK RATE OF RETURN

We pointed out that net present value and internal rate of return are both discounted cash flow measures. In other words, each measure depends only on the project's cash flows and the opportunity cost of capital. But when companies report to shareholders on their performance, they do not show simply the cash flows. Instead they report the firm's book income and book assets.

book rate of return
Accounting income divided by book value. Also called *accounting rate of return*.

Shareholders and financial managers sometimes use these accounting numbers to calculate a **book rate of return** (also called the *accounting rate of return*). In other words, they look at the company's book income (i.e., accounting profits) as a proportion of the book value of the assets:

$$\text{Book rate of return} = \frac{\text{book income}}{\text{book assets}} \qquad (7.2)$$

EXAMPLE 7.3	**BOOK RATE OF RETURN**

Salad Daze invests $90,000 in a vegetable washing machine. The machine will increase cash flows by $50,000 a year for 3 years, when it will need to be replaced. The contribution to accounting profits equals this cash flow less an allowance for depreciation of $30,000 a year. (We ignore taxes to keep things simple.) The book return on this project in each year can be calculated as follows:

Book Value, Start of Year ($000s)	Net Income during Year ($000s)	Book Value, End of Year ($000s)	Book Rate of Return = Income/Book Value at Start of Year
90	50 – 30 = 20	60	20/90 = .222 = 22.2%
60	50 – 30 = 20	30	20/60 = .333 = 33.3%
30	50 – 30 = 20	0	20/30 = .667 = 66.7%

We have already seen that cash flows and accounting income may be very different. For example, the accountant labels some cash outflows as *capital investments* and others as *operating expenses*. The operating expenses are deducted immediately from each year's income, while the capital investment is depreciated over a number of years. Thus the book rate of return depends on which items the accountant chooses to treat as capital investments and how rapidly they are depreciated. Book rate of return is not generally the same as the internal rate of return and, as you can see in Check Point 7.4, the difference between the two can be considerable. Book rate of return therefore can easily give a misleading impression of the attractiveness of a project.

---

[6] There may be *fewer* IRRs than the number of sign changes. You may even encounter projects for which there is *no* IRR. For example, there is no IRR for a project that has cash flows of +$1,000 in Year 0, –$3,000 in Year 1, and +$2,500 in Year 2. If you don't believe us, try plotting NPV for different discount rates. Can such a project ever have a negative NPV?

[7] We will examine more pitfalls in Sections 7.3 when we reevaluate the IRR rule in the context of mutually exclusive projects.

Managers seldom make investment decisions nowadays on the basis of accounting numbers. But they know that the company's shareholders pay considerable attention to book measures of profitability, and therefore, naturally, they look at how major projects would affect the company's book rate of return.

> ✓ **Check Point 7.4**
>
> Suppose that a company invests $60,000 in a project. The project generates a cash inflow of $30,000 a year for each of 3 years and nothing thereafter. Book income in each year is equal to this cash flow less an allowance for depreciation of $20,000 a year. For simplicity, we assume there are no taxes.
> a. Calculate the project's internal rate of return. (If you do not have a financial calculator or spreadsheet program, this will require a little trial and error.)
> b. Now calculate the book rate of return in each year by dividing the book income for that year by the book value of the assets at the start of the year.

7.3   MUTUALLY EXCLUSIVE PROJECTS

The projects we have considered so far involve take-it-or-leave-it decisions. But almost all real-world decisions about capital expenditures involve either–or choices. You could build an apartment block on that vacant site rather than build an office block. You could build a 5-story office block or a 50-story one. You could heat it with oil or with natural gas. You could build it today, or wait a year to start construction. Such choices are said to be **mutually exclusive**.

mutually exclusive projects
Two or more projects that cannot be pursued simultaneously.

> When you need to choose between mutually exclusive projects, the decision rule is simple. Calculate the NPV of each project and, from those options that have a positive NPV, choose the one whose NPV is highest.

EXAMPLE 7.4   CHOOSING BETWEEN TWO PROJECTS

It has been several years since your office last upgraded its office networking software. Two competing systems have been proposed. Both have an expected useful life of three years, at which point it will be time for another upgrade. One proposal is for an expensive cutting-edge system, which will cost $800,000 and increase firm cash flows by $350,000 a year through increased productivity. The other proposal is for a cheaper, somewhat slower system. This system would cost only $700,000 but would increase cash flows by only $300,000 a year. If the cost of capital is 7 percent, which is the better option?

The following table summarizes the cash flows and the NPVs of the two proposals:

	Cash Flows, $000s				
System	C_0	C_1	C_2	C_3	NPV at 7%
Faster	−800	+350	+350	+350	+ 118.5
Slower	−700	+300	+300	+300	+ 87.3

In both cases, the software systems are worth more than they cost, but the faster system would make the greater contribution to value and therefore should be your preferred choice.

Mutually exclusive projects, such as our two proposals to update the networking system, involve a project interaction, since taking one project forecloses the other. Unfortunately, not every project interaction is as simple to evaluate as the choice between the two networking projects, but we will explain how to tackle three important decisions:

- *The investment timing decision.* Should you buy a computer now or wait and think again next year? (Here today's investment is competing with possible future investments.)
- *The choice between long- and short-lived equipment.* Should the company save money today by installing cheaper machinery that will not last as long? (Here today's decision would accelerate a later investment in machine replacement.)
- *The replacement decision.* When should existing machinery be replaced? (Using it another year could delay investment in machine replacement.)

INVESTMENT TIMING

Let us return to Example 7.1, where Obsolete Technologies was contemplating the purchase of a new computer system. The proposed investment has a net present value of almost $20,000, so it appears that the cost savings would easily justify the expense of the system. However, the financial manager is not persuaded. She reasons that the price of computers is continually falling and therefore proposes postponing the purchase, arguing that the NPV of the system will be even higher if the firm waits until the following year. Unfortunately, she has been making the same argument for 10 years and the company is steadily losing business to competitors with more efficient systems. Is there a flaw in her reasoning?

This is a problem in investment timing. When is it best to commit to a positive-NPV investment? Investment timing problems all involve choices among mutually exclusive investments. You can either proceed with the project now, or you can do so later. You can't do both.

Table 7.2 lays out the basic data for Obsolete. You can see that the cost of the computer is expected to decline from $50,000 today to $45,000 next year, and so on. The new computer system is expected to last for four years from the time it is installed. The present value of the savings *at the time of installation* is expected to be $70,000. Thus if Obsolete invests today, it achieves an NPV of $70,000 − $50,000 = $20,000; if it invests next year, it will have an NPV of $70,000 − $45,000 = $25,000.

Isn't a gain of $25,000 better than one of $20,000? Well, not necessarily—you may prefer to be $20,000 richer *today* rather than $25,000 richer *next year*. The better choice depends on the cost of capital. The fifth column of Table 7.2 shows the value today (Year 0) of those net present values at a 10 percent cost of capital. For example, you can see that the discounted value of that $25,000 gain is $25,000/1.10 = $22,700. The financial manager has a point. It is worth postponing investment in the computer, but it should not be postponed indefinitely. You maximize net present value today by buying the computer in Year 3.

Notice that you are involved in a trade-off. The sooner you can capture the $70,000 savings the better, but if it costs you less to realize those savings by postponing the investment, it may pay you to do so. If you postpone the purchase by 1 year, the gain from buying a computer rises from $20,000 to $25,000, an increase of 25 percent. Since the cost of capital is only 10 percent, it pays to postpone at least until Year 1. If you postpone from Year 3 to Year 4, the gain rises from $34,000 to $37,000, a rise of just under 9 percent. Since this is less than the cost of capital, it is not worth waiting any longer.

TABLE 7.2
Obsolete Technologies: the gain from purchase of a computer is rising, but the NPV today is highest if the computer is purchased in Year 3 (figures in $000s).

Year of Purchase	Cost of Computer	PV Savings	NPV at Year of Purchase ($r = 10\%$)	NPV Today	
0	$50	$70	$20	$20.0	
1	45	70	25	22.7	
2	40	70	30	24.8	
3	36	70	34	25.5	← optimal
4	33	70	37	25.3	purchase
5	31	70	39	24.2	date

> The decision rule for investment timing is to choose the investment date that results in the highest net present value today.

Check Point 7.5

Unfortunately, Obsolete Technology's business is shrinking as the company dithers and dawdles. Its chief financial officer realizes that the savings from installing the new computer will likewise shrink by $4,000 per year, from a present value of $70,000 now to $66,000 next year, then to $62,000, and so on. Redo Table 7.2 with this new information. When should Obsolete buy the new computer?

LONG- VERSUS SHORT-LIVED EQUIPMENT

Suppose the firm is forced to choose between two machines, D and E. The two machines are designed differently but have identical capacity and do exactly the same job. Machine D costs $15,000 and will last 3 years. It costs $4,000 per year to run. Machine E is an "economy" model, costing only $10,000, but it will last only 2 years and costs $6,000 per year to run.

Because the two machines produce exactly the same product, the only way to choose between them is on the basis of cost. Suppose we compute the present value of the costs:

	Costs, $000s				
Year:	0	1	2	3	PV at 6%
Machine D	15	4	4	4	25.69
Machine E	10	6	6	—	21.00

Should we take machine E, the one with the lower present value of costs? Not necessarily. All we have shown is that machine E offers 2 years of service for a lower cost than 3 years of service from machine D. But is the annual cost of using E lower than that of D?

Suppose the financial manager agrees to buy machine D and pay for its operating costs out of his budget. He then charges the plant manager an annual amount for use of the machine. There will be three equal payments starting in Year 1. Obviously, the financial manager has to make sure that the present value of these payments equals the present value of the costs of machine D, $25,690. The payment stream with such a present value when the discount rate is 6 percent turns out to be $9,610 a year. In other words, the cost of buying and operating machine D is equivalent to an annual charge of $9,610 a year for 3 years. This figure is therefore termed the **equivalent annual cost** of machine D.

equivalent annual cost   The cost per period with the same present value as the cost of buying and operating a machine.

	Costs, $000s				
Year:	0	1	2	3	PV at 6%
Machine D	15	4	4	4	25.69
Equivalent Annual Cost		9.61	9.61	9.61	25.69

How did we know that an annual charge of $9,610 has a present value of $25,690? The annual charge is a three-year annuity. So we calculate the value of this annuity and set it equal to $25,690:

Equivalent annual cost × 3-year annuity factor = PV cost of D = $25,690

If the cost of capital is 6 percent, the 3-year annuity factor is 2.673. So

$$\text{Equivalent annual cost} = \frac{\text{present value of costs}}{\text{annuity factor}} \tag{7.3}$$

$$= \frac{\$25,690}{\text{3-year annuity factor}} = \frac{\$25,690}{2.673} = \$9,610$$

If we make a similar calculation of costs for machine E, we get

		Costs, $000s		
Year:	0	1	2	PV at 6%
Machine E	10	6	6	21.00
Equivalent				
2-year annuity		11.45	11.45	21.00

We see now that machine D is better, because its equivalent annual cost is less ($9,610 for D versus $11,450 for E). In other words, the financial manager could afford to set a lower *annual* charge for the use of D.

> We thus have a rule for comparing assets of different lives: Select the machine that has the lowest equivalent annual cost.

Think of the equivalent annual cost as the level annual charge[8] necessary to recover the present value of investment outlays and operating costs. The annual charge continues for the life of the equipment. Calculate equivalent annual cost by dividing the appropriate present value by the annuity factor.

EXAMPLE 7.5   **EQUIVALENT ANNUAL COST**

You need a new car. You can either purchase one outright for $15,000 or lease one for 7 years for $3,000 a year. If you buy the car, it will be worth $500 to you in 7 years. The discount rate is 10 percent. Should you buy or lease? What is the maximum lease you would be willing to pay?

The present value of the cost of purchasing is

$$PV = \$15,000 - \frac{\$500}{(1.10)^7} = \$14,743$$

The equivalent annual cost of purchasing the car is therefore the annuity with this present value:

$$\text{Equivalent annual cost} \times \frac{\text{7-year annuity}}{\text{factor at 10\%}} = \frac{\text{PV cost}}{\text{of buying}} = \$14,743$$

$$\text{Equivalent annual cost} = \frac{\$14,743}{\text{7-year annuity factor}} = \frac{\$14,743}{4.8684} = \$3,028$$

Therefore, the annual lease payment of $3,000 is less than the equivalent annual cost of buying the car. You should be willing to pay up to $3,028 annually to lease.

REPLACING AN OLD MACHINE

The previous example took the life of each machine as fixed. In practice, the point at which equipment is replaced reflects economics, not physical collapse. *We* usually decide when to replace. The machine will rarely decide for us.

Here is a common problem. You are operating an old machine that will last two more years before it gives up the ghost. It costs $12,000 per year to operate. You can replace it now with a new machine, which costs $25,000 but is much more efficient ($8,000 per year in operating costs) and will last for 5 years. Should you replace it now or wait a year? The opportunity cost of capital is 6 percent.

---

[8] We have implicitly assumed that inflation is zero. If that is not the case, it would be better to calculate the equivalent annuities for machines D and E in real terms, using the real rate of interest to calculate the annuity factor.

We can calculate the NPV of the new machine and its equivalent annual cost, that is, the five-year annuity that has the same present value.

	Costs, $000s						
Year:	0	1	2	3	4	5	PV at 6%
New machine	25	8	8	8	8	8	58.70
Equivalent 5-year annuity		13.93	13.93	13.93	13.93	13.93	58.70

The cash flows of the new machine are equivalent to an annuity of $13,930 per year. So we can equally well ask at what point we would want to replace our old machine, which costs $12,000 a year to run, with a new one costing $13,930 a year. When the question is posed this way, the answer is obvious. As long as your old machine costs only $12,000 a year, why replace it with a new machine that costs $1,930 more?[9]

Check Point 7.6

Machines F and G are mutually exclusive and have the following investment and operating costs. Note that machine F lasts for only two years:

Year:	0	1	2	3
F	10,000	1,100	1,200	—
G	12,000	1,100	1,200	1,300

Calculate the equivalent annual cost of each investment using a discount rate of 10 percent. Which machine is the better buy?

Now suppose you have an existing machine. You can keep it going for only one more year, but it will cost $2,500 in repairs and $1,800 in operating costs. Is it worth replacing now with either F or G?

MUTUALLY EXCLUSIVE PROJECTS AND THE IRR RULE

We have seen that the NPV rule deals easily with mutually exclusive projects. But what about the rate of return rule? Would it make sense to just choose the project that offers the highest internal rate of return? Unfortunately, no. Mutually exclusive projects involve an additional pitfall for users of the IRR rule.[10]

Pitfall 3: Mutually Exclusive Projects.   We have seen that firms are seldom faced with take-it-or-leave-it projects. Usually they need to choose from a number of mutually exclusive alternatives. Given a choice between competing projects, you should accept the one that adds most to shareholder wealth. This is the one with the higher NPV. However, it won't necessarily be the project with the higher internal rate of return. So the IRR rule can lead you astray when choosing between projects.

Think once more about the two office-block proposals from Section 7.1. You initially intended to invest $350,000 in the building and then sell it at the end of the year for $400,000. Under the revised proposal, you plan to rent out the offices for 3 years at a fixed annual rent of $16,000 and then sell the building for $450,000. Here are the cash flows, their IRRs, and their NPVs:

---

[9] In our discussion, we have ignored tax-law implications, such as those applicable to the amortization of assets. We will take up this discussion in Chapter 8 when we will examine Canada's Capital Cost Allowance system in detail.

[10] The other rules we've considered, such as payback or book rate of return, give poor guidance even in the much simpler case of the accept/reject decision of a project considered in isolation. They are of no help in choosing among mutually exclusive projects.

| | Cash Flows, $000s | | | | | |
Project	C_0	C_1	C_2	C_3	IRR	NPV at 7%
H: Initial proposal	−350	+400			+14.29	+$24,000
I: Revised proposal	−350	+16	+16	+466	+12.96	+$59,000

Both projects are good investments; both offer a positive NPV. But the revised proposal has the higher net present value and therefore is the better choice. Unfortunately, the superiority of the revised proposal doesn't show up as a higher rate of return. The IRR rule seems to say you should go for the initial proposal because it has the higher IRR. If you follow the IRR rule, you have the satisfaction of earning a 14.29 percent rate of return; if you use NPV, you are $59,000 richer.

Figure 7.5 shows why the IRR rule gives the wrong signal. The figure plots the NPV of each project as a function of the discount rate. These two NPV profiles cross at an interest rate of 12.26 percent. So if the opportunity cost of capital is higher than 12.26 percent, the initial proposal, with its rapid cash inflow, is the superior investment. If the cost of capital is lower than 12.26 percent, then the revised proposal dominates. Depending on the discount rate, either proposal may be superior. For the 7 percent cost of capital that we have assumed, the revised proposal is the better choice.

Now consider the IRR of each proposal. The IRR is simply the discount rate at which NPV equals zero, that is, the discount rate at which the NPV profile crosses the horizontal axis in Figure 7.5. As noted, these rates are 14.29 percent for the initial proposal and 12.96 percent for the revised proposal. However, as you can see from Figure 7.5, the higher IRR for the initial proposal does not mean that it has a higher NPV.

In our example both projects involved the same outlay, but the revised proposal had the longer life. The IRR rule mistakenly favoured the quick-payback project, with the high percentage return but the lower NPV.

> Remember, a high IRR is not an end in itself. You want projects that increase the value of the firm. Projects that earn a good rate of return for a long time often have higher NPVs than those that offer high percentage rates of return but die young.

FIGURE 7.5
The initial proposal offers a higher IRR than the revised proposal, but its NPV is lower if the discount rate is less than 12.26 percent

Check Point 7.7

A rich, friendly, and probably slightly unbalanced benefactor offers you the opportunity to invest $1 million in two mutually exclusive ways. The payoffs are
a. $2 million after 1 year, a 100 percent return.
b. $300,000 a year forever.
   Neither investment is risky, and safe securities are yielding 7.5 percent. Which investment will you take? You can't take both, so the choices are mutually exclusive. Do you want to earn a high percentage return or do you want to be rich? By the way, if you really had this investment opportunity, you'd have no trouble borrowing the money to undertake it.

Pitfall 3a: Mutually Exclusive Projects Involving Different Outlays.   A similar misranking also may occur when comparing projects with the same lives but different outlays. In this case the IRR may mistakenly favour small projects with high rates of return but low NPVs.

Check Point 7.8

Your wacky benefactor now offers you the choice of two opportunities:
a. Invest $1,000 today and quadruple your money—a 300 percent return—in 1 year, with no risk.
b. Invest $1 million for 1 year at a guaranteed 50 percent return.
   Which will you take? Do you want to earn a wonderful rate of return (300 percent) or do you want to be rich? Safe securities now yield 8 percent.

7.4   CAPITAL RATIONING

A firm maximizes its shareholders' wealth by accepting every project that has a positive net present value. But this assumes that the firm can raise the funds needed to pay for these investments. This is usually a good assumption, particularly for major firms that can raise very large sums of money on fair terms and short notice. Why then does top management sometimes tell subordinates that capital is limited and that they may not exceed a specified amount of capital spending? There are two reasons.

SOFT RATIONING

capital rationing Limit set on the amount of funds available for investment.

For many firms the limits on capital funds are "soft." By this we mean that the **capital rationing** is not imposed by investors. Instead the limits are imposed by top management. For example, suppose that you are an ambitious, upwardly mobile junior manager. You are keen to expand your part of the business and, as a result, you tend to overstate the investment opportunities. Rather than trying to determine which of your many bright ideas really are worthwhile, upper management may find it simpler to impose a limit on the amount that you and other junior managers can spend. This limit forces you to set your own priorities.

   Even if capital is not rationed, other resources may be. For example, very rapid growth can place considerable strains on management and the organization. A somewhat rough-and-ready response to this problem is to ration the amount of capital that the firm spends.

HARD RATIONING

Soft rationing should never cost the firm anything. If the limits on investment become so tight that truly good projects are being passed up, then upper management should raise more money and relax the limits it has imposed on capital spending.

   But what if there is "hard rationing," meaning that the firm actually cannot raise the money it needs? In that case, it may be forced to pass up positive-NPV projects.

With hard rationing you may still be interested in net present value, but you now need to select the package of projects that is within the company's resources and yet gives the highest net present value.

Let us illustrate. Suppose that the opportunity cost of capital is 10 percent, that the company has total resources of $20 million, and that it is presented with the following project proposals:

Project	Cash Flows, $ Millions			PV at 10%	NPV
	C_0	C_1	C_2		
L	−3	+2.2	+2.42	$ 4	$1
M	−5	+2.2	+4.84	6	1
N	−7	+6.6	+4.84	10	3
O	−6	+3.3	+6.05	8	2
P	−4	+1.1	+4.84	5	1

All five projects have a positive NPV. Therefore, if there were no shortage of capital, the firm would like to accept all five proposals. But with only $20 million available, the firm needs to find the package that gives the highest possible NPV within the budget.

The solution is to pick the projects that give the highest net present value per dollar of investment. The ratio of net present value to initial investment is known as the **profitability index**.[11]

profitability index
Ratio of present value to initial investment.

$$\text{Profitability index} = \frac{\text{net present value}}{\text{initial investment}} \qquad (7.4)$$

For our five projects the profitability index is calculated as follows:

Project	PV	Investment	NPV	Profitability Index
L	$ 4	$3	1	1/3 = 0.33
M	6	5	1	1/5 = 0.20
N	10	7	3	3/7 = 0.43
O	8	6	2	2/6 = 0.33
P	5	4	1	1/4 = 0.25

Project N offers the highest ratio of net present value to investment (0.43) and therefore N is picked first. Next come projects L and O, which tie with a ratio of 0.33, and after them comes P. These four projects use up exactly the $20 million budget. Between them they offer shareholders the highest attainable gain in wealth.[12]

Check Point 7.9   Which projects should the firm accept if its capital budget is only $10 million?

PITFALLS OF THE PROFITABILITY INDEX

The profitability index is sometimes used to rank projects even when there is no soft or hard capital rationing. In this case the unwary user may be led to favour small projects over larger projects with higher NPVs. The profitability index was designed to select the projects with the most bang per buck—the greatest NPV per dollar spent. That's the right objective when bucks are limited. When they are not, a bigger bang is always better than a smaller one, even when more bucks are spent. Check Point 7.10 is a numerical example.

---

[11] Sometimes the profitability index is defined as the ratio of present value to required investment. By this definition, all the profitability indexes calculated below are increased by 1.0. For example, Project L's index would be PV/investment = 4/3 = 1.33. Note that project rankings under either definition are identical.

[12] Unfortunately, when capital is rationed in more than one period, or when personnel, production capacity, or other resources are rationed in addition to capital, it isn't always possible to get the NPV-maximizing package just by ranking projects on their profitability index. Tedious trial and error may be called for, or linear programming methods may be used.

Calculate the profitability indexes of the two pairs of mutually exclusive investments in Check Points 7.7 and 7.8. Use a 7.5 percent discount rate. Does the profitability index give the right ranking in each case?

7.5   A LAST LOOK

We've covered several investment criteria, each with its own nuances. If your head is spinning, you might want to take a look at Table 7.3, which gives an overview and summary of these decision rules.

Clearly, NPV is the gold standard. It is designed to tell you whether an investment will increase the value of the firm and by how much it will do so. It is the only rule that consistently can be used to rank and choose among mutually exclusive investments. The only instance in which NPV fails as a decision rule is when the firm faces capital rationing. In this case, it may not be possible to take every project with positive NPV, and the firm must then rank projects by profitability ratio, that is, net present value per dollar invested.

IRR is a handy and widely used measure that indicates rate of return on investment. Despite its potential pitfalls, it will generally give the correct answer about project viability.

TABLE 7.3
A comparison of investment decision rules

Criterion	Definition	Investment Rule	Comments
Net present value (NPV)	Present value of cash inflows minus present value of cash outflows	Accept project if NPV is positive. For mutually exclusive projects, choose the one with the highest (positive) NPV.	The "gold standard" of investment criteria. Only criterion necessarily consistent with maximizing the value of the firm. Provides proper rule for choosing among mutually exclusive investments. Only pitfall involves capital rationing, when one cannot accept all positive-NPV projects.
Internal rate of return (IRR)	The discount rate at which project NPV equals zero	Accept project if IRR is greater than opportunity cost of capital	Results in same accept/reject decision as NPV in the absence of project interactions. However, beware of the following pitfalls: IRR cannot rank mutually exclusive projects—the project with higher IRR may have lower NPV; IRR rule cannot be used in cases of multiple IRRs or upward-sloping NPV profile.
Payback period	Time until sum of project cash flows equals the initial investment	Accept project if payback period is less than some specified number of years	A quick and dirty rule of thumb, with several critical pitfalls. Ignores cash flows beyond the acceptable payback period. Ignores discounting. Tends to improperly reject long-lived projects.
Discounted payback period	Time until sum of project's discounted cash flow equals the initial investment.	Accept project if discounted payback period is less than some specified number of years	Discounting cash flows is an improvement on the payback period. The other critical pitfalls of the payback period still remain.
Profitability index	Ratio of net present value to initial investment	Accept project if profitability index is greater than 0. In case of capital rationing, accept projects with highest profitability index.	Results in same accept/reject decision as NPV in the absence of project interactions. Useful for ranking projects in case of capital rationing, but misleading in the presence of interactions. Cannot rank mutually exclusive projects.

7.6   SUMMARY

1. **What is the net present value of an investment, and how do you calculate it?**

The **net present value** of a project measures the difference between its value and cost. NPV is therefore the amount that the project will add to shareholder wealth. A company maximizes shareholder wealth by accepting all projects that have a positive NPV.

2. **How is the internal rate of return of a project calculated, and what must one look out for when using the internal rate of return rule?**

Instead of asking whether a project has a positive NPV, many businesses prefer to ask whether it offers a higher return than shareholders could expect to get by investing in the capital market. Return is usually defined as the discount rate that would result in a zero NPV. This is known as the **internal rate of return**, or IRR. The project is attractive if the IRR exceeds the **opportunity cost of capital**.

There are some pitfalls in using the internal rate of return rule. Be careful about using the IRR when (1) the early cash flows are positive, (2) there is more than one change in the sign of the cash flows, or (3) you need to choose between two **mutually exclusive projects**.

3. **Why don't the payback and discounted payback rules and the book rate of return rule always make shareholders better off?**

The net present value rule and the rate of return rule both properly reflect the time value of money. But companies sometimes use rules of thumb to judge projects. One is the payback rule, which states that a project is acceptable if you get your money back within a specified period. The payback rule takes no account of any cash flows that arrive after the payback period and fails to discount cash flows within the payback period.

The discounted payback rule improves upon the payback rule by examining discounted cash flows. It states that a project is acceptable if the discounted cash flows recover your initial investment within a specified period.

Book (or accounting) rate of return is the income of a project divided by the book value. Unlike the internal rate of return, book rate of return does not depend just on the project's cash flows. It also depends on which cash flows are classified as capital investments and which as operating expenses. Managers often keep an eye on how projects would affect book rate of return.

4. **How can the net present value rule be used to analyze three common problems that involve competing projects: when to postpone an investment expenditure; how to choose between projects with equal lives; and when to replace equipment?**

Sometimes a project may have a positive NPV if undertaken today but an even higher NPV if the investment is delayed. Choose between these alternatives by comparing their NPVs *today*.

When you have to choose between projects with different lives, you should put them on an equal footing by comparing the **equivalent annual cost** or benefit of the two projects. When you are considering whether to replace an aging machine with a new one, you should compare the cost of operating the old one with the equivalent annual cost of the new one.

5. **How is the profitability index calculated, and how can it be used to choose between projects when funds are limited?**

If there is a shortage of capital, companies need to choose projects that offer the highest net present value per dollar of investment. This measure is known as the **profitability index**.

Related Web Links

http://www.asbdc.ualr.edu/bizfacts/1518.asp How net present value analysis helps answer business questions

http://www.channeltunnel.co.uk Web site of the Eurotunnel system

http://www.tbs-sct.gc.ca/fin/sigs/Revolving_Funds/bcag/BCA2_E.asp A cost benefit analysis guide prepared by the Treasury Board of Canada Secretariat

Key Terms

Questions and Problems

*Answers in Appendix B

BASIC

Problems 1–10 refer to two projects with the following cash flows:

Year	Project A	Project B
0	–$100	–$100
1	40	50
2	40	50
3	40	50
4	40	

*1. **IRR/NPV.** If the opportunity cost of capital is 11 percent, which of these projects is worth pursuing?

2. **Mutually Exclusive Investments.** Suppose that you can choose only one of these projects. Which would you choose? The discount rate is still 11 percent.

*3. **IRR/NPV.** Which project would you choose if the opportunity cost of capital were 16 percent?

4. **IRR.** What are the internal rates of return on projects A and B?

*5. **Investment Criteria.** In light of your answers to problems 2 to 4, is there any reason to believe that the project with the higher IRR is the better project?

6. **Profitability Index.** If the opportunity cost of capital is 11 percent, what is the profitability index for each project? Does the profitability index rank the projects correctly?

*7. **Payback.** What is the payback period of each project?

8. **Discounted Payback.** What is the discounted payback for each project if the opportunity cost of capital is 11 percent?

9. **Investment Criteria.** Considering your answers to problems 2, 3, and 7, is there any reason to believe that the project with the lower payback period is the better project?

EXCEL

10. **Book Rate of Return.** Accountants have set up the following depreciation schedules for the two projects:

Year:	1	2	3	4
Project A	$25	$25	$25	$25
Project B	33.33	33.33	33.34	

Calculate book rates of return for each year. Are these book returns the same as the IRR?

11. **NPV and IRR.** A project that costs $3,000 to install will provide annual cash flows of $800 for each of the next 6 years. Is this project worth pursuing if the discount rate is 10 percent? How high can the discount rate be before you would reject the project?

12. **Payback.** A project that costs $2,500 to install will provide annual cash flows of $600 for the next 6 years. The firm accepts projects with payback periods of less than five years. Will the project be accepted?

*13. **Profitability Index.** What is the profitability index of a project that costs $10,000 and provides cash flows of $3,000 in years 1 and 2 and $5,000 in years 3 and 4? The discount rate is 10 percent.

14. **Discounted Payback.** A project that costs $3,000 to install will provide annual cash flows of $800 for each of the next 6 years. The firm accepts projects with a discounted payback

of 5 years or less. Should this project be pursued if the discount rate is 2 percent? What if the discount rate is 12 percent? Will the firm's decision change as the discount rate changes?

15. **NPV.** A proposed nuclear power plant will cost $2.2 billion to build and then will produce cash flows of $300 million a year for 15 years. After that period (in Year 15), it must be decommissioned at a cost of $900 million. What is project NPV if the discount rate is 6 percent? What if it is 16 percent?

PRACTICE

*16. **NPV/IRR.** Consider projects A and B:

	Cash Flows, $			
Project	C_0	C_1	C_2	NPV at 10%
A	−30,000	21,000	21,000	+$6,446
B	−50,000	33,000	33,000	+$7,273

Calculate IRRs for A and B. Which project does the IRR rule suggest is best? Which project is really best?

*17. **IRR.** You have the chance to participate in a project that produces the following cash flows:

C_0	C_1	C_2
+$5,000	+$4,000	−$11,000

The internal rate of return is 13.6 percent. If the opportunity cost of capital is 12 percent, would you accept the offer?

*18. **NPV/IRR.**
   a.   Calculate the net present value of the following project for discount rates of 0, 50, and 100 percent:

C_0	C_1	C_2
+$6,750	+$4,500	−$18,000

   b.   What is the IRR of the project?

19. **IRR.** Marielle Machinery Works forecasts the following cash flows on a project under consideration. It uses the internal rate of return rule to accept or reject projects. Should this project be accepted if the required return is 12 percent?

C_0	C_1	C_2	C_3
+$10,000	0	−$7,500	−$8,500

*20. **NPV/IRR.** A new computer system will require an initial outlay of $20,000 but it will increase the firm's cash flows by $4,000 a year for each of the next 8 years. Is the system worth installing if the required rate of return is 9 percent? What if it is 14 percent? How high can the discount rate be before you would reject the project?

21. **Investment Criteria.** If you insulate your office for $1,000, you will save $100 a year in heating expenses. These savings will last forever.
   a.   What is the NPV of the investment when the cost of capital is 8 percent? 10 percent?
   b.   What is the IRR of the investment?
   c.   What is the payback period on this investment?
   d.   What is the discounted payback period on this investment when the cost of capital is 8 percent? 10 percent?

EXCEL

22. **NPV versus IRR.** Here are the cash flows for two mutually exclusive projects:

Project	C_0	C_1	C_2	C_3
A	−$20,000	+$8,000	+$8,000	+$8,000
B	−$20,000	0	0	+$25,000

a.   At what interest rates would you prefer project A to B? *Hint*: Try drawing the NPV profile of each project.

b.   What is the IRR of each project?

*23. **Payback and NPV.** A project has a life of 10 years and a payback period of 10 years. What must be true of project NPV?

24. **IRR/NPV.** Consider this project with an internal rate of return of 13.1 percent. Should you accept or reject the project if the discount rate is 12 percent?

Year	Cash Flow
0	+$100
1	−60
2	−60

*25. **Payback, Discounted Payback, and NPV.** A firm is considering the following projects. Its opportunity cost of capital is 10 percent.

Project	Time: 0	Cash Flows, $			
		1	2	3	4
A	−5,000	+1,000	+1,000	+3,000	0
B	−1,000	0	+1,000	+2,000	+3,000
C	−5,000	+1,000	+1,000	+3,000	+5,000

a.   What are the payback period and discounted payback period on each project?

b.   Given that you wish to use the payback rule with a cutoff period of two years, which projects would you accept?

c.   If you use a cutoff period of three years with the discounted payback rule, which projects would you accept?

d.   Which projects have positive NPVs?

e.   "Payback gives too much weight to cash flows that occur after the cutoff date." True or false?

26. **Book Rate of Return.** Consider these data on a proposed project:

Original investment = $200

Straight-line depreciation of $50 a year for 4 years

Project life = 4 years

Year:	0	1	2	3	4
Book value	$200	—	—	—	—
Sales		100	110	120	130
Costs		30	35	40	45
Depreciation		—	—	—	—
Net income		—	—	—	—

a.   Fill in the blanks in the table.

b.   Find the book rate of return of this project in each year.

c.   Find project NPV if the discount rate is 20 percent.

27. **Book Rate of Return.** A machine costs $8,000 and is expected to produce profit before depreciation of $2,500 in each of years 1 and 2 and $3,500 in each of years 3 and 4. Assuming that the machine is depreciated at a constant rate of $2,000 a year and that there are no taxes, what is the average return on book?

EXCEL

28. **Book Rate of Return.** A project requires an initial investment of $10,000, and over its 5-year life it will generate annual cash revenues of $5,000 and cash expenses of $2,000. The firm will use straight-line depreciation, but it does not pay taxes.

*a.   Find the book rates of return on the project for each year.

*b.   Is the project worth pursuing if the opportunity cost of capital is 8 percent?

c.   What would happen to the book rates of return if half the initial $10,000 outlay were treated as an expense instead of a capital investment? *Hint*: Instead of depreciating all of the $10,000, treat $5,000 as an expense in the first year.

*d.   Does NPV change as a result of the different accounting treatment proposed in (c)?

29. **Profitability Index.** Consider the following projects:

Project	C_0	C_1	C_2
A	−$2,100	+$2,000	+$1,200
B	− 2,100	+ 1,440	+ 1,728

a.   Calculate the profitability index for A and B assuming a 20 percent opportunity cost of capital.

b.   Use the profitability index rule to determine which project(s) you should accept (1) if you could undertake both and (2) if you could undertake only one.

30. **Capital Rationing.** You are a manager with an investment budget of $8 million. You may invest in the following projects. Investment and cash flow figures are in millions of dollars.

Project	Discount Rate, %	Investment	Annual Cash Flow	Project Life, Years
A	10	3	1	5
B	12	4	1	8
C	8	5	2	4
D	8	3	1.5	3
E	12	3	1	6

a.   Why might these projects have different discount rates?

b.   Which projects should the manager choose?

c.   Which projects will be chosen if there is no capital rationing?

EXCEL

31. **Profitability Index versus NPV.** Consider these two projects:

Project	C_0	C_1	C_2	C_3
A	−$18	+$10	+$10	+$10
B	−$50	+$25	+$25	+$25

a.   Which project has the higher NPV if the discount rate is 10 percent?

b.   Which has the higher profitability index?

c.   Which project is most attractive to a firm that can raise an unlimited amount of funds to pay for its investment projects? Which project is most attractive to a firm that is limited in the funds it can raise?

*32. **Mutually Exclusive Investments.** Here are the cash flow forecasts for two mutually exclusive projects:

	Cash Flows, $	
Year	Project A	Project B
0	−$100	−$100
1	30	49
2	50	49
3	70	49

a.   Which project would you choose if the opportunity cost of capital is 2 percent?

b.   Which would you choose if the opportunity cost of capital is 12 percent?

c.   Why does your answer change?

33. **Investment Criteria.** Elm City Electronics is considering two mutually exclusive projects that differ greatly on the required investment and projected cash flows. The initial investment required for Project I is $250,000 while for Project II it is $25,000. Projected after-tax cash flows are shown below:

	Cash Flows, $	
Year	Project I	Project II
1	12,000	15,000
2	18,000	8,000
3	18,000	6,000
4	30,000	6,000
5	250,000	500

The opportunity cost of capital for Elm City is 6 percent.

a. Decide which project you would choose by applying each of the following decision criteria separately. Explain your reasoning in each case: (1) payback period, (2) discounted payback period, (3) NPV, (4) IRR, and (5) profitability index.

b. Which project would you eventually choose? Explain your answer.

*34. **Equivalent Annual Cost.** A precision lathe costs $10,000 and will cost $20,000 a year to operate and maintain. If the discount rate is 12 percent and the lathe will last for 5 years, what is the equivalent annual cost of the tool?

35. **Equivalent Annual Cost.** A firm can lease a truck for 4 years at a cost of $30,000 annually. It can instead buy a truck at a cost of $80,000, with annual maintenance expenses of $10,000. The truck will be sold at the end of 4 years for $20,000. Which is the better option if the discount rate is 12 percent?

36. **Multiple IRR.** Consider the following cash flows:

C_0	C_1	C_2	C_3	C_4
−22	+20	+20	+20	−40

a. Confirm that one internal rate of return on this project is (a shade above) 7 percent, and that the other is (a shade below) 34 percent.

*b. Is the project attractive if the discount rate is 5 percent?

*c. What if it is 20 percent? 40 percent?

d. Why is the project attractive at mid-range discount rates but not at very high or very low rates?

EXCEL

37. **Equivalent Annual Cost.** Econo-cool air conditioners cost $300 to purchase, result in electricity bills of $150 per year, and last for 5 years. Luxury Air models cost $500, result in electricity bills of $100 per year, and last for 8 years. The discount rate is 21 percent.

a. What are the equivalent annual costs of the Econo-cool and Luxury Air models?

b. Which model is more cost effective?

c. Now you remember that the inflation rate is expected to be 10 percent per year for the foreseeable future. Redo parts (a) and (b).

38. **Investment Timing.** You can purchase an optical scanner today for $400. The scanner provides benefits worth $60 a year. The expected life of the scanner is 10 years. Scanners are expected to decrease in price by 20 percent per year. Suppose the discount rate is 10 percent. Should you purchase the scanner today or wait to purchase? When is the best purchase time?

39. **Replacement Decision.** You are operating an old machine that is expected to produce a cash inflow of $5,000 in each of the next 3 years before it fails. You can replace it now with a new machine that costs $20,000 but is much more efficient and will provide a cash flow of $10,000 a year for 4 years. Should you replace your equipment now? The discount rate is 15 percent.

*40. **Replacement Decision.** A forklift will last for only two more years. It costs $5,000 a year to maintain. For $20,000 you can buy a new lift that can last for 10 years and should require maintenance costs of only $2,000 a year.
    a. If the discount rate is 5 percent per year, should you replace the forklift?
    b. If the discount rate is 10 percent per year? Why does your answer change?

41. **Internet.** Go to the Industry Canada Web site at **http://strategis.ic.gc.ca** and click on the icon for "Economic Analysis, Statistics." You will be able to reach a number of publications providing analyses and statistics on a wide range of economic, demographic, trade-related, and other issues. From these publications, can you find the amount of business investment in machinery and equipment as of the fourth quarter of 2004? Also, what was the percentage capacity utilization of different industry sectors such as Food, Paper, Plastic and Rubber Products, and Machinery in the fourth quarter of 2004? From which publications did you obtain the information? Does the percentage capacity utilization provide an indicator of the likelihood of future capital spending?

CHALLENGE

EXCEL

42. **NPV/IRR.** Growth Enterprises believes its latest project, which will cost $80,000 to install, will generate a perpetual growing stream of cash flows. Cash flow at the end of this year will be $5,000, and cash flows in future years are expected to grow indefinitely at an annual rate of 5 percent.
    a. If the discount rate for this project is 10 percent, what is the project NPV?
    b. What is the project IRR?

43. **Investment Timing.** A classic problem in management of forests is determining when it is most economically advantageous to cut a tree for lumber. When the tree is young, it grows very rapidly. As it ages, its growth slows. Why is the NPV-maximizing rule to cut the tree when its growth rate equals the discount rate?

44. **Multiple IRRs.** Strip Mining, Inc., can develop a new mine at an initial cost of $5 million. The mine will provide a cash flow of $30 million in 1 year. The land then must be reclaimed at a cost of $28 million in the second year.
    a. What are the IRRs of this project?
    b. Should the firm develop the mine if the discount rate is 10 percent? 20 percent? 350 percent? 400 percent?

45. **Replacement Decision.** The Faculty of Business at Old Renowned University wishes to buy new personal computers for its 20 full-time faculty members. The university is a non-profit institution and does not pay any taxes. The Faculty can buy 20 Ultra Fast PCs, each costing $2,500. It is estimated that the annual cost of each PC will be $150. The Ultra Fast PCs will be scheduled for replacement at the end of 5 years, at which time they can be resold for $450 each. As an alternative to the Ultra Fast brand, the Faculty can also buy the more moderately priced Medium Fast PC for $2,000 apiece with annual servicing cost of $300 each. If the Faculty does decide on the Medium Fast PC, it will buy 25 units for all its full and part-time faculty members. The Medium Fast PCs are expected to be replaced at the end of 4 years with an estimated resale value of $250 each.

    The Dean of the Faculty of Business has approached you to conduct an analysis and make a recommendation. You have been informed that the opportunity cost of funds to the Faculty for investments of this nature is 12 percent.
    a. Based on your analysis, would you recommend buying the Ultra Fast or the Medium Fast brand?
    b. Suppose now that the PCs will not be resold at the time of replacement but will instead be donated for free to an international charitable organization. Rework your analysis to see whether your recommendation will change based on this new information.

c.   The Dean has informed you that if a new superior model, the Hyper 3MM, appears in the market in the near future then this model will be the preferred choice for replacement purposes. In this case, the Faculty will replace all its existing PCs with the Hyper brand at the end of four years. Would you now recommend the Ultra Fast or the Medium Fast brand until the end of Year 4?

46. **Comprehensive.** Visionary Inc. is examining two projects, A and B. Project A has a lower initial investment than Project B and is expected to generate a steady stream of cash flows over its economic life. Project B is expected to generate lower cash flows in earlier years and higher cash flows in later years relative to Project A. Details regarding the initial investment projected at time 0 and subsequent cash flows for the two projects are provided below:

	Cash Flows	
	Project A	**Project B**
Year	**$**	**$**
0	–10,000	–15,000
1	6,000	3,000
2	6,000	5,000
3	6,000	7,000
4	6,000	8,000

Assume that the cost of capital for both projects is 10 percent.

a.   Calculate the payback and discounted payback period for each project. Which project appears to be preferable using these methods? Give reasons. What are the major flaws in these methods?

b.   Calculate the net present value of each project. Which project is preferable using this method?

c.   Calculate the profitability index for each project. Which project would you select using this method?

d.   Calculate the IRR for each project. Which project would you choose using the IRR rule? Try to calculate the IRR for Project B using interpolation and see if you are able get an answer close to the one you would get by using a financial calculator or a software package.

e.   Does the question provide sufficient information to help us determine whether the projects are independent or mutually exclusive? How would you distinguish between the two categories?

f.   Are you able to reach the same decision by applying the different decision criteria? If not, which criterion would you rely on? Why?

47. **Comprehensive.** You wish to start a new line of software. Your initial investment in the project will be $100,000. You do not expect to generate any cash flows for the first two years. However, cash flows in Year 3 are expected to be $16,000 and are expected to increase by 15 percent every year till Year 7, after which time they will decline by 2 percent until Year 9. You do not expect any growth in cash flows beyond Year 9. However, you expect your business to generate constant cash flows into the foreseeable future.

a.   Assuming that your cost of capital is 8 percent per year, should you pursue the project if your objective is to accept projects only when they are worth more than their cost?

b.   Explain your answer to part (a) above. What technique did you use in your answer to part (a)?

c.   By what time frame do you expect to recover your initial investment in the project: (1) ignoring the time value of money, and (2) taking into account the time value of money? Name the techniques you have used for your computation. What are the benefits and drawbacks to these techniques?

d.   Can you find the IRR for this project?

48. **Comprehensive.** You have joined the Projects division of GrowMore Inc. Your first job is to analyze two projects, which you have code named "alpha" and "beta." Both projects will require the same initial investment of $100,000 and are expected to generate the following cash flows over an expected economic life of 4 years.

	Project "Alpha"	Project "Beta"
Year	$	$
1	70,000	40,000
2	32,000	40,000
3	32,000	40,000
4	9,000	40,000

Assuming that GrowMore Inc.'s cost of capital for these projects is 10 percent:

a. Calculate its (1) payback period, and (2) discounted payback period. Which project would you select under these methods? Explain your answer.

b. Calculate net present values for each project and indicate which one you would undertake using this decision rule.

c. Calculate internal rates of return for each project. Which project would you select using the IRR rule?

d. Calculate the profitability index for each project and indicate your decision using this rule.

e. Can you think of any situations where, because of a change in the cost of capital, you might be confronted with conflicting decisions using the NPV and IRR rules? Show how this might happen.

49. **Replacement.** You are thinking of purchasing a new machine (NEW) for your business operations and replacing the existing machine (OLD), which you have used for the past three years. The new machine will cost $75,000 and will be useful to your business for five years after which it can be sold to fetch a salvage value of $9,000. The new machine will be depreciated straight-line to 0 over 5 years. The old machine was purchased for $70,000 and is also being depreciated straight-line to 0 over 5 years. The old machine can be sold today for $30,000, but if you waited for 5 years it will be worth only $6,500 at that time.

The new machine is expected to significantly boost the efficiency of your business operations. Annual savings in operating costs are expected to be $12,000. Also your net working capital requirement will decline annually by $4,000. Your business pays tax at the rate of 35 percent and has a cost of capital rate of 12 percent. Does it make sense for you to replace the OLD machine with the NEW machine?

Solutions to Check Points

7.1   Even if construction costs are $355,000, NPV is still positive:

$$NPV = PV - \$355,000 = \$357,143 - \$355,000 = \$2,143$$

Therefore, the project is still worth pursuing. The project is viable as long as construction costs are less than the PV of the future cash flow, that is, as long as construction costs are less than $357,143. However, if the opportunity cost of capital is 20 percent, the PV of the $400,000 sales price is lower and NPV is negative:

$$PV = \$400,000 \times \frac{1}{1.20} = \$333,333$$

$$NPV = PV - \$355,000 = -\$21,667$$

The present value of the future cash flow is not as high when the opportunity cost of capital is higher. The project would need to provide a higher payoff in order to be viable in the face of the higher opportunity cost of capital.

7.2   The payback period is $3,000/$660 = 4.6 years. We find the discounted payback period and NPV as follows:

Year	Cash Flows	Discount Factor	Discounted Cash Flows	Cumulative Discounted Cash Flows
0	−3,000	1.0000	−3,000	
1	660	0.9434	623	−2,377
2	660	0.8900	587	−1,790
3	660	0.8396	554	−1,236
4	660	0.7921	523	−713
5	660	0.7473	493	−220
6	660	0.7050	465	245
7	660	0.6651	439	**684** ↓ NPV

Notice the cumulative discounted cash flows are negative until Year 5 and positive from Year 6. This means that the discounted payback period = 5 years + 220/465 = 5.5 years. The cumulative discounted cash flow for Year 7 is also the NPV, $684.

You can also calculate NPV by taking the present value of a $660 annuity for 7 years at 6 percent:

PV annuity = $3,684

NPV = −$3,000 + $3,684 = $684

The project should be accepted.

7.3   The IRR is now about 8.9 percent because

$$NPV = -\$350{,}000 + \frac{\$16{,}000}{1.089} + \frac{\$16{,}000}{(1.089)^2} + \frac{\$416{,}000}{(1.089)^3} = 0$$

Note in Figure 7.6 that NPV falls to zero as the discount rate reaches 8.9 percent.

7.4   a. IRR = 23% (i.e., −60 + 30/1.23 + 30/1.23² + 30/1.23³ = 0)
       b. Year 1: Income/book value at start of Year 1 = (30 − 20)/60 = .17, or 17%
           Year 2: Income/book value at start of Year 2 = (30 − 20)/40 = .25, or 25%
           Year 3: Income/book value at start of Year 3 = (30 − 20)/20 = .50, or 50%

FIGURE 7.6
NPV falls to zero at an interest rate of 8.9 percent

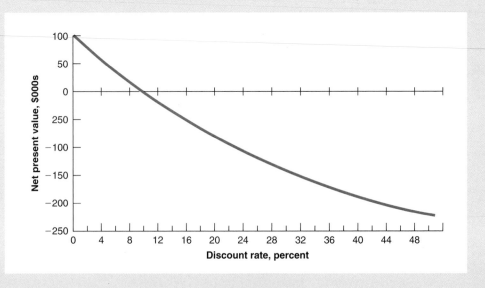

7.5	Year of Purchase	Cost of Computer	PV Savings	NPV at Year of Purchase	NPV Today
	0	50	70	20	20
	1	45	66	21	19.1
	2	40	62	22	18.2
	3	36	58	22	16.5
	4	33	54	21	14.3
	5	31	50	19	11.8

Purchase the new computer now.

7.6

Year:	0	1	2	3	PV of Costs
F. Cash flows	10,000	1,100	1,200		11,992
Equivalent annual cost		6,910	6,910		11,992
G. Cash flows	12,000	1,100	1,200	1,300	14,968
Equivalent annual cost		6,019	6,019	6,019	14,968

Machine G is the better buy. However, it's still better to keep the old machine going one more year. That costs $4,300, which is less than G's equivalent annual cost, $6,019.

7.7 You want to be rich. The NPV of the long-lived investment is much larger.

$$\text{Short: NPV} = -\$1 + \frac{\$2}{1.075} = +\$.8605 \text{ million}$$

$$\text{Long: NPV} = -\$1 + \frac{\$.3}{.075} = +\$3 \text{ million}$$

7.8 You want to be rich. The second alternative generates greater value at any reasonable discount rate. For example, other risk-free investments offer 8 percent. Then

$$\text{NPV} = -\$1,000 + \frac{\$4,000}{1.08} = +\$2,703$$

$$\text{NPV} = -\$1,000,000 + \frac{\$1,500,000}{1.08} = +\$388,888$$

7.9 Rank each project in order of profitability index as in the following table:

Project	Profitability Index	Investment
N	0.43	$7
L	0.33	3
O	0.33	6
P	0.25	4
M	0.20	5

Starting from the top, we run out of funds after accepting projects N and L. While L and O have equal profitability indexes, project O could not be chosen because it would force total investment above the limit of $10 million.

7.10 The profitability index gives the correct ranking for the first pair, the wrong ranking for the second:

Project	PV	Investment	NPV	Profitability Index (NPV/Investment)
Short	$1,860,000	$1,000,000	$ 860,000	0.86
Long	4,000,000	1,000,000	3,000,000	3.0
Small	$ 3,703	$ 1,000	$ 2,703	2.7
Large	1,388,888	1,000,000	388,888	0.39

USING DISCOUNTED CASH FLOW ANALYSIS TO MAKE INVESTMENT DECISIONS

Think of the problems that General Motors faces when considering whether to introduce a new model. How much will we need to invest in new plant and equipment? What will it cost to market and promote the new car? How soon can we get the car into production? What is the projected production cost? What do we need in the way of inventories of raw materials and finished cars? How many cars can we expect to sell each year and at what price? What credit arrangements will we need to give our dealers? How long will the model stay in production? What happens at the end of that time? Can we use the plant and equipment elsewhere in the company? All of these issues affect the level and timing of project cash flows. In this chapter we continue our analysis of the capital budgeting decision by turning our focus to how the financial manager should prepare cash flow estimates for use in net present value analysis.

In Chapter 7 we used the net present value rule to make a simple capital budgeting decision. You tackled the problem in four steps:

Step 1:   Forecast the project cash flows.

Step 2:   Estimate the opportunity cost of capital—that is, the rate of return that your shareholders could expect to earn if they invested their money in the capital market.

Step 3:   Use the opportunity cost of capital to discount the future cash flows. The project's present value (PV) is equal to the sum of the discounted future cash flows.

Step 4: Net present value (NPV) measures whether the project is worth more than it costs. To
           calculate NPV you need to subtract the required investment from the present value of
           the future payoffs:

$$NPV = PV - \text{required investment}$$

You should proceed with the project if it has a positive NPV.

We now need to consider how to apply the net present value rule to practical investment problems. The first step is to decide what to discount. We know the answer in principle: discount cash flows. This is why capital budgeting is often referred to as *discounted cash flow*, or *DCF*, analysis. But useful forecasts of cash flows do not arrive on a silver platter. Often the financial manager has to make do with raw data supplied by specialists in product design, production, marketing, and so on, and must adjust such data before they are useful. In addition, most financial forecasts are prepared in accordance with accounting principles that do not necessarily recognize cash flows when they occur. These data must also be adjusted.

We start this chapter with a discussion of the principles governing the cash flows that are relevant for discounting. We then present an example designed to show how standard accounting information can be used to compute those cash flows and why cash flows and accounting income usually differ. The example will lead us to various further points, including the links between depreciation and taxes, and the importance of tracking investments in working capital.

After studying this chapter you should be able to
- Identify the cash flows properly attributable to a proposed new project.
- Calculate the cash flows of a project from standard financial statements.
- Understand how the company's tax bill is affected by depreciation and how this affects project value.
- Understand how changes in working capital affect project cash flows.

8.1   DISCOUNT CASH FLOWS, NOT PROFITS

Up to this point we have been concerned mainly with the mechanics of discounting and with the various methods of project appraisal. We have had almost nothing to say about the problem of what you should discount. The first and most important point is this: to calculate net present value you need to discount cash flows, *not* accounting profits.

We stressed the difference between cash flows and profits in Chapter 3. Here we stress it again. Income statements are intended to show how well the firm has performed. They do not track cash flows.

If the firm lays out a large amount of money on a big capital project, you would not conclude that the firm performed poorly that year, even though a lot of cash is going out the door. Therefore, the accountant does not deduct capital expenditure when calculating the year's income but instead depreciates it over several years.

That is fine for computing year-by-year profits, but it could get you into trouble when working out net present value. For example, suppose that you are analyzing an investment proposal. It costs $2,000 and is expected to bring in a cash flow of $1,500 in the first year and $500 in the second. You think that the opportunity cost of capital is 10 percent and so calculate the present value of the cash flows as follows:

$$PV = \frac{\$1,500}{1.10} + \frac{\$500}{(1.10)^2} = \$1,776.86$$

The project is worth less than it costs; it has a negative NPV:

$$NPV = \$1,776.86 - \$2,000 = -\$223.14$$

The project costs $2,000 today, but accountants would not treat that outlay as an immediate expense. They would depreciate that $2,000 over 2 years and deduct the depreciation from the cash flow to obtain accounting income:

	Year 1	Year 2
Cash inflow	+ $1,500	+$ 500
Less depreciation	– 1,000	– 1,000
Accounting income	+ 500	– 500

Thus an accountant would forecast income of $500 in Year 1 and an accounting loss of $500 in Year 2.

Suppose you were given this forecast income and loss and naively discounted them. Now NPV *looks* positive:

$$\text{Apparent NPV} = \frac{\$500}{1.10} + \frac{-\$500}{(1.10)^2} = \$41.32$$

Of course we know that this is nonsense. The project is obviously a loser; we are spending money today ($2,000 cash outflow) and we are simply getting our money back ($1,500 in Year 1 and $500 in Year 2). We are earning a zero return when we could get a 10 percent return by investing our money in the capital market.

The message of the example is this:

> When calculating NPV, recognize investment expenditures when they occur, not later when they show up as depreciation. Projects are financially attractive because of the cash they generate, either for distribution to shareholders or for reinvestment in the firm. Therefore, the focus of capital budgeting must be on cash flow, not profits.

Here is another example of the distinction between cash flow and accounting profits. Accountants try to show profit as it is earned, rather than when the company and the customer get around to paying their bills. For example, an income statement will recognize revenue when the sale is made, even if the bill is not paid for months. This practice also results in a difference between accounting profits and cash flow. The sale generates immediate profits, but the cash flow comes later.

EXAMPLE 8.1	**SALES BEFORE CASH**

Reggie Hotspur, ace computer salesperson, closed a $500,000 sale on December 15, just in time to count it toward his annual bonus. How did he do it? Well, for one thing he gave the customer 180 days to pay. The income statement will recognize Hotspur's sale in December, even though cash will not arrive until June. But a financial analyst tracking cash flows would concentrate on the latter event.

The accountant takes care of the timing difference by adding $500,000 to accounts receivable in December, then reducing accounts receivable when the money arrives in June. (The total of accounts receivable is just the sum of all cash due from customers.)

You can think of the increase in accounts receivable as an investment—it's effectively a 180-day loan to the customer—and therefore a cash outflow. That investment is recovered when the customer pays. Thus financial analysts often find it convenient to calculate cash flow as follows:

December		June	
Sales	$500,000	Sales	0
Less investment in accounts receivable	–$500,000	Plus recovery of accounts receivable	+$500,000
Cash flow	0	Cash flow	$500,000

Note that this procedure gives the correct cash flow of $500,000 in June.

It is not always easy to translate accounting data back into actual dollars. If you are in doubt about what is a cash flow, simply count the dollars coming in and take away the dollars going out.

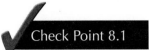

Check Point 8.1

A regional supermarket chain is deciding whether to install a tewgit machine in each of its stores. Each machine costs $250,000. Projected income per machine is as follows:

Year:	1	2	3	4	5
Sales	$250,000	$300,000	$300,000	$250,000	$250,000
Operating expenses	200,000	200,000	200,000	200,000	200,000
Depreciation	50,000	50,000	50,000	50,000	50,000
Accounting income	0	50,000	50,000	0	0

Why would the stores continue to operate a machine in years 4 and 5 if it produces no profits? What are the cash flows from investing in a machine? Assume each tewgit machine is completely depreciated and has no salvage value at the end of its five-year life.

8.2   DISCOUNT INCREMENTAL CASH FLOWS

A project's present value depends on the extra cash flows that it produces. Forecast the firm's cash flows first if you proceed with the project. Then forecast the cash flows if you don't accept the project. Take the difference and you have the extra (or incremental) cash flows produced by the project:

$$\frac{\text{Incremental}}{\text{cash flow}} = \frac{\text{cash flow}}{\text{with project}} - \frac{\text{cash flow}}{\text{without project}} \qquad (8.1)$$

EXAMPLE 8.2   **LAUNCHING A NEW PRODUCT**

Consider the decision by Intel to launch its Pentium 4 microprocessor. A successful launch could mean the sale of millions of processors a year and several billion dollars in profits.

But are these profits all incremental cash flows? Certainly not. Our with-versus-without principle reminds us that we also need to think about what the cash flows would be without the new processor. Intel recognized that if it went ahead with the Pentium III, demand for its older Pentium II processors would be reduced. The incremental cash flows are therefore

Cash flow with Pentium 4		Cash flow without Pentium 4
(including lower cash flow	–	(with higher cash flow
from Pentium 3 processors)		from Pentium 3 processors)

The trick in capital budgeting is to trace all the incremental flows from a proposed project. Here are some things to look out for.

INCLUDE ALL INDIRECT EFFECTS

Intel's new processor illustrates a common indirect effect. New products often damage sales of an existing product. Of course, companies frequently introduce new products anyway, usually because they believe that their existing product line is under threat from competition. Even if you don't go ahead with a new product, there is no guarantee that sales of the existing product line will continue at their present level. Sooner or later they will decline.

Sometimes a new project will *help* the firm's existing business. Suppose that you are the financial manager of an airline that is considering opening a new short-haul route from Prince George, B.C. to Vancouver International Airport. When considered in isolation, the new route may have a negative NPV. But once you allow for the additional business that the new route brings to your other traffic out of Vancouver, it may be a very worthwhile investment.

> To forecast incremental cash flow, you must trace out all indirect effects of accepting the project.

Some capital investments have very long lives once all indirect effects are recognized. Consider the introduction of a new jet engine. Engine manufacturers often offer attractive pricing to achieve early sales, because once an engine is installed, 15 years' sales of replacement parts are almost assured. Also, since airlines prefer to reduce the number of different engines in their fleet, selling jet engines today improves sales tomorrow as well. Later sales will generate further demands for replacement parts. Thus the string of incremental effects from the first sales of a new model engine can run out 20 years or more.

FORGET SUNK COSTS

Sunk costs are like spilled milk: they are past and irreversible outflows.

> Sunk costs remain the same whether or not you accept the project. Therefore, they do not affect project NPV.

Unfortunately, often managers are influenced by sunk costs. For example, in 1971 Lockheed sought a federal guarantee for a bank loan to continue development of the Tristar airplane. Lockheed and its supporters argued that it would be foolish to abandon a project on which nearly $1 billion had already been spent. This was a poor argument, however, because the $1 billion was sunk. The relevant questions were how much more needed to be invested and whether the finished product warranted the incremental investment.

Lockheed's supporters were not the only ones to appeal to sunk costs. Some of its critics claimed that it would be foolish to continue with a project that offered no prospect of a satisfactory return on that $1 billion. This argument too was faulty. The $1 billion was gone, and the decision to continue with the project should have depended only on the return on the incremental investment.

INCLUDE OPPORTUNITY COSTS

Resources are almost never free, even when no cash changes hands. For example, suppose a new manufacturing operation uses land that could otherwise be sold for $100,000. This resource is costly; by using the land you pass up the opportunity to sell it. There is no out-of-pocket cost but there is an **opportunity cost**, that is, the value of the forgone alternative use of the land.

opportunity cost Benefit or cash flow forgone as a result of an action.

This example prompts us to warn you against judging projects "before versus after" rather than "with versus without." A manager comparing before versus after might not assign any value to the land because the firm owns it both before and after:

Before	Take Project	After	Cash Flow, Before versus After
Firm owns land	⟶	Firm still owns land	0

The proper comparison, *with versus without*, is as follows:

Before	Take Project	After	Cash Flow, with Project
Firm owns land	⟶	Firm still owns land	0

Before	Do Not Take Project	After	Cash Flow, without Project
Firm owns land	⟶	Firm sells land for $100,000	$100,000

Comparing the cash flows with and without the project, we see that $100,000 is given up by undertaking the project. The original cost of purchasing the land is irrelevant—that cost is sunk.

> The opportunity cost equals the cash that could be realized from selling the land now, and therefore is a relevant cash flow for project evaluation.

When the resource can be freely traded, its opportunity cost is simply the market price.[1] However, sometimes opportunity costs are difficult to estimate. Suppose that you go ahead with a project to develop Computer Nouveau, pulling your software team off their work on a new operating system that some existing customers are not-so-patiently awaiting. The exact cost of infuriating those customers may be impossible to calculate, but you'll think twice about the opportunity cost of moving the software team to Computer Nouveau.

RECOGNIZE THE INVESTMENT IN WORKING CAPITAL

net working capital   Current assets minus current liabilities.

Net working capital (often referred to simply as *working capital*) is the difference between a company's short-term assets and liabilities. The principal short-term assets are cash, accounts receivable (customers' unpaid bills), and inventories of raw materials and finished goods. The principal short-term liabilities are accounts payable (bills that you have not paid), notes payable, and accruals (liabilities for items such as wages or taxes that have recently been incurred but have not yet been paid).

Most projects entail an additional investment in working capital. For example, before you can start production, you need to invest in inventories of raw materials. Then, when you deliver the finished product, customers may be slow to pay and accounts receivable will increase. (Remember Reggie Hotspur's computer sale, described in Example 8.1. It required a $500,000, 6-month investment in accounts receivable.) Next year, as business builds up, you may need a larger stock of raw materials and you may have even more unpaid bills.

> Investments in working capital, just like investments in plant and equipment, result in cash outflows.

We find that working capital is one of the most common sources of confusion in forecasting project cash flows.[2] Here are the most common mistakes:

1. *Forgetting about working capital entirely.* We hope that you never fall into that trap.
2. *Forgetting that working capital may change during the life of the project.* Imagine that you sell $100,000 of goods per year and customers pay on average 6 months late. You will therefore have $50,000 of unpaid bills. Now you increase prices by 10 percent, so that revenues increase to $110,000. If customers continue to pay 6 months late, unpaid bills increase to $55,000, and therefore, you need to make an *additional* investment in working capital of $5,000.
3. *Forgetting that working capital is recovered at the end of the project.* When the project comes to an end, inventories are run down, any unpaid bills are (you hope) paid off, and you can recover your investment in working capital. This generates a cash *inflow*.

BEWARE OF ALLOCATED OVERHEAD COSTS

We have already mentioned that the accountant's objective in gathering data is not always the same as the investment analyst's. A case in point is the allocation of overhead costs such as rent, heat, or

---

[1] If the value of the land to the firm were less than the market price, the firm would sell it. On the other hand, the opportunity cost of using land in a particular project cannot exceed the cost of buying an equivalent parcel to replace it.

[2] If you are not clear why working capital affects cash flow, look back to Chapter 3, where we gave a primer on working capital and a couple of simple examples.

electricity. These overhead costs may not be related to a particular project, but they must be paid for nevertheless. Therefore, when the accountant assigns costs to the firm's projects, a charge for overhead is usually made. But our principle of incremental cash flows says that in investment appraisal we should include only the extra expenses that would result from the project.

> A project may generate extra overhead costs, but then again, it may not. We should be cautious about assuming that the accountant's allocation of overhead costs represents the *incremental* cash flow that would be incurred by accepting the project.

Check Point 8.2

A firm is considering an investment in a new manufacturing plant. The site is already owned by the company, but existing buildings would need to be demolished. Which of the following should be treated as incremental cash flows?

a. The market value of the site.
b. The market value of the existing buildings.
c. Demolition costs and site clearance.
d. The cost of a new access road put in last year.
e. Lost cash flows on other projects due to executive time spent on the new facility.
f. Future depreciation of the new plant.

8.3   DISCOUNT NOMINAL CASH FLOWS BY THE NOMINAL COST OF CAPITAL

The distinction between nominal and real cash flows and interest rates is crucial in capital budgeting. Interest rates are usually quoted in *nominal* terms. If you invest $100 in a bank deposit offering 6 percent interest, then the bank promises to pay you $106 at the end of the year. It makes no promises about what that $106 will buy. The real rate of interest on the bank deposit depends on inflation. If inflation is 2 percent, that $106 will buy you only 4 percent more goods at the end of the year than your $100 could buy today. The real rate of interest is therefore about 4 percent.[3]

If the discount rate is nominal, consistency requires that cash flows be estimated in nominal terms as well, taking into account trends in selling price, labour and materials costs, and so on. This calls for more than simply applying a single assumed inflation rate to all components of cash flow. Some costs or prices increase faster than inflation, some slower. For example, perhaps you have entered into a five-year fixed-price contract with a supplier. No matter what happens to inflation over this period, this part of your costs is fixed in nominal terms.

Of course, there is nothing wrong with discounting real cash flows at the real interest rate, although this is not commonly done. We saw in Chapter 4 that real cash flows discounted at the real discount rate give exactly the same present values as nominal cash flows discounted at the nominal rate.

---

[3] Remember from Chapter 4,

$$\text{Real rate of interest} \approx \text{nominal rate of interest} - \text{inflation rate}$$

The exact formula is

$$1 + \text{real rate of interest} = \frac{1 + \text{nominal rate of interest}}{1 + \text{inflation rate}}$$

$$= \frac{1.06}{1.02} = 1.0392$$

Therefore, the real interest rate is .0392, or 3.92 percent.

> It should go without saying that you cannot mix and match real and nominal quantities. Real cash flows must be discounted at a real discount rate, nominal cash flows at a nominal rate. Discounting real cash flows at a nominal rate is a big mistake.

While the need to maintain consistency may seem like an obvious point, analysts sometimes forget to account for the effects of inflation when forecasting future cash flows. As a result, they end up discounting real cash flows at a nominal interest rate. This can grossly understate project values.

EXAMPLE 8.3   **CASH FLOWS AND INFLATION**

City Consulting Services is considering moving into a new office building. The cost of a 1-year lease is $8,000, but this cost will increase in future years at the annual inflation rate of 3 percent. The firm believes that it will remain in the building for four years. What is the present value of its rental costs if the discount rate is 10 percent?

The present value can be obtained by discounting the nominal cash flows at the 10 percent discount rate as follows:

Year	Cash Flow	Present Value at 10% Discount Rate		
1	8,000	8,000/1.10	=	7,272.73
2	8,000 × 1.03 = 8,240	8,240/1.10^2	=	6,809.92
3	8,000 × 1.03^2 = 8,487.20	8,487.20/1.10^3	=	6,376.56
4	8,000 × 1.03^3 = 8,741.82	8,741.82/1.10^4	=	5,970.78
				$26,429.99

Alternatively, the real discount rate can be calculated as $1.10/1.03 - 1 = .067961 = 6.7961$ percent. The present value of the cash flows can also be computed by discounting the real cash flows at the real discount rate as follows:

Year	Real Cash Flow		Present Value at 6.7961% Discount Rate		
1	8,000/1.03	= 7,766.99	7,766.99/1.067961	=	7,272.73
2	8,240/1.03^2	= 7,766.99	7,766.99/1.067961^2	=	6,809.92
3	8,487.20/1.03^3	= 7,766.99	7,766.99/1.067961^3	=	6,376.56
4	8,741.82/1.03^4	= 7,766.99	7,766.99/1.067961^4	=	5,970.78
					$26,429.99

Notice the real cash flow is a constant, since the lease payment increases at the rate of inflation. The present value of *each* cash flow is the same regardless of the method used to discount. The sum of the present values is also identical, of course.

Check Point 8.3

Nasty Industries is closing down an outmoded factory and throwing all of its workers out on the street. Nasty's CEO, Cruella DeLuxe, is enraged to learn that it must continue to pay for workers' health insurance for four years. The cost per worker next year will be $2,400 per year, but the inflation rate is 4 percent, and health costs have been increasing at 3 percentage points faster than inflation. What is the present value of this obligation? The (nominal) discount rate is 10 percent.

8.4 SEPARATE INVESTMENT AND FINANCING DECISIONS

When we calculate the cash flows from a project, we ignore how that project is financed. The company may decide to finance partly by debt, but even if it did, we would neither subtract the debt proceeds from the required investment nor recognize the interest and principal payments as cash outflows. Regardless of the actual financing, we should view the project as if it were all-equity financed, treating all cash outflows required for the project as coming from shareholders and all cash inflows as going to them.

We do this to separate the analysis of the investment decision from the financing decision. We first measure whether the project has a positive net present value, assuming all-equity financing. Then we can undertake a separate analysis of the financing decision. We discuss financing decisions later in the book.

8.5 CALCULATING CASH FLOW

A project cash flow is the sum of three components: investment in fixed assets such as plant and equipment, investment in working capital, and cash flow from operations:

$$\text{Total cash flow} = \begin{array}{l} \text{cash flow from investment in plant and equipment} \\ + \text{ cash flow from investment in working capital} \\ + \text{ cash flow from operations} \end{array} \qquad (8.2)$$

Let's examine each of these in turn.

CAPITAL INVESTMENT

To get a project off the ground, a company will typically need to make considerable up-front investments in plant, equipment, research, marketing, and so on. For example, Gillette spent about $750 million to develop and build the production line for its Mach3 razor cartridge and an additional $300 million in its initial marketing campaign, largely before a single razor was sold. These expenditures are negative cash flows—negative because they represent a cash outflow from the firm.

Conversely, if a piece of machinery can be sold when the project winds down, the sales price (net of any taxes on the sale) represents a positive cash flow to the firm.

EXAMPLE 8.4	CASH FLOW FROM INVESTMENTS

Gillette's competitor, Slick, invests $800 million to develop the Mock4 razor blade. The specialized blade factory will run for 7 years, until it is replaced by more advanced technology. At that point, the machinery will be sold for scrap metal, for a price of $50 million. Taxes of $10 million will be assessed on the sale.

Therefore, the initial cash flow from investment is –$800 million, and in 7 years, the cash flow from the disinvestment in the production line will be $50 million – $10 million = $40 million.

INVESTMENT IN WORKING CAPITAL

We pointed out earlier in the chapter that when a company builds up inventories of raw materials or finished product, the company's cash is reduced; the reduction in cash reflects the firm's investment in inventories. Similarly, cash is reduced when customers are slow to pay their bills—in this case, the firm makes an investment in accounts receivable. Investment in working capital, just like investment in plant and equipment, represents a negative cash flow. On the other hand, later in the life of a project, when inventories are sold off and accounts receivable are collected, the firm's investment in working capital is reduced as it converts these assets into cash.

EXAMPLE 8.5	**CASH FLOW FROM INVESTMENTS IN WORKING CAPITAL**

Slick makes an initial (Year 0) investment of $10 million in inventories of plastic and steel for its blade plant. Then in Year 1 it accumulates an additional $20 million of raw materials. The total level of inventories is now $10 million + $20 million = $30 million, but the cash expenditure in Year 1 is simply the $20 million addition to inventory. The $20 million investment in additional inventory results in a cash flow of –$20 million.

Later on, say in Year 5, the company begins planning for the next-generation blade. At this point, it decides to reduce its inventory of raw material from $20 million to $15 million. This reduction in inventory investment frees up $5 million of cash, which is a positive cash flow. Therefore, the cash flows from inventory investment are –$10 million in Year 0, –$20 million in Year 1, and +$5 million in Year 5.

In general,

An *increase* in working capital is an investment, and therefore implies a *negative* cash flow; a decrease implies a positive cash flow. The cash flow is measured by the change in working capital, not the *level* of working capital.

CASH FLOW FROM OPERATIONS

The third component of project cash flow is cash flow from operations. There are several ways to work out this component.

Method 1. Take only the items from the income statement that represent cash flows. We start with cash revenues and subtract cash expenses and taxes paid. We do not, however, subtract a charge for depreciation because depreciation is an accounting entry, not a cash expense. Thus

$$\text{Cash flow from operations} = \text{revenues} - \text{cash expenses} - \text{taxes paid}$$

Method 2. Alternatively, you can start with accounting profits and add back any deductions that were made for non-cash expenses such as depreciation. (Remember from our earlier discussion that you want to discount cash flows, not profits.) By this reasoning,

$$\text{Cash flow from operations} = \text{net profit} + \text{depreciation}$$

Method 3. Although the depreciation deduction is not a cash expense, it does affect net profits and therefore taxes paid, which is a cash item.[4] For example, if the firm's tax bracket is 35 percent, each additional dollar of depreciation reduces taxable income by $1. Tax payments therefore fall by $.35, and cash flow increases by the same amount. The total **depreciation tax shield** equals the product of depreciation and the tax rate:

depreciation tax shield
Reduction in taxes attributable to the depreciation allowance.

$$\textbf{Depreciation tax shield} = \textbf{depreciation} \times \textbf{tax rate} \qquad (8.3)$$

This suggests a third way to calculate cash flow from operations. First, calculate net profit *assuming* zero depreciation. This item would be (revenues – cash expenses) × (1 – tax rate). Now add back the tax shield created by depreciation. We then calculate operating cash flow as follows:

$$\text{Cash flow from operations} = (\text{revenues} - \text{cash expenses}) \times (1 - \text{tax rate}) + (\text{depreciation} \times \text{tax rate})$$

---

[4] The discussion here is general, without reference to the tax laws of any country. In Section 8.6 we will examine the treatment of depreciation in Canadian tax law.

At this point, it would be worthwhile to pause and review some generally accepted terminology. The term *depreciation* is often used by accountants while referring to the periodic charge against revenue for the cost of tangible assets. When capital assets include tangible and intangible assets as well as natural resources and long-term deferred charges, the more appropriate all-encompassing term is *amortization*.[5] Since our discussion mostly deals with tangible assets, we will continue to use the term *depreciation* in this and other chapters on capital budgeting.

The following example confirms that the three methods for estimating cash flow from operations all give the same answer.

EXAMPLE 8.6

CASH FLOW FROM OPERATIONS

A project generates revenues of $1,000, cash expenses of $600, and depreciation charges of $200 in a particular year. The firm's tax bracket is 35 percent. Net income is calculated as follows:

	Revenues	$1,000
−	Cash expenses	600
−	Depreciation expense	200
=	Profit before tax	200
−	Tax at 35%	70
=	Net income	130

Methods 1, 2, and 3 all show that cash flow from operations is $330:

Method 1: Cash flow from operations = revenues − cash expenses − taxes
$$= 1,000 - 600 - 70 = 330$$

Method 2: Cash flow from operations = net profit + depreciation
$$= 130 + 200 = 330$$

Method 3: Cash flow from operations = (revenues − cash expenses) × (1 − tax rate)
$$+ \text{(depreciation} \times \text{tax rate)}$$
$$= (1,000 - 600) \times (1 - .35) + (200 \times .35) = 330$$

Check Point 8.4

A project generates revenues of $600, expenses of $300, and depreciation charges of $200 in a particular year. The firm's tax bracket is 35 percent. Find the operating cash flow of the project using all three approaches.

In many cases, a project will seek to improve efficiency or cut costs. A new computer system may provide labour savings. A new heating system may be more energy efficient than the one it replaces. These projects also contribute to the operating cash flow of the firm—not by increasing revenue, but by reducing costs. As the next example illustrates, we calculate the addition to operating cash flow on cost-cutting projects just as we would for projects that increase revenues.

EXAMPLE 8.7

OPERATING CASH FLOW ON COST-CUTTING PROJECTS

Suppose the new heating system costs $100,000 but reduces heating expenditures by $30,000 a year. The system will be depreciated straight-line over a 5-year period, so the annual depreciation

---

[5] For a good exposition of these issues, you may refer to T.H. Beechy and J.E.D. Conrad, *Intermediate Accounting: Volume One*, 3rd ed. (2005), McGraw-Hill Ryerson.

charge will be $20,000. The firm's tax rate is 35 percent. We calculate the incremental effects on revenues, expenses, and depreciation charges as follows. Notice that the reduction in expenses increases revenues minus cash expenses.

$$
\begin{array}{ll}
\text{Increase in (revenues minus expenses)} & \$30,000 \\
- \text{ Additional depreciation expense} & -\ 20,000 \\
= \text{ Incremental profit before tax} & =\ 10,000 \\
- \text{ Incremental tax at 35\%} & -\ \ 3,500 \\
= \text{ Change in net income} & =\ \ 6,500
\end{array}
$$

Therefore, the increment to operating cash flow can be calculated by *method 1* as

Increase in (revenues – cash expenses) – additional taxes
$$= \$30,000 - \$3,500$$
$$= \$26,500$$

or by *method 2*:

Increase in net profit + additional depreciation
$$= \$6,500 + \$20,000$$
$$= \$26,500$$

or by *method 3*:

Increase in (revenues – cash expenses) $\times$ (1 – tax rate) + (additional depreciation $\times$ tax rate)
$$= \$30,000 \times (1 - .35) + (\$20,000 \times .35)$$
$$= \$26,500$$

8.6

BUSINESS TAXES IN CANADA AND THE CAPITAL BUDGETING DECISION

DEPRECIATION AND CAPITAL COST ALLOWANCE

capital cost allowance (CCA) The amount of write-off on depreciable assets allowed by Canada Revenue Agency (CRA) against taxable income.

While calculating profit before tax, or taxable income, the business is allowed to deduct an amount for depreciation on its depreciable assets. This deduction, called the **capital cost allowance (CCA)** in Canada, enables the business to recover the original amount invested in the asset over a period of time, free of tax. In a general sense,

$$\textbf{Taxable income = revenues – expenses – CCA} \qquad \textbf{(8.4)}$$

undepreciated capital cost (UCC) The balance remaining in an asset class that has not yet been depreciated in that year.

The CCA for each year is calculated by multiplying the balance on the asset, called the **undepreciated capital cost (UCC)**, by the appropriate tax rate.[6] Although the CCA itself is a non-cash charge, it does affect cash flow to the extent that it reduces the taxes paid. This tax saving, called the **CCA tax shield**, or sometimes the *depreciation tax shield*, is discussed in more detail later in the chapter.

CCA tax shield Tax savings arising from the capital cost allowance charge.

It is important to remember that although the terms *depreciation* and *CCA* are often used interchangeably, they are not necessarily the same. In fact, the depreciation figure shown in a company's income statement is often calculated in a different manner than the CCA it reports to Canada Revenue Agency (CRA). We should note that only the CCA amount has an effect on the company's cash flows since it determines its tax bill.

THE ASSET CLASS SYSTEM

asset class Eligible depreciable assets are grouped into specified asset classes by CRA. Each asset class has a prescribed CCA rate.

All eligible depreciable assets are grouped into one of over 30 CCA **asset classes**. Each asset class has been assigned a CCA rate by CRA. Table 8.1 provides details regarding some of the asset

---

[6] We can define UCC as the total cost of all assets in an asset class minus the accumulated CCA in that class. It is similar to the concept of "net fixed assets" under GAAP.

TABLE 8.1
CCA rates and classes

Class number	Description	CCA rate
	The following is a partial list describing the most common capital cost allowance (CCA) classes.	
1	Most buildings made of brick, stone, or cement acquired after 1987, including their component parts such as electric wiring, lighting fixtures, plumbing, heating and cooling equipment, elevators, and escalators	4%
3	Most buildings made of brick, stone, or cement acquired before 1988, including their component parts as listed in Class 1 above	5%
7	Canoes, boats, and most other vessels, including their furniture, fittings, or equipment	15%
9	Aircraft, including furniture, fittings, or equipment attached, and their spare parts	25%
10	Automobiles (except taxis and those used for lease or rent), vans, wagons, trucks, buses, tractors, trailers, drive-in theatres, general-purpose electronic data-processing equipment (e.g., personal computers) and systems software, and timber-cutting and -removing equipment	30%
12	Chinaware, cutlery, linen, uniforms, dies, jigs, moulds or lasts, computer software (except systems software), cutting or shaping parts of a machine, certain production costs associated with making a motion picture film, such as apparel or costumes, videotape cassettes, ….	100%
13	Property that is leasehold interest (the maximum CCA rate depends on the type of the leasehold and the terms of the lease)	N/A
38	Most power-operated movable equipment acquired after 1987 used for moving, excavating, placing, or compacting earth, rock, concrete, or asphalt	30%
39	Machinery and equipment acquired after 1987 that is used in Canada primarily to manufacture and process goods for sale or lease	25%
43	Manufacturing and processing machinery and equipment acquired after February 25, 1992, described in Class 39 above	30%

Source: "CCA Rates and Classes," Canada Revenue Agency Web site, www.cra-arc.gc.ca. Reproduced with permission of the Minister of Public Works and Government Services Canada.

classes. We note that buildings are generally included in asset classes 1 and 3 and allowed a lower CCA rate. For instance, most buildings acquired after 1987 would fall in Class 1, and a firm that owned such buildings would be entitled to a CCA amount equal to 4 percent of the value of this class. At the other extreme, chinaware, cutlery, most computer software, and videotape cassettes used for rental purposes fall into asset class 12, which is allowed a 100 percent CCA rate. CCA rate can change periodically. For instance, the 2004 federal budget has proposed some changes in CCA rates pertaining to information and communications technology equipment. The budget proposes an increase in the CCA rate applicable to computer equipment from 30 to 45 percent. Also, the CCA rate applicable to broadband Internet and other data network infrastructure equipment is proposed to be raised from 20 to 30 percent. For up-to-date information on CCA rates, you may check out Canada Revenue Agency's Web site at **www.ccra-adrc.gc.ca**. For most assets, CCA is calculated by applying the appropriate asset class rate against the declining asset balance (UCC amount). Intangible assets such as leasehold improvements (a Class 13 asset) or patents (a Class 14 asset) follow the **straight-line depreciation** method for computing CCA. For such assets, CCA essentially represents an annuity series.

Under the asset class system, all assets within a particular CCA class are depreciated for tax purposes as if they were a single asset. To understand how the asset class system works, suppose that you have started a business as a tourbus operator and have invested $100,000 in a new bus. This would be a Class 10 asset for which the CCA is computed using a **declining balance depreciation** method and the applicable CCA rate is 30 percent. Suppose, in the second year, you decide to expand your business and buy another bus for $100,000. To keep things simple, let us

straight-line depreciation
Constant depreciation for each year of the asset's accounting life.

declining balance depreciation This is computed by applying the depreciation rate to the asset balance for each year.

TABLE 8.2

Undepreciated capital cost (UCC) and capital cost allowance (CCA) (without the half-year rule)

Year	Cost of Buses	Beginning of Year UCC	CCA	End of Year UCC
1	$100,000	$100,000	$30,000[1]	$ 70,000
2	$100,000	$170,000	$51,000	$119,000

[1] $100,000 × .30.

Reproduced with permission of the Minister of Public Works and Government Services Canada.

half-year rule Only one-half of the purchase cost of the asset is added to the asset class and used to compute CCA in the year of purchase.

ignore the **half-year rule** for now.[7] Your CCA claims at the end of the first and second years are provided in Table 8.2.

You would reduce your taxable income in the first year by $30,000. You begin the next year with an undepreciated balance (the *undepreciated capital cost, UCC*) of $70,000 to which you would add the purchase cost of the second bus of $100,000 for a total UCC amounting to $170,000. In the second year you would be entitled to a CCA deduction from your taxable income of $51,000. The UCC remaining at the end of the second year is $119,000.

Let us now introduce the half-year rule for the illustration above. As shown in Table 8.3, the CCA for asset Class 10 is $15,000 in Year 1 and $40,500 in Year 2. Taxable income is reduced by these amounts in the two years. In the first year, CCA is calculated on one-half of the purchase cost of the asset or $.5 \times \$100,000 \times .30$. In the second year, the total CCA of $40,500 for the asset class is calculated as follows: for the asset purchased in the first year, CCA computed on the UCC balance is $85,000 × .30, or $25,500, whereas the half-year rule applies to the second year's purchase, and the eligible CCA is $.5 \times \$100,000 \times .30$, or $15,000. Notice that, for Year 3, if you do not make any further additions to this asset class, CCA will be calculated on the UCC balance of $144,500 at the applicable rate of 30 percent.

SALE OF ASSETS

A company is entitled to a CCA as long as it owns at least one asset in the asset class. When a depreciable asset is sold, the undepreciated capital cost of its asset class is reduced by either the asset's sale price or its initial cost, whichever is less. The result is called the *adjusted cost of disposal*. In the example in Table 8.3, if the bus purchased in Year 1 for $100,000 is sold in Year 3 for $80,000, the adjusted cost of disposal is $80,000 and gets deducted from the UCC of Class 10 in Year 3.

In any given year, the company may buy new assets and sell old assets from within the same asset class. In this case, we would apply the *net acquisitions rule*. That is, we would determine the total cost of all additions to an asset class and then subtract the adjusted cost of disposal of all assets in that class. If the net acquisition is positive, we would apply the half-year rule and calculate CCA as shown earlier. Continuing with our tourbus operator example, suppose in Year 3, in addition to selling the bus bought in Year 1 for $80,000, we buy another luxury coach for $150,000. Our net acquisition in Year 3 will be $150,000 – $80,000, or $70,000. To calculate CCA for Year 3, we will apply the half-year rule on $70,000. This result will be added to the CCA computed on the UCC balance of $144,500 to get the overall CCA for Year 3. If, on the other hand, the net acquisition is negative, we do not adjust for the half-year rule. Instead, we will subtract the negative net acquisition amount from the beginning UCC balance of the asset class. CCA for the year will be calculated by applying the CCA rate on this net amount.

TABLE 8.3

Undepreciated capital cost (UCC) and capital cost allowance (CCA) (with the half-year rule)

Year	Cost of Buses	Beginning of Year UCC	CCA	End of Year UCC
1	$100,000	$100,000	$15,000	$85,000
2	$100,000	$185,000	$40,500	$144,500

Reproduced with permission of the Minister of Public Works and Government Services Canada.

---

[7] The half-year rule, which applies to most assets, will allow your firm to include one-half of the purchase cost of the asset for calculating the year's CCA in that asset class in the year the asset is purchased. This is the case regardless of what part of the year the asset is purchased. The remaining half of the purchase cost is added to the asset class in the next year.

Check Point 8.5

In Year 1 of your new business as a boat rental company, you have bought a motorboat for $100,000 and a sailboat for $80,000. In Year 2, you sell the motorboat for $110,000 and the sailboat for $75,000. You also buy a speedboat in Year 2 for $150,000. For CCA purposes, the boats are grouped in Class 7, which carries a 15 percent CCA rate. Calculate the CCA for years 1 and 2. What is the UCC balance at the end of Year 2?

TERMINATION OF ASSET POOL

terminal loss   When an asset class has a positive balance following the disposal of all assets in the class, this balance is called terminal loss. The UCC of the asset class is set to zero after a terminal loss is recognized.

recaptured depreciation
If the sale of an asset causes a negative balance in an asset class, the amount of the negative balance is known as recaptured depreciation and is added to taxable income.

What happens if the company disposes of its entire pool of assets in an asset class? Once again, we determine the adjusted cost of disposal (as the lower of the sale proceeds or the initial cost of this pool of assets) and subtract this amount from the undepreciated capital cost of the asset class. If this leaves a positive balance in the asset class and there are *no other assets remaining* in the class, this remaining balance is called a **terminal loss** and is deducted from taxable income. Also, the UCC then becomes zero, and the asset class ceases to generate CCA tax shields.[8]

If, on the other hand, we arrive at a negative balance after deducting the adjusted cost of disposal from the UCC of the asset class, this amount is called **recaptured depreciation** and is added back to taxable income. Once again, the undepreciated capital cost of the asset class becomes zero.

When an asset is sold for more than its initial cost, the difference between the sale price and initial cost is called a capital gain. Presently capital gains, net of any capital losses, are taxed at 50 percent of the firm's applicable marginal tax rate.

EXAMPLE 8.8   **RECAPTURED DEPRECIATION**

Remember our example where you bought two buses in years 1 and 2, respectively, each costing $100,000. To calculate CCA, the buses fall into Class 10 and are eligible for a 30 percent CCA rate. From Table 8.3, we saw that after taking 2 years of CCA, the undepreciated capital cost in the asset class is $144,500. Suppose you now decide to end your career as a tourbus operator and terminate the pool of assets in this class by selling both buses. You sell each bus for $120,000 for a total sale value of $240,000. Notice that because the sale price of the buses exceeds their purchase cost, they have actually appreciated in value instead of depreciating. The adjusted cost of disposal is their total purchase cost of $200,000. In such a situation, CRA will determine that you have taken $200,000 – $144,500 = $55,500 depreciation that did not reflect the economic depreciation on the assets. Therefore, this amount ($55,500) will be "recaptured" and added to your income to calculate tax. In addition, you have a capital gain of $240,000 – $200,000 = $40,000. The capital gain will be taxed at 50 percent of your firm's applicable marginal tax rate.

Suppose that instead of selling the two buses, you sell only one bus for $120,000 and continue running your business using the other bus. Notice that because one bus still remains in the asset class, the asset pool is not terminated. The UCC of $144,500 gets reduced by the adjusted cost of disposal of $100,000[9] but is still a positive amount of $44,500 and so there is no recaptured depreciation. You have also made a capital gain on the sale of $120,000 – $100,000 = $20,000.

Check Point 8.6

Think again about Example 8.8. Suppose that instead of selling the two buses for $120,000 each, you sell the bus bought in Year 1 for $65,000 and the one bought in Year 2 for $70,000. What are the tax consequences of this transaction, assuming that the firm has no other Class 10 assets?

---

[8] We should note that if the asset pool is not completely terminated—that is, there are other assets remaining in the asset class—then a positive balance would simply become the UCC of the class and continue to generate CCA tax shields.

[9] This amount, representing the initial purchase cost, is lower than the sale price of $120,000.

PRESENT VALUES OF CCA TAX SHIELDS

Suppose we start a new asset class by buying an asset. We'll use the following notation for our subsequent discussion:

C = capital cost of an asset acquired at the beginning of Year 1
d = CCA rate for the asset class to which the asset belongs
UCC_t = undepreciated capital cost in Year t after deducting CCA for the year
T_c = the firm's tax rate
r = discount rate
S = salvage amount from the sale of the asset at the end of Year t

To properly evaluate a project and calculate its present value, we need to compute the present value of the CCA tax shields accruing from capital investments in the project. As we show later in our discussion of Example 8.9, an asset can continue to generate CCA tax shields for the firm even after it is sold, provided there are other assets remaining in its class and the total UCC balance for the asset class is positive. This suggests that the CCA tax shield from investing in an asset can continue in perpetuity, since we are essentially deducting a fraction of the remaining UCC balance over an infinite period. Equation 1 below can be used to compute the present value of a perpetual tax shield.[10]

$$\frac{CdT_c}{r+d}\left[\frac{1+.5r}{1+r}\right] \tag{1}$$

Let us now introduce a residual or salvage value arising from the sale of an asset into the discussion. We would deduct this salvage value from the UCC of the asset class, and thereby reduce the CCA deductions and CCA tax shields for later years. Let us assume that other assets remain in the asset class and the total UCC exceeds the salvage value.[11] If the asset is sold at the end of Year t for a salvage amount, S, then the total tax shield lost is a perpetuity with a present value at the end of Year t of

$$\frac{SdT_c}{r+d}$$

When we discount this back to the present, we get the present value of lost CCA tax shields due to salvage value:

$$\left[\frac{SdT_c}{r+d}\right]\left[\frac{1}{(1+r)^t}\right] \tag{2}$$

Combining equations 1 and 2 enables us to provide a general formula for the present value of the CCA tax shield:

Present value of CCA tax shield =

$$\left[\frac{CdT_c}{r+d}\right]\left[\frac{1+.5r}{1+r}\right] - \left[\frac{SdT_c}{r+d}\right]\left[\frac{1}{(1+r)^t}\right] \tag{3}$$

We can now look at an example of how to get the present value of the tax shields. Keep in mind that we are looking for incremental changes in CCA and UCC that arise because of the purchase (or sale) of assets for the project. From Chapter 3, we know that the combined federal and provincial tax rate varies from province to province. Also, the tax rate could be different depending on whether the firm is a large corporation or a small business, and, also, whether it is in manufacturing and processing or some other industry. To illustrate the calculation of taxes, we will assume that the company pays a total of 35 percent of its taxable income to the federal and provincial government.

---

[10] A detailed discussion of how this equation is obtained follows in Appendix 8A.

[11] Notice that, otherwise, we may have to consider recapture of CCA and capital gains or terminal losses.

EXAMPLE 8.9	**PV OF CCA TAX SHIELDS**

Suppose that in Year 1 you buy heavy equipment for your factory for an amount C of $250,000. The equipment belongs to asset class 39 with a CCA rate $d = .25$. You intend to sell the equipment in Year 8 for a salvage value, S, of $8,000. At the time of sale, you still anticipate having other assets in the class and a UCC that exceeds the salvage value of the asset, so you will not have to deal with recaptured CCA or a terminal loss. Your tax rate is 35 percent and your discount rate is 12 percent. You want to know the present value of the incremental tax shields generated from owning and eventually selling the asset.

To calculate the present value of such incremental tax shields, we would have to reduce the present value of CCA tax shields by the present value of the tax shields lost due to the sale of the asset in Year 8.

$$\text{PV of CCA tax shields} = \begin{array}{c}\text{PV of perpetual tax}\\\text{shield on asset acquired}\\\text{in Year 1}\end{array} - \begin{array}{c}\text{PV of perpetual tax}\\\text{shield on salvage}\\\text{value in Year 8}\end{array}$$

$$= \left[\frac{CdT_c}{r + d}\right]\left[\frac{1 + .5r}{1 + r}\right] - \left[\frac{SdT_c}{r + d}\right]\left[\frac{1}{(1 + r)^t}\right]$$

$$= \left[\frac{250,000 \times .25 \times .35}{.12 + .25}\right]\left[\frac{1 + (.5 \times .12)}{1 + .12}\right]$$

$$- \left[\frac{8,000 \times .25 \times .35}{.12 + .25}\right]\left[\frac{1}{(1 + .12)^8}\right]$$

$$= \left[\frac{21,875}{.37}\right]\left[\frac{1.06}{1.12}\right] - \left[\frac{700}{.37}\right]\left[\frac{1}{2.48}\right]$$

$$= 55,954 - 763 = 55,191$$

From Table 8.4, note that the UCC generated by the machinery after 8 years of CCA tax shields is $29,200. Even *after* selling the equipment in Year 8, you will continue to depreciate $29,200 − $8,000 = $21,200 over future years. This example shows us a unique feature of Canadian tax law, that it is possible for an asset to generate CCA tax shields for the firm even after it is sold. Notice that two basic conditions have to be met for this to happen: (1) there are other assets remaining in its class and (2) the proceeds from disposing of any such assets are less than the total UCC for the asset class.

Check Point 8.7

You are evaluating a project that requires an investment of $5,000 and generates revenues of $3,000 and expenses of $1,500. CCA on the project will be based on a declining balance system with an applicable rate of 15 percent. The project will last for five years, at which time the machinery will be worthless and the firm will no longer produce cash flows. The firm's tax bracket is 35 percent.
a. Find the relevant cash flows for the first five years.
b. Assume that depreciation is on a straight-line basis over five years. What is the yearly depreciation charge? How would this change the cash flows for the first 5 years?

TABLE 8.4
CCA and UCC generated
by the heavy equipment
until Year 8

Year	1	2	3	4	5	6	7	8
C	250,000							
CCA	31,250	54,688	41,016	30,762	23,071	17,303	12,978	9,732
UCC	218,750	164,062	123,046	92,284	69,213	51,910	38,932	29,200

Reproduced with permission of the Minister of Public Works and Government Services Canada.

8.7

EXAMPLE: BLOOPER INDUSTRIES

Now that we have examined many of the pieces of a cash flow analysis, let's try to put them together into a coherent whole. As the newly appointed financial manager of Blooper Industries, you are about to analyze a proposal for mining and selling a small deposit of high-grade magnoosium ore.[12] You are given the forecasts shown in Table 8.5. We will walk through the lines in the table.

Capital Investment (line 1). The project requires an investment of $10 million in mining machinery. At the end of five years the machinery has no further value. The machinery falls into asset class 38, which has a CCA rate of 30 percent. The company owns other assets that also fall into this asset class. These other assets will remain in the asset class even after the magnoosium project ceases to exist after five years.

Working Capital (lines 2 and 3). Line 2 shows the level of working capital. As the project gears up in the early years, working capital increases, but later in the project's life, the investment in working capital is recovered.

Line 3 shows the change in working capital from year to year. Notice that in years 1 to 4 the change is positive; in these years the project requires a continuing investment in working capital. Starting in Year 5 the change is negative; there is a disinvestment as working capital is recovered.

Revenues (line 4). The company expects to be able to sell 750,000 kilograms of magnoosium a year at a price of $20 a kilogram in Year 1. That points to initial revenues of $750,000 \times 20 = $15,000,000$. But be careful: inflation is running at about 5 percent a year. If magnoosium prices keep pace with inflation, you should up your forecast of the second-year revenues by 5 percent.

TABLE 8.5
Financial projections for
Blooper's magnoosium
mine ($000s)

Year:	0	1	2	3	4	5	6
1. Capital investment	10,000						
2. Working capital	1,500	4,075	4,279	4,493	4,717	3,039	0
3. Change in working capital	1,500	2,575	204	214	225	−1,678	−3,039
4. Revenues		15,000	15,750	16,538	17,364	18,233	
5. Expenses		10,000	10,500	11,025	11,576	12,155	
6. CCA of mining equipment (asset class 38, $d = 30\%$)		1,500[1]	2,550	1,785	1,250	875	612 ...
7. Pretax profit		3,500	2,700	3,728	4,538	5,203	
8. Tax (35%)		1,225	945	1,305	1,588	1,821	
9. Profit after tax		2,275	1,755	2,423	2,950	3,382	

[1]In the first year, CCA is computed using the half-year rule.
Note: Some entries are subject to rounding error.

___

[12] Readers have inquired whether magnoosium is a real substance. Here, now, are the facts. Magnoosium was created in the early days of TV, when a splendid-sounding announcer closed a variety show by saying, "This program has been brought to you by Blooper Industries, proud producer of aleemium, magnoosium, and stool." We forget the company, but the blooper really happened.

Third-year revenues should increase by a further 5 percent, and so on. Line 4 in Table 8.5 shows revenues rising in line with inflation.

The sales forecasts in Table 8.5 are cut off after five years. That makes sense if the ore deposit will run out at that time. But if Blooper could make sales for Year 6, you should include them in your forecasts. We have sometimes encountered financial managers who assume a project life of (say) 5 years, even when they confidently expect revenues for 10 years or more. When asked the reason, they explain that forecasting beyond five years is too hazardous. We sympathize, but you just have to do your best. Do not arbitrarily truncate a project's life.

Expenses (line 5).   We assume that the expenses of mining and refining also increase in line with inflation at 5 percent per year.

CCA (line 6).   Mining equipment falls in asset class 38, which has a CCA rate of 30 percent. We compute CCA using the declining balance method, which is prescribed by CRA for this asset class. Notice from Table 8.6, that even though the magnoosium mine stops producing in Year 5, an undepreciated capital cost (UCC) balance of $2.04 million remains at the end of Year 5. This suggests that the initial investment has not been completely depreciated. In fact, computing with the declining balance system will continue to provide smaller CCA values each year over an infinite period. To get around this problem, we will use a method of computing the present value of the CCA tax shields under the declining balance system we described with Equation 3, page 255. Even after the magnoosium mine shuts its operations in Year 5, we assume that the company has other assets in Class 38 and that the asset pool will not be terminated.

Pretax Profits (line 7).   Profit after depreciation equals (revenues – expenses – CCA).

Tax (line 8). Company taxes are 35 percent of pretax profits. For example, in Year 1,
$$\text{Tax} = .35 \times 3{,}500 = 1{,}225, \text{ or } \$1{,}225{,}000$$

Profit after Tax (line 9).   Profit after tax is simply equal to pretax profit less taxes.

CALCULATING BLOOPER'S PROJECT CASH FLOWS

Table 8.5 provides most of the information you need to figure out the cash flows on the magnoosium project. These cash flows are the sum of three broad components: investment in plant and equipment, investment in working capital, and cash flows from operations. In turn, cash flows from operations comprise (1) operating cash flows excluding depreciation (CCA) and (2) the CCA tax shield.

> Cash flow from investment in plant and equipment
> + Cash flow from investment in working capital
> + Cash flow from operations, including
>   • Operating cash flows
>   • CCA tax shield
> = Total project cash flows

Table 8.7 provides calculations for yearly operating cash flows excluding CCA tax shields, Table 8.8 sets out the project cash flows excluding the CCA tax shield, and Table 8.9 provides details by year regarding the CCA tax shield. First, let's see where these figures come from.

TABLE 8.6
Computation of CCA and UCC balances for Blooper's magnoosium mine ($000s)

Year	Capital Investment UCC	CCA	End of Year (UCC)
1	10,000	1,500	8,500
2	8,500	2,550	5,950
3	5,950	1,785	4,165
4	4,165	1,250	2,915
5	2,915	875	2,040
6	2,040	612	1,428

TABLE 8.7
Operating cash flows
excluding CCA tax shields
for Blooper's magnoosium
mine ($000s)

Year:	0	1	2	3	4	5	6
Revenues		15,000	15,750	16,538	17,364	18,233	
− Expenses		10,000	10,500	11,025	11,576	12,155	
= Profit before tax		5,000	5,250	5,513	5,788	6,078	
− Tax at 35%		1,750	1,838	1,930	2,026	2,127	
= Operating cash flows (excluding CCA tax shield)		3,250	3,412	3,583	3,762	3,951	

Capital Investment.   Investment in plant and equipment is taken from line 1 of Table 8.5. Blooper's initial investment is a negative cash flow of –$10 million shown in line 1 of Table 8.8.

Investment in Working Capital.   We've seen that investment in working capital, just like investment in plant and equipment, produces a negative cash flow. For instance, when the company builds up inventories of refined magnoosium, the company's cash is reduced, or when customers are slow to pay their bills, cash is reduced. An increase in working capital implies a negative cash flow; a decrease implies a positive cash flow.

The numbers required for these calculations come from lines 2 and 3 of Table 8.5. Line 2 shows the amount or level of working capital whereas line 3 shows the change in working capital. Notice the cash flow is measured by the *change* in working capital, not the level of working capital. For instance, from Table 8.5, line 2, we see that Blooper makes an initial (Year 0) investment of $1,500,000 in working capital, which goes up to $4,075,000 in Year 1. This *total* level of working capital in Year 1 is arrived at by an additional investment in working capital of $2,575,000 in Year 1 to Year 0's investment, that is, $1,500,000 + $2,575,000 = $4,075,000. The additional investment in Year 1 of $2,575,000 is shown in line 3, Table 8.5, and results in a negative cash flow by this amount (line 2, Table 8.8).

Cash Flows from Operations.   The third component of project cash flows is cash flow from operations. As we have discussed earlier, we can segregate this component into two parts: (1) operating cash flows, excluding CCA, and (2) the CCA tax shield. Let us discuss these one by one.

- *Operating cash flows, excluding CCA*: Table 8.5 has the necessary data to calculate such operating cash flows. The details, in thousands of dollars, are provided in Table 8.7.

    The cash flow amounts for Blooper's magnoosium mine are in line 3 of Table 8.8. Line 4 provides the yearly total cash flows excluding the CCA tax shield. Notice that the table does not fully capture the entire amount of cash flows for the project since the CCA tax shield is not included. Let us now examine the CCA tax shield.
- *CCA Tax Shield*: In Section 8.6, we saw that CCA has an important effect on cash flows because it reduces taxable income and the firm's tax bill. For any year, this tax shield is calculated as the product of the CCA and tax rate.

$$\text{CCA tax shield} = \text{CCA} \times \text{tax rate} \qquad (8.5)$$

TABLE 8.8
Cash flows for Blooper's
magnoosium mine ($000s)

Year:	0	1	2	3	4	5	6
1. Capital investment	−10,000						
2. Change in working capital	−1,500	−2,575	−204	−214	−225	1,678	3,039
3. Cash flows from operations (excluding CCA tax shield)		3,250	3,412	3,583	3,762	3,951	
4. Total cash flows (excluding CCA tax shield)	−11,500	675	3,208	3,369	3,537	5,629	3,039

TABLE 8.9
Computation by year of CCA tax shields for Blooper's magnoosium mine ($000s)

Year:	0	1	2	3	4	5	6
CCA		1,500	2,550	1,785	1,250	875	612
× Tax Rate		.35	.35	.35	.35	.35	.35
= CCA Tax Shield		525	893	625	438	306	214

For Blooper, which pays tax at a rate of 35 percent, this means that each additional dollar of CCA reduces taxable income by $1 and taxes owed by 35 cents. Table 8.9 provides details regarding the CCA tax shields for Blooper. Notice that both the CCA and the CCA tax shield increase between years 1 and 2 but, thereafter, are represented by a series of declining balances. This is because in Year 1 when Blooper purchases the machine, the half-year rule applies, but all subsequent CCA tax shield calculations use a declining balance system. Also, CCA tax shields from the project will continue to be generated beyond Year 5, assuming that Blooper will have other assets in Class 38 after the magnoosium mine is shut down.

CALCULATING THE NPV OF BLOOPER'S PROJECT

Table 8.10 sets out the calculations for the total present value of cash flows excluding the CCA tax shield. Assume that investors expect a return of 12 percent from investments in the capital market with the same risk as the magnoosium project. This is the opportunity cost of the shareholders' money that Blooper is proposing to invest in the project. Therefore, to calculate NPV you need to discount the cash flows at 12 percent. Remember that to calculate the present value of a cash flow in Year t you can divide the cash flow by $(1 + r)^t$ or you can multiply by a discount factor that is equal to $1/(1 + r)^t$.

The total present value in Table 8.10 is not the net present value of the project because we still have to deal with the CCA tax shield. We deal with the tax shields separately because even though the magnoosium project terminates in Year 5 and we have computed cash flows till Year 6, from Table 8.6 we have noted that there is still a UCC balance at the end of Year 6 on which CCA can be computed for future years.[13] To compute the present value of the CCA tax shield, we use Equation 3, page 255. Notice that in the example we have assumed a zero salvage value, S, at the end of the project's life.

$$\text{PV of CCA tax shield} = \left[\frac{CdT_c}{r + d}\right]\left[\frac{1 + .5r}{1 + r}\right] - \left[\frac{SdT_c}{r + d}\right] \times \left[\frac{1}{(1 + r)^t}\right]$$

$$= \left[\frac{10,000 \times .3 \times .35}{.12 + .3}\right]\left[\frac{1 + (.5 \times .12)}{1 + .12}\right]$$

$$- \left[\frac{0 \times .3 \times .35}{.12 + .3}\right]\left[\frac{1}{(1 + .12)^6}\right]$$

$$= \$2,366$$

We now have all the necessary information to determine the net present value of Blooper's magnoosium project. It is the sum of the total present value excluding CCA tax shields in Table 8.10 and the present value of the CCA tax shield, that is

NPV = total PV excluding CCA tax shields + PV of CCA tax shield
    = $1,040 + $2,366 = $3,406

We see that when all cash flows are discounted and added up, the magnoosium project offers a positive net present value of about $3.4 million.

Now let's consider a small point that often causes confusion. To calculate the present value of the first year's cash flow, we divide by $(1 + r) = 1.12$. Strictly speaking, this makes sense only if

---

[13] Of course, this assumes that the firm has other assets in the asset class.

TABLE 8.10

Cash flows and total present value of Blooper's project excluding the CCA tax shield ($000s)

Year:	0	1	2	3	4	5	6
Total cash flow excluding tax shields	−11,500	675	3,208	3,369	3,537	5,629	3,039
Discount factor	1.0000	.8929	.7972	.7118	.6355	.5674	.5066
Present value (excluding CCA tax shields)	−11,500	603	2,557	2,398	2,248	3,194	1,540
Total present value (excluding CCA tax shields)	1,040						

all the sales and all the costs occur exactly 365 days, 0 hours, and 0 minutes from now. But, of course, the year's sales don't all take place on the stroke of midnight December 31. However, when making capital budgeting decisions, companies are usually happy to pretend that all cash flows occur at one-year intervals—for one reason only—simplicity. When sales forecasts are sometimes little more than intelligent guesses, it may be pointless to inquire how the sales are likely to be spread out during the year.[14]

FURTHER NOTES AND WRINKLES ARISING FROM BLOOPER'S PROJECT

Before we leave Blooper and its magnoosium project, we should cover a few extra wrinkles.
How to Deal with Salvage Value. So far, we have assumed that Blooper will not receive any salvage value from the mining equipment when the magnoosium mine is closed. But suppose Blooper forecasts that the equipment can be sold for $1.5 million in Year 6.

You recorded the initial $10 million investment as a negative cash flow. Now, in Year 6, you have a forecast return of $1.5 million of that investment. That is a positive cash flow estimate, which has a present value of

$$\frac{S}{(1+r)^6} = \frac{1.5}{(1.12)^6} = .76$$

The salvage value will also reduce future tax shields, and therefore, the present value of the CCA tax shield as follows:[15]

$$\frac{1}{(1+r)^6} \times \frac{SdT_c}{(r+d)} = \frac{1}{(1.12)^6} \times \frac{1.5 \times .3 \times .35}{(.12+.3)} = .19$$

So we see that while the sale of the mining equipment increases the net present value of the project by $760,000, the present value of the lost tax shield from the salvage will reduce net present value by $190,000. Overall, net present value of the project will increase by $760,000 − $190,000 = $570,000.

A Further Note on CCA. We warned you earlier not to assume that all cash flows are likely to increase with inflation. The CCA tax shield is a case in point because CRA lets companies depreciate only the amount of the original investment. For example, if you go back to CRA to explain that inflation mushroomed since you made the investment and you should be allowed to depreciate more, CRA won't listen. The *nominal* amount of CCA is fixed, and therefore, the higher the rate of inflation, the lower the *real* value of the CCA that you can claim.

---

[14] Financial managers sometimes assume cash flows arrive in the middle of the calendar year, that is, the end of June. This also makes NPV a mid-year number. If you are standing at the start of the year, the NPV must be discounted for a further half-year. To do this, divide the mid-year NPV by the square root of $(1 + r)$.

This mid-year convention is roughly equivalent to assuming cash flows are distributed evenly throughout the year. This is a bad assumption for some industries. In retailing, for example, most of the cash flow comes late in the year as the holiday season approaches.

[15] Remember that we have assumed that Blooper has other machines in this asset class so the sale will not close out the asset class.

A Spreadsheet Model for Blooper (Formula Inserts)

	A	B	C	D	E	F	G	H
1	Year:	0	1	2	3	4	5	6
2	Capital investment	10,000						
3	Working capital	=0.15*C6+2/12*B5	=0.15*D6+2/12*C5	=0.15*E6+2/12*D5	=0.15*F6+2/12*E5	=0.15*G6+2/12*F5	=0.15*H6+2/12*G5	=0.15*I6+2/12*H5
4	Change in working capital	=B3	=C3-B3	=D3-C3	=E3-D3	=F3-E3	=G3-F3	=H3-G3
5	Revenues		15000	=C5*1.05	=D5*1.05	=E5*1.05	=F5*1.05	
6	Expenses		10000	=C6*1.05	=D6*1.05	=E6*1.05	=F6*1.05	
7	Profit before tax (excluding CCA tax shield)		=C5-C6	=D5-D6	=E5-E6	=F5-F6	=G5-G6	
8	Tax (35%)		=C7*0.35	=D7*0.35	=E7*0.35	=F7*0.35	=G7*0.35	
9	Operating cash flows (excluding CCA tax shield)		=C7-C8	=D7-D8	=E7-E8	=F7-F8	=G7-G8	
10	Salvage value							0
11	Total cash flow (excluding CCA tax shield)	=-B2-B4	=C2-C4+C9	=D2-D4+D9	=E2-E4+E9	=F2-F4+F9	=G2-G4+G9	=H2-H4+H9+H10
12	PV of cash flow (excluding CCA tax shield)	=B11/(1.12)^B1	=C11/(1.12)^C1	=D11/(1.12)^D1	=E11/(1.12)^E1	=F11/(1.12)^F1	=G11/(1.12)^G1	=H11/(1.12)^H1
13	Total present value (excluding CCA tax shield) (A)	=SUM(B12:H12)						
14	CCA		=0.5*B2*0.3	=(B2-C14)*0.3	=D14*0.7	=E14*0.7	=F14*0.7	=G14*0.7
15	CCA tax shield		=10000*0.3/2*0.35	=8500*0.3*0.35	=5950*0.3*0.35	=4165*0.3*0.35	=2916*0.3*0.35	=2041*0.3*0.35
16	PV of CCA tax shield (B)	=(B2*0.3*0.35/(0.12+0.3))*((1+(0.5*0.12))/(1+0.12))-(H10*0.3*0.35/(0.3+0.12)*(1/(1+0.12)^H1))						
17	Total net present value (A) + (B)	=(B13+B16)						

You might have guessed that discounted cash flow analysis such as that of the Blooper case is tailor-made for spreadsheets. The worksheet directly above shows the formulas from the Excel spreadsheet that we used to generate the Blooper example. The first spreadsheet shows the resulting values, which appear in the text in tables 8.5 through 8.10. This model assumes that there is no salvage value on Blooper's equipment. We have also included a spreadsheet model in which we assume a salvage value of $1.5 million in Year 6.

The assumed values are the capital investment (cell B2), the initial level of revenues (cell C5), and expenses (cell C6). Rows 5 and 6 show that each entry for revenues and expenses equals the previous value times (1 + inflation rate), or 1.05. Row 3, which is the amount of working capital, is the sum of inventories and accounts receivable. To capture the fact that inventories tend to rise with production, we set working capital equal to .15 times the following year's expenses. Similarly, accounts receivable rise with sales, so we assumed that accounts receivable would be 1/6 times the current year's revenues. Each entry in row 3 is the sum of these two quantities.[16] Net investment in working capital (row 4) is the increase in working capital from one year to the next. Total cash flow excluding the CCA tax shield (row 11) is capital investment plus change in working capital plus profit after tax, which we have called operating cash flows. Cell H10 includes a provision for salvage value in Year 6 that is set at zero in the first spreadsheet model and $1.5 million in the second model. In row 12, we discount the cash flow amounts at a 12 percent discount rate and in cell B13 we add the present value of each cash flow to find the total present value excluding the CCA tax shield. Row 14 includes CCA values. Notice that the first year's CCA in cell C14 is computed using the half-year rule, whereas the subsequent CCA amounts follow the declining balance system. Row 15 includes the yearly CCA tax shields and row 16 incorporates the present value of the CCA tax shield. The project's net present value is provided in cell B17 as the sum of the total present value excluding the CCA tax shield (cell B13) and the present value of the CCA tax shield (cell B16).

Once the spreadsheet is up and running it is easy to do various sorts of "what if" analysis. Also, we can do some comparative analysis involving straight-line and declining balance calculations. Keep in mind that so far we have used declining balance CCA. But what if we used straight-line depreciation instead? Here are a few questions to try your hand.

Questions (Answers on page 3 of Appendix 8A found at www.mcgraw hill.ca/college/brealey.)

1. Suppose the firm can economize on working capital by managing inventories more efficiently. If the firm can reduce inventories from 15 percent to 10 percent of next year's cost of goods sold, what will be the effect on project NPV?

2. What happens to NPV if the inflation rate falls from 5 percent to zero and the discount rate falls from 12 percent to 7 percent? Given that the real discount rate is almost unchanged, why does project NPV increase?

3. Suppose that Blooper's mining equipment could be depreciated on a 5-year, straight-line basis. What is the present value of the depreciation tax shield? What happens to cash flow in each year and to the project NPV?

[16] For convenience we assume that Blooper pays all its bills immediately and therefore accounts payable equals zero. If it didn't, working capital would be reduced by the amount of the payables.

A Spreadsheet Model for Blooper (without Salvage Value)[1]

	A	B	C	D	E	F	G	H	I
1	Year:	0	1	2	3	4	5	6	...∞
2	Capital investment	10,000							
3	Working capital	1,500	4,075	4,279	4,493	4,717	3,039	0	
4	Change in working capital	1,500	2,575	204	214	225	−1,679	−3,039	
5	Revenues		15,000	15,750	16,538	17,364	18,233		
6	Expenses		10,000	10,500	11,025	11,576	12,155		
7	Profit before tax (excluding CCA tax shield)		5,000	5,250	5,513	5,788	6,078		
8	Tax (35%)		1,750	1,838	1,930	2,026	2,127		
9	Operating cash flows (excluding CCA tax shield)		3,250	3,412	3,583	3,762	3,950		
10	Salvage value							0	
11	Total cash flow (excluding CCA tax shield)	−11,500	675	3,208	3,369	3,538	5,629	3,039	
12	PV of cash flow (excluding CCA tax shield)	−11,500	603	2,558	2,398	2,248	3,194	1,540	
13	Total present value (excluding CCA tax shield) (A)	1,041							
14	CCA[2]		1,500	2,550	1,785	1,250	875	612	′0
15	CCA tax shield[2]		525	893	625	437	306	214	′0
16	PV of CCA tax shield[2] (B)	2,366							
17	Total net present value (A) + (B)	3,407							

Notes: [1] Some entries in this table may differ from those in tables 8.5 to 8.10 due to rounding error.
[2] The CCA and the CCA tax shield (lines 14 and 15) will continue even after Year 6.
The PV of the CCA tax shield (line 16) has been calculated assuming that the CCA
and the CCA tax shield will continue in perpetuity.

A Spreadsheet Model for Blooper (with Salvage Value)[1]

	A	B	C	D	E	F	G	H	I
1	Year:	0	1	2	3	4	5	6	...∞
2	Capital investment	10,000							
3	Working capital	1,500	4,075	4,279	4,493	4,717	3,039	0	
4	Change in working capital	1,500	2,575	204	214	225	−1,679	−3,039	
5	Revenues		15,000	15,750	16,538	17,364	18,233		
6	Expenses		10,000	10,500	11,025	11,576	12,155		
7	Profit before tax (excluding CCA tax shield)		5,000	5,250	5,513	5,788	6,078		
8	Tax (35%)		1,750	1,838	1,930	2,026	2,127		
9	Operating cash flows (excluding CCA tax shield)		3,250	3,412	3,583	3,762	3,950		
10	Salvage value							1,500	
11	Total cash flow (excluding CCA tax shield)	−11,500	675	3,208	3,369	3,538	5,629	4,539	
12	PV of cash flow (excluding CCA tax shield)	−11,500	603	2,558	2,398	2,248	3,194	2,299	
13	Total present value (excluding CCA tax shield) (A)	1,801							
14	CCA[2]		1,500	2,550	1,785	1,250	875	612	′0
15	CCA tax shield[2]		525	893	625	437	306	214	′0
16	PV of CCA tax shield[2] (B)	2,176							
17	Total net present value (A) + (B)	3,977							

Notes: [1] Some entries in this table may differ from those in tables 8.5 to 8.10 due to rounding error.
[2] The CCA and the CCA tax shield (lines 14 and 15) will continue even after Year 6. The PV
of the CCA tax shield (line 16) has been calculated assuming that the CCA and the CCA tax
shield will continue in perpetuity.

8.8   SUMMARY

1. How should the cash flows properly attributable to a proposed new project be calculated?

Here is a checklist to bear in mind when forecasting a project's cash flows:

- Discount cash flows, not profits.
- Estimate the project's incremental cash flows—that is, the difference between the cash flows with the project and those without the project.
- Include all indirect effects of the project, such as its impact on the sales of the firm's other products.
- Forget sunk costs.
- Include **opportunity costs**, such as the value of land that you could otherwise sell.
- Beware of allocated overhead charges for heat, light, and so on. These may not reflect the incremental effects of the project on these costs.
- Remember the investment in working capital. As sales increase, the firm may need to make additional investments in working capital and, as the project finally comes to an end, it will recover these investments.
- Do not include debt interest or the cost of repaying a loan. When calculating NPV, assume that the project is financed entirely by the shareholders and that they receive all the cash flows. This isolates the investment decision from the financing decision.

2. How can the cash flows of a project be computed from standard financial statements?

Project cash flow does not equal profit. You must allow for changes in working capital as well as non-cash expenses such as depreciation. Also, if you use a nominal cost of capital, consistency requires that you forecast *nominal* cash flows—that is, cash flows that recognize the effect of inflation.

3. How is the company's tax bill affected by capital cost allowance (CCA) and how does this affect project value?

CCA is not a cash flow. However, because CCA reduces taxable income, it reduces taxes. This tax reduction is called the **CCA tax shield**. For computing tax depreciation in Canada, assets are assigned into different **asset classes**, which have specified CCA rates. Most asset classes follow a declining balance system for computing CCA, and, therefore, most assets continue to generate CCA tax shields over an infinite time frame. Because of this, we find the present value of operating cash flows separately from the present value of the CCA tax shields to determine the net present value of a project.

4. How do changes in working capital affect project cash flows?

Increases in **net working capital**, such as accounts receivable or inventory, are investments and, therefore, use cash. That is, they reduce the net cash flow provided by the project in that period. When working capital is run down, cash is freed up, so cash flow increases.

Related Web Links

www.4pm.com/articles/palette.html Try the on-line demonstration here to see how good business judgment is used to formulate cash flow projections

www.acfa-cashflow.com Web site of the American Cash Flow Association, which manages the infrastructure of the cash flow industry in the United States and Canada

www.acfi-online.com Web site of the American Cash Flow Institute, which provides training on cash flows and income streams

www.cra-arc.gc.ca Canada Revenue Agency Web site; provides tax information including information on CCA regulations and rates

www.irs.ustreas.gov/businesses/index.html Web site maintained by the U.S. Internal Revenue Service; provides tax information for businesses from the U.S. standpoint

Key Terms

opportunity cost	244	undepreciated capital cost		declining balance	
net working capital	245	(UCC)	251	depreciation	252
depreciation tax shield	249	CCA tax shield	251	half-year rule	253
capital cost allowance		asset class	251	terminal loss	254
(CCA)	251	straight-line depreciation	252	recaptured depreciation	254

Questions and Problems

*Answers in Appendix B

BASIC

1. **Cash Flows.** A new project will generate sales of $74 million, costs of $42 million, and depreciation expense of $10 million in the coming year. The firm's tax rate is 35 percent. Calculate cash flows for the year using all three methods discussed in the chapter and confirm that they are equal.

2. **Cash Flows.** Canyon Tours showed the following components of working capital last year:

	Beginning	End of Year
Accounts receivable	$24,000	$22,500
Inventory	12,000	13,000
Accounts payable	14,500	16,500

   a.   What was the change in net working capital during the year?
   b.   If sales were $36,000 and costs were $24,000, what was cash flow for the year? Ignore taxes.

*3. **Cash Flows.** Tubby Toys estimates that its new line of rubber ducks will generate sales of $7 million, operating costs of $4 million, and a depreciation expense of $1 million. If the tax rate is 40 percent, what is the firm's operating cash flow? Show that you get the same answer using all three methods to calculate operating cash flow.

4. **Cash Flows.** We've emphasized that the firm should pay attention only to cash flows when assessing the net present value of proposed projects. Depreciation is a non-cash expense. Why then does it matter whether we assume straight-line depreciation or declining balance CCA depreciation when we assess project NPV?

*5. **Proper Cash Flows.** Quick Computing currently sells 10 million computer chips each year at a price of $20 per chip. It is about to introduce a new chip, and it forecasts annual sales of 12 million of these improved chips at a price of $25 each. However, demand for the old chip will decrease, and sales of the old chip are expected to fall to 3 million per year. The old chip costs $6 each to manufacture, and the new ones will cost $8 each. What is the proper cash flow to use to evaluate the present value of the introduction of the new chip?

6. **Calculating Net Income.** The owner of a bicycle repair shop forecasts revenues of $160,000 a year. Variable costs will be $45,000, and rental costs for the shop are $35,000 a year. Depreciation on the repair tools will be $10,000. Prepare an income statement for the shop based on these estimates. The tax rate is 35 percent.

7. **Cash Flows.** Calculate the operating cash flow for the repair shop in the previous problem using all three methods suggested in the chapter: (a) net income plus depreciation; (b) cash inflow/cash outflow analysis; and (c) the depreciation tax shield approach. Confirm that all three approaches result in the same value for cash flow.

*8. **Cash Flows and Working Capital.** A house-painting business had revenues of $16,000 and expenses of $9,000. There were no depreciation expenses. However, the business reported the following changes in various components of working capital:

	Beginning	End
Accounts receivable	$1,200	$4,500
Accounts payable	600	200

   Calculate net cash flow for the business for this period.

9. **Incremental Cash Flows.** A corporation donates a valuable painting from its private collection to an art museum. Which of the following are incremental cash flows associated with the donation?
   a. The price the firm paid for the painting.
   b. The current market value of the painting.
   c. The deduction from income that it declares for its charitable gift.
   d. The reduction in taxes due to its declared tax deduction.

EXCEL

*10. **Operating Cash Flows.** Laurel's Lawn Care, Ltd., has a new mower line that can generate revenues of $120,000 per year. Direct production costs are $40,000 and the fixed costs of maintaining the lawn mower factory are $15,000 a year. The factory originally cost $1 million and is included in an asset class with a CCA rate of 5 percent. Calculate the operating cash flows of the project for the next 6 years if the firm's tax bracket is 35 percent.

PRACTICE

*11. **Operating Cash Flows.** Talia's Tutus bought a new sewing machine for $40,000 that will be depreciated in asset class 39, which has a CCA rate of 30 percent. This firm's tax bracket is 35 percent.
   a. Find the CCA amount each year for the next three years.
   b. If the sewing machine is sold after 3 years for $20,000, what will be the after-tax proceeds on the sale if the firm's tax bracket is 35 percent? Assume that Talia's Tutus has other assets in Class 39.
   c. Now rework your calculations assuming that Talia's Tutus has no other assets in Class 39 and the asset class will be terminated upon the sale of the sewing machine in Year 3.

12. **Proper Cash Flows.** Conference Services Inc. has leased a large office building for $4 million per year. The building is larger than the company needs: two of the building's eight stories are almost empty. A manager wants to expand one of her projects, but this will require using one of the empty floors. In calculating the net present value of the proposed expansion, upper management allocates one-eighth of $4 million of building rental costs (i.e., $.5 million) to the project expansion, reasoning that the project will use one-eighth of the building's capacity.
   a. Is this a reasonable procedure for the purposes of calculating NPV?
   b. Can you suggest a better way to assess the cost of the office space used by the project?

13. **Cash Flows and Working Capital.** A firm had net income last year of $1.2 million. Its depreciation expenses were $.5 million, and its total cash flow was $1.2 million. What happened to net working capital during the year?

14. **Cash Flows and Working Capital.** The only capital investment required for a small project is investment in inventory. Profits this year were $10,000, and inventory increased from $4,000 to $5,000. What was the cash flow from the project?

EXCEL

15. **Cash Flows and Working Capital.** A firm's balance sheets for year-ends 2000 and 2001 contain the following data. What happened to investment in net working capital during 2001? All items are in millions of dollars.

	Dec. 31, 2000	Dec. 31, 2001
Accounts receivable	32	35
Inventories	25	30
Accounts payable	12	25

*16. **Salvage Value.** Quick Computing (from problem 5) installed its previous generation of computer chip manufacturing equipment three years ago. Some of that older equipment will become unnecessary when the company goes into production of its new product. The obsolete equipment, which originally cost $40 million, has been depreciated straight-line over an assumed tax life of 5 years, but it can now be sold for $18 million. The firm's tax rate is 35 percent. What is the after-tax cash flow from the sale of the equipment?

17. **Salvage Value.** Your firm purchased machinery for $10 million. The machinery falls into asset class 38, which has a CCA rate of 25 percent. The project will end after five years. If the equipment can be sold for $4 million at the completion of the project and your firm's tax rate is 35 percent, what is the after-tax cash flow from the sale of the machinery? Assume that the firm has no other assets in Class 38 and the asset class will be terminated upon the sale of the machinery.

EXCEL

*18. **CCA, Depreciation, and Project Value.** Bottoms Up Diaper Service is considering the purchase of a new industrial washer. It can purchase the washer for $6,000 and sell its old washer for $2,000. The new washer will last for 6 years and save $1,500 a year in expenses. If the old washer is retained, it will also last for 6 more years after which it will have to be junked. The washers fall into an asset class with a CCA rate of 30 percent. Bottoms Up owns other washing machines that also fall into this asset class. The opportunity cost of capital is 15 percent, and the firm's tax rate is 40 percent.
   a. If the salvage value of the washer is expected to be zero at the end of its six-year life, what are the cash flows of the project in years 0 to 6?
   b. What is the project NPV?
   c. What will the NPV and IRR be if the firm uses straight-line depreciation with a 6-year tax life?

19. **Equivalent Annual Cost.** What is the equivalent annual cost of the washer in the previous problem if the firm uses straight-line depreciation?

20. **Cash Flows and NPV.** Johnny's Lunches is considering purchasing a new, energy-efficient grill. The grill will cost $20,000 and will be depreciated in an asset class that carries a CCA rate of 30 percent. It will be sold for scrap metal after 3 years for $5,000. The grill will have no effect on revenues but will save Johnny's $10,000 in energy expenses. The firm has other assets in this asset class. The tax rate is 35 percent.
   a. What are the operating cash flows in years 1 to 3?
   b. What are total cash flows in years 1 to 3?
   c. If the discount rate is 12 percent, should the grill be purchased?

EXCEL

21. Project Evaluation. Revenues generated by a new fad product are forecast as follows:

Year	Revenues
1	$40,000
2	30,000
3	20,000
4	10,000
Thereafter	0

Expenses are expected to be 40 percent of revenues, and working capital required in each year is expected to be 20 percent of revenues in the following year. The product requires an immediate investment of $50,000 in plant and equipment.
   a. What is the initial investment in the product? Remember working capital.
   b. If the plant and equipment are in an asset class that has a CCA rate of 25 percent, and the firm's tax rate is 40 percent, what are the project cash flows in each year?
   c. If the opportunity cost of capital is 10 percent, what is the project NPV?

22. **Buy versus Lease.** You can buy a car for $25,000 and sell it in 5 years for $5,000. Or you can lease the car for 5 years for $5,000 a year. The discount rate is 10 percent per year.
   a. Which option do you prefer?
   b. What is the maximum amount you should be willing to pay to lease rather than buy the car?

*23. **Project Evaluation.** Kinky Copies may buy a high-volume copier. The machine costs $100,000 and will be depreciated straight-line over 5 years to a salvage value of $20,000. Kinky anticipates that the machine can be sold in 5 years for $30,000. The machine will save

$20,000 a year in labour costs but will require an increase in working capital, mainly paper supplies, of $10,000. The firm's marginal tax rate is 35 percent. Ignore the CCA system and assume that the straight-line depreciation method adopted by Kinky Copies will suffice for tax purposes. Should Kinky buy the machine? The discount rate is 8 percent.

24. **Project Evaluation.** Fireplaces Etc. is about to launch a new range of wood stoves, priced at $110 per unit. The unit cost of the wood stoves is $65. The firm expects to sell the wood stoves over the next five years. The venture will require an initial investment in plant and equipment of $25,000. Assume that the investment will be in an asset class with a CCA rate of 15 percent. At the end of five years, the plant and equipment will have a zero salvage value but Fireplaces Etc. will continue to have other assets in this asset class. Sales projections for the wood stoves are as follows:

Year	Unit Sales
1	300
2	350
3	400
4	500
5	500

The net working capital requirement (including the initial working capital needed in Year 0) is expected to be 20 percent of the following year's sales. The firm's tax rate is 35 percent. Using a discount rate of 15 percent, calculate the net present value of the project.

*25. **Project Evaluation.** Blooper Industries must replace its magnoosium purification system. Quick & Dirty Systems sells a relatively cheap purification system for $10 million. The system will last five years. Do-It-Right sells a sturdier but more expensive system for $12 million; it will last for 8 years. Both systems entail $1 million in operating costs; both will be depreciated in an asset class that has a CCA rate of 30 percent; neither will have any salvage value at the end of its life. The firm's tax rate is 35 percent, and the discount rate is 12 percent. Which system should Blooper install?

26. **Project Evaluation.** The following table presents sales forecasts for Golden Gelt Giftware. The unit price is $40. The unit cost of the giftware is $25.

Year	Unit Sales
1	22,000
2	30,000
3	14,000
4	5,000
Thereafter	0

It is expected that net working capital will amount to 25 percent of sales in the following year. For example, the store will need an initial (Year 0) investment in working capital of .25 × 22,000 × $40 = $220,000. Plant and equipment necessary to establish the giftware business will require an additional investment of $200,000. This investment will be depreciated in an asset class with a CCA rate of 25 percent. We will assume that the firm has other assets in this asset class. After four years, the equipment will have an economic and book value of zero. The firm's tax rate is 35 percent. The discount rate is 20 percent. What is the net present value of the project?

*27. **Project Evaluation.** Ilana Industries, Inc., needs a new lathe. It can buy a new high-speed lathe for $1 million. The lathe will cost $35,000 to run, will save the firm $125,000 in labour costs, and will be useful for 10 years. Suppose that for tax purposes, the lathe will be in an asset class with a CCA rate of 25 percent. Ilana has many other assets in this asset class. The lathe is expected to have a 10-year life with a salvage value of $100,000. The actual market value of the lathe at that time will also be $100,000. The discount rate is 10 percent and the corporate tax rate is 35 percent. What is the NPV of buying the new lathe?

28. **Internet.** Go to the Canada Revenue Agency Web site at **http://www.cra-arc.gc.ca/ menu-e.html** and try to get to relevant documents describing the Capital Cost Allowance system. One quick way is to do a search on the Web site with the keywords "Capital Cost Allowance." Read the prescribed rules and regulations that govern Capital Cost Allowance. How many asset classes are there? What are the minimum and maximum eligible CCA rates? Most asset classes have declining balance rates. Can you identify the asset classes that involve straight-line computation? Why do you think the rate structure is not declining balance for these asset classes?

29. **Go to Market Insight (www.mcgrawhill.ca/edumarketinsight).** Find the net capital expenditures, capital expenditures less sales of plant and equipment, and total sales for Rogers Communications (CLB.RG) and Microsoft (MSFT). What were the ratios of net capital expenditure to sales for the last three years for both companies? What were the sales and net capital expenditures relative to total assets? What might explain the variation in these ratios for these two large corporations? Did the company make an investment or disinvestment in working capital in each of the three years?

CHALLENGE

30. **Project Evaluation.** The efficiency gains resulting from a just-in-time inventory management system will allow a firm to reduce its level of inventories permanently by $250,000. What is the most the firm should be willing to pay for installing the system?

31. **Project Evaluation.** You are considering investing in a new line of entertainment products. The project has an estimated economic life of five years. You anticipate some immediate start-up costs amounting to $25,000. In addition, you will be investing $100,000 in new plant and equipment. Assume, for tax purposes, that the machinery and equipment will be depreciated straight-line over its economic life. Also assume that the initial start-up costs are fully tax-deductible.

In the first year of operation you are anticipating sales revenues of $60,000. These revenues are expected to grow by five percent per year until Year 4, however, the revenues are expected to decline by five percent in the fifth year. First year operating costs will be $10,000; in subsequent years, these are expected to grow in proportion to sales revenues. The tax rate applicable to your business will be 34 percent. Also, at the end of the project's economic life, your plant and equipment will not have any salvage value. Your cost of capital is 12 percent.

Assuming that you will be able to expense the project's start-up costs,

a. Calculate its payback period, discounted payback period, internal rate of return, net present value, and profitability index.

b. Using the net present value and internal rate of return criteria, do you think it is worthwhile for you to pursue this project? Explain your answer.

c. Now, assume that for CCA purposes, your plant and equipment actually belong to asset Class 39. Recompute the project's net present value, assuming that you have other assets in asset Class 39 that will be continued even after the economic life of this project is over. Work out your calculations separately assuming (1) a zero salvage value and (2) a $10,000 salvage value, at the end of the project's economic life. Would you pursue the project under these new conditions? Explain your answer.

*32. **Project Evaluation.** Better Mousetraps has developed a new trap. It can go into production for an initial investment in equipment of $6 million. The equipment will be depreciated straight-line over 5 years to a value of zero, but in fact it can be sold after 5 years for $500,000. The firm believes that working capital at each date must be maintained at a level of 10 percent of next year's forecast sales. The firm estimates production costs equal to $1.50 per trap and believes that the traps can be sold for $4 each. Sales forecasts are given in the following table. The project will come to an end in five years, when the trap becomes technologically obsolete. The firm's tax bracket is 35 percent, and the required rate of return on the project is 12 percent. What is project NPV?

Year:	0	1	2	3	4	5	Thereafter
Sales (millions of traps)	0	.5	.6	1.0	1.0	.6	0

33. **Working Capital Management.** Return to the previous problem. Suppose the firm can cut its requirements for working capital in half by using better inventory control systems. By how much will this increase project NPV?

34. **Project Evaluation.** PC Shopping Network may upgrade its modem pool. It last upgraded 2 years ago, when it spent $115 million on equipment with an assumed life of 5 years and an assumed salvage value of $15 million for tax purposes. The firm uses straight-line depreciation. The old equipment can be sold today for $80 million. A new modem pool can be installed today for $150 million. This will have a 3-year life, and will be depreciated to zero using straight-line depreciation. The new equipment will enable the firm to increase sales by $25 million per year and decrease operating costs by $10 million per year. At the end of 3 years, the new equipment will be worthless. Assume the firm's tax rate is 35 percent and the discount rate for projects of this sort is 12 percent.
   a. What is the net cash flow at time 0 if the old equipment is replaced?
   b. What are the incremental cash flows in Years 1, 2, and 3?
   *c. What are the NPV and IRR of the replacement project?
   *d. Now ignore straight-line depreciation and assume that both new and old equipment are in an asset class with a CCA rate of 30 percent. PC Shopping Network has other assets in this asset class. What is the NPV of the replacement project? For this part, assume that the new equipment will have a salvage value of $30 million at the end of 3 years.

35. **Integrative.** You are exploring the possibility of starting a project involving production of an assortment of spicy curried pickles. You had approached a marketing consultant to conduct market research and do a one-year feasibility study for $25,000. The recommendations of the study are positive, and you have decided to begin work on the project. You expect the life of the project to be six years.

    The initial investment in the project is expected to be as follows:

    • Land: $150,000

    • Buildings: $350,000

    • Manufacturing equipment: $250,000

    • Net working capital: $40,000

    For CCA computation, the buildings belong to asset Class 1 and the manufacturing equipment is in asset Class 39. At the end of the project's economic life, you expect to be able to sell the buildings and land for $450,000 (the value of the land is expected to remain unchanged). The manufacturing equipment is, however, expected to have a salvage value of only $125,000. Net working capital requirements for each year are expected to increase by 10 percent from the previous year. Your business will be taxed at 35 percent.

    In the first year, you expect to sell 30,000 units of the gourmet pickles in bottled jars. In each subsequent year, unit sales are expected to increase by 4 percent. You have decided to price the pickles at $8.50 for each jar in the first year. You intend to adjust the price in subsequent years to keep up with inflation, which you expect to be about 1.5 percent per year over the life of the project. Variable costs are expected at $16,000 in the first year and are expected to grow in proportion to sales in each subsequent year. Fixed costs are estimated at $40,000 per year.

    Based on your estimates of the cost of financing the project, you have decided that the appropriate discount rate to evaluate the project's cash flows should be 12 percent. Conduct an NPV analysis to determine whether your decision to go ahead with the project is correct.

36. **Project Evaluation.** Virtual Printing Inc. has devised a new technology based on which it plans to launch a new line of print media products. The firm intends to spend $160,000 in new plant and equipment and $40,000 in expanding its building facilities to house the project. The project has an estimated economic life of eight years. Assume, for tax purposes, that the machinery and equipment and building will be depreciated straight-line over its economic life.

In the first year of operation, Virtual Printing expects to generate sales revenues of $60,000. These revenues are expected to stay at the same level until Year 3 but are subsequently expected to grow by 10 percent annually until Year 6, after which the revenues are expected to decline by 5 percent per year. First-year operating costs will be $15,000; in subsequent years, these are expected to grow in proportion to sales revenues. The tax rate applicable to Virtual Printing's business will be 34 percent. Also, at the end of the project's economic life, the plant and equipment will not have any salvage value. The expanded building facilities also cannot be sold, leased, or rented to another business entity without compromising the firm's existing operations. Virtual Printing's cost of capital is 12 percent.

a. Should Virtual Printing's finance manager recommend accepting the project if the firm's objective is to accept projects only when they are worth more than their cost?

b. Explain your answer to part (a) above. What technique did you use in your answer to part (a)?

c. By what time frame can Virtual Printing expect to recover its initial investment in the project: (1) ignoring the time value of money, and (2) taking into account the time value of money? Name the techniques you have used for your computation. What are the benefits and drawbacks to these techniques?

d. What is the IRR for this project?

e. Now, assume that for CCA purposes, the plant and equipment actually belong to asset Class 39 and the buildings belong to asset Class 1. Recompute the project's net present value, assuming that Virtual Printing has other assets in both asset classes that will be continued even after the economic life of this project is over. Work out your calculations assuming a zero salvage value for the building expansion and a $10,000 salvage value for the plant and equipment, at the end of the project's economic life. Would you pursue the project under these new conditions? Explain your answer.

Solutions to Check Points

8.1 Remember, discount cash flows, not profits. Each tewgit machine costs $250,000 right away; recognize that outlay, but forget accounting depreciation. Cash flows per machine are

Year:	0	1	2	3	4	5
Investment (outflow)	–250,000					
Sales		250,000	300,000	300,000	250,000	250,000
Operating expenses		–200,000	–200,000	–200,000	–200,000	–200,000
Cash flow	–250,000	+ 50,000	+100,000	+100,000	+ 50,000	+ 50,000

Each machine is forecast to generate $50,000 of cash flow in years 4 and 5. Thus it makes sense to keep operating for five years.

8.2   a., b. The site and buildings could have been sold or put to another use. Their values are opportunity costs, which should be treated as incremental cash outflows.

c. Demolition costs are incremental cash outflows.

d. The cost of the access road is sunk and not incremental.

e. Lost cash flows from other projects are incremental cash outflows.

f. Depreciation is not a cash expense and should not be included, except as it affects taxes. (Taxes are discussed later in this chapter.)

8.3   Actual health costs will be increasing at about 7 percent a year.

Year:	1	2	3	4
Cost per worker	$2,400	$2,568	$2,748	$2,940

The present value at 10 percent is $9,214 if the first payment is made immediately. If it is delayed a year, present value falls to $8,377.

8.4   The tax rate is T = 35 percent. Taxes paid will be

$$T \times (\text{revenue} - \text{expenses} - \text{depreciation}) = .35 \times (600 - 300 - 200) = \$35$$

Operating cash flow can be calculated as follows.

a. Revenue − expenses − taxes = 600 − 300 − 35 = $265

b. Net profit + depreciation = (600 − 300 − 200 − 35) + 200
$$= 65 + 200 = 265$$

c. (Revenues − cash expenses) $\times$ (1 − tax rate) + (depreciation $\times$ tax rate)
$$= (600 - 300) \times (1 - .35) + (200 \times .35) = 265$$

8.5

	Year 1	Year 2
Beginning UCC	—	$166,500
Net Acquisition	$180,000	(25,000)
CCA	13,500	21,225
Ending UCC	166,500	120,275

Calculations:

Year 1: CCA = $180, 000 $\times$ .5 $\times$ .15 = $13,500

Year 2: Adjusted cost of disposal = $100,000 + 75,000 = $175,000

Net acquisition = Total cost of additions − Adjusted cost of disposal
$$= \$150,000 - \$175,000 = -\$25,000$$

CCA = $141,500 $\times$ .15 = $21,225

Ending UCC = $141,500 − $21,225 = $120,275

8.6   Adjusted cost of disposal = $65,000 + $70,000 = $135,000
UCC is reduced by this amount to $144,500 − $135,000 = $9,500.

If the firm has no other assets in Class 10, then the asset pool will be terminated, and the amount of $9,500 will be treated as a terminal loss.

8.7   a.   All figures in dollars

Year:	0	1	2	3	4	5
1. Capital investment	−5,000					
2. Revenues		3,000	3,000	3,000	3,000	3,000
3. Expenses		1,500	1,500	1,500	1,500	1,500
4. Profit before tax (2 − 3)		1,500	1,500	1,500	1,500	1,500
5. Tax at 35%		525	525	525	525	525
6. Operating cash flow excluding CCA tax shield (4 − 5)		975	975	975	975	975
7. UCC		4,625	3,931	3,341	2,840	2,414
8. CCA		375	694	590	501	426
9. CCA tax shield (.35 × 8)		131	243	207	175	149
10. Total yearly cash flows including CCA tax shield (1 + 6 + 9)	5,000	1,106	1,218	1,182	1,150	1,124

Notice that the amounts in row 10 do not reflect all cash flows, since there remains a UCC balance of $2,414 in Year 5, which should continue to provide CCA tax shields beyond Year 5 if there are other assets in the asset class.

b.   If depreciation is on a straight-line basis over five years, we would change items 8, 9, and 10 of the table in part (a) above as follows:

$

Year:	0	1	2	3	4	5
8. Depreciation		1,000	1,000	1,000	1,000	1,000
9. Depreciation tax shield (.35 × 8)		350	350	350	350	350
10. Total yearly cash flows including depreciation tax shield (1 + 6 + 9)	−5,000	1,325	1,325	1,325	1,325	1,325

MINICASE

Jack Tar, CFO of Sheetbend & Halyard, Inc., opened the company confidential envelope. It contained a draft of a competitive bid for a contract to supply duffel canvas to the Canadian Armed Forces. The cover memo from Sheetbend's CEO asked Mr. Tar to review the bid before it was submitted.

The bid and its supporting documents had been prepared by Sheetbend's sales staff. It called for Sheetbend to supply 100,000 yards of duffel canvas per year for 5 years. The proposed selling price was fixed at $30 per yard.

Mr. Tar was not usually involved in sales, but this bid was unusual in at least two respects. First, if accepted by the forces, it would commit Sheetbend to a fixed price, long-term contract. Second, producing the duffel canvas would require an investment of $1.5 million to purchase machinery and to refurbish Sheetbend's plant in Saint John, New Brunswick.

Mr. Tar set to work and by the end of the week had collected the following facts and assumptions:

- The plant in Saint John was built in the early 1900s and is now idle. The plant was fully depreciated on Sheetbend's books, except for the purchase cost of the land (in 1947) of $10,000.
- Now that the land was valuable shorefront property, Mr. Tar thought the land and the idle plant could be sold, immediately or in the future, for $600,000.
- Refurbishing the plant would cost $500,000. This investment would be depreciated for tax purposes in an asset class that has a CCA rate of 5 percent.
- The new machinery would cost $1 million. This investment could be depreciated in an asset class that has a CCA rate of 30 percent.

- The refurbished plant and new machinery would last for many years. However, the remaining market for duffel canvas was small, and it was not clear that additional orders could be obtained once the Forces contract was finished. The machinery was custom built and could be used only for duffel canvas. Its second-hand value at the end of five years was probably zero.
- Table 8.11 shows the sales staff's forecasts of income from the navy contract. Mr. Tar reviewed this forecast and decided that its assumptions were reasonable, except that the forecast used book, not tax, depreciation.
- But the forecast income statement contained no mention of working capital. Mr. Tar thought that working capital would average about 10 percent of sales.

Armed with this information, Mr. Tar constructed a spreadsheet to calculate the NPV of the duffel canvas project, assuming that Sheetbend's bid would be accepted by the Forces.

He had just finished debugging the spreadsheet when another confidential envelope arrived from Sheetbend's CEO. It contained a firm offer from a New Brunswick real estate developer to purchase Sheetbend's Saint John land and plant for $1.5 million in cash.

Should Mr. Tar recommend submitting the bid to the Forces at the proposed price of $30 per yard? The discount rate for this project is 12 percent.

TABLE 8.11

Forecast income statement for the navy duffel canvas project (dollar figures in thousands, except price per yard)

Year	1	2	3	4	5
1. Yards sold	100.00	100.00	100.00	100.00	100.00
2. Price per yard	30.00	30.00	30.00	30.00	30.00
3. Revenue (1 × 2)	3,000.00	3,000.00	3,000.00	3,000.00	3,000.00
4. Cost of goods sold	2,100.00	2,184.00	2,271.36	2,362.21	2,456.70
5. Operating cash flow (3 − 4)	900.00	816.00	728.64	637.79	543.30
6. Depreciation	250.00	250.00	250.00	250.00	250.00
7. Income (5 − 6)	650.00	566.00	478.64	387.79	293.30
8. Tax at 35%	227.50	198.10	167.52	135.72	102.65
9. Net income (7 − 8)	$422.50	$367.90	$311.12	$252.06	$190.64

Notes:

1. Yards sold and price per yard would be fixed by contract.
2. Cost of goods includes fixed cost of $300,000 per year plus variable costs of $18 per yard. Costs are expected to increase at the inflation rate of 4 percent per year.
3. Depreciation: A $1 million investment in machinery is depreciated straight-line over 5 years ($200,000 per year). The $500,000 cost of refurbishing the Saint John plant is depreciated straight-line over 10 years ($50,000 per year).

CHAPTER 9

PROJECT ANALYSIS

It helps to use discounted cash-flow techniques to value new projects, but good investment decisions also require good data. Therefore, we start this chapter by thinking about how firms organize the capital budgeting operation to get the kind of information they need. In addition, we look at how they try to ensure that everyone involved works together toward a common goal.

Project evaluation should never be a mechanical exercise in which the financial manager takes a set of cash flow forecasts and cranks out a net present value. Cash flow estimates are just that—estimates. Financial managers need to look behind the forecasts to try to understand what makes the project tick and what could go wrong with it. A number of techniques have been developed to help managers identify the key assumptions in their analysis. These techniques involve asking a number of "what if" questions. What if your market share turns out to be higher or lower than you forecast? What if interest rates rise during the life of the project? In the second part of this chapter we show how managers use the techniques of sensitivity analysis, scenario analysis, and break-even analysis to help answer these "what if" questions.

Books about capital budgeting sometimes create the impression that once the manager has made an investment decision, there is nothing to do but sit back and watch the cash flows develop. But since cash flows rarely proceed as anticipated, companies constantly need to modify their operations. If cash flows are better than anticipated, the project may be expanded; if they are worse, it may be scaled back or abandoned altogether. In the third section of this chapter we describe how good managers take account of these options when they analyze a project and why they are willing to pay money today to build in future flexibility.

After studying this chapter you should be able to
- Appreciate the practical problems of capital budgeting in large corporations.
- Use sensitivity, scenario, and break-even analyses to see how project profitability would be affected by an error in your forecasts and understand why an overestimate of sales is more serious for projects with high operating leverage.
- Recognize the importance of managerial flexibility in capital budgeting.

9.1

HOW FIRMS ORGANIZE THE INVESTMENT PROCESS

For most sizable firms, investments are evaluated in two separate stages.

STAGE 1: THE CAPITAL BUDGET

capital budget   List of planned investment projects.

Once a year, the head office generally asks each of its divisions and plants to provide a list of the investments that they would like to make.[1] These are gathered into a proposed **capital budget**.

This budget is then reviewed and pruned by senior management and other staff specializing in planning and financial analysis. Usually there are negotiations between the firm's senior management and its divisional management, and there may also be special analyses of major outlays or ventures into new areas. Once the budget has been approved, it generally remains the basis for planning over the ensuing year.

Many investment proposals bubble up from the bottom of the organization. But sometimes the ideas are likely to come from higher up. For example, the managers of plants A and B cannot be expected to see the potential benefits of closing their plants and consolidating production at a new plant C. We expect divisional management to propose plant C. Similarly, divisions 1 and 2 may not be eager to give up their own data processing operations to a large central computer. That proposal would come from senior management.

Senior management's concern is to see that the capital budget matches the firm's strategic plans. It needs to ensure that the firm is concentrating its efforts in areas where it has a real competitive advantage. As part of this effort, management must also identify declining businesses that should be sold or allowed to run down.

The firm's capital investment choices should reflect both "bottom-up" and "top-down" processes—capital budgeting and strategic planning, respectively. The two processes should complement each other. Plant and division managers, who do most of the work in bottom-up capital budgeting, may not see the forest for the trees. Strategic planners may have a mistaken view of the forest because they do not look at the trees.

STAGE 2: PROJECT AUTHORIZATIONS

The annual budget is important because it allows everybody to exchange ideas before attitudes have hardened and personal commitments have been made. However, the fact that your pet project has been included in the annual budget doesn't mean you have permission to go ahead with it. At a later stage you will need to draw up a detailed proposal describing particulars of the project, engineering analyses, cash-flow forecasts, and present value calculations. If your project is large, this proposal may have to pass a number of hurdles before it is finally approved.

The type of backup information that you need to provide depends on the project category. For example, some firms use a fourfold breakdown:

1. Outlays required by law or company policy; for example, for pollution control equipment. These outlays do not need to be justified on financial grounds. The main issue is whether requirements are satisfied at the lowest possible cost. The decision is therefore likely to hinge on engineering analyses of alternative technologies.
2. Maintenance or cost reduction, such as machine replacement. Engineering analysis is also important in machine replacement, but new machines have to pay their own way. In this category of the proposal the firm faces the classical capital budgeting problems described in chapters 7 and 8.
3. Capacity expansion in existing businesses. Projects in this category are less straightforward; these decisions may hinge on forecasts of demand, possible shifts in technology, and the reac-

---

[1] Large firms may be divided into several divisions. For example, International Paper has divisions that specialize in printing paper, packaging, specialty products, and forest products. Each of these divisions may be responsible for a number of plants.

tions of competitors.

4. Investment for new products. Projects in this category are most likely to depend on strategic decisions. The first projects in a new area may not have positive NPVs if considered in isolation, but they may give the firm a valuable option to undertake follow-up projects. More about this later in the chapter.

PROBLEMS AND SOME SOLUTIONS

Valuing capital investment opportunities is hard enough when you can do the entire job yourself. In most firms, however, capital budgeting is a cooperative effort, and this brings with it some challenges.

Ensuring that Forecasts Are Consistent. Inconsistent assumptions often creep into investment proposals. For example, suppose that the manager of the furniture division is bullish (optimistic) on housing starts but the manager of the appliance division is bearish (pessimistic). This inconsistency makes the projects proposed by the furniture division look more attractive than those of the appliance division.

To ensure consistency, many firms begin the capital budgeting process by establishing forecasts of economic indicators, such as inflation and the growth in national income, as well as forecasts of particular items that are important to the firm's business, such as housing starts or the price of raw materials. These forecasts can then be used as the basis for all project analyses.

Eliminating Conflicts of Interest. In Chapter 1 we pointed out that while managers want to do a good job, they are also concerned about their own futures. If the interests of managers conflict with those of shareholders, the result is likely to be poor investment decisions. For example, new plant managers naturally want to demonstrate good performance right away. To this end, they might propose quick-payback projects even if NPV is sacrificed. Unfortunately, many firms measure performance and reward managers in ways that encourage such behaviour. If the firm always demands quick results, it is unlikely that plant managers will concentrate only on NPV.

Reducing Forecast Bias. Someone who is keen to get a project proposal accepted is also likely to look on the bright side when forecasting the project's cash flows. Such overriding optimism is a common feature in financial forecasts. For example, think of large public expenditure proposals. How often have you heard of a new missile, dam, or highway that actually cost less than was originally forecast? Think back to the Eurotunnel project introduced in Chapter 7. The final cost of the project was about 50 percent higher than initial forecasts. It is probably impossible to ever eliminate bias completely, but if senior management is aware of why bias occurs, it is at least partway to solving the problem.

Project sponsors are likely to overstate their case deliberately only if the head office encourages them to do so. For example, if middle managers believe that success depends on having the largest division rather than the most profitable one, they will propose large expansion projects that they do not believe have the largest possible net present value. Or if divisions must compete for limited resources, they will try to outbid each other for those resources. The fault in such cases is with top management—if lower-level managers are not rewarded based on net present value and contribution to firm value, it should not be surprising that they focus their efforts elsewhere.

Other problems stem from sponsors' eagerness to obtain approval for their favourite projects. As the proposal travels up the organization, alliances are formed. Thus once a division has screened its own plants' proposals, the plants in that division unite in competing against outsiders. The result is that the head office may receive several thousand investment proposals each year, all essentially sales documents presented by united fronts and designed to persuade. The forecasts have been doctored to ensure that NPV appears positive.

Since it is difficult for senior management to evaluate each specific assumption in an investment proposal, capital investment decisions are effectively decentralized whatever the rules say. Some firms accept this; others rely on head office staff to check capital investment proposals.

Sorting the Wheat from the Chaff. Senior managers are continually bombarded with requests for funds for capital expenditures. All these requests are supported with detailed analyses showing that the projects have positive NPVs. How then can managers ensure that only worthwhile projects make the grade? One response of senior managers to the problem of poor information is to impose rigid expenditure limits on individual plants or divisions. These limits force the subunits to choose among projects. The firm ends up using capital rationing not because capital is unobtainable but as a way of decentralizing decisions.[2]

Senior managers might also ask some searching questions about why the project has a positive NPV. After all, if the project is so attractive, why hasn't someone already undertaken it? Will others copy your idea if it is so profitable? Positive NPVs are plausible only if your company has some competitive advantage.

Such an advantage can arise in several ways. You may be smart enough or lucky enough to be the first to the market with a new or improved product for which customers will pay premium prices. Your competitors eventually will enter the market and squeeze out excess profits, but it may take them several years to do so. Or you may have a proprietary technology or production cost advantage that competitors cannot easily match. You may have a contractual advantage such as the distributorship for a particular region. Or your advantage may be as simple as a good reputation and an established customer list.

Analyzing competitive advantage can also help ferret out projects that incorrectly appear to have a negative NPV. If you are the lowest cost producer of a profitable product in a growing market, then you should invest to expand along with the market. If your calculations show a negative NPV for such an expansion, then you have probably made a mistake.

9.2

SOME "WHAT IF" QUESTIONS

SENSITIVITY ANALYSIS

Uncertainty means that more things can happen than *will* happen. Therefore, whenever managers are given a cash flow forecast, they try to determine what else might happen and the implications of those possible events. This is called **sensitivity analysis**.

sensitivity analysis Analysis of the effects of changes in sales, costs, and so on, on project profitability.

Put yourself in the well-heeled shoes of the financial manager of the Finefodder supermarket chain. Finefodder is considering opening a new superstore in Gravenstein and your staff members have prepared the figures shown in Table 9.1. The figures are fairly typical for a new supermarket, except that to keep the example simple we have assumed no inflation. We have also assumed that the entire investment can be depreciated straight-line for tax purposes, we have neglected the working capital requirement, and we have ignored the fact that at the end of the 12 years you could sell off the land and buildings.

TABLE 9.1
Cash flow forecasts for Finefodder's new superstore

	Year 0	Years 1–12
Investment	−$5,400,000	
1. Sales		$ 16,000,000
2. Variable costs		13,000,000
3. Fixed costs		2,000,000
4. Depreciation		450,000
5. Pretax profit (1 − 2 − 3 − 4)		550,000
6. Taxes (at 40%)		220,000
7. Profit after tax		330,000
8. Cash flow from operations (4 + 7)		780,000
Net cash flow	−$5,400,000	$ 780,000

---

[2] We discussed capital rationing in Chapter 7.

As an experienced financial manager, you recognize immediately that these cash flows constitute an annuity, and therefore, you calculate present value by multiplying the $780,000 cash flow by the 12-year annuity factor. If the cost of capital is 8 percent, present value is

$$PV = \$780,000 \times \text{12-year annuity factor}$$
$$= \$780,000 \times 7.536 = \$5.878 \text{ million}$$

Subtract the initial investment of $5.4 million and you obtain a net present value of $478,000:

$$NPV = PV - \text{investment}$$
$$= \$5.878 \text{ million} - \$5.4 \text{ million} = \$478,000$$

Before you agree to accept the project, however, you want to delve behind these forecasts and identify the key variables that will determine whether the project succeeds or fails.

Some of the costs of running a supermarket are fixed. For example, regardless of the level of output, you still have to heat and light the store and pay the store manager. These **fixed costs** are forecast to be $2 million per year.

fixed costs Costs that do not depend on the level of output.

Other costs vary with the level of sales. In particular, the lower the sales, the less food you need to buy. Also, if sales are lower than forecast, you can operate a lower number of checkouts and reduce the staff needed to restock the shelves. The new superstore's variable costs are estimated at 81.25 percent of sales. Thus **variable costs** = .8125 × $16 million = $13 million.

variable costs Costs that change as the level of output changes.

The initial investment of $5.4 million will be depreciated on a straight-line basis over the 12-year period, resulting in annual depreciation of $450,000. Profits are taxed at a rate of 40 percent.

These seem to be the important things you need to know, but look out for things that may have been forgotten. Perhaps there will be delays in obtaining planning permission, or perhaps you will need to undertake costly landscaping. The greatest dangers often lie in these unknown unknowns, or "unk-unks," as scientists call them.

Having found no unk-unks (no doubt you'll find them later), you look at how NPV may be affected if you have made a wrong forecast of sales, costs, and so on. To do this, you first obtain optimistic and pessimistic estimates for the underlying variables. These are set out in the left-hand columns of Table 9.2.

Next you see what happens to NPV under the optimistic or pessimistic forecasts for each of these variables. You recalculate project NPV under these various forecasts to determine which variables are most critical to NPV.

EXAMPLE 9.1	**SENSITIVITY ANALYSIS**

The right-hand side of Table 9.2 shows the project's NPV if the variables are set one at a time to their optimistic and pessimistic values. For example, if fixed costs are $1.9 million rather than the forecast $2.0 million, annual cash flows are increased by (1 − tax rate) × ($2.0 million − $1.9 million) = .6 × $100,000 = $60,000. If the cash flow increases by $60,000 a year for 12 years, then

TABLE 9.2

Sensitivity analysis for superstore project

Variable	Range			NPV		
	Pessimistic	Expected	Optimistic	Pessimistic	Expected	Optimistic
Investment ($)	6,200,000	5,400,000	5,000,000	−121,000	+478,000	+778,000
Sales ($)	14,000,000	16,000,000	18,000,000	−1,218,000	+478,000	+2,174,000
Variable cost as percentage of sales (Range: %; NPV: $)	83	81.25	80	−788,000	+478,000	+1,382,000
Fixed cost ($)	2,100,000	2,000,000	1,900,000	+26,000	+478,000	+930,000

the project's present value increases by $60,000 times the 12-year annuity factor, or $60,000 × 7.536 = $452,000. Therefore, NPV increases from the expected value of $478,000 to $478,000 + $452,000 = $930,000, as shown in the bottom right corner of the table. The other entries in the three columns on the right in Table 9.2 similarly show how the NPV of the project changes when each input is changed.

Your project is by no means a sure thing. The principal uncertainties appear to be sales and variable costs. For example, if sales are only $14 million rather than the forecast $16 million (and all other forecasts are unchanged), then the project has an NPV of –$1.218 million. If variable costs are 83 percent of sales (and all other forecasts are unchanged), then the project has an NPV of –$788,000.

Check Point 9.1   Recalculate cash flow as in Table 9.1 if variable costs are 83 percent of sales. Confirm that NPV will be –$788,000.

Value of Information. Now that you know the project could be thrown badly off course by a poor estimate of sales, you might like to see whether it is possible to resolve some of this uncertainty. Perhaps your worry is that the store will fail to attract sufficient shoppers from neighbouring towns. In that case, additional survey data and more careful analysis of travel times may be worthwhile.

On the other hand, there is less value to gathering additional information about fixed costs. Because the project is marginally profitable even under pessimistic assumptions about fixed costs, you are unlikely to be in trouble if you have estimated that variable incorrectly.

Limits to Sensitivity Analysis. Your analysis of the forecasts for Finefodder's new superstore is known as a *sensitivity analysis*. Sensitivity analysis expresses cash flows in terms of unknown variables and then calculates the consequences of incorrectly estimating those variables. It forces the manager to identify the underlying factors, indicates where additional information would be most useful, and helps to expose confused or inappropriate forecasts.

Of course, there is no law stating which variables you should consider in your sensitivity analysis. For example, you may wish to look separately at labour costs and the costs of the goods sold. Or, if you are concerned about a possible change in the corporate tax rate, you may wish to look at the effect of such a change on the project's NPV.

One drawback to sensitivity analysis is that it gives somewhat ambiguous results. For example, what exactly do *optimistic* and *pessimistic* mean? One department may be interpreting the terms in a different way from another. Ten years from now, after hundreds of projects, hindsight may show that one department's pessimistic limit was exceeded twice as often as the other's, but hindsight won't help you now while you're making the investment decision.

Another problem with sensitivity analysis is that the underlying variables are likely to be interrelated. For example, if sales exceed expectations, demand will likely be stronger than you anticipated and your profit margins will be wider. Or, if wages are higher than your forecast, both variable costs and fixed costs are likely to be at the upper end of your range.

Because of these connections, you cannot push one-at-a-time sensitivity analysis too far. It is impossible to obtain expected, optimistic, and pessimistic values for total project cash flows from the information in Table 9.2. Still, it does give a sense of which variables should be most closely monitored.

SCENARIO ANALYSIS

scenario analysis Project analysis given a particular combination of assumptions.

When variables are interrelated, managers often find it helpful to look at how their project would fare under different scenarios. **Scenario analysis** allows them to look at different but *consistent* combinations of variables. Forecasters generally prefer to give an estimate of revenues or costs under a particular scenario rather than giving some absolute optimistic or pessimistic value.

TABLE 9.3
Scenario analysis, NPV of Finefodder's Gravenstein superstore with scenario of new competing store in nearby Salome

	Cash Flows Years 1–12	
	Base Case	**Competing Store Scenario**[a]
1. Sales	$16,000,000	$13,600,000
2. Variable costs	13,000,000	11,152,000
3. Fixed costs	2,000,000	2,000,000
4. Depreciation	450,000	450,000
5. Pretax profit (1 − 2 − 3 − 4)	550,000	−2,000
6. Taxes (40%)	220,000	−800
7. Profit after tax	330,000	−1,200
8. Cash flow from operations (4 + 7)	780,000	448,800
Present value of cash flows	5,878,000	3,382,000
NPV	478,000	−2,018,000

[a] *Assumptions*: Competing store causes (1) a 15 percent reduction in sales and (2) variable costs to increase to 82 percent of sales.

EXAMPLE 9.2   **SCENARIO ANALYSIS**

You are worried that Stop and Scoff may decide to build a new store in nearby Salome. That would reduce sales in your Gravenstein store by 15 percent and you might be forced into a price war to keep the remaining business. Prices might be reduced to the point that variable costs equal 82 percent of revenue. Table 9.3 shows that under this scenario of lower sales and smaller margins your new venture would no longer be worthwhile.

simulation analysis
Estimation of the probabilities of different possible outcomes, e.g., from an investment project.

An extension of scenario analysis is called **simulation analysis**. Here, instead of specifying a relatively small number of scenarios, a computer generates several hundred or thousand possible combinations of variables according to probability distributions specified by the analyst. Each combination of variables corresponds to one scenario. Project NPV and other outcomes of interest can be calculated for each combination of variables, and the entire probability distribution of outcomes can be constructed from the simulation results.

Check Point 9.2   What is the basic difference between sensitivity analysis and scenario analysis?

9.3	# BREAK-EVEN ANALYSIS

When we undertake a sensitivity analysis of a project or when we look at alternative scenarios, we are asking how serious it would be if we misestimated sales or costs. Managers sometimes prefer to rephrase this question and ask how far off the estimates could be before the project begins to lose money. This exercise is known as **break-even analysis**.

break-even analysis   Analysis of the level of sales at which the company breaks even.

For many projects, the make-or-break variable is sales volume. Therefore, managers most often focus on the break-even level of sales. However, you might also look at other variables, for example, at how high costs could be before the project goes into the red.

As it turns out, "losing money" can be defined in more than one way. Most often, the break-even condition is defined in terms of accounting profits. More properly, however, it should be defined in terms of net present value. We will start with accounting break-even, show that it can lead you astray, and then show how NPV break-even can be used as an alternative.

ACCOUNTING BREAK-EVEN ANALYSIS

The *accounting break-even* point is the level of sales at which profits are zero or, equivalently, at which total revenues equal total costs. As we have seen, some costs are fixed regardless of the level of output. Other costs vary with the level of output.

When you first analyzed the superstore project, you came up with the following estimates:

Sales	$16	million
Variable cost	13	million
Fixed costs	2	million
Depreciation	0.45	million

Notice that variable costs are 81.25 percent of sales. So, for each additional dollar of sales, costs increase by only $.8125. We can easily determine how much business the superstore needs to attract to avoid losses. If the store sells nothing, the income statement will show fixed costs of $2 million and depreciation of $450,000. Thus there will be a loss of $2.45 million. Each dollar of sales reduces this loss by $1.00 − $.8125 = $.1875. Therefore, to cover fixed costs plus depreciation, you need sales of 2.45 million/.1875 = $13.067 million. At this sales level, the firm will break even. More generally,

$$\text{Break-even level of revenues} = \frac{\textbf{fixed costs including depreciation}}{\textbf{additional profit from each additional dollar of sales}} \quad (9.1)$$

Table 9.4 shows how the income statement looks with only $13.067 million of sales.

Figure 9.1 shows how the break-even point is determined. The 45-degree line shows accounting revenues. The cost line shows how costs vary with sales. If the store doesn't sell a cent, it still incurs fixed costs and depreciation amounting to $2.45 million. Each extra dollar of sales adds $.8125 to these costs. When sales are $13.067 million, the two lines cross, indicating that costs equal revenues. For lower sales, revenues are less than costs and the project is in the red; for higher sales, revenues exceed costs and the project moves into the black.

Is a project that breaks even in accounting terms an acceptable investment? If you are not sure about the answer, this may be an easier question: Would you be happy about an investment in a stock that after five years gave you a total rate of return of zero? We hope not. You might break even on such a stock but a zero return does not compensate you for the time value of money or the risk that you have taken.

> A project that simply breaks even on an accounting basis gives you your money back but does not cover the opportunity cost of the capital tied up in the project. A project that breaks even in accounting terms will surely have a negative NPV.

Let's check this with the superstore project. Suppose that in each year the store has sales of $13.067 million—just enough to break even on an accounting basis. What would be the cash flow from operations?

$$\text{Cash flow from operations} = \text{profit after tax} + \text{depreciation}$$
$$= 0 + \$450,000 = \$450,000$$

The initial investment is $5.4 million. In each of the next 12 years, the firm receives a cash flow of $450,000. So the firm gets its money back:

TABLE 9.4
Income statement, break-even sales volume

Item	$ 000s	
Revenues	13,067	
Variable costs	10,617	(81.25% of sales)
Fixed costs	2,000	
Depreciation	450	
Pretax profit	0	
Taxes	0	
Profit after tax	0	

FIGURE 9.1
Accounting break-even
analysis

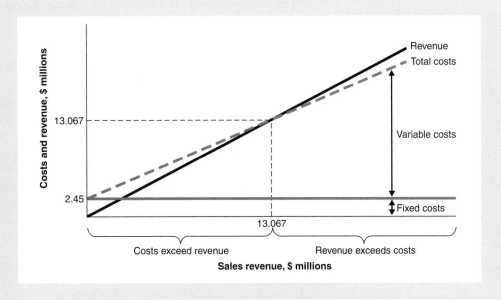

Total cash flow from operations = initial investment
12 × $450,000 = $5.4 million

But revenues are not sufficient to repay the opportunity cost of that $5.4 million investment.
NPV is negative.

ECONOMIC VALUE ADDED AND BREAK-EVEN ANALYSIS

The source of the problem with accounting break-even calculations is the fact that accounting earnings are calculated after the deduction of all costs *except the opportunity cost of the capital that is invested in the project*. Think again of how a firm creates value for its investors. It can either invest in new plant and equipment or it can return the cash to investors, who can then invest the money for themselves by buying stocks and bonds in the capital market. A firm that earns more than the cost of capital makes its investors better off: it is earning them a higher return than they could obtain for themselves. Naturally, therefore, financial managers are concerned with whether earnings are positive after deduction of the cost of capital.

Accounting for the cost of capital is simple, at least in principle—when calculating income, you should deduct the opportunity cost of the capital employed, just as you deduct other costs. Income that is measured after deduction of the cost of capital is often known as *economic profit*, or more commonly, **economic value added** or **EVA**.[3] A project that has a positive EVA adds to firm value; one with a negative EVA reduces firm value.

economic value added or EVA® Income that is measured after deduction of the cost of capital.

Think back to our superstore project, which involves an initial investment of $5.4 million and is expected to last for 12 years. Suppose for a moment that the cost of capital is zero. Then the equivalent annual cost of this investment is simply $5.4 million/12 = $450,000. In this case the accountant's deduction for depreciation correctly measures the cost of the capital invested.

However, if the cost of capital is positive, shareholders will not be happy with a project that simply gives them their money back. By ignoring the opportunity cost of capital, the depreciation allowance of $450,000 understates the true annual cost of the capital investment. A better measure of that cost is the equivalent annual annuity of the investment. A project that returns a cash flow over its life equal to that equivalent annual annuity will have an NPV of zero. We call the level of sales consistent with this cash flow the **economic break-even** (as opposed to *accounting* break-even) **point**.

economic break-even point Minimum level of sales needed to cover all costs including the cost of capital.

---

[3] The terms are used by Stern-Stewart, the consulting firm, which has done much to promote the measure. With Stern-Stewart's permission, we omit the copyright symbol in what follows.

To find the economic break-even point, we solve for the annual annuity, received over the 12-year life of the project, that will give the project an NPV of zero. For the superstore project, the equivalent annual annuity is

$$\frac{\text{Initial investment}}{\text{12-year annuity factor at 8 percent}} = \frac{\$5.4 \text{ million}}{7.536} = \$716,553$$

Notice that the actual depreciation allowance understates the appropriate charge for capital by $716,553 − $450,000 = $266,553. The economic profit, or equivalently the economic value added, equals the accounting profit minus this adjustment for the capital charge. For the superstore, economic profit = accounting profit − $266,553. While the superstore is expected to produce an annual after-tax accounting profit of $330,000, each year's profit adds only $330,000 − $266,553 = $63,447 to shareholder value. This is the project's expected annual economic value added.

Now we can perform our break-even calculation, asking how large sales would need to be before the project adds value for the shareholders. The superstore's EVA depends on sales as follows:

1. Variable costs	81.25% of sales
2. Fixed costs	$2 million
3. Depreciation	$450,000
4. Pretax profit	$(.1875 \times \text{sales}) - \$2.45$ million
5. Tax (at 40%)	$.40 \times (.1875 \times \text{sales} - \$2.45$ million)
6. After-tax accounting profit	$.60 \times (.1875 \times \text{sales} - \$2.45$ million)
7. Cost of capital over and above allowed depreciation[4]	$266,553
8. Economic value added (EVA) (= line 6 − line 7)	$.60 \times (.1875 \times \text{sales} - \$2.45$ million) $- \$266,553$

The project will have zero EVA when

$.60 \times (.1875 \times \text{sales} - \$2.45$ million$) - \$266,553 = 0$
$.1125 \times \text{sales} = \$1,736,553$
$\text{sales} = \$15,436,027$, or about $15.4 million

This implies that the store needs sales of about $15.4 million a year before it creates value for shareholders, that is, before it achieves economic break-even. This is more than 18 percent higher than the point at which the project has zero accounting profit. These days companies are increasingly aware that capital has an opportunity cost and therefore they think of break-even in terms of EVA rather than accounting profits.

Check Point 9.3   A project that has zero EVA creates no value. In other words, it has an NPV of zero. Confirm that, if the superstore generates sales of $15.436 million a year, it will also have zero NPV.

Figure 9.2 is a plot of the after-tax cash flow from the superstore as a function of annual sales. The cash flow equals the equivalent annual annuity of the initial investment when sales are $15.4 million. This is the point at which the project has zero EVA. As long as sales are greater than this, the project cash flow exceeds the equivalent annual annuity and the project has a positive EVA.

Check Point 9.4   What would be the economic break-even level of sales if the capital investment was only $5 million?

---

[4] Note that Canada Revenue Agency will allow the firm to deduct only the $450,000 cost of the investment. The additional $266,553 that is needed to satisfy shareholders must be earned after payment of tax.

FIGURE 9.2
NPV break-even
analysis

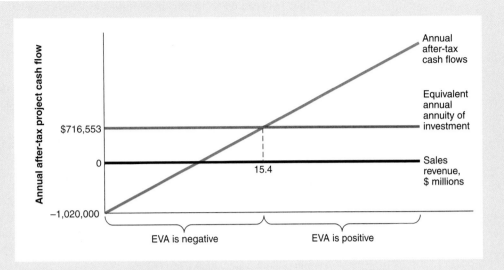

EXAMPLE 9.3   **BREAK-EVEN ANALYSIS**

We have said that projects that break even on an accounting basis are really making a loss—they are losing the opportunity cost of their investment. Here is a dramatic example. Lophead Aviation is contemplating investment in a new passenger aircraft, code-named the Trinova. Lophead's financial staff has gathered the following estimates:

1. The cost of developing the Trinova is forecast at $900 million, and this investment can be depreciated in six equal annual amounts.
2. Production of the plane is expected to take place at a steady annual rate over the following six years.
3. The average price of the Trinova is expected to be $15.5 million.
4. Fixed costs are forecast at $175 million a year.
5. Variable costs are forecast at $8.5 million a plane.
6. The tax rate is 50 percent.
7. The cost of capital is 10 percent.

Lophead's financial manager has used this information to construct a forecast of the profitability of the Trinova program. This is shown in rows 1 to 7 of Table 9.5 (ignore row 8 for a moment).

How many aircraft does Lophead need to sell to break even? The answer depends on what is meant by "break even." In accounting terms the venture will break even when net profit (row 7 in the table) is zero. In this case

$$(3.5 \times \text{planes sold}) - 162.5 = 0$$
$$\text{Planes sold} = 162.5/3.5 = 46.4$$

TABLE 9.5
Forecast profitability for
production of the Trinova
airliner (figures in $ millions)

	Year 0	Years 1–6
Investment	$900	
1. Sales		15.5 × planes sold
2. Variable costs		8.5 × planes sold
3. Fixed costs		175
4. Depreciation		900/6 = 150
5. Pretax profit (1 − 2 − 3 − 4)		(7 × planes sold) − 325
6. Taxes (at 50%)		(3.5 × planes sold) − 162.5
7. Net profit (5 − 6)		(3.5 × planes sold) − 162.5
8. Net cash flow (4 + 7)	−$900	(3.5 × planes sold) − 12.5

Thus Lophead needs to sell about 46 planes a year, or a total of 280 planes over the 6 years to show a profit. With a price of $15.5 million a plane, Lophead will break even in accounting terms with annual revenues of 46.4 × $15.5 million = $719 million.

We would have arrived at the same answer if we had used our formula to calculate the break-even level of revenues. Notice that the variable cost of each plane is $8.5 million, which is 54.8 percent of the $15.5 million sale price. Therefore, each dollar of sales increases pretax profits by $1 − $.548 = $.452. Now we use the formula for the accounting break-even point:

$$\text{Break-even revenues} = \frac{\text{fixed costs including depreciation}}{\text{additional profit from each additional dollar of sales}}$$
$$= \frac{\$325 \text{ million}}{.452} = \$719 \text{ million}$$

If Lophead sells about 46 planes a year, it will recover its original investment, but it will not earn any return on the capital tied up in the project. Companies that earn a zero return on their capital can expect some unhappy shareholders. Shareholders will be content only if the company's investments earn at least the cost of the capital invested. True break-even occurs when the projects have zero economic value added.

How many planes must Lophead sell to break even in terms of economic value added? Development of the Trinova costs $900 million. If the cost of capital is 10 percent, the 6-year annuity factor is 4.355. So the equivalent annual annuity of the capital invested in the project is $900 million/4.355 = $206.6 million. This is $56.6 million more than the allowance for depreciation. So the company needs to earn $56.6 million after tax each year just to cover the cost of the capital employed. We can now find how many planes Lophead needs to sell to break even in terms of EVA:

$$\begin{aligned}
\text{EVA} &= \text{accounting profit} - \text{additional cost of capital} = 0 \\
(\$3.5 \times \text{planes sold} &- \$162.5) - \$56.6 &&= 0 \\
\text{Planes sold} &&&= 219.1/3.5 = 62.6
\end{aligned}$$

Thus Lophead can recover its initial investment with sales of 46.4 planes a year (about 280 in total), but it needs to sell 62.6 a year (or about 375 in total) to recover the cost of the capital invested in the project.

Our example may seem fanciful but it is based loosely on reality. In 1971 Lockheed was in the middle of a major program to bring out the L-1011 TriStar airliner. This program was to bring Lockheed to the brink of failure and it tipped Rolls-Royce (supplier of the TriStar engine) over the brink. In giving evidence to the U.S. Congress, Lockheed argued that the TriStar program was commercially attractive and that sales would eventually exceed the break-even point of about 200 aircraft. But in calculating this break-even point Lockheed appears to have ignored the opportunity cost of the huge capital investment in the project. Lockheed probably needed to sell about 500 aircraft to reach a zero net present value.[5]

Check Point 9.5   What is the basic difference between sensitivity analysis and break-even analysis?

OPERATING LEVERAGE

A project's break-even point depends on both its *fixed costs*, which do not vary with sales, and the profit on each extra sale. Managers often face a trade-off between these variables. For example, we typically think of rental expenses as fixed costs. But supermarket companies sometimes rent stores with contingent rent agreements. This means that the amount of rent the company

---

[5] The true break-even point for the TriStar program is estimated in U. E. Reinhardt, "Break-Even Analysis for Lockheed's TriStar: An Application of Financial Theory," *Journal of Finance* 28 (September 1973), pp. 821–38.

pays is tied to the level of sales from the store. Rent rises and falls along with sales. The store thus replaces a fixed cost with a *variable cost* that rises along with sales. Because a greater proportion of the company's expenses will fall when its sales fall, its break-even point is reduced.

Of course, a high proportion of fixed costs is not all bad. The firm whose costs are largely fixed fares poorly when demand is low, but it may make a killing during a boom. Let us illustrate.

Finefodder has a policy of hiring long-term employees who will not be laid off except in the most dire circumstances. For all intents and purposes, these salaries are fixed costs. Its rival, Stop and Scoff, has a much smaller permanent labor force and uses expensive temporary help whenever demand for its product requires extra staff. A greater proportion of its labour expenses are therefore variable costs.

Suppose that if Finefodder adopted its rival's policy, fixed costs in its new superstore would fall from $2 million to $1.56 million but variable costs would rise from 81.25 to 84 percent of sales. Table 9.6 shows that with the normal level of sales, the two policies fare equally. In a slump a store that relies on temporary labour does better since its costs fall along with revenue. In a boom the reverse is true and the store with the higher proportion of fixed costs has the advantage.

If Finefodder follows its normal policy of hiring long-term employees, each extra dollar of sales increases pre-tax profits by $1.00 - \$.8125 = \$.1875$. If it uses temporary labour, an extra dollar of sales increases profits by only $1.00 - \$.84 = \$.16$. As a result, a store with high fixed costs is said to have high **operating leverage**. High operating leverage magnifies the effect on profits of a fluctuation in sales.

We can measure a business's operating leverage by asking how much profits change for each 1 percent change in sales. The **degree of operating leverage**, often abbreviated as **DOL**, is this measure.

$$\text{DOL} = \frac{\text{percentage change in profits}}{\text{percentage change in sales}}$$

For example, Table 9.6 shows that as the store moves from normal conditions to boom, sales increase from $16 million to $19 million, a rise of 18.75 percent. For the policy with high fixed costs, profits increase from $550,000 to $1,112,000, a rise of 102.2 percent. Therefore,

$$\text{DOL} = \frac{102.2}{18.75} = 5.45$$

The percentage change in sales is magnified more than fivefold in terms of the percentage impact on profits.

Now look at the operating leverage of the store if it uses the policy with low fixed costs but high variable costs. As the store moves from normal times to boom, profits increase from $550,000 to $1,030,000, a rise of 87.3 percent. Therefore,

$$\text{DOL} = \frac{87.3}{18.75} = 4.65$$

Because some costs remain fixed, a change in sales still generates a large percentage change in profits, but the degree of operating leverage is lower.

operating leverage   Degree to which costs are fixed.

degree of operating leverage (DOL)   Percentage change in profits given a 1 percent change in sales.

TABLE 9.6

A store with high operating leverage performs relatively badly in a slump but flourishes in a boom (figures in $000s)

	High Fixed Costs			High Variable Costs		
	Slump	Normal	Boom	Slump	Normal	Boom
Sales	13,000	16,000	19,000	13,000	16,000	19,000
− Variable costs	10,563	13,000	15,438	10,920	13,440	15,960
− Fixed costs	2,000	2,000	2,000	1,560	1,560	1,560
− Depreciation	450	450	450	450	450	450
= Pretax profit	−13	550	1,112	70	550	1,030

In fact, one can show that degree of operating leverage depends on fixed charges (including depreciation) in the following manner:[6]

$$DOL = 1 + \frac{\text{fixed costs}}{\text{profits}}$$

This relationship makes it clear that operating leverage increases with fixed costs.

EXAMPLE 9.4   **OPERATING LEVERAGE**

Suppose the firm adopts the high-fixed-cost policy. Then fixed costs including depreciation will be $2.00 + .45 = \$2.45$ million. Since the store produces profits of $.55 million at a normal level of sales, DOL should be

$$DOL = 1 + \frac{\text{fixed costs}}{\text{profits}} = 1 + \frac{2.45}{.55} = 5.45$$

This value matches the one we obtained by comparing the actual percentage changes in sales and profits.

> The risk of a project depends on operating leverage. If a large proportion of costs is fixed, a shortfall in sales has a magnified effect on profits.

We will have more to say about risk in the next three chapters.

Check Point 9.6   Suppose that sales increase by 10 percent from the values in the normal scenario. Compute the percentage change in pretax profits from the normal level for both policies in Table 9.6. Compare your answers to the values predicted by the DOL formula.

9.4   # REAL OPTIONS AND THE VALUE OF FLEXIBILITY

When you use discounted cash flow (DCF) to value a project, you implicitly assume that the firm will hold the assets passively. But managers are not paid to be dummies. After they have invested in a new project, they do not simply sit back and watch the future unfold. If things go well, the project may be expanded; if they go badly, the project may be cut back or abandoned altogether. Projects that can easily be modified in these ways are more valuable than those that don't provide such flexibility. The more uncertain the outlook, the more valuable this flexibility becomes.

---

[6] This formula for DOL can be derived as follows. If sales increase by 1 percent, then variable costs also should increase by 1 percent, and profits will increase by $.01 \times (\text{sales} - \text{variable costs}) = .01 \times (\text{profits} + \text{fixed costs})$. Now recall the definition of DOL:

$$DOL = \frac{\text{percentage change in profits}}{\text{percentage change in sales}} = \frac{\text{change in profits/level of profits}}{.01}$$

$$= 100 \times \frac{\text{change in profits}}{\text{level of profits}} = 100 \times \frac{.01 \times (\text{profits} + \text{fixed costs})}{\text{level of profits}}$$

$$= 1 + \frac{\text{fixed costs}}{\text{profits}}$$

THE OPTION TO EXPAND

The scientists at MacCaugh have developed a diet whisky and the firm is ready to go ahead with pilot production and test-marketing. The preliminary phase will take a year and cost $200,000. Management feels that there is only a 50-50 chance that the pilot production and market tests will be successful. If they are, then MacCaugh will build a $2 million production plant that will generate an expected annual cash flow in perpetuity of $480,000 after taxes. Given an opportunity cost of capital of 12 percent, project NPV in this case will be $-\$2$ million $+ \$480,000/.12 = \$2$ million. If the tests are not successful, MacCaugh will discontinue the project and the cost of the pilot production will be wasted.

Notice that MacCaugh's expenditure on the pilot program buys a valuable managerial option. The firm is not obliged to enter full production, but it has the option to do so depending on the outcome of the tests. If there is some doubt as to whether the project will take off, expenditure on the pilot operation could help the firm to avoid a costly mistake. Therefore, when it proposed the expenditure, MacCaugh's management was simply following the fundamental rule of swimmers: If you know the water temperature (and depth), dive in; if you don't, try putting a toe in first.

When faced with projects like this that involve future decisions, it is often helpful to draw a **decision tree** as in Figure 9.3. You can think of the problem as a game between MacCaugh and fate. Each square represents an action or decision by the company. Each circle represents an outcome revealed by fate. MacCaugh starts the play at the left-hand square. If it decides to test, then fate will cast the enchanted dice and decide the results of the test. Once the results are known, MacCaugh faces a second decision: Should it wind up the project, or should it invest $2 million and start full-scale production?

The second-stage decision is obvious: *Invest if the tests indicate that NPV is positive, and stop if they indicate that NPV is negative.* So now MacCaugh can move back to consider whether it should invest in the test program. This first-stage decision boils down to a simple problem: Should MacCaugh invest $200,000 now to obtain a 50 percent chance of a project with an NPV of $2 million a year later? At any reasonable discount rate the test program has a positive NPV.

> The option to walk away once the results are revealed introduces a valuable asymmetry. Good outcomes can be exploited, while bad outcomes can be limited by cancelling the project.

Here is another example of an apparently unprofitable investment that has value because of the flexibility it gives to make further follow-on investments. Some of the world's largest oil

decision tree Diagram of sequential decisions and possible outcomes.

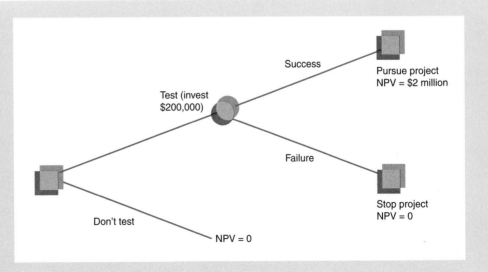

FIGURE 9.3
Decision tree for the Diet Whisky project

Buoyed by market and political momentum, Syncrude Canada Ltd., the consortium that runs northern Alberta's largest oil sands operation, will seek owner approval by July for the next and largest stage of its $8 billion expansion.

The Imperial Oil–led plant has also begun work on Stage 4, the final stage of its Syncrude 21 suite of projects, which may be larger than originally planned, Eric Newell, chairperson and chief executive, said in an interview.

"We continue at Syncrude to spend between $30 million and $40 million a year on research and development and we are continuing to find better ways. And who knows, you may see that investment even larger," he said. "The oil sands has a tremendous future and Syncrude is going to continue to be a major player."

Under current estimates, Stage 4 calls for investment of about $2.3 billion to boost production by about 100,000 barrels a day to raise Syncrude's output to 465,000 barrels a day, or 25 percent of Canada's crude oil requirements, upon the project's completion at the end of the decade.

Shell Canada Ltd.'s own expansion, which peaks this year, was scheduled to be near completion by mid-2002, while Suncor Energy, Inc.'s is already past its peak and wrapping up this year.

Shell has said the cost of its $3.5 billion Athabasca oil sands project could escalate by about 15 percent because of a tight market for skilled labour. Suncor suggested similar cost pressures could further increase its expansion costs, which have already jumped to $2.8 billion from original estimates of about $2 billion.

Newell said he is encouraged by political attention but said new development must wait until those projects already underway were completed.

"In 1995, we didn't have any projects going ahead, and now we have $51 billion in terms of announced projects," he said. "It's hard for me to imagine that we could entertain more right now." He added that the oil sands reserves, which rival those of Saudi Arabia, offer opportunities for more expansion as long as governments stand aside and let the market work.

Source: Excerpted from Claudia Cattaneo, "Syncrude Staged for $8 Billion Expansion: Consortium to Seek Approval for Go-Ahead in July," *The National Post*, March 25, 2002, p. C7.

reserves are found in the Athabasca tar sands of Alberta. Until recently, the cost of extracting oil from the sands was substantially higher than the current market price, and almost certainly higher than most people's estimate of the likely price in the future. Yet oil companies were prepared to pay considerable sums for these tracts of barren land. Why?

The answer is that ownership of these tracts gives the companies an option. They are not obliged to extract the oil. If oil prices remain below the cost of extraction, the Athabasca sands remain undeveloped. But if prices rise above the cost of extraction, those land purchases could prove very profitable. In the last few years, oil companies such as Suncor Energy and Shell Canada have made investment commitments of billions of dollars in oil sands projects (see the Finance in Action box above).

SEE BOX ABOVE ▷

Notice that the option to develop the tar sands is valuable because the future price of oil is uncertain. If, when oil prices were low, we *knew* they would remain at that level, nobody would pay a cent for the tar sands. It is the possibility that oil prices will fluctuate sharply that gives the option value.[7]

As a general rule, flexibility is most valuable when the future is most uncertain. The ability to change course as events develop and new information becomes available is most valuable when it is hard to predict with confidence what the best action ultimately will turn out to be.

You can probably now think of many other investments that take on added value because of the options they provide to expand in the future. For example

- When designing a factory, it can make sense to provide extra land or floor space to reduce the future cost of a second production line.
- When building a four-lane highway, it may pay to build six-lane bridges so that the road can be converted later to six lanes if traffic proves higher than expected.

SEE BOX P. 291 ▷

- An airline may acquire an option to buy a new aircraft (the nearby Finance in Action box explains how Federal Express bought options on the Airbus superjumbo).

---

[7] Oil prices sometimes move very sharply. They roughly halved between the beginning of 1997 and the end of 1998. By 2005, they had almost risen fourfold.

FedEx Buys an Option

In 2000 FedEx placed an order for 10 Airbus A380 superjumbo transport planes for delivery in the years 2008–2011. Each flight of an A380 freighter will be capable of carrying 200,000 pounds of goods and therefore the plane could have a huge impact on FedEx's worldwide business.

If FedEx's long-haul airfreight business continues to expand and the superjumbo is efficient and reliable, the company will need more superjumbos. But it cannot be sure they will be needed. Therefore, rather than placing further firm orders in 2000, FedEx has secured a place in the Airbus production line by acquiring options to buy a "substantial number" of additional aircraft at a predetermined price. These options do not commit the company to expand but give it the flexibility to do so.

real options Options to invest, modify, or dispose of a capital investment project.

In each of these cases you are paying out money today to give you the option to invest in real assets at some time in the future. Managers therefore often refer to such options as **real options**. These options do not show up in the assets that the company lists in its balance sheet, but investors are very aware of their existence. If a company has valuable real options that allow it to invest in profitable future projects, its market value will be higher than the value of its physical assets now in place.

Check Point 9.7

Goody Foods has developed choc-o-spice cookies with a distinct flavour it believes will be popular with young people. The product will be test-marketed in Atlantic Canada for two years. It requires an initial investment of $2 million, and because of heavy promotional expenses, it is not expected to generate any positive cash flows after tax (CFAT) during the first two years. There is a 60 percent chance that demand for the choc-o-spice cookies will be satisfactory; if that is so, a further investment cost of $5 million will be incurred in Year 2 to market the cookies nationwide. The subsequent CFATs expected are $4 million, $7 million, and $6 million, in years 3, 4, and 5, respectively. The cookies will be withdrawn from the market if the test-market results are unfavourable (a 40 percent chance) in Year 2.

Goody Foods considers the project to be of average risk, with a 14 percent opportunity cost of capital. The company intends to use net present value analysis to determine whether it will be worthwhile to go forward with the project. What decision should the company make?

SEE BOX P. 292

Large capital budgeting projects are, however, very often inherently complex and fraught with uncertainty. The nearby Finance in Action box describes the recent problems associated with huge unexpected cost overruns at Syncrude Canada's oil sands expansion project. Sometimes, when management is confronted with acute and unanticipated challenges, a sensible choice may be the decision to bail out. In our next section, therefore, we describe another real option; namely, the option to abandon.

A SECOND REAL OPTION: THE OPTION TO ABANDON

If the option to expand has value, what about the decision to bail out? Projects don't just go on until assets expire of old age. The decision to terminate a project is usually taken by management, not by nature. Once the project is no longer profitable, the company will cut its losses and exercise its option to abandon the project.

Some assets are simpler to bail out of than others. Tangible assets are usually easier to sell than intangible ones. It helps to have active secondhand markets, which really exist only for standardized items. Real estate, airplanes, trucks, and certain machine tools are likely to be relatively easy to sell. On the other hand, the knowledge accumulated by a software company's research and development program is a specialized intangible asset and probably would not have significant abandonment value. (Some assets, such as old mattresses, even have *negative* abandonment value; you have to pay to get rid of them. It is costly to decommission nuclear power plants or to reclaim land that has been strip-mined.)

Syncrude Consortium's Plans to Revitalize Its Oil Sands Operations Following Cost Overruns

The partners in Syncrude Canada Ltd. will be meeting early next week to hammer out a plan to revitalize the oil sands operator following massive cost overruns on a planned expansion and disappointing operating results last year.

The meeting, scheduled for Monday and Tuesday in Victoria, will be the first for the joint-venture partners since Syncrude revealed two weeks ago that its latest expansion would cost $2.1 billion more than previously expected—for a total price tag of $7.8 billion.

The so-called Stage Three expansion, which includes major upgrader enhancements and a new train at the open-pit mine in northern Alberta, will also be delayed nearly a year—pushing the anticipated startup to 2006.

"All the partners have the same degree of disappointment with this project," Marcel Coutu, president of the Canadian Oil Sands Trust and Syncrude's new chairman, said yesterday. "If anybody's most disappointed, it's probably us because we don't have any other assets that cushion the blow." Canadian Oil Sands is the country's largest income trust, and biggest single Syncrude shareholder, with more than 35 per cent of the project.

Stage Three was announced in July 2001, at an estimated cost of $4.1-billion. With current figures, the project will be about 93 per cent over the initial budget. While saying that nobody would have purposefully low-balled the original cost estimates, Mr. Coutu said it's likely the project would not have occurred if the partners had known at the start it would have a price tag of nearly $8-billion.

"It's a pretty definite chance that we would not have gotten all or maybe even any of these partners to go along, because at the time, people were using price schedules" of $20 (U.S.) oil. Current oil prices are hovering at 13-year record highs of nearly $38 a barrel. "And that just wouldn't support that kind of capital." Eric Newell, the former Syncrude chairman and chief executive who retired last December, told Canadian Press this week that the company simply didn't realize how complex it was to make large additions to the existing oil sands operation, already the biggest in the world.

"I think we underestimated," Mr. Newell said from Edmonton. "I'm not throwing stones here, but with all the brains looking at it, we just didn't piece together the magnitude."

Mr. Newell said that as the complexity of the project increases, unexpected things crop up like a work camp that's too small, or unexpected traffic delays caused by huge pieces of machinery clogging up the one road in to Fort McMurray, Alta.

Source: Excerpted from J. Stevenson "Syncrude Plans Revitalization Strategy Sessions: Partners to Meet Next Week Following Major Cost Overruns on Planned Expansion," *The Globe and Mail*, March 20, 2004, page B4. With permission of the Canadian Press.

EXAMPLE 9.5 | **ABANDONMENT OPTION**

Suppose that the Widgeon Company must choose between two technologies for the manufacture of a new product, a Wankel-engined outboard motor:

1. Technology A uses custom-designed machinery to produce the complex shapes required for Wankel engines at low cost. But if the Wankel engine doesn't sell, this equipment will be worthless.

2. Technology B uses standard machine tools. Labour costs are much higher, but the tools can easily be sold if the motor doesn't sell.

Technology A looks better in an NPV analysis of the new product, because it is designed to have the lowest possible cost at the planned production volume. Yet you can sense the advantage of technology B's flexibility if you are unsure whether the new outboard will sink or swim in the marketplace.

Check Point 9.8 — Draw a decision tree showing how the choices open to the Widgeon Company depend on demand for the new product. Pick some plausible numbers to illustrate why it might make sense to adopt the more expensive technology B.

When you are unsure about the success of a venture, you may wish to choose a flexible technology with a good resale market to preserve the option to abandon the project at low cost.

Check Point 9.9   Consider a firm operating a copper mine that incurs both variable and fixed costs of production. Suppose the mine can be shut down temporarily if copper prices fall below the variable cost of mining copper. Why is this a valuable operating option? How does it increase the NPV of the mine to the operator?

A THIRD REAL OPTION: THE TIMING OPTION

Suppose that you have a project that could be a big winner or a big loser. The project's upside potential outweighs its downside potential, and it has a positive NPV if undertaken today. However, the project is not "now-or-never." So should you invest right away or wait? It's hard to say. If the project turns out to be a winner, waiting means the loss or deferral of its early cash flows. But if it turns out to be a loser, it may pay to wait and get a better fix on the likely demand.

You can think of any project proposal as giving you the *option* to invest today. You don't have to exercise that option immediately. Instead you need to weigh the value of the cash flows lost by delaying against the possibility that you will pick up some valuable information. Suppose, for example, you are considering development of a new oil field. At current oil prices the investment has a small positive NPV. But oil prices are highly volatile, occasionally halving or doubling in the space of a couple of years. If a small decline in crude prices could push your project into the red, it might be better to wait a little before investing.

Our example illustrates why companies sometimes turn down apparently profitable projects. For example, suppose you approach your boss with a proposed project. It involves spending $1 million and has an NPV of $1,000. You explain to him how carefully you have analyzed the project, but nothing seems to convince him that the company should invest. Is he being irrational to turn down a positive-NPV project?

Faced by such marginal projects, it often makes sense to wait. One year later you may have much better information about the prospects for the project and it may become clear whether it is really a winner or a loser. In the former case you can go ahead with confidence, but, if it looks like a loser, the delay will have helped you to avoid a bad mistake.

A FOURTH REAL OPTION: FLEXIBLE PRODUCTION FACILITIES

A sheep is not a flexible production facility. It produces mutton and wool in roughly fixed proportions. If the price of mutton suddenly rises and that of wool falls, there is little that the farmer with a flock of sheep can do about it. Many manufacturing operations are different, for they have built-in flexibility to vary their output mix as demand changes. Since we have mentioned sheep, we might point to the knitwear industry as a case in which manufacturing flexibility has become particularly important in recent years. Fashion changes have made the pattern of demand in the knitwear industry notoriously difficult to predict, and firms have increasingly invested in computer-controlled knitting machines, which provide an option to vary the product mix as demand changes.

Companies also try to avoid becoming dependent on a single source of raw materials. For example, at current prices gas-fired industrial boilers may be cheaper to operate than oil-fired ones. Yet most companies prefer to buy boilers that can use *either* oil or natural gas, even though these dual-fired boilers cost more than a gas-fired boiler. The reason is obvious. If gas prices rise relative to oil prices, the dual-fired boiler gives the company a valuable option to exchange one asset (an oil-fired boiler) for another (a gas-fired boiler).

Check Point 9.10   Investments in new products or production capacity often include an option to expand. What are the other major types of option encountered in capital investment decisions?

CAPITAL BUDGETING PRACTICES OF FIRMS IN CANADA AND THE UNITED STATES

How do Canadian firms make their capital budgeting decisions? Over the years, several studies have attempted to answer this question. A survey of the capital budgeting practices of large Canadian firms and foreign firms operating in Canada in the 1990s concluded that most firms used multiple capital budgeting methods to assess capital investments.[8] Table 9.7 provides partial results from the survey.

The study notes that discounted cash flow (DCF) methods, including NPV and IRR techniques, were used by more than 75 percent of respondents to evaluate different types of projects, such as expansion of existing operations, expansion into new operations, foreign operations, and leasing. The propensity to use DCF techniques increased with the complexity of the project decision. Of the DCF methods, IRR was used more frequently than NPV in every instance except leasing. The payback method was also common and noticeably more frequent when it was employed in conjunction with DCF methods as part of a multiple criteria evaluation.

For purposes of cash-flow forecasting, quantitative methods—particularly sensitivity analysis—were used by 39.5 percent of respondents. This may reflect the popularity among firms of PC-based spreadsheet programs. Most of these respondents also indicated that they used quantitative methods together with qualitative methods, such as management's subjective estimates, which suggests the importance of strategic considerations in capital budgeting decisions. Surprisingly, 18 percent of the respondents did not use any quantitative methods at all, and at least one-quarter of the respondents did not have a formal risk analysis technique in use.

A more recent study of large U.S. and Canadian firms also concludes that for managers in the field, discounted cash flow analysis is in fact the dominant tool for project evaluation. The survey[9] found that 75 percent of firms either always or almost always use both NPV and IRR to evaluate projects. The dominance of these criteria was even stronger among larger firms. Despite the clear advantages of the NPV rule, however, firms do use other investment criteria to evaluate projects. For example, just over half of corporations will always or almost always compute a project's payback period. Profitability index is routinely computed by about 12 percent of firms.

What explains such wide use of presumably inferior decision rules? To some extent, these rules present rough reality checks on the project. As we noted in the introduction to the chapter, managers might want to consider some simple ways to describe project profitability, even if they present obvious pitfalls. For example, managers talk casually about quick-payback projects in the same way that investors talk about high-P/E stocks. The fact that they talk about payback does not mean that the payback rule governs their decisions.

TABLE 9.7
Propensity to use various capital budgeting techniques[1]

Models Used	Replacement Projects (%)	Existing Operations (%)	Expansion— New Operations (%)	Expansion— Foreign Operations (%)	Abandonment (%)	Leasing (%)
ARR/Book Rate of Return	14.9	17.5	19.9	14.6	15.2	9.3
IRR	51.2	64.3	65.1	67.0	28.3	44.9
NPV	38.0	42.9	47.6	47.6	41.3	53.3
Payback	53.7	52.4	50.0	50.0	21.7	17.8
DCF Methods	66.1	80.9	84.9	80.5	53.3	77.6

[1] The numbers indicate the percentage of respondents citing the use of a particular technique either alone or in combination with other techniques.
Source: V. M. Jog and A. K. Srivastava, "Capital Budgeting Practices in Corporate Canada," *Financial Practice and Education* 5 (Fall/Winter 1995), pp. 37–43.

[8] See V. M. Jog and A. K. Srivastava, "Capital Budgeting Practices in Corporate Canada," *Financial Practice and Education* 5 (Fall/Winter 1995), pp. 37–43.

[9] J. R. Graham and C. R. Harvey, "The Theory and Practice of Corporate Finance: Evidence from the Field," *Journal of Financial Economics* 60 (May–June 2001), pp. 187–243.

9.6   SUMMARY

1. What are some of the practical problems of capital budgeting in large corporations?

For most large corporations there are two stages in the investment process: the preparation of the **capital budget**, which is a list of planned investments, and the authorization process for individual projects. This process is usually a cooperative effort.

Investment projects should never be selected through a purely mechanical process. Managers need to ask why a project should have a positive NPV. A positive NPV is plausible only if the company has some competitive advantage that prevents its rivals from stealing most of the gains.

2. How are sensitivity, scenario, and break-even analyses used to see the effects of forecasting errors on project profitability? Why is an overestimate of sales more serious for projects with high operating leverage?

Good managers realize that the forecasts behind NPV calculations are imperfect. Therefore, they explore the consequences of a poor forecast and check whether it is worth doing some more homework. They use the following principal tools to answer these "what if" questions:

- **Sensitivity analysis**, where one variable at a time is changed.
- **Scenario analysis**, where the manager looks at the project under alternative scenarios.
- **Simulation analysis**, an extension of scenario analysis in which a computer generates hundreds or thousands of possible combinations of variables.
- **Break-even analysis**, where the focus is on how far sales could fall before the project begins to lose money. Often the phrase "lose money" is defined in terms of accounting losses, but it makes more sense to define it as "failing to cover the opportunity cost of capital"—in other words, as a negative NPV.
- **Operating leverage**, the degree to which costs are fixed. A project's break-even point will be affected by the extent to which costs can be reduced as sales decline. If the project has mostly **fixed costs**, it is said to have *high operating leverage*. High operating leverage implies that profits are more sensitive to changes in sales.

3. Why is managerial flexibility important in capital budgeting?

Some projects may take on added value because they give the firm the option to bail out if things go wrong or to capitalize on success by expanding. These options are known as **real options**, which include options to expand, abandon, delay investment, or make use of flexible production facilities. We showed how **decision trees** may be used to set out the possible choices.

4. How do Canadian firms make their capital budgeting decisions?

A survey reports that most firms use multiple capital budgeting methods to assess capital investments, including the NPV, IRR, and payback rules. For purposes of cash-flow forecasting, firms use quantitative methods, such as sensitivity analysis, as well as qualitative methods, such as management's subjective estimates. Strategic considerations are very important in capital budgeting decisions.

Related Web Links

www.windpower.dk/tour/econ/econ.htm Evaluation of a sample energy-saving project

www.palisade.com Software for Monte Carlo analysis

www.suncor.com Web site of Suncor Energy

www.lockheedmartin.com Web site of Lockheed Martin

Key Terms

capital budget	276	break-even analysis	281	degree of operating	
sensitivity analysis	278	economic value		leverage (DOL)	287
fixed costs	279	added (EVA)	283	decision tree	289
variable costs	279	economic break-even		real options	291
scenario analysis	280	point	283		
simulation analysis	281	operating leverage	287		

Questions and Problems

*Answers in Appendix B

BASIC

*1. **Fixed and Variable Costs.** In a slow year, Wimpy's Burgers will produce 1 million hamburgers at a total cost of $1.75 million. In a good year, it can produce 2 million hamburgers at a total cost of $2.25 million. What are the fixed and variable costs of hamburger production?

2. **Average Cost.** Reconsider Wimpy's Burgers from problem 1.
   a. What is the average cost per burger when the firm produces 1 million hamburgers?
   b. What is average cost when the firm produces 2 million hamburgers?
   c. Why is average cost lower when more burgers are produced?

3. **Sensitivity Analysis.** A project currently generates sales of $10 million, variable costs equal to 50 percent of sales, and fixed costs of $2 million. The firm's tax rate is 35 percent. What are the effects of the following changes on after-tax profits and cash flows?
   a. Sales increase from $10 million to $11 million.
   b. Variable costs increase to 60 percent of sales.

PRACTICE

4. **Sensitivity Analysis.** The project in problem 3 will last for 10 years. The discount rate is 12 percent.
   a. What is the effect on project NPV of each of the changes considered in the problem?
   b. If project NPV under the base-case scenario is $2 million, how much can fixed costs increase before NPV turns negative?
   c. How much can fixed costs increase before accounting profits turn negative?

*5. **Sensitivity Analysis.** Emperor's Clothes Fashions can invest $5 million in a new plant for producing invisible makeup. The plant has an expected life of 5 years, and expected sales are 6 million jars of makeup a year. Fixed costs are $2 million a year, and variable costs are $1 per jar. The product will be priced at $2 per jar. The plant will be depreciated straight-line over five years to a salvage value of zero. The opportunity cost of capital is 12 percent, and the tax rate is 40 percent.
   a. What is project NPV under these base-case assumptions?
   b. What is NPV if variable costs turn out to be $1.20 per jar?
   c. What is NPV if fixed costs turn out to be $1.5 million per year?
   d. At what price per jar would the project NPV equal zero?

6. **Scenario Analysis.** The most likely outcomes for a particular project are estimated as follows:

Unit price:	$50
Variable cost:	$30
Fixed cost:	$300,000
Expected sales:	30,000 units per year

   However, you recognize that some of these estimates are subject to error. Suppose that each variable may turn out to be either 10 percent higher or 10 percent lower than the initial estimate. The project will last for 10 years and requires an initial investment of $1 million, which will be depreciated straight-line over the project life to a final value of zero. The firm's tax rate is 35 percent and the required rate of return is 14 percent. What is project NPV in the "best-case" scenario, that is, assuming all variables take on the best possible value? What about the "worst-case" scenario?

7. **Scenario Analysis.** Reconsider the best- and worst-case scenarios in the previous problem. In terms of the combination of variables, do the best- and worst-case outcomes seem reasonable when each variable is treated independently? For example, if price is higher than predicted, is it more or less likely that cost is higher than predicted? What other relationships may exist among the variables?

8. **Break-Even.** The following estimates have been prepared for a project under consideration:

Fixed costs: $20,000
Depreciation: $10,000
Price: $2
Accounting break-even: 60,000 units

What must be the variable cost per unit?

EXCEL

*9. **Break-Even.** Dime a Dozen Diamonds makes synthetic diamonds by treating carbon. Each diamond can be sold for $100. The materials cost for a standard diamond is $30. The fixed costs incurred each year for factory upkeep and administrative expenses are $200,000. The machinery costs $1 million and is depreciated straight-line over 10 years to a salvage value of zero.
   a. What is the accounting break-even level of sales in terms of number of diamonds sold?
   b. What is the NPV break-even level of sales assuming a tax rate of 35 percent, a 10-year project life, and a discount rate of 12 percent?

10. **Break-Even.** Turn back to problem 9.
   a. Would the accounting break-even point in the first year of operation increase or decrease if the machinery were depreciated over a five-year period?
   b. Would the NPV break-even point increase or decrease if the machinery were depreciated over a five-year period?

*11. **Break-Even.** You are evaluating a project that will require an investment of $10 million that will be depreciated over a period of seven years. You are concerned that the corporate tax rate will increase during the life of the project. Would such an increase affect the accounting break-even point? Would it affect the NPV break-even point?

*12. **Break-Even.** Define the *cash-flow break-even point* as the sales volume (in dollars) at which cash flow equals zero. Is the cash-flow break-even level of sales higher or lower than the zero-profit break-even point?

13. **Break-Even and NPV.** If a project operates at cash-flow break-even (see problem 12) for its entire life, what must be true of the project's NPV?

14. **Break-Even.** Modern Artifacts can produce keepsakes that will be sold for $80 each. Non-depreciated fixed costs are $1,000 per year and variable costs are $60 per unit.
   a. If the project requires an initial investment of $3,000 and is expected to last for 5 years and the firm pays no taxes, what are the accounting and NPV break-even levels of sales? The initial investment will be depreciated straight-line over 5 years to a final value of zero, and the discount rate is 10 percent.
   b. How do your answers change if the firm's tax rate is 40 percent?

*15. **Break-Even.** A financial analyst based in the United States has computed both accounting and NPV break-even sales levels for a project under consideration using straight-line depreciation over a six-year period. The project manager wants to know what will happen to these estimates if the firm uses depreciation calculated on the basis of the Modified Accelerated Cost Recovery System (MACRS). Firms in the United States are allowed by the Internal Revenue Service to depreciate their equipment for tax purposes using this system. The capital investment will be in a five-year recovery period class under MACRS rules. Under the rules, applicable percentage depreciation rates over years 1 to 6 will be 20, 32, 19.20, 11.52, 11.52, and 5.76, so the firm will be able to use higher rates in earlier years. The firm is in a 35 percent tax bracket.
   a. What (qualitatively) will happen to the accounting break-even level of sales in the first years of the project?
   b. What (qualitatively) will happen to the NPV break-even level of sales?
   c. If you were advising the analyst, would the answer to (a) or (b) be important to you? Specifically, would you say that the switch to MACRS makes the project more or less attractive?

16. **Break-Even. Reconsider Finefodder's new superstore.** Suppose that by initially investing an additional $600,000 in more efficient checkout equipment, Finefodder could reduce variable costs to 80 percent of sales.
    a. Using the base-case assumptions (Table 9.1), find the NPV of this alternative scheme. *Hint*: Remember to focus on the *incremental* cash flows from the project.
    b. At what level of sales will accounting profits be unchanged if the firm invests in the new equipment? Assume the equipment receives the same 12-year straight-line depreciation treatment as in the original example. *Hint*: Focus on the project's incremental effects on fixed and variable costs.
    c. What is the NPV break-even point?

*17. **Break-Even and NPV.** If the superstore project (see the previous problem) operates at accounting break-even, will net present value be positive or negative?

18. **Operating Leverage.** You estimate that your cattle farm will generate $1 million of profits on sales of $4 million under normal economic conditions, and that the degree of operating leverage is 7.5. What will profits be if sales turn out to be $3.5 million? What if they are $4.5 million?

19. **Operating Leverage.**
    a. What is the degree of operating leverage of Modern Artifacts (in problem 14) when sales are $8,000?
    b. What is the degree of operating leverage when sales are $10,000?
    c. Why is operating leverage different at these two levels of sales?

*20. **Operating Leverage.** What is the lowest possible value for the degree of operating leverage for a profitable firm? Show with a numerical example that if Modern Artifacts (see problem 14a) has zero fixed costs, then DOL = 1, and in fact, sales and profits are directly proportional so that a 1 percent change in sales results in a 1 percent change in profits.

EXCEL

21. **Operating Leverage.** A project has fixed costs of $1,000 per year, depreciation charges of $500 a year, revenue of $6,000 a year, and variable costs equal to two-thirds of revenues.
    a. If sales increase by 5 percent, what will be the increase in pretax profits?
    b. What is the degree of operating leverage of this project?
    c. Confirm that the percentage change in profits equals DOL times the percentage change in sales.

EXCEL

22. **Project Options.** Your midrange guess as to the amount of oil in a prospective field is 10 million barrels, but in fact there is a 50 percent chance that the amount of oil is 15 million barrels, and a 50 percent chance of 5 million barrels. If the actual amount of oil is 15 million barrels, the present value of the cash flows from drilling will be $8 million. If the amount is only 5 million barrels, the present value will be only $2 million. It costs $3 million to drill the well. Suppose that a seismic test that costs $100,000 can verify the amount of oil under the ground. Is it worth paying for the test? Use a decision tree to justify your answer.

*23. **Project Options.** A silver mine can yield 10,000 ounces of copper at a variable cost of $8 per ounce. The fixed costs of operating the mine are $10,000 per year. In half the years, silver can be sold for $12 per ounce; in the other years, silver can be sold for only $6 per ounce. Ignore taxes.
    a. What is the average cash flow you will receive from the mine if it is always kept in operation and the silver is always sold in the year it is mined?
    b. Now suppose you can shut down the mine in years of low silver prices. What happens to the average cash flow from the mine?

24. **Project Options.** An auto plant that costs $100 million to build can produce a new line of cars that will produce cash flows with a present value of $140 million if the line is

successful, but only $50 million if it is unsuccessful. You believe that the probability of success is only about 50 percent.

a. Would you build the plant?

b. Suppose that the plant can be sold for $90 million to another automaker if the auto line is not successful. Now would you build the plant?

c. Illustrate the option to abandon in (b) using a decision tree.

25. **Production Options.** Explain why options to expand or contract production are most valuable when forecasts about future business conditions are most uncertain.

26. **Standard & Poor's.** Go to Market Insight (**www.mcgrawhill.ca/edumarketinsight**).

a. Can you guess Dell's incremental cost for producing one computer? You probably have that amount in your wallet or purse! Let's estimate the sales break-even point and degree of operating leverage for Dell Computer (DELL). Go to the annual income statement. With reference to Table 9.4, treating S&GA and depreciation expense as our proxy for fixed costs, and costs of goods sold as variable costs, estimate the break-even level of sales for Dell for the last year (annual).

b. Estimate Dell's degree of operating leverage (DOL) by calculating the percentage change in operating profits compared to the previous year and dividing that by the percentage change in sales. How does that compare to the result you would obtain for operating leverage using the formula DOL = 1 + fixed costs/profits? Why is there a difference when using these two approaches?

27. **Decision Tree.** Zoom Technologies, Inc., is considering expanding its operations into digital music devices. Zoom anticipates an initial investment of $1.3 million and, at best, an operational life of 3 years for the project. Zoom's management team has considered several probable outcomes over the life of the project, which it has labelled as either "successes" or "failures." Accordingly, Zoom anticipates that in the first year of operations there is a 65 percent chance of "success," with after-tax cash flow of $800,000, or a 35 percent chance of "failure," with a meagre $1,000 cash flow after tax.

If the project "succeeds" in the first year, Zoom expects three probable outcomes regarding net cash flows after tax in the second year. These outcomes are $2.2 million, $1.8 million, or $1.5 million, with probabilities of 0.3, 0.5, and 0.2, respectively. In the third and final year of operation, the net cash flows after tax are expected to be either $35,000 more or $55,000 less than they were in Year 2, with an equal chance of occurrence.

If, on the other hand, the project "fails" in Year 1, there is a 60 percent chance that it will produce net cash flows after tax of only $1,500 in years 2 and 3. There is also a 40 percent chance that it will really fail and Zoom will earn nothing in Year 2, and will get out of this line of business, terminating the project and resulting in no net cash flows after tax in Year 3.

The opportunity cost of capital for Zoom Technologies is 10 percent.

a. Construct a decision tree representing the possible outcomes.

b. Determine the joint probability of each possible sequence of events.

c. What is the project's expected NPV?

*28. **Abandonment Option.** Hit or Miss Sports is introducing a new product this year. If its see-at-night soccer balls are a hit, the firm expects to be able to sell 50,000 units a year at a price of $60 each. If the new product is a bust, only 30,000 units can be sold at a price of $55. The variable cost of each ball is $30 and fixed costs are zero. The cost of the manufacturing equipment is $6 million, and the project life is estimated at 10 years. The firm will use straight-line depreciation over the 10-year life of the project. The firm's tax rate is 35 percent and the discount rate is 12 percent.

    a.   If each outcome is equally likely, what is the expected NPV? Will the firm accept the project?

    b.   Suppose now that the firm can abandon the project and sell off the manufacturing equipment for $5.4 million if demand for the balls turns out to be weak. The firm will make the decision to continue or abandon after the first year of sales. Does the option to abandon change the firm's decision to accept the project?

29. **Expansion Option.** Now suppose that Hit or Miss Sports from the previous problem can expand production if the project is successful. By paying its workers overtime, it can increase production by 20,000 units; the variable cost of each ball will be higher, equal to $35 per unit. By how much does this option to expand production increase the NPV of the project?

Solutions to Check Points

9.1   Cash flow forecasts for Finefodder's new superstore:

	Year 0	Years 1–12
Investment	–5,400,000	
1. Sales		16,000,000
2. Variable costs		13,280,000
3. Fixed costs		2,000,000
4. Depreciation		450,000
5. Pretax profit (1 – 2 – 3 – 4)		270,000
6. Taxes (at 40%)		108,000
7. Profit after tax		162,000
8. Cash flow from operations (4 + 7)		612,000
Net cash flow	–5,400,000	612,000

$$\text{NPV} = -\$5.4 \text{ million} + (7.536 \times \$612,000) = -\$788,000$$

9.2   Both calculate how NPV depends on input assumptions. Sensitivity analysis changes inputs one at a time, whereas scenario analysis changes several variables at once. The changes should add up to a consistent scenario for the project as a whole.

9.3   Cash flow = net income + depreciation. From the table on page 284, we see that net income (i.e., after-tax accounting profit) is $.60 \times (.1875 \times \text{sales} - \$2.45 \text{ million})$, and depreciation is $.45 million. Therefore,

        Cash flow = $.60 \times (.1875 \times \text{sales} - \$2.45) + .45 = .1125 \times \text{sales} - \$1.02$ million.

    For a sales level of $15.436 million, cash flow will be $.71655 million. The 12-year annuity factor for an interest rate of 8 percent is 7.536. Therefore, the present value of project cash flows is $.71655 \times 7.536 = \$5.4$ million, just equal to the initial investment. Project NPV = 0.

9.4   With the lower initial investment, depreciation is also lower; it now equals $417,000 per year. Cash flow is now as follows:

1. Variable costs	81.25 percent of sales
2. Fixed costs	$2 million
3. Depreciation	$417,000
4. Pretax profit	$(.1875 \times \text{sales}) - \$2.417$ million
5. Tax (at 40%)	$.4 \times (.1875 \times \text{sales} - \$2.417$ million$)$
6. Profit after tax	$.6 \times (.1875 \times \text{sales} - \$2.417$ million$)$
7. Cash flow (3 + 6)	$.6 \times (.1875 \times \text{sales} - \$2.417$ million$) + \$417,000$
	$= .1125 \times \text{sales} - \$1.033$ million

Break-even occurs when

$$\begin{array}{ll} \text{PV (cash inflows)} & = \text{investment} \\ 7.536 \times (.1125 \times \text{sales} - \$1.033 \text{ million}) & = \$5.0 \text{ million} \end{array}$$

and sales = $15.08 million.

9.5   Break-even analysis finds the level of sales or revenue at which NPV = 0. Sensitivity analysis changes these and other input variables to optimistic and pessimistic values and recalculates NPV.

9.6   Reworking Table 9.6 for the normal level of sales and 10 percent higher sales gives the following:

	High Fixed Costs		**High Variable Costs**	
	Normal	**10% Higher Sales**	**Normal**	**10% Higher Sales**
Sales	16,000	17,600	16,000	17,600
– Variable costs	13,000	14,300	13,440	14,784
– Fixed costs	2,000	2,000	1,560	1,560
– Depreciation	450	450	450	450
= Pretax profit	550	850	550	806

For the high-fixed-cost policy, profits increase by 54.5 percent, from $550,000 to $850,000. For the low-fixed-cost policy, profits increase by 46.5 percent. In both cases the percentage increase in profits equals DOL times the percentage increase in sales. This illustrates that DOL measures the sensitivity of profits to changes in sales.

9.7   A decision tree model for Goody Foods' choc-o-spice cookie project is provided below:

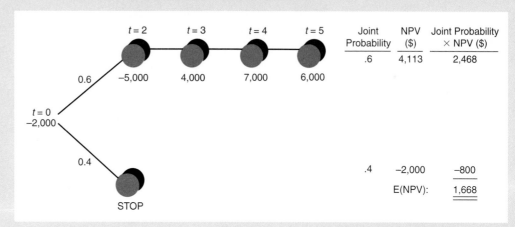

NPV analysis for satisfactory outcome ($000s)

Year	Cash Flows ($)	Present Value = 1/(1.14)^t	Discounted Cash Flows ($)
0	–2,000	1.0000	–2,000
1	—	.8772	
2	–5,000	.7695	–3,848
3	4,000	.6750	2,700
4	7,000	.5921	4,145
5	6,000	.5194	3,116
		NPV	4,113

9.8   See Figure 9.4. Note that while technology A delivers the higher NPV if demand is high, technology B has the advantage of a higher salvage value if demand is unexpectedly low.

FIGURE 9.4
Example of a decision tree for Widgeon Company

9.9   The option to shut down is valuable because the mine operator can avoid incurring losses when copper prices are low. If the shut-down option were not available, cash flow in the low-price periods would be negative. With the option, the worst cash flow is zero. By allowing managers to respond to market conditions, the option makes the worst-case cash flow better than it would be otherwise. The average cash flow (that is, averaging over all possible scenarios) therefore must improve, which increases project NPV.

9.10   Abandonment options, options due to flexible production facilities, and investment timing options.

MINICASE

Maxine Peru, the CEO of Peru Resources, hardly noticed the plate of savoury quenelles de brochet and the glass of Corton Charlemagne '94 on the table before her. She was absorbed by the engineering report handed to her just as she entered the executive dining room.

The report described a proposed new mine on the North Ridge of Mt. Zircon. A vein of transcendental zirconium ore had been discovered there on land owned by Peru's company. Test borings indicated sufficient reserves to produce 340 tonnes per year of transcendental zirconium over a 7-year period.

The vein probably also contained hydrated zircon gemstones. The amount and quality of these zircons were hard to predict, since they tended to occur in "pockets." The new mine might come across one, two, or dozens of pockets. The mining engineer guessed that 150 pounds per year might be found. The current price for high-quality hydrated zircon gemstones was $3,300 per pound.

Peru Resources was a family-owned business with total assets of $45 million, including cash reserves of $4 million. The outlay required for the new mine would be a major commitment. Fortunately, Peru Resources was conservatively financed, and CEO Peru believed that the company could borrow up to $9 million at an interest rate of about 8 percent.

The mine's operating costs were projected at $900,000 per year, including $400,000 of fixed costs and $500,000 of variable costs. Peru thought these forecasts were accurate. The big question marks seemed to be the initial cost of the mine and the selling price of transcendental zirconium.

Opening the mine, and providing the necessary machinery and ore-crunching facilities, was supposed to cost $10 million, but cost overruns of 10 percent or 15 percent were common in the mining business. In addition, new environmental regulations, if enacted, could increase the cost of the mine by $1.5 million.

There was a cheaper design for the mine, which would reduce its cost by $1.7 million and eliminate much of the uncertainty about cost overruns. Unfortunately, this design would require much higher fixed operating costs. Fixed costs would increase to $850,000 per year at planned production levels.

The current price of transcendental zirconium was $10,000 per tonne, but there was no consensus about future prices.[10] Some experts were projecting rapid price increases to as much as $14,000 per tonne. On the other hand, there were pessimists saying that prices could be as low as $7,500 per tonne. Peru did not have strong views either way: her best guess was that price would just increase with inflation at about 3.5 percent per year. (Mine operating costs would also increase with inflation.)

Peru had wide experience in the mining business, and she knew that investors in similar projects usually wanted a forecast nominal rate of return of at least 14 percent.

You have been asked to assist Peru in evaluating this project. Lay out the base-case NPV analysis and undertake sensitivity, scenario, or break-even analyses as appropriate. Assume that Peru Resources pays tax at a 35 percent rate. For simplicity, also assume that the investment in the mine could be depreciated for tax purposes straight-line over seven years.

What forecasts or scenarios should worry Peru the most? Where would additional information be most helpful? Is there a case for delaying construction of the new mine?

[10] There were no traded forward or futures contracts on transcendental zirconium. See Chapter 26.

PART THREE
Risk

CHAPTER 10

INTRODUCTION TO RISK, RETURN, AND THE OPPORTUNITY COST OF CAPITAL

We have thus far skirted the issue of project risk; now it is time to confront it head-on. We can no longer be satisfied with vague statements like "The opportunity cost of capital depends on the risk of the project." We need to know how to measure risk and we need to understand the relationship between risk and the cost of capital. These are the topics of the next two chapters.

Think for a moment what the cost of capital for a project means. It is the rate of return that shareholders could expect to earn if they invested in equally risky securities. So one way to estimate the cost of capital is to find securities that have the same risk as the project and then estimate the expected rate of return on these securities.

We start our analysis by looking at the rates of return earned in the past from different investments, concentrating on the *extra* return that investors have received for investing in risky rather than safe securities. We then show how to measure the risk of a portfolio by calculating its standard deviation and we look again at past history to find out how risky it is to invest in the stock market.

Finally, we explore the concept of diversification. Most investors do not put all their eggs into one basket—they diversify. Thus investors are not concerned with the risk of each security in isolation; instead they are concerned with how much it contributes to the risk of a diversified portfolio. We therefore need to distinguish between the risk that can be eliminated by diversification and the risk that cannot be eliminated.

After studying this chapter you should be able to
- Estimate the opportunity cost of capital for an "average risk" project.
- Calculate the standard deviation of returns for individual common stocks or for a stock portfolio.
- Understand why diversification reduces risk.
- Distinguish between unique risk, which can be diversified away, and market risk, which cannot.

10.1 RATES OF RETURN: A REVIEW

When investors buy a stock or a bond, their return comes in two forms: (1) a dividend or interest payment, and (2) a capital gain or a capital loss. For example, suppose you bought the stock of Le Château at the beginning of 2004 when its price was about $12.50 a share. By the end of the year the value of that investment had appreciated to $24, giving a capital gain of $24 − 12.50 = $11.50. In addition, in 2004 Le Château paid a dividend of $.55 a share.

The *percentage* return on your investment was therefore

$$\text{Percentage return} = \frac{\text{capital gain} + \text{dividend}}{\text{initial share price}} \tag{10.1}$$

$$= \frac{\$11.50 + \$.55}{\$12.50} = .964, \text{ or } 96.4\%$$

The percentage return can also be expressed as the sum of the dividend yield and percentage capital gain. The dividend yield is the dividend expressed as a percentage of the stock price at the beginning of the year:

$$\text{Dividend yield} = \frac{\text{dividend}}{\text{initial share price}} \tag{10.2}$$

$$= \frac{\$.55}{\$12.50} = .044, \text{ or } 4.4\%$$

Similarly, the percentage capital gain is

$$\text{Percentage capital gain} = \frac{\text{capital gain}}{\text{initial share price}} \tag{10.3}$$

$$= \frac{\$11.50}{\$12.50} = .92, \text{ or } 92\%$$

Thus the total return is the sum of 4.4% + 92% = 96.4%.

EXAMPLE 10.1   **EQUIVALENT ANNUAL RATE OF RETURN**

Although a rate of return can be calculated over any time period—a day, a month, five years—the convention is to report annual rates of return. As we saw in Chapter 4, we need to calculate the *equivalent annual rate*. For example, suppose you bought a share of Canfor for $11.27 at the end of 2003 and sold it at the end of July 2004, when the stock was at $15.30 per share. The capital gain was $15.30 − $11.27 or $4.03. No dividends were paid. The percentage rate of return was $4.03/$11.27 or 35.8 percent. How does this compare with the 96.4 percent earned on Le Château over 12 months? Convert the seven-month Canfor return to its annual equivalent. First, calculate the monthly equivalent rate: $(1 + \text{7-month rate})^{1/7} - 1 = (1.358)^{1/7} - 1 = .04469$. Next, convert the monthly rate to an annual rate: $(1 + \text{1-month rate})^{12} - 1 = (1.04469)^{12} - 1 = .69$, or 69 percent per year.[1] We have not compared the riskiness of the two stocks so we can't say which investment was better.

Remember that in Chapter 4 we made a distinction between the *nominal* rate of return and the *real* rate of return. The nominal return measures how much more money you will have at the end of the year if you invest today. The 2004 return that we just calculated for Le Château stock is therefore a nominal return. The real rate of return tells you how much more you will be able to *buy* with your money at the end of the year. To convert from a nominal to a real rate of return, we use the following relationship:

---

[1] We could have jumped directly to the annual equivalent rate by recognizing that a year is 12/7 of a 7-month period, making the annual equivalent rate equal to $(1.358)^{12/7} - 1$, or 69.0 percent.

$$1 + \text{real rate of return} = \frac{1 + \text{nominal rate of return}}{1 + \text{inflation rate}} \qquad (10.4)$$

In 2004, inflation was 2 percent. So we calculate the real rate of return on Le Château stock as follows:

$$1 + \text{real rate of return} = \frac{1.964}{1.02} = 1.925$$

Therefore, the real rate of return equals .925, or 92.5 percent. Fortunately, inflation in 2004 was moderate; the real return was only slightly less than the nominal return.

Check Point 10.1

Suppose you buy a bond for $1,020 with a 15-year maturity paying an annual coupon of $80. A year later interest rates have dropped and the bond's price has increased to $1,050. What are your nominal and real rates of return? Assume the inflation rate is 4 percent.

10.2   SEVENTY-NINE YEARS OF CAPITAL MARKET HISTORY

When you invest in a stock, you don't know what return you will earn. But by looking at the history of security returns, you can get some idea of the return that investors might reasonably expect from investments in different types of securities and of the risks that they face. Let us look, therefore, at the risks and returns that investors have experienced in the past.

MARKET INDEXES

market index   Measure of the investment performance of the overall market.

S&P/TSX Composite Index Index of the investment performance of a portfolio of the major stocks listed on the Toronto Stock Exchange. Also called the TSX. Formerly called the TSE 300.

Investors can choose from an enormous number of different securities. Currently common shares, preferred shares, income trust units, and convertible debentures of almost 1,400 large, established companies are listed for trading on the Toronto Stock Exchange (TSX, **www.tsx.com**). Common shares of about 2,300 new and smaller companies trade on the Toronto Venture Exchange.[2] In addition, Canadian investors are free to cross-border shop in the U.S. and overseas markets. The New York Stock Exchange (NYSE), the major U.S. stock exchange, lists about 3,000 common stocks. Over 4,000 common stocks are traded through Nasdaq, a network of dealers linked by computer terminals and telephones. The London Stock Exchange lists common shares of about 2,800 companies; it is Europe's largest stock exchange.

Financial analysts can't track every stock, so they rely on **market indexes** to summarize the return on different classes of securities. The primary stock market index in Canada is the **S&P/TSX Composite Index**, based on a portfolio of the largest TSX stocks.[3] It is a value-weighted index, measuring the performance of a portfolio that holds shares in each firm in proportion to the number of shares that have been issued to investors. Weighting shares by their relative value rather than giving equal weight per share is a better way to measure market performance. For example, in 2004 there were 653 million Royal Bank common shares outstanding and only 57 million shares of

---

[2] The TSX Venture Exchange was created through the merger of the Vancouver and Alberta Stock Exchanges and is owned by the TSX Group, which also owns the TSX. The Bourse de Montréal, formerly known as the Montreal Exchange, no longer lists stocks (it once listed over 800 common shares) but is Canada's exclusive derivative securities market.

[3] In 2002, the TSX index replaced the *TSE 300 Composite Index*, which consisted of exactly 300 stocks. Companies must be of a minimum size and liquidity to be included in the TSX index. As of December 2004, the TSX index contained 223 stocks.

Cameco. So on average, investors did *not* hold the same number of shares of the two firms. A value-weighted index shows the *average* performance of investors in the stocks.[4]

The index is calculated by multiplying the current share prices by the number of outstanding shares.[5] The number is then divided by the original value of the index, arbitrarily taken from January 1975, and multiplied by 1,000. An index value of 8,000 says that the TSX stocks have increased 8 times from their 1975 value. If the index rises by 80 points to end the day at 8,080, the portfolio makes a capital gain of 80/8,000 = .01, or 1 percent.

TSX Total Return Index Value (TRIV)   Measure of the composite index based on the prices plus dividends paid by the stocks in the S&P/TSX Composite Index. Formerly the TSE 300 Total Return Index.

To know the total rate of return (capital gains plus dividends) on the TSX index stocks, use the **TSX Total Return Index Value (TRIV)**, which includes dividends paid to stocks in the index. For example, in November 2004, the S&P/TSX Composite Index increased from 8,870.97 to 9,030.50 points, or a 1.80 percent capital gain. Over the same period, the TSX Total Return Index Value increased from 20,494.96 to 20,892.76 points, for a total return of 1.94 percent. The higher rate of return on the TRIV comes from dividends earned during the month. Use the TRIV rate of return to compare the total rate of return on a stock to the market's return.

The fact that the TSX index is value-weighted created an interesting situation during 1999–2000 when the market value of one of its stocks, Nortel Networks, soared. At one point, Nortel accounted for more than 30 percent of the index's value. Since the index is used to assess the performance of investment portfolios, portfolio managers, especially those legally restricted to not hold more than 10 percent of their portfolio in any one company, argued that the TSX was an inappropriate benchmark. Consequently, the **S&P/TSX Capped Composite Index** was created and limited the weight on any one company to less than 10 percent. Nortel's share price has since fallen and in 2004 accounted for about 2 percent of the TSX; Manulife Financial had the highest weighting, at 4.88 percent of the index value.

S&P/TSX Capped Composite Index   Index based on the prices of the TSX stocks, with no stock weighted more than 10 percent. Formerly the TSE 300 Capped Index.

Dow Jones Industrial Average   U.S. index of the investment performance of a portfolio of 30 "blue-chip" stocks.

The best-known stock market index in the United States is the **Dow Jones Industrial Average**, generally known as *the Dow*. The Dow tracks the performance of a portfolio that holds one share in each of 30 large firms.

However, the Dow is far from the best measure of the performance of the U.S. stock market. First, with only 30 large industrial stocks, it is not representative of the performance of stocks generally. Second, unlike the TSX, it is an equal-weighted index. Despite the fact that in 2004 there were 10.6 billion shares in General Electric and only 1 billion shares of DuPont, the index gave equal weight to each company. An equal-weighted portfolio cannot reflect the average performance of investors in the stocks.

Standard & Poor's Composite Index   U.S. index of the investment performance of a portfolio of 500 large stocks. Also called the S&P 500.

The **Standard & Poor's Composite Index**, better known as the *S&P 500*, includes the stocks of 500 major U.S. companies and is therefore a more comprehensive index than the Dow. Like the TSX index, it measures the performance of a portfolio that holds shares in each firm in proportion to the number of shares that have been issued to investors.[6]

Only a small proportion of the thousands of publicly traded companies are represented in the TSX or the S&P 500. However, these firms are among the largest in Canada and the United States, respectively, and they account for roughly 70 percent of the stocks traded. Therefore, success for professional investors usually means "beating the TSX" or "beating the S&P."

Market indexes track performance of stock markets around the world. The main index of the London Stock Exchange, the world's third largest stock market after the NYSE and Nasdaq, is

---

[4] Although Royal had about 11.5 times the number of shares of Cameco, the Royal Bank index weight was 4.582 percent and Cameco's weight was .7223 percent, giving a Royal common share about 6.34 (= 4.582/.7223) times more weight than a Cameco share. This reflects the fact that Royal Bank shares were trading around $63 per share and Cameco's shares were worth about $114 per share. The relative value of Royal Bank's common stock to Cameco's was $63 × 653 million/$114 × 57 million, or 6.33 times.

[5] For some stocks, a portion of shares is not available to investors for trading, such as shares held by a control group, founding family, another company, or a government. If 20 percent or more of the shares are held by controlling shareholders, these shares are subtracted from the total number of shares to determine the *float* shares. The weights for the S&P/TSX index stocks are based on the number of float shares.

[6] As of September 2005, the S&P 500 and all other U.S. S&P stock indexes will be calculated based on the number of float shares (shares outside control groups), similar to the way the TSX index is calculated. For details see **www.spglobal.com**.

the Financial Times Stock Exchange Index, FTSE 100, or the "footsie." The Tokyo Stock Exchange market index is the Nikkei 225. Many other indexes have been created to measure performance of special groups of stock, such as the S&P/TSX SmallCap Index based on smaller companies listed on the TSX. Morgan Stanley Capital International (MSCI) even computes a world stock market index and Standard & Poor's produces many indexes for markets around the world. Visit the S&P Web site at **www.spglobal.com** to learn more.

THE HISTORICAL RECORD

The historical returns of stock or bond market indexes can give us an idea of the typical performance of different investments. Using data prepared by the Canadian Institute of Actuaries and Statistics Canada (CANSIM),[7] we can measure the investment performance of three portfolios of securities since 1925:

1. A portfolio of 91-day government securities, known as Treasury bills.[8]
2. A portfolio of long-term Canadian government bonds.
3. A portfolio of stocks of large Canadian companies.[9]

These portfolios are not equally risky. Treasury bills are about as safe an investment as you can make. Because they are issued by the government, you can be sure that you will get your money back. Their short-term maturity means that their prices are relatively stable. In fact, investors who wish to lend money for three months can achieve a certain payoff by buying three-month Treasury bills. Of course, they can't be sure what that money will buy; there is still some uncertainty about inflation.

Long-term government bonds are also certain to be repaid when they mature, but the prices of these bonds fluctuate more as interest rates vary. When interest rates fall, the value of long-term bonds rises; when rates rise, the value of the bonds falls.

Common stocks are the riskiest of the three groups of securities. When you invest in common stocks, there is no promise that you will get your money back. As a part-owner of the corporation, you receive whatever is left over after the bonds and any other debts have been repaid.

Figure 10.1 shows the performance of the three groups of securities assuming that all dividend or interest income had been reinvested in the portfolio. You can see that the performance of the portfolios fits our intuitive risk ranking. Common stocks were the riskiest investment but they also offered the greatest gains. One dollar invested at the end of 1925 in a portfolio of common stocks would have grown to $1,595 by 2004. At the other end of the spectrum, an investment of $1 in a Treasury bill would have accumulated to only $36.25.

Table 10.1 shows the average of the annual returns from each of these portfolios. These rates of return are comparable to the return that we calculated for Le Château. In other words, they include (1) dividends or interest and (2) any capital gains or losses.

maturity premium Extra average return from investing in long-term bonds versus short-term Treasury securities.

The safest investment, Treasury bills, had the lowest rates of return—they averaged 4.7 percent a year. Long-term government bonds gave slightly higher returns than Treasury bills. This difference is called the **maturity premium**. Common stocks were in a class by themselves. Investors who accepted the risk of common stocks received on average an extra return of 6.7 percent a year over the return on Treasury bills. This compensation for taking on the risk of common stock ownership is known as the **market risk premium**:

risk premium Expected return in excess of risk-free return as compensation for risk.

---

[7] The main data source was the Canadian Institute of Actuaries Report on Canadian Economic Statistics 1924–2003, retrieved May 18, 2004, from **www.actuaries.ca/publications/documents_reports_e.html**. 2004 Government of Canada Long Bond Index V122587 and 91-day Treasury Bill V122541 data from CANSIM, retrieved June 17, 2004, from Statistics Canada Web site, **www.statscan.ca**.

[8] Canada did not have Treasury bills until 1934. We used U.S. Treasury bill data from Ibbotson Associates adjusted for the U.S.–Canada exchange rate for the years 1926 to 1933.

[9] Stock data used in the *Report on Canadian Economic Statistics* comes from different sources. A stock index from M.C. Urquhart and K.A.H. Buckley, *Historical Statistics of Canada* (Toronto: Macmillan, 1965) is used for 1926 to 1934. The TSE Industrial Index is used for 1935 to 1956. In 1956, the TSE 300 index began and then was replaced by S&P/TSX index in 2002. For convenience, we refer to this portfolio as the TSX.

FIGURE 10.1
The value to which a $1 investment made at the end of 1925 would have grown by the end of 2004 (index values plotted on log scale)

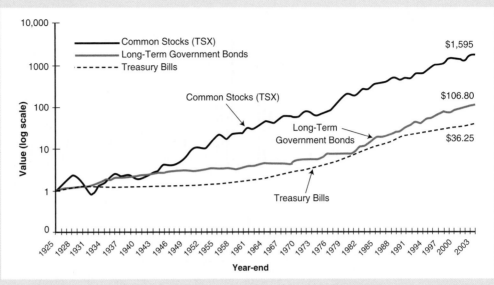

Adapted from Statistics Canada CANSIM database http://cansim2.statcan.ca. Series V122620, V122587, and V122541.

$$\text{Rate of return} \atop \text{on common stocks} = {\text{interest rate on} \atop \text{Treasury bills}} + {\text{market risk} \atop \text{premium}} \qquad (10.5)$$

> The historical record shows that investors have received a risk premium for holding risky assets. Average returns on high-risk assets are higher than those on low-risk assets.

You may ask why we look back over such a long period to measure average rates of return. The reason is that annual rates of return for common stocks fluctuate so much that averages taken over short periods are extremely unreliable. In some years investors in common stocks had a disagreeable shock and received a substantially lower return than they expected. In other years they had a pleasant surprise and received a higher-than-expected return. By averaging the returns across both the rough years and the smooth ones, we should get a fair idea of the typical return that investors might justifiably expect.

While common stocks have offered the highest average returns, they have also been riskier investments. Figure 10.2 shows the 79 annual rates of return for the stock portfolio. The fluctuations in year-to-year returns on common stocks are remarkably wide. There were 2 years (1933 and 1950) when investors earned a return of around 50 percent. However, Figure 10.2 shows that you can also lose money by investing in the stock market. The most dramatic case was the world stock market crash of 1929/1932. Between 1929 and 1932, the Canadian stock markets fell 64 percent and the U.S. stock market fell almost 90 percent.

TABLE 10.1
Average rates of return on Treasury bills, government bonds, and common stocks, 1926–2004 (figures in percent per year)

Portfolio	Average Annual Rate of Return	Average Risk Premium (Extra Return versus Treasury Bills)
Treasury bills	4.7	
Long-term government bonds	6.4	1.7
Common stocks	11.4	6.7

Source: Authors' calculations using data from Canadian Institute of Actuaries, *Report on Canadian Economic Statistics 1924–2003*. Adapted from Statistics Canada CANSIM database http://cansim2.statcan.ca. Series V122620, V122587, and V122541.

FIGURE 10.2
Rates of return on common stock, 1926–2004

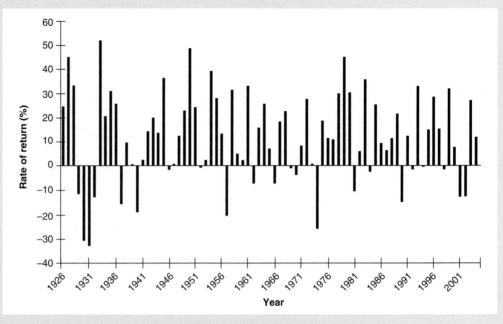

Source: Authors' calculations using data from Canadian Institute of Actuaries, *Report on Canadian Economic Statistics 1924–2003*. Adapted from Statistics Canada CANSIM database http://cansim2.statcan.ca. Series V122620, V122587, and V122541.

The period between 1999 and 2002 was another time of extreme volatility. With massive business investment in new information-based technologies, the value of telecommunications, technology, and dot-com stocks boomed. This fuelled double-digit increases in prices on world stock markets between 1999 and mid-2000. The TSX index rose almost 32 percent in 1999 and reached an all-time high by September 2000, giving more than a 35 percent increase in the first 8 months of 2000. With its heavier concentration in technology and dot-com stocks, the Nasdaq index increased nearly 103 percent from the start of 1999 to its peak in March of 2000. The gains were not sustained, with stock prices falling more than 12 percent in both 2001 and 2002. The market rebounded again, with the TSX earning more than 26 percent in 2003 and 11.5 percent in 2004.

Bond prices also fluctuate, but far less than stock prices. The worst year for investors in our long-term bond portfolio was 1994; their return that year was –10.5 percent.

Check Point 10.2

Here are the average rates of return for common stocks, government bonds, and Treasury bills for three different periods:

	1926–1949	1950–1975	1976–2004
Stocks	9.8	11.6	12.6
Government bonds	4.8	2.7	11.1
Treasury bills	1.2	3.9	8.4

What were the risk premium on stocks and the maturity premium on government bonds for each period?

USING HISTORICAL EVIDENCE TO ESTIMATE TODAY'S COST OF CAPITAL

Think back now to Chapter 7, where we showed how firms calculate the present value of a new project by discounting the expected cash flows by the opportunity cost of capital. The opportunity cost of capital is the return that the firm's shareholders are giving up by investing in the project rather than in comparable risk alternatives.

Measuring the cost of capital is easy if the project is a sure thing. Since shareholders can obtain a sure-fire payoff by investing in a Government of Canada Treasury bill, the firm should invest in a risk-free project only if it can at least match the rate of interest on such a loan. If the project is risky—and most projects are—then the firm needs to at least match the return that shareholders could expect to earn if they invested in securities of similar risk. It is not easy to put a precise figure on this, but our skim through history provides an idea of the average return an investor might expect to earn from an investment in risky common stocks.

Suppose there is an investment project that you *know*—don't ask how—has the same risk as an investment in the portfolio of stocks in the S&P/TSX Composite Index. We will say that it has the same degree of risk as the *market portfolio* of common stocks.[10]

Instead of investing in the project, your shareholders could invest directly in this market portfolio of common stocks. Therefore, the opportunity cost of capital for your project is the return that the shareholders could expect to earn on the market portfolio. This is what they are giving up by investing money in your project.

The problem of estimating the project cost of capital boils down to estimating the currently expected rate of return on the market portfolio. One way to estimate the expected market return is to assume that the future will be like the past and that today's investors expect to receive the average rates of return shown in Table 10.1. In this case, you would judge that the expected market return today is 11.4 percent, the average of past market returns.

Unfortunately, this is not the way to do it. Investors are not likely to demand the same return each year on an investment in common stocks. For example, we know that the interest rate on safe Treasury bills varies over time. At their peak in 1981, Treasury bills offered a return of 20 percent, more than 15 percentage points above the 4.7 percent average return on bills shown in Table 10.1.

What if you were called upon to estimate the expected return on common stocks in 1981? Would you have said 11.4 percent? That doesn't make sense. Who would invest in the risky stock market for an expected return of 11.4 percent when you could get a safe 20 percent from Treasury bills?

A better procedure is to take the current interest rate on Treasury bills plus 6.7 percent, the average *risk premium* shown in Table 10.1. In 1981, when the rate on Treasury bills was 20 percent, that would have given

$$\begin{matrix} \text{Expected market} \\ \text{return (1981)} \end{matrix} = \begin{matrix} \text{interest rate on} \\ \text{Treasury bills (1981)} \end{matrix} + \begin{matrix} \text{normal risk} \\ \text{premium} \end{matrix}$$
$$= \ 20\% + 6.7\% = 26.7\%$$

The first term on the right-hand side tells us the time value of money in 1981; the second term measures the compensation for risk.

> The expected return on an investment provides compensation to investors both for waiting (the time value of money) and for worrying (the risk of the particular asset).

What about today? As we write this in early 2005, Treasury bills offer a return of only 2.5 percent. This suggests that investors in common stocks are looking for a return of just over 9 percent:[11]

$$\begin{matrix} \text{Expected market} \\ \text{return (2005)} \end{matrix} = \begin{matrix} \text{interest rate on} \\ \text{Treasury bills (2005)} \end{matrix} + \begin{matrix} \text{normal risk} \\ \text{premium} \end{matrix}$$
$$= \ 2.5\% + 6.7\% = 9.2\%$$

These calculations assume that there is a normal, stable risk premium on the market portfolio, so that the expected *future* risk premium can be measured by the average past risk premium.

---

[10] This is speaking a bit loosely, because the TSX does not include all stocks traded in Canada, much less in world markets.

[11] In practice, things might be a bit more complicated. We've mentioned the yield curve, the relationship between bond maturity and yield. When firms consider investments in long-lived projects, they usually think about risk premiums relative to long-term bonds. In this case, the risk-free rate would be taken as the current long-term bond yield less the average maturity premium on such bonds.

But even with 79 years of data, we cannot estimate the market risk premium exactly; moreover, we cannot be sure that investors today are demanding the same reward for risk that they were in the 1940s or 1960s. All this leaves plenty of room for argument about what the risk premium *really* is. Many financial managers and economists believe that long-run historical returns are the best measure available and therefore settle on a risk premium of about 6 to 7 percent. Others have a gut instinct that investors don't need such a large risk premium to persuade them to hold common stocks and so shade downward their estimate of the expected future risk premium.

10.3   MEASURING RISK

You now have some benchmarks. You know that the opportunity cost of capital for safe projects must be the rate of return offered by safe Treasury bills and you know that the opportunity cost of capital for "average risk" projects must be the expected return on the market portfolio. But you *don't* know how to estimate the cost of capital for projects that do not fit these two simple cases. Before you can do this you need to understand more about investment risk.

The average fuse time for army hand grenades is seven seconds, but that average hides a lot of potentially relevant information. If you are in the business of throwing grenades, you need some measure of the variation around the average fuse time.[12] Similarly, if you are in the business of investing in securities, you need some measure of how far the returns may differ from the average.

One way to present the spread of possible investment returns is by using histograms, such as the ones in Figure 10.3. The bars in each histogram show the number of years between 1926 and 2004 that the investment's return fell within a specific range. Look first at the performance of common stocks. Their risk shows up in the wide spread of outcomes. For example, you can see that in one year the return was between +50 and +55 percent but in two other years, investors lost between 30 and 35 percent.

The corresponding histograms for government bonds and Treasury bills show that unusually high or low returns are much less common. Investors in these securities face a smaller range of outcomes than do investors in common stocks.

VARIANCE AND STANDARD DEVIATION

Investment risk depends on the dispersion or spread of possible outcomes. For example, Figure 10.3 shows that on past evidence there is a greater uncertainty about the possible returns from common stocks than about the returns from Treasury bills or bonds. Sometimes a picture like Figure 10.3 tells you all you need to know about (past) dispersion. But in general, pictures do not suffice. The financial manager needs a numerical measure of dispersion. The standard measures are **variance** and **standard deviation**. More variable returns imply greater investment risk. This suggests that some measure of dispersion will provide a reasonable measure of risk, and dispersion is precisely what is measured by variance and standard deviation.

variance   Average value of squared deviations from mean. A measure of volatility.

standard deviation   Square root of variance. Another measure of volatility.

Here is a very simple example showing how variance and standard deviation are calculated. Suppose that you are offered the chance to play the following game. You start by investing $100. Then two coins are flipped. For each head that comes up your starting balance will be *increased* by 20 percent, and for each tail that comes up your starting balance will be *reduced* by 10 percent. There are four equally likely outcomes:

- Head + head: You make 20 + 20 = 40%
- Head + tail: You make 20 − 10 = 10%
- Tail + head: You make −10 + 20 = 10%
- Tail + tail: You make −10 − 10 = −20%

---

[12] We can reassure you; the variation around the standard fuse time is very small.

FIGURE 10.3
Historical returns on major asset classes, 1926–2004

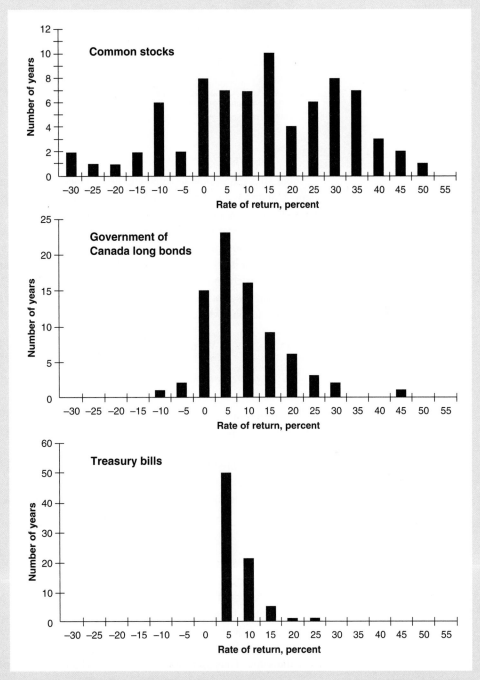

Source: Authors' calculations using data from Canadian Institute of Actuaries, *Report on Canadian Economic Statistics 1924–2003*. Adapted from Statistics Canada CANSIM database http://cansim2.statcan.ca. Series V122620, V122587, and V122541.

There is a chance of 1 in 4, or .25, that you will make 40 percent; a chance of 2 in 4, or .5, that you will make 10 percent; and a chance of 1 in 4, or .25, that you will lose 20 percent. The game's expected return is therefore a weighted average of the possible outcomes:

Expected return = probability-weighted average of possible outcomes   (10.6)

$$= (.25 \times 40) + (.5 \times 10) + (.25 \times -20) = +10\%$$

If you play the game a very large number of times, your average return should be 10 percent.

TABLE 10.2

The coin-toss game: calculating variance and standard deviation when there are equal probabilities of each outcome

(1) Percent Rate of Return	(2) Deviation from Expected Return	(3) Squared Deviation
+40	+30	900
+10	0	0
+10	0	0
−20	−30	900

Variance = average of squared deviations = 1,800/4 = 450

Standard deviation = square root of variance = $\sqrt{450}$ = 21.2, about 21%

Table 10.2 shows how to calculate the variance and standard deviation of the returns on your game. Column 1 shows the four equally likely outcomes. In column 2 we calculate the difference between each possible outcome and the expected outcome. You can see that at best the return could be 30 percent higher than expected; at worst it could be 30 percent lower.

These deviations in column 2 illustrate the spread of possible returns. But if we want a measure of this spread, it is no use just averaging the deviations in column 2—the average is always going to be zero. To get around this problem, we square the deviations in column 2 before averaging them. These squared deviations are shown in column 3. The variance is the weighted average of the squared deviations, where the weights are the probabilities. It is a useful measure of dispersion.

$$\text{Variance} = \frac{\textbf{probability-weighted average of squared}}{\textbf{deviations around the expected return}} \qquad (10.7)$$

$$= (.25 \times 900) + (.25 \times 0) + (.25 \times 0) + (.25 \times 900)$$
$$= 450$$

When each of the outcomes is equally likely, the variance is just the average of the squared deviations. Taking the average of the squared deviations in column 3 of Table 10.2, you get 1,800/4 or 450.

When we squared the deviations from the expected return, we changed the units of measurement from percentages to percentages squared. Our last step is to get back to percentages by taking the square root of the variance. This is the standard deviation:

$$\textbf{Standard deviation} = \textbf{square root of variance} \qquad (10.8)$$
$$= \sqrt{450} = 21\%$$

Because standard deviation is simply the square root of variance, it too is a natural measure of risk. If the outcome of the game had been certain, the standard deviation would have been zero because there would then be no deviations from the expected outcome. The actual standard deviation is positive because we *don't* know what will happen.

When we calculated variance in Table 10.2 we recorded each of the four possible outcomes separately. An alternative would have been to recognize that in two of the cases the outcomes were the same. Thus there was a 50 percent chance of a 10 percent return from the game, a 25

TABLE 10.3

The coin-toss game: calculating variance and standard deviation when there are different probabilities of each outcome

(1) Percent Rate of Return	(2) Probability of Return	(3) Deviation from Expected Return	(4) Probability × Squared Deviation
+40	.25	+30	.25 × 900 = 225
+10	.50	0	.50 × 0 = 0
−20	.25	−30	.25 × 900 = 225

Variance = sum of squared deviations weighted by probabilities = 225 + 0 + 225 = 450

Standard deviation = square root of variance = $\sqrt{450}$ = 21.2, about 21%

percent chance of a 40 percent return, and a 25 percent chance of a –20 percent return. We calculate variance by weighting each squared deviation by the probability and then summing the results. Table 10.3 confirms that this method gives the same answer.

Now think of a second game. It is the same as the first except that each head means a 35 percent gain and each tail means a 25 percent loss. Again there are four equally likely outcomes:

- Head + head: You gain 70%
- Head + tail: You gain 10%
- Tail + head: You gain 10%
- Tail + tail: You lose 50%

For this game, the expected return is 10 percent, the same as that of the first game, but it is more risky. For example, in the first game, the worst possible outcome is a loss of 20 percent, which is 30 percent worse than the expected outcome. In the second game the downside is a loss of 50 percent, or 60 percent below the expected return. This increased spread of outcomes shows up in the standard deviation, which is double that of the first game, 42 percent versus 21 percent. By this measure the second game is twice as risky as the first.

Check Point 10.3   Calculate the expected return, the variance, and the standard deviation of this second coin-toss game in the same formats as Tables 10.2 and 10.3.

MEASURING THE VARIATION IN STOCK RETURNS

When estimating the spread of possible outcomes from investing in the stock market, most financial analysts start by assuming that the spread of returns in the past is a reasonable indication of what could happen in the future. Therefore, they calculate the variance and standard deviation of past returns. However, this situation is not the same as the previous coin-toss example, where the probability of each possible outcome was known, and variance was calculated as the probability-weighted average of the squared deviations. In the coin-toss example, we calculated the *population* variance and the *population* standard deviation. When you have a sample of observed rates of return, the probability of each possible return is unknown.[13] For a sample of observations, we calculate the *sample* variance. As before, the squared deviations from the average rate of return are calculated. The sample variance is the sum of the squared deviations around the estimated average rate of return, divided by the number of observations minus one:

$$\text{Variance based on a sample of observations} = \frac{\text{sum of the squared deviations around the average}}{\text{number of observations} - 1}$$

The sample standard deviation is the square root of the sample variance.

Although there are two different definitions of variance, people often call them both variance. However, you can always tell which variance is being used. If you know the probability of each possible value, you have the population variance, as in the coin-toss example. If you have a group of observed values, the sample variance is calculated using the formula above.

To illustrate, suppose that you were presented with the data for stock market returns shown in Table 10.4. The average return over the 6 years from 1999 to 2004 was 8.7 percent. This is just the sum of the returns over the 6 years divided by 6 (52.4/6 = 8.7 percent).

---

[13] In terms of statistics, we are drawing a distinction between calculating the variance of a population, where you know the probability of every possible outcome (the coin-toss example), and estimating the variance of a population with a sample of observations. We use the sample variance to infer what is the true but unknown variance of the population. That is why the sample variance is also called the *estimated* variance of the population.

TABLE 10.4

The average return and standard deviation of stock market returns, 1999–2004

Year	Rate of Return	Deviation from Average Return	Squared Deviation
1999	31.7	23.0	528.4
2000	7.4	−1.3	1.7
2001	−12.6	−21.3	453.7
2002	−12.4	−21.2	448.0
2003	26.7	18.0	323.9
2004	11.5	2.8	7.9
Total	52.4		1,763.6

Average rate of return = 52.4/6 = 8.7%

Variance = sum of squared deviations/(number of observations − 1) = 1,763.6/(6 − 1) = 352.7

Standard deviation = square root of variance $\sqrt{352.7}$ = 18.8%

Source: Authors' calculations using data from Canadian Institute of Actuaries, *Report on Canadian Economic Statistics 1924–2003*. Adapted from Statistics Canada CANSIM database http://cansim2.statcan.ca. Series V122620, V122587, and V122541.

Column 2 in Table 10.4 shows the difference between each year's return and the average return. For example, in 1999 the return of 31.7 percent on common stocks was above the 6-year average by 23 percent (31.7 − 8.7 = 23 percent). In column 3 we square these deviations from the average. The variance is the sum of these squared deviations divided by the number of observations minus one:

$$\textbf{Variance = sum of squared deviations/(number of observations – 1)} \qquad \textbf{(10.9)}$$

$$=\frac{1,763.6}{6-1} = 352.7$$

Since standard deviation is the square root of the variance,

$$\textbf{Standard deviation = square root of variance} \qquad \textbf{(10.10)}$$

$$= \sqrt{352.7} = 18.8\%$$

With Excel, sample variance and standard deviation can be quickly calculated using the VAR and STDEV functions. If six stock returns from Table 10.4 were in cells A1 to A6, the variance and standard deviations of the returns would be calculated as VAR(A1:A6) and STDEV(A1:A6).

It is difficult to measure the risk of securities on the basis of just six past outcomes. Therefore, Table 10.5 lists the annual standard deviations for our three portfolios of securities over the period from 1926 to 2004. As expected, Treasury bills were the least variable security, and common stocks were the most variable. Long-term government bonds hold the middle ground.

Of course, there is no reason to believe that the market's variability should stay the same over many years. Indeed, many people believe that in recent years the stock market has become more volatile due to irresponsible speculation by … [fill in the name of your preferred guilty party]. Figure 10.4 provides a chart of the volatility of the Canadian and U.S. stock markets for each year from 1926 to 2004.[14] You can see that there are periods of unusually high variability, but there is no long-term upward trend.

TABLE 10.5

Standard deviation of rates of return, 1926–2004

Portfolio	Standard Deviation, %
Treasury bills	4.2
Long-term government bonds	9.0
Common stocks	18.6

Source: Authors' calculations using data from Canadian Institute of Actuaries, *Report on Canadian Economic Statistics 1924–2003*. Adapted from Statistics Canada CANSIM database http://cansim2.statcan.ca. Series V122620, V122587, and V122541.

---

[14] We converted the monthly variance to an annual variance by multiplying by 12. In other words, the variance of annual returns is 12 times that of monthly returns. The longer you hold a security, the more risk you have to bear. Monthly data for the TSX begins in 1956.

FIGURE 10.4
Canadian and U.S.
stock market volatility,
1926–2004

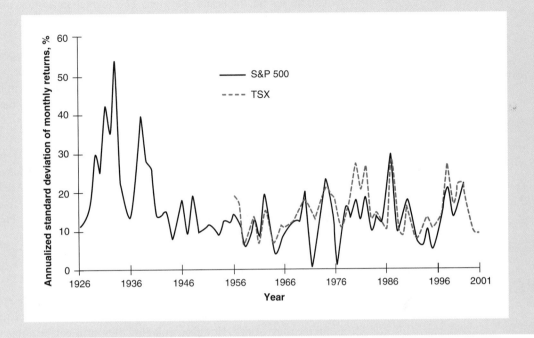

10.4

RISK AND DIVERSIFICATION

DIVERSIFICATION

We can calculate our measures of variability equally well for individual securities and portfolios of securities. Of course, the level of variability over 79 years is less interesting for specific companies than for the market portfolio because it is a rare company that faces the same business risks today as it did in 1926.

Table 10.6 presents estimated standard deviations for the common stocks of 11 Canadian companies for a recent 5-year period.[15] Do these standard deviations look high to you? They should. Remember that the market portfolio's standard deviation was about 19 percent over the entire 1926 to 2004 period. Of our individual stocks, none had a standard deviation of less than 19 percent! Most stocks are substantially more variable than the market portfolio; only a handful are less variable.

TABLE 10.6
Standard deviations for
selected common stocks,
January 1999–December 2003

Stock	Standard Deviation, %
Biomira	108.7
CanWest Global Communications	56.0
Inco	47.1
Cameco	38.9
Four Seasons Hotels	38.4
Alcan Aluminum	33.4
Barrick Gold	30.5
BCE	30.4
Canadian National Railway	26.9
Magna International	25.6
Royal Bank	19.2

---

[15] We pointed out earlier that six annual observations are insufficient to give a reliable estimate of variability. Therefore, these estimates are derived from 60 monthly rates of return and then the monthly variance is multiplied by 12.

diversification Strategy designed to reduce risk by spreading the portfolio across many investments.

This raises an important question: The market portfolio comprises individual stocks, so why isn't its variability equal to the average variability of its components? The answer is that **diversification** reduces variability.

Selling umbrellas is a risky business; you may make a killing when it rains but you are likely to lose your shirt in a heat wave. Selling ice cream is no safer; you do well in a heat wave but business is poor in the rain. Suppose, however, that you invest in both an umbrella shop and an ice cream shop. By diversifying your investment across the two businesses you make an average level of profit come rain or shine.

> Portfolio diversification works because prices of different stocks do not move exactly together. Statisticians make the same point when they say that stock price changes are less than perfectly correlated. Diversification works best when the returns are negatively correlated, as is the case for our umbrella and ice cream businesses. When one business does well, the other does badly. Unfortunately, in practice, stocks that are negatively correlated are extremely rare.

ASSET VERSUS PORTFOLIO RISK

The history of returns on different asset classes provides compelling evidence of a risk–return trade-off and suggests that the variability of the rates of return on each asset class is a useful measure of risk. However, volatility of returns can be a misleading measure of risk for an individual asset held as part of a portfolio. To see why, consider the following example.

Suppose there are three equally likely outcomes, or *scenarios*, for the economy: a recession, normal growth, and a boom. An investment in an auto stock will have a rate of return of –8 percent in a recession, 5 percent in a normal period, and 18 percent in a boom. Auto firms are cyclical: they do well when the economy does well. In contrast, gold firms are often said to be *countercyclical*, meaning that they do well when other firms do poorly. Suppose that stock in a gold mining firm will provide a rate of return of 20 percent in a recession, 3 percent in a normal period, and –20 percent in a boom. These assumptions are summarized in Table 10.7.

It appears that gold is the more volatile investment. The difference in return across the boom and bust scenarios is 40 percent (–20 percent in a boom versus +20 percent in a recession) compared to a spread of only 26 percent for the auto stock. In fact, we can confirm the higher volatility by measuring the variance or standard deviation of returns of the two assets. The calculations are set out in Table 10.8.

Since all three scenarios are equally likely, the expected return on each stock is simply the average of the three possible outcomes.[16] For the auto stock the expected return is 5 percent; for the gold stock it is 1 percent. The variance is the average of the squared deviations from the expected return, and the standard deviation is the square root of the variance.

Check Point 10.4

Suppose the probabilities of the recession or boom are .30, while the probability of a normal period is .40. Would you expect the variance of returns on these two investments to be higher or lower? Why? Confirm by calculating the standard deviation of the auto stock.

TABLE 10.7
Rate of return assumptions for two stocks

Scenario	Probability	Rate of Return, % Auto Stock	Gold Stock
Recession	1/3	–8	+20
Normal	1/3	+5	+3
Boom	1/3	+18	–20

---

[16] If the probabilities were not equal, we would need to weight each outcome by its probability in calculating the expected outcome and the variance.

TABLE 10.8 Expected return and volatility for two stocks

Scenario	Auto Stock			Gold Stock		
	Rate of Return, %	Deviation from Expected Return, %	Squared Deviation	Rate of Return, %	Deviation from Expected Return, %	Squared Deviation
Recession	−8	−13	169	+20	+19	361
Normal	+5	0	0	+3	+2	4
Boom	+18	+13	169	−20	−21	441
Expected return	$\frac{1}{3}(-8 + 5 + 18) = 5\%$			$\frac{1}{3}(+20 + 3 - 20) = 1\%$		
Variance[a]	$\frac{1}{3}(169 + 0 + 169) = 112.7$			$\frac{1}{3}(361 + 4 + 441) = 268.7$		
Standard deviation (= √variance)	$\sqrt{112.7} = 10.6\%$			$\sqrt{268.7} = 16.4\%$		
Covariance[b]	$= \frac{1}{3}(-13 \times 19) + \frac{1}{3}(0 \times 2) + \frac{1}{3}(13 \times -21) = -173.3$					
Correlation[c]	$= \dfrac{-173.3}{(10.6)(16.4)} = -.997$, or about −1					

[a] Variance = probability–weighted average of squared deviations from the expected value

[b] Covariance = probability – weighted average of the product of each stock's deviation from its expected value, for each possible scenario.

[c] Correlation $= \dfrac{\text{covariance}}{\text{Standard deviation of auto} \times \text{Standard deviation of gold}}$

The gold mining stock offers a lower expected rate of return than the auto stock, and *more* volatility—a loser on both counts, right? Would anyone be willing to hold gold mining stocks in an investment portfolio? The answer is a resounding Yes.

To see why, suppose you do believe that gold is a lousy asset, and therefore, hold your entire portfolio in the auto stock. Your expected return is 5 percent and your standard deviation is 10.6 percent. We'll compare that portfolio to a partially diversified one, invested 75 percent in autos and 25 percent in gold. For example, if you have a $10,000 portfolio, you could put $7,500 in autos and $2,500 in gold.

First, we need to calculate the return on this portfolio in each scenario. The portfolio return is the weighted average of returns on the individual assets with weights equal to the proportion of the portfolio invested in each asset. For a portfolio formed from only two assets,

$$\begin{array}{l}\text{Portfolio rate} \\ \text{of return}\end{array} = \left(\begin{array}{c}\text{fraction of portfolio} \\ \text{in first asset}\end{array} \times \begin{array}{c}\text{rate of return} \\ \text{on first asset}\end{array}\right) \\ + \left(\begin{array}{c}\text{fraction of portfolio} \\ \text{in second asset}\end{array} \times \begin{array}{c}\text{rate of return} \\ \text{on second asset}\end{array}\right) \qquad \text{(10.11)}$$

For example, autos have a weight of .75 and a rate of return of −8 percent in the recession, and gold has a weight of .25 and a return of 20 percent in a recession. Therefore, the portfolio return in the recession is the following weighted average:[17]

$$\text{Portfolio return in recession} = [.75 \times (-8\%)] + [.25 \times 20\%]$$
$$= -1\%$$

---

[17] Let's confirm this. Suppose you invest $7,500 in autos and $2,500 in gold. If the recession hits, the rate of return on autos will be −8 percent, and the value of the auto investment will fall by 8 percent to $6,900. The rate of return on gold will be 20 percent, and the value of the gold investment will rise 20 percent to $3,000. The value of the total portfolio falls from its original value of $10,000 to $6,900 + $3,000 = $9,900, which is a rate of return of −1 percent. This matches the rate of return given by the formula for the weighted average.

TABLE 10.9
Rates of return for two stocks and a portfolio

Scenario	Probability	Rate of Return, % Auto Stock	Gold Stock	Portfolio Return, %[a]
Recession	1/3	−8	+20	−1%
Normal	1/3	+5	+3	+4.5
Boom	1/3	+18	−20	+8.5
Expected return		5%	1%	4%
Variance		112.7	268.7	15.2
Standard deviation		10.6%	16.4%	3.9%

[a] Portfolio return = (.75 × auto stock return) + (.25 × gold stock return).

Table 10.9 expands Table 10.7 to include the portfolio of the auto and gold mining stocks. The expected returns and volatility measures are summarized at the bottom of the table. The surprising finding is this: When you shift funds from the auto stock to the more volatile gold mining stock, your portfolio variability actually *decreases*. In fact, the volatility of the auto-plus-gold stock portfolio is considerably less than the volatility of either stock separately. This is the payoff to diversification.

We can understand this more clearly by focusing on asset returns in the two extreme scenarios, boom and recession. In the boom, when auto stocks do best, the poor return on gold reduces the performance of the overall portfolio. However, when auto stocks are stalling in a recession, gold shines, providing a substantial positive return that boosts portfolio performance. The gold stock offsets the swings in the performance of the auto stock, reducing the best-case return but improving the worst-case return. The inverse relationship between the returns on the two stocks means that the addition of the gold mining stock to an all-auto portfolio stabilizes returns.

A gold stock is really a *negative-risk* asset to an investor starting with an all-auto portfolio. Adding it to the portfolio reduces the volatility of returns. The *incremental* risk of the gold stock (that is, the *change* in overall risk when gold is added to the portfolio) is negative despite the fact that gold returns are highly volatile.

In general, the incremental risk of a stock depends on whether its returns tend to vary with or against the returns of the other assets in the portfolio. Incremental risk does not just depend on a stock's volatility. If returns do not move closely with those of the rest of the portfolio, the stock will reduce the volatility of portfolio returns.

We can summarize as follows:

1. Investors care about the expected return and risk of their *portfolio* of assets. The risk of the overall portfolio can be measured by the volatility of the portfolio returns, that is, the variance or standard deviation.

2. The standard deviation of the returns of an individual security measures how risky that security would be if held in isolation. But an investor who holds a portfolio of securities is interested only in how each security affects the risk of the entire portfolio. The contribution of a security to the risk of the portfolio depends on how the security's returns vary with the investor's other holdings. Thus a security that is risky if held in isolation may nevertheless serve to reduce the variability of the portfolio, as long as its returns vary inversely with those of the rest of the portfolio.

EXAMPLE 10.2

MAGNA INTERNATIONAL AND CAMECO

Suppose at the beginning of July 2003 you split your savings evenly between the shares of Magna International, a major auto parts manufacturer, and Cameco, a leading uranium producer. The blue bars in Figure 10.5 show the next six months' returns from your investment in Magna, while the gold bars show the corresponding returns from Cameco. Both stocks had their ups and downs, but on occasion a decline in the value of one stock was reduced by the rise in the price of the other. You can see from the

FIGURE 10.5
Monthly returns
July–December 2003 from
stocks of Magna International
and Cameco. A portfolio
invested equally in the two
stocks would have had lower
variability

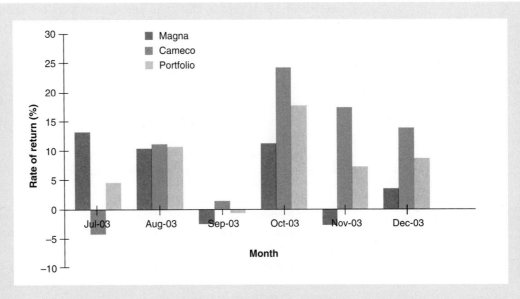

	7/31/2003	8/29/2003	9/30/2003	10/31/2003	11/28/2003	12/31/2003
Magna	13.0965	10.3312	−2.5021	11.1989	−2.9291	3.237
Cameco	−4.3077	11.0932	1.2947	24.133	17.1323	13.7688
Portfolio	4.3944	10.7122	−0.6037	17.66595	7.1016	8.5029

grey bars in Figure 10.5 that the return on your portfolio would have much less variable than the returns of the individual holdings. The peaks are lower and the valleys are less deep.

We have hit here on a six-month period when the returns of Magna and Cameco tended to move in opposite directions. Of course, that won't generally be the case. If the market falls, there is a fair bet that both Magna and Cameco will fall too. But because the two stocks don't move in exact lockstep, there is still an opportunity to reduce risk by diversification.

Check Point 10.5

An investor is currently fully invested in gold mining stocks. Which action would do more to reduce portfolio risk: diversification into silver mining stocks or automotive stocks? Why?

CORRELATION

We have given you an intuitive idea of how diversification reduces risk: Combining assets into a portfolio reduces risk because the assets' prices do not move in exact lockstep. When one stock is doing poorly, another may be doing well, helping to offset the negative impact of the stock with the poorer performance on the portfolio return. However, to understand portfolio diversification more fully we need to look in more detail at *correlation*.

correlation coefficient
Measure of how closely two
variables move together.

The **correlation coefficient**—always a number between −1 and 1—measures the degree to which two variables move together. If the correlation coefficient is greater than zero, the two variables tend to move in the same direction; they are *positively* correlated. The higher the correlation coefficient the stronger the relationship is between the two variables. When the correlation coefficient equals 1, the variables are perfectly positively correlated and the variables move in lockstep. On the other hand, if the correlation coefficient is less than zero, the two variables tend to move in the opposite direction; they are *negatively* correlated. With a correlation coefficient equal to −1, the variables are perfectly negatively correlated. If the correlation coefficient equals zero, a change in one variable does not tell you anything about the likely change in the other; the variables are said to be *uncorrelated*.

Check Point 10.6

Are each of the following pairs of variables likely to be positively correlated, negatively correlated, or uncorrelated? Briefly explain why.
a. The number of hours of sunshine per day and the average daily air temperature.
b. The number of hours of television you watch per day and your grade on your finance final.
c. The flying time from Vancouver to St. John's and the quality of the in-flight movie.
d. The level of interest rates in the United States and the level of interest rates in Canada.

Correlation is a useful concept for measuring how stocks move relative to each other. In the previous example, we said that auto firms were cyclical: they tend to do well when the economy is doing well. In other words, the return on auto stocks is positively correlated with the economy. On the other hand, gold stocks were said to be countercyclical, tending to do well when the economy is doing poorly. Thus the return on gold stocks tends to have low correlation with the economy.

MEASURING CORRELATION

How correlated are Magna's and Cameco's stock returns in Example 10.2? The Excel function CORREL can figure it out for you. If the return data for one stock is in cells A1 to A6 and the returns for the other stock are in cells B1 to B6, their correlation is calculated with CORREL(A1:A6, B1:B6). For the 6 pairs of stock returns for Magna and Cameco, the correlation coefficient is –5.8 percent. Just as we noticed in Figure 10.5, these two stocks were negatively correlated during the period. Using the 60 monthly stock returns from January 1999 to December 2003, the correlation between the two stocks is 30 percent. As long as the correlation is less than 1, diversification is possible.

The mathematical definition of correlation between two variables is their *covariance* divided by the product of their standard deviations:

$$\text{Correlation between } x \text{ and } y = \frac{\text{Covariance between } x \text{ and } y}{\text{Standard deviation of } x \times \text{Standard deviation of } y} \quad (10.12)$$

Covariance of a population is equal to the probability-weighted average of the product of each variable's difference from its mean, for each possible future event. At the bottom of Table 10.8 are covariance and correlation calculations for the auto and gold stocks. The correlation is approximately –1, indicating that the two stocks move almost exactly opposite to each other. To calculate the covariance of set of observations, use the Excel function COVAR or see a basic statistics text for the details.

CORRELATION AND PORTFOLIO DIVERSIFICATION

The degree of correlation among assets determines the extent to which risk is reduced through portfolio diversification. To illustrate, we will create a portfolio of two stocks, Steelco (S), manufacturer of construction steel, and Gold Bear (G), a gold mine and refinery. The expected return on Steelco shares, r_S, is 15 percent, and the expected return on Gold Bear shares, r_G, is 9 percent. The standard deviation of return on Steelco is 12 percent and the standard deviation of return on Gold Bear is 18 percent. What are the expected return and standard deviation of return for a portfolio of these two stocks?

The expected return on the portfolio of Steelco and Gold Bear stocks will depend on the fraction of funds invested in each. Let x_S be the fraction of the total funds invested in shares of Steelco and x_G be the fraction invested in shares of Gold Bear Mine. The expected return on the portfolio is the weighted average of the expected returns on the two stocks, where the weights equal the fraction invested in each, so

$$r_p = x_S \times 15\% + x_G \times 9\%$$

If 100 percent of the funds are invested in Steelco, $x_S = 1$ and $x_G = 0$, the portfolio expected return is 15 percent, the expected return on Steelco. If 25 percent of the funds are invested in Steelco ($x_S = .25$) and 75 percent are invested in Gold Bear ($x_G = .75$), the expected portfolio return is

$$r_p = .25 \times 15\% + .75 \times 9\% = 10.5\%$$

The general formula for expected return of a portfolio is simply the weighted average of the expected return on the assets in the portfolio, where the weights are the fractions invested in each stock:

$$\text{Portfolio expected return} = r_p = x_S r_S + x_G r_G$$

Is the portfolio standard deviation equal to the weighted average of the standard deviations of assets in the portfolio? The answer depends on the correlation between the assets in the portfolio. If the assets' returns are perfectly positively correlated, there is no benefit from diversification and the portfolio standard deviation is simply the weighted average of the individual stocks' standard deviations. However, if the stocks are less than perfectly correlated, diversification reduces portfolio risk—the portfolio standard deviation will be less than the weighted average of the assets' standard deviations.

To show you how this works, we need a bit of notation. The commonly used symbol for standard deviation is the Greek letter σ ("sigma"). Thus the standard deviation of the return on Steelco is σ_S, and for Gold Bear, σ_G. We use the Greek letter ρ ("rho") to represent the correlation coefficient. Thus ρ_{SG} is the correlation coefficient for Steelco and Big Bear. The expression for the standard deviation of a portfolio with two stocks is

$$\textbf{Portfolio standard deviation} = \sigma_p = \sqrt{x_S^2 \sigma_S^2 + x_G^2 \sigma_G^2 + 2 x_S x_G \rho_{SG} \sigma_S \sigma_G} \qquad \textbf{(10.13)}$$

Notice that the portfolio standard deviation depends on the individual stocks' standard deviations and also on their correlation to one another.

Suppose the returns on Steelco and Gold Bear are perfectly positively correlated, $\rho_{SG} = 1$. The standard deviation of a portfolio with 25 percent invested in Steelco ($X_S = .25$) and 75 percent in Gold Bear ($X_G = .75$)

$$\sigma_p = \sqrt{(.25)^2(.12)^2 + (.75)^2(.18)^2 + 2(.25)(.75)(1)(.12)(.18)} = .165$$

This is also the weighted average of Steelco's and Gold Bear's standard deviations: $(.25)(.12) + (.75)(.18) = .165$. Only if the stocks are perfectly positively correlated, $\rho_{SG} = 1$, will there be no benefit from diversification. Table 10.10 shows portfolio standard deviation for other possible correlation coefficients. See how as the correlation gets lower, the benefit from diversification increases.

Can portfolio risk (portfolio standard deviation) be reduced to zero through diversification? If some assets are negatively correlated with the others, it is mathematically possible to reduce

TABLE 10.10

Relationship between correlation and portfolio standard deviation

Correlation Coefficient, ρ_{SG}	Portfolio Standard Deviation $= \sigma_p = \sqrt{x_S^2 \sigma_S^2 + x_G^2 \sigma_G^2 + 2 x_S x_G \rho_{SG} \sigma_S \sigma_G}$ $= \sqrt{(.25)^2(.12)^2 + (.75)^2(.18)^2 + 2(.25)(.75)\rho_{SG}(.12)(.18)}$
1.0	.165
0.8	.160
0.2	.144
0	.138
−0.3	.129
−0.7	.116
−1.0	.105

the portfolio risk to zero. In our example, if the correlation coefficient was −.3, and you invested about 65 percent in Steelco and 35 percent in Gold Bear, the portfolio standard deviation would be close to zero.

Unfortunately, assets with negative correlation with the economy are hard to find. Although some assets have low correlation with other assets (gold, for instance), all assets' returns tend to be positively correlated. Portfolio diversification can reduce risk up to a point but cannot remove all risks.

✓ **Check Point 10.7**	Go back to the auto and gold stock example. Calculate the correlation between their returns, using the portfolio standard deviation formula, Equation 10.13. The stocks' variances, standard deviations, the portfolio weights, and portfolio variance are found in Table 10.9.

MARKET RISK VERSUS UNIQUE RISK

Our examples illustrate that even a little diversification can provide a substantial reduction in variability. Suppose you calculate and compare the standard deviations of randomly chosen one-stock portfolios, two-stock portfolios, five-stock portfolios, and so on. You can see from Figure 10.6 that diversification can cut the variability of returns by about half. But you can get most of this benefit with relatively few stocks: the improvement is slight when the number of stocks is increased beyond, say, 15.

Figure 10.6 also illustrates that no matter how many securities you hold, you cannot eliminate all risk. There remains the danger that the market—including your portfolio—will plummet.

unique risk Risk factors affecting only the particular firm. Also called diversifiable risk.

market risk Economywide (macroeconomic) sources of risk that affect the overall stock market. Also called systematic risk.

The risk that can be eliminated by diversification is called **unique risk**. This is the same as saying that stock returns tend to be less than perfectly positively correlated. The risk that you can't avoid—regardless of how much you diversify—is generally known as **market risk**, or *systematic risk*. Thus, although stocks are less than perfectly positively correlated, they are nonetheless positively correlated, and portfolio standard deviation cannot be reduced to zero.

> *Unique risk* arises because many of the perils that surround an individual company are peculiar to that company and perhaps its direct competitors. Market risk stems from economywide perils that threaten all businesses. *Market risk* explains why stocks have a tendency to move together, so that even well-diversified portfolios are exposed to market movements.

FIGURE 10.6
Diversification reduces risk (standard deviation) rapidly at first, then more slowly

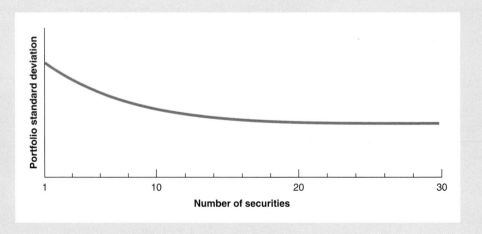

FIGURE 10.7
Diversification
eliminates unique risk.
But there is some risk
that diversification
cannot eliminate. This
is called market risk.

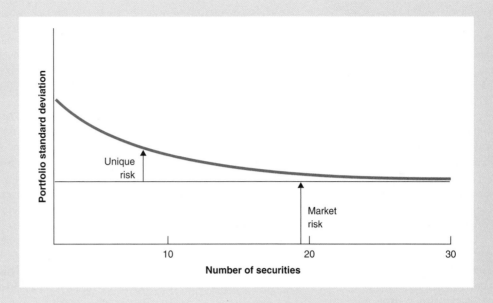

Figure 10.7 divides risk into its two parts—unique risk and market risk. If you have only a single stock, unique risk is very important; but once you have a portfolio of 30 or more stocks, diversification has done most of what it can to eliminate risk.

For a reasonably well-diversified portfolio, only market risk matters.

EXAMPLE 10.3   **INTERNATIONAL PORTFOLIO DIVERSIFICATION**

If holding a portfolio of Canadian stocks reduces investors' risk without sacrificing return, holding a portfolio of Canadian and foreign stocks should further reduce risk. Investing internationally yields benefits to investors from increased diversification; that is, the decreased portfolio standard deviation that results from including an international component within their portfolios. The ability to reduce risk without sacrificing return arises because not all markets move up or down at the same time. Due to this less than perfect positive correlation between the Canadian financial markets and financial markets in other countries, losses in the domestic market can often be offset by gains in those foreign markets that have a low correlation to our markets. By diversifying internationally, the investor hopes to have international investments that are doing well when the Canadian portion of the portfolio is not, and vice versa.

Look back at Figure 10.4. You will see that the standard deviations of the TSX and the S&P 500 tend to move together but not perfectly. The correlation coefficient between the annual rates of return of the two market indexes over the period 1956 to 2004 is about 70 percent. By holding both stock indexes, you can reduce portfolio risk, since the markets are not perfectly correlated. But the high degree of integration between the U.S. and Canadian economies and stock markets means that the correlation coefficient is far from zero, reflecting the common market risk.

You can add stocks from other countries to further reduce the portfolio risk provided that their returns are less than perfectly correlated with the U.S. and Canadian markets. See the nearby **SEE BOX P. 328** Finance in Action box for a discussion of globalization and the opportunities for international portfolio diversification.

Academic researchers and investment advisers have been strongly recommending that investors diversify their portfolios by investing in international equities. Supported by extensive academic research that has proclaimed the risk reduction advantages of international diversification, increasing numbers of investors look for international equity components within the asset allocation of their portfolios. Here are some thoughts on opportunities for international diversification from a well-known financial economist, Burton Malkiel, as reported in Benefits Canada, *a trade journal for pension fund managers.*

The importance of international diversification is critical for institutional investors in Canada. This country represents less than 3 percent of the global economy for heaven's sake. Too significant a reliance on domestic stocks and bonds is a recipe for disaster.

Canadian pension fund executives have understood this for years. The assets of Canada's top 100 pension funds have never been as internationally diversified as they are now. The global equity holdings held by the country's 100 largest funds jumped almost $9 billion in 2000 alone.

But while the importance of international diversification is understood, its effectiveness has to be seen within the context of this emerging global economy. Just as globalization helps Canadian pension fund managers develop international investment portfolios, it may also reduce the diversification benefits those portfolios offer.

That warning comes from one of the world's most influential economists. Burton Malkiel, the Chemical Bank chairperson, professor of economics at Princeton University, and author of *A Random Walk Down Wall Street*, says it is time to reexamine the assumption that international markets don't move in lockstep.

"Our global markets are much more closely tied and the correlations among markets are much higher than they have been in the past," says Malkiel. He made his comments during an interview with *Benefits Canada* last month. "The diversification benefits are likely to be a little less."

Malkiel isn't suggesting Canadian pension asset managers buck the international investment trend. In fact he describes himself as a "big believer in globalization." But Malkiel warns you can't assume a level of diversification that isn't there.

Globalization lends stability to international markets—it encourages higher correlations. For example, we need look only as far as British Columbia to understand the international impact of a financial crisis in Asia.

What is Malkiel's recommendation? There's more to investing than geography.

"There are three asset classes where correlations have not increased," he says. "One is real estate—global real estate as well. The second is bonds. I consider high yield bonds to be an equity type of asset. You're really getting paid to take those risks in the bond market, and the correlations don't seem to have gone up. Third, I think the risk of inflation is going to be a worldwide phenomenon. One asset class that is uncorrelated with both equities and real estate are inflation-protection securities such as are issued by the U.S. and Canadian federal governments."

Adapted from "A Small World After All," Kevin Press.

Source: *Benefits Canada* 25/5 (May 2001), p. 7.

10.5   THINKING ABOUT RISK

How can you tell which risks are unique and diversifiable? Where do market risks come from? Here are three messages to help you think clearly about risk.

MESSAGE 1: SOME RISKS LOOK BIG AND DANGEROUS BUT REALLY ARE DIVERSIFIABLE

Managers confront risks "up close and personal." They must make decisions about particular investments. The failure of such an investment could cost a promotion, bonus, or a steady job. Yet that same investment may not seem risky to an investor who can stand back and combine it in a diversified portfolio with many other assets or securities.

EXAMPLE 10.4	WILDCAT OIL WELLS

You have just been promoted to director of exploration, Western Hemisphere, of MPS Oil. The manager of your exploration team in far-off Costaguana has appealed for $20 million extra to drill in an even steamier part of the Costaguanan jungle. The manager thinks there may be an "elephant" field worth

$500 million or more hidden there. But the chance of finding it is at best one in 10, and yesterday, MPS's CEO sourly commented on the $100 million already "wasted" on Costaguanan exploration.

Is this a risky investment? For you it probably is; you may be a hero if oil is found, and a goat otherwise. But MPS drills hundreds of wells worldwide; for the company as a whole, it's the *average* success rate that matters. Geologic risks (is there oil or not?) should average out. The risk of a worldwide drilling program is much less than the apparent risk of any single wildcat well.

Back up one step and think of the investors who buy MPS stock. The investors may hold other oil companies, too, as well as companies producing steel, computers, clothing, cement, and breakfast cereal. They naturally—and realistically—assume that your successes and failures in drilling oil wells will average out with the thousands of independent bets made by the companies in their portfolio.

Therefore, the risks you face in Costaguana do not affect the rate of return they demand for investing in MPS Oil. Diversified investors in MPS stock will be happy if you find that elephant field, but they are unlikely to notice if you fail and lose your job. In any case, they will not demand a higher *average* rate of return for worrying about geologic risks in Costaguana.

EXAMPLE 10.5   **FIRE INSURANCE**

Would you be willing to write a $100,000 fire insurance policy on your neighbour's house? The neighbour is willing to pay you $100 for a year's protection, and experience shows that the chance of fire damage in a given year is substantially less than one in a thousand. But if your neighbour's house is damaged by fire, you would have to pay up.

Few of us have deep enough pockets to insure our neighbours, even if the odds of fire damage are very low. Insurance seems a risky business if you think policy by policy. But a large insurance company, which may issue a million policies, is concerned only with average losses, which can be predicted with excellent accuracy.

Check Point 10.8

Imagine a laboratory at IBM, late at night. One scientist speaks to another.

"You're right, Watson, I admit this experiment will consume all the rest of this year's budget. I don't know what we'll do if it fails. But if this yttrium–magnoosium alloy superconducts, the patents will be worth millions."

Would this be a good or bad investment for IBM? Can't say. But from the ultimate investors' viewpoint this is not a risky investment. Explain why.

MESSAGE 2: MARKET RISKS ARE MACRO RISKS

We have seen that diversified portfolios are not exposed to the unique risks of individual stocks but are exposed to the uncertain events that affect the entire securities market and the entire economy. These are macroeconomic, or "macro," factors such as changes in interest rates, industrial production, inflation, foreign exchange rates, and energy costs. These factors affect most firms' earnings and stock prices. When the relevant macro risks turn generally favourable, stock prices rise and investors do well; when the same variables go the other way, investors suffer.

You can often assess relative market risks just by thinking through exposures to the business cycle and other macro variables. The following businesses have substantial macro and market risks:

- *Airlines*. Because business travel falls during a recession, and individuals postpone vacations and other discretionary travel, the airline industry is subject to the swings of the business cycle. On the positive side, airline profits really take off when business is booming and personal incomes are rising.
- *Machine tool manufacturers*. These businesses are especially exposed to the business cycle. Manufacturing companies that have excess capacity rarely buy new machine tools to expand. During recessions, excess capacity can be quite high.

Here, on the other hand, are two industries with less than average macro exposures:

- *Food companies*. Companies selling staples, such as breakfast cereal, flour, and dog food, find that demand for their products is relatively stable in good times and bad.
- *Electric utilities*. Business demand for electric power varies somewhat across the business cycle, but by much less than demand for air travel or machine tools. Also, many electric utilities' profits are regulated. Regulation cuts off upside profit potential but also gives the utilities the opportunity to increase prices when demand is slack.

> Remember, investors holding diversified portfolios are mostly concerned with macroeconomic risks. They do not worry about microeconomic risks peculiar to a particular company or investment project. Micro risks wash out in diversified portfolios. Company managers may worry about both macro and micro risks, but only the former affect the cost of capital.

Check Point 10.9

Which company of each of the following pairs would you expect to be more exposed to macro risks?
a. A luxury Montreal restaurant or an established Burger Queen franchise?
b. A paint company that sells through small paint and hardware stores to do-it-yourselfers, or a paint company that sells in large volumes to Ford, GM, and Honda?

MESSAGE 3: RISK CAN BE MEASURED

Air Canada clearly has more exposure to macro risks than food companies such as Westons or Kraft. These are easy cases. But is IBM stock a riskier investment than Imperial Oil? That's not an easy question to reason through. We can, however, *measure* the risk of IBM and Imperial Oil by looking at how their stock prices fluctuate.

We've already hinted at how to do this. Remember that diversified investors are concerned with market risks. The movements of the stock market sum up the net effects of all relevant macroeconomic uncertainties. If the market portfolio of all traded stocks is up in a particular month, we conclude that the net effect of macroeconomic news is positive. Remember, the performance of the market is barely affected by a firm-specific event. These cancel out across thousands of stocks in the market.

How do we measure the risk of a single stock, like IBM or Imperial Oil? We do not look at the stocks in isolation, because the risks that loom when you're up close to a single company are often diversifiable. Instead we measure the individual stock's sensitivity to the fluctuations of the overall stock market. We will show you how this works in the next chapter.

10.6   SUMMARY

1. How can one estimate the opportunity cost of capital for an "average risk" project?

Over the past 79 years the calculated return on the **TSX Total Return Index Value** of common stocks has averaged about 6.7 percent a year higher than the return on safe Treasury bills. This is the **risk premium** that investors have received for taking on the risk of investing in stocks. Long-term bonds have offered a higher return than Treasury bills but less than stocks.

If the risk premium in the past is a guide to the future, we can estimate the expected return on the market today by adding that 6.7 percent expected risk premium to today's interest rate on Treasury bills. This would be the opportunity cost of capital for an average-risk project, that is, one with the same risk as a typical share of common stock.

2. How is the standard deviation of returns for individual common stocks or a stock portfolio calculated?

The spread of outcomes on different investments is commonly measured by the **variance** or **standard deviation** of the possible outcomes. The variance is the average of the squared deviations around the average outcome, and the standard deviation is the square root of the variance. The standard deviation of the returns on a market portfolio of common stocks has averaged about 19 percent per year.

3. Why does diversification reduce risk?

The standard deviation of returns is generally higher on individual stocks than it is on the market. Because individual stocks do not move in exact lockstep, much of their risk can be diversified away. Stock returns are less than perfectly correlated. By spreading your portfolio across many investments you smooth out the risk of your overall position. The risk that can be eliminated through diversification is known as **unique risk**.

4. What is the difference between unique risk, which can be diversified away, and market risk, which cannot?

Even if you hold a well-diversified portfolio, you will not eliminate all risk. You will still be exposed to macroeconomic changes that affect most stocks and the overall stock market. This means that stock returns are positively correlated. These macro risks combine to create **market risk**—that is, the risk that the market as a whole will slump.

Stocks are not all equally risky. But what do we mean by a "high risk" stock? We don't mean a stock that is risky if held in isolation; we mean a stock that makes an above-average contribution to the risk of a diversified portfolio. In other words, investors don't need to worry much about the risk that they can diversify away; they do need to worry about risk that can't be diversified. This depends on the stock's sensitivity to macroeconomic conditions.

Related Web Links

www.financialengines.com Some good introductory material on risk, return, and inflation

www.stern.nyu.edu/~adamodar This New York University site contains some historical data on market risk and return

www.tsx.ca Toronto Stock Exchange and TSX Venture Exchange

www.nyse.com New York Stock Exchange

www.spglobal.com Standard & Poor's indexes, including S&P/TSX Composite Index

Key Terms

Questions and Problems

BASIC

*1. **Rate of Return.** A stock is selling today for $40 per share. At the end of the year, it pays a dividend of $2 per share and sells for $44. What is the total rate of return on the stock? What are the dividend yield and capital gains yield?

2. **Rate of Return.** Return to problem 1. Suppose the year-end stock price after the dividend is paid is $36. What are the dividend yield and capital gains yield in this case? Why is the dividend yield unaffected?

3. **Real versus Nominal Returns.** You purchase 100 shares of stock for $40 a share. The stock pays a $2 per share dividend at year-end. What is the rate of return on your investment for these end-of-year stock prices? What is your real (inflation-adjusted) rate of return? Assume an inflation rate of 5 percent.
   *a. $38
   b. $40
   c. $42

4. **Real versus Nominal Returns.** The Costaguanan stock market provided a rate of return of 95 percent. The inflation rate in Costaguana during the year was 80 percent. In Canada, in contrast, the stock market return was only 14 percent, but the inflation rate was only 3 percent. Which country's stock market provided the higher *real* rate of return?

*5. **Real versus Nominal Returns.** The inflation rate in Canada between 1926 and 2004 averaged 3.2 percent. What was the average real rate of return on Treasury bills, government bonds, and common stocks in that period? Use the data in Table 10.1.

6. **Real versus Nominal Returns.** Do you think it is possible for risk-free Treasury bills to offer a negative nominal interest rate? Might they offer a negative *real* expected rate of return?

EXCEL

7. **Market Indexes.** The accompanying table shows the complete history of stock prices on the Polish stock exchange for nine weeks in 1991. At that time only five stocks were traded. Construct two stock market indexes, one using equal weights, the other using value weights.

Prices (in zlotys) for the first nine weeks of trading on the Warsaw Stock Exchange, beginning in April 1991. There was one trading session per week. Only five stocks were listed in the first nine weeks.

			Stock		
	Tonsil	**Prochnik**	**Krosno**	**Exbud**	**Kable**
	(Electronics)	**(Garments)**	**(Glass)**	**(Construction)**	**(Electronics)**
Week	**1,500***	**1,500***	**2,200***	**1,000***	**1,000***
1	85	56	59.5	149	80
2	76.5	51	53.5	164	80
3	69	46	49	180	80
4	62.5	41.5	47	198	79.5
5	56.5	38	51.5	217	80
6	56	41.5	56.5	196	80
7	61.5	45.5	62	177	80
8	67.5	50	60	160	80.5
9	61	45.5	54	160	72.5

* Number of shares outstanding.
Source: We are indebted to Professor Mary M. Cutler for providing these data.

EXCEL

8. **Stock Market History.** Using the data in problem 7, calculate the average rate of return and standard deviation of return for each stock as well as for an equal-weighted portfolio of all the stocks using Excel. Do you observe any benefits from diversification?

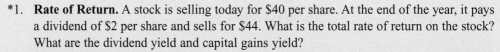

9. **Risk Premiums.** Here are annual stock market, Government of Canada bond, and bill percentage returns between 2000 and 2004:

Year	TSX Return	T-Bill Return	Government Long Bond Return
2000	7.41	5.63	13.64
2001	–12.57	4.14	3.92
2002	–12.44	2.55	10.09
2003	26.72	2.93	8.06
2004	11.53	2.28	8.82

a. What were the risk premiums on the TSX and on long-term government bonds in each year?

*b. What were the average risk premiums for the TSX and long-term government bonds?

*c. Calculate the standard deviation of each risk premium using the approach in Table 10.4. Do they make sense?

10. **Market Indexes.** In 1990, the Dow Jones Industrial Average was at a level of about 2,600. In 2004, it was about 10,500. Would you expect the Dow in 2004 to be more or less likely to move up or down by more than 40 points in a day than in 1990? Does this mean the market was riskier in 2004 than it was in 1990?

11. **Maturity Premiums.** Investments in long-term government bonds produced a negative average return during the period 1977–1981. How should we interpret this? Did bond investors in 1977 expect to earn a negative maturity premium? What do these five years of bond returns tell us about the normal future maturity premium?

12. **Risk Premiums.** What will happen to the opportunity cost of capital if investors suddenly become especially conservative and less willing to bear investment risk?

13. **Risk Premiums and Discount Rates.** You believe that a stock with the same market risk as the TSX will sell at year-end at a price of $50. The stock will pay a dividend at year-end of $2. What price will you be willing to pay for the stock today? *Hint:* Start by checking today's three-month Treasury bill rate.

EXCEL

*14. **Scenario Analysis.** The common stock of Leaning Tower of Pita, Inc., a restaurant chain, will generate the following payoffs to investors next year:

	Probability	Dividend	Stock Price
Boom	.3	$5	$195
Normal economy	.5	2	100
Recession	.2	0	0

The company goes out of business if a recession hits. Calculate the expected rate of return and standard deviation of return to Leaning Tower of Pita shareholders. The stock is selling today for $90.

15. **Portfolio Risk.** Who would view the stock of Leaning Tower of Pita (see problem 14) as a risk-reducing investment—the owner of a gambling casino or a successful bankruptcy lawyer? Explain.

16. **Scenario Analysis.** The common stock of Escapist Films sells for $25 a share and offers the following payoffs next year:

	Probability	Dividend	Stock Price
Boom	.3	$0	$18
Normal economy	.5	1	26
Recession	.2	3	34

Calculate the expected return and standard deviation of Escapist. Then calculate the expected return and standard deviation of a portfolio half invested in Escapist and half in

Leaning Tower of Pita (from problem 14). Show that the portfolio standard deviation is lower than either stock's. Explain why this happens.

17. **Scenario Analysis.** Consider the following scenario analysis:

		Rate of Return	
Scenario	Probability	Stocks	Bonds
Recession	.2	−5%	+14%
Normal economy	.6	+15	+8
Boom	.2	+25	+4

    a. Is it reasonable to assume that bonds will provide higher returns in recessions than in booms?

  *b. Calculate the expected rate of return and standard deviation for each investment.

    c. Which investment would you prefer?

18. **Portfolio Analysis.** Use the data in the previous problem and consider a portfolio with weights of .60 in stocks and .40 in bonds.

    a. What is the rate of return on the portfolio in each scenario?

    b. What is the expected rate of return and standard deviation of the portfolio?

    c. Would you prefer to invest in the portfolio, in stocks only, or in bonds only?

    d. Calculate the correlation coefficient for the bond and stock returns.

19. **Risk Premium.** If the stock market return in 2010 turns out to be −20 percent, what will happen to our estimate of the "normal" risk premium? Does this make sense?

20. **Diversification.** In which of the following situations would you get the largest reduction in risk by spreading your portfolio across two stocks? In each case, is the correlation less than, greater than, or equal to zero?

    a. The stock returns vary with each other.

    b. The stock returns are independent.

    c. The stock returns vary against each other.

*21. **Market Risk.** Which firm from each pair would you expect to have greater market risk? Explain your choice.

    a. General Steel or General Food Supplies.

    b. Club Med or General Cinemas.

22. **Risk and Return.** A stock will provide a rate of return of either −20 percent or +30 percent.

    a. If both possibilities are equally likely, calculate the expected return and standard deviation.

    b. If Treasury bills yield 5 percent, and investors believe that the stock offers a satisfactory expected return, what must be the market risk of the stock?

23. **Unique versus Market Risk.** Sassafras Oil is staking all its remaining capital on wildcat exploration off the Côte d'Huile. There is a 10 percent chance of discovering a field with reserves of 50 million barrels. If it finds oil, it will immediately sell the reserves to Big Oil, at a price depending on the state of the economy. Thus the possible payoffs are as follows:

	Value of Reserves, per Barrel	Value of Reserves, 50 Million Barrels	Value of Dryholes
Boom	$4.00	$200,000,000	0
Normal economy	$5.00	$250,000,000	0
Recession	$6.00	$300,000,000	0

Is Sassafras Oil a risky investment for a diversified investor in the stock market—compared, say, to the stock of Leaning Tower of Pita, described in problem 14? Explain.

24. **Portfolio Risk and Return.** The expected return on Big Time Toys is 9 percent and its standard deviation is 20 percent. The expected return on Chemical Industries is 8 percent and its standard deviation is 25 percent.

a. Suppose the correlation coefficient for the two stocks' returns is .2. What is the expected return and standard deviation of a portfolio with 30 percent invested in Big Time Toys and the rest in Chemical Industries?

b. If the correlation coefficient is .7, recalculate the portfolio expected return and standard deviation, assuming the portfolio weights are unchanged.

c. Explain the difference between your answers to (a) and (b).

*25. **Portfolio Risk and Return.** Using the data in problem 9,

a. Calculate the average rate of return and standard deviation of return for the TSX, government bonds, and Treasury bills between 2000 and 2004.

b. Form a portfolio with one-third in each of the three securities and calculate its average rate of return and standard deviation. Can you see any benefit from diversification?

EXCEL

26. **Correlation.** Using the Excel function CORREL, calculate the correlation between the return on Tonsil and each of the other five stocks mentioned in problem 7. Which stock offers the best diversification benefit?

27. **Internet.** Go to the Web site of the Institute of Canadian Actuaries at **www.actuaries.ca/publications/documents_reports_e.html** and find the most recent *Report on Canadian Economic Statistics*. Click on "Tables" and then look at Table 1-A, which contains the annual rates of return for various financial indexes. Using the data, calculate the arithmetic average for the annual return and standard deviation for stocks, Canada long-term bonds, mortgages, and Treasury bills from 1952. For each index, calculate its excess return over Treasury bills. Also, adjust each series by inflation to calculate the real rates of return. Do the average returns, standard deviations, and spreads over Treasury bills make sense? Repeat for successive 10-year periods. Do the calculated values still make sense? Why might using only a few years of data not be a smart idea when estimating the market risk premium?

28. **Internet.** Rates of return on U.S. stock, bond, and bill indexes are available to download for free at **www.globalfindata.com**. Click on Sample Data and download the NYSE Composite, United States Government Bonds Total Return Index, and United States Treasury Bills Total Return Index into a spreadsheet. Calculate the annual rate of return for each series. Then calculate the average market risk premium for the NYSE stocks, using the Treasury bill as the risk-free security for successive 10-year periods and for the entire period. Repeat, using the long-term government bond as the risk-free security.

a. Is the overall market risk premium bigger or smaller when the risk-free security is the Treasury bill or the long-term government bond?

b. Compare the risk premiums over time. Do you think the results suggest that the risk premium may have been changing? Explain.

29. **Internet.** A large variety of mutual funds are available to Canadian investors. Some, called sector funds, specialize in particular industries; others, known as index funds, simply invest in the market index. Go to **www.globefund.com**, click on "Reports" and look up TD Canadian Index fund. Click on the fund name and find its three-year risk (the standard deviation of its monthly return). Now find the three-year risk (standard deviation) for four other mutual funds for different industry (sector) funds. Are they larger or smaller than the Index fund? How do you interpret your results?

STANDARD
&POOR'S

30. **Standard & Poor's.** Using Market Insight (**www.mcgrawhill.ca/edu.marketinsight**) download stock prices for Magna International (MGA) by clicking on Excel Analytics, then on Monthly Data, and finally on the "Mthly. Adj. Prices" link. Find the December closing stock price the most recent five years. Use the income statement to get the annual dividend per share. Calculate the annual dividend yield, capital gains yield, and rate of

return for each year. Repeat for the Ford Motor Company (F) and Microsoft (MSFT). Describe the main business activities of these companies and compare their rates of return, dividend yields, and capital gains yields.

31. **Standard & Poor's.** Using Market Insight (**www.mcgrawhill.ca/edu.marketinsight**) "Mthly. Adj. Prices," download the monthly rates of return over a two-year period for five companies of your choice. Form an equally weighted portfolio of the five stocks (i.e., a portfolio with equal investment in each stock). What is the rate of return each month on your portfolio? Compare the mean and standard deviation of the monthly portfolio returns to that of each stock and to the average standard deviation across the five stocks. What evidence of portfolio diversification do you find? Use the CORREL function to calculate the correlation coefficient for each stock with the S&P 500. Describe what you find.

Solutions to Check Points

10.1   The bond price at the end of the year is $1,050. Therefore, the capital gain on each bond is $1,050 – $1,020 = $30. Your dollar return is the sum of the income from the bond, $80, plus the capital gain, $30, or $110. The rate of return is

$$\frac{\text{Income plus capital gain}}{\text{Original price}} = \frac{80 + 30}{1,020} = .108, \text{ or } 10.8\%$$

Real rate of return is

$$\frac{1 + \text{nominal return}}{1 + \text{inflation rate}} - 1 = \frac{1.108}{1.04} - 1 = .065, \text{ or } 6.5\%$$

10.2   The risk premium on stocks is the average return in excess of Treasury bills. It was 8.6 percent in period 1, 7.7 percent in period 2, and 4.2 percent in period 3. The maturity premium is the average return on Canada long bonds minus the return on Treasury bills. It was 3.6 percent in period 1, –1.2 percent in period 2, and 2.7 percent in period 3.

10.3   Expected return = $(.25 \times 70) + (.5 \times 10) + (.25 \times -50) = +10\%$

Variance and standard deviation calculation with equal probabilities:

Rate of Return	Deviation	Squared Deviation
+70%	+60%	3,600
+10	0	0
+10	0	0
–50	–60	3,600

Variance = average of squared deviations = 7,200/4 = 1,800

Standard deviation = square root of variance = $\sqrt{1,800}$ = 42.4, or about 42%

Variance and standard deviation calculation with unequal probabilities:

(1) Rate of Return (%)	(2) Probability of Return	(3) Deviations from Expected Return (%)	(4) Probability × Squared Deviation
+70	.25	+60	.25 × 3600 = 900
+10	.50	0	.50 × 0 = 0
–50	.25	–60	.25 × 3600 = 900

Variance = sum of squared deviations weighted by probabilities = 900 + 0 + 900 = 1,800

Standard deviation = square root of variance = $\sqrt{1,800}$ = 42.4, or about 42%

10.4   The standard deviation should decrease because there is now a lower probability of the more extreme outcomes. The expected rate of return on the auto stock is now

$$[.3 \times (-8\%)] + [.4 \times 5\%] + [.3 \times 18\%] = 5\%$$

The variance is

$$[.3 \times (-8 - 5)^2] + [.4 \times (5 - 5)^2] + [.3 \times (18 - 5)^2] = 101.4$$

The standard deviation is $\sqrt{101.4} = 10.07$ percent, which is lower than the value assuming equal probabilities of each scenario.

10.5   The gold mining stock's returns are more highly correlated with the silver mining company than with a car company. As a result, the automotive firm will offer a greater diversification benefit. The power of diversification is lowest when rates of return are highly correlated or performing well or poorly in tandem. Shifting the portfolio from one such firm to another has little impact on overall risk.

10.6   a. Since sunshine heats the air, the number of hours of sunshine per day and average daily temperature will be positively correlated. However, they will not be perfectly positively correlated because other factors affect air temperature such as latitude, altitude, and season.

b. The more television watched, the less time you have to study and the lower will be your grade in finance. Thus these two variables will be negatively correlated.

c. The quality of the in-flight movie has no relationship with the flying time. Thus these two variables are uncorrelated. Of course, if the movie is boring, the trip will *seem* to take longer!

d. The connectedness of the Canadian and U.S. economies and financial markets leads to a positive correlation between interest rates in Canada and the United States.

10.7   Let the auto stock be stock 1 and the gold stock be stock 2. Portfolio standard deviation formula for stocks 1 and 2 is

$$\sigma_p = \sqrt{x_1^2\sigma_1^2 + x_2^2\,\sigma_2^2 + 2x_1x_2\rho_{12}\sigma_1\sigma_2}$$

The known values are $x_1 = .75$, $x_2 = .25$, $\sigma_1 = .106$, $\sigma_2 = .164$, and $\sigma_\rho = .039$. The unknown is the correlation coefficient, ρ_{12}.

Substitute in all of the known values and solve for ρ_{12}:

$$\rho_{12} = [(.039)^2 - (.75)^2(.106)^2 - (.25)^2(.164)^2]/[(2)(.75)(.25)(.106)(.164)] = -.994$$

10.8   The success of this project depends on the experiment. Success does *not* depend on the performance of the overall economy. The experiment creates a diversifiable risk. A portfolio of many stocks will embody "bets" on many such unique risks. Some bets will work out and some will fail. Because the outcomes of these risks do not depend on common factors, such as the overall state of the economy, the risks will tend to cancel out in a well-diversified portfolio.

10.9   a. The luxury restaurant will be more sensitive to the state of the economy because expense account meals will be curtailed in a recession. Burger Queen meals should be relatively recession-proof.

b. The paint company that sells to the auto producers will be more sensitive to the state of the economy. In a downturn, auto sales fall dramatically as consumers stretch the lives of their cars. In contrast, in a recession, more people "do it themselves," which makes paint sales through small stores more stable and less sensitive to the economy.

RISK, RETURN, AND CAPITAL BUDGETING

In Chapter 10 we began to come to grips with the topic of risk. We made the distinction between *unique risk* and macro, or *market*, risk. Unique risk arises from events that affect only the individual firm or its immediate competitors; it can be eliminated by diversification. But regardless of how much you diversify, you cannot avoid the macroeconomic events that create market risk. This is why investors do not require a higher rate of return to compensate for unique risk but do need a higher return to persuade them to take on market risk.

How can you measure the market risk of a security or a project? We will see that market risk is usually measured by the sensitivity of the investment's returns to fluctuations in the market. We will also see that the risk premium investors demand should be proportional to this sensitivity. This relationship between risk and return is a useful way to estimate the return that investors expect from investing in common stocks.

Finally, we will distinguish between the risk of the company's securities and the risk of an individual project. We will also consider what managers should do when the risk of the project is different from that of the company's existing business.

After studying this chapter you should be able to
- Measure and interpret the market risk, or beta, of a security.
- Relate the market risk of a security to the rate of return that investors demand.
- Calculate the opportunity cost of capital for a project.

11.1   MEASURING MARKET RISK

market portfolio Portfolio of all assets in the economy. In practice, a broad stock market index, such as the S&P/TSX or S&P 500 Composite Index, is used to represent the market.

Changes in interest rates, government spending, monetary policy, oil prices, foreign exchange rates, and other macroeconomic events affect almost all companies and the returns on almost all stocks. We can therefore assess the impact of "macro" news by tracking the rate of return on a **market portfolio** of all securities. If the market is up on a particular day, then the net impact of macroeconomic changes must be positive. We know the performance of the market reflects only macro events, because firm-specific events—that is, unique risks—average out when we look at the combined performance of thousands of companies and securities.

In principle, the market portfolio should contain all assets in the world economy—not just stocks, but bonds, foreign securities, real estate, and so on. In practice, however, financial analysts make do with indexes of the stock market, such as the S&P/TSX Composite Index (TSX) or the Standard & Poor's Composite Index (the S&P 500).[1]

beta Sensitivity of a stock's return to the return on the market portfolio.

Our task here is to define and measure the risk of *individual* common stocks. You can probably see where we are headed. Risk depends on exposure to macroeconomic events and can be measured as the sensitivity of a stock's returns to fluctuations in returns on the market portfolio. This sensitivity is called the stock's **beta**. Beta is often written as the Greek letter β.

MEASURING BETA

In the last chapter we looked at the variability of individual securities. Biomira had the highest standard deviation and Royal Bank the lowest. If you had held Biomira on its own, your returns would have varied almost six times as much as if you had held Royal Bank. But wise investors don't put all their eggs in just one basket: they reduce their risk by diversification. An investor with a diversified portfolio will be interested in the effect each stock has on the risk of the entire portfolio.

Diversification can eliminate the risk that is unique to individual stocks, but not the risk that the market as a whole may decline, carrying your stocks with it.

Some stocks are less affected than others by market fluctuations. Investment managers talk about "defensive" and "aggressive" stocks. Defensive stocks are not very sensitive to market fluctuations. In contrast, aggressive stocks amplify any market movements. If the market goes up, it is good to be in aggressive stocks; if it goes down, it is better to be in defensive stocks (and better still to have your money in the bank).

Aggressive stocks have high betas, betas greater than 1.0, meaning that their returns tend to respond more than one-for-one to changes in the return of the overall market. The betas of defensive stocks are less than 1.0. The returns of these stocks vary less than one-for-one with market returns. The average beta of all stocks is—no surprises here—1.0 exactly.

Now we'll show you how betas are measured.

EXAMPLE 11.1   **MEASURING BETA FOR TURBOT-CHARGED SEAFOODS**

Suppose we look back at the trading history of Turbot-Charged Seafoods and pick out 6 months when the return on the market portfolio was plus or minus 1 percent.

Month	Market Return, %	Turbot-Charged Seafood's Return, %	
1	+1	+ .8	
2	+1	+1.8	Average = +.8%
3	+1	− .2	
4	−1	−1.8	
5	−1	+ .2	Average = −.8%
6	−1	− .8	

---

[1] We discussed the most popular stock market indexes in Section 10.2.

Look at Figure 11.1, where these observations are plotted. We've drawn a line through the average performance of Turbot when the market is up or down by 1 percent. *The slope of this line is Turbot's beta.* You can see right away that the beta is .8, because on average Turbot stock gains or loses .8 percent when the market is up or down by 1 percent. Notice that a 2-percentage-point difference in the market return (–1 to +1) generates on average a 1.6-percentage-point difference for Turbot shareholders (–.8 to +.8). The ratio, 1.6/2 = .8, is beta.

In four months, Turbot's returns lie above or below the line in Figure 11.1. The distance from the line shows the response of Turbot's stock returns to news or events that affected Turbot but did not affect the overall market. For example, in Month 2, investors in Turbot stock benefited from good macroeconomic news (the market was up 1 percent) and also from some favourable news specific to Turbot. The market rise gave a boost of .8 percent to Turbot stock (beta of .8 times the 1 percent market return). Then firm-specific news gave Turbot shareholders an extra 1 percent return, for a total return that month of 1.8 percent.

> As this example illustrates, we can break down common stock returns into two parts: the part explained by market returns and the firm's beta, and the part due to news that is specific to the firm. Fluctuations in the first part reflect market risk; fluctuations in the second part reflect unique risk.

Of course, diversification can get rid of the unique risks. That's why wise investors, who don't put all their eggs in one basket, will look to Turbot's less-than-average beta and call its stock "defensive."

Check Point 11.1

Here are six months' returns to shareholders in the Anchovy Queen restaurant chain:

Month	Market Return, %	Anchovy Queen Return, %
1	+1	+2
2	+1	+0
3	+1	+1
4	–1	–1
5	–1	+0
6	–1	–2

Draw a figure like Figure 11.1 and check the slope of the fitted line. What is Anchovy Queen's beta?

FIGURE 11.1

This figure is a plot of the data presented in the table from Example 11.1. Each point shows the performance of Turbot-Charged Seafoods stock when the overall market is either up or down by 1 percent. On average, Turbot-Charged moves in the same direction as the market, but not as far. Therefore, Turbot-Charged's beta is less than 1.0. We can measure beta by the slope of a line fitted to the points in the figure. In this case it is .8.

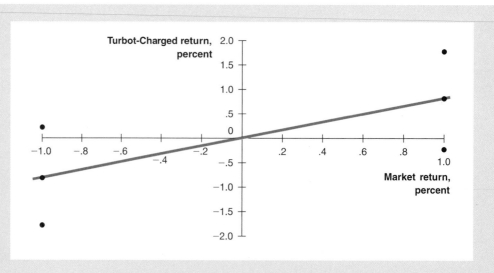

Real life doesn't serve up numbers quite as convenient as those in our examples so far. However, the procedure for measuring real companies' betas is exactly the same:

1. Observe rates of return, usually monthly, for the stock and the market.
2. Plot the observations as in Figure 11.1.
3. Fit a line showing the average return to the stock at different market returns.

Beta is the slope of the fitted line.

This may sound like a lot of work but in practice computers do it for you. In Excel, the SLOPE function will give you the slope of a fitted line. Suppose you have 60 monthly rates of return for a stock and for the TSX. If the stock returns are in cells A1 to A60 and the market returns are in cells B1 to B60, the beta of the stock is SLOPE(A1:A60,B1:B60).

You can also calculate the beta of a stock if you know the correlation of the stock's return with the market's return, and the standard deviations of the stock and market returns. Using the notation from Chapter 10, let $\rho_{j,m}$ be the correlation coefficient for the return on stock j with the market; σ_j, the standard deviation of the return on stock j; and σ_m, the standard deviation of the return on the market. The beta of stock j is the correlation coefficient times the stock's standard deviation, divided by the market's standard deviation:

$$\textbf{Beta of stock j} = \beta_j = \frac{\rho_{j,m}\sigma_j}{\sigma_m} \tag{11.1}$$

For example, if a stock has a correlation coefficient with the market equal to .7 and the stock return's standard deviation is 30 percent and the market return's standard deviation is 20 percent, the beta of the stock is $.7 \times .3/.2 = 1.05$. If the stock's correlation with the market is only .3, its beta will be much lower: $.3 \times .3/.2 = .45$.

Another way to measure the relatedness of changes in one random variable with another is *covariance*. The correlation between two variables equals their covariance divided by the product of their standard deviations: $\rho_{j,m} = \text{cov}(r_j, r_m)/\sigma_j\sigma_m$. If we replace correlation with this expression, we get another expression for beta: covariance between the return on the stock, r_j, and the market, r_m, divided by the variance of the market return, σ_m^2:

$$\textbf{Beta of stock j} = \beta_j = \frac{\text{cov}(r_j, r_m)}{\sigma_m^2} \tag{11.2}$$

This formula for beta is consistent with our estimation of beta as the slope of the fitted line. Consult any basic statistics text and you will see that the slope of a fitted line can be expressed in terms of covariance and variance.

Here are two real examples of how to estimate stock betas.

BETAS FOR INCO AND ROYAL BANK

Each point in Figure 11.2*a* shows the return on Inco stock and the return on the market index in a different month. For example, the circled point shows that in the month of June 1999 Inco stock price rose by 26 percent, whereas the market index rose by 5.1 percent. Notice that more often than not Inco outperformed the market when the index rose and underperformed the market when the index fell. Thus Inco was a relatively aggressive, high-beta stock.

We have drawn a line of best fit through the points in the figure.[2] The slope of this line is 1.47. For each extra 1 percent rise in the market, Inco stock price moved on average an extra 1.47 percent. For each extra 1 percent fall in the market, Inco stock price fell an extra 1.47 percent. Thus Inco's beta was 1.47.

---

[2] The line of best fit is usually known as a *regression* line. The slope of the line can be calculated using *ordinary least squares* regression. The dependent variable is the return on the stock (Inco). The independent variable is the return on the market index, in this case, a value-weighted market index from the Center for Research in Security Prices (CRSP). We chose not to use the S&P/TSX Composite Index return because in 1999 and 2000 it became heavily weighted in Nortel stocks and was not a widely diversified portfolio.

FIGURE 11.2

(a) Each point in this figure shows the returns on Inco common stock and the overall market in a particular month. Sixty months are plotted in all. Inco's beta is the slope of the line fitted to these points. Inco has a relatively high beta of 1.47.

(b) In this plot of 60 months' returns for Royal Bank and the overall market, the slope of the fitted line is much less than Inco's beta in (a). Royal Bank has a relatively low beta of .49.

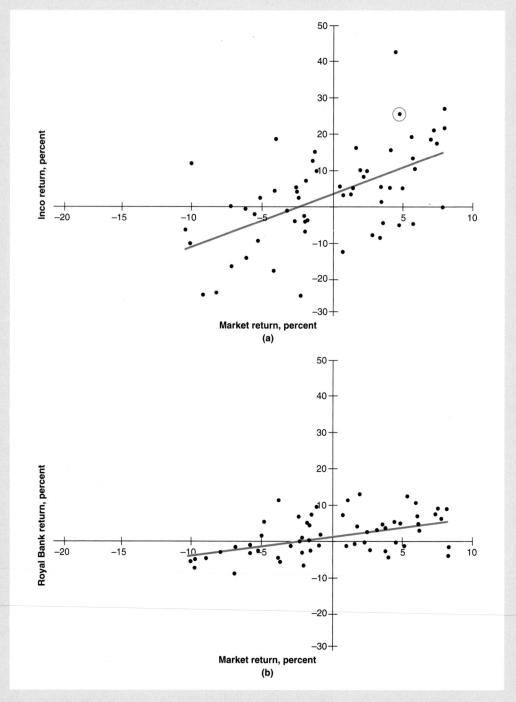

Market return, percent
(a)

Market return, percent
(b)

Source: Author's calculations, using stock returns from CRSP, Center for Research in Security Prices, Graduate School of Business, The University of Chicago (2003). Used with permission. All rights reserved. **www.crsp.uchicago.edu**

Of course, Inco's stock returns are not perfectly related to market returns. The company was also subject to unique risk, which shows up in the scatter of points around the line. Sometimes Inco flew south while the market went north, or vice versa.

Figure 11.2b shows a similar plot of the monthly returns for Royal Bank. In contrast to Inco, Royal Bank was a defensive, low-beta stock. It was not highly sensitive to market movements, usually lagging when the market rose and yet doing better (or not as badly) when the market fell. The slope of the line of best fit shows that on average an extra 1 percent change in the index resulted in an extra .49 percent change in the price of Royal Bank stock. Thus Royal Bank's beta was .49.

TABLE 11.1
Betas for selected common stocks, January 1999–December 2003

Stock	Beta
Biomira	2.23
CanWest Global Communications	1.89
Inco	1.47
Cameco	0.46
Four Seasons Hotel	1.29
Alcan Aluminum	1.17
Barrick Gold	0.16
BCE	0.86
Canadian National Railway	0.63
Magna International	0.50
Royal Bank	0.49

Note: Betas are calculated with five years of monthly returns.
Source: Author's calculations, using stock returns from CRSP, Center for Research in Security Prices, Graduate School of Business, The University of Chicago (2003). Used with permission. All rights reserved. **www.crsp.uchicago.edu**

Table 11.1 shows how past market movements have affected the stocks from Table 10.6. The stocks are sorted by the *standard deviation* of their return, not by beta. Table 11.1 shows that high variability of returns does not necessarily imply high sensitivity to market movements. Royal Bank, with the lowest standard deviation of 19.2 percent, had a low beta of .49. However, Barrick Gold, with a standard deviation of 30.5 percent, had the lowest beta. Its stock return is only .16 times as sensitive as the average stock to market movements. Much of Barrick Gold stock's variability is from unique risk, uncorrelated with the market, resulting in a very low beta. Biomira, with the highest standard deviation, also had the highest beta; its return was 2.23 times as sensitive as the average stock market movements.

PORTFOLIO BETAS

Diversification decreases variability from unique risk but not from market risk. The beta of a portfolio is just an average of the betas of the securities in the portfolio, weighted by the investment in each security. For example, a portfolio comprising only two stocks would have a beta as follows:

> **Beta of portfolio = (fraction of portfolio in first stock × beta of first stock)**
> **+ (fraction of portfolio in second stock × beta of second stock)**

Thus a portfolio invested 50-50 in Inco and Royal Bank would have a beta of (.5 × 1.47) + (.5 × .49) = .98.

A well-diversified portfolio of stocks all with betas of 1.47, like Inco, would still have a portfolio beta of 1.47. However, most of the individual stocks' unique risk would be diversified away. The market risk would remain, and such a portfolio would end up 1.47 times as variable as the market. For example, if the market has an annual standard deviation of 19 percent (about the historical average reported in Chapter 10), a fully diversified portfolio with beta of 1.47 has a standard deviation of 1.47 × 19 = 27.9 percent.

Portfolios with betas between 0 and 1.0 tend to move in the same direction as the market but not as far. A well-diversified portfolio of low-beta stocks like Royal Bank, all with betas of .49, has almost no unique risk and is relatively unaffected by market movements. Such a portfolio is .49 times as variable as the market.

Of course, on average, stocks have a beta of 1. A well-diversified portfolio including all kinds of stocks, with an average beta of 1, has the same variability as the market index.

Check Point 11.2   Say you invested an equal amount in each of the stocks shown in Table 11.1. Calculate the beta of your portfolio.

EXAMPLE 11.2	**HOW RISKY ARE MUTUAL FUNDS?**

You don't have to be wealthy to own a diversified portfolio. You can buy shares in one of the more than 6,000 mutual funds in Canada.

Investors buy shares of the funds, and the funds use the money to buy portfolios of securities. The returns on the portfolios are passed back to the funds' owners in proportion to their shareholdings. Therefore, the funds act like investment cooperatives, offering even the smallest investors diversification and professional management at low cost.

Let's look at the betas of two mutual funds that invest in stocks. Figure 11.3a plots the monthly returns of TD's Precious Metals mutual fund and the S&P/TSX Composite index from December 1999 to November 2004. You can see that the stocks in the Precious Metals fund had below-average sensitivity to market changes: on average they had a beta of .40.

If the Precious Metals fund had no unique risk, its portfolio would have been .40 times as variable as the market portfolio. But the fund had not diversified away quite all the unique risk; there is still some scatter about the line in Figure 11.3a. As a result, the variability of the fund was more than .40 times that of the market.

Figure 11.3b shows the same sort of plot for TD Canadian Index mutual fund. Notice that this fund has a beta of .98 and only a tiny residual of unique risk—the fitted line fits almost exactly because an *index fund* is designed to track the market as closely as possible. The managers of the fund do not attempt to pick good stocks but just work to achieve full diversification at very low cost. (The TD Canadian Index fund takes investments of as little as $1,000 outside an RRSP and $100 inside one, and manages the fund for an annual fee of .85 percent of the fund's assets.) The index fund is *fully diversified*. Investors in this fund buy the market as a whole and don't have to worry at all about unique risk.

Check Point 11.3

Suppose you could achieve full diversification in a portfolio constructed from stocks with an average beta of .5. If the standard deviation of the market is 20 percent per year, what is the standard deviation of the portfolio return?

11.2   RISK AND RETURN

In Chapter 10 we looked at past returns on selected investments. The least risky investment was Treasury bills. Since the return on Treasury bills is fixed, it is unaffected by what happens to the market. Thus the beta of Treasury bills is zero. The *most* risky investment that we considered was the market portfolio of common stocks. This has average market risk: its beta is 1.0.

Wise investors don't run risks just for fun. They are playing with real money and therefore require a higher return from the market portfolio than from Treasury bills. The difference between the expected return on the market and the interest rate on Treasury bills is termed the **market risk premium**. Over the past 79 years the average market risk premium has been just under 7 percent a year. Of course, there is plenty of scope for argument as to whether the past 79 years constitute a typical period, but we will just assume here that 7 percent is the normal risk premium; that is, the additional return that an investor could reasonably expect from investing in the stock market rather than Treasury bills.

In Figure 11.4a we plotted the risk and expected return from Treasury bills and the market portfolio. You can see that Treasury bills have a beta of zero and a risk-free return; we'll assume that return is 4 percent. The market portfolio has a beta of 1.0 and an assumed expected return of 11 percent.[3]

market risk premium Risk premium of market portfolio. Expected extra return on the market portfolio relative to the return on risk-free Treasury bills.

---

[3] On past evidence the risk premium on the market is 7 percent. With a 4 percent Treasury bill rate, the expected market return would be $4 + 7 = 11$ percent.

FIGURE 11.3

(a) The slope of the fitted line shows that investors in the TD Precious Metals mutual fund bore market risk less than that of the TSX portfolio. TD Precious Metals' beta was .40. This was the average beta of the individual common stocks held by the fund. They also bore some unique risk, however: note the scatter of TD Precious Metals' returns above and below the fitted line.

(b) The TD Canadian Index Fund is a fully diversified index fund designed to track the performance of the market. Note the fund's beta (.98) and the absence of unique risk. The fund's returns lie almost precisely on the fitted line, relating its returns to those of the TSX portfolio.

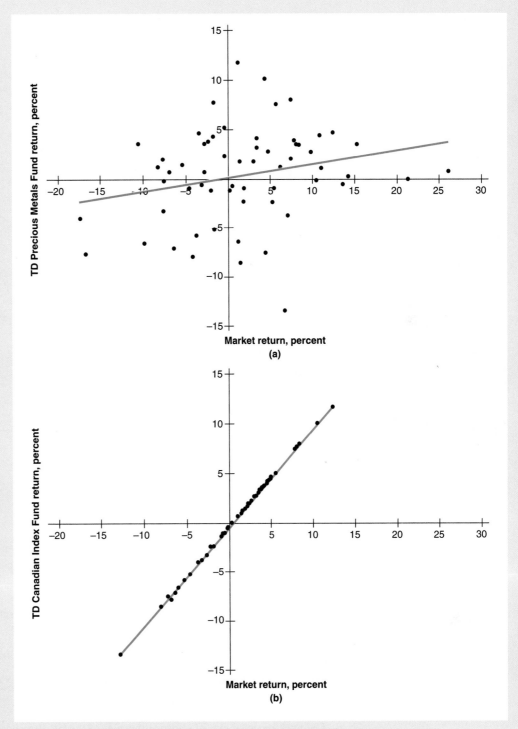

Source: Author's calculations, using data from **www.GlobeinvestorGOLD.com**, retrieved December 3, 2004.

Now, given these two benchmarks, what expected rate of return should an investor require from a stock or portfolio with a beta of .5? Halfway between, of course. Thus in Figure 11.4*b* we drew a straight line through the Treasury bill return and the expected market return and marked with an X the expected return for a beta of .5, that is, 7.5 percent. This includes a risk premium of 3.5 percent above the Treasury bill return of 4 percent.

FIGURE 11.4

(a) Here we begin the plot of expected rate of return against beta. The first benchmarks are Treasury bills (beta = 0) and the market portfolio (beta = 1.0). We assume a Treasury bill rate of 4 percent and a market return of 11 percent. The market risk premium is 11 − 4 = 7 percent.

(b) A portfolio split evenly between Treasury bills and the market will have beta = .5 and an expected return of 7.5 percent (point X). A portfolio invested 80 percent in the market and 20 percent in Treasury bills has beta = .8 and an expected rate of return of 9.6 percent (point Y). Note that the expected rate of return on any portfolio mixing Treasury bills and the market lies on a straight line. The risk premium is proportional to the portfolio beta.

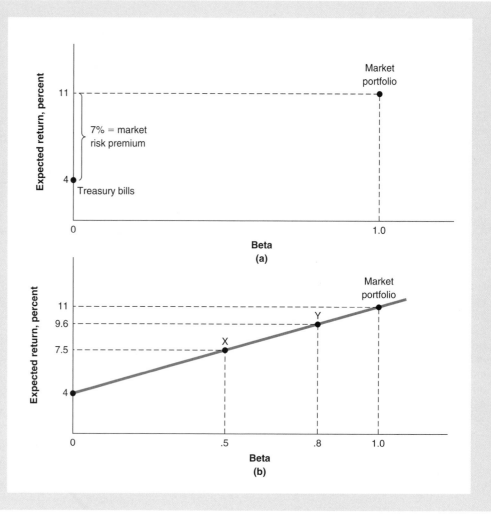

You can calculate this return as follows: start with the difference between the expected market return r_m and the Treasury bill rate r_f. This is the expected market risk premium.

$$\text{Market risk premium} = r_m - r_f = 11\% - 4\% = 7\%$$

Beta measures risk relative to the market. Therefore, the expected risk premium on any asset equals beta times the market risk premium:

Risk premium on any asset $= r - r_f = \beta(r_m - r_f)$ (11.3)

With a beta of .5 and a market risk premium of 7 percent,

$$\text{Risk premium} = \beta(r_m - r_f) = .5 \times 7 = 3.5\%$$

The total expected rate of return is the sum of the risk-free rate and the risk premium:

Expected return = risk-free rate + risk premium (11.4)
$$r = r_f + \beta(r_m - r_f)$$
$$= 4\% + 3.5\% = 7.5\%$$

You could have calculated the expected rate of return in one step from this formula:

$$\text{Expected return} = r = r_f + \beta(r_m - r_f)$$
$$= 4\% + (.5 \times 7\%) = 7.5\%$$

capital asset pricing model (CAPM) Theory of the relationship between risk and return that states that the expected risk premium on any security equals its beta times the market risk premium.

This formula states the basic risk–return relationship called the **capital asset pricing model**, or **CAPM**. The CAPM has a simple interpretation:

> The expected rates of return demanded by investors depend on two things: (1) compensation for the time value of money (the risk-free rate, r_f) and (2) a risk premium, which depends on beta and the market risk premium.

Note that the expected rate of return on an asset with $\beta = 1$ is just the expected market return. With a risk-free rate of 4 percent and market risk premium of 7 percent,

$$r = r_f + \beta(r_m - r_f)$$
$$= 4\% + (1 \times 7\%) = 11\%$$

Check Point 11.4

What are the risk premium and expected rate of return on a stock with $\beta = 1.5$? Assume a Treasury bill rate of 6 percent and a market risk premium of 7 percent.

WHY THE CAPM WORKS

The CAPM assumes that the stock market is dominated by well-diversified investors who are concerned only with market risk. That makes sense in a stock market where trading is dominated by large institutions and even small fry can diversify at very low cost.

EXAMPLE 11.3

HOW WOULD YOU INVEST $1 MILLION?

Have you ever daydreamed about receiving a $1 million cheque, no strings attached, from an unknown benefactor? Let's daydream about how you would invest it.

We have two good candidates: Treasury bills, which offer an absolutely safe return, and the market portfolio (possibly via the TD Canadian Index fund discussed earlier in this chapter). The market has generated superior returns on average, but those returns have fluctuated a lot. (Look back to Figure 10.3.) So your investment policy will depend on your tolerance for risk.

If you're a cautious soul, you may invest only part of your money in the market portfolio and lend the remainder to the government by buying Treasury bills. Suppose that you invest 80 percent of your money in the market portfolio and lend out the other 20 percent to the government by buying Treasury bills. Then the beta of your portfolio will be a mixture of the beta of the market ($\beta_{\text{market}} = 1.0$) and the beta of the Treasury bills ($\beta_{\text{T-bills}} = 0$):

$$\text{Beta of portfolio} = \left(\begin{array}{c} \text{proportion} \\ \text{in market} \end{array} \times \begin{array}{c} \text{beta of} \\ \text{market} \end{array} \right) + \left(\begin{array}{c} \text{proportion} \\ \text{in T-bills} \end{array} \times \begin{array}{c} \text{beta of} \\ \text{T-bills} \end{array} \right)$$
$$\beta = (.8 \times \beta_{\text{market}}) \qquad\qquad + (.2 \times \beta_{\text{T-bills}})$$
$$= (.8 \times 1.0) \qquad\qquad + (.2 \times 0) = .80$$

The fraction of funds that you invest in the market also affects your return. If you invest your entire million in the market portfolio, you earn the full market risk premium. But if you invest only 80 percent of your money in the market, you earn only 80 percent of the risk premium.

$$\begin{array}{c} \text{Expected} \\ \text{risk premium} \\ \text{on portfolio} \end{array} = \left(\begin{array}{c} \text{proportion in} \\ \text{T-bills} \end{array} \times \begin{array}{c} \text{risk premium} \\ \text{on T-bills} \end{array} \right) + \left(\begin{array}{c} \text{proportion in} \\ \text{market} \end{array} \times \begin{array}{c} \text{market risk} \\ \text{premium} \end{array} \right)$$
$$= (.2 \times 0) + (.8 \times \text{expected market risk premium})$$
$$= .8 \times \text{expected market risk premium}$$
$$= .8 \times 7 = 5.6\%$$

The expected return on your portfolio is equal to the risk-free interest rate plus the expected risk premium:

$$\text{Expected portfolio return} = r_{\text{portfolio}} = 4 + 5.6 = 9.6\%$$

In Figure 11.4*b* we show the beta and expected return on this portfolio by the letter *Y*.

THE SECURITY MARKET LINE

security market line
Relationship between expected return and beta.

Example 11.3 illustrates a general point: by investing some proportion of your money in the market portfolio and lending (or borrowing)[4] the balance, you can obtain any combination of risk and expected return along the sloping line in Figure 11.5. This line is generally known as the **security market line**.

Check Point 11.5

How would you construct a portfolio with a beta of .25? What is the expected return to this strategy? Assume Treasury bills yield 6 percent and the market risk premium is 7 percent.

> The security market line describes the expected returns and risks from investing different fractions of your funds in the market. It also sets a standard for other investments. Investors will be willing to hold other investments only if they offer equally good prospects. Thus the required risk premium for *any* investment is given by the security market line:
>
> Risk premium on investment = beta × expected market risk premium

FIGURE 11.5
The security market line shows how expected rate of return depends on beta. According to the capital asset pricing model, expected rates of return for all securities and all portfolios lie on this line.

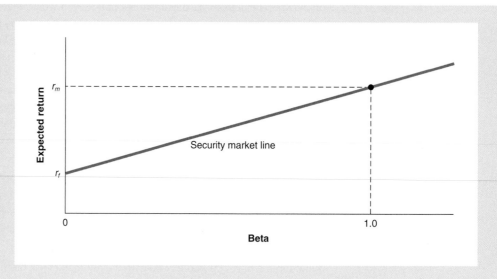

---

[4] Notice that the security market line extends above the market return at $\beta = 1$. How would you generate a portfolio with, say, $\beta = 2$? It's easy, but it's risky. Suppose you borrow $1 million at the risk-free rate and invest the loan plus $1 million in the market portfolio. That gives you $2 million invested and a $1 million liability. Your portfolio now has a beta of 2:

$$\text{Beta of portfolio} = (\text{proportion in market} \times \text{beta of market}) + (\text{proportion in loan} \times \text{beta of loan})$$
$$\beta = (2 \times \beta_{\text{market}}) + (-1 \times \beta_{\text{loan}})$$
$$= (2 \times 1.0) + (-1 \times 0) = 2$$

Notice that the proportion in the loan is negative because you are borrowing, not lending, money.

By the way, borrowing from a bank or stockbroker would not be difficult or unduly expensive as long as you put up your $2 million stock portfolio as security for the loan.

Can you calculate the risk premium and the expected rate of return on this borrow-and-invest strategy?

Look back to Figure 11.4*b*, which asserts that an individual common stock with $\beta = .5$ must offer a 7.5 percent expected rate of return when Treasury bills yield 4 percent and the market risk premium is 7 percent. You can now see why this has to be so. If that stock offered a lower rate of return, nobody would buy even a little of it—they could get 7.5 percent just by investing 50-50 in Treasury bills and the market. And if nobody wants to hold the stock, its price has to drop. A lower price means a better buy for investors, that is, a higher rate of return. The price will fall until the stock's expected rate of return is pushed up to 7.5 percent. At that price and expected return the CAPM holds.

If, on the other hand, our stock offered more than 7.5 percent, diversified investors would want to buy more of it. That would push the price up and the expected return down to the levels predicted by the CAPM.

This reasoning holds for stocks with any beta. That's why the CAPM makes sense, and why the expected risk premium on an investment should be proportional to its beta.

Check Point 11.6

Suppose you invest $400,000 in Treasury bills and $600,000 in the market portfolio. What is the return on your portfolio if Treasury bills yield 6 percent and the expected return on the market is 15 percent? What does the return on this portfolio imply for the expected return on individual stocks with betas of .6?

HOW WELL DOES THE CAPM WORK?

The basic idea behind the capital asset pricing model is that investors expect a reward for both waiting and worrying. The greater the worry, the greater the expected return. If you invest in a risk-free Treasury bill, you just receive the rate of interest. That's the reward for waiting. When you invest in risky stocks, you can expect an extra return or risk premium for worrying. The capital asset pricing model states that this risk premium is equal to the stock's beta times the market risk premium. Therefore,

$$\text{Expected return on stock} = \text{risk-free interest rate} + (\text{beta} \times \text{market risk premium})$$
$$r = r_f + \beta(r_m - r_f)$$

How well does the CAPM work in practice? Do the returns on stocks with betas of .5 on average lie halfway between the return on the market portfolio and the interest rate on Treasury bills? Unfortunately, the evidence is conflicting. Let's look back to the actual returns earned by investors in low-beta stocks and in high-beta stocks.

Imagine that in 1931 ten investors gathered in a Wall Street bar to discuss their portfolios. Each agreed to follow a different strategy. Each year investor 1 opted to buy the 10 percent of New York Stock Exchange stocks with the lowest betas; investor 2 chose the 10 percent with the next-lowest betas; and so on, up to investor 10, who agreed to buy the stocks with the highest betas. They also agreed that they or their heirs would return 70 years later to compare results, and so they parted with much cordiality and good wishes.

Although the 10 investors all passed away, their heirs agreed to meet in the same bar, early in 2002, to compare the performance of the portfolios. Figure 11.6 shows how they fared. Investor 1's portfolio turned out to be much less risky than the market; its beta was only .35. However, investor 1 also realized the lowest return, 10.1 percent above the risk-free rate of interest. At the other extreme, the beta of investor 10's portfolio was 1.68, about 4.8 times that of investor 1's portfolio. But investor 10 was rewarded with the highest return, averaging 18.6 percent above the interest rate. So over this 70-year period, returns did indeed increase with beta.

As you can see from Figure 11.6, the market portfolio over the same 70-year period provides an average return of 14 percent above the interest rate[5] and (of course) had a beta of 1.0. The CAPM predicts that the risk premium should lie on the upward-sloping security market line in Figure 11.6. Since the market provided a risk premium of 14 percent, investor 1's portfolio, with a beta of .35, should have provided a risk premium of a shade under 5 percent, and investor 10's portfolio, with a beta of 1.68, should have given a premium of a shade over 23 percent. You can see that while high-beta stocks performed better than low-beta stocks, the difference was not as great as the CAPM predicts.

Figure 11.6 provides broad support for the CAPM, though it suggests that the line relating return to beta has been too flat. But recent years have been less kind to the CAPM. For example, if the 10 friends had invested their cash in 1966 rather than 1931, there would have been very little relation between their portfolio returns and beta. Does this imply that there has been a fundamental change in the relation between risk and return in the last 35 years or did high-beta stocks just happen to perform worse during these years than investors expected? It is hard to be sure.

There is little doubt that the CAPM is too simple to capture everything that is going on in the stock market. For example, look at Figure 11.7, which shows the cumulative return on three portfolios. The dark blue line shows that a dollar invested in the U.S. equity market at the end of 1926 would have grown to just over $1,600 by 2001. The gold line shows how you would have fared if you had invested in a portfolio of the stocks of small firms. By 2001 your wealth would have swelled to over $4,000. Finally, the light blue line shows your performance if you had invested only in stocks with a high ratio of book value to market value. Investors often refer to such stocks as "value stocks" in contrast to "growth stocks," which have a low ratio of book to market. Each dollar invested in a portfolio of value stocks would have appreciated to more than $13,000 by 2001.

The superior performance of small-firm stocks and value stocks does not fit well with the CAPM, which predicts that beta is the only reason that expected returns differ. If investors *expected* the returns to depend on firm size or book-to-market ratios, then the simple version of the capital asset pricing model cannot be the whole truth.

FIGURE 11.6

The capital asset pricing model states that the expected risk premium from any investment should lie on the security market line. The dots show the actual average risk premiums from portfolios with different betas. The high-beta portfolios generated higher average returns, just as predicted by the CAPM. But the high-beta portfolios plotted below the security market line, and four of the five low-beta portfolios plotted above. A line fitted to the 10 portfolio returns would be flatter than the market line.

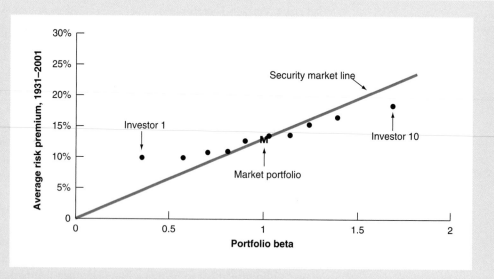

[5] In Figure 11.6 the stocks in the "market portfolio" are weighted equally. Since the stocks of small firms have provided higher average returns than those of large firms, the risk premium on an equally weighted index is higher than on a value-weighted index. This is one reason for the difference between the 14 percent market risk premium in Figure 11.6 and the 7 percent premium reported in Table 10.1. Also, this study is based on U.S. market data and covers a different time period than we used in Chapter 10.

FIGURE 11.7 An investment in 1926 in the stocks of small firms or those with high book-to-market ratios would have resulted in above-average returns (U.S. data).

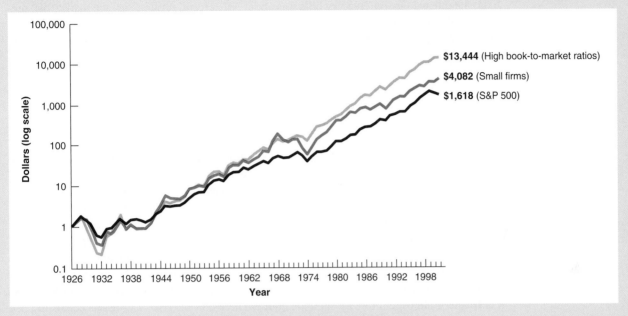

$13,444 (High book-to-market ratios)
$4,082 (Small firms)
$1,618 (S&P 500)

Source: Kenneth French's Web page, **http://mba.tuck.dartmouth.edu/pages/faculty/ken.french/**

What's going on here? It is hard to say. Defenders of the capital asset pricing model emphasize that it is concerned with *expected* returns, whereas we can observe only actual returns. Actual returns reflect expectations, but they also embody lots of "noise"—the steady flow of surprises that conceal whether on average investors have received the returns that they expected. Thus, when we observe that in the past small-firm stocks and value stocks have provided superior performance, we can't be sure whether this was simply a coincidence or whether investors have required a higher return to hold these stocks.

Such debates have prompted headlines like "Is Beta Dead?" and "Is Beta Dead Again?"in the business and academic press.[6] It is not the first time that beta has been declared dead, but the CAPM remains the leading model for estimating required returns. Only strong theories can have more than one funeral.

The CAPM is not the only model of risk and return. It has several brothers and sisters as well as cousins. These other models, including the multi-factor CAPM and Arbitrage Pricing Theory (APT), argue that the risk of a stock depends on more than its correlation with the market index. Although much of a stock's risk does depend on the general movement of the market, stock risk may also be affected by the growth rate of GDP, the yield spread between long- and short-term bonds, and relative firm size.[7] Researchers have examined these other factors and some believe that beta and the CAPM are not enough to capture all the systematic (non-diversifiable) risks.[8] However, the CAPM captures two fundamental ideas in a simple way. First, almost everyone agrees that investors require some extra return for taking on risk. Second, investors appear to be concerned principally with the market risk that they cannot eliminate by diversification. That is why financial managers rely on the capital asset pricing model as a good rule of thumb.

---

[6] A. Wallace, "Is Beta Dead?" *Institutional Investor* 14 (July 1980), pp. 22–30 and R. Grinold, "Is Beta Dead Again?," *Financial Analyst Journal* 49 (July/August 1993), pp. 28–34.

[7] To learn more about models of stock returns, see Z. Bodie, A. Kane, A. J. Marcus, S. Perrakis, and P. Ryan, *Investments* (5th ed.) (Toronto: McGraw-Hill Ryerson, 2005).

[8] Visit **www.ibbotson.com**, the Web site of Ibbotson Associates, to see how one company estimates and sells CAPM betas and other risk measures. Click on "Cost of Capital Center" and explore the sample information.

USING THE CAPM TO ESTIMATE EXPECTED RETURNS

To calculate the returns that investors are expecting from particular stocks, we need three numbers—the risk-free interest rate, the expected market risk premium, and the beta. In December 2004, the interest rate on Treasury bills was about 3.0 percent. Assume that the market risk premium is about 7 percent. Finally, look back to Table 11.1, where we gave you betas of several stocks. Table 11.2 puts these numbers together to give an estimate of the expected return from each stock. Let's take Inco as an example:

$$\text{Expected return on Inco} = \text{risk-free interest rate} + \left(\text{beta} \times \begin{array}{c} \text{expected market} \\ \text{risk premium} \end{array} \right)$$

$$r = 3.0\% + (1.47 \times 7\%)$$
$$= 13.29\%$$

You can also use the capital asset pricing model to find the discount rate for a new capital investment. For example, suppose you are asked to analyze a proposal by Biomira to expand its operations. At what rate should you discount the forecast cash flows? According to Table 11.2 investors are looking for a return of 18.6 percent from investments with the risk of Biomira stock. That is the opportunity cost of capital for Biomira's expansion project.

In practice, choosing a discount rate is seldom this easy. (After all, you can't expect to become a captain of finance simply by plugging numbers into a formula.) For example, you must learn how to estimate the return demanded by the company's investors when the company has issued both equity and debt securities. We could ignore this complication in the case of Biomira because it is financed almost entirely by common equity. Therefore, the risk of its assets equals the risk of its equity. Most companies, however, finance themselves with a mix of debt and equity. We will come to such refinements later.

EXAMPLE 11.4   **COMPARING PROJECT RETURNS AND THE OPPORTUNITY COST OF CAPITAL**

You have forecast the cash flows on a project and calculated that its internal rate of return is 12 percent. Suppose that Treasury bills offer a return of 4 percent and the expected market risk premium is 7 percent. Should you go ahead with the project?

To answer this question you need to figure out the opportunity cost of capital r. This depends on the project's beta. For example, if the project is a sure thing, the beta is zero and the cost of capital equals the interest rate on Treasury bills:

TABLE 11.2
Expected rates of return

Stock	Expected return, %
Biomira	18.6
CanWest Global Communications	16.2
Inco	13.3
Cameco	6.2
Four Seasons Hotel	12.0
Alcan Aluminum	11.2
Barrick Gold	4.1
BCE	9.0
Canadian National Railway	7.4
Magna International	6.5
Royal Bank	6.4

Note: Expected return = $r = r_f + \beta(r_m - r_f) = 3\% + (\beta \times 7\%)$.

Source: Author's calculations, using stock returns from CRSP, Center for Research in Security Prices, Graduate School of Business, The University of Chicago (2003). Used with permission. All rights reserved.
www.crsp.uchicago.edu

$$r = 4 + (0 \times 7) = 4\%$$

If your project offers a return of 12 percent when the cost of capital is 4 percent, you should obviously go ahead.[9]

Sure-fire projects rarely occur outside finance texts. So let's think about the cost of capital if the project has the same risk as the market portfolio. In this case beta is 1 and the cost of capital is the expected return on the market:

$$r = 4 + (1 \times 7) = 11\%$$

The project appears less attractive than before, but still worth doing.

What if the project has even higher risk? Suppose, for example, that it has a beta of 1.5. What is the cost of capital in this case? To find the answer, we plug a beta of 1.5 into our formula for r:

$$r = 4 + (1.5 \times 7) = 14.5\%$$

A project this risky would need a return of at least 14.5 percent to justify going ahead. The 12 percent project should be rejected.

This rejection occurs because, as Figure 11.8 shows, the project's expected rate of return plots below the security market line. The project offers a lower return than investors can get elsewhere, so it is a negative-NPV investment.

The security market line provides a standard for project acceptance. If the project's return lies above the security market line, then the return is higher than investors could expect to get by investing their funds in the capital market and, therefore, is an attractive investment opportunity.

Check Point 11.7

Suppose that Biomira's expansion project is forecast to produce cash flows of $50 million a year for each of 10 years. What is its present value? Use data from Table 11.2. What would the present value be if the beta of the investment were .7 and the risk-free rate were 3 percent?

FIGURE 11.8
The expected return of this project is less than the expected return one could earn on stock market investments with the same market risk (beta). Therefore, the project's expected return–risk combination lies below the security market line, and the project should be rejected.

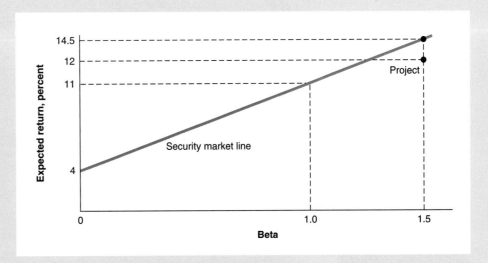

---

[9] In Chapter 7 we described some special cases where you should prefer projects that offer a *lower* internal rate of return than the cost of capital. We assume here that your project is a "normal" one, and that you prefer high IRRs to low ones.

11.3   CAPITAL BUDGETING AND PROJECT RISK

COMPANY VERSUS PROJECT RISK

Long before the development of modern theories linking risk and return, smart financial managers adjusted for risk in capital budgeting. They realized intuitively that, other things being equal, risky projects are less desirable than safe ones and must provide higher rates of return.

company cost of capital
Expected rate of return demanded by investors in a company, determined by the average risk of the company's assets and operations.

Many companies estimate the rate of return required by investors in their securities and use this **company cost of capital** to discount the cash flows on all new projects. Since investors require a higher rate of return from a risky company, risky firms will have a higher company cost of capital and will set a higher discount rate for their new investment opportunities. For example, we showed in Table 11.1 that on past evidence Biomira has a beta of 2.23 and the corresponding expected rate of return (see Table 11.2) is about 18.6 percent. According to the company cost of capital rule, Biomira should use a 18.6 percent cost of capital to calculate project NPVs.

This is a step in the right direction, but we must take care when the firm has issued securities other than equity. Moreover, this approach can get a firm in trouble if its new projects do not have the same risk as its existing business. Biomira's beta reflects investors' estimate of the risk of the business, and its company cost of capital is the return that investors require for taking on this risk. If Biomira is considering an expansion of its regular business, it makes sense to discount the forecast cash flows by the company cost of capital. But suppose that Biomira is wondering whether to branch out into the broadcasting business. Its beta tells us nothing about the **project cost of capital.** That depends on the risk of the broadcasting business and the return that shareholders require from investing in such a business.

project cost of capital
Minimum acceptable expected rate of return on a project given its risk.

The concept of measuring the project's cost of capital on the basis of the project's risk seems straightforward to us. However, sometimes managers seriously miscalculate a project's required rate of return because they ignore the fact that the project's risk is very different than the firm's overall risk. To avoid that mistake, ask yourself: If this project were a mini-firm, separate from our company, what rate of return would investors require to be willing to invest in it? When a firm evaluates an investment, it must use a required rate of return that corresponds to the risk of the investment.

The principle of assessing the required rate of return on the basis of the risk of the investment applies to your own investment activities. Suppose you take money from your savings account, which is currently paying 1 percent annual interest, and invest in shares of Inco. You would not be happy if your expected return on the Inco shares was only 1 percent. You would expect to earn a higher rate of return to compensate for the substantially higher market risk associated with Inco, right? The same applies to a firm's investment decisions: the project's required rate of return depends on the project's risk.

> The project cost of capital depends on the use to which that capital is put. Therefore, it depends on the risk of the project and not on the risk of the company. If a company invests in a low-risk project, it should discount the cash flows at a correspondingly low cost of capital. If it invests in a high-risk project, those cash flows should be discounted at a high cost of capital.

SEE BOX P. 355

The nearby Finance in Action box discusses how companies decide on the discount rate. It notes, for example, that Siemens, a German industrial giant, uses 16 different discount rates, depending on the riskiness of each line of its business.

✓ Check Point 11.8

The company cost of capital for Biomira is about 18.6 percent (see Table 11.2); for CanWest Global Communications it is about 16.2 percent. What would be the more reasonable discount rate for Biomira to use for its proposed broadcasting division? Why?

It did raise some eyebrows at first. Two months ago, when Aegon, a Dutch life insurer known for taking care of its shareholders, bought Transamerica, a San Francisco–based insurer, Aegon said it was expecting a return of only 9% from the deal, well below the 11% "hurdle rate" it once proclaimed as its benchmark. Had this darling of the stock market betrayed its devoted investors for the sake of an eye-catching deal?

Not at all. Years of falling interest rates and rising equity valuations have shrunk the cost of capital for firms such as Aegon. So companies that regularly adjust the hurdle rates they use to evaluate potential investment projects and acquisitions are not cheating their shareholders. Far from it: they are doing their investors a service. Unfortunately, such firms are rare in Europe. "I don't know many companies at all who lowered their hurdle rates in line with interest rates, so they're all underinvesting," says Greg Milano, a partner at Stern Stewart, a consultancy that helps companies estimate their cost of capital.

This has a huge impact on corporate strategy. Companies generally make their investment decisions by discounting the net cash flows a project is estimated to generate to their present value. If the net present value is positive, the project should make shareholders better off.

Generally speaking, says Paul Gibbs, an analyst at J.P. Morgan, an American bank, finance directors in America often review their hurdle rates; in continental Europe they do so sometimes, and in Britain, rarely. As a result, the Confederation of British Industry, a big-business lobby, worries about underinvestment, and officials at the Bank of England grumble about firms' reluctance to lower hurdles. This reluctance seems surprising, since companies with high hurdle rates will tend to lose out in bidding for business assets or firms. The hurdle rate should reflect not only interest rates but also the riskiness of each individual project. For instance, Siemens, a German industrial giant, last year started assigning a different hurdle rate to each of its 16 businesses, ranging from household appliances to medical equipment and semiconductors. The hurdle rates—from 8% to 11%—are based on the volatility of shares in rival companies in the relevant industry, and are under constant review.

Source: "How High a Hurdle?" *The Economist*, May 8, 1999, p. 82. © 1999 The Economist Newspaper Group, Inc. Reprinted with permission. Further reproduction prohibited. **www.economist.com**.

DETERMINANTS OF PROJECT RISK

We have seen that the company cost of capital is the correct discount rate for projects that have the same risk as the company's existing business, but *not* for those projects that are safer or riskier than the company's average. How do we know whether a project is unusually risky? Estimating project risk is never going to be an exact science, but here are a few things to bear in mind.

First, we saw in Chapter 9 that operating leverage increases the risk of a project. When a large fraction of your costs is fixed, any change in revenues can have a dramatic effect on earnings. Therefore, projects that involve high fixed costs tend to have higher betas.

Second, many people intuitively associate risk with the variability of earnings. But much of this variability reflects diversifiable risk. Lone prospectors in search of gold look forward to extremely uncertain future earnings, but whether they strike it rich is not likely to depend on the performance of the rest of the economy. These investments have a high standard deviation but a low beta.

Third, look at the risk and required rate of return of a similar risk project outside the firm. (We saw this in Check Point 11.8). Biomira uses the required rate of return of a company already in the broadcasting industry—CanWest Global—to assess its investment in a broadcasting division. Using CanWest's cost of capital is an application of the **pure-play approach** to determine project risk. *Pure play* is a term used by investors to refer to companies exclusively involved in a single line of business. If you wanted a pure play in silver, you would invest in a silver mining company and not in diversified company that owns a silver mine.

pure-play approach
Estimating project cost of capital using the cost of capital of another company involved exclusively in the same type of project.

The key to the pure-play approach is finding the beta and market-required rate of return of a company exclusively involved in the type of project under consideration. If the comparable company is publicly traded, its beta may be available from a company specializing in financial analysis such as Bloomberg or Ibbotson. You can also estimate the beta yourself using the stock's monthly rates of return, as we did for Figure 11.2. If the comparable company is not publicly traded, you may wish to estimate its beta with rates of return based on accounting earnings or cash flow.[10]

---

[10] For example, see W. H. Beaver and J. Manegold, "The Association between Market-Determined and Accounting-Determined Measures of Systematic Risk: Some Further Evidence," *Journal of Financial and Quantitative Analysis*, 10 (June 1975), pp. 231–284.

It may be difficult to find a suitable pure play for comparison. Many companies are involved in several different businesses and hence their betas reflect the risks of all of the businesses. Like any portfolio, the beta of a company is the sum of the betas of its businesses, each weighted by its fraction of the firm's total value. Even if a comparable company is found, determining the appropriate risk and discount rate may be complicated by a different capital structure. We will have more to say about this in Chapter 12.

You cannot hope to measure the systematic risk of a project with any precision, but good managers examine any project from a variety of angles and look for clues to its riskiness. They know that high market risk is a characteristic of cyclical ventures and of ventures with high fixed costs. They think about the major uncertainties affecting the economy and how projects are affected by these uncertainties. Experience at assessing risks plays an important role too. Regrettably, we have no magic formula for determining a project's risk. On the other hand, if such a formula existed, no one would pay financial managers handsomely for their expertise.

> What matters is the strength of the relationship between the firm's earnings and the aggregate earnings of all firms. Thus cyclical businesses, whose revenues and earnings are strongly dependent on the state of the economy, tend to have high betas and a high cost of capital. By contrast, businesses that produce essentials, such as food, beer, and cosmetics, are less affected by the state of the economy. They tend to have low betas and a low cost of capital.

DON'T ADD FUDGE FACTORS TO DISCOUNT RATES

Risk to an investor arises because an investment adds to the spread of possible portfolio returns. To a diversified investor, risk is predominantly market risk. But in everyday usage risk simply means "bad outcome." People think of the "risks" of a project as the things that can go wrong. For example,

- A geologist looking for oil worries about the risk of a dry hole.
- A pharmaceutical manufacturer worries about the risk that a new drug that reverses balding may not be approved by Health Canada.
- The owner of a hotel in a politically unstable part of the world worries about the political risk of expropriation.

Managers sometimes add fudge factors to discount rates to account for worries such as these.

This sort of adjustment makes us nervous. First, the bad outcomes we cited appear to reflect diversifiable risks that would not affect the expected rate of return demanded by investors. Second, the need for an adjustment in the discount rate usually arises because managers fail to give bad outcomes their due weight in cash flow forecasts. They then try to offset that mistake by adding a fudge factor to the discount rate. For example, if a manager is worried about the possibility of a bad outcome, such as a dry hole in oil exploration, he or she may reduce the value of the project by using a higher discount rate. This approach is unsound, however. Instead, the possibility of the dry hole should be included in the calculation of the expected cash flows to be derived from the well. Suppose that there is a 50 percent chance of a dry hole and a 50 percent chance that the well will produce oil worth $20 million. Then the *expected* cash flow is not $20 million but $(.5 \times 0) + (.5 \times 20) = \$10$ million. You should discount the $10 million expected cash flow at the opportunity cost of capital: it does not make sense to discount the $20 million using a fudged discount rate.

> Expected cash flow forecasts should already reflect the probabilities of all possible outcomes, good and bad. If the cash flow forecasts are prepared properly, the discount rate should reflect only the market risk of the project. It should not have to be fudged to offset errors or biases in the cash flow forecast.

11.4   SUMMARY

1. **How can you measure and interpret the market risk, or beta, of a security?**

   The contribution of a security to the risk of a diversified portfolio depends on its market risk. But not all securities are equally affected by fluctuations in the market. The sensitivity of a stock to market movement is known as **beta**. Stocks with a beta greater than 1.0 are particularly sensitive to market fluctuations. Those with a beta of less than 1.0 are not so sensitive to such movements. The average beta of all stocks is 1.0.

2. **What is the relationship between the market risk of a security and the rate of return that investors demand of that security?**

   The extra return that investors require for taking risk is known as the risk premium. The **market risk premium**—that is, the risk premium on the **market portfolio**—averaged 7 percent between 1926 and 2004. The **capital asset pricing model** states that the expected risk premium of an investment should be proportional to both its beta and the market risk premium. The expected rate of return from any investment is equal to the risk-free interest rate plus the risk premium, so the **CAPM** boils down to

$$r = r_f + \beta(r_m - r_f)$$

The **security market line** is the graphical representation of the CAPM equation. The security market line relates the expected return investors demand of a security to the beta.

3. **How can a manager calculate the opportunity cost of capital for a project?**

   The opportunity cost of capital is the return that investors give up by investing in the project rather than in securities of equivalent risk. Financial managers use the capital asset pricing model to estimate the opportunity cost of capital. The **company cost of capital** is the expected rate of return demanded by investors in a company, determined by the average risk of the company's assets and operations.

   The opportunity cost of capital depends on the use to which the capital is put. Therefore, required rates of return are determined by the risk of the project, not by the risk of the firm's existing business. The **project cost of capital** is the minimum acceptable expected rate of return on a project given its risk.

   Your cash flow forecasts should already factor in the chances of pleasant and unpleasant surprises. Potential bad outcomes should be reflected in the discount rate only to the extent that they affect beta.

Related Web Links

http://finance.yahoo.com Includes stock betas as well as other risk measures and company profiles

www.ibbotson.com Click on the Cost of Capital Center to learn about its products and methodology

Key Terms

market portfolio	339	capital asset pricing model		company cost of capital	354
beta	339	(CAPM)	347	project cost of capital	354
market risk premium	344	security market line	348	pure-play approach	355

Questions and Problems

*Answers in Appendix B

BASIC

*1. **Risk and Return.** True or false? Explain or qualify as necessary.
  a.   Investors demand higher expected rates of return on stocks with more variable rates of return.
  b.   The capital asset pricing model predicts that a security with a beta of zero will provide an expected return of zero.
  c.   An investor who puts $10,000 in Treasury bills and $20,000 in the market portfolio will have a portfolio beta of 2.
  d.   Investors demand higher expected rates of return from stocks with returns that are highly exposed to macroeconomic changes.

e. Investors demand higher expected rates of return from stocks with returns that are very sensitive to fluctuations in the stock market.

2. **Diversifiable Risk.** In light of what you've learned about market versus diversifiable (unique) risks, explain why an insurance company has no problem selling life insurance to individuals but is reluctant to issue policies insuring against flood damage to residents of coastal areas. Why don't the insurance companies simply charge coastal residents a premium that reflects the actuarial probability of damage from hurricanes and other storms?

3. **Unique vs. Market Risk.** Figure 11.9 plots monthly rates of return from 2001 to 2004 for the Snake Oil mutual fund. Was this fund well diversified? Explain.

4. **Risk and Return.** Suppose that the risk premium on stocks and other securities did in fact rise with total risk (that is, the variability of returns) rather than just market risk. Explain how investors could exploit the situation to create portfolios with high expected rates of return but low levels of risk.

EXCEL

5. **CAPM and Hurdle Rates.** A project under consideration has an internal rate of return of 14 percent and a beta of .6. The risk-free rate is 4 percent and the expected rate of return on the market portfolio is 11 percent.
   a. Should the project be accepted?
   b. Should the project be accepted if its beta is 1.6?
   c. Does your answer change? Why or why not?

PRACTICE

6. **CAPM and Valuation.** You are considering acquiring a firm that you believe can generate expected cash flows of $10,000 a year forever. However, you recognize that those cash flows are uncertain.
   a. Suppose you believe that the beta of the firm is .4. How much is the firm worth if the risk-free rate is 5 percent and the expected rate of return on the market portfolio is 11 percent?
   b. By how much will you misvalue the firm if its beta is actually .6?

*7. **CAPM and Expected Return.** If the risk-free rate is 4 percent and the expected rate of return on the market portfolio is 11 percent, is a security with a beta of 1.25 and an expected rate of return of 11 percent overpriced or underpriced?

8. **Using Beta.** Investors expect the market rate of return this year to be 14 percent. A stock with a beta of .8 has an expected rate of return of 12 percent. If the market return this year turns out to be 10 percent, what is your best guess as to the rate of return on the stock?

FIGURE 11.9
Monthly rates of return for the Snake Oil mutual fund and the S&P/TSX Composite Index (See problem 3)

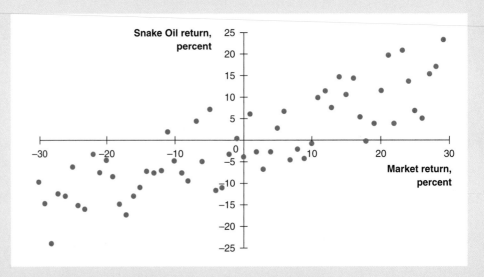

*9. **Unique versus Market Risk.** Figure 11.10 shows plots of monthly rates of return on three stocks versus the stock market index. The beta and standard deviation of each stock is given beside its plot.

 a. Which stock is riskiest to a diversified investor?

 b. Which stock is riskiest to an undiversified investor who puts all her funds in one of these stocks?

 c. Consider a portfolio with equal investments in each stock. What would this portfolio's beta have been?

 d. Consider a well-diversified portfolio made up of stocks with the same beta as Exxon. What are the beta and standard deviation of this portfolio's return? The standard deviation of the market portfolio's return is 20 percent.

 e. What is the expected rate of return on each stock? Use the capital asset pricing model with a market risk premium of 7 percent. The risk-free rate of interest is 4 percent.

EXCEL

10. **Calculating Beta.** Following are several months' rates of return for Tumblehome Canoe Company. Prepare a plot like Figure 11.1. What is Tumblehome's beta? Check your answers using the Excel SLOPE function.

Month	Market Return, %	Tumblehome Return, %
1	0	+1
2	0	−1
3	−1	−2.5
4	−1	−0.5
5	+1	+2
6	+1	+1
7	+2	+4
8	+2	+2
9	−2	−2
10	−2	−4

EXCEL

*11. **Expected Returns.** An economy has two scenarios: boom or bust. The returns in each scenario for the market portfolio, an aggressive stock A, and a defensive stock D are

	Rate of Return		
Scenario	Market	Aggressive Stock A	Defensive Stock D
Bust	−8%	−10%	−6%
Boom	32	38	24

 a. Find the beta of each stock. In what way is stock D defensive?

 b. If each scenario is equally likely, find the expected rate of return on the market portfolio and on each stock.

 c. If the Treasury bill rate is 4 percent, what does the CAPM say about the fair expected rate of return on the two stocks?

 d. Which stock seems to be a better buy based on your answers to (a) through (c)?

EXCEL

12. **CAPM and Cost of Capital.** Draw the security market line when the Treasury bill rate is 4 percent and the market risk premium is 7 percent. What are the project costs of capital for new ventures with betas of .75 and 1.75? Which of the following capital investments have positive NPVs?

Project	Beta	Internal Rate of Return, %
P	1.0	11
Q	0.0	6
R	2.0	17
S	0.4	7
T	1.6	16

FIGURE 11.10
These plots show
monthly rates of return
for (a) Exxon, (b)
Polaroid, (c) Nike, and
the market portfolio.
See problem 9.

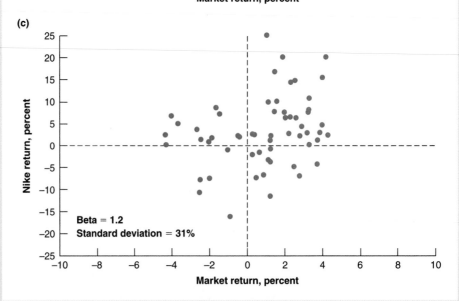

*13. **CAPM and Valuation.** You are a consultant to a firm evaluating an expansion of its current business. The annual cash flow forecasts (in millions of dollars) for the project are

Years	Annual Cash Flow
0	−100
1–10	+ 15

Based on the behaviour of the firm's stock, you believe that the beta of the firm is 1.4. Assuming that the rate of return available on risk-free investments is 4 percent and that the expected rate of return on the market portfolio is 11 percent, what is the net present value of the project?

14. **CAPM and Cost of Capital.** Reconsider the project in the preceding problem. What is the project IRR? What is the cost of capital for the project? Does the accept–reject decision using IRR agree with the decision using NPV?

*15. **CAPM and Valuation.** A share of stock with a beta of .75 now sells for $50. Investors expect the stock to pay a year-end dividend of $2. The Treasury bill rate is 4 percent, and the market risk premium is 7 percent. If the stock is perceived to be fairly priced today, what must be investors' expectation for the price of the stock at the end of the year?

EXCEL

16. **CAPM and Expected Return.** Reconsider the stock in the preceding problem. Suppose investors actually believe the stock will sell for $54 at year-end. Is the stock a good or bad buy? What will investors do? At what point will the stock reach an "equilibrium" at which it again is perceived as fairly priced?

17. **Portfolio Risk and Return.** Suppose that the TSX, with a beta of 1.0, has an expected return of 13 percent and Treasury bills provide a risk-free return of 5 percent.
    a. What would be the expected return and beta of portfolios constructed from these two assets with weights in the TSX of (1) 0; (2) .25; (3) .5; (4) .75; (5) 1.0?
    b. Based on your answer to (a), what is the trade-off between risk and return, that is, how does expected return vary with beta?
    c. What does your answer to (b) have to do with the security market line relationship?

18. **Portfolio Risk and Return.** Suppose that the TSX, with a beta of 1.0, has an expected return of 10 percent and Treasury bills provide a risk-free return of 5 percent.
    a. Construct a portfolio from these two assets with an expected return of 8 percent. What is the beta of this portfolio?
    b. Construct a portfolio from these two assets with a beta of .4. Calculate the portfolio's expected return.
    c. Show that the risk premiums of the portfolios in (a) and (b) are proportional to their betas.

*19. **CAPM and Valuation.** You are considering the purchase of real estate that will provide perpetual income that should average $50,000 per year. How much will you pay for the property if you believe its market risk is the same as the market portfolio's? The Treasury bill rate is 5 percent, and the expected market return is 12.5 percent.

20. **Risk and Return.** According to the CAPM, would the expected rate of return on a security with a beta less than zero be more or less than the risk-free interest rate? Why would investors be willing to invest in such a security? *Hint*: Look back to the auto and gold example in Chapter 10.

21. **CAPM and Expected Return.** The following table shows betas for several companies. Calculate each stock's expected rate of return using the CAPM. Assume the risk-free rate of interest is 4 percent. Use a 7 percent risk premium for the market portfolio.

Company	Beta
ATI Technologies	2.48
Nova Chemicals	.95
Quebecor World	.41
Shaw Communications	.9

22. **CAPM and Expected Return.** Stock A has a beta of .5 and investors expect it to return 5 percent. Stock B has a beta of 1.5 and investors expect it to return 13 percent. Use the CAPM to find the market risk premium and the expected rate of return on the market.

*23. **CAPM and Expected Return.** If the expected rate of return on the market portfolio is 14 percent and Treasury bills yield 6 percent, what must be the beta of a stock that investors expect to return 10 percent?

24. **Internet.** Free online betas are hard to find for stocks listed on the TSX unless they are also listed on the NYSE, ASE, or Nasdaq. For a U.S.–listed company's beta, go to **http://finance.yahoo.com**, enter the stock's ticker symbol, then click on "More Key Statistics" to find the beta.

   To find Canadian stocks listed on the NYSE, go to **www.nyse.com**, click on "International," and then "Non–U.S. Listed Company Directory." For Nasdaq-listed companies, go to **www.nasdaq.com/asp/nonusoutput.asp?page=c**.

   Using this method, find the beta estimates for five different Canadian stocks and estimate their required rates of return. Use the current 3-month Treasury bill yield, available at **www.bankofcanada.ca/en/rates/tbill.html**, as the risk-free rate and a 7 percent market risk premium.

25. **Project Cost of Capital.** Suppose Shaw Communications, a major Canadian cable television, Internet, and satellite services provider, is considering a new investment in graphics hardware for computers. Which of the betas shown in problem 21 is most relevant in determining the required rate of return for this venture? Explain why the others are NOT appropriate.

26. **Risk and Return.** True or false? Explain or qualify as necessary.
   a. The expected rate of return on an investment with a beta of 2 is twice as high as the expected rate of return of the market portfolio.
   b. The contribution of a stock to the risk of a diversified portfolio depends on the market risk of the stock.
   c. If a stock's expected rate of return plots below the security market line, it is underpriced.
   d. A diversified portfolio with a beta of 2 is twice as volatile as the market portfolio.
   e. An undiversified portfolio with a beta of 2 is twice as volatile as the market portfolio.

27. **CAPM and Expected Return.** A mutual fund manager expects her portfolio to earn a rate of return of 9 percent this year. The beta of her portfolio is .8. If the rate of return available on risk-free assets is 4 percent and you expect the rate of return on the market portfolio to be 11 percent, should you invest in this mutual fund?

28. **Required Rate of Return.** Reconsider the mutual fund manager in the previous problem. Explain how you would use a stock index mutual fund and a risk-free position in Treasury bills (or a money-market mutual fund) to create a portfolio with the same risk as the manager's but with a higher expected rate of return. What is the rate of return on that portfolio?

29. **Required Rate of Return.** In view of your answer to the preceding problem, explain why a mutual fund must be able to provide an expected rate of return in excess of that predicted by the security market line for investors to consider the fund an attractive investment opportunity.

EXCEL

30. **CAPM.** We Do Bankruptcies is a law firm that specializes in providing advice to firms in financial distress. It prospers in recessions when other firms are struggling. Consequently, its beta is negative, –0.2.
   a. If the interest rate on Treasury bills is 5 percent and the expected return on the market portfolio is 12 percent, what is the expected return on the shares of the law firm according to the CAPM?

b. Suppose you invested 90 percent of your wealth in the market portfolio and the remainder of your wealth in the shares in the law firm. What would be the beta of your portfolio?

CHALLENGE

31. **Leverage and Portfolio Risk.** Footnote 4 in the chapter asks you to consider a borrow-and-invest strategy in which you use $1 million of your own money and borrow another $1 million at the risk-free rate to invest $2 million in a market index fund. If the risk-free interest rate is 4 percent and the expected rate of return on the market index fund is 12 percent, what is the risk premium and expected rate of return on the borrow-and-invest strategy? Why is the risk of this strategy twice that of simply investing your $1 million in the market index fund?

32. **Integrative.** BigCo has a market value of $1 billion and a beta of .9. It has three divisions: chemical processing, oil and gas distribution, and plastic products. The company is thinking about buying another chemical producer, ChemCo. ChemCo is expected to earn cash flows of $9 million this year and cash flows are expected to grow 4 percent per year thereafter. The beta of ChemCo is 1.4. Currently, the risk-free rate is 4 percent and the expected rate of return on the market portfolio is 11 percent.
   a. What is the expected rate of return for BigCo?
   b. What discount rate should BigCo use to evaluate ChemCo and why?
   c. How much is ChemCo worth?
   d. Suppose BigCo acquires ChemCo for the price in (c). What will be BigCo's new beta after adding ChemCo?

33. **Integrative.** Food Express is a well-established grocery chain. Computer Power is an up-and-coming computer software developer for business. Bridge Steel is an integrated steel producer, focusing on steel for buildings and bridges. Some information about the companies was provided by an investment banking company:

Firm	Beta	Expected Cash Flow Year 1	Expected Cash Flow Growth Rate Years 2 to 5	Year 6 and on
Food Express	.85	$ 7 million	3%	3%
Computer Power	.95	2 million	8%	4%
Bridge Steel	1.3	10 million	2%	3%

   a. If the risk-free rate is 4 percent and the expected return on the market portfolio is 10 percent, what is each firm worth?
   b. If you owned all three companies, what would be the beta of your stock portfolio?

34. **Comprehensive.** Conglomerated Industries has four divisions, each worth about one-quarter of the firm's market value. The following chart summarizes the possible returns on the divisions as well as on the market portfolio.

State of the Economy	Probability	Division Internal Rates of Return				Market Portfolio
		A	B	C	D	
Recession	.20	8%	–10%	–1%	–4%	–3%
Normal	.60	8%	15%	7%	15%	11%
Boom	.20	9%	30%	10%	20%	22%
Correlation with the market portfolio		0.730	0.995	0.970	0.945	1

   a. Calculate the expected rate of return and standard deviation of return for each division, the firm, and the market.
   b. What is the beta of the divisions, the firm, and the market?
   c. According to the CAPM, what rate of return do investors require for each division?

    d.   If the company was thinking of selling the underperforming divisions, which one(s) should it consider selling? Explain your answer.

35. **Standard & Poor's.** Use data from Market Insight (**www.mcgrawhill.ca/edu marketinsight**) to calculate the beta of Alliance Atlantis Communications. Get the monthly rates of return for Alliance and the S&P 500 from the "Mthly Adj. Price" link for the most recent four years. Use the Excel SLOPE function to estimate the beta.

36. **Standard & Poor's.** The "Mthly Val. Data" link at Market Insight (**www.mcgrawhill.ca/ edumarketinsight**) provides betas, updated monthly, for companies. Pick five companies in five different industries and compare their most recent equity betas. Think about the market risks faced by each of the companies. Would you expect their betas to be greater or less than one? Does your intuition match the calculated betas?

Solutions to Check Points

11.1 See Figure 11.11. Anchovy Queen's beta is 1.

11.2 A portfolio's beta is just a weighted average of the betas of the securities in the portfolio. In this case the weights are equal, since an equal amount is assumed invested in each of the stocks in Table 11.1. The average beta of these stocks is (2.23 + 1.89 + 1.47 + .46 + 1.29 + 1.17 + .16 + .86 + .63 + .50 + .49)/11 = 1.01.

11.3 The standard deviation of a fully diversified portfolio's return is proportional to its beta. The standard deviation in this case is .5 × 20 = 10 percent.

11.4 $r = r_f + \beta(r_m - r_f)$
$ = 6 + (1.5 \times 7) = 16.5\%$

11.5 Put 25 percent of your money in the market portfolio and the rest in Treasury bills. The expected market return is 6% + 1 × 7% = 13%. The portfolio's beta is .25 and its expected return is

$$r_{portfolio} = (.75 \times 6) + (.25 \times 13) = 7.75\%$$

11.6 $r_{portfolio} = (.4 \times 6) + (.6 \times 15) = 11.4\%$

This portfolio's beta is .6, since $600,000, which is 60 percent of the investment, is in the market portfolio. Investors would not buy a stock with a beta of .6 it unless it also offered a rate of return of 11.4 percent, and would rush to buy if it offered more. The stock price would adjust until the stock's expected rate of return was 11.4 percent.

FIGURE 11.11

Each point shows the performance of Anchovy Queen stock when the market is up or down by 1 percent. On average, Anchovy Queen stock follows the market; it has a beta of 1.

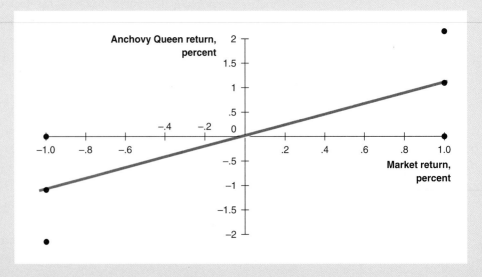

11.7   Present value = $50 million $\times$ 10-year annuity factor at 18.6%

                      = $220.0 million

If β = .7, then the cost of capital falls to

$$r = 3\% + (.7 \times 7\%) = 7.9\%$$

and the value of the 10-year annuity increases to $337.02 million.

11.8   Biomira should use CanWest's cost of capital. Biomira's cost of capital tells us what expected rate of return investors demand from the biotechnology business. This is not the appropriate project cost of capital for Biomira's venture into broadcasting. Note that we have ignored the fact that CanWest is financed with a mix of debt and equity. And we have not considered whether Biomira's proposed new venture makes any business sense. We shall deal with these issues in due course.

THE COST OF CAPITAL

In the last chapter you learned how to use the capital asset pricing model to estimate the expected return on a company's common stock. If the firm is financed wholly by common stock, then the shareholders own all the firm's assets and are entitled to all the cash flows. In this case, the expected return required by investors in the common stock equals the company cost of capital.[1]

Most companies, however, are financed by a mixture of securities, including common stock, bonds, and often preferred stock or other securities. Each of these securities has different risks and therefore people who invest in them look for different rates of return. In these circumstances, the company cost of capital is no longer the same as the expected return on the common stock. It depends on the expected return from all the securities that the company has issued. It also depends on taxes because interest payments made by a corporation are tax-deductible expenses.

Therefore, the company cost of capital is usually calculated as a weighted average of the *after-tax* interest cost of debt financing and the "cost of equity"; that is, the expected rate of return on the firm's common stock. The weights are the fractions of debt and equity in the firm's capital structure. Managers refer to the firm's *weighted-average cost of capital*, or *WACC* (rhymes with "quack").

Managers use the weighted-average cost of capital to evaluate average-risk capital investment projects. "Average risk" means that the project's risk matches the risk of the firm's existing assets and operations. This chapter explains how the weighted-average cost of capital is calculated in practice.

---

[1] Investors will invest in the firm's securities only if they offer the same expected return as that of other equally risky securities. When securities are properly priced, the return that investors can *expect* from their investments is therefore also the return that they *require*.

After studying this chapter you should be able to

- Calculate a firm's capital structure.
- Estimate the required rates of return on the securities issued by the firm.
- Calculate the weighted-average cost of capital.
- Understand when the weighted-average cost of capital is—or isn't—the appropriate discount rate for a new project.

Managers calculating WACC can get bogged down in formulas. We want you to understand *why* WACC works, not just how to calculate it. Let's start with "why?" We'll listen in as a young financial manager struggles to recall the rationale for project discount rates.

12.1   GEOTHERMAL'S COST OF CAPITAL

Jo Ann Cox, a recent graduate of a prestigious Canadian business school, poured a third cup of black coffee and tried again to remember what she once knew about project hurdle rates. Why hadn't she paid more attention in Finance 101? Why had she sold her finance text the day after passing the finance final?

Costas Thermopolis, her boss and CEO of Geothermal Corporation, had told her to prepare a financial evaluation of a proposed expansion of Geothermal's production. She was to report at 9 o'clock Monday morning. Thermopolis, whose background was geophysics, not finance, not only expected a numerical analysis, but also expected her to explain it to him.

Thermopolis had founded Geothermal in 1993 to produce electricity from geothermal energy trapped deep under Alberta. The company had pioneered this business and had been able to obtain perpetual production rights for a large tract on favourable terms from the Canadian government. When the 2008 oil shock drove up energy prices worldwide, Geothermal became an exceptionally profitable company. It was currently reporting a rate of return on book assets of 25 percent per year.

Now, in 2012, production rights are no longer cheap. The proposed expansion would cost $30 million and should generate a perpetual after-tax cash flow of $4.5 million annually. The projected rate of return is 4.5/30 = .15, or 15 percent, much less than the profitability of Geothermal's existing assets. However, once the new project is up and running, it will be no riskier than Geothermal's existing business.

Jo Ann realized that 15 percent is not necessarily a bad return—though, of course, 25 percent would have been better. Fifteen percent might still exceed Geothermal's cost of capital, that is, exceed the expected rate of return that outside investors would demand to invest money in the project. If the cost of capital was less than the 15 percent expected return, expansion would be a good deal and would generate net value for Geothermal and its shareholders.

Jo Ann remembered how to calculate the cost of capital for companies that use only common stock financing. Briefly she sketched the argument.

"I need the expected rate of return investors would require from Geothermal's real assets— the wells, pumps, generators, etc. That rate of return depends on the assets' risk. However, the assets aren't traded in the stock market, so I can't observe how risky they have been. I can observe only the risk of Geothermal's common stock.

"But if Geothermal issues only stock—no debt—then owning the stock means owning the assets, and the expected return demanded by investors in the stock must also be the cost of capital for the assets." She jotted down the following identities:

Value of business = value of stock

Risk of business = risk of stock

Rate of return on business = rate of return on stock

Investors' required return from business = investors' required return from stock

Unfortunately, Geothermal had borrowed a substantial amount of money; its shareholders did *not* have unencumbered ownership of Geothermal's assets. The expansion project would also

capital structure A firm's mix of long-term financing.

justify some extra debt finance. Jo Ann realized that she would have to look at Geothermal's **capital structure**—its mix of debt and equity financing—and consider the required rates of return of debt as well as equity investors.

Geothermal had issued 22.65 million shares, now trading at $20 each. Thus shareholders valued Geothermal's equity at $20 × 22.65 million = $453 million. In addition, the company had issued bonds with a market value of $194 million. The market value of the company's debt and equity was therefore $194 + $453 = $647 million. Debt was 194/647 = .3, or 30 percent of the total.

"Geothermal's worth more to investors than either its debt or its equity," Jo Ann mused. "But I ought to be able to find the overall value of Geothermal's business by adding up the debt and equity." She sketched a rough balance sheet:

Assets		Liabilities and Shareholders' Equity		
Market value of assets = value		Market value of debt	$194	(30%)
of Geothermal's existing business	$647	Market value of equity	$453	(70%)
Total value	$647	Total value	$647	(100%)

"Holy Toledo, I've got it!" Jo Ann exclaimed. "If I bought all the securities issued by Geothermal, debt as well as equity, I'd own the entire business. That means …" She jotted again:

$$\text{Value of business} = \text{value of portfolio of all the firm's} \quad (12.1)$$
$$\text{debt and equity securities}$$

$$\text{Risk of business} = \text{risk of portfolio} \quad (12.2)$$

$$\text{Rate of return on business} = \text{rate of return on portfolio} \quad (12.3)$$

$$\text{Investors' required return on business} = \text{investors' required return on} \quad (12.4)$$
$$\text{(company cost of capital)} \quad \text{portfolio}$$

"All I have to do is calculate the expected rate of return on a portfolio of all the firm's securities. That's easy. The debt's yielding 8 percent, and Fred, the banker, says that equity investors want 14 percent. Suppose he's right. The portfolio would contain 30 percent debt and 70 percent equity, so …"

$$\text{Portfolio return} = (.3 \times 8\%) + (.7 \times 14\%) = 12.2\%$$

It was all coming back to her now. The company cost of capital is just a weighted average of returns on debt and equity, with weights depending on relative market values of the two securities.

"But there's one more thing. Interest is tax-deductible. If Geothermal pays $1 of interest, taxable income is reduced by $1, and the firm's tax bill drops by 35 cents (assuming a 35 percent tax rate). The net cost is only 65 cents. So the cost of debt is not 8 percent, but .65 × 8 = 5.2 percent.

"Now I can finally calculate the weighted-average cost of capital:

$$\text{WACC} = (.3 \times 5.2\%) + (.7 \times 14\%) = 11.4\%$$

"Looks like the expansion's a good deal. Fifteen's better than 11.4. But I sure need a break."

12.2   THE WEIGHTED-AVERAGE COST OF CAPITAL

SEE BOX P. 369

Jo Ann's conclusions were important. It should be obvious by now that the choice of the discount rate can be crucial, especially when the project involves large capital expenditures or is long-lived. The nearby Finance in Action box describes how a major investment in a power station—an investment with both a large capital expenditure and very long life—turned on the choice of the discount rate.

Think again what the company cost of capital is, and what it is used for. We *define* it as the opportunity cost of capital for the firm's existing assets; we *use* it to value new assets that have the same risk as the old ones. The weighted-average cost of capital is a way of estimating the company cost of capital; it also incorporates an adjustment for the taxes a company saves when it borrows.

Shortly before the British government began to sell off the electricity industry to private investors, controversy erupted over the industry's proposal to build a 1,200-megawatt nuclear power station known as Hinkley Point C. The government argued that a nuclear station would both diversify the sources of electricity generation and reduce sulphur dioxide and carbon dioxide emissions. Protesters emphasized the dangers of nuclear accidents and attacked the proposal as "bizarre, dated and irrelevant."

At the public inquiry held to consider the proposal, opponents produced some powerful evidence that the nuclear station was also a very high cost option. Their principal witness, Professor Elroy Dimson, argued that the government-owned power company had employed an unrealistically low figure for the opportunity cost of capital. Had the government-owned industry used a more plausible figure, the cost of building and operating the nuclear station would have been higher than that of a comparable station based on fossil fuels.

The reason why the choice of discount rate was so important was that nuclear stations are expensive to build but cheap to operate. If capital is cheap (i.e., the discount rate is low), then the high up-front cost is less serious. But if the cost of capital is high, then the high initial cost of nuclear stations made them uneconomic.

Evidence produced at the inquiry suggested that the construction cost of a nuclear station was £1,527 million (or about $2.3 billion), while the cost of a comparable non-nuclear station was only £895 million. However, power stations last about 40 years and, once built, nuclear stations cost much less to operate than non-nuclear stations. If operated at 75 percent of theoretical capacity, the running costs of the nuclear station would be about £63 million a year, compared with running costs of £168 million a year for the non-nuclear station.

The following table shows the cost advantage of the nuclear power station at different (real) discount rates. At a 5 percent discount rate, which was the figure used by the government, the present value of the costs of the nuclear option was nearly £1 billion lower than that of a station based on fossil fuels. But with a discount rate of 16 percent, which was the figure favoured by Professor Dimson, the position was almost exactly reversed, so that the

government could save nearly £1 billion by refusing the power company permission to build Hinkley Point C and relying instead on new fossil-fuel power stations.

Thirteen years after the inquiry, the proposal to construct Hinkley Point C has not been implemented. However, British Energy, the privatized electric utility, has suggested that it is time to build new nuclear power stations. To do so, they need the approval of the British government—and more hearings may take place—which means discussion may well resume about the appropriate discount rate for the project.

Present value of the cost advantage to a nuclear rather than a fossil-fuel station (figures in billions of pounds)

Real Discount Rate	Present Value of the Cost Advantage of the Nuclear Station
5%	0.9
8	0.2
10	−0.1
12	−0.4
14	−0.7
16	−0.9
18	−1.2

Technical Notes:

1. Present values are measured at the date that the power station comes into operation.
2. The above table assumes for simplicity that construction costs for nuclear stations are spread evenly over the 8 years before the station comes into operation, while the costs for fossil-fuel stations are assumed to be spread evenly over the 4 years before operation. As a result, the present value of the costs of the two stations may differ slightly from the more precise estimates produced by Professor Dimson.

Source: Adapted with permission from *Energy Economics*, July 1989, E. Dimson, "The Discount Rate for a Power Station," 1989, Elsevier Science Ltd., Oxford, England.

CALCULATING COMPANY COST OF CAPITAL AS A WEIGHTED AVERAGE

Calculating the company cost of capital is straightforward, though not always easy, when only common stock is outstanding. For example, a financial manager could estimate beta and calculate shareholders' required rate of return using the capital asset pricing model (CAPM). This would be the expected rate of return investors require on the company's existing assets and operations and also the expected return they will require on new investments that do not change the company's market risk.

But most companies issue debt as well as equity.

The company cost of capital is a *weighted average* of the returns demanded by debt and equity investors. The weighted average is the expected rate of return investors would demand on a portfolio of all the firm's outstanding securities.

Let's review Jo Ann Cox's calculations for Geothermal. To avoid complications, we'll ignore taxes for the next couple of pages. The total market value of Geothermal, which we denote as V, is the sum of the values of the outstanding debt D and the equity E. Thus firm value is $V = D + E = \$194$ million + \$453 million = \$647 million. Debt accounts for 30 percent of the value and equity accounts for the remaining 70 percent. If you held all the shares and all the debt, your investment in Geothermal would be $V = \$647$ million. Between them, the debt and equity holders own all the firm's assets. So V is also the value of these assets—the value of Geothermal's existing business.

Suppose that Geothermal's equity investors require a 14 percent rate of return on their investment in the stock. What rate of return must a new project provide in order that all investors—both debtholders and shareholders—earn a fair rate of return? The debtholders require a rate of return of $r_{debt} = 8$ percent. So each year the firm will need to pay interest of $r_{debt} \times D = .08 \times \$194$ million = \$15.52 million. The shareholders, who have invested in a riskier security, require a return of $r_{equity} = 14$ percent on their investment of \$453 million. Thus in order to keep shareholders happy, the company needs additional income of $r_{equity} \times E = .14 \times \$453$ million = \$63.42 million. To satisfy both the debtholders and the shareholders, Geothermal needs to earn \$15.52 million + \$63.42 million = \$78.94 million. This is equivalent to earning a return of $r_{assets} = 78.94/647 = .122$, or 12.2 percent.

Figure 12.1 illustrates the reasoning behind our calculations. The figure shows the amount of income needed to satisfy the debt and equity investors. Notice that debtholders account for 30 percent of Geothermal's capital structure but receive less than 30 percent of its expected income. On the other hand, they bear less than a 30 percent share of risk, since they have first cut at the company's income, and also first claim on its assets if the company gets in trouble. Shareholders expect a return of more than 70 percent of Geothermal's income because they bear correspondingly more risk.

However, if you buy *all* Geothermal's debt and equity, you own its assets lock, stock, and barrel. You receive all the income and bear all the risks. The expected rate of return you would require on this portfolio of securities is the same return you would require from unencumbered ownership of the business. This rate of return—12.2 percent, ignoring taxes—is therefore the company cost of capital and the required rate of return from an equal-risk expansion of the business.

The bottom line (still ignoring taxes) is

Company cost of capital = weighted average of debt and equity returns   (12.5)

The underlying algebra is simple. Debtholders need income of $(r_{debt} \times D)$ and the equity investors need income of $(r_{equity} \times E)$. The *total* income that is needed is $(r_{debt} \times D) + (r_{equity} \times E)$. The amount of their combined existing investment in the company is V. So to calculate the return that is needed on the assets, we simply divide the income by the investment:

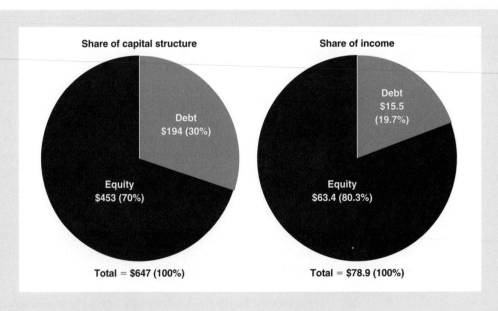

FIGURE 12.1
Geothermal's debtholders account for 30 percent of the company's capital structure, but they get a smaller share of income because their return is guaranteed by the company. Geothermal's shareholders bear more risk and receive, on average, greater return. Of course, if you buy all the debt and all the equity, you get all the income.

Share of capital structure

Debt
$194 (30%)

Equity
$453 (70%)

Total = $647 (100%)

Share of income

Debt
$15.5
(19.7%)

Equity
$63.4 (80.3%)

Total = $78.9 (100%)

$$r_{assets} = \frac{\text{total income}}{\text{value of investment}} \qquad (12.6)$$

$$= \frac{(D \times r_{debt}) + (E \times r_{equity})}{V} = \left(\frac{D}{V} \times r_{debt}\right) + \left(\frac{E}{V} \times r_{equity}\right)$$

For Geothermal,

$$r_{assets} = (.30 \times 8\%) + (.70 \times 14\%) = 12.2\%$$

This figure is the expected return demanded by investors in the firm's assets.

Check Point 12.1

Hot Rocks Corp., one of Geothermal's competitors, has issued long-term bonds with a market value of $50 million and an expected return of 9 percent. It has 4 million shares outstanding trading for $10 each. At this price the shares offer an expected return of 17 percent. What is the weighted-average cost of capital for Hot Rocks' assets and operations? Assume Hot Rocks pays no taxes.

MARKET VERSUS BOOK WEIGHTS

The company cost of capital is the expected rate of return that investors demand from the company's assets and operations.

> The cost of capital must be based on what investors are actually willing to pay for the company's outstanding securities—that is, based on the securities' *market* values.

Market values usually differ from the values recorded by accountants in the company's books. The book value of Geothermal's equity reflects money raised in the past from shareholders or reinvested by the firm on their behalf. If investors recognize Geothermal's excellent prospects, the market value of equity may be much higher than book value, and the debt ratio will be lower when measured in terms of market values rather than book values.

Financial managers use book debt-to-value ratios for various other purposes, and sometimes they unthinkingly look to the book ratios when calculating weights for the company cost of capital. That's a mistake, because the company cost of capital measures what investors want from the company, and it depends on how *they* value the company's securities. That value depends on future profits and cash flows, not on accounting history. Book values, while useful for many other purposes, measure only net cumulative historical outlays; they don't generally measure market values accurately.

Check Point 12.2

Here is a book-value balance sheet for Rhodes Construction Company. Figures are in millions.

Assets		Liabilities and Shareholders' Equity	
Assets (book value)	$75	Debt	$25
		Equity	50
	$75		$75

Unfortunately, the company has fallen on hard times. The 6 million shares are trading for only $4 apiece, and the market value of its debt securities is 20 percent below the face (book) value. Because of the company's large cumulative losses, it will pay no taxes on future income.

Suppose shareholders now demand a 20 percent expected rate of return. The bonds are now yielding 14 percent. What is the weighted-average cost of capital?

TAXES AND THE WEIGHTED-AVERAGE COST OF CAPITAL

Thus far in this section our examples have ignored taxes. Taxes are important because interest payments are deducted from income before tax is calculated. Therefore, the cost to the company of an interest payment is reduced by the amount of this tax saving.

The interest rate on Geothermal's debt is r_{debt} = 8 percent. However, with a corporate tax rate of T_c = .35, the government bears 35 percent of the cost of the interest payments. The government doesn't send the firm a cheque for this amount, but the income tax that the firm pays is reduced by 35 percent of its interest expense.

Therefore, Geothermal's after-tax cost of debt is only $100 - 35 = 65$ percent of the 8 percent pretax cost:

$$\text{After-tax cost of debt} = \textbf{pretax cost} \times \textbf{(1 - tax rate)} \qquad (12.7)$$
$$= r_{debt} \times (1 - T_c)$$
$$= 8\% \times (1 - .35) = 5.2\%$$

We can now adjust our calculation of Geothermal's cost of capital to recognize the tax saving associated with interest payments:

$$\text{Company cost of capital, after-tax} = (.3 \times 5.2\%) + (.7 \times 14\%) = 11.4\%$$

Check Point 12.3   Criss-cross Industries has earnings before interest and taxes (EBIT) of $10 million. Interest payments are $2 million and the corporate tax rate is 35 percent. Construct a simple income statement to show that the debt interest reduces the taxes the firm owes to the government. How much more tax would Criss-cross pay if it were financed solely by equity?

weighted-average cost of capital (WACC) Expected rate of return on a portfolio of all the firm's securities, adjusted for tax savings due to interest payments.

Now we're back to the **weighted-average cost of capital**, or **WACC**. The general formula is

$$\text{WACC} = \left[\frac{D}{V} \times (1 - T_c)r_{debt}\right] + \left[\frac{E}{V} \times r_{equity}\right] \qquad (12.8)$$

Check Point 12.4   Calculate WACC for Hot Rocks (Check Point 12.1) and Rhodes Construction (Check Point 12.2) assuming the companies face a 35 percent corporate income tax rate.

WHAT IF THERE ARE THREE (OR MORE) SOURCES OF FINANCING?

We have simplified our discussion of the cost of capital by assuming the firm has only two classes of securities: debt and equity. Even if the firm has issued other classes of securities, our general approach to calculating WACC remains unchanged. You simply calculate the weighted-average after-tax return of each security type.

For example, suppose the firm also has outstanding preferred stock. Preferred stock has some of the characteristics of both common stock and fixed-income securities. Like bonds, preferred stock promises to pay a given, usually level, stream of dividends. Unlike bonds, however, there is no maturity date for the preferred stock. The promised dividends constitute a perpetuity as long as the firm stays in business. Moreover, a failure to come up with the cash to pay the dividends does not push the firm into bankruptcy. Instead, dividends owed simply cumulate; the common shareholders do not receive dividends until the accumulated preferred dividends have been paid. Finally, unlike interest payments, preferred stock dividends are not considered tax-deductible expenses.

How would we calculate WACC for a firm with preferred stock as well as common stock and bonds outstanding? Using P to denote preferred stock, we simply generalize the formula for WACC as follows:

$$\text{WACC} = \left[\frac{D}{V} \times (1 - T_c)r_{\text{debt}}\right] + \left[\frac{P}{V} \times r_{\text{preferred}}\right] + \left[\frac{E}{V} \times r_{\text{equity}}\right] \qquad (12.9)$$

Let's try an example to make this concrete.

| EXAMPLE 12.1 | **WEIGHTED-AVERAGE COST OF CAPITAL FOR EXECUTIVE FRUIT** |

Unlike Geothermal, Executive Fruit has issued three types of securities—debt, preferred stock, and common stock. The debtholders require a return of 6 percent, the preferred shareholders require an expected return of 12 percent, and the common shareholders require 18 percent. The debt is valued at $4 million ($D = 4$), the preferred stock at $2 million ($P = 2$), and the common stock at $6 million ($E = 6$). The corporate tax rate is 35 percent. What is Executive's weighted-average cost of capital?

Don't be put off by the third security, preferred stock. We simply work through the following three steps.

Step 1. Calculate the value of each security as a proportion of the firm's value. Firm value is $V = D + P + E = 4 + 2 + 6 = \$12$ million. So $D/V = 4/12 = .33$; $P/V = 2/12 = .17$; and $E/V = 6/12 = .5$

Step 2. Determine the required rate of return on each security. We have already given you the answers: $r_{\text{debt}} = 6\%$, $r_{\text{preferred}} = 12\%$, and $r_{\text{equity}} = 18\%$[2]

Step 3. Calculate a weighted average of the cost of the after-tax return on debt and the return on the preferred and common stock:

$$\begin{aligned}\text{Weighted-average} \atop \text{cost of capital} &= \left[\frac{D}{V} \times (1 - T_c)r_{\text{debt}}\right] + \left[\frac{P}{V} \times r_{\text{preferred}}\right] + \left[\frac{E}{V} \times r_{\text{equity}}\right] \\ &= [.33 \times (1 - .35)\, 6\%] + [.17 \times 12\%] + [.5 \times 18\%] \\ &= 12.3\% \end{aligned}$$

WRAPPING UP GEOTHERMAL

We now turn one last time to Jo Ann Cox and Geothermal's proposed expansion. We want to make sure that she—and you—know how to *use* the weighted-average cost of capital.

Remember that the proposed expansion cost $30 million and should generate a perpetual cash flow of $4.5 million per year. A simple cash flow worksheet might look like this:[3]

Revenue	$10.0 million
− Operating expenses	− 3.08
= Pretax operating cash flow	6.92
− Tax at 35%	− 2.42
After-tax cash flow	$ 4.5 million

Note that these cash flows do not include the tax benefits of using debt.

Geothermal's managers and engineers forecast revenues, costs, and taxes as if the project was to be all-equity financed. The interest tax shields generated by the project's actual debt financing are not forgotten, however. They are accounted for by using the *after-tax* cost of debt in the weighted-average cost of capital.

Project net present value is calculated by discounting the cash flow (which is a perpetuity) at Geothermal's 11.4 percent weighted-average cost of capital:

$$\text{NPV} = -30 + \frac{4.5}{.114} = +\$9.5 \text{ million}$$

Expansion will thus add $9.5 million to the net wealth of the owners of Geothermal's assets, Geothermal's debtholders and shareholders.

---

[2] Financial managers often use "equity" to refer to *common* stock, even though a firm's equity strictly includes both common and preferred stocks. We continue to use r_{equity} to refer specifically to the expected return on the common stock.

[3] For this example we ignore depreciation, a non-cash but tax-deductible expense. (If the project were really perpetual, why depreciate?)

CHECKING OUR LOGIC

Any project offering a rate of return more than 11.4 percent will have a positive NPV, assuming that the project has the same risk and financing as Geothermal's business. A project offering exactly 11.4 percent would be just break-even; it would generate just enough cash to satisfy both debtholders and shareholders.

Let's check that out. Suppose the proposed expansion had revenues of only $8.34 million and after-tax cash flows of $3.42 million:

Revenue	$8.34 million
− Operating costs	− 3.08
= Pretax operating cash flow	5.26
− Tax at 35%	− 1.84
After-tax cash flow	$3.42 million

With an investment of $30 million, the internal rate of return on this perpetuity is exactly 11.4 percent:

$$\text{Rate of return} = \frac{3.42}{30} = .114, \text{ or } 11.4\%$$

NPV is exactly zero:

$$\text{NPV} = -30 + \frac{3.42}{.114} = 0$$

When we calculated Geothermal's weighted-average cost of capital, we recognized that the company's debt ratio was 30 percent. When Geothermal's analysts use the weighted-average cost of capital to evaluate the new project, they are assuming that the $30 million additional investment would support the issue of additional debt equal to 30 percent of the investment, or $9 million. The remaining $21 million is provided by the shareholders.

The following table shows how the cash flows would be shared between the debtholders and shareholders. We start with the pretax operating cash flow of $5.26 million:

Cash flow before tax and interest	$5.26 million
− Interest payment (.08 × $9 million)	− .72
= Pretax cash flow	4.54
− Tax at 35%	− 1.59
Cash flow after tax	$2.95 million

Project cash flows before tax and interest are forecast to be $5.26 million. Out of this figure, Geothermal needs to pay interest of 8 percent of $9 million, which comes to $.72 million. This leaves a pretax cash flow of $4.54 million, on which the company must pay tax. Taxes equal .35 × 4.54 = $1.59 million. Shareholders are left with $2.95 million, just enough to give them the 14 percent return that they need on their $21 million investment. (Note that 2.95/21 = .14, or 14 percent.) Therefore, everything checks out.

> If a project has zero NPV when the expected cash flows are discounted at the weighted-average cost of capital, then the project's cash flows are just sufficient to give debtholders and shareholders the returns they require.

12.3   MEASURING CAPITAL STRUCTURE

We have explained the formula for calculating the weighted-average cost of capital. We will now look at some of the practical problems in applying that formula. Suppose that the financial manager of Big Oil has asked you to estimate the firm's weighted-average cost of capital. Your first step is to work out Big Oil's capital structure. But where do you get the data?

Financial managers usually start with the company's accounts, which show the book value of debt and equity, whereas the weighted-average cost of capital formula calls for their market values. A little work and a dash of judgment are needed to go from one to the other.

Table 12.1 shows the debt and equity issued by Big Oil. The firm has borrowed $200 million from banks and has issued a further $200 million of long-term bonds. These bonds have a coupon rate of 8 percent and mature at the end of 12 years. Finally, there are 100 million shares of common stock outstanding, originally issued at $1.00 per share. But the accounts also recognize that Big Oil has in past years plowed back into the firm $300 million of retained earnings. The total book value of the equity shown in the accounts is $100 million + $300 million = $400 million.

The figures shown in Table 12.1 are taken from Big Oil's annual accounts and are therefore book values. Sometimes the differences between book values and market values are negligible. For example, consider the $200 million that Big Oil owes the bank. The interest rate on bank loans is usually linked to the general level of interest rates. Thus if interest rates rise, the rate charged on Big Oil's loan also rises to maintain the loan's value. As long as Big Oil is reasonably sure to repay the loan, the loan is worth close to $200 million. Most financial managers most of the time are willing to accept the book value of bank debt as a fair approximation of its market value.

What about Big Oil's long-term bonds? Since the bonds were originally issued, long-term interest rates have risen to 9 percent.[4] We can calculate the value today of each bond as follows.[5] There are 12 coupon payments of .08 × 200 = $16 million, and then repayment of face value 12 years out. Thus the final cash payment to the bondholders is $216 million. All the bond's cash flows are discounted back at the *current* interest rate of 9 percent.

$$PV = \frac{16}{1.09} + \frac{16}{(1.09)^2} + \frac{16}{(1.09)^3} + \ldots + \frac{216}{(1.09)^{12}} = \$185.7$$

Therefore, the bonds are worth only $185.7 million, 92.8 percent of their face value.

If you used the book value of Big Oil's long-term debt rather than its market value, you would be a little bit off in your calculation of the weighted-average cost of capital, but probably not seriously so.

The really big errors are likely to arise if you use the book value of equity rather than its market value. The $400 million book value of Big Oil's equity measures the total amount of cash that the firm has raised from shareholders in the past or has retained and invested on their behalf. But perhaps Big Oil has been able to find projects that were worth more than they originally cost or perhaps the value of the assets has increased with inflation. Perhaps investors see great future investment opportunities for the company. All these considerations determine what investors are willing to pay for Big Oil's common stock.

If in September 2006 Big Oil stock was $12 a share, the total *market value* of the stock would be

Number of shares × share price = 100 million × $12 = $1,200 million

In Table 12.2 we show the market value of Big Oil's debt and equity. You can see that debt accounts for 24.3 percent of company value (D/V = .243) and equity accounts for 75.7 percent

TABLE 12.1

The book value of Big Oil's debt and equity ($ millions)

Bank debt	$200	25.0%
Long-term bonds (12-year maturity, 8% coupon)	200	25.0
Common stock (100 million shares)	100	12.5
Retained earnings	300	37.5
Total	$800	100.0%

---

[4] If Big Oil's bonds are traded, you can simply look up their price. But many bonds are not traded regularly, and in such cases you need to infer their price by calculating the bond's value using the rate of interest offered by similar bonds.

[5] We assume that coupon payments are annual. Most bonds in Canada and the United States actually pay interest twice a year.

TABLE 12.2
The market value of Big Oil's
debt and equity ($ millions)

Bank debt	$ 200	12.6%
Long-term bonds	185.7	11.7
Total debt	385.7	24.3
Common stock, 100 million shares at $12	1,200	75.7
Total	$1,585.7	100%

($E/V = .757$). These are the proportions to use when calculating the weighted-average cost of capital. Notice that if you looked only at the book values shown in the company accounts, you would mistakenly conclude that debt and equity each accounted for 50 percent of value.

Check Point 12.5   Here is the capital structure shown in Executive Fruit's *book* balance sheet:

Debt	$4.1 million	45 %
Preferred stock	2.2	24.2
Common stock	2.8	30.8
Total	$9.1 million	100 %

Explain why the percentage weights given above should *not* be used in calculating Executive Fruit's WACC.

12.4   CALCULATING REQUIRED RATES OF RETURN

To calculate Big Oil's weighted-average cost of capital, you also need the rate of return that investors require from each security.

THE EXPECTED RETURN ON BONDS

We know that Big Oil's bonds offer a yield to maturity of 9 percent. As long as the company does not go belly-up, that is the rate of return investors can expect to earn from holding Big Oil's bonds. If there is any chance that the firm may be unable to repay the debt, however, the yield to maturity of 9 percent represents the most favourable outcome and the *expected* return is lower than 9 percent.

For most large and healthy firms, the probability of bankruptcy is sufficiently low that financial managers are content to take the promised yield to maturity on the bonds as a measure of the expected return. But beware of assuming that the yield offered on the bonds of Fly-by-Night Corporation is the return that investors could *expect* to receive.

THE EXPECTED RETURN ON COMMON STOCK

Estimates Based on the Capital Asset Pricing Model

In Chapter 11 we showed you how to use the capital asset pricing model to estimate the expected rate of return on common stock. The capital asset pricing model tells us that investors demand a higher rate of return from stocks with high betas. The formula is

$$\begin{array}{l} \text{Expected return} \\ \text{on stock} \end{array} = \begin{array}{l} \text{risk-free} \\ \text{interest rate} \end{array} + \left[\begin{array}{l} \text{stock's} \\ \text{beta} \end{array} \times \begin{array}{l} \text{expected market} \\ \text{risk premium} \end{array} \right]$$

Financial managers and economists measure the risk-free rate of interest by the yield on Treasury bills. To measure the expected market risk premium, they usually look back at capital market history, which suggests that investors have received an extra 6 to 8 percent a year from investing in common stocks rather than Treasury bills. Yet wise financial managers use this evidence with considerable humility, for who is to say whether investors in the past received more or less than they expected, or whether investors today require a higher or lower reward for risk than their parents did?

Let's suppose Big Oil's common stock beta is estimated at .95, the risk-free interest rate of r_f is 6 percent, and the expected market risk premium $(r_m - r_f)$ is 7 percent. Then the CAPM would put Big Oil's cost of equity at

$$\text{Cost of equity} = r_{\text{equity}} = r_f + \beta(r_m - r_f)$$
$$= 6\% + .95(7\%) = 12.65\%$$

Of course no one can estimate expected rates of return to two decimal places, so we'll just round to 12.7 percent.

Check Point 12.6

Jo Ann Cox decides to check whether Fred, the banker, was correct in claiming that Geothermal's cost of equity is 14 percent. She estimates Geothermal's beta at 1.2. The risk-free interest rate in 2012 is 6 percent, and the long-run average market risk premium is 7 percent. What is the expected rate of return on Geothermal's common stock, assuming of course that the CAPM is true? Recalculate Geothermal's weighted-average cost of capital.

Dividend Discount Model Cost of Equity Estimates

Whenever you are given an estimate of the expected return on a common stock, always look for ways to check whether it is reasonable. One check on the estimates provided by the CAPM can be obtained from the dividend discount model (DDM). In Chapter 6 we showed you how to use the constant-growth DDM formula to estimate the return that investors expect from different common stocks. *Remember the formula*: If dividends are expected to grow indefinitely at a constant rate g, then the price of the stock is equal to

$$P_0 = \frac{\text{DIV}_1}{r_{\text{equity}} - g}$$

where P_0 is the current stock price, DIV_1 is the forecast dividend at the end of the year, and r_{equity} is the expected return from the stock. We can rearrange this formula to provide an estimate of r_{equity}.

$$r_{\text{equity}} = \frac{\text{DIV}_1}{P_0} + g$$

In other words, the expected return on equity is equal to the dividend yield (DIV_1/P_0) plus the expected perpetual growth rate in dividends (g).

This constant-growth dividend discount model is widely used in estimating expected rates of return on common stocks of public utilities. Utility stocks have a fairly stable growth pattern and are therefore tailor-made for the constant-growth formula.

Remember that the constant-growth formula will get you into trouble if you apply it to firms with very high current rates of growth. Such growth cannot be sustained indefinitely.

Using the formula in these circumstances will lead to an overestimate of the expected return.

Beware of False Precision

Do not expect estimates of the cost of equity to be precise. In practice you can't know whether the capital asset pricing model fully explains expected returns or whether the assumptions of the dividend discount model hold exactly. Even if your formulas were right, the required inputs would be "noisy" and subject to error. Thus a financial analyst who can confidently locate the cost of equity in a band of two or three percentage points is doing pretty well. In this endeavour it is perfectly OK to conclude that the cost of equity is, say, "about 15 percent" or "somewhere between 14 and 16 percent."[6]

Sometimes accuracy can be improved by estimating the cost of equity or WACC for an industry or a group of comparable companies. This cuts down the "noise" that plagues single-company estimates. Suppose, for example, that Jo Ann Cox is able to identify three companies with investments and operations similar to Geothermal's. The average WACC for these three companies would be a valuable check on her estimate of WACC for Geothermal alone.

Or suppose that Geothermal is contemplating investment in oil refining. For this venture, Geothermal's existing WACC is probably not right; it needs a discount rate reflecting the risks of the refining business. It could therefore try to estimate WACC for a sample of oil refining companies. If too few "pure-play" refining companies were available—most oil companies invest in production and marketing as well as refining—an industry WACC for a sample of large oil companies could be a useful check or benchmark.

The Expected Return on Preferred Stock

Preferred stock that pays a fixed annual dividend can be valued from the perpetuity formula:

$$\text{Price of preferred} = \frac{\text{dividend}}{r_{\text{preferred}}}$$

where $r_{\text{preferred}}$ is the appropriate discount rate for the preferred stock. Therefore, we can infer the required rate of return on preferred stock by rearranging the valuation formula to

$$r_{\text{preferred}} = \frac{\textbf{dividend}}{\textbf{price of preferred}} \qquad (12.10)$$

For example, if a share of preferred stock sells for $20 and pays a dividend of $2 per share, the expected return on preferred stock is $r_{\text{preferred}} = \$2/\$20 = 10$ percent, which is simply the dividend yield.

12.5   CALCULATING THE WEIGHTED-AVERAGE COST OF CAPITAL

Now that you have worked out Big Oil's capital structure and estimated the expected return on its securities, you need only simple arithmetic to calculate the weighted-average cost of capital. Table 12.3 summarizes the necessary data. Now all you need to do is plug the data from Table 12.3 into the weighted-average cost of capital formula:

$$\text{WACC} = \left[\frac{D}{V} \times (1 - T_c)r_{\text{debt}}\right] + \left[\frac{E}{V} \times r_{\text{equity}}\right]$$
$$= [.243 \times (1 - .35)\ 9\%] + [.757 \times 12.7\%] = 11.0\%$$

Suppose that Big Oil needed to evaluate a project with the same risk as its existing business that would also support a 24.3 percent debt ratio. The 11.0 percent weighted-average cost of capital is the appropriate discount rate for the cash flows.

TABLE 12.3
Data needed to calculate Big Oil's weighted-average cost of capital ($ millions)

Security Type	Capital Structure		Required Rate of Return
Debt	$D = \$\ \ 385.7$	$D/V = .243$	$r_{\text{debt}}\ \ = .09$, or 9%
Common stock	$E = \$1,200$	$E/V = .757$	$r_{\text{equity}} = .127$, or 12.7%
Total	$V = \$1,585.7$		

Note: Corporate tax rate = $T_c = .35$.

---

[6] The calculations in this chapter have been done to one or two decimal places only to avoid confusion from rounding.

12.6

INTERPRETING THE WEIGHTED-AVERAGE COST OF CAPITAL

WHEN YOU CAN AND CAN'T USE WACC

We first discussed the company cost of capital in Chapter 11, but at that stage we did not know how to measure the company cost of capital when the firm issues different types of securities or how to adjust for the tax-deductibility of interest payments. The weighted-average cost of capital formula solves those problems.

> The weighted-average cost of capital is the rate of return that the firm must expect to earn on its average-risk investments in order to provide a fair expected return to all its security holders. We use it to value new assets that have the same risk as the old ones and that support the same ratio of debt. Strictly speaking, the weighted-average cost of capital is an appropriate discount rate only for a project that is a carbon copy of the firm's existing business. But often it is used as a company-wide benchmark discount rate; the benchmark is adjusted upward for unusually risky projects and downward for unusually safe ones.

There is a good musical analogy here. Most of us, lacking perfect pitch, need a well-defined reference point, like middle C, before we can sing on key. But anyone who can carry a tune gets *relative* pitches right. Businesspeople have good intuition about *relative* risks (at least in industries they are used to) but not about absolute risk or required rates of return. Therefore, they set a company- or industry-wide cost of capital as a benchmark. This is not the right hurdle rate for everything the company does, but good judgment adjustments can be used to make for more or less risky ventures.

SOME COMMON MISTAKES

One danger with the weighted-average formula is that it tempts people to make logical errors. Think back to your estimate of the cost of capital for Big Oil:

$$\text{WACC} = \left[\frac{D}{V} \times (1 - T_c)r_{\text{debt}}\right] + \left[\frac{E}{V} \times r_{\text{equity}}\right]$$
$$= [.243 \times (1 - .35)\, 9\%] + (.757 \times 12.7\%) = 11.0\%$$

Now you might be tempted to say to yourself, "Aha! Big Oil has a good credit rating. It could easily push up its debt ratio to 50 percent. If the interest rate is 9 percent and the required return on equity is 12.7 percent, the weighted-average cost of capital would be

$$\text{WACC} = [.50 \times (1 - .35)\, 9\%] + [.50 \times 12.7\%] = 9.3\%$$

"At a discount rate of 9.3 percent, we can justify a lot more investment."

That reasoning will get you into trouble. First, if Big Oil increased its borrowing, the lenders would almost certainly demand a higher rate of interest on the debt. Second, as the borrowing increased, the risk of the common stock would also increase and therefore the shareholders would demand a higher return.

> There are actually two costs of debt finance. The explicit cost of debt is the rate of interest that bondholders demand. But there is also an implicit cost, because borrowing increases the required return to equity.

When you jumped to the conclusion that Big Oil could lower its weighted-average cost of capital to 9.3 percent by borrowing more, you were recognizing only the explicit cost of debt and not the implicit cost.

Check Point 12.7

Jo Ann Cox's boss has pointed out that Geothermal proposes to finance its expansion entirely by borrowing at an interest rate of 8 percent. He argues that this is therefore the appropriate discount rate for the project's cash flows. Is he right?

HOW CHANGING CAPITAL STRUCTURE AFFECTS EXPECTED RETURNS

We will illustrate how changes in capital structure affect expected returns by focusing on the simplest possible case, where the corporate tax rate T_c is zero.

Think back to our earlier example of Geothermal. Geothermal, you may remember, has the following market-value balance sheet:

Assets		Liabilities and Shareholders' Equity		
Assets = value of Geothermal's existing business	$647	Debt	$194	(30%)
		Equity	$453	(70%)
Total value	$647	Value	$647	(100%)

Geothermal's debtholders require a return of 8 percent and the shareholders require a return of 14 percent. Since we assume here that Geothermal pays no corporate tax, its weighted-average cost of capital is simply the expected return on the firm's assets:

$$\text{WACC} = r_{\text{assets}} = (.3 \times 8\%) + (.7 \times 14\%) = 12.2\%$$

This is the return you would expect if you held all Geothermal's securities and therefore owned all its assets.

Now think what will happen if Geothermal borrows an additional $97 million and uses the cash to buy back and retire $97 million of its common stock. The revised market-value balance sheet is

Assets		Liabilities and Shareholders' Equity		
Assets = value of Geothermal's existing business	$647	Debt	$291	(45%)
		Equity	356	(55%)
Total value	$647	Value	$647	(100%)

If there are no corporate taxes, the change in capital structure does not affect Geothermal's assets nor the total cash that Geothermal pays out to its security holders nor the risk of those cash flows. Therefore, if investors require a return of 12.2 percent on the total package of debt and equity before the financing, they must require the same 12.2 percent return on the package afterward. The weighted-average cost of capital is therefore unaffected by the change in the capital structure. More on this topic appears in Chapter 15.

Although the required return on the *package* of the debt and equity is unaffected, the change in capital structure does affect the required return on the individual securities. Since the company has more debt than before, the debt is riskier and debtholders are likely to demand a higher return. Increasing the amount of debt also makes the equity riskier and increases the return that shareholders require.

HOW CHANGING CAPITAL STRUCTURE AFFECTS BETA

We have looked at how changes in capital structure affect expected return. Let us now look at the effect on risk.

Both shareholders and debtholders receive a share of the company's cash flow from its assets and both bear part of the risk. For example, if the firm's assets turn out to be worthless, there will be no cash to pay either of them. But debtholders bear much less risk than shareholders. Interest and principal payments are made to debtholders before shareholders are paid dividends. If the company fails to pay the promised interest and principal payments, the debtholders have the right to force the company into bankruptcy and can take over the company. The risk of the debt of large blue chip firms is close to zero—close enough that many financial analysts assume that beta of the debt, β_{debt}, is zero.

If you owned a portfolio consisting of all the firm's securities, you wouldn't share the firm's cash flows with anyone. You wouldn't share the risks with anyone either; you would bear them all. Thus the asset beta, that is, the beta of all the firm's assets, is equal to the beta of a portfolio of all of the firm's debt and all its equity. This is just a weighted average of the debt and equity betas:

$$\beta_{assets} = \frac{D}{V} \times \beta_{debt} + \frac{E}{V} \times \beta_{equity} \qquad \textbf{(12.11)}$$

Think back to our Geothermal example. Assume that the risk-free rate of interest is 6 percent and the expected market risk premium is 7 percent. If Geothermal's debtholders require an 8 percent return and its shareholders require 14 percent, what must be the betas of debt and equity? Using the CAPM,

$$\text{Stock's beta} = \frac{\text{expected return on stock} - \text{risk-free rate}}{\text{expected market risk premium}} = \frac{14\% - 6\%}{7\%} = 1.14$$

Likewise, the CAPM can be used to calculate the debt's beta:

$$\text{Debt's beta} = \frac{\text{expected return on debt} - \text{risk-free rate}}{\text{expected market risk premium}} = \frac{8\% - 6\%}{7\%} = .29$$

Thus, Geothermal's asset beta is

$$\beta_{assets} = (.3 \times .29) + (.7 \times 1.14) = .89$$

What happens after the proposed refinancing, where Geothermal borrows an additional $97 million and retires $97 million of equity? The assets of the company are unchanged. Thus the risk of the package of debt and equity is unaffected but both the debt and the equity are now riskier. Suppose that the debt beta increases to .3. We can work out the new equity beta:

$$\beta_{assets} = \frac{D}{V} \times \beta_{debt} + \frac{E}{V} \times \beta_{equity}$$
$$.89 = .45 \times .3 + (.55 \times \beta_{equity})$$
$$\beta_{equity} = 1.37$$

The riskiness of the equity has increased from 1.14 to 1.37 due to the additional leverage. By rearranging Equation 12.11, the beta of a firm's equity, in the absence of corporate taxes, can be expressed as

$$\beta_{equity} = \beta_{assets} + (\beta_{assets} - \beta_{debt})\frac{D}{E} \qquad \textbf{(12.12)}$$

Often it is reasonable to assume that the beta of debt is zero and equation 12.12 reduces to

$$\beta_{equity} = \beta_{assets} \times \left(1 + \frac{D}{E}\right) \qquad \textbf{(12.13)}$$

If the corporate tax rate is zero, you can use Equation 12.12 or 12.13 to assess the effect of a change in capital structure on the riskiness of equity.

Check Point 12.8

Tollbar Cookies Inc. is 80 percent equity financed, its common stock beta, β_{equity}, is .8 and its debt beta is .1. The corporate tax rate is zero. The risk-free rate is 4 percent and the market risk premium is 7 percent. What would be the equity beta if Tollbar is 50 percent debt? Assume the debt beta is .14 at 50 percent debt. Calculate Tollbar's WACC for both capital structures. Explain what you find.

WHAT HAPPENS IF CAPITAL STRUCTURE CHANGES AND THE CORPORATE TAX RATE IS NOT ZERO?

We have shown that when there are no corporate taxes the weighted-average cost of capital is unaffected by a change in capital structure. Unfortunately, taxes can complicate the picture.

Since interest paid on the debt is tax-deductible, increasing leverage reduces the company's tax bill and hence increases the company's total cash flows. In this situation, changing the capital structure of the firm can change the value of the firm's assets and also their risk. We will show you the details in Chapter 15. For now, we will show you the implications for the equity beta.

The risk of the firm's equity has two sources: business risk and financial risk. Business risk arises from the nature of the firm's operating business. Financial risk exists because shareholders are paid dividends only after debtholders receive their promised interest and principal. Increasing leverage, by raising the debt-equity ratio, increases the financial risk of shareholders. If the firm is unlevered (debt free), the shareholders bear only the risk of the operating business and no financial risk. We call the equity beta of a debt-free firm the **unlevered beta**, β_u. With leverage, the shareholders not only bear business risk but also the added risk from financial leverage. The **levered equity beta**, $\beta_{levered}$, is a function of the unlevered beta, β_u, the beta of the debt, β_{debt}, and the degree of financial leverage, D/E:

unlevered beta   Beta of equity of a debt-free firm, reflecting the risk arising from the firm's operating business.

levered equity beta   Beta of equity of a firm that has debt, reflecting both the risk arising from the firm's operating business and the risk created by the leverage (debtholders are entitled to be paid principal and interest before shareholders are paid dividends).

$$\beta_{levered} = \beta_u + (\beta_u - \beta_{debt})(1 - T_C)\frac{D}{E} \qquad (12.14)$$

If it is reasonable to assume that the debt is riskless, the debt beta is zero and the equation becomes

$$\beta_{levered} = \beta_u \times \left[1 + (1 - T_C) \times \frac{D}{E}\right] \qquad (12.15)$$

A word of warning: these formulas are based on assumptions that you will learn more about in Chapter 15. However, analysts and investment bankers often use them to unlever and relever equity betas when assessing the impact of a change in capital structure. In Example 12.2, we show you how to do it and, in the next section, we will show you how unlevering and relevering betas can be useful when hunting for the appropriate beta for a project.

EXAMPLE 12.2	**SUPER BIKES' CAPITAL STRUCTURE AND EQUITY BETA**

Super Bikes, a bicycle manufacturer, is currently 30 percent debt financed. Its levered equity beta is 1.1 and its debt beta is 0. What would be the impact on the riskiness of its equity if debt financing is increased to be 50 percent of the firm value? Assume the debt beta remains 0. The company's tax rate is 35 percent.

First rearrange Equation 12.15 to find Super Bikes' unlevered beta[7]:

$$\beta_u = \frac{\beta_{levered}}{1 + D/E \times (1 - T_C)} \qquad (12.16)$$

$$= \frac{1.1}{1 + (.3/.7) \times (1 - .35)} = .86$$

---

[7] If the debt beta is not zero, the equation for the unlevered beta is
$$\beta_u = \frac{\beta_{levered} + \beta_{debt} \times D/E \times (1 - T_C)}{1 + D/E \times (1 - T_C)}$$

Without the added risk from leverage, the unlevered beta is .86. The new levered equity beta, if leverage is increased to 50 percent is

$$\beta_{\text{levered}} = \beta_u \times \left[1 + (1 - T_C)\frac{D}{E}\right] = .86 \times (1 + (1 - .35) \times (.5/.5)) = 1.42$$

We see that by increasing the leverage from 30 percent debt to 50 percent debt the beta of the equity increases from 1.1 to 1.42.

To summarize, whether or not there are corporate taxes, you should remember

- The weighted-average cost of capital is the right discount rate for average-risk capital investment projects.
- The weighted-average cost of capital is the return the company needs to earn after tax in order to satisfy all its security holders.
- If the firm increases its debt ratio, both the debt and the equity will become more risky. The debtholders and equity holders require higher rates of return to compensate for the increased risk. Exactly how the risk increases depends on whether or not the company pays taxes.

REVISITING THE PROJECT COST OF CAPITAL

In Chapter 11 we introduced the project cost of capital: the minimum acceptable expected rate of return on a project, given its risks. When funds are invested in a project, the required rate of return on the investment depends on the project's *risk*, not the source of funds. In Chapter 11 we discussed ways of finding a suitable estimate of a project's cost of capital. We now must extend that analysis to consider a project's weighted-average cost of capital.

We use the weighted-average cost of capital because, typically, firms are financed by a mix of securities. The weighted-average cost of capital depends on the expected return on all of the securities issued by the company. In our analysis so far, we have not answered an important question: Why are firms financed this way? We have shown that when there are no corporate taxes, a company's cost of capital is unaffected by how it is financed. With taxes, the analysis is more complex. We will deal with the details in Chapter 15. In the meantime we can say that a firm selects its capital structure to maximize the firm's or project's value. Consequently, the determination of the cost of capital appropriate for a project has two components. First, the risks of the project's cash flows must be assessed; that is, the project's unlevered beta must be determined. Second, the best financing mix must be selected. This will determine the added financial risk for shareholders and the levered equity beta. The project's weighted-average cost of capital will reflect the project's overall risk and the best securities mix for the project.

We now know that the pure-play approach to assessing the project's risk is complicated by the choice of capital structure. As a first step, you may want to use the pure-play company's weighted-average cost of capital as a proxy for the project's weighted-average cost of capital. This assumes that the pure-play company's choice of financing mix is also the best mix of financing for the project. However, you can also use the formula for levered equity beta to change the pure-play equity beta to your chosen capital structure. Of course, this presupposes that you have picked the appropriate capital structure for the project.

EXAMPLE 12.3	ESTIMATING THE COST OF CAPITAL FOR A NEW VENTURE

Snow Fun Inc., a manufacturer of skis and snowboards, is contemplating entering a new line of business: bicycle manufacturing. The company's analysts have estimated the project's cash flows but need to determine the project cost of capital. Snow Fun analysts assess that the capital structure for their new bicycle division will be 40 percent debt.

Super Bike, in Example 12.2, is a pure play in bicycle manufacturing and is 30 percent debt financed. Analysts at Snow Fun use Super Bike's unlevered equity of .86 and relever it to their chosen capital structure:

$$\beta_{levered} = \beta_u \times \left(1 + (1 - T)\frac{D}{E}\right) = .86 \times \left(1 + (1 - .35) \times (.4/.6)\right) = 1.23$$

Given that the cost of debt is 6 percent, the risk-free rate is 4 percent, and the market risk premium is 7 percent, the project cost of equity is

$$r_{equity} = r_f + \beta_{levered} \times \text{market risk premium} = 4\% + 1.23 \times 7\% = 12.61\%$$

The project cost of capital is

$$\text{Project cost of capital} = \frac{D}{V} \times (1 - T_c)\, r_{debt} + \frac{E}{V} \times r_{equity}$$

$$= .4 \times (1 - .35) \times 6\% + .6 \times 12.61\% = 9.13\%, \text{ or about 9.1 percent}$$

12.7

FLOTATION COSTS AND THE COST OF CAPITAL

To raise the necessary cash for a new project, the firm may need to issue stocks, bonds, or other securities. The costs of issuing these securities to the public can easily amount to 5 percent of funds raised. For example, a firm issuing $100 million in new equity may net only $95 million after incurring the costs of the issue. We will examine flotation costs, that is, the costs of "floating" new securities to the public, in Chapter 14.

Flotation costs involve real money. A new project is less attractive if the firm must spend large sums on issuing new securities. To illustrate, consider a project that will cost $900,000 to install and is expected to generate a level perpetual cash flow stream of $90,000 a year. At a required rate of return of 10 percent, the project is just barely viable, with an NPV of zero: –$900,000 + $90,000/.10 = 0.

Now suppose that the firm needs to raise equity to pay for the project, and that flotation costs are 10 percent of funds raised. To raise $900,000, the firm actually must sell $1 million of equity. Since the installed project will be worth only $90,000/.10 = $900,000, NPV including flotation costs is actually –$1 million + $900,000 = –$100,000.

In our example, we recognized flotation costs as one of the incremental costs of undertaking the project. But instead of recognizing these costs explicitly, some companies attempt to cope with flotation costs by increasing the cost of capital used to discount project cash flows. By using a higher discount rate, project present value is reduced.

This procedure is flawed on practical as well as theoretical grounds. First, on a purely practical level, it is far easier to account for flotation costs as a negative cash flow than to search for an adjustment to the discount rate that will give the right NPV. Finding the necessary adjustment is easy only when cash flows are level or will grow indefinitely at a constant trend rate. This is almost never the case in practice, however. Of course, there always exists some discount rate that will give the right measure of the project's NPV, but this rate could no longer be interpreted as the rate of return available in the capital market for investments with the same risk as the project.

> The cost of capital depends only on interest rates, taxes, and the risk of the project. Flotation costs should be treated as incremental (negative) cash flows; they do not increase the required rate of return.

12.8   SUMMARY

1. Why do firms compute weighted-average costs of capital?

They need a standard discount rate for average-risk projects. An "average risk" project is one that has the same risk as the firm's existing assets and operations.

2. What about projects that are not average?

The **weighted-average cost of capital** can still be used as a benchmark. The benchmark is adjusted up for unusually risky projects and down for unusually safe ones.

3. How do firms compute weighted-average costs of capital?

Here's the WACC formula one more time:

$$\text{WACC} = \frac{D}{V} \times (1 - T_c)\, r_{\text{debt}} + \frac{E}{V} \times r_{\text{equity}}$$

The WACC is the expected rate of return on the portfolio of debt and equity securities issued by the firm. The required rate of return on each security is weighted by its proportion of the firm's total market value (not book value). Since interest payments reduce the firm's income tax bill, the required rate of return on debt is measured after tax, as $(1 - T_c)r_{\text{debt}}$.

This WACC formula is usually written assuming the firm's capital structure includes just two classes of securities: debt and equity. If there is another class, say preferred stock, the formula expands to include it. In other words, we would estimate $r_{\text{preferred}}$, the rate of return demanded by preferred shareholders, determine P/V, the fraction of market value accounted for by preferred, and add $r_{\text{preferred}} \times P/V$ to the equation. Of course, the weights in the WACC formula always add up to 1.0. In this case, $D/V + P/V + E/V = 1.0$.

4. How are the costs of debt and equity calculated?

The cost of debt (r_{debt}) is the market interest rate demanded by bondholders. In other words, it is the rate that the company would pay on new debt issued to finance its investment projects. The cost of preferred ($r_{\text{preferred}}$) is just the preferred dividend divided by the market price of a preferred share.

The tricky part is estimating the cost of equity (r_{equity}), the expected rate of return on the firm's shares. Financial managers use the capital asset pricing model to estimate expected return. But for mature, steady-growth companies, it can also make sense to use the constant-growth dividend discount model. Remember, estimates of expected return are less reliable for a single firm's stock than for a sample of comparable-risk firms. Therefore, some managers also consider WACCs calculated for industries.

5. What happens when capital structure changes?

The rates of return on debt and equity will change. For example, increasing the debt ratio will increase the risk borne by both debt and equity investors and cause them to demand higher returns. However, this does not necessarily mean that the overall WACC will increase, because more weight is put on the cost of debt, which is less than the cost of equity. In fact, if we ignore taxes, the overall cost of capital will stay constant as the fractions of debt and equity change. This is discussed further in Chapter 15.

6. Should WACC be adjusted for the costs of issuing securities to finance a project?

No. If acceptance of a project would require the firm to issue securities, the flotation costs of the issue should be added to the investment required for the project. This reduces project NPV dollar for dollar. There is no need to adjust WACC.

Related Web Links

www.pwcglobal.com/Extweb/pwcpublications.nsf/docid/748F5814D61CC2618525693A007EC870
Cost of capital of New Zealand companies, by PricewaterhouseCoopers, New Zealand.

Key Terms

capital structure	368	weighted-average cost of capital (WACC)	372
		unlevered beta	382
		levered equity beta	382

Questions and Problems

*Answers in Appendix B

BASIC

*1. **Cost of Debt.** Micro Spinoffs, Inc., issued 20-year debt a year ago at par value, with a coupon rate of 9 percent paid annually. Today, the debt is selling at $1,050. If the firm's tax bracket is 35 percent, what is its after-tax cost of debt?

2. **Cost of Preferred Stock.** Micro Spinoffs also has preferred stock outstanding. The stock pays a dividend of $4 per share and the stock sells for $40. What is the cost of preferred stock?

*3. **Calculating WACC.** Suppose Micro Spinoffs's cost of equity is 12.5 percent. What is its WACC if equity is 50 percent, preferred stock is 20 percent, and debt is 30 percent of total capital?

*4. **Cost of Equity.** Reliable Electric is a regulated public utility, and it is expected to provide steady growth of dividends of 5 percent per year for the indefinite future. Its last dividend was $5 per share; the stock sold for $60 per share just after the dividend was paid. What is the company's cost of equity?

5. **Calculating WACC.** Reactive Industries has the following capital structure. Its corporate tax rate is 35 percent. What is its WACC?

Security	Market Value	Required Rate of Return
Debt	$20 million	8%
Preferred stock	$10 million	10%
Common stock	$50 million	15%

*6. **Company versus Project Discount Rates.** Geothermal's WACC is 11.4 percent. Executive Fruit's WACC is 12.3 percent. Now Executive Fruit is considering an investment in geothermal power production. Should it discount project cash flows at 12.3 percent? Why or why not?

7. **Flotation Costs.** A project costs $10 million and has NPV of +$2.5 million. The NPV is computed by discounting at a WACC of 15 percent. Unfortunately, the $10 million investment will have to be raised by a stock issue. The issue would incur flotation costs of $1.2 million. Should the project be undertaken?

PRACTICE

*8. **WACC.** The common stock of Buildwell Conservation & Construction, Inc., has a beta of .8. The Treasury bill rate is 4 percent and the market risk premium is estimated at 8 percent. BCCI's capital structure is 30 percent debt paying a 5 percent interest rate, and 70 percent equity. What is BCCI's cost of equity capital? Its WACC? Buildwell pays no taxes.

9. **WACC and NPV.** BCCI (see problem 8) is evaluating a project with an internal rate of return of 12 percent. Should it accept the project? If the project will generate a cash flow of $100,000 per year for 7 years, what is the most BCCI should be willing to pay to initiate the project?

EXCEL

*10. **Calculating WACC.** Find the WACC of William Tell Computers. The total book value of the firm's equity is $10 million; book value per share is $20. The stock sells for a price of $30 per share, and the cost of equity is 15 percent. The firm's bonds have a par value of $5 million and sell at a price of 110 percent of par. The yield to maturity on the bonds is 9 percent, and the firm's tax rate is 40 percent.

11. **WACC.** Nodebt, Inc., is a firm with all-equity financing. Its equity beta is .8. The Treasury bill rate is 5 percent and the market risk premium is expected to be 10 percent. What is Nodebt's asset beta? What is Nodebt's weighted-average cost of capital? The firm is exempt from paying taxes.

12. **Cost of Capital.** A financial analyst at Dawn Chemical notes that the firm's total interest payments this year were $10 million while total debt outstanding was $80 million, and he concludes that the cost of debt was 12.5 percent. What is wrong with this conclusion?

13. **Cost of Equity.** Bunkhouse Electronics is a recently incorporated firm that makes electronic entertainment systems. Its earnings and dividends have been growing at a rate of 30 percent, and the current dividend yield is 2 percent. Its beta is 1.2, the market risk premium is 8 percent, and the risk-free rate is 4 percent.
    a. Calculate two estimates of the firm's cost of equity.
    b. Which estimate seems more reasonable to you? Why?

EXCEL

14. **Cost of Debt.** Olympic Sports has two issues of debt outstanding. One is a 9 percent coupon bond with a face value of $20 million, a maturity of 10 years, and a yield to maturity of 10 percent. The coupons are paid annually. The other bond issue has a maturity of 15 years, with coupons also paid annually, and a coupon rate of 10 percent. The face value of the issue is $25 million, and the issue sells for 92.8 percent of par value. The firm's tax rate is 35 percent.
    *a. What is the before-tax cost of debt for Olympic?
    b. What is Olympic's after-tax cost of debt?

EXCEL

15. **Capital Structure.** Examine the following book-value balance sheet for University Products, Inc. What is the capital structure of the firm based on market values? The preferred stock currently sells for $15 per share and the common stock for $20 per share. There are one million common shares outstanding.

BOOK VALUE BALANCE SHEET
($ millions)

Assets		Liabilities and Net Worth	
Cash and short-term securities	$1	Bonds, coupon = 8%, paid annually (maturity = 10 years, current yield to maturity = 9%)	$10
Accounts receivable	3	Preferred stock (par value $20 per share)	2
Inventories	7	Common stock	10
Plant and equipment	21	Retained earnings	10
Total	$32	Total	$32

*16. **Calculating WACC.** Turn back to University Products's balance sheet from problem 15. If the preferred stock pays a dividend of $2 per share, the beta of the common stock is 1.5, the market risk premium is 7 percent, the risk-free rate is 4 percent, and the firm's tax rate is 40 percent, what is University's weighted-average cost of capital?

17. **Integrative.** University Products is evaluating a new venture into home computer systems (see problems 15 and 16). The internal rate of return on the new venture is estimated at 13.4 percent. WACCs of firms in the personal computer industry tend to average around 14 percent. Should the new project be pursued? Will University Products make the correct decision if it discounts cash flows on the proposed venture at its own WACC?

EXCEL

18. **Comprehensive.** The total market value of Muskoka Real Estate Company is $6 million, and the total value of its debt is $2 million. The treasurer estimates that the beta of the stock is currently 1.5 and that the expected risk premium on the market is 7 percent. The Treasury bill rate is 4 percent.
    a. What is the required rate of return on Muskoka stock?
    b. What is the beta of the company's existing portfolio of assets? The debt is perceived to be virtually risk-free.
    c. Estimate the weighted-average cost of capital assuming a tax rate of 40 percent.
    d. Estimate the discount rate for an expansion of the company's present business.
    e. Suppose the company wants to diversify into the manufacture of rose-coloured glasses. The beta of optical manufacturers with no debt outstanding is 1.2. What is the required rate of return on Muskoka's new venture?

19. **Integrative.** Big Door Company has 10 million shares outstanding, which are currently trading for about $15 per share and have an equity beta of 1.2. Big Door has 20,000 outstanding bonds, with a 6 percent coupon rate, payable semi-annually and due in 10 years. The bonds are rated BBB. Currently the credit spread for BBB is 95 basis points over equivalent-maturity Government of Canada debt. The current yield on 10-year Canada bonds is 4 percent, compounded semi-annually. The risk-free interest rate is 2.5 percent, and the market risk premium is 6.5 percent. The company has a 35 percent tax rate.
   a. Calculate Big Door's WACC.
   b. Calculate Big Door's unlevered beta, using the formula in footnote 7.
   c. If Big Door was 50 percent debt financed, what would be its WACC? Assume that the beta of its debt is unchanged by the capital structure change.

20. **Comprehensive.** Two ambitious business graduates, Boris and Isabelle, are considering purchasing Premier Pizza, a frozen pizza manufacturer. Forecasted annual sales for the coming year are $10 million, with operating costs equal to 75 percent of sales, including taxes, and required annual investment in new equipment of 5 percent of sales. Sales and costs are expected to grow 4 percent in perpetuity. Based on their analysis of the industry, Boris and Isabelle anticipate financing their company with 30 percent debt. The required rate of return on the debt will be 6 percent and the required rate of return on the equity will be 15 percent. Premier Pizza's corporate tax rate is 35 percent. The risk-free interest rate is 3 percent and the market risk premium is 7 percent.
   a. What is the maximum price Boris and Isabelle should be willing to pay for Premier Pizza? Explain your answer.
   b. A national grocery chain, Fresh Foods, is also considering making an offer for Premier Pizza. The levered equity beta of the grocery chain is .8, its cost of debt is 5 percent, it is 40 percent debt financed, and it has a 35 percent tax rate. What is the maximum price that Fresh Foods should be willing to pay for Premier Pizza? Assume that Fresh Foods' forecast for Premier's cash flows are the same as Boris and Isabelle's. Explain your answer.

CHALLENGE

21. **Changes in Capital Structure.** Look again at our calculation of Big Oil's WACC. Suppose Big Oil is excused from paying taxes. How would its WACC change? Now suppose Big Oil makes a large stock issue and uses the proceeds to pay off all its debt. How would the cost of equity change?

EXCEL

22. **Changes in Capital Structure.** Refer back to problem 21. Suppose Big Oil starts from the financing mix in Table 12.3, and then borrows an additional $200 million from the bank. It then pays out a special $200 million dividend, leaving its assets and operations unchanged. What happens to Big Oil's WACC, still assuming it pays no taxes? What happens to the cost of equity?

23. **WACC and Taxes.** "The after-tax cost of debt is lower when the firm's tax rate is higher; therefore, the WACC falls when the tax rate rises. Thus, with a lower discount rate, the firm must be worth more if its tax rate is higher." Explain why this argument is wrong.

24. **Cost of Capital.** An analyst at Dawn Chemical notes that its cost of debt is far below that of equity. He concludes that it is important for the firm to maintain the ability to increase its borrowing because if it cannot borrow, it will be forced to use more expensive equity to finance some projects. This might lead it to reject some projects that would have seemed attractive if evaluated at the lower cost of debt. Comment on this reasoning.

25. **Internet.** Use the required rates of return calculated in Chapter 11, problem 24, to estimate the weighted-average cost of capital for the five companies. For their capital structures, go to **http://finance.yahoo.com**, click on "Key Statistics" and record the "Market Cap," the current market value of equity, and the book value of debt, near the bottom of the page. Estimating the yield on the debt is trickier. If you are lucky, the bonds are rated at

www.moodys.com, **www.dbrs.com**, or **www.standardandpoors.com**. If you cannot find a debt rating, assume that the debt is BBB rated. Assume that each company's debt has an average maturity of seven years. Assume that the credit spread (i.e., the extra yield over the equivalent term government bond) for AA-rated debt is 44 basis points, for A-rated debt is 71 basis points, for BBB-rated debt is 125 basis points, and for BB-rated debt is 265 basis points. (One basis point is .01 percentage points.) Add each spread to the current yield on 7-year Government of Canada bonds, found at **www.bankofcanada.ca/en/rates/bonds.html**. Assume that the companies have a 35 percent corporate tax rate. Now calculate the WACCs.

STANDARD &POOR'S

26. **Standard & Poor's.** Calculate the WACC for a company using information from Market Insight (**www.mcgrawhill.ca/edumarketinsight**). Find the bond rating for your selected company at the "Financial Hlts" (Financial Highlights) link. Calculate the bond's required rate of return using the credit spreads at **www.bondsonline.com/Search_Quote__Center/ Corporate_Agency_Bonds/Spreads/** and the current U.S. government bond rate at **www.bloomberg.com/market/rates/**. Assume the debt has an average maturity of 10 years and the company's tax rate is 40 percent. Estimate the cost of equity two ways:
   a. The constant dividend growth valuation model, given the current price, current dividend, and the five-year dividend growth rate.
   b. The CAPM using the 3-month U.S. Treasury bill rate as your risk-free rate. Get the company's beta at the "Mthly Val. Data" link at Market Insight (**www.mcgrawhill.ca/ edumarketinsight**) and use the U.S. historical market risk premium of 7.7 percent.

To find the weights, use the book value of interest bearing debt from the Annual Balance Sheet link (short/current long-term debt plus long-term debt). Market value of equity (market capitalization) is found at "Financial Highlights."

Solutions to Check Points

12.1 Hot Rocks' 4 million common shares are worth $40 million. Its market value balance sheet is

Assets		Liabilities and Shareholders' Equity		
Assets	$90	Debt	$50	(56%)
		Equity	40	(44%)
Value	$90	Value	$90	

WACC = (.56 × 9%) + (.44 × 17%) = 12.5%

We use Hot Rocks' pretax return on debt because the company pays no taxes.

12.2 Rhodes' 6 million shares are now worth only 6 million × $4 = $24 million. The debt is selling for 80 percent of book, or $20 million. The market value balance sheet is

Assets		Liabilities and Shareholders' Equity		
Assets	$44	Debt	$20	(45%)
		Equity	24	(55%)
Value	$44	Value	$44	

WACC = (.45 × 14%) + (.55 × 20%) = 17.3%

Note that this question ignores taxes.

12.3 Compare the two income statements ($ millions), one for Criss-cross Industries as it currently is and the other for Criss-cross with no debt in its capital structure.

	Criss-cross	Criss-Cross with No Debt
EBIT	$10.0	$10.0
Interest expense	2.0	0.0
Taxable income	8.0	10.0
Taxes owed	2.8	3.5
Net income	5.2	6.5
Total income accruing to debt and equity holders	7.2	6.5

Notice that Criss-cross with no debt pays $.7 million (= 3.5 million – 2.8 million) more in taxes than it does with debt. Accordingly, the total income available to debt and equity holders is $.7 million higher when Criss-cross is financed with both debt and equity.

12.4   For Hot Rocks,

$$\text{WACC} = [.56 \times 9 \times (1 - .35)] + (.44 \times 17) = 10.76\%$$

For Rhodes Construction,

$$\text{WACC} = [.45 \times 14 \times (1 - .35)] + (.55 \times 20) = 15.1\%$$

12.5   WACC measures the expected rate of return demanded by debt and equity investors in the firm (plus a tax adjustment capturing the tax-deductibility of interest payments). Thus the calculation must be based on what investors are actually paying for the firm's debt and equity securities. In other words, it must be based on market values.

12.6   From the CAPM:

$$r_{equity} = r_f + \beta_{equity}(r_m - r_f)$$
$$= 6\% + 1.20(7\%) = 14.4\%$$
$$\text{WACC} = .3(1 - .35)\ 8\% + .7(14.4\%) = 11.64\%$$

12.7   Jo Ann's boss is wrong. The ability to borrow at 8 percent does not mean that the cost of capital is 8 percent. This analysis ignores the side effects of the borrowing; for example, that at the higher indebtedness of the firm the equity will be riskier, and therefore, the equityholders will demand a higher rate of return on their investment.

12.8   Using equation 12.11, find Tollbar's asset beta:

$$\beta_{assets} = \frac{D}{V} \times \beta_{debt} + \frac{E}{V} \times \beta_{equity} = .2 \times .1 + .8 \times .8 = .66$$

Using equation 12.12, if Tollbar is 50 percent debt financed, its new equity beta will be

$$\beta_{equity} = \beta_{assets} + (\beta_{assets} - \beta_{debt})\frac{D}{E} = .66 + (.66 - .14)\frac{.5}{.5} = 1.18$$

WACC at original capital structure

$$r_{debt} = r_f + \beta_{debt} \times \text{MRP} = 4\% + .1 \times 7\% = 4.7\%$$
$$r_{equity} = r_f + \beta_{equity} \times \text{MRP} = 4\% + .8 \times 7\% = 9.6\%$$
$$\text{WACC} = \frac{D}{V} \times r_{debt} + \frac{E}{V} \times r_{equity} = .2 \times 4.7\% + .8 \times 9.6\% = 8.62\%$$

WACC at new capital structure

$$r_{debt} = r_f + \beta_{debt} \times \text{MRP} = 4\% + .14 \times 7\% = 4.98\%$$
$$r_{equity} = r_f + \beta_{equity} \times \text{MRP} = 4\% + 1.18 \times 7\% = 12.26\%$$
$$\text{WACC} = \frac{D}{V} \times r_{debt} + \frac{E}{V} \times r_{equity} = .5 \times 4.98\% + .5 \times 12.16\% = 8.62\%$$

MINICASE

Bernice Mountaindog was glad to be back at Sea Shore Salt. Employees were treated well. When she had asked a year ago for a leave of absence to complete her degree in finance, top management promptly agreed. When she returned with an honours degree, she was promoted from administrative assistant (she had been secretary to Joe-Bob Brinepool, the president) to treasury analyst.

Bernice thought the company's prospects were good. Sure, table salt was a mature business, but Sea Shore Salt had grown steadily at the expense of its less well-known competitors. The company's brand name was an important advantage, despite the difficulty most customers had in pronouncing it rapidly.

Bernice started work on January 2, 2006. The first two weeks went smoothly. Then Mr. Brinepool's cost of capital memo (see Figure 12.2) assigned her to explain Sea Shore Salt's weighted-average cost of capital to other managers. The memo came as a surprise to Bernice, so she stayed late to prepare for the questions that would surely come the next day.

Bernice first examined Sea Shore Salt's most recent balance sheet, summarized in Table 12.4. Then she jotted down the following additional points:

- The company's bank charged interest at current market rates, and the long-term debt had just been issued. Book and market values could not differ by much.
- But the preferred stock had been issued 35 years ago, when interest rates were much lower. The preferred stock was now trading for only $70 per share.
- The common stock traded for $40 per share. Next year's earnings per share would be about $4.00 and dividends per share,

probably $2.00. Sea Shore Salt had traditionally paid out 50 percent of earnings as dividends and plowed back the rest.

- Earnings and dividends had grown steadily at 6 to 7 percent per year, in line with the company's sustainable growth rate:

$$\begin{aligned} \frac{\text{Sustainable}}{\text{growth rate}} &= \frac{\text{return}}{\text{on equity}} \times \frac{\text{plowback}}{\text{ratio}} \\ &= 4.00/30 \times .5 \\ &= .067, \text{ or } 6.7\% \end{aligned}$$

- Sea Shore Salt's beta had averaged about .5, which made sense, Bernice thought, for a stable, steady-growth business. She made a quick cost of equity calculation using the capital asset pricing model (CAPM). With current interest rates of about 7 percent, and a market risk premium of 8 percent,

$$\text{CAPM cost of equity} = r_E = r_f + \beta(r_m - r_f)$$
$$= 7\% + .5(8\%) = 11\%$$

This cost of equity was significantly less than the 16 percent decreed in Mr. Brinepool's memo. Bernice scanned her notes apprehensively. What if Mr. Brinepool's cost of equity was wrong? Was there some other way to estimate the cost of equity as a check on the CAPM calculation? Could there be other errors in his calculations?

Bernice resolved to complete her analysis that night. If necessary, she would try to speak with Mr. Brinepool when he arrived at his office the next morning. Her job was not just finding the right number. She also had to figure out how to explain it all to Mr. Brinepool.

TABLE 12.4
Sea Shore Salt's balance sheet, taken from the company's 2005 balance sheet ($ millions)

Assets		Liabilities and Net Worth	
Working capital	$200	Bank loan	$120
Plant and equipment	360	Long-term debt	80
Other assets	40	Preferred stock	100
		Common stock, including retained earnings	300
Total	$600	Total	$600

Notes:
1. At year-end 2005, Sea Shore Salt had 10 million common shares outstanding.
2. The company had also issued 1 million preferred shares with book value of $100 per share. Each share receives an annual dividend of $6.00.

FIGURE 12.2 Mr. Brinepool's cost of capital memo

Sea Shore Salt Company
Salt Spring Island, British Columbia

CONFIDENTIAL MEMORANDUM

DATE: January 15, 2006
TO: S.S.S. Management
FROM: Joe-Bob Brinepool, President
SUBJECT: Cost of Capital

This memo states and clarifies our company's long-standing policy regarding hurdle rates for capital investment decisions. There have been many recent questions, and some evident confusion, on this matter.

Sea Shore Salt evaluates replacement and expansion investments by discounted cash flow. The discount or hurdle rate is the company's after-tax weighted-average cost of capital.

The weighted-average cost of capital is simply a blend of the rates of return expected by investors in our company. These investors include banks, bondholders, and preferred stock investors in addition to common shareholders. Of course, many of you are, or soon will be, shareholders of our company.

The following table summarizes the composition of Sea Shore Salt's financing:

	Amount ($ millions)	Percent of Total	Rate of Return (%)
Bank loan	$120	20%	7.75%
Bond issue	80	13.3	8
Preferred stock	100	16.7	6
Common stock	300	50	16
	$600	100%	

The rates of return on the bank loan and bond issue are, of course, just the interest rates we pay. However, interest is tax-deductible, so the after-tax interest rates are lower than shown above. For example, the after-tax cost of our bond financing, given our 35% tax rate, is $8(1 - .35) = 5.2\%$.

The rate of return on preferred stock is 6%. Sea Shore Salt pays a $6 dividend on each $100 preferred share.

Our target rate of return on equity has been 16% for many years. I know that some newcomers think this target is too high for the safe and mature salt business. But we must all aspire to superior profitability.

Once this background is absorbed, the calculation of Sea Shore Salt's weighted-average cost of capital (WACC) is elementary:

$$\text{WACC} = 7.75(1 - .35)(.2) + 8(1 - .35)(.133) + 6(.167) + 16(.50) = 10.7\%$$

The official corporate hurdle rate is therefore 10.7%.

If you have further questions about these calculations, please direct them to our new treasury analyst, Bernice Mountaindog. It is a pleasure to have Bernice back at Sea Shore Salt after a year's leave of absence to complete her degree in finance.

PART FOUR
Financing

AN OVERVIEW OF CORPORATE FINANCING

This chapter begins our analysis of long-term financing decisions. In later chapters this will involve a careful look at some classic finance problems, such as how much firms should borrow and what dividends they should pay their shareholders. But before getting down to specifics, we will provide a brief overview of the types of long-term finance.

It is customary to classify sources of finance as debt or equity. When the firm borrows, it promises to repay the debt with interest. If it doesn't keep its promise, the debtholders may force the firm into bankruptcy. However, no such commitments are made to the equityholders. They are entitled to whatever is left over after the debtholders have been paid off. For this reason, equity is called a *residual claim* on the firm.

However, a simple division of sources of finance into debt and equity would miss the enormous *variety* of financing instruments that companies use today. For example, Table 13.1 shows the many securities issued by George Weston Limited. Yet George Weston has not come close to exhausting the menu of possible securities.

This chapter introduces you to the principal families of securities and explains how they are used by corporations. We also draw attention to some of the interesting aspects of firms issuing these securities.

After studying this chapter you should be able to
- Describe the major classes of securities issued by firms to raise capital.
- Summarize recent trends in the use made by firms of different sources of finance.

TABLE 13.1
Large firms use many different kinds of securities. Look at the variety of securities issued by George Weston Limited, Ltd.

Equity	Debt
Common stock	Debentures
Preferred stock	Medium-term notes
Exchangeable Debentures	Notes payable
	Commercial paper
	Capital lease
	Bank loan

Source: Adapted from George Weston Limited Annual Report 2003.
Note: You can also retrieve this annual report at **www.sedar.com**. The Web site for the System for Electronic Document Analysis and Retrieval (SEDAR) provides a variety of information including annual reports and proxy forms for most publicly traded Canadian companies.

13.1   COMMON STOCK

Most major corporations are far too large to be owned by one investor. For example, you would need to lay your hands on over $13 billion if you wanted to own all of George Weston, Ltd. (GW).

GW is owned by about 1,200 different investors, each of whom holds a number of shares of common stock. These investors are therefore known as *shareholders* or *stockholders*. Altogether GW has outstanding about 129 million shares of common stock. Thus if you were to buy one GW share, you would own 1/129,433,442, or about .0000008 percent of the company. Of course, a large pension fund, such as the Ontario Teachers' Pension Plan, might hold many thousands of GW shares.

issued shares Shares that have been issued by the company.

The 129 million shares held by investors at the end of 2003 represents the number of outstanding or **issued** and **outstanding shares** of GW.[1] If GW wishes to raise more money, it can sell more shares. The maximum number of shares that can be issued is known as the **authorized share capital**; looking at Table 13.2, for GW, this is unlimited. However, many firms set a limit to their authorized share capital, which is specified in the firm's articles of incorporation and can be changed only with the permission of the shareholders. Votes on proposed changes to the *articles of incorporation* occur at shareholders' meetings.

outstanding shares Shares that have been issued by the company and are held by investors.

authorized share capital
Maximum number of shares that the company is permitted to issue as specified in the firm's articles of incorporation.

Table 13.2 shows how the investment by GW's shareholders is recorded in the company's books. The value of new shares issued by GW is shown in the common shares account. As of December 31, 2003, this is $120 million. In the past, a company issuing new shares would specify a monetary value, called **par value**, for such shares. The par value was an arbitrarily set number and almost always lower than the actual sale price of the new shares. The difference was recorded as **additional paid-in capital**, *paid-in surplus*, *capital surplus* or *contributed surplus*. The Canadian Business Corporations Act has since been changed to stop this practice, and today common shares mostly do not have a par value.[2]

par value Value of security shown on certificate.

additional paid-in capital
Difference between issue price and par value of stock, also called capital surplus.

Besides buying new stock, shareholders also indirectly contribute new capital to the firm whenever profits that could be paid out as dividends are instead plowed back into the company. Table 13.2 shows that the cumulative amount of such **retained earnings** is about $4,046 million.

retained earnings Earnings not paid out as dividends.

A negative amount of $192 million is shown in Table 13.2 for *foreign currency translation adjustments*, representing currency translation losses from GW's foreign operations. In this chapter we will ignore foreign exchange accounting.

The sum of common shares, retained earnings, and foreign currency translation adjustment gains is known as the *net common equity* of the firm. It equals the total amount contributed directly by common shareholders when the firm issued new stock, and indirectly, when it plowed back part of its earnings.

---

[1] Of course, only about 49 million of these common shares are available for public trading. The remaining shares are closely held.

[2] The practice of setting par value and using the additional paid-in capital account is still followed in the United States.

TABLE 13.2
Book value of common stockholders' equity of George Weston, Ltd., December 31, 2003 (Figures in millions)

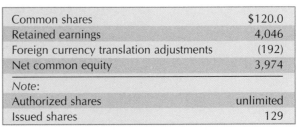

Common shares	$120.0
Retained earnings	4,046
Foreign currency translation adjustments	(192)
Net common equity	3,974
Note:	
Authorized shares	unlimited
Issued shares	129

Source: Adapted from George Weston, Ltd., 2003 *Annual Report.*

During 2003, GW repurchased a little over 2.8 million of its shares, which it had issued in the past.[3] In the United States, when a company repurchases some of its shares, it can continue to hold them as its own stock. These shares would appear in the balance sheet as treasury stock. In Canada treasury stock is not allowed. Instead, any shares repurchased must be cancelled. This is done by reducing the company's net equity account to the extent of the amount paid for any shares repurchased.[4] The common shares account is reduced by the average issue price. Any amount in excess of the average issue price is subtracted from retained earnings or, sometimes, from the paid-in surplus account. For example, suppose 1,000 shares are repurchased for $30 per share and the average issue price was $25 per share. To cancel the repurchased shares, the overall net equity account is reduced by $30 × $1,000 = $30,000. This comprises a reduction to the common shares account by $25 × $1,000 = $25,000 and a reduction to retained earnings by the remaining $5,000. The repurchase of the 2.8 million shares cost GW $275 million. It cancelled these shares by charging $2 million to its common shares account and about $273 million to its retained earnings account.

Check Point 13.1

Generic Products has had one stock issue in which it sold 100,000 shares to the public at $15 per share. Can you fill in the following table?

Common shares	_____
Retained earnings	_____
Common equity	$3,000,000

BOOK VALUE VERSUS MARKET VALUE

We discussed the distinction between book and market value in Chapters 3 and 6, but it bears repeating.

> Book value is a backward-looking measure. It tells us how much capital the firm has raised from shareholders in the past. It does not measure the value that investors place on those shares today. The market value of the firm is forward looking; it depends on the future dividends that shareholders expect to receive.

GW's common equity has a book value of $3,974 million. With 129 million shares outstanding, this translates to a book value of $3974/129 million = $30.81 per share. But on December 31, 2003, GW shares were priced at about $103.71 each. So the total *market* value of the common stock was 129 million shares × $103.71 per share = $13.4 billion, nearly 236 percent more than the book value.

Market value is usually greater than book value. This is partly because inflation has driven the value of many assets above what they originally cost. Also, firms raise capital to invest in

---

[3] We will look into why companies repurchase their shares in Chapter 16.

[4] For this reason, in Canada, the number of shares issued always equals the number outstanding.

projects with present values that exceed initial cost. These positive-NPV projects made the shareholders better off. So we would expect the market value of the firm to be higher than the amount of money put up by the shareholders.

However, sometimes projects do go awry and companies fall on hard times. In this case, market value can fall below book value.

Check Point 13.2   No-Name News can be established by investing $10 million in a printing press. The newspaper is expected to generate a cash flow of $2 million a year for 20 years. If the cost of capital is 10 percent, is the firm's market or book value greater? What if the cost of capital is 20 percent?

DIVIDENDS

Shareholders hope to receive a series of dividends on their investment. However, the company is not obliged to pay any dividends and the decision is up to the board of directors. In Chapter 16, we will discuss how that decision affects the value of the stock.

Because dividends are discretionary, they are not considered to be a business expense. Therefore, companies are not allowed to deduct dividend payments when they calculate their taxable income.

SHAREHOLDERS' RIGHTS

Ultimately, shareholders have control of the company's affairs. Occasionally companies need shareholder approval before they can take certain actions. For example, they need approval to increase the authorized capital or to merge with another company.

> On most other matters, shareholder control boils down to the right to vote on appointments to the board of directors.

The board usually consists of the company's top management as well as *non-executive directors*, who are not employed by the firm. In principle, the board is elected as an agent of the shareholders. It appoints and oversees the management of the firm and meets to vote on such matters as new share issues. Most of the time the board will go along with management, but in crisis situations it can be very independent. For example, when management of RJR Nabisco, the giant American tobacco and food company, announced that it wanted to take over the company, the outside directors stepped in to make sure that the company was sold to the highest bidder. When serious accounting and managerial irregularities were found with Livent, the Toronto-based production company, which staged such hits as *Phantom of the Opera*, its board of directors fired the company's two co-founders and also filed a multimillion dollar civil suit against them. Recently, Chicago-based Hollinger International filed a $1.25 billion lawsuit against its former chairman and CEO as well as its former chief operating officer for improperly taking millions of dollars in management fees and other payments from the company.

VOTING PROCEDURES

majority voting   Voting system in which each director is voted on separately.

cumulative voting   Voting system in which all the votes one shareholder is allowed to cast can be cast for one candidate for the board of directors.

In most companies shareholders elect directors by a system of **majority voting**. In this case each director is voted on separately, and shareholders can cast one vote for each share they own. In some companies directors are elected by **cumulative voting**. The directors are then voted on jointly and the shareholders can, if they choose, cast all their votes for just one candidate. For example, suppose there are five directors to be elected and you own 100 shares. You therefore have a total of 5 × 100 = 500 votes. Under majority voting you can cast a maximum of 100 votes for any one candidate. With a cumulative voting system, you can cast all 500 votes for your favourite candidate. Cumulative voting makes it easier for a minority group of the shareholders to elect a director to represent their interests. That is why minority groups devote so much effort to campaigning for cumulative voting.

On many issues a simple majority of the votes cast is enough to carry the day, but there are some decisions that require a "supermajority" of between two-thirds and 80 percent of those eligible to vote. For example, a supermajority vote of two-thirds of the shareholders of record is usually needed to approve a merger. This requirement makes it difficult for the firm to be taken over and therefore helps to protect the incumbent management.

proxy contest Takeover attempt in which outsiders compete with management for shareholders' votes.

Shareholders can either vote in person or appoint a proxy to vote. The issues on which they are asked to vote are rarely contested, particularly in the case of large, publicly traded firms. Occasionally, however, there are **proxy contests** in which outsiders compete with the firm's existing management and directors for control of the corporation. But the odds are stacked against the outsiders because the insiders can get the firm to pay all the costs of presenting their case and obtaining votes.

In some special situations involving important corporate decisions such as mergers, or selling the firm's assets, the votes of most of the minority shareholders must be received. For example, the Ontario Securities Commission has introduced regulations that are intended to give the minority shareholders the opportunity to prevent majority shareholders and management from doing deals that reduce the value of the minority shareholders' shares. Sometimes powerful minority shareholders can successfully prevent takeover decisions made by the company's management or majority shareholders.

In 2000, a deal valued at $5.7 billion was struck to sell the Montreal-based cable company Groupe Videotron Ltée to Rogers Communications, Inc., of Toronto. The powerful Caisse de dépôt et placement du Québec, Canada's biggest pension fund manager, which held a 10 percent minority voting stake in Videotron, opposed the deal because it wanted Videotron to remain in Québec. Caisse de dépôt broke ranks with the Chagnon family, which built Videotron into Québec's largest cable operator and held 71 percent of its votes. Instead, Caisse de dépôt engineered a competing bid with Montreal-based printing and publishing giant Quebecor, Inc., worth $5.9 billion. Videotron was eventually acquired by Quebecor.

CLASSES OF STOCK

Many companies issue just one class of common stock. Sometimes, however, a firm may have two or more classes outstanding, which differ in their right to vote or receive dividends.[5] Suppose that a firm needs fresh capital but its present shareholders do not want to give up control of the firm. The existing shares could be labelled Class A, and then Class B shares could be issued to outside investors. The Class B shares could have limited voting rights, although they would probably sell for less as a result.

For instance, in April 2004, Bombardier had listed about 342 million Class A shares and over 1,408 million Class B shares on the Toronto Stock Exchange.[6] The Class A shares carry 10 votes per share whereas the Class B shares carry only one vote per share. The Bombardier family controlled, through holding companies, over 82 percent of the Class A shares, or about 58 percent of the total voting rights of Bombardier.

Common shares without full voting rights are called *restricted shares*. There are various types of restricted shares. If the restricted shares have no votes, they are called *non-voting*. If the restricted shares have fewer votes per share than another class of common shares, they are called *subordinate voting*. You can also own *limited voting* shares that also carry fewer voting rights relative to another class of common shares. As of December 2003, 126 different classes of restricted shares were trading on the TSX. These included 43 non-voting shares, 75 subordinate voting shares, 4 limited voting shares, and 4 restricted voting shares. How do we figure out the type of class? If a share is denoted as Class B *nv*, *nv* stands for non-voting, if it is denoted as *sv*, it is sub-

---

[5] In the United States, most companies issue one class of common stock and follow the practice of "one share, one vote."
[6] Bombardier's Class B shares are also traded in stock exchanges in Brussels, Belgium, and Frankfurt, Germany.

ordinate voting, *lv* stands for limited voting, *rv* stands for restricted voting. In addition to Bombardier, other large Canadian companies such as Power Corporation, Quebecor, Inc., and Magna International have also issued restricted voting shares. For instance, Power Corporation has issued subordinate voting shares, and Allstream Inc. (formerly AT&T, Canada) has issued Class B Limited Voting Shares. Table 13.3 shows some large multivoting share Canadian companies. From Table 13.3, notice that although AGF Management Ltd.'s Class A shares carry one vote per share, only shareholders holding this category of shares are eligible to vote. The company also has a large number of Class B non-voting shares. Similarly, only the common shares at Canadian Tire carry voting rights—albeit at one vote per share—although the company has a large issue of non-voting Class A shares outstanding.

Canadian securities regulators are also making it more difficult for a firm to convert an existing common share class into two share classes with different voting rights. In order to convert, most of the minority shareholders must approve. Also, the stock exchanges will not list a new class of non-voting or subordinate voting shares unless the shares have the right to participate in takeover bids. This right is called a *coattail provision*.

The following example illustrates how coattail provisions may be valuable.[7] In 1986 a group of independent dealers from Canadian Tire stores offered to purchase 49 percent of Canadian Tire common (voting) shares for $160.24 each, which were then trading at $40, while making no offer for the Class A non-voting stock, which traded at about $14.50. This offer, if accepted, would give them control of the firm since they already owned about 17 percent of the voting stock. However, the Class A non-voting stock had a coattail provision in place, which stated that in the event of a bid for all or substantially all of the voting common shares, the Class A shareholders would be entitled to tender their shares to the bidder as well. The Class A non-voting shareholders felt that a bid for 49 percent of the common stock meant "substantially all" of the voting shares, so the coattail provision should be triggered. Therefore, they took the view that they should also be allowed to sell their shares for $160.24 per share. The Ontario Securities Commission disallowed the transaction after holding a hearing. Their decision, in favour of the Class A non-voting shareholders, was later upheld by the court and the takeover bid was withdrawn.

CORPORATE GOVERNANCE IN CANADA AND ELSEWHERE

In many large corporations, shareholders own the company but they don't manage it. For instance, the aluminum products giant, Alcan Inc., is owned by about 18,000 different shareholders. Management is delegated to a team of professional managers. Each shareholder owns only a small fraction of Alcan's shares and can exert little influence on the way the company is

TABLE 13.3
Some Large Multivoting Share Companies in Canada

	Other Share Class	Votes per Share	Major Shareholder	% of Total Shares	% of Total Votes
AGF Management Ltd.	Class A	1	Goldring Capital	0.1	80
Bombardier Inc.	Class A	10	Bombardier family	16.1	58.3
Canadian Tire Corp. Ltd.	Common	1	Martha Billes	3.5	61.4
CanWest Global Communications Corp.	Multiple	10	Asper family	45.8	89.1
The Jean Coutu Group (PJC) Inc.	Class B	10	Jean Coutu	55.2	92.4
Magna International Inc.	Class B	500	Stronach Trust	0.7	56.5
Power Corp. of Canada	Partic.Pref.	10	Paul Desmarais	30.2	64.7
Quebecor Inc.	Class A	10	Péladeau family	27.1	65.1
Rogers Communications Inc.	Class A	25	Ted Rogers	21.9	90.9

Source: Excerpted from "FP500 Corporate Structure: Largest Multi-Voting Share Companies," *National Post*, Business, June 2004.

---

[7] See also E. Maynes, C. Robinson, and A. White, "How Much Is a Share Vote Worth," *Canadian Investment Review* (Spring 1990), Volume III, pp. 49–55.

run. If shareholders do not like the policies the management team pursues, they can try to vote in another board of directors who will bring about a change in policy. But such attempts are rarely successful, and the shareholders' simplest solution is to sell the shares.

The separation between ownership and management in major Canadian corporations creates a potential conflict between shareholders (the principals who own the company) and managers (their agents who make the decisions). We noted in Chapter 1 several mechanisms that have evolved to mitigate this conflict:

- Shareholders elect a board of directors, which then appoints the managers, oversees them, and, on occasion, fires them.
- Managers' remuneration is tied to their performance.
- Poorly performing companies are taken over and the management is replaced by a new team.[8]

SEE BOX P. 401

These principles of corporate governance provide for a healthy and ethical business environment. However, as the nearby Finance in Action box shows, a perception of excessive emphasis on governance can cause a climate of risk aversion among business leaders. Rules of corporate governance may differ across nations. Canada, the United States, Britain, Australia, and other English-speaking countries all have broadly similar systems, but other countries do not. In Japan industrial and financial companies are often linked together in a group called a *keiretsu*. For example, the Mitsubishi keiretsu contains 29 core companies, which includes two banks, two insurance companies, an automobile manufacturer, a steel producer, and a cement company. Members of the keiretsu are tied together in several ways. First, managers may sit on the boards of directors of other group companies, and a "president's council" of chief executives meets regularly. Second, each company in the group holds shares in many of the other companies. And third, companies generally borrow from the keiretsu's bank or from elsewhere within the group. These links may have several advantages. Companies can obtain funds from other members of the group without the need to reveal confidential information to the public, and if a member of the group runs into financial difficulties, its problems can be worked out with other members of the group rather than in the bankruptcy court.

The more stable and concentrated shareholder base of large Japanese corporations may make it easier for them to resist pressures for short-term performance and allow them to focus on securing long-term advantages. But the Japanese system of corporate governance also has its disadvantages: The lack of market discipline can promote a life that's too cozy, and allow lagging or inefficient Japanese corporations to put off painful surgery.

Keiretsus are found only in Japan. Similar structures exist in other Asian countries; for instance, South Korea has large, powerful *chaebols*. Large companies in continental Europe are linked in some similar ways. For example, banks and other companies often own or control large blocks of shares and can push hard for changes in the management or strategy of poorly performing firms. (Banks in the United States are prohibited from large or permanent holdings of the stock of non-financial corporations.) Thus oversight and control are entrusted largely to banks and other corporations. Hostile takeovers of poorly performing companies are rare in Germany and virtually impossible in Japan.

> For large corporations, separation of ownership and control is seen the world over. In Canada and the United States, control of large public companies is exercised through the board of directors and pressure from the stock market. In other countries the stock market is less important, and control shifts to major shareholders, typically banks and other companies.

[8] Lately, corporate governance has been a popular theme of study among academic researchers, particularly in the United States. A recent study of large Canadian firms finds little evidence of a relationship between corporate governance and firm performance, and, indeed, between performance and CEO pay that appears to be associated more with firm size. See V. Jog and S. Dutta, "Searching for the Governance Trail: Is There a Link between the Quality of Corporate Governance and a Firm's Performance or CEO Compensation?" *Canadian Investment Review* (Spring 2004), Volume 17 (1), pp. 33-43.

Has Corporate Governance Run Amok and Made Company Directors Too Risk Averse?

FINANCE IN ACTION

Corporate governance concerns have reached "hysterical" proportions, leaving directors of public companies more averse to risk, Power Corp. of Canada chairman and co-chief executive Paul Desmarais Jr. said yesterday.

"I think the corporate governance pendulum is swinging at its maximum. People are getting hysterical over just about everything," Mr. Desmarais said following the conglomerate's annual meeting. "There's so much second guessing. I am worried generally about corporations ... And I think what's happening is you're going to start getting a bit of gridlock on boards and everybody second-guessing and [watching] their backs."

Mr. Desmarais said he's worried that with the pressure being applied by pension funds and other groups to enact governance changes that corporations will be afraid to take the normal sorts of risks required to make their businesses grow and prosper.

Mr. Desmarais' comments follow the stark admission last week by Placer Dome Inc. chief executive Jay Taylor that he's not keen to join boards after he retires this fall because "the role of a director is almost 90% governance ... Watching people and looking for infractions and fraud and embezzlement is not what it's all about for me."

Since the Enron meltdown in 2001, governance has been the top buzzword at public companies, resulting in more work and stiffer requirements for boards.

Stephen Jarislowsky, cofounder of the Canadian Coalition for Good Governance, said that "Desmarais should set an example rather than bitch about it. It may not bother them, but it bothers everybody else.

"Directors weren't gridlocked before when there were too many guys who were stealing from their companies, and there have been a hell of a lot of boards that never carried out their responsibilities. The investor was never regarded except as an idiot who gave cash to companies."

Mr. Jarislowsky said Power has been "very good to shareholders." But he criticized its dual class share structure and the rich award of

options in the past by the company and its subsidiaries.

Like other public companies, Power—which indirectly controls insurance giant Great West Lifeco Inc. and Canada's largest mutual fund company, IGM Financial Inc., and has other holdings in Asia, Europe and North America—follows a long list of governance guidelines. A majority of directors are independent; there are no related directors on the audit and compensation committees.

But Power also maintains an "executive committee of the board"—which creates a two-tier board, in the eyes of critics—and hasn't separated the roles of chairman and CEO.

In addition, Paul Desmarais Sr. has 65% voting control despite owning just 30% of Power's equity. That's because the 77-year-old billionaire's stake of 24.1 million "participating preferred shares," carry 10 votes each, compared with one vote for each of the 197 million subordinate voting shares.

Dual share classes are another bugbear for governance critics.

Paul Desmarais Jr. has argued in the past there shouldn't be a one-size-fits-all governance standard, pointing to his company's long-term returns as evidence there is nothing wrong with Power's approach.

"What we're worried about is having one [governance] system that would be designated for every single corporation, when we believe quite fundamentally that our system has worked well for our corporation," his brother, co-CEO André said yesterday.

Shareholders heard yesterday Power's 10-year total shareholder return (stock price appreciation plus dividends) to March was 20.7% compounded annually, far exceeding the Toronto Stock Exchange index. To bolster its case, Power yesterday increased its quarterly dividend for the ninth straight year, to $1.15 annually, up 18%. The company also reported it earned $207 million (90¢ per share) in net income during the first quarter ended March 31, a 24% rise over the same period last year.

Source: Excerpted from S. Silcoff, "Governance Run Amok: Desmarais," *Financial Post*, May 13, 2004, p. FP1, 5.

13.2 PREFERRED STOCK

Usually when investors talk about equity or stock, they are referring to common stock. But as of December 31, 2003, GW had also issued 9.4 million shares of 5.65 percent cumulative redeemable preferred shares, Series I, for $228 million. In addition, GW had issued 10.6 million 5.15 percent cumulative redeemable preferred shares, Series II, which will be convertible to GW's common shares on and after July 1, 2009, for $260 million. The sum of GW's common equity and **preferred stock** is known as **net worth**. This amounts to $3,974 million + $488 million = $4,462 million.

preferred stock Stock that takes priority over common stock in regard to dividends.

For most companies preferred stock is much less important than common stock. However, it can be a useful method of financing in mergers and certain other special situations.

net worth Book value of common shareholders' equity plus preferred stock.

Like debt, most preferred stock promises a series of fixed payments to the investor and with relatively rare exceptions preferred dividends are paid in full and on time. For instance, GW promises a *fixed* annual dividend of $1.2875 on its preferred shares Series II. This dollar amount can be obtained as the product of the fixed dividend rate of 5.15 percent and the value per share of $25. Nevertheless, preferred stock is legally an equity security. This is because payment of a preferred dividend is almost invariably within the discretion of the directors. The only obligation is that no dividends can be paid on the common stock until the preferred dividend has been paid.[9] If the company goes out of business, the preferred shareholders get in the queue after the debtholders but before the common shareholders.

Notice that GW's Series II preferred shares are *cumulative*. If the board of directors decides to skip a dividend payment on these shares, the unpaid dividend will be in *arrears*. In such a situation, the company may not pay dividends on common shares or redeem any preferred shares until all arrears are paid. If, on the other hand, a preferred share is *non-cumulative* then the investor is entitled to payment of a dividend only if the board of directors declares a dividend. Arrears do not accrue on non-cumulative preferred shares.

Like common stock, preferred stock usually does not have a final repayment However, a sizable number of issues tend to be *redeemable*. This means the company has the right to acquire the shares at a set amount known as the *call price*. GW's preferred shares are redeemable at $25 per share. Sometimes, preferred shares can also be *retractable*, in which case the investor can force the company to buy back the share at a specified date.

Some preferred shares are *convertible*, which means that the shares can be converted into another class of shares—usually common shares—at a predetermined price (the exercise price) and for a certain period of time. For example, Bank of Montreal has issued Class B preferred shares, Series 10 U.S.F, which will be convertible into a specified number of common shares on or after February 25, 2012. To discourage investors from simply buying convertible preferred shares and immediately converting them, such shares usually trade at a premium. Investors like the convertibility option especially when the company's common stock has the potential for price appreciation, since investors will want to convert if the price of the common shares rises above the exercise price.

How do you tell whether a share is common or preferred? This is fairly easy to do because usually the stock symbols for preferred shares will have a special extension. For example, when preferred shares are listed on the TSX, the stock symbol ends in ".PR."

SEE BOX P. 403 ▶

Preferred stock rarely confers full voting privileges. This is an advantage to firms that want to raise new money without sharing control of the firm with the new shareholders. The nearby Finance in Action box suggests that many Canadian firms appear to issue preferred shares for this reason. However, if there is any matter that affects their place in the queue, preferred shareholders usually get to vote on it. Most issues also provide the holder with some voting power if the preferred dividend is skipped.

Companies cannot deduct preferred dividends when they calculate taxable income. However, dividend income is generally not taxed when received by Canadian corporations and is taxed at reduced rates when received by individuals who are eligible to a dividend tax credit.[10] Thus, in Canada, corporations tend to invest more in preferred shares than individual investors. Firms paying little or no tax could have a tax-based incentive to issue preferred shares rather than debt. For example, suppose XYZ Company pays no tax. The company wishes to obtain financing from a bank that has offered it a loan at an 8 percent annual interest rate. If the bank's marginal tax rate is 35 percent, then after paying tax on the interest, the bank will receive a net return of $(1 - .35) \times 8\% = 5.2\%$. The bank can earn the same return by buying XYZ's preferred shares with a dividend yield of 5.2 percent, since the bank pays no tax on the preferred share dividends. Now consider XYZ's point of view. The company cannot use the interest deduction from the bank loan to reduce its tax since it pays no tax, so its before- and after-tax costs of the bank loan are 8 percent. On the other hand, if it sells preferred shares with a 5.2 percent dividend yield, it has reduced its cost of funds from 8 percent to 5.2 percent. It is much cheaper for XYZ to raise the needed money by selling preferred shares than by borrowing. The Government of Canada has made it more difficult for banks to buy preferred stock from other corporations. For instance, in 1987, the federal government

---

[9] These days this obligation is usually cumulative. In other words, before the common shareholders get a cent, the firm must pay any preferred dividends that have been missed in the past.

[10] We discussed this issue in Chapter 3 and will also discuss it later in Chapter 16.

Is There Too Much Concentration of Power in Canadian Corporations?

Money managers and analysts are calling for an overhaul of investing laws to allow Canadians to invest more of their money in foreign firms in hopes of forcing uncompetitive and unaccountable domestic companies to respect the rights of minority shareholders.

As the Canadian market slowly loses its best companies to foreign takeovers, investors are being forced to choose from a slew of other stocks that are either controlled by family voting trusts, mired in various unrelated businesses, or drowning in red ink, analysts say.

Because Canadian investors can only invest up to 30 percent of their RRSP portfolio in foreign stocks and bonds, institutional investors must put 70 percent of their assets in Canadian securities if they want to sell to the retirement savings market. Despite this, Canada represents only about 2 percent of the world economy.

The laws were designed to protect Canadian industries and jobs from foreign competition and ensure most of Canada's wealth was kept within the country.

But investors and analysts say the rules have backfired, fostering an environment in which a small corporate elite can keep voting control of their companies while silencing common shareholders who have little choice but to invest in Canada.

Too many Canadian firms, such as Bombardier, Inc., Alliance Atlantis Communications, Inc., Chum, Ltd., and Shaw Communications, Inc., use preferred shares to let insiders control the majority of votes, although they may own just a fraction of the company's equity.

The restrictions are particularly onerous given the fact that such arrangements are almost unheard of in the United States.

What's more worrying is the fact that insider control and preferred voting structures are becoming more common, said Bill Mackenzie, president of Fairvest Proxy Monitor, which provides corporate governance advice to institutional shareholders.

In 1997, 23 percent of companies listed in the TSE 300 had a single shareholder holding more than half the voting shares. This year, that number rose to 30 percent, said Mr. Mackenzie.

Similarly in 1997, 17.7 percent of the companies in the index had preferred shares giving insiders with minority-equity stakes voting control. This year, that number jumped to 22.7 percent.

The laws ultimately hurt more than just big institutional investors, Mr. Mackenzie said. He argues that the concentration of power in Canada's corporate elite affects the entire Canadian market and every person with money invested in it.

Source: Excerpted from S. Maich, "Investing Rules Attacked: Pressure to Overhaul Foreign Content Laws," *The Financial Post* (August 16, 2001), pp. C1, C8.

introduced measures to reduce the tax loophole by requiring issuers of preferred shares to pay a 40 percent tax on preferred dividends.[11] The tax is refunded if the issuer is taxable.

Individual U.S. investors do not have the dividend tax credit of Canadian investors and must pay the full personal tax on dividend income. U.S. corporations enjoy some tax relief on dividend income. If one corporation buys another's stock, only 30 percent of the dividends it receives are taxed. This rule applies to both common and preferred stock but is most important for preferred for which returns are dominated by dividends rather than capital gains. Also, regulated American public utilities, which can take tax payments into account when negotiating the rates they charge to customers, can effectively pass the tax disadvantage of preferred stock on to the consumer. As a result, a large fraction of the dollar value of American offerings of non-convertible preferred stock consists of issues by utilities. Overall, preferred share financing is used less in the United States than in Canada, due to lower tax incentives.

If you invest your firm's spare cash in a preferred stock, you will want to make sure that when it is time to sell the stock it won't have plummeted in value. One problem with garden-variety preferred stock that pays a fixed dividend is that the preferreds' market prices go up and down as interest rates change (because present values fall when rates rise). So one ingenious banker had an idea: Why not link the dividend on the preferred stock to interest rates so that it goes up when interest rates rise, and vice versa? The result is known as floating-rate preferred. If you own **floating-rate preferred**, the dividend rate could be tied to the prime rate of interest. You know that any change in interest rates will be counterbalanced by a change in the dividend payment, so the value of your investment is protected. For instance, Alcan Aluminum's preferred shares, Series C and E, carry floating dividend rates.

floating-rate preferred
Preferred stock paying dividends that vary with short-term interest rates.

---

[11] See I. Fooladi, P. A. McGraw, and G. S. Roberts, "Preferred Share Rule Freezes Out the Individual Investor," *CA Magazine* (April 11, 1988), pp. 38–41.

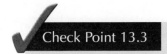

A company in a 35 percent tax bracket can buy a bond yielding 10 percent or a preferred stock of the same firm that is priced to yield 8 percent. Which will provide the higher after-tax yield? What if the purchaser is a private individual in a 35 percent tax bracket?

13.3   CORPORATE DEBT

When companies borrow money, they promise to make regular interest payments and to repay the principal (that is, the original amount borrowed).

However, corporations have limited liability. By this we mean that the promise to repay the debt is not always kept. If the company gets into deep water, the company has the right to default on the debt and to hand over the company's assets to the lenders.

Clearly the company will choose bankruptcy only if the value of the assets is less than the amount of the debt. In practice, when companies go bankrupt, this handover of assets is far from straightforward. For example, when Eaton's, the venerated department store, went into bankruptcy, there were a large number of creditors all jostling for a place in the queue. Some fashion companies reportedly sent their employees to the store locations to seize their merchandise. Sorting out these problems is left to the bankruptcy court.

Because lenders are not regarded as owners of the firm, they don't normally have any voting power. Also, the company's payments of interest are regarded as a cost and are therefore deducted from taxable income. Thus interest is paid out of *before-tax* income, whereas dividends on common and preferred stock are paid out of *after-tax* income. This means that the government provides a tax subsidy on the use of debt, which it does not provide on stock.

DEBT COMES IN MANY FORMS

An orderly scheme of classification is essential to cope with the almost endless variety of debt issues. We will walk you through the major distinguishing characteristics.

Interest Rate

The interest payment, or *coupon*, on most long-term loans is fixed at the time of issue. If a $1,000 bond is issued with a coupon of 10 percent, the firm continues to pay $100 a year regardless of how interest rates change. As we pointed out in Chapters 4 and 5, you sometimes encounter zero-coupon bonds. In this case the firm does not make a regular interest payment. It just makes a single payment at maturity. Obviously, investors pay less for zero-coupon bonds.

prime rate   Benchmark interest rate charged by banks.

Most loans from a bank and some long-term loans carry a *floating interest rate*. For example, your firm may be offered a loan at "1 percent over prime." The **prime rate** is the benchmark interest rate charged by banks to large customers with good to excellent credit. (But the largest and most creditworthy corporations can, and do, borrow at less than prime.) The prime rate is adjusted up and down with the general level of interest rates. When the prime rate changes, the interest on your floating-rate loan also changes.

Floating-rate loans are not always tied to the prime rate. Often they are tied to the rate at which international banks lend to one another. This is known as the *London Interbank Offered Rate*, or *LIBOR*.

Would you expect the price of a 10-year floating-rate bond to be more or less sensitive to changes in interest rates than the price of a 10-year maturity fixed-rate bond?

Maturity

long-term debt   Debt with more than one year remaining to maturity.

Long-term debt is any debt repayable more than one year from the date of issue. Debt due in less than a year is termed *short term* and is carried on the balance sheet as a current liability. Short-term debt is often described as unfunded debt, and long-term debt is described as funded, although it is clearly artificial to call a 364-day debt short term and a 366-day debt long term.

There are corporate bonds of nearly every conceivable maturity. For example, Walt Disney Co. has issued bonds with a 100-year maturity. Before it broke up into separately traded companies, Canadian Pacific, Ltd. had issued perpetual debentures—that is, bonds that may survive forever (see the nearby Finance in Action box). Of course, the survival of the debentures depended on the survival of the company. At the other extreme we find firms borrowing literally overnight.

SEE BOX P. 406

Repayment Provisions

sinking fund   Fund established to retire debt before maturity.

Long-term loans are commonly repaid in a steady regular way, perhaps after an initial grace period. For bonds that are publicly traded, this is done by means of a **sinking fund**. Each year the firm puts aside a sum of cash into a sinking fund that is then used to buy back the bonds. When there is a sinking fund, investors are prepared to lend at a lower rate of interest. They know that they are more likely to be repaid if the company sets aside some cash each year than if the entire loan has to be repaid on a specific day.

callable bond   Bond that may be repurchased by the firm before maturity at a specified call price.

Firms issuing debt to the public sometimes reserve the right to call the debt—that is, issuers of **callable bonds** may buy back the bonds before the final maturity date. The price at which the firm can call the bonds is set at the time that the bonds are issued. Call provisions usually come into effect after several years have elapsed since the bond issue. For instance, a bond issue may stipulate that it remain *call protected* during its first five years, in which case, the company may not issue a call during this time frame.

refunding   When an old bond issue is replaced with a new one by the firm. Often, this is done when interest rates decline, and the firm can save on the interest cost of the new issue.

This option to call the bond is attractive to the issuer. If interest rates decline and bond prices rise, the issuer may repay the bonds at the specified call price and borrow the money back at a lower rate of interest. This would be a bond **refunding** decision by the company and would be made by looking at present values of the costs associated with calling the existing bond and the benefits associated with lower coupon payments on the new bond. The analysis would be conducted using a net present value framework. We will discuss the bond refunding decision later in Appendix 13A.

The call provision comes at the expense of bondholders because it limits investors' capital gain potential. If interest rates fall and bond prices rise, holders of callable bonds may find their bonds bought back by the firm for the call price.

Check Point 13.5

Suppose GW is considering two issues of 20-year maturity coupon bonds; one issue will be callable, the other not. For a given coupon rate, will the callable or non-callable bond sell at the higher price? If both the bonds are to be sold to the public at par value, which bond must have the higher coupon rate?

Seniority

subordinated debt   Debt that may be repaid in bankruptcy only after senior debt is paid.

Some debts are **subordinated**. In the event of default the subordinated lender gets in line behind the firm's general creditors. The subordinated lender holds a junior claim and is paid only after all senior creditors are satisfied.

When you lend money to a firm, you can assume that you hold a senior claim unless the debt agreement says otherwise. However, this does not always put you at the front of the line because the firm may have set aside some of its assets specifically for the protection of other lenders. This brings us to our next classification.

Security

When you borrow to buy your home, the bank or trust company will take out a mortgage on the house. The mortgage acts as security for the loan. If you default on the loan payments, the bank can seize your home.

CP Debenture Investors Want Vote

Investors holding Canadian Pacific, Ltd.'s historic consolidated debenture stock are asking for a right to vote on the company's breakup this fall, which is expected to create five separate companies.

Their application will be heard in court on July 9.

Calgary-based CP has scheduled a special shareholders' meeting for late September to approve the breakup, but it argues that investors holding the consolidated debenture stock shouldn't get a say.

The obscure bonds, which were issued late in the 19th century and early 20th century, are supposed to pay 4 percent interest in perpetuity in gold coin. But using gold coin to pay interest was outlawed in the 1930s in Canada and the United States, so holders are paid in cash.

Holders of the special stock were unsuccessful in a bid to overturn CP's previous restructuring in the 1990s. In that case, they argued that the debenture stock originally had first charge on all CP assets. But as a result of the earlier restructuring, the securities were backed only by the company's railway assets.

In February, CP ended years of speculation by announcing that it would break into separately traded companies in order to boost the overall value of those units.

When the transaction occurs, investors will be handed shares in five companies: Pan Canadian Petroleum, Ltd., Canadian Pacific Railway Co., Canadian Pacific Hotels & Resorts, Inc., Fording, Inc., and CP Ships Holdings, Inc.

As part of the plan, CP's preferred shareholders will be able to either tender their shares for $26 each or receive shares in a special fund scheduled for redemption in 2004.

Source: Excerpted from K. McArthur, "CP Debenture Investors Want Vote," *The Globe and Mail* (July 4, 2001), p. B3. Reprinted with permission from *The Globe and Mail*.

---

secured debt Debt that has first claim on specified collateral in the event of default.

When companies borrow, they also may set aside certain assets as security for the loan. These assets are termed *collateral* and the debt is said to be **secured**. In the event of default, the secured lender has first claim on the collateral; unsecured lenders have a general claim on the rest of the firm's assets but only a junior claim on the collateral.

Default Risk

Seniority and security do not guarantee payment. A debt can be senior and secured but still as risky as a dizzy tightrope walker—it depends on the value and the risk of the firm's assets. In Chapter 5 we showed how the safety of most corporate bonds can be judged from bond ratings provided by Dominion Bond Rating Service, Moody's, and Standard & Poor's. Bonds that are rated AAA or triple-A seldom default. At the other extreme, many speculative-grade bonds (or junk bonds) may be teetering on the brink.

As you would expect, investors demand a high return from low-rated bonds. We saw evidence of this in Chapter 5, where Figure 5.9 showed yields on Canadian long-term bonds. The lower-rated bonds did, in fact, offer higher promised yields to maturity.

Country and Currency

These days capital markets know few national boundaries and many large firms, in particular, those with sizable foreign operations, borrow abroad. For example, a Canadian company may choose to finance a new plant in Switzerland by borrowing Swiss francs from a Swiss bank, or it may expand its Dutch operation by issuing a bond in Holland.

In addition to these national capital markets, there is also an international capital market centred mainly in London. There are about 500 banks in London from over 70 different countries, which include such giants as Citicorp, Union Bank of Switzerland, Deutsche Bank, Bank of Tokyo–Mitsubishi, Banque Nationale de Paris, and Barclays Bank. One reason they are there is to collect deposits in the major currencies. For example, suppose an Arab sheikh has just received payment in dollars for a large sale of oil to the United States. Rather than depositing the cheque in the United States, he may choose to open a U.S. dollar account with a bank in London. Dollars held in a bank outside the United States came to be known as **eurodollars**. Similarly, yen held outside Japan were termed euroyen, and so on). When the new European currency was named the euro, the term *eurodollars* became confusing. Doubtlessly, in time, bankers will

eurodollars Dollars held on deposit in a bank outside the United States.

dream up a new name for dollars held outside the United States; until they do, we'll just call them *international dollars*.

The London bank branch that is holding the sheikh's U.S. dollar deposit may temporarily lend those dollars to a company in the same way that a bank in the United States may relend U.S. dollars that have been deposited with it. Thus a company can either borrow U.S. dollars from a bank in the United States or borrow U.S. dollars from a bank in London.[12]

If a firm wants to make an issue of long-term bonds, it can choose to do so in Canada. Alternatively, it can sell the bonds to investors in several countries. These bonds have traditionally been known as **eurobonds**, but *international bonds* may be a less misleading term. Although these bonds are sold to investors in different countries, they are typically denominated in the currency of the issuer. For example, a Canadian company could issue bonds denominated in Canadian dollars to investors in other countries. The payments on these bonds may be fixed in dollars, euros, or any other major currency. Companies usually sell these bonds to the London branches of the major international banks, which then resell them to investors throughout the world.

Sometimes companies may issue **foreign bonds**, which are issued in another country and denominated in the currency of that country. For instance, Alcan has long-term debt issues in several different currencies including the U.S. dollar, Swiss franc, and the euro.

Public versus Private Placements

Publicly issued bonds are sold to anyone who wishes to buy, and once they have been issued, they can be freely traded in the securities markets. In a **private placement**, the issue is sold directly to a small number of banks, insurance companies, or other investment institutions. Privately placed bonds generally cannot be resold to individuals in Canada but only to other qualified institutional investors. However, there is increasingly active trading among these investors.

There is more information about the difference between public issues and private placements in the next chapter.

Protective Covenants

When investors lend to a company, they know that they might not get their money back. But they expect that the company will use their money well and not take unreasonable risks. To help ensure this, lenders usually impose a number of conditions, or **protective covenants**, on companies that borrow from them. An honest firm is willing to accept these conditions because it knows that they enable the firm to borrow at a reasonable rate of interest.

Companies that borrow in moderation are less likely to get into difficulties than those that are up to the gunwales in debt. So lenders usually restrict the amount of extra debt that the firm can issue. Lenders are also eager to prevent others from pushing ahead of them in the queue if trouble occurs, so they will not allow the company to create new debt that is senior to them or to put aside assets for other lenders.

Another possible hazard for lenders is that the company will pay a bumper dividend to the shareholders, leaving no cash for the debtholders. Therefore, lenders sometimes limit the size of the dividends that can be paid.

The story of Marriott in the nearby Finance in Action box shows what can happen when bondholders are not sufficiently careful about the conditions they impose. In the wake of the large losses suffered by Marriott bondholders, several observers predicted that investors would demand more restrictive bond covenants in future transactions.

SEE BOX P. 408

---

[12] Because the Federal Reserve requires banks in the United States to keep interest-free reserves, there is a tax on U.S. dollar deposits in the United States. U.S. dollar deposits made overseas are free of this tax, and therefore, banks can afford to charge the borrower slightly lower interest rates.

eurobond   Bond that is denominated in the currency of one country but issued to investors in other countries.

foreign bond   Bond issued in the currency of its country but the borrower is from another country.

private placement   Sale of securities to a limited number of investors without a public offering.

protective covenant   Restriction on a firm to protect bondholders.

Marriott Plan Enrages Holders of Its Bonds

Marriott Corp. has infuriated bond investors with a restructuring plan that may be a new way for companies to pull the rug out from under bondholders.

Prices of Marriott's existing bonds have plunged as much as 30 percent in the past two days in the wake of the hotel and food-services company's announcement that it plans to separate into two companies, one burdened with virtually all of Marriott's debt.

On Monday, Marriott said that it will divide its operations into two separate businesses. One, Marriott International, Inc., is a healthy company that will manage Marriott's vast hotel chain; it will get most of the old company's revenue, a larger share of the cash flow and will be nearly debt-free.

The second business, called Host Marriott Corp., is a debt-laden company that will own Marriott hotels along with other real estate and retain essentially all of the old Marriott's $3 billion of debt.

The announcement stunned and infuriated bondholders, who watched nervously as the value of their Marriott bonds tumbled and as Moody's Investors Service, Inc., downgraded the bond to the junk-bond category from investment grade.

Price Plunge

In trading, Marriott's 10 percent bonds that mature in 2012, which Marriott sold to investors just six months ago, were quoted yesterday at about $.80 on the dollar, down from $1.10 Friday. The price decline translates into a stunning loss of $300 for a bond with a $1,000 face amount.

Marriott officials concede that the company's spinoff plan penalizes bondholders. However, the company notes that, like all public corporations, its fiduciary duty is to stockholders not bondholders. Indeed, Marriott's stock jumped 12 percent Monday. (It fell a bit yesterday.)

Bond investors and analysts worry that if the Marriott spinoff goes through, other companies will soon follow suit by separating debt-laden units from the rest of the company. "Any company that fears it has underperforming divisions that are dragging down its stock price is a possible candidate" for such a restructuring, says Dorothy K. Lee, an assistant vice president at Moody's.

If the trend heats up, investors said, the Marriott restructuring could be the worst news for corporate bondholders since RJR Nabisco, Inc.'s managers shocked investors in 1987 by announcing they were taking the company private in a record $25 billion leveraged buy-out. The move, which loaded RJR with debt and tanked the value of RJR bonds, triggered a deep slump in prices of many investment-grade corporate bonds as investors backed away from the market.

Strong Covenants May Re-Emerge

Some analysts say the move by Marriott may trigger the re-emergence of strong covenants, or written protections, in future corporate bond issues to protect bondholders against such restructurings as the one being engineered by Marriott. In the wake of the RJR buy-out, many investors demanded stronger covenants in new corporate bond issues.

Some investors blame themselves for not demanding stronger covenants. "It's our own fault," said Robert Hickey, a bond fund manager at Van Kampen Merritt. In their rush to buy bonds in an effort to lock in yields, many investors have allowed companies to sell bonds with covenants that have been "slim to none," Mr. Hickey said.

✔ **Check Point 13.6**

In 1988, RJR Nabisco, the food and tobacco giant, had $5 billion (US) of A-rated debt outstanding. In that year the company was taken over, and $19 billion (US) of debt was issued and used to buy back equity. The debt ratio skyrocketed, and the debt was downgraded to a BB rating. The holders of the previously issued debt were furious, and one filed a lawsuit claiming that RJR had violated an implicit obligation not to undertake major financing changes at the expense of existing bondholders. Why did these bondholders believe they had been harmed by the massive issue of new debt? What type of explicit restriction would you have wanted if you had been one of the original bondholders?

A Debt by Any Other Name

The word *debt* sounds straightforward, but companies enter into a number of financial arrangements that look suspiciously like debt yet are treated differently in the accounts. Some of these obligations are easily identifiable. For example, accounts payable are simply obligations to pay for goods that have already been delivered and are therefore like short-term debt.

Other arrangements are not so easy to spot. For example, instead of borrowing money to buy equipment, many companies **lease** or rent it on a long-term basis. In this case the firm promises to make a series of payments to the lessor (the owner of the equipment). This is just like the obligation to make payments on an outstanding loan. What if the firm can't make the payments? The lessor can then take back the equipment, which is precisely what would happen if the firm had

lease Long-term rental agreement.

borrowed money from the lessor, using the equipment as collateral for the loan. We will discuss the analysis of leasing in detail in Chapter 22.

EXAMPLE 13.1	**THE TERMS OF ALCAN'S BOND ISSUE**

Now that you are familiar with some of the jargon, you might like to look at an example of a bond issue. Table 13.4 is a summary of the terms of a bond issue by Alcan. We have added some explanatory notes.

INNOVATION IN THE DEBT MARKET

We have discussed domestic bonds and eurobonds, fixed-rate and floating-rate loans, secured and unsecured loans, senior and junior loans, and much more. You might think that this gives you all the options you need. Yet almost every day, companies and their advisers dream up a new type of debt. Here are some examples of unusual bonds.

Indexed Bonds

We saw in Chapter 5 how the Canadian government has issued bonds whose payments rise in line with inflation. Occasionally borrowers have linked the payments on their bonds to the price of a

TABLE 13.4
Alcan's bond issue

Comments	Description of bond
1. A debenture is an unsecured bond.	**Alcan Aluminum, Ltd., 6.450% debentures, due 2011**
2. Coupon is 6.450 percent. Thus each bond makes an annual interest payment of .0645 × $1,000= $64.50	
3. Moody's bond rating is A2 and Standard and Poor's is A–.	**Rating: A2 and A–**
4. Alcan has issued and has outstanding $400 million (US) of the bonds.	Outstanding: $400,000,000 (US).
5. The bond was issued in March 2001 and is to be repaid in March 2011.	Dated: March 23, 2001. Due: March 15, 2011.
6. Interest is payable at six-month intervals on March and September 15.	Interest: March and September 15.
7. The bonds can be held in multiples of $1,000.	Denomination: $1,000 (US) and integral multiples thereof.
8. Unlike some bond issues, this issue does not give the company an option to call (i.e., repurchase) the bonds before maturity at specific prices. Thus the bond is not redeemable prior to maturity.	Early redemption: The debentures are not redeemable prior to maturity.
9. The bonds are not secured, that is, no assets have been set aside to protect the bondholders in the event of default.	Security: not secured.
10. The bonds were sold at a price of 99.748 percent of face value. The company will have to deduct the payment to the underwriters before it receives any money from the bond issue.	Offered: $400,000,000 (US) debenture offerings are priced at 99.748% of their principal amount to yield 6.485%. Morgan Stanley & Co. Inc., Credit Suisse First Boston Corporation, RBC Dominion Securities Corporation, Salomon Smith Barney, Inc., Scotia Capital (U.S.A.), Inc., CIBC World Markets Corp., and Toronto Dominion Securities (U.S.A.) are co-underwriters of the offerings, which are to be made by prospectus only.
11. A trustee is appointed to look after the bondholder's interest.	
12. The bonds are registered. The registrar keeps a record of who owns the bonds.	

Source: **www.bondsonline.com**; *Financial Post* Historical Reports at **www.fpdata.finpost.com**; **www.alcan.com**.

Canadian Tire Securitizes Credit Card Receivables in a Public Offering

Canadian Tire Corp. has joined the small but growing list of Canadian issuers that have securitized some of their credit card receivables in a public offering.

The issuer, along with Tim Hortons, is a defining symbol of Canada and raised $300 million from the offering of 5-year AAA-rated term notes and placed $15 million of subordinated notes.

Stan Pasternak, Canadian Tire treasurer, said the securities will be priced at 46 basis points over comparable Canada bonds.

Source: Excerpted from B. Critchley, "Canadian Tire Deal No Retread," The Financial Post (July 6, 2001), p. D3.

particular commodity. For example, Mexico, which is a large oil producer, has issued billions of dollars worth of bonds that provide an extra payoff if oil prices rise. Mexico reasons that oil-linked bonds reduce its risk. If the price of oil is high, it can afford the higher payments on the bond. If oil prices are low, its interest payments will also be lower. The Swiss insurance company Winterthur has also issued an unusual bond with varying interest payments. The payments on the bonds are reduced if there is a hailstorm in Switzerland that damages at least 6,000 cars that have been insured by Winterthur.[13] The bondholders receive a higher interest rate but take on some of the company's risk.

Asset-Backed Bonds

The rock star David Bowie earns royalties from a number of successful albums such as *The Rise and Fall of Ziggy Stardust* and *Diamond Dogs*. But instead of waiting to receive these royalties, Bowie decided that he would prefer the money upfront. The solution was to issue $55 million 10-year bonds and to set aside the future royalty payments from the singer's albums to make the payments on these bonds. Such bonds are known as *asset-backed securities*; the borrower sets aside a group of assets and the income from these assets is then used to service the debt.

The Bowie bonds are an unusual example of an asset-backed security, but billions of dollars of house and commercial mortgages, credit card loans, personal lines of credit, and receivables are packaged each year, or *securitized*, and resold as asset-backed bonds. According to Dominion Bond Rating Service, Canada's outstanding asset-backed securities stood at about $88.2 billion at the end of 2002 compared with about $10 billion in the mid 1990s. For the most part, these securities comprised assets financed by short-term unsecured debt such as commercial paper.[14] Mostly such securities are high quality investments with good credit ratings. Investors in asset-backed securities include money market mutual funds, pension funds, corporations, financial institutions, and governments. Securitization can be done through multiseller or single-seller programs that are typically offered by large investment dealers such as BMO Nesbitt Burns, TD Securities, or CIBC World Markets. For instance, a multiseller program that securitizes receivables may pool such receivables from a variety of providers and then finance those purchases by issuing commercial paper securities. Two Finance in Action boxes discuss the securitization market. The first nearby Finance In Action box describes a recent public offering by Canadian Tire through the securitization of some of its credit card receivables. The second Finance in Action box describes the securitization of $1.5 billion of credit card receivables by Toronto Dominion bank in July 2003. In contrast, a single-seller program would involve a single provider.

SEE BOX ABOVE

SEE BOX P. 411

Similarly, commercial mortgage-backed securities can be securitized as single-asset and multi-asset offerings, the former involving one building and the latter involving several buildings. Brookfield Properties, a large Canadian real estate company, raised $432 (US) million from refinancing its One Liberty Plaza building in New York and a further $500 (US) million from refinancing another Manhattan building. In both deals, investors purchased securities known as

---

[13] The Winterthur bond is an example of a *catastrophe* (or *CAT*) *bond.* Its payments are linked to the occurrence of a natural catastrophe. CAT bonds are discussed in M. S. Cantor, J. B. Cole, and R. L. Sandor, "Insurance Derivatives: A New Asset Class for the Capital Markets and a New Hedging Tool for the Insurance Industry," *Journal of Applied Corporate Finance* 10 (Fall 1997), pp. 69–83.

[14] We will discuss commercial paper in more detail in Chapter 19.

"The summer doldrums have yet to settle into the asset-backed securities market," BMO Nesbitt Burns Inc. said in a recent report.

Toronto-Dominion Bank, through its financing arm York Receivables Trust III, securitized $1.5 billion (Canadian) of credit card receivables in late July.

The trust was set up to issue securities such as fixed-rate and floating-rate notes backed by credit card receivables.

The transaction was the largest single asset-backed security transaction ever done in Canada, with the largest number of investors, said Bill Furlong, managing director of asset securitization for TD Securities Inc.

"Considering that it has been more than two years since the last public credit card issue by one of Canada's big five Schedule A banks, the market was well set up to absorb the transaction," BMO Nesbitt Burns' asset-backed and mortgaged-back securities desk stated in a report. Yields in that sector of the credit market were unaffected despite the size of the issue, it said.

There was a slew of other sizable financings as well, as companies moved to take advantage of low interest rates. The note market was particularly active, with about $2.6 billion borrowed by companies seeking to take advantage of low interest rates. The issuers tapping the market included Alliance Pipeline LP ($300 million); Caisse Centrale Desjardins du Québec ($310 million); Canadian Pacific Railway Ltd. ($350 million); Citigroup Finance Canada Inc. ($500 million); Household Financial Corp. ($400 million); Hydro One Inc. ($500 million); and John Deere Credit Inc. ($200 million).

Source: Excerpted from Allan Robinson, "Summer Sizzles in Capital Markets," *The Globe and Mail*, August 13, 2003, at **www.globeinvestor.com**. Reprinted with permission from *The Globe and Mail*.

multiclass mortgage pass-through certificates, which ranged from being AAA rated to just investment grade (BBB-).[15]

Reverse Floaters

Floating-rate bonds that pay a higher rate of interest when other interest rates fall and a lower rate when other rates rise are called *reverse floaters*. They are riskier than normal bonds. When interest rates rise, the prices of all bonds fall, but the prices of reverse floaters suffer a double whammy because the coupon payments on the bonds fall as the discount rate rises. In 1994, Orange County, California, learned this the hard way when it invested heavily in reverse floaters. Robert Citron, the treasurer, was betting that interest rates would fall. He was wrong; interest rates rose sharply and partly because of its investment in reverse floaters, the county lost $1.7 billion (US).

These three examples illustrate the great variety of potential security designs. As long as you can convince investors of its attractions, you can issue a callable, subordinated, floating-rate bond denominated in euros. Rather than combining features of existing securities, you may be able to create an entirely new one. We can imagine a copper mining company issuing preferred shares where the dividend fluctuates with the world copper price. We know of no such security, but it is perfectly legal to issue it and, who knows, it might generate considerable interest among investors.

Variety is intrinsically good. People have different tastes, levels of wealth, rates of tax, and so on. Why not offer them a choice? Of course, the problem is the expense of designing and marketing new securities. But if you can think of a new security that will appeal to investors, you may be able to issue it on especially favourable terms, and thus, increase the value of your company.

13.4 CONVERTIBLE SECURITIES

warrant Right to buy shares from a company at a stipulated price before a set date.

We have seen that companies sometimes have the option to repay an issue of bonds before maturity. There are also cases in which investors have an option. The most dramatic case is provided by a **warrant**, which really is an option. Companies often issue warrants and bonds in a package.

---

[15] See also, B. Critchley, "Asset-Backed Market Soaring: Value of Securities up Eightfold from Five Years Ago," *Financial Post* (March 21, 2001), p. D3. See also, B. Critchley, "Brookfield Taps into U.S. MBS Market: Raises US$932 Million with New York Refinancings," *Financial Post* (March 19, 2001), p. C8. Following the tragic events of September 11, 2001, at New York's World Trade Center, the One Liberty Plaza complex had to be temporarily vacated. The building has since been reopened to tenants.

| EXAMPLE 13.2 | **WARRANTS** |

Macaw Bill wishes to make a bond issue, which could include some warrants as a "sweetener." Each warrant might allow you to purchase one share of Macaw stock at a price of $50 any time during the next 5 years. If Macaw's stock performs well, that option could turn out to be very valuable. For instance, if the stock price at the end of the 5 years is $80, then you pay the company $50 and receive in exchange a share worth $80. Of course, an investment in warrants also has its perils. If the price of Macaw stock fails to rise above $50, then the warrants expire and are worthless.

convertible bond Bond that the holder may exchange for a specified amount of another security.

A **convertible bond** gives its owner the option to exchange the bond for a predetermined number of common shares. The convertible bondholder hopes that the company's share price will zoom up so that the bond can be converted at a big profit. But if the shares zoom down, there is no obligation to convert; the bondholder remains just that. Not surprisingly, investors value this option to keep the bond or exchange it for shares, and therefore, a convertible bond sells at a higher price than a comparable bond that is not convertible.

The convertible is like a package of a bond and a warrant. But there is an important difference: When the owners of a convertible wish to exercise their options to buy shares, they do not pay cash—they just exchange the bond for shares of the stock.

Companies may also issue convertible preferred stock. In this case the investor receives preferred stock with fixed dividend payments but has the option to exchange this preferred stock for the company's common stock. The preferred stock issued by the Bank of Montreal is convertible into common stock. In December 2003, 95 convertible preferred stock issues were listed on the TSX.

These examples do not exhaust the options encountered by the financial manager. In fact once you read Chapter 25 and learn how to analyze options, you will find that they are all around you.

13.5 PATTERNS OF CORPORATE FINANCING

We have now completed our tour of corporate securities. You may feel like the tourist who has just gone through 12 cathedrals in 5 days. But there will be plenty of time in later chapters for reflection and analysis. For now, let's look at how firms use these sources of finance.

Firms have two broad sources of cash: They can raise money from external sources by an issue of debt or equity, or they can plow back part of their profits. When the firm retains cash rather than paying the money out as dividends, it is increasing shareholders' investment in the firm.

internally generated funds Cash reinvested in the firm: depreciation plus earnings not paid out as dividends.

Figure 13.1 summarizes the sources of capital for Canadian corporations. The most striking aspect of this figure is the dominance of **internally generated funds**, defined as depreciation plus earnings that are not paid out as dividends.[16] For much of this period, over half of the total funding requirement of corporations was met from internally generated funds.

DO FIRMS RELY TOO HEAVILY ON INTERNAL FUNDS?

Gordon Donaldson, in a classic survey of corporate debt policies, encountered several firms that acknowledged "that it was their long-term objective to hold to a rate of growth which was consistent with their capacity to generate funds internally." A number of other firms appeared to think less about expenditure proposals that could be financed internally.[17]

---

[16] Remember that depreciation is a non-cash expense.

[17] See G. Donaldson, *Corporate Debt Capacity*, Division of Research, Graduate School of Business Administration, Harvard University, Boston, 1961, Chapter 3, especially pp. 51–56.

FIGURE 13.1
Sources of financing
for non-financial
private corporations

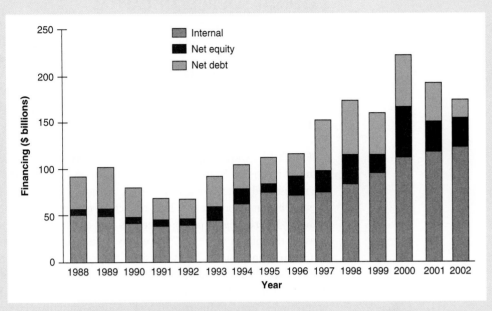

Source: Adapted from Statistics Canada CANSIM database http://cansim2.statcan.ca. Table 378-0004 and Matrix 0702.

At first glance, this behaviour doesn't make sense. As we have already noted, retained profits are additional capital invested by shareholders and represent, in effect, a compulsory issue of shares. A firm that retains $1 million could have paid out the cash as dividends and then sold new common shares to raise the same amount of additional capital. The opportunity cost of capital ought not to depend on whether the project is financed by retained profits or a new stock issue.

Why then do managers have an apparent preference for financing by retained earnings? Perhaps managers are simply taking the line of least resistance, dodging the discipline of the securities markets.

Think back to Chapter 1, where we pointed out that a firm is a team, consisting of managers, shareholders, debtholders, and so on. The shareholders and debtholders would like to monitor management to make sure that it is pulling its weight and truly maximizing market value. It is costly for individual investors to keep checks on management. However, large financial institutions are specialists in monitoring, so when the firm goes to the bank for a large loan or makes a public issue of stocks or bonds, managers know that they had better have all the answers. If they want a quiet life, they will avoid going to the capital market to raise money, and they will retain sufficient earnings to be able to meet unanticipated demands for cash.

We do not mean to paint managers as loafers. There are also rational reasons for relying on internally generated funds. The costs of new securities are avoided, for example. Moreover, the announcement of a new equity issue is usually bad news for investors, who worry that the decision signals lower profits.[18] Raising equity capital from internal sources avoids the costs and the bad omens associated with equity issues.

Check Point 13.7

"Since internal funds provide the bulk of industry's needs for capital, the securities markets serve little function." Does the speaker have a point?

---

[18] Managers do have insiders' insights and naturally are tempted to issue stock when the stock price looks good to them, that is, when they are less optimistic than outside investors. The outside investors realize all this and will buy a new issue only at a discount from the preannouncement price. Stock issues are discussed further in the next chapter.

EXTERNAL SOURCES OF CAPITAL

Of course, firms don't rely exclusively on internal funds. They also issue securities and retire them, sometimes in big volume. For example, since the mid 1990s, GW has steadily increased its reliance on new debt by issuing considerable amounts of bonds. Between 2000 and 2001, its outstanding long-term debt increased by about 64 percent. At the same time, since the mid 1990s, GW has been consistently buying back shares from the public. So, for instance, over the period 1995-1999, and between 2002 and 2003, GW had *negative* net stock issues.

It is, therefore, not surprising that GW's ratio of long-term debt to the book value of equity has risen consistently since 1996, barring 2002 when the ratio declined from the 2001 level.

Figure 13.2 shows the book value of GW's long-term debt to both the book value and market value of its equity. Notice that the ratio based on market value has consistently been lower than the ratio based on the book value. Also, the ratio of long-term debt to the market value of equity was, by far, more stable. This reflects a general optimistic outlook of investors about the company's performance and prospects as well as a rise in stock market values in the 1990s, which allowed the market value of GW's equity to keep up with its issues of long-term debt.

GW was not alone in its use of share repurchases since the mid-1990s. Other Canadian companies were repurchasing their shares as well during this period, often by making large issues of debt and using part of the money to buy back common stock. We see from Figure 13.1 that the proportion of net debt financing[19] by Canadian non-financial firms generally went up in the final years of the 1990s, but from Figure 13.3, their average debt-to-equity ratios actually came down in this period. The high profit levels during this period resulted in record-setting levels of internally generated funds. As a result, despite the share repurchases, common equity rose more than debt, resulting in lower debt-to-equity ratios. Notice, from Figure 13.3, an increase in average

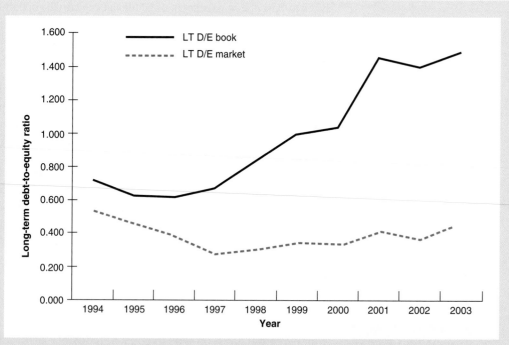

FIGURE 13.2

Long-term debt-to-equity ratios for George Weston Limited

Note: 1. LT D/E ratio (book) = Long-term debt/Common shareholder's equity
2. LT D/E ratio (market) = Long-term debt/(Average number of common shares × average stock price).
Source: Financial Post Online Historical Report and FP Analyzer. Retrieved June 17, 2004, from **www.fpinfomart.ca**.

---

[19] This includes long-term and short-term debt.

FIGURE 13.3
Average debt-to-equity ratio, Canadian non-financial enterprises, 1993–2003

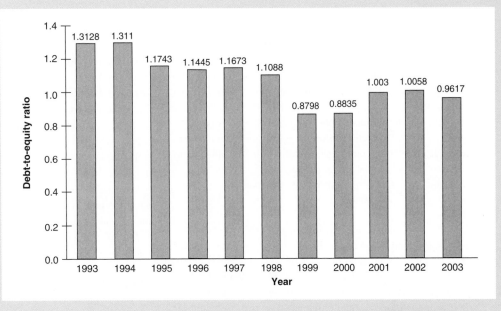

Notes:
1. The annual debt-to-equity ratios were calculated by taking the average of the quarterly debt-to-equity ratios reported for each year. Debt includes loans and accounts with affiliates plus borrowings. Equity is total equity.
2. Debt-to-equity ratios were calculated using the latest available data; for instance, where possible, the first quarter report of a subsequent year was used to calculate the average debt-to-equity ratio for the previous year. Otherwise, fourth-quarter reports were used to calculate the average debt-to-equity ratio for a given year.

Source: Adapted from Statistics Canada publication, *Quarterly Financial Statistics for Enterprises*, Catalogue 61–008, 1993–2003.

debt-to-equity ratios for Canadian non-financial enterprises in 2001 and 2002; this was also the period when corporate profits and internally generated funds declined somewhat. Average debt-to-equity ratios in 2003 declined somewhat from 2002.

However, share repurchase programs among Canadian and U.S. companies have recently been declining following the downturn in stock market prices. For instance, the number of share buyback programs in place for TSX-listed companies fell to 352 in July 2001 from 420 in July 2000. There has been a similar decline in share buyback programs among companies in the United States.

The net effect of these financing policies is shown in Figure 13.3, which confirms that debt-to-equity ratios for Canadian firms in the 1990s and the first three years after 2000 were relatively stable in book-value terms.

Canadian corporations are carrying more debt than they did 30 years ago. The nearby Finance in Action box articles show that Canadian companies have recently issued record levels of new bonds. Should we be worried? It is true that higher debt ratios mean that more companies are likely to fall into financial distress when a serious recession hits the economy. But all companies live with this risk to some degree, and it does not follow that less risk is better. Finding the optimal debt ratio is like finding the optimal speed limit: We can agree that accidents at 60 kilometres per hour are less dangerous, other things being equal, than accidents at 100 kilometres per hour, but we do not therefore set the national speed limit at 60. Speed has benefits as well as risks. So does debt, as we will see in Chapter 15.

SEE BOXES P. 416

Are Canadian Companies on a Borrowing Binge?

Canadian companies issued a record level of new bonds last quarter, spurring the debt market ... even as new stock offerings and corporate deals continue to slump.

Canadian corporate debt issues in the second quarter jumped to a record high of $24.2 billion in the gross amount of issues in the second quarter.

"There's been a lot of uncertainty about stocks. By comparison, corporate bonds have offered investors attractive spreads [in yields] relative to the government bond market," said Rob Palombi, a senior fixed-income analyst at Standard & Poor's MMS in Toronto.

Among the recent offerings galvanizing the market have been Quebecor, Inc.'s $1 billion bond issue and Hydro One, Inc.'s $550 million issue.

Telus Corp. solidified much of the bond market's recent enthusiasm with its mammoth and well-received $5 billion issue in late May.

The $24.2 billion in gross corporate debt issues in Canada in the second quarter surpassed the latest high of $21.2 billion in the second quarter of 1998, according to data from the Bank of Canada.

When taking into account the offsetting effect of $7.8 billion in corporate bonds that came due, and which companies therefore had to pay back to investors, total net bond issues were $16.4 billion in the last quarter. This was still a new record, beating the previous high of $15.6 billion in the second quarter of 1999.

As another example of the buoyant activity, net Canadian corporate debt in both the first and second quarter in this year was $26.8 billion, far stronger than the $12.7 billion in corporate debt issues in the first half of 2000.

Canadian debt also continued to attract a heavy level of foreign interest. While nearly $8.2 billion net corporate debt was issued in Canadian dollars in the second quarter, Canadian companies issued roughly the same amount in U.S. dollars and euros in the quarter.

As another comparison, Canadian corporations had issued only $2.4 billion in net foreign-denominated debt in the first six months of 2000. This year they issued $12.3 billion.

Falling interest rates have helped. Action by the Bank of Canada, and particularly, the U.S. Federal Reserve Board to spur the economy by lowering interest rates has led to a general decline in all bond yields across the board (and a consequential increase in bond prices, which automatically move in the opposite direction as yields do).

But even with corporate bond yields falling, they remain, as ever, higher than Government of Canada bond yields.

Corporate bonds with riskier ratings from debt-rating agencies, such as Telus's triple-B-plus rating from Standard & Poor's, and the accompanying higher yields these bonds have to offer are increasingly attracting investors.

With a wave of Government of Canada bonds recently coming due, investors have been looking for other bonds in which to put their money, helping to spark even more demand for corporate debt.

Source: Excerpted from G. Dixon, "Bond Issues Hit High in Second Quarter," *The Globe and Mail* (July 9, 2001), p. B1. Reprinted with permission from *The Globe and Mail.*

The Binge Continues in 2003

Canadian companies are raising money at a record pace, with the flood of stock and bond sales expected to continue as investors regain their faith in rising markets ...

Equity financings totalled $12.7-billion in the third quarter, up 35 per cent from the previous year, according to the Investment Dealers Association of Canada. It's the strongest quarter seen in the four years that the IDA has been compiling this data ...

Corporate debt markets are also on fire, as companies borrow or refinance during a period when short-term interest rates are at historic lows. Canadian companies have raised $46.3 billion in 225 debt offerings through the first 10 months of the year, according to statistics compiled by Bloomberg. In all of 2002, corporate debt sales totalled $34.5 billion, done with 177 offerings.

Source: Excerpted from Andrew Willis, "Firms Raising Money at Record Pace," *The Globe and Mail*, November 8, 2003, B1. Retrieved June 28, 2005, from **www.globeandmail.com**. Reprinted with permission from *The Globe and Mail.*

13.6   SUMMARY

1. What are the major classes of securities issued by firms to raise capital?

Companies may raise money from shareholders by issuing more shares. They also raise money indirectly by plowing back cash that could otherwise have been paid out as dividends.

Preferred stock offers a fixed dividend but the company has the discretion not to pay it. It can't, however, then pay a dividend on the common stock. Despite its name, preferred stock is not a popular source of finance, but it is useful in special situations.

When companies issue debt, they promise to make a series of interest payments and to repay the principal. However, this liability is limited. Shareholders have the right to default on their obligation and to hand over the assets to the debtholders. Unlike dividends on common stock and preferred stock, the interest payments on debt are regarded as a cost and therefore they are paid out of before-tax income. Here are some forms of debt:

- Fixed-rate and floating-rate debt
- Long-term (funded) and short-term (unfunded) debt
- Callable and sinking-fund debt
- Senior and subordinated debt
- Secured and unsecured debt
- Investment grade and junk debt

- Domestic and international debt
- Publicly traded debt and private placements

The fourth source of finance consists of options and optionlike securities. The simplest option is a warrant, which gives its holder the right to buy a share from the firm at a set price by a set date. Warrants are often sold in combination with other securities. **Convertible bonds** give the holder the right to convert the bond to shares. They therefore resemble a package of straight debt and a warrant.

2. What are recent trends in firms' use of different sources of finance?

Internally generated cash is the principal source of company funds. Some people worry about that; they think that if management does not go to the trouble of raising money, it may be profligate in spending it.

In the late 1990s, net equity issues were negative; that is, companies repurchased more equity than they issued. At the same time companies issued large quantities of debt. However, large levels of **internally generated funds** in this period allowed book equity to increase despite the share repurchases, with the result that the ratio of long-term debt to book value of equity was fairly stable. Moreover, the stock market boom of the 1990s meant that the ratio of debt to the market value of equity actually fell considerably during this period.

Related Web Links

www.ashtonanalytics.com Information about the debt markets

www.finpipe.com See "Bonds" for information on bonds

www.hoovers.com Information about corporations and corporate financing

www.lacaisse.com Caisse de dépôt et placement du Québec

www.canadiantire.ca

www.weston.ca George Weston

www.cp.ca Canadian Pacific

www.osc.gov.on.ca Ontario Securities Commission

www.bondsonline.com Informative Web site on bonds

www.alson.com Alcan

Key Terms

issued shares	395	net worth	401	eurobond	407
outstanding shares	395	floating-rate preferred	403	foreign bond	407
authorized share capital	395	prime rate	404	private placement	407
par value	395	long-term debt	405	protective covenant	407
additional paid-in capital	395	sinking fund	405	lease	408
retained earnings	395	callable bond	405	warrant	411
majority voting	397	refunding	405	convertible bond	412
cumulative voting	397	subordinated debt	405	internally generated funds	412
proxy contest	398	secured debt	406		
preferred stock	401	eurodollars	406		

Questions and Problems

*Answers in Appendix B

BASIC

EXCEL

*1. **Equity Accounts.** The authorized share capital of the Alfred Cake Company is 100,000 shares. Currently 20,000 shares are issued and outstanding. The equity is currently shown in the company's books as follows:

Common stock	$ 60,000
Retained earnings	30,000
Common equity	90,000

  a. How many more shares can be issued without the approval of shareholders?

  b. If the company issues 10,000 shares at $5 a share, show how this will appear in the company's books.

2. **Equity Accounts.** Look back at problem 1. What would happen to the company's books if instead it bought back 1,000 shares at $5 per share? The average issue price of these shares was $5.

3. **Financing Terms.** Fill in the blanks by choosing the appropriate term from the following list: lease, funded, floating-rate, eurobond, convertible, subordinated, call, sinking fund, prime rate, private placement, public issue, senior, unfunded, eurodollar rate, warrant, debentures, term loan.

  *a. Debt maturing in more than one year is often called _____ debt.

  *b. An issue of bonds that is sold simultaneously in several countries is traditionally called a(n) _____.

  c. If a lender ranks behind the firm's general creditors in the event of default, the loan is said to be _____.

  *d. In many cases a firm is obliged to make regular contributions to a(n) _____, which is then used to repurchase bonds.

  e. Most bonds give the firm the right to repurchase or _____ the bonds at specified prices.

  *f. The benchmark interest rate that banks charge to their customers with good to excellent credit is generally termed the _____.

  *g. The interest rate on bank loans is often tied to short-term interest rates. These loans are usually called _____ loans.

  *h. Where there is a(n) _____, securities are sold directly to a small group of institutional investors. These securities cannot be resold to individual investors. In the case of a(n) _____, debt can be freely bought and sold by individual investors.

  i. A long-term rental agreement is called a(n) _____.

  j. A(n) _____ bond can be exchanged for shares of the issuing corporation.

  k. A(n) _____ gives its owner the right to buy shares in the issuing company at a predetermined price.

4. **Financing Trends.** Are the following statements true or false? Explain.

  a. In several recent years, non-financial corporations in Canada have repurchased more stock than they have issued.

  b. A corporation pays tax on only 30 percent of the common or preferred dividends it receives from other corporations.

  c. Because of the tax advantage, a large fraction of preferred shares is held by corporations.

5. **Preferred Stock.** In what ways is preferred stock like long-term debt? In what ways is it like common stock?

PRACTICE

*6. **Voting for Directors.** If there are 10 directors to be elected and a shareholder owns 90 shares, indicate the maximum number of votes that he or she can cast for a favourite candidate under

  a. majority voting

  b. cumulative voting

EXCEL

*7. **Voting for Directors.** The shareholders of the Pickwick Paper Company need to elect five directors. There are 400,000 shares outstanding. How many shares do you need to own to ensure that you can elect at least one director if the company has

  a. majority voting

  b. cumulative voting

Hint: How many votes in total will be cast? How many votes are required to ensure that at least a fifth of votes are cast for your choice?

EXCEL

8. **Equity Accounts.** Look back at Table 13.2.

  a. Suppose that George Weston issues 10 million shares at $55 a share. Rework Table 13.2 to show the company's equity after the issue.

  b. Suppose that George Weston *subsequently* repurchased 500,000 shares at $60 a share. Rework part (a) to show the effect of the further change. Take the average issue price of the shares to be $30.

9. **Protective Covenants.** Why might a bond agreement limit the amount of assets that the firm can lease?

10. **Bond Yields.** Other things being equal, will the following provisions increase or decrease the yield to maturity at which a firm can issue a bond?

  a. a call provision

  b. a restriction on further borrowing

  c. a provision of specific collateral for the bond

  d. an option to convert the bonds into shares

*11. **Income Bonds.** *Income bonds* are unusual. Interest payments on such bonds may be skipped or deferred if the firm's income is insufficient to make the payment. In what way are these bonds like preferred stock? Why might a firm choose to issue an income bond instead of preferred stock?

12. **Preferred Stock.** Preferred stock of financially strong firms sometimes sells at lower yields than the bonds of those firms. For weaker firms, the preferred stock has a higher yield. What might explain this pattern?

13. **Internet.** In Table 13.1, we showed examples of securities issued by George Weston, Ltd. Try to construct a similar table for another company, say Alcan Inc., by looking up its annual report on the Web. An easy way to do this is to go to Alcan's Web site at **www.alcan.com**, click on "Investors," and see a variety of information about the company, including its annual reports. You can also retrieve Alcan's annual report from **www.sedar.com**.

14. **Internet.** Now try to retrieve the annual report of another large company, Bell Canada Inc., by either going to its Web site or through the Sedar site. You can always search and find the Web site of Bell Canada through a search engine such as Yahoo (**www.yahoo.com**) or Google (**www.google.com**). How many issued and outstanding common shares did the company have in 2003 and 2004? Has the company in the past raised more money by new issues of shares or by plowing back earnings? Is that typical of Canadian public companies?

15. **Internet.** In Figure 13.2, we calculated the book and market long-term debt-to-equity ratios of George Weston Ltd. Using Alcan's annual report calculate the company's book long-term debt-to-equity ratio for 2002 and 2003. See if you can use other resources on the web (hint: try the Yahoo! Finance Web site) to calculate a recent market long-term debt-to-equity ratio estimate for the company.

STANDARD &POOR'S

16. **Standard & Poor's.** Go to Market Insight (**www.mcgrawhill.ca/edumarketinsight**). Compare the major sources and uses of funds (Annual Cash Flow Report and Balance Sheet) for INCO Ltd. (N) and Falconbridge Ltd. (FAL). What factors might explain the differences in financing patterns for the two companies?

CHALLENGE

17. **Comprehensive.**
    a. Go to Market Insight (**www.mcgrawhill.ca/edumarketinsight**). Anheuser-Busch Inc. (BUD) used internal and external sources to fund its tremendous growth in the late 1990s. Examine Anheuser-Busch's internal and external sources of funds and then compare your findings with Figure 13.2 in this chapter. (See Annual Cash Flow Statement.) What was Anheuser-Busch's primary use of funds?
    b. Using book values, balance sheet debt ratios (Ratios Report) increased significantly for Anheuser-Busch Inc. (BUD) in the last few years. How has the debt ratio changed if one calculates debt ratios using the market value of equity?
    c. Locate a Canadian company, preferably in the same industry as Anheuser-Busch, and redo the calculations required in parts (a) and (b) for this company. What insights do you get when you compare the results for this company with that of Anheuser-Busch?

Solutions to Check Points

13.1 The paid-in capital to the extent of common shares sold to the public is $15 × 100,000 shares = $1,500,000. Since book value is $3,000,000, retained earnings must be $1,500,000. Therefore, the accounts look like this:

Common shares:	
Paid-in capital	1,500,000
Retained earnings	1,500,000
Common equity	$3,000,000

13.2 Book value is $10 million. At a discount rate of 10 percent, the market value of the firm ought to be $2 million × 20-year annuity factor at 10% = $17 million, which exceeds book value. At a discount rate of 20 percent, market value falls to $9.7 million, which is below book value.

13.3 The corporation's after-tax yield on the bonds is 10% − (.35 × 10%) = 6.5%. The after-tax yield on the preferred is 8% − [.35 × (.30 × 8%)] = 7.16%. The preferred stock provides the higher after-tax rate despite its lower before-tax rate. For the individual, the tax rate on both the preferred and the bond is equal to 35 percent, so the investment with the higher before-tax rate also provides the higher after-tax rate.

13.4 Because the coupon on floating-rate debt adjusts periodically to current market conditions, the bondholder is less vulnerable to changes in market yields. The coupon rate paid by the bond is not locked in for as long a period of time. Therefore, prices of floaters should be less sensitive to changes in market interest rates.

13.5 The callable bond will sell at a lower price. Investors will not pay as much for the callable bond since they know that the firm may call it away from them if interest rates fall. Thus they know that their capital gains potential is limited, which makes the bond less valuable. If both bonds are to sell at par value, the callable bond must pay a higher coupon rate as compensation to the investor for the firm's right to call the bond.

13.6 The extra debt makes it more likely that the firm will not be able to make good on its promised payments to its creditors. If the new debt is not junior to the already-issued debt, then the original bondholders suffer a loss when their bonds become more susceptible to default risk. A protective covenant limiting the amount of new debt that the firm can issue would have prevented this problem. Investors, having witnessed the problems of the RJR bondholders, generally demanded the covenant on future debt issues.

13.7 Capital markets provide liquidity for investors. Because individual shareholders can always lay their hands on cash by selling shares, they are prepared to invest in companies that retain earnings rather than pay them out as dividends. Well-functioning capital markets allow the firm to serve all its shareholders simply by maximizing value. Capital markets also provide managers with information. Without this information, it would be very difficult to determine opportunity costs of capital or to assess financial performance.

13.7

APPENDIX 13.A: THE BOND REFUNDING DECISION

We saw in Section 13.3 that corporate bonds often include a call provision that allows the company to pay back the debt early. If interest rates fall and bond prices rise, the option to buy back the bond at a fixed price can be very attractive to the company. The company can buy back the existing bond and issue a new one at a higher price and a lower interest rate.

The refunding decision would involve an analysis of whether it is profitable for the firm to replace an existing issue of higher-interest cost bonds with a new issue of lower-interest cost bonds.[20] The approach used is similar to the analysis done in a replacement capital-budgeting situation. This involves determining the net present value (NPV) of the proposed refunding after considering incremental after-tax cash flows from the new issue relative to the old issue. The analysis will typically be conducted for the period remaining until the maturity of the existing issue. A refunding project yielding a positive net present value would be taken up, while a negative net-present-value project will be rejected.

Let us examine the issues involved in a refunding project through the analysis conducted by the finance manager of Strike-a-Deal, Inc.

EXAMPLE 13.A

The finance manager of Strike-a-Deal, Inc. has been closely watching interest rates with a view to refunding the company's 20-year, $100 million outstanding callable bonds, which were issued at par 5 years ago but still have 15 years remaining to maturity. The bonds have a par value of $1,000 and carry a 10 percent coupon interest rate. Flotation costs of $3 million were incurred when the bonds were issued. The bonds carry a call premium of 10 percent. The finance manager feels that because of a drop in long-term interest rates, the firm can sell an additional $100 million of new 15-year bonds at a coupon interest rate of 7.7 percent. To ensure the availability of funds to refund the outstanding bonds, the new bonds will have to be sold one month before the old issue is called. The finance manager is well aware that interest will have to be paid on both issues for one month, but feels that the proceeds of the new issue can be invested for this period in money market funds to yield 5 percent annually. The estimated flotation cost on the new issue is $2.5 million. Strike-a-Deal's marginal tax rate is 35 percent. Should it refund its outstanding bonds?

As we have mentioned earlier, to determine the NPV of the proposed refunding, we would look at incremental after-tax cash flows from the new issue. To do this, we would compare, in present-value terms, the net investment required to refund the bond issue with the incremental savings generated from lower interest payments on the new issue. To arrive at present values, we would discount all such after-tax cash flows by the after-tax cost of the new issue. This would be the appropriate discount rate. Refunding projects are of low risk to the firm since they involve only the replacement of one issue by another, so using the higher weighted average cost of capital rate would not be appropriate.

NET INVESTMENT COSTS ASSOCIATED WITH REFUNDING

Let us first look at the incremental investment required to refund the bond issue. For Strike-a-Deal, this will include the call premium to be paid on the old bonds, flotation costs, and net additional interest costs for the overlapping month when both new and old bond issues are in

---

[20] The refunding decision can also be applied to preferred stock issues. For instance, a company may decide to replace an existing issue of preferred stock with a new issue carrying a lower dividend rate.

place. Tax implications of such incremental costs will also have to be considered, so our objective will be to arrive at the overall after-tax investment costs.

Call Premium. This works out to 0 .1 × $100,000,000 = $10,000,000. The call premium is not a tax-deductible expense to the firm.

Flotation Costs. For tax purposes, flotation costs must be amortized over the life of the new bond or five years, whichever is less. The flotation cost on the old bond would have been amortized by now. However, the annual tax deduction on the flotation cost on the new bond issue will have to be computed.

So annual tax deduction on flotation cost of new issue = $2,500,000/5 = $500,000

Using Strike-a-Deal's marginal tax rate of 35 percent, the tax savings in each of the 5 years will be 0.35 × $500,000 = $175,000. This represents an annuity series over the five-year period. The present value of these deductions will have to be computed. As discussed earlier, the appropriate discount rate here is the after-tax cost of the new debt issue:

$$\text{After-tax cost of new debt} = 7.7\% \ (1 - \ \text{tax rate})$$
$$= 7.7\% \ (1 - 0.35)$$
$$= 5.005\%$$

We compute the present value of the tax saving by applying the annuity formula that we studied in Chapter 4:

$$\$175,000 \left[\frac{1 - [1/(1.05005)^5]}{0.05005} \right] = \$757,554$$

When, from the gross flotation cost, we subtract the present value of the tax saving from amortizing such costs, we get the net after-tax flotation cost on the new issue:

Gross flotation costs on new issue	$2,500,000
Less: Present value of associated tax savings	− 757,554
Net after-tax flotation cost on new issue	$1,742,446

Additional Interest. The new bond issue will have to be sold one month before the old bonds are replaced, so for this month Strike-a-Deal will have to incur interest costs on both issues. The additional cost during this month will be the interest that will have to be paid on the old issue. Because this interest is tax deductible, we will consider the after-tax interest cost on the old issue.

$$\text{Additional after-tax interest cost} = \text{Dollar amount of old issue} \times$$
$$(1/12 \times \text{old interest rate})(1 - T)$$
$$= \$100,000,000 \times (1/12 \times 0.1)(1 - 0.35)$$
$$= \$541,667$$

Keep in mind that the proceeds of the new issue can also be invested for a month. Strike-a-Deal has decided to invest in the money market for this period. Because any interest earned on this investment will incur tax, we compute the after-tax interest earned:

$$\text{After-tax interest earned} = \text{Dollar amount of new issue} \times$$
$$(1/12 \times \text{new interest rate})(1 - T)$$
$$= \$100,000,000 \times (1/12 \times 0.05)(1 - T)$$
$$= \$270,833$$

The net after-tax additional interest cost to Strike-a-Deal is the difference between the after-tax additional interest paid on the old issue and the after-tax interest earned on the new issue, or

$$\$541,667 - \$270,833 = \$270,834$$

Total After-Tax Investment Costs. We have now figured out the different after-tax component costs. When we add them up, we arrive at the total present value of net investments costs associated with the refunding decision.

Call premium	= $10,000,000
Net after-tax flotation cost on new issue	= $ 1,742,446
Net after-tax additional interest	= $ 270,834
Total present value of net investment costs	= $12,013,280

NET SAVINGS ASSOCIATED WITH REFUNDING

If Strike-a-Deal goes forward with the refunding, it will save every year on lower interest payments on the new issue. To determine the extent of the annual savings, we will have to take the difference between the yearly after-tax interest costs on the two issues. These savings will continue to be generated every year over the life of the new issue and can, therefore, be represented by a 15-year annuity.

The annual after-tax interest cost on the old issue is $100,000,000 \times 0.10 \times (1 - 0.35) = $6,500,000. For the new issue, the annual after-tax interest cost is $100,000,000 \times 0.077 \times (1 - 0.35) = $5,005,000. So, the yearly interest savings from going forward with refunding is $6,500,000 - $5,005,000 = $1,495,000. To find the present value of this stream of yearly savings, we, once again, discount the annuity by the after-tax interest cost of the new issue:

$$\$1,495,000 \left[\frac{1 - 1/(1.05005)^{15}}{0.05005} \right] = \$15,512,346$$

The present value of the net savings from refunding is, therefore, $15,512,346.

NET PRESENT VALUE ASSOCIATED WITH REFUNDING

Having figured out, in present value terms, the net savings and investment costs, we are now in a position to compute the NPV of the proposed refunding:

NPV of refunding = present value of net savings – net investment cost
= $15,512,346 – $12,013,280 = $3,499,066

Since NPV is positive, the finance manager of Strike-a-Deal concludes that it will be profitable for the company to refund the existing bond issue.

You may have noticed that the analysis of bond refunding is tailor-made for spreadsheets. The spreadsheet on page 424 recreates our analysis of Strike-a-Deal's proposed bond refunding. The worksheet that follows shows the formulas that were used to generate relevant values for the spreadsheet. Once we have the spreadsheet, we can try various sorts of "what-if analysis" to aid in our decision.

BOND REFUNDING WITH THE CANADA CALL OR DOOMSDAY CALL FEATURE

Our example above assumed a fixed call price based on a conventional call provision. In this situation, a sufficient decline in interest rates will make refunding profitable to the issuer. However, as we saw in Chapter 5, in Canada corporate bonds seldom have conventional call provisions. Callable bonds in Canada often come with a feature known as a Canada call or a Doomsday call. With this feature, if a bond is called back by the issuer before its maturity, it can be redeemed at a price that is set to provide a yield that is equivalent to the yield on a Canada bond of the same maturity plus a premium for default risk determined at the time of the bond issue. The bondholder is paid the Canada yield price, which is the higher of (a) the price calculated on the basis of the Canada bond yield plus default risk premium or (b) its par value. When interest rates fall, the call price goes up, resulting in a higher call premium. With the Canada call feature, therefore, any savings to the issuer from refunding associated with a decline in interest rates is offset by a higher call price. It is no wonder then that bonds with Canada calls rarely get called.

To see why the Canada call makes refunding less attractive, let us rework Example 13A assuming now that Strike-a-Deal's bonds are redeemable at the greater of Canada Yield Price (Canada

Yield plus .7 percent) and par. You will recall, from Chapter 5, that the Canada Yield is the yield to maturity for a Government of Canada bond with the same maturity date as the Strike-a-Deal bond. At the time the finance manager is contemplating refunding the bond issue, the yield to maturity of 15-year Canada bonds is 7 percent. To determine the call price on Strike-a-Deal's bonds, its remaining cash flows will have to be discounted at the Canada yield plus .7 percent. On our calculator, we set FV=1,000, PMT=100, n=15, I=7.7, and compute PV=1200.526. The call price is, therefore, $1,200.526. Given a par value of $1,000, the call premium per bond is now $1,200.526 – $1,000 = $200.526. With 100,000 bonds outstanding, the total call premium is 100,000 × $200.526 = $20,052,600. Notice that the call premium is now $10,052,600 higher than the call premium with the conventional call. When we add this additional call premium to the total present value of net investment costs that we computed earlier for the conventional call, we get $10,052,600 + $12,013,280 = $22,065,880.

$$\text{NPV of refunding} = \text{present value of net savings} - \text{present value of net investment costs}$$
$$= \$15,512,346 - \$22,065,880 = -\$6,553,534.$$

Notice that, with the Canada call feature, NPV is now negative, and refunding the bonds is no longer worthwhile for Strike-a-Deal.

A SPREADSHEET MODEL FOR STRIKE-A-DEAL'S PROPOSED BOND REFUNDING WITH A CONVENTIONAL CALL

	A	B	C	D
		Rate	Time period (years)	Dollar amount ($)
1				
2	Outstanding bond issue		0	100,000,000
3	Coupon interest rate on old issue	10%		
4	New bond issue		0	100,000,000
5	Coupon interest rate on new issue	7.7%		
6	After-tax coupon interest rate on new issue	5.0%		
7	Short-term money market investment yield	5.0%		
8	Marginal tax rate	35%		
9	**Present Value of Net Investment Costs**			
10	Call premium on outstanding bond issue	10%	0	10,000,000
11	Flotation cost on new issue		0	2,500,000
12	Flotation cost amortized for tax purposes		1–5	500,000
13	Annual tax savings on amortized flotation cost		1–5	175,000
14	PV of tax savings on flotation cost		0	757,554
15	Net after-tax flotation cost on new issue		0	1,742,446
16	Additional interest cost on old issue		0	541,667
17	Interest earned on short-term investment of new issue (after tax)		0	270,833
18	Net after-tax additional interest		0	270,833
19	Total PV of after-tax investment costs (D10 + D15 + D18)		0	12,013,280
20	**Net Savings from Refunding**			
21	Annual after-tax interest on old issue		1–15	6,500,000
22	Annual after-tax interest on new issue		1–15	5,005,000
23	Net annual savings in interest cost		1–15	1,495,000
24	PV of total interest cost savings over 15 years		0	15,512,346
25	**Net Present Value (NPV) from Bond Refunding (D24 – D19)**		0	**3,499,066**

FORMULA INSERTS FOR STRIKE-A-DEAL'S PROPOSED BOND REFUNDING SPREADSHEET MODEL WITH A CONVENTIONAL CALL

	A	B	C	D
1		Rate	Time period (years)	Dollar amount ($)
2	Outstanding bond issue		0	100,000,000
3	Coupon interest rate on old issue	0.1		
4	New bond issue		0	100,000,000
5	Coupon interest rate on new issue	0.077		
6	After-tax coupon interest rate on new issue	=B5*(1–B8)		
7	Short-term money market investment yield	0.05		
8	Marginal tax rate	0.35		
9	**Present Value of Net Investment Costs**			
10	Call premium on outstanding bond issue	0.1	0	=D2*B10
11	Flotation cost on new issue		0	2,500,000
12	Flotation cost amortized for tax purposes		1–5	=D11/5
13	Annual tax savings on amortized flotation cost		1–5	=D12*B8
14	PV of tax savings on flotation cost		0	=D13*(1–(1/(B6+1)^5))/B6
15	Net after-tax flotation cost on new issue		0	=D11–D14
16	Additional interest cost on old issue		0	=D2*(1/12*B3)(1–B8)
17	Interest earned on short-term investment of new issue (after tax)		0	=D4*(1/12*B7)(1–B8)
18	Net after-tax additional interest		0	=D16–D17
19	Total PV of after-tax investment costs (D10 + D15 + D18)		0	=D10 + D15 + D18
20	**Net Savings from Refunding**			
21	Annual after-tax interest on old issue		1–15	=D2*B3*(1–B8)
22	Annual after-tax interest on new issue		1–15	=D4*B5*(1–B8)
23	Net annual savings in interest cost		1–15	=D21–D22
24	PV of total interest cost savings over 15 years		0	=D23*(1–(1/(B6+1)^15))/B6
25	**Net Present Value (NPV) from Bond Refunding** (D24 – D19)		0	**=D24 – D19**

A SPREADSHEET MODEL FOR STRIKE-A-DEAL'S PROPOSED BOND REFUNDING (WITH CANADA CALL FEATURE)

	A	B	C	D
1		Rate	Time period (years)	Dollar amount ($)
2	Outstanding bond issue		0	100,000,000
3	Par value per bond			1,000
4	Coupon interest rate on old issue	10%		
5	New bond issue		0	100,000,000
6	Coupon interest rate on new issue	7.7%		
7	After-tax coupon interest rate on new issue	5.005%		
8	Short-term money market investment yield	5.0%		
9	Marginal tax rate	35%		
10	**Present Value of Net Investment Costs**			
11	Call price per bond			1200.526
12	Call premium per bond			200.526
13	Call premium on outstanding bond issue			20,052,600
14	Flotation cost on new issue		0	2,500,000
15	Flotation cost amortized for tax purposes		1–5	500,000
16	Annual tax savings on amortized flotation cost		1–5	175,000
17	PV of tax savings on flotation cost		0	757,554
18	Net after-tax flotation cost on new issue		1,742,446	
19	Additional interest cost on old issue		0	541,667
20	Interest earned on S-T investment of new issue (after tax)		0	270,833
21	Net after-tax additional interest		0	270,833
22	Total PV of after-tax investment costs (D10 + D15 + D18)		0	22,065,880
23	**Net Savings from Refunding**			
24	Annual after-tax interest on old issue		1–15	6,500,000
25	Annual after-tax interest on new issue		1–15	5,005,000
26	Net annual savings in interest cost		1–15	1,495,000
27	PV of total interest cost savings over 15 years		0	15,512,346
28	**Net Present Value (NPV) from bond refunding** (D24-D19)		0	**–6,553,534**

FORMULA INSERTS FOR STRIKE-A-DEAL'S PROPOSED BOND REFUNDING SPREADSHEET MODEL WITH A CONVENTIONAL CALL

	A	B	C	D
1		Rate	Time period (years)	Dollar amount ($)
2	Outstanding bond issue		0	100,000,000
3	Par value per bond			1,000
4	Coupon interest rate on old issue	0.1		
5	New bond issue		0	100,000,000
6	Coupon interest rate on new issue	0.077		
7	After-tax coupon interest rate on new issue	=B6*(1-B9)		
8	Short-term money market investment yield	0.05		
9	Marginal tax rate	0.35		
10	**Present Value of Net Investment Costs**			
11	Call price per bond			=100*(1–1/1.077)^15/0.077)+1,000/(1.077)^{15}
12	Call premium per bond			=D11–D3
13	Call premium on outstanding bond issue			=D12*D2/D3
14	Flotation cost on new issue		0	2,500,000
15	Flotation cost amortized for tax purposes		1–5	=D14/5
16	Annual tax savings on amortized flotation cost		1–5	=D15*B9
17	PV of tax savings on flotation cost		0	=D16*(1–(1/(B7+1)^5)/B7
18	Net after-tax flotation cost on new issue		0	=D14–D17
19	Additional interest cost on old issue		0	=D2*(1/12*B4)*(1–B9)
20	Interest earned on S-T investment of new issue (after tax)		0	=D5*(1/12*B8)*(1–B9)
21	Net after-tax additional interest		0	=D19–D20
22	Total PV of after-tax investment costs (D10 + D15 + D18)		0	=D13+D18+D21
23	**Net Savings from Refunding**			
24	Annual after-tax interest on old issue		1–15	=D2*B4*(1–B9)
25	Annual after-tax interest on new issue		1–15	=D5*B6*(1–B9)
26	Net annual savings in interest cost		1–15	=D24–D25
27	PV of total interest cost savings over 15 years		0	=D26*(1–(1/(B7+1)^15)/B7
28	**Net Present Value (NPV) from bond refunding** (D24–D19)		0	**=D27–D22**

Practice Problems

13.A1. **Bond Refunding.** E-Books.com currently has a 10-year $1 million bond issue outstanding (5 years remaining to maturity) with an 11 percent coupon interest rate and a $1,000 par value. The call premium on these bonds is 5 percent. Because of a decline in interest rates, the firm would be able to refund the issue with a $1 million issue of 9 percent 5-year bonds. The flotation costs for refunding the issue are $25,000. The new bonds will have to be issued one month before the old bonds are called. The present return on short-term government securities is 5 percent annually. E-books has a marginal tax rate of 25 percent. Assume that there are no other costs associated with refunding. Should the firm refund the bond issue?

13.A2. **Bond Refunding.** Food-Galore, Inc. has a $10 million outstanding bond issue, carrying a 12 percent coupon interest rate with 20 years remaining to maturity. This issue was sold 5 years ago and can be called by the company at a premium of 7 percent over its par value. Currently new 20-year bonds can be floated at a coupon interest rate of 9 percent. To ensure the availability of funds to pay off the old debt, the new bonds would be sold one month before the old issue is called, so for one month, interest would have to be paid on both issues. Flotation costs, comprising mainly issuing and underwriting expenses, for the new debt would be $150,000. Currently, short-term interest rates are at 10 percent per annum. Food-Galore's marginal tax rate is 35 percent. Based on discounted cash flow analysis, should refunding take place?

Challenge Problem

13.A3.   **Bond Refunding.** Universal Heavy Equipment is looking into the possibility of refunding its 30-year $100 million outstanding bond issue, carrying a 14 percent coupon rate, which was sold 10 years ago. If the company goes ahead with the refunding, it can sell a new 20-year issue at a lower coupon rate of 10 percent, given current low interest rates in the economy. A call premium of 12 percent will have to be paid to retire the old bonds, while flotation costs on the new issue are expected to be $5 million. The company's marginal tax rate is 35 percent. The new bonds will have to be issued one month before the old bonds are called. Short-term government securities are currently providing a return of 6 percent annually. Universal's management is aware that the low interest rates may not last for very long and may, in fact, go up if the economy continues to grow very rapidly and creates inflationary pressures.

1. Provide a complete bond refunding analysis and compute the NPV of the proposed refunding.

2. Create a spreadsheet model of your analysis and also provide detailed formula inserts.

3. Now assume that the bonds have a Canada call feature and are callable at the greater of Canada Yield Price (Canada Yield plus 0.50 percent) and par. The yield to maturity on a 20-year Government of Canada bond is 9.5 percent. Rework the bond refunding analysis. How does the Canada Call feature affect the NPV of the proposed refunding? Create a new spreadsheet model for this analysis and provide detailed formula inserts.

HOW CORPORATIONS ISSUE SECURITIES

Bill Gates and Paul Allen founded Microsoft in 1975 when they were both around 20. Eleven years later, Microsoft shares were sold to the public for $21 a share and immediately zoomed to $35. The largest shareholder was Bill Gates whose shares in Microsoft then were worth $350 million (US).

In 1976 two college dropouts, Steve Jobs and Steve Wozniak, sold their most valuable possessions: a van and a couple of calculators, and used the cash to start manufacturing computers in a garage. In 1980 when Apple Computer went public, the shares were offered to investors at $22 and jumped to $36. At that point, the shares owned by the company's two founders were worth $414 million (US).

In 1994 Marc Andreesen, a 24-year-old from the University of Illinois, joined with an investor, James Clark, and founded Netscape Communications. Just over a year later, Netscape stock was offered to the public at $28 a share and immediately leapt to $71. At this price James Clark's shares were worth $566 million (US), while Marc Andreesen's shares were worth $245 million (US).

Mike Lazardis quit his studies in electrical engineering at the University of Waterloo at 23. In 1984 he started Research In Motion (RIM) with two friends.[1] RIM went public in 1997, offering 13.8 million common shares at $7.25 each on the Toronto Stock Exchange. RIM's product, the BlackBerry e-mail pager-cum-computer, was such a success that by early 2000 its shares were trad-

---

[1] While it is true that some of these highly successful entrepreneurs dropped out of college or university, we do not want to give the impression that quitting school had anything to do with their success.

ing at $260. Mike Lazardis became a billionaire, and recently shared an Academy Award for technical achievement with a co-worker for designing a device that quickened the pace of film editing.

Such stories illustrate that the most important asset of a new firm may be a good idea. But that is not all you need. To take an idea from the drawing board to a prototype and through to large-scale production requires ever greater amounts of capital.

To get a new company off the ground, entrepreneurs may rely on their own savings and personal bank loans. But this is unlikely to be sufficient to build a successful enterprise. Venture capital firms specialize in providing new equity capital to help firms over the awkward adolescent period before they are large enough to "go public." In the first part of this chapter, we will explain how venture capital firms do this.

If the firm continues to be successful, there is likely to come a time when it needs to tap a wider source of capital. At this point it will make its first public issue of common stock. This is known as an *initial public offering*, or IPO. In the second section of the chapter we will describe what is involved in an IPO.

A company's initial public offering is seldom its last. In Chapter 13 we saw that internally generated cash is not usually sufficient to satisfy the firm's needs. Established companies make up the deficit by issuing more equity or debt. The remainder of this chapter looks at this process.

After studying this chapter you should be able to
- Understand how venture capital firms design successful deals.
- Understand how firms make initial public offerings and the costs of such offerings.
- Know what is involved when established firms make a general cash offer or a private placement of securities.
- Explain the role of the underwriter in an issue of securities.

14.1   VENTURE CAPITAL

You have taken a big step. With a couple of friends, you have formed a corporation to open a number of fast food outlets, offering innovative combinations of international dishes such as sushi with sauerkraut, curry Bolognese, and chow mein with Yorkshire pudding. Breaking into the fast food business costs money, but after pooling your savings and borrowing to the hilt from the bank, you have raised $100,000 and purchased one million shares in the new company. At this *zero-stage* investment, your company's assets are $100,000 plus the *idea* for your new product.

That $100,000 is enough to get the business off the ground, but if the idea takes off, you will need more capital to pay for new restaurants. You therefore decide to look for an investor who is prepared to back an untried company in return for part of the profits. Equity capital in young businesses is known as **venture capital**, and it is provided by specialized venture capital firms, financial and investment institutions such as banks and pension funds, and government agencies. If you need very early stage financing for your new enterprise, you may seek financing from an **angel** investor. "Angels" are wealthy individual investors who can play a critical role in the creation of new ventures by making small-scale investments in local start-ups and early-stage ventures. They also bring a significant hands-on contribution to such business ventures. We will describe these venture capital providers in more detail in Appendix 14A.

venture capital Money invested to finance a new firm.

angel A wealthy individual investor in early-stage ventures.

Most entrepreneurs are able to spin a plausible yarn about their company. But it is as hard to convince a venture capitalist to invest in your business as it is to get a first novel published. Your first step is to prepare a *business plan*. This describes your product, the potential market, the production method, and the resources—time, money, employees, facilities, and equipment—needed for success. It helps if you can point out that you are prepared to put your money where your mouth is. By staking all your savings in the company, you signal your faith in the business.

The venture capital company knows that the success of a new business depends on the effort its managers put in. Therefore, it will try to structure a deal where you have a strong incentive to work hard. For example, if you agree to accept a modest salary (and look forward instead to increasing the value of your investment in the company's stock), the venture capital company knows you will be committed to working hard. However, if you insist on a watertight employment contract and a fat salary, you won't find it easy to raise venture capital.

You are unlikely to persuade a venture capitalist to give you as much money as you need all at once. Rather, the firm will probably give you enough to reach the first major checkpoint. Suppose you can convince the venture capital company to buy one million new shares for $.50 each. This means it owns half of the firm: It owns one million shares, and you and your friends also own one million shares. Because the venture capitalist is paying $500,000 for a claim to half your firm, it is placing a $1 million value on the business. After this *first-stage* financing, your company's balance sheet looks like this:

First-Stage Market-Value Balance Sheet
($ millions)

Assets		Liabilities and Shareholders' Equity	
Cash from new equity	$ .5	New equity from venture capital	$ .5
Other assets	.5	Your original equity	.5
Value	$1.0	Value	$1.0

Check Point 14.1

Why might the venture capital company prefer to put up only part of the funds upfront? Would this affect the amount of effort put in by you, the entrepreneur? Is your willingness to accept only part of the venture capital that will eventually be needed a good signal of the likely success of the venture?

Suppose that 2 years later your business has grown to the point where it needs a further injection of equity. This *second-stage* financing might involve the issue of another one million shares at $1 each. Some of these shares might be bought by the original backers and some by other venture capital firms. The balance sheet after the new financing would then be as follows:

Second-Stage Market-Value Balance Sheet
($ millions)

Assets		Liabilities and Shareholders' Equity	
Cash from new equity	$1.0	New equity from second-stage financing	$1.0
Other assets	2.0	Equity from first stage	1.0
		Your original equity	1.0
Value	$3.0	Value	$3.0

Notice that the value of the initial one million shares owned by you and your friends has now been marked up to $1 million. Is this beginning to sound like a money machine? It works only if you have made a success of the business and new investors are prepared to pay $1 to buy a share in the business. When you started out, it wasn't clear that sushi and sauerkraut would catch on. If it hadn't caught on, the venture capital firm could have refused to put up more funds.

You are not yet in a position to cash in on your investment, but your gain is real. The second-stage investors have paid $1 million for a one-third share in the company. (There are now three million shares outstanding, and the second-stage investors hold one million shares.) Therefore, at least these impartial observers—who are willing to back up their opinions with a large investment—must have decided that the company was worth at least $3 million. Your one-third share is therefore also worth $1 million.

For every 10 first-stage venture capital investments, only two or three may survive as successful, self-sufficient businesses, and only one may pay off big. From these statistics come two rules of success in venture capital investment: First, don't shy away from uncertainty; accept a low probability of success. But don't buy into a business unless you can see the *chance* of a big, public company in a profitable market. There's no sense taking a big risk unless the reward is big if you win. Second, cut your losses; identify losers early, and if you can't fix the problem—by replacing management, for example—don't throw good money after bad.

The same advice holds for any backer of a risky start-up business—after all, only a fraction of new businesses are funded by card-carrying venture capitalists. Some start-ups are funded directly by managers or by their friends and families. Some grow using bank loans and reinvested earnings. But if your start-up combines high risk, sophisticated technology, and substantial investment, you will probably try to find venture capital financing.

14.2   THE INITIAL PUBLIC OFFERING

Very few new businesses make it big, but those that do can be very profitable. For example, an investor who provided $1,000 of first-stage financing for Intel would by mid-2000 have reaped $43 million (US). So venture capitalists and angel investors keep sane by reminding themselves of the success stories[2]—those who got in on the ground floor of firms like Intel, Lotus Development Corporation, and Research In Motion.[3]

Some very large companies, such as Levi Strauss or Cargill in the United States or McCain Foods in Canada, have been able to continue and prosper as independent private businesses. But for many other successful start-ups there comes a time when they need more capital than can comfortably be provided by a small number of individuals or venture capitalists. At this point one solution is to sell the business to a larger firm. But many entrepreneurs do not easily fit into a corporate bureaucracy and would prefer instead to remain the boss. In this case, the company may choose to raise money by selling shares to the public.

initial public offering (IPO)
First offering of stock to the general public.

> A firm is said to go *public* when it sells its first issue of shares in a general offering to investors. This first sale of stock is called an **initial public offering**, or **IPO**.

An IPO is called a *primary* offering when new shares are sold to raise additional cash for the company. It is a *secondary* offering when the company's founders and the venture capitalist cash in on some of their gains by selling shares. A secondary offer, therefore, is no more than a sale of shares from the early investors to new investors, and the cash raised in a secondary offer does not flow to the company. Of course, IPOs can be and commonly are both primary and secondary: The firm raises new cash at the same time that some of the already-existing shares in the firm are sold to the public. Some of the biggest secondary offerings have involved governments selling off stock in nationalized enterprises. For example, the Japanese government raised $12.6 billion (US) by selling its stock in Nippon Telegraph and Telephone, and the British government took in $9 billion (US) from its sale of British Gas. The Canadian government received about $2.2 billion in 1996 in the biggest initial public offering in Canadian history—when 84 million shares of the newly privatized Canadian National Railway hit the stock market. The world's largest IPO took place in 1999 when the Italian government raised $19.3 billion (US) from the sale of shares in the state-owned electricity company, Enel.

ARRANGING A PUBLIC ISSUE

Once a firm decides to go public, the first task is to select the underwriters.

underwriter   Firm that buys an issue of securities from a company and resells it to the public.

> **Underwriters** are investment dealers that act as financial "midwives" to a new issue. Usually they play a triple role—first providing the company with procedural and financial advice, then buying the stock, and finally reselling it to the public.

---

[2] Fortunately, the successes have outweighed the failures. The National Venture Capital Association (NVCA) estimated that net returns on venture capital funds averaged 25 percent a year for the 10 years ending December 2003.

[3] The founder of Lotus took a class from one of the authors. Within five years the student had become a multimillionaire. Perhaps that will make you feel better about the cost of this book.

A small IPO may have only one underwriter, but larger issues usually requires a syndicate of underwriters who buy the issue and resell it. For example, the initial public offering by Microsoft involved a total of 114 underwriters.

In the typical underwriting arrangement, called a *firm commitment*, the underwriters buy the securities from the firm and then resell them to the public. The underwriters receive payment in the form of a **spread**—that is, they are allowed to sell the shares at a slightly higher price than they paid for them. But the underwriters also accept the risk that they won't be able to sell the stock at the agreed offering price. If that happens, they will be stuck with unsold shares and must get the best price they can for them. In the more risky cases, the underwriter may not be willing to enter into a firm commitment and will handle the issue on a *best efforts* basis. In this case the underwriter agrees to sell as much of the issue as possible but does not guarantee the sale of the entire issue. Because fees tend to be less in a best efforts distribution, it might also be favoured by a high-quality issuer wishing to reduce issuing expenses.

Before any stock can be sold to the public, the company must satisfy the requirements of provincial securities laws and regulations.[4] Five provinces including Ontario, Québec, Alberta, Manitoba, and British Columbia have commissions while other provinces have securities acts. The stock may have to be registered with an appropriate securities commission. For instance, companies listed on the Toronto Stock Exchange (TSX) come under the purview of the Ontario Securities Commission (OSC), which administers the *Ontario Securities Act*. Generally, securities laws tend to be similar across provinces with the OSC playing a leadership role, given the overall importance of the TSX.

The first part of the registration statement is distributed to the public in the form of a preliminary **prospectus**. The preliminary prospectus contains some financial information that will also be included in the final prospectus, the company's history and its plans for the future, but it does not provide the price at which the security will be offered. It is sometimes called a *red herring* because it contains a printed disclaimer in red letters, which claims that it is not a final document and is subject to amendments because the securities commission has neither approved nor disapproved the registration statement.

One function of the prospectus is to warn investors about the risks involved in any investment in the firm. Some investors have joked that if they read prospectuses carefully, they would never dare buy a new issue. Appendix 14B is an example prospectus for your fast food business.

The securities commission, while reviewing the preliminary prospectus, may require it to be revised before approving it. Recent Canadian prospectuses can be found at the System for Electronic Documents and Retrieval (SEDAR) Web site (**www.sedar.com**).

The company and its underwriters also need to set the issue price. To gauge how much the stock is worth, they may undertake discounted cash flow calculations like those described in Chapter 6. They also look at the price-earnings ratios of the shares of the firm's principal competitors.

Before settling on the issue price, the underwriters may arrange a "roadshow," which gives the underwriters and the company's management an opportunity to talk to potential investors. These investors may then offer their reaction to the issue, suggest what they think is a fair price, and indicate how much stock they would be prepared to buy. This allows the underwriters to build up a book of likely orders. Although investors are not bound by their indications, they know that if they want to remain in the underwriters' good books, they must be careful not to renege on their expressions of interest.

The managers of the firm are eager to secure the highest possible price for their stock, but the underwriters are likely to be cautious because they will be left with any unsold stock if they overestimate investor demand. As a result, underwriters typically try to underprice the initial public

spread   Difference between public offer price and price paid by underwriter.

prospectus   Formal summary that provides information on an issue of securities.

---

[4] In contrast, in the U.S., all securities regulation is handled at the federal level by the Securities and Exchange Commission (SEC).

underpricing Issuing securities at an offering price set below the true value of the security.

offering. **Underpricing**, they argue, is needed to tempt investors to buy stock and to reduce the cost of marketing the issue to customers.

> Underpricing represents a cost to the existing owners since the new investors are allowed to buy shares in the firm at a favourable price. The cost of underpricing may be very large.

It is common to see the stock price increase substantially from the issue price in the days following an issue. Such immediate price jumps indicate the amount by which the shares were underpriced compared to what investors were willing to pay for them. A study by Ibbotson, Sindelar, and Ritter of approximately 9,000 new issues from 1960 to 1987 found average underpricing of 16 percent.[5] Sometimes new issues are dramatically underpriced. In January 2000, for example, six million shares in 724 Solutions were sold in an IPO simultaneously on the Toronto and Nasdaq stock exchanges, priced at $37.29 and $26 (US), respectively, per share. When the issue opened, the stock started trading at $108 on the TSX and $73 (US) on Nasdaq. Greg Wolfond, the co-founder of 724 Solutions, owned eight million shares in the company and ended the day $828 million richer than when he woke up that morning. Unfortunately, the bonanza did not last. By July 2001, the stock price had fallen to a little over $10 on the TSX.

SEE BOX P. 434

The nearby Finance in Action box reports on the phenomenal performance of Internet IPOs in the late 1990s.

| **EXAMPLE 14.1** | **UNDERPRICING OF IPO'S** |

Suppose an IPO is a secondary issue, and the firm's founders sell part of their holding to investors. Clearly, if the shares are sold for less than their true worth, the founders will suffer an opportunity loss.

But what if the IPO is a primary issue that raises new cash for the company? Do the founders care whether the shares are sold for less than their market value? The following example illustrates that they do care.

Suppose Cosmos.com has two million shares outstanding and now offers a further one million shares to investors at $50. On the first day of trading, the share price jumps to $80, so that the shares that the company sold for $50 million are now worth $80 million. The total market capitalization of the company is 3 million × $80 = $240 million.

The value of the founders' shares is equal to the total value of the company less the value of the shares that have been sold to the public—in other words, $240 – $80 = $160 million. The founders might justifiably rejoice at their good fortune. However, if the company had issued shares at a higher price, it would have needed to sell fewer shares to raise the $50 million that it needs, and the founders would have retained a larger share of the company. For example, suppose that the outside investors, who put up $50 million, received shares that were *worth* only $50 million. In that case the value of the founders' shares would be $240 – $50 = $190 million.

The effect of selling shares below their true value is to transfer $30 million of value from the founders to the investors who buy the new shares.

Unfortunately, underpricing does not mean that anyone can become wealthy by buying stock in IPOs. If an issue is underpriced, everybody will want to buy it and the underwriters will not have enough stock to go around. You are therefore likely to get only a small share of these hot issues. If

---

[5] R. G. Ibbotson, J. L. Sindelar, and J. R. Ritter, "Initial Public Offerings," *Journal of Applied Corporate Finance* 1 (Summer 1988), pp. 37–45. Note, however, that initial underpricing does not mean that IPOs are superior long-run investments. In fact, IPO returns over the first three years of trading have been less than a control sample of matching firms. See J. R. Ritter, "The Long-Run Performance of Initial Public Offerings," *Journal of Finance* 46 (March 1991), pp. 3–27.

Internet Shares: Loopy.com?

The tiny images are like demented postage stamps coming jerkily to life; the sound is prone to break up and at times could be coming from a bathroom plughole. Welcome to the Internet's live broadcasting experience. However, despite offering audio-visual quality that would have been unacceptable in the pioneering days of television, a small, loss-making company called Broadcast.com broke all previous records when it made its Wall Street debut on July 17th.

Shares in the Dallas-based company were offered at $18 and reached as high as $74 before closing at $62.75—a gain of nearly 250 percent on the day after a feeding frenzy in which 6.5 million shares changed hands. After the dust had settled, Broadcast.com was established as a $1 billion company, and its two 30-something founders, Mark Cuban and Todd Wagner, were worth nearly $500 million between them.

In its three years of existence, Broadcast.com, formerly known as AudioNet, has lost nearly $13 million, and its offer document frankly told potential investors that it had absolutely no idea when it might start to make money. So has Wall Street finally taken leave of its senses?

The value being placed on Broadcast.com is not obviously loopier than a number of other gravity-defying Internet stocks, particularly the currently fashionable "portals"—gateways to the Web—such as Yahoo! and America Online. Yahoo!, the Internet's leading content aggregator, has nearly doubled in value since June. On the back of revenue estimates of around $165 million, it has a market value of $8.7 billion.

Mark Hardie, an analyst with the high-tech consultancy Forrester Research, does not believe, in any case, that the enthusiasm for Broadcast.com has been overdone. He says, "There are no entrenched players in this space. The 'old' media are aware that the intelligence to exploit the Internet lies outside their organizations and are standing back waiting to see what happens. Broadcast.com is well-positioned to be a service intermediary for those companies and for other content owners." Persuaded?

Note: The dollar amounts are in U.S. currency.
Source: © 1998 The Economist Newspaper Group, Inc. Reprinted with permission. Further reproduction prohibited. **www.economist.com**.

it is overpriced, other investors are unlikely to want it, and the underwriter will be only too delighted to sell it to you. This phenomenon is known as the *winner's curse*.[6] It implies that, unless you can spot which issues are underpriced, you are likely to receive a small proportion of the cheap issues and a large proportion of the expensive ones. Since the dice are loaded against uninformed investors, they will play the game only if there is substantial underpricing on average.

EXAMPLE 14.2   UNDERPRICING OF IPOs AND INVESTOR RETURNS

Suppose that an investor will earn an immediate 10 percent return on underpriced IPOs and lose 5 percent on overpriced IPOs. But because of high demand, you may get only half the shares you bid for when the issue is underpriced. Suppose you bid for $1,000 of shares in two issues, one overpriced and the other underpriced. You are awarded the full $1,000 of the overpriced issue, but only $500 worth of shares in the underpriced issue. The net gain on your two investments is $(.10 \times \$500) - (.05 \times \$1,000) = 0$. Your net profit is zero, despite the fact that on average, IPOs are underpriced. You have suffered the winner's curse: You "win" a larger allotment of shares when they are overpriced.

 Check Point 14.2   What is the percentage profit earned by an investor who can identify the underpriced issues in Example 14.2? Who are such investors likely to be?

flotation costs   The costs incurred when a firm issues new securities to the public.

The costs of a new issue are termed **flotation costs**. Underpricing is not the only flotation cost. In fact, when people talk about the cost of a new issue, they often think only of the *direct costs* of the issue. For example, preparation of the registration statement and prospectus involves management, legal counsel, and accountants, as well as underwriters and their advisers. There is

---

[6] The highest bidder in an auction is the participant who places the highest value on the auctioned object. Therefore, it is likely that the winning bidder has an overly optimistic assessment of true value. Winning the auction suggests that you have overpaid for the object—this is the winner's curse. In the case of IPOs, your ability to "win" an allotment of shares may signal that the stock is overpriced.

FIGURE 14.1

Direct cost as a percent of total proceeds (by size category, figures in millions, U.S. dollars)

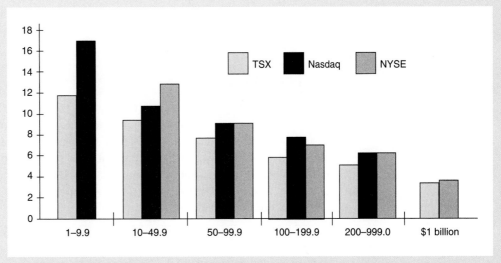

Source: Financial Post DataGroup, Securities Data Company. Excerpted from T. Shutt and H. Williams, "Going to Market: The Cost of IPOs in Canada and the United States," The Conference Board of Canada (June 2000), pp. 1–4.

also the underwriting spread. (Remember, underwriters make their profit by selling the issue at a higher price than they paid for it.)

According to the Toronto Stock Exchange, Canadian companies raised over $38 billion in new equity financing in 2004, including about $16 billion through 115 initial public offerings. Figure 14.1 summarizes the results of a study that compared the direct costs of going public, expressed as a percentage of total proceeds for IPOs on the TSX, Nasdaq, and NYSE over the period of January 1, 1998, and September 30, 1999.[7] Direct costs include underwriting commissions, legal, accounting, and other administrative costs. In general, larger IPO issues have lower direct costs as a percentage of total proceeds. For a small IPO of no more than $10 million, the underwriting spread and administrative costs are likely to absorb over 11 to 17 percent of the proceeds from the issue depending on the exchange. For the very largest IPOs, these direct costs may amount to only 3.5 percent of the proceeds.

Figure 14.2 details the extent of underpricing on the three exchanges for a sub-sample of the group of IPOs discussed above. This is estimated by calculating the percentage difference between

FIGURE 14.2

Degree of underpricing

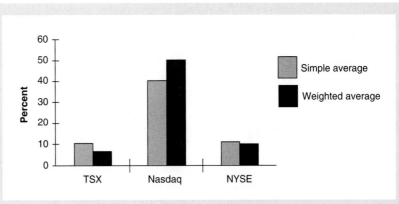

Source: Financial Post DataGroup, Securities Data Company. Excerpted from T. Shutt and H. Williams, "Going to Market: The Cost of IPOs in Canada and the United States," The Conference Board of Canada (June 2000), pp. 1–4.

---

[7] For complete details of the study, see T. Shutt and H. Williams, "Going to Market: The Costs of IPOs in Canada and the United States," The Conference Board of Canada (June 2000), p. 1–4.

the offer price of the share and its closing price after the first day of trading. For the TSX, the simple average of the underpricing was 10 percent while the weighted average was 5.8 percent. For the American exchanges, the numbers were found to be higher.

EXAMPLE 14.3   **COSTS OF AN IPO**

When the American investment bank Goldman Sachs went public in 1999, the sale was partly a primary issue (the company sold new shares to raise cash) and partly a secondary one (two large existing shareholders cashed in some of their shares). The underwriters acquired a total of 69 million Goldman Sachs shares for $50.75 (US) each and sold them to the public at an offering price of $53.[8] The underwriters' spread was therefore $53 – $50.75 = $2.25. The firm and its shareholders also paid a total of $9.2 million in legal fees and other costs. By the end of the first day's trading, Goldman's stock price had risen to $70.

Here are the direct costs of the Goldman Sachs issue:

Direct Expenses	(US$ in millions)
Underwriting spread	69 million × $2.25 = $155.25
Other expenses	9.2
Total direct expenses	$164.45

The total amount of money raised by the issue was 69 million × $53 = $3,657 million. Of this sum, 4.5 percent was absorbed by direct expenses (that is, 164.45/3,657 = .045).

In addition to these direct costs, there was underpricing. The market valued each share of Goldman Sachs at $70, so the cost of underpricing was 69 million × ($70 – $53) = $1,173 million, resulting in total costs of $164.45 + $1,173 = $1,337.45 million. Therefore, while the total market value of the issued shares was 69 million × $70 = $4,830 million, direct costs and the costs of underpricing absorbed nearly 28 percent of the market value of the shares.

SEE BOX P. 437   The nearby Finance in Action box describes plans for an initial public offering by the well-known Internet firm, Google. As the box shows, Google intends to use an unconventional electronic auction to price and sell its shares directly to the investing public.

Check Point 14.3   Suppose that the underwriters acquired Goldman Sachs shares for $60 (US) and sold them to the public at an offering price of $64. If all other features of the offer were unchanged (and investors still valued the stock at $70 a share), what would have been the direct costs of the issue and the costs of underpricing? What would have been the total costs as a proportion of the market value of the shares?

14.3   # THE UNDERWRITERS

We have described underwriters as playing a triple role—providing advice, buying a new issue from the company, and reselling it to investors. Underwriters don't just help the company make its initial public offering; they are called in whenever a company wishes to raise cash by selling securities to the public.

---

[8] No prizes for guessing which investment bank acted as lead underwriter.

Google's IPO

Six-year-old Google Inc. put a price tag on its initial public share offering yesterday, valuing itself at a cool $29 billion to $36 billion (U.S.), but the founders are taking extraordinary steps to ensure that no one gets rich flipping the stock in the most anticipated Internet IPO in years.

In the latest example of how Google is turning the investing process on its ear, the Mountain View, Calif.-based company warned investors not to expect to be able to sell their shares for a profit in the near term. Google is using an unconventional electronic auction process to price and sell its stock directly to investors rather than to a select group of investment bankers and insiders.

As part of the process, interested investors must log on to a Google website and register to bid in advance of the offering. In a filing with the U.S. Securities and Exchange Commission yesterday, the company warned it will reject bids that it decides "have the potential to manipulate or disrupt the bidding process."

In Canada, investors don't have access to the auction as the stock is made available only through private placement, a method that exempts the company and the selling stockholders from filing a prospectus with regulatory authorities.

The company has taken unusual steps to try to preserve a number of principles the company's co-founders have set out (which includes the mantra "Don't Be Evil"). Google says it will not provide regular earnings guidance and will forgo quarterly stability in favour of pursuing long-term strategies.

Several large underwriters have recently taken the uncommon step of pulling out of the IPO process, walking away from a deal expected to generate about $90 million in fees. The U.S. securities subsidiary of Royal Bank of Canada, and SunTrust Robinson Humphrey were the latest underwriters to pull out, at a time when IPO business is slow on Wall Street, Merrill Lynch & Co. removed itself from the process last month.

"The fees are pretty thin," complained one industry source, who asked not to be identified. The auction process removes the selling concession usually set aside for the brokers who distribute regular IPO shares, he said.

The combination of lower-than-normal fees and the risk associated with the uncertainty about how the market will respond to Google has made the deal unattractive for some investment firms. In addition, some firms don't want to deal with partial blocks that will likely emerge from the pricing structure, the source said.

In its filing, Google set a price range of between $108 and $135 a share. Companies normally split their shares before they reach that price to make it easier for retail investors to buy in blocks of 100 shares. Google has set the minimum size of any bid at five shares.

Despite the unusual nature of Google's offering, there are still 28 firms listed as part of underwriting, led by Morgan Stanley and Credit Suisse First Boston. Google said several shareholders and the company expect to sell 24.6 million shares, valuing the initial public offering between $2.7 billion and $3.3 billion. At that price, the company would be worth almost as much as rival, Yahoo Inc., and possibly more than such corporate stalwarts as Ford Motor Co. Ltd. or McDonald's Corp.

Co-founders Sergey Brin, 30, and Larry Page, 31—who abandoned PhD studies at Stanford University to launch their company—plan to sell a sliver of their holdings as part of the IPO and could pocket as much as $130 million based on yesterday's filing.

In yesterday's prospectus, however, they warned investors not to expect immediate big gains. "As part of this auction process, we are attempting to assess the market demand for our class A common stock and to set the size and price to the public of this offering to meet that demand. As a result, buyers should not expect to be able to sell their shares for a profit shortly after our class A common stock begins trading."

The class A shares carry one vote each, while the class B stock, already held by employees and early investors, will each have 10 votes. Google said this dual-class voting structure will give Mr. Brin and Mr. Page strategic control of the company.

Google said it expects to raise $1.7 billion from the public offering. The funds will be used for general corporate purposes, including working capital and possibly acquisitions. The company said it does not expect to pay any dividends "in the foreseeable future."

Unlike many of the Internet IPOs that preceded it, Google has been profitable for several years. It said yesterday that second-quarter profit rose to $79.1 million from $64 million in the first quarter. Revenue climbed 7.5 per cent to $700.2 million from $651.6 million.

As much as $3.3 billion U.S. in Google stock could be sold at the company's IPO, making it the eighth largest in U.S. history.

Source: Excerpted from Simon Avery, "Google turns investing world on its ear with IPO auction. Internet search company valuing itself at between $29 billion and $36 billion (U.S.)," *The Globe and Mail*, July 27, 2004. Reprinted with permission from *The Globe and Mail*.

Most companies raise capital only occasionally, but underwriters are in the business all the time. Established underwriters are careful of their reputation and will not handle a new issue unless they believe the facts have been presented fairly to investors. Thus, in addition to handling the sale of an issue, the underwriters, in effect, give it their seal of approval. This implied endorsement may be worth quite a bit to a company that is coming to the market for the first time.

For large issues, a group of underwriters called a *syndicate* or *banking group* will usually be formed to handle the sale. Syndication helps to market and distribute the issue more widely and also to spread its risks. The principal underwriter acts as the lead manager to the issue while other underwriters in the group are also responsible for buying and reselling the security, but play *non-lead roles*.

Underwriting is not always fun. On October 15, 1987, the British government finalized arrangements to sell its holding of British Petroleum (BP) shares at £3.30 a share. This huge issue involving more than $12 billion was underwritten by an international group of underwriters and simultaneously marketed in a number of countries. Four days after the underwriting arrangement was finalized, the October stock market crash occurred and stock prices nose-dived. The underwriters appealed to the British government to cancel the issue but the government hardened its heart and pointed out that the underwriters knew the risks when they agreed to handle the sale.[9] By the closing date of the offer, the price of BP stock had fallen to £2.96, and the underwriters had lost more than $1 billion (US). Needless to say, the business is very competitive resulting, at times, in participants being accused of unethical behaviour. As the nearby Finance in Action box describes, this is what happened when Canadian Imperial Bank of Commerce (CIBC) recently sued some high-profile former employees who defected from the bank to form Genuity Capital Markets, a new investment banking firm. CIBC alleged that the employees had taken with them privileged information from the bank when they left.

SEE BOX P. 439 ▷

WHO ARE THE UNDERWRITERS?

Since underwriters play such a crucial role in new issues, we should look at who they are. Several hundred investment banks, security dealers, and brokers are, at least, sporadically involved in underwriting. However, the market for the larger issues is dominated by the major investment dealers, which specialize in underwriting new issues, dealing in securities, and arranging mergers. These firms enjoy great prestige, experience, and financial muscle.

Table 14.1 lists some of the largest Canadian firms, ranked by total value of issues in 2003.[10] Notice that each of the firms has acted as a lead underwriter and also in a non-lead capacity within a syndicate. RBC Capital Markets, the winner, raised a total of $27,072 million. Of course, only a small proportion of these issues was for companies that were coming to the market for the first time. Table 14.2 lists the top 10 Canadian corporate equity issues in 2003. Notice the large

TABLE 14.1
Canada's Top Underwriters for Equity and Debt, 2003 (dollar figures in millions)

Underwriter	Lead Number	Lead Amount	Total Number	Total Amount
1 RBC Capital Markets	200	18,705	479	27,072
2 CIBC World Markets Inc.	218	13,873	495	21,686
3 TD Securities Inc.	159	12,801	477	21,345
4 Scotia Capital Inc.	143	12,085	437	20,785
5 BMO Nesbitt Burns Inc.	119	8,215	446	17,148
6 Merrill Lynch & Co.	60	9,062	154	12,594
7 Natl. Bank Financial Inc.	92	4,525	387	10,204
8 Salomon Smith Barney Inc.	44	5,927	55	6,379
9 HSBC Securities	11	2,575	149	5,867
10 Deutsche Bank AG	20	5,129	39	5,675

Source: *Financial Post*, January 26, 2004.

---

[9] The government's only concession was to put a floor on the underwriters' losses by giving them the option to resell their stock to the government at £2.80 a share. The BP offering is described and analyzed in C. Muscarella and M. Vetsuypens, "The British Petroleum Stock Offering: An Application of Option Pricing," *Journal of Applied Corporate Finance* 1 (1989), pp. 74–80.

[10] This table is based on a formula of bonus credit to the lead underwriter, also called book runner. With this formula, the book runner receives two shares of the transaction while each of the other syndicate members receives one share. For more details, see Barry Critchley "How Much of the Pie They Ate," *Financial Post*, January 29, 2004, DM8.

Allegations of Unethical Conduct: The Controversy Surrounding Ex-Employees of CIBC and Genuity Capital Markets

Canadian Imperial Bank of Commerce is suing another three former employees who defected to Genuity Capital Markets, and has accused some partners at the fledgling brokerage firm of masterminding a "conspiracy" to poach colleagues from the bank.

CIBC filed a statement of claim against Genuity late Friday, and added David Morrison, Ted Hirst and Gunnar Eggertson to its original list of defendants. The bitter legal battle erupted this month when CIBC sued six former employees, including star investment banker David Kassie and several other top deal makers, for allegedly taking confidential information from the bank and planning a "scheme" to lure co-workers to Genuity. The bank is asking an Ontario court to force the departed executives to return any bonuses received last year prior to embarking for Genuity.

Mr. Morrison was head of institutional equity sales at CIBC World Markets Inc. before he resigned from the bank's brokerage arm in mid-December, shortly after year-end bonuses were paid. Mr. Hirst and Mr. Eggertson are a Vancouver-based investment-banking team specializing in the mining sector, and are among the more than 20 CIBC traders, analysts, and bankers who have already left for Genuity.

Marie Cordero, a business specialist at the bank, is the only member of the Genuity defendants who CIBC has not accused of participating in the alleged conspiracy. The bank claims Ms. Cordero copied files before she departed that may have contained privileged information relating to the bank's clients.

CIBC now claims that Ms. Cordero was induced to duplicate these files.

Ms. Cordero has denied taking any material from the bank, and Genuity partners maintained recently that she was merely compiling an invitation list for an anniversary celebration next month at CIBC Wood Gundy.

Alan Lenczner, a lawyer for Genuity, said he was not surprised that CIBC has added more names to the suit.

"They're just making sure they get everyone [included] that they want to get," he said.

Despite the conspiracy allegations, he played down the latest legal manoeuvring as routine, and said he expects to file a statement of defence in the next few weeks.

A spokesman for CIBC declined to comment on the matter.

The original filing spanned more than 600 pages, much of it filled with e-mail discussions between Genuity's founding partners and other CIBC employees that the bank cited as evidence of a "well-orchestrated" recruitment scheme.

Genuity's founders have denied CIBC's allegations.

In a recent interview, Mr. Kassie insisted he did not recruit former colleagues or spirit away confidential information from the bank, pointing out that potential employees signed confidentiality agreements with Genuity in which they confirmed they had not been solicited. However, the bank is still seeking a court-imposed injunction that would prevent Genuity from soliciting any of its staff.

Mr. Kassie, an aggressive deal maker once regarded as the heir successor to CIBC chief executive officer John Hunkin, was ousted as head of CIBC World Markets last February as the bank attempted to overhaul its culture and lower its risk profile following a settlement with U.S. regulators over its involvement with disgraced Enron Corp.

Genuity officially opened for business earlier this month, and is regarded as the largest startup investment-banking boutique in Bay Street history. Last week it unveiled its first major deal: an advisory role on Cedara Software Corp.'s planned $477-million merger with Merge Technologies Inc. of Milwaukee.

In addition to Mr. Kassie, CIBC is suing Phil Evershed, who was the bank's head of mergers and acquisitions; Dan Daviau, a high-ranking investment banker specializing in technology and media; former vice-chair Earl Rotman, one of the architects of CIBC's push into income trusts; and John Esteireiro, who ran the trading operations.

Source: Excerpted from S. Stewart "CIBC Names 3 More in Lawsuit," *Canadian News*, January 24, 2005. **www.digitaldefence.ca/html/printer_707.shtml**

TABLE 14.2
Top 10 IPO Issues

Rank 2003		Gross Proceeds Raised $000s	Lead Underwriter(s)
1	Yellow Pages Income Fund	935,000	CIBC World Markets; Scotia Capital
2	Brompton Equal Weight Income Fund	400,000	RBC Capital Markets; CIBC World Markets
3	UE Waterheater Income Fund	361,000	CIBC World Markets; TD Securities
4	Indexplus Income Fund	325,000	CIBC World Markets; RBC Capital Markets
5	Series S-1 Income Fund	325,000	CIBC World Markets; TD Securities
6	SCITI Trust	300,000	Scotia Capital
7	Select 50 S-1 Income Trust	300,000	National Bank Financial; CIBC World Markets
8	Citadel Multi-Sector Income Fund	270,557	CIBC World Markets; BMO Nesbitt Burns
9	Chartwell Seniors Housing REIT	210,000	RBC Capital Markets
10	Northbridge Financial Corp.	201,000	BMO Nesbitt Burns; Scotia Capital

Source: *National Post Business*, June 2004, p. 122.

TABLE 14.3
Top five underwriters of debt, equity, and equity-related issues in 2003 ($ millions [U.S.] dollars)

Global		
Underwriter	**Proceeds**	**No. of Issues**
Citigroup	542,748.5	1,872
Morgan Stanley	394,779.8	1,365
Merrill Lynch	380,318.9	1,914
Lehman Brothers	354,145.8	1,264
JP Morgan	353,900.5	1,417
Top 5 Totals	**2,025,893.5**	**7,832**
Industry Totals	**5,326,243.5**	**19,706**

Source: Thomson Financial, December 31, 2003, **www.thomson.com/league**.

SEE BOX P. 441

number of income funds and income trusts in the table. These financial instruments have recently become very popular with the investing public in Canada. We will describe these in more detail in the next chapter. As the nearby Finance in Action box shows, investors were busy buying equity and bond issues in 2003.

Some of the largest debt and equity issues are in the United States. In Chapter 13, we pointed out that instead of issuing bonds in Canada, corporations can issue eurobonds in London, which are then sold to investors outside Canada. In addition, new equity issues by large multinational companies are increasingly marketed to investors throughout the world. Since these securities are sold in a number of countries, many of the major international banks are involved in underwriting the issues. Have a look at Table 14.3. It shows the names of principal underwriters of global debt and equity issues in 2003.

14.4   LISTING ON THE STOCK MARKET

When a firm decides on an initial public offering of its stocks, it has to decide where its newly issued shares should be traded. As we have discussed in Chapters 2 and 6, stock markets can be either organized exchanges with centralized physical locations or over-the-counter markets consisting of a network of security dealers who trade with each other over the phone and increasingly over electronic networks. Most trading in the shares of large Canadian corporations takes place on the Toronto Stock Exchange (TSX), while shares of smaller and emerging companies are traded through the TSX Venture Exchange (TSXV). Electronic trading in shares can also be done through Nasdaq Canada, which has operations in Montreal for the purpose of trading in shares listed on the Nasdaq stock market. Table 14.4 provides details regarding the trading activity for May 2004 of the Toronto Stock Exchange and the TSX Venture Exchange.

In order to list its stock issue on a stock exchange, the firm will have to meet the exchange's listing requirements and pay the requisite listing fee. These tend to vary; generally, the larger and more prestigious stock exchanges also tend to have stricter listing requirements and higher listing fees. Table 14.5 summarizes major listing requirements of the TSX for profitable industrial companies.

TABLE 14.4
Trading activity on Canadian stock exchanges

	Trading Activity, May 2004	
Stock Exchange	**Value of Shares (Millions of Dollars)**	**Volume of Shares (Millions of Shares)**
Toronto Stock Exchange	$61,917	4,478
TSX Venture Exchange	562	964

Source: The Toronto Stock Exchange and the TSX Venture Exchange Web site at **www.tsx.com**.

A Buying Spree for Equity and Bonds in 2003

Canadian companies are raising money at a record pace, with the flood of stock and bond sales expected to continue as investors regain their faith in rising markets.

Equity financings totaled $12.7 billion in the third quarter, up 35 per cent from the previous year, according to the Investment Dealers Association of Canada. It's the strongest quarter seen in the four years that the IDA has been compiling this data.

"I don't see any sign of a slowdown," said Jon Cockerline, director of capital markets at the IDA. "There are strong fundamentals that the market is responding to. It looks like we're starting the up-leg of the next bull market."

Investors are being enticed back into the market by the 20-percent year-over-year rise in the S&P/TSX composite index, Mr. Cockerline said. He added that for the first time in three years, underwriting activity is balanced between common stock and income trust deals, compared with the dominance of trust issues in preceding quarters.

From June through September, common stock offerings accounted for $5.3-billion, while there was $5.8-billion of new trust units, the strongest quarter ever for the sector. The remaining financings were preferred share offerings.

Great-West Lifeco Inc., which took over Canada Life Financial Corp., was the single largest stock issuer, raising a total of $900 million. In the trust sector, the initial public offering of Yellow Pages Income Fund rang in at $935 million.

New equity offerings have certainly continued to hit the market at a steady pace. This week saw the first high-tech IPO in three years as Workbrain Inc. kicked off what's expected to be a $40-million IPO. And the merge-deals continued, with investors stepping up for $1-billion worth of Shoppers Drug Mart Corp. stock.

"Short of ringing a great big bell, there couldn't be a better signal that the market is open than the success of Shoppers and the first tech IPO since 2000," said an executive at one Canadian brokerage house involved in the drugstore underwriting. He estimated that at least $2-billion of equity sales are poised to come to market in the next two months …

The financing activity comes as merger and acquisition activity picks up. The value of takeovers announced in the third quarter spiked upward to $34.1 billion on 194 takeovers, according to merchant bank Crosbie & Co. That compares with the $12.8 billion on 219 deals in the previous quarter.

In the past three months, Manulife Financial Corp. made a $15 billion bid for John Hancock Financial Services, and Alcan Inc. made its $6.3 billion offer for Pechiney SA.

"The combination of improved operating performance by potential strategic buyers, forecasts of good economic growth, valuation multiples generally in line with historical norms and capital pools seeking homes for their ample cash resources, augurs well for activity," said Mel Margolese, a partner at Crosbie & Co.

In addition to buying shares, investors are trading with a passion. The Toronto Stock Exchange saw record volumes in recent months, with 14.1 billion shares changing hands in the third quarter. Through the end of October, TSX trading volume was up 17.9 per cent from the same period last year.

Source: Excerpted from Andrew Willis, "Firms raising money at record pace," *The Globe and Mail*, November 8, 2003, B1. Reprinted with permission from *The Globe and Mail.*

TABLE 14.5

Toronto Stock Exchange: major listing requirements for profitable industrial companies[1]

(i) *Assets*: Net tangible assets of $2,000,000.

(ii) *Earnings*: Earnings from ongoing operations of at least $200,000 before taxes and extraordinary items in the fiscal year immediately preceding the filing of the listing application.

(iii) *Cash Flow*: Pre-tax cash flow of $500,000 in the immediately preceding fiscal year.

(iv) *Working Capital and Capital Structure*: Adequate working capital to carry on the business and an appropriate capital structure.

(v) *Public Distribution*: At least 1,000,000 freely tradeable shares having an aggregate market value of $4,000,000 must be held by at least 300 public holders, each holding one board lot or more shares.[2]

(vi) *Management*: Management (including the company's board of directors) should have adequate experience and technical expertise relevant to the company's business and industry and adequate public company experience. Companies will be required to have at least two Canadian directors.

[1] The requirements vary with the type of industrial companies, that is profitable companies, companies forecasting profitability, technology companies, or research and development companies. Different requirements also exist for mining, and oil and gas companies. Complete details regarding all listing requirements are provided on the TSX Web site at **www.tsx.com**.

[2] A board lot comprises 100 shares for securities selling at $1 and more. See **www.tsx.com**.

RIGHTS ISSUES AND GENERAL CASH OFFERS BY PUBLIC COMPANIES

After the initial public offering, a successful firm will continue to grow and from time to time it will need to raise more money by issuing stock or bonds. An issue of additional stock by a company whose stock already is publicly traded is called a **seasoned offering**. Any issue of securities needs to be formally approved by the firm's board of directors. If a stock issue requires an increase in the company's authorized capital, it also needs the consent of the shareholders.

Public companies can issue securities either by making a general cash offer to investors at large or by making a **rights issue**, which is limited to existing shareholders. Let us first concentrate on the mechanics of the rights issue.

RIGHTS ISSUES

In a rights issue, the company offers the shareholders the opportunity, or *right*, to buy more shares at an "attractive" subscription price. For example, if the current stock price is $100, the company might offer investors an additional share at $50 for each share they hold. Suppose that before the issue an investor has one share worth $100 and $50 in the bank. If the investor takes up the offer of a new share, that $50 of cash is transferred from the investor's bank account to the company's. The investor now has two shares that are a claim on the original assets worth $100 and on the $50 cash that the company has raised. So the two shares are worth a total of $150, or $75 each.

By directly offering a new share issue to existing shareholders, a company could hope to save on issuing and underwriting expenses. Also, shareholders do not run a risk of dilution of their proportional shareholding and are able to retain their voting position on the company's major business decisions. Of course, shareholders will have an incentive to exercise their rights only if the subscription price stays below the market price of the shares. Otherwise, if the share price falls, the full issue of new shares may not be taken up. To protect against this possibility, the firm may enter into a **standby underwriting agreement** with an investment dealer. Under this arrangement, the underwriter stands ready to purchase any unsold shares and receives a *standby fee* and possible additional amounts depending on the extent of unsold shares. Also, the company may give its shareholders an **oversubscription privilege** under which they will be able to purchase any unsold shares at the subscription price. Of course, a small proportion of shareholders may not exercise their rights, perhaps because they are away on vacation or for other personal reasons.

In some countries, rights issues are the most common or only method for issuing common stock. In Canada, they are less common. Sometimes, a preemptive right is contained in the firm's articles of incorporation, in which case, the firm has to offer any new issue of common stock to its existing shareholders.

In a rights offering, existing shareholders receive one right for each share of stock held. To take advantage of the rights offering, shareholders will have to exercise the right within a specified period of time by submitting a completed subscription form to the company's subscription agent. If rights are not exercised within the period stipulated, they will expire.

seasoned offering   Sale of securities by a firm that is already publicly traded.

rights issue   Issue of securities offered only to current shareholders.

standby underwriting agreement   The underwriter stands ready to purchase any unsold shares.

oversubscription privilege   Given to shareholders in a rights issue, enabling them to purchase any unsold shares at the subscription price.

EXAMPLE 14.4	RIGHTS ISSUES

Easy Writer Word Processing Company has one million shares outstanding, selling at $20 a share. To finance the development of a new software package, it plans a rights issue, allowing one new share to be purchased for each 10 shares currently held. The purchase price will be $10 a share. How many shares will be issued? How much money will be raised? What will be the stock price after the rights issue?

The firm will issue one new share for every 10 old ones, or 100,000 shares. So shares outstanding will rise to 1.1 million. The firm will raise $10 × 100,000 = $1 million. Therefore, the total value of the firm will increase from $20 million to $21 million, and the stock price will fall to $21 million/1.1 million shares = $19.09 per share.

The standard procedure for issuing rights involves the firm announcing the issue and setting a **holder-of-record date**. This is the date on which existing shareholders, as listed in the company's records, are entitled to the stock rights. Actually, to comply with stock exchange rules, the stock will usually go *ex-rights* four trading days before the holder-of-record date. If the stock is sold before this date, the new owner will receive the rights, and so, its value will be with *rights*, *rights-on*, or *cum-rights*. If the stock is sold after the **ex-rights date**, the buyer will no longer be entitled to the rights.

Since rights offerings enable shareholders to buy shares at a favourable price, they clearly have value. How would you arrive at the value of a right? Notice that to buy one new share, the existing shareholder will have to use 10 rights and pay the purchase price of $10. However, the market price of the share after the rights issue, that is the ex-rights price, is $19.09. We can, therefore, formulate an equation that will give the theoretical value of a right.

$$\text{Value of one right} = \frac{\text{Market value of share, ex-rights} - \text{subscription price}}{\text{Number of rights required to purchase a share}}$$

$$= \frac{\$19.09 - \$10}{10} = \frac{\$9.09}{10} = \$0.91$$

You can also arrive at the theoretical value of a right by using the price of the stock during the cum-rights period.

$$\text{Value of one right} = \frac{\text{Market value of share, rights on} - \text{subscription price}}{\text{Number of rights required to purchase a share} + 1}$$

$$= \frac{\$20 - \$10}{10 + 1} = \frac{\$10}{11} = \$0.91$$

Suppose Easy Writer Word Processing Company announces the terms of its rights offering on May 31, stating that the rights would be mailed to shareholders of record as of July 15. In this case, the ex-rights date is July 11, and so shareholders who own the stock until July 10 are entitled to receive the rights. The rights-on price of the shares is $20 and it drops to the ex-rights price of $19.09. Notice that the share price drops by $.91, that is, to the extent of the value of a right.

GENERAL CASH OFFERS

When a public company makes a **general cash offer** of debt or equity, it essentially follows the same procedure used when it first went public. This means that it must first register the issue in compliance with the regulations of relevant provincial commissions. The issue is then sold to an underwriter under a firm-commitment arrangement or on a best-effort basis.[11] The underwriter (or syndicate of underwriters), in turn, offers the securities to the public.

Many underwriting agreements, including those involving firm commitments, may contain a *market-out clause*, which limits the underwriters' risk. This clause can enable the underwriter to terminate the underwriting agreement without penalty under extraordinary circumstances or even if the underwriter judges that the state of the financial market is not good for the security issue. In Canada, competition for lucrative underwriting deals and a dislike of the market-out clause among investors has created an environment for **bought deals**, which are often used by large, well-known companies for their seasoned equity issues. Here, the investment dealer buys the entire offering from the issuing company and then decides how to sell it to investors. This is advantageous to the company because it is able to obtain a relatively quick and firm commitment on its securities. Bought deals are not commonly used in the United States.

holder-of-record date   The date on which shareholders appearing on company records are entitled to receive the stock rights.

ex-rights date   This date is usually four business days before the holder-of-record date.

general cash offer   Sale of securities open to all investors by an already-public company.

bought deal   The underwriter buys securities from the issuing company and sells them to investors.

[11] A large issue will typically be handled by a syndicate of underwriters.

prompt offering prospectus (POP) system   Allows qualified firms quicker access to capital markets by enabling them to use a short-form filing process rather than a full prospectus.

shelf registration   A procedure followed in the United States that allows firms to file one registration statement for several issues of the same security.

Usually the large issuers in Canada who go for bought deals can also take advantage of the **prompt offering prospectus (POP) system**, which allows short-form filing since much of the information contained in the regular prospectus is already expected to have been filed annually. Thus under the POP system, only material changes and financial statements have to be provided to regulators who are able to give their clearance within about five days—instead of several weeks required for a full prospectus. The investing public must still be provided with a regular prospectus. In the United States, companies can take advantage of **shelf registration**, which allows them to file a single registration statement covering financing plans for up to two years into the future. Within this time period, companies do not need to prepare a separate registration statement every time they issue new securities.

COSTS OF THE GENERAL CASH OFFER

Whenever a firm makes a cash offer, it incurs substantial administrative costs. Also, the firm needs to compensate the underwriters by selling them securities below the price that they expect to receive from investors. Figure 14.3 shows the average underwriting spread and administrative costs for several types of security issues in the United States.[12]

The figure clearly shows the economies of scale in issuing securities. Costs may absorb 15 percent of a small IPO or seasoned equity issue of no more than $10 million (U.S.). This occurs because a large part of the issue cost is fixed. The costs are similar in Canada.[13]

Figure 14.3 shows that issue costs are higher for equity than for debt securities—the costs for both types of securities, however, show the same economies of scale. Issue costs are higher for equity than for debt because administrative costs are somewhat higher, and also because underwriting stock is riskier than underwriting bonds. The underwriters demand additional compensation for the greater risk they take in buying and reselling equity.

FIGURE 14.3

Total direct costs as a percentage of gross proceeds. The total direct costs for initial public offerings (IPOs), seasoned equity offerings (SEOs), convertible bonds, and straight bonds are composed of underwriter spreads and other direct expenses.

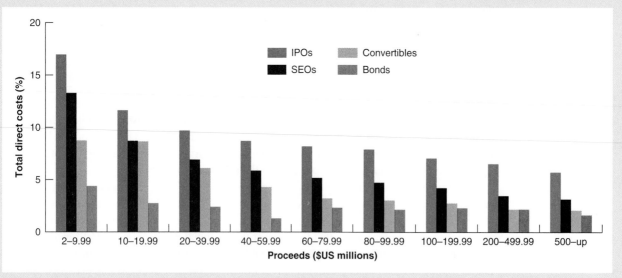

Source: I. Lee, S. Lochhead, J. Ritter, and Q. Zhao, "The Costs of Raising Capital," *Journal of Financial Research* 19 (Spring 1996), pp. 59–74. Copyright © 1996. Reprinted by permission.

---

[12] These figures do not capture all administrative costs. For example, they do not include management time spent on the issue.

[13] A recent study finds that average Canadian underwriter fees for medium-sized IPOs ($10 to 50 million) average 6 percent, compared with a U.S. average of 7 percent. See L. Kryzanowski and I. Rakita "Is the U.S. 7 percent Solution Equivalent to the Canadian 6 percent Solution?" *Canadian Investment Review* (Fall 1999), Volume 2, pp. 27–34.

Use Figure 14.3 to compare the costs of 10 issues of $15 million (US) of stock in a seasoned offering versus one issue of $150 million (US).

MARKET REACTION TO STOCK ISSUES

Because stock issues usually throw a sizable number of new shares onto the market, it is widely believed that they must temporarily depress the stock price. If the proposed issue is very large, this price pressure may, it is thought, be so severe as to make it almost impossible to raise money.

This belief in price pressure implies that a new issue depresses the stock price temporarily below its true value. However, that view doesn't appear to fit very well with the notion of market efficiency. If the stock price falls solely because of increased supply, then that stock would offer a higher return than comparable stocks, and investors would be attracted to it like ants to a picnic.

Economists who have studied new issues of common stock have generally found that the announcement of the issue *does* result in a decline in the stock price. For industrial issues in the United States, this decline amounts to about 3 percent.[14] While this may not sound overwhelming, such a price drop can be a large fraction of the money raised. Suppose that a company with a market value of equity of $5 billion announces its intention to issue $500 million of additional equity and thereby causes the stock price to drop by 3 percent. The loss in value is .03 × $5 billion, or $150 million. That's 30 percent of the amount of money raised (.30 × $500 million = $150 million).

What's going on here? Is the price of the stock simply depressed by the prospect of the additional supply? Possibly, but here is an alternative explanation.

Suppose managers (who have better information about the firm than outside investors) know that their stock is undervalued. If the company sells new stock at this low price, it will give the new shareholders a good deal at the expense of the old shareholders. In these circumstances managers might be prepared to forgo the new investment rather than sell shares at too low a price.

If managers know that the stock is overvalued, the position is reversed. If the company sells new shares at the high price, it will help its existing shareholders at the expense of the new ones. Managers might be prepared to issue stock even if the new cash were just put in the bank.

Of course, investors are not stupid. They can predict that managers are more likely to issue stock when they think it is overvalued, and therefore, they mark the price of the stock down accordingly.

> The tendency for stock prices to decline at the time of an issue may have nothing to do with increased supply. Instead, the stock issue may simply be a signal that well-informed managers believe the market has overpriced the stock.[15]

14.6   THE PRIVATE PLACEMENT

private placement Sale of securities to a limited number of investors without a public offering.

Whenever a company makes a public offering, it must register the issue with the relevant provincial commission. It could avoid this costly process by selling the issue privately. There are no hard and fast definitions of a **private placement**. Most private sales of debt and equity are to exempt institutions such as large pension funds or insurance companies, which are considered to be knowledgeable buyers and will not require all the information provided in a regular prospectus. Currently, the

---

[14] See, for example, P. Asquith and D. W. Mullins, "Equity Issues and Offering Dilution," *Journal of Financial Economics* 15 (January–February 1986), pp. 61–90; R. W. Masulis and A. N. Korwar, "Seasoned Equity Offerings: An Empirical Investigation," *Journal of Financial Economics* 15 (January–February 1986), pp. 91–118; W. H. Mikkelson and M. M. Partch, "Valuation Effects of Security Offerings and the Issuance Process," *Journal of Financial Economics* 15 (January–February 1986), pp. 31–60. There appears to be a smaller price decline for utility issues. Also Marsh observed a smaller decline for rights issues in the United Kingdom; see P. R. Marsh, "Equity Rights Issues and the Efficiency of the UK Stock Market," *Journal of Finance* 34 (September 1979), pp. 839–862.

[15] This explanation was developed in S. C. Myers and N. S. Mailuf's "Corporate Financing and Investment Decisions When Firms Have Information That Investors Do Not Have," *Journal of Financial Economics* 13 (1984), pp. 187–222.

minimum investment requirement for a private placement is $150,000, which effectively shuts out average investors, although some wealthy individuals do participate as buyers.

One disadvantage of a private placement is that the investor cannot easily resell the security. This is less important to institutions such as insurance companies, which invest huge sums of money in corporate debt for the long haul.

As you would expect, it costs less to arrange a private placement than to make a public issue. That might not be so important for the very large issues where costs are less significant, but it is a particular advantage for companies making smaller issues.

Another advantage of the private placement is that the debt contract can be custom-tailored for firms with special problems or opportunities. Also, if the firm wishes later to change the terms of the debt, it is much simpler to do this with a private placement where only a few investors are involved.

Therefore, it is not surprising that private placements occupy a particular niche in the corporate debt market, namely, loans to small- and medium-sized firms. These are the firms that face the highest costs in public issues, that require the most detailed investigation, and that may require specialized, flexible loan arrangements.

We do not mean that large, safe, and conventional firms should rule out private placements. Enormous amounts of capital are sometimes raised by this method. For example, Air Canada borrowed $400 million through a private placement of senior unsecured debt. Norske Skog Canada Ltd., a large pulp and paper company based in Western Canada, had a $250 million (U.S.) private placement offering targeted at investors in the United States and some Canadian provinces. Nevertheless, the advantages of private placement—avoiding registration costs and establishing a direct relationship with the lender—are generally more important to smaller firms.

Of course, these advantages are not free. Lenders in private placements have to be compensated for the risks they face and for the costs of research and negotiation. They also have to be compensated for holding an asset that is not easily resold. All these factors are rolled into the interest rate paid by the firm. It is difficult to generalize about the differences in interest rates between private placements and public issues, but a typical yield differential could be on the order of half a percentage point.

14.7   SUMMARY

1. How do venture capital firms design successful deals?

Infant companies raise **venture capital** to carry them through to the point where they can make their first public issue of stock. More established publicly traded companies can issue additional securities in a **general cash offer**.

Financing choices should be designed to avoid conflicts of interest. This is especially important in the case of a young company that is raising venture capital. If both managers and investors have an important equity stake in the company, they are likely to pull in the same direction. The willingness to take that stake also signals management's confidence in the new company's future. Therefore, most deals require that the entrepreneur maintain large stakes in the firm. In addition, most venture financing is done in stages that keep the firm on a short

leash and force it to prove, at several crucial points, that it is worthy of additional investment.

2. How do firms make initial public offerings and what are the costs of such offerings?

The **initial public offering** is the first sale of shares in a general offering to investors. The sale of the securities is usually managed by an underwriting firm that buys the shares from the company and resells them to the public. The **underwriter** helps to prepare a **prospectus**, which describes the company and its prospects. The costs of an IPO include direct costs such as legal and administrative fees as well as the underwriting spread—the difference between the price the underwriter pays to acquire the shares from the firm and the price the public pays the underwriter for those shares. Another major implicit cost is the **underpricing** of the issue—that is, shares are typically sold to the public somewhat below the true value of the security. This discount is reflected in abnormally high average returns to new issues on the first day of trading.

3. **What are some of the significant issues that arise when established firms make a rights issue, a general cash offer, or a private placement of securities?**

There are always economies of scale in issuing securities. It is cheaper to go to the market once for $100 million than to make two trips for $50 million each. Consequently, firms "bunch" security issues. This may mean relying on short-term financing until a large issue is justified. Or it may mean issuing more than is needed at the moment to avoid another issue later.

A **seasoned offering** may depress the stock price. The extent of this price decline varies, but for issues of common stocks by industrial firms, the fall in the value of the existing stock may amount to a significant proportion of the money raised. The likely explanation for this pressure is the information the market reads into the company's decision to issue stock.

The **prompt offering prospectus (POP) system** often makes sense for equity or debt issues by well-established companies. It allows short-form filing to regulators and, thereby, reduces the time taken to arrange a new issue.

Private placements are well suited for small, risky, or unusual firms. Of course, established and conventional firms also often raise large sums of capital by this method. The special advantages of private placement stem from avoiding registration expenses and getting a more direct relationship with the lender.

4. **What is the role of the underwriter in an issue of securities?**

The underwriter manages the sale of the securities for the issuing company. The underwriting firms have expertise in such sales because they are in the business all the time, whereas the company raises capital only occasionally. Moreover, the underwriters may give an implicit seal of approval to the offering. Because the underwriters will not want to squander their reputation by misrepresenting facts to the public, the implied endorsement may be quite important to a firm coming to the market for the first time.

Related Web Links

www.ipohome.com/default.asp News and statistics on the IPO market

www.cbs.marketwatch.com Information on new IPOs in the United States

www.tfibcm.com Information on underwriting activity

www.FreeEDGAR.com Information on registration of new securities offerings in the United States

www.cob.ohio-state.edu/~fin/resources_education/credit.htm The changing mix of corporate financing

www.vnpartners.com/ Venture capital as a source of project financing

www.strategis.ic.gc.ca Industry Canada

www.bdc.ca Business Development Bank of Canada

www.rim.com Research In Motion

www.osc.gov.on.ca Ontario Securities Commission

www.sedar.com Information on document filings by Canadian companies including for new securities

www.724.com 724 Solutions

www.cvca.ca Canadian Venture Capital Association (CVCA)

www.canadavc.com Venture capital information; Web site of Macdonald and Associates Ltd.

www.iclub.com/investorama.html Products and services targeted at investment clubs

www.canadait.com Venture capital and angel investor information

http://bear.cba.ufl.edu/ritter Web page of Jay Ritter, the well-known finance professor; includes some great data on IPOs

www.ventureeconomics.com News and statistics on the U.S. venture capital industry

Key Terms

Questions and Problems

*Answers in Appendix B

BASIC

*1. **Underwriting.**
   a. Is a rights issue more likely to be used for an initial public offering or for subsequent issues of stock?
   b. Is a private placement more likely to be used for issues of seasoned stock or seasoned bonds by an industrial company?
   c. Is the Prompt Offering Prospectus (POP) system more likely to be used for issues of unseasoned stocks or bonds by a large industrial company?

2. **Underwriting.** Each of the following terms is associated with one of the events beneath. Can you match them up?
   a. Red herring
   b. Firm commitment
   c. Rights issue
   A. The underwriter agrees to buy the issue from the company at a fixed price.
   B. The company offers to sell stock to existing stockholders.
   C. The company issues a preliminary prospectus for distribution to the public.

*3. **Underwriting Costs.** For each of the following pairs of issues state which of the two you would expect to involve the lower proportionate underwriting and administrative costs, other things being equal:
   a. a large issue/a small issue
   b. a bond issue/a common stock issue
   c. a small private placement of bonds/a small general cash offer of bonds

*4. **IPO Costs.** Why are the issue costs for debt issues generally less than those for equity issues?

5. **Venture Capital.** Why do venture capital companies prefer to advance money in stages?

6. **IPOs.** Your broker calls and says that you can get 500 shares of an imminent IPO at the offering price. Should you buy? Are you worried about the fact that your broker called you?

PRACTICE

*7. **IPO Underpricing.** Having heard about IPO underpricing, I put in an order to my broker for 1,000 shares of every IPO he can get for me. After three months, my investment record is as follows:

IPO	Shares Allocated to Me	Price per Share	Initial Return
A	500	$10	7%
B	200	20	12
C	1,000	8	−2
D	0	12	23

   a. What is the average underpricing of this sample of IPOs?
   b. What is the average initial return on my "portfolio" of shares purchased from the four IPOs I bid on? Calculate the average initial return, weighting by the amount of money invested in each issue.

c.   Why have I performed so poorly relative to the average initial return on the full sample of IPOs? What lessons do you draw from my experience?

8. **IPO Costs.** Moonscape has just completed an initial public offering. The firm sold three million shares at an offer price of $8 per share. The underwriting spread was $.50 a share. The price of the stock closed at $11 per share at the end of the first day of trading. The firm incurred $100,000 in legal, administrative, and other costs. What were flotation costs as a fraction of funds raised?

9. **IPO Costs.** Look at the illustrative new-issue prospectus in Appendix 14B.

a.   Is this issue a primary offering, a secondary offering, or both?

b.   What are the direct costs of the issue as a percentage of the total proceeds? Are these more than the average for an issue of this size?

c.   Suppose that on the first day of trading the price of Hotch Pot's stock is $15 a share. What are the *total* costs of the issue as a percentage of the market price?

d.   After paying her share of the expenses, how much will the firm's president, Emma Lucullus, receive from the sale? What will be the value of the shares that she retains in the company?

*10. **Flotation Costs.** "For small issues of common stock, the costs of flotation amount to about 15 percent of the proceeds. This means that the opportunity cost of external equity capital is about 15 percentage points higher than that of retained earnings." Does this make sense?

EXCEL

11. **Flotation Costs.** When Microsoft went public, the company sold two million new shares (the primary issue). In addition, existing shareholders sold .8 million shares (the secondary issue) and kept 21.1 million shares. The new shares were offered to the public at $21, and the underwriters received a spread of $1.31 a share. At the end of the first day's trading, the market price was $35 a share.

a.   How much money did the company receive before paying its portion of the direct costs?

b.   How much did the existing shareholders receive from the sale before paying their portion of the direct costs?

c.   If the issue had been sold to the underwriters for $30 a share, how many shares would the company have needed to sell to raise the same amount of cash?

d.   How much better off would the existing shareholders have been?

*12. **Flotation Costs.** The market value of the marketing research firm Fax Facts is $600 million. The firm issues an additional $100 million of stock, but as a result the stock price falls by 2 percent. What is the cost of the price drop to existing shareholders as a fraction of the funds raised?

13. **Flotation Costs.** Young Corporation stock currently sells for $30 per share. There are one million shares currently outstanding. The company announces plans to raise $3 million by offering shares to the public at a price of $30 per share.

a.   If the underwriting spread is 8 percent, how many shares will the company need to issue in order to be left with net proceeds of $3 million?

b.   If other administrative costs are $60,000, what is the dollar value of the total direct costs of the issue?

c.   If the share price falls by 3 percent at the announcement of the plans to proceed with a seasoned offering, what is the dollar cost of the announcement effect?

14. **Private Placements.** You need to choose between the following types of issues:

A public issue of $10 million face value of 10-year debt. The interest rate on the debt would be 8.5 percent and the debt would be issued at face value. The underwriting spread would be 1.5 percent and other expenses would be $80,000.

A private placement of $10 million face value of 10-year debt. The interest rate on the private placement would be 9 percent, but the total issuing expenses would be only $30,000.

a. What is the difference in the proceeds to the company net of expenses?

b. Other things being equal, which is the better deal?

c. What other factors beyond the interest rate and issue costs would you wish to consider before deciding between the two offers?

*15. **Rights.** In 2001, Pandora, Inc., makes a rights issue at a subscription price of $5 a share. One new share can be purchased for every four shares held. Before the issue there were 10 million shares outstanding, and the share price was $6.

a. What is the total amount of new money raised?

b. What is the expected stock price after the rights are issued?

16. **Rights.** Problem 15 contains details of a rights offering by Pandora. Suppose that the company had decided to issue the new stock at $4 instead of $5 a share. How many new shares would it have needed to raise the same sum of money? Recalculate the answers to problem 15. Show that Pandora's shareholders are just as well off if it issues the shares at $4 a share rather than $5.

EXCEL

17. **Rights.** Consolidated Jewels needs to raise $2 million to pay for its Diamonds in the Rough campaign. It will raise the funds by offering 200,000 rights, each of which entitles the owner to buy one new share. The company currently has one million shares outstanding priced at $20 each.

*a. What must be the subscription price on the rights the company plans to offer?

*b. What will be the share price after the rights issue?

*c. What is the value of a right to buy one share?

*d. How many rights would be issued to an investor who currently owns 1,000 shares?

e. Show that the investor who currently holds 1,000 shares is unaffected by the rights issue. Specifically, show that the value of the rights plus the value of the 1,000 shares after the rights issue equals the value of the 1,000 shares before the rights issue.

18. **Rights.** Associated Breweries is planning to market unleaded beer. To finance the venture it proposes to make a rights issue with a subscription price of $10. One new share can be purchased for each two shares held. The company currently has 100,000 shares outstanding priced at $40 a share. Assuming that the new money is invested to earn a fair return, give values for the

a. number of new shares

b. amount of new investment

c. total value of company after issue

d. total number of shares after issue

e. share price after the issue

CHALLENGE

STANDARD
&POOR'S

19. **Standard & Poor's.** Go to Market Insight (**www.mcgrawhill.ca/edumarketinsight**). Click on the "Excel Analytics" icon and review the Monthly Valuation Data Report for Georgia Pacific (GP) and Domtar, Inc. (DTC). Which company has the higher price-earnings ratio? What variables (for example, financial ratios or growth rates) might explain the P/E differential?

20. **Internet.** Jay Ritter's home page (**http://bear.cba.ufl.edu/ritter**) is a mine of information on IPOs. Look up the number of IPOs during the 1999–2000 period and compare this with the number of IPOs during the 2002–2003 period. What is the average first day return on IPOs and money left on the table for the two periods? From his table of "money-left-on-the-table," which company provided the greatest one-day dollar gains to investors?

EXCEL

21. **Venture Capital.** Here is a difficult question. Pickwick Electronics is a new high-tech company financed entirely by one million ordinary shares, all of which are owned by George Pickwick. The firm needs to raise $1 million now for stage one and, assuming all goes well, a further $1 million at the end of 5 years for stage two.

First Cookham Venture Partners is considering two possible financing schemes:

1. Buying two million shares now at their current valuation of $1.
2. Buying one million shares at the current valuation and investing a further $1 million at the end of 5 years at whatever the shares are worth.

The outlook for Pickwick is uncertain, but as long as the company can secure the additional financing for stage two, it will be worth either $2 million or $12 million after completing stage two. (The company will be valueless if it cannot raise the funds for stage two.) Show the possible payoffs for Mr. Pickwick and First Cookham and explain why one scheme might be preferred. Assume an interest rate of zero.

22. **Internet.** In Appendix 14B we provide a flavour of an IPO prospectus, but you can see what an actual prospectus or registration statement looks like by using the System for Electronic Document Analysis and Retrieval (Sedar) Web site at **www.sedar.com** for Canadian companies or the SEC's huge database on **www.freeedgar.com** for U.S. companies. You can also log in to **www.nasdaq.com**, click on "IPOs" to find a company, and then click on "Filings," which will take you to the correct SEC form. Pick a recent prospectus filing of a Canadian company from **www.sedar.com**. On the basis of this prospectus, do you think the stock looks like an attractive investment? Which parts of the statement appear most useful? Which seem the least useful?

Solutions to Check Points

14.1 Unless the firm can secure second-stage financing, it is unlikely to succeed. If the entrepreneur will reap any reward on his own investment, he needs to put in enough effort to get further financing. By accepting only part of the necessary venture capital, management increases its own risk and reduces that of the venture capitalist. This decision would be costly and foolish if management lacked confidence that the project would be successful enough to get past the first stage. A credible signal by management is one that only managers who are truly confident can afford to provide. However, words are cheap and there is little to be lost by *saying* that you are confident (although if you are proved wrong, you may find it difficult to raise money a second time).

14.2 If an investor can distinguish between overpriced and underpriced issues, she will bid only on the underpriced ones. In this case she will purchase only issues that provide a 10 percent gain. However, the ability to distinguish these issues requires considerable insight and research. The return to the informed IPO participant may be viewed as a return on the resources expended to become informed.

14.3

Direct expenses	($ millions)
Underwriting spread = 69 million × $4	276.0
Other expenses	9.2
Total direct expenses	285.2
Underpricing = 69 million × ($70 – $64)	414.0
Total expenses	699.2
Market value of issue = 69 million × $70	4,830.0

Expenses as proportion of market value = 699.2/4,830 = .145 = 14.5%.

14.4 Ten issues of $15 million each will cost about 9 percent of proceeds, or .09 × $150 million = $13.5 million. One issue of $150 million will cost only 4 percent of $150 million, or $6 million.

MINICASE

Mutt.Com was founded in 2000 by two graduates of the University of Wisconsin with help from Georgina Sloberg, who had built up an enviable reputation for backing new start-up businesses. Mutt.Com's user-friendly system was designed to find buyers for unwanted pets. Within 3 years the company was generating revenues of $3.4 million a year, and despite racking up sizable losses, was regarded by investors as one of the hottest new e-commerce businesses. The news that the company was preparing to go public therefore generated considerable excitement.

The company's entire equity capital of 1.5 million shares was owned by the two founders and Ms Sloberg. The initial public offering involved the sale of 500,000 shares by the three existing shareholders, together with the sale of a further 750,000 shares by the company in order to provide funds for expansion.

The company estimated that the issue would involve legal fees, auditing, printing, and other expenses of $1.3 million, which would be shared proportionately between the selling shareholders and the company. In addition, the company agreed to pay the underwriters a spread of $1.25 per share.

The roadshow had confirmed the high level of interest in the issue, and indications from investors suggested that the entire issue could be sold at a price of $24 a share. The underwriters, however, cautioned about being too greedy on price.

They pointed out that indications from investors were not the same as firm orders. Also, they argued, it was much more important to have a successful issue than to have a group of disgruntled shareholders. They therefore suggested an issue price of $18 a share.

That evening Mutt.Com's financial manager decided to run through some calculations. First she worked out the net receipts to the company and the existing shareholders, assuming that the stock was sold for $18 a share. Next she looked at the various costs of the IPO and tried to judge how they stacked up against the typical costs for similar IPOs. That brought her up against the question of underpricing. When she had raised the matter with the underwriters that morning, they had dismissed the notion that the initial day's return on an IPO should be considered part of the issue costs. One of the members of the underwriting team had asked: "The underwriters want to see a high return and a high stock price. Would Mutt.Com prefer a low stock price? Would that make the issue less costly?" Mutt.Com's financial manager was not convinced but felt that she should have a good answer. She wondered whether underpricing was a problem only because the existing shareholders were selling part of their holdings. Perhaps the issue price would not matter if they had not planned to sell.

14.8   APPENDIX 14.A: THE FINANCING OF NEW AND SMALL ENTERPRISES

VENTURE CAPITAL IN CANADA

We saw in Section 14.1 that venture capital is an important source of equity for start-up companies that have the potential to develop into significant economic contributors. Venture capitalists make risky investments with the expectation of earning high rewards if the young ventures become successful. Often, their investments pay off handsomely, as in the case of companies such as Microsoft, Intel, or Research In Motion, which are today established leaders in their respective industries. Of course, venture capitalists may seek to lessen the risk of venture investing in a number of ways. For instance, before making investment decisions, they try to carefully screen the technical and business merits of the proposed company and usually end up investing in only a small percentage of the businesses they review. They also like to actively work with managements of companies they invest in by contributing their business knowledge and experience, gained from helping other companies with similar growth challenges. Often, they diversify their investments by developing a portfolio of young companies in a single venture fund. Many times they will co-invest with other professional venture capital firms in syndicated investment arrangements. In addition, many venture capitalists manage multiple funds together. Table 14.A1 lists some of the important attributes of classic venture capital investing.

TABLE 14.A1
Attributes of classic venture capital investing

1. Create new businesses or expand or revitalize existing ones.
2. The investor, usually the venture capital (VC) fund's general manager and associates, are involved in the management of their portfolio companies, providing a great deal of "value added" to their companies.
3. The *potential* return from the investment is quite large due to investing in high-risk/high-reward situations.
4. Only a few investments are made each year after many candidates have been screened and a handful have been fully analyzed.
5. Negotiate appropriate financial structures using individualized investment instruments.
6. Take a long-term orientation toward their portfolio companies because of the illiquidity of their investments.
7. Try to maximize the growth of their funds since the VC receives, as incentive, compensation as a percentage of the capital gains after return of capital.
8. Venture capitalists often diversify their risk by syndicating their investment with other VC funds.

Based on information in K. W. Rind, "The Role of Venture Capital in Corporate Development," *Strategic Management Journal* (April–June 1981), pp. 169–180.
Source: A. Best and D. Mitra, "The Venture Capital Industry in Canada," *Journal of Small Business Management* (April 1997), Vol. 35, No. 2, pp. 105–110.

TYPES OF VENTURE CAPITAL FUNDS

In Canada, venture capital activity has grown significantly since 1990. For instance, in 1990 there were 34 venture funds with $3.3 billion worth of capital under management. By 2004, the number of venture capital investment firms had grown to 138. Together, these funds had over $20 billion worth of capital under management.

Canada's venture capital funds can be grouped into one of five categories: private independent, labour-sponsored, corporate, government and hybrid.[16] *Private independent firms* typically have no affiliations with any other financial institution. Some large private independent funds have been very active although in recent years the level of activity of this category of funds has slowed somewhat. For instance, in 2004, about $1.7 billion of new capital flowed into the industry across all fund types, with private independent funds attracting $500 million of new capital, far less than the $1.1 billion raised by such funds in 2002. Fund raising was generally quite sluggish in 2004, down by 15 percent from the $2.0 billion of 2003.

Labour-sponsored funds, or retail funds, are venture capital pools formed with the help of provincial and federal governments. These funds were mostly introduced in the late 1980s to facilitate business and economic growth. By 2000, these had about 50 percent of the money invested in the venture capital industry, mainly because of generous tax incentives given to investors in such funds. Despite a decline in investment activity in recent years, these funds were the largest investors when compared with all other categories until 2003. However, in 2004, their share of capital under management dropped to third place at 21 percent. Currently, investors receive a 15 percent tax credit from both the federal government and participating provincial governments. Moreover, the investment is Registered Retirement Savings Plan (RRSP) eligible, and, therefore, provides the investor an additional tax benefit in the form of a tax deferral depending on her income level. Labour-sponsored funds are structured in a similar fashion to mutual funds. Individuals are able to buy shares in the fund, allowing investment by those who are not wealthy. The fund pools the money with the objective

[16] These classifications are used by Canada's Venture Capital and Private Equity Association (CVCA) to provide periodic reports on venture capital activity. The reports are available on its Web site at **www.cvca.ca**. Data for these reports is often compiled by Macdonald and Associates Ltd., which is the best-known data source on Canadian venture capital activity.

[17] Recently, Macdonald and Associates has created a new category, namely "provincial venture capital corporations," which operate primarily in British Columbia and Québec.

of investing in enterprises that have yet to go public instead of purchasing stocks and bonds. Three large and active labour-sponsored funds are GrowthWorks, Fonds de Solidarité du Travailleurs du Québec, and Triax Growth Fund.[17]

A number of *corporate venture capital funds* also exist in Canada. These could include financial corporation funds, which tend to be venture capital affiliates or subsidiaries set up by large Canadian banks. For instance, RBC Capital Partners is a subsidiary of the RBC Financial Group. The financial institution can provide a range of financial services to entrepreneurs and enhance their credibility with suppliers and customers. You could also have subsidiaries of large manufacturing companies such as Dow Chemical Corporate Venture Capital, or subsidiaries of utility and power corporations such as Hydro-Québec Capitech Inc. Goals of corporate venture capital funds tend to be strategically tied to the parent organization; they often prefer to invest in ventures that will give them access to new technologies or provide a competitive advantage. For instance, Chrysalix Energy LP is an early-stage venture capital firm focusing on fuel cell and related fuelling technology companies and was formed jointly by Ballard Power Systems and several large multinational companies such as Boeing, Mitsubishi Corporation, and Shell Hydrogen.

Federal or provincial governments run government funds by employing professional venture capital fund managers. For instance, the federal Business Development Corporation (BDC) has an active venture capital division that, for the end of fiscal year March, 2004, had a total commitment of venture capital investments of $491 million. The BDC has focused on using venture capital to generate growth in new economy industries such as biotechnology, medical/health-related, information technology, and electronics. Much of the financing goes to companies in early stages of development and considered to be high risk. Some crown corporations such as Export Development Canada have venture capital operations as well. Provincial governments have also sponsored their own funds with goals of nurturing small businesses and also providing financing to high-technology firms, for instance, Crown Investments Corporation of Saskatchewan.

Hybrid funds can be formed jointly by the government and private investors or in response to a government incentive. Until recently, Halifax-based ACF Equity Atlantic Inc. was a hybrid fund. Government and hybrid funds have profit-maximizing objectives similar to private and labour-sponsored funds.

Table 14.A2 lists some Canadian venture capital funds and describes their investment preferences.

STAGES OF DEVELOPMENT FINANCED BY CANADIAN VENTURE CAPITAL FIRMS

New enterprises can be at different stages of development. Described below are some of the stages firms may go through after they are started.

- *Seed Stage*: the very early stage when the new enterprise may seek to test a concept or build a product prototype and develop a product.
- *Start-Up Stage*: the enterprise may have a product being developed, but not yet marketed and sold commercially.
- *Expansion Stage*: the firm requires significant capital for plant expansion, marketing, and initiation of full commercial production and sales.
- *Acquisition/Buyout Stage*: the management of the firm acquires a product line, a division, or a company.
- *Turnaround Stage*: the firm was once profitable but is now earning less than its cost of capital.

Generally the seed and start-up stages are considered to be the early stages of development. During their life cycle, all firms will go through the seed, start-up, and expansion stages, but not all will experience the buyout or turnaround stages. From Table 14.A3, we see that Canadian venture capital firms tend to finance enterprises across different stages of development. Over $871 million, or roughly 49 percent of all investments, went to financing 324 early-stage enterprises including seed, start-up, and other early-stage firms in 2004. In total, these young companies represented 53

TABLE 14.A2
Some representative Canadian venture capital firms

Firm	Type of Firm	Capital under Management ($ millions)	Geographic Preference	Industry Preference
ACF Equity Atlantic Inc.	Private venture capital fund[1]	$30	Within Canada	Information technology, life science, and other technologies. Businesses not considered are real estate and retail.
Ventures West Management Inc.	Private venture capital fund	$600	Within Canada	Information technology, life science, and other technologies
GrowthWorks	Labour-sponsored venture capital fund	$774	Within Canada	All sectors except real estate
Hydro-Québec CapiTech Inc.	Corporate investor (100% owned by Hydro-Quebec)	$240	Canada	Energy technologies or related products. Businesses excluded: non-energy-related technologies
Scotia Merchant Capital Corporation	Bank (Wholly owned by Bank of Nova Scotia)	$250	Canada or USA	Businesses excluded: Real estate, mining, oil & gas

Source: CVCA—Canada's Venture Capital & Private Equity Association and Macdonald & Associates Ltd.
[1] Until very recently, this fund was classified as a hybrid fund.

percent of the aggregate. In 2003 and 2004, compared with past years, there was a higher emphasis on new ventures or those in early stages of development. For instance, in 2002 early-stage firms obtained 44 percent of all disbursements, whereas in 2003 early-stage firms received 50 percent of all disbursements. Some recent examples of big early-stage deals include BelAir Networks, Q1 Labs, and Xanthus Life Sciences. Follow-on and expansion-stage investments amounted to about $754 million, or 43 percent of all disbursements, received by 228 firms in 2004. This was slightly lower than 2003, where expansion stage firms received 46 percent of the total disbursement. Unlike in the United States, where expansion and later-stage transactions have been gaining momentum, in Canada such investments have been proportionately less.

TABLE 14.A3
Venture capital investment activity by stage of development in 2003 and 2004

Stage	2004 Amount ($ millions)	2004 Percentage of Total	2003 Amount ($ millions)	2003 Percentage of Total
Early Stage	871	49	836	50
Expansion	754	43	762	46
Acquisition/Buyout	83	5	27	2
Turnaround	16	1	18	1
Other	38	2	19	1
Total	**1,762**	**100**	**1,662**	**100**

Source: CVCA—Canada's Venture Capital & Private Equity Association and Macdonald & Associates Ltd.

RECENT VENTURE CAPITAL INVESTMENT ACTIVITY

Just a few years ago, Canada's venture capital firms had been very active, with record investments of $5.8 billion in 2000 disbursed to 1,006 companies.[18] Since then, investment activity has considerably declined and, in 2004, a little under $1.76 billion was disbursed to 612 firms. Table 14.A4 provides sector-wise details regarding where the venture capital firms invested in 2004. We see that 82 percent of the investing has focussed on large deals involving technology companies, particularly in life sciences, computer and Internet-related sectors, communications, and electronics. Topping the list were firms in the information technology sector, accounting for 258 companies that absorbed about $900 million or 52 percent of total disbursement. In this sector, firms in software and semiconductor-related sectors received $398 million, followed by those in the communications industry with $350 million, while firms in the electronics and computer hardware industry received $80 million. Biotechnology and health science firms received 25 percent representing 118 firms. Companies in traditional industries such as manufacturing or consumer-related received only 18 percent of venture capital investments.

Table 14.A5 provides details on the top 10 venture capital deals for 2003. Notice the very large amounts invested in some life science firms. However, there were only a few such mega deals in 2003; in fact, only 43 of these amounted to $10 million or more. On average, the size of financing was much less, at $2.4 million in 2003, and well below the average of $3.7 million for 2002. About $660 million, or 44 percent of the total invested, went to 165 Ontario-based firms, particularly to technology-intensive enterprises in the Greater Toronto and Ottawa Valley regions. Quebec-based companies captured the second largest portion of total spending—about 39 percent.

TABLE 14.A4
Venture capital investment activity by sector

Stage	2004 Amount ($ millions)	2004 Percentage of Total	2003 Amount ($ millions)	2003 Percentage of Total
Technology				
Biotechnology	334	19	345	21
Medical/Health Related	111	6	96	6
Communications	350	20	228	14
Electronics and Computer Hardware	80	4.5	141	8
Internet Related	69	4	88	5
Software & Semiconductors	398	23	412	25
Others	96	5.5	58	3
Total	**1,438**	**82**	**1,368**	**82**
Traditional				
Consumer Related	149	8	164	10
Manufacturing	118	7	43	3
Miscellaneous	56	3	88	5
Total	**323**	**18**	**295**	**18**
TOTAL	**1,761**	**100**	**$ 1,663**	**100**

Source: CVCA—Canada's Venture Capital & Private Equity Association and Macdonald & Associates Ltd.

[18] In contrast, the American venture capital industry reported a 14.8 percent increase in investment activity in 2004 from the previous year, with investments totalling $20.9 billion (US) disbursed to 2,876 company deals. This increase in investment activity reversed a period of yearly declines that culminated in a six-year low of $18.9 billion (US) in 2003. For more information on venture capital activity in the United States, go the National Venture Capital Association Web site at **www.nvca.ca**.

TABLE 14.A5

Top 10 venture capital deals in 2003

Rank 2003		Invested $000s	Sector	Investors
1	NeuroMed Technologies Inc., Vancouver	44,800	Neurological disorder drugs	BDC Venture Capital, Cogene Biotech Ventures, GrowthWorks, MDS Capital, MPM Capital, Neuro Discovery, RBC Capital Partners, TriFund Capital (VCC)
2	Xanthus Life Sciences Inc., Montreal	43,120	Anti-cancer medicines	CDIB BioScience Ventures, CDP Capital, China Development Indust. Bank, GeneChem, GIMV NV, Hambrecht & Quist, Healthcare Ventures, Kestrel Mgmt., Oxford Bioscience, Yasuda, Still River
3	Tropic Networks Inc., Ottawa	30,000	Optical IP services	Celtic House Venture Partners, Crescendo Ventures, Goldman Sachs Canada, Kodiac Venture Partners, Teachers' Merchant Bank
4	Medicago Inc., Sainte-Foy, Que.	28,000	Plant biology	Innovatech Québec et Chaudière-Appalaches, Investissement Québec, Société générale de financement du Québec and others
5	Engim Canada, Kanata, Ont.	27,750	Wireless technology	Adams Street Partners, Benchmark Capital, Bessemer Venture Partners, Matrix Partners
6	Silicon Optix Inc., Toronto	25,200	Warping integrated circuits	Canaan Partners, Firsthand Capital, Focus Ventures, Origin Partners, Polaris Venture Partners, Primaxis Technology Venutres
7	Axcan Pharma Inc., Saint-Hilaire, Que.	22,110	Gastroenterology products	Fonds de solidarité des travailleurs du Québec (FTQ)
8	BelAir Networks, Kanata, Ont.	21,000	Mobile networking	BDC Venture Capital, JPMorgan Partners, VenGrowth Capital Partners and others
9	YottaYotta Inc., Edmonton	21,000	Data hardware	Bank of America Investment, Bombardier Trust UK, Grosvenor Venture Partners III, Optical Capital, TechnoCap, Technology Partnerships Canada
10	Adherex Technologies Inc., Ottawa	21,000	Therapeutic products	HBM Bioventures, OrbiMed Advisors, VenGrowth Capital Partners

Source: *National Post Business*, June 2004, p. 180.

VENTURE CAPITAL EXITS

Venture capitalists provide a combination of unique services to companies in which they invest. In addition to financial capital they also help with a variety of advisory services. The investee firm also benefits indirectly when a reputed venture capital organization invests in it. By making the investment, the venture capitalist is, in a sense, signalling its approval of the firm's business plan, growth and profit potential, and future prospects. Once information gets out about the venture capitalist's interest in the firm, other service providers such as advertisement agencies or accounting firms also become eager to do business with the firm and are, often, willing to provide significant discounts on fees and other charges during its early-growth phase. As the investee firm matures and becomes more established, the value of services provided to it by the venture capitalist diminishes. It becomes important, therefore, for the venture capitalist to exit from the firm and to recycle its investment into another young venture.[19]

---

[19] For further discussion, see B.S. Black and R. J. Gilson (1998). "Venture Capital and the Structure of Capital Markets: Banks versus Stock Markets," *Journal of Financial Economics*, Vol. 47, 243–277.

The venture capitalist can exit from an investment through a variety of means including (a) acquisition by a third party, (b) company buyback by the entrepreneur, (c) initial public offering, (d) merger with another entity and, in the event that all other options fail, (e) write-off. According to a recent study, company buybacks by entrepreneur/managers from venture capitalists appear to be the predominant mode of venture capital exits in Canada followed by initial public offerings.[20] Acquisition by a third party is also a popular exit route. Unfortunately, a sizeable number of exits occur through write-offs as well. The average duration of successful venture capital investments before exiting through a company buyback or an initial public offering is close to six years. Venture capitalists appear to be able to spot failures earlier on; the average duration of investments that are written off is a little over four years.

ANGEL INVESTING

Although the organized venture capital industry plays an important role in the creation of new ventures, those seeking very early-stage financing for small and new enterprises often have to resort to informal financing sources. In this context, wealthy individual investors, known as angels, can play a critical role by making small-scale investments in local start-ups and early-stage ventures, and by bringing a significant hands-on contribution to such business ventures.

The angel investor, typically a millionaire or a multimillionaire, may invest on average between $100,000 and $250,000 in a start-up, and prefers to be involved with the project. According to some estimates, there are about 200,000 angel investors in Canada.[21] Angels can play either *active* or *passive* roles in the investee firms. "Active" angels are often highly motivated ex-entrepreneurs who are skilled at picking good management teams and good ideas. They help companies arrange additional financing, hire top management, and recruit knowledgeable board members. "Passive" angels provide only money and rarely monitor the firm closely; they are often part of an informal network led by one or more active angels who find deals and manage the investments. A number of organized services exist that are designed to match angel investors with entrepreneurs looking to fund their new ventures. These angel-network services include Ottawa Capital Network, VentureDrive.com, the Montreal-based InvestAngel Network, the Ottawa-based eValhalla.com, and Angel Investors Canada, which is the Toronto chapter of the International Angel Investors Group.

OTHER SOURCES OF SMALL BUSINESS FINANCING

FINANCING UNDER THE CANADA SMALL BUSINESS FINANCING ACT[22]

These are term loans and capital leases of up to 10 years available through all chartered banks, most credit unions and caisses populaires, and many trust and insurance companies, and are guaranteed by the federal government if taken for specific purposes and limits. The loans or leases are available under the federal government's Canada Small Business Financing Act (CSBFA) to small businesses in Canada that have gross revenues of $5 million or less in the year of application for the loan. The loans can be used to finance up to 90 percent of the purchase or improvement of eligible assets such as land, premises, and equipment. The loans cannot be used to buy shares or provide working capital. Capital leases (with an option to purchase) can be used to finance the cost of a variety of new and used equipment including vehicles, hotel and restaurant equipment, medical and health services equipment, computer hardware and software, telecommunications, and

---

[20] See D.J. Cummings and J.G. MacIntosh "A Cross-Country Comparison of Full and Partial Venture Capital Exits," *Journal of Banking and Finance* 27 (2003), pp. 511–548.

[21] See, for instance, *The Globe and Mail* "Startups Angle for Angels" (June 29, 2000), p. T1.

[22] Details are available at the Industry Canada Web site, **http://strategis.ic.gc.ca**.

manufacturing equipment. CSBFA loans and leases are made to small businesses in a variety of industries such as communication, construction, manufacturing, transportation, and wholesale trade. The loans and leases are not available to farming, charitable, or religious enterprises.

BUSINESS DEVELOPMENT BANK OF CANADA

The Business Development Bank of Canada (BDC) is a Crown financial institution that specializes in providing financial and other support services to small- and medium-sized businesses in Canada. BDC's major activities include term lending, giving loan guarantees, and providing venture capital financing. It is also involved in lease financing and providing consultancy services. As of the fiscal year ending March 2004, BDC had over 22,900 customers to whom the total financing committed exceeded $8.8 billion. During the fiscal year March 2004, total financing authorized had reached a record $2.1 billion. In recent years, BDC supports new ventures in fields such as medical technologies, telecommunications, information technology etc. BDC continued to provide financing in support of new ventures with direct investment of $87 million as of the fiscal year ending March 2004. It also plays an active role in the First Peoples' market and in supporting female entrepreneurs.

REGIONAL AND PROVINCIAL LENDING PROGRAMS

There are a number of regional agencies across Canada that have lending and other assistance programs, designed to nurture and grow small businesses. Some of the important regional agencies and initiatives include Atlantic Canada Opportunities Agency (ACOA), Federal Economic Development Initiative in Northern Ontario (FedNor); Canada Economic Development for Québec Regions: Financing; and Western Economic Diversification Canada: Financing. For descriptions of such agencies and details regarding the services provided by them, go to the Industry Canada Web site at **http://strategis.ic.gc.ca**.

Practice Problems

1. **Internet.** This chapter has provided Web site information for several venture capital sources and angel investing networks. Use the Internet to explore these Web sites. Also, see whether you can identify other interesting Web sites that will provide useful information on venture capital and angel investing activity.

2. **Venture Capital.** Based on your Internet research in question 1, can you answer the following?
   a. We described different types of venture capital funds that exist in Canada. What are the main differences in investment goals and characteristics between these funds? Do some types of funds appear to participate more in earlier stage financing than others?
   b. Do some venture capitalists appear to specialize by investing in only a few selected industries, while others are more diversified in their investment activity? Can you think of some good reasons for firms pursuing either of the two strategies?
   c. Venture capitalists have geographical preferences for their investment activity. Can you discern some common motivations for such preferences?

3. **Venture Capital and Angel Investing.** Venture capitalists and many angel investors are often actively involved with the ventures in which they invest. How does this benefit the entrepreneur? Does this benefit the venture capitalist and angel investor as well?

4. **Internet.** To find out what is happening in the venture capital industry in the United States, look at the recent news on **www.ventureeconomics.com**. Now click on "Statistics" and look at the recent U.S. national data. How does the level of deals compare with the boom year of 2000? Which industries are attracting the most venture capital? Is the money going into new start-ups or expansion of existing businesses?

14.9

APPENDIX 14.B: HOTCH POT'S NEW ISSUE PROSPECTUS[23]

PROSPECTUS

800,000 Shares
Hotch Pot, Inc.
Common Stock

Of the 800,000 shares of Common Stock offered hereby, 500,000 shares are being sold by the Company and 300,000 shares are being sold by the Selling Shareholders. See "Principal and Selling Shareholders." The Company will not receive any of the proceeds from the sale of shares by the Selling Shareholders.

Before this offering there has been no public market for the Common Stock. **These securities involve a high degree of risk. See "Certain Factors."**

THESE SECURITIES HAVE NOT BEEN APPROVED OR DISAPPROVED BY A SECURITIES COMMISSION NOR HAS ANY COMMISSION PASSED ON THE ACCURACY OR ADEQUACY OF THIS PROSPECTUS. ANY REPRESENTATION TO THE CONTRARY IS A CRIMINAL OFFENSE.

	Price to Public	Underwriting Discount	Proceeds to Company[1]	Proceeds to Selling Shareholders
Per share	$12.00	$1.30	$10.70	$10.70
Total	$9,600,000	$1,040,000	$5,350,000	$3,210,000

[1] Before deducting expenses payable by the Company estimated at $400,000, of which $250,000 will be paid by the Company and $150,000 by the Selling Stockholders.

The Common Shares are offered, subject to prior sale, when, as, and if delivered to and accepted by the Underwriters and subject to approval of certain legal matters by their counsel and by counsel for the Company and the Selling Shareholders. The Underwriters reserve the right to withdraw, cancel, or modify such offers and reject orders in whole or in part.

Silverman Pinch Inc.   **April 1, 2004**

No person has been authorized to give any information or to make any representations, other than as contained therein, in connection with the offer contained in this Prospectus, and, if given or made, such information or representations must not be relied upon. This Prospectus does not constitute an offer of any securities other than the registered securities to which it relates or an offer to any person in any jurisdiction where such an offer would be unlawful. The delivery of this Prospectus at any time does not imply that information herein is correct as of any time subsequent to its date.

IN CONNECTION WITH THIS OFFERING, THE UNDERWRITER MAY OVER ALLOT OR EFFECT TRANSACTIONS WHICH STABILIZE OR MAINTAIN THE MARKET PRICE OF THE COMMON SHARES OF THE COMPANY AT A LEVEL ABOVE THAT WHICH MIGHT OTHERWISE PREVAIL IN THE OPEN MARKET. SUCH STABILIZING, IF COMMENCED, MAY BE DISCONTINUED AT ANY TIME.

---

[23] Most prospectuses have content similar to that of the Hotch Pot prospectus but go into considerably more detail. Also, we have omitted from the Hotch Pot prospectus the company's financial statements. You can get a better impression of the contents of a prospectus by looking at some real ones. These are available at the system for Electronic Document Analysis and Retrieval (SEDAR) Web site at **www.sedar.com**. For instance, you can read the preliminary prospectus of Ripple Lake Diamonds Inc., which was filed on August 26, 2004.

PROSPECTUS SUMMARY

The following summary information is qualified in its entirety by the detailed information and financial statements appearing elsewhere in this Prospectus.

The Company: Hotch Pot, Inc. operates a chain of 140 fast food outlets in Canada, offering unusual combinations of dishes.

The Offering: Common Shares offered by the Company 500,000 shares;
Common Shares offered by the Selling Shareholders 300,000 shares;
Common Shares to be outstanding after this offering 3,500,000 shares.

Use of Proceeds: For the construction of new restaurants and to provide working capital.

THE COMPANY

Hotch Pot, Inc. operates a chain of 140 fast food outlets in Ontario, Québec, and British Columbia. These restaurants specialize in offering an unusual combination of foreign dishes.

The Company was organized in Ontario in 1994.

USE OF PROCEEDS

The Company intends to use the net proceeds from the sale of 500,000 shares of Common Stock offered hereby, estimated at approximately $5 million, to open new outlets in the Atlantic provinces and to provide additional working capital. It has no immediate plans to use any of the net proceeds of the offering for any other specific investment.

DIVIDEND POLICY

The company has not paid cash dividends on its Common Stock and does not anticipate that dividends will be paid on the Common Stock in the foreseeable future.

CERTAIN FACTORS

Investment in the Common Stock involves a high degree of risk. The following factors should be carefully considered in evaluating the Company:

Substantial Capital Needs.   The Company will require additional financing to continue its expansion policy. The Company believes that its relations with its lenders are good, but there can be no assurance that additional financing will be available in the future.

Competition.   The Company is in competition with a number of restaurant chains supplying fast food. Many of these companies are substantially larger and better capitalized than the Company.

CAPITALIZATION

The following table sets forth the capitalization of the Company as of December 31, 2003, and is adjusted to reflect the sale of 500,000 shares of Common Stock by the Company.

	Actual	As Adjusted
	($ 000s)	
Long-term debt	$ —	$ —
Stockholders' equity		
Common shares: 3,000,000 shares outstanding,	2,000	7,350
3,500,000 shares outstanding, as adjusted		
Retained earnings	3,200	3,200
Total shareholders' equity	5,200	10,550
Total capitalization	$ 5,200	$10,550

SELECTED FINANCIAL DATA

[The Prospectus typically includes a summary income statement and balance sheet.]

MANAGEMENT'S ANALYSIS OF RESULTS OF OPERATIONS AND FINANCIAL CONDITION

Revenue growth for the year ended December 31, 2003, resulted from the opening of 10 new restaurants in the Company's existing geographic area and from sales of a new range of desserts, notably crêpe suzette with custard. Sales per customer increased by 20% and this contributed to the improvement in margins.

During the year the Company borrowed $600,000 from its banks at an interest rate of 2% above the prime rate.

BUSINESS

Hotch Pot, Inc. operates a chain of 140 fast food outlets in Ontario, Québec, and British Columbia. These restaurants specialize in offering an unusual combination of international dishes. Fifty percent of the company's revenues were derived from the sale of two dishes, sushi and sauerkraut, and curry bolognese. All dishes are prepared in three regional centres and then frozen and distributed to the individual restaurants.

MANAGEMENT

The following table sets forth information regarding the Company's directors, executive officers, and key employees:

Name	Age	Position
Emma Lucullus	28	President, Chief Executive Officer, and Director
Ed Lucullus	33	Treasurer & Director

Emma Lucullus   Emma Lucullus established the Company in 1994 and has been its Chief Executive Officer since that date.

Ed Lucullus   Ed Lucullus has been employed by the Company since 1994.

EXECUTIVE COMPENSATION

The following table sets forth the cash compensation paid for services rendered for the year 2003 by the executive officers:

Name	Capacity	Cash Compensation
Emma Lucullus	President and Chief Executive Officer	$ 130,000
Ed Lucullus	Treasurer	$ 95,000

CERTAIN TRANSACTIONS

At various times between 1994 and 2003, First Cookham Venture Partners invested a total of $1.5 million in the Company. In connection with this investment, First Cookham Venture Partners was granted certain rights to registration under the Ontario Securities Act, including the right to have their shares of Common Stock registered at the Company's expense with the Ontario Securities Commission.

PRINCIPAL AND SELLING STOCKHOLDERS

The following table sets forth certain information regarding the beneficial ownership of the Company's voting Common Stock as of the date of this prospectus by (i) each person known by the Company to be the beneficial owner of more than 5% of its voting Common Stock, and (ii) each director of the Company who beneficially owns voting Common Stock. Unless otherwise indicated, each owner has sole voting and dispositive power over his or her shares.

Name of Beneficial Owner	Shares Beneficially Owned prior to Offering		Shares to Be Sold	Shares Beneficially Owned after Offering	
	Number	Percent		Number	Percent
Emma Lucullus	400,000	13.3	25,000	375,000	10.7
Ed Lucullus	400,000	13.3	25,000	375,000	10.7
First Cookham Venture Partners	1,700,000	56.7	250,000	1,450,000	41.4
Hermione Kraft	200,000	6.7	—	200,000	5.7

DESCRIPTION OF CAPITAL STOCK

The Company's authorized capital stock consists of 10,000,000 shares of voting Common Stock.

As of the date of this Prospectus, there are four holders of record of the Common Stock.

Under the terms of one of the Company's loan agreements, the Company may not pay cash dividends on Common Stock except from net profits without the written consent of the lender.

UNDERWRITING

Subject to the terms and conditions set forth in the Underwriting Agreement, the Underwriter, Silverman Pinch, Inc., has agreed to purchase from the Company and the Selling Stockholders 800,000 shares of Common Stock.

There is no public market for the Common Stock. The price to the public for the Common Stock was determined by negotiation between the Company and the Underwriter, and was based on, among other things, the Company's financial and operating history and condition, its prospects, and the prospects for its industry in general, the management of the Company, and the market prices of securities for companies in businesses similar to that of the Company.

LEGAL MATTERS

The validity of the shares of Common Stock offered by the Prospectus is being passed on for the Company by Blair, Kohl, and Chirac, and for the Underwriter by Chretien Howard.

LEGAL PROCEEDINGS

Hotch Pot was served in January 2004 with a summons and complaint in an action commenced by a customer who alleged that consumption of the Company's products caused severe nausea and loss of feeling in both feet. The Company believes that the complaint is without foundation.

EXPERTS

The consolidated financial statements of the Company have been so included in reliance on the reports of Hooper Firebrand, independent accountants, given on the authority of that firm as experts in auditing and accounting.

FINANCIAL STATEMENTS

[*Text and tables omitted.*]

PART FIVE

Capital Structure and Dividend Policy

THE CAPITAL STRUCTURE DECISION

A firm's basic financial resource is the stream of cash flows produced by its assets and operations. When the firm is financed entirely by common stock, all those cash flows belong to the shareholders. When it issues both debt and equity, the firm splits the cash flows into two streams, a relatively safe stream that goes to the debtholders and a more risky one that goes to the shareholders.

The firm's mix of securities is known as its capital structure. Look at Table 15.6. You can see that in some industries companies borrow much more heavily than in others. Most high-tech firms, such as Research In Motion and Ballard Power, rely almost wholly on equity finance, as do most biotech, software, and Internet companies. At the other extreme, debt accounts for a substantial part of the market value of retailers, utilities, and banks. For instance, ATCO's total debt is higher than its total equity.

Capital structure is not immutable. Firms change their capital structure, sometimes almost overnight. For instance, Alliance Atlantis Communications recently announced a $131.5 million offering of Class B non-voting common shares that will be used to pay down some of the firm's debt. In the 1990s, DuPont Canada generated large amounts of cash flows and used the money to pay off its long-term debt. Later in the chapter you will see how an American company, Sealed Air Corporation, benefited from changing its capital structure.

Shareholders want management to choose the mix of securities that maximizes firm value. But does this optimal capital structure exist? We must consider the possibility that no combination has any greater appeal than any other. Perhaps the really important decisions concern the company's assets, and decisions about capital structure are mere details—matters to be attended to but not worried about.

In the first part of the chapter, we will look at examples in which capital structure doesn't matter. After that we will put back some of the things that *do* make a difference, such as taxes, bankruptcy, and the signals that your financing decisions may send to investors. At the end of the chapter, we will draw up a checklist for financial managers who need to decide on the firm's capital structure.

After studying this chapter you should be able to
- Analyze the effect of debt finance on the risk and required return of equityholders.
- Appreciate the advantages and disadvantages of debt finance.
- Cite the various costs of financial distress.
- Explain why the debt-equity mix varies across firms and across industries.

15.1   HOW BORROWING AFFECTS VALUE IN A TAX-FREE ECONOMY

It is after the ball game and the pizza man is delivering a pizza to Yogi Berra. "Should I cut it into four slices as usual, Yogi?" asks the pizza man. "No," replies Yogi, "Cut it into eight; I'm hungry tonight."

capital structure   A firm's mix of long-term financing.

If you understand why more slices won't sate Yogi's appetite, you will have no difficulty understanding why a company's choice of **capital structure** can't increase the underlying value of the cash flows generated by its real assets and operations.

Think of a simple balance sheet with all entries expressed as current market values:

Assets	Liabilities and Stockholders' Equity
Value of cash flows from the firm's real assets and operations	Market value of debt
	Market value of equity
Value of firm	Value of firm

The right- and left-hand sides of a balance sheet are always equal. (Balance sheets have to balance!) Therefore, if you add up the market value of all the firm's debt and equity securities, you can calculate the value of the future cash flows from the real assets and operations.

In fact the value of those cash flows determines the value of the firm and therefore determines the aggregate value of all the firm's outstanding debt and equity securities. If the firm changes its capital structure, say by using more debt and less equity financing, overall value should not change.

Think of the left-hand side of the balance sheet as the size of the pizza; the right-hand side determines how it is sliced. A company can slice its cash flow into as many parts as it likes, but the value of those parts will always sum back to the value of the unsliced cash flow. (Of course, we have to make sure that none of the cash flow stream is lost in the slicing. We cannot say that the value of a pizza is independent of how it is sliced if the slicer is also a nibbler.)

The basic idea here (the value of a pizza does not depend on how it is sliced) has various applications. Yogi Berra got friendly chuckles for his misapplication. Franco Modigliani and Merton Miller received Nobel prizes for applying it to corporate financing. Modigliani and Miller, always referred to as "MM," showed in 1958 that the value of a firm does not depend on how its cash flows are "sliced." More precisely, they demonstrated the following proposition:

> When there are no taxes and well-functioning capital markets exist, the market value of a company does not depend on its capital structure. In other words, financial managers cannot increase value by changing the mix of securities used to finance the company.

Of course this MM proposition rests on some important simplifying assumptions. For example, capital markets have to be "well functioning." That means that investors can trade securities without restrictions and can borrow or lend on the same terms as the firm. It also means that capital markets are efficient, so that securities are fairly priced given the information available to investors. (We discussed market efficiency in Chapter 6.) MM's proposition also assumes that there are no distorting taxes, and it ignores the costs encountered if a firm borrows too much and lands in financial distress.

The firm's capital structure decision can matter if these assumptions are not true or if other practical complications are encountered. But the best way to start thinking about capital structure is to work through MM's argument. *To keep things as simple as possible, we will ignore taxes until further notice.*

MM'S ARGUMENT

Cleo, the president of River Cruises, is reviewing the firm's capital structure with Antony, the financial manager. Table 15.1 shows the current position. The company has no debt and all its operating income is paid as dividends to the shareholders. The *expected* earnings and dividends per share are $1.25, but this figure is by no means certain—it could turn out to be more or less than $1.25. For example, earnings could fall to $.75 in a slump, or they could jump to $1.75 in a boom.

The price of each share is $10. The firm expects to produce a level stream of earnings and dividends in perpetuity. With no growth forecast, shareholders' expected return is equal to the dividend yield—that is, the expected dividend per share divided by the price, $1.25/$10 = .125, or 12.5 percent.

Cleo has come to the conclusion that shareholders would be better off if the company had equal proportions of debt and equity. She therefore proposes to issue $500,000 of debt at an interest rate of 10 percent and to use the proceeds to repurchase 50,000 shares. This is called a **restructuring**. Notice that the $500,000 raised by the new borrowing does not stay in the firm. It goes right out the door to shareholders in order to repurchase and retire 50,000 shares. Therefore, the assets and investment policy of the firm are not affected. Only the financing mix changes.

What would MM say about this new capital structure? Suppose the change is made. Operating income is the same, so the value of the "pie" is fixed at $1 million. With $500,000 in new debt outstanding, the remaining common shares must be worth $500,000, that is, 50,000 shares at $10 per share. The total value of the debt and equity is still $1 million.

Since the value of the firm is the same, common shareholders are no better or worse off than before. River Cruises' shares still trade at $10 each. The overall value of River Cruises' equity falls from $1 million to $500,000, but shareholders have also received $500,000 in cash.

Antony points all this out. "The restructuring doesn't make our shareholders any richer or poorer, Cleo. Why bother? Capital structure doesn't matter."

restructuring   Process of changing the firm's capital structure without changing its assets.

✓ Check Point 15.1

Suppose River Cruises issues $350,000 of new debt (rather than $500,000) and uses the proceeds to repurchase and retire common stock. How does this affect price per share? How many shares will be left outstanding?

TABLE 15.1
River Cruises is entirely equity financed. Although it expects to have an income of $125,000 in perpetuity, this income is not certain. This table shows the return to the shareholders under different assumptions about operating income. No taxes are assumed.

Data			
Number of shares	100,000		
Price per share	$10		
Market value of shares	$1 million		

	State of the Economy		
	Slump	Normal	Boom
Operating income	$75,000	125,000	175,000
Earnings per share	$.75	1.25	1.75
Return on shares	7.5%	12.5%	17.5%
		Expected outcome	

TABLE 15.2
River Cruises is wondering whether to issue $500,000 of debt at an interest rate of 10 percent and repurchase 50,000 shares. This table shows the return to the shareholder under different assumptions about operating income. Returns to shareholders are increased in normal and boom times but fall in slumps.

Data	
Number of shares	50,000
Price per share	$10
Market value of shares	$500,000
Market value of debt	$500,000

Outcomes			
	State of the Economy		
	Slump	Normal	Boom
Operating income	$75,000	125,000	175,000
Interest	$50,000	50,000	50,000
Equity earnings	$25,000	75,000	125,000
Earnings per share	$.50	1.50	2.50
Return on shares	5%	15%	25%
		Expected outcome	

HOW BORROWING AFFECTS EARNINGS PER SHARE

Cleo is unconvinced. She prepares Table 15.2 and Figure 15.1 to show how borrowing $500,000 could increase earnings per share. Comparison of tables 15.1 and 15.2 shows that "normal" earnings per share increase to $1.50 (versus $1.25) after the restructuring. Table 15.2 also shows more "upside" (earnings per share of $2.50 versus $1.75) and more "downside" ($.50 versus $.75).

The blue line in Figure 15.1 shows how earnings per share would vary with operating income under the firm's current all-equity financing. It is therefore simply a plot of the data in Table 15.1. The gold line shows how earnings per share would vary if the company moves to equal proportions of debt and equity. It is therefore a plot of the data in Table 15.2.

Cleo reasons as follows: "It is clear that debt could either increase or reduce the return to the equityholder. In a slump the return to the equityholder is reduced by the use of debt, but otherwise it is increased. We could be heading for a recession, but it doesn't look likely. Maybe we could help our shareholders by going ahead with the debt issue."

As financial manager, Antony replies as follows: "I agree that borrowing will increase earnings per share as long as there's no slump. But we're not really doing anything for shareholders

FIGURE 15.1
Borrowing increases River Cruises' earnings per share (EPS) when operating income is greater than $100,000 but reduces it when operating income is less than $100,000. Expected EPS rises from $1.25 to $1.50.

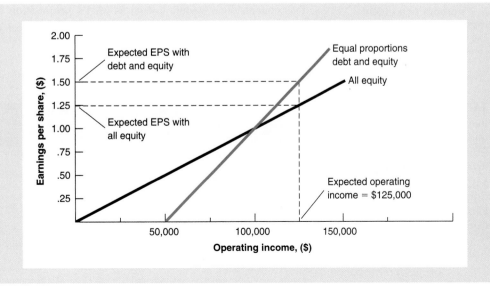

TABLE 15.3
Individual investors can replicate River Cruises' borrowing by borrowing on their own. In this example, it is assumed that River Cruises has not restructured. However, the investor can put up $10 of her own money, borrow $10 more, and buy two shares at $10 apiece. This generates the same rates of return as in Table 15.2.

	State of the Economy		
	Slump	Normal	Boom
Earnings on two shares	$1.50	2.50	3.50
Less interest at 10%	$1.00	1.00	1.00
Net earnings on investment	$ .50	1.50	2.50
Return on $10 investment	5%	15%	25%
		Expected outcome	

that they can't do on their own. Suppose River Cruises does not borrow. In that case an investor could go to the bank, borrow $10, and then invest $20 in two shares. Such an investor would put up only $10 of her own money. (Table 15.3 shows how the payoffs on this $10 investment vary with River Cruises' operating income.) You can see that these payoffs are exactly the same as the investor would get by buying one share in the company after the restructuring. (Compare the last two lines of tables 15.2 and 15.3.) It makes no difference whether shareholders borrow directly or whether River Cruises borrows on their behalf. Therefore, if River Cruises goes ahead and borrows, it will not allow investors to do anything that they could not do already, and so it cannot increase the value of the firm."

"We can run the same argument in reverse and show that investors won't be worse off after the restructuring either. Imagine an investor who owns two shares in the company before the restructuring. If River Cruises borrows money, there is some chance that the return on the shares will be lower than before. If that possibility is not to our investor's taste, he can buy one share in the restructured company and also invest $10 in the firm's debt. (Table 15.4 shows how the payoff on this investment varies with River Cruises' operating income.) You can see that these payoffs are exactly the same as the investor got before the restructuring. (Compare the last lines of tables 15.1 and 15.4.) By lending half of his capital (by investing in River Cruises' debt), the investor offsets the company's borrowing exactly. So if River Cruises goes ahead and borrows, it won't *stop* investors from doing anything that they could previously do."

This recreates MM's original argument.[1] As long as investors can borrow or lend on their own account on the same terms as the firm, they are not going to pay more for a firm that has borrowed on their behalf. The value of the firm after the restructuring must be the same as before.

> In other words, the value of the firm must be unaffected by its capital structure.

MM's proposition I (debt irrelevance proposition)
The value of a firm is unaffected by its capital structure.

This conclusion is widely known as **MM's proposition I**. It is also called the **MM debt irrelevance proposition**, because it shows that under ideal conditions the firm's debt policy shouldn't matter to shareholders.

TABLE 15.4
Individual investors can also undo the effects of River Cruises' borrowing. Here the investor buys one share for $10 and lends out $10 more. Compare these rates of return to the original returns of River Cruises in Table 15.1.

	State of the Economy		
	Slump	Normal	Boom
Earnings on one share	$ .50	1.50	2.50
Plus interest at 10%	$1.00	1.00	1.00
Net earnings on investment	$1.50	2.50	3.50
Return on $20 investment	7.5%	12.5%	17.5%
		Expected outcome	

---

[1] There are many more general—and technical—proofs of the MM proposition. We will not pursue them here.

Check Point 15.2

Suppose that River Cruises had issued $750,000 of debt and uses the proceeds to buy back stock.
a. What would be the impact of a $50,000 change in operating income on earnings per share?
b. Show how a conservative investor could "undo" the change in River Cruises' capital structure by varying the investment strategy shown in Table 15.4. *Hint*: The investor will have to lend $3 for every dollar invested in River Cruises' stock.

HOW BORROWING AFFECTS RISK AND RETURN

Figure 15.2 summarizes the implications of MM's debt irrelevance proposition for River Cruises. The upper circles represent firm value, the lower circles expected, or "normal," operating income. Restructuring does not affect the size of the circles, because the amount and risk of operating income are unchanged. Thus if the firm raises $500,000 in debt and uses the proceeds to repurchase and retire shares, the remaining shares *must* be worth $500,000, and the total value of debt and equity must stay at $1 million.

The two bottom circles in Figure 15.2 are also the same size. But notice that the bottom right circle shows that shareholders can expect to earn more than half of River Cruises' normal operating income. They get more than half of the expected "income pie." Does that mean shareholders are better off? MM say no. Why not? The answer is that shareholders bear more risk.

operating risk or business risk Risk in a firm's operating income.

Look again at tables 15.1 and 15.2. Restructuring does not affect operating income, regardless of the state of the economy. Therefore, debt financing does not affect the **operating risk** or, equivalently, the **business risk** of the firm. But with less equity outstanding, a change in operating income has a greater impact on earnings per share. Suppose operating income drops from $125,000 to $75,000. Under all-equity financing, there are 100,000 shares; so earnings per share fall by $.50. With 50 percent debt, there are only 50,000 shares outstanding; so the same drop in operating income reduces earnings per share by $1.

FIGURE 15.2
"Slicing the pie" for River Cruises. The circles on the left assume the company has no debt. The circles on the right reflect the proposed restructuring. The restructuring splits firm value (top circles) 50-50. Shareholders get more than 50 percent of expected, or "normal," operating income (bottom circles), but only because they bear financial risk. Note that restructuring does not affect total firm value or operating income.

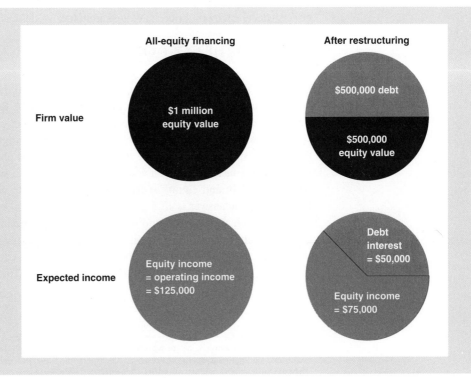

financial leverage Debt financing to amplify the effects of changes in operating income on the returns to stockholders.

You can see now why the use of debt finance is known as **financial leverage**, and a firm that has issued debt is described as a *levered firm*. The debt increases the uncertainty about percentage stock returns. If the firm is financed entirely by equity, a decline of $50,000 in operating income reduces the return on the shares by 5 percent. If the firm issues debt, then the same decline of $50,000 in operating income reduces the return on the shares by 10 percent. (Compare tables 15.1 and 15.2.) In other words, the effect of leverage is to double the magnitude of the upside and downside in the return on River Cruises' shares. Whatever the beta of the firm's shares before the restructuring, it would be twice as high afterward.

financial risk Risk to shareholders resulting from the use of debt.

> Debt finance does not affect the operating risk but it does add **financial risk**. With only half the equity to absorb the same amount of operating risk, risk per share must double.[2]

Consider now the implications of MM's proposition I for the expected return on River Cruises' stock. Before the proposed debt issue, the expected stream of earnings and dividends per share is $1.25. Since investment in the shares is risky, the shareholders require a return of 12.5 percent, or 2.5 percent above the interest rate. So the share price (which for a perpetuity is equal to the expected dividends divided by the required return) is $1.25/.125 = $10. The good news is that after the debt issue, expected earnings and dividends rise to $1.50. The bad news is that the risk of the shares has now doubled. So instead of being content with a return of 2.5 percent above the interest rate, shareholders now demand a return of 5 percent more than the interest rate—that is, a required return of 10 + 5 = 15 percent. The benefit from the rise in dividends is exactly cancelled out by the rise in the required return. The share price after the debt issue is $1.50/.15 = $10—exactly the same as before.

	Current Structure: All Equity	Proposed Structure: Equal Debt and Equity
Expected earnings per share	$1.25	$1.50
Share price	$10	$10
Expected return on share	12.5%	15.0%

Thus leverage increases the expected return to shareholders but it also increases the risk. The two effects cancel each other out, leaving shareholder value unchanged.

DEBT AND THE COST OF EQUITY

What is River Cruises' cost of capital? With all-equity financing, the answer is easy. Shareholders pay $10 per share and expect earnings per share of $1.25. If the earnings per share are paid out in a perpetual stream, the expected return is $1.25/10 = .125, or 12.5 percent. This is the cost of equity capital, r_{equity}, and also, r_{assets}, the expected return and cost of capital for the firm's assets.

Since the restructuring does not change operating earnings or firm value, it should not change the cost of capital either. Suppose the restructuring takes place. Also, by a grand stroke of luck you simultaneously become an Internet billionaire. Flush with cash, you decide to buy all the outstanding debt and equity of River Cruises. What rate of return should you expect on this investment? The answer is 12.5 percent, because once you own all the debt and equity, you will effectively own all the assets and receive all the operating income.

You will indeed get 12.5 percent. Table 15.2 shows expected earnings per share of $1.50, and share price is still $10. Therefore, the expected return on equity is $1.50/10 = .15, or 15 percent (r_{equity} = .15). The return on debt is 10 percent (r_{debt} = .10). Your overall return is

$$(.5 \times .10) + (.5 \times .15) = .125 = r_{assets}$$

---

[2] Think back to Section 9.3, where we showed that fixed costs increase the variability in a firm's profits. These fixed costs are said to provide *operating leverage*. It is exactly the same with debt. Debt interest is a fixed cost and therefore debt magnifies the variability of profits after interest. These fixed interest charges create financial leverage.

There is obviously a general principle here: The appropriate weighted average of r_{debt} and r_{equity} takes you to r_{assets}, the opportunity cost of capital for the company's assets. The formula is

$$r_{assets} = (r_{debt} \times D/V) + (r_{equity} \times E/V)$$

where D and E are the amounts of outstanding debt and equity and V equals overall firm value, the sum of D and E. Remember that D, E, and V are market values, not book values.

This formula does not match the weighted-average cost of capital (WACC) formula presented in Chapter 12.[3] Don't worry, we'll get to WACC in a moment. (Remember, we're still ignoring taxes.) First let's look at the implications of MM's debt irrelevance proposition for the cost of equity.

MM's proposition I states that the firm's choice of capital structure does not affect the firm's operating income or the value of its assets. So r_{assets}, the expected return on the package of debt and equity, is unaffected.

However, we have just seen that leverage does increase the risk of the equity and the return that shareholders demand. To see how the expected return on equity varies with leverage, we simply rearrange the formula for the company cost of capital as follows:

$$r_{equity} = r_{assets} + \frac{D}{E}(r_{assets} - r_{debt})$$

which in words says that

$$
\begin{array}{ccc}
\begin{array}{c}\textbf{Expected}\\\textbf{return}\\\textbf{on equity}\end{array}
=
\begin{array}{c}\textbf{expected}\\\textbf{return}\\\textbf{on assets}\end{array}
+
\left[
\begin{array}{c}\textbf{debt-}\\\textbf{equity}\\\textbf{ratio}\end{array}
\times
\left(
\begin{array}{c}\textbf{expected}\\\textbf{return on}\\\textbf{assets}\end{array}
-
\begin{array}{c}\textbf{expected}\\\textbf{return on}\\\textbf{debt}\end{array}
\right)
\right]
\end{array}
\qquad (15.1)
$$

MM's proposition II The required rate of return on equity increases as the firm's debt-equity ratio increases.

This is **MM's proposition II**. It states that the expected rate of return on the common stock of a leveraged firm increases in proportion to the debt-equity ratio (D/E), expressed in market values. Note that $r_{equity} = r_{assets}$ if the firm has no debt.

EXAMPLE 15.1	RIVER CRUISES' COST OF EQUITY

We can check out MM's proposition II for River Cruises. Before the decision to borrow

$$r_{equity} = r_{assets} = \frac{\text{expected operating income}}{\text{market value of all securities}}$$

$$= \frac{125,000}{1,000,000} = .125, \text{ or } 12.5\%$$

If the firm goes ahead with its plan to borrow, the expected return on assets, r_{assets}, is still 12.5 percent. So the expected return on equity is

$$r_{equity} = r_{assets} + \frac{D}{E}(r_{assets} - r_{debt})$$

$$= .125 + \frac{500,000}{500,000}(.125 - .10)$$

$$= .15, \text{ or } 15\%$$

We pointed out in Chapter 12 that you can think of a debt issue as having an explicit cost and an implicit cost. The explicit cost is the rate of interest charged on the firm's debt.

Debt also increases financial risk and causes shareholders to demand a higher return on their investment. Once you recognize this implicit cost, debt is no cheaper than equity—the return that investors require on their assets is unaffected by the firm's borrowing decision.

---

[3] See sections 12.1 and 12.2.

FIGURE 15.3

MM's proposition II with a fixed interest rate on debt. The expected return on River Cruises' equity rises in line with the debt-equity ratio. The weighted average of the expected returns on debt and equity is constant, equal to the expected return on assets.

Check Point 15.3   When the firm issues debt, why does r_{assets}, the company cost of capital, remain fixed, while the expected return on equity, r_{equity}, changes? Why is it not the other way around?

The implications of MM's proposition II are shown in Figure 15.3. No matter how much the firm borrows, the expected return on the package of debt and equity, r_{assets}, is unchanged, but the expected rate of return on the separate parts of the package does change. How is this possible? Because the proportions of debt and equity in the package are also changing. More debt means that the cost of equity increases, but at the same time the amount of equity is less.

In Figure 15.3 we have drawn the rate of interest on the debt as constant no matter how much the firm borrows. That is not wholly realistic. It is true that most large, conservative companies could borrow a little more or less without noticeably affecting the interest rate that they pay. But at higher debt levels lenders become concerned that they may not get their money back, and they demand higher rates of interest. Figure 15.4 modifies Figure 15.3 to take account of this. You can see that as

---

FIGURE 15.4

MM's proposition II, when debt is not risk-free. As the debt-equity ratio increases, debtholders demand a higher expected rate of return to compensate for the risk of default. The expected return on equity increases more slowly when debt is risky because the debtholders take on part of the risk. The expected return on the package of debt and equity, r_{assets}, remains, constant.

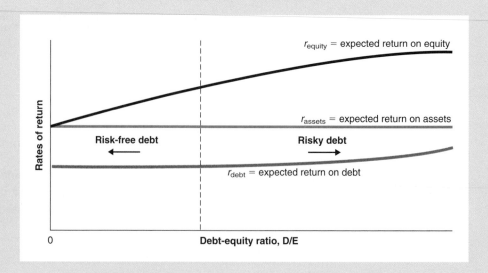

the firm borrows more, the risk of default increases and the firm has to pay higher rates of interest. Proposition II continues to predict that the expected return on the package of debt and equity does not change. However, the slope of the r_{equity} line now tapers off as D/E increases. Why? Essentially because holders of risky debt begin to bear part of the firm's operating risk. As the firm borrows more, more of that risk is transferred from shareholders to bondholders.

Figures 15.3 and 15.4 wrap up our discussion of MM's leverage irrelevance proposition. Because overall firm value is constant, the average return on the firm's debt and equity securities is also constant, regardless of the fraction of debt financing. This result follows from MM's assumptions that capital markets are well functioning and taxes are absent. Now it's time to put taxes back into the picture.

15.2 CAPITAL STRUCTURE AND CORPORATE TAXES

The MM propositions suggest that debt policy should not matter. Yet financial managers do worry about debt policy, and for good reasons. Now we are ready to see why.

If debt policy were *completely* irrelevant, actual debt ratios would vary randomly from firm to firm and from industry to industry. Yet almost all airlines, utilities, banks, and real estate development companies rely heavily on debt. And so do many firms in capital-intensive industries like steel, aluminum, chemicals, petroleum, and mining. On the other hand, it is rare to find a drug company or advertising agency that is not predominantly equity-financed. Glamorous growth companies seldom use much debt, despite rapid expansion and often heavy requirements for capital.

The explanation of these patterns lies partly in the things that we have so far left out of our discussion. Now we will put all these things back in, starting with taxes.

DEBT AND TAXES AT RIVER CRUISES

Debt financing has one important advantage. The interest that the company pays is a tax-deductible expense but equity income is subject to corporate tax.

To see the advantage of debt finance, let's look once again at River Cruises. Table 15.5 shows how expected income is reduced if profits are taxed at a rate of 35 percent. The left-hand column sets out the position if River Cruises is financed entirely by equity. The right-hand column shows what happens if the firm issues $500,000 of debt at an interest rate of 10 percent.

Notice that the combined income of the debtholders and equityholders is higher by $17,500 when the firm is levered. This is because the interest payments are tax-deductible. Thus every dollar of interest reduces taxes by $.35. The total amount of tax savings is simply .35 × interest payments. In the case of River Cruises, the **interest tax shield** is .35 × $50,000 = $17,500 each year. In other words, the "pie" of after-tax income to be shared by debt and equity investors increases by $17,500 relative to the zero-debt case. Since the debtholders receive no more than the going rate of interest, the benefit of this interest tax shield is captured by the shareholders.

The interest tax shield is a valuable asset. Let's see how much it could be worth. Suppose that River Cruises plans to replace its bonds when they mature and to keep "rolling over" the debt indefinitely. It therefore looks forward to a permanent stream of tax savings of $17,500 per year.

interest tax shield Tax savings resulting from deductibility of interest payments.

TABLE 15.5
Since debt interest is tax-deductible, River Cruises' debtholders and equity-holders expect to receive a higher combined income when the firm is leveraged.

	Zero Debt	$500,000 of Debt
Expected operating income	$125,000	$125,000
Debt interest at 10%	0	50,000
Before-tax income	125,000	75,000
Tax at 35%	43,750	26,250
After-tax income	81,250	48,750
Combined debt and equity income (debt interest + after-tax income)	81,250	98,750

These savings depend only on the corporate tax rate and on the ability of River Cruises to earn enough to cover interest payments. So the risk of the tax shield is likely to be small. Therefore, if we wish to compute the present value of all the future tax savings associated with permanent debt, we should discount the interest tax shields at a relatively low rate.

But what rate? The most common assumption is that the risk of the tax shields is the same as that of the interest payments generating them. Thus we discount at 10 percent the expected rate of return demanded by investors who are holding the firm's debt. If the debt is permanent, then the firm can look forward to an annual savings of $17,500 in perpetuity. Their present value is

$$\text{PV tax shield} = \frac{\$17,500}{.10} = \$175,000$$

This is what the tax savings are worth to River Cruises.

How does company value change? We continue to assume that if the firm is all-equity financed, the shareholders will demand a 12.5 percent return and, therefore, the company will be valued at $81,250/.125 = $650,000.[4] But if River Cruises issues $500,000 of permanent debt, the package of all the firm's securities increases by the value of the tax shield to $650,000 + $175,000 = $825,000.

Let us generalize. The interest payment each year equals the rate of interest times the amount borrowed, or $r_{debt} \times D$. The annual tax savings is the corporate tax rate, T_c, times the interest payment. Therefore,

$$\text{Annual tax shield} = \text{corporate tax rate} \times \text{interest payment}$$
$$= T_c \times (r_{debt} \times D)$$

If the tax shield is perpetual, we use the perpetuity formula to calculate its present value:

$$\textbf{PV tax shields} = \frac{\textbf{annual tax shield}}{r_{debt}} = \frac{T_c \times (r_{debt} \times D)}{r_{debt}} = T_c D \qquad (15.2)$$

Of course, the present value of the tax shield is less if the firm does not plan to borrow permanently or if it may not be able to use the tax shields in the future.[5] This present value ($T_c D$) is actually the maximum possible value. However, we will continue to use this value in the rest of this chapter in order to keep the argument and illustrations simple.

Check Point 15.4

In 2003, BCE, Inc. paid out $1,093 million as debt interest. How much more tax would BCE have paid if the firm was entirely equity financed? What is the present value of BCE's interest tax shield if BCE planned to keep its borrowing permanently at the 2003 level? Assume an interest rate of 8 percent and a corporate tax rate of 35 percent.

HOW INTEREST TAX SHIELDS CONTRIBUTE TO THE VALUE OF SHAREHOLDERS' EQUITY

MM's proposition I amounts to saying that "the value of the pizza does not depend on how it is sliced." The pizza is the firm's assets, and the slices are the debt and equity claims. If we hold the pizza constant, then a dollar more of debt means a dollar less of equity value.

But there is really a third slice—the government's. MM would still say that the value of the pizza—in this case the company value *before taxes*—is not changed by slicing. But anything the firm can do to reduce the size of the government's slice obviously leaves more for the others. One

---

[4] The firm was worth $1 million when the corporate tax rate was zero (see Table 15.1). It is worth only $650,000 when all-equity financed because 35 percent of income is lost to taxes.

[5] The value of the interest tax shield is also reduced if the future level of debt is not fixed, but it is increased when the firm does well and paid down when it does poorly. In this case the future interest tax shields are correlated with the firm's performance and are therefore risky.

way to do this is to borrow money. This reduces the firm's tax bill and increases the cash payments to the investors. The value of their investment goes up by the present value of the tax savings.

In a no-tax world, MM's proposition I states that the value of the firm is unaffected by capital structure. But MM also modified proposition I to recognize corporate taxes:

Value of levered firm = value if all-equity financed + present value of tax shield

In the special case of permanent debt,

Value of levered firm = value if all-equity financed + T$_c$D

This "corrected" formula is illustrated in Figure 15.5. It implies that borrowing increases firm value and shareholders' wealth.

CORPORATE TAXES AND THE WEIGHTED-AVERAGE COST OF CAPITAL

We have shown that when there are corporate taxes, debt provides the company with a valuable tax shield. Few companies explicitly calculate the present value of interest tax shields associated with a particular borrowing policy. The tax shields are not forgotten, however, because they show up in the discount rate used to evaluate capital investments.

Since debt interest is tax-deductible, the government in effect pays 35 percent of the interest cost. So to keep its investors happy, the firm has to earn the *after-tax* rate of interest on its debt and the return required by shareholders. Once we recognize the tax benefit of debt, the weighted-average cost of capital formula (see Chapter 12 for a review if you need one) becomes

$$\text{WACC} = (1 - T_c)\, r_{\text{debt}} \left(\frac{D}{D + E} \right) + r_{\text{equity}} \left(\frac{E}{D + E} \right) \tag{15.3}$$

Notice that when we allow for the tax advantage of debt, the weighted-average cost of capital depends on the *after-tax* rate of interest, $(1 - T_c) \times r_{\text{debt}}$.

EXAMPLE 15.2	**WACC AND DEBT POLICY**

We can use the weighted-average cost of capital formula to see how leverage affects River Cruises' cost of capital if the company pays corporate tax. When a company has no debt, the weighted-average cost of capital and the return required by shareholders are identical. In the case of River Cruises, the WACC with all-equity financing is 12.5 percent, and the value of the firm is $650,000.

Now let us calculate the weighted-average cost of capital if River Cruises issues $500,000 of permanent debt (D = $500,000). Company value increases by PV tax shield = $175,000, from $650,000

FIGURE 15.5
The blue line shows how the availability of interest tax shields affects the market value of the firm. Additional borrowing decreases corporate income tax payments and increases the cash flows available to lenders and shareholders; thus, market value increases.

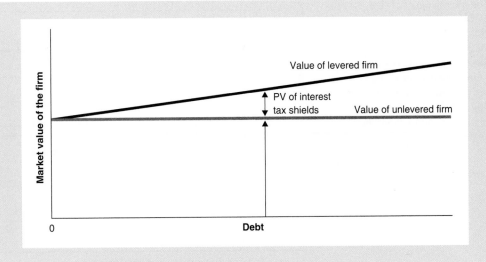

to $825,000 (meaning that $D + E = \$825,000$). Therefore the value of equity must be $825,000 − $500,000 = $325,000 ($E = \$325,000$).

To calculate River Cruises' weighted-average cost of capital, we would need to know its cost of equity after issuing debt. We can take some guidance from MM Proposition II with corporate taxes, which tells us that for a levered firm the expected rate of return to shareholders, or the cost of equity, should be

$$r_{equity} = r_{assets} + (D/E)(1 - T_c)(r_{assets} - r_{debt})$$

We get, $r_{equity} = .125 + (500,000/325,000)(1 - .35)(.125 - .10) = .15$.

Table 15.5 shows that when River Cruises borrows, the expected equity income is $48,750. So the expected return to shareholders is $48,750/\$325,000 = 15$ percent ($r_{equity} = .15$).[6] The interest rate is 10 percent ($r_{debt} = .10$) and the corporate tax rate is 35 percent ($T_c = .35$). This is all the information we need to see how leverage affects River Cruises' weighted-average cost of capital:

$$WACC = (1 - T_c)r_{debt}\left(\frac{D}{D + E}\right) + r_{equity}\left(\frac{E}{D + E}\right)$$

$$= (1 - .35) .10\left(\frac{500,000}{825,000}\right) + .15\left(\frac{325,000}{825,000}\right) = .0985, \text{ or } 9.85\%$$

We saw earlier that if there are no corporate taxes, the weighted-average cost of capital is unaffected by borrowing. But when there are corporate taxes, debt provides the company with a new benefit—the interest tax shield. In this case leverage reduces the weighted-average cost of capital (in River Cruises' case from 12.5 percent to 9.85 percent).

Figure 15.6 repeats Figure 15.3 except that now we have allowed for the effect of taxes on River Cruises' cost of capital. You can see that as the company borrows more, the expected return on equity rises, but the rise is less rapid than in the absence of taxes. The after-tax cost of debt is only 6.5 percent. As a result, the weighted-average cost of capital declines. For example, if the company has debt of $500,000, the equity is worth $325,000, and the debt-equity ratio (D/E) is $500,000/\$325,000 = 1.54$. Figure 15.6 shows that with this amount of debt the weighted-average cost of capital is 9.85 percent, the same figure that we calculated above.

FIGURE 15.6

Changes in River Cruises' cost of capital with increased leverage, when there are corporate taxes. The after-tax cost of debt is assumed to be constant at $(1 − .35)10 = 6.5$ percent. With increased borrowing the cost of equity rises, but more slowly than in the no-tax case (see Figure 15.3). The weighted-average cost of capital (WACC) declines as the firm borrows more.

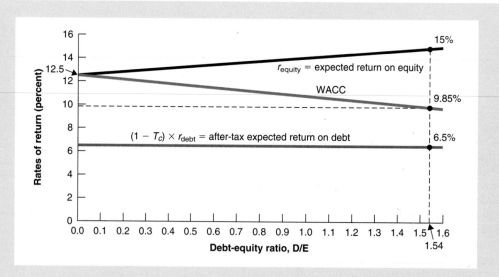

THE IMPLICATIONS OF CORPORATE TAXES FOR CAPITAL STRUCTURE

If borrowing provides an interest tax shield, the implied optimal debt policy appears to be embarrassingly extreme: All firms should borrow to the hilt. This maximizes firm value and minimizes the weighted-average cost of capital.

MM were not that fanatical about it. No one would expect the gains to apply at extreme debt ratios. For example, if a firm borrows heavily, all its operating income may go to pay interest, and, therefore, there are no corporate taxes to be paid. There is no point in such firms borrowing any more.

There may also be some tax *disadvantages* to borrowing because bondholders have to pay personal income tax on any interest they receive. Shareholders, on the other hand, can get a tax break because some of their returns come as capital gains. Capital gains are not taxed until the stock is sold and, currently, only 50 percent of such capital gains are taxed.[7]

All this suggests that there may come a point at which the tax savings from debt level off and may even decline. But it doesn't explain why highly profitable companies with large tax bills often thrive with little or no debt. There are clearly factors besides tax to consider. One such factor is the likelihood of financial distress.

15.3

COSTS OF FINANCIAL DISTRESS

Financial distress occurs when promises to creditors are broken or honoured with difficulty. Sometimes financial distress leads to bankruptcy. Sometimes it only means skating on thin ice.

costs of financial distress
Costs arising from bankruptcy or distorted business decisions before bankruptcy.

As we will see, financial distress is costly. Investors know that levered firms may run into financial difficulty, and they worry about the **costs of financial distress**. That worry is reflected in the current market value of the levered firm's securities. Even if the firm is not now in financial distress, investors factor the potential for future distress into their assessment of current value. This means that the overall value of the firm is

$$\begin{matrix} \text{Overall market} \\ \text{value} \end{matrix} = \begin{matrix} \text{value if all-equity} \\ \text{financed} \end{matrix} + \begin{matrix} \text{PV tax} \\ \text{shield} \end{matrix} - \begin{matrix} \text{PV costs of} \\ \text{financial distress} \end{matrix} \qquad (15.4)$$

The present value of the costs of financial distress depends both on the probability of distress and on the magnitude of the costs encountered if distress occurs.

Figure 15.7 shows how the trade-off between the tax benefits of debt and the costs of distress determines optimal capital structure. Think of a firm like River Cruises, which starts with no debt but considers moving to higher and higher debt levels, holding its assets and operations constant.

> At moderate debt levels the probability of financial distress is trivial and therefore the tax advantages of debt dominate. But at some point the probability of financial distress increases rapidly with additional borrowing, and the potential costs of distress begin to take a substantial bite out of firm value. The theoretical optimum is reached when the present value of tax savings due to additional borrowing is just offset by increases in the present value of costs of distress.

trade-off theory   Debt levels are chosen to balance interest tax shields against the costs of financial distress.

This is called the **trade-off theory** of optimal capital structure. The theory says that managers will try to increase debt levels to the point where the value of additional interest tax shields is offset by the additional costs of financial distress exactly.

An enterprise that maximizes firm value should also minimize its weighted-average cost of capital. It follows that a particular debt-to-equity ratio represents the *optimal capital structure*

---

[7] Recall from Chapter 3 that combined federal and provincial tax rates on ordinary income can be close to 50 percent in most provinces. But, as we have just discussed, capital gains are taxed at one-half of the regular personal tax rate.

FIGURE 15.7
The trade-off theory of capital structure. The curved gold line shows how the market value of the firm initially increases as the firm borrows but decreases as the costs of financial distress become more and more important. The optimal capital structure balances the costs of financial distress against the value of the interest tax shields generated by borrowing.

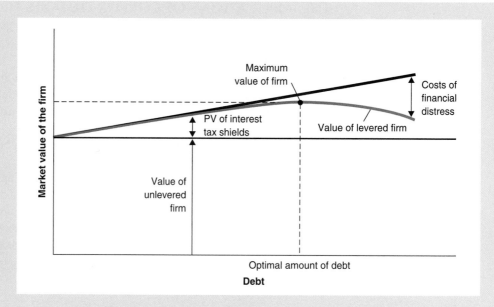

if it results in the lowest possible weighted-average cost of capital, keeping in mind the potential costs of financial distress and bankruptcy that can result from excessive debt. We see this in Figure 15.8.

Now let's take a closer look at financial distress.

BANKRUPTCY COSTS

In principle, bankruptcy is merely a legal mechanism for allowing creditors (that is, lenders) to take over the firm when the decline in the value of its assets triggers a default on outstanding debt. If the company cannot pay its debts, the company is turned over to the creditors, who become the new owners; the old shareholders are left with nothing. Bankruptcy is not the *cause* of the decline in the value of the firm. It is the result.

FIGURE 15.8
The figure shows that an optimum capital structure is consistent with a minimum WACC for the firm.

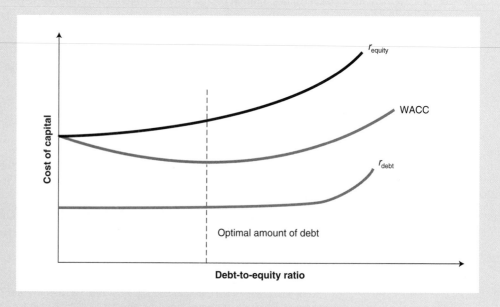

In practice, of course, anything involving courts and lawyers cannot be free. The fees involved in a bankruptcy proceeding are paid out of the remaining value of the firm's assets. Creditors end up with only what is left after paying the lawyers and other court expenses. If there is a possibility of bankruptcy, the current market value of the firm is reduced by the present value of these potential costs.

It is easy to see how increased leverage affects the costs of financial distress. The more the firm owes, the higher the chance of default and therefore the greater the expected value of the associated costs. This reduces the current market value of the firm.

Creditors foresee the costs and realize that if default occurs, the bankruptcy costs will come out of the value of the firm. For this they demand compensation in advance in the form of a higher promised interest rate. This reduces the possible payoffs to shareholders and reduces the current market value of their shares.

Check Point 15.5   Suppose investors foresee $2 million of legal costs if the firm defaults on its bonds. How does this affect the value of the firm's bonds if bankruptcy occurs? How does the possibility of default affect the interest rate demanded by bondholders today? How does this possibility affect today's value of the firm's common stock?

EVIDENCE ON BANKRUPTCY COSTS

When large firms file for bankruptcy, they usually do so under regulations provided in the *Bankruptcy and Insolvency Act* of 1992. Some companies are also governed by the *Companies' Creditors Arrangement Act* and the *Winding-up and Restructuring Act*.[8] The purpose of these statutes is to nurse the firm back to health and enable it to face the world again. This requires approval of a reorganization plan for who gets what; under the plan each class of creditors needs to give up its claim in exchange for new securities or a mixture of new securities and cash. The challenge is to design a new capital structure that will satisfy the creditors and allow the firm to solve the business problems that got it into trouble in the first place. Sometimes it proves possible to satisfy both demands and the patient emerges fit and healthy. Often, however, the proceedings involve costly delays and legal tangles, and the business continues to deteriorate.

Bankruptcy costs can add up quickly. Manville, which declared bankruptcy in 1982 because of expected liability for asbestos-related health claims, spent $200 million (US) on bankruptcy fees before it emerged from bankruptcy in 1988.[9] The legal and professional fees of the Braniff International Corporation bankruptcy were reported to be $12 million (US); legal fees in the Continental Airlines bankruptcy were running $2 million (US) a month. Daunting as such numbers seem, they may not be a large *percentage* of the total prebankruptcy value of the firm. A recent study of troubled, highly leveraged firms found costs of financial distress amounting to 10 to 20 percent of predistress market value.[10] But the percentage costs can be much higher when smaller companies get into trouble.

DIRECT VERSUS INDIRECT COSTS OF BANKRUPTCY

Thus far we have discussed only the *direct* (that is, legal and administrative) costs of bankruptcy. The *indirect* costs reflect the difficulties of running a company while it is going through bankruptcy. Management's efforts to prevent further deterioration in the firm's business are often undermined by the delays and legal tangles that go with bankruptcy. When Eastern Airlines entered bankruptcy in 1989, it was in severe financial trouble, but it still had some valuable, profit-making routes and readily saleable assets such as planes and terminal facilities. After

---

[8] We will discuss bankruptcy in more detail in Chapter 21.

[9] S. P. Sherman, "Bankruptcy's Spreading Blight," *Fortune* (June 3, 1991), pp. 123–132.

[10] G. Andrade and S. N. Kaplan, "How Costly Is Financial (Not Economic) Distress? Evidence from Highly Leveraged Transactions that Became Distressed," *Journal of Finance* 53 (October 1998), pp. 1443–1493.

SEE BOX P. 483 ▶

SEE BOX P. 484 ▶

nearly two years under the "protection" of a bankruptcy court, which allowed Eastern to continue loss-making operations, there was hardly anything of value left when it was finally forced to liquidate in 1991. Another illustration of the indirect costs of bankruptcy is provided in the nearby Finance in Action box, which describes the disruption to Penn Central Railroad's business. A more recent example of disruptions and costs associated with bankruptcy is provided in the Finance in Action box describing the actions of Jetsgo's creditors, after the Canadian discount airline filed for bankruptcy protection in March 2005.

We don't know how much these indirect costs add to the expenses of bankruptcy. We suspect it is a significant number, particularly when bankruptcy proceedings are prolonged. Perhaps the best evidence is the reluctance of creditors to force a firm into bankruptcy. In principle, they would be better off to end the agony and seize the assets as soon as possible. But instead creditors often overlook defaults in the hope of nursing the firm over a difficult period. They do this in part to avoid the costs of bankruptcy. There is an old financial saying, "Borrow $1,000 and you've got a banker. Borrow $10,000,000 and you've got a partner."

FINANCIAL DISTRESS WITHOUT BANKRUPTCY

Not every firm that gets into trouble goes bankrupt. As long as the firm can scrape up enough cash to pay the interest on its debt, it may be able to postpone bankruptcy for many years. Eventually the firm may recover, pay off its debt, and escape bankruptcy altogether.

A narrow escape from bankruptcy does not mean that costs of financial distress are avoided. When a firm is in trouble, suppliers worry that they may not be paid, potential customers fear that the firm will not be able to honour its warranties, and employees start contemplating their next job. While all firms suffer in times of financial trouble, manufacturers of relatively expensive, durable products requiring regular after-sales service, such as automobile or computer companies, can have particularly high costs associated with financial distress. Similarly, the perception that an airline company is in financial trouble may scare away customers concerned about the maintenance and safety of the aircraft and its ability to honour frequent flyer programs. For instance, before Canadian Airlines was taken over by Air Canada, there were concerns about its growing financial difficulties, which caused business travellers to switch to other airlines.

In 2004, Air Canada's own financial woes caused similar concerns amongst travellers as the troubled airline struggled to restructure itself under court-ordered bankruptcy protection. Indeed, there is good reason for concern because an insolvent airline can cause a lot of turmoil for its customers, suppliers, and generally anyone doing business with it. Once again, take the case of Jetsgo. In March 2005, the discount airline sought bankruptcy protection and, without any warning, cancelled all its flights. An estimated 17,000 passengers, including many travelling on spring break, found that their tickets were no good and were left stranded. Many of these passengers were forced to make alternate arrangements with other carriers, providing brisk business to competitors such as Air Canada and WestJet.

The firm's bondholders and stockholders both want the company to recover, but in other respects their interests may be in conflict. In times of financial distress the security holders are like many political parties—united on generalities but threatened by squabbling on any particular issue.

> Financial distress is costly when conflicts get in the way of running the business. Shareholders are tempted to forsake the usual objective of maximizing the overall market value of the firm; they pursue their self-interests instead. They are tempted to play games at the expense of their creditors. These games add to the costs of financial distress.

Think of a company—call it Double-R Nutting—which is teetering on the brink of bankruptcy. It has large debts and large losses. Double-R's assets have little value, and if its debts were due today, Double-R would default, leaving the firm bankrupt. The assets would then be sold off, the debtholders would perhaps receive a few cents on the dollar, and the shareholders would be left with nothing.

The Penn Central Railroad went under in June 1970. It was the largest and most dramatic corporate failure up to that time. Four years later, with bankruptcy proceedings nowhere near completion, *Business Week* published an article called "Why the Penn Central Is Falling Apart." The article noted that

> although the railroad needed to invest huge sums of money to rebuild its facilities and continue operations, its creditors were more concerned with getting their own money back, even if that meant shutting down the railroad. In a chicken-and-egg type of problem, the capital necessary to make the railroad viable would not be forthcoming unless Penn Central could convince investors that it could be reorganized as a viable corporation.

Penn Central could have raised money by selling off some of its assets, but its creditors naturally opposed this. As the *Business Week* article put it:

Agonizingly for everyone on the Penn Central, there is a tremendous source of capital that cannot be touched. For example, just about every abandoned mine branch in the Allegheny Mountains is chock full of old Penn Central cars destined for scrap. With today's scrap prices, they are a potential gold mine. But the creditors will not allow this asset to be turned into cash that will be reinvested in the estate, since that estate is eroding everyday.

Penn Central's problems show that some of the most important costs of bankruptcy are difficult to measure. The disruption of business activity is less visible but can be far more costly than the firm's legal bills.

Source: Quotations from *Business Week*, October 12, 1974.

But suppose the debts are not due yet. That grace period explains why Double-R's shares still have value. There could be a stroke of luck that will rescue the firm and allow it to pay off its debts with something left over. That's a long shot—unless firm value increases sharply, the stock will be valueless. But the owners have a secret weapon: They control investment and operating strategy.

The First Game: Bet the Bank's Money

Suppose Double-R has the opportunity to take a wild gamble. If it can't pull it off, the shareholders will be no worse off, the company will probably go under anyway. But if the gamble does succeed, there will be more than enough assets to pay off the debt, and the surplus will go into the shareholders' pockets. You can see why management might want to take the chance. In taking the gamble, they are essentially betting the debtholders' money, but if Double-R does hit the jackpot, the equityholders get most of the loot.

One owner-manager of a small bankrupt company called KenDavis Industries put the point this way: "Everyone agrees there is no shareholder equity—so *we've* got *nothing* to lose. The *banks* have it all on the line now—not us." In another case, the managers of the failing firm took the incentive to gamble literally. They went to Las Vegas and bet the company's money, hoping to win enough to pay off the creditors. The effects of such distorted incentives to take on risk are usually not this blatant, but the results can be the same. For example, Sambo's Restaurants borrowed against unencumbered assets while in bankruptcy proceedings and used the funds to pay for a risky marketing initiative, changing the name and concept of its restaurants. When the gamble failed, unsecured creditors suffered most of the loss: They received only $.11 of each dollar owed to them.[11]

These kinds of warped capital investment strategies clearly are costly for the bondholders and for the firm as a whole. Why do we say they create costs of financial distress? Because the temptation to follow such strategies is strongest when the odds of default are high. A healthy firm would never invest in Double-R's negative-NPV gamble, since it would be gambling with its own money, not the bondholders'. A healthy firm's creditors would not be vulnerable to this type of game.

The Second Game: Don't Bet Your Own Money

We have just seen how shareholders, acting in self-interest, may take on risky, unprofitable projects. These are errors of commission. We will now illustrate how conflicts of interest may also lead to errors of omission.

---

[11] These cases are cited in Lynn M. LoPucki, "The Trouble with Chapter 11," *Wisconsin Law Review* (1993), pp. 729–760.

Costs of Insolvency

Eight airport authorities across Canada have joined forces in a bid to recoup nearly $3 million owed to them by insolvent Jetsgo Corp.

At stake are Jetsgo's fleet of 29 aircraft, consisting of 15 company-owned Fokker 100s and 14 leased Boeing MD-83s, with creditors seeking to seize the Fokkers.

The eight authorities have hired Montreal law firm Langlois Kronstrom Desjardins LLP to represent them in Quebec Superior Court.

The group said yesterday that Jetsgo collected but failed to remit certain airport improvement fees (AIF). In total, the airports say they are owed $1.1 million in such fees and $1.7 million in other airport charges, such as landing and terminal fees. Some of the airports also want to recover monthly rental fees normally charged for storing Jetsgo aircraft.

Banding together in court are: Aéroports de Montréal, Vancouver International Airport Authority, Ottawa Macdonald-Cartier International Airport Authority, Winnipeg Airports Authority, Aéroport de Québec, Edmonton Regional Airports Authority, Calgary Airport Authority and Halifax International Airport Authority.

Total amounts owed for AIF and other airport charges range from $178,203 (Halifax) to $922,083 (Montreal).

Gerald Apostolatos, a senior partner at Langlois Kronstrom Desjardins, said he expects the case to come up for discussion in today's court proceedings in Montreal.

Others seeking court dates for their own claims against Montreal-based Jetsgo, which filed for bankruptcy protection March 11, include the Greater Toronto Airports Authority, overseer of Pearson International Airport, and NAV CANADA, operator of the country's air traffic control system.

The GTAA says it is owed $5.5 million and NAV CANADA is claiming $1.6 million.

NordTech Aerospace Inc., an aircraft maintenance firm, is also part of the list of creditors trying to recover debts through actions such as requesting that the court issue an order that would pave the way for seizing the fleet of Fokkers in Quebec City. Supervisors at Jetsgo, which is controlled by discount airline entrepreneur Michel Leblanc, directed the bulk of Fokker pilots to fly the planes to Quebec City on the night of March 10, under the guise of maintenance checks.

The Fokkers, with an average age of $12\frac{1}{2}$ years, have become a prized commodity, with the GTAA, the group of eight authorities, NAV Canada and NordTech all attempting to seize them.

Twelve of the Fokkers are on the Quebec City airport's premises, while another five (including two spare jets for parts) are on property leased to NordTech in the Quebec capital, court documents show. Eight of the MD-83s are parked in Toronto, and the rest are in Vancouver and Montreal.

Jetsgo leases space at airports in Montreal, Vancouver, Quebec City and Halifax. Those four airports normally would be collecting a total of $6,159 in monthly rental fees from Jetsgo and another $22,301 in monthly aircraft parking charges.

Jetsgo has court protection from creditors until April 11.

Source: Excerpted from B. Jang, *The Globe and Mail*, "Airports Seek Compensation for Jetsgo Fees: Group of Eight Claim $3 Million Owed," March 24, 2005. Reprinted with permission from *The Globe and Mail*.

Suppose Double-R uncovers a relatively safe project with a positive NPV. Unfortunately, the project requires a substantial investment. Double-R will need to raise this extra cash from its shareholders. Although the project has a positive NPV, the profits may not be sufficient to rescue the company from bankruptcy. If that is so, all the profits from the new project will be used to help pay off the company's debt, and the shareholders will get no return on the cash they put up. Although it is in the firm's interest to go ahead with the project, it is not in the owners' interest, and the project will be passed up.

Again, our example illustrates a general point. The value of any investment opportunity to the firm's *shareholders* is reduced because project benefits must be shared with the bondholders. Thus it may not be in the shareholders' interest to contribute fresh equity capital even if that means forgoing positive-NPV opportunities.

These two games illustrate potential conflicts of interest between shareholders and debtholders. These conflicts, which theoretically affect all levered firms, become much more serious when firms are staring bankruptcy in the face.

> If the probability of default is high, managers and shareholders will be tempted to take excessively risky projects. At the same time, shareholders may refuse to contribute more equity capital even if the firm has safe, positive-NPV opportunities. Shareholders would rather take money out of the firm than put new money in.

The more the firm borrows, the greater the temptation to play such games. The increased odds of poor decisions in the future prompt investors to reduce today's assessment of the market value of the firm. Potential lenders, realizing that games may be played at their expense in the future, protect themselves by demanding better terms on the money they lend today. So the fall in value comes out of shareholders' pockets. This is the reason that it is ultimately in the shareholders' interest to avoid temptation. The easiest way to do this is to limit borrowing to levels at which the firm's debt is safe or close to it.

Frequently, agreements between shareholders and bondholders, called *protective covenants*, are incorporated as part of the loan document. These covenants are designed to safeguard the interests of bondholders. While many covenants carry restrictive clauses that can reduce flexibility in managerial decision making, these agreements can also have the effect of lowering interest rates.

We do not mean to leave the impression that managers and shareholders always succumb to temptation unless restrained. Usually they refrain voluntarily, not only from a sense of fair play but also on pragmatic grounds: A firm or individual that makes a killing today at the expense of a creditor will be coldly received when the time comes to borrow again. Aggressive game playing is done only by out-and-out crooks and by firms in extreme financial distress. Firms limit borrowing precisely because they don't wish to be in distress and exposed to the temptation to play.

Check Point 15.6

We have described two games that might be played by firms in financial distress. Why are the games costly? How does the possibility that the game might be played at some point in the future affect today's capital structure decisions?

COSTS OF DISTRESS VARY WITH TYPE OF ASSET

Suppose your firm's only asset is a large downtown hotel, Heartbreak Hotel, mortgaged to the hilt. A recession hits, occupancy rates fall, and the mortgage payments cannot be met. The lender takes over and sells the hotel to a new owner and operator. The stock is worthless and you use the firm's stock certificates for wallpaper.

What is the cost of bankruptcy? In this example, probably very little. The value of the hotel is, of course, much less than you hoped, but that is due to the lack of guests not bankruptcy. Bankruptcy does not damage the hotel itself. The direct bankruptcy costs are restricted to items such as legal and court fees, real estate commissions, and the time the lender spends sorting things out.

Suppose we repeat the story of Heartbreak Hotel for Fledgling Electronics. Everything is the same, except for the underlying assets. Fledgling is a high-tech going concern and much of its value reflects investors' beliefs that its research team will come up with profitable ideas. Fledgling is a "people business"; its most important assets go down in the elevator and into the parking lot every night.

If Fledgling gets into trouble, the shareholders may be reluctant to put up money to cash in on those profitable ideas—why should they put up cash that will simply go to pay off the banks? Failure to invest is likely to be much more serious for Fledgling than for a company like Heartbreak Hotel.

If Fledgling finally defaults on its debt, the lender would find it much more difficult to cash in by selling off the assets. In fact, if trouble comes, many of those assets may drive into the sunset and never come back.

Some assets, like good commercial real estate, can pass through bankruptcy and reorganization largely unscathed; the values of other assets are likely to be considerably diminished. The losses are greatest for intangible assets that are linked to the continuing prosperity of the firm. An important determinant of debt capacity is the availability of collateral. When a firm faces financial distress, certain assets such as plants, land, and equipment are more readily valued and sold than patents, brand names, and other intangibles. That may be why debt ratios are low in the pharmaceutical industry, where company values depend on continued success in research and development. It may also explain the low debt ratios in many service companies, whose main asset is their skilled labour. On the other hand, capital-intensive manufacturing firms or wholesale and retail businesses with sizable tangible assets tend to have higher debt ratios. Table 15.6 provides debt-

TABLE 15.6
Debt-to-equity ratios for a
sample of Canadian firms
and industries in 2003

Firm	Debt-to-Equity Ratio	Industry	Industry Average Debt-to-Equity Ratio
QLT, Inc.	0.30	Biotechnology	0.00
Stantec, Inc.	0.38	Capital goods	0.49
Research In Motion, Ltd.	0.02	Communications equipment	0.09
Gildan Activewear, Inc.	0.28	Consumer durable and apparel	0.81
Power Financial Corp.	0.31	Diversified financials	0.47
Maple Leaf Foods, Inc.	0.90	Food, beverage and tobacco	1.21
Loblaw Companies, Ltd.	0.99	Food and staples retailing	0.59
Barrick Gold Corporation	0.14	Gold	0.28
Extendicare, Inc.	2.24	Health care equipment services	0.27
Rogers Communications, Inc.	3.35	Media	1.59
Imperial Oil, Ltd.	0.25	Oil and gas	0.50
Abitibi-Consolidated, Inc.	1.63	Paper and forest products	1.12
Canadian National Railway Company	0.72	Transportation	1.20
ATCO, Ltd.	1.05	Utilities	1.47

Source: *Financial Post Analyzer*, Industry Reports and Investor Report. Retrieved April 5, 2004, from **www.fpinfomart.ca**.

to-equity ratios for some representative Canadian firms in different industries as well as industry average debt-to-equity ratios. Notice the very low debt-to-equity ratio of the communications equipment company, Research In Motion, Ltd., but the relatively high debt-to-equity ratio of Loblaw, the large grocery chain. The moral of these examples is

> Do not think only about whether borrowing is likely to bring trouble. Think also of the value that may be lost if trouble comes.

Check Point 15.7

For which of the following companies would the costs of financial distress be most serious? Why?
- A three-year-old biotech company. So far the company has no products approved for sale, but its scientists are hard at work developing a breakthrough drug.
- An oil production company with 50 producing wells and 20 million barrels of existing oil reserves.

We have now completed our review of the building blocks of the trade-off theory of optimal capital structure. In the next section we will sum up that theory and briefly cover a competing "pecking order" theory.

15.4   EXPLAINING FINANCING CHOICES

THE TRADE-OFF THEORY

Financial managers often think of the firm's debt-equity decision as a trade-off between interest tax shields and the costs of financial distress. Of course, there is controversy about how valuable interest tax shields are and what kinds of financial trouble are most threatening, but these disagreements are only variations on a theme. Thus Figure 15.7 illustrates the debt-equity trade-off.

This trade-off theory predicts that target debt ratios will vary from firm to firm. Companies with safe, tangible assets and plenty of taxable income to shield should have high target ratios. Unprofitable companies with risky, intangible assets should rely primarily on equity financing.

All in all, this trade-off theory of capital structure tells a comforting story. It avoids extreme predictions and rationalizes moderate debt ratios. But what are the facts? Can the trade-off theory of capital structure explain how companies actually behave?

The answer is yes and no. On the yes side, the trade-off theory successfully explains many industry differences in capital structure. For example, high-tech growth companies, whose assets are risky and mostly intangible, normally use relatively little debt. Utilities or retailers can and do borrow heavily because their assets are tangible and relatively safe. From Table 15.6, compare the low debt-to-equity ratio of the high-tech company Research In Motion with the much higher debt-to-equity ratio of the utility company, ATCO. Notice that in general, the company ratios are consistent with their respective industry averages.

On the no side, there are other things the trade-off theory cannot explain. It cannot explain why some of the most successful companies thrive with little debt. Consider, for example, the large American pharmaceutical company Johnson & Johnson, which is basically all-equity financed. Granted, Johnson & Johnson's most valuable assets are intangible—the fruits of its research and development. We know that intangible assets and conservative capital structures should go together. But Johnson & Johnson also has a very large corporate income tax bill ($3.1 billion in 2003) and the highest possible credit rating. It could borrow enough to save tens of millions of tax dollars without raising a whisker of concern about possible financial distress.

Our example illustrates an odd fact about real-life capital structures: The most profitable companies generally borrow the least. Here the trade-off theory fails because it predicts exactly the reverse. Under the trade-off theory, high profits should mean more debt-servicing capacity and more taxable income to shield and therefore should give a higher debt ratio.

Check Point 15.8   Rank these industries in order of predicted debt ratios under the trade-off theory of capital structure (1) Internet software, (2) auto manufacturing, and (3) regulated electric utilities.

A PECKING-ORDER THEORY

There is an alternative theory that could explain why profitable companies borrow less. It is based on *asymmetric information*—managers know more than outside investors about the profitability and prospects of their firm. Thus investors may not be able to assess the true value of a new issue of securities by the firm. They may be especially reluctant to buy newly issued common stock, because they worry that the new shares will turn out to be overpriced.

Such worries can explain why the announcement of a stock issue can drive down the stock price.[12] If managers know more than outside investors, the manager will be tempted to time stock issues when their companies' stock is overpriced—in other words, when the managers are relatively pessimistic. On the other hand, optimistic managers will see their companies' shares as underpriced and decide not to issue. You can see why investors would learn to interpret the announcement of a stock issue as a "pessimistic manager" signal and mark down the stock price accordingly. You can also see why optimistic financial managers—and most managers are optimistic!—would view a common stock issue as a relatively expensive source of financing.

All these problems are avoided if the company can finance with internal funds, that is, with earnings retained and reinvested. But if external financing is required, the path of least resistance is debt, not equity. Issuing debt seems to have a trifling effect on stock prices. There is less scope for debt to be misvalued and therefore a debt issue is a less worrisome signal to investors.

pecking-order theory Firms prefer to issue debt rather than equity if internal finance is insufficient.

These observations suggest a **pecking-order theory** of capital structure. It goes like this:

1. Firms prefer internal finance because these funds are raised without sending any adverse signals that may lower the stock price.

---

[12] We described this "announcement effect" in Chapter 14.

2. If external finance is required, firms issue debt first and issue equity only as a last resort. This pecking order arises because an issue of debt is less likely than an equity issue to be interpreted by investors as a bad omen.

In this story, there is no clear target debt-equity mix, because there are two kinds of equity, internal and external. The first is at the top of the pecking order and the second is at the bottom. The pecking order explains why the most profitable firms generally borrow less; it is not because they have low target debt-ratios but because they don't need outside money. Less profitable firms issue debt because they do not have sufficient internal funds for their capital investment program and because debt is first in the pecking order for *external* finance.

The pecking order theory does not deny that taxes and financial distress can be important factors in the choice of capital structure. However, the theory says that these factors are less important than managers' preference for internal over external funds and for debt financing over new issues of common stock.

We saw in Chapter 13 that for most Canadian corporations, internal funds finance the majority of new investment, and most external financing comes from debt. These aggregate financing patterns are consistent with the pecking-order theory. Yet the pecking order seems to work best for mature firms. Fast-growing high-tech firms often resort to a series of common stock issues to finance their investments. For this type of firm, common stock often comes at the *top* of the pecking order. The reasons the pecking-order theory works for some firms and not others are not well understood.

THE TWO FACES OF FINANCIAL SLACK

Other things being equal, it's better to be at the top of the pecking order than at the bottom. Firms that have worked down the pecking order and need external equity may end up living with excessive debt or bypassing good investments because shares can't be sold at what managers consider a fair price.

financial slack Ready access to cash or debt financing.

In other words, financial slack is valuable. Having **financial slack** means having cash, marketable securities, readily saleable real assets, and ready access to the debt markets or to bank financing. Ready access basically requires conservative financing so that potential lenders see the company's debt as a safe investment.

In the long run, a company's value rests more on its capital investment and operating decisions than on financing. Therefore, you want to make sure your firm has sufficient financial slack so that financing is quickly available for good investments. Financial slack is most valuable to firms with plenty of positive-NPV growth opportunities. That is another reason growth companies usually aspire to conservative capital structures.

There is also a dark side to financial slack. Too much of it may encourage managers to take it easy, expand their perks, or empire build with cash that should be paid back to shareholders. Michael Jensen has stressed the tendency of managers with ample free cash flow (or unnecessary financial slack) to plow too much cash into mature businesses or ill-advised acquisitions. "The problem," Jensen says, "is how to motivate managers to disgorge the cash rather than investing it below the cost of capital or wasting it in organizational inefficiencies."[13]

If that's the problem, then maybe debt is an answer. Scheduled interest and principal payments are contractual obligations of the firm. Debt forces the firm to pay out cash. Perhaps the best debt level would leave just enough cash in the bank after debt service to finance all positive-NPV projects, with not a penny left over.

We do not recommend this degree of fine-tuning, but the idea is valid and important. For some firms, the threat of financial distress may have a good effect on managers' incentives. After all, skating on thin ice can be useful if it makes the skater concentrate. Likewise, managers of

---

[13] M.C. Jensen, "Agency Costs of Free Cash Flow, Corporate Finance and Takeovers," *American Economic Review* 26 (May 1986), p. 323.

How Sealed Air's Change in Capital Structure Acted as a Catalyst to Organizational Change

Sealed Air Corporation manufactures a wide variety of packaging materials such as plastic packing bubbles and Jiffy padded envelopes.

As it entered 1989, Sealed Air was very conservatively financed with $33 million in total debt and over $54 million in cash. Thus, rather than borrowing cash, the company was actually a net lender. However, in June of that year, Sealed Air dramatically changed its capital structure by paying a special one-time dividend of $40 a share. With about 8.25 million shares trading, the total cash payout amounted to almost $330 million, or close to 90 percent of the total market value of the firm's common stock. To help finance this special dividend, the company borrowed a total of $307 million. Thus, the company went overnight from being a net lender to being a very heavy borrower. Debt now amounted to 125 percent of the book value of the assets and 65 percent of their market value.

Until the change in capital structure Sealed Air's performance was no better than that of the industry as a whole. But the change was a prelude to a sharp improvement in the company's operating performance. In the following 5 years, operating profit increased by 70 percent while the asset base grew by only 9 percent. This improvement in profitability was more than matched by the company's stock market performance. The initial effect of Sealed Air's announced change in capital structure was a jump of 10 percent in the stock price. Over the next 5.5 years the stock outperformed the market by 400 percent.

What, then, motivated the change in capital structure and what role, if any, did this change play in the company's subsequent performance?

Some of the gains from the change in capital structure may have come from the fact that the company was able to offset the interest payments against tax. But this does not appear to have been a primary motive. Instead, the change appears to have been management's response to the realization that life at Sealed Air was in many respects too comfortable. For years patents had insulated the company from competition. Cash was plentiful. So the company never needed to think hard about requests to invest in new projects, and there was no sense of urgency in removing inefficiencies. In the management's view, it would take nothing less than a crisis to shake employees out of their complacency. The change in capital structure was just such a crisis.

The sharp increase in debt levels meant that cash was no longer abundant for it was now needed to pay the debtholders and was literally essential to the company's survival. Thus, managers now felt under pressure to make those efficiency gains that previously had not seemed worthwhile. As employees became aware of the need for more effective operations, it was possible to decentralize decision making within the company and to install a more effective system of performance measurement and compensation. The result was a sharp increase in profit margins and a reduction in the working capital and fixed assets employed to generate each dollar of sales. It seemed that the capital structure change had succeeded in kick-starting a remarkable improvement in Sealed Air's performance.

Source: Adapted from K. H. Wruck, "Financial Policy as a Catalyst for Organizational Change: Sealed Air Corporation's Leveraged Special Dividend," *Journal of Applied Corporate Finance* 7 (Winter 1995), pp. 20–37.

SEE BOX ABOVE ▷

highly levered firms are more likely to work harder, run a leaner operation, and think more carefully before they spend money.

The Finance in Action box above tells the story of how Sealed Air Corporation borrowed more than $300 million (US), using the proceeds of the loan to pay a special cash dividend to shareholders. The net effect was to increase debt from a trivial level to a full 65 percent of the total value of the firm. The dramatic increase in debt committed the firm to pay out large sums of money as interest, leaving it with little opportunity to fritter its cash away in pursuit of a comfortable life. Sealed Air showed great improvements in efficiency after the change in capital structure.

15.5 SUMMARY

1. What is the goal of the capital structure decision? What is the financial manager trying to do?

The goal is to maximize the overall market value of all the securities issued by the firm. Think of the financial manager as taking all the firm's real assets and selling them to investors as a package of securities. Some financial managers choose the simplest package possible: all-equity financing. Others end up issuing dozens of types of debt and equity securities. The financial manager must try to find the particular combination that maximizes the market value of the firm. If firm value increases, common shareholders will benefit.

2. Does firm value increase when more debt is used?

Not necessarily. Modigliani and Miller's (MM) famous **debt irrelevance proposition** states that firm value can't be increased by changing **capital structure**. Therefore, the proportions of debt and equity financing don't matter. **Financial leverage** does increase the expected rate of return to shareholders, but the risk of their shares increases proportionally. MM show that the extra return and extra risk balance out, leaving shareholders no better or worse off.

Of course, MM's argument rests on simplifying assumptions. For example, the argument assumes efficient, well-functioning capital markets, and ignores taxes and costs of financial distress. But even if these assumptions are incorrect in practice, MM's proposition is important. It exposes logical traps that financial managers sometimes fall into, particularly the idea that debt is "cheap financing" because the explicit cost of debt (the interest rate) is less than the cost of equity. Debt has an implicit cost too, because increased borrowing increases **financial risk** and cost of equity. When both costs are considered, debt is not cheaper than equity. MM show that if there are no corporate income taxes, the firm's weighted-average cost of capital does not depend on the amount of debt financing.

3. How do corporate income taxes modify MM's leverage irrelevance proposition?

Debt interest is a tax-deductible expense. Thus borrowing creates an **interest tax shield**, which equals the marginal corporate tax rate, T_c, times the interest payment $r_{debt} \times D$. Future interest tax shields are usually valued by discounting at the borrowing rate r_{debt}. In the special case of permanent debt,

$$\text{PV tax shield} = \frac{T_c\,(r_{debt} \times D)}{r_{debt}} = T_c D$$

Of course, interest tax shields are valuable only for companies that are making profits and paying taxes.

4. If interest tax shields are valuable, why don't all tax-paying firms borrow as much as possible?

The more they borrow, the higher the odds of financial distress. The **costs of financial distress** can be broken down as follows:

- Direct bankruptcy costs, primarily legal and administrative costs.
- Indirect bankruptcy costs, reflecting the difficulty of managing a company when it is in bankruptcy proceedings.
- Costs of the threat of bankruptcy, such as poor investment decisions resulting from conflicts of interest between debtholders and shareholders.

5. Suppose I add interest tax shields and costs of financial distress to MM's leverage irrelevance proposition. What's the result?

The **trade-off theory** of optimal capital structure. The trade-off theory says that financial managers should increase debt to the point where the value of additional interest tax shields is just offset by additional costs of possible financial distress.

The trade-off theory says that firms with safe, tangible assets and plenty of taxable income should operate at high debt levels. Less profitable firms, or firms with risky, intangible assets, should borrow less.

6. What's the pecking-order theory?

The **pecking-order theory** says that firms prefer internal financing (that is, earnings retained and reinvested) over external financing. If external financing is needed, they prefer to issue debt rather than issue new shares. The pecking-order theory starts with the observation that managers know more than outside investors about the firm's value and prospects. Therefore, investors find it difficult to value new security issues, particularly issues of common stock. Internal financing avoids this problem. If external financing is necessary, debt is the first choice.

The pecking-order theory says that the amount of debt a firm issues will depend on its need for external financing. The theory also suggests that financial managers should try to maintain at least some **financial slack**, that is, a reserve of ready cash or unused borrowing capacity.

7. Is financial slack always valuable?

Not if it leads to slack managers. High debt levels (and the threat of financial distress) can create strong incentives for managers to work harder, conserve cash, and avoid negative-NPV investments.

8. Is there a rule for finding optimal capital structure?

Sorry, there are no simple answers for capital structure decisions. Debt may be better than equity in some cases, worse in others. But there are at least four dimensions for the financial manager to think about.

- *Taxes.* How valuable are interest tax shields? Is the firm likely to continue paying taxes over the full life of a debt issue? Safe, consistently profitable firms are most likely to stay in a tax-paying position.
- *Risk.* Financial distress is costly even if the firm survives it. Other things being equal, financial distress is more likely for firms with high business risk. That is why risky firms typically issue less debt.

• *Asset type.* If distress does occur, the costs are generally greatest for firms whose value depends on intangible assets. Such firms generally borrow less than firms with safe, tangible assets.

• *Financial slack.* How much is enough? More slack makes it easy to finance future investments, but it may weaken incentives for managers. More debt, and therefore less slack, increases the odds that the firm may have to issue stock to finance future investments.

Related Web Links

www.investinginbonds.com This Bond Market Association site has extensive information about bond markets and bond pricing

www.bondsonline.com/Bond_Ratings_Definitions.php Information on bond ratings from a variety of sources

http://finance.yahoo.com Information on the capital structure of individual firms and industries

Key Terms

capital structure	467	financial leverage	472	pecking-order theory	487
restructuring	468	financial risk	472	financial slack	488
MM's proposition I (debt		MM's proposition II	473		
irrelevance proposition)	470	interest tax shield	475		
operating risk or business		costs of financial distress	479		
risk	471	trade-off theory	479		

Questions and Problems

*Answers in Appendix B

BASIC

1. **MM's Leverage Irrelevance Proposition.** True or false? MM's leverage irrelevance proposition says that
   a. the value of the firm does not depend on the fraction of debt versus equity financing.
   b. as financial leverage increases, the value of the firm increases by just enough to affect the additional financial risk absorbed by equity.
   c. the cost of equity increases with financial leverage only when the risk of financial distress is high.
   d. if the firm pays no taxes, the weighted-average cost of capital does not depend on the debt ratio.

2. **Effects of Leverage.** Increasing financial leverage can increase both the cost of debt, (r_{debt}), and the cost of equity, (r_{equity}). How can the overall cost of capital stay constant? (Assume the firm pays no taxes.)

3. **Tax Shields.** What is an interest tax shield? How does it increase the "pie" of after-tax income shareholders? Explain. *Hint*: Construct a simple numerical example showing how financial leverage affects the total cash flow available to debt and equity investors. Be sure to hold pretax operating income constant.

*4. **Value of Tax Shields.** Establishment Industries borrows $800 million at an interest rate of 7.6 percent. It expects to maintain this debt level into the far future. What is the present value of interest tax shields? Establishment will pay tax at an effective rate of 37 percent.

5. **Trade-off Theory.** What is the trade-off theory of optimal capital structure? How does it define the optimal debt ratio?

6. **Financial Distress.** Give three examples of the types of costs incurred by firms in financial distress.

7. **Pecking-Order Theory.** What is the pecking-order theory of optimal capital structure? If the theory is correct, what types of firms would you expect to operate at high debt levels?

8. **Financial Slack.** Why is financial slack valuable? *Hint*: What does the pecking-order theory say about financial slack? Are there circumstances where too much financial slack might actually reduce the market value of the firm?

9. **Earnings and Leverage.** Suppose that River Cruises, which currently is all-equity financed, issues $250,000 of debt and uses the proceeds to repurchase 25,000 shares. Assume the firm pays no taxes, and that debt finance has no impact on its market value. Rework Table 15.2 to show how earnings per share and share return now vary with operating income.

10. **Debt Irrelevance.** Suppose an investor is unhappy with River Cruises' decision to borrow $250,000 (see the previous problem). What modifications can she make to her own investment portfolio to offset the effects of the firm's additional borrowing?

*11. **Leverage and P/E Ratio.** Calculate the ratio of price to expected earnings for River Cruises both before and after it borrows the $250,000. Why does the P/E ratio fall after the increase in leverage?

12. **Tax Shields.** Now suppose that the corporate tax is $T_c = .35$. Demonstrate that when River Cruises borrows the $250,000, the combined after-tax income of its debtholders and equityholders increases (compared to all-equity financing) by 35 percent of the firm's interest expense regardless of the state of the economy.

PRACTICE

13. **Equity Return and Leverage.** The common stock and debt of Northern Sludge are valued at $70 million and $30 million, respectively. Investors currently require a 16 percent return on the common stock and an 8 percent return on the debt. If Northern Sludge issues an additional $10 million of common stock and uses this money to retire debt, what happens to the expected return on the stock? Assume that the change in capital structure does not affect the risk of the debt and that there are no taxes.

EXCEL

14. **Earnings and Leverage.** Reliable Gearing currently is all-equity financed. It has 10,000 shares of equity outstanding, selling at $100 a share. The firm is considering a capital restructuring. The low-debt plan calls for a debt issue of $200,000 with the proceeds used to buy back stock. The high-debt plan would exchange $400,000 of debt for equity. The debt will pay an interest rate of 10 percent. The firm pays no taxes.
   a. What will be the debt-to-equity ratio after each possible restructuring?
   b. If earnings before interest and tax (EBIT) will be either $90,000 or $130,000, what will earnings per share be for each financing mix for both possible values of EBIT? If both scenarios are equally likely, what is expected (i.e., average) EPS under each financing mix? Is the high-debt mix preferable?
   c. Suppose that EBIT is $100,000. What is EPS under each financing mix? Why are they the same in this particular case?

EXCEL

15. **Leverage and Risk Premiums.** Schuldenfrei A.G. is financed entirely by common stock and has a beta of 1.0. The firm pays no taxes. The stock has a price-earnings multiple of 10 and is priced to offer a 10 percent expected return. The company decides to repurchase half the common stock and substitute an equal value of debt. If the debt yields a risk-free 5 percent, calculate
   a. the beta of the common stock after the refinancing.
   b. the required return and risk premium on the common stock before the refinancing.
   c. the required return and risk premium on the common stock after the refinancing.
   d. the required return on the debt.
   e. the required return on the company (i.e., stock and debt combined) after the refinancing.

   Assume that the operating profit of the firm is expected to remain constant. Give

   f. the percentage increase in earnings per share after the refinancing.
   g. the new price-earnings multiple. *Hint*: Has anything happened to the stock price?

*16. **Leverage and Capital Costs.** Hubbard's Pet Foods is financed 80 percent by common stock and 20 percent by bonds. The expected return on the common stock is 12 percent and the rate of interest on the bonds is 6 percent. Assume that the bonds are default-free and that there are no taxes. Now assume that Hubbard's issues more debt and uses the proceeds to retire equity. The new financing mix is 40 percent equity and 60 percent debt. If the debt is still default-free, what happens to the expected rate of return on equity? What happens to the expected return on the package of common stock and bonds?

17. **Leverage and Capital Costs.** "MM totally ignore the fact that as you borrow more, you have to pay higher rates of interest." Explain carefully whether this is a valid objection.

18. **Debt Irrelevance.** What's wrong with the following arguments?
    a. As the firm borrows more and debt becomes risky, both share- and bondholders demand higher rates of return. Thus by *reducing* the debt ratio we can reduce both the cost of debt and the cost of equity, making everybody better off.
    b. Moderate borrowing doesn't significantly affect the probability of financial distress or bankruptcy. Consequently, moderate borrowing won't increase the expected rate of return demanded by shareholders.
    c. A capital investment opportunity offering a 10 percent internal rate of return is an attractive project if it can be 100 percent debt-financed at an 8 percent interest rate.
    d. The more debt the firm issues, the higher the interest rate it must pay. That is one important reason firms should operate at conservative debt levels.

EXCEL

19. **Leverage and Capital Costs.** A firm currently has a debt-equity ratio of 1/2. The debt, which is virtually riskless, pays an interest rate of 6 percent. The expected rate of return on the equity is 12 percent. What would happen to the expected rate of return on equity if the firm reduced its debt-equity ratio to 1/3? Assume the firm pays no taxes.

20. **Leverage and Capital Costs.** If an increase in the debt-equity ratio makes both debt and equity more risky, how can the cost of capital remain unchanged?

21. **Tax Shields.** Look back to Table 3.2 where we provided a summary 2004 income statement for Maple Leaf Foods. If the tax rate is 35 percent, what is Maple Leaf Foods' annual interest tax shield? What is the present value of the annual tax shield if the company plans to maintain its current debt level indefinitely? Assume a discount rate of 8 percent.

*22. **WACC.** Here is Establishment Industries' market-value balance sheet ($ millions):

Net working capital	$ 550	Debt	$ 800
Long-term assets	$2,150	Equity	$1,900
Value of firm	$2,700		$2,700

The debt is yielding 7.6 percent and the cost of equity is 14 percent. The tax rate is 37 percent. Investors expect this level of debt to be permanent.
    a. What is Establishment's WACC?
    b. Write out a market-value balance sheet assuming Establishment has no debt. Use your answer to problem 4.

*23. **Tax Shields and WACC.** Here are book- and market-value balance sheets of the United Frypan Company:

BOOK-VALUE BALANCE SHEET

Net working capital	$ 20	Debt	$40
Long-term assets	80	Equity	60
	$100		$100

MARKET-VALUE BALANCE SHEET

Net working capital	$ 20	Debt	$ 40
Long-term assets	140	Equity	120
	$160		$160

Assume that MM's theory holds except for taxes. There is no growth and the $40 of debt is expected to be permanent. Assume a 35 percent corporate tax rate.

   a.   How much of the firm's value is accounted for by the debt-generated tax shield?

   b.   What is United Frypan's after-tax weighted-average cost of capital (WACC)?

   c.   Now suppose that Parliament passes a law that eliminates the deductibility of interest for tax purposes after a grace period of five years. What will be the new value of the firm, other things being equal? Assume an 8 percent borrowing rate.

*24. **Bankruptcy.** What are the drawbacks of operating a firm that is close to bankruptcy? Give some examples.

25. **Costs of Financial Distress.** The Salad Oil Storage Company (SOS) has financed a large part of its facilities with long-term debt. There is a significant risk of default, but the company is not on the ropes yet. Explain why

   a.   SOS shareholders could lose by investing in a positive-NPV project financed by an equity issue.

   b.   SOS shareholders could gain by investing in a highly risky, negative-NPV project.

26. **Financial Distress.** Explain how financial distress can lead to conflicts of interest between debt and equity investors. Then explain how these conflicts can lead to costs of financial distress.

27. **Costs of Financial Distress.** For which of the following firms would you expect the costs of financial distress to be highest? Explain briefly.

   a.   a computer software company that depends on skilled programmers to produce new products.

   b.   a shipping company that operates a fleet of modern oil tankers.

28. **Trade-off Theory.** Smoke and Mirrors currently has EBIT of $25,000 and is all-equity financed. EBIT is expected to stay at this level indefinitely. The firm pays corporate taxes equal to 35 percent of taxable income. The discount rate for the firm's projects is 10 percent.

   a.   What is the market value of the firm?

   b.   Now assume the firm issues $50,000 of debt paying interest of 6 percent per year and uses the proceeds to retire equity. The debt is expected to be permanent. What will happen to the total value of the firm (debt plus equity)?

   c.   Recompute your answer to part (b) under the following assumptions; the debt issue raises the possibility of bankruptcy; the firm has a 30 percent chance of going bankrupt after 3 years; if it does go bankrupt, it will incur bankruptcy costs of $200,000. The discount rate is 10 percent. Should the firm issue the debt?

29. **Pecking-Order Theory.** Alpha Corp. and Beta Corp. both produce turbo encabulators. Both companies' assets and operations are growing at the same rate and their annual capital expenditures are about the same. However, Alpha Corp. is the more efficient producer and is consistently more profitable. According to the pecking-order theory, which company should have the higher debt ratio? Explain.

30. **Financial Slack.** Look back to the Sealed Air example in the Finance in Action box on page 489. What was the value of financial slack to Sealed Air before its restructuring? What does the success of the restructuring say about optimal capital structure? Would you recommend that all firms restructure as Sealed Air did?

31. **Internet.** Log in to **http://finance.yahoo.com** and find the profile for Magna International (MGA). Construct the debt ratio, debt/(debt + equity), for the firm. Now calculate Magna's debt ratio by using the market value of equity, but assuming that book value of debt approximates its market value. How does debt as a proportion of firm value change as you switch from book to market value?

32. **Standard & Poor's.** Go to Market Insight (**www.mcgrawhill.ca/edumarketinsight**). Review the Ratio and Profitability reports for one or more of the following companies: American Airlines (AMRI), Nortel Networks (NT), and Kmart (KMRT). Are you able to

see a trend toward financial distress for these companies in 2003 and 2004? If so, what factors seem to be associated with their financial distress?

CHALLENGE

33. **Internet.**
    a. Go to **http://finance.yahoo.com** and find the profiles for PepsiCo (PEP) and IBM (IBM) and then look at each firm's annual balance sheet and income statement under "Highlights." Calculate the present value of the interest tax shield contributed by each company's long-term debt. Assume a 34 percent tax rate for both companies. Now suppose that each issues $3 billion more of long-term debt and uses the proceeds to re-purchase equity. How would the interest tax shield change?
    b. While you are logged in to the Yahoo! page for PepsiCo or IBM, move down and click on the "Industry" in the left-hand column. This will give you a table of financial ratios for different industries in the United States. Compare the debt-equity ratios for different industries. Can you account for the differences? Are they better explained by the trade-off theory or the pecking-order theory?

*34. **Costs of Financial Distress.** Let's go back to the Double-R Nutting Company. Suppose that Double-R's bonds have a face value of $50. Its current market-value balance sheet is

Assets		Liabilities and Equity	
Net working capital	$20	Bonds outstanding	$25
Fixed assets	10	Common stock	5
Total assets	$30	Total liabilities and shareholders' equity	$30

Who would gain or lose from the following manoeuvres?
    a. Double-R pays a $10 cash dividend.
    b. Double-R halts operations, sells its fixed assets for $6, and converts net working-capital into $20 cash. It invests its $26 in Treasury bills.
    c. Double-R encounters an investment opportunity requiring a $10 initial investment with NPV = $0. It borrows $10 to finance the project by issuing more bonds with the same security, seniority, and so on, as the existing bonds.
    d. Double-R finances the investment opportunity in part (c) by issuing more common stock.

35. **Trade-off Theory.** Ronald Masulis[14] has analyzed the stock price impact of *exchange offers* of debt for equity, or vice versa. In an exchange offer, the firm offers to trade freshly issued securities for seasoned securities in the hands of investors. Thus a firm that wanted to move to a higher debt ratio could offer to trade new debt for outstanding shares. A firm that wanted to move to a more conservative capital structure could offer to trade new shares for outstanding debt securities. Masulis found that debt-for-equity exchanges were good news (stock price increased on announcement) and equity-for-debt exchanges were bad news.
    a. Are these results consistent with the trade-off theory of capital structure?
    b. Are the results consistent with the evidence that investors regard announcements of (1) stock issues as bad news, (2) stock repurchases as good news, and (3) debt issues as no news, or at most trifling disappointments?

36. **Pecking-Order Theory.** Construct a simple example to show that a firm's existing shareholders gain if they can sell overpriced stock to new investors and invest the cash in a zero-NPV project. Who loses from these actions? If investors are aware that managers are likely to issue stock when it is overpriced, what will happen to the stock price when the issue is announced?

---

[14] R.W. Masulis, "The Effects of Capital Structure Change on Security Prices: A Study of Exchange Offers," *Journal of Financial Economics* 8 (June 1980), pp. 139–177 and "The Impact of Capital Structure Change on Firm Value," *Journal of Finance* 38 (March 1983), pp. 107–126.

37. **Pecking-Order Theory.** When companies announce an issue of common stock, the share price typically falls. When they announce an issue of debt, there is typically only a negligible change in the stock price. Can you explain why?

38. **Taxes.** MM's proposition I suggests that in the absence of taxes it makes no difference whether the firm borrows on behalf of its shareholders or whether they borrow directly. However, if there are corporate taxes, this is no longer the case. Construct a simple example to show that with taxes it is better for the firm to borrow than for the shareholders to do so.

39. **Taxes.** MM's proposition I, when modified to recognize corporate taxes, suggests that there is a tax advantage to firm borrowing. If there is a tax advantage to firm borrowing, there is also a tax disadvantage to firm lending. Explain why.

Solutions to Check Points

15.1   Price per share will stay at $10, so with $350,000, River Cruises can repurchase 35,000 shares, leaving 65,000 outstanding. The remaining value of equity will be $650,000. Overall firm value stays at $1 million. Shareholders' wealth is unchanged: They start with shares worth $1 million, receive $350,000, and retain shares worth $650,000.

15.2   a. Data:

Number of shares	25,000
Price per share	$10
Market value of shares	$250,000
Market value of debt	$750,000

	State of the Economy		
	Slump	**Normal**	**Boom**
Operating income	$75,000	125,000	175,000
Interest	$75,000	75,000	75,000
Equity earnings	$ 0	50,000	100,000
Earnings per share	$ 0	2	4
Return on shares	0%	20%	40%

Every change of $50,000 in operating income leads to a change in the return to equity-holders of 20 percent. This is double the swing in equity returns when debt was only $500,000.

b. The shareholder should lend out $3 for every $1 invested in River Cruises' stock. For example, he could buy one share for $10 and then lend $30. The payoffs are

	State of the Economy		
	Slump	**Normal**	**Boom**
Earnings on one share	$0	2	4
Plus interest at 10%	$3	3	3
Net earnings	$3	5	7
Return on $40 investment	7.5%	12.5%	17.5%

15.3   Business risk is unaffected by capital structure. As the financing mix changes, whatever equity is outstanding must absorb the fixed business risk of the firm. The less equity, the more risk absorbed per share. Therefore, as capital structure changes, r_{assets} is held fixed while r_{equity} adjusts.

15.4   BCE, Inc.'s borrowing reduced taxable profits by $1,093 million. With a tax rate of 35 percent, tax was reduced by $.35 \times \$1,093 = \$382.6$ million. If the borrowing is permanent, BCE, Inc., will save this amount of tax each year. The present value of the tax saving would be $382.6/.08 = \$4,782.5$ million.

15.5   In bankruptcy bondholders will receive $2 million less. This lowers the expected cash flow from the bond and reduces its present value. Therefore, the bonds will be priced lower and must offer a higher interest rate. This higher rate is paid by the firm today. It comes out of shareholders' income. Thus common stock value falls.

15.6   The conflicts are costly because they lead to poor investment decisions. The more debt the firm has today, the greater the chance of poor decisions in the future. Investors foresee this possibility and reduce today's market value of the firm.

15.7   Financial distress would be most costly for the biotech company. Its assets are all intangible. If bankruptcy threatens and the best scientists accept job offers from other firms, there may not be much value remaining for the biotech company's debt and equity investors. On the other hand, bankruptcy would have little or no effect on the value of 50 producing oil wells and of the oil reserves still in the ground.

15.8   The electric utility has the most stable cash flow. It also has the highest reliance on tangible assets that would not be impaired by a bankruptcy. It should have the highest debt ratio. The software firm has the least dependence on tangible assets and the most on assets that have value only if the firm continues as an ongoing concern. It probably also has the most unpredictable cash flows. It should have the lowest debt ratio.

MINICASE

In March 2004, the management team of Londonderry Air (LA) met to discuss a proposal to purchase five short-haul aircraft at a total cost of $25 million. There was general enthusiasm for the investment, and the new aircraft were expected to generate an annual cash flow of $4 million for 20 years.

The focus of the meeting was on how to finance the purchase. LA had $20 million in cash and marketable securities (see table on the following page), but Ed Johnson, the chief financial officer, pointed out that the company needed at least $10 million in cash to meet normal outflow and as a contingency reserve. This meant that there would be a cash deficiency of $15 million, which the firm would need to cover either by the sale of common stock or by additional borrowing. While admitting that the arguments were finely balanced, Johnson recommended an issue of stock. He pointed out that the airline industry was subject to wide swings in profits, and the firm should be careful to avoid the risk of excessive borrowing. He estimated that in market-value terms the long-term debt ratio was about 62 percent and that a further debt issue would raise the ratio to 64 percent.

Johnson's only doubt about making a stock issue was that investors might jump to the conclusion that management believed the stock was overpriced, in which case the announcement might prompt an unjustified selloff by investors. He stressed therefore that the company needed to explain carefully the reasons for the issue. Also, he suggested that demand for the issue would be enhanced if at the same time LA increased its dividend payment. This would provide a tangible indication of management's confidence in the future.

These arguments cut little ice with LA's chief executive. "Ed," she said, "I know that you're the expert on all this, but everything you say flies in the face of common sense. Why should we want to sell more equity when our stock has fallen over the past year by nearly a fifth? Our stock is currently offering a dividend yield of 6.5 percent, which makes equity an expensive source of capital. Increasing the dividend would simply make it more expensive. What's more, I don't see the point of paying out more money to the shareholders at the same time that we are asking *them* for cash. If we hike the dividend, we will need to increase the amount of the stock issue; so we will just be paying the higher dividend out of the shareholders' own pockets. You're also ignoring the question of dilution. Our equity currently has a book value of $12 a share; it's not playing fair by our existing shareholders if we now issue stock for around $10 a share.

"Look at the alternative. We can borrow today at 5 percent. We get a tax break on the interest, so the after-tax cost of borrowing is .65 × 5 = 3.25 percent. That's about half the cost of equity. We expect to earn a return of 15 percent on these new aircraft. If we can raise money at 3.25 percent and invest it at 15 percent, that's a good deal in my book.

"You finance guys are always talking about risk, but as long as we don't go bankrupt, borrowing doesn't add any risk at all. In any case, my calculations show that the debt ratio is only 45 percent, which doesn't sound excessive to me.

"Ed, I don't want to push my views on this—after all, you're the expert. We don't need to make a firm recommendation to the board until next month. In the meantime, why don't you get one of your new business graduates to look at the whole issue of how we should finance the deal and what return we need to earn on these planes."

Summary financial
statements for Londonderry
Air, 2003 (figures are book
values, $ millions)

Balance Sheet			
Bank debt	$ 50	Cash	$ 20
Other current liabilities	20	Other current assets	20
10% bond, due 2023[1]	100	Fixed assets	250
Stockholders' equity[2,3]	120		
Total liabilities	$ 290	Total assets	$ 290

Income Statement	
Gross profit	57.5
Depreciation	20.0
Interest	7.5
Pretax profit	30.0
Tax	10.5
Net profit	19.5
Dividend	6.5

Notes:
1. The yield to maturity on LA debt currently is 5 percent.
2. LA has 10 million shares outstanding and a market price of $10 a share.
3. LA's equity beta is estimated at 1.25, the market risk premium is 8 percent, and the
   Treasury bill rate is 4 percent.

15.6   APPENDIX 15.A: A NOTE ON INCOME TRUSTS

WHAT ARE INCOME TRUSTS?

In recent years, income trusts have become very popular with the investing public in Canada. We feel
that it is only appropriate to spend some time discussing these entities and to describe some of their
unique attributes. In the process, we will also examine some of their capital structure implications.

An income trust sells units in the trust to investors and uses the funds to purchase revenue-gen-
erating assets, often by investing in the entire equity of an operating company. While ideally such
assets should belong to mature industries that generate stable cash flows and require little incremental capital expenditure such as natural gas processing and distribution or mining, in practice
income trusts exist for businesses as diverse as manufacturing, telecommunications, and restaurants.

Income trusts have a unique "tax efficient" structure that is geared toward reducing the incidence of double taxation of dividend income, which we discussed in Chapter 3, whereby business
profits are taxed first at the corporate level, and dividend payments to shareholders are taxed subsequently in their hands. This happens because the trust is taxed as an individual legal entity. If,
however, it distributes the income it receives from the operating company to its unitholders, it is
permitted to deduct such distributions from its taxable income. So, for instance, if the trust pays
out all of its income from investments to the unitholders, it can, in effect, end up not paying any
income tax. Tax efficiency may be further enhanced by having the operating company borrow
from the trust and using the interest on the loan to reduce the operating company's tax liability.
Reducing or eliminating taxes at the corporate level in turn enables higher dividend payments to
unitholders than would have been possible from an equivalent corporate entity. Of course, the
income distributed by the trust to unitholders is taxed in their hands. The extent of income tax
levied on an individual unitholder would depend on the nature of the distributed income—i.e. dividend, interest, or some other type of income—and the unitholder's tax status.

For instance, if the distributed income represents interest or royalty, it will be taxed at the
unitholder's full tax rate. If, on the other hand, the distributed income represents dividends, the

unitholder could be entitled to a dividend tax credit. which would then result in a lower tax liability. At times, unitholders may receive a return of capital. This would happen if the cash distributions by the operating company are higher than its taxable income. Sometimes, the use of capital cost allowance or other accelerated tax deductions may enable cash distributions to unitholders that are in excess of the operating company's taxable income. While return of capital is tax deferred, it could result in capital gains and attract capital gains tax for the unitholder if the unitholder chooses to sell the units. Similar to equity securities, income trust units can be held as eligible investments in registered retirement savings plans (RRSPs) and pension accounts.

Income trusts have two key differences with corporate entities. First, the income trust is set up as a separate legal entity that acts as a "flow-through" between the equity investor and the operating company. Investors own units in the income trust, which in turn owns all of the equity in the operating company. For tax purposes, an income trust can treat some or all of its investment in the equity of the operating company as debt.[15] The operating company generates cash flows from the use of its assets. These cash flows are distributed to unitholders in the form of interest, dividend, royalty, or some other form of income. Notice that the equity that is treated as debt by the income trust is generally subordinated to other creditor claims and treated as equity for all purposes except tax. Sometimes, the income trust can simply be set up as a limited partnership that owns the assets of the underlying operating business. Investors buy units of the limited partnership, which may trade on a stock exchange such as the TSX. The business assets are managed by a general partner, who is often closely related to the sponsor of the partnership. Inter Pipelines or TransCanada Power are examples of limited partnership trusts.

Also, unlike in a corporation where governance is the responsibility of the board of directors, many income trusts appoint trustees to supervise the operating company on behalf of unitholders.[16] The trustee makes decisions pertaining to cash distributions to unitholders of the income trust. Day-to-day management decisions of the operating company are typically delegated to its management who are often full-time professional managers. Figure 15A.1 compares the general structure of an income trust with that of a corporation. Panel A of the figure shows the corporate structure. From Panel A, notice that shareholders invest directly in the equity of the operating company and receive periodic dividends. The overall supervision of the operating company is with its board of directors. The operating company may raise funds by issuing bonds and taking loans for which it pays interest to creditors and repays the principal amount when the bond matures or when the loan becomes due. Panel B shows that within an income trust framework, investors purchase units in the income trust, which in turn invests in the operating company. The operating company can distribute cash flows to the income trust through a variety of means including royalties, business income, interest, or dividends. The income trust, in turn, passes on the cash distribution to its unitholders. Typically, the trust may own all of the equity of the operating company and may assume overall supervision of its key decision-making including decisions pertaining to the extent of cash distribution. In practice, the day-to-day running of the operating company is usually delegated to its managers. Of course, multiple layers of administration associated with an income trust structure could result in higher administrative costs relative to a corporate structure.

Income trusts can take various forms depending on the nature of the business such as oil and gas royalty trusts, or real estate investment trusts (REITs). *Oil and Gas Royalty Trusts* distribute nearly all (say 99 percent) of net cash flows generated by the oil and gas operating business. Given the nature of business operations, assets of the producing company are being depleted over time and need to be replenished through capital expenditures on exploration and development. Often, the operating company pays a tax-deductible royalty to the trust that can significantly reduce or even eliminate its income tax liability. Examples of such royalty trusts include PrimeWest Energy Trust, and ARC Energy Trust. *Real Estate Investment Trusts* (REITs) can take various forms depending on the nature of real estate investment by the income trust. For instance,

---

[15] For a good discussion see Michael King, "Income Trusts: A Growing Asset Class," *Canadian Investment Review*, Spring 2004, 17(1), pp. 8–18.

[16] Some income trusts also have boards of directors.

FIGURE 15.A1
Corporate Structure

a. Corporate Structure

b. Income Trust Structure

Source: Michael R. King "Income Trusts—Understanding the Issues" Bank of Canada, Working Papers 2003–25.

REITs could be set up as office REITs, apartment REITs, retail REITs, or hotel and health care REITs. Examples of REITs include Canadian Hotel Income Properties and Legacy Hotels.

In recent years, income trusts have become increasingly popular with Canadian investors, particularly since the decline in stock market activity following the "hi-tech market meltdown." Their main strength is supposedly in their ability to provide sizeable and stable cash distributions. As such, they account for a large proportion of the Canadian IPO and secondary issue markets. In fact, income trusts accounted for 94 percent of all Canadian IPOs in 2002 and 80 percent in 2003. In 1997, there were 46 trusts in 18 separate business lines with a market capitalization of $10 billion. In 2003, there were 114 companies in 49 separate operating businesses which had adopted income trust structures with a market capitalization in excess of $50 billion.[17] Currently with a market capitalization of about $90 billion, representing roughly 7 percent of the market capitalization of traded stocks, trusts are an entrenched and established business structure. Table 15A.1 shows the total revenues, percentage dividend yields, and cash flows per share of some large income trusts in 2002. Notice the rather large dividend yields that investors would have found to be quite attractive.

Income trusts are owned mostly by individual investors although institutional investors are gradually increasing their investment in such funds as well. For instance, Ontario Teachers Pension Plan has started a special-purpose fund to invest in income trusts. The lack of limited liability is considered to be an important deterrent to investing by pension funds and large institutional investors in such trusts. As the nearby Finance in Action Box shows, concerns about proper corporate governance have, to date, prevented the deep-pocketed institutional investors from putting large sums of money into such entities. Also, with the burgeoning of income trusts in the marketplace, there are concerns about an investment bubble. It has been suggested that trust units are sometimes intentionally misrepresented and marketed as debt because they pay interest income but they lack the security and rights of bondholders. For instance, in the typical trust structure, the payment of cash

SEE BOX P. 502

---

[17] See, for instance, *Income Trust Primer—Update* (June 2003) prepared by the Equity Research Division of Canaccord Capital Corporation.

TABLE 15.A1
10 Large Income Trusts in 2002

Rank	Company and Year End	Total Revenue $000	% Change	Profit $000	% Change	Dividend Yield %	Cash Flow Per Share
1	Gaz Métropolitain & Co. LP	1,607,700	−22	154,580	10	7.07	2.59
2	Fording Canadian Coal Trust	882,300	−12	−70,900	−175	9.45	2.73
3	North West Co. Fund	749,759	6	34,469	19	7.50	3.70
4	Canadian Oil Sands Trust	728,175	8	269,928	84	5.26	5.63
5	TransForce Income Fund	444,684	48	26,590	126	15.00	1.19
6	Legacy Hotels REIT	649,686	7	55,105	3	10.21	0.99
7	Retirement Residences REIT	643,863	298	42,080	106	10.25	1.14
8	Superior Plus Income Fund	640,900	−19	68,800	84	10.10	2.16
9	Enerplus Resources Fund	622,009	−3	115,876	−36	11.84	4.03
10	Parkland Income Fund	260,228	18	9,413	58	13.49	2.19

Source: "50 Top Income Trusts," Canada's Power Book: Special 20th Annual Issue, *The Globe and Mail*, Report on Business, July 2003. Reprinted with permission from *The Globe and Mail*.

distributions is tied to the ability of the assets of the operating business to continue to generate consistent cash flows. There is no contractual or legal obligation to pay such distributions. Some also wonder whether the tax efficiency advantages of these entities are too good to be true and may be plugged by the federal government to prevent loss of tax revenues. There is some evidence to this effect; for instance, the recent federal budget has imposed some restrictions on the ability of pension funds to invest in income trusts. According to the budget proposal, pension funds are limited to having 1 percent of their assets in business income trusts and may hold no more than 5 percent of the assets of any single business trust.

The growth in income trusts has occurred through initial public offerings, secondary offerings, private placements, and also conversion of existing public entities into income trusts. Table 15A.2 provides details for different types of income trust issues for all four quarters of 2003.

CAPITAL STRUCTURE IMPLICATIONS OF INCOME TRUSTS

In our earlier discussion, we have seen that "tax efficiency" is one of the main perceived attractions of income trusts since corporate taxes are reduced or eliminated, thereby reducing double taxation of income. It follows that by assuming an income trust structure, a business enterprise may choose to increase its financial leverage with the expectation that the higher interest tax shield would reduce corporate taxes and thereby increase overall enterprise value. Also, the higher interest burden will, in effect, reduce the amount of "free cash flow" of the enterprise, providing its management with fewer opportunities to pursue frivolous or negative net present value projects. Notice that the

TABLE 15.A2
Quarterly Comparison of Income Trust Issues

Quarter	Total Issuance Value ($ billions)	Number of Deals	Initial Public Offerings Value ($ billions)	Number of Deals	Secondary Issues Value ($ billions)	Number of Deals	Private Placements Value ($ billions)	Number of Deals
Q1/03	$2.718	22	$0.834	8	$1.490	10	$0.395	4
Q2/03	$3.189	30	$1.837	12	$1.332	17	$0.021	1
Q3/03	$5.498	42	$3.571	16	$1.819	19	$0.107	7
Q4/03	$6.067	50	$2.944	20	$2.966	24	$0.156	6

Source: Investment Dealers Association of Canada Web site at **www.ida.ca**.

The Need to Improve Governance Rules in Income Trusts

Income trusts should not be included in the Toronto Stock Exchange's flagship index until they meet minimum standards of corporate governance, says the head of a powerful shareholder activist group.

"Because of their convoluted structure, a lot of work has to be done," David Beatty, managing director of the Canadian Coalition for Good Governance, told the Institute of Corporate Directors at a meeting in Toronto yesterday. "We'd be flying blind if we put trusts into the TSX index until we get a handle on their governance."

The market value of the burgeoning income trust sector totaled $63.3 billion at the end of 2003, up 44 per cent from a year earlier, according to the Investment Dealers Associations of Canada. In the fourth quarter of last year, $5.9 billion in trust financings hit the market, almost double those from a year earlier.

Unlike corporations, income trusts distribute most of their cash flow to their unitholders and do not pay taxes.

Mr. Beatty said in an interview that income trusts as a class need their own set of governance rules that would take into account their structure. Under trust law, the investors elect the trustees of an income trust who, in turn, appoint the directors to oversee the operating business. These directors are the primary decision makers for the trust.

"I would be hopeful that they would not be accepted into the index until such time as those standards are established and some policing is put in place," he said.

Stephen Probyn, chairman of the Canadian Association of Income Funds, said the sector wants a level playing field with publicly traded corporations on governance. "We believe that governance standards are very high in the sector."

However, Mr. Probyn acknowledged that there are structural issues with income trusts that must be taken into account. "Often, the mind and management of the trust is the board of what is effectively a subsidiary."

While income trusts have been a huge hit with individual investors, they are still fighting for acceptance by deep-pocketed institutional investors. The coalition Mr. Beatty runs represents a who's who of major Canadian institutional investors—its 30 members manage more than $500 billion in assets.

Once the problem of unlimited liability is addressed, the last impediment to income trusts being a problem asset for institutional investors will be removed, Mr. Beatty said. "Demand for them is going to continue to explode when we haven't even got our arms around the governance issues."

The Ontario government introduced legislation in December to protect income trust unitholders from being forced to pay personal damages for wrongs committed by the trust. Demand for trusts could spike if investors no longer have to worry about the theoretical possibility of being held liable for the actions of a trust whose units they own.

The legislation could also pave the way for the inclusion of large trusts in the S&P/TSX benchmark composite index.

Canadian securities regulators put the burgeoning income trust sector under the microscope last October with a proposed policy calling for greater scrutiny of marketing materials, more thorough disclosure and more explicit statements of investment risks.

A recent review of the disclosure practices of 40 income trusts by provincial securities regulators turned up problems among all but nine of the trusts. Two of the trusts were required to re-file their disclosure documents as a result of the review and 29 made commitments to change their disclosure practices, according to a notice published in a recent Ontario Securities Commission weekly bulletin.

Mr. Beatty also said in his speech that companies need to cast a wider net in the selection of directors. He said the coalition plans to ask the OSC to consider whether companies should introduce succession planning for directors. Many already have such plans in place for selecting a chief executive officer.

He said succession planning could end many companies' knee-jerk reaction of selecting board members from the "old boys' list" and create a larger pool of potential directors.

"I think it's a responsibility of the board members today to look beyond their immediate circle of friends."

Source: K. Howlett, "Governance rules urged for trusts before TSX entry: Shareholder activist calls for standards," February 19, 2004, *The Globe and Mail*. Reprinted with permission from *The Globe and Mail*.

problem of free cash flows is lessened in an income trust structure since it often requires most of the cash flows of the operating company to be distributed to unitholders.

Of course, there could also be some drawbacks to making large cash distributions. Firstly, this could reduce the flexibility of the operating company's management to respond to unexpected changes and events, and funds may not be readily available to undertake unexpected projects. Also, pressure to pay the cash distributions may force management to make unwise decisions, such as excessive borrowing from a third party, or not undertaking the project at all. As we have seen earlier in this chapter, excessive third-party borrowing can lead to higher bankruptcy and financial distress costs.

There is also the issue of limited liability. We have seen in Chapter 1 that the limited liability feature of corporations means that shareholders are not personally liable for the corporation's debts beyond their initial investment. But are unitholders granted the same legal protection in an income trust structure? This issue remains a grey area with differing opinions among legal experts.

Questions and Problems

*Answers in Appendix B

PRACTICE

1. **Income Trusts.** Describe some key features of income trusts that distinguish them from corporations. Why have income trusts been so popular with individual investors and issuers of securities? A number of business entities have chosen a trust structure as opposed to a corporate structure. Are there any potential drawbacks associated with a trust structure?

2. **Internet.** The Investment Dealers Association of Canada Web site at **www.ida.ca** contains updated quarterly statistics on new income trust activity. Go to the Web site and check out the most recent numbers for new income trust issues. From these statistics do you see increasing or declining investment activity in the trust sector? What type of issue (i.e., IPO, secondary offering, private placement, etc.) appears to be the most popular with investors and issuers? Which industry sectors appear to be raising the most funding through income trust issues?

DIVIDEND POLICY

In this chapter we explain how companies set their dividend payments, and we discuss the controversial question of how dividend policy affects value.

Why should you care about these issues? Of course, if you are responsible for deciding on your company's dividend payment, you will want to know how it affects the value of your stock. But there is a more general reason. When we discussed the company's investment decision, we assumed that it was not affected by financing policy. In that case, a good project is a good project, no matter how it is ultimately financed. If dividend policy does not affect value, this still holds true. But suppose that it *does* affect value. Then the attractiveness of a project would depend on where the money was coming from. For example, if investors prefer companies with high dividend payouts, then these firms might be reluctant to take on new projects that required them to cut back dividends.

We start the chapter with a discussion of how dividends are paid. We then show that in an ideal world, the value of a firm would be independent of its dividend policy. This demonstration is in the same spirit as the Modigliani and Miller debt-irrelevance proposition of the previous chapter.

That leads us to look at the real-world complications that might favour one dividend policy over another. These complications include transaction costs, taxes, and the signals that investors might read into the firm's dividend announcement.

After studying this chapter you should be able to
- Describe how dividends are paid and how companies decide on dividend payments.
- Explain why dividend policy would not affect firm value in an ideal world.
- Show how differences in the tax treatment of dividends and capital gains might affect dividend policy.
- Explain why dividends may be used by management to signal the prospects of the firm.

16.1

HOW DIVIDENDS ARE PAID

CASH DIVIDENDS

cash dividend Payment of cash by the firm to its shareholders.

On October 23, 2003, Maple Leaf Foods Inc. (MLF) announced a regular quarterly **cash dividend** of $.04 per share, making a total payment of $.16 for the year; soon after, its board of directors met and approved the decision. The term *regular* indicates that MLF expected to maintain the payment in the future. If it did not want to give that kind of assurance, it could have declared both a regular and an *extra dividend*. In July 2004, Microsoft did just that. As the nearby Finance in Action box describes, the cash-rich software giant declared a whopping $32 billion (US) *special dividend* because it could not find any other way to spend its sizeable cash flows. As the box shows, the company also declared a $3.5 billion (US) regular quarterly dividend, and still had $20 billion cash on hand. Investors realize that extra dividends are less likely to be repeated.[1]

SEE BOX P. 506 ▶

Who receives the MLF dividend? That may seem an obvious question, but because shares trade constantly, the firm's records of who owns its shares can never be fully up to date. So MLF announced that it would send a dividend cheque to all shareholders recorded in its books on December 12. This is known as the *record date*.

The *payment date* for MLF's dividend was December 31. On that date the dividend cheques were mailed to investors. If MLF's records were not up to date, some of those cheques would be sent to the wrong investor. To handle this problem, stock exchanges fix a cut-off date, called the **ex-dividend date**, two business days prior to the record date. If you owned MLF stock on the *with-dividend date*, which in this case was December 9, you were entitled to the dividend. If MLF mistakenly sent that dividend to someone else, that person was obliged to pass it on to you. If you acquired the stock after December 9, you were not entitled to the dividend. If MLF sent you that dividend by mistake, you had to send it on to the previous owner.

ex-dividend date Date that determines whether a stockholder is entitled to a dividend payment; anyone holding stock before this date is entitled to a dividend.

Through December 9, MLF stock was said to be trading "with dividend" or "cum dividend." Beginning on December 10, the stock traded "ex dividend." The only difference between buying MLF before and after the ex-dividend date is that in the second case you miss out on the dividend. Other things being equal, the stock is worth more when it is with dividend. Thus when the stock "goes ex," we would expect the stock price to drop by the amount of the dividend.

Figure 16.1 illustrates the sequence of the key dividend dates. This sequence is the same whenever companies pay a dividend (though of course the actual dates will differ).

Some of MLF's shareholders may have desired the cash payment, but others preferred to reinvest the dividend in the company. To help these investors, MLF had an automatic dividend reinvestment plan. If a shareholder belonged to this plan, his or her dividends were automatically used to buy additional shares.[2]

✓ Check Point 16.1

Mick Milekin buys 100 shares of Junk Bombs, Inc., on Tuesday, June 2. The company has declared a dividend of $1 per share payable on June 30 to shareholders on record as of Friday, June 5. If the ex-dividend date is June 1, is Mick entitled to the dividend? When will the cheques go out in the mail?

SOME LEGAL LIMITATIONS ON DIVIDENDS

Suppose that an unscrupulous board decided to sell all the firm's assets and distribute the money as dividends. That would not leave anything in the kitty to pay the company's debts. Therefore, bondholders often guard against this danger by placing limits on dividend payments.

---

[1] Companies also use the term "special dividend" for payments that are unlikely to be repeated.

[2] Often the new shares in an automatic dividend investment plan are issued at a small discount from the market price; the firm offers this sweetener because it saves the underwriting costs of a regular share issue. Sometimes 10 percent or more of total dividends will be reinvested under such plans.

Microsoft Issues a Special Dividend

Microsoft, with more than $50 billion on hand, announced yesterday that it would bestow on its shareholders a special one-time dividend of $3 a share, a payout worth $32 billion.

Although other companies have paid special dividends in the past, the size of Microsoft's payout is far and away the largest cash grant in corporate history.

Bill Gates, the company's chairman and largest shareholder, will receive $3.3 billion of that one-time dividend. Mr. Gates, already one of the world's richest men, will also see an extra $180 million a year from an increase in the quarterly dividends, also announced yesterday.

Mr. Gates pledged to give all of the one-time dividend to the Bill and Melinda Gates Foundation, which focuses on global health and education issues. The contribution will increase the size of the foundation's assets by 11 percent, to $30 billion, making it roughly three times the size of the next largest foundation in the United States.

In addition to the special dividend, Microsoft said it would double its quarterly dividend to 8 cents a share, a move that translates into an additional $3.5 billion a year paid to shareholders.

The company also announced that it would buy back as much as $30 billion of its own stock over the next four years.

"The magnitude of the action being taken here is breathtaking," said Rick G. Sherlund, an analyst with Goldman, Sachs.

A large cash distribution to shareholders had been expected, according to Wall Street analysts, given investor pressures. Microsoft shares soared in the 1990s, but have been treading water in recent years as the revenue growth has slowed.

At the same time, there has been mounting pressure on the company to do something about its mounting hoard of cash, which has ballooned to $56 billion. The $32 billion payout, which will be paid in December, will leave the company with more than $20 billion on hand.

"This has been a low- to medium-grade issue for at least a year now, and a high-grade issue in the last couple of months," said Charles J. di Bona, an analyst with Sanford C. Bernstein & Company. "Most investors would ask what took so long."

Microsoft generates roughly $1 billion in extra cash each month. "I don't know any company out there that generates that kind of excess cash," Mr. di Bona said.

Fifteen months ago, Microsoft announced that it would pay a quarterly dividend, a rare decision by a technology company. That decision was cast as tacit acknowledgement that Microsoft was making the transition from hot stock to a more steady, investor-friendly blue-chip stock.

The announcement that the company would raise its quarterly dividend "puts us on course to be one of the largest dividend payers in any industry," said John Connors, Microsoft's chief financial officer. According to Standard & Poor's, the move will make Microsoft the 10th-largest dividend payer in the S&P 500.

"When you're generating cash at that pace, you have to keep distributing it out," Mr. di Bona said.

The company currently invests its excess cash in a variety of investment vehicles, from bonds to mortgage-backed securities and holdings in individual stocks, Mr. Connors said. The company has earned roughly 7 percent a year over the last several years on its surplus cash.

Analysts had expected Microsoft to announce an aggressive stock buyback plan and to increase its quarterly dividend payment.

The surprise in yesterday's announcement was that the company was spending over half its cash on hand in a one-time giveaway, which could even give a modest boost to the economy.

"The story here isn't that they're doing something about all that money they have," Mr. Sherlund said. "It's that they're being big and bold in how they're choosing to spend it."

Microsoft announced its plans after the close of the markets. Shares of Microsoft rose 37 cents, to $28.32, at the close of the market. In after-hours trading, shares spiked more than 5 percent, to $29.91.

The one-time cash dividend, Mr. Sherlund said, provides "immediate gratification" for shareholders who have been restless over a stock price that has barely budged in the last couple of years, despite a modest rebound in technology stocks. At the same time, he noted, the company leaves itself "with a sizable war chest moving forward."

"Most companies hold debt," Mr. Sherlund said. "This is a company with all this excess cash. This in no way inhibits its future growth opportunity."

But because of its recent antitrust troubles, the company is limited in its ability to spend on acquisitions because of heightened scrutiny from the government.

Still, Steven A. Ballmer, Microsoft's chief executive, was bullish about growth in a conference call with analysts and reporters. "As I look out over the next several years," Mr. Ballmer said, "I'm confident we have some of the greatest dollar growth prospects of any company in the world. No doubt about it. Period." Mr. Ballmer stands to receive $1.2 billion in the one-time dividend.

Microsoft officials said the motivation for the announcement was the resolution of lawsuits and legal challenges against the company, many involving antitrust claims in both the United States and abroad, rather than pressures from investors.

"Over the past two years or so, we've been focused on resolving our legal issues from the past and creating stronger relationships within the industry," said Bradford L. Smith, the company's general counsel. On June 30, a federal appeals court handed Microsoft a convincing victory in ending its domestic antitrust problems, upholding the settlement the company reached with the government two years ago.

The company has also resolved three-quarters of the state class-action suits filed, Mr. Smith said. The company's appeal of a $603 million fine the European Commission imposed in March is still pending, "but at least we have a better sense of the known risk," Mr. Connors said.

In recent months, the company has also resolved several high-profile legal disputes with competitors, including Sun Microsystems, a settlement that cost Microsoft nearly $2 billion.

"We had committed to investors that once we had resolved these issues, we'd announce our plans," Mr. Connors said.

The company decided to make its announcement yesterday rather than waiting until tomorrow, when the company will issue its quarterly earnings results.

"There's already enough news and important analysis that analysts and investors are required to do without this much-anticipated announcement," Mr. Connors said.

The plan, which the Microsoft board approved Tuesday morning, is subject to shareholder approval at the annual meeting in November.

"We had a lot of different scenarios we looked at," Mr. Connors said. "We decided this scenario is one that met the interests and inputs of all the different constituencies.

"I don't think you're going to see much opposition when you're talking about a $3-a-share one-time dividend," Mr. Sherland said. "That works out to a 10 percent premium given where the stock price has been."

Mr. Connors said: "The special dividend satisfied the input we received from shareholders who wanted the cash. The buyback met the input of those who thought a large-scale buyback was the appropriate action for building value." As for that quarterly dividend increase, Mr. Connors said that was what "investors told us they wanted."

And under the tax law enacted last year, investors will be able to keep even more of their dividends in their pockets. The law cut the maximum tax rate on dividends to 15 percent, down from the maximum 35 percent that stockholders would pay on ordinary income.

The stock buyback will mean fewer shares outstanding, which will increase the earnings per share—a number that is all important on Wall Street.

"This is all things to all people," said Mr. di Bona, who added that he was by and large impressed with the company's three-part plan.

"Bearish people will say the increase in the dividend is an admission that the company has matured and sees limited growth in the future," Mr. di Bona said. "I vehemently disagree. I think all this reflects is recognition that Microsoft has created a business model that create "more cash than anything we've ever seen before."

Source: Excerpted from G. Rivlin *The New York Times*, July 21, 2004, at **www.nytimes.com**.

Federal law under the *Canadian Business Corporations Act* as well as provincial acts may include provisions prohibiting firms from paying dividends under certain conditions. The intent of such provisions is to protect the firm's creditors against excessive dividend payments, which could push the firm toward insolvency. For example, payment of dividends could be prohibited if it results in the firm being unable to pay its liabilities when they become due, or if such liabilities exceed the firm's assets. Similarly, restrictions may be imposed when the dividend exceeds retained earnings, or when the dividend would be paid from the firm's invested capital.[3] Essentially, the spirit of such regulations is that dividends should be paid from retained earnings. Under certain conditions, firms are allowed to pay a "liquidating dividend." The laws give most corporations a large degree of flexibility in deciding what to pay out, but they help prevent unscrupulous managers from gutting the firm by paying out all its assets as dividends and then escaping creditors.

STOCK DIVIDENDS, STOCK SPLITS, AND REVERSE SPLITS

stock dividend Distribution of additional shares to a firm's shareholders.

MLF's dividend was in the form of cash, but companies often declare **stock dividends**. For example, the Bank of Montreal declared a 100 percent stock dividend in January 2001, doubling the number of common shares. The American company Archer Daniels Midland has paid a yearly stock dividend of 5 percent for two decades. That means it sends each shareholder five additional shares for every 100 shares that are currently owned.

stock split Issue of additional shares to firm's shareholders.

A stock dividend is very much like a **stock split**. In both cases the shareholder is given a fixed number of new shares for each share held. For example, in a two-for-one split, each investor

FIGURE 16.1
The key dates for Maple Leaf Foods Inc, quarterly dividend

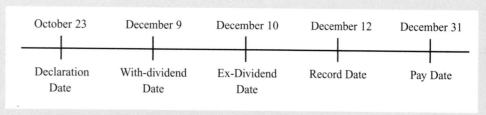

Note: Maple Leaf Foods' present dividend rate is $ .16 per common share per annum paid in regular quarterly payments of $.04 per share. The above time line is for MLF's fourth-quarter payout of 2003.
Source: *Financial Post Online*, FP Dividends. Retrieved from **www.fpinfomart.ca**.

---

[3] Invested capital consists of part or all the receipts from the issue of shares.

would receive one additional share for each share already held. The investor ends up with two shares rather than one. For instance, a recent two-for-one stock split by Canadian Natural Resources Ltd. is therefore like a 100 percent stock dividend.[4] Both result in a doubling of the number of outstanding shares, but neither changes the total assets held by the firm. In both cases, therefore, we would expect the stock price to fall by half, leaving the total market value of the firm (price per share times shares outstanding) unchanged.[5]

More often than not, however, the announcement of a stock split does result in a rise in the market value of the firm, even though investors are aware that the company's assets and business are not affected. The reason: Investors take the decision to split as a signal of management's confidence in the company's propects.[6]

EXAMPLE 16.1

STOCK DIVIDENDS AND SPLITS

Amoeba Products has issued two million shares currently selling at $15 each. Thus investors place a total market value on Amoeba of $30 million. The company now declares a 50 percent stock dividend. This means that each shareholder will receive one new share for every two shares that are currently held. So the total number of Amoeba shares will increase from two million to three million. The company's assets are not changed by this paper transaction and are still worth $30 million. The value of each share after the stock dividend is therefore $30/3 = $10.

If Amoeba split its stock three-for-two, the effect would be the same.[7] In this case two shares would split into three. (Amoeba's motto is "divide and conquer.") So each shareholder has 50 percent more shares with the same total value. Share price must decline by a third.

There are other types of non-cash dividends. For example, companies sometimes send shareholders a sample of their product. The British company Dundee Crematorium once offered its more substantial shareholders a discount cremation. Needless to say, you were not *required* to receive this dividend.

reverse split Issue of new shares in exchange for old shares, which results in the reduction of outstanding shares.

Sometimes a firm may decide to opt for a **reverse split**, which would effectively reduce its number of outstanding shares. For instance, in a one-for-two reverse split, shareholders would exchange two existing shares for one new share. Reverse splits occur much more infrequently than stock splits. An important consideration in a reverse-split decision appears to be an expectation of the resultant increase in share price. A company may wish to achieve such a share price increase in order to maintain minimum price per share requirements of the stock exchange (or exchanges) listing its stock. Also, for a low-priced stock, bringing the share price up to a higher, more acceptable trading range could increase its market participation and improve its liquidity. A more dubious reason could be to ease out minority shareholders who may end up with less than a required minimum number of shares following the reverse split.

---

[4] The Bank of Montreal's stock dividend effectively achieved a two-for-one stock split.

[5] One American survey of managers indicated that 93.7 percent of splits are motivated by the desire to bring the stock price into an acceptable "trading range." They seem to believe that if the price is too high, investors won't be able to afford to buy a "round lot" of 100 shares. Of course that might be a problem for you or us, but it isn't a worry for the Prudential or GM pension funds. See J. Lakonishok and B. Lev, "Stock Splits and Stock Dividends: Why, Who, and When," *Journal of Finance* 42 (September 1987), pp. 913–932.

[6] The insight that stock splits provide a signal to investors was proposed in E. F. Fama, L. Fisher, M. Jensen, and R. Roll, "The Adjustment of Stock Prices to New Information," *International Economic Review* 10 (February 1969), pp. 1–21. For evidence that companies that split their stock have above-average earnings prospects, see P. Asquith, P. Healy, and K. Palepu, "Earnings and Stock Splits," *Accounting Review* 64 (July 1989), pp. 387–403.

[7] The distinction between stock dividends and stock splits is a technical one. A stock dividend is shown on the balance sheet as a transfer from retained earnings to par value and additional paid-in capital, whereas a split is shown as a proportional reduction in the par value of each share. Neither affects the total book value of shareholders' equity.

DIVIDEND REINVESTMENT PLANS AND SHARE PURCHASE PLANS

dividend reinvestment plan
Enables shareholders to reinvest dividends into additional new shares.

share purchase plan Allows shareholders to make cash contributions toward the acquisition of new shares.

Nowadays many firms offer their shareholders additional means of investing in new shares through **dividend reinvestment plans** and **share purchase plans**. Shareholders have the choice of reinvesting their dividend receipts into additional shares of the firm through a *dividend reinvestment plan (DRIP)*. The reinvested proceeds may initially translate only into new fractional shares; however, those shareholders who continue to reinvest over a period of time could acquire sizeable amounts of new shares. Notice that DRIPs can be useful to firms looking for ways to finance valuable investment opportunities, which is why companies may sometimes offer discounts on the cost of acquiring additional shares through DRIPs. One should note that by investing through a DRIP, the shareholder does not necessarily get any tax advantage since reinvested amounts are treated on par with cash dividends for tax purposes and taxed as ordinary income. Firms also provide shareholders the choice of acquiring additional shares through *share purchase plans (SPP)* into which they can make cash contributions. By investing through DRIPs or SPPs, investors are able to save on brokerage costs. Also, costs associated with administering the plans are typically borne by the firms.

16.2

SHARE REPURCHASE

stock repurchase Firm buys back stock from its shareholders.

When a firm wants to pay cash to its shareholders, it usually declares a cash dividend. But an alternative and increasingly popular method is for the firm to repurchase its own stock. In a **stock repurchase**, the company pays cash to repurchase shares from its shareholders.

To see why share repurchase is similar to a dividend, look at panel A of Table 16.1, which shows the market value of Hewlard Pocket's assets and liabilities. Shareholders hold 100,000 shares worth, in total, $1 million, so price per share equals $1 million/100,000 = $10.

Pocket is proposing to pay a dividend of $1 per share. With 100,000 shares outstanding, that amounts to a total payout of $100,000. Panel B shows the effect of this dividend payment. The cash account is reduced by $100,000, and the market value of the firm's assets falls to $900,000. Since there are still 100,000 shares outstanding, share price falls to $9. Suppose that before the

TABLE 16.1
Cash dividend versus share repurchase. Hewlard Pocket's market-value balance sheet

Assets		Liabilities and Shareholders' Equity	
A. Original balance sheet			
Cash	$ 150,000	Debt	$ 0
Other assets	850,000	Equity	1,000,000
Value of firm	$ 1,000,000	Value of firm	$ 1,000,000
Shares outstanding = 100,000			
Price per share = $1,000,000/100,000 = $10			
B. After-cash dividend			
Cash	$ 50,000	Debt	$ 0
Other assets	850,000	Equity	900,000
Value of firm	$ 900,000	Value of firm	$ 900,000
Shares outstanding =100,000			
Price per share = $900,000/100,000 = $9			
C. After-stock repurchase			
Cash	$ 50,000	Debt	$ 0
Other assets	850,000	Equity	900,000
Value of firm	$ 900,000	Value of firm	$ 900,000
Shares outstanding = 90,000			
Price per share = $900,000/90,000 = $10			

dividend payment you owned 1,000 shares of Pocket worth $10,000. After the payment you would have $1,000 in cash and 1,000 shares worth $9,000.

Rather than paying out $100,000 as a dividend, Pocket could use the cash to buy back 10,000 shares at $10 each. Panel C shows what happens. The firm's assets fall to $900,000 just as in panel B, but only 90,000 shares remain outstanding, so price per share remains at $10. If you owned 1,000 shares before the repurchase, you would own 1 percent of the company. If you then sold 100 of your shares to Pocket, you would still own 1 percent of the company. Your sale would put $1,000 cash in your pocket and you would keep 900 shares worth $9,000. This is precisely the position that you would have been in if Pocket had paid a dividend of $1 per share.

It is not surprising that a cash dividend and a share repurchase are equivalent transactions. In both cases, the firm pays out some of its cash, which then goes into the shareholders' pockets. The assets that are left in the company are the same regardless of whether that cash was used to pay a dividend or to buy back shares. Later, however, we will see that how the company chooses to pay out cash may affect the tax that the investor is obliged to pay.

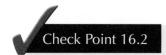

Check Point 16.2   What would Table 16.1 look like if the dividend changes to $1.50 per share and the share repurchase to $150,000?

THE ROLE OF SHARE REPURCHASES

Share repurchases are generally used to make major adjustments to the firm's capital. For example, in May 2003, Canada's largest gold producer, Barrick Gold Corp., announced plans to spend $500 million (US) to repurchase up to $35 million of its outstanding shares, or approximately 7 percent of the company's overall stock. The repurchase plan was expected to reduce Barrick's cost of capital and improve its capital structure.

Since the 1980s share repurchases have have increased sharply. Recently such programs have been announced by Johnson & Johnson ($5 billion), IBM ($3.5 billion), Dell Computer ($2.5 billion), and Metropolitan Life ($1 billion).

Repurchases are like bumper dividends; they cause large amounts of cash to be paid to investors. But they don't *substitute* for dividends. Most companies that repurchase stock are mature, profitable companies that also pay dividends. When a company announces a repurchase program, it is not making a long-term commitment to distribute more cash. Repurchases are therefore much more volatile than dividends. They tend to mushroom during boom times as firms accumulate excess cash and to wither in recessions. Firms occasionally use share repurchases when their cash resources have outrun good investment opportunities.

Suppose that a company has a large amount of unwanted cash or wishes to change its capital structure by replacing equity with debt. It will usually do so by repurchasing stock rather than by paying out large dividends. For example, consider the case of U.S. banks. In 1997 large bank holding companies paid out just under 40 percent of their earnings as dividends. There were few profitable investment opportunities for the remaining income, but the banks did not want to commit themselves in the long run to any larger dividend payments. They therefore returned the cash to shareholders not by increasing the dividend rate, but by repurchasing $16 billion (US) of shares.

Shareholders often worry that excess cash will be frittered away on unprofitable ventures. So, when firms announce that they will use the cash to repurchase shares, the stock price generally rises. Of course, investors would be less thrilled if the management of their favourite growth company suddenly announced that it could not think of anything better to do with the cash.

REPURCHASES AND SHARE VALUATION

Now here is a question that often causes confusion. We stated in Chapter 6 that the value of a share is equal to the discounted value of the stream of dividends paid on that stock. If companies also hand back cash to their shareholders in the form of repurchases, does our simple dividend discount model still hold?

The answer is yes, but we need to explain why. Suppose that you hold one share. As long as you continue to hold it, you will be entitled to receive any dividend that the company pays. However, if you sell your share either to another investor or to the company itself, you receive cash from the sale, but of course you lose out on any *subsequent* dividends that the company may pay. You can, therefore, either value the share by assuming that you continue to hold it (i.e., discount a continuing stream of dividends) or by assuming that you sell the share back to the company (i.e., discount both the dividend stream *up to the time of sale* and the price at which the share is sold). As long as the company buys your share at a fair price, the two methods are equivalent.

Here is a simple example. Company X has outstanding 100,000 shares and pays a dividend of $10 a share. Investors expect this dividend to be maintained indefinitely and require a return of 10 percent on their investment. Therefore share price today is

$$PV(\text{share}) = 10/1.10 + 10/1.10^2 + \ldots = 10/.10 = \$100$$

Since the dividend stream is not expected to grow, the share price is forecast to remain at $100.

Now suppose that the company announces that it plans to repurchase 1,000 shares in the market just after it has paid the next dividend. The announcement does not change investors' forecast of future dividends per share. So those shareholders who do not plan to sell their shares back to the company can continue to look forward to dividends of $10 per share each year and will be happy to pay $100 today for the share. But what about those shareholders who *do* plan to sell their shares? They will receive at the end of the year an expected dividend of $10, plus the $100 that the company must pay to repurchase their shares. The value of the shares today for these shareholders is $(10 + 100)/1.10 = \$100$. Thus, it does not matter whether we consider the cash flows for the shareholder who continues to hold the shares or the cash flows for the shareholder who resells her shares to the company. As long as the company pays a fair price for the share, both methods give the same value. It would, however, be double-counting to assume that a shareholder could both sell her share *and* continue to receive dividends.

As long as X's announcement does not lead investors to revise their view of company prospects, it will not affect today's company value. But after the repurchase has taken place, there will be 1,000 fewer shares outstanding. Since each share is worth $100, the *total* value of the company's shares will fall by $1,000 \times \$100 = \$100,000$.

16.3   HOW DO COMPANIES DECIDE ON DIVIDEND PAYMENTS?

What does the board of directors think about when it sets the dividend? To help answer this question, John Lintner conducted a classic series of interviews with corporate managers about their dividend policies.[8] His description of how dividends are determined can be summarized in four "stylized facts":

dividend payout ratio
Percentage of earnings paid out as dividends.

1. Firms have long-run target **dividend payout ratios**. This ratio is the fraction of earnings paid out as dividends.
2. Managers focus more on dividend *changes* than on absolute levels. Thus paying a $2 dividend is an important financial decision if last year's dividend was $1, but it's no big deal if last year's dividend was $2.
3. Dividend changes follow shifts in long-run, sustainable levels of earnings rather than short-run changes in earnings. Managers are unlikely to change dividend payouts in response to temporary variations in earnings. Instead, they "smooth" dividends.
4. Managers are reluctant to make dividend changes that might have to be reversed. They are particularly worried about having to rescind a dividend increase.

---

[8] J. Lintner, "Distribution of Incomes of Corporations among Dividends, Retained Earnings, and Taxes," *American Economic Review* 46 (May 1956), pp. 97–113.

A firm that always stuck to its target payout ratio would have to change its dividend whenever earnings changed. But the managers in Lintner's survey were loath to do this. They believed that shareholders prefer a steady progression in dividends. Therefore, even if circumstances appeared to warrant a large increase in their company's dividend, they would move only partway toward their target payment.

An extensive study by Fama and Babiak confirms Lintner's survey.[9] They found that if the company enjoys a good year, dividends may increase but to a lesser extent than earnings. Managers wait to see that the earnings increase is permanent before the dividend is fully adjusted.

If managers are reluctant to make dividend changes that might have to be reversed, we should also expect them to take *future* prospects into account when setting the payment. And that is what we find. When companies pay unexpectedly low dividends, earnings on the average subsequently decline. When they pay unexpectedly high dividends, earnings subsequently increase.[10] That is why investors pay close attention to the dividend decision.

To see Lintner's model at work, consider Figure 16.2, which plots the dividends and earnings per share of MLF. While earnings per share fluctuate quite erratically, dividends per share do not. Dividends declined from $.38 per share in 1994 to $.22 in 1995 and $.16 in 1996. Since 1996, dividends have remained steady at $.16 per share right through to 2003. Notice that management continued to pay a dividend of $.22 per share in 1995 despite losses incurred in that year. Similarly, although earnings per share in 1998 were negative, dividends were maintained at the previous year's level of $.16 per share.

16.4   WHY DIVIDEND POLICY SHOULD NOT MATTER

The first step toward understanding dividend policy is to recognize that the phrase means different things to different people. Therefore, we must start by defining what we mean by it.

FIGURE 16.2

Maple Leaf Foods Inc: Earnings and dividends per common share

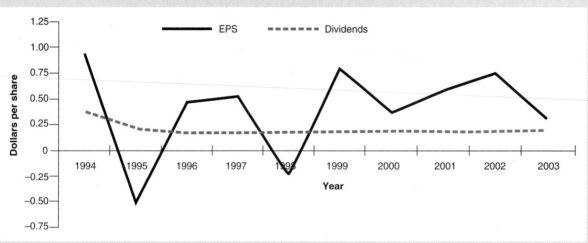

Source: *Financial Post Adviser*, FP analyzer database at **www.fpinfomart.ca**

---

[9] E. F. Fama and H. Babiak, "Dividend Policy: An Empirical Analysis," *Journal of the American Statistical Association* 63 (December 1968), pp. 1132–1161.

[10] See, for example, R. Watts, "The Information Content of Dividends," *Journal of Business* 46 (April 1973), pp. 191–211, for an analysis of the information effects in the United States.

A firm's decisions about dividends are often intertwined with other financing and investment decisions. Some firms pay low dividends because management is optimistic about the firm's future and wishes to retain earnings for expansion. In this case the dividend is a byproduct of the firm's capital budgeting decision. Another firm might finance capital expenditures largely by borrowing. This frees up cash for dividends. In this case the firm's dividend is a byproduct of the borrowing decision.

We wish to isolate dividend policy from other problems of financial management. The precise question we should ask is "What is the effect of a change in cash dividends paid, *given the firm's capital budgeting and borrowing decisions?*" Of course, the cash used to finance a dividend increase has to come from somewhere. If we fix the firm's investment outlays and borrowing, there is only one possible source—an issue of shares.

> We define *dividend policy* as the trade-off between retaining earnings on the one hand and paying out cash and issuing shares on the other.

One nice feature of economics is that it can accommodate not just two, but three opposing points of view—and so it is with dividend policy. On one side there is a group that believes high dividends increase firm value. On the other side there is a group that believes high dividends bring high taxes and therefore reduce firm value. And in the centre there is a middle-of-the-road party that believes dividend policy makes no difference.

DIVIDEND POLICY IS IRRELEVANT IN COMPETITIVE MARKETS

The middle-of-the-road party was founded in 1961 by Modigliani and Miller (MM)[11]—the same two who showed that in idealized conditions capital structure is also irrelevant.

We can illustrate MM's views about dividend policy by considering the Pickwick Paper Company, which had set aside $100 million in cash to construct a new paper mill. But Pickwick's directors now propose to use the $100 million to increase the dividend payment. If Pickwick is to continue to build its new mill, that cash needs to be replaced. If the borrowing is fixed, there is only one place the money can come from, and that is the sale of new shares. The combination of the dividend payment and the new issue of shares leaves Pickwick and its shareholders in exactly the same position they started from. All that has happened is that Pickwick has put an extra $100 million in investors' pockets (the dividend payment) and then taken it out again (the share issue). In other words, Pickwick is simply recycling cash. To suggest that this makes investors better off is like advising the cook to cool the kitchen by leaving the refrigerator door open.

After Pickwick pays the additional dividend and replaces the cash by selling new shares, the company value is unchanged. The old shareholders now have an extra $100 million cash in their pockets, but they have given up a stake in the firm to those investors who buy the newly issued shares. The new shareholders are putting up $100 million and therefore will demand to receive shares *worth* $100 million. Since the total value of the company is the same, the value of the old shareholders' stake in the company falls by this $100 million. Thus the extra dividend that the old shareholders receive just offsets the loss in the value of the shares that they hold.

Does it make any difference to the old shareholders that they receive an extra dividend payment plus an offsetting capital loss? It might if that were the only way they could get their hands on the cash. But as long as there are efficient capital markets, they can raise cash by selling shares. Thus Pickwick's old shareholders can "cash in" either by persuading the management to pay a higher dividend or by selling some of their shares. In either case there will be the same transfer of value from the old to the new shareholders.

---

[11] M. H. Miller and F. Modigliani, "Dividend Policy, Growth and the Valuation of Shares," *Journal of Business* 34 (October 1961), pp. 411–433.

> Because investors do not need dividends to convert their shares to cash, they will not pay higher prices for firms with higher dividend payouts. In other words, dividend policy will have no impact on the value of the firm.

MM dividend-irrelevance proposition   Under ideal conditions, the value of the firm is unaffected by dividend policy.

This conclusion is known as the **MM dividend-irrelevance proposition**.

The example of the Pickwick Paper Company showed that the firm cannot make shareholders better off by simply increasing the proportion of earnings paid out as dividends. But what about the reverse? Can a firm increase its value by *reducing* the dividend payout?

In the case of Pickwick, the extra cash paid out as a dividend needed to be replaced by a sale of stock. The same argument works in reverse: If investment and borrowing are held constant, any *reduction* in dividends must be balanced by a *purchase* of stock. For example, suppose that Old Curiosity Shops has $100 million surplus cash, which it had been proposing to pay out to shareholders as a dividend. If Old Curiosity now decides not to pay this dividend, then the surplus cash can be used only to buy back some of the company's shares. The shareholders miss out on $100 million of dividend payments, but they receive $100 million from the sale to the company of part of their shareholdings. Thus MM's dividend-irrelevance proposition holds true both for increases in dividends and for reductions.

> As these examples illustrate, dividend policy is a trade-off between cash dividends and the issue or repurchase of common shares. In a perfect capital market, dividend choice would have no impact on firm value.

These examples may seem artificial at first because we do not observe firms scheduling a stock issue with every dividend payment. But there are many firms that pay dividends and also issue stock from time to time. They could avoid the stock issues by paying lower dividends and retaining more funds in the firm. Many other firms restrict dividends so that they *do not* have to issue shares. They could instead issue shares occasionally and increase the dividend.

Of course, our demonstrations of dividend irrelevance have ignored taxes, issue costs, and a variety of other real-world complications. We will turn to these intricacies shortly, but before we do, we note that the crucial assumption in our proof is that the sale or purchase of shares occurs at a fair price. The shares that Pickwick sells to raise $100,000 must actually be worth $100,000; those that Old Curiosity buys for $100,000 must also be worth that figure. In other words, dividend irrelevance assumes efficient capital markets.

EXAMPLE 16.2   DIVIDEND IRRELEVANCE

The columns labelled "Old Dividend Plan" in Table 16.2 show that Consolidated Pasta is expected to pay annual dividends of $10 per share in perpetuity. Shareholders expect a 10 percent rate of return from Consolidated stock, and therefore the value of each share is

$$PV = \frac{10}{1.10} + \frac{10}{1.10^2} + \frac{10}{1.10^3} + \ldots = \frac{10}{.10} = \$100$$

Consolidated has issued one million shares. So the total forecast dividend payment in each year is 1 million $\times$ $10 = $10 million, and the total value of Consolidated Pasta equity is 1 million $\times$ $100 = $100 million. The president, Al Dente, has read that the value of a share depends on the dividends it pays. That suggests an easy way to keep shareholders happy—increase next year's dividend to $20 per share. That way, he reasons, share price should rise by the present value of the increase in the first-year dividend to a new value of

$$PV = \frac{20}{1.10} + \frac{10}{1.10^2} + \frac{10}{1.10^3} + \ldots = \frac{10}{1.10} + \frac{10}{.10} = \$109.91$$

	Old Dividend Plan		Revised Dividend Plan	
	Year 1	Year 2 on	Year 1	Year 2 on
Total dividend payments ($ million)	10	10	20	10
Total dividends paid to old shareholders ($ million)	10	10	20	9
Total dividends paid to new shareholders ($ million)	—	—	—	1

TABLE 16.2
Consolidated Pasta is currently expected to pay a dividend of $10 million in perpetuity. However, the president is proposing to pay a one-time bumper dividend of $20 million in Year 1. To replace the lost cash, the firm will need to issue more shares, and the dividends that will need to be diverted to the new shareholders will exactly offset the effect of the higher dividend in Year 1.

Note: New shareholders are putting up $10 million cash at the end of Year 1. Since they require a return of 10 percent, the total dividends paid to the new shares (starting in Year 2) must be 10 percent of $10 million, or $1 million.

The president's heart is obviously in the right place. Unfortunately, his head isn't. Let's see why.

Consolidated is proposing to pay out an extra $10 million in dividends. It can't do that and earn the same profits in the future, unless it also replaces the lost cash by an issue of shares. The new shareholders who provide this cash will require a return of 10 percent on their investment. So Consolidated will need to pay $1 million per year of dividends to the new shares ($1 million/$10 million = .10, or 10%). This is shown in the last line of Table 16.2.

As long as the company replaces the extra cash it pays out, it will continue to earn the same profits and to pay out $10 million of dividends each year from Year 2. However, $1 million of this total will be needed to satisfy the new shareholders, leaving only $9 million (or $9 per share) for the original shareholders. Now recalculate the value of the original shares under the revised dividend plan:

$$PV = \frac{20}{1.10} + \frac{9}{1.10^2} + \frac{9}{1.10^3} + \ldots = \frac{11}{1.10} + \frac{9}{.10} = \$100$$

The value of the shares is unchanged. The extra cash dividend in Year 1 is exactly offset by the reduction of dividends per share in later years. This reduction is necessary because some of the money paid out as dividends in later years is diverted to the new shareholders.[12]

 Check Point 16.3   Suppose that Consolidated Pasta had issued $10 million in preferred stock rather than common stock to pay the extra dividend. What would be the stock price?

THE ASSUMPTIONS BEHIND DIVIDEND IRRELEVANCE

Many shareholders and businesspeople find it difficult to accept the suggestion that dividend policy is irrelevant. When faced with MM's argument, they often reply that dividends are cash in hand while capital gains are at best in the bush. It may be true, they say, that the recipient of an extra cash dividend forgoes an equal capital gain, but if the dividend is safe and the capital gain is risky, isn't the shareholder ahead?

It's correct that dividends are more predictable than capital gains. Managers can stabilize dividends but they cannot control stock price. From this it seems a small step to conclude that increased

---

[12] Notice that at the end of Year 1, when the new shareholders purchase their shares, the dividend per share they can look forward to receiving will be $9; since this dividend is expected to be a perpetuity, the share price at that time will be $9/.10 = $90. So the new shareholders will receive $10,000,000/$90 = 111,111 shares. Consistent with Table 16.2, the new shareholders therefore will receive total dividend payments of 111,111 × $9 = $1 million, and the old shareholders will receive total dividend payments of 1 million × $9 = $9 million. Notice also that after the extra $10 million dividend is paid in Year 1, the share price falls to $90, and the value of the shares held by the original shareholders falls by exactly $10 million to $90 million.

dividends make the firm less risky.[13] But the important point is, once again, that as long as investment policy and borrowing are held constant, a firm's *overall* cash flows are the same regardless of payout policy. The risks borne by *all* the firm's shareholders are likewise fixed by its investment and borrowing policies and unaffected by dividend policy.

If we really believed that existing shareholders are better off by trading a risky asset for cash, then we would also have to argue that the new shareholders—those who trade cash for the newly issued shares—are worse off. But this doesn't make sense: The new shareholders are bearing risk, but they are getting paid for it. They are willing to buy because the new shares are priced to offer an expected return adequate to compensate for the risk.

MM's argument for the irrelevance of dividend policy does not assume a world of certainty; it assumes an efficient capital market. Market efficiency means that the transfers of ownership created by shifts in dividend policy are carried out on fair terms. And since the overall value of (old and new) shareholders' equity is unaffected, nobody gains or loses.

16.5   WHY DIVIDENDS MAY INCREASE FIRM VALUE

MARKET IMPERFECTIONS

Most economists believe that MM's conclusions are correct, given their assumptions of perfect and efficient capital markets. However, nobody claims their model is an exact description of the so-called real world. Thus the impact of dividend policy finally boils down to arguments about imperfections and inefficiencies.

Those who believe that dividends are good argue that some investors have a natural preference for high-payout stocks. For example, some financial institutions are legally restricted from holding stocks lacking established dividend records. Trusts and endowment funds may prefer high-dividend stocks because dividends are regarded as spendable "income," whereas capital gains are "additions to principal," which may not be spent.[14]

In addition, many investors look to their stock portfolios for a steady source of cash to live on. In principle this cash can be generated from stocks paying no dividends at all; the investor can just sell off a small fraction of her holdings from time to time. For example, an investor who holds 1,000 shares of BCE stock can sell 10 shares (1 percent of the total holdings) this year. This "homemade dividend" is equivalent to an increase of one percentage point in BCE's annual dividend yield.

However, instead of BCE's shareholders making regular sales, it is simpler and cheaper for the company to send them a dividend cheque. The costs of trading small numbers of shares can be extremely high. BCE's regular dividends relieve many of its shareholders of these transaction costs and considerable inconvenience.

All this is undoubtedly true, but it does not follow that you can increase the value of your firm by increasing the dividend payout. Smart managers already have recognized that there is a clientele of investors who would be prepared to pay a premium for high-payout stocks. High-payout fans already have a wide variety of stocks to choose from.

> There are natural clienteles for high-payout stocks, but it does not follow that any particular firm can benefit by increasing its dividends. The high-dividend clienteles already have plenty of high-dividend stocks to choose from.

You don't hear businesspeople argue that because there is a clientele of car buyers, their company should manufacture cars. So why should you believe that because there is a clientele

---

[13] In that case one might also argue that interest payments are even more predictable, so that a company's risk would be reduced by increasing the proportion of profits paid out as interest. How would you respond to that suggestion?

[14] Many colleges and universities are legally free to spend capital gains from their endowments, but this is rarely done.

of investors who like high payouts, your company can increase value by manufacturing a high payout? That clientele was probably satisfied long ago.

Check Point 16.4   Suppose an investor in BCE does not need a regular income. What could she do to offset BCE's "overly generous" payout policy? If there were no trading costs, would she have any reason to care about BCE's dividend payout policy? What if there is a brokerage fee on the purchase of new shares? What if BCE has a dividend reinvestment plan that allows the investor to buy shares at a 5 percent discount?

DIVIDENDS AS SIGNALS

Another line of argument for high payouts does not rely on market imperfections like trading costs. Think of a market in which investors receive very little reliable information about a firm's earnings. Such markets exist in some countries where a passion for secrecy and a tendency to construct many-layered corporate organizations produce earnings figures that are next to meaningless. Some people say that the situation is little better in the United States or Canada, thanks to creative accounting.

How might an investor in such a world separate marginally profitable firms from the real money makers? One clue is dividends. A firm that reports good earnings and pays a generous dividend is putting its money where its mouth is. Accounting numbers may lie, but dividends require the firm to come up with hard cash. We can understand why investors would favour firms with established dividend records. We can also see how investors would value the information content of dividends. Investors would refuse to believe a firm's reported earnings announcements unless they were backed up by an appropriate dividend policy.

Of course, firms can cheat in the short run by overstating earnings and scraping up cash to pay a generous dividend. But it is hard to cheat in the long run because a firm that is not making money will not have the cash flow to pay out. Only the firms with sufficient cash flow will find that it pays to signal their good fortune by choosing a high-dividend level. If a firm chooses a high-dividend payout without the cash flow to back it up, that firm ultimately will have to cut back on investment or turn to investors for additional debt or equity financing. All of these consequences are costly. Therefore, most managers don't increase dividends until they are confident that sufficient cash will flow in to pay them.

Investors can't read managers' minds, but they learn from managers' actions. When dividends increase, they infer managers' confidence in the firm's cash flow and earnings.

> Because a high-dividend payout policy will be costly to firms that do not have the cash flow to support it, dividend increases signal a company's good fortune and its managers' confidence in future cash flow.

Healy and Palepu report that between 1970 and 1979 companies that made a dividend payment for the first time experienced relatively flat earnings growth until the year before the announcement.[15] In that year earnings grew by an average 43 percent. If managers thought that this was a temporary windfall, they might have been cautious about committing themselves to paying out cash. But it looks as if they had good reason to be confident about prospects, because over the next 4 years earnings grew by a further 164 percent.

Since dividends anticipate future earnings, it is no surprise to find that announcements of dividend cuts are usually taken as bad news (stock price typically falls) and that dividend increases are good news (stock price rises). This is called the **information content of dividends**.

information content of dividends   Dividend increases send good news about cash flow and earnings. Dividend cuts send bad news.

[15] P. Healy and K. Palepu, "Earnings Information Conveyed by Dividend Initiations and Omissions," *Journal of Financial Economics* 21 (1988), pp. 149–175.

It's important not to jump to the conclusion that investors like higher dividends for their own sake. A dividend initiation or increase may be welcomed *only* as a sign of higher future earnings. Even investors who prefer low-dividend policies might find that a drop in the dividend is unwelcome news about the firm's prospects.[16] Sometimes, companies could begin paying dividends long after they have achieved high earnings. In such instances, the announcement of a dividend initiation is not always greeted as good news by investors. For instance, when Microsoft initiated dividend payments in 2003, investors reacted negatively to the news and the company's shares fell by 4.7 percent. At that time the company had built up a cash surplus of $43 billion (US).

SEE BOX P. 519

The nearby Finance in Action box illustrates the signalling power of dividends and describes the effects of a dividend cut by the Florida Power & Light Company. When Florida Power & Light cut its dividend, the firm stressed that the cut was not a response to low or uncertain profits but part of a rethinking of its financial strategy for a deregulated world. Despite these reassurances, the stock price fell. The market apparently paid more attention to what the firm did than to what its management said. The stock price recovered only later as the market became convinced that the prospects of the firm were in fact fine.

Occasionally, when a company cuts dividends, investors react negatively and penalize it as well as others in the same industry. When TransCanada PipeLines shocked investors in December 1999 by cutting its dividend to $.80 from $1.12, its share price dropped to $11.65 from $23. The share price of TransAlta Corp., which didn't cut dividends, fell along with TransCanada despite assurances from top management that the company had no intention of cutting its dividend. More recently, Abitibi Consolidated Inc. reduced its quarterly dividend by 75 percent and warned that the loss for the second quarter of 2003 would be larger than expected. The company's stock price price fell by 10 percent the following day despite reassurances from its CEO that the second half of the year would show better results.

Check Point 16.5

In 1974 Consolidated Edison announced that it would omit its regular $.45 per share cash quarterly dividend. It cited losses due to increased oil prices following the OPEC oil embargo. The stock price fell by about 30 percent in one day, from about $18 (US) per share to $12 per share. Why would omission of a $.45 per share dividend result in a stock price drop of $6 per share?

16.6   WHY PAY DIVIDENDS? A LOOK AT TAX LAW IMPLICATIONS

DIVIDENDS VERSUS CAPITAL GAINS

Could paying dividends reduce firm value? If dividends are taxed more heavily than capital gains, any tax-paying investor would be attracted to companies that can convert dividends to capital gains by shifting their dividend policies. Firms should then pay the lowest cash dividend they can get away with. Available cash should be retained and reinvested or used to repurchase shares.

In Chapter 3, we discussed the treatment of income from dividends and capital gains under Canadian tax laws. Canadian public corporations do not pay any tax on dividend income received from another Canadian corporation, whereas individual investors receive some tax relief through a *dividend tax credit* (DTC). The dividend tax credit reduces the burden of double taxation on shareholder income, which occurs because the cash flows that produce such income are taxed at both

---

[16] For example, in an article in *Fortune,* Carol Loomis tells the story of General Public Utilities, "A Case for Dropping Dividends," *Fortune* (June 15, 1968), p. 181ff. In 1968 its management decided to reduce its cash dividend to avoid a stock issue. Despite the company's assurances, it encountered considerable opposition. Individual shareholders advised the president to see a psychiatrist, institutional holders threatened to sell their stock, the share price fell nearly 10 percent, and eventually management capitulated.

The Dividend Cut Heard 'Round the World

On May 9, 1994, FPL Group, the parent company of Florida Power & Light Company, announced a 32 percent reduction in its quarterly dividend payout, from $.62 per share to $.42. This was the first-ever dividend cut by a healthy utility. A number of utilities had reduced their dividends in the past, but only after cash flow problems—often associated with heavy investment in nuclear plants—had given them no other choice.

In its announcement, FPL stressed that it had studied the situation carefully and that, given the prospect of increased competition in the electric utility industry, the company's high-dividend payout ratio (which had averaged 90 percent in the past 4 years) was no longer in the shareholders' best interests. The new policy resulted in a dividend payout of about 60 percent of the prior year's earnings. Management also announced that, starting in 1995, the dividend payout would be reviewed in February instead of May to reinforce the linkage between dividends and annual earnings. In doing so, the company wanted to minimize unintended "signalling effects" from any future changes in the dividend.

At the same time it announced this change in dividend policy, FPL Group's board authorized the repurchase of up to 10 million shares of common stock over the next 3 years. FPL's management said that four million shares would be repurchased over the next 12 months, depending on market conditions. In adopting this strategy, the company noted that changes in the U.S. tax code since 1990 had made capital gains more attractive than dividends to shareholders.

Besides providing a more tax-efficient means of distributing excess capital to its shareholders, FPL's substitution of stock repurchases for dividends was also designed to increase the company's financial flexibility in preparation for a new era of deregulation and heightened competition among utilities. Although much of the cash savings from the dividend cut would be returned to investors in the form of stock repurchases, the rest would be used to retire debt at Florida Power & Light and so reduce the company's leverage ratio. This deleveraging and strengthening of FPL's financial condition were intended to prepare the company for an increase in business risk and to provide the financial resources to take advantage of future growth opportunities.

The stock market's initial reaction to FPL's announcement was negative. On the day of the announcement, the company's stock price fell from $31.88 to $27.50, a drop of nearly 14 percent. But, as analysts digested the news and considered the reasons for the reduction, they concluded that the action was not a signal of financial distress but rather a strategic decision that would improve the company's long-term financial flexibility and prospects for growth. This view spread throughout the financial community, and FPL's stock began to recover.

On May 31, less than a month after the announcement, FPL's stock closed at $32.17 (adjusted for the quarterly dividend of $.42), or about $.30 higher than the preannouncement price. By the middle of June, at least 15 major brokerage houses had placed FPL's common stock on their "buy" lists. On May 9, 1995—exactly one year after the announcement of the cut—FPL's stock price closed at $37.75, giving shareholders a one-year post-announcement return (including dividends) of 23.8 percent, more than double the 11.2 percent of the S&P Index and well above the 14.2 percent of the S&P utilities index over the same period.

Source: Modified from D. Soter, E. Brigham, and P. Evanson, "The Dividend Cut 'Heard 'Round the World': The Case of FPL," *Journal of Applied Corporate Finance* 9 (Spring 1996), pp. 4–15.

corporate and personal levels. On the other hand, corporations and individual investors pay tax on capital gains that are realized when the asset is sold. Currently, only 50 percent of such realized capital gains are taxable. Tax law is on the side of capital gains in another important respect. Taxes on dividends have to be paid immediately, but taxes on capital gains can be deferred until shares are sold and capital gains are realized. Stockholders can choose when to sell their shares and thus when to pay the capital gains tax.[17] Other countries have also sought to ameliorate the effects of double taxation of dividend income. Recently, the United States has also moved to reduce the burden of double taxation on dividend income under legislation introduced in 2003. Now, dividends received from domestic U.S. companies and some qualified foreign corporations will be taxed at a maximum rate of 15 percent and not at ordinary income tax rates. The new legislation will provide relief to recipients of dividend income, particularly those in high income tax brackets, whose tax rates on ordinary income can go up to 35 percent.

Overall, for some investors, dividends are taxed more heavily than capital gains, whereas for others, capital gains suffer more tax than dividends. For instance, refer back to the solution to Check Point 3.7. Notice that a British Columbia–based investor in the lowest tax bracket (combined tax rate of 22.05 percent) has a dividend tax rate of 4.52 percent, but a higher capital gains tax rate of 11.03 percent. On the other hand, the investor in the highest tax bracket with a

---

[17] Suppose the discount rate is 8 percent, and an investor in a combined 40 percent federal and provincial tax bracket has a $100 capital gain. If the stock is sold today, the tax on capital gain will be $20 (that is, $.5 \times .4 \times 100$), but by virtue of delaying the sale for a year, the present value of the tax falls to $20/1.08 = \$18.52$. The effective tax rate falls to 18.52 percent. The longer the sale is deferred, the lower the effective tax rate.

combined tax rate of 43.7 percent has a dividend tax rate of 31.59 percent, but a lower capital gains tax rate of 21.85 percent.[18]

From the discussion above, some investors have a tax reason for preferring income from dividend instead of capital gains. These would include investors in low tax brackets and Canadian corporations. Suppose we call this group "Clientele D." There would also be a group of investors, particularly those in high tax brackets, who would prefer capital gains to dividends. We call this group "Clientele C."

Table 16.3 illustrates how taxes can affect firm value. It assumes that dividends and capital gains are taxed at rates applicable to the BC–based high-tax bracket investor, that is, a tax rate on dividends of 31.59 percent, but a lower capital gains tax rate of 21.85 percent. For convenience, we have rounded off these rates to 30 percent and 20 percent, respectively.

The table shows stocks of firms A and B, which are equally risky. Investors demand an expected after-tax rate of return of 10 percent on each. Investors expect A to be worth $112.50 per share next year. The share price of B is expected to be only $102.50, but a $10 dividend is also forecast, so the total pretax payoff is the same, $112.50.

Both stocks offer the same pretax dollar payoff. Yet, B's stock sells for less than A's and therefore offers a higher pretax rate of return. The reason is obvious: Investors are willing to buy stock A because its return comes in the form of low-taxed capital gains. After tax, each stock offers the same 10 percent return.[19]

In this example, we have assumed tax rates on income from dividends and capital gains from the point of view of the Clientele C group of investors. Notice that we would have arrived at the opposite conclusion if we had assumed tax rates from the standpoint of the Clientele D investor. Does either one of these clienteles play a dominant role in the market? If so, then the dominant clientele should have an influence on whether high-dividend yield stocks should sell for more or less than low-dividend yield stocks on the basis of taxes. Researchers have tried to find answers by examining whether high-yield stocks provide different expected rates of return than low-yield stocks. Unfortunately, it is difficult to measure such clientele effects, and the researchers have not been able to come up with definitive answers.[20]

Also, we must keep in mind that tax laws tend to change over time and the relationship between dividends and pretax rates of return should change as well. Capital gains were taxed for the first time

TABLE 16.3

Effects of a shift in dividend policy when dividends are taxed more heavily than capital gains. The high-payout stock (firm B) must sell at a lower price in order to provide the same after-tax return.

	Firm A	Firm B
Next year's price	$112.50	$102.50
Dividend	$ 0	$ 10.00
Total pretax payoff	$112.50	$112.50
Today's stock price	$100	$ 98.90
Capital gain	$ 12.50	$ 3.60
Before-tax rate of return (%)	$\frac{12.5}{100} = .125 = 12.5\%$	$\frac{13.60}{98.90} = 0.138 = 13.8\%$
Tax on dividend at 30%	$0	$.30 \times \$10 = \$3.00$
Tax on capital gain at 20%	$.20 \times \$12.50 = \$2.50$	$.20 \times \$3.60 = \$.72$
Total after-tax income (dividends plus capital gains less taxes)	$(0 + 12.50) - 2.50 = \$10.00$	$(10 + 3.60) - (3.00 + .72) = \$9.88$
After-tax rate of return (%)	$\frac{10}{100} = .10 = 10\%$	$\frac{9.88}{98.90} \cong .10 = 10\%$

[18] See Chapter 3, Table 3.6, for a table of tax rates on ordinary income.

[19] Actually, stock B's after-tax return is being rounded off to 10 percent.

[20] Some important early studies that provide insights on the issues involved in this research include F. Black and M. Scholes, "The Effects of Dividend Yield and Dividend Policy on Common Stock Prices and Returns," *Journal of Financial Economics* 1 (May 1974), pp. 1–22; R. H. Litzenberger and K. Ramaswamy, "The Effects of Dividends on Common Stock Prices: Tax Effects or Information Effect," *Journal of Finance* 37 (May 1982), pp. 429–443; and M. H. Miller, "Behavioural Rationality in Finance: The Case of Dividends," *Journal of Business* 59 (October 1986), pp. 451–468.

in Canada in 1972. Before that year, many investors were taxed at higher rates on dividend income than on capital gains income. Consequently, we would expect high-dividend–paying stocks to earn a higher pretax rate of return to compensate for the extra taxes. Since the 1980s, new reforms have increased the tax on capital gains. For example, a $100,000 lifetime capital gain exemption, introduced in the mid-1980s, was ended in 1994. In 2000, the federal budget lowered the taxable portion of capital gains from 75 percent to 50 percent. The net effect of these changes has been to reduce the difference in the taxes on dividends and capital gains. We would expect that the pretax rate of return on high-dividend–paying stocks would get smaller.[21] While there may have been a predominance of Clientele D investors in Canada before the tax reforms, the tax savings from moving between the high- and low-dividend stocks are perhaps not as high as they used to be.

Check Point 16.6

Look again at Table 16.3. What would happen to the price and pretax rate of return on stock B if the tax on capital gains were eliminated?

DIVIDEND CLIENTELE EFFECTS

From our discussion above, we have seen that some groups of investors, such as rich individuals, prefer to receive capital gains and little or no dividends, while other groups, such as corporate investors, may prefer high-dividend payouts. Different investor groups, or clienteles, therefore prefer different payouts; this is the **dividend clientele effect**. The dividend-clientele effect argument is that changing the dividend policy of the firm would attract a new investor clientele but may not change the value of the firm. Suppose a firm with a low dividend payout switches to a high-dividend payout policy. It will now attract clienteles seeking high-dividend payout stocks. However, its share price may not go up as long as enough firms satisfy the demand for high-dividend–paying stocks. Essentially, this is a supply and demand argument. If the demand from investor clienteles is more for high-dividend–paying stocks relative to the supply of such stocks, the prices of high-dividend–paying stocks should rise. However, low dividend paying firms will now find it advantageous to switch to high dividend–payout policies until prices stabilize and the "market for dividends" is in equilibrium. In such an environment, a dividend policy change by an individual firm will have no effect on its share value.

dividend clientele effect
Different investor groups prefer different dividend yields. Changing the firm's dividend policy may attract a new investor clientele but may not change firm value.

SHARE REPURCHASES INSTEAD OF CASH DIVIDENDS?

Many Canadian firms have active share repurchase programs in place. For example, Research In Motion's share repurchase program allows it to buy up to 5 percent of its outstanding common shares at prevailing market prices on the TSX and the Nasdaq National Market where its shares are listed. Other companies have similar programs in place.

Companies may repurchase their shares for a variety of reasons. A company may decide to repurchase some of its stock if it wishes to distribute temporary excess cash to its shareholders as an alternative form of dividend. Notice that a share repurchase can also reduce the firm's future cash dividend requirement. Sometimes a company's management may decide to repurchase shares because they feel that the stock is undervalued, given their knowledge of the firm's future prospects. Share repurchases can be used to achieve other corporate goals such as "leveraging up" and altering the firm's capital structure, or as a takeover defence.

From the firm's point of view, a share repurchase is similar to paying a cash dividend. However, the tax treatment for shareholders may be quite different. When a company pays a cash dividend, the investor has no choice but to receive it and pay any applicable tax that may become due. However, if shares are repurchased on the open market, the shareholder pays taxes only if she has decided to

---

[21] Although a study by I. G. Morgan, "Dividends and Stock Price Behaviour in Canada," *Journal of Business Administration* 12 (Fall 1980), pp. 91–106, found no difference in the before-tax rates of return between high- and low-dividend paying stocks between 1972 and 1977. Another study has examined the issue: B. Amoako-adu, M. Rashid, and M. Stebbens, "Capital Gains Tax and Equity Values: Empirical Test of Stock Price Reaction to the Introduction and Reduction of Capital Gains Tax Exemption," *Journal of Banking and Finance* 16 (1992), pp. 275–287.

Whatever Happened to Dividends?

"The only thing that gives me pleasure," John D. Rockefeller once said, "is to see my dividends coming in." But Mr. Rockefeller would have less fun today, for many of America's corporate stars, such as Microsoft, Cisco, Sun Microsystems, Dell, and America Online, have never paid a dividend. In the 1950s, nine out of 10 American companies paid dividends. Today only one in five does. Dividends are disappearing so fast that professors Eugene Fama and Kenneth French have looked into the phenomenon.

Part of their explanation for it is straightforward: The sorts of companies that are traded on America's stock markets have changed radically. Until the early 1970s, an exchange listing was, by and large, the preserve of large, profitable firms—firms that one would expect to pay a dividend. All this changed after 1971, when the New York Stock Exchange was joined by a new rival, Nasdaq, which imposed less stringent listing conditions. The result was that many less profitable companies began to obtain a listing. Newly listed companies made returns on equity of about 18% in the 1970s, but only 3% in the mid-1990s, compared with 11% for corporate America as a whole. By 1997, only about half the new listings made any profits at all. Since then, as some cynics on Wall Street joke, making profits for any self-respecting "dot.com," has become uncool.

Companies that are making losses are ill-advised to pay a dividend. But even a company with profits should choose to retain them if it thinks that its own investment opportunities are better than those available to shareholders elsewhere. For both reasons, more "growth" companies will tend to mean fewer dividend-payers.

Even so, there is a puzzle about the disappearing dividend. It is not just growth companies that are opting out of dividends, but all companies, including those enjoying healthy flows of free cash.

Among very profitable companies, only 32% pay dividends, half the proportion that did 20 years ago.

One possible explanation is that shareholders do not want dividends. These represent income, which is taxed at a top federal rate of 39.6%. By leaving profits in the firm, investors can defer this tax, and, if need be, cash in a capital gain, which is taxed at only 20%. But taxes do not in themselves explain the decline in dividend-paying. After all, income tax has long been higher than capital gains tax; it is unlikely that American investors have only just noticed.

Another theory says that dividends have not disappeared, but assumed a new guise: companies' purchases of their own shares. Such buybacks have risen from 3 to 5% of annual corporate profits during the 1970s to 26% in the 1980s and 1990s. But share buybacks are not replacing dividends as such, because most of the companies buying back shares also pay dividends. Mr. Fama and Mr. French find no evidence that companies stop paying dividends (or do not start) because they can buy back shares instead.

That does not mean dividends have become irrelevant. But it may mean that they have become less relevant. For most of the century the dividend yield was one of the most watched measures in the stock market. Whenever it dropped to 3% or less, traders assumed the market was overvalued and sold their holdings. Yet today the dividend yield on the S&P 500 shares is 1.2%. Optimists might argue that since dividends no longer play the role they once did, this does not, of itself, mean the market is wildly overvalued. But, given the uncertainty over what role dividends precisely play now, that is scarcely reassuring.

Source: Abridged from *The Economist*, November 20, 1999. © 1999 The Economist Newspaper Group, Inc. Reprinted with permission, **www.economist.com**.

sell the shares and incurs a taxable capital gain on the sale. As we have discussed earlier, by deferring a sale, the investor can lower the present value of the capital gains tax liability.

Sometimes, the investor could sell shares to another company making a tender offer to take over a target firm. In this case, any amount paid by the company for the repurchase of shares that exceeds their paid-up capital value is treated by the *Income Tax Act* as "deemed dividend" in the hands of investors. This removes any tax advantage of stock repurchases over dividends.

Shareholders who pay higher taxes on dividends than on capital gains (Clientele C) might be happy to sell some shares to the firm and receive income as capital gains. They will avoid paying the higher tax on the dividend income. We must caution firms to *not* stop paying dividends altogether and only make regular share repurchases. A firm that eliminates dividends and starts repurchasing stock on a regular basis may find that Canada Revenue Agency (CRA) would recognize the repurchase program for what it really is and would tax the payments accordingly. That is why financial managers have never announced that they are repurchasing shares to save shareholders taxes; they give some other reason.[22]

Nevertheless, one could argue that firms that pay dividends, and as a result have to issue shares from time to time, are making a serious mistake. Any such firm is essentially financing its dividends by issuing stock; it should cut its dividends at least to the point where stock issues are unnecessary. This would not only save taxes for shareholders, but also avoid the transaction costs of stock issues.

SEE BOX ABOVE ▶ The above Finance in Action box notes that dividend payouts have, in fact, drastically declined in the last few decades, and it explores some explanations for this phenomenon.

---

[22] They might say, "Our stock is a good investment," or "The repurchase program will enhance shareholder value." What do you think of these rationales?

16.7   SUMMARY

1.   How are dividends paid and how do companies decide on dividend payments?

Dividends come in many forms. The most common is the regular **cash dividend**, but sometimes companies pay an extra cash dividend, and sometimes they pay a **stock dividend**. A firm is not free to pay dividends at will. For example, it may have accepted restrictions on dividends as a condition for borrowing money.

Most managers seem to have a target **dividend payout ratio**. But if firms simply applied this target payout rate to each year's earnings, dividends could fluctuate wildly. Managers therefore try to smooth dividends by moving only partway toward the target payout in each year. Also, they don't look just at past earnings: They try to look into the future when they set the payment. Investors are aware of this and they know that a dividend increase is usually a sign of optimism on the part of management.

2.   How are repurchases used to distribute cash to shareholders?

Companies also pay out money to shareholders by repurchasing their shares. **Share repurchases** have grown rapidly in recent years, but they do not substitute for dividends. Instead, they are generally used to make major one-off changes to the firm's capital structure, particularly when cash resources have outrun good investment opportunities. Repurchases can be like bumper dividends; they cause large amounts of cash to be paid to investors when the firm buys back their shares.

3.   Why would dividend policy not affect firm value in an ideal world?

If we hold the company's investment policy and capital structure constant, then dividend policy is a trade-off between cash dividends and the issue or repurchase of common stock. In an ideally simple and perfect world, the choice would have no effect on market value. This is the **MM dividend-irrelevance proposition**. The dividend controversy centres on the effects of dividend policy in our flawed world. A common—though by no means universal—view is that high payout enhances share price. For example, this could occur if there were unsatisfied clienteles for high-payout stocks.

4.   How might differences in the tax treatment of dividends and capital gains affect dividend policy?

Instead of paying dividends, the company can repurchase its own stock. The Canada Revenue Agency (CRA) taxes shareholders on the capital gains that they realize as a result of the repurchase.

Are capital gains taxed at lower rates than dividend income? For some investor groups, dividend income can offer some tax advantages over realized capital gains income. However, investors who do not realize capital gains can defer, and thereby lower, the present value of any capital gains tax liability. This suggests the existence of different investor clienteles preferring different dividend payouts. The **dividend-clientele-effect** argument is that changing the dividend policy of the firm would attract a new investor clientele but may not change the value of the firm.

If dividends are seriously tax-disadvantaged for some investors, we would expect such investors to demand a higher before-tax return on high-payout stocks. Instead of paying high dividends, companies should then use the cash to repurchase shares or to reduce the amount of share issues. In this way, the company would in effect convert dividend income into capital gains. This is one reason a low-dividend policy might be preferred.

5.   Why may dividends be used by management to signal the prospects of the firm?

A firm that chooses a high-dividend policy without the cash flow to back it up will find that it ultimately has to either cut back on investments or turn to capital markets for additional debt or equity financing. Because this is costly, managers do not increase dividends unless they are confident that the firm is generating enough cash to pay them. This is the principal reason that we say that there is an **information content of dividends**—that is, dividend changes are liable to be interpreted as signals of a change in the firm's prospects.

If a sharp dividend change is necessary, then the company should provide as much forewarning and explanation as possible. Moreover, a firm should adopt a target payout that is sufficiently low to minimize its reliance on external equity. Why pay out cash to shareholders if that requires issuing new shares to get the cash back? It's better to hold on to the cash in the first place.

Related Web Links

www.cfonews.com Current dividend news

www.dripcentral.com Information about dividend reinvestment plans

www.companyboardroom.com Data on recent dividend declarations

www.ndir.com/SI/DRPs.shtml Information on Canadian dividend reinvestment plans and share purchase plans

Key Terms

cash dividend	505	share purchase plan	509	information content		
ex-dividend date	505	stock repurchase	509	of dividends	517	
stock dividend	507	dividend payout ratio	511	dividend clientele effect	521	
stock split	507	MM dividend-irrelevance				
reverse split	508	proposition	514			
dividend reinvestment						
plan	509					

Questions and Problems

*Answers in Appendix B

BASIC

1. **Dividend Sequence.** Cash Cow International paid a regular quarterly dividend of $.075 a share.
   a. Connect each of the following dates to the correct term:

May 7	Record date
June 6	Payment date
June 7	Ex-dividend date
June 11	Last with-dividend date
July 2	Declaration date

   *b. On one of these dates the stock price is likely to fall by about the value of the dividend. Why?
   *c. The stock price in early January was $27. What was the prospective dividend yield?
   *d. The earnings per share were forecast at around $1.90. What was the percentage payout rate?
   *e. Suppose that the company paid a 10 percent stock dividend. What would be the expected fall in the stock price?

2. **Institutional Background.** True or false? If false, correct the statement.
   a. A company may not generally pay a dividend out of legal capital.
   b. A company may not generally pay a dividend if it is insolvent.
   c. The *effective* tax rate on capital gains can be less than the stated tax rate on such gains.
   d. Corporations are not taxed on dividends received from other corporations.

*3. **Splits and Dividends.** Shares in Raven Products are selling for $40 per share. There are one million shares outstanding. What will be the share price in each of the following situations? Ignore taxes.
   a. The stock splits five-for-four.
   b. The company pays a 25 percent stock dividend.
   c. The company repurchases 100,000 shares.

4. **Dividend Irrelevance.** You own 1,000 shares of Patriot Corporation, which is about to raise its dividend from $.75 to $1 per share. The share price is currently $50. You would prefer that the dividend remain at its current level. What would you do to offset the effects of the increase in the dividend?

5. **DRIPs.** A firm considers initiating an aggressive dividend reinvestment plan (DRIP) in which it allows its investors to use dividends to buy shares at a discount of 40 percent from current market value. The firm's financial manager argues that the policy will benefit shareholders by giving them the opportunity to buy additional shares at a deep discount and will benefit the firm by providing a source of cash. Is the manager correct?

PRACTICE

6. **Dividends and Repurchases.** While dividend yields in the United States in the late 1990s were at historically low levels, share repurchases were at historical highs. Was this a coincidence?

7. **Dividend Irrelevance.** Respond to the following comment: "It's all very well saying that I can sell shares to cover cash needs, but that may mean selling at the bottom of the market. If the company pays a regular dividend, investors avoid the risk."

8. **Cash Dividends.** The stock of Payout Corp. will go ex-dividend tomorrow. The dividend will be $1 per share, and there are 20,000 shares of stock outstanding. The market-value balance sheet for Payout is shown below.
   a. What price is Payout stock selling for today?
   b. What price will it sell for tomorrow? Ignore taxes.

Assets		Liabilities and Equity	
Cash	$100,000	Equity	$1,000,000
Fixed assets	900,000		

EXCEL

*9. **Repurchases.** Now suppose that Payout from problem 8 announces its intention to repurchase $20,000 worth of stock instead of paying out the dividend.
   a. What effect will the repurchase have on an investor who currently holds 100 shares and sells two of those shares back to the company in the repurchase?
   b. Compare the effects of the repurchase to the effects of the cash dividend that you worked out in problem 8.

10. **Stock Dividend.** Now suppose that Payout again changes its mind and decides to issue a 2 percent stock dividend instead of either issuing the cash dividend or repurchasing 2 percent of the outstanding stock. How would this action affect a shareholder who owns 100 shares of stock? Compare with your answers to problems 8 and 9.

*11. **Dividend Irrelevance.** Suppose Mr. Dente from Example 16.2 changes his mind and cuts out Consolidated's Year 1 dividend entirely, instead spending $10 million to buy back stock. Are shareholders any better or worse off than if Consolidated had paid out $10 million as cash dividends? Hints: How many shares will be repurchased? The purchase price at Year 1 will be $110.

*12. **Dividends and Taxes.** Suppose that the tax rate on dividends is 28 percent, and the tax rate on capital gains is zero. Eagle Net Resources is about to pay a $2 per share dividend.
   a. By how much will Eagle Net's share price fall when the stock goes ex-dividend?
   b. Will anything happen to the share price on the payment date when the dividend cheques are sent out?

*13. **Stock Dividends and Splits.** Suppose that you own 1,000 shares of Nocash Corp., and the company is about to pay a 25 percent stock dividend. The stock currently sells at $50 per share.
   a. What will be the number of shares that you hold and the total value of your equity position after the dividend is paid?
   b. What will happen to the number of shares that you hold and the value of your equity position if the firm splits five-for-four instead of paying the stock dividend?

*14. **Dividends and Taxes.** Good Values, Inc., is all-equity financed. The total market value of the firm currently is $100,000, and there are 2,000 shares outstanding.
   a. The firm has declared a $5 per share dividend. The stock will go ex-dividend tomorrow. At what price will the stock sell today? Ignore taxes.
   b. Now assume that the federal marginal tax rate is 26 percent and the provincial marginal tax rate is 13.39 percent, the federal dividend tax credit is 13.33 percent of the grossed-up dividend, and the provincial dividend tax credit is 5.1 percent of grossed-up dividend. The applicable gross-up for dividend tax credits is 25 percent. What is the dividend tax rate?
   c. Using your result for the dividend tax rate from part (b) and assuming a capital gains tax rate of zero, at what price will the stock sell today?

EXCEL

15. **Repurchases and Taxes.** Now suppose that instead of paying a dividend, Good Values (from problem 14) plans to repurchase $10,000 worth of stock.
   a. What will be the stock price before and after the repurchase?

b. Suppose an investor who holds 200 shares sells 20 of her shares back to the firm. If there are no taxes on dividends or capital gains, show that she should be indifferent toward the repurchase and the dividend.

c. For this part, use the dividend tax rate from your answer to part (b) in problem 14 and assume that capital gains are not taxed. Is the value of the firm higher or lower if it pursues the share repurchase instead of the dividend?

EXCEL

*16. **Dividends and Taxes.** Investors require an after-tax rate of return of 10 percent on their stock investments. Assume that the tax rate on dividends is 28 percent while capital gains escape taxation. A firm will pay a $2 per share dividend 1 year from now, after which it is expected to sell at a price of $20.

a. Find the current price of the stock.

b. Find the expected before-tax rate of return for a one-year holding period.

c. Now suppose that the dividend will be $3 per share. If the expected after-tax rate of return is still 10 percent, and investors still expect the stock to sell at $20 in 1 year, at what price must the stock now sell?

d. What is the before-tax rate of return? Why is it now higher than in part (b)?

17. **Internet.**

a. Log in to a search engine such as Yahoo or Google and search the news section to find information on recent or planned stock repurchases. What reasons have the companies given for the repurchases? Look up the companies on **http://finance.yahoo.com**. Do the repurchase programs appear to be a substitute for dividends?

b. Log into **www.ndir.com/SI/DRPs.shtml** and look under Canadian DRPs and SPPs to find out which companies offer dividend reinvestment plans and share purchase plans. What are the advantages and drawbacks to investing in such plans?

c. Log in to **www.companyboardroom.com** and click on "Dividends" to find a recent list of dividend declarations. Can you explain what each of the dates means? What is the typical interval between each event?

18. **Dividends and Taxes.** Suppose all investments offered the same expected return *before* tax. Consider two equally risky shares, Hi and Lo. Hi shares pay a generous dividend and offer low expected capital gains. Lo shares pay low dividends and offer high expected capital gains. Which of the following investors would prefer the Lo shares? Which would prefer the Hi shares? Which wouldn't care? Explain. Assume that any stock purchased will be sold after one year.

a. a pension fund

b. an individual

c. a corporation

19. **Signalling.** It is well documented that stock prices tend to rise when firms announce an increase in their dividend payouts. How then can it be said that dividend policy is irrelevant?

20. **Dividend Policy.** Here are several assertions about typical corporate dividend policies. Which of them are true? Write out a corrected version of any false statements.

a. Most companies set a target dividend payout ratio.

b. They set each year's dividend equal to the target payout ratio times that year's earnings.

c. Managers and investors seem more concerned with dividend changes than dividend levels.

d. Managers often increase dividends temporarily when earnings are unexpectedly high for a year or two.

21. **Dividend Policy.** For each of the following four groups of companies, state whether you would expect them to distribute a relatively high or low proportion of current earnings and whether you would expect them to have a relatively high or low price-earnings ratio.

a. high-risk companies

b. companies that have recently experienced a temporary decline in profits

c.   companies that expect to experience a decline in profits

d.   "growth" companies with valuable future investment opportunities

22. **Dividend Policy.** "Risky companies tend to have lower target payout ratios and more grad-
     ual adjustment rates." Explain what is meant by this statement. Why do you think it is so?

23. **Standard & Poor's.** Go to Market Insight (**www.mcgrawhill.ca/edumarketinsight**).
     Review the dividend policy of Alcan (AL), BCE (BCE), and Biovail (BVF) in the
     Profitability and Monthly Valuation Data reports. Review the dividend yield, dividend
     payout ratio, and retention rate for each firm. What factors might explain the differences
     in dividend policies among the companies? Review the "Financial Highlights" page.

CHALLENGE

EXCEL

24. **Dividends and Taxes.** The expected pretax return on three stocks is divided between
     dividends and capital gains in the following way:

Stock	Expected Dividend	Expected Capital Gain
A	$ 0	$10
B	5	5
C	10	0

a.   If each stock is priced at $100, what are the expected net returns on each stock to (1) a
     pension fund that does not pay taxes; (2) an Ontario corporation engaged in manufac-
     turing activity, paying tax at a combined federal and provincial rate of 36.12 percent; and
     (3) an individual based in Ontario, paying a federal marginal tax rate of 29 percent and
     a provincial marginal tax rate of 11.16 percent. The gross-up for dividend tax credits is
     25 percent. The federal dividend tax credit is 13.33 percent of the grossed-up dividend,
     and the provincial dividend tax credit is 5.1 percent of grossed-up dividend.

b.   Suppose that stocks A, B, and C were priced to yield an 8 percent after-tax return to
     individual investors paying federal tax of 16 percent and provincial tax of 6.2 percent.
     The gross-up for dividend tax credits is 25 percent. The federal dividend tax credit is
     13.33 percent of the grossed-up dividend and the provincial dividend tax credit is 5.1
     percent of grossed-up dividend. What would A, B, and C each sell for?

25. **Dividends versus Repurchases.** Big Industries has the following market-value balance
     sheet. The stock currently sells for $20 a share, and there are 1,000 shares outstanding. The
     firm will either pay a $1 per share dividend or repurchase $1,000 worth of stock. Ignore taxes.

Assets		Liabilities and Equity	
Cash	$ 2,000	Debt	$10,000
Fixed assets	28,000	Equity	20,000

*a. What will be the price per share under each alternative (dividend versus repurchase)?

*b. If total earnings of the firm are $2,000 a year, find earnings per share under each
     alternative.

*c. Find the price-earnings ratio under each alternative.

d.   Adherents of the "dividends-are-good" school sometimes point to the fact that stocks
     with high dividend payout ratios tend to sell at above-average price-earnings multi-
     ples. Is this evidence convincing? Discuss this argument with regard to your answers
     to parts (a) through (c).

**Solutions to
Check Points**

16.1   The ex-dividend date is June 1. Therefore Mick buys the stock ex-dividend and will not
       receive the dividend. The cheques will be mailed on June 30.

16.2

Assets		Liabilities and Equity	
After-cash dividend			
Cash	$ 0	Debt	$ 0
Other assets	850,000	Equity	850,000
Value of firm	$850,000	Value of firm	$850,000

Shares outstanding = 100,000
Price per share = $850,000/100,000 = $8.50

Assets		Liabilities and Equity	
After-stock repurchase			
Cash	$ 0	Debt	$ 0
Other assets	850,000	Equity	850,000
Value of firm	$850,000	Value of firm	$850,000

Shares outstanding = 85,000
Price per share = $850,000/85,000 = $10

If a dividend is paid, the stock price falls by the amount of the dividend. If the company instead uses the cash for a share repurchase, the stock price remains unchanged, but with fewer shares left outstanding, the market value of the firm falls by the same amount as if the dividend had been paid. If a shareholder wants to receive the same amount of cash as if the firm had paid a dividend, he or she must sell shares, and the market value of the remaining stock will be the same as if the firm had paid a dividend.

16.3 The total value of the firm remains at $100 million. Since the firm issues $10 million in new preferred stock and the total value of the firm is fixed, the total value of common equity must fall by $10 million, which translates into the same $1 per share price drop as when equity was issued. If the firm starts out all-equity financed, the market-value balance sheet of the firm will be as follows (in millions):

Assets		Liabilities and Equity	
Assets	$100	Preferred stock	$ 10
		Common equity	90
Value of firm	$100	Value of firm	$100

Shares outstanding = 1 million
Price per share = $90 million/1 million = $90

16.4 An investor who prefers a zero-dividend policy can reinvest any dividends received. This will cause the value of the shares held to be unaffected by payouts. The price drop on the ex-dividend date is offset by the reinvestment of the dividends. However, if the investor had to pay brokerage fees on the newly purchased shares, she would be harmed by a high-payout policy since part of the proceeds of the dividends would go toward paying the broker. On the other hand, if the firm offers a dividend reinvestment plan (DRIP) with a 5 percent discount, she is better off with a high-dividend policy. The DRIP is like a "negative trading cost." She can increase the value of her stock by 5 percent of the dividend just by participating in the DRIP.

16.5 The stock price dropped by more than the dividend because investors interpreted the news as a signal that in addition to omitting the current dividend Consolidated Edison would have to reduce future dividends. The omitted dividend conveyed bad news about the future prospects of the firm.

16.6 The price of the stock will equal the after-tax cash flows discounted by the required (after-tax) rate of return:

$$P = \frac{102.5 + 10 \times (1 - .3)}{1.10} = \$99.55$$

Notice that the after-tax proceeds from the stock would increase by the amount that previously went to pay capital gains taxes, $.20 \times \$3.60 = \$.72$. The present value of this tax savings is $\$.72/1.10 = \$.65$. Therefore, the price increases to $\$98.90 + \$.65 = \$99.55$. The pretax rate of return falls to $(102.50 - 99.55 + 10)/99.55 = .1301$, or 13.01 percent, but the after-tax rate remains at 10 percent.

PART SIX
Financial Planning

FINANCIAL STATEMENT ANALYSIS

Divide and conquer. That is the only practical strategy for presenting a complex topic like financial management. For that reason we have broken down the financial manager's job into separate areas: capital budgeting, dividend policy, equity financing, and debt policy. Ultimately the financial manager has to consider the combined effects of decisions in each of these areas on the firm as a whole. Therefore, we devote all of Part Six to financial planning. We begin in this chapter by looking at the analysis of financial statements.

Why do companies provide accounting information? Public companies have a variety of stakeholders: shareholders, bondholders, bankers, suppliers, employees, and management, for example. These stakeholders all need to monitor how well their interests are being served. They rely on the company's periodic financial statements to provide basic information on the profitability of the firm.

In this chapter we look at how you can use financial statements to analyze a firm's overall performance and assess its current financial standing. You may wish to understand the policies of a competitor or the financial health of a customer. Or you may need to check your own firm's financial performance in meeting standard criteria and determine where there is room for improvement.

We will look at how analysts summarize the large volume of accounting information by calculating some key financial ratios. We will then describe these ratios and look at some interesting relationships among them. Next we will show how the ratios are used and note the limitations of the accounting data on which most ratios are based. Finally, we will look at some measures of firm performance. Some of these are expressed in ratio form; some measure how much value the firm's decisions have added.

After studying this chapter you should be able to
- Calculate and interpret measures of a firm's leverage, liquidity, efficiency, and profitability.
- Use the DuPont formula to understand the determinants of the firm's return on its assets and equity.
- Examine the statement of cash flows.
- Evaluate the potential pitfalls of ratios based on accounting data.
- Understand some key measures of firm performance such as market value added and economic value added.

17.1   FINANCIAL RATIOS

We have all heard stories of whizzes who can take a company's accounts apart in minutes, calculate a few financial ratios, and discover the company's innermost secrets. The truth, however, is that financial ratios are no substitute for a crystal ball. They are just a convenient way to summarize large quantities of financial data and to compare firms' performance. Ratios help you to ask the right questions: they seldom answer them.

We will describe and calculate four types of financial ratios:

- *Leverage ratios* show how heavily the company is in debt.
- *Liquidity ratios* measure how easily the firm can lay its hands on cash.
- *Efficiency* or *turnover ratios* measure how productively the firm is using its assets.
- *Profitability ratios* are used to measure the firm's return on its investments.

Before diving headlong into the numbers, you need to learn about the company. Without an understanding of the business, reading the financial statements is like trying to put together a puzzle without knowing what it is a picture of; you may fit some pieces together but it's a slow and difficult job. Start by reading the entire annual report, not just the financial statements. Don't forget the notes to the financial statements—they have important information on how the accountants put the statements together and other details about the company not included in the financial statements. Also read management's discussion and analysis, "MD&A," where management provides its view on the company's performance.

Another excellent information source is the company's annual information form, containing details on the business. Annual reports, annual information forms and other corporate documents are freely available at **www.sedar.com**.[1] Finance and business Web sites such as **www.globe investor.com** provide stock prices, press releases, and access to analysts' opinions. Industry Canada's Web site, Strategis at **http://strategis.ic.gc.ca**, is useful for industry information.

In this chapter, we will be analyzing the financial statements of Le Château (LC). LC management describes the company as "a leading Canadian specialty retailer offering fashion-forward apparel, accessories, and footwear to style-conscious women and men."[2] LC operates 170 retail stores in Canada and 4 in the New York City area. The company researches, designs, and manufactures 45 percent of the clothing sold in LC stores and imports the rest.

You'll find LC's income statements and balance sheets for recent years in Tables 17.1 and 17.3. Note that LC, like many retailers, selects the end of January for its fiscal year-end. This allows a given year's Christmas sales to be in one set of financial statements. When we refer to 2005 revenues, we mean the revenues earned in the one-year period ending January 31, 2005, even though 11 of the 12 months were in 2004. LC reports this information in its 2004 Annual Report. By contrast, Reitmans, another retailer, reports on the same time period in its 2005 Annual Report. To avoid mistakes, use the date on the financial statements, not on the annual report.

The **income statement** summarizes the firm's revenues and expenses and the difference between the two, which is the firm's profit. You can see in Table 17.1 that LC sold $241.131 million of clothing in 2005, a 6.3 percent increase over 2004 revenues. The costs of this clothing include the costs of producing or buying it, rent, and expenses for the retail sales staff, advertising and other marketing costs, and head-office expenses (i.e., the "selling, general, and administrative expenses"). After deducting these expenses, LC had earnings before interest, taxes, depreciation, and amortization (EBITDA) of $35.214 million, 36.9 percent more than 2004. In the process of making these sales, LC also used its fixed assets, including its retail stores, cash registers, and manufacturing facilities, and charged itself $9.062 million for depreciation and amortization of these assets. After deducting these charges, LC had earnings before interest and taxes (EBIT) of $25.010 million, a 43.2 percent increase over 2004.

income statement

Financial statement that shows the revenues, expenses, and net income of a firm over a period of time

---

[1] SEDAR, the System for Electronic Document Analysis and Retrieval, is a public Web site where Canadian public companies and mutual funds post their corporate documents, press releases, and other information releases, as required by the Canadian securities commissions.

[2] Le Château's 2004 Annual Report and Annual Information Form are found at **www.sedar.com**.

TABLE 17.1
Income statement

INCOME STATEMENT FOR LE CHÂTEAU INC., 2005 AND 2004 ($000s)		
	2005	**2004**
Sales	241,131	226,766
Cost of sales and selling, general and administrative	205,917	201,048
Earnings before interest, taxes, depreciation, and amortization (EBITDA)	35,214	25,718
Depreciation and amortization	9,062	7,745
Write-off of fixed assets	1,142	511
Earnings before interest and taxes (EBIT)	25,010	17,462
Interest	674	339
Earnings before taxes	24,336	17,123
Provision for income taxes	8,450	6,475
Net earnings	15,886	10,648
Allocation of net earnings		
Dividends	3,423	2,072
Addition to retained earnings	12,463	8,576

Source: Le Château, Inc., *Annual Report*, 2004.

In addition to the expenses of operating the business, LC paid $.674 million in interest to its lenders and set aside $8.45 million for taxes. The $15.886 million in net earnings belonged to the shareholders. However, only $3.423 million was paid out as dividends, with the rest plowed back into the business.[3]

How do analysts make sense of the data presented in income statements? One way is to calculate the change from the previous year. LC's sales were 6.3 percent (= $241,131/$226,766 − 1) higher in 2005, EBIT was 43.2 percent higher, and net earnings were 49.2 percent higher than in 2004. When making comparison between years and between firms, analysts also calculate a **common-size income statement**. Rather than showing the number of dollars earned, the common-size income statement expresses all items as a percentage of revenues. Table 17.2 is LC's common-size income statement. You can see that the cost of sales and selling, and general and administrative expenses,

common-size income statement Income statement that presents items as a percentage of revenues.

TABLE 17.2
Common-size income statement

COMMON-SIZE INCOME STATEMENT FOR LE CHÂTEAU INC. 2005 AND 2004 (all items expressed as percentage of year's revenues)		
	2005	**2004**
Sales	100.0	100.0
Cost of sales and selling, general and administrative	85.4	88.7
Earnings before interest, taxes, depreciation, and amortization (EBITDA)	14.6	11.3
Depreciation and amortization	3.8	3.2
Write-off of fixed assets	0.4	0.2
Earnings before interest and taxes (EBIT)	10.4	7.7
Interest	0.3	0.1
Earnings before taxes	10.1	7.6
Provision for income taxes	3.5	2.9
Net earnings	6.6	4.7
Allocation of net earnings		
Dividends	1.4	0.9
Addition to retained earnings	5.2	3.8

Source: Author's calculations based on Le Château Inc. *Annual Report*, 2004.

---

[3] This is in addition to the $9.062 million earmarked for depreciation and amortization.

consumed 85.4 percent of revenues in 2005. In contrast, these operating costs as a percentage of sales were higher in 2004. Thus not only were sales higher but costs, relative to sales, were lower, making 2005 a more profitable year than 2004.

balance sheet Financial statement that shows the value of the firm's assets and liabilities at a particular time.

Whereas the income statement summarizes activity during a period, the **balance sheet** presents a "snapshot" of the firm at a given moment. For example, the balance sheet in Table 17.3 is a snapshot of LC's assets and liabilities at the end of January 2004 and 2005.

As we pointed out in Chapter 3, the accountant lists first the assets that are most likely to be turned into cash in the near future. They include cash itself, short-term securities, receivables (that is, bills that have not yet been paid by the firm's customers), and inventories of raw materials, work-in-process, and finished goods. These assets are all known as *current assets*. The second main group of assets consists of *long-term assets* such as buildings, land, machinery, and equipment. Remember that the balance sheet does not show the market value of each asset. Instead, the accountant records the amount that the asset originally cost and then, in the case of plant and equipment, deducts an annual charge for depreciation. LC also owns many valuable assets, such as its brand name, that are not shown on the balance sheet.

LC's liabilities show the claims on the firm's assets. These also are classified as current and long term. *Current liabilities* are bills that the company expects to pay in the near future. They include

TABLE 17.3
Balance sheet

BALANCE SHEET FOR LE CHÂTEAU INC., AS OF JANUARY 31 ($000s)		
Assets	**2005**	**2004**
Current assets		
Cash and cash equivalents	45,985	22,067
Accounts receivable and prepaid expenses	2,089	1,394
Inventories	29,393	26,075
Other current assets	—	566
Total current assets	77,467	50,102
Fixed assets		
Property, plant, and equipment, gross	81,935	76,327
Less accumulated depreciation	31,204	31,883
Net property, plant, and equipment	50,731	44,444
Total assets	128,198	94,546
Liabilities and Shareholders' Equity	**2005**	**2004**
Current liabilities		
Accounts payable and accrued liabilities	22,397	20,148
Current portion of capital lease obligations	1,399	1,525
Current portion of long-term debt	2,940	914
Other current liabilities	2,950	2,528
Total current liabilities	29,686	25,115
Capital lease obligations	2,329	3,728
Long-term debt	6,757	852
Other long-term liabilities	4,182	3,689
Total liabilities	42,954	33,384
Shareholders' equity		
Capital stock	26,393	14,774
Retained earnings	58,851	46,388
Total shareholders' equity	85,244	61,162
Total liabilities and shareholders' equity	128,198	94,546

Source: Le Château, Inc., *Annual Report*, 2004.

debts that are due to be repaid within the next year and payables (that is, amounts the company owes to its suppliers). In addition to these short-term debts, LC has borrowed money that will not be repaid for several years. These are shown as *long-term liabilities*. Of the long-term debt, $2.94 million is to be repaid within one year and is included with the short-term liabilities. Total outstanding long-term debt is $9.697 million, the sum of the current ($2.94 million) and long-term ($6.757 million) portions of the long-term debt. As well, LC has entered into long-term rental agreements for fixed assets, such as cash registers and computer equipment. These leases are quite similar to debt because LC has committed to make fixed regular payments. Under GAAP, the present value of these lease payments is reported as a long-term liability called *capital lease obligations*. LC has committed to repay an amount with a present value of $3.728 million to the leasing companies, the sum of the current portion and the long-term capital lease obligation. Likewise, LC's fixed assets include the value of the leased assets. Just as it depreciates the fixed assets it purchases, LC depreciates these leased assets.[4]

After taking account of all the firm's liabilities, the remaining assets belong to the common shareholders. The *shareholders' equity* is simply the total value of the assets less the current and long-term liabilities.[5] It is also equal to the amount that the firm has raised from shareholders ($26.393 million) plus the earnings that have been retained and reinvested on their behalf ($58.851 million).

Just as it is sometimes useful to provide a common-size income statement, so we can also calculate a **common-size balance sheet**. In this case all items are re-expressed as a percentage of total assets. Table 17.4 is LC's common-size balance sheet. The table shows, for example, that inventories, a major asset for retailers, decreased from 27.6 percent of total assets to 22.9 percent in 2005. LC's cash and cash equivalents increased from 23.3 percent to 35.9 percent of assets.

common-size balance sheet
Balance sheet that presents items as a percentage of total assets.

LEVERAGE RATIOS

When a firm borrows money, it promises to make a series of interest payments and then to repay the amount that it has borrowed. If profits rise, the debtholders continue to receive a fixed interest payment, so that all the gains go to the shareholders. Of course, the reverse happens if profits fall. In this case shareholders bear all the pain. If times are sufficiently hard, a firm that has borrowed heavily may not be able to pay its debts. The firm is then bankrupt and shareholders lose their entire investment. Because debt increases returns to shareholders in good times and reduces them in bad times, it is said to create *financial leverage*. Leverage ratios measure how much financial leverage the firm has taken on.

Debt Ratio

Financial leverage is usually measured by the ratio of long-term debt to total long-term capital. Some analysts use a narrow definition of long-term debt and consider only bonds and other borrowings. Our definition of long-term debt includes the value of long-term leases. Total long-term capital, sometimes called total capitalization, is the sum of long-term debt, preferred equity, and common equity. Thus for LC,

$$\text{Long-term debt ratio} = \frac{\text{long-term debt} + \text{value of leases}}{\text{long-term debt} + \text{value of leases} + \text{preferred equity} + \text{common equity}}$$

$$= \frac{9,697 + 3,728}{9,697 + 3,728 + 85,244} = .136$$

---

[4] Not all leases are capitalized. As we shall soon see, LC does not capitalize leases for its retail space. You can find a more detailed look at leasing in Chapter 22.

[5] If LC had also issued preferred stock, we would also need to deduct this before calculating the equity that belonged to the common shareholders.

TABLE 17.4
Common-size balance
sheet

COMMON-SIZE BALANCE SHEET FOR LE CHÂTEAU INC., 2000 AND 1999 (all items expressed as a percentage of year's total assets)		
Assets	**2005**	**2004**
Current assets		
Cash and cash equivalents	35.9	23.3
Accounts receivables and prepaid expenses	1.6	1.5
Inventories	22.9	27.6
Other current assets	—	0.6
Total current assets	60.4	53.0
Fixed assets		
Property, plant, and equipment, gross	63.9	80.7
Less accumulated depreciation	24.3	33.7
Net property, plant, and equipment	39.6	47.0
Total assets	100.0	100.0
Liabilities and Shareholders' Equity	**2005**	**2004**
Current liabilities		
Accounts payable and accrued liabilities	17.5	21.3
Current portion of capital lease obligations	1.1	1.6
Current portion of long-term debt	2.3	1.0
Other current liabilities	2.3	2.7
Total current liabilities	23.2	26.6
Capital lease obligations	1.8	3.9
Long-term debt	5.3	0.9
Other long-term liabilities	3.3	3.9
Total liabilities	33.5	35.3
Shareholders' equity		
Capital stock	20.6	15.6
Retained earnings	45.9	49.1
Total shareholders' equity	66.5	64.7
Total liabilities and shareholders' equity	100.0	100.0

Source: Author's calculations based on Le Château Inc. *Annual Report*, 2004.

This means that 13.6 cents of every dollar of long-term capital is in the form of long-term debt. Another way to express leverage is in terms of the company's debt-equity ratio:

$$\text{Debt-equity ratio} = \frac{\text{long-term debt} + \text{value of leases}}{\text{equity}} = \frac{9,697 + 3,728}{85,244} = .157$$

These ratios might leave you with the impression that Le Château has low leverage. However, as is often the case when analyzing financial statements, first looks can be deceiving. If you read the notes to the financial statements, you will discover that LC rents all of its retail space and has entered into significant long-term leases that are not reported on its balance sheet. These leases are classified as operating leases and expensed, and are therefore a form of off-balance-sheet financing.[6] For example, its minimum operating lease payment was $24.363 million in 2006. If all of the reported future operating lease payments are capitalized by calculating their present

---

[6] LC is following GAAP when it capitalizes some of its leases but not others. If a company bears substantially all of the economic risk and reward associated with owning the asset it leases, then it must capitalize the lease. Otherwise, it can expense the lease payments like other operating expenses. As shopping malls last for many years, even a 10-year lease would not be consider a capital lease because is short, relative to the expected life of the mall.

value, we get a value of $109.86 million.[7] That is, LC has an obligation with a present value of about $110 million over the next 6 years. If we include this with the other long-term liabilities, the long-term debt ratio increases substantially to $(9,697 + 3,728 + 109,860)/(9,697 + 3,728 + 109,860 + 85,244) = .591$. About 59 cents of every dollar of long-term capital is in the form of long-term debt and leases, or equivalently, the debt-equity ratio is 1.44.

What do you think is a better measure of LC's financial leverage: including the value of the operating leases or not? If you were a loans officer at a bank considering a $5 million loan to LC, you would be very interested to know the extent of the operating leases. Just because the assets are leased does not mean that LC can ignore the payments. Be warned: financial statement analysis is a tricky business!

Notice that these measures make use of book (that is, accounting) values rather than market values.[8] The market value of the company determines whether the debtholders get their money back, so you would expect analysts to look at the face amount of the debt as a proportion of the total *market value* of debt and equity. One reason that they don't do this is that market values are often not readily available. Does it matter much? Perhaps not; after all, the market value of the firm includes the value of intangible assets generated by research and development, advertising, staff training, and so on. These assets are not readily saleable and, if the company falls on hard times, the value of these assets may disappear altogether. Thus when banks demand that a borrower keep within a maximum debt ratio, they are usually content to define this debt ratio in terms of book values and to ignore the intangible assets that are not shown in the balance sheet.

Notice also that these measures of leverage take account only of long-term debt. Managers sometimes also define debt to include all liabilities. Including the operating leases gives[9]

$$\text{Total debt ratio} = \frac{\text{total liabilities}}{\text{total assets}} = \frac{42,954 + 109,860}{128,198 + 109,860} = .64$$

Therefore, LC is financed 64 percent with debt, both long term and short term, and 36 percent with equity. We could also say that its ratio of total debt to equity is $(42,954 + 109,860)/85,244 = 1.79$.

Managers sometimes refer loosely to a company's debt ratio, but we have just seen that the debt ratio may be measured in several different ways. For example, LC could be said to have a debt ratio of .136 (the long-term debt ratio ignoring operating leases) or .64 (the total debt ratio including operating leases). The general point is there are a variety of ways to define most financial ratios and there is no law stating how they should be defined. Our advice: Don't accept a ratio at face value without understanding how it was calculated.

Times Interest Earned Ratio

Another measure of financial leverage is the extent to which interest is covered by earnings. Banks prefer to lend to firms whose earnings are far in excess of interest payments. Therefore, analysts often calculate the ratio of earnings before interest and taxes (EBIT) to interest payments. For LC,

$$\text{Times interest earned (TIE)} = \frac{\text{EBIT}}{\text{interest payments}} = \frac{25,010}{674} = 37.1$$

LC's profits would need to fall dramatically before they were insufficient to cover the interest payment.

---

[7] The reported minimum payments from 2006 to 2010, in millions of dollars are $24.363, $22.704, $20.860, $17.865, and $14.204, respectively, and $39.729 for 2011 and beyond. The payments were discounted at an assumed 7 percent required rate of return.

[8] As we have seen, in the case of leased assets, accountants estimate the present value of the lease commitments. In the case of long-term debt they simply show the face value. This can sometimes be very different from present values. For example, the present value of low-coupon debt may be only a fraction of its face value.

[9] If operating leases are excluded, the total debt ratio becomes 42,954/128,198 or .335.

The regular interest payment is a hurdle that companies must keep jumping if they are to avoid default. The times interest earned ratio (also called the interest cover ratio) measures how much clear air there is between hurdle and hurdler.

Cash Coverage Ratio

We have pointed out that depreciation and amortization are deducted when calculating the firm's earnings, even though no cash goes out the door. Thus, rather than asking whether earnings are sufficient to cover interest payments, it might be more interesting to calculate the extent to which interest is covered by the cash flow from operations. This is measured by the cash coverage ratio. For LC,

$$\text{Cash coverage ratio} = \frac{\text{EBIT} + \text{depreciation and amortization}}{\text{interest payments}} = \frac{25,010 + 10,204}{674} = 52.2$$

These two ratios tell only part of the story. For instance, they don't tell us whether LC is generating enough cash to repay debt as it comes due, or whether it can make its capital lease obligations. Other possible fixed charges include preferred share sinking-fund payments and preferred share dividends. A *fixed-charge coverage ratio* shows how many times greater EBIT plus depreciation and amortization is relative to the fixed charges the company is obliged to make.

When creating a fixed-charge coverage ratio, watch out for fixed payments that are made from after-tax earnings (or after-tax cash flows). Such non-tax-deductible payments include debt principal repayment and payments to preferred shares. You must convert these payments to a before-tax basis by dividing by (1 – corporate tax rate). For example, if a company is obligated to pay $3 million in preferred share dividends and its tax rate is 35 percent, it must earn $3 million/(1 – .35) = $4.615 million in before-tax dollars.

In LC's case, we use a fixed charge coverage ratio that includes both its current portion of long-term debt and capital lease obligations. From the balance sheet, we see the current portion of long-term debt is $2.94 million and current lease obligation is $1.399 million. With a 35 percent corporate tax rate,

Fixed charge coverage ratio =

$$\frac{\text{EBIT} + \text{depreciation and amortization}}{\text{Interest payments} + (\text{current debt repayment} + \text{current lease obligations})/(1 - \text{tax rate})}$$

$$= \frac{25,010 + 10,204}{674 + (2,940 + 1,399)/(1 - .35)} = 4.79$$

The cash flow from LC's operations was 4.79 times greater than its fixed charges, indicating sufficient cash flow to cover its fixed charges. Analysts often compare debt and coverage ratios over time for a firm as well as between firms in the same industry, to assess whether the debt level is manageable.

Check Point 17.1

A firm repays $10 million par value of outstanding debt and issues $10 million of new debt with a lower rate of interest. What happens to its long-term debt ratio? What happens to its times interest earned and cash coverage ratios?

LIQUIDITY RATIOS

If you are extending credit to a customer or making a short-term bank loan, you are interested in more than the company's leverage. You want to know whether it will be able to lay its hands on the cash to repay you. That is why credit analysts and bankers look at several measures of **liquidity**. Liquid assets can be converted into cash quickly and cheaply.

liquidity Ability of an asset to be converted to cash quickly at low cost.

Think, for example, what you would do to meet a large, unexpected bill. You might have some money in the bank or some investments that are easily sold, but you would not find it so simple to convert your old sweaters into cash. Companies also own assets with different degrees of liquidity. For example, accounts receivable and inventories of finished goods are generally quite liquid. As inventories are sold and customers pay their bills, money flows into the firm. At the other extreme, real estate may be quite *illiquid*. It can be hard to find a buyer, negotiate a fair price, and close a deal at short notice.

Managers have another reason to focus on liquid assets: the accounting figures are more reliable. The book value of a catalytic cracker may be a poor guide to its true value, but at least you know what cash in the bank is worth.

Liquidity ratios also have some *less* desirable characteristics. Because short-term assets and liabilities are easily changed, measures of liquidity can rapidly become outdated. You might not know what the catalytic cracker is worth, but you can be fairly sure that it won't disappear overnight. Also, companies often choose a slack period for the end of their financial year. For example, like many other retailers, LC ends its financial year in January after the Christmas boom. At these times, the companies are likely to have more cash and less short-term debt than during busier seasons.

Net Working Capital to Total Assets Ratio

We have seen that current assets are those that the company expects to meet in the near future. The difference between the current assets and current liabilities is known as *net working capital*. It roughly measures the company's potential reservoir of cash. Net working capital is usually positive; however, it can be negative. For LC,

$$\text{Net working capital} = 77{,}467 - 29{,}686 = 47{,}781$$

Managers often express net working capital as a proportion of total assets. For LC,

$$\frac{\text{Net working capital}}{\text{Total assets}} = \frac{47{,}781}{128{,}198} = .37$$

Current Ratio

Another measure that serves a similar purpose is the current ratio:

$$\text{Current ratio} = \frac{\text{current assets}}{\text{current liabilities}} = \frac{77{,}467}{29{,}686} = 2.61$$

So LC has $2.61 in current assets for every $1 in current liabilities.

Rapid decreases in the current ratio sometimes signify trouble. For example, a firm that drags out its payables by delaying payment of its bills will suffer an increase in current liabilities and a decrease in the current ratio.

Changes in the current ratio can be misleading, however. For example, suppose that a company borrows a large sum from the bank and invests it in marketable securities. Current liabilities rise and so do current assets. Therefore, if nothing else changes, net working capital is unaffected but the current ratio changes. For this reason, it is sometimes preferable to net short-term investments against short-term debt when calculating the current ratio.

EXAMPLE 17.1	CURRENT RATIO

Suppose Le Chateau borrows $1,000,000 to invest in marketable securities. Its current liabilities increase to $30,686,000, while its current assets increase to $78,467,000. The current ratio falls from 2.61 to 78,467/30,686 = 2.56.

Quick (or Acid-Test) Ratio

Some assets are closer to cash than others. If trouble comes, inventory may not sell at anything above fire-sale prices. (Trouble typically comes *because* the firm can't sell its finished-product inventory for more than the production cost.) Thus managers often exclude inventories and other less liquid components of current assets when comparing current assets to current liabilities. They focus instead on cash, marketable securities, and bills that customers have not yet paid. This results in the quick ratio:

$$\text{Quick ratio} = \frac{\text{cash} + \text{marketable securities} + \text{receivables}}{\text{current liabilities}} = \frac{45,985 + 2,089}{29,686} = 1.62$$

Check Point 17.2

a. A firm has $1.2 million in current assets and $1.0 million in current liabilities. If it uses $.5 million of cash to pay off some of its accounts payable, what will happen to the current ratio? What happens to net working capital?

b. A firm uses cash on hand to pay for additional inventories. What will happen to the current ratio? To the quick ratio?

Interval Measure

Instead of looking at a firm's liquid assets relative to its current liabilities, it may be useful to measure whether liquid assets are large relative to the firm's regular outgoings. We ask how long the firm could keep up with its bills using only its cash and other liquid assets. This is called the interval measure, which is computed by dividing liquid assets by daily expenditures:

$$\text{Interval measure} = \frac{\text{cash} + \text{marketable securities} + \text{receivables}}{\text{average daily expenditures from operations}}$$

For LC,

$$\text{Interval measure} = \frac{45,985 + 2,089}{(205,917)/365} = 85.2$$

LC has enough liquid assets to finance operations for 85 days if it does not sell another pair of pants or another shirt.

Cash Ratio

A company's most liquid assets are its holdings of cash and marketable securities. That is why analysts also look at the cash ratio:

$$\text{Cash ratio} = \frac{\text{cash} + \text{marketable securities}}{\text{current liabilities}} = \frac{45,985}{29,686} = 1.55$$

A low cash ratio may not matter if the firm can borrow on short notice. Who cares whether the firm has actually borrowed from the bank or whether it has a guaranteed line of credit that lets it borrow whenever it chooses? None of the standard liquidity measures takes the firm's "reserve borrowing power" into account.

EFFICIENCY RATIOS

Financial analysts employ another set of ratios to judge how efficiently the firm is using its assets.

Asset Turnover Ratio

The asset turnover, or sales-to-assets, ratio shows how hard the firm's assets are being put to use. For LC, each dollar of assets produced $1.88 of sales:

$$\frac{\text{Sales}}{\text{Total assets}} = \frac{241,131}{128,198} = 1.88$$

A high ratio compared with other firms in the same industry could indicate that the firm is working close to capacity. It may prove difficult to generate further business without additional investment.

You may have noticed that the asset turnover ratio is calculated with a balance sheet variable (total assets) and an income statement variable (sales). Balance sheet variables are snapshot figures, measured at a point in time, but income statement variables are flow figures, measured over a period of time, typically one year. When using both a flow figure and snapshot figure in a ratio, the analyst must consider the possible impact of the time difference between the two variables. Suppose the company has grown substantially over the year. The end-of-year asset level may be much higher than at the start of the year, reflecting the need for higher assets to support the higher sales rate and be mismatched to the sales measured over the year. A common approach taken in this situation is to replace end-of-year total assets with the *average* of the assets at the beginning and end of the year. For any efficiency ratio, you can replace the end-of-year balance sheet figure with its average, if you assess that the company has grown (or shrunk) substantially over the year. LC sales grew about 6 percent in 2005, which is moderate growth, and we will use the end-of-year asset values in our definitions of the ratios.

Instead of looking at the ratio of sales to total assets, managers sometimes look at how hard particular types of capital are being put to use. For example, they might look at the value of sales per dollar invested in fixed assets. Or they might look at the ratio of sales to net working capital.

Thus for LC each dollar of fixed assets generated $4.75 of sales:

$$\frac{\text{Sales}}{\text{Fixed assets}} = \frac{241{,}131}{50{,}731} = 4.75$$

Both the total-asset and fixed-asset turnover ratios are affected by the choice of lease accounting. For example, if Le Château's retail space leases were capitalized, an additional fixed asset, perhaps called "leased rental space," would show up on the balance sheet to reflect the present value of the lease payments. This increase in the fixed assets would produce lower asset turnover even though the firm's operations had not changed. This is important to remember if you are comparing two companies with very different leasing activities.

Average Collection Period

The average collection period measures the speed with which customers pay their bills. It expresses accounts receivable in terms of daily sales:

$$\text{Average collection period} = \frac{\text{receivables}}{\text{average daily sales}} = \frac{2{,}089}{241{,}131/365} = 3.2 \text{ days}$$

LC's average collection period is only 3.2 days.

Often a comparatively low figure indicates a highly efficient collections department. Not this time; here is another example of the importance of knowing the nature of the company's business. LC is a retailer and most of its sales are by cash or credit card. Cash has a zero collection period, and with electronic credit-card billing, retailers are able to receive cash from the credit card companies quickly. The average collection period for credit card companies such as Visa and MasterCard will be much longer. If we knew LC's credit sales, we could measure its average collection period more sensibly. Note, too, that sometimes a low average collection period, especially when low compared to the firm's competitors, results from an unduly restrictive credit policy in which the firm offers credit only to customers who are certain to pay promptly. Again, this is not the case for Le Château.

Inventory Turnover Ratio

Managers may also monitor the rate at which the company is turning over its inventories. The balance sheet shows the cost of inventories rather than what the finished goods will eventually sell for. So, ideally, we compare the cost of inventories with the cost of goods sold, which is the value of the goods drawn out of inventory. Unfortunately, some firms lump together various costs on the income statement, making it difficult to identify the cost of the goods sold. LC discloses the sum of its cost of sales, and its selling, general, and administrative expenses. This is LC's operating costs, not its cost of goods sold. In this situation, analysts are forced to calculate inventory turnover as the ratio of operating costs to inventory or even as sales to inventory. The important principle to remember is to be consistent: when comparing inventory turnover of two companies, be sure to calculate the ratios the same way for each company. Using LC's operating costs as a proxy for its cost of goods sold, LC's inventory turnover is

$$\text{Inventory turnover} = \frac{\text{cost of goods sold}}{\text{inventory}} = \frac{205,917}{29,393} = 7.01$$

Efficient firms turn over their inventory rapidly and don't tie up more capital than they need in raw materials or finished goods. But firms that are living from hand to mouth may also cut their inventories to the bone.

Managers sometimes also look at how many days' sales are represented by inventories. This is equal to the inventory divided by the daily cost of goods sold:

$$\text{Days' sales in inventories} = \frac{\text{inventory}}{\text{cost of goods sold}/365} = \frac{29,393}{205,917/365} = 52.1 \text{ days}$$

You could say that on average LC has sufficient inventories to maintain sales for 52 days.[10]

Check Point 17.3   The average collection period measures the number of days it takes LC to collect its bills. But LC also delays *paying* its own bills. Use the information in tables 17.1 and 17.3 to calculate the average number of days that it takes the company to pay its bills.

PROFITABILITY RATIOS

Profitability ratios focus on the firm's earnings, giving an overall indication of the firm's performance. One group of profitability measures, known as *profit margins*, looks at profit or earnings as a fraction of sales. The other group, called *return ratios*, measures profits earned as a fraction of the assets used or the funds invested in the firm.

The definition of profits (or earnings or income) used in a profitability ratio depends on what you want to measure. Let's look at a few profit margins and return ratios for Le Château.

Net Profit Margin

If you want to know the proportion of revenue that finds its way to profits, you look at the net profit margin. This is commonly defined as

$$\text{Net profit margin} = \frac{\text{net income}}{\text{sales}} = \frac{15,886}{241,131} = 0.0659, \text{ or } 6.59\%$$

For every dollar of sales, LC's shareholders earned 6.59 cents.

Operating Profit Margin

When companies are partly financed by debt, the profits are divided between the debtholders and the shareholders. We would not want to say that such a firm is less profitable simply because it employs debt finance and pays out part of its profits as interest. Therefore, when calculating the profit margin, it seems appropriate to add back the debt interest to net income. This gives another profit margin that also has wide acceptance and which we will call the operating profit margin.

$$\text{Operating profit margin} = \frac{\text{net income} + \text{interest}}{\text{sales}} = \frac{15,886 + 674}{241,131} = 0.0687, \text{ or } 6.87\%$$

For every dollar of sales, LC's debtholders and shareholders together earn 6.87 cents.

Another way to think about the operating profit margin is in terms of the operating profits generated by the company, rather than the earnings of debtholders and shareholders. We define

---

[10] This is a loose statement, because it ignores the fact that LC may have more than 52 days' supply of some materials and less of others. Futhermore, the days' worth of inventory is understated because we divide by daily operating costs, not daily COGS.

operating profit as sales revenue minus operating expenses, which include cost of sales, selling, general and administrative expenses, and taxes, or EBIT minus taxes. Look back to Table 17.1 and you will see that net income equals EBIT − interest − taxes. This equation can be rearranged to show that net income + interest = EBIT − taxes. In other words, operating profit can be calculated as EBIT − taxes, or as the earnings of debtholders and shareholders, net income + interest. Thus, for LC

$$\text{Operating profit} = \text{EBIT} - \text{taxes} = 25{,}010 - 8{,}450 = 16{,}560$$

$$\text{Operating profit} = \text{Net income} + \text{interest} = 15{,}886 + 674 = 16{,}560$$

Whether the operating profit margin is calculated as the ratio of EBIT minus taxes to sales or as the sum of net income and interest to sales, the answer is the same.[11]

Holding everything constant, a firm would naturally prefer a high profit margin. But all else cannot be held constant. A high-price and high-margin strategy typically will result in lower sales. So while Holt Renfrew might have a higher margin than Wal-Mart, it will not necessarily enjoy higher profits. A low-margin but high-volume strategy can be quite successful. We return to this issue later.

Return on Assets (ROA)

Another way to assess a firm's profitability is to measure profits as a percentage of assets or funds invested. A commonly used measure is the ratio of net income to total assets, known as return on assets, ROA. For LC,

$$\text{Return on assets} = \frac{\text{net income}}{\text{total assets}} = \frac{15{,}886}{128{,}198} = .124, \text{ or } 12.4\%$$

However, because net income measures profits net of interest expense, ROA makes the apparent profitability of a firm a function of its financing choices as well as it operating decisions. It is better to use operating profits, net income plus interest, because we are measuring the return on all of the firm's assets, not just its equity investment. We call this the *operating return on assets*:[12]

$$\text{Operating return on assets} = \frac{\text{net income} + \text{interest}}{\text{total assets}} = \frac{15{,}886 + 674}{128{,}198} = .129, \text{ or } 12.9\%$$

As LC has relatively little interest-bearing debt, its return on assets is almost the same as its operating return on assets.

Return on Invested Capital (ROIC)

This ratio focuses on the return earned on total capital: debt, and capital leases, plus preferred and common equity invested in the company. Again the numerator should be the firm's earnings:

$$\text{Return on invested capital} = \frac{\text{net income} + \text{interest}}{\text{short-term and long-term debt} + \text{preferred and common equity}}$$

$$= \frac{15{,}886 + 674}{1{,}399 + 2{,}940 + 2{,}329 + 6{,}757 + 85{,}244} = \frac{16{,}560}{98{,}699} = .168, \text{ or } 16.8\%$$

---

[11] A word of warning: if a company has sources of income and expenses other than from operating activities, the interest and net income may not add up to EBIT less taxes. Pick the definition best suited to your goals. To compare operating profits of different firms, you will likely want to use EBIT − taxes and ignore the other income statement items. However, if you want overall performance, net income plus interest is a better measure.

[12] To compare operating performance of firms with different capital structure, a modified definition of operating return on assets can be used. Firms with more interest pay less in taxes. Thus to measure operating profits alone, adjust for leverage by subtracting that part of operating profit generated by interest tax shields (interest payments × marginal tax rate). This gives the operating profit that the firm would earn if were all-equity financed.

The assets in a company's books are valued on the basis of their original cost (less any depreciation). A high return on assets does not always mean that you could buy the same assets today and get a high return. Nor does a low return imply that the assets could be employed better elsewhere. But it does suggest that you should ask some searching questions.

In a competitive industry, firms can expect to earn only their cost of capital. Therefore, a high return on assets is sometimes cited as an indication that the firm is taking advantage of a monopoly position to charge excessive prices. For example, when a public utility commission tries to determine whether a utility is charging a fair price, much of the argument will centre on a comparison between the cost of capital and the return that the utility is earning (its ROA).

Return on Equity (ROE)

Another measure of profitability focuses on the return on the shareholders' equity:

$$\text{Return on equity} = \frac{\text{net income}}{\text{equity}} = \frac{15,886}{85,244} = .186, \text{ or } 18.6\%$$

ROE for 2004 was 17.4 percent.

Payout Ratio

The payout ratio measures the proportion of earnings that is paid out as dividends. Thus,

$$\text{Payout ratio} = \frac{\text{dividends}}{\text{earnings}} = \frac{3,423}{15,886} = .215, \text{ or } 21.5\%$$

The 2004 payout ratio was 19.5 percent. We saw in Section 16.3 that managers don't like to cut dividends because of a shortfall in earnings. Therefore, if a company's earnings are particularly variable, management is likely to play it safe by setting a low average payout ratio.

When earnings fall unexpectedly, the payout ratio is likely to rise temporarily. Likewise, if earnings are expected to rise next year, management may feel that it can pay somewhat more generous dividends than it would otherwise have done.

In LC's case, dividends were increased 5 cents a share in March 2004, contributing to the higher payout ratio.

Earnings not paid out as dividends are retained, or plowed back into the business. The proportion of earnings reinvested in the firm is called the *plowback ratio*:

$$\text{Plowback ratio} = 1 - \text{payout ratio} = \frac{\text{earnings} - \text{dividends}}{\text{earnings}}$$

If you multiply this figure by the return on equity, you can see how rapidly shareholders' equity is growing as a result of plowing back part of its earnings each year. In 2005 earnings plowed back into the firm increased the book value of equity by 20.4 percent:

$$\begin{aligned}
\text{Growth in equity from plowback} &= \frac{\text{earnings} - \text{dividends}}{\text{equity}} \\
&= \frac{\text{earnings} - \text{dividends}}{\text{earnings}} \times \frac{\text{earnings}}{\text{equity}} \\
&= \text{plowback ratio} \times \text{ROE} \\
&= .785 \times .26 = .204, \text{ or } 20.4\%
\end{aligned}$$

If LC could continue to earn 26 percent on its book equity and plow back 78.5 percent of earnings, both earnings and equity would grow at 20.4 percent a year.[13]

---

[13] Analysts sometimes refer to this figure as the *sustainable rate of growth*. Notice that, when calculating the sustainable rate of growth, ROE is properly measured by earnings (in LC's case, $15.886 million) as a proportion of equity at the *start* of the year (in LC's case, $61.162 million), rather than the equity at the end of the year. We discussed the sustainable rate of growth in Chapter 6 and we will return to it again in Chapter 18.

Is this a reasonable prospect? We saw in Chapter 6 that such high growth rates are unlikely to persist. In the long run, it is difficult for companies to grow faster than the economy. Add the competition from the many other clothing retailers, and LC is unlikely to sustain this growth rate for more than a couple of years.

17.2

DuPont system
A breakdown of ROE and ROA into component ratios.

THE DUPONT SYSTEM

Some profitability or efficiency measures can be linked in useful ways. These relationships are often referred to as the **DuPont system**, in recognition of the chemical company that popularized them.

The first relationship links the return on assets (ROA) with the firm's turnover ratio and its net profit margin:

$$\text{ROA} = \frac{\text{net income}}{\text{assets}} = \underset{\underset{\text{turnover}}{\text{asset}}}{\underbrace{\frac{\text{sales}}{\text{assets}}}} \times \underset{\underset{\text{margin}}{\text{net profit}}}{\underbrace{\frac{\text{net income}}{\text{sales}}}} \qquad (17.1)$$

A similar decomposition can be done on the company's operating return on capital, in which case the operating return on capital is decomposed into the asset turnover times the operating profit margin.

All firms would like to earn a higher return on their assets, but their ability to do so is limited by competition. If the expected return on assets is fixed by competition, firms face a trade-off between the turnover ratio and the profit margin. Thus we find that fast-food chains, which have high turnover, also tend to operate on low profit margins. Hotels have relatively low turnover ratios but tend to compensate for this with higher margins. Table 17.5 illustrates the trade-off. Both the fast-food chain and the hotel have the same return on assets. However, their profit margins and turnover ratios are entirely different.

Firms often seek to improve their profit margins by acquiring a supplier. The idea is to capture the supplier's profit as well as their own. Unfortunately, unless they have some special skill in running the new business, they are likely to find that any gain in profit margin is offset by a decline in the asset turnover.

A few numbers may help to illustrate this point. Table 17.6 shows the sales, profits, and assets of Admiral Motors and its components supplier Diana Corporation. Both earn a 10 percent return on assets, though Admiral has a lower profit margin (20 percent versus Diana's 25 percent). Since all of Diana's output goes to Admiral, Admiral's management reasons that it would be better to merge the two companies. That way the merged company would capture the profit margin on both the auto components and the assembled car.

The bottom line of Table 17.6 shows the effect of the merger. The merged firm does indeed earn the combined profits. Total sales remain at $20 million, however, because all the components produced by Diana are used within the company. With higher profits and unchanged sales, the profit margin increases. Unfortunately, the asset turnover ratio is reduced by the merger since the merged firm operates with higher assets. This exactly offsets the benefit of the higher profit margin. The return on assets is unchanged.

TABLE 17.5
Fast-food chains and hotels may have similar returns on assets but different asset turnover ratios and profit margins

	Asset Turnover	× Profit Margin	= Return on Assets
Fast-food chains	2.0	5%	10%
Hotels	0.5	20	10

TABLE 17.6

Merging with suppliers or customers will generally increase the profit margin, but this will be offset by a reduction in the turnover ratio

	$ Millions			Asset Turnover	Profit Margin	ROA
	Sales	Profits	Assets			
Admiral Motors	$20	$4	$40	.50	20%	10%
Diana Corp.	8	2	20	.40	25	10
Diana Motors (the merged firm)	20	6	60	.33	30	10

We can also break down financial ratios to show how the return on equity (ROE) depends on the return on assets and leverage:

$$ROE = \frac{\text{earnings available for common stock}}{\text{equity}} = \frac{\text{net income}}{\text{equity}}$$

Multiply ROE by assets/assets × sales/sales and rearrange to get

$$ROE = \underset{\substack{\uparrow \\ \text{leverage} \\ \text{ratio}}}{\frac{\text{assets}}{\text{equity}}} \times \underset{\substack{\uparrow \\ \text{asset} \\ \text{turnover}}}{\frac{\text{sales}}{\text{assets}}} \times \underset{\substack{\uparrow \\ \text{net profit} \\ \text{margin}}}{\frac{\text{net income}}{\text{sales}}} = \frac{\text{assets}}{\text{equity}} \times ROA \qquad (17.2)$$

The decomposition of ROE reveals the key drivers of shareholders' return: operating efficiency (as measured by the net profit margin), efficiency of asset use (as measured by asset turnover) and leverage (as measured by the asset/equity ratio). If a company can earn more income on its sales, say by cutting operating costs, its net profit margin will increase, raising ROE. If it can increase the volume of sales generated by its existing assets, its asset turnover will increase and so too will ROE. Finally, increasing leverage will increase ROE, provided that the firm's return on assets is higher than its cost of debt.

Check Point 17.4

a. Sappy Syrup has a net profit margin below the industry average, but its ROA equals the industry average. How is this possible?

b. Sappy Syrup's ROA equals the industry average, but its ROE exceeds the industry average. How is this possible?

OTHER IMPORTANT FINANCIAL RATIOS

Each of the financial ratios that we have described involves accounting data only. But managers also compare accounting numbers with the values that are established in the marketplace. For example, they may compare the total market value of the firm's shares with the book value (the amount that the company has raised from shareholders or reinvested on their behalf). If managers have been successful in adding value for shareholders, the *market-to-book ratio* should be greater than 1.0. In Chapter 6 we also discussed two other ratios that use accounting data, the *price-earnings ratio* and the *dividend yield*. These ratios provide additional measures of how highly the company is valued by investors.

You can probably think of a number of other ratios that could provide useful insights into a company's health. For example, a retail chain might compare its sales per square foot with those of its competitors, a steel producer might look at the cost per ton of steel produced, and an airline might look at revenues per passenger mile flown. A little thought and common sense should suggest which measures are likely to provide insights into your own company's efficiency.

ANALYSIS OF THE STATEMENT OF CASH FLOWS

Like a corporate version of a bank statement, the cash flow statement tracks the cash coming into and flowing out of a corporation over the year. By contrast, the income statement, based on accrual accounting, matches expenses to current-period sales and gives a better sense of the long-run profitability of the firm. However, with accrual accounting, a healthy-looking income statement can miss a current cash crunch that would be quite apparent on the cash flow statement.

Consider a firm that spends $3 million in the year on a new production facility. The cash outflow is reported on that year's cash flow statement as an investment activity reducing cash by $3 million. The income statement won't show the $3 million expenditure. Instead, once production starts, the cost of the building will be expensed as depreciation, gradually over the expected life of the building, perhaps 30 years. The company might look quite profitable while experiencing a severe shortage of cash.

The statement of cash flows for Le Château is in Table 17.7. As we saw in Chapter 3, cash flows are divided into three distinct categories: operating activities, investing activities, and financing activities. Each section reveals important information on where the cash came from and where it went.

An important cash flow number is the cash generated by the firm's operations after all of the necessary investments in net working capital and fixed assets. As we saw in Chapter 3, this is called either *cash flow from assets* or *free cash flow*.[14]

In Chapter 3, we showed you a fast way to measure free cash flow by rearranging the statement of cash flows. Using the information in Table 17.7, the following are LC's 2004 and 2005 free cash flows in millions of dollars:

	2005	2004
Cash flows from operating activities	$ 24.739	$19.639
Cash flows from (used in) investing activities	(16.491)	(14.438)
= Cash flows from assets (free cash flow)	8.248	5.201

In 2005, LC generated $8.248 million in cash flow from its assets, even after spending $16.491 million on new long-term assets. In other words, it had sufficient cash flow from its operating activities to fund its investment requirements.

Where did the $8.248 million of cash generated by the business go? From the financing activities section of the statement of cash flows, we see that LC received $15.67 million from bondholders and shareholders, largely through the sale of shares. So, LC not only generated cash through its business operations, but also raised cash from investors, totalling $23.918 million. Where did it all go? Check the bank account: LC's cash and equivalents increased $23.918 million over the year. In the coming years, LC will have to decide what to do with all of its cash. Nice problem to have!

It is not unusual for firms to have negative free cash flow during a growth period or in periods of poor performance. Often, firms need to make significant investments in assets before they can produce goods to sell and generate cash. In 1999, LC added 13 new stores and renovated others and had negative free cash flows. In 2000, LC continued to make significant investments in its facilities, largely to renovate existing stores, but also had poor sales, leading to negative free cash flows. Had the negative free cash flows continued, LC might have gone bankrupt if investors refused to put more cash into the business. Fortunately, LC's business picked up and it now has no cash flow problem. The nearby Finance in Action box presents a discussion of free cash flow in the chemical industry.

SEE BOX P. 548

---

[14] No standard definition of cash flows from assets or free cash flows exists. A common variation of free cash flow treats interest expense as a cash flow to bondholders and not as an operating expense. To do this, add back interest expense to cash flows from assets. For LC, interest in 2005 was only $0.674 million, making adjusted cash flow from assets $8.92 million. If you want to remove any impact of the choice of financing, add back interest expense but also subtract the interest tax shield. Then include after-tax interest expense as a cash flow to bondholders.

TABLE 17.7
Statement of cash flows

STATEMENT OF CASH FLOWS FOR LE CHÂTEAU INC. 2005 AND 2004 ($000s)		
	2005	**2004**
Operating Activities		
Net earnings	15,886	10,648
Adjustments to determine net cash from operating activities		
Depreciation and amortization	9,062	7,745
Write-off of fixed assets	1,142	511
Other adjustments	493	(112)
Cash provided by operations	26,583	18,792
Net change in non-cash working capital items related to operations	(1,844)	847
Cash flows from operating activities	24,739	19,639
Investing Activities		
Additions to fixed assets	(16,491)	(14,438)
Cash flows from (used in) investing activities	(16,491)	(14,438)
Financing Activities		
Repayment of loan to director	566	
Proceeds of capital leases		5,620
Retirement of capital lease obligations	(1,525)	(1,355)
Proceeds of long-term debt	9,991	
Retirement of long-term debt	(2,060)	(1,483)
Issue of capital stock	11,619	1,094
Dividends paid	(2,921)	(2,050)
Cash flows from (used in) financing activities	15,670	1,826
Increase (decrease) in cash and cash equivalents	23,918	7,027
Cash and cash equivalents, beginning of year	22,067	15,040
Cash and cash equivalents, end of year	45,985	22,067

Source: Le Château Inc. *Annual Report*, 2004 .

In addition to measuring free cash flow, analysts also calculate ratios using information from the statement of cash flows. Bond rating agencies often include cash flow ratios in their assessment of the quality of firm's debt. For example, in Table 17.10 (page 553), one of the key financial ratios used by Standard and Poor's is the ratio of free operating cash flow to total debt. This ratio tells what fraction of the outstanding debt could be paid for with the current year's operating cash flow. However, unlike the ratios based on the income statement and balance sheet, cash-flow–based ratios have not become standardized. We think this will change given the increasing interest analysts and investors are paying to companies' cash flows.[15]

17.4   USING FINANCIAL RATIOS

ACCOUNTING PRINCIPLES AND FINANCIAL RATIOS

Accounting rules are designed to provide investors with a fair view of the company's earnings, assets, and liabilities. Accountants are continually revising these rules but, inevitably, no summary set of numbers can hope to capture the financial position of a large and complex business. So, when you calculate financial ratios, it is important to look below the surface and understand

---

[15] See J. Mills and J. Yamamura, "The Power of Cash Flow Ratios," *Journal of Accountancy* (October 1998), p. 53, for some other cash flow ratios.

Focus Shifts to Free Cash Flow in Return to Value Investing

When it comes to finance and investing, "cash is king," they say. To determine how much excess cash a company generates from its operations after capital expenditures and other expenses, it pays to look at the metric free cash flow (FCF). The chemical industry, despite all the doom and gloom, tends to generate healthy amounts of FCF. As traditional investing becomes more fashionable in the wake of the ongoing massacre in the technology sector, the issue of FCF is getting pushed into the spotlight.

"Investors appear to be seeking safe havens where there is little risk of additional compression of P/E multiples, and where the general level of cash flow and free cash flow are both healthy and stable," says JP Morgan analyst Jeffrey Zekauskas. As one portfolio manager put it, "I am not interested in stories; I am interested in cash flow."

While Wall Street and investors tend to focus on net income and earnings per share, a truer metric for actual cash generation is FCF. Although just about every analyst has a slightly different definition for FCF, we will define it as net income plus depreciation and amortization minus capital expenditures minus change in working capital.

The benefit of using FCF is that it accounts for capital expenditures and working capital as uses of cash and adds back noncash expenses (D&A) to net income to get a clear picture of how much actual cash the business generated.

"For the chemical industry in general, earnings are often misleading as far as cash-flow generation capability of the companies because noncash charges are so large," Mr. Zekauskas points out. "Free cash flow provides a clearer picture of the quality of the cash flow that the company is throwing off."

"Looking at free cash flow instead of reported earnings per share is a better indicator of the kind of real value being created by the entity instead of clouding the underlying cash flow by accounting rules," says Lehman Brothers analyst Timothy Gerdeman. "It just gives you a better idea of the underlying cash the business is generating."

The difference between reported earnings and free cash flow can be substantial in many cases. For example, Lyondell Chemical Company posted 2000 adjusted net income of $70 million, or 59 cents per share.

However, to get a better sense of actual cash generation, take net income of $70 million, add $279 million in depreciation and amortization (noncash expenses), subtract $104 million in capital expenditures (cash expense) and add $254 million from the reduction in working capital (current assets minus current liabilities) from $865 million in 1999 to $611 million in 2000.

Lyondells total free cash flow generation for 2000 comes out to $499 million, or $4.24 per share, of which $106 million paid shareholders' dividends. Much of the rest was used to pay off debt.

In addition to dividends and paying down debt, FCF can be used to make acquisitions, buy back stock or invest in new projects or expansions. Measuring FCF gives investors an idea of what projects companies can fund just from the cash it generates.

Certain institutional investors look at free cash flow on a yield basis—that is, FCF per share divided by share price to get a percentage. "There are some institutions out there, primarily value investors, that really focus on FCF yield," notes Bank of America securities analyst Mark Gulley.

Despite its usefulness, there are some drawbacks to FCF as there are with all financial metrics. In any given year, a surge or sharp decline in capital expenditures or working capital could distort the picture.

"Let's say a new management comes in and slashes capital expenditures and works really hard on reducing working capital," says Bank of America's Mr. Gulley. "You could have one year of great FCF, but that would be a head fake." On the other hand, sharp increases in capital expenditures or working capital can reduce FCF to lower than normalized levels. For example, in 2000, Rohm and Haas' working capital increased by $570 million, leading to FCF of $33 million compared to net income of $381 million.

In the case of Lyondell, FCF of $499 million in 2000 benefited from a reduction in working capital of $254 million related to the sale of its polyols business in March 2000. Excluding the impact of the sale, working capital would have actually increased $98 million, according to the company, leading to an adjusted FCF figure of $147 million.

Because of the magnitude of the changes in capital expenditures and working capital from year to year, institutional investors tend to use normalized levels of capital expenditures and working capital in their FCF calculations, notes Bank of America's Mr. Gulley.

Source: Excerpted from Joseph Chang, "Chemical Cash Generation Capability Clouded by EPS," *Chemical Market Reporter*, March 19, 2001, p.1.

---

some of the limitations in the accounting numbers. Remember our earlier comment that financial ratios are just a starting point and help you to ask the right questions.

Here are a few examples of things that can make simple comparisons of financial ratios misleading.

1. *Goodwill.* The assets shown in Maple Leaf's 2004 balance sheet in Chapter 3 include a figure of $.899 million for "goodwill and other intangibles." Goodwill is the difference between the amount that Maple Leaf paid when it acquired several companies and the book value of their assets. If the estimated value of this goodwill ever falls below the amount shown in the balance sheet, the figure in the balance sheet must be adjusted downward and the write-off deducted from that year's earnings. We don't want to debate here whether goodwill is really an asset, but we should warn you about the dangers of comparing ratios of firms whose balance sheets include a substantial goodwill element with those that do not.

2. *Research and Development.* LC spent an unreported amount on research and development (R&D). Large pharmaceutical companies often spend billions on R&D. This research and development is an investment that, it is hoped, will pay off in the form of higher future cash flows, but, unlike an investment in plant and equipment, R&D does not show up on the balance sheet. Instead, expenditures on R&D are treated as a current expense. This makes it difficult to compare the profitability of companies with very different levels of expenditure on research and development.

3. *Pensions.* For many firms their largest debts consist of the pension promises that they have made to their employees. In the case of Maple Leaf, whose financial statements are in Chapter 3, the present value of the pensions benefits that it has undertaken to pay amounted to about $1 billion in 2004. This debt is shown in the notes to the accounts but not in the balance sheet. Instead, balance sheets show a liability only when there are insufficient assets in the pension fund to cover the pension promises. In the case of Maple Leaf, the pension plan had a surplus that was lumped in with "other assets." By contrast, Stelco Inc. filed for bankruptcy protection in January 2004, in part due to a $1.25 billion unfunded pension liability. Many Canadian and U.S. companies with defined benefit pension plans, which promise workers a certain level of income in retirement, are struggling to meet their pension obligations. Dealing with the pension issues can have a dramatic effect on corporate earnings and shareholder returns.

CHOOSING A BENCHMARK

We have shown you how to calculate the principal financial ratios for LC. In practice you may not need to calculate all of them, because many measure essentially the same thing. For example, often one debt ratio and one coverage ratio are sufficient to characterize the situation. However, for LC, debt ratios change dramatically with the treatment of the off-balance-sheet operating leases.

Once you have selected and calculated the important ratios, you still need some way of judging whether they are high or low. A good starting point is to compare them to the equivalent figures for the same company in earlier years. For example, the first two columns in Table 17.8 show selected financial ratios for LC in 2004 and 2005. Overall, LC's use of debt did not change substantially, although its times interest earned is substantially lower, falling from 51.5 times to 37.1. However, earnings that are 37.1 times interest are not a cause for concern. Given the large operating lease commitments, fixed charge coverage should also be examined. LC's liquidity also increased, with all of its liquidity ratios improving over 2004. A possible area of concern is the decline in the efficiency ratios. All of the asset turnover ratios fell, indicating that the company produced fewer sales per dollar of assets. LC took longer to collect receivables but also took longer to pay its suppliers. Despite the marginal decline in efficiency, LC's profitability increased. LC made more profit per sale, seen by the higher net and operating profit margins, and also generated more profit per dollar invested. All together, LC's financial performance in 2005 was better than 2004.

It is also helpful to compare LC's financial position with that of other firms. However, you would not expect companies in different industries to have similar ratios. For example, a soft drink manufacturer is unlikely to have the same profit margin as a jeweller or the same leverage as a finance company. It makes sense, therefore, to limit comparison to other firms in the same industry. For example, the third and fourth columns of Table 17.8 show the financial ratios for Reitmans (Canada) Ltd., a Canadian retailer of clothing for women with a network of six retail banners, including Reitmans, Smart Set, Penningtons, Thyme, RW & Co., and Addition-Elle.

When making these comparisons remember our earlier warning about the need to dig behind the figures. For example, you might wonder why LC's inventory turnover is about half that of Reitmans'. Is LC less efficient in managing its inventory? Although this may be true, it is also the case that LC manufactures about 45 percent of its goods but Reitmans manufactures none. We would expect LC to hold more inventory per dollar of COGS than Reitmans because the production process takes time.

Financial ratios for industries are published by StatsCanada, the *Financial Post*, Dun & Bradstreet, Robert Morris Associates, and others. Table 17.9 contains ratios for some major industry groups. This should give you a feel for some of the differences between industries.

TABLE 17.8
Financial ratios

FINANCIAL RATIOS FOR LE CHÂTEAU AND REITMANS (CANADA) 2005 AND 2004	Le Château		Reitmans	
	2005	**2004**	**2005**	**2004**
Leverage Ratios				
Long-term debt ratio, excluding operating leases	0.136	0.103	0.052	0.255
Long-term debt ratio, including operating leases	0.591	0.611	0.487	0.581
Total debt ratio, including operating leases	0.642	0.667	0.566	0.636
Times interest earned	37.1	51.5	46.1	10.6
Liquidity Ratios				
Net working capital to assets	0.37	0.26	0.15	0.18
Current ratio	2.61	1.99	1.71	1.71
Quick ratio	1.62	0.96	1.05	1.16
Cash ratio	1.55	0.88	1.02	1.12
Interval measure (days)	85.2	42.6	48.3	50.4
Efficiency Ratios				
Asset turnover	1.88	2.4	1.95	1.81
Fixed asset turnover	4.75	5.1	4.91	4.80
Average collection period (days)	3.2	2.2	0.97	1.70
Inventory turnover[a]	7.0	7.7	13.3	12.7
Average payables period (days)[a]	39.7	36.6	37.7	35.7
Profitability Ratios				
Net profit margin (%)	6.6	4.7	7.3	4.7
Operating profit margin (%)	6.9	4.8	7.5	5.3
Return on assets (%)	12.4	11.3	14.3	8.5
Return on invested capital (%)	16.9	16.1	19.7	12.1
Return on equity (%)	18.6	17.4	20.2	14.5

[a] Neither Le Château nor Reitmans reports cost of sales separately. Inventory turnover and average payables period are based on cost of sales plus selling, general, and administrative expense.

Source: Author's calculations based on Le Château Inc. *Annual Report*, 2004, and Reitmans (Canada) Inc., *Annual Report*, 2005.

TABLE 17.9 Financial ratios

Financial Ratios for Selected Industry Groups, 2004	Retailing	Computers and Electronic Equipment	Food and Beverage	Telecommunications	Automobiles and Components	Oil and Gas	Steel
Long-term debt ratio[a]	−1.1	0.2	0.7	0.85	0	0.4	0.42
Cash flow from operations/total debt (%)	101.9	79.5	70.5	32.2	57.8	89.4	90.5
Times interest earned	50.4	63.2	37	4.3	25	16.6	11.7
Current ratio	2.2	2.9	2	1.3	1.8	2	2.9
Quick ratio	0.9	2	0.9	1	1.2	1.6	1.5
Total asset turnover	2.1	1.3	1.6	0.8	1.3	0.4	1.3
Operating profit margin (%)	10.5	6.9	10.5	28.2	−4.0	28	18.7
Operating return on assets (%)	14.8	−1.4	5.7	4.52	−1.9	5.9	14.5
Return on equity (%)	4.2	−10.4	6.7	3.5	−2.1	10.3	24.22

[a] (Short-term + Long-term debt)/equity
Source: Various Industry Reports, retrieved June 15, 2005, from **FPinfomart.ca**.

Check Point 17.5 Look at the financial ratios shown in Table 17.9. The retail industry has a higher asset turnover and a lower operating profit margin than steel manufacturers. What do you think accounts for these differences?

17.5   MEASURING COMPANY PERFORMANCE

The book value of the company's equity is equal to the total amount that the company has raised from its shareholders or retained and reinvested on their behalf. If the company has been successful in adding value, the market value of the equity will be higher than the book value. So investors are likely to look favourably on the managers of firms that have a high ratio of market to book value and to frown upon firms whose market value is less than book value. Of course, the market to book ratio does not tell you just how much richer the shareholders have become. Take Inco, for example. At the end of 2004 the book value of Inco's equity was $5,457 million, but investors valued its shares at $10,914 million. So every dollar that Inco invested on behalf of its shareholders had increased 2 times in value ($10,914/$5,457 = 2). The difference between the market value of shares and their book value is often called the **market value added**. Inco had added $10,914 – $5,457 = $5,457 million to the equity capital that it had invested.

Measures of company performance that are based on market values have two disadvantages. First, the market value of the company's shares reflects investors' expectations. Investors placed a high value on Inco's shares partly because they believed that its management would *continue* to find profitable investments in the future. However, if expectations of growth diminished, Inco's MVA would fall. Second, market values cannot be used to judge the performance of companies that are privately owned, or the performance of divisions or plants that are part of larger companies. Therefore, financial managers also calculate accounting measures of performance.

Think again of how a firm creates value for its investors, both debtholders and shareholders. It can either invest in new plant and equipment or it can return the cash to investors, who can then invest the money for themselves by buying stocks and bonds in the capital market. The return that investors could expect to earn if they invested in the capital market is called the *cost of capital*.[16] A firm that earns *more* than the cost of capital makes its investors better off: it is earning them a higher return than they could obtain for themselves. A firm that earns *less* than the cost of capital makes investors worse off: they could earn a higher return simply by investing their cash in the capital market. Therefore, naturally, financial managers are concerned whether the firm's return on its assets exceeds or falls short of the cost of capital.

Financial managers can assess how much better off are the bondholders and shareholders by measuring the firm's **residual income**. It is also known as **economic value added**, or **EVA®**, a term coined by Stern Stewart, a company that has done much to develop and promote the concept. The residual income is the difference between the after-tax operating profits of the firm and the cost of using bondholders' and shareholders' money, the company's cost of capital times the invested capital:

Residual income = After-tax operating profit – cost of capital × invested capital   (17.3)

The after-tax operating profit is sometimes calculated by multiplying the return on invested capital, ROIC, by invested capital, giving another expression for residual income:

Residual income = (ROIC – cost of capital) × invested capital   (17.4)

market value added The difference between the market value of the firm's equity and its book value.

residual income (also called economic value added or EVA®) The net profit of a firm or division after deducting the cost of the capital employed.

economic value added (EVA®) See residual income.

---

[16] The cost of capital is also called the *weighted average* cost of capital, or WACC, reflecting the mix of debt and equity financing of the company. See Chapter 12.

EXAMPLE 17.2	MEGA TOY'S RESIDUAL INCOME

The book value of Mega Toys Inc.'s debt is $15 million and the book value of its equity is $40 million, giving it invested capital of $55 million. Its return on invested capital, ROIC, is 15 percent and its cost of capital is 9.5 percent. Its after-tax operating profit is ROIC × invested capital = .15 × $55 million, or $8.25 million. The return that investors in Mega Toys expect is cost of capital × invested capital = .095 × $55 million, or $5.225 million. Thus Mega Toy's residual income is

$$\text{Residual income} = 8.25 - 5.225 = \$3.025 \text{ million}$$

In other words, Mega Toys has generated $3.025 million for its bondholders and shareholders, over the year. If Mega Toy's ROIC were less than its cost of capital, the company has generated negative residual income.

Residual income or EVA is a better measure of a company's performance than accounting profits. Profits are calculated after deducting all costs *except* the cost of capital. EVA recognizes that companies need to cover their cost of capital before they add value. If a plant or division is not earning a positive EVA, its management is likely to face some pointed questions about whether the assets could be better employed elsewhere—or by fresh management. Therefore, a growing number of firms now calculate EVA and tie managers' compensation to it.

17.6   THE ROLE OF FINANCIAL RATIOS

Before we end this chapter it might be helpful to emphasize the role of such accounting measures. Whenever two managers get together to discuss the state of the business, there is a good bet they will refer to financial ratios. Let's drop in on two conversations. See if you understand what they are talking about.

Conversation 1. The CEO was musing out loud: "How are we going to finance this expansion? Would the banks be happy to lend us the $30 million that we need?"

"I've been looking into that," the financial manager replies. "Currently our debt ratio is .3. If we borrow the full cost of the project, the ratio would be about .45. When we took out our last loan from the bank, we agreed that we would not allow our debt ratio to get above .5. So if we borrow to finance this project, we wouldn't have much leeway to respond to possible emergencies. Also, the rating agencies currently give our bonds an investment-grade rating. They, too, look at a company's leverage when they rate its bonds. I have a table here [Table 17.10] which shows that, when firms are highly leveraged, their bonds receive a lower rating. I don't know whether the rating agencies would downgrade our bonds if our debt ratio increased to .45, but they might. That wouldn't please our existing bondholders, and it could raise the cost of any new borrowing.

"We also need to think about our interest cover, which is beginning to look a bit thin. Debt interest is currently covered three times and, if we borrowed the entire $30 million, interest cover would fall to about two times. Sure, we expect to earn additional profits on the new investment but it could be several years before they come through. If we run into a recession in the meantime, we could find ourselves short of cash."

"Sounds to me as if we should be thinking about a possible equity issue," concluded the CEO.

Conversation 2. The CEO was not in the best of moods after her defeat at the company golf tournament by the manager of the packaging division: "I see our stock was down again yesterday," she growled. "It's now selling below book value, and the stock price is only six times earnings. I work my socks off for this company; you would think that our shareholders would show a little more gratitude."

"I think I can understand a little of our shareholders' worries," the financial manager replies. "Just look at our return on assets. It's only 6 percent, well below the cost of capital. Sure we are

TABLE 17.10

Key financial ratios for U.S. Long-Term Industrial Debt as identified by Standard & Poor's

Key Industrial Financial Ratios, Long-Term Debt Ratings							
Three-year (2001 to 2003) medians	**AAA**	**AA**	**A**	**BBB**	**BB**	**B**	**CCC**
1. EBIT interest coverage (×)	23.8	13.6	6.9	4.2	2.3	0.9	0.4
2. EBITDA interest coverage (×)	25.3	17.1	9.4	5.9	3.1	1.6	0.9
3. Free operating cash flow/total debt (%)	104.1	41.1	25.4	16.9	7.9	2.6	(0.9)
4. Return on capital (%)	35.1	26.9	16.8	13.4	10.3	6.7	2.3
5. Total debt/capital (%)	6.2	34.8	39.8	45.6	57.2	74.2	101.2

FORMULA FOR KEY RATIOS

1. EBIT interest coverage $= \dfrac{\text{Earnings from continuing operations* before interest and taxes}}{\text{Gross interest incurred before subtracting capitalized interest and interest income}}$

2. EBITDA interest coverage $= \dfrac{\text{Adjusted earnings from continuing operations** before interest, taxes, depreciation, and amortization}}{\text{Gross interest incurred before subtracting capitalized interest and interest income}}$

3. Free operating cash flow/total debt $= \dfrac{\substack{\text{Funds from operations – capital expenditures, – (+)} \\ \text{the increase (decrease) in working capital (excluding changes} \\ \text{in cash, marketable securities, and short-term debt)}}}{\substack{\text{Long-term debt*** + current maturities, commercial paper,} \\ \text{and other short-term borrowings}}}$

4. Return on capital $= \dfrac{\text{EBIT}}{\substack{\text{Average of beginning-of-year and end-of-year capital, including} \\ \text{short-term debt, current maturities, long-term debt***,} \\ \text{non-current deferred taxes, minority interest, and equity}}}$

5. Total debt/capital $= \dfrac{\substack{\text{Long-term debt*** + current maturities, commercial paper,} \\ \text{and other short-term borrowings}}}{\substack{\text{Long-term debt*** + current maturities, commercial paper, and other short-term} \\ \text{borrowings + shareholders' equity (including preferred stock) + minority interest}}}$

* Including interest income and equity earnings; excluding non-recurring items.

** Excludes interest income, equity earnings, and non-recurring items; also excludes rental expense that exceeds the interest component of capitalized operating leases.

*** Including amounts for operating lease, debt equivalents, and debt associated with accounts receivable sales/securitization programs.

Source: 2005 Corporate Criteria Book, **www.standardandpoors.com**, retrieved June 14, 2005.

making a profit, but that profit does not cover the cost of the funds that investors provide. Our economic value added is actually negative. Of course, this doesn't necessarily mean that the assets could be used better elsewhere, but we should certainly be looking carefully at whether any of our divisions should be sold off or the assets redeployed.

"In some ways we're in good shape. We have very little short-term debt and our current assets are three times our current liabilities. But that's not altogether good news because it also suggests that we may have more working capital than we need. I've been looking at our main competitors. They turn over their inventory 12 times a year compared with our figure of just 8 times. Also, their customers take an average of 45 days to pay their bills. Ours take 67. If we could just match their performance on these two measures, we would release $300 million that could be paid out to shareholders."

"Perhaps we could talk more about this tomorrow," said the CEO. "In the meantime, I intend to have a word with the production manager about our inventory levels and see the credit manager about our collections policy. You've also got me thinking about whether we should sell off our packaging division. I've always worried about the divisional manager there. Spends too much time practising his backswing and not enough worrying about his return on assets."

17.7   SUMMARY

1. **What are the standard measures of a firm's leverage, liquidity, profitability, asset management, and market valuation? What is the significance of these measures?**

If you are analyzing a company's financial statements, there is a danger of being overwhelmed by the sheer volume of data contained in the **income statement**, **balance sheet**, and statement of cash flows. Managers use a few salient ratios to summarize the firm's leverage, liquidity, efficiency, and profitability. They may also combine accounting data with other data to measure the esteem in which investors hold the company or the efficiency with which the firm uses its resources.

Table 17.11 summarizes the four categories of financial ratios that we have discussed in this chapter. Remember though that financial analysts define the same ratio in different ways or use different terms to describe the same ratio.

Leverage ratios measure the indebtedness of the firm. Liquidity ratios measure how easily the firm can obtain cash. Efficiency ratios measure how intensively the firm is using its assets. Profitability ratios measure the firm's return on its investments. Be selective in your choice of these ratios. Different ratios often tell you similar things.

Financial ratios crop up repeatedly in financial discussions and arrangements. For example, banks and bondholders commonly place limits on the borrower's leverage ratios. Ratings agencies also look at leverage ratios when they decide how highly to rate the firm's bonds.

2. **How does the DuPont formula help identify the determinants of the firm's return on its assets and equity?**

The **DuPont system** provides a useful way to link ratios to explain the firm's return on assets and equity. The formula states that the return on equity is the product of the firm's leverage ratio, asset turnover, profit margin, and debt burden. Return on assets is the product of the firm's asset turnover and profit margin.

3. **What are some potential pitfalls of ratio analysis based on accounting data?**

Financial ratio analysis will rarely be useful if practised mechanically. It requires a large dose of good judgment. Financial ratios seldom provide answers but they do help you ask the right questions. Moreover, accounting data do not necessarily reflect market values properly, and so must be used with caution. You need a benchmark for assessing a company's financial position. Therefore, we typically compare financial ratios with the company's ratios in earlier years and with the ratios of other firms in the same business.

4. **How do measures such as market value added and economic value added help to assess the firm's performance?**

The ratio of the market value of the firm's equity to its book value indicates how far the value of the shareholders' investment exceeds the money that they have contributed. The *difference* between the market and book values is known as **market value added** and measures the number of dollars of value that the company has added.

Managers often compare the company's return on assets with the cost of capital, to see whether the firm is earning the return that investors require. It is also useful to deduct the cost of the capital employed from the company's profits to see how much profit the company has earned after all costs. This measure is known as **residual income**, and also called **economic value added**, or **EVA**. Managers of divisions or plants are often judged and rewarded by their business's economic value added.

Related Web Links

www.onlinewbc.gov/docs/finance Basics of financial analysis, with tutorials and tools

www.corporateinformation.com Detailed information on 350,000 companies worldwide

www.sedar.com Annual reports, prospectuses, and other documents of Canadian companies

www.reportgallery.com Annual reports on thousands of companies

http://ca.finance.yahoo.com Useful financial profiles on thousands of Canadian firms

www.globeinvestor.com Detailed information on publicly traded Canadian companies

www.sternstewart.com Articles on economic value added

www.strategis.ic.gc.ca Canadian business information, tools, and links, operated by Industry Canada

TABLE 17.11

Leverage ratios

Long-term debt ratio $= \dfrac{\text{long-term debt}}{\text{long-term debt + equity}}$

Debt–equity ratio $= \dfrac{\text{long-term debt}}{\text{equity}}$

Total debt ratio $= \dfrac{\text{total liabilities}}{\text{total assets}}$

Times interest earned $= \dfrac{\text{EBIT}}{\text{interest payments}}$

Cash coverage ratio $= \dfrac{\text{EBIT + depreciation}}{\text{interest payments}}$

Fixed-charge coverage ratio $= \dfrac{\text{EBIT + depreciation}}{\text{interest payments} + (\text{debt repayment})/(1 - \text{tax rate})}$

Liquidity ratios

NWC to assets $= \dfrac{\text{net working capital}}{\text{total assets}}$

Current ratio $= \dfrac{\text{current assets}}{\text{current liabilities}}$

Quick ratio $= \dfrac{\text{cash + marketable securities + receivables}}{\text{current liabilities}}$

Interval measure $= \dfrac{\text{cash + marketable securities + receivables}}{\text{average daily expenditures from operations}}$

Cash ratio $= \dfrac{\text{cash + marketable securities}}{\text{current liabilities}}$

Efficiency ratios

Total asset turnover $= \dfrac{\text{sales}}{\text{total assets}}$

Average collection period $= \dfrac{\text{receivables}}{\text{average daily sales}}$

Inventory turnover $= \dfrac{\text{cost of goods sold}}{\text{inventory}}$

Days' sales in inventories $= \dfrac{\text{inventory}}{\text{cost of goods sold}/365}$

Average payment period $= \dfrac{\text{payables}}{\text{average daily expenses}}$

Profitability ratios

Net profit margin $= \dfrac{\text{net income}}{\text{sales}}$

Return on assets $= \dfrac{\text{net income}}{\text{assets}}$

Operating profit margin $= \dfrac{\text{net income + interest}}{\text{sales}}$

Operating return on assets $= \dfrac{\text{net income + interest}}{\text{total assets}}$

Return on invested capital $= \dfrac{\text{net income + interest}}{\text{debt + preferred equity + common equity}}$

Return on equity $= \dfrac{\text{net income}}{\text{equity}}$

Payout ratio $= \dfrac{\text{dividends}}{\text{earnings}}$

Plowback ratio $= 1 - \text{payout ratio}$

Growth in equity from plowback $= \text{plowback ratio} \times \text{ROE}$

Key Terms

Questions and Problems

*Answers in Appendix B

BASIC

*1. **Calculating Ratios.** Here are simplified financial statements of Phone Corporation from a recent year:

BALANCE SHEET
($millions)

	End of Year	Start of Year
Assets		
Cash and marketable securities	89	158
Receivables	2,382	2,490
Inventories	187	238
Other current assets	867	932
Total current assets	3,525	3,818
Net property, plant, and equipment	19,973	19,915
Other long-term assets	4,216	3,770
Total assets	27,714	27,503
Liabilities and shareholders' equity		
Payables	2,564	3,040
Short-term debt	1,419	1,573
Other current liabilities	811	787
Total current liabilities	4,794	5,400
Long-term debt and leases	7,018	6,833
Other long-term liabilities	6,178	6,149
Shareholders' equity	9,724	9,121
Total liabilities and shareholders' equity	27,714	27,503

INCOME STATEMENT
($millions)

Net sales	13,194
Cost of goods sold	4,060
Other expenses	4,049
Depreciation	2,518
Earnings before interest and taxes (EBIT)	2,566
Interest expenses	685
Income before tax	1,881
Taxes	570
Net income	1,311
Dividends	856

Calculate the following financial ratios:

a. Long-term debt ratio
b. Total debt ratio
c. Times interest earned
d. Cash coverage ratio
e. Current ratio
f. Quick ratio
g. Net profit margin
h. Inventory turnover

i. Days' sales in inventory
j. Average collection period
k. Return on equity
l. Return on assets
m. Payout ratio
n. Operating profit margin
o. Operating return on assets
p. Return on invested capital

2. **Interval Measure.** Suppose that Phone Corp. shut down operations. For how many days could it pay its bills?

*3. **Gross Investment.** What was Phone Corp.'s gross investment in plant and other equipment?

4. **Market Value Ratios.** If the market value of Phone Corp. stock was $17.2 billion at the end of the year, what was the market-to-book ratio? If there were 205 million shares outstanding, what were earnings per share? The price-earnings ratio?

5. **Common-Size Balance Sheet.** Prepare a common-size balance sheet for Phone Corp. using its balance sheet from problem 1.

6. **DuPont Analysis.** Use the data for Phone Corp. to confirm that ROA = asset turnover × net profit margin.

7. **DuPont Analysis.** Use the data for Phone Corp., to demonstrate that ROE = leverage ratio × asset turnover ratio × net profit margin.

EXCEL

PRACTICE

8. **Asset Turnover.** In each case, choose the firm that you expect to have a higher asset turnover ratio.
   a. Economics Consulting Group or Stelco
   b. Catalogue Shopping Network or Hudson's Bay
   c. Electric Utility Co. or Standard Supermarkets

9. **Defining Ratios.** There are no universally accepted definitions of financial ratios, but some of the following ratios make no sense at all. Substitute the correct definitions.
   a. Debt-equity ratio $= \dfrac{\text{long-term debt}}{\text{long-term debt + equity}}$

   b. Return on equity $= \dfrac{\text{EBIT} - \text{tax}}{\text{equity}}$

   c. Net profit margin $= \dfrac{\text{net income + interest}}{\text{sales}}$

   d. Inventory turnover $= \dfrac{\text{total assets}}{\text{inventory}}$

   e. Current ratio $= \dfrac{\text{current liabilities}}{\text{current assets}}$

   f. Interval measure $= \dfrac{\text{current assets} - \text{inventories}}{\text{average daily expenditure from operations}}$

   g. Average collection period $= \dfrac{\text{sales}}{\text{receivables/365}}$

   h. Quick ratio $= \dfrac{\text{cash + marketable securities + receivables}}{\text{current liabilities}}$

10. **Current Liabilities.** Suppose that at year-end LC had unused lines of credit that would have allowed it to borrow a further $10 million. Suppose also that it used this line of credit to borrow $10 million and invested the proceeds in marketable securities. Would the company have appeared to be (a) more or less liquid, (b) more or less highly leveraged? Calculate the appropriate ratios using Tables 17.1 and 17.3.

11. **Current Ratio.** How would each of the following actions affect a firm's current ratio?
    a. Inventory is sold at cost.
    b. The firm takes out a bank loan to pay its accounts due.
    c. A customer pays its accounts receivable.
    d. The firm uses cash to purchase additional inventories.

*12. **Liquidity Ratios.** A firm uses $1 million in cash to purchase inventories. What will happen to its current ratio? Its quick ratio?

13. **Receivables.** Chik's Chickens has accounts receivable of $6,333. Sales for the year were $9,800. What is its average collection period?

*14. **Inventory.** Salad Daze maintains an inventory of produce worth $400. Its total bill for produce over the course of the year was $73,000. On average, how old is the lettuce it serves its customers?

EXCEL

15. **Inventory Turnover.** If a firm's inventory level of $10,000 represents 30 days' sales, what is the annual cost of goods sold? What is the inventory turnover ratio?

*16. **Leverage Ratios.** Lever Age pays an 8 percent coupon on outstanding debt with face value $10 million. The firm's EBIT was $1 million and its tax rate was 40 percent.
   a. What is times interest earned?
   b. If depreciation is $200,000, what is cash coverage?
   c. If the firm must retire $300,000 of debt for the sinking fund each year, what is its fixed-charge coverage ratio?

17. **DuPont Analysis.** Keller Cosmetics maintains a net profit margin of 5 percent and asset turnover ratio of 3.
   a. What is its ROA?
   b. If its debt-equity ratio is 1.0, its interest payments are $8,000, its taxes are $3,600, and its EBIT is $20,000, what is its ROE?

*18. **DuPont Analysis.** Torrid Romance Publishers has total receivables of $3,000, which represent 20 days' sales. Total assets are $75,000. The firm's net profit margin is 5 percent. Find the firm's ROA and asset turnover ratio.

19. **Leverage.** A firm has a long-term debt-equity ratio of .4. Shareholders' equity is $1 million. Current assets are $200,000 and the current ratio is 2.0. The only current liabilities are notes payable. What is the total debt ratio?

*20. **Leverage Ratios.** A firm has a debt-to-equity ratio of .5 and an equity market-to-book ratio of 2.0. What is the ratio of the book value of debt to the market value of equity?

21. **Times Interest Earned.** In the past year, TVG had revenue of $3 million, cost of goods sold of $2.5 million, and depreciation expense of $200,000. The firm has a single issue of debt outstanding with face value of $1 million, market value of $.92 million, and a coupon rate of 8 percent. What is the firm's times interest earned ratio?

22. **DuPont Analysis.** CFA Corp. has a debt-equity ratio that is lower than the industry average, but its cash coverage ratio is also lower than the industry average. What might explain this seeming contradiction?

23. **Leverage.** Suppose that a firm has both floating-rate and fixed-rate debt outstanding. What effect will a decline in market interest rates have on the firm's times interest earned ratio? On the market value debt-to-equity ratio? Based on these answers, would you say that leverage has increased or decreased?

*24. **Interpreting Ratios.** In each of the following cases, explain briefly which of the two companies is likely to be characterized by the higher ratio:
   a. Debt-equity ratio: a shipping company or a computer software company
   b. Payout ratio: United Foods Inc. or Computer Graphics Inc.
   c. Ratio of sales to assets: an integrated pulp and paper manufacturer or a grocery store
   d. Average collection period: Regional Electric Power Company or Z-Mart Discount Outlets
   e. Price-earnings multiple: Basic Sludge Company or Fledgling Electronics

25. **Using Financial Ratios.** For each category of financial ratios discussed in this chapter, give some examples of who would be likely to examine these ratios and why.

CHALLENGE

26. **Comprehensive.** As you can see, someone has spilled ink over some of the entries in the balance sheet and income statement of Transylvania Railroad. Can you use the following information to work out the missing entries?

Long-term debt ratio	0.5
Times interest earned	6.125
Current ratio	1.4
Quick ratio	1.0
Return on assets	21.39%
Return on equity	82%
Inventory turnover	5.5
Average collection period	80.3 days

INCOME STATEMENT
($millions)

Net sales	•••
Cost of goods sold	•••
Selling, general, and administrative expenses	10
Depreciation	20
Earnings before interest and taxes (EBIT)	•••
Interest expense	•••
Income before tax	•••
Tax	•••
Net income	•••
Dividends	•••

BALANCE SHEET
($millions)

Assets	
Cash and marketable securities	11
Receivables	•••
Inventories	•••
Total current assets	•••
Net property, plant, and equipment	•••
Total assets	•••
Liabilities and shareholders' equity	
Accounts payable	25
Notes payable	30
Total current liabilities	•••
Long-term debt	•••
Shareholders' equity	•••
Total liabilities and shareholders' equity	115

27. **Comprehensive.** BusyBee Nursery operates in suburban Toronto and its owner is wondering how well the company is performing. The stated objectives of its owner are an operating profit margin of 6 percent and operating expense of not more than 25 percent of sales. BusyBee's strategy is to provide high quality service at a fair price. Staff are well trained and the company encourages environmentally friendly gardening practices.

    a. Evaluate BusyBee's financial performance and compare it to the industry medians. What do you think of its stated financial goals?

    b. Using the Dupont analysis, evaluate BusyBee's ROE and the industry median ROE. Where are the differences?

    c. Discuss possible changes to BusyBee that may improve its financial performance.

BALANCE SHEET
as of year end, 2006

Assets	
Cash	$8,150
Accounts receivable	32,600
Inventory	195,600
Total current assets	236,350
Fixed assets, net	89,650
Total assets	326,000
Liabilities and Shareholders' Equity	
Accounts payable	40,750
Notes payable	32,600
Total current liabilities	73,350
Long-term debt	105,950
Common stock	48,900
Retained earnings	97,800
Shareholders' equity	146,700
Total liabilities and shareholders' equity	$326,000

INCOME STATEMENT

Sales	$652,000
Cost of goods sold	326,000
Selling, general and administrative expense	290,140
Depreciation	6,520
Earnings before interest and taxes	29,340
Interest	8,150
Earnings before taxes	21,190
Taxes	3,179
Net earnings	18,012
Dividends	8,150
Addition to retained earnings	9,862

INDUSTRY MEDIAN RATIOS

Current ratio	1.7 ×
Total asset turnover	2.4 ×
Cost of sales/inventory	6.5 ×
Net profit margin	2.3%
Operating profit margin	3%
ROE	14.9%
Interest-bearing debt/equity	1.7 ×

28. **Comprehensive.** Start with *operating* return on assets and decompose it into its components as we did for ROA. Then decompose ROE to include operating return on assets. Using these two formulas, analyze BusyBee's return on operating assets and ROE, with the data from problem 27. Compare your findings to the decompositions in problem 27 (b).

29. **Internet.** Go to **www.sedar.com** and select "Search Database," then "Public Company." Select "Annual Report" as document type and pick an annual report to analyze. Read the report and its footnotes, and then calculate the financial ratios in Table 17.11 and any other ratios you think would be useful. What did you learn about your company's financial performance?

30. **Internet.** Investors can use financial ratios to screen stocks. Go to **www.globe investor.com** and select "Filter." Click on "Company Financials Filter" and select an industry, such as broadcasting and click on "Go." Click on "Ratios" beneath the Financial tab and identify the reported ratios. Why might investors be interested in these ratios? Check on the ratio definitions by clicking on the ratios at the bottom of the page. Pick three companies from the same industry and three from different industries and compare their ratios. What do you learn about the companies and industries?

31. **Internet.** Financial ratios and performance measures are often used to provide incentives to employees to work in the shareholders' interests. Read the following two articles available at the Web site of *CFO Magazine*. The first deals with the DuPont model (**www.cfo.com/ article.cfm/2990236**), and the second with more recent value-based measures such as economic value added (**www.cfo.com/article.cfm/2991941**). Identify the issues associated with using financial ratios and value metrics for providing incentives to employees.

STANDARD &POOR'S

32. **Standard & Poor's.** Go to Market Insight (**www.mcgrawhill.ca/edumarketinsight**) and click on the Industry button and select a GICS Sub-Industry, such as Apparel Retail or Brewers, and click on its most current S&P industry survey. Be aware that industry surveys are unavailable for a few sub-industries. Read the survey and pay particular attention to the section on how to analyze a company in the industry. Note the key business factors and financial ratios that S&P identifies as important. Select a second, unrelated GICS Sub-Industry. Compare and contrast the business factors and financial ratios for these two industries.

STANDARD &POOR'S

33. **Standard & Poor's.** Lowes (LOW) and The Home Depot (HD) have been in a tremendous race for the homeowner's dollar in the last few years. Who is winning? Review the company profile (also review the industry information under "Home Improvement Retail," financial highlights, annual ratios, profitability, and monthly valuation data reports. What company performance information supports your view as to which company is winning the race in the home improvement industry? Has the stock market picked a winner in this race?

STANDARD &POOR'S

34. **Standard & Poor's.** Compare the components of return on equity (using the Du Pont formula) for Rogers (RG) and Shaw (SJR). Examine both levels and trends in these variables. Review the trends in net profit margin, total asset turnover, and leverage. What factors tend to explain the performance differential between these two competing communications companies? Do they operate in the same businesses? How has the market reacted to their operating performance?

Solutions to Check Points

17.1 Nothing will happen to the long-term debt ratio computed using book values, since the face values of the old and new debt are equal. However, times interest earned and cash coverage ratios will increase since the firm will reduce its interest expense.

17.2 a. The current ratio starts at 1.2/1.0 = 1.2. The transaction will reduce current assets to $.7 million and current liabilities to $.5 million. The current ratio increases to .7/.5 = 1.4. Net working capital is unaffected: current assets and current liabilities fall by equal amounts.

b. The current ratio is unaffected, since the firm merely exchanges one current asset (cash) for another (inventories). However, the quick ratio will fall since inventories are not included among the most liquid assets.

17.3 Average daily expenses are 205,917/365 = $564.16 million. Accounts payable are $22,397 million. The average payment delay is therefore 22,397/564.16 = 39.7 days.

17.4 a. The firm must compensate for its below-average profit margin with an above-average turnover ratio. Remember that ROA is the product of margin × turnover.

b. If ROA equals the industry average but ROE exceeds the industry average, the firm must have above-average leverage. As long as ROA exceeds the borrowing rate, leverage will increase ROE.

17.5 Retailers' profit margin on sales is relatively low, but they make up for that low margin by turning over goods rapidly. The high asset turnover allows retailers to earn an adequate return on assets even with a low profit margin, and competition prevents them from increasing prices and margins to a level that would provide a better ROA. In contrast, manufacturing firms have low turnover, and therefore, need higher profit margins to remain viable.

MINICASE

Burchetts Green had enjoyed the bank training course, but it was good to be starting his first real job in the corporate lending group. Earlier that morning the boss had handed him a set of financial statements for The Hobby Horse Company, Inc. (HH). "Hobby Horse," she said, "has got a $45 million loan from us due at the end of September, and it is likely to ask us to roll it over. The company seems to have run into some rough weather recently and I have asked Furze Platt to go down there this afternoon and see what is happening. It might do you good to go along with her. Before you go, take a look at these financial statements and see what you think the problems are. Here's a chance for you to use some of that stuff they taught you in the training course."

Burchetts was familiar with the HH story. Founded in 1990, it had rapidly built up a chain of discount stores selling materials for crafts and hobbies. However, last year a number of new store openings coinciding with a poor Christmas season had pushed the company into a loss. Management had halted all new construction and put 15 of its existing stores up for sale.

Burchetts decided to start with the 6-year summary of HH's balance sheet and income statement (Table 17.12). Then he turned to examine the latest position in more detail (Tables 17.13 and 17.14).

TABLE 17.12
Financial highlights for The Hobby Horse Company, Inc., year ending March 31

	2006	2005	2004	2003	2002	2001
Net sales	3,351	3,314	2,845	2,796	2,493	2,160
EBIT	−9	312	256	243	212	156
Interest	37	63	65	58	48	46
Taxes	3	60	46	43	39	34
Net income	−49	189	145	142	125	76
Earnings per share	−.15	.55	.44	.42	.37	.25
Current assets	669	469	491	435	392	423
Net fixed assets	923	780	753	680	610	536
Total assets	1,573	1,249	1,244	1,115	1,002	959
Current liabilities	680	365	348	302	276	320
Long-term debt	217	159	159	311	319	315
Shareholders' equity	676	725	599	502	407	324
Number of stores	240	221	211	184	170	157
Employees	13,057	11,835	9,810	9,790	9,075	7,825

TABLE 17.13
Income statement

INCOME STATEMENT FOR THE HOBBY HORSE COMPANY, INC., year ending March 31, 2006 ($ millions)	
Net sales	3,351
Cost of goods sold	1,990
Selling, general, and administrative expenses	1,211
Depreciation expense	159
Earnings before interest and taxes (EBIT)	–9
Net interest expense	37
Taxable income	–46
Income taxes	3
Net income	–49
Allocation of net income	
Addition to retained earnings	–49
Dividends	0

Note: Column sums subject to rounding error.

TABLE 17.14
Consolidated balance sheet

CONSOLIDATED BALANCE SHEET FOR THE HOBBY HORSE COMPANY, INC. ($ millions)		
Assets	**Mar. 31, 2006**	**Mar. 31, 2005**
Current assets		
Cash and marketable securities	14	72
Receivables	176	194
Inventories	479	203
Total current assets	669	469
Fixed assets		
Property, plant, and equipment, gross	1,813	1,511
Less accumulated depreciation	890	731
Net fixed assets	923	780
Total assets	1,592	1,249
Liabilities and Shareholders' Equity	**Mar. 31, 2006**	**Mar. 31, 2005**
Current liabilities		
Debt due for repayment	484	222
Accounts payable	94	58
Other current liabilities	102	85
Total current liabilities	680	365
Long-term debt	236	159
Shareholders' equity		
Common stock	155	155
Addition to retained earnings	521	570
Total shareholders' equity	676	725
Total liabilities and shareholders' equity	1,592	1,249

FINANCIAL PLANNING

It's been said that a camel looks like a horse designed by committee. If a firm made all its financial decisions piecemeal, it would end up with a financial camel. Therefore, smart financial managers consider the overall effect of future investment and financing decisions. This process is called *financial planning*, and the end result is called a *financial plan*.

New investments need to be paid for. So investment and financing decisions cannot be made independently. Financial planning forces managers to think systematically about their goals for growth, investment, and financing. Planning should reveal any inconsistencies in these goals.

Planning also helps managers avoid some surprises and think about how they should react to those surprises that *cannot* be avoided. In Chapter 9 we stressed that good financial managers insist on understanding what makes projects work and what could go wrong with them. The same approach should be taken when investment and financing decisions are considered as a whole.

Finally, financial planning helps establish goals to motivate managers and provide standards for measuring performance.

We start the chapter by summarizing what financial planning involves and we describe the contents of a typical financial plan. We then discuss the use of financial models in the planning process. Finally, we examine the relationship between a firm's growth and its need for new financing.

After studying this chapter you should be able to
- Describe the contents and uses of a financial plan.
- Construct a simple financial planning model.
- Estimate the effect of growth on the need for external financing.

WHAT IS FINANCIAL PLANNING?

Financial planning involves

1. Analyzing the investment and financing choices open to the firm.
2. Projecting the future consequences of current decisions.
3. Deciding which alternatives to undertake.
4. Measuring performance against the goals set out in the financial plan.

Notice that financial planning is not designed to minimize risk. Instead it is a process of deciding which risks to take and which risks are unnecessary or not worth taking.

Firms must plan for both the short term and the long term. Short-term planning rarely looks ahead further than the next 12 months. It is largely the process of ensuring that the firm has enough cash to pay its bills and that short-term borrowing and lending are arranged to the best advantage. We discuss short-term planning in Chapter 19.

planning horizon Time horizon for a financial plan.

Here we are more concerned with long-term planning, where a typical **planning horizon** is 5 years (although some firms look ahead 10 years or more). For example, it can take at least 10 years for an electric utility to design, obtain approval for, build, and test a major power-generating plant.

FINANCIAL PLANNING FOCUSES ON THE BIG PICTURE

Many of the firm's capital expenditures are proposed by plant managers. But the final budget must also reflect strategic plans made by senior management. Positive-NPV opportunities occur in those businesses where the firm has a real competitive advantage. Strategic plans identify such businesses and look to expand them. These plans also seek to identify businesses to sell or liquidate as well as businesses that should be allowed to run down.

Strategic planning involves capital budgeting on a grand scale. In this process, financial planners try to look at the investment by each line of business and avoid getting bogged down in details. Of course, some individual projects are large enough to have significant individual impact. When Walt Disney announced its intention to build a new theme park in Hong Kong at a cost of $4 billion, you can bet that this project was explicitly analyzed as part of Disney's long-range financial plan. Normally, however, financial planners do not work on a project-by-project basis. Smaller projects are aggregated into a unit that is treated as a single project.

At the beginning of the planning process the corporate staff might ask each division to submit three alternative business plans covering the next five years:

1. A *best case* or *aggressive growth* plan calling for heavy capital investment and rapid growth of existing markets.
2. A *normal growth* plan in which the division grows with its markets but not significantly at the expense of its competitors.
3. A plan of *retrenchment* if the firm's markets contract. This is planning for lean economic times.

The plan will contain a summary of capital expenditures, working-capital requirements, and strategies to raise funds for these investments.

WHY BUILD FINANCIAL PLANS?

Firms spend considerable energy, time, and resources building elaborate financial plans. What do they get for this investment?

Contingency Planning

Planning is not just forecasting. Forecasting concentrates on the most likely outcomes, but planners need to worry about unlikely events as well as likely ones. If you think ahead about what could go wrong, then you are less likely to ignore the danger signals and you can respond faster to trouble.

Companies have developed a number of ways of asking "what if" questions about both individual projects and the overall firm. For example, planners often work through the consequences of the plan under different scenarios. One scenario might envisage high interest rates contributing to a slowdown in world economic growth and lower commodity prices. A second scenario might involve a buoyant domestic economy, high inflation, and a weak currency.

The idea is to formulate responses to inevitable surprises. What will you do, for example, if sales in the first year turn out to be 10 percent below forecast? A good financial plan should help you adapt as events unfold. The nearby Finance in Action box describes how Georgia Power Company used scenario analysis to help plan for the unexpected.

SEE BOX P. 567

Considering Options

Planners need to determine whether there are opportunities for the company to exploit its existing strengths by moving into a wholly new area. Often they may recommend entering a market for "strategic" reasons—that is, not because the immediate investment has a positive net present value but because it establishes the firm in a new market and creates options for possibly valuable follow-on investments.

As an example, think of the decision by IBM to acquire Lotus Corporation for $3.3 billion. Lotus added less than $1 billion in revenues, but it had considerable experience in helping computers talk to each other. This know-how gave IBM an *option* to produce and market new products in the future.

Forcing Consistency

Financial plans draw out the connections between the firm's plans for growth and the financing requirements. For example, a forecast of 25 percent growth might require the firm to issue securities to pay for necessary capital expenditures while a 5 percent growth rate might enable the firm to finance capital expenditures by using only reinvested profits.

Financial plans should help to ensure that the firm's goals are mutually consistent. For example, the chief executive might say that she is shooting for a profit margin of 10 percent and sales growth of 20 percent, but financial planners need to think whether the higher sales growth may require price cuts that will reduce profit margin.

Moreover, a goal that is stated in terms of accounting ratios is not operational unless it is translated back into what that means for business decisions. For example, a higher profit margin can result from higher prices, lower costs, or a move into new, high-margin products. Why then do managers define objectives in this way? In part, such goals may be a code to communicate real concerns. For example, a target profit margin may be a way of saying that in pursuing sales growth, the firm has allowed costs to get out of control.

The danger is that everyone may forget the code and the accounting targets may be seen as goals in themselves. No one should be surprised when lower-level managers focus on the goals for which they are rewarded. For example, when Volkswagen set a goal of 6.5 percent profit margin, some VW groups responded by developing and promoting expensive, high-margin cars. Less attention was paid to marketing cheaper models, which had lower profit margins but higher sales volume. In 2002 Volkswagen announced that it would de-emphasize its profit margin goal and would instead focus on return on investment. This, it hoped, would encourage managers to get the most profit out of every dollar of invested capital.

> Financial plans help managers ensure that their financing strategies are consistent with their capital budgets. They highlight the financing decisions necessary to support the firm's production and investment goals.

18.2   FINANCIAL PLANNING MODELS

Financial planners often use a financial planning model to help them explore the consequences of alternative financial strategies. These models range from simple models, such as the one presented later in this chapter, to models that incorporate hundreds of equations.

Contingency Planning at Georgia Power Company

The oil price hikes in 1973/1974 and 1979 caused consternation in the planning departments of electric utilities. Planners, who had assumed steady growth in energy usage and prices, found that their assumptions could no longer be relied on.

The planning department of Georgia Power Company responded by developing a number of possible scenarios and exploring their implications for Georgia Power's business over the next 10 years. In planning for the future, the company was not simply interested in the most likely outcome; it also needed to develop contingency plans to cover any unexpected occurrences.

Georgia Power's planning process involved three steps: (1) identify the key factors affecting the company's prospects; (2) determine a range of plausible outcomes for each of these factors; and (3) consider whether a favourable outcome for one factor was likely to be matched by a favourable outcome for the other factors.

This exercise generated three principal scenarios. For example, in the most rosy scenario, the growth in gross national product was expected to exceed 3.2 percent a year. This higher economic growth

was likely to be accompanied by high productivity growth and lower real interest rates as the baby boom generation matured. However, high growth was also likely to mean that economic prosperity would be more widely spread, so that the net migration to Georgia and the other sunbelt states was likely to decline. The average price of oil would probably remain below $18 a barrel as the power of OPEC weakened, and this would encourage industry to substitute oil for natural gas. The government was likely to pursue a free-market energy policy, which would tend to keep the growth in electricity prices below the rate of inflation.

Georgia Power's planners explored the implications of each scenario for energy demand and the amount of investment the company needed to make. That in turn allowed the financial managers to think about how the company could meet the possible demands for cash to finance the new investment.

Source: Georgia Power Company's use of scenario analysis is described in D. L. Goldfarb and W. R. Huss, "Building Scenarios for an Electric Utility," *Long Range Planning* 21 (1988), pp. 78–85.

Financial planning models support the financial planning process by making it easier and cheaper to construct forecast financial statements. The models automate an important part of planning that would otherwise be boring, time consuming, and labour intensive.

Programming these financial planning models used to consume large amounts of computer time and high-priced talent. These days, standard spreadsheet programs such as Microsoft Excel are regularly used to solve complex financial planning problems.

COMPONENTS OF A FINANCIAL PLANNING MODEL

A completed financial plan for a large company is a substantial document. A smaller corporation's plan has the same elements but less detail. For the smallest, youngest businesses, financial plans may be entirely in the financial manager's head. However, the basic elements of the plans will be similar for firms of any size.

Financial plans include three components: inputs, the planning model, and outputs. The relationship among these components is represented in Figure 18.1. Let's look at these components in turn.

Inputs

The inputs to the financial plan consist of the firm's current financial statements and its forecasts about the future. Usually, the principal forecast is the likely growth in sales, since many of the other variables such as labour requirements and inventory levels are tied to sales. These forecasts

FIGURE 18.1
The components of a financial plan

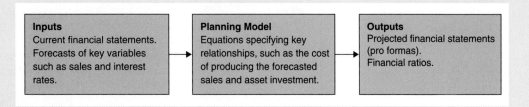

Inputs	Planning Model	Outputs
Current financial statements. Forecasts of key variables such as sales and interest rates.	Equations specifying key relationships, such as the cost of producing the forecasted sales and asset investment.	Projected financial statements (pro formas). Financial ratios.

are only in part the responsibility of the financial manager. Obviously, the marketing department will play a key role in forecasting sales. Their analysis of sales potential is based on their market research, including their assessment of competitors' plans. In addition, because sales will depend on the state of the overall economy, large firms will seek forecasting help from firms that specialize in preparing macroeconomic and industry forecasts.

The Planning Model

The financial planning model calculates the implications of the manager's forecasts for profits, new investment, and financing. The model consists of equations relating output variables to forecasts. For example, the equations can show how a change in sales is likely to affect costs, working capital, fixed assets, and financing requirements. The financial model could specify that the total cost of goods produced will increase by 80 cents for every $1 increase in total sales, that accounts receivable will be a fixed proportion of sales, and that the firm will need to increase fixed assets by 8 percent for every 10 percent increase in sales.

Outputs

pro formas   Projected or forecast financial statements.

The output of the financial model consists of financial statements such as income statements, balance sheets, and cash flow statements. These statements are called **pro formas**, which means that they are forecasts based on the inputs and the assumptions built into the plan. Usually the output of financial models also includes many of the financial ratios we discussed in the last chapter. These ratios indicate whether the firm will be financially fit and healthy at the end of the planning period.

AN EXAMPLE OF A PLANNING MODEL

We can illustrate the basic components of a planning model with a very simple example. In the next section we will start to add some complexity.

Executive Cheese's balance sheet and income statement for the year just ended are shown in Table 18.1. The firm's financial planners forecast that total sales over the next year will increase by 10 percent from this year's level. They expect that costs will be a fixed proportion of sales, so they too will increase by 10 percent. Almost all the forecasts for Executive Cheese are proportional to the forecast of sales. Such models are therefore called **percentage-of-sales models**. The result is the pro forma, or forecast, income statement in Table 18.2, which shows that next year's income will be $200 \times 1.10 = 220$.

percentage-of-sales models
Planning model in which sales forecasts are the driving variables and most other variables are proportional to sales.

Executive Cheese has no spare capacity, and in order to sustain this higher level of output, it must increase plant and equipment by 10 percent, or $200. Therefore, the left-hand side of the balance sheet, which lists total assets, must increase to $2,200. What about the right-hand side? The firm must decide how it intends to finance its new assets. Suppose it decides to maintain its current debt-equity ratio. To do this, both debt and equity must be increased by the same percentage. We have already figured out that assets must grow by 10 percent, and since the balance sheet must balance, both debt and equity must also grow by 10 percent. This implies the firm must issue $80 in additional debt, 10 percent of the original debt of $800. Also, equity must increase by $120, 10 percent of the original $1,200 in equity. However, no new equity needs to

TABLE 18.1
Financial statements of Executive Cheese Company for the past year

INCOME STATEMENT		
Sales		$1,200
Costs		1,000
Net income		$ 200
BALANCE SHEET, YEAR-END		
Assets	$2,000	Debt	$ 800
		Equity	1,200
Total	$2,000	Total	$2,000

TABLE 18.2
Pro forma financial statements of Executive Cheese for the next year, with fixed debt-equity ratio

PRO FORMA INCOME STATEMENT	
Sales	$1,320
Costs	1,100
Net income	$ 220

PRO FORMA BALANCE SHEET			
Assets	$2,200	Debt	$ 880
		Equity	1,320
Total	$2,200	Total	$2,200

be issued. The 10 percent increase in equity can be accomplished by retaining $120 of net income. The pro forma balance sheet for this financing plan is in Table 18.2.[1]

This raises a question, however. If income is forecast at $220, why does equity increase by only $120? The answer is that the firm must be planning to pay a dividend of $220 − $120 = $100. Notice that this dividend payment is not chosen independently but is a *consequence* of the other decisions. Given the company's need for funds and its decision to maintain the debt-equity ratio, dividend policy is completely determined. Any other dividend payment would be inconsistent with the two conditions that (1) the right-hand side of the balance sheet increase by $200, and (2) both debt and equity

balancing item   Variable that adjusts to maintain the consistency of a financial plan. Also called the plug.

increase by 10 percent. For this reason we call dividends the **balancing item**, or plug. The balancing item is the variable that adjusts to make the sources of funds equal to the uses.

Of course, most firms would be reluctant to vary dividends simply because they have a temporary need for cash; instead, they like to maintain a steady progression of dividends. In this case Executive Cheese could commit to some other dividend payment and allow the debt-equity ratio to vary. The amount of debt would therefore become the balancing item.

EXAMPLE 18.1

BALANCING ITEM

Suppose the firm commits to a dividend level of $180, and raises any extra money it needs by an issue of debt. In this case the amount of debt becomes the balancing item. With the dividend set at $180, addition to retained earnings would be only $40, so the firm would have to issue $160 in new debt to help pay for the additional $200 of assets. Table 18.3, panel A, is the new balance sheet.

Now suppose instead that the firm commits to the $180 dividend but decides that it will issue at most $100 in new debt. In that case, new equity issue becomes the balancing item. With $40 of earnings retained, and $100 of new debt, an additional $60 of equity needs to be raised to support the total addition of $200 to the firm's assets. Table 18.3, panel B, is the resulting balance sheet.

Is one of these plans better than the others? It's hard to give a simple answer. The choice of dividend payment depends partly on how investors will interpret the decision. If last year's dividend was only $50, investors might regard a dividend payment of $100 as a sign of a confident management; if last year's dividend was $150, investors might not be so content with a payment of $100. The alternative of paying $180 in dividends and making up the shortfall by issuing more debt leaves the

TABLE 18.3
Pro forma balance sheets. A: Dividends fixed and debt is the balancing item. B: Dividends and debt are fixed and equity issues is the balancing item.

Panel A				Panel B			
Assets	$2,200	Debt	$ 960	Assets	$2,200	Debt	$ 900
		Equity	1,240			Equity	1,300
Total	$2,200	Total	$ 2,200	Total	$2,200	Total	$ 2,200

---

[1] The new financing required can be figured out another way. If the debt-equity ratio is fixed, so too is the debt-asset ratio. The current debt-asset ratio is 800/2,000, or 40 percent. This tells us that the $200 increase in assets must be financed with 40 percent new debt, .4 × $200 = $80, and 60 percent new equity, .6 × $200 = $120, the same values we found above.

company with a debt-equity ratio of 77 percent. That is unlikely to make your bankers edgy but you may worry about how long you can continue to finance expansion predominantly by borrowing.

Our example shows how experiments with a financial model, including changes in the model's balancing item, can raise important financial questions. But the model does not answer these questions.

> Financial models ensure consistency between growth assumptions and financing plans, but they do not identify the best financing plan.

✓ Check Point 18.1

Suppose that the firm decides to maintain its debt-equity ratio at 800/1,200 = 2/3. It is committed to increasing assets by 10 percent to support the forecast increase in sales, and it strongly believes that a dividend payment of $180 is in the best interests of the firm. What must be the balancing items? What is the implication for the firm's financing activities in the next year?

AN IMPROVED MODEL

Now that you have grasped the idea behind financial planning models, we can move on to a more sophisticated example.

Table 18.4 shows the financial statements for Executive Fruit Company. The balance sheet contains values at the *start* of 2005. The income statement is for activities *during* 2005. Judging by these figures, the company is ordinary in almost all respects. Its earnings before interest and taxes, EBIT, were 10 percent of sales revenue. Net income was $96,000 after payment of taxes and 10 percent interest on $400,000 of long-term debt. The company paid out two-thirds of its net income as dividends.

Next to each item on the financial statements in Table 18.4 we have entered a comment about the relationship between that variable and sales. In most cases, the comment gives the value of each item as a percentage of sales. This may be useful for forecasting purposes. For example, it would be rea-

TABLE 18.4
Financial statements for
Executive Fruit Co., 2005

INCOME STATEMENT for the period of Jan. 1, 2005–Dec. 31, 2005 ($000s)		
		Comment
Revenue	$ 2,000	
Cost of goods sold	1,800	90% of sales
EBIT	200	Difference = 10% of sales
Interest	40	10% of debt at start of year
Earnings before taxes	160	EBIT – interest
Corporate tax	64	40% of (EBIT – interest)
Net income	$ 96	EBIT – interest – taxes
Dividends	$ 64	Payout ratio = 2/3
Addition to retained earnings	$ 32	Net income – dividends
BALANCE SHEET as of Jan. 1, 2005		
Assets		
Net working capital	$ 200	10% of sales
Fixed assets	800	40% of sales
Total assets	$ 1,000	50% of sales
Liabilities and shareholders' equity		
Long-term debt	$ 400	
Shareholders' equity	600	
Total liabilities and shareholders' equity	$ 1,000	Equals total assets

sonable to assume that cost of goods sold will remain at 90 percent of sales even if sales grow by 10 percent next year. Similarly, it is reasonable to assume that net working capital will remain at 10 percent of sales.

On the other hand, the fact that long-term debt currently is 20 percent of sales does not mean that we should assume that this ratio will continue to hold next period. Many alternative financing plans with varying combinations of debt issues, equity issues, and dividend payouts may be considered without affecting the firm's operations.

Now suppose that you are asked to prepare pro forma financial statements for Executive Fruit for 2006. You are told to assume that (1) sales are expected to be up 10 percent over 2005, (2) 2006 operating costs are expected to be the same percentage of sales as in 2005, (3) interest rates will remain at their current level, (4) the firm will stick to its traditional dividend policy of paying out two-thirds of earnings, and (5) there is zero excess capacity so the firm must increase its fixed assets and net working capital[2] to support the larger sales volume, and the new assets must be in place at the beginning of 2006. The 2006 asset/sales ratio will be same as the ratio of assets to sales in 2005. The assumption that the costs and asset requirements are the same percentage of sales in 2006 as in 2005 is equivalent to assuming that costs and assets will grow at the sales growth rate.

In Table 18.5 we present the resulting first-stage pro forma calculations for Executive Fruit. These calculations show what would happen if the size of the firm increases along with sales, but at this preliminary stage, the plan does not specify a particular mix of new security issues.

Without any new financing, the balance sheet at the start of the year will not balance: assets will increase to $1,100,000 while debt plus shareholders' equity will amount to only $1,032,000. Somehow the firm will need to raise an extra $68,000 to help pay for the increase in assets that is necessary to support the higher projected level of sales. In this first pass, external financing is

TABLE 18.5
First-stage pro forma statements for Executive Fruit Co., 2006

PRO FORMA INCOME STATEMENT FOR JAN. 1, 2006 TO DEC. 31, 2006 ($000s)		
		Comment
Revenue	$ 2,200	10% higher
Cost of goods sold	1,980	90% of sales
EBIT	220	10% higher
Interest	40	Unchanged
Earnings before taxes	180	EBIT – interest
Corporate tax	72	40% of (EBIT – interest)
Net income	$ 108	EBIT – interest – taxes
Dividends	$ 72	2/3 of net income
Addition to retained earnings	$ 36	Net income - dividends
PRO FORMA BALANCE SHEET AS OF JAN. 1, 2006		
Assets		
Net working capital	$ 220	10% of sales
Fixed assets	880	40% of sales
Total assets	$ 1,100	10% higher
Liabilities and shareholders' equity		
Long-term debt	$ 400	Temporarily held fixed
Shareholders' equity	632	Increased by addition to retained earnings
Total liabilities and shareholders' equity	$ 1,032	Sum of debt plus equity
Required external financing	$ 68	Balancing item or plug (= $1,100 – $1,032)

---

[2] Net working capital is current assets minus current liabilities. However, include only current assets and current liabilities directly related to sales, such as operating cash, accounts receivable, inventories, accounts payable, and accruals. Short-term loans, excess cash and marketable securities, or other financing items, are typically considered as part of the financing plans.

the balancing item. Given the firm's growth forecasts and its dividend policy, the financial plan calculates how much money the firm needs to raise.

In the second-stage pro forma, the firm must decide on the financing mix that best meets its needs for additional funds. It must choose some combination of new debt and/or new equity that supports the contemplated acquisition of additional assets. For example, it could issue $68,000 of equity or debt, or it could choose to maintain its long-term debt-equity ratio at two-thirds by issuing both debt and equity.

Table 18.6 shows the second-stage pro forma balance sheet if the required funds are raised by issuing $68,000 of debt. Therefore, in Table 18.6, debt is treated as the balancing item. Notice that while the plan requires the firm to specify a financing plan *consistent* with its growth projections, it does not provide guidance as to the *best* financing mix.

Table 18.7 sets out the firm's sources and uses of funds for the period of January 1, 2005, to January 1, 2006. It shows that the firm needs an investment of $20,000 in working capital and an investment of $80,000 in fixed assets at the start of 2006 to support the planned 2006 sales. To finance this $100,000 investment, the firm reinvests $32,000 of the profits from 2005 and must raise the remaining $68,000 from the capital markets. Under the financing plan presented in Table 18.6, the firm borrows the entire $68,000.

Another way to describe the flow of funds is to calculate the cash flow from assets and the financing flows, as shown in Chapter 3. In Table 18.8 is the cash flow from assets. Executive Fruit generated $4,000 less cash flow from its operating activities than it needed to invest in net working capital and fixed assets. Table 18.9 shows how it financed the shortfall. It borrowed $68,000 to both pay for the $64,000 dividend and provide the additional $4,000 needed to fund its investments.

We have spared you the trouble of actually calculating the figures necessary for all these tables. The calculations do not take more than a few minutes for this simple example, *provided* you set up

TABLE 18.6
Second-stage pro forma balance sheet for Executive Fruit Co., at the start of 2006, with debt as the balancing item

PRO FORMA BALANCE SHEET AS OF JAN. 1, 2006 ($000s)		
		Comment
Assets		
Net working capital	$ 220	10% of sales
Fixed assets	880	40% of sales
Total assets	$ 1,100	10% higher
Liabilities and shareholders' equity		
Long-term debt	$ 468	16% higher (new borrowing = $68; this is the balancing item)
Shareholders' equity	$ 632	Increased by 2005 addition to retained earnings
Total liabilities and shareholders' equity	$ 1,100	Again equals total assets

TABLE 18.7
Pro forma statement of sources and uses of funds for Executive Fruit, for the period from the beginning of 2005 to the beginning of 2006

PRO FORMA SOURCES AND USES OF FUNDS ($000s)			
Sources		**Uses**	
Addition to retained earnings	$ 32	Investment in net working capital	$ 20
New borrowing	68	Investment in fixed assets	80
Total sources	$ 100	Total uses	$ 100

TABLE 18.8
Pro forma cash flow from assets for Executive Fruit, for the period from the beginning of 2005 to the beginning of 2006

PRO FORMA CASH FLOW FROM ASSETS ($000s)	
Net income	$96
Investment in net working capital	(20)
Investment in fixed assets	(80)
Total cash flow from assets	($ 4)

TABLE 18.9

Pro forma cash flow to bondholders and shareholders for Executive Fruit for the period from the beginning of 2005 to the beginning of 2006

PRO FORMA CASH FLOW TO BONDHOLDERS AND SHAREHOLDERS ($000s)	
New borrowing	($68)
Dividends	64
Total cash flow to bondholders and shareholders	($ 4)

the calculations correctly and make no arithmetic mistakes. If that time requirement seems trivial, remember that in reality you probably would be asked for four similar sets of statements covering each year from 2006 to 2009. Probably you would be asked for alternative projections under different assumptions (for example, 5 percent instead of 10 percent growth rate of revenue) or different financial strategies (for example, freezing dividends at their 2005 level of $64,000). This would be far more time consuming. Moreover, actual plans will have many more line items than this simple one. Building a model and letting the computer toil in your place has obvious attractions.

Figure 18.2 is the spreadsheet we used for the Executive Fruit model. Column E contains the values that appear in Table 18.4 except now we have recognized that additional debt issued at

FIGURE 18.2 Executive Fruit spreadsheet

	A	B	C	D	E	F	G	H
1	**Model Inputs**				Base year			Formula
2				Income Statement	2005	2006	2007	for column G
3	Sales growth rate	0.1		Revenue	2,000	2,200.0	2,420.0	F3*(1+B3)
4	Tax rate	0.4		Cost of goods sold	1,800	1,980.0	2,178.0	G3*B8
5	Interest rate	0.1		EBIT	200	220.0	242.0	G3–G4
6	NWC/sales	0.1		Interest expense	40	46.8	54.3	B5*G20
7	Fixed assets/sales	0.4		Earnings before taxes	160	173.2	187.7	G5–G6
8	COGS/sales	0.9		Taxes	64	69.3	75.1	B4*G7
9	Payout ratio	2/3		Net income	96	103.9	112.6	G7–G8
10				Dividends	64	69.3	75.1	G9*B9
11				Addition to retained earnings	32	34.6	37.5	G9–G10
12								
13				**Balance Sheet (start of year)**				
14				Assets				
15				Net working capital	200	220.0	242.0	B6*G3
16				Fixed assets	800	880.0	968.0	B7*G3
17				Total assets	1,000	1,100.0	1,210.0	G15+G16
18								
19				Liabilities and equity				
20				Long-term debt (note a)	400	468.0	543.4	F20+G24
21				Shareholders' equity (note b)	600	632.0	666.6	F21+F11
22				Total liab. & share. equity	1,000	1,100.0	1,210.0	G20+G21
23								
24				Required external financing		68.0	75.4	G17–F17–F11
25								
26								
27	**Notes**							
28	(a): Long-term debt, the balancing item, increases by required external financing.							
29	(b): Shareholders' equity at the start of year equals its value at start of previous year plus earnings							
30	retained during the year.							

the start of 2006 will result in increased interest expenses in that year. Column G extends the analysis out one more year so that you can see the balance sheet at the start of 2007. Column H presents the formulas used to obtain each value. Notice that we assume the firm will maintain its dividend payout ratios at 2/3 (for 2006, cell F10) and that debt will be the balancing item, increasing in each year by required external financing (cell F20). Required external financing in 2006 equals total assets required to support that year's sales (cell F17) minus the previous year's assets (cell E17) minus earnings retained in the previous year (cell E11). Shareholders' equity (cell F21) equals its previous value plus retained earnings from the previous year (cell E11).

Now that the spreadsheet is set up, it is easy to explore the consequences of various assumptions. For example, you can change the assumed sales growth rate (cell B3) or experiment with different policies, such as changing the dividend payout ratio or forcing debt or equity finance (or both) to absorb the required external financing.

| EXAMPLE 18.2 | **WHAT HAPPENS IF THE GROWTH RATE CHANGES?** |

Let's use the spreadsheet to explore the effect of sales growth on the need for external financing. We can alter the assumed growth rate in cell B3 and see the effect on required external finance in cell F24. For example, we saw in Figure 18.2 that when the sales growth rate was 10 percent, required external finance was $68. In our model, assets are proportional to sales, so as we assume a higher growth rate of sales, assets also increase at a higher rate. The additional funds necessary to pay for those additional assets imply greater external finance.

If the firm pays a dividend of $64,000 in 2005, leaving $32,000 to be reinvested in the firm, assets increase by 32/1,000 = 3.2 percent. Thus, retained earnings are sufficient to support a 3.2 percent growth in sales in 2006. Table 18.10 shows how the required external finance changes if the firm wishes to grow sales at a slower or faster rate. Notice that at a 3.2 percent growth rate, required external finance is indeed zero. At higher growth rates, the firm requires external finance; at lower rates, retained earnings exceed the addition to assets and there is a surplus of funds from internal sources; this shows up as negative required external financing. Later in the chapter, we will explore the limits to internal growth more systematically.

 Check Point 18.2

a. Suppose that Executive Fruit is committed to its expansion plans and to its dividend policy. It also wishes to maintain its debt-equity ratio at two-thirds. What are the implications for external financing at the beginning of 2006?

b. If the company is prepared to reduce dividends paid in 2005 to $60,000, how much external financing would be needed?

TABLE 18.10
Required external financing for Executive Fruit. Notice that with $1 million in assets, each one percentage point increase in the assumed growth rate increases required external finance by .01 × $1 million = $10,000.

Growth Rate (%)	Required External Finance ($000s)
0	−32
2	−12
3.2	0
5	18
10	68
15	118
20	168

PLANNERS BEWARE

PITFALLS IN MODEL DESIGN

The Executive Fruit model is still too simple for practical application. You probably have already noticed several ways to improve it. For example, we ignored the capital cost allowance, CCA, associated with the fixed asset. CCA is important because it provides a tax shield. If Executive Fruit deducts CCA before calculating its tax bill, it could plow back more money into new investments and would need to borrow less. Also, in the first-stage pro formas in Table 18.5, we ignored the fact that there would likely be some interest to pay in 2006 on the new borrowing, which would cut into the cash for new investments. We corrected this omission in Figure 18.2.

Imbedded in the model design is the timing of new asset purchases. Although investments can occur at any point during the year, typically it is sufficient to assume that the investments occur either at the beginning or at the end of the forecast year. For example, the Executive Cheese asset investment occurred at the end of the forecast year. We know this because we forecasted the end-of-year pro forma balance sheet with the asset investment paid in part by the profits generated over the forecast year and in part with new financing arranged at the end of the forecast year. By contrast, investment in assets for Executive Fruit occurred at the beginning of the forecast year, before any new sales were generated. That is why we worked with the balance sheet as of the start of 2006, used the profits from 2005 to help fund the investment, and arranged the new financing at the beginning of 2006. Neither assumption is better—pick the one that best suits the business reality.

You would certainly want to make the obvious improvements. But beware: there is always the temptation to make a model bigger and more detailed. You may end up with an exhaustive model that is too cumbersome for routine use.

Excessive detail gets in the way of the intended use of corporate planning models, which is to project the financial consequences of a variety of strategies and assumptions. The fascination of detail, if you give in to it, distracts attention from crucial decisions like stock issues and dividend policy and allocation of capital by business area.

THE ASSUMPTION IN PERCENTAGE-OF-SALES MODELS

A key factor in any planning exercise is the sales forecast. Ensure the plan reflects reality. For example, if a plan is based on aggressive growth and increase in market share, ask where the sales growth will come from. Put yourself in your competitors' shoes and think how they are likely to react. Although the firm will never have perfectly accurate sales forecasts, managers must strive for the best forecasts possible.

The percentage-of-sales forecasting method assumes that costs and assets increase proportionately with sales. In Executive Fruit's forecast, the 2006 percentage-of-sales forecasting factors are taken from the 2005 sales, costs, and assets. These forecasting assumptions are listed as the "Model Inputs" in Column A of Figure 18.2. Are these sensible forecasting factors? When building planning models, financial managers do not naively accept the previous year's percent-of-sales factors as necessarily valid for the future. They recognize that their specific expansion plans may change the cost-to-sales ratios and the need for assets. For example, suppose Executive Fruit's management expects the ratio of cost of goods sold to sales (COGS/sales) to be 85 percent in 2006, reflecting expected improvements in production. The COGS/sales value in cell B8 would be changed from .9 to .85.

When forecasting Executive Fruit's capital requirements, we assumed that both fixed assets and working capital increase proportionately with sales. For example, line (a) in Figure 18.3 shows that net working capital is a constant 10 percent of sales.

Percentage-of-sales models are useful first approximations for financial planning. However, in reality, assets may not be proportional to sales. For example, we will see in Chapter 20 that important components of working capital such as inventories and cash balances will generally rise less than proportionately with sales. Suppose that Executive Fruit looks back at past variations in sales and estimates that on average a $1 rise in sales requires only a $.075 increase in net

FIGURE 18.3

Net working capital (NWC) as a function of sales: line (a) shows net working capital equal to .10 × sales. Line (b) depicts net working capital as $50,000 + (.075 × sales), so that NWC increases less than proportionately with sales.

working capital. Line (b) in Figure 18.3 shows the level of working capital that would now be needed for different levels of sales. To allow for this in the Executive Fruit model, we would need to set net working capital equal to ($50,000 + .075 × sales).

A further complication is that typically fixed assets such as plant and equipment are not added in small increments as sales increase. Instead, the picture is more likely to resemble Figure 18.4. If Executive Fruit's factories are operating at less than full capacity (point A, for example), then the firm can expand sales without any additional investment in plant. Ultimately, however, if sales continue to increase, say beyond point B, Executive Fruit will need to add new capacity. This is shown by the occasional large changes to fixed assets in Figure 18.4. These "lumpy" changes to fixed assets need to be recognized when devising the financial plan. If there is considerable excess capacity, even rapid sales growth may not require big additions to fixed assets. On the other hand, if the firm is already operating at capacity, even small sales growth may call for large investment in plant and equipment.

FIGURE 18.4

If factories are operating below full capacity, sales can increase without investment in fixed assets (point A). Beyond some sales level (point B), new capacity must be added.

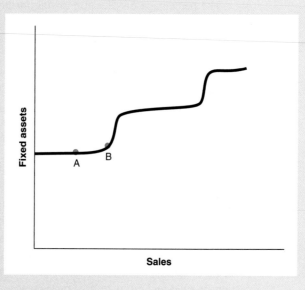

EXAMPLE 18.3   **REQUIRED EXTERNAL FUNDS AND EXCESS CAPACITY**

Suppose that Carter Tools has $50 million invested in fixed assets and generates sales of $60 million. The company is currently working at 80 percent of capacity. Suppose that a 50 percent increase in sales is forecast. How much investment in fixed assets would be required?

Sales can increase *without* the need for new investments in fixed assets until the company is at 100 percent of capacity. Therefore, sales can increase to $60 million × 100/80 = $75 million before the firm reaches full capacity given its current level of fixed assets. At full capacity, therefore, the ratio of assets to sales would be $50 million/$75 million = 2/3.

The 50 percent increase in forecast sales would imply a sales level of $60 million × 1.5 = $90 million. To support this level of sales, the company needs at least $90 million × 2/3 = $60 million of fixed assets. This calls for a $10 million investment in additional fixed assets.

✔ **Check Point 18.3**

Suppose that at its current level of assets and sales, Carter Tools in Example 18.3 is working at 75 percent of capacity.
a. How much can sales expand without any further investment in fixed assets?
b. How much investment in fixed assets would be required to support a 50 percent expansion in sales?

THE ROLE OF FINANCIAL PLANNING MODELS

Models such as the one that we constructed for Executive Fruit help the financial manager avoid surprises. If the planned rate of growth will require the company to raise external finance, the manager can start planning how best to do so.

We commented earlier that financial planners are concerned about unlikely events as well as likely ones. For example, Executive Fruit's manager may wish to consider how the company's capital requirement would change if profit margins come under pressure and the company generated less cash from its operations. Planning models make it easy to explore the consequences of such events.

However, there are limits to what you can learn from planning models. Although they help to trace through the consequences of alternative plans, they do not tell the manager which plan is best. For example, we saw that Executive Fruit is proposing to grow its sales and earnings per share. Is that good news for shareholders? Well, not necessarily; it depends on the opportunity cost of the additional capital that the company needs to achieve that growth. In 2006 the company proposes to invest $100,000 in fixed assets and working capital. Table 18.5 showed that this extra investment is expected to generate $12,000 of additional net income,[3] equivalent to a return of 12 percent on the new investment. If the cost of that capital is less than 12 percent, the new investment will have a positive NPV and will add to shareholder wealth. But suppose that the cost of capital is higher at, say, 15 percent. In this case Executive Fruit's investment makes shareholders *worse off*, even though the company is recording steady growth in earnings per share and dividends. Executive Fruit's planning model tells us how much money the firm must raise to fund the planned growth, but it cannot tell us whether that growth contributes to shareholder value. Nor can it tell us whether the company should raise the cash by issuing new debt or equity.

✔ **Check Point 18.4**

Which of the following questions will a financial plan help to answer?
a. Is the firm's assumption for asset growth consistent with its plans for debt and equity issues and dividend policy?
b. Will accounts receivable increase in direct proportion to sales?
c. Will the contemplated debt-equity mix maximize the value of the firm?

---

[3] In Figure 18.2 we recognized that the increased borrowing will result in higher interest payments and also a higher interest tax shield. In this case, the investment resulted in increased interest payments plus net income, $6,800 + $7,900 = $14,700. Part of the gain is from the project itself and part is from how it is financed.

18.4

SEE BOX P. 579

EXTERNAL FINANCING AND GROWTH

Financial *plans* force managers to be consistent in their goals for growth, investments, and financing. The nearby Finance in Action box describes how one company was brought to its knees when it did not plan sufficiently for the cash that would be required to support its ambitions.

Financial models, such as the one that we have developed for Executive Fruit, can help managers trace through the financial consequences of their growth plans and avoid such disasters. But there is a danger that the complexities of a full-blown financial model can obscure the basic issues. Therefore, managers also use some simple rules of thumb to draw out the relationship between a firm's growth objectives and its requirement for external financing.

Recall that in 2005 Executive Fruit started the year with $1,000,000 of fixed assets and net working capital and it had $2,000,000 of sales. In other words, each dollar of sales required $.50 of net assets. The company forecasts that sales next year will increase by $200,000. Therefore, if the ratio of sales to net assets remains constant, assets will need to rise by .50 × 200,000 = $100,000.[4] Part of this increase can be financed by additional retained earnings, which in 2005 are $32,000. So the amount of external finance needed is

$$\text{Required external financing} = \begin{array}{l}(\text{net assets/sales}) \times \text{increase in sales} \\ - \text{addition to retained earnings}\end{array}$$

$$= .50 \times 200,000 - 32,000 = \$68,000$$

Sometimes it is useful to write this calculation in terms of growth rates. Executive Fruit's forecasted increase in sales is equivalent to a rise of 10 percent. So, if net assets are a constant proportion of sales, the higher sales volume will also require a 10 percent addition to net assets. Thus

$$\text{New investment} = \text{growth rate} \times \text{initial assets}$$
$$\$100,000 = .10 \times \$1,000,000$$

Part of the funds to pay for the new assets will be provided by the addition to retained earnings. The remainder must come from external financing. Therefore,

$$\textbf{Required external financing} = \textbf{new investment} - \begin{array}{l}\textbf{addition to} \\ \textbf{retained earnings}\end{array} \quad \textbf{(18.1)}$$

$$= (\textbf{growth rate} \times \textbf{assets}) - \begin{array}{l}\textbf{addition to} \\ \textbf{retained earnings}\end{array}$$

This simple equation highlights that the amount of external financing depends on the firm's projected growth. The faster the firm grows, the more it needs to invest and therefore the more it needs to raise new capital.

In the case of Executive Fruit,

$$\text{Required external financing} = (.10 \times \$1,000,000) - \$32,000$$
$$= \$100,000 - \$32,000 = \$68,000$$

If Executive Fruit's assets remain a constant percentage of sales, then the company needs to raise $68,000 to produce a 10 percent addition to sales.

The sloping line in Figure 18.5 illustrates how required external financing increases with the growth rate. At low growth rates, the firm generates more funds than necessary for expansion. In this sense, its requirement for further external funds is negative. It may choose to use its surplus to pay off some of its debt or buy back its stock. In fact, the vertical intercept in Figure 18.5, at zero growth, is the negative of the addition to retained earnings. When growth is zero, no funds are needed for expansion, so all the additions to retained earnings are surplus.

---

[4] However, remember our earlier warning that the ratio of sales to net assets may change as the firm grows.

The Bankruptcy of W.T. Grant: A Failure in Planning

W.T. Grant was the largest and one of the most successful department store chains in the United States with 1,200 stores, 83,000 employees, and $1.8 billion of sales. Yet, in 1975, the company filed for bankruptcy, in what *BusinessWeek* termed "the most significant bankruptcy in U.S. history."

The seeds of Grant's difficulties were sown in the mid-1960s when the company foresaw a shift in shopping habits from inner-city areas to out-of-town centres. The company decided to embark on a rapid expansion policy that involved opening new stores in suburban areas. In addition to making a substantial investment in new buildings, the company needed to ensure that the new stores were stocked with merchandise and it encouraged customers by extending credit more freely. As a result, the company's investment in inventories and receivables more than doubled between 1967 and 1974.

W.T. Grant's expansion plan led to impressive growth. Sales grew from $900 million in 1967 to $1.8 billion in 1974. For a while, profits also boomed, growing from $63 million in 1967 to a peak of $90 million in 1970. Shareholders were delighted. By 1971 the share price had reached a high of $71, up from $20 in 1967.

To achieve the growth in sales, W.T. Grant needed to invest a total of $650 million in fixed assets, inventories, and receivables. However, it takes time for new stores to reach full profitability, so while profits initially increased, the return on capital fell. At the same time, the company decided to increase its dividends in line with earnings. This meant that the bulk of the money to finance the new investment had to be raised from the capital market. W.T. Grant was reluctant to sell more shares and chose instead to raise the money by issuing more than $400 million of new debt.

By 1974 Grant's debt-equity ratio had reached 1.8. This figure was high, but not alarmingly so. The problem was that rapid expansion combined with recession to eat into profits. Almost all the operating cash flows in 1974 were used to service the company's debt. Yet the company insisted on maintaining the dividend on its common stock. Effectively, it was borrowing to pay the dividend. By the next year, W.T. Grant could no longer service its mountain of debt and had to seek postponement of payments on a $600 million bank loan.

W.T. Grant's failure was partly a failure of financial planning. It did not recognize and plan for the huge cash drain involved in its expansion strategy.

As the firm's projected growth rate increases, more funds are needed to pay for the necessary investments. Therefore, the plot in Figure 18.5 is upward sloping. For high rates of growth the firm must issue new securities to pay for new investments.

Where the sloping line crosses the horizontal axis, external financing is zero: the firm is growing as fast as possible without resorting to new security issues. This is called the **internal growth rate**. The growth rate is "internal" because it can be maintained without resort to additional external sources of capital.

internal growth rate
Maximum rate of growth without external financing.

Notice that if we set required external financing to zero, we can solve for the internal growth rate as

$$\text{Internal growth rate} = \frac{\text{addition to retained earnings}}{\text{assets}} \tag{18.2}$$

FIGURE 18.5
External financing and growth

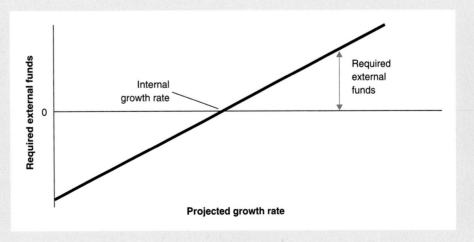

579

Thus the firm's rate of growth without additional external sources of capital will equal the ratio of the addition to retained earnings to assets. This means that a firm with a high volume of retained earnings relative to its assets can generate a higher growth rate without needing to raise more capital.

We can gain more insight into what determines the internal growth rate by multiplying the top and bottom of the expression for internal growth by net income and equity as follows:

$$\textbf{Internal growth rate} = \frac{\textbf{addition to retained earnings}}{\textbf{net income}} \times \frac{\textbf{net income}}{\textbf{equity}} \times \frac{\textbf{equity}}{\textbf{assets}} \quad \textbf{(18.3)}$$

$$= \textbf{plowback ratio} \times \textbf{return on equity} \times \frac{\textbf{equity}}{\textbf{assets}}$$

A firm can achieve a higher growth rate without raising external capital if (1) it plows back a high proportion of its earnings, (2) it has a high return on equity (ROE), and (3) it has a low debt-to-asset ratio.

Instead of focusing on the maximum growth rate that can be supported without any external financing, firms also may be interested in the growth rate that can be sustained without additional equity issues. Of course, if the firm is able to issue enough debt, virtually any growth rate can be financed. However, it makes more sense to assume that the firm has settled on an optimal capital structure that it will maintain even as equity is augmented by the addition to retained earnings. The firm issues only enough debt to keep its debt-equity ratio constant. The **sustainable growth rate** is the highest growth rate the firm can maintain without increasing its financial leverage. It turns out that the sustainable growth rate depends only on the plowback ratio and return on equity:[5]

sustainable growth rate
Steady rate at which a firm can grow without changing leverage; plowback ratio × return on equity.

$$\textbf{Sustainable growth rate} = \textbf{plowback ratio} \times \textbf{return on equity} \quad \textbf{(18.4)}$$

You may remember this formula from Chapter 6, where we first used it when we looked at the valuation of the firm and the dividend discount model.

---

[5] Here is proof:

Required equity issues = growth rate × assets – addition to retained earnings – new debt issues

We find the sustainable growth rate by setting required new equity issues to zero and solving for growth:

$$\text{Sustainable growth rate} = \frac{\text{addition to retained earnings} + \text{new debt issues}}{\text{assets}}$$

$$= \frac{\text{addition to retained earnings} + \text{new debt issues}}{\text{debt} + \text{equity}}$$

However, because both debt and equity are growing at the same rate, new debt issues must equal the additional retained earnings multiplied by the ratio of debt to equity, D/E. Therefore, we can write the sustainable growth rate as

$$\text{Sustainable growth rate} = \frac{\text{addition to retained earnings} \times (1 + D/E)}{\text{debt} + \text{equity}}$$

$$= \frac{\text{addition to retained earnings} \times (1 + D/E)}{\text{equity} \times (1 + D/E)} = \frac{\text{addition to retained earnings}}{\text{equity}}$$

$$= \frac{\text{addition to retained earnings}}{\text{net income}} \times \frac{\text{net income}}{\text{equity}} = \text{plowback} \times \text{ROE}$$

| EXAMPLE 18.4 | INTERNAL AND SUSTAINABLE GROWTH FOR EXECUTIVE FRUIT |

Executive Fruit has chosen a plowback ratio of one-third. As Table 18.4 shows, at the beginning of 2005, the outstanding assets were $1,000 and outstanding equity was $600. Because net income during 2005 was $96, Executive Fruit's return on equity[6] is ROE = 96/600 = .16. Its ratio of equity to assets is 600/1,000 = .60. If it is unwilling to raise new capital, its maximum growth rate is

$$\text{Internal growth rate} = \text{plowback ratio} \times \text{ROE} \times \frac{\text{equity}}{\text{assets}}$$
$$= \frac{1}{3} \times .16 \times .60 = .032, \text{ or } 3.2\%$$

This is much less than the 10 percent growth it projects, which explains its need for external financing.

If Executive Fruit is prepared to maintain its current ratio of equity to total assets, it can issue an additional 40 cents of debt for every 60 cents of retained earnings. In this case, the maximum growth rate would be

$$\text{Substainable growth rate} = \text{plowback ratio} \times \text{ROE}$$
$$= \frac{1}{3} \times .16 = .0533, \text{ or } 5.33\%$$

Executive Fruit's planned growth rate of 10 percent requires not only new borrowing but also an increase in the debt-equity ratio. In the long run the company will need to either issue new equity or cut back its rate of growth.[7]

Check Point 18.5   Suppose Executive Fruit reduces the dividend payout ratio to 25 percent. Calculate its growth rate assuming (a) that no new debt or equity will be issued and (b) the firm maintains its equity-to-asset ratio at .60. For each case, check that the calculated growth rate is correct.

---

[6] Note that when we calculate internal or sustainable growth rates, ROE is properly measured by earnings as a proportion of equity at the *start* of the year rather than as a proportion of either end-of-year equity or the average of outstanding equity at the start and end of the year.

[7] As the firm issues more debt, its return on equity also changes. But Executive would need to have a very high debt-equity ratio before it could support a growth rate of 10 pecent a year and maintain a constant debt ratio.

18.5   SUMMARY

1.   What are the contents and uses of a financial plan?

Most firms take financial planning seriously and devote considerable resources to it. The tangible product of the planning process is a financial plan describing the firm's financial strategy and projecting its future consequences by means of **pro forma** balance sheets, income statements, and statements of sources and uses of funds. The plan establishes financial goals and is a benchmark for evaluating subsequent performance. Usually it also describes why that strategy was chosen and how the plan's financial goals are to be achieved.

Planning, if it is done right, forces the financial manager to think about events that could upset the firm's progress and to devise strategies to be held in reserve for counterattack when unfortunate surprises occur. Planning is more than forecasting, because forecasting deals with the most likely outcome. Planners also have to think about events that may occur even though they are unlikely.

In long-range, or strategic, planning, the **planning horizon** is usually five years or more. This kind of planning deals with aggregate decisions; for example, the planner would worry about whether the broadax division should commit to heavy capital investment and rapid growth, but not whether the division should choose machine tool A versus tool B. In fact, planners must be constantly on guard against the fascination of detail, because giving in to it means slighting crucial issues like investment strategy, debt policy, and the choice of a target dividend payout ratio.

The plan is the end result. The process that produces the plan is valuable in its own right. Planning forces the financial manager to consider the combined effects of all the firm's investment and financing decisions. This is important because these decisions interact and should not be made independently.

2. How are financial planning models constructed?

There is no theory or model that leads straight to the optimal financial strategy. Consequently, financial planning proceeds by trial and error. Many different strategies may be projected under a range of assumptions about the future before one strategy is finally chosen. The dozens of separate projections that may be made during this trial-and-error process generate a heavy load of arithmetic and paperwork. Firms have responded by developing corporate planning models to forecast the financial consequences of specified strategies and assumptions about the future.

One very simple starting point may be a **percentage-of-sales** model in which many key variables are assumed to be directly proportional to sales. Planning models are efficient and widely used. But remember that there is not much finance in them. Their primary purpose is to produce accounting statements. The models do not search for the best financial strategy but only trace out the consequences of a strategy specified by the model user.

3. What is the effect of growth on the need for external financing?

Higher growth rates will lead to greater need for investments in fixed assets and working capital. The **internal growth rate** is the maximum rate that the firm can grow if it relies entirely on reinvested profits to finance its growth, that is, the maximum rate of growth without requiring external financing. The **sustainable growth rate** is the rate at which the firm can grow without changing its leverage ratio.

Related Web Links

www.bsa.cbsc.org Government of Canada gateway to information on starting a business in Canada

www.jaxworks.com/bpindex.htm Helpful materials on development of a financial plan

Key Terms

planning horizon	565	percentage-of-sales		balancing item	569
pro formas	568	models	568	internal growth rate	579
				sustainable growth rate	580

Questions and Problems

*Answers in Appendix B

BASIC

1. **Financial Planning.** True or false? Explain.
    a. Financial planning should attempt to minimize risk.
    b. The primary aim of financial planning is to obtain better forecasts of future cash flows and earnings.
    c. Financial planning is necessary because financing and investment decisions interact and should not be made independently.
    d. Firms' planning horizons rarely exceed three years.
    e. Individual capital investment projects are not considered in a financial plan unless they are very large.
    f. Financial planning requires accurate and consistent forecasting.
    g. Financial planning models should include as much detail as possible.

2. **Financial Models.** What are the dangers and disadvantages of using a financial model? Discuss.

3. **Using Financial Plans.** Corporate financial plans are often used as a basis for judging subsequent performance. What can be learned from such comparisons? What problems might arise and how might you cope with such problems?

*4. **Growth Rates.** Find the sustainable and internal growth rates for a firm with the following ratios: asset turnover = 1.40; net profit margin = 6 percent; interest/sales = 1 percent; payout ratio = 25 percent; equity/assets = .60.

5. **Percentage-of-Sales Models.** Percentage-of-sales models often assume that costs, fixed assets, and working capital all increase at the same rate as sales. When do you think that these assumptions do not make sense? Would you feel happier using a percentage-of-sales model for short-term or long-term planning?

6. **Relationships among Variables.** Comebaq Computers is aiming to increase its market share by slashing the price of its new range of personal computers. Are costs and assets likely to increase or decrease as a proportion of sales? Explain.

*7. **Balancing Items.** What are the possible choices of balancing items when using a financial planning model? Discuss whether some are generally preferable to others.

8. **Financial Targets.** Managers sometimes state a target growth rate for sales or earnings per share. Do you think that either one makes sense as a corporate goal? If not, why do you think that managers focus on them?

PRACTICE

*9. **Percentage-of-Sales Models.** Here are the abbreviated financial statements for Planners Peanuts:

INCOME STATEMENT, 2006

Sales	$2,000
Costs	1,500
Net income	$ 500

BALANCE SHEET, YEAR-END

	2005	2006		2005	2006
Assets	$2,500	$3,000	Debt	$ 833	$1,000
			Equity	1,667	2,000
Total	$2,500	$3,000	Total	$2,500	$3,000

If sales increase by 20 percent in 2007, and the company uses a strict percentage-of-sales planning model (meaning that all items on the income and balance sheet also increase by 20 percent), and purchases new assets at the end of 2007, what must be the balancing item? What will be its value?

EXCEL

10. **Required External Financing.** If the dividend payout ratio in problem 9 is fixed at 50 percent, calculate the required total external financing for growth rates in 2007 of 15 percent, 20 percent, and 25 percent.

*11. **Feasible Growth Rates.** What is the maximum possible growth rate in 2007 for Planners Peanuts (see problem 9) if the payout ratio remains at 50 percent and
   a.   no external debt or equity is to be issued?
   b.   the firm maintains a fixed debt ratio but issues no equity?

12. **Using Percentage of Sales.** Eagle Sports Supply has the following financial statements. Assume that Eagle's assets are proportional to its sales and asset purchases are made at the end of 2007.

INCOME STATEMENT, 2006

Sales	$950
Costs	250
EBIT	700
Taxes	200
Net income	$500

BALANCE SHEET, YEAR-END

	2005	2006		2005	2006
Assets	$2,700	$3,000	Debt	$ 900	$1,000
			Equity	1,800	2,000
Total	$2,700	$3,000	Total	$2,700	$3,000

a. Find Eagle's required external funds if it maintains a dividend payout ratio of 60 percent and plans a growth rate of 15 percent in 2007.

b. If Eagle chooses not to issue new shares of stock, what variable must be the balancing item? What will its value be?

c. Now suppose that the firm plans instead to increase long-term debt only to $1,100 and does not wish to issue any new shares of stock. Why must the dividend payment now be the balancing item? What will its value be? What is the dividend payout ratio?

13. **Feasible Growth Rates.**

a. What is the 2007 internal growth rate of Eagle Sports (see problem 12) if the dividend payout ratio is fixed at 60 percent and the equity-to-asset ratio is fixed at two-thirds?

b. What is the 2007 sustainable growth rate?

14. **Building Financial Models.** How would Executive Fruit's financial model change if the dividend payout ratio were cut to one-third? Use the revised model to generate a new financial plan for 2006 assuming that debt is the balancing item. Show how the financial statements given in Table 18.6 would change. What would be required external financing?

EXCEL

*15. **Required External Financing.** Executive Fruit's financial manager believes that sales in 2006 could rise by as much as 20 percent or by as little as 5 percent.

a. Recalculate the first-stage pro forma financial statements (Table 18.5) under these two assumptions. How does the rate of growth in revenues affect the firm's need for external funds?

b. Assume any required external funds will be raised by issuing long-term debt and that any surplus funds will be used to retire such debt. Prepare the completed (second-stage) pro forma balance sheet. In the second-stage pro forma, ignore the interest payments on the new debt.

EXCEL

16. **Building Financial Models.** The following tables contain financial statements for Dynastatics Corporation. Although the company has not been growing, it now plans to expand and will increase net fixed assets (that is, assets net of depreciation) by $200,000 per year at the end of the next 5 years and forecasts that the ratio of revenues to total assets will remain at 1.5. Net working capital will equal 50 percent of end-of-year net fixed assets. Annual depreciation is 10 percent of net fixed assets at the start of the year. Fixed costs are expected to remain at $56,000 and variable costs at 80 percent of revenue. The company's policy is to pay out two-thirds of net income as dividends and to maintain a book debt ratio of 25 percent of total capital.

INCOME STATEMENT 2006
($000s)

Revenue	$1,800
Fixed costs	56
Variable costs (80% of revenue)	1,440
Depreciation	80
Interest (8% of beginning-of-year debt)	24
Taxable income	200
Taxes (at 40%)	80
Net income	$ 120

Dividends	$80	
Addition to retained earnings	$40	

BALANCE SHEET, YEAR-END
($000s)

	2006
Assets	
Net working capital	$ 400
Net fixed assets	800
Total assets	$1,200
Liabilities and shareholders' equity	
Debt	$ 300
Equity	900
Total liabilities and shareholders' equity	$1,200

a.   Produce a set of financial statements for 2007.

b.   Now assume that the balancing item is debt, and that no equity is to be issued. Prepare a completed pro forma balance sheet for 2007. What is the projected debt ratio for 2007?

*17.   **Sustainable Growth.** Plank's Plants had net income of $2,000 on sales of $50,000 last year. The firm paid a dividend of $500. Total assets at the end of last year were $100,000, of which $40,000 was financed by debt.

a.   What is the firm's sustainable growth rate?

b.   If the firm grows at its sustainable growth rate, how much debt will be issued in the coming year?

c.   What would be the maximum possible growth rate if the firm did not issue any debt in the coming year?

18.   **Sustainable Growth.** A firm has decided that its optimal capital structure is 100 percent equity financed. It perceives its optimal dividend policy to be a 40 percent payout ratio. Asset turnover is sales/assets = .8, the net profit margin is 10 percent, and the firm has a target growth rate of 5 percent.

a.   Is the firm's target growth rate consistent with its other goals?

b.   If not, by how much does it need to increase asset turnover to achieve its goals?

c.   How much would it need to increase the profit margin instead?

19.   **Internal Growth.** Go Go Industries is growing at 30 percent per year. It is all-equity financed and has total assets of $1 million. Its return on equity is 25 percent. Its plowback ratio is 40 percent.

a.   What is the internal growth rate?

b.   What is the firm's need for external financing this year?

c.   By how much would the firm increase its internal growth rate if it reduced its payout ratio to zero?

d. By how much would such a move reduce the need for external financing? What do you conclude about the relationship between dividend policy and requirements for external financing?

20. **Sustainable Growth.** A firm's net profit margin is 10 percent and its asset turnover ratio is .6. It has no debt, has net income of $10 per share, and pays dividends of $4 per share. What is the sustainable growth rate?

*21. **Internal Growth.** An all-equity-financed firm plans to grow at an annual rate of at least 10 percent. Its return on equity is 18 percent. What is the maximum possible dividend pay-out rate the firm can maintain without resorting to additional equity issues?

22. **Internal Growth.** Suppose the firm in the previous question has a debt-equity ratio of one-third. What is the maximum dividend payout ratio it can maintain without resorting to any external financing?

*23. **Internal Growth.** A firm has an asset turnover ratio of 2.0. Its plowback ratio is 50 percent, and it is all-equity financed. What must its net profit margin be if it wishes to finance 10 percent growth using only internally generated funds?

24. **Internal Growth.** If the net profit margin of the firm in the previous problem is 6 percent, what is the maximum payout ratio that will allow it to grow at 8 percent without resorting to external financing?

*25. **Internal Growth.** If the net profit margin of the firm in problem 23 is 6 percent, what is the maximum possible growth rate that can be sustained without external financing?

26. **Using Percentage of Sales.** The 2006 financial statements for Growth Industries are presented here. Sales and costs in 2007 are projected to be 20 percent higher than in 2006. Both current assets and accounts payable are projected to rise in proportion to sales. The firm is currently operating at full capacity, so it plans to increase fixed assets in proportion to sales. What external financing will be required by the firm? Interest expense in 2007 will equal 10 percent of long-term debt outstanding at the start of the year. The firm will maintain a dividend payout ratio of .4.

INCOME STATEMENT, 2006

Sales	$200,000
Costs	150,000
EBIT	50,000
Interest expense	10,000
Taxable income	40,000
Taxes (at 35%)	14,000
Net income	$ 26,000
Dividends	10,400
Addition to retained earnings	15,600

BALANCE SHEET, 2006

Assets		Liabilities	
Current assets		Current liabilities	
Cash	$ 3,000	Accounts payable	$ 10,000
Accounts receivable	8,000	Total current liabilities	10,000
Inventories	29,000	Long-term debt	100,000
Total current assets	$ 40,000	Shareholders' equity	
Net plant and equipment	160,000	Common stock	15,000
		Retained earnings	75,000
		Total liabilities and	
Total assets	$200,000	shareholders' equity	$200,000

CHALLENGE

EXCEL

EXCEL

27. **Capacity Use and External Financing.** Now suppose that the fixed assets of Growth Industries (from the previous problem) are operating at only 75 percent of capacity. What is required external financing over the next year?

28. **Capacity Use and External Financing.** If Growth Industries from problem 26 is operating at only 75 percent of capacity, how much can sales grow before the firm will need to raise any external funds? Assume that once fixed assets are operating at capacity, they will need to grow thereafter in direct proportion to sales.

29. **Internal Growth.** We will see in Chapter 20 that for many firms, cash and inventory needs may grow less than proportionally with sales. When we recognize this fact, will the firm's internal growth rate be higher or lower than the level predicted by the formula

$$\text{Internal growth rate} = \frac{\text{addition to retained earnings}}{\text{assets}} ?$$

30. **Spreadsheet Problem.** Use a spreadsheet like that in Figure 18.2 to answer the following questions about Executive Fruit:
    a. What would be required external financing if the growth rate is 15 percent and the dividend payout ratio is 60 percent?
    b. Given the assumptions in part (a), what would be the amount of debt and equity issued if the firm wants to maintain its debt-equity ratio at a level of two-thirds?
    c. What formulas would you put in cells H20 and H21 (as well as the corresponding cells in columns F and G) of the spreadsheet in Figure 18.2 to maintain the debt-equity ratio at two-thirds, while forcing the balance sheet to balance (that is, forcing debt + equity = total assets)?

31. **Integrative.** Using the spreadsheet from the previous problem, examine the effect on leverage (debt ratio and interest coverage) and profitability (operating profit margin, ROA, return on invested capital, and ROE) of the following scenarios. Unless otherwise stated, use the forecasting assumptions from the original Executive Fruit problem, as seen in Figure 18.2. Forecast annual pro forma statements for 2006 to 2010.
    a. Annual sales growth is 10 percent and all required external financing will be debt. Will the company breach the bank's requirement that the company's debt ratio not exceed 60 percent?
    b. Same scenario as (a), except that the interest rate on all debt increases from 10 to 15 percent.
    c. Same scenario as (a), except that Executive Fruit keeps its debt ratio at 40 percent.
    d. Same scenario as (a), except that asset investments in 2006 are based on forecasted sales growth of 10 percent but actual sales growth for 2006 is only 5 percent. Forecasted annual sales growth rate for 2007–2010 is 10 percent.

32. **Comprehensive.** Starting with the financial statements for Dynastatics, problem 16, build a spreadsheet like that in Figure 18.2. Assume that the company is operating at full capacity and will invest $200,000 in fixed assets (gross, not net) per year at the start of each of the next five years. Net working capital at the start of each year will equal 50 percent of the beginning-of-year net fixed assets. Create the 2007 beginning-of-year balance sheet by adding the investments in fixed assets and net working capital to the 2006 year-end balance sheet. Dynastatics forecasts that the ratio of revenues to beginning-of-year total assets will be 1.5. Annual depreciation is 10 percent of net fixed assets at the start of the year. Fixed costs are expected to remain at $56,000 and variable costs at 80 percent of revenues. The interest rate is 8 percent, based on the beginning-of-year debt, and the company's tax rate is 40 percent. Hint: At the beginning of 2008, net fixed assets will equal 2007 beginning-of-year net fixed assets plus the 2008 capital expenditures of $200,000, minus 2007 depreciation. Add to the spreadsheet the financial ratios listed in problem 31.

a. Assuming that Dynastatics pays out two-thirds of net income as dividends and maintains a book debt ratio of 25 percent of total capital, produce financial statements for 2007 to 2011.

b. Maintaining the two-thirds dividend payout, but assuming that the balancing item is debt, prepare the five years of pro formas and compare the financial ratios to those in (a).

33. **Integrative.** As shown in Chapter 3, determine the cash flow from assets and financing flows for each forecast year in the previous problem. Assume that interest is a financing expense. Discuss how the different financing assumptions affect the cash flow from assets and the financing flows.

34. **Standard & Poor's.** Go to Market Insight (**www.mcgrawhill.ca/edumarketinsight**). Calculate and compare Canadian National Railway's (CNI) and Canadian Pacific Railway's (CP) internal growth rate and sustainable growth rate by using recent annual data. Calculate the addition to retained earnings as the change in total retained earnings, using retained earnings from the balance sheet. What is the forecasted sales growth rate used by S&P in its Forecasted Values Report for CNR and CP? Are the forecasts consistent with the past performance of each firm?

35. **Standard & Poor's.** Go to Market Insight (**www.mcgrawhill.ca/edumarketinsight**) and copy the balance sheet and income statement for Agrium into Excel. Calculate the average annual sales growth for the past two years. Forecast its pro forma statements for the next two years, assuming that the annual growth rate is double your calculated growth rate. In addition, calculate appropriate leverage, liquidity, and profitability ratios. Assume all assets are acquired at the start of the year and that the interest rate on all debt is 9 percent. Any financial shortfall will be met by issuing new debt. Surplus earnings will pay down debt. Make any other assumptions necessary to complete the forecast.

36. **Internet.** The Web site at **www.strategis.ic.gc.ca/sc_mangb/stepstogrowth/engdoc/ homepage.php** is designed to help entrepreneurs raise funding to grow their businesses. The nine steps in the process of raising financing are summarized at **www.strategis.ic.gc.ca/ sc_mangb/stepstogrowth/engdoc/stepover/ssg-overview4.php**. Click on the first step, "Identify Your Financial Needs" and read the pages. Also read the first step of the accompanying case study, New Tech, starting at **www.strategis.ic.gc.ca/sc_mangb/stepstogrowth/ engdoc/newtech/nt-0-1.php**. The link to the projected financial statements and assumptions for NewTech are found at **www.strategis.ic.gc.ca/sc_mangb/stepstogrowth/engdoc/ newtech/nt-1-1.php**. Outline the details of this step and describe the important role played by financial planning.

37. **Internet.** Thinking about starting a business? Click on the Canadian Banker's Association Guide, Getting Started in Business, at **www.cba.ca/en/publication_list.asp**, to assess whether you are suited to run your own business.

Solutions to Check Points

18.1 Total assets will rise to $2,200. The debt-equity ratio is to be maintained at 2/3. Therefore, debt rises by $80 to $880 and equity rises by $120 to $1,320. Net income will be $220. (See Table 18.2.) If the dividend is fixed at $180, addition to retained earnings will be $40. Therefore, the firm needs to issue $120 − $40 = $80 of new equity and $80 of new debt.

18.2 a. The *total amount* of external financing is unchanged, since the dividend payout is unchanged. The $100,000 increase in total assets will now be financed by a mixture of debt and equity. If the debt-equity ratio is to remain at two-thirds, the firm will need to increase equity by $60,000 and debt by $40,000. Since addition to retained earnings already increases shareholders' equity by $32,000, the firm needs to issue an additional $28,000 of new equity and $40,000 of debt.

b. If dividends are reduced to $60,000 then the required external funds fall by $4,000 to $64,000.

18.3 a. The company currently runs at 75 percent of capacity given the current level of fixed assets. Sales can increase until the company is at 100 percent of capacity; therefore, sales can increase to $60 million × (100/75) = $80 million.

b. If sales were to increase by 50 percent to $90 million, new fixed assets would need to be added. The ratio of assets to sales when the company is operating at 100 percent of capacity (from part a) is $50 million/$80 million = 5/8. Therefore, to support sales of $90 million, the company needs at least $90 million × 5/8 = $56.25 million of fixed assets. This calls for a $6.25 million investment in additional fixed assets.

18.4 a. This question is answered by the planning model. Given assumptions for asset growth, the model will show the need for external financing, and this value can be compared to the firm's plans for such financing.

b. Such a relationship may be assumed and built into the model. However, the model does not help to determine whether it is a reasonable assumption.

c. Financial models do not shed light on the best capital structure. They can tell us only whether contemplated financing decisions are consistent with asset growth.

18.5 a. If the payout ratio were reduced to 25 percent, the maximum growth rate assuming no external financing would be .75 × 16 percent × .6 = 7.2 percent. With a growth rate of 7.2 percent, the forecast increase in assets is .072 × 1,000 = $72. Since no new debt is raised, this increase in assets must be financed with equity. Equity must increase $72. Does the firm produce sufficient additional retained earnings?

Since forecast ROE is 16 percent and starting equity $2,000, net income is forecast to be .16 × 2,000 = $96. Plowback is 75 percent, giving additional retained earnings of .75 × 96 = $72. So the company can grow at 7.2 percent if it uses only its internally generated funds (addition to retained earnings).

b. If the firm also can issue enough debt to maintain its equity-to-asset ratio unchanged, the sustainable growth rate will be .75 × 16 percent = 12 percent. At 12 percent growth, additional assets of .12 × $1,000 = 120 are needed. Of this increase in assets, 40 percent is financed with new debt. Equity must increase 120 − .4 × 120 = $72. Does the firm produce sufficient additional retained earnings?

In (a) we know that the forecast addition to retained earnings is 72. So the firm can grow at 12 percent if it borrows to maintain its capital structure and uses the additional retained earnings.

MINICASE

Zoe Ashtropova, CEO and sole shareholder of Dog Delights, pored over the brochure showing the fully automated baking system capable of producing 1,000 dog biscuits an hour. "Wow!" she thought, "If we had that equipment, we could double our annual production. Just think of all the dog biscuits we could make!" Then reality returned. The equipment cost $1.2 million and would be completely worn out in 10 years. How could the company finance such a huge expenditure? On the other hand, production was at capacity. Without new equipment, sales would grow only with inflation, expected to be 2 percent per year.

Zoe turned her attention to the recent financial statements of her company, shown in Tables 18.11 to 18.13. What would be the impact of the equipment purchase on the company's financial performance? She would prepare annual pro forma financial statements, ending December 31, 2009, and use them to consider different scenarios.

Considering first the sales forecast, Zoe decided she would have to hire a new salesperson and increase the advertising budget. She estimated that sales would increase 20 percent in each of the next 2 years and a further 10 percent in the third year. She figured the incremental annual cost of the salesperson and additional advertising would be $100,000.

With the new equipment, operating costs would be lower. She estimated that 2 percentage points could be shaved off the current COGS/sales ratio. Depreciation on the existing assets would be about $19,000 a year and the depreciation on the new equipment would add an additional $50,000 per year. The company's tax rate was 35 percent.

Turning her attention to the balance sheet, Zoe decided to assume that the new equipment would be purchased immediately. She would create a balance sheet for the beginning of 2007 by adding the $1.2 million equipment expenditure to the 2006 balance sheet. To finance the expenditure, she would draw $200,000 from the bank account and raise the rest from external sources, as detailed below.

Working capital would not be increased until the end of each year. Operating cash requirements were about 1.254 percent of sales. Although the company's stated credit terms were net 35 days, what was the actual average collection period? Furthermore, their competitors were offering 40 days credit. She would start by with the current average collection period and then consider changing it to 40 days. She expected that the new equipment would not change inventory requirements and would forecast inventories using the current inventory/sales ratio. She would do the same for accounts payable and other current liabilities.

Zoe then turned her attention to financing the purchase and any subsequent investments.

The manager of MoneyBank had said she could borrow at 8 percent if the debt-equity ratio was less than .6. Any borrowing beyond that would carry a 10 percent interest rate. And Dog Delights had to continue to repay $10,000 on December 31 on the existing 6 percent loan from Friendly Bank.

Zoe could ask her wealthy Uncle George for equity financing. He liked dividends and Zoe figured he would ask for dividends equal to 5 percent of his investment. On the other hand, he might want to meddle in the operation of the business. Did she really want to put up with him? The more of his money she used, the worse it would be.

Zoe decided to prepare pro formas for several financing scenarios and look at key financial ratios for each. First, she would assume that the equipment purchase was financed with debt. Then she would assume she took her uncle's equity financing. Then she would consider a third option of half-debt and half-equity financing for the purchase. If she needed more financing in any other year, she would assume she could arrange a bank loan. If she had excess financing, she would pay down debt. For each financing scenario, she would also consider the impact on financial performance of Dog Delights achieving only 5 percent annual sales growth. In addition, she would examine the past financial performance of Dog Delights. With all this information, she would evaluate the pros and cons of each financing alternative and decide which one was best for her.

TABLE 18.11

INCOME STATEMENT FOR DOG DELIGHTS FOR THE YEARS ENDED DECEMBER 31, 2004 TO 2006 ($000s)			
	2004	**2005**	**2006**
Sales	2,500	2,774	3,190
Cost of goods sold	1,850	2,081	2,488
Selling, general, and administrative expenses	250	305	383
Depreciation expense	16	18	19
Earnings before interest and taxes (EBIT)	384	370	300
Interest expense	27	26	26
Taxable income	357	344	274
Income taxes	125	120	96
Net income	232	224	178
Allocation of net income			
Addition to retained earnings	202	194	148
Dividends	30	30	30

TABLE 18.12

BALANCE SHEET FOR DOG DELIGHTS as at December 31, 2004 to 2006 ($000s)			
Assets	**2004**	**2005**	**2006**
Current assets			
Cash and marketable securities	50	176	240
Receivables	274	342	481
Inventories	313	370	456
Total current assets	636	888	1,176
Fixed assets			
Property, plant, and equipment	900	900	900
Less accumulated depreciation	187	205	224
Net fixed assets	713	695	676
Total assets	1,349	1,583	1,852
Liabilities and Shareholders' Equity	**2002**	**2003**	**2004**
Current liabilities			
Debt due for repayment	10	10	10
Accounts payable	152	200	327
Other current liabilities	26	28	32
Total current liabilities	188	238	369
Long-term debt	440	430	420
Shareholders' equity			
Common stock	70	70	70
Retained earnings	651	845	993
Total shareholders' equity	721	915	1,063
Total liabilities and shareholders' equity	1,349	1,582	1,852

TABLE 18.13

CASH FLOW FROM ASSETS AND FINANCING FLOWS for the years ended January 31, 2005, and 2006 ($000s)		
Cash flow from assets	**2005**	**2006**
Net income	224	178
Depreciation	18	19
Interest	26	26
Cash flow from operations	268	223
Cash provided by (used in) non-cash net working capital	(76)	(93)
Cash provided by (used in) capital expenditures	(0)	(0)
Cash flow from assets	192	130
Financing Flows		
Interest	26	26
Repayment of debt	10	10
Dividends	30	30
Increase in cash	126	64
Total financing flow	192	130

CHAPTER 19

WORKING CAPITAL MANAGEMENT AND SHORT-TERM PLANNING

Much of this book is devoted to long-term financial decisions such as capital budgeting and the choice of capital structure. These are called *long-term* decisions for two reasons. First, they usually involve long-lived assets or liabilities. Second, they are not easily reversed and thus may commit the firm to a particular course of action for several years.

Short-term financial decisions generally involve short-lived assets and liabilities, and usually they are easily reversed. Compare, for example, a 60-day bank loan for $50 million with a $50 million issue of 20-year bonds. The bank loan is clearly a short-term decision. The firm can repay it two months later and be right back where it started. A firm might conceivably issue a 20-year bond in January and retire it in March, but it would be extremely inconvenient and expensive to do so. In practice, such a bond issue is a long-term decision, not only because of the bond's 20-year maturity, but because the decision to issue it cannot be reversed on short notice.

A financial manager responsible for short-term financial decisions does not have to look far into the future. The decision to take the 60-day bank loan could properly be based on cash flow forecasts for the next few months only. The bond-issue decision will normally reflect forecast cash requirements 5, 10, or more years into the future.

Short-term financial decisions do not involve many of the difficult conceptual issues encountered elsewhere in this book. In a sense, short-term decisions are easier than long-term decisions—but they are not less important. A firm can identify extremely valuable capital investment opportunities, find the precise optimal debt ratio, follow the perfect dividend policy, and yet founder because no one bothers to raise the cash to pay this year's bills. Hence the need for short-term planning.

In this chapter, we will review the major classes of short-term assets and liabilities, show how long-term financing decisions affect the firm's short-term financial planning, and describe how financial managers trace changes in cash and working capital. We will also describe how managers forecast month-by-month cash requirements or surpluses and how they develop short-term investment and financing strategies.

After studying this chapter you should be able to

- Understand *why* the firm needs to invest in net working capital.
- Show how long-term financing policy affects short-term financing requirements.
- Trace a firm's sources and uses of cash and evaluate its need for short-term borrowing.
- Develop a short-term financing plan that meets the firm's need for cash.

19.1   WORKING CAPITAL

THE COMPONENTS OF WORKING CAPITAL

Short-term, or *current*, assets and liabilities are collectively known as working capital. Table 19.1 Panel A gives a breakdown of current assets and liabilities for all non-financial industries in Canada in the third quarter of 1998. Total current assets were over $391 billion and total current liabilities were $335 billion.

Current Assets

One important current asset is *accounts receivable*. Accounts receivable arise because companies do not usually expect customers to pay for their purchases immediately. These unpaid bills are a valuable asset that companies expect to be able to turn into cash in the near future. The bulk of accounts receivable consists of unpaid bills from sales to other companies and are known as *trade credit*. The remainder arises from the sale of goods to the final consumer. These are known as *consumer credit*.

Another important current asset is *inventory*. Inventories may consist of raw materials, work in process, or finished goods awaiting sale and shipment. Table 19.1 Panel A shows that firms in Canada had about 8 percent more invested in accounts receivable than in inventories in 1998. From Panel B of the table, we see that by 2003, investments in accounts receivables were about 20 percent more than in inventories.

The remaining current assets are cash and other current assets. The cash consists partly of dollar bills, but most of the cash is in the form of bank deposits. These may be *demand deposits*

TABLE 19.1, PANEL A

Current assets and liabilities of the Canadian non-financial industry sector, third quarter 1998 ($ millions)

Current Assets		Current Liabilities	
Cash	$ 60,485	Accounts payable and accrued liabilities	$196,580
Accounts receivable	169,706	Other current liabilities	138,657
Inventories	156,331		
Other current assets	5,122		
Total	$391,644	Total	$335,237

Note: Net working capital (current assets − current liabilities) equals $391,644 − $335,650 = $56,407 million.
Source: Adapted from Statistics Canada CANSIM database **http://cansim2.statcan.ca** Table 187-0001.

TABLE 19.1, PANEL B

Important current assets and liabilities of the Canadian non-financial industry sector, third quarter 2003 ($ millions)

Current Assets		Current Liabilities	
Cash	$ 98,897	Accounts payable and accrued liabilities	$ 318,313
Account receivables	261,739	Other current liabilities	106,478
Inventories	217,275		

Source: Adapted from Statistics Canada CANSIM database **http://cansim2.statcan.ca** Table 187-0001.

(money in chequing accounts that the firm can pay out immediately) and *time deposits* (money in savings accounts that can be paid out only with a delay). Other current assets include items such as marketable securities. The principal marketable security is *commercial paper* (short-term unsecured debt sold by other firms). Other securities include *Treasury bills*, which are short-term debts sold by the Canadian government, and provincial and local government securities.

In managing their cash, companies face much the same problem you do. There are always advantages to holding large amounts of ready cash—they reduce the risk of running out of cash and having to borrow more on short notice. On the other hand, there is a cost to holding idle cash balances rather than putting the money to work earning interest. In Chapter 20 we will tell you how the financial manager collects and pays out cash and decides on an optimal cash balance.

Current Liabilities

We have seen that a company's principal current asset consists of unpaid bills. One firm's credit must be another's debit. Therefore, it is not surprising that a company's principal current liability consists of accounts payable—that is, outstanding payments due to other companies.

The other major current liability consists of short-term borrowing. We will have more to say about this later in the chapter.

WORKING CAPITAL AND THE CASH CONVERSION CYCLE

net working capital   Current assets minus current liabilities. Often called working capital.

The difference between current assets and current liabilities is known as **net working capital**, but financial managers often refer to the difference simply (but imprecisely) as *working capital*. Usually current assets exceed current liabilities—that is, firms have positive net working capital. In 1998, for Canadian non-financial companies, current assets were on average about 17 percent higher than current liabilities.

To see why firms need net working capital, imagine a small company, Simple Souvenirs, that makes small novelty items for sale at gift shops. It buys raw materials such as leather, beads, and rhinestones for cash, processes them into finished goods like wallets or costume jewelry, and then sells these goods on credit. Figure 19.1 shows the whole cycle of operations.

If you prepare the firm's balance sheet at the beginning of the process, you see cash (a current asset). If you delay a little, you find the cash replaced first by inventories of raw materials and then by inventories of finished goods (also current assets). When the goods are sold, the inventories give way to accounts receivable (another current asset), and finally, when the customers pay their bills, the firm takes out its profit and replenishes the cash balance.

The components of working capital constantly change with the cycle of operations, but the amount of working capital is fixed. This is one reason net working capital is a useful summary measure of current assets or liabilities.

FIGURE 19.1
Simple cycle of operations

FIGURE 19.2
Cash conversion cycle

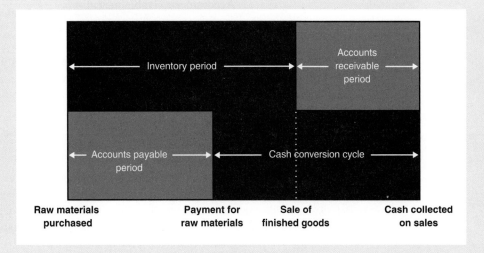

Figure 19.2 depicts four key dates in the production cycle that influence the firm's investment in working capital. The firm starts the cycle by purchasing raw materials, but it does not pay for them immediately. This delay is the *accounts payable period*. The firm processes the raw material and then sells the finished goods. The delay between the initial investment in inventories and the sale date is the *inventory period*. Some time after the firm has sold the goods its customers pay their bills. The delay between the date of sale and the date at which the firm is paid is the accounts *receivable period*.

The top part of Figure 19.2 shows that the *total* delay between initial purchase of raw materials and ultimate payments from customers is the sum of the inventory and accounts receivable periods: first the raw materials must be purchased, processed, and sold, and then the bills must be collected. However, the net time that the company is out of cash is reduced by the time it takes to pay its own bills. The length of time between the firm's payment for its raw materials and the collection of payment from the customer is known as the firm's **cash conversion cycle**. To summarize,

cash conversion cycle
Period between firm's payment for materials and collection on its sales.

$$\text{Cash conversion cycle} = (\text{inventory period} + \text{receivables period}) \quad (19.1)$$
$$- \text{ accounts payable period}$$

The longer the production process, the more cash the firm must keep tied up in inventories. Similarly, the longer it takes customers to pay their bills, the higher the value of accounts receivable. On the other hand, if a firm can delay paying for its own materials, it may reduce the amount of cash it needs. In other words, accounts payable *reduce* net working capital.

In Chapter 17 we showed you how the firm's financial statements can be used to estimate the inventory period, also called days' sales in inventory:

$$\text{Inventory period } = \frac{\text{average inventory}}{\text{annual cost of goods sold}/365} \quad (19.2)$$

The denominator in this equation is the firm's daily output. The ratio of inventory to daily output measures the average number of days from the purchase of the inventories to the final sale.

We can estimate the accounts receivable period and the accounts payable period in a similar way:[1]

---

[1] Because inventories are valued at cost, we divide inventory levels by cost of goods sold rather than sales revenue to obtain the inventory period. This way, both numerator and denominator are measured by cost. The same reasoning applies to the accounts payable period. On the other hand, because accounts receivable are valued at product price, we divide average receivables by daily sales revenue to find the receivables period.

$$\text{Accounts receivable period} = \frac{\text{average accounts receivable}}{\text{annual sales}/365} \qquad (19.3)$$

$$\text{Accounts payable period} = \frac{\text{average accounts payable}}{\text{annual cost of goods sold}/365} \qquad (19.4)$$

EXAMPLE 19.1

CASH CONVERSION CYCLE

Table 19.2 provides the information necessary to compute the cash conversion cycle for non-financial firms in Canada in 2004. We can use the table to answer four questions: How long on average does it take Canadian non-financial firms to produce and sell their product? How long does it take to collect bills? How long does it take to pay bills? And what is the cash conversion cycle?

The delays in collecting cash are given by the inventory and receivables period. The delay in paying bills is given by the payables period. The net delay in collecting payments is the cash conversion cycle. We calculate these periods as follows:

$$\text{Inventory period} = \frac{\text{average inventory}}{\text{annual cost of goods sold}/365} \qquad (19.5)$$

$$= \frac{(218,896 + 222,513)/2}{2,104,620/365} \qquad = 38.3 \text{ days}$$

$$\text{Receivables period} = \frac{\text{average accounts receivable}}{\text{annual sales}/365} \qquad (19.6)$$

$$= \frac{(264,622 + 264,733)/2}{2,144,891/365} \qquad = 45.1 \text{ days}$$

$$\text{Payables period} = \frac{\text{average accounts payable}}{\text{annual cost of goods sold}/365} \qquad (19.7)$$

$$= \frac{(318,058 + 325,240)/2}{2,104,620/365} \qquad = 55.8 \text{ days}$$

The cash conversion cycle is

Inventory period + receivables period − accounts payable period
= 38.3 + 45.1 − 55.8 = 27.6 days

It is therefore taking Canadian non-financial enterprises an average of 28 days, or almost a month, from the time they lay out money on inventories to collect payment from their customers.

TABLE 19.2
These data can be used to calculate the cash conversion cycle for Canadian non-financial enterprises ($ millions)

Income Statement Data		Balance Sheet Data		
Year Ending First Quarter 2004			**End of First Quarter 2003**	**End of First Quarter 2004**
Sales	$ 2,144,891	Inventory	$ 218,896	$ 222,513
Cost of goods sold	2,104,620	Accounts receivable	264,622	264,733
		Accounts payable	318,058	325,240

Source: Adapted from Statistics Canada CANSIM database **http://cansim2.statcan.ca**. Series V634677, V634678, V634688, V634695, and V634715.

Check Point 19.1

a. Suppose Canadian non-financial enterprises are able to reduce inventory levels to a year-average value of $150,000 million and average accounts receivable to $200,000 million. By how many days will this reduce the cash conversion cycle?
b. Suppose that with the same level of inventories, accounts receivable, and accounts payable, Canadian non-financial enterprises can increase production and sales by 10 percent. What will be the effect on the cash conversion cycle?

THE WORKING CAPITAL TRADE-OFF

Of course, the cash conversion cycle is not cast in stone. To a large extent it is within management's control. Working capital can be *managed*. For example, accounts receivable are affected by the terms of credit the firm offers to its customers. You can cut the amount of money tied up in receivables by getting tough with customers who are slow in paying their bills. (You may find, however, that in the future they take their business elsewhere.) Similarly, the firm can reduce its investment in inventories of raw materials. (Here the risk is that it may one day run out of inventories and production will grind to a halt.)

These considerations show that investment in working capital has both costs and benefits. For example, the cost of the firm's investment in receivables is the interest that could have been earned if customers had paid their bills earlier. The firm also forgoes interest income when it holds idle cash balances rather than putting the money to work in marketable securities. The cost of holding inventory includes not only the opportunity cost of capital but also storage and insurance costs and the risk of spoilage or obsolescence. All of these **carrying costs** encourage firms to hold current assets to a minimum.

carrying costs   Costs of maintaining current assets, including opportunity cost of capital.

While carrying costs discourage large investments in current assets, too low a level of current assets makes it more likely that the firm will face **shortage costs**. For example, if the firm runs out of inventory of raw materials, it may have to shut down production. Similarly, a producer holding a small finished goods inventory is more likely to be caught short, unable to fill orders promptly. There are also disadvantages to holding small "inventories" of cash. If the firm runs out of cash, it may have to sell securities and incur unnecessary trading costs. The firm may also maintain too low a level of accounts receivable. If the firm tries to minimize accounts receivable by restricting credit sales, it may lose customers.

shortage costs   Costs incurred from shortages in current assets.

> An important job of the financial manager is to strike a balance between the costs and benefits of current assets, that is, to find the level of current assets that minimizes the sum of carrying costs and shortage costs.

The trade-off between carrying costs and shortage costs is depicted in Figure 19.3. The figure measures the amount of current assets on the horizontal axis and dollar costs on the vertical axis. With zero current assets, there are no carrying costs. However, as investment in current assets goes up, there is a corresponding increase in carrying costs. Shortage costs, on the other hand, are high at low levels of current assets but decline steadily as current assets increase. Total costs, shown as the sum of carrying costs and shortage costs, are lowest (at TC*) when the investment in current assets is at CA*. This is also the optimal level of investment in current assets.

In Chapter 17 we pointed out that in recent years many managers have tried to make their staff more aware of the cost of the capital that is used in the business. So, when they review the performance of each part of their business, they deduct the cost of the capital employed from its profits. This measure is known as *residual income* or *economic value added (EVA)*, which is the term coined by the consulting firm Stern Stewart. Firms that employ EVA to measure performance have often discovered that they can make large savings on working capital. Herman Miller

FIGURE 19.3
The working capital
trade-off and the
optimal investment in
current assets

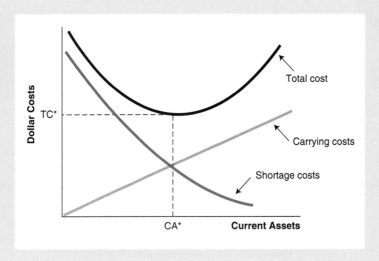

Corporation, the U.S. furniture manufacturer, found that after it introduced EVA, employees became much more conscious of the cash tied up in inventories. One sewing machine operator commented:

> *We used to have these stacks of fabric sitting here on the tables until we needed them . . . We were going to use the fabric anyway, so who cares that we're buying it and stacking it up there? Now no one has excess fabric. They only have stuff we're working on today. And it's changed the way we connect with suppliers, and we're having [them] deliver fabric more often.*[2]

The company also started to look at how rapidly customers paid their bills. It found that, any time an item was missing from an order, the customer would delay payment until all the pieces had been delivered. When the company cleared up the problem of missing items, it made its customers happier and it collected the cash faster.[3]

We will look more carefully at the costs and benefits of working capital in the next two chapters.

Check Point 19.2

How will the following affect the size of the firm's optimal investment in current assets?
a. The interest rate rises from 6 percent to 8 percent.
b. A just-in-time inventory system is introduced that reduces the risk of inventory shortages.
c. Customers pressure the firm for a more lenient credit sales policy.

19.2

LINKS BETWEEN LONG-TERM AND SHORT-TERM FINANCING

Businesses require capital—that is, money invested in plant, machinery, inventories, accounts receivable, and all the other assets it takes to run a company efficiently. Typically, these assets are not purchased all at once but are obtained gradually over time as the firm grows. The total cost of these assets is called the firm's *total capital requirement*.

When we discussed long-term planning in Chapter 18, we showed how the firm needs to develop a sensible strategy that allows it to finance its long-term goals and weather possible setbacks.

---

[2] A. Ehrbar, *EVA: The Real Key to Creating Wealth* (New York: John Wiley & Sons, 1998), pp. 130–131.

[3] A. Ehrbar and G. Bennett Stewart III, "The EVA Revolution," *Journal of Applied Corporate Finance* 12 (Summer 1999), pp. 18–31.

But the firm's total capital requirement does not grow smoothly and the company must be able to meet temporary demands for cash. This is the focus of short-term financial planning.

Figure 19.4 illustrates the growth in the firm's total capital requirements. The upward-sloping line shows that as the business grows, it is likely to need additional fixed assets and current assets. You can think of this trendline as showing the base level of capital that is required. In addition to this base capital requirement, there may be seasonal fluctuations in the business that require an additional investment in current assets. Thus the wavy line in the illustration shows that the total capital requirement peaks late in each year. In practice, there would also be week-to-week and month-to-month fluctuations in the capital requirement, but these are not shown in Figure 19.4.

The total capital requirement can be met through either long- or short-term financing. When long-term financing does not cover the total capital requirement, the firm must raise short-term capital to make up the difference. When long-term financing more than covers the total capital requirement, the firm has surplus cash available for short-term investment. Thus the amount of long-term financing raised, given the total capital requirement, determines whether the firm is a short-term borrower or lender.

The three panels in Figure 19.5 illustrate alternate approaches of long-term versus short-term financing. Each depicts a different long-term financing strategy. The "relaxed strategy" in panel (a) always implies a short-term cash surplus. This surplus will be invested in marketable securities. The "restrictive" policy illustrated in panel (c) implies a permanent need for short-term borrowing. Finally, panel (b) illustrates an intermediate strategy: the firm has spare cash, which it can lend out during the part of the year when total capital requirements are relatively low, but it is a borrower during the rest of the year when capital requirements are relatively high.

What is the best level of long-term financing relative to the total capital requirement? It is hard to say. We can make several practical observations, however.

1. *Matching Maturities.* Most financial managers attempt to "match maturities" of assets and liabilities. That is, they finance long-lived assets like plant and machinery with long-term borrowing and equity. Short-term assets like inventory and accounts receivable are financed with short-term bank loans or by issuing short-term debt like commercial paper.
2. *Permanent Working-Capital Requirements.* Most firms have a permanent investment in net working capital (current assets less current liabilities). By this we mean that they plan to have a positive amount of working capital at all times. This is financed from long-term sources. This is an extension of the maturity-matching principle. Since the working capital is permanent, it is funded with long-term sources of financing.

FIGURE 19.4
The firm's total capital requirement grows over time. It also exhibits seasonal variation around the trend.

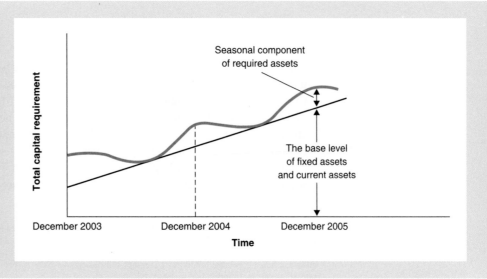

FIGURE 19.5

Alternative approaches to long- versus short-term financing.

(a) Relaxed strategy, where the firm is always a short-term lender

(b) Middle-of-the-road policy

(c) Restrictive policy, where the firm is always a short-term borrower

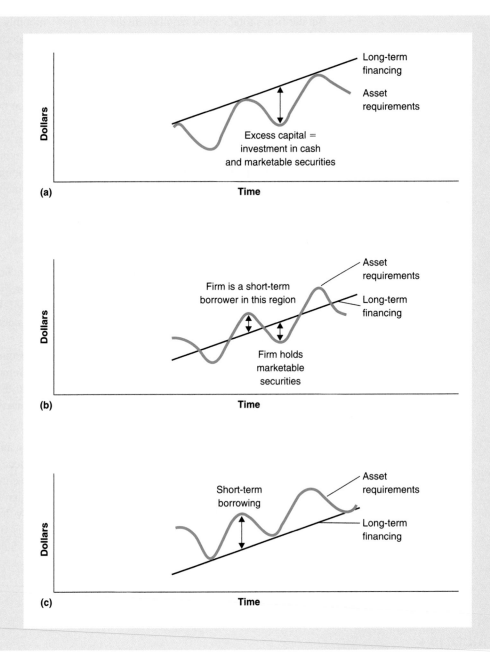

3. *The Comforts of Surplus Cash.* Many financial managers would feel more comfortable under the relaxed strategy illustrated in Figure 19.5a than the restrictive strategy in panel (c). Consider, for example, General Motors. At the end of 2001 it was sitting on a cash mountain of over $8 billion (US), almost certainly far more than it needed to meet any seasonal fluctuations in its capital requirements. Firms with such a surplus of long-term financing never have to worry about borrowing to pay next month's bills. But is the financial manager paid to be comfortable? Firms usually put surplus cash to work in Treasury bills or other marketable securities. This is at best a zero-NPV investment for a tax-paying firm.[4] Thus we think that

---

[4] Why do we say *at best* zero NPV? Not because we worry that the Treasury bills may be overpriced. Instead, we worry that when the firm holds Treasury bills, the interest income is subject to double taxation, first at the corporate level, and then again at the personal level when the income is passed through to investors as dividends. The extra layer of taxation can make corporate holdings of Treasury bills a negative-NPV investment, even if the bills would provide a fair rate of interest to an individual investor.

firms with a permanent cash surplus ought to go on a diet, retiring long-term securities to reduce long-term financing to a level at or below the firm's total capital requirement. That is, if the firm is described by panel (a), it ought to move down to panel (b), or perhaps even lower.

19.3 TRACING CHANGES IN CASH AND WORKING CAPITAL

Table 19.3 compares 2003 and 2004 year-end balance sheets for Dynamic Mattress Company. Table 19.4 shows the firm's income statement for 2004. Note that Dynamic's cash balance increases from $4 million to $5 million in 2004. What caused this increase? Did the extra cash come from Dynamic Mattress Company's additional long-term borrowing? From reinvested earnings? From cash released by reducing inventory? Perhaps it came from extra credit extended by Dynamic's suppliers. (Note the increase in accounts payable.)

The correct answer? All of the above. There is rarely any point in linking a particular source of funds with a particular use. Instead, financial analysts list the various sources and uses of cash in a statement like the one shown in Table 19.5. The statement shows that Dynamic *generated* cash from the following sources:

1. It issued $7 million of long-term debt.
2. It reduced inventory, releasing $1 million.
3. It increased its accounts payable, in effect borrowing an additional $7 million from its suppliers.
4. By far the largest source of cash was Dynamic's operations, which generated $16 million. Note that the $12 million net income reported in Table 19.4 understates cash flow because depreciation is deducted in calculating income. Depreciation is not a cash outlay. Thus it must be added back in order to obtain operating cash flow.

TABLE 19.3
Year-end balance sheets for Dynamic Mattress Company ($ millions)

Assets	2003	2004	Liabilities and Shareholders' Equity	2003	2004
Current assets			Current liabilities		
Cash	$ 4	$ 5	Bank loans	$ 5	$ 0
Marketable securities	0	5	Accounts payable	20	27
Inventory	26	25	Total current liabilities	$ 25	$ 27
Accounts receivable	25	30	Long-term debt	5	12
Total current assets	$ 55	$ 65	Net worth (equity and retained earnings)	65	76
Fixed assets			Total liabilities and owners' equity	$ 95	$ 115
Gross investment	$ 56	$ 70			
Less depreciation	16	20			
Net fixed assets	$ 40	$ 50			
Total assets	$ 95	$115			

TABLE 19.4
Income statement for Dynamic Mattress Company, 2004 ($ millions)

Sales	$ 350
Operating costs	321
Depreciation	4
EBIT	25
Interest	1
Pretax income	24
Tax at 50 percent	12
Net income	$ 12

Note: Dividend = $1 million; retained earnings = $11 million.

TABLE 19.5
Sources and uses of cash for Dynamic Mattress Company, 2004 ($ millions)

Sources		
Issued long-term debt	$	7
Reduced inventories		1
Increased accounts payable		7
Cash from operations		
Net income		12
Depreciation		4
Total sources	$	31
Uses		
Repaid short-term bank loan	$	5
Invested in fixed assets		14
Purchased marketable securities		5
Increased accounts receivable		5
Dividend		1
Total uses	$	30
Increase in cash balance	$	1

Dynamic *used* cash for the following purposes:

1. It paid a $1 million dividend. (Note: The $11 million increase in Dynamic's equity is due to retained earnings: $12 million of equity income, less the $1 million dividend.)
2. It repaid a $5 million short-term bank loan.
3. It invested $14 million. This shows up as the increase in gross fixed assets in Table 19.3.
4. It purchased $5 million of marketable securities.
5. It allowed accounts receivable to expand by $5 million. In effect, it lent this additional amount to its customers.

Check Point 19.3

How will the following affect cash and net working capital?
a. The firm takes out a short-term bank loan and uses the funds to pay off some of its accounts payable.
b. The firm uses cash on hand to buy raw materials.
c. The firm repurchases outstanding shares of stock.
d. The firm sells long-term bonds and puts the proceeds in its bank account.

19.4   CASH BUDGETING

The financial manager's task is to forecast *future* sources and uses of cash. These forecasts serve two purposes. First, they alert the financial manager to future cash needs. Second, the cash flow forecasts provide a standard, or budget, against which subsequent performance can be judged.

There are several ways to produce a quarterly cash budget. Many large firms have developed elaborate "corporate models"; others use a spreadsheet program to plan their cash needs. The procedures of smaller firms may be less formal. But no matter what method is chosen, there are three common steps to preparing a cash budget:

Step 1.   Forecast the sources of cash. The largest inflow of cash comes from payments by the firm's customers.
Step 2.   Forecast uses of cash.
Step 3.   Calculate whether the firm is facing a cash shortage or surplus.

The financial plan sets out a strategy for investing a cash surplus or financing any deficit. We will illustrate these issues by continuing the example of Dynamic Mattress.

FORECAST SOURCES OF CASH

Most of Dynamic's cash inflow comes from the sale of mattresses. We therefore start with a sales forecast by quarter for 2005:[5]

Quarter:	First	Second	Third	Fourth
Sales, millions of dollars	87.5	78.5	116	131

However, unless customers pay cash on delivery, sales become accounts receivable before they become cash. Cash flow comes from *collections* on accounts receivable.

Most firms keep track of the average time it takes customers to pay their bills. From this they can forecast what proportion of a quarter's sales is likely to be converted into cash in that quarter and what proportion is likely to be carried over to the next quarter as accounts receivable. This proportion depends on the lags with which customers pay their bills. For example, if customers wait one month to pay their bills, then on average one-third of each quarter's bills will not be paid until the following quarter. If the payment delay is two months, then two-thirds of quarterly sales will be collected in the following quarter.

Suppose that 80 percent of sales are collected in the immediate quarter and the remaining 20 percent in the next. Table 19.6 shows forecast collections under this assumption.

In the first quarter, for example, collections from current sales are 80 percent of $87.5 million, or $70 million. But the firm also collects 20 percent of the previous quarter's sales, or .20 × $75 million = $15 million. Therefore, total collections are $70 million + $15 million = $85 million.

Dynamic started the first quarter with $30 million of accounts receivable. The quarter's sales of $87.5 million were *added* to accounts receivable, but $85 million of collections was *subtracted*. Therefore, as Table 19.6 shows, Dynamic ended the quarter with accounts receivable of $30 million + $87.5 million − $85 million = $32.5 million. The general formula is

$$\text{Ending accounts receivable} = \frac{\text{beginning accounts receivable}}{+ \text{ sales} - \text{collections}} \tag{19.8}$$

The top section of Table 19.7 shows forecast sources of cash for Dynamic Mattress. Collection of receivables is the main source but it is not the only one. Perhaps the firm plans to dispose of some land or expects a tax refund or payment of an insurance claim. All such items are included as "other" sources. It is also possible that you may raise additional capital by borrowing or selling stock, but we don't want to prejudge that question. Therefore, for the moment we just assume that Dynamic will not raise further long-term finance.

TABLE 19.6
Dynamic Mattress's collections on accounts receivable, 2005 ($ millions)

		Quarter			
		First	Second	Third	Fourth
1.	Receivables at start of period	$ 30	$ 32.5	$ 30.7	$ 38.2
2.	Sales	87.5	78.5	116	131
3.	Collections				
	Sales in current period (80%)	70	62.8	92.8	104.8
	Sales in last period (20%)	15[a]	17.5	15.7	23.2
	Total collections	$ 85	$ 80.3	$108.5	$128
4.	Receivables at end of period (4 = 1 + 2 − 3)	$ 32.5	$ 30.7	$ 38.2	$ 41.2

[a] Sales in the fourth quarter of the previous year were $75 million.

[5] For simplicity, we present a quarterly forecast. However, most firms would forecast by month instead of by quarter. Sometimes weekly or even daily forecasts are made.

TABLE 19.7
Dynamic Mattress's cash
budget for 2005 ($ millions)

	Quarter			
	First	Second	Third	Fourth
Sources of cash				
Collections on accounts receivable	$ 85	$ 80.3	$ 108.5	$128
Other	1.5	0	12.5	0
Total sources of cash	$ 86.5	$ 80.3	$ 121	$128
Uses of cash				
Payments of accounts payable	$ 65	$ 60	$ 55	$ 50
Labour and administrative expenses	30	30	30	30
Capital expenditures	32.5	1.3	5.5	8
Taxes, interest, and dividends	4	4	4.5	5
Total uses of cash	$131.5	$ 95.3	$ 95	$ 93
Net cash inflow equals sources minus uses	–$ 45	–$ 15	+$ 26	+$ 35

FORECAST USES OF CASH

There always seem to be many more uses for cash than there are sources. The second section of Table 19.7 shows how Dynamic expects to use cash. For simplicity, in Table 19.7 we condensed the uses into four categories:

1. *Payments of Accounts Payable.* Dynamic has to pay its bills for raw materials, parts, electricity, and so on. The cash flow forecast assumes all these bills are paid on time, although Dynamic could probably delay payment to some extent. Delayed payment is sometimes called stretching your payables. Stretching is one source of short-term financing, but for most firms it is an expensive source, because by stretching they lose discounts given to firms that pay promptly. (This is discussed in more detail in Chapter 21.)
2. *Labour, Administrative, and Other Expenses.* This category includes all other regular business expenses.
3. *Capital Expenditures.* Note that Dynamic Mattress plans a major outlay of cash in the first quarter to pay for a long-lived asset.
4. *Taxes, Interest, and Dividend Payments.* This includes interest on currently outstanding long-term debt and dividend payments to shareholders.

THE CASH BALANCE

The forecast net inflow of cash (sources minus uses) is shown on the bottom row of Table 19.7. Note the large negative figure for the first quarter: a $45 million forecast *outflow*. There is a smaller forecast *outflow* in the second quarter and then substantial cash inflows in the second half of the year.

Table 19.8 calculates how much financing Dynamic will have to raise if its cash flow forecasts are right. It starts the year with $5 million in cash. There is a $45 million cash outflow in the first quarter, and so Dynamic will have to obtain at least $45 million – $5 million = $40 million of additional financing. This would leave the firm with a forecast cash balance of exactly zero at the start of the second quarter.

TABLE 19.8
Short-term financing
requirements for Dynamic
Mattress ($ millions)

	First	Second	Third	Fourth
Cash at start of period	$ 5	–$40	–$55	–$29
+ Net cash inflow (from Table 19.7)	– 45	– 15	+ 26	+ 35
= Cash at end of period[a]	– 40	– 55	– 29	+ 6
Minimum operating cash balance	5	5	5	5
Cumulative short-term financing required (minimum cash balance minus cash at end of period)[b]	$45	$60	$34	–$ 1

[a] Of course, firms cannot literally hold a negative amount of cash. This line shows the amount of cash the firm will have to raise to pay its bills.
[b] A negative sign indicates that no short-term financing is required. Instead the firm has a cash surplus.

Most financial managers regard a planned cash balance of zero as driving too close to the edge of the cliff. They establish a *minimum operating cash balance* to absorb unexpected cash inflows and outflows. We will assume that Dynamic's minimum operating cash balance is $5 million. That means it will have to raise $45 million instead of $40 million in the first quarter, and $15 million more in the second quarter. Thus its *cumulative* financing requirement is $60 million in the second quarter. Fortunately, this is the peak; the cumulative requirement declines in the third quarter when its $26 million net cash inflow reduces its cumulative financing requirement to $34 million. (Notice that the change in cumulative short-term financing in Table 19.8 equals the net cash inflow in that quarter from Table 19.7.) In the final quarter Dynamic is out of the woods. Its $35 million net cash inflow is enough to eliminate short-term financing and actually increase cash balances above the $5 million minimum acceptable balance.

Before moving on, we offer two general observations about this example:

1. The large cash outflows in the first two quarters do not necessarily spell trouble for Dynamic Mattress. In part they reflect the capital investment made in the first quarter: Dynamic is spending $32.5 million, but it should be acquiring an asset worth that much or more. The cash outflows also reflect low sales in the first half of the year; sales recover in the second half.[6] If this is a predictable seasonal pattern, the firm should have no trouble borrowing to help it get through the slow months.
2. Table 19.7 is only a best guess about future cash flows. It is a good idea to think about the *uncertainty* in your estimates. For example, you could undertake a sensitivity analysis, in which you inspect how Dynamic's cash requirements would be affected by a shortfall in sales or by a delay in collections.

Check Point 19.4   Calculate Dynamic Mattress's quarterly cash receipts, net cash inflow, and cumulative short-term financing required if customers pay for only 60 percent of purchases in the current quarter and pay the remaining 40 percent in the following quarter.

Our next step will be to develop a short-term financing plan that covers the forecast requirements in the most economical way possible. Before presenting such a plan, however, we should pause briefly to point out that short-term financial planning, like long-term planning, is best done on a computer. The nearby Excel Spreadsheet box presents the spreadsheets underlying tables 19.6 to 19.8. The spreadsheet on the top presents the data appearing in the tables; the one on the bottom presents the underlying formulas. Examine those formulas and note which items are inputs (for example, rows 15–18) and which are calculated from equations. The formulas also indicate the links from one table to another. For example, in the spreadsheet, collections of receivables are calculated in Table 19.6 (row 6), and passed through as inputs in Table 19.7 (row 11). Similarly, net cash inflow in Table 19.7 (row 20) is passed along to Table 19.8 (row 24).

SEE BOX P. 606

Once the spreadsheet is set up, it becomes easy to explore the consequences of many what-if questions. For example, Check Point 19.4 asks you to recalculate the quarterly cash receipts, net cash inflow, and cumulative short-term financing required if the firm's collections on accounts receivable slow down. You can obviously do this by hand, but it is quicker and easier to do it in a spreadsheet—especially when there might be dozens of scenarios that you must work through!

19.5   A SHORT-TERM FINANCING PLAN

OPTIONS FOR SHORT-TERM FINANCING

Suppose that Dynamic can borrow up to $40 million from the bank at an interest cost of 8 percent per year or 2 percent per quarter. Dynamic can also raise capital by putting off paying its

---

[6] Maybe people buy more mattresses late in the year when the nights are longer.

	A	B	C	D	E
1	Quarter:	First	Second	Third	Fourth
2					
3	**Accounts receivable (Table 19.6)**				
4	Receivables (beginning period)	30.0	32.5	3.7	38.2
5	Sales	87.5	78.5	116.0	131.0
6	Collections	85.0	80.3	108.5	128.0
7	Receivables (end period)	32.5	30.7	38.2	41.2
8					
9	**Cash budget (Table 19.7)**				
10	**Sources of cash**				
11	Collections of accounts receivable	85.0	80.3	108.5	128.0
12	Other	1.5	0.0	12.5	0.0
13	Total sources	86.5	80.3	121.0	128.0
14	**Uses**				
15	Payments of accounts payable	65.0	60.0	55.0	50.0
16	Labour & administrative expenses	30.0	30.0	30.0	30.0
17	Capital expenses	32.5	1.3	5.5	8.0
18	Taxes, interest, & dividends	4.0	4.0	4.5	5.0
19	Total uses	131.5	95.3	95.0	93.0
20	**Net cash inflow**				
21					
22	**Short-term financing requirements (Table 19.8)**				
23	Cash at start of period	5.0	–40.0	–55.0	–29.0
24	+ Net cash inflow	–45.0	–15.0	26.0	35.0
25	= Cash at end of period	–40.0	–55.0	–29.0	6.0
26	Minimum operating balance	5.0	5.0	5.0	5.0
27	Cumulative short-term financing required	45.0	60.0	34.0	–1.0

	A	B	C	D	E
1	Quarter:	First	Second	Third	Fourth
2					
3	**Accounts receivable (Table 19.6)**				
4	Receivables (beginning period)	30	=B7	=C7	=D7
5	Sales	87.5	78.5	116.0	131.0
6	Collections	=75*0.2+B5*0.8	=B5*0.2+C5*0.8	=C5*0.2+D5*0.8	=D5*0.2+E5*0.8
7	Receivables (end period)	=B4+B5+B6	=C4+C5+C6	=D4+D5+D6	=E4+E5+E6
8					
9	**Cash budget (Table 19.7)**				
10	**Sources of cash**				
11	Collections of accounts receivable	=B6	=C6	=D6	=E6
12	Other	1.5	0.0	12.5	0.0
13	Total sources	=B11+B12	=C11+C12	=D11+D12	=E11+E12
14	**Uses**				
15	Payments of accounts payable	65.0	60.0	55.0	50.0
16	Labour & administrative expenses	30.0	30.0	30.0	30.0
17	Capital expenses	32.5	1.3	5.5	8.0
18	Taxes, interest, & dividends	4.0	4.0	4.5	5.0
19	Total uses	=SUM(B15:B18)	=SUM(C15:C18)	=SUM(D15:D18)	=SUM(E15:E18)
20	**Net cash inflow**	=B13-B19	=C13-C19	=D13-D19	=E13-E19
21					
22	**Short-term financing requirements (Table 19.8)**				
23	Cash at start of period	5.0	=B25	=C25	=D25
24	+ Net cash inflow	=B20	=C20	=D20	=E20
25	= Cash at end of period	=B23+B24	=C23+C24	=D23+D24	=E23+E24
26	Minimum operating balance	5.0	=B26	=C26	=D26
27	Cumulative short-term financing required	=B26-B25	=C26-C25	=D26-D25	=E26-E25

bills and thus increasing its accounts payable. In effect, this is taking a loan from its suppliers. The financial manager believes that Dynamic can defer the following amounts in each quarter:

Quarter:	First	Second	Third	Fourth
Amount deferrable, millions of dollars	52	48	44	40

That is, $52 million can be saved in the first quarter by not paying bills in that quarter. (Note that Table 19.7 was prepared assuming these bills are paid in the first quarter.) If deferred, these payments *must* be made in the second quarter. Similarly, $48 million of the second quarter's bills can be deferred to the third quarter and so on.

Stretching payables is often costly, however, even if no ill will is incurred.[7] This is because many suppliers offer discounts for prompt payment, so that Dynamic loses the discount if it pays late. In this example we assume the lost discount is 5 percent of the amount deferred. In other words, if a $52 million payment is delayed in the first quarter, the firm must pay 5 percent more, or $54.6 million in the next quarter. This is like borrowing at an annual interest rate of over 20 percent ($1.05^4 - 1 = .216$, or 21.6 percent).

With these two options, the short-term financing strategy is obvious: use the lower-cost bank loan first. Stretch payables only if you can't borrow enough from the bank.

Table 19.9 shows the resulting plan. The first panel (cash requirements) sets out the cash that needs to be raised in each quarter. The second panel (cash raised) describes the various sources of financing the firm plans to use. The third and fourth panels describe how the firm will use net cash inflows when they turn positive.

TABLE 19.9
Dynamic Mattress's financing plan ($ millions)

		Quarter		
	First	Second	Third	Fourth
Cash requirements				
1. Cash required for operations[a]	$ 45	$15	–$ 26	–$35
2. Interest on bank loan[b]	0	0.8	0.8	0.6
3. Interest on stretched payables[c]	0	0	0.8	0
4. Total cash required	$ 45	$15.8	–$ 24.4	–$34.4
Cash raised				
5. Bank loan	$ 40	$ 0	$ 0	$ 0
6. Stretched payables	0	15.8	0	0
7. Securities sold	5	0	0	0
8. Total cash raised	$ 45	$15.8	$ 0	$ 0
Repayments				
9. Of stretched payables	0	0	$ 15.8	$ 0
10. Of bank loan	0	0	8.6	$31.4
Increase in cash balances				
11. Addition to cash balances	$ 0	$ 0	$ 0	$ 3
Line of credit				
12. Beginning of quarter	$ 0	$40	$ 40	$31.4
13. End of quarter	40	40	31.4	0

[a] From Table 19.7, bottom line. A negative cash requirement implies positive cash flow from operations.
[b] The interest rate on the bank loan is 2 percent per quarter applied to the bank loan outstanding at the start of the quarter. Thus the interest due in the second quarter is .02 × $40 million = $.8 million.
[c] The "interest" cost of the stretched payables is 5 percent of the amount of payment deferred. For example, in the third quarter, 5 percent of the $15.8 million stretched in the second quarter is about $.8 million.

---

[7] In fact, ill will is likely to be incurred. Firms that stretch payments risk being labelled as credit risks. Since stretching is so expensive, suppliers reason that only customers that cannot obtain credit at reasonable rates elsewhere will resort to it. Suppliers naturally are reluctant to act as the lender of last resort.

In the first quarter, the plan calls for borrowing the full amount available from the bank ($40 million). In addition, the firm sells the $5 million of marketable securities it held at the end of 2004. Thus, under this plan, it raises the necessary $45 million in the first quarter.

In the second quarter, an additional $15 million must be raised to cover the net cash outflow predicted in Table 19.7. In addition, $.8 million must be raised to pay interest on the bank loan. Therefore, the plan calls for Dynamic to maintain its bank borrowing and to stretch $15.8 million in payables. Notice that in the first two quarters, when net cash flow from operations is negative, the firm maintains its cash balance at the minimum acceptable level. Additions to cash balances are zero. Similarly, repayments of outstanding debt are zero. In fact, outstanding debt rises in each of these quarters.

In the third and fourth quarters, the firm generates a cash flow surplus, so the plan calls for Dynamic to pay off its debt. First it pays off stretched payables, as it is required to do, and then it uses any remaining cash flow surplus to pay down its bank loan. In the third quarter, all of the net cash inflow is used to reduce outstanding short-term borrowing. In the fourth quarter, the firm pays off its remaining short-term borrowing and uses the extra $3 million to increase its cash balances.

Check Point 19.5

Revise Dynamic Mattress's short-term financial plan assuming it can borrow up to $45 million through its line of credit. Assume that the firm will still sell its $5 million of short-term securities in the first quarter.

EVALUATING THE PLAN

Does the plan shown in Table 19.9 solve Dynamic's short-term financing problem? No—the plan is feasible but Dynamic can probably do better. The most glaring weakness of this plan is its reliance on stretching payables, an extremely expensive financing device. Remember that it costs Dynamic 5 percent *per quarter* to delay paying bills—20 percent per year at simple interest. This first plan should merely stimulate the financial manager to search for cheaper sources of short-term borrowing.

The financial manager would ask several other questions as well. For example:

1. Does Dynamic need a larger reserve of cash or marketable securities, say, to guard against its customers stretching *their* payables (thus slowing down collections on accounts receivable)?
2. Does the plan yield satisfactory current and quick ratios?[8] Its bankers may be worried if these ratios deteriorate.
3. Are there hidden costs to stretching payables? Will suppliers begin to doubt Dynamic's creditworthiness?
4. Does the plan for 2005 leave Dynamic in good financial shape for 2006? (Here the answer is yes, since Dynamic will have paid off all short-term borrowing by the end of the year.)
5. Should Dynamic try to arrange long-term financing for the major capital expenditure in the first quarter? This seems sensible, following the rule of thumb that long-term assets deserve long-term financing. It would also dramatically reduce the need for short-term borrowing. A counterargument is that Dynamic is financing the capital investment *only temporarily* by short-term borrowing. By year-end, the investment is paid for by cash from operations. Thus Dynamic's initial decision not to seek immediate long-term financing may reflect a preference for ultimately financing the investment with retained earnings.
6. Perhaps the firm's operating and investment plans can be adjusted to make the short-term financing problem easier. Is there any easy way of deferring the first quarter's large cash outflow? For example, suppose that the large capital investment in the first quarter is for new

---

[8] These ratios are discussed in Chapter 17.

mattress-stuffing machines to be delivered and installed in the first half of the year. The new machines are not scheduled to be ready for full-scale use until August. Perhaps the machine manufacturer could be persuaded to accept 60 percent of the purchase price on delivery and 40 percent when the machines are installed and operating satisfactorily.

> Short-term financing plans must be developed by trial and error. You lay out one plan, think about it, then try again with different assumptions about financing and investment alternatives. You continue until you can think of no further improvements.

19.6 SOURCES OF SHORT-TERM FINANCING

We suggested that Dynamic's manager might want to investigate alternative sources of short-term borrowing. Here are some of the possibilities.

BANK LOANS

line of credit Agreement by a bank that a company may borrow at any time up to an established limit.

The simplest and most common source of short-term financing is an unsecured loan from a bank. For example, Dynamic might have a standing arrangement with its bank allowing it to borrow up to $40 million. The firm can borrow and repay whenever it wants so long as it does not exceed the credit limit. This kind of arrangement is called a **line of credit**.

commitment fee Fee charged by the lender on the unused portion of a line of credit.

Lines of credit are typically reviewed annually, and it is possible that the bank may seek to cancel it if the firm's creditworthiness deteriorates. If the firm wants to be sure that it will be able to borrow, it can enter into a *revolving credit agreement* with the bank. Revolving credit arrangements usually last for a few years and formally commit the bank to lending up to the agreed limit. In return the bank will require the firm to pay a **commitment fee**; for example, it could be .25 percent of the unused amount.

EXAMPLE 19.2   **COMMITMENT FEES**

Goofy Eatery Inc. has entered into a $1,000,000 revolving credit arrangement with its bank with a commitment fee of 0.5 percent, which will apply on the average unused portion of the loan. The interest on any funds borrowed will be 6 percent per year. At the end of the year, it is determined that the firm has, on average, used up only $600,000 of its credit limit. The interest on the loan for the year is, therefore, $600,000 \times 0.06 = $36,000. In addition, a commitment fee is applicable on the average funds unused, that is $1,000,000 - $600,000 = $400,000. This works out to 0.5 percent of $400,000, or $2,000. The interest and commitment fee together total $36,000 + $2,000 = $38,000.

---

term loans Loans that last for several years.

Most bank loans have durations of only a few months. For example, Dynamic may need a loan to cover a seasonal increase in inventories, and the loan is then repaid as the goods are sold. However, banks also make **term loans**, which last for several years. These term loans sometimes involve huge sums of money, and in this case they may be parcelled out among a syndicate of banks. For example, when Eurotunnel needed to arrange more than $10 billion (US) of borrowing to construct the tunnel between Britain and France, a syndicate of more than 200 international banks combined to provide the cash.

syndicated loans Loans provided by a group of banks that combine to provide the loan amount.

In a syndicated loan arrangement, a group of commercial and investment banks combine to put together the loan; however, one bank usually plays the role of lead financial institution. **Syndicated loans** generally tend to be of medium-term maturity (that is, up to five years), although lenders have arranged for such loans for periods ranging from three months to

20 years.[9] This market is very large in the United States, which accounts for 60 percent of all global syndicated loan issues. Canada's share of this market, at roughly 4 percent, is much smaller. The big Canadian banks are quite active with syndicated loans, particularly in the United States. Major international banks often are confronted with borrowers requiring large-size loans, which they may have difficulty servicing on their own. On the other hand, smaller, regional banks may have excess funds on hand after meeting the needs of regional borrowers. By joining forces and lending as a syndicate, the larger and smaller banks can create a flexible source of financing that is beneficial to lenders and borrowers alike. In Canada, there is no market that facilitates the trading of syndicated loans. In the United States, there is a secondary market where such loans are traded. The New York–based Loans Syndications and Trading Association is a not-for-profit organization that seeks to promote the development of a fair, efficient, liquid and professional trading market for such loans. The association's Web site at **www.lsta.org** provides details regarding the daily trading activity of selected syndicated loans.

COMMERCIAL PAPER

When banks lend money, they provide two services. They match up would-be borrowers and lenders, and they check that the borrower is likely to repay the loan. Banks recover the costs of providing these services by charging borrowers on average a higher interest rate than they pay to lenders. These services are less necessary for large, well-known companies that regularly need to raise large amounts of cash. These companies have increasingly found it profitable to bypass the bank and to sell short-term debt, known as **commercial paper**, directly to large investors. Banks have been forced to respond by reducing the interest rates on their loans to blue-chip customers.

commercial paper Short-term unsecured notes issued by firms.

In Canada, commercial paper can sometimes have a maturity of a year, although corporations mostly issue these instruments for periods of one, two or three months. Commercial paper is not secured, but companies generally back up their issue of paper by arranging a special line of credit with a bank. This guarantees that they can find the money to repay the paper and the risk of default is therefore small.

Some companies regularly sell commercial paper in huge amounts. For example, the giant U.S. financial services company GE Capital Corporation had about $111 billion (US) of commercial paper in use at the end of 2001. George Weston had about $696 million of outstanding commercial paper in 2003.

Rating organizations often provide information to investors regarding the quality and risk of different commercial paper issues. For instance, Dominion Bond Rating Service provides the following categories of ratings for commercial paper issues:[10]

R-1 (high, medium, or low): Prime credit quality securities
R-2 (high, medium, or low): Adequate credit quality securities
R-3 (high, medium, or low): Speculative securities
D: Securities in, or likely to be in, arrears

An R-1 (high) rating indicates the best possible credit rating whereas an R-3 (low) rating signifies a highly speculative issue. Firms with R-3–rated issues are likely to have unstable earnings and low profitability. If a security is rated D, it means that the issuer has missed a scheduled payment, such as interest, or is going to miss such a payment in the near future. The rate of return, or yield, on commercial paper tends to differ according to the issue's credit rating. Higher-rated issues carry lower yields than lower-rated ones. Commercial paper issues may carry yields of one or two percentage points below the prime rate, which tends to fluctuate with changing economic conditions and general levels of interest rates.

---

[9] Our discussion of syndicated loans is based on J. Armstrong "The Syndicated Loan Market: Developments in the North American Market," *Financial System Review* (June 2003), Bank of Canada, pp. 69-73. The paper is available at the Bank of Canada Web site: **www.bank-banque-canada.ca**.

[10] For details, see Dominion Bond Rating Service's Web site at **www.dbrs.com**.

| EXAMPLE 19.3 | **COST OF COMMERCIAL PAPER** |

Suppose Maya Entertainment has issued commercial paper with a face value of $500,000 that will mature in 60 days. The present market value of the paper is $492,000. Interest on the paper is, therefore, $500,000 − $492,000 = $8,000. Over a 60-day period, the effective interest rate is $8,000/$492,000 = 1.63 percent. The annualized rate is calculated by solving for i in the following equation:

Face value of the commercial paper = Price $\times$ [1+ ($i \times t$)/365]. Inserting numbers, we get $500,000 = $492,000 $\times$ [1 + ($i \times$ 60)/365]. With some algebraic manipulation, we get $i = (8,000 \times 365)/(492,000 \times 60)$, which works out to 0.0989 or 9.89 percent.

BANKER'S ACCEPTANCE

banker's acceptance
A firm's time draft that has been accepted by a bank and may be sold to investors as a short-term unsecured note issued by the firm and guaranteed by the bank.

A firm may also seek short-term financing through a **banker's acceptance**. This instrument is created when a firm submits a time draft (which is much like a post-dated cheque) to the bank for acceptance. When the bank stamps "accepted" on the draft, it becomes a *banker's acceptance* and represents an unconditional promise of the bank to pay the amount stated on the draft when it matures. As such, a banker's acceptance becomes the bank's IOU and can be sold to portfolio investors in the acceptance market. Such investors may include money market funds, pension funds, and banks.

SECURED LOANS

Many short-term loans are unsecured, but sometimes the company may offer assets as security. Since the bank is lending on a short-term basis, the security generally consists of liquid assets such as receivables, inventories, or securities. For example, a firm may decide to borrow short-term money secured by its accounts receivable. When its customers pay their bills, it can use the cash collected to repay the loan. Banks will not usually lend the full value of the assets that are used as security. For example, a firm that puts up $100,000 of receivables as security may find that the bank is prepared to lend only $75,000. The safety margin (or haircut, as it is called) is likely to be even larger in the case of loans that are secured by inventory.

Accounts Receivable Financing

account receivable pledging
A firm assigns its accounts receivable as a security to the lender to obtain a loan.

When a loan is secured by receivables, the firm *assigns* or *pledges* the receivables to the bank. If the firm fails to repay the loan, the bank can collect the **accounts receivables pledged** from the firm's customers and use the cash to pay off the debt. However, the firm is still responsible for the loan even if ultimately the receivables cannot be collected. The risk of default on the receivables is therefore borne by the firm. Depending on the arrangement between the borrowing firm and the bank, the customer whose receivable has been assigned may or may not be notified about such a pledge. Typically, in such an arrangement, in addition to the interest on the loan, the bank may also charge a service fee to cover administrative costs. For instance, the interest rate could be set at a premium of, say, 3 percent above the prime rate while the service fee could be at 2 percent of the receivables amount pledged. Since accounts receivables tend to be relatively liquid current assets, pledging them provides good collateral value to the lender.

| EXAMPLE 19.4 | **ACCOUNT RECEIVABLES PLEDGING** |

Suppose Mid-life Gym Equipment is negotiating a bank loan by assigning its receivables totalling $150,000. The bank has agreed to lend to the extent of 70 percent of the amount pledged at an interest rate of 3 percent points above the prime rate, which is currently at 5 percent. In this instance, the bank has also agreed to waive the service fee as a goodwill gesture to Mid-life Gym. Mid-life

Gym's average collection period is 30 days. Here, we calculate the amount of the bank loan as $150,000 × 0.7 = $105,000. Interest costs, at an annual percentage rate of 8 percent are calculated over the average collection period as $105,000 × 0.08 × 30/365 = $690.41.

factoring   A firm sells its accounts receivable at a discount for the purpose of obtaining short-term financing.

An alternative procedure is **factoring**, that is, to *sell* the receivables at a discount to a financial institution known as a factor and let it collect the money. In other words, some companies solve their financing problem by borrowing on the strength of their current assets; others solve it by selling their current assets. Once the firm has sold its receivables, the factor bears all the responsibility for collecting on the accounts. Therefore, the factor plays three roles: it administers collection of receivables, takes responsibility for bad debts, and provides finance.

EXAMPLE 19.5	FACTORING

To illustrate factoring, suppose that the firm sells its accounts receivables to a factor at a 2 percent discount. This means that the factor pays 98 cents for each dollar of accounts receivable. If the average collection period is 1 month, then in a month the factor should be able to collect $1 for every 98 cents it paid today. Therefore, the implicit interest rate is 2/98 = 2.04 percent per month, which corresponds to an effective annual interest rate of $(1.0204)^{12} - 1 = .274$, or 27.4 percent.

While factoring would appear to be an expensive source of financing for the firm, from this example, part of the apparently steep interest rate represents payment for the assumption of default risk as well as for the cost of running the credit operation.

Inventory Financing

Banks also lend on the security of inventory, but they are choosy about the inventory they will accept. They want to make sure that they can identify and sell it if you default. Automobiles and other standardized, non-perishable commodities are good security for a loan; work in progress and ripe strawberries are poor collateral.

Banks need to monitor companies to be sure they don't sell their assets and run off with the money. Consider, for example, the story of the great salad oil swindle. Fifty-one banks and companies made loans for nearly $200 million (US) to the Allied Crude Vegetable Oil Refining Corporation in the belief that these loans were secured on valuable salad oil. Unfortunately, they did not notice that Allied's tanks contained false compartments that were mainly filled with seawater. When the fraud was discovered, the president of Allied went to jail and the 51 lenders were

SEE BOX P. 613

left out in the cold looking for their $200 million. The nearby Finance in Action box presents a similar story that illustrates the potential pitfalls of secured lending. Here, too, the loans were not as "secured" as they appeared: the supposed collateral did not exist.

To protect themselves against this sort of risk, lenders often insist on *field warehousing*. An independent warehouse company hired by the bank supervises the inventory pledged as collateral for the loan. As the firm sells its product and uses the revenue to pay back the loan, the bank directs the warehouse company to release the inventory back to the firm. If the firm defaults on the loan, the bank keeps the inventory and sells it to recover the debt.

SEE BOX P. 614

Now that we have reviewed various types of secured loans, read the nearby Finance in Action box, which discusses the growing popularity of asset-based lending in Canada.

19.7   THE COST OF BANK LOANS

Bank loans often extend for several years. Interest payments on these loans are sometimes fixed for the term of the loan but more commonly they are adjusted up or down as the general level of interest rates changes.

The National Safety Council of Australia's Victoria Division had been a sleepy outfit until John Friedrich took over. Under its new management, NSC members trained like commandos and were prepared to go anywhere and do anything. They saved people from drowning, they fought fires, found lost bushwalkers, and went down mines. Their lavish equipment included 22 helicopters, 8 aircraft, and a mini-submarine. Soon the NSC began selling its services internationally.

Unfortunately the NSC's paramilitary outfit cost millions of dollars to run—far more than it earned in revenue. Friedrich bridged the gap by borrowing $236 million (AUD) of debt. The banks were happy to lend because the NSC's debt appeared well secured. At one point the company showed $107 million (AUD) of receivables (that is, money owed by its customers), which it pledged as security for bank loans. Later checks revealed that many of these customers did not owe the NSC a cent. In other cases, banks took comfort in the fact that their loans were secured by containers of valuable rescue gear. There were more than 100 containers stacked around the NSC's main base. Only a handful contained any equipment, but these were the ones that the bankers saw when they came to check

that their loans were safe. Sometimes a suspicious banker would ask to inspect a particular container. Friedrich would then explain that it was away on exercise, fly the banker across the country in a light plane and point to a container well out in the bush. The container would of course be empty, but the banker had no way to know that.

Six years after Friedrich was appointed CEO, his massive fraud was uncovered. But a few days before a warrant could be issued, Friedrich disappeared. Although he was eventually caught and arrested, he shot himself before he could come to trial. Investigations revealed that Friedrich was operating under an assumed name, having fled from his native Germany where he was wanted by the police. Many rumours continued to circulate about Friedrich. He was variously alleged to have been a plant of the CIA and the KGB, and the NSC was said to have been behind an attempted countercoup in Fiji. For the banks there was only one hard truth. Their loans to the NSC, which had appeared so well secured, would never be repaid.

Source: Adapted from Chapter 7 of T. Sykes, *The Bold Riders* (St. Leonards, NSW, Australia: Allen & Unwin, 1994).

The interest rate on bank loans of less than a year is almost invariably fixed for the term of the loan. However, you need to be careful when comparing rates on these shorter-term bank loans, for the rates may be calculated in different ways.

SIMPLE INTEREST

The interest rate on bank loans frequently is quoted as simple interest. For example, if the bank quotes an annual rate of 12 percent on a simple interest loan of $100,000 for 1 month, then at the end of the month you would need to repay $100,000 plus 1 month's interest. This interest is calculated as

$$\text{Amount of loan} \times \frac{\text{annual interest rate}}{\text{number of periods in the year}} = \$100,000 \times \frac{.12}{12} = \$1,000$$

Your total payment at the end of the month would be

$$\text{Repayment of face value } plus \text{ interest} = \$100,000 + \$1,000 = \$101,000$$

In Chapter 4 you learned to distinguish between simple interest and compound interest. We have just seen that your 12 percent simple interest bank loan costs 1 percent per month. One percent per month compounded for 1 year cumulates to $1.01^{12} = 1.1268$. Thus the compound, or *effective*, annual interest rate on the bank loan is 12.68 percent, not the quoted rate of 12 percent.

The general formula for the equivalent compound interest rate on a simple interest loan is

$$\text{Effective annual rate} = \left(\frac{1 + \text{quoted annual interest rate}}{m}\right)^m - 1$$

where the annual interest rate is stated as a fraction (.12 in our example) and m is the number of periods in the year (12 in our example).

DISCOUNT INTEREST

The interest rate on a bank loan is often calculated on a discount basis. Similarly, when companies issue commercial paper, they also usually quote the interest rate as a discount. With a discount inter-

The Growth of Asset-Based Lending in Canada

When Leitch Technology went looking for cash last year, it wasn't because the video-equipment maker was in dire straits. Despite losing money for four straight quarters, Leitch's balance sheet was solid, and it had no debt on the books. Still, the Toronto company (TSX: LTV) linked a three-year, $20 million asset-based loan with CIT Business Credit Canada. Leitch didn't really need the money, but it wanted a ready supply of cheap capital just in case it decided it had to move quickly on an acquisition. The deal puts "powder in the keg," says John Jazwinski, a vice-president at Deloitte who helps mid-market companies secure funds. "They have access to $20 million in cheap capital to pull the trigger on a deal."

Once the near-last resort of companies in trouble, asset-based loans (ABLs) are becoming all the rage for mid-size businesses interested more in tapping potential growth opportunities than stopping the bleeding. ABLs—which are based on the quality and quantity of a company's receivables and inventories rather than balance-sheet dynamics—have typically made headlines only when industry giants like Algoma Steel and Air Canada have used them to smooth their passage out of bankruptcy protection. But a growing number of mid-market retailers, manufacturers, distributors, and others are turning to ABLs instead of more traditional—and more expensive—forms of financing, such as mezzanine and other covenant-based financing, venture capital and debt issues.

The Leitch transaction is the kind of mid-market deal that signals the mainstream acceptance of ABLs in Canada. Companies recognize they can access cheaper capital—and more of it—at a time when the major banks seem more interested in safe money streams like cash management services. ABLs have been a hit since the 1970s in the United States, where some 900 asset-based lenders manage a US$325 billion portfolio. Indeed, 50% of all US commercial loans are asset-based. Canadian banks have been slow to catch on, but US firms such as Bank of America, Congress Financial and LaSalle Business Credit are making inroads into this country, and the Canadian portfolio of ABLs now accounts for roughly $7 billion in commercial loans. Part of the reason asset-based lending hasn't caught fire already is the lack of maturity of Canadian financial markets. But ABLs have also historically had a negative connotation. "Asset-based loans were considered maybe not a lender of last resort, but somewhere just above that," says Robert Hickey, a managing director at Deloitte.

That's not surprising when you consider that asset-based lending grew out of encyclopedia salesmen financing their own encyclopedias, says Kevin Morley, a partner at Ogilvy Renault in Toronto and chair of the firm's ABL team, which has represented lenders in connection with more than $3 billion in transactions over the past three years. But the industry is shaking off its past. That's not to suggest ABLs aren't still attractive to companies in turnaround mode or on the brink of bankruptcy. Just ask Air Canada, which signed an ABL last year with GE Capital, using the planes GE leases to the airline as collateral. But smaller businesses, such as Leitch and tiny Baffin Footwear Technology, are getting in on the action as well.

For small and mid-size businesses, a primary attraction is that the terms are usually more accommodating than other forms of financing. "ABLs are very flexible to accommodate changes in the business plan because they haven't tied a bunch of financial covenants to the plan," says Morley. Those contract terms often make cash-flow-based loans, which rely on metrics such as historical and projected future performance, unwieldy for borrowers. They're more limited in what they can do with the funds, because cash flow loans are based on the ability to service the debt. Anything that is perceived to be a threat to that capability is turned down. ABLs, on the other hand, are based on the estimated liquidation or recovery value of a company's assets, rather than the ability to pay back the loan from earnings. That makes them a good option for companies with seasonal or unpredictable cash flows.

But before any chief financial officer goes hopping down to the local ABL shop, there are a few issues to consider. The most important thing an ABL candidate needs is marquee-quality assets, either finished goods or raw materials that can be easily collected on, and non-foreign receivables that are due in the next 90 days. Asset-based lenders don't like to see a lot of work in progress and generally won't consider soft assets like intellectual property (although some US banks are getting creative about that).

Assuming a company has solid assets, its primary concern should be reporting. Depending on the nature of the assets, there may be a fair amount of reporting required to secure and maintain the loan. Be prepared to make at least monthly, but probably weekly or even daily, reports to the lender. That means small and mid-sized businesses may have to invest in more sophisticated financial reporting systems.

ABLs are also usually linked up with cash management, so the lender will require that the company deposit receivables in a lock-box account or to a particular bank where they have control over them to pay down the debt as monies are collected. Robin Schwill, an insolvency and restructuring lawyer at Toronto firm Osler, Hoskin & Harcourt, advises chief financial officers to make sure they're comfortable with the asset-based lender's banking relationships and the sophistication of their IT systems. There may also be landlord and possessor waivers, especially if the assets are spread out at many different warehouses, processors and locations.

And don't get sucked in by marketing messages that equate ABLs with another form of asset capital called factoring. Factoring is the sale of your receivables at a discount to a third party who will be responsible for collecting. It's not really a form of borrowing, says Schwill, and the fees could end up in the neighbourhood of credit card interest rates, depending on how often and how quickly you strike such deals. That's because you're effectively paying, say a 2% margin on each factoring arrangement. "No asset-based lender is in the business of being a collateral liquidator," says Schwill. "They're looking for a return and an expectation that it's a relationship they will continue for a significant period of time."

Which asset-based lender to choose comes down to who you feel most comfortable with poking around your accounts. Competition has pushed fees down to around the same level, so it could be as simple as who's offering the right amount of money at the lowest cost. Be prepared to deal with US lenders, but there shouldn't be any cross-border concerns.

Source: Excerpted from Andy Holloway, "Nice Assets, Here's Cash," *Canadian Business*, March 15, 2004, at **www.canadianbusiness.com**.

est loan, the bank deducts the interest up front. For example, suppose that you borrow $100,000 on a discount basis for 1 year at 12 percent. In this case the bank hands you $100,000 less 12 percent, or $88,000. Then at the end of the year you repay the bank the $100,000 face value of the loan. This is equivalent to paying interest of $12,000 on a loan of $88,000. The effective interest rate on such a loan is therefore $12,000/$88,000 = .1364, or 13.64 percent.

Now suppose that you borrow $100,000 on a discount basis for 1 month at 12 percent. In this case the bank deducts 1 percent up-front interest and hands you

$$\text{Face value of loan} \times \left(1 - \frac{\text{quoted annual interest rate}}{\text{number of periods in the year}}\right)$$

$$= \$100,000 \times \left(1 - \frac{.12}{12}\right) = \$99,000$$

At the end of the month you repay the bank the $100,000 face value of the loan, so you are effectively paying interest of $1,000 on a loan of $99,000. The *monthly* interest rate on such a loan is $1,000/$99,000 = 1.01 percent and the compound, or effective, annual interest rate on this loan is $1.0101^{12} - 1 = .1282$, or 12.82 percent. The effective interest rate is higher than on the simple interest rate loan because the interest is paid at the beginning of the month rather than the end.

The general formula for the equivalent compound interest rate on a discount interest loan is

$$\text{Effective annual rate on a discount loan} = \left(\frac{1}{1 - \dfrac{\text{quoted annual interest rate}}{m}}\right)^{m} - 1$$

where the quoted annual interest rate is stated as a fraction (.12 in our example) and m is the number of periods in the year (12 in our example).

INTEREST WITH COMPENSATING BALANCES

Occasionally, bank loans require the firm to maintain some amount of money on balance at the bank. This is called a *compensating balance*. For example, a firm might have to maintain a balance of 20 percent of the amount of the loan. In other words, if the firm borrows $100,000, it gets to use only $80,000, because $20,000 (20 percent of $100,000) must be left on deposit in the bank.[11]

If the compensating balance does not pay interest (or pays a below-market rate of interest), the actual interest rate on the loan is higher than the stated rate. The reason is that the borrower must pay interest on the full amount borrowed but has access to only part of the funds. For example, we calculated above that a firm borrowing $100,000 for 1 month at 12 percent simple interest must pay interest at the end of the month of $1,000. If the firm gets the use of only $80,000, the effective monthly interest rate is $1,000/$80,000 = .0125, or 1.25 percent. This is equivalent to a compound annual interest rate of $1.0125^{12} - 1 = .1608$, or 16.08 percent.

In general, the compound annual interest rate on a loan with compensating balances is

$$\text{Effective annual rate on a loan with compensating balances} = \left(1 + \frac{\text{actual interest paid}}{\text{borrowed funds available}}\right)^{m} - 1$$

where m is the number of periods in the year (again, 12 in our example).

Check Point 19.6

Suppose that Dynamic Mattress needs to raise $20 million for 6 months. Bank A quotes a simple interest rate of 7 percent but requires the firm to maintain an interest-free compensating balance of 20 percent. Bank B quotes a simple interest rate of 8 percent but does not require any compensating balances. Bank C quotes a discount interest rate of 7.5 percent and also does not require compensating balances. What is the effective (or compound) annual interest rate on each of these loans?

---

[11] It is worth noting that the *Bank Act* does not allow banks operating in Canada to mandate that their customers maintain compensating balances. Banks operating in the United States, on the other hand, can impose compensating balance requirements on their customers.

19.8   SUMMARY

1. Why do firms need to invest in net working capital?

Short-term financial planning is concerned with the management of the firm's short-term, or *current*, assets and liabilities. The most important current assets are cash, marketable securities, inventory, and accounts receivable. The most important current liabilities are bank loans and accounts payable. The difference between current assets and current liabilities is called **net working capital**.

Net working capital arises from lags between the time the firm obtains the raw materials for its product and the time it finally collects its bills from customers. The **cash conversion cycle** is the length of time between the firm's payment for materials and the date that it gets paid by its customers. The cash conversion cycle is partly within management's control. For example, it can choose to have a higher or lower level of inventories. Management needs to trade off the benefits and costs of investing in current assets. Higher investments in current assets entail higher **carrying costs** but lower expected **shortage costs**.

2. How does long-term financing policy affect short-term financing requirements?

The nature of the firm's short-term financial planning problem is determined by the amount of long-term capital it raises. A firm that issues large amounts of long-term debt or common stock, or that retains a large part of its earnings, may find that it has permanent excess cash. Other firms raise relatively little long-term capital and end up as permanent short-term debtors. Most firms attempt to find a golden mean by financing all fixed assets and part of current assets with equity and long-term debt. Such firms may invest cash surpluses during part of the year and borrow during the rest of the year.

3. How do the firm's sources and uses of cash relate to its need for short-term borrowing?

The starting point for short-term financial planning is an understanding of sources and uses of cash. Firms forecast their net cash requirement by forecasting collections on accounts receivable, adding other cash inflows, and subtracting all forecast cash outlays. If the forecast cash balance is insufficient to cover day-to-day operations and to provide a buffer against contingencies, you will need to find additional finance. For example, you may borrow from a bank on an unsecured **line of credit**, you may borrow by offering receivables or inventory as security, or you may issue your own short-term notes known as **commercial paper**. You may also seek a short-term financing through a **banker's acceptance**.

4. How do firms develop a short-term financing plan that meets their need for cash?

The search for the best short-term financial plan inevitably proceeds by trial and error. The financial manager must explore the consequences of different assumptions about cash requirements, interest rates, limits on financing from particular sources, and so on. Firms are increasingly using computerized financial models to help in this process. Remember the key differences between the various sources of short-term financing—for example, the differences between bank lines of credit and commercial paper. Remember too that firms often raise money on the strength of their current assets, especially accounts receivable and inventories.

Related Web Links

www.lsta.org The Loan Syndications and Trading Association

www.businessfinancemag.com Business Finance magazine has resources and software reviews for financial planning

www.toolkit.cch.com Financial planning resources of all kinds

www.ibcdata.com/index.html Short-term investment and money fund rates

www.dbrs.com Dominion Bond Rating Service

http://pages.stern.nyu.edu/~adamodar Aswath Damodaran's home page, includes data on working-capital requirements by U.S. industry sector

www.gecapital.com Information on types of short-term finance

www.treasuryandrisk.com Web site of Treasury & Risk Management

www.americanbanker.com Host of information for bankers and finance professionals

www.intltreasurer.com Contain articles on short-term financial management

Key Terms

net working capital	594	commitment fee	609	account receivable	
cash conversion cycle	595	term loans	609	pledging	611
carrying costs	597	syndicated loans	609	factoring	612
shortage costs	597	commercial paper	610		
line of credit	609	banker's acceptance	611		

Questions and Problems

*Answers in Appendix B

BASIC

1. **Working Capital Management.** Indicate how each of the following six different transactions that Dynamic Mattress might make would affect (1) cash and (2) net working capital:
   *a.   Paying out a $2 million cash dividend.
   *b.   A customer paying a $2,500 bill resulting from a previous sale.
   c.   Paying $5,000 previously owed to one of its suppliers.
   d.   Borrowing $1 million long term and investing the proceeds in inventory.
   e.   Borrowing $1 million short term and investing the proceeds in inventory.
   *f.   Selling $5 million of marketable securities for cash.

*2. **Short-Term Financial Plans.** Fill in the blanks in the following statements:
   a.   A firm has a cash surplus when its _____ exceeds its _____. The surplus is normally invested in _____.
   b.   In developing the short-term financial plan, the financial manager starts with a(n) _____ budget for the next year. This budget shows the _____ generated or absorbed by the firm's operations and also the minimum _____ needed to support these operations. The financial manager may also wish to invest in _____ as a reserve for unexpected cash requirements.

3. **Sources and Uses of Cash.** State how each of the following events would affect the firm's balance sheet. State whether each change is a source or use of cash.
   a.   An automobile manufacturer increases production in response to a forecast increase in demand. Unfortunately, the demand does not increase.
   b.   Competition forces the firm to give customers more time to pay for their purchases.
   c.   The firm sells a parcel of land for $100,000. The land was purchased 5 years earlier for $200,000.
   d.   The firm repurchases its own common stock.
   e.   The firm pays its quarterly dividend.
   f.   The firm issues $1 million of long-term debt and uses the proceeds to repay a short-term bank loan.

4. **Cash Conversion Cycle.** What effect will the following events have on the cash conversion cycle?
   a.   Higher financing rates induce the firm to reduce its level of inventory.
   b.   The firm obtains a new line of credit that enables it to avoid stretching payables to its suppliers.
   c.   The firm factors its accounts receivable.
   d.   A recession occurs, and the firm's customers increasingly stretch their payables.

*5. **Managing Working Capital.** A new computer system allows your firm to more accurately monitor inventory and anticipate future inventory shortfalls. As a result, the firm feels more able to pare down its inventory levels. What effect will the new system have on working capital and on the cash conversion cycle?

6. **Cash Conversion Cycle.** Calculate the accounts receivable period, accounts payable period, inventory period, and cash conversion cycle for the following firm:

   Income statement data:

Sales	5,000
Cost of goods sold	4,200

Balance sheet data:

	Beginning of Year	End of Year
Inventory	500	600
Accounts receivable	100	120
Accounts payable	250	290

7. **Cash Conversion Cycle.** What effect will the following have on the cash conversion cycle?
   *a.   Customers are given a larger discount for cash transactions.
   *b.   The inventory turnover ratio falls from 8 to 6.
   *c.   New technology streamlines the production process.
   d.   The firm adopts a policy of reducing outstanding accounts payable.
   e.   The firm starts producing more goods in response to customers' advance orders instead of producing for inventory.
   f.   A temporary glut in the commodity market induces the firm to stock up on raw materials while prices are low.

PRACTICE

8. **Compensating Balances.** Suppose that Dynamic Sofa (a subsidiary of Dynamic Mattress) has a line of credit with a stated interest rate of 10 percent and a compensating balance of 25 percent. The compensating balance earns no interest.
   a.   If the firm needs $10,000, how much will it need to borrow?
   b.   Suppose that Dynamic's bank offers to forget about the compensating balance requirement if the firm pays interest at a rate of 12 percent. Should the firm accept this offer? Why or why not?
   c.   Redo part (b) if the compensating balance pays interest of 4 percent. *Warning*: You cannot use the formula in the chapter for the effective interest rate when the compensating balance pays interest. Think about how to measure the effective interest rate on this loan.

*9. **Compensating Balances.** The stated bank loan rate is 8 percent, but the loan requires a compensating balance of 10 percent on which no interest is earned. What is the effective interest rate on the loan? What happens to the effective rate if the compensating balance is doubled to 20 percent?

10. **Factoring.** A firm sells its accounts receivables to a factor at a 1.5 percent discount. The average collection period is one month. What is the implicit effective annual interest rate on the factoring arrangement? Suppose the average collection period is 1.5 months. How does this affect the implicit effective annual interest rate?

*11. **Discount Loan.** A discount bank loan has a quoted annual rate of 6 percent.
   a.   What is the effective rate of interest if the loan is for one year and is paid off in one payment at the end of the year?
   b.   What is the effective rate of interest if the loan is for one month?

EXCEL

12. **Compensating Balances.** A bank loan has a quoted annual rate of 6 percent. However, the borrower must maintain a balance of 25 percent of the amount of the loan, and the balance does not earn any interest.
   a.   What is the effective rate of interest if the loan is for one year and is paid off in one payment at the end of the year?
   b.   What is the effective rate of interest if the loan is for one month?

13. **Forecasting Collections.** Here is a forecast of sales by National Bromide for the first 4 months of 2006 (figures in thousands of dollars):

Month:	1	2	3	4
Cash sales	15	24	18	14
Sales on credit	100	120	90	70

On average, 50 percent of credit sales are paid for in the current month, 30 percent in the next month, and the remainder in the month after that. What are expected cash collections in months 3 and 4?

EXCEL

14. **Forecasting Payments.** If a firm pays its bills with a 30-day delay, what fraction of its purchases will be paid for in the current quarter? In the following quarter? What if its payment delay is 60 days?

EXCEL

*15. **Short-Term Planning.** Paymore Products places orders for goods equal to 75 percent of its sales forecast in the next quarter. What will be orders in each quarter of the year if the sales forecasts for the next five quarters are

	Quarter in Coming Year				Following Year
	First	**Second**	**Third**	**Fourth**	**First Quarter**
Sales forecast	$372	$360	$336	$384	$384

16. **Forecasting Payments.** Calculate Paymore's cash payments to its suppliers under the assumption that the firm pays for its goods with a one-month delay. Therefore, on average, two-thirds of purchases are paid for in the quarter that they are purchased and one-third are paid in the following quarter.

17. **Forecasting Collections.** Now suppose that Paymore's customers pay their bills with a two-month delay. What is the forecast for Paymore's cash receipts in each quarter of the coming year? Assume that sales in the last quarter of the previous year were $336.

18. **Forecasting Net Cash Flow.** Assuming that Paymore's labour and administrative expenses are $65 per quarter and that interest on long-term debt is $40 per quarter, work out the net cash inflow for Paymore for the coming year using a table like Table 19.7.

*19. **Short-Term Financing Requirements.** Suppose that Paymore's cash balance at the start of the first quarter is $40 and its minimum acceptable cash balance is $30. Work out the short-term financing requirements for the firm in the coming year using a table like Table 19.8. The firm pays no dividends.

20. **Short-Term Financing Plan.** Now assume that Paymore can borrow up to $100 from a line of credit at an interest rate of 2 percent per quarter. Prepare a short-term financing plan. Use Table 19.9 to guide your answer.

21. **Short-Term Plan.** Recalculate Dynamic Mattress's financing plan (Table 19.9) assuming that the firm wishes to maintain a minimum cash balance of $10 million instead of $5 million. Assume the firm can convince the bank to extend its line of credit to $45 million.

22. **Internet.** Industries differ substantially in the amount of working capital that they need to hold. Which industries would you expect to involve large investments in working capital? Which would involve small investments in working capital? Now check your answers by looking at the table of working-capital requirements by industry sector on Professor Aswath Damodaran's home page (**http://pages.stern.nyu.edu/~adamodar**).

23. **Internet.** GE Capital's Web site, **www.gecapital.com**, contains a lot of information on types of short-term finance. Suppose that you need to finance your investment in inventory. What are the possible options? Do some make more sense than others?

24. **Internet.** We mentioned that the interest rate on longer-term bank loans is not usually fixed for the term of the loan, but is adjusted up or down as the general level of interest rates changes. Often the interest rate is linked to the bank's prime rate or to the London Interbank Offered Rate (LIBOR), which is the interest rate at which major international banks lend to one another. Suppose you are offered the choice between a 3-year loan at the bank's prime rate or at 1 percent above LIBOR. Which would you prefer based on information about current rates? Log in to **www.bloomberg.com** to find current rates.

EXCEL

*25. **Sources and Uses of Cash.** The accompanying tables show Dynamic Mattress's year-end 2002 balance sheet and its income statement for 2003. Use these tables (and Table 19.3) to work out a statement of sources and uses of cash for 2003.

YEAR-END BALANCE SHEET FOR 2002
($ millions)

Assets		Liabilities	
Current assets		Current liabilities	
Cash	4	Bank loans	4
Marketable securities	2	Accounts payable	15
Inventory	20	Total current liabilities	19
Accounts receivable	22	Long-term debt	5
Total current assets	48	Net worth (equity and retained earnings)	60
Fixed assets			
Gross investment	50		
Less depreciation	14	Total liabilities and net worth	84
Net fixed assets	36		
Total assets	84		

INCOME STATEMENT FOR 2003
($ millions)

Sales	300
Operating costs	−285
	15
Depreciation	−2
EBIT	13
Interest	−1
Pretax income	12
Tax at 50 percent	−6
Net income	6

Note: Dividend = $1 million and retained earnings = $5 million.

CHALLENGE

26. **Standard and Poor's.** Go to **www.mcgrawhill.ca/edumarketinsight**. Wal-Mart Stores and Sears Holding Corp. are two retailers at opposite ends of the performance scale. Calculate the net working capital and the cash conversion cycle, discussed in Section 19.1, for each firm. By how much would the investment in working capital fall if each firm could reduce its cash conversion cycle by one day? Compare and contrast the level and trend of the "per employee" ratios for each company. Which company has higher employee efficiency? Use the most recent year-end Balance Sheet Report, Income Statement Report, Annual Ratio Report, and Profitability Report from Market Insight. Based on the Profitability Report, how has the market reacted to the performance differences between the companies?

STANDARD
&POOR'S

*27. **Cash Budget.** The following data are from the budget of Ritewell Publishers. Half the company's sales are transacted on a cash basis. The other half are paid for with a one-month delay. The company pays all of its credit purchases with a one-month delay. Credit purchases in January were $30 and total sales in January were $180.

	February	March	April
Total sales	200	220	180
Cash purchases	70	80	60
Credit purchases	40	30	40
Labour and administrative expenses	30	30	30
Taxes, interest, and dividends	10	10	10
Capital expenditures	100	0	0

Complete the following cash budget:

	February	March	April
Sources of cash			
Collections on current sales			
Collections on accounts receivable			
Total sources of cash			
Uses of cash			
Payments of accounts payable			
Cash purchases			
Labour and administrative expenses			
Capital expenditures			
Taxes, interest, and dividends			
Total uses of cash			
Net cash inflow			
Cash at start of period	100		
+ Net cash inflow			
= Cash at end of period			
+ Minimum operating cash balance	100	100	100
= Cumulative short-term financing required			

Solutions to Check Points

19.1 a. The new values for the accounts receivable period and inventory period are

$$\text{Days in inventory} = \frac{150,000}{2,104,620/365} = 26 \text{ days}$$

This is a reduction of 12.3 days from the original value of 38.3 days.

$$\text{Days in receivables} = \frac{200,000}{2,144,891/365} = 34 \text{ days}$$

This is a reduction of 11.1 days from the original value of 45.1 days

The cash conversion cycle falls by a total of 12.3 + 11.1 = 23.4 days.

b. The inventory period, accounts receivable period, and accounts payable period will all fall by a factor of 1.10. (The numerators are unchanged, but the denominators are higher by 10 percent.) Therefore, the conversion cycle will fall from 27.6 days to 27.6/1.10 = 25.1 days.

19.2 a. An increase in the interest rate will increase the cost of carrying current assets. The effect is to reduce the optimal level of such assets.

b. The just-in-time system lowers the expected level of shortage costs and reduces the amount of goods the firm ought to be willing to keep in inventory.

c. If the firm decides that more lenient credit terms are necessary to avoid lost sales, it must then expect customers to pay their bills more slowly. Accounts receivable will increase.

19.3 a. This transaction merely substitutes one current liability (short-term debt) for another (accounts payable). Neither cash nor net working capital is affected.

b. This transaction will increase inventory at the expense of cash. Cash falls but net working capital is unaffected.

c. The firm will use cash to buy back the stock. Both cash and net working capital will fall.

d. The proceeds from the sale will increase both cash and net working capital.

19.4 Quarter:	First	Second	Third	Fourth
Accounts receivable (Table 19.6)				
Receivables (beginning period)	30	35	31.4	46.4
Sales	87.5	78.5	116	131
Collections[a]	82.5	82.1	101	125
Receivables (end period)	35	31.4	46.4	52.4
Cash budget (Table 19.7)				
Sources of cash				
Collections of accounts receivable	82.5	82.1	101	125
Other	1.5	0	12.5	0
Total sources	84	82.1	113.5	125
Uses				
Payments of accounts payable	65	60	55	50
Labour and administrative expenses	30	30	30	30
Capital expenses	32.5	1.3	5.5	8
Taxes, interest, and dividends	4	4	4.5	5
Total uses	131.5	95.3	95	93
Net cash inflow	−47.5	−13.2	18.5	32
Short-term financing requirements (Table 19.8)				
Cash at start of period	5	−42.5	−55.7	−37.2
+ Net cash inflow	−47.5	−13.2	18.5	32
= Cash at end of period	−42.5	−55.7	−37.2	−5.2
Minimum operating balance	5	5	5	5
Cumulative short-term financing required	47.5	60.7	42.2	10.2

[a] Sales in fourth quarter of the previous year totalled $75 million.

19.5   The major change in the plan is the substitution of the extra $5 million of borrowing via the line of credit (bank loan) in the second quarter and the corresponding reduction in the stretched payables. This substitution is advantageous because the bank loan is a cheaper source of funds. Notice that the cash balance at the end of the year is higher under this plan than in the original plan.

Quarter:	First	Second	Third	Fourth
Cash requirements				
1. Cash required for operations	45	15	−26.0	−35
2. Interest on line of credit	0	0.8	0.9	0.6
3. Interest on stretched payables	0	0	0.5	0
4. Total cash required	45	15.8	−24.6	−34.4
Cash raised				
5. Bank loan	40	5	0	0
6. Stretched payables	0	10.8	0	0
7. Securities sold	5	0	0	0
8. Total cash raised	45	15.8	0	0
Repayments				
9. Of stretched payables	0	0	10.8	0
10. Of bank loan	0	0	13.8	31.2
Increase in cash balances				
11. Addition to cash balances	0	0	0	3.2
Bank loan				
12. Beginning of quarter	0	40	45	31.2
13. End of quarter	40	45	31.2	0

19.6   Bank A: The interest paid on the $20 million loan over the 6-month period will be $20 million $\times$ .07/2 = $.7 million. With a 20 percent compensating balance, $16 million is available to the firm. The effective annual interest rate is

$$\text{Effective annual rate on a loan with compensating balances} = \left(1 + \frac{\text{actual interest paid}}{\text{borrowed funds available}}\right)^m - 1$$

$$= \left(1 + \frac{\text{\$.7 million}}{\text{\$16 million}}\right)^2 - 1 = .0894, \text{ or } 8.94\%$$

Bank B: The compound annual interest rate on the simple loan is

$$\text{Effective annual rate} = \left(1 + \frac{\text{quoted interest rate}}{m}\right)^m - 1$$

$$= \left(1 + \frac{.08}{2}\right)^2 - 1 = 1.04^2 - 1 = .0816, \text{ or } 8.16\%$$

Bank C: The compound annual interest rate is

$$\text{Effective annual rate on a discount loan} = \left(\frac{1}{1 - \dfrac{\text{annual interest rate}}{m}}\right)^m - 1$$

$$= \left(\frac{1}{1 - \dfrac{.075}{2}}\right)^2 - 1 = \left(\frac{1}{.9625}\right)^2 - 1 = .0794, \text{ or } 7.94\%$$

MINICASE

Capstan Autos operated a dealership in the Maritime provinces for a major Japanese car manufacturer. Capstan's owner, Sidney Capstan, attributed much of the business's success to its no-frills policy of competitive pricing and immediate cash payment. The business was basically a simple one—the firm imported cars at the beginning of each quarter and paid the manufacturer at the end of the quarter. The revenues from the sale of these cars covered the payment to the manufacturer and the expenses of running the business, as well as providing Sidney Capstan with a good return on his equity investment.

By the fourth quarter of 2007, sales were running at 250 cars a quarter. Since the average sale price of each car was about $20,000, this translated into quarterly revenues of 250 $\times$ $20,000 = $5 million. The average cost to Capstan of each imported car was $18,000. After paying wages, rent, and other recurring costs of $200,000 per quarter and deducting depreciation of $80,000, the company was left with earnings before interest and taxes (EBIT) of $220,000 a quarter and net profits of $140,000.

The year 2008 was not a happy year for car importers in Canada. Recession led to a general decline in auto sales, while the fall in the value of the dollar shaved profit margins for many dealers in imported cars. Capstan, more than most

firms, foresaw the difficulties ahead and reacted at once by offering six months' free credit while holding the sale price of its cars constant. Wages and other costs were pared by 25 percent to $150,000 a quarter and the company effectively eliminated all capital expenditures. The policy appeared successful. Unit sales fell by 20 percent to 200 units a quarter, but the company continued to operate at a satisfactory profit (see table).

The slump in sales lasted for six months, but as consumer confidence began to return, auto sales began to recover. The company's new policy of six months' free credit was proving sufficiently popular that Sidney Capstan decided to maintain the policy. In the third quarter of 2008, sales had recovered to 225 units; by the fourth quarter they were 250 units; and by the first quarter of the next year they had reached 275 units. It looked as if the company could expect to sell 300 cars by the second quarter of 2009. Earnings before interest and tax were already in excess of their previous high and Sidney Capstan was able to congratulate himself on weathering what looked to be a tricky period. Over the 18-month period the firm had earned net profits of over half a million dollars, and the equity had grown from just under $1 million to about $2 million.

Sidney Capstan was first and foremost a superb salesman and always left the financial aspects of the business to his financial manager. However, there was one feature of the financial statements that disturbed Sidney Capstan—the mounting level of debt, which had reached $9.7 million by the end of the first quarter of 2009. This unease turned to alarm when the financial manager phoned to say that the bank was reluctant to extend further credit and was even questioning its current level of exposure to the company.

Capstan found it impossible to understand how such a successful year could have landed the company in financial difficulties. The company had always had good relationships with its bank, and the interest rate on its bank loans was a rea-

sonable 8 percent per year (or about 2 percent per quarter). Surely, Capstan reasoned, when the bank saw the projected sales growth for the rest of 2009, it would realize that there were plenty of profits to enable the company to start repaying its loans.

Questions

1. Is Capstan Autos in trouble?
2. Is the bank correct to withhold further credit?
3. Why is Capstan's indebtedness increasing if its profits are higher than ever?

SUMMARY INCOME STATEMENT
(all figures except unit sales in $000s)

Year:	2007	2008				2009
Quarter:	4	1	2	3	4	1
1. Number of cars sold	250	200	200	225	250	275
2. Unit price	20	20	20	20	20	20
3. Unit cost	18	18	18	18	18	18
4. Revenues (1 × 2)	5,000	4,000	4,000	4,500	5,000	5,500
5. Cost of goods sold (1 × 3)	4,500	3,600	3,600	4,050	4,500	4,950
6. Wages and other costs	200	150	150	150	150	150
7. Depreciation	80	80	80	80	80	80
8. EBIT (4 − 5 − 6 − 7)	220	170	170	220	270	320
9. Net interest	4	0	76	153	161	178
10. Pretax profit (8 − 9)	216	170	94	67	109	142
11. Tax (.35 × 10)	76	60	33	23	38	50
12. Net profit (10 − 11)	140	110	61	44	71	92

SUMMARY BALANCE SHEETS
($000s)

	End of 3rd Quarter 2007	End of 1st Quarter 2008
Cash	10	10
Receivables	0	10,500
Inventory	4,500	5,400
Total current assets	4,510	15,910
Fixed assets, net	1,760	1,280
Total assets	6,270	17,190
Bank loan	230	9,731
Payables	4,500	5,400
Total current liabilities	4,730	15,131
Shareholders' equity	1,540	2,059
Total liabilities	6,270	17,190

PART SEVEN

Short-Term Financial Decisions

CASH AND INVENTORY MANAGEMENT

In August 2004 citizens and corporations in Canada held nearly $164 billion in cash. This included about $35 billion held in demand deposits (chequing accounts) of commercial banks. Cash pays no interest. Why, then, do sensible people hold it? Why, for example, don't you take all your cash and invest it in interest-bearing securities? The answer is that cash gives more *liquidity* than securities. By this we mean it can be used it to buy things. It is hard enough getting Toronto cab drivers to give you change for a $50 bill, but try asking them to split a Treasury bill. There could be myriad reasons for firms wanting to hold cash balances, but we can categorize the main ones as follows:

- *Meet Transactions Needs.* Firms have to carry certain minimum cash balances to meet day-to-day cash expenditures, which include routine items such as paying monthly bills or spending on regular supplies. Cash is also needed for major recurring expenses such as wage and salary disbursements as well as tax and dividend payments.
- *Hedge Against Uncertain Future.* Firms often hold some additional cash over and above their transaction requirement as a provision for the future. These funds are typically held as marketable securities. Alternatively, firms may choose to hedge against uncertainty by obtaining a line of credit. With a line of credit from a bank, the firm can borrow up to a specified maximum amount over a stipulated period of time. However, lines of credit generally require a commitment fee, whether they are used or not.
- *Speculation.* Firms may hold liquid assets in anticipation of taking advantage of unforeseen opportunities.
- *Compensating Balance Requirement.* We saw in Chapter 19 that although this requirement is not prevalent in Canada, a firm in the United States may be required to maintain a specified amount on deposit in its chequing account in lieu of loans and services provided by its bank. Usually, the amount of the compensating balance is determined by the size of the loan and the amount and range of services provided.

Of course, rational investors will not hold an asset like cash unless it provides the same benefit on the margin as other assets such as Treasury bills. The benefit from holding Treasury bills is the interest received; the benefit of holding cash is convenience of liquidity. When you have only a small proportion of your assets in cash, a little extra liquidity can be extremely useful; when you have a substantial holding, any additional liquidity is not worth much. Therefore, financial managers want to hold cash balances up to the point where the value of any additional liquidity is equal to the value of the interest forgone.

Cash is simply a raw material that companies need to carry out production. As we will explain later, the financial manager's decision to stock up on cash is in many ways similar to the production manager's decision to stock up on inventories of raw materials. We will therefore look at the problem of managing inventories and then show how this helps us to understand how much cash should be held.

But first you need to learn about the mechanics of cash collection and disbursement. This may seem a rather humdrum topic, but you will find that it involves some interesting and important decisions.

After studying this chapter you should be able to
- Measure float and explain why it arises and how it can be controlled.
- Calculate the value of changes in float.
- Understand the costs and benefits of holding inventories.
- Cite the costs and benefits of holding cash.
- Explain why an understanding of inventory management can be useful for cash management.
- Identify where firms can invest excess funds.

20.1 CASH COLLECTION, DISBURSEMENT, AND FLOAT

Companies don't keep their cash in a little tin box; they keep it in a bank deposit. To understand how they can make best use of that deposit, you need to understand what happens when companies withdraw money from their accounts or pay money into them.

FLOAT

Suppose that the United Carbon Company has $1 million in a demand deposit (chequing account) with its bank. It now pays one of its suppliers by writing and mailing a cheque for $200,000. The company's records are immediately adjusted to show a cash balance of $800,000. Thus the company is said to have a *ledger balance* of $800,000.

But the company's bank won't learn anything about this cheque until it has been received by the supplier, deposited at the supplier's bank, and finally presented to United Carbon's bank for payment. During this time United Carbon's bank continues to show in its ledger that the company has a balance of $1 million.

While the cheque is clearing, the company obtains the benefit of an extra $200,000 in the bank. This sum is often called disbursement float, or **payment float**.

payment float   Cheques written by a company that have not yet cleared.

Company's ledger balance $800,000	+	Payment float $200,000

equals

Bank's ledger balance $1,000,000

Float sounds like a marvelous invention; every time you spend money, it takes the bank a few days to catch on. Unfortunately it can also work in reverse. Suppose that in addition to paying its supplier, United Carbon *receives* a cheque for $120,000 from a customer. It first processes the cheque and then deposits it in the bank. At this point both the company and the bank increase the ledger balance by $120,000:

But this money isn't available to the company immediately. The bank doesn't actually have the money in hand until it has sent the cheque to the customer's bank and received payment. Since the bank has to wait, it makes United Carbon wait too—usually one or two business days. In the meantime, the bank will show that United Carbon still has an available balance of only $1 million. The extra $120,000 has been deposited but is not yet available. It is therefore known as **availability float**.

availability float   Cheques already deposited that have not yet been cleared.

Notice that the company gains as a result of the payment float and loses as a result of availability float. The **net float** available to the firm is the difference between payment and availability float:

net float   Difference between payment float and availability float.

$$\textbf{Net float = payment float – availability float}$$

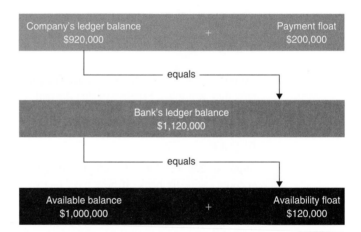

In our example, the net float is $80,000. The company's available balance is $80,000 greater than the balance shown in its ledger.

Check Point 20.1

Your bank account currently shows a balance of $940. You deposit $100 into the account and write a cheque for $40.
a. What is the ledger balance in your account?
b. What is the availability float?
c. What is payment float?
d. What is the bank's ledger balance?
e. Show that your ledger balance plus payment float equals the bank's ledger balance, which in turn equals the available balance plus availability float.

VALUING FLOAT

Float results from the delay between writing a cheque and the reduction in the bank balance. The amount of float will therefore depend on the size of the cheque and the delay in collection.

EXAMPLE 20.1	FLOAT

Suppose that your firm writes cheques worth $6,000 per day. It may take three days to mail these cheques to your suppliers, who then take a day to process the cheques and deposit them into their banks. Finally, it may be a further three days before the suppliers' banks send the cheques to your bank, which then debits your account. The total delay is 7 days and the payment float is $7 \times \$6,000 = \$42,000$. On average, the available balance at the bank will be $42,000 more than what is shown in your firm's ledger.

As a financial manager your concern is with the available balance, not with the company's ledger balance. If you know that it is going to be a week before some of your cheques are presented for payment, you may be able to get by on a smaller cash balance. The smaller you can keep your cash balance, the more funds you can hold in interest-earning accounts or securities. This game is often called *playing the float*.

You can increase your available cash balance by increasing your net float. This means ensuring that cheques received from customers are cleared rapidly and those paid to suppliers are cleared slowly. Perhaps this may sound like small potatoes, but think what it could mean to a company like General Motors of Canada (GM). GM's daily sales average is over $100 million. If it could speed up collections by 1 day, and the interest rate is .02 percent per day (about 7.6 percent per year), it would increase earnings by $.0002 \times \$100$ million = $20,000 per day.

What would be the present value to GM if it could *permanently* reduce its collection period by one day? The extra interest income would then be a perpetuity, and the present value of the income would be $20,000/.0002 = $100 million, exactly equal to the reduction in float.

Why should this be? Think about the company's cash flow stream. It receives $100 million per day. At any time, suppose that four days' worth of payments are deposited and "in the pipeline." When the company speeds up the collection period by a day, the pipeline will shrink to three days' worth of payments. At that point, GM receives an extra $100 million cash flow: it receives the "usual" payment of $100 million, and it also receives the $100 million for which it ordinarily would have had to wait an extra day. From that day forward, it continues to receive $100 million per day, exactly as before. So the net effect of reducing the payment pipeline from 4 days to 3 is that GM gets an extra up-front payment equal to 1 day of float, or $100 million. Therefore, the present value of a permanent reduction in float is simply the amount by which float is reduced.

However, be careful not to become overenthusiastic about managing the float. Writing cheques on your account for the sole purpose of creating float and earning interest is called *cheque kiting* and is illegal. In 1985 the American brokerage firm E. F. Hutton pleaded guilty to 2,000 separate counts of mail and wire fraud. Hutton admitted that it had created nearly $1 billion of float by shuffling funds between its branches and through various accounts at different banks.

Check Point 20.2

Suppose Ford's stock price is $14 (US) per share, and there are 1.83 billion shares of Ford outstanding. Assume that the daily sales average is $470 million (US). Now suppose that technological improvements in the cheque-clearing process reduce availability float from four days to two days. What would happen to the stock price? How much should Ford be willing to pay for a new computer system that would reduce availability float by two days?

20.2   CANADA'S PAYMENTS SYSTEM

Every day, Canadians withdraw cash from banking machines; use cheques, debit cards, and preauthorized payments; or make other payments totalling, on average, more than $147 billion. Typically, these transactions result in financial institutions owing money to one another and settling payments over 18 million times daily. Canada's payments system includes the set of rules and procedures that guide the clearing, exchange, and mechanism for settling all of these different types of payments. The system is run by the Canadian Payments Association, a non-profit organization, which was created by an act of Parliament in 1980. Its members are institutions such as banks, trust companies, credit unions, and caisses populaires that take deposits and offer chequing privileges. All members belong to deposit-insurance plans, which are statutory or regulated under special federal legislation.

The Bank of Canada and the Canadian Payments Association are responsible for clearing cheques and other types of payment. The CPA owns and operates two major payment systems in Canada, the *Automated Clearing Settlement System (ACSS)* and the *Large Value Transfer System (LVTS)*. The ACSS is the system by which cheques and certain types of automated payments (such as direct deposits) are cleared and settled. LVTS, introduced in 1999, is an electronic wire transfer system, which can be used by Canadian companies for their domestic and international payments.

There are essentially three steps in the process of clearing and settling payments:[1]

Step 1: Payment by cheque, debit card, direct deposit, or other means.

Step 2: Clearing, or the daily process by which CPA members exchange deposited payment items and then determine the net amounts owed to each other.

Step 3: Settlement, or the procedure by which CPA members use funds on deposit at the Bank of Canada to meet their net payment obligations to other member institutions.

For example, when you deposit a cheque at your bank, which is drawn on another financial institution, it is sent together with other cheques for sorting and clearance to a data centre operated by one of the Canadian Payments Association's (CPA) member financial institutions. These *direct clearers* clear their own cheques and have contracts to clear items on behalf of other financial institutions. After your cheque gets sorted, it will be forwarded to the data centre of the financial institution where the cheque is drawn. Most cheques, regardless of how far they have to travel, are received at the branch level no later than two days after they are deposited. Canadians usually receive credit immediately for the cheques they deposit, even if they do so at another branch on the other side of the country. The computerized network enables same-day settlement for cheques, keeping transit float to a minimum. In contrast, in the United States, a cheque may be placed on hold till it is verified that the person who wrote it has the funds in his or her account. In the United Kingdom, it could take an average of four days for a cheque to clear.[2]

20.3   MANAGING FLOAT

Several kinds of delay create float, so people in the cash management business refer to several kinds of float. Figure 20.1 shows the three sources of float:

- the time it takes to mail a cheque
- the time it takes the company to process the cheque after it has been received
- the time it takes the bank to clear the cheque and adjust the firm's account[3]

The total collection time is the sum of these three sources of delay.

> Delays that help the payer hurt the recipient. Recipients try to speed up collections. Payers try to slow down disbursements. Both attempt to minimize net float.

---

[1] Much of our discussion here and elsewhere in this section is based on information provided on the Canadian Payment Association's Web site at **www.cdnpay.ca**.

[2] See "Introduction to the Canadian Payments Association," (August 2003), **www.cdnpay.ca**.

[3] In the earlier discussion of Canada's payments system, we saw that Canadians often receive immediate credit for the cheques they deposit, and so this type of float is not significant here. However, this may be important if you are doing business in other countries such as the United States or the United Kingdom where the delay could be longer.

FIGURE 20.1
Delays create float. Each arrow represents a source of delay. Recipients try to reduce delay to get available cash sooner. Payers prefer delay so they can use their cash longer.

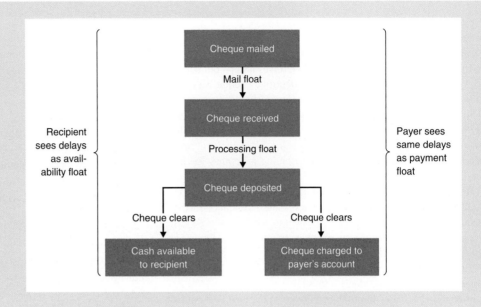

You probably have come across attempts by companies to reduce float in your own financial transactions. For example, many stores now encourage you to pay bills with your bank debit card instead of a credit card. The payment is automatically debited from your bank account on the day of the transaction, which eliminates the considerable float you otherwise would enjoy until you were billed by your credit card company and paid your bill. The stores save on any transaction costs that would have been payable to the credit card companies. Also, by receiving payment through debit cards, the stores have almost immediate use of cash and are able to eliminate accounts receivables. Similarly, many companies now arrange *preauthorized payments* or *preauthorized debits (PADs)* with their customers. For example, if you have a mortgage payment on a house, the lender can arrange to have your bank account debited by the amount of the payment each month. The funds are automatically transferred to the lender. You save the work of paying the bill by hand, and the lender saves the float time during which your cheque would have been processed through the banking system. In Section 20.2, we saw that in Canada the amount of float time saved would not be much as Canadians often receive immediate credit for deposited cheques, unlike other countries where it can take several days. The nearby Finance in Action box discusses tactics that American banks use to maximize their income from float.

SEE BOX P. 632

Traditionally, insurance companies and mortgage providers, such as banks, have offered PADs as a convenient way for their customers to meet monthly premium and loan payments. In recent years, other businesses such as utility companies, and satellite and cable TV suppliers have realized the convenience and efficiency of this type of payment and are also offering PAD services. Many firms routinely deposit employees' paycheques directly into their bank accounts, which saves the employees a few days of float.

SPEEDING UP COLLECTIONS

concentration banking
System whereby customers make payments to a regional collection centre that transfers funds to a principal bank.

One way to speed up collections is by a method known as **concentration banking**. In this case customers in a particular area make payments to a local branch office rather than to company headquarters. The local branch office then deposits the cheques into a local bank account. Surplus funds are periodically transferred to a concentration account at one of the company's principal banks.

Concentration banking reduces float in two ways. First, because the branch office is nearer to the customer, mailing time is reduced. Second, because the customers are local, there is a good chance that they have local bank accounts, and therefore, the time taken to clear their cheques is also reduced. Another advantage is that concentration brings many small balances together in

High-Tech Tactics Let Banks Keep the "Float"

If anybody knows time is money, it's banks.

And in the electronic age, banks are becoming more expert at the movement of money: racing it to themselves faster—but sometimes slamming on the brakes when you deposit a cheque. So don't expect your funds to be available to you any quicker.

To zip cheques along and reduce the "float"—or the downtime between when a cheque is written and when the funds are actually drawn from an account—banks are turning to everything from speedier cheque-reading machines to zooming jet planes loaded with bundles of cheques.

First Union Corp., for one, has begun installing scanning devices at HairCuttery salons, so when a patron hands over an ordinary cheque for a shampoo and cut, a machine reads it and swiftly deducts the amount from the chequing account—just as debit cards currently do.

But when it comes to moving funds into a customer's account, sometimes the pace is suddenly a lot slower.

There is big business in playing traffic cop to the flow of cheques. At any given moment, an estimated $140 billion in cheques are en route to a bank—a mountain of paper that could earn roughly $20 million in interest every day, estimates David Medeiros, an analyst at Tower Group, a bank consultancy in Needham, Mass.

Responding to the accelerated movement of money, the government may clamp down on banks. A pending Federal Reserve Board proposal, which banks oppose, would cut the maximum number of days a bank can put a hold on most cheques to four business days

from the current five-day limit. The Fed started putting limits on how long banks can hold customers' funds about a decade ago, in response to numerous customer complaints that deposits were being tied up for no reason.

Clearly, paper cheques are moving faster now. About 83% of cheques currently arrive back at their bank of origin within five business days, up from 73% in 1990, according to the Fed. Major banks now use a fleet of 30 Lear jets owned by AirNet Systems Inc. of Columbus, Ohio to whiz cheques across the country.

But other bank-policy changes are reducing the breathing room people have long enjoyed with cheques. One new tactic is requiring that loan payments be received by their due date; in the past, banks usually considered a payment made if it was postmarked by the due date.

For the time being, the vast majority of cheques are covered by the Fed's five-day rule, but a cheque may be held longer by the bank under certain circumstances. A cheque, for instance, might be unusually large or it might be deposited by a customer who has repeatedly overdrawn his account. But even in those cases, the bank must notify the customer when a deposit will be held for a week or longer and explain exactly when the funds will be available for withdrawal.

Source: Rick Brooks, "High-Tech Tactics Let Banks Keep the 'Float,'" *The Wall Street Journal* (June 3, 1999), p. B1. Reprinted with permission of *The Wall Street Journal*. Copyright 1999 Dow Jones & Company. All Rights Reserved Worldwide.

one large, central balance, which then can be invested in interest-paying assets through a single transaction. For example, when Amoco streamlined its U.S. bank accounts, it was able to reduce its daily bank balances in non-interest-bearing accounts by almost 80 percent.[4]

Unfortunately, concentration banking also involves additional costs. First, the company is likely to incur additional administrative costs. Second, the company's local bank needs to be paid for its services. Third, there is the cost of transferring the funds to the concentration bank. The fastest but most expensive arrangement is *wire transfer*; funds are transferred from one account to another via computer entries in the accounts. A slower but cheaper method is a *depository transfer cheque*, or *DTC*. This is a preprinted cheque used to transfer funds between specified accounts. The funds will become available within 2 days.

Wire transfer makes more sense when large funds are being transferred. For example, at a daily interest rate of .02 percent, the daily interest on a $10 million payment would be $2,000. Suppose a wire transfer costs $10. It clearly would pay to spend $10 to save 2 days' float. On the other hand, it would not be worth using wire transfer for just $5,000. The extra 2 days' interest that you pick up amounts to only $2, not nearly enough to justify the extra expense of the wire transfer.

EXAMPLE 20.2　　　**BREAK-EVEN WIRE TRANSFER AMOUNT**

Suppose the daily interest rate is .02 percent and that a wire transfer saves 2 days of float but costs $10 more than a depository transfer cheque. How large a transfer is necessary to justify the additional cost of a wire transfer?

---

[4] "Amoco Streamlines Treasury Operations," The *Citibank Globe* (November/December 1998).

The interest savings are .02 percent per day × 2 days × funds to be transferred. So the break-even level of funds to be transferred is found by solving

$$.0004 \times \text{size of transfer} = \$10$$

$$\text{Size of transfer} = \frac{\$10}{.0004} = \$25,000$$

The cost of the wire transfer can be justified for any transfer above this amount.

lock-box system System whereby customers send payments to a post office box and a local bank collects and processes cheques.

Often concentration banking is combined with a **lock-box system**. In a lock-box system, you pay the local bank to take on the administrative chores. It works as follows: The company rents a locked post office box in each principal region. All customers within a region are instructed to send their payments to the post office box. The local bank empties the box at regular intervals (as often as several times per day) and deposits the cheques in your company's local account. Surplus funds are transferred periodically to one of the company's principal banks.

How many collection points do you need if you use a lock-box system or concentration banking? The answer depends on where your customers are and on the speed of Canada Post.

EXAMPLE 20.3

LOCK-BOX SYSTEMS

Suppose that you are thinking of opening a lock box. The local bank shows you a map of mail delivery times. From that and knowledge of your customers' locations, you come up with the following data:

Average number of daily payments to lock box	= 150
Average size of payment	= $1,200
Rate of interest *per day*	= .02 percent
Saving in mailing time	= 1.2 days
Saving in processing time	= .8 of a day

On this basis, the lock box would reduce collection float by

$$150 \text{ items per day} \times \$1,200 \text{ per item} \times (1.2 + .8) \text{ days saved} = \$360,000$$

Invested at .02 percent per day, that gives a daily return of

$$.0002 \times \$360,000 = \$72$$

The bank's charge for operating the lock-box system depends on the number of cheques processed. Suppose that the bank charges $.26 per cheque. That works out to 150 × $.26 = $39 per day. You are ahead by $72 – $39 = $33 per day, plus whatever your firm saves from not having to process the cheques itself.

Our example assumes that the company has only two choices. It can do nothing or it can operate the lock box. But maybe there is some other lock-box location or some mixture of locations that would be still more effective. Of course, you can always find this out by working through all possible combinations, but many banks have computer programs that find the best locations for lock boxes.[5]

Check Point 20.3

How will the following conditions affect the price that a firm should be willing to pay for a lock-box service?
a. The average size of its payments increases.
b. The number of payments per day increases (with no change in average size of payments).
c. The interest rate increases.
d. The average mail time saved by the lock-box system increases.
e. The processing time saved by the lock-box system increases.

---

[5] These usually involve linear programming. Linear programming is an efficient method of hunting through the possible solutions to find the optimal one.

CONTROLLING DISBURSEMENTS

Speeding up collections is not the only way to increase the net float. You can also do this by slowing down disbursements. One tempting strategy is to increase mail time. For example, United Carbon could pay its Halifax suppliers with cheques mailed from Prince George, B.C., and its Vancouver suppliers with cheques mailed from Charlottetown, P.E.I.

But on second thought you realize that these kinds of post office tricks are unlikely to help you. Suppose you have promised to pay a Halifax supplier on March 29. Does it matter whether you mail the cheque from Prince George on the 26th or from Halifax on the 28th? Such mailing games would buy you time only if your creditor cares more about the date you mailed the cheque than the day it arrives. This is unlikely: With the notable exception of tax returns sent to Canada Revenue Agency, mailing dates are irrelevant. Of course, you could use a remote mailing address as an *excuse* to pay late, but that's a trick easily seen through. If you have to pay late, you might as well mail late.

Remote Disbursement

You could try to pay the Toronto supplier with a cheque drawn on your account at the Prince George branch of your bank. This technique, known as *remote disbursement*, works in the United States where banks do not have widespread branches and the process for clearing cheques tends to be slow. Some American firms even maintain disbursement accounts in different parts of the country. The computer looks up each supplier's zip code and automatically produces a cheque on the most distant bank.[6] However, as we saw in Section 20.2 when we described Canada's payments system, this may not be of much use in Canada where most cheques are settled on the same day, and there is little scope for creating float through the clearing system.

Zero-Balance Accounts

A Toronto bank receives several cheque deliveries each day. Thus, if United Carbon uses a Toronto bank for paying its suppliers, it will not know at the beginning of the day how many cheques will be presented for payment. Either it must keep a large cash balance to cover contingencies or it must be prepared to borrow.

However, instead of having a disbursement account with, say, TD Canada Trust in Toronto, United Carbon could open a **zero-balance account** with TD Canada Trust's affiliated bank in Sackville, New Brunswick. Because it is *not* in a major banking centre, this affiliated bank receives almost all cheque deliveries in the form of a single, early-morning delivery. Therefore, it can let the cash manager at United Carbon know early in the day exactly how much money will be paid out that day. The cash manager then arranges for this sum to be transferred from the company's concentration account to the disbursement account. Thus by the end of the day (and at the start of the next day), United Carbon has a zero balance in the disbursement account.

United Carbon's Sackville account has two advantages. First, by choosing a remote location, the company has gained several days of float. Second, because the bank can forecast early in the day how much money will be paid out, United Carbon does not need to keep extra cash in the account to cover contingencies. The nearby Finance in Action box describes how one company has been able to economize on the use of cash by means of a zero-balance account.

ELECTRONIC FUNDS TRANSFER

Many cash payments involve pieces of paper, such as dollar bills or cheques. But, as shown in Table 20.1, the use of paper transactions is on the decline. In recent years, there has been a steady increase in the use of *electronic payment systems* or **electronic funds transfers**, which help

zero-balance account
Regional bank account to which just enough funds are transferred daily to pay each day's bills.

SEE BOX P. 635

electronic funds transfer
Payments made electronically instead of using paper-based cheques.

---

[6] This way, the company hopes to gain a few days of additional float. However, the suppliers won't object to these machinations because the U.S. Federal Reserve guarantees a maximum clearing time of two days on all cheques cleared through the Federal Reserve system. Therefore, the supplier never gives up more than two days of float; instead, the victim of remote disbursement is the Federal Reserve, which loses float if it takes more than two days to collect funds. The Fed has been trying to prevent remote disbursement.

How Laidlaw Restructured Its Cash Management

The Canadian company Laidlaw Inc., has more than 4,000 facilities throughout America, operating school bus services, ambulance services, and Greyhound coaches. During the 1990s the company expanded rapidly through acquisition, and its number of banking relationships multiplied until it had 1,000 separate bank accounts with more than 2,000 different banks. The head office had no way of knowing how much cash was stashed away in these accounts until the end of each quarter, when it was able to construct a consolidated balance sheet.

To economize on the use of cash, Laidlaw's financial manager sought to cut the company's average float from five days to two. At the same time management decided to consolidate cash management at five key banks. This enabled cash to be zero-balanced to a single account for each division and swept daily to Laidlaw's disbursement bank. Because the head office could obtain daily reports of the company's cash position, cash forecasting was improved and the company could reduce its cash needs still further.

Source: Cash management at Laidlaw is described in G. Mann and S. Hutchinson, "Driving Down Working Capital: Laidlaw's Story," *Canadian Treasurer Magazine*, August/September 1999.

---

electronic data interchange (EDI) Direct, electronic information exchange between enterprises, eliminating the mailing and handling of paper invoices.

debit card An automated-teller-machine card that allows retail customers to transfer funds directly from their bank accounts to a retailer's account.

businesses facilitate payments electronically. There is a growing practice of the exchange of financial information, or **Electronic Data Interchange (EDI)**, between enterprises. By making electronic payments, companies are eliminating the use of paper invoices and cheques, thereby avoiding the mail. Many firms deposit employees' paycheques directly into their bank accounts. Also, there is widespread use of **debit cards** among consumers, allowing retail customers to transfer funds directly from their bank account to a retailer's account. Firms using this system eliminate accounts receivables and virtually have immediate use of cash. Electronic payment options, such as automated payments under the ACSS and electronic wire transfers through the LVTS, have enabled businesses to become more efficient in their cash management procedures. In the first half of 2004, total electronic remittances in Canada were valued at about $613 billion.[7]

For companies that are "wired" to their banks, electronic payment systems have several advantages:

- Record keeping and routine transactions are easy to automate when money moves electronically. For example, the Campbell Soup Company discovered it could handle cash management and short-term borrowing and lending with a total staff of seven.[8] The company's domestic cash flow was about $5 billion (US).

TABLE 20.1
Percentage of paper versus electronic items flowing through the ACSS

Year		Paper	Electronic
2004	Volume	24.0	76.0
	Value	69.7	30.3
2003	Volume	26.5	73.5
	Value	73.2	26.8
2002	Volume	29.3	70.7
	Value	80.5	19.5
2001	Volume	31.5	68.5
	Value	83.1	16.9
2000	Volume	35.0	65.0
	Value	85.6	14.4
1999	Volume	38.6	61.4
	Value	91.0	9.0
1998	Volume	43.3	56.7
	Value	96.9	3.1

Source: Copyright 2005 Canadian Payments Association.

---

[7] For details, visit the Canadian Payment Association's Web site at **www.cdnpay.ca**.

[8] J. D. Moss, "Campbell Soup's Cutting-Edge Cash Management," *Financial Executive* 8 (September/October 1992), pp. 39–42.

- The marginal cost of transactions on ACSS and LVTS is very low. For example, it can cost less than $10 to transfer huge sums of money through electronic wire transfers.
- Float is drastically reduced. This can generate substantial savings. For example, cash managers at Occidental Petroleum found that one plant was paying out about $8 million (US) per month, several days early, to avoid any risk of late fees if cheques were delayed in the mail. The solution was obvious: The plant's managers switched to paying large bills electronically, that way they could ensure cheques arrived exactly on time.[9]

20.4   INVENTORIES AND CASH BALANCES

So far we have focused on managing the *flow* of cash efficiently. We have seen how efficient float management can improve a firm's income and its net worth. Now we turn to the management of the *stock* of cash that a firm chooses to keep on hand and ask: How much cash does it make sense for a firm to hold?

> Recall that cash management involves a trade-off. If the cash were invested in securities, it would earn interest. On the other hand, you can't use securities to pay the firm's bills. If you had to sell those securities every time you needed to pay a bill, you would incur heavy transactions costs. The art of cash management is to balance these costs and benefits.

If that seems more easily said than done, you may be comforted to know that production managers must make a similar trade-off. Ask yourself why they carry inventories of raw materials, work in progress, and finished goods. They are not obliged to carry these inventories; for example, they could simply buy materials day by day, as needed. But then they would pay higher prices for ordering in small numbers, and they would risk production delays if the materials were not delivered on time. That is why they order more than the firm immediately needs. Similarly, the firm holds inventories of finished goods to avoid the risk of running out of product and losing a sale because it cannot fill an order.

But there are costs to holding inventories: Money tied up in inventories does not earn interest, storage and insurance must be paid for, and often there is spoilage and deterioration. Production managers must try to strike a sensible balance between the costs of holding too little inventory and holding too much.

In this sense, cash is just another raw material needed for production. There are costs to keeping an excessive inventory of cash (lost interest) and costs to keeping an inventory too small (the cost of repeated sales of securities).

MANAGING INVENTORIES

Let us take a look at what economists have had to say about managing inventories and then see whether some of these ideas can help us manage cash balances. Here is a simple inventory problem.

A builder's merchant faces a steady demand for engineering bricks. Every so often when the merchant runs out of inventory, it replenishes the supply by placing an order for more bricks from the manufacturer.

There are two costs associated with the merchant's inventory of bricks. First, there is the *order cost*. Each order placed with a supplier involves a fixed handling expense and delivery charge.[10] The second type of cost is the *carrying cost*. This includes the cost of space, insurance, and

---

[9] R. J. Pisapia, "The Cash Manager's Expanding Role: Working Capital," *Journal of Cash Management* 10 (November/December 1990), pp. 11–14.

[10] Some components of order costs, such as delivery charges, may at times include a variable component as well. For simplicity, we assume order costs, in general, to be fixed.

losses due to spoilage or theft. The opportunity cost of the capital tied up in the inventory is also part of the carrying cost.

Here is the kernel of the inventory problem:

> As the firm increases its order size, the number of orders falls and therefore the order costs decline. However, an increase in order size also increases the average amount in inventory, so that the carrying cost of inventory rises. The trick is to strike a balance between these two costs.

Let's insert some numbers to illustrate this point. Suppose that the merchant plans to buy 1 million bricks over the coming year. Each order that it places costs $90, and the annual carrying cost of the inventory is $.05 per brick. To minimize order costs, the merchant would need to place a single order for the entire 1 million bricks on January 1 and would then work off the inventory over the remainder of the year. The *average* inventory over the year would be 500,000 bricks and therefore carrying costs would be 500,000 × $.05 = $25,000. The first row of Table 20.2 shows that if the firm places just this one order, total costs are $25,090:

$$\text{Total costs} = \text{order costs} + \text{carrying costs}$$
$$\$25,090 = \$90 + \$25,000$$

To minimize *carrying costs*, the merchant would need to minimize inventory by placing a large number of very small orders. For example, the bottom row of Table 20.2 shows the costs of placing 100 orders a year for 10,000 bricks each. The average inventory is now only 5,000 bricks, and therefore the carrying costs are only 5,000 × $.05 = $115. But the order costs have risen to 100 × $90 = $9,000.

Each row in Table 20.2 illustrates how changes in the order size affect the inventory costs. You can see that as the order size decreases and the number of orders rises, total inventory costs decline at first because carrying costs fall faster than order costs rise. Eventually, however, the curve turns up as order costs rise faster than carrying costs fall. Figure 20.2 illustrates this graphically. The downward-sloping curve charts annual order costs, and the upward-sloping straight line charts carrying costs. The U-shaped curve is the sum of these two costs. Total costs are minimized in this example when the order size is 60,000 bricks. About 17 times per year the merchant should place an order for 60,000 bricks, and it should work off this inventory over a period of about three weeks. Its inventory will therefore follow the sawtoothed pattern in Figure 20.3.

Note that it is worth increasing order size as long as the decrease in total order costs outweighs the increase in carrying costs. The optimal order size is the point at which these

TABLE 20.2
How inventory costs vary with the number of orders

Order Size =	Orders per Year =	Average Inventory =	Order Costs =	Carrying Costs =	Total Costs =
					Order Costs plus
Bricks per Order	Annual Purchases / Bricks per Order	Order Size / 2	$90 per Order	$.05 per Brick	Carrying Costs
1,000,000	1	500,000	$ 90	$ 25,000	$ 25,090
500,000	2	250,000	180	12,500	12,680
200,000	5	100,000	450	5,000	5,450
100,000	10	50,000	900	2,500	3,400
60,000	16.7	30,000	1,500	1,500	3,000
50,000	20	25,000	1,800	1,250	3,050
20,000	50	10,000	4,500	500	5,000
10,000	100	5,000	9,000	250	9,250

FIGURE 20.2
Determination of
optimal order size

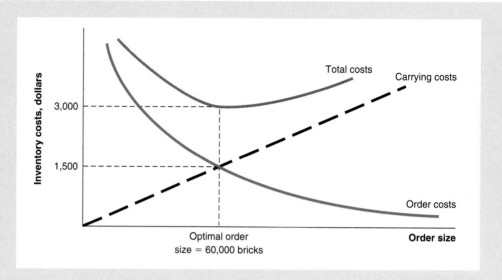

economic order quantity
Order size that minimizes total
inventory costs.

two effects offset each other. This order size is called the **economic order quantity**. There is a formula for calculating the economic order quantity:

$$\text{Economic order quantity} = \sqrt{\frac{2 \times \text{annual sales} \times \text{cost per order}}{\text{carrying cost}}} \qquad (20.1)$$

In the present example,

$$\text{Economic order quantity} = \sqrt{\frac{2 \times 1,000,000 \times 90}{.05}} = 60,000 \text{ bricks}$$

You have probably already noticed several unrealistic features in our simple example. First, rather than allowing inventories of bricks to decline to zero, the firm would want to allow for the time it takes to fill an order. If it takes five days before the bricks can be delivered and the builder's merchant waits until it runs out of stock before placing an order, it will be out of stock for five days. In this case the firm should reorder when its stock of bricks falls to a five-day supply.

The firm also might want to recognize that the rate at which it sells its goods is subject to uncertainty. Sometimes business may be slack; on other occasions, the firm may land a large

FIGURE 20.3
The builder's merchant
minimizes inventory costs by
placing about 17 orders per
year for 60,000 bricks each.
That is, it places orders at
about 3-week intervals.

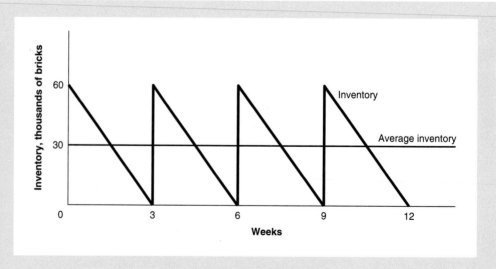

order. In this case it should maintain a minimum *safety stock* below which it would not want inventories to drop.

The number of bricks the merchant plans to buy in the course of the year, in this case 1 million, is also a forecast that is subject to uncertainty. The optimal order size is proportional to the square root of the forecast of annual sales.

The economic order quantity is a simplified, and even simplistic, version of the inventory management process in real firms, but it does capture the four essential features of inventory management:

- Optimal inventory levels involve a trade-off between carrying costs and order costs.
- Carrying costs include the cost of storing goods as well as the cost of capital tied up in inventory.
- Inventory levels will be lower when storage or interest costs are high and will be higher when restocking costs are high.
- Inventory level does not rise in direct proportion to sales. As sales increase, the optimal inventory level rises, but less than proportionately.

✔ **Check Point 20.4**

The builder's merchant has experienced an increase in demand for engineering bricks. It now expects to sell 1.25 million bricks a year. Unfortunately, interest rates have risen and the annual carrying cost of the inventory has increased to $.09 per brick. Order costs have remained steady at $90 per order.
a. Rework Table 20.2 for each of the eight order sizes shown in the table.
b. Has the optimal inventory level risen or fallen? Explain why.

JUST-IN-TIME INVENTORY MANAGEMENT

just-in-time inventory management A system of inventory management in which materials are delivered to the firm just when needed.

In recent years a number of firms have used a technique known as **just-in-time inventory management** to make dramatic reductions in inventory levels. This technique, first implemented by Toyota Motor Corp. in Japan, is particularly useful to manufacturers that produce a variety of different products. Firms that use the just-in-time system receive a nearly continuous flow of deliveries with no more than two or three hours' worth of parts inventory on hand at any time. For these firms the extra cost of restocking is completely outweighed by the savings in carrying cost. Just-in-time inventory management entails detailed and careful planning of material requirements and much greater coordination with suppliers to avoid the costs of stock-outs, however. Suppliers should be able to maintain frequent deliveries of smaller orders with meticulous timing.

Just-in-time inventory management also can reduce costs by allowing suppliers to produce and transport goods on a steadier schedule. However, just-in-time systems rely heavily on the predictability of the production process. A firm with shaky labour relations, for example, would adopt a just-in-time system at its peril; because it essentially has no inventory on hand, it would be particularly vulnerable to a strike.

SEE BOX P. 640 We must now return to the problem of managing the firm's inventory of cash, but see the nearby Finance in Action box, which describes how automobile manufacturers have been able to use just-in-time and other systems to reduce their inventories of parts and finished product.

MANAGING INVENTORIES OF CASH

William Baumol was the first to notice that this simple inventory model can tell us something about the management of cash balances.[11] Suppose that you keep a reservoir of cash that is

---

[11] See W. J. Baumol, "The Transactions Demand for Cash: An Inventory Theoretic Approach," *Quarterly Journal of Economics* 66 (November 1952), pp. 545–556.

Cutting That Wasteful Inventory

Inventories tie up capital, they take up floor space, and they deteriorate. So it is not surprising that managers are constantly looking for ways to reduce these costs. Twenty-five years ago inventories held by U.S. manufacturing companies accounted for 20 percent of their total assets. Today that figure is about 10 percent.

One way that companies have reduced inventories is by moving to a just-in-time (JIT) approach. JIT was pioneered by Toyota in Japan but has since been adopted by other companies throughout the world. With JIT a company calls up supplies only when needed. For example, deliveries to Toyota plants are made throughout the day at intervals as short as one hour for air-conditioners and heaters, and as long as a day for wipers, seat belts, and trim parts. Toyota's largest supplier, Denso Corp., makes hundreds of shipments each day to the automaker's assembly plants throughout Japan. Denso's Nishio plant alone dispatches 16 truckloads of air-conditioners and heaters to Takaoka, nearly one every hour, covering a distance of 15 miles.

To keep the production line running requires careful planning and coordination between Toyota and its suppliers. A strike at a supplier's plant or transportation difficulties in delivering components can cause havoc. For example, Toyota once had to shut down its Georgetown, KY, plant for nearly a day because an ice storm in the Midwest left roads impassable. Toyota's response was to hire a

forecasting company to monitor weather conditions between the Georgetown plant and its 330 suppliers.

Just-in-time systems have helped to reduce inventories of parts and materials. At the same time many firms are cutting inventories of finished goods by building their products to order. For example, in the automobile industry the traditional policy has been to produce batches of different colours or with different options, based on forecasts of likely demand. The cost of producing cars in this way to meet a demand that sometimes never materializes has been estimated at $80 billion a year. So automobile manufacturers are increasingly trying to reduce unwanted inventory by building cars in response to customer orders. They observe how a similar policy of build-to-order enabled Dell Computer to become the largest producer of personal computers. Dell customers use the Internet to specify what features they want on their PC. The machine is then assembled to order and dispatched, usually arriving within three days.

Sources: These examples of just-in-time and build-to-order production are taken from T. Murphy, "JIT: When ASAP Isn't Good Enough," *Ward's Auto World*, May 1999, pp. 67–73; R. Schreffler, "Alive and Well," *Ward's Auto World*, May 1999, pp. 73–77; "A Long March: Mass Customisation," *The Economist*, July 14, 2001, pp. 63–65.

steadily drawn down to pay bills. When it runs out, you replenish the cash balance by selling short-term securities. In these circumstances your inventory of cash also follows a sawtoothed pattern like the pattern for inventories we saw in Figure 20.3.

In other words, your cash management problem is just like the problem of finding the optimal order size faced by the builder's merchant. You simply need to redefine the variables. Instead of bricks per order, the order size is defined as the value of short-term securities that are sold whenever the cash balance is replenished. Total cash outflow takes the place of the total number of bricks sold. Cost per order becomes the cost per sale of securities, and the carrying cost is just the interest rate. Our formula for the number of securities to be sold or, equivalently, the initial cash balance is therefore

$$\text{Initial cash balance} = \sqrt{\frac{2 \times \text{annual cash outflows} \times \text{cost per sale of securities}}{\text{interest rate}}} \qquad (20.2)$$

Baumol's model of optimal cash balances illustrates the basic trade-offs that managers must make:

- When the cost of selling securities is high, you should hold larger average cash balances.
- When interest rates are high, you should hold smaller cash balances.
- When annual cash outflows increase, the optimal level of cash increases less than proportionally.

EXAMPLE 20.4	THE OPTIMAL CASH BALANCE

Suppose that you can invest spare cash in Canadian Treasury bills at an interest rate of 8 percent, but every sale of bills costs you $20. Your firm pays out cash at a rate of $105,000 per month, or $1,260,000 per year. Our formula for the initial cash balance tells us that the optimal number of Treasury bills that you should sell at one time is

$$\sqrt{\frac{2 \times 1,260,000 \times 20}{.08}} = \$25,100$$

Thus your firm would sell approximately $25,000 of Treasury bills four times a month—about once a week. Its average cash balance will be $25,000/2, or $12,500.

In Baumol's model a higher interest rate implies smaller sales of bills. In other words, when interest rates are high, you should hold more of your funds in interest-bearing securities and make small sales of these securities when you need the cash. On the other hand, if you use up cash at a high rate or there are high costs to selling securities, you want to hold large average cash balances. Think about that for a moment. *You can hold too little cash.* Many financial managers proudly point out the extra interest that they have earned; these benefits are highly visible. The costs are less visible but they can be very high. When you allow for the time that a manager spends in monitoring the cash balance, it may make some sense to forgo some of that extra interest.

 Check Point 20.5

Suppose now that the interest rate is only 4 percent. How will this affect the optimal initial cash balance derived in Example 20.4? What will be the average cash balance? What will be annual trading costs? Explain why the optimal cash position now involves fewer trades.

UNCERTAIN CASH FLOWS

Baumol's model stresses the essential similarity between the inventory problem and the cash management problem. It also demonstrates the relationship between the optimal cash balance on the one hand, and the level of interest rates and the cost of transactions on the other. However, it is clearly too simple for practical use. For example, firms do not pay out cash at a steady rate day after day and week after week. Sometimes the firm may collect a large unpaid bill and therefore receive a net *inflow* of cash. On other occasions it may pay its suppliers and so incur a net *outflow* of cash.

Economists and management scientists have developed a variety of more elaborate and realistic models that allow for the possibility of both cash inflows and outflows. For example, Figure 20.4 illustrates how the firm should manage its cash balance if it cannot predict day-to-day cash inflows and outflows. You can see that the cash balance meanders unpredictably until it reaches an upper limit, which we denote as U. At this point the firm buys enough securities to return the cash balance to a more normal level, C^*. The firm will move $U–C^*$ dollars from its cash holdings into securities.

FIGURE 20.4
If cash flows are unpredictable, the cash balance should be allowed to meander until it hits an upper or lower limit. At this point the firm buys or sells securities to restore the balance to the return point, which is the lower limit plus one-third of the spread between the upper and lower limits.

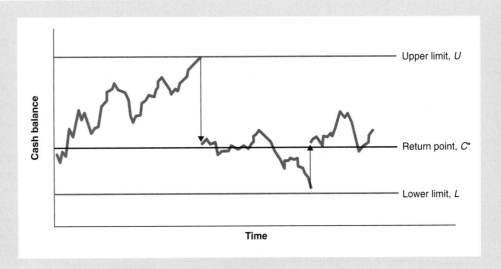

Once again the cash balance is allowed to meander until this time it hits a lower limit, L. This may be zero, a minimum safety margin above zero, or a balance necessary to keep the bank happy. When the cash balance hits the lower limit, the firm *sells* enough securities to restore the balance to a normal level. In this instance, the amount of securities sold is given by C^*–L dollars. Thus the rule is to allow the cash holding to wander freely until it hits an upper or lower limit. When this happens, the firm should buy or sell securities to regain the desired balance.

How far should the firm allow its cash balance to wander? The answer depends on three factors. If the day-to-day variability in cash flows is large or if the cost of buying and selling securities is high, then the firm should set the upper and lower limits far apart. The firm allows wider limits when cash flow volatility is high to keep down the frequency of costly security sales and purchases. Similarly, the firm tolerates wider limits if the cost of security transactions is high. Conversely, if the rate of interest is high and the incentives to manage cash are correspondingly more important, the firm will set the limits close together.[12]

Have you noticed one odd feature about Figure 20.4? The cash balance does not return to a point halfway between the lower and upper limits. It always comes back to a point one-third of the distance from the lower to the upper limit. Always starting at this return point means the firm hits the lower limit more often than the upper limit. This does not minimize the number of transactions—that would require always starting exactly at the middle of the spread. However, always starting at the middle would mean a higher average cash balance and higher interest costs. The lower return point minimizes the sum of transaction costs and interest costs.

If F represents the fixed cost per transaction of buying and selling marketable securities, and I is the interest rate per period on marketable securities,[13] then, according to the Miller-Orr model, the upper limit to the amount of cash, U, the target cash balance, C^*, and the average cash balance, $AvgC^*$, can be represented by the following equations:

$$U = [(3 \times C^*) - (2 \times L)]$$
$$C^* = L + (3/4 \times F \times \sigma^2/I)^{1/3}$$
$$AvgC^* = [4 \times (C^* - L)]/3$$

Where σ^2 is the variance of the firm's monthly net cash flows.

To illustrate, suppose $F = \$8$ and $I = 0.75$ percent per month. Also, assume that the lower limit to the firm's target cash balance, L, is \$150 and the standard deviation of its monthly net cash flows, σ, is \$125. The variance, $\sigma^2 = (\$125)^2 = \$15,625$. Inserting the numbers into our equations for U, C^*, and $AvgC^*$, we get

$$C^* = \$150 + (3/4 \times \$8 \times \$15,625/0.0075)^{1/3}$$
$$\text{Or, } C^* = \$150 + (\$12,500,000)^{1/3} = \$150 + \$231 = \$381.$$
$$U = 3 \times \$381 - 2 \times \$150 = \$1,143 - \$300 = \$843.$$
$$AvgC^* = (4 \times \$381 - \$150)/3 = \$308.$$

Recognizing uncertainty in cash flows is realistic, but few managers would concede that cash inflows and outflows are entirely unpredictable. The manager of Toys"R"Us knows that there will be substantial cash inflows around Christmas. Financial managers know when dividends will be paid and when taxes will be due. In Chapter 19 we described how firms forecast cash inflows and outflows and how they arrange short-term investment and financing decisions to supply cash when needed and put cash to work earning interest when it is not needed.

This kind of short-term financial plan is usually designed to produce a cash balance that is stable at some lower limit. But there are always fluctuations that financial managers cannot plan for, certainly not on a day-to-day basis. You can think of the decision rule depicted in Figure 20.4 as a way to cope with the cash inflows and outflows, which cannot be predicted or that are not *worth* predicting. Trying to predict *all* cash flows would chew up enormous amounts of management time.

---

[12] See M. H. Miller and D. Orr, "A Model of the Demand for Money by Firms," *Quarterly Journal of Economics* 80 (August 1966), pp. 413–435.

[13] I can also be regarded as the opportunity cost of holding cash.

You should therefore think of these cash management rules as helping us understand the problem of cash management. But they are not generally used for day-to-day management and would probably not yield substantial savings compared with policies based on a manager's judgment, providing of course that the manager understands the trade-offs we have discussed.

Check Point 20.6

How would you expect the firm's cash balance to respond to the following changes?
a. Interest rates increase.
b. The volatility of daily cash flow decreases.
c. The transaction cost of buying or selling marketable securities goes up.

CASH MANAGEMENT IN THE LARGEST CORPORATIONS

For very large firms, the transaction costs of buying and selling securities become trivial compared with the opportunity cost of holding idle cash balances. Suppose that the interest rate is 4 percent per year, or roughly 4/365 = .011 percent per day. Then the daily interest earned on $1 million is .00011 × $1,000,000 = $110. Even at a cost of $50 per transaction, which is generous, it pays to buy Treasury bills today and sell them tomorrow rather than leave $1 million idle overnight.

A corporation with $1 billion of annual sales has an average daily cash flow of $1,000,000,000/365, about $2.7 million. Firms of this size end up buying or selling securities once a day, every day, unless by chance they have only a small positive cash balance at the end of the day.

Why do such firms hold any significant amounts of cash? For two reasons. First, cash may be left in non-interest-bearing accounts to compensate banks for the services they provide. Second, large corporations may have, literally, hundreds of accounts with dozens of different banks. It is often less expensive to leave idle cash in some of these accounts than to monitor each account daily and make daily transfers between them.

One major reason for the proliferation of bank accounts is decentralized management. You cannot give a subsidiary operating freedom to manage its own affairs without giving it the right to spend and receive cash.

Good cash management nevertheless implies some degree of centralization. You cannot maintain your desired inventory of cash if all the subsidiaries in the group are responsible for their own private pools of cash. And you certainly want to avoid situations in which one subsidiary is investing its spare cash at 8 percent while another is borrowing at 10 percent. It is not surprising, therefore, that even in highly decentralized companies, generally, there is central control over cash balances and bank relations.

INVESTING IDLE CASH: THE MONEY MARKET

We have seen that when firms have excess funds, they can invest the surplus in interest-bearing securities. Treasury bills are only one of many securities that might be appropriate for such short-term investments. More generally, firms may invest in a variety of securities in the **money market**, the market for short-term financial assets. Larger firms usually invest directly in these securities. However, smaller firms often park their spare cash in a money market mutual fund, which holds a portfolio of money market investments.

money market   Market for short-term financial assets.

Only fixed-income securities with maturities less than one year are considered to be part of the money market. In fact, however, most instruments in the money market have considerably shorter maturity. Limiting maturity has two advantages for the cash manager. First, short-term securities entail little interest rate risk. Recall from Chapter 5 that price risk due to interest rate fluctuations increases with maturity. Very short-term securities, therefore, have almost no interest rate risk. Second, it is far easier to gauge financial stability over very short horizons. It isn't necessary to worry as much about deterioration in financial strength over a 90-day horizon compared to the 30-year life of a bond. These considerations imply that high-quality money market securities are a safe "parking spot" to keep idle balances until they are converted back to cash.

Most money market securities are also highly marketable, or *liquid*, meaning that it is easy and cheap to sell the asset for cash. This property, too, is an attractive feature of securities used as temporary investments until cash is needed. Some important money market instruments are described below.[14] Also, Table 20.3 provides information on recent rates for some Canadian money market securities.

Treasury Bills

These are the most liquid of assets and are traded actively over-the-counter by banks and security dealers. Treasury bills are issued by the Canadian government with original maturities ranging from one month to a year. These securities are sold at weekly auctions.

Commercial Paper

This is the short-term, usually unsecured, debt of large and well-known companies. While maturities can range up to 365 days, commercial paper usually is issued with maturities ranging from 1 to 3 months. Because there is no active trading in commercial paper, it has low marketability. Therefore, it would not be an appropriate investment for a firm that could not hold it until maturity.[15] Dominion Bond Rating Service rates commercial paper in terms of the default risk of the issuer.

Certificates of Deposit

CDs are time deposits at banks, usually in denominations greater than $100,000. Unlike demand deposits (chequing accounts), time deposits cannot be withdrawn from the bank on demand: The bank pays interest and principal only at the maturity of the deposit. However, short-term CDs (maturities less than three months) are actively traded, so a firm can easily sell the security if it needs cash.

TABLE 20.3
Money rates

Administered Rates	%
Bank of Canada	2.25
Target overnight rate	2.00
Central bank operating band	1.75–2.25
Canadian prime	3.75
Money Market Rates	
(for transactions of $1 million or more)	
3-month Treasury bills	2.24
6-month Treasury bills	2.42
1-year Treasury bills	2.68
10-year Canadian bonds	4.61
30-year Canadian bonds	5.12
1-month banker's acceptance	2.17
2-month banker's acceptance	2.22
3-month banker's acceptance	2.29
Commercial Paper (R-1 Low)	
1-month	2.14
3-month	2.25
Call money	2.00

Source: Reprinted with permission from *The Globe and Mail.*

---

[14] We have not included a discussion of the *banker's acceptance* here. This instrument is discussed in detail in chapters 19 and 21.

[15] Firms that issue commercial paper often repurchase it directly before maturity.

Repurchase Agreements

Also known as repos, or buybacks, repurchase agreements are in effect collateralized loans. A government bond dealer sells Treasury bills to an investor, with an agreement to repurchase them at a later date at a higher price. The increase in price serves as implicit interest, so the investor, in effect, is lending money to the dealer, first giving money to the dealer and later getting it back with interest. The bills serve as collateral for the loan: If the dealer fails and cannot buy back the bill, the investor can keep it. Repurchase agreements are usually very short term, with maturities of only a few days and sometimes overnight. These are usually transacted in minimum denominations of $100,000.

20.5   SUMMARY

1. What is float and why can it be valuable?

The cash shown in the company ledger is not the same as the available balance in its bank account. When you write a cheque, it takes time before your bank balance is adjusted downward. This is **payment float**. During this time the available balance will be larger than the ledger balance. When you deposit a cheque, there is a delay before it gets credited to your bank account. In this case the available balance will be smaller than the ledger balance. This is **availability float**. The difference between payment float and availability float is the **net float**. If you can predict how long it will take cheques to clear, you may be able to "play the float" and get by on a smaller cash balance. The interest you can thereby earn on the net float is a source of value.

2. What are some tactics to increase net float?

You can manage the float by speeding collections and slowing payments. One way to speed collections is by **concentration banking**. Customers make payments to a regional office, which then pays the cheques into a local bank account. Surplus funds are transferred from the local account to a concentration bank. A related technique is **lock-box banking**. In this case customers send their payments to a local post office box. A local bank empties the box at regular intervals and clears the cheques. Concentration banking and lock-box banking reduce mailing time and the time required to clear cheques. Finally, a **zero-balance account** is a regional bank account to which just enough funds are transferred each day to pay that day's bills.

3. What are the costs and benefits of holding inventories?

The benefit of higher inventory levels is the reduction in order costs associated with restocking and the reduced chances of running out of material. The costs are the carrying costs, which include the cost of space, insurance, spoilage, and the opportunity cost of the capital tied up in inventory. The **economic order quantity** is the order size that minimizes the sum of order costs plus carrying costs.

4. What are the costs and benefits of holding cash?

Cash provides liquidity, but it doesn't pay interest. Securities pay interest, but you can't use them to buy things. As financial manager, you want to hold cash up to the point where the incremental or marginal benefit of liquidity is equal to the cost of holding cash, that is, the interest that you could earn on securities.

5. Why is an understanding of inventory management useful for cash management?

Cash is simply a raw material—like inventories of other goods—that you need to do business. Capital that is tied up in large inventories of *any* raw material rather than earning interest is expensive. So why do you hold inventories at all? Why not order materials when you need them? The answer is that placing many small orders is also expensive. The principles of optimal inventory management and optimal cash management are similar.

Try to strike a balance between holding an inventory of cash that's too large (and losing interest on the money) and making too many small adjustments to your inventory (and incurring additional transaction or administrative costs). If interest rates are high, you want to hold relatively small inventories of cash. If your cash needs are variable and your transaction or administrative costs are high, you will want to hold relatively large inventories.

6. Where do firms invest excess funds until they are needed to pay bills?

Firms can invest idle cash in the **money market**, the market for short-term financial assets. These assets tend to be short term, low risk, and highly liquid, making them ideal instruments in which to invest funds for short periods of time before cash is needed.

Related Web Links

www.smallbusinessbc.ca Guide to preparing a cash flow forecast

www.fpsc.com Web site of Financial Publishing Services. Provides useful and current information for treasury management professionals.

www.ioma.com An on-line management library with some articles on cash management

www.nacha.org Automated collection systems for cash management

www.cdnpay.ca Canadian Payments Association

www.gmcanada.com General Motors of Canada

www.federalreserve.gov Information on money market and interest rates

www.ny.frb.org Interest rates and payment systems

www.phoenixhecht.com A comprehensive Web site on cash management with useful links

www.treasuryandrisk.com Web site of Treasury & Risk Management

www.americanbanker.com This site provides a host of information for bankers and finance professionals

www.intltreasurer.com Articles on short-term financial management

Key Terms

payment float	627	zero-balance account	634	economic order quantity	638
availability float	628	electronic funds transfer	634	just-in-time inventory	
net float	628	electronic data interchange		management	639
concentration banking	631	(EDI)	635	money market	643
lock-box system	633	debit card	635		

Questions and Problems

*Answers in Appendix B

BASIC

*1. **Float.** On January 25, Coot Company has $250,000 deposited with a local bank. On January 27, the company writes and mails cheques of $20,000 and $60,000 to suppliers. At the end of the month, Coot's financial manager deposits a $45,000 cheque received from a customer in the morning mail and picks up the end-of-month account summary from the bank. The manager notes that only the $20,000 payment of the 27th has cleared the bank. What are the company's ledger balance and payment float? What is the company's net float?

2. **Float.** A company has the following cash balances:

Company's ledger balance = $600,000

Bank's ledger balance = $625,000

Available balance = $550,000

   a. Calculate the payment float and availability float.
   b. Why does the company gain from the payment float?
   c. Suppose the company adopts a policy of writing cheques on a remote bank. How is this likely to affect the three measures of cash balance?

3. **Float.** General Products writes cheques that average $20,000 daily. These cheques take an average of six days to clear. It receives payments that average $22,000 daily. It takes three days before these cheques are available to the firm.
   a. Calculate payment float, availability float, and net float.
   b. What would be General Products' annual savings if it could reduce availability float to two days? The interest rate is 6 percent per year. What would be the present value of these savings?

4. **Lock Boxes.** Anne Teak, the financial manager of a furniture manufacturer, is considering operating a lock-box system. She forecasts that 300 payments per day will be made to

lock boxes with an average payment size of $1,500. The bank's charge for operating the lock boxes is $.40 per cheque. The interest rate is .015 percent per day.

a. If the lock box saves two days in collection float, is it worthwhile to adopt the system?

b. What minimum reduction in the time to collect and process each cheque is needed to justify use of the lock-box system?

5. **Cash Management.** Complete the following passage by choosing the appropriate term from the following list: lock-box banking, wire transfer, payment float, concentration banking, availability float, net float, depository transfer cheque.

The firm's available balance is equal to its ledger balance plus the _____ and minus the _____. The difference between the available balance and the ledger balance is often called the _____. Firms can increase their cash resources by speeding up collections. One way to do this is to arrange for payments to be made to regional offices that pay the cheques into local banks. This is known as _____. Surplus funds are then transferred from the local bank to one of the company's main banks. Transfer may be by the quick but expensive _____ or by the slightly slower but cheaper _____. Another technique is to arrange for a local bank to collect the cheques directly from a post office box. This is known as _____.

PRACTICE

*6. **Lock Boxes.** Sherman's Sherbet currently takes about six days to collect and deposit cheques from customers. A lock-box system could reduce this time to four days. Collections average $10,000 daily. The interest rate is .02 percent per day.

a. By how much will the lock-box system reduce collection float?

b. What is the daily interest savings of the system?

c. Suppose the lock-box service is offered for a fixed monthly fee instead of payment per cheque. What is the maximum monthly fee that Sherman's should be willing to pay for this service? (Assume a 30-day month.)

EXCEL

7. **Lock Boxes.** The financial manager of JAC Cosmetics is considering opening a lock box in Calgary. Cheques cleared through the lock box will amount to $300,000 per month. The lock box will make cash available to the company three days earlier.

a. Suppose that the bank offers to run the lock box for a $20,000 compensating balance. Is the lock box worthwhile?

b. Suppose that the bank offers to run the lock box for a fee of $.10 per cheque cleared instead of a compensating balance. What must the average cheque size be for the fee alternative to be less costly? Assume an interest rate of 6 percent per year.

c. Why did you need to know the interest rate to answer (b) but not to answer (a)?

*8. **Collection Policy.** Major Manufacturing has a big market for its products in the United States. It currently has one bank account located in New York to handle all of its collections. The firm keeps a compensating balance of $300,000 (US) to pay for these services (see Section 19.7). It is considering opening a bank account with West Coast National Bank to speed collections from its many California-based customers. Major estimates that the West Coast account would reduce collection time by 1 day on the $1 million a day of business that it does with its California-based customers. If it opens the account, it can reduce the compensating balance with its New York bank to $200,000 since it will do less business in New York. However, West Coast also will require a compensating balance of $200,000. Should Major open the new account?

EXCEL

9. **Economic Order Quantity.** Assume that Everyman's Bookstore uses up cash at a steady rate of $200,000 per year. The interest rate is 2 percent and each sale of securities costs $20.

a. How many times a year should the store sell securities?

b. What is its average cash balance?

*10. **Economic Order Quantity.** Genuine Gems orders a full month's worth of precious stones at the beginning of every month. Over the course of the month, it sells off its stock, at which point it restocks inventory for the following month. It sells 200 gems per month, and the monthly carrying cost is $1 per gem. The fixed order cost is $20 per order. Should the firm adjust its inventory policy? If so, should it order smaller stocks more frequently or larger stocks less frequently?

11. **Economic Order Quantity.** Patty's Pancakes orders pancake mix once a week. The mix is used up by the end of the week, at which point more is reordered. Each time Patty orders pancake mix, she spends about a half hour of her time, which she estimates is worth $20. Patty sells 200 pounds of reconstituted pancake each week. The carrying cost of each pound of the mix is $.05 per week. Should Patty restock more or less frequently? What is the cost-minimizing order size? How many times per month should Patty restock?

EXCEL

12. **Economic Order Quantity.** A large consulting firm orders photocopying paper by the carton. The firm pays a $30 delivery charge on each order. The total cost of storing the paper, including forgone interest, storage space, and deterioration comes to about $1.50 per carton per month. The firm uses about 1,000 cartons of paper per month.

a.   Fill in the following table:

	Order Size			
	100	200	250	500
Orders per month				
Total order cost				
Average inventory				
Total carrying costs				
Total inventory costs				

b.   Calculate the economic order quantity. Is your answer consistent with your findings in part (a)?

*13. **Economic Order Quantity.** Micro-Encapsulator Corp. (MEC) expects to sell 7,200 miniature home encapsulators this year. The cost of placing an order from its supplier is $250. Each unit costs $50 and carrying costs are 20 percent of the purchase price.

a.   What is the economic order quantity?

b.   What are total costs—order costs plus carrying costs—of inventory over the course of the year?

14. **Inventory Management.** Suppose now that the supplier in the previous problem offers a 1 percent discount on orders of 1,800 units or more. Should MEC accept the supplier's offer?

*15. **Inventory Management.** A just-in-time inventory system reduces the cost of ordering additional inventory by a factor of 100. What is the change in the optimal order size predicted by the economic order quantity model?

*16. **Cash Management.** A firm maintains a separate account for cash disbursements. Total disbursements are $100,000 per month, spread evenly over the month. Administrative and transaction costs of transferring cash to the disbursement account are $10 per transfer. Marketable securities yield 1 percent per month. Determine the size and number of transfers that will minimize the cost of maintaining the special account.

17. **Float Management in the United States and Canada.** The Automated Clearinghouse (ACH) system in the United States uses electronic communication to provide next-day delivery of payments. The processing cost of making a payment through the ACH system is roughly half the cost of making the same payment by cheque.

a.   Why then do American firms often rationally choose to make payments by cheque?

b.   Two major payment systems in Canada are the Automated Clearing Settlement System (ACSS) and the Large Value Transfer System (LVTS). Would your answer in the context of Canada's payment system be different from part (a) above?

18. **Float Management.** A parent company settles the collection account balances of its subsidiaries once a week. (That is, each week it transfers any balances in the accounts to a central account.) The cost of a wire transfer is $10. A depository transfer cheque costs $.80. Cash transferred by wire is available the same day, but the parent must wait three days for depository transfer cheques to clear. Cash can be invested at 12 percent per year. How much money must be in a collection account before it pays to use a wire transfer?

*19. **Float Management.** Knob, Inc., is a nationwide distributor of furniture hardware. The company now uses a central billing system for credit sales of $182.5 million annually. The Bank of Montreal, Knob's principal bank, offers to establish a new concentration banking system for a flat fee of $100,000 per year. The bank estimates that mailing and collection time can be reduced by three days.
   a.   By how much will Knob's availability float be reduced under the new system?
   b.   How much extra interest income will the new system generate if the extra funds are used to reduce borrowing under Knob's line of credit with the Bank of Montreal? Assume the interest rate is 12 percent.
   c.   Finally, should Knob accept the Bank of Montreal's offer if collection costs under the old system are $40,000 per year?

20. **Cash Management.** If cash flows change unpredictably, the firm should allow the cash balance to move within limits.
   *a.   What three factors determine how far apart these limits are?
   *b.   How far should the firm adjust its cash balance when it reaches the upper or lower limit?
   c.   Why does it not restore the cash balance to the halfway point?

*21. **Optimal Cash Balances.** Suppose that your weekly cash expenses are $80. Every time you withdraw money from the automated teller at your bank, you are charged $.15. Your bank account pays interest of 3 percent annually.
   a.   How often should you withdraw funds from the bank?
   b.   What is the optimal-sized withdrawal?
   c.   What is your average amount of cash on hand?

*22. **Cash Management.** Suppose that the rate of interest increases from 4 to 8 percent per year. Would firms' cash balances go up or down relative to sales? Explain.

23. **Cash and Inventory Management.** According to the economic-order-quantity-inventory model and the Baumol model of cash management, what will happen to cash balances and inventory levels if the firm's production and sales both double? What is the implication of your answer for percentage-of-sales financial planning models (see Section 18.2)?

24. **Internet.** Log in to the web page of a major bank such as TD Canada Trust (**www.tdcanada trust.com**) or Scotiabank (**www.scotiabank.com**). How do these banks help corporations to manage their cash?

25. **Internet.** Your company has some spare cash to invest for three months. You are wondering whether to invest it in Canadian or U.S. Treasury bills, commercial paper, or certificates of deposit (CDs). CDs can either be with a bank in Canada, the United States, or England (this is called a euro-dollar deposit). Log in to the Bank of Canada Web site (**www.bank-banque-canada.ca/en**) or the U.S. Federal Reserve System Web site (**www.federal reserve.gov**) and find the latest rates on these investments. Why might you not choose to take the investment offering the highest rate?

26. **Identify the Model.** The Asian Tigers Conglomerate is seeking appropriate ways to manage its cash balances. The firm has established a lower limit with regard to its cash balance

holdings of $40,000. It faces quite a bit of volatility in its daily cash flows, with a variance of $300,000. The annual interest rate on marketable securities is 6 percent. The fixed cost per transaction of buying and selling securities is $50.

a. Calculate the target cash balance and the upper limit to holding cash for the firm.

b. Which cash balance model did you use for your computation?

Go to **www.mcgrawhill.ca/edumarketinsight**.

STANDARD &POOR'S

27. **Inventory.** Look at the financial statements of Ann Taylor Stores (ANN) and Buckle, Inc. (BKE), two fashion-clothing retailers. Compare the inventory level and turnover of each. What might explain the differences you uncover?

STANDARD &POOR'S

28. **Inventory Management.** Check out the recent performance of two very nice coffee shops with attached free reading rooms: Barnes & Noble, Inc. (BKS), and Borders Group (BGP). These firms are sometimes characterized as "inventory businesses." Why? How does their inventory management compare?

CHALLENGE

29. **Float Management.** Some years ago, Merrill Lynch, the American investment bank, increased its float by mailing cheques drawn on West Coast banks to customers in the east and cheques drawn on East Coast banks to customers in the west. A subsequent class action suit against Merrill Lynch revealed that in 28 months from September 1976, Merrill Lynch disbursed $1.25 billion (US) in 365,000 cheques to New York State customers alone. The plaintiff's lawyer calculated that by using a remote bank Merrill Lynch had increased its average float by 1.5 days.[16]

a. How much did Merrill Lynch disburse per day to New York State customers?

b. What was the total gain to Merrill Lynch over the 28 months, assuming an interest rate of 8 percent?

c. What was the present value of the increase in float, if the benefits were expected to be permanent?

d. Suppose that the use of remote banks had involved Merrill Lynch in extra expenses. What was the maximum extra cost per cheque that Merrill Lynch would have been prepared to pay?

Solutions to Check Points

20.1   a. The ledger balance is $940 + $100 − $40 = $1,000.

b. Availability float is $100, since you do not yet have access to the funds you have deposited.

c. Payment float is $40, since the cheque that you wrote has not yet cleared.

d. The bank's ledger balance is $940 + $100 = $1,040. The bank is aware of the cheque you deposited but is not aware of the cheque you wrote.

e. Ledger balance plus payment float = $1,000 + $40 = $1,040, which equals the bank's ledger balance. Available balance + availability float = $940 + $100 = $1,040, also equal to the bank's ledger balance.

20.2   The current market value of Ford is $25.6 billion. The 2-day reduction in float is worth $940 million. This increases the value of Ford to $26.54 billion. The new stock price will be 26.54/1.83 = $14.50 per share. Ford should be willing to pay up to $940 million for the system, since the present value of the savings is $940 million. (All amounts are in U.S. dollars.)

20.3   The benefit of the lock-box system, and the price the firm should be willing to pay for the system, is higher when

a. Payment size is higher (since interest is earned on more funds).

---

[16] See I. Ross, "The Race Is to the Slow Player," *Fortune* (April 1983), pp. 75–80.

b. Payments per day are higher (since interest is earned on more funds).

c. The interest rate is higher (since the cost of float is higher).

d. Mail time saved is higher (since more float is saved).

e. Processing time saved is higher (since more float is saved).

20.4   a.

Order Size	Orders per Year	Average Inventory	Order Costs	Carrying Costs	Total Costs
Bricks per Order	$\dfrac{1{,}250{,}000}{\text{Bricks per Order}}$	$\dfrac{\text{Order Size}}{2}$	$90 per Order	$.09 per Brick	Order Costs plus Carrying Costs
1,000,000	1.25	500,000	$ 113	$45,000	$45,113
500,000	2.50	250,000	225	22,500	22,725
200,000	6.25	100,000	563	9,000	9,563
100,000	12.50	50,000	1,125	4,500	5,625
60,000	20.83	30,000	1,875	2,700	4,575
50,000	25.00	25,000	2,250	2,250	4,500
20,000	62.50	10,000	5,625	900	6,525
10,000	125.00	5,000	11,250	450	11,700

b. The optimal order size decreases to 50,000 bricks:

$$\text{Economic order quantity} = \sqrt{\frac{2 \times \text{annual sales} \times \text{costs per order}}{\text{carrying cost}}}$$

$$= \sqrt{\frac{2 \times 1{,}250{,}000 \times 90}{.09}} = 50{,}000$$

Therefore, the average inventory level will fall to 25,000 bricks. The effect of the higher carrying costs more than offsets the effect of the higher sales.

20.5   At an interest rate of 4 percent, the optimal initial cash balance is

$$\sqrt{\frac{2 \times 1{,}260{,}000 \times 20}{.04}} = \$35{,}496$$

The average cash balance will be one-half this amount, or $17,748. The firm will need to sell securities 1,260,000/35,496 = 35.5 times per year. Therefore, annual trading costs will be 35.5 × $20 = $710 per year. Because the interest rate is lower, the firm is willing to hold larger cash balances.

20.6   a. Higher interest rates will lead to lower cash balances.

b. Higher (lower) volatility will lead to higher (lower) cash balances.

c. Higher transaction costs will lead to higher cash balances.

CREDIT MANAGEMENT AND COLLECTION

When companies sell their products, they sometimes demand cash on delivery, but in most cases they allow a delay in payment. The customers' promises to pay for their purchases constitute a valuable asset; therefore, the accountant enters these promises in the balance sheet as accounts receivable. If you turn back to the balance sheet in Panel A of Table 19.1, you can see that accounts receivable constitute, on the average, more than one-third of a firm's current assets. These receivables include both trade credit to other firms and consumer credit to retail customers. The former is by far the larger and will therefore be the main focus of this chapter.

Customers may be attracted by the opportunity to buy goods on credit, but there is a cost to the seller who provides the credit. Take Maple Leaf, for example. In Chapter 3 we saw that in 2004, Maple Leaf had sales of $6,365 million, or about $17 million a day. Receivables during the year averaged $267 million.[1] Thus Maple Leaf's customers were taking an average of 267/17 = 15.7 days to pay their bills. Suppose that Maple Leaf could collect this cash one day earlier without affecting sales. In that case receivables would decline by $17 million, and Maple Leaf would have an extra $17 million in the bank, which it could either hand back to shareholders or invest to earn interest.

Credit management involves the following steps, which we will discuss in turn.

First, you must establish the *terms of sale* on which you propose to sell your goods. How long are you going to give customers to pay their bills? Are you prepared to offer a cash discount for prompt payment?

Second, you must decide what evidence you need to have that shows the customer owes you money. Do you just ask the buyer to sign a receipt, or do you insist on a more formal IOU?

Third, you must consider which customers are likely to pay their bills. This is called *credit analysis*. Do you judge this from the customer's past payment record or past financial statements? Do you also rely on bank references?

---

[1] This is an average of receivables at the start of the year and at the end of the year.

Fourth, you must decide on *credit policy*. How much credit are you prepared to extend to each customer? Do you play it safe by turning down any doubtful prospects? Or do you accept the risk of a few bad debts as part of the cost of building up a large, regular clientele?

Fifth, after you have granted credit, you have the problem of collecting the money when it becomes due. This is called *collection policy*. How do you keep track of payments and pursue slow payers? If all goes well, this is the end of the matter. But sometimes you will find that the customers go bankrupt and cannot pay. In this case you need to understand how bankruptcy works.

After studying this chapter you should be able to

- Identify the steps in credit management.
- Measure the implicit interest rate on credit.
- Understand when it makes sense to ask the customer for a formal IOU.
- Explain how firms can assess the probability that a customer will pay, and decide whether it makes sense to grant credit to that customer.
- Summarize the bankruptcy procedures when firms cannot pay their creditors.

21.1   TERMS OF SALE

terms of sale   Credit, discount, and payment terms offered on a sale.

Whenever you sell goods, you need to set the **terms of sale**. For example, if you are supplying goods to a wide variety of irregular customers, you may require cash on delivery (COD). And if you are producing goods to the customer's specification or incurring heavy delivery costs, then it may be sensible to ask for cash before delivery (CBD).

Some contracts provide for *progress payments* as work is carried out. For example, a large consulting contract might call for 30 percent payment after completion of field research, 30 percent more on submission of a draft report, and the remaining 40 percent when the project is finally completed.

In many other cases, payment is not made until after delivery, so the buyer receives *credit*. Each industry seems to have its own typical credit arrangements. These arrangements have a rough logic. For example, the seller will naturally demand earlier payment if its customers are financially less secure, if their accounts are small, or if the goods are perishable or quickly resold.

When you buy goods on credit, the supplier will state a final payment date. To encourage you to pay *before* the final date, it is common to offer a cash discount for prompt settlement. For example, a manufacturer may require payment within 30 days but offer a 5 percent discount to customers who pay within 10 days. These terms would be referred to as 5/10, net 30:

5	/	10,		net 30
↑		↑		↑
percent discount for early payment		number of days that discount is available		number of days before payment is due

Similarly, if a firm sells goods on terms of 2/30, net 60, customers receive a 2 percent discount for payment within 30 days or else must pay in full within 60 days. If the terms are simply net 30, then customers must pay within 30 days of the invoice date, and no discounts are offered for early payment.

Check Point 21.1

Suppose that a firm sells goods on terms of 2/10, net 20. On May 1 you buy goods from the company with an invoice value of $20,000. How much would you need to pay if you took the cash discount? What is the latest date on which the cash discount is available? By what date should you pay for your purchase if you decide not to take the cash discount?

For many items that are bought regularly, it is inconvenient to require separate payment for each delivery. A common solution is to pretend that all sales during the month in fact occur at the end of the month (EOM). Thus goods may be sold on terms of 8/10, EOM, net 60. This allows the customer a cash discount of 8 percent if the bill is paid within 10 days of the end of the month; otherwise, the full payment is due within 60 days of the invoice date.

When purchases are subject to seasonal fluctuations, manufacturers often encourage customers to take early delivery, allowing them to delay payment until the usual order season. This practice is known as *season dating*. For example, summer products might have terms of 2/10, net 30, but the invoice might be dated May 1, even if the sale takes place in February. The discount is then available until May 11, and the bill is not due until May 31.

> A firm that buys on credit is in effect borrowing from its supplier. It saves cash today but will have to pay later. This, of course, is an implicit loan from the supplier.

Of course, a free loan is always worth having. But if you pass up a cash discount, then the loan may prove to be very expensive. For example, a customer who buys on terms of 3/10, net 30, may decide to forgo the cash discount and pay on the 30th day. The customer obtains an extra 20 days' credit by deferring payment from 10 to 30 days after the sale but pays about 3 percent more for the goods. This is equivalent to borrowing money at a rate of 74.3 percent a year. To see why, consider an order of $100. If the firm pays within 10 days, it gets a 3 percent discount and pays only $97. If it waits the full 30 days, it pays $100. The extra 20 days of credit increase the payment by the fraction $3/97 = .0309$, or 3.09 percent. Therefore, the implicit interest charged to extend the trade credit is 3.09 percent *per 20 days*. There are $365/20 = 18.25$ twenty-day periods in a year, so the effective annual rate of interest on the loan is $(1.0309)^{18.25} - 1 = .743$, or 74.3 percent.

The general formula for calculating the implicit annual interest rate for customers who do not take the cash discount is

$$\text{Effective annual rate} = \left(1 + \frac{\textbf{discount}}{\textbf{discounted price}} \right)^{365/\text{extra days credit}} - 1 \qquad (21.1)$$

The discount divided by the discounted price is the percentage increase in price paid by a customer who forgoes the discount. In our example, with terms of 3/10, net 30, the percentage increase in price is $3/97 = .0309$, or 3.09 percent. This is the per-period implicit rate of interest. The period of the loan is the number of extra days of credit that you can obtain by forgoing the discount. In our example, this is 20 days. To annualize this rate, we compound the per-period rate by the number of periods in a year.

Of course, any firm that delays payment beyond day 30 gains a cheaper loan but damages its reputation for creditworthiness.

EXAMPLE 21.1   **TRADE CREDIT RATES**

What is the implied interest rate on the trade credit if the discount for early payment is 5/10, net 60?

The cash discount in this case is 5 percent and customers who choose not to take the discount receive an extra $60 - 10 = 50$ days credit. So the effective annual interest is

$$\text{Effective annual rate} = \left(1 + \frac{\text{discount}}{\text{discounted price}} \right)^{365/\text{extra days credit}} - 1$$

$$= \left(1 + \frac{5}{95} \right)^{365/50} - 1 = .454, \text{ or } 45.4\%$$

In this case the customer who does not take the discount is effectively borrowing money at an annual interest rate of 45.4 percent.

You might wonder why the effective interest rate on trade credit is typically so high. Part of the rate should be viewed as compensation for the costs the firm anticipates in collecting from slow payers. After all, at such steep effective rates, most purchasers will choose to pay early and receive the discount. Therefore, you might interpret the choice to stretch payables and not to take the cash discount as a sign of financial difficulties. It makes sense that the charged interest rate should be high.

Check Point 21.2   What would be the effective annual interest rate in Example 21.1 if the terms of sale were 5/10, net 50? Why is the rate higher?

21.2   CREDIT AGREEMENTS

open account Agreement whereby sales are made with no formal debt contract.

The terms of sale define the amount of credit but not the nature of the contract. Repetitive sales are almost always made on **open account** and involve only an implicit contract. There is simply a record in the seller's books and a receipt signed by the buyer.

Sometimes you might want a more formal agreement stating that the customer owes you money. When the order is very large and there is no complicated cash discount, the customer may be asked to sign a *promissory note*. This is just a straightforward IOU, worded along the following lines:

> Vancouver
> April 1, 2004
>
> Sixty days after date, ABC, Inc., promises to pay to the order of the XYZ Company ten thousand dollars ($10,000) for value received.
>
> Signature

Such an arrangement is not common but it does eliminate the possibility of any subsequent disputes about the amount and existence of the debt; the customer knows that he may be sued immediately for failure to pay on the due date.

If you want a clear commitment from the buyer, it is more useful to have it *before* you deliver the goods. In this case the common procedure is to arrange a *commercial draft*. This is simply jargon for an order to pay.[2] It works as follows. The seller prepares a draft ordering payment by the customer and sends this draft to the customer's bank. If immediate payment is required, the draft is termed a *sight draft*; otherwise it is known as a *time draft*. Depending on whether it is a sight or a time draft, the customer either tells the bank to pay up or acknowledges the debt by adding the word *accepted* and a signature. Once accepted, a time draft is like a postdated cheque and is called a *trade acceptance*. This trade acceptance is then forwarded to the seller, who holds it until the payment becomes due.

If the customer's credit is for any reason suspect, the seller may ask the customer to arrange for her bank to accept the time draft. In this case, the bank guarantees the customer's debt and the draft is called a *banker's acceptance*. Banker's acceptances are often used in overseas trade. They are actively bought and sold in the money market, the market for short-term high-quality debt.

If you sell goods to a customer who proves unable to pay, you cannot get your goods back. You simply become a general creditor similar to other unfortunate companies. You can avoid this situation by making a *conditional sale*, so that ownership of the goods remains with the seller until full payment is made. The conditional sale is common in Europe. In Canada it is used only for goods that are bought on instalment. In this case, if the customer fails to make the agreed number of payments, then the equipment can be immediately repossessed by the seller.

---

[2] For example, a cheque is an example of a draft. Whenever you write a cheque, you are ordering the bank to make a payment.

CREDIT ANALYSIS

credit analysis   Procedure to determine the likelihood a customer will pay its bills.

There are a number of ways to find out whether customers are likely to pay their debts, that is, to carry out **credit analysis**. The most obvious indication is whether they have paid promptly in the past. Prompt payment is usually a good omen, but beware of the customer who establishes a high credit limit based on small payments, and then disappears, leaving you with a large unpaid bill.

If you are dealing with a new customer, you will probably check with a credit agency. Dun & Bradstreet, which is by far the largest of these agencies, provides credit ratings on several million American and international firms, including more than 1 million Canadian businesses. In addition to its rating service, Dun & Bradstreet provides, on request, a full credit report on a potential customer. Similarly Trans Union Canada offers consumer credit-related products and services throughout Canada to its subscribers.

Credit agencies usually report the experience that other firms have had with your customer, but you can also get this information by contacting those firms directly or through a credit bureau.

Your bank can also make a credit check. It will contact the customer's bank and ask for information on the customer's average bank balance, access to bank credit, and general reputation.

In addition to checking with your customer's bank, it might make sense to check what everybody else in the financial community thinks about your customer's credit standing. Does that sound expensive? Not if your customer is a public company. You just look at Dominion Bond Rating Service's or Standard & Poor's rating for the customer's bonds.[3] You can also compare prices of these bonds to the prices of other firms' bonds. (Of course, the comparisons should be between bonds of similar maturity, coupon, and so on.) Finally, you can look at how the customer's stock price has been behaving recently. A sharp fall in price doesn't mean that the company is in trouble, but it does suggest that prospects are less bright than they were formerly.

FINANCIAL RATIO ANALYSIS

We have suggested a number of ways to check whether your customer is a good risk. You can ask your collection manager, a specialized credit agency, credit bureau, banker, or the financial community at large. But if you don't like relying on the judgment of others, you can do your own homework. Ideally this would involve a detailed analysis of the company's business prospects and financing, but this is usually too expensive. Therefore, credit analysts concentrate on the company's financial statements, using rough rules of thumb to judge whether the firm is a good credit risk. The rules of thumb are based on *financial ratios*. Chapter 17 described how these ratios are calculated and interpreted.

NUMERICAL CREDIT SCORING

Analyzing credit risk is like detective work. You have a lot of clues—some important, some fitting into a neat pattern, others contradictory. You must weigh these clues to come up with an overall judgment.

When the firm has a small, regular clientele, the credit manager can easily handle the process informally and make a judgment about what are often termed the *five Cs of credit*:

1. customer's *character*
2. customer's *capacity to pay*
3. customer's *capital*
4. *collateral* provided by the customer[4]
5. *condition* of the customer's business

---

[3] A few years ago, Standard & Poor's acquired Canadian Bond Rating Service, which used to be a major Canadian rating organization. Of course, many Canadian companies borrow regularly in the United States and other countries, and their bonds are rated by other prominent rating firms such as Moody's. We described bond ratings in Chapter 5, Section 5.2.

[4] For example, the customer can offer bonds as collateral. These bonds can then be seized by the seller if the customer fails to pay.

When the company is dealing directly with consumers or with a large number of small trade accounts, some streamlining is essential. In these cases it may make sense to use a scoring system to prescreen credit applications.

For example, if you apply for a credit card or a bank loan, you will be asked about your job, home, and financial position. The information that you provide is used to calculate an overall credit score. Applicants who do not make the grade on the score are likely to be refused credit or subjected to more detailed analysis.

Banks and the credit departments of industrial firms also use mechanical credit scoring systems to cut the costs of assessing commercial credit applications. One bank claimed that by introducing a credit scoring system, it cut the cost of reviewing loan applications by two-thirds. It cited the case of an application for a $5,000 credit line from a small business. A clerk entered information from the loan application into a computer and checked the firm's deposit balances with the bank, as well as the owner's personal and business credit files. Immediately the loan officer could see the applicant's score: 240 on a scale of 100 to 300, well above the bank's cut-off figure. All that remained for the bank was to check that there was nothing obviously suspicious about the application. "We don't want to lend to set up an alligator farm in the desert," said one bank official.[5]

Firms use several statistical techniques to separate the creditworthy customers from the impecunious ones. One common method employs *multiple discriminant analysis* to produce a measure of solvency called a *Z score*. For example, a study by Edward Altman suggested the following relationship between a firm's financial ratios and its creditworthiness (*Z*):[6]

$$Z = 3.3 \frac{\text{EBIT}}{\text{total assets}} + 1.0 \frac{\text{sales}}{\text{total assets}} + .6 \frac{\text{market value of equity}}{\text{total book debt}}$$

$$+ 1.4 \frac{\text{retained earnings}}{\text{total assets}} + 1.2 \frac{\text{working capital}}{\text{total assets}}$$

Here EBIT is earnings before interest and taxes. This equation did a good job at distinguishing between the bankrupt and non-bankrupt firms. Of the former, 94 percent had *Z* scores *less* than 2.7 before they went bankrupt. In contrast, 97 percent of the non-bankrupt firms had *Z* scores *above* this level.[7]

EXAMPLE 21.2

CREDIT SCORING

Consider a firm with the following financial ratios:

$$\frac{\text{EBIT}}{\text{total assets}} = .12 \qquad \frac{\text{sales}}{\text{total assets}} = 1.4 \qquad \frac{\text{market equity}}{\text{book debt}} = .9$$

$$\frac{\text{retained earnings}}{\text{total assets}} = .4 \qquad \frac{\text{working capital}}{\text{total assets}} = .12$$

The firm's *Z* score is thus

$$(3.3 \times .12) + (1.0 \times 1.4) + (.6 \times .9) + (1.4 \times .4) + (1.2 \times .12) = 3.04$$

This score is above the cut-off level for predicting bankruptcy and, thus, would be considered favourable in terms of evaluating the firm's creditworthiness.

SEE BOX P. 658

The nearby Finance in Action box describes how statistical scoring systems similar to the *Z* score can provide timely first-cut estimates of creditworthiness. These assessments can streamline the credit decision and free up labour for other, less mechanical tasks. These scoring systems

---

[5] Quoted in S. Hansell, "Need a Loan? Ask the Computer; 'Credit Scoring' Changes Small-Business Lending," the *New York Times* (April 18, 1995), p. D1.

[6] E. I. Altman, "Financial Ratios, Discriminant Analysis and the Prediction of Corporate Bankruptcy," *Journal of Finance* 23 (September 1968), pp. 589–609.

[7] This equation was fitted with hindsight. The equation did slightly less well when used to *predict* bankruptcies after 1965.

To hear bankers tell it, credit scoring is the best thing to happen to small-business borrowers since the invention of compound interest. Forget haggling over things like how well your business is doing or what your competitors are up to. Just hand in some predetermined data about yourself and your company, let the computer crunch the numbers, and voila: Out comes a "credit score" that predicts the chances that you'll actually pay off the loan. Score high enough, and you get approved, sometimes within minutes.

Scoring is already ubiquitous in consumer lending, and 22 of the 25 biggest players in the small-business loan market use the system, according to Fair, Isaac & Co., a pioneer in the development of credit-scoring software. Almost any loan of $50,000 or less issued by a national financial services company will have gone through a credit-scoring system.

Credit-scoring models assign points for up to 20 factors. The more points you get, the better credit risk you represent. The best-known credit-scoring models are provided by Fair, Isaac. The score on its Small Business Scoring Service ranges from 50 to 350, with most small businesses falling into the 150 to 250 area. While lenders set their own cutoff points, if you score above 220, that's generally good, while scores below 170 are considered high risk.

The overriding factor in a small-business credit score is your personal credit history. Specifically, the system looks at whether you pay your personal bills on time. The later you pay, the fewer points you get, and the more bills you pay late, the more your score gets knocked down.

The next key input is how much credit you've already got access to and balances on your accounts. If lines of credit are maxed out, lenders worry that there is little room to maneuver if the business runs into trouble. Other major red flags include bankruptcies, debts turned over to a collection agency, liens, and even overdue child-support payments. You can even get penalized for shopping too hard for credit.

Finally, specific business characteristics are weighed. They include the size of the company; its age; the industry in which it does business; and whether it's a corporation, partnership, or sole proprietorship. A sole prop gets fewer points than a partnership, and a partnership gets fewer points than a corporation. After all, if you're a sole proprietor and you get hit by a bus, all bets are off on your business. By the same token, a manufacturer gets higher points than bars or restaurants because it's less likely to go under quickly.

Source: V. M. Kahn, "Credit Scoring: What Your Lender Won't Tell You," *BusinessWeek*, May 22, 2000, p. F30.

can be used in conjunction with large databases, such as Dun & Bradstreet's, to provide quick credit scores for thousands of firms.

WHEN TO STOP LOOKING FOR CLUES

We told you earlier where to start looking for clues about a customer's creditworthiness, but we never said anything about when to stop. A detailed credit analysis costs money, so you need to keep the following basic principle in mind:

> Credit analysis is worthwhile only if the expected savings exceed the cost.

This simple rule has two immediate implications:

1. *Don't undertake a full credit analysis unless the order is big enough to justify it.* If the maximum profit on an order is $100, it is foolish to spend $200 to check whether the customer is a good prospect. Rely on a less detailed credit check for the smaller orders and save your energy and your money for the big orders.
2. *Undertake a full credit analysis for the doubtful orders.* If a preliminary check suggests that a customer is almost certainly a good prospect, then searching further is unlikely to justify the costs. That is why many firms use a numerical credit scoring system to identify borderline applicants, who are then the subject of a full-blown detailed credit check. Other applicants are either accepted or rejected without further question.

21.4   THE CREDIT DECISION

credit policy Standards set to determine the amount and nature of credit to extend to customers.

You have taken the first three steps toward an effective credit operation. In other words, you have fixed your terms of sale; you have decided whether to sell on open account or to ask your customers to sign an IOU; and you have established a procedure for estimating the probability of customers paying up. Your next step is to decide on **credit policy**.

FIGURE 21.1
If you refuse credit, you make neither profit nor loss. If you offer credit, there is a probability (*p*) that the customer will pay and you will make REV – COST; there is a probability (1 – *p*) that the customer will default and you will lose COST.

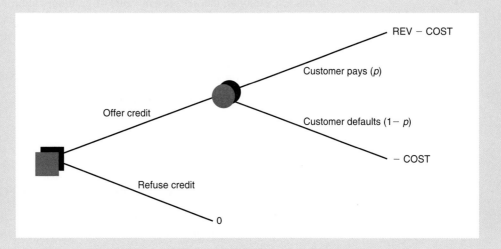

If there is no possibility of repeat orders, the credit decision is relatively simple. Figure 21.1 summarizes your choice. On the one hand, you can refuse credit and pass up the sale. In this case you make neither profit nor loss. The alternative is to offer credit. If you offer credit and the customer pays, you benefit by the profit margin on the sale. If the customer defaults, you lose the cost of the goods delivered.

> The decision to offer credit depends on the probability of payment. You should grant credit if the expected profit from doing so is greater than the profit from refusing.

Suppose that the probability that the customer will pay up is p. If the customer does pay, you receive additional revenues (REV), and you deliver goods that you incurred costs to produce; your net gain is the present value of REV – COST. Unfortunately, you can't be certain that the customer will pay; there is a probability $(1 - p)$ of default. Default means you receive nothing but still incur the additional costs of the delivered goods. The *expected profit*[8] from the two sources of action is therefore as follows:

$$\textbf{Refuse credit: 0}$$
$$\textbf{Grant credit: } p \times \textbf{PV(REV} - \textbf{COST)} - (1 - p) \times \textbf{PV(COST)} \tag{21.2}$$

You should grant credit if the expected profit from doing so is positive.

EXAMPLE 21.3   **THE CREDIT DECISION**

Consider the case of the Cast Iron Company. On each non-delinquent sale, Cast Iron receives revenues with a present value of $1,200 and incurs costs with a present value of $1,000. Therefore, the company's expected profit if it offers credit is

$$p \times \text{PV(REV} - \text{COST)} - (1 - p) \times \text{PV(COST)} = p \times 200 - (1 - p) \times 1,000$$

If the probability of collection is 5/6, Cast Iron can expect to break even:

$$\text{Expected profit} = 5/6 \times 200 - (1 - 5/6) \times 1,000 = 0$$

Thus Cast Iron's policy should be to grant credit whenever the chances of collection are better than 5 out of 6.

---

[8] Notice that we use the present values of costs and revenues. This is because there sometimes are significant lags between costs incurred and revenues generated. Also, while we follow convention in referring to the "expected profit" of the decision, it should be clear that our equation for expected profit is, in fact, the net present value of the decision to grant credit. As we emphasized in Chapter 1, the manager's task is to add value, not to maximize accounting profits.

In this last example, the net present value of granting credit is positive if the probability of collection exceeds 5/6. In general, this break-even probability can be found by setting the net present value of granting credit equal to zero, and solving for p. It turns out that the formula for the break-even probability is simply the ratio of the present value of costs to revenues:

$$p \times PV(REV - COST) - (1 - p) \times PV(COST) = 0$$

Break-even probability of collection, then, is

$$p = \frac{PV(Cost)}{PV(REV)}$$

and the break-even probability of *default* is

$$(1 - p) = 1 - PV(COST)/PV(REV) = PV(PROFIT)/PV(REV)$$

In other words, the break-even probability of default is simply the profit margin on each sale. If the default probability is larger than the profit margin, you should not extend credit.

Think what this implies. Companies that operate on low profit margins should be cautious about granting credit to high-risk customers. Firms with high margins can afford to deal with more doubtful ones.

Check Point 21.3

What is the break-even probability of collection if the present value of the revenues from the sale is $1,100 rather than $1,200? Why does the break-even probability increase? Use your answer to decide whether firms that sell high-profit-margin or low-margin goods should be more willing to issue credit.

CREDIT DECISIONS WITH REPEAT ORDERS

What effect does the possibility of repeat orders have on your credit decision? One of the reasons for offering credit today is that you may get yourself a good, regular customer.

Cast Iron has been asked to extend credit to a new customer. You can find little information on the firm, and you believe that the probability of payment is no better than .8. If you grant credit, the expected profit on this order is

$$\text{Expected profit on initial order} = p \times PV(REV - COST) - (1 - p) \times PV(COST)$$
$$= (.8 \times 200) - (.2 \times 1,000) = -\$40$$

You decide to refuse credit.

This is the correct decision *if* there is no chance of a repeat order. But now consider the future. If the customer does pay up, there will be a reorder next year. Having paid once, the customer will seem less of a risk. For this reason, any repeat orders are very profitable.

Think back to Chapter 9, and you will recognize that the credit decision bears many similarities to our earlier discussion of real options. By granting credit now, the firm retains the option to grant credit on an entire sequence of potentially profitable repeat sales. This option can be very valuable and can tilt the decision toward granting credit. Even a dubious prospect may warrant some initial credit if there is a chance that it will develop into a profitable steady customer.

| **EXAMPLE 21.4** | **CREDIT DECISIONS WITH REPEAT ORDERS** |

To illustrate, let's look at an extreme case. Suppose that if a customer pays up on the first sale, you can be *sure* you will have a regular and completely reliable customer. In this case, the value of such a customer is not the profit of one order but an entire stream of profits from repeat purchases. For example, suppose that the customer will make one purchase each year from Cast Iron. If the discount rate is 10 percent and the profit on each order is $200 per year, then the present value of an indefinite stream of business from a good customer is not $200 but $200/.10 = $2,000. There is a probability (p) that Cast Iron will secure a good customer with a value of $2,000. There is a probability of ($1 - p$) that the customer will default, resulting in a loss of $1,000. So, once we recognize the benefits of securing a good and permanent customer, the expected profit from granting credit is

Expected profit = ($p \times 2,000$) – ($1 - p$) $\times$ 1,000

This is positive for any probability of collection above .33. Thus the break-even probability falls from 5/6 to 1/3.

> If one sale may lead to profitable repeat sales, the firm should be inclined to grant credit on the initial purchase.

Check Point 21.4

How will the break-even probability vary with the discount rate? Try a rate of 20 percent in Example 21.4. What is the thinking behind your answer?

EXAMPLE 21.5

THE CREDIT DECISION: A COMPREHENSIVE LOOK

Careerbuild Publishers sells motivational guides on how to be successful at different careers. The books are priced at $125. The present value of the cost of producing one such career enhancement book is $100. Careerbuild sells the books on terms of net 30 and estimates that about 10 percent of all orders will not be collectible. If the interest rate is 1 percent per month, should the firm extend credit for a one-time order?

To work through this problem, we need to first determine present values of production costs and revenues. We know the present value of production costs to be $100. The present value of revenues is $125/1.01 = $123.76. The expected profit from a sale will be

$$.9(\$123.76 - \$100) - .1(\$100)$$
$$= \$21.38 - \$10 = \$11.38.$$

What would be the steps to figure out the breakeven probability of collection? We know that breakeven probability, which we denote as p, implies zero expected profits. We solve for p as follows:

$$p(\$123.76 - \$100) - (1 - p)(\$100) = 0$$
$$\text{or, } 23.76p - \$100 + 100p = 0$$
$$\text{or, } p = 100/123.76 = 0.808$$

Let us now see what happens with repeat orders. In such instances, a paying customer will potentially generate a perpetuity of profits of $123.76 – $100 = $23.76 per month. At an interest rate of 1 percent per month, the present value of the perpetuity is $23.76/.01 = $2,376. If we continue to assume a 10 percent default rate, the present value of a sale will work out to

$$.9 (\$2,376) - .1 (\$100) = \$2,138.4 - \$10 = \$2,128.4.$$

Notice that for repeat orders it is much easier to justify extending credit to paying customers.

To calculate the breakeven probability of collection, p, in the case of repeat orders, we solve for

$$p(\$2,376) - (1 - p)(\$100) = 0$$
$$\text{or, } 2,376p - \$100 + 100p = 0$$
$$\text{or, } p = 100/2,476 = .04$$

So, for repeat orders, the probability of payments needs to be greater than only 4 percent to justify extending credit.

EVALUATING A CREDIT POLICY SWITCH

Let us look at an example to help us evaluate the efficacy of switching from a cash-only policy to a new credit policy.

| EXAMPLE 21.6 | THE CREDIT DECISION: EVALUATING A CREDIT POLICY SWITCH |

Start-me-up Inc. specializes in manufacturing a type of component used in automotive transmissions. To help boost its unit sales, the firm is contemplating switching from a cash-only policy to a new credit policy of net 30 days on sales. The cost of capital rate for Start-me-up is 1 percent per month. The firm's price per unit of automotive transmission parts is $120, and variable cost per unit is $95. These numbers are likely to remain unchanged even after a switch to a new credit policy. The new credit policy is, however, likely to increase unit sales from 900 to 1,000 per month. Notice that by introducing the new credit policy, Start-me-up has, in effect, increased its sales by 100 additional units per month in perpetuity. The incremental cash inflows each month from the extra sales is 100($120 – $95) = $2,500. Since this amount is expected to be generated in perpetuity, the present value of this perpetuity is $2,500/.01 = $250,000.

What about the cost of switching to the new credit policy? One component of this cost is the variable cost associated with producing the extra units; that is, 100 × $95 = $9,500. Another component of the cost is the monthly sales revenue under the old policy, which, with the new policy, will no longer be available to Start-me-up in the same month but only in the following month; this works out to $120 × 900 = $108,000. The total cost of the switch is, therefore, $9,500 + $ 108,000 = $117,500.

The net present value of the credit policy switch is $250,000 – $117,500 = $132,500. Clearly, in this instance, the switch in credit policy is worthwhile to Start-me-up.

SOME GENERAL PRINCIPLES

Real-life situations are generally far more complex than our simple examples. Customers are not all good or all bad. Many pay late consistently; you get your money, but it costs more to collect, and you lose a few months' interest. And estimating the probability that a customer will pay up is far from an exact science.

Like almost all financial decisions, credit allocation involves a strong dose of judgment. Our examples are intended as reminders of the issues involved rather than as "cookbook" formulas. Here are the basic things to remember:

1. *Maximize Profit.* As credit manager, your job is not to minimize the number of bad accounts; it is to maximize profits. You are faced with a trade-off. The best that can happen is that the customer pays promptly; the worst is default. In the one case the firm receives the full additional revenues from the sale less the additional costs; in the other it receives nothing and loses the costs. You must weigh the chances of these alternative outcomes. If the margin of profit is high, you are justified in a liberal credit policy; if it is low, you cannot afford many bad debts.
2. *Concentrate on the Dangerous Accounts.* You should not expend the same effort on analyzing all credit decisions. If an application is small or clear-cut, your decision should be largely routine; if it is large or dubious, you might do better to move forward to a detailed credit appraisal. Most credit managers don't make credit decisions on an order-by-order basis. Instead they set a credit limit for each customer. The sales representative is required to refer the order for approval only if the customer exceeds this limit.
3. *Look Beyond the Immediate Order.* Sometimes it may be worth accepting a relatively poor risk as long as there is a likelihood that the customer will grow into a regular and reliable buyer. (This is why credit card companies are eager to sign up university and college students even though few students can point to an established credit history.) New businesses must be prepared to incur more bad debts than established businesses because they have not yet formed relationships with low-risk customers. This is part of the cost of building up a good customer list.

21.5

COLLECTION POLICY

It would be nice if all customers paid their bills by the due date. But they don't, and since you may also "stretch" your payables, you can't really blame them.

Slow payers impose two costs on the firm. First, they require the firm to spend more resources in collecting payments. They also force the firm to invest more in working capital. Recall from Chapter 17 that accounts receivable are proportional to the average collection period (also known as days' sales in receivables):

$$\text{Accounts receivable} = \text{daily sales} \times \text{average collection period}$$

collection policy Procedures to collect and monitor receivables.

When your customers stretch payables, you end up with a longer collection period and a greater investment in accounts receivable. Thus you must establish a **collection policy**.

The credit manager keeps a record of payment experiences with each customer. In addition, the manager monitors overdue payments by drawing up a schedule of the aging of receivables. The **aging schedule** classifies accounts receivable by the length of time they are outstanding. This may look similar to Table 21.1. The table shows that customer A, for example, is fully current: There are no bills outstanding for more than a month. Customer Z, however, might present problems, as there are $15,000 in bills that have been outstanding for more than 3 months.

aging schedule Classification of accounts receivable by time outstanding.

When a customer is in arrears, the usual procedure is to send a *statement of account* and to follow this at intervals with increasingly insistent letters, telephone calls, or fax messages. If none of these has any effect, most companies turn the debt over to a collection agency or an attorney.

✓ **Check Point 21.5**

Suppose a customer who buys goods on terms 1/10, net 45, always forgoes the cash discount and pays on the 45th day after sale. If the firm typically buys $10,000 of goods per month, spread evenly over the month, what will the aging schedule look like?

There is always a potential conflict of interest between the collection department and the sales department. Sales representatives commonly complain that they no sooner win new customers than the collection department frightens them off with threatening letters. The collection manager, on the other hand, bemoans the fact that the sales force is concerned only with winning orders and does not care whether the goods are subsequently paid for. This conflict is another example of the agency problem introduced in Chapter 1.

Good collection policy balances conflicting goals. The company wants cordial relations with its customers. It also wants them to pay their bills on time.

There are instances of cooperation between sales managers and the financial managers who worry about collections. For example, the specialty chemicals division of a major pharmaceutical company actually made a business loan to an important customer that had been suddenly cut off by its bank. The pharmaceutical company bet that it knew its customer better than the customer's bank did—and the pharmaceutical company was right. The customer arranged

TABLE 21.1
An aging schedule of receivables

Customer's Name	Less than 1 Month	1–2 Months	2–3 Months	More than 3 Months	Total Owed
A	$ 10,000	$ 0	$ 0	$ 0	$ 10,000
B	8,000	3,000	0	0	11,000
•	•	•	•	•	•
•	•	•	•	•	•
•	•	•	•	•	•
Z	5,000	4,000	6,000	15,000	30,000
Total	$ 200,000	$ 40,000	$ 15,000	$ 43,000	$298,000

alternative bank financing, paid back the pharmaceutical company, and became more of a loyal customer. It is a nice example of financial management supporting sales.

21.6

BANKRUPTCY

We have reviewed some of the techniques that firms use to evaluate the creditworthiness of their customers and to decide whether to issue credit. It would be helpful if these techniques were refined enough to distinguish between customers that will pay their bills and those that will go belly-up, but this is not realistic. In any event, we have seen that granting credit to a financially shaky customer may pay off if there is a chance that the offer will lead to a profitable future relationship. Therefore, it is not uncommon for firms to have to deal with an insolvent customer.

bankruptcy The reorganization or liquidation of a firm that cannot pay its debts.

According to the Office of the Superintendent of Bankruptcy (OSB), about 84,000 individuals and 8,200 businesses filed for bankruptcy in 2004. Individual liabilities totalled $4.75 billion while business liabilities were roughly $3.06 billion.[9] Our focus here is on business **bankruptcy**. Business bankruptcies account for only about 9 percent of the total number of bankruptcies, but because they are larger than individual bankruptcies, they involve about 40 percent of all claims by value. When the U.S. telecommunications giant WorldCom went bankrupt in 2002, it had over $30 billion of long-term debt. There are also more complications when a business declares bankruptcy compared to when an individual does. Table 21.2 provides details regarding business bankruptcies by type of industry in 2004.

BANKRUPTCY PROCEDURES

workout Agreement between a company and its creditors establishing the steps the company must take to avoid bankruptcy.

A corporation that cannot pay its debts will often try to come to an informal agreement with its creditors. This is known as a **workout**. A workout may take several forms. For example, the firm may negotiate an *extension*, that is, an agreement with its creditors to delay payments. Or the firm may negotiate a *composition*, in which the firm makes partial payments to its creditors in exchange for relief of its debts.

The advantage of a negotiated agreement is that the costs and delays of formal bankruptcy are avoided. However, the larger the firm, and the more complicated its capital structure, the less likely it is that a negotiated settlement can be reached. (For example, the American firm, Wickes Corp. tried—and failed—to reach a negotiated settlement with its 250,000 creditors.)

liquidation Sale of a bankrupt firm's assets.

Regulations pertaining to bankruptcies are provided in the *Bankruptcy and Insolvency Act, 1992*. Some companies are also governed by the *Companies' Creditors Arrangement Act* and the *Winding-up and Restructuring Act*. These laws provide mechanisms by which the firm's assets can be **liquidated**—that is, sold—and the proceeds used to pay creditors. Liquidation usually involves a process wherein a petition is first filed in a federal court, either voluntarily by the debtor company, or involuntarily, if it is filed on behalf of the company by its creditors. A trustee in bankruptcy is then elected by the creditors to take over and liquidate the assets of the company. Proceeds from liquidating the assets are distributed among the creditors after paying bankruptcy administration costs. If any assets remain after meeting expenses and payments to creditors, they are distributed to preferred and common shareholders. This priority for distribution of claims may not always be followed at the discretion of the courts. Secured creditors are paid from the proceeds of sales of assets to which they have title, while unsecured creditors share in what is left over. If, however, the sale of the secured property does not generate sufficient cash to cover the amount owed, the secured creditors join with the unsecured creditors in dividing the liquidated value of remaining assets. In contrast, if secured assets are liquidated for proceeds greater than the secured claim, the net proceeds are used to pay unsecured creditors and others. In large bankruptcies involving numerous secured and unsecured claimants, creditors sometimes take controversial actions in their attempt at securing a piece

---

[9] These and other statistics are available at OSB's Web site, **www.osb-bsf.gc.ca**.

TABLE 21.2
Business bankruptcies reported in the calendar year 2004, by type of industry

Type of Industry	Number of Cases	Total Assets $	Total Liabilities $	Total Deficiency $
Agriculture, Forestry, Fishing, and Hunting	412	109,236,496	304,814,023	195,577,527
Mining and Oil and Gas Extraction	67	7,872,224	53,699,347	45,827,123
Utilities	12	84,678	3,041,408	2,956,730
Construction	1,344	91,256,660	326,886,976	235,630,317
Manufacturing	739	169,791,635	692,212,328	522,420,693
Wholesale Trade	390	60,298,493	235,093,225	174,794,732
Retail Trade	1,204	96,283,087	279,347,430	183,064,343
Transportation and Warehousing	803	52,046,353	181,183,773	129,137,420
Information and Cultural Industries	140	11,134,856	221,918,699	210,783,842
Finance and Insurance	118	8,622,983	49,872,084	41,249,100
Real Estate and Rental and Leasing	175	23,156,724	81,808,568	58,651,844
Professional, Scientific, and Technical Services	512	34,566,906	145,730,078	111,163,173
Management of Companies and Enterprises	39	5,997,132	46,289,230	40,292,098
Administrative and Support, Waste Management and Remediation Services	332	22,210,498	84,785,730	62,575,232
Educational Services	51	3,265,482	16,205,857	12,940,376
Health Care and Social Assistance	136	10,693,370	24,938,049	14,244,679
Arts, Entertainment, and Recreation	174	11,639,735	48,386,521	36,746,786
Accommodation and Food Services	932	44,274,246	169,313,260	125,039,014
Other Services (except Public Administration)	542	29,026,240	87,532,686	58,506,446
Public Administration	6	1,106,271	2,416,433	789,559
Total	**8,128**	**792,564,067**	**3,055,475,704**	**2,262,911,637**

Source: Office of the Superintendent of Bankruptcy Canada, *Annual Statistical Report for the 2004 calendar year*, at **www.osb-bsf.gc.ca**.

SEE BOX P. 666

of a shrinking asset pool. The nearby Finance in Action box describes the controversy surrounding Enron, the energy giant, and one of its large lenders, Citigroup, after Enron's bankruptcy filing.

There is also a pecking order of unsecured creditors. First come claims for expenses that arise after bankruptcy is filed, such as attorneys' fees or employees' compensation earned after the filing. If such post-filing claims did not receive priority, no firm in bankruptcy proceedings could continue to operate. Next come claims for wages and employee benefits earned in the period immediately prior to the filing. Taxes are next in line, together with debts to some government agencies such as the Workers' Compensation Board. Finally come general unsecured claims such as bonds or unsecured trade debt.

reorganization Restructuring of financial claims on a failing firm to allow it to keep operating.

The alternative to a liquidation is to seek a **reorganization**, which keeps the firm as a going concern and usually compensates creditors with new securities, often including equity, in the reorganized firm. Such reorganizations are generally in the shareholders' interests—they have little to lose if things deteriorate further and everything to gain if the firm recovers.

Firms attempting reorganization may seek refuge under specific provisions of the *Bankruptcy and Insolvency Act, 1992*, the *Companies' Creditors Arrangement Act*, or the *Winding-up and Restructuring Act*. Such provisions are designed to keep the firm alive and operating and to protect the value of its assets while a plan of reorganization is being worked out. During this period, other proceedings against the firm are halted, and the company is operated by existing management or by a court-appointed trustee.[10]

Recently, Ivaco, Inc., a leading Canadian steel manufacturer, filed for and obtained protection under the *Companies' Creditors Arrangement Act* from the Ontario Superior Court,

---

[10] In the United States, firms attempting to reorganize would seek protection under Chapter 11 of the *Bankruptcy Reform Act*.

Citigroup's Enron Financing Challenged by Other Lenders

When Enron Corp. turned to its bankers for money in late October, the energy company needed a quick, big loan to restore investor confidence in its finances.

Citigroup, Inc., came up with the cash—but with a catch.

Enron owed Citigroup $250 million (US) in unsecured debt that was coming due in early December; just one portion of the overall debt Enron owes the bank. So Citigroup told Enron it would provide $600 million of a new $1 billion loan—as long as $250 million was used to pay back existing Citigroup debt, according to people familiar with the transaction.

Now, a number of bankers in the lending syndicate are crying foul. Citigroup, they say, used its influence as a new secured lender to improve the standing of unsecured loans it had already extended at the expense of other lenders. The bankers say they discovered, only later, that part of the loan facility was used to prop a Citigroup debt position. Thus, the bankers are likely to challenge Citigroup's arrangement as part of Enron's bankruptcy filing in a New York bankruptcy court.

Few can blame Citigroup for trying to reduce its exposure to Enron. But some analysts say the manoeuvre raises questions about whether Citigroup moved unfairly to grab assets. And the deal effectively reduced the pool of collateral available to all of Enron's other creditors in the bankruptcy proceedings.

At a minimum, the controversy over the Citigroup financing underscores how contentious Enron's bankruptcy process could become, as numerous creditors fight to secure a piece of a shrinking asset pie. In addition, it continues to raise more questions about the multiple hats worn by large lenders such as Citigroup, and the conflicts that may be created with Enron's other creditors.

In most bankruptcy cases, unsecured creditors examine all loans extended before the filing to see whether the collateral was granted properly.

If an unsecured debt was to be paid off, or turned into a secured debt within 90 days of a bankruptcy, that lender is sometimes accused of receiving a "preference" over other lenders.

Because such "preferences" clash with a basic aim of bankruptcy law—to stop a race to the courthouse by treating all similarly situated creditors the same—they can be challenged in court.

If the Citigroup financing is successfully challenged, the $250 million claim would once again become unsecured, freeing up the collateral for the potential pool of assets to be divided up by unsecured creditors.

Source: Reprinted with permission from *The Wall Street Journal*.

SEE BOX P. 667

effectively putting its creditors on hold. The nearby Finance in Action box describes the restructuring and survival efforts of Laidlaw, Inc., as it prepared to seek protection from its creditors in Canadian and U.S. courts.

Although such court-ordered reorganization keeps creditors at bay, shareholders may not always feel that protection under the *Companies' Creditors Arrangement Act* is in their best interest. Take the case of Stelco, Inc., another large Canadian steel maker, which has been trying to restructure itself under protection from the *Companies' Creditors Arrangement Act* since January

SEE BOX P. 668

2004 when there was a general glut in steel prices. As the nearby Finance in Action box shows, an increase in the price of steel has since led some shareholders to question the need for such court-ordered protection.

The responsibility for developing a plan of reorganization may fall on the debtor firm. Otherwise, a plan may also be submitted by others—for example, a trustee, if appointed, or a committee of creditors.

The reorganization plan is basically a statement of who gets what; each class of creditors gives up its claim in exchange for new securities. (Sometimes creditors receive cash as well.) The problem is to design a new capital structure for the firm that will (1) satisfy the creditors, and (2) allow the firm to solve the *business* problems that got the firm into trouble in the first place. Sometimes only a plan of baroque complexity can satisfy these two requirements. When the Penn Central Corporation was finally reorganized in the United States in 1978 (7 years after it became the largest railroad bankruptcy ever), more than a dozen new securities were created and parcelled out among 15 classes of creditors.

The reorganization plan goes into effect if it is accepted by creditors and confirmed by the court. Acceptance requires approval by a majority of each class of creditor. Once a plan is accepted, the court normally approves it, provided that *each* class of creditors has approved it and that the creditors will be better off under the plan than if the firm's assets were liquidated and dis-

SEE BOX P. 669

tributed. The nearby Finance in Action box describes Air Canada's recent restructuring plan and its strategic implications for the future.

Struggling Laidlaw, Inc., will seek bankruptcy court protection here and in the U.S. during the next few days in its reorganization and survival efforts. The Burlington-based transportation giant will apply to courts in Toronto and Buffalo for protection from creditors, so the company can proceed with a vote on a reorganization and repayment plan, sources said yesterday.

"There's an 80 to 90 percent chance it may come down (today)," said one insider familiar with the negotiations.

The source said creditors would get between $.70 and $.80 on the dollar under the proposal.

It would come in the form of $.17 in cash, $.25 in new notes and the remainder in shares in a newly restructured Laidlaw company.

Most of the senior creditors, including Canadian banks, support the plan, according to the source.

The company, which is trying to overcome the weight of a huge debt load, has been working on restructuring debts of more than $3.4 billion (US) and a reorganization plan since last year.

Laidlaw indicated late last year the company would likely complete a plan by spring and then apply for a brief period under bankruptcy court protection, in both countries, for further negotiations and a creditors' vote on the plan.

Laidlaw, North America's biggest public and school bus operator, ran into serious debt problems after an expansion drive during the last decade.

The acquisitions included interests in U.S. health-care operations, primarily in ambulance and hospital emergency services.

The company lost $90 million on revenues of $1.56 billion in the six months ended Feb. 28.

In fiscal 2000, Laidlaw reported an operating loss of $961 million on revenues of $2.92 billion.

Laidlaw reports its results in U.S. dollars.

However, Laidlaw's net loss climbed to a whopping $2.23 billion as the company wrote down investments in its health-care holdings and Safety-Kleen Corp.

Safety-Kleen, which is trying to overcome lawsuits and an accounting scandal, filed for bankruptcy protection last year.

Laidlaw suspended interest payments on its bank and bond debt more than a year ago. The company closed a $150 million (Cdn) financing deal to help provide working capital for all its operating companies, except the Greyhound Lines division early this year.

Laidlaw completed the deal with a group of banks, led by the Canadian Imperial Bank of Commerce, for a $100 million line of credit. It also secured another $50 million in short-term financing.

Greyhound, the biggest intercity bus line on the continent, got its own $125 million credit line last fall.

Laidlaw won't have to hold its annual meeting until Jan. 15, 2002, because of the restructuring efforts after receiving permission from the Ontario Court of Justice. Laidlaw's stock has traded as high as $.93 in the last year but is currently languishing at less than $.20 a share.

The stock closed at $.18 on the Toronto Stock Exchange yesterday.

Source: T. Van Alphen and S. Josey, "Laidlaw to Seek Bankruptcy Protection, Sources Say," the *Toronto Star Syndicate* (June 27, 2001) p. E01.

The court may, under certain conditions, confirm a plan even if one or more classes of creditors vote against it. This is known as a *cram-down*. The terms of a cram-down are open to negotiation among all parties. For example, unsecured creditors may threaten to slow the process as a way of extracting concessions from secured creditors. The secured creditors may take less than 100 cents on the dollar and give something to unsecured creditors in order to expedite the process and reach an agreement.

Restructuring efforts under court protection are often successful, and the patient emerges fit and healthy. But in other cases, cures prove impossible and the assets are sold or liquidated. Sometimes the firm may emerge from bankruptcy protection for a brief period before it is once again submerged by disaster and back in bankruptcy. For example, the American airline company TWA came out of Chapter 11 bankruptcy at the end of 1993 and was back again less than two years later, prompting jokes about "Chapter 22." The once successful Canadian clothing retailer Dylex emerged from bankruptcy protection in 1995. Five years later, the company was once again on the brink of bankruptcy and had sold most of its well-known retail outlets, such as BiWay, Tip Top Tailors, Thriftys, and Braemar.

THE CHOICE BETWEEN LIQUIDATION AND REORGANIZATION

Here is an idealized view of the bankruptcy decision. Whenever a payment is due to creditors, management checks the value of the firm. If the firm is worth more than the promised payment, the firm pays up (if necessary, raising the cash by an issue of shares). If not, the equity is worthless, and the firm defaults on its debt and petitions for bankruptcy. If in the court's judgment the assets of the bankrupt firm can be put to better use elsewhere, the firm is liquidated and the

Stelco Shareholders Challenge Company's Insolvency

A group of Stelco Inc. shareholders jumped into the steel maker's restructuring Friday, demanding an independent evaluation of the company, a meeting of shareholders and an end to protection under the *Companies' Creditors Arrangement Act*.

Pollitt and Co. Inc., which holds 670,000 class A Stelco shares and says it represents holders of another 2.3 million, said Friday that shareholder value is in danger of being extinguished and the Ontario Superior Court needs to prevent that from happening.

"It is my firm belief that Stelco is not presently insolvent and I am gravely concerned with the prospect that these proceedings and the actions being undertaken by the current management of Stelco will lead to Stelco shareholders being wiped out," Murray Pollitt, the investment firm's president, said in court documents filed Friday.

Circumstances have changed since Stelco was granted CCAA protection on Jan. 29, Mr. Pollitt said, echoing arguments the United Steelworkers of America has made almost since the beginning of the company's restructuring.

His motion to overturn the CCAA proceedings is the second move by common shareholders, who have watched the value of

their shares jump to more than $1 in recent months after bottoming out at 48 cents in June. The key change in the environment is the huge jump in steel prices this year, Mr. Pollitt said in the filing. He also noted that the methodology Stelco's chief restructuring officer Hap Stephen used to put on the company's assets in February is no longer valid.

Based on changes in the business landscape last week when International Steel Group Inc. (ISG) agreed to a merger with privately held Dutch steel maker LNM Group, Mr. Pollitt said Stelco's two major mills are worth about $1.3 billion (Canadian), rather than the $353 million assessment Mr. Stephen originally made. The ISG deal covers many of the same steel-producing assets evaluated by Mr. Stephen.

The jump in steel prices has eliminated any danger the company will run out of cash, as it feared in January. "There is now no reasonable basis whatsoever to believe that Stelco will run out of money on or before Nov. 30," Mr. Pollitt said. "There is also no reasonable basis to expect that it will run out of money at any time."

Source: Reprinted with permission from *The Globe and Mail*.

SEE BOX P. 670

proceeds are used to pay off the creditors. Otherwise, the creditors simply become the new owners and the firm continues to operate.

In practice, matters are rarely so simple. For example, we observe that firms often petition for bankruptcy even when the equity has a positive value. And firms are often reorganized even when the assets could be used more efficiently elsewhere. The nearby Finance in Action box about Eastern Airlines provides a striking example. There are several reasons.

First, although the reorganized firm is legally a new entity, it is entitled to any tax-loss carry-forwards belonging to the old firm. If the firm is liquidated rather than reorganized, any tax-loss carry-forwards disappear. Thus there is an incentive to continue in operation even if assets are better used by another firm.

Second, if the firm's assets are sold off, it is easy to determine what is available to pay the creditors. However, when the company is reorganized, it needs to conserve cash as far as possible. Therefore, claimants are generally paid in a mixture of cash and securities. This makes it less easy to judge whether they have received their entitlement. For example, each bondholder may be offered $300 in cash and $700 in a new bond, which pays no interest for the first 2 years and a low rate of interest thereafter. A bond of this kind in a company that is struggling to survive may not be worth much, but the bankruptcy court usually looks at the face value of the new bonds and may decide that the bondholders have received as much as they would have if the firm was liquidated and, therefore, regard them as paid in full.

Senior creditors who know they are likely to get a raw deal in a reorganization are likely to press for a liquidation. Shareholders and junior creditors prefer a reorganization. They hope that the court will not interpret the pecking order too strictly and that they will receive some crumbs.

Third, although shareholders and junior creditors are at the bottom of the pecking order, they have a secret weapon: They can play for time. Bankruptcies of large companies often take several years before a plan is presented to the court and agreed to by each class of creditor. The bankruptcy proceedings of the Missouri Pacific Railroad, in the United States, took a total of 22 years. When they use delaying tactics, the junior claimants are betting on a turn of fortune that will rescue their investment. On the other hand, the senior creditors know that time is working against them, so they may be prepared to accept a smaller payoff as part of the price for getting

Air Canada's Reorganization Strategy

An Ontario court is expected to grant an order today approving Air Canada's comeback strategy, allowing the beleaguered airline to revamp its fleet, boost international routes and prepare to spin off subsidiaries.

Mr. Justice James Farley of Ontario Superior Court is scheduled to consider an Air Canada motion seeking the court's blessing for the company's restructuring plan.

The spotlight for the past 17 months has been on Montreal-based Air Canada's efforts to attract financing and get creditors outside. Now that investors and lenders are lined up, and creditors have agreed to forgive a large portion of debt owed by Air Canada, the nuts and bolts of the carrier's business plan will soon take centre stage.

Air Canada, having reduced labour expenses by wringing wage concessions from unionized employees, intends to further shrink costs while gaining passengers.

The court sanctioning order expected today will pave the way for Air Canada to emerge from bankruptcy protection on Sept. 30.

The goal is to run the airline efficiently and, eventually, profitably. With oil prices last week flirting near $50 (U.S.) a barrel and jet fuel prices soaring, however, the carrier has a steep path to recovery.

Creditors, who gave the green light last week to Air Canada's reorganization plan despite typically reaping just a dime on a dollar owed, will be keenly watching how well the airline can execute its business strategy. Creditors are poised to effectively assume an 88 percent interest in Air Canada, which sought court protection under the *Companies' Creditors Arrangement Act* (CCAA) on April 1, 2003.

"It's been a long, tough road and it's encouraging for all of us to have the end in sight," Air Canada chief executive officer Robert Milton said in a tape-recorded message to employees last week. Two key executives helping Mr. Milton are Montie Brewer, executive vice-president of commercial operations, and Stephen Smith, recently named to the newly created position of senior vice-president of customer experience.

It's Mr. Brewer's task to shape competitive and simplified fares, while Mr. Smith, a former WestJet Airlines Ltd. executive, seeks to motivate employees to provide the best service possible to consumers.

Mr. Milton emphasizes that he senses momentum building for Air Canada to implement its strategy, and he's optimistic about delivering a "winning performance."

Air Canada already has eliminated from its fleet dozens of aircraft deemed old and inefficient. It's now ready to remove aircraft such as the Boeing 737-200 and the BAE 146 while phasing out the oldest Dash-8s in its regional Jazz operation. New aircraft costing $2 billion will be purchased, notably regional jets from Brazil's Embraer SA and Montreal's Bombardier Inc., with delivery starting next month.

As well, the much-ballyhooed Zip fleet in Western Canada, launched nearly two years ago as Air Canada's discount rival to Calgary-based WestJet, will be retired. Zip employees are set to be integrated into Air Canada's mainline operation within a month.

On the international front, Air Canada will be seeking to build on its strength on global routes. The airline wants to expand its service to destinations abroad while looking for gains in efficiency by being careful to match the right aircraft with appropriate routes.

Markets in Latin America and the Caribbean are seen as growth areas, including flights to Lima, Peru, starting this November. Last month, the airline introduced its service to Bogota and Caracas.

Canada–U.S. routes will be another key component of Air Canada's restructuring plan.

While Air Canada boasts the most transborder flights into the United States of any carrier, the competition for customers is fierce and will get even tougher. WestJet, for instance, plans to expand into several U.S. markets by the end of this year.

Domestically, Air Canada's regional Jazz subsidiary will remain under the Air Canada banner. But eventually, Jazz could be one of several entities spun off as separate, publicly traded firms.

Douglas Reid, a professor at Queen's University's school of business, said it will be difficult for Air Canada to carry out its game plan in a profitable manner. While Air Canada has come a long way, "it's still in a frail state financially" because rising fuel prices will place greater pressure on the airline to find cost savings elsewhere and perhaps stretch employees too thin, Prof. Reid said.

"I don't want to sound like I'm raining on Air Canada's parade, and I feel very bad about saying this, but objectively, I don't understand how they'll be able to assemble the winning conditions needed to create profits" any time soon. Prof. Reid envisages Air Canada continuing to post annual losses through 2006. A new parent company for Air Canada, Ace Aviation Holdings Inc., is set to be created next month, and it's ACE that would control Jazz and other subsidiaries such as the Aeroplan loyalty program and the technical services unit, which oversees aircraft maintenance.

Just how much control ACE will maintain over the subsidiaries is unclear since ACE's new directors will need time to decide if and when to sell off minority stakes in, for example, Aeroplan and Jazz.

Rupert Duchesne, Aeroplan's president and CEO, said the expansion of the rewards program—beyond the staples of hotels and car rentals—will help restore consumer confidence in Air Canada.

He said Air Canada is on the verge of receiving court approval for its restructuring plan, so consumers should be "very reassured that their Aeroplan mileage is safe to carry on accumulating more."

Source: Reprinted with permission from *The Globe and Mail*.

---

a plan accepted. Also, prolonged bankruptcy cases are costly (the liquidators handling the Eaton's bankruptcy reportedly received $80 million). Senior claimants may see their money seeping into lawyers' pockets and therefore decide to settle quickly.

Fourth, while a reorganization plan is being drawn up, the company is allowed to buy goods on credit and borrow money. Post-petition creditors (those who extend credit to a firm already in

The Grounding of Eastern Airlines

Chapter 11 bankruptcy proceedings often involve a conflict between the objective of keeping the company afloat and that of protecting the interests of the lenders. Seldom has that conflict been more apparent than in the case of Eastern Airlines.

Eastern Airlines operated in the very competitive East Coast corridor and had services to South America and the Caribbean. For some years before it filed for bankruptcy, the company had had a record of high operating costs and poor labour relations. Its boss, Frank Lorenzo, had a reputation for union busting and one trade unionist had termed him "the Typhoid Mary of organized labour." Lorenzo's attempts to force Eastern's employees to take a wage cut led to a strike by machinists in March 1989 and almost immediately Eastern filed for bankruptcy under Chapter 11.

When Eastern filed for bankruptcy, it had saleable assets, such as planes and gates, worth over $4 billion. This would have been more than sufficient to pay off the company's creditors and preferred stockholders. But the bankruptcy judge decided that it was important to keep Eastern flying at all costs for the sake of its customers and employees.

Eastern did keep flying, but the more it flew, the more it lost. Management presented the bankruptcy court with three different plans to reorganize the company, but each time it immediately became clear that the plan was not viable. Eventually, the creditors' patience with management ran out, and they demanded the appointment of an independent trustee to run the company. However, the deficits continued to accumulate. In less than two years the airline had piled up additional losses of nearly $1.3 billion. Eventually, Eastern could no longer raise the cash to continue flying, and in January 1991 its planes were finally grounded.

Nearly four more years were to elapse before the court was able to settle on a plan to pay off Eastern's creditors and a further year passed before the last of the company's assets were sold. A large part of the proceeds from asset sales had been eaten up by the operating losses and just over $100 million had seeped away in legal costs. Less than $900 million was left to pay off the creditors. The secured creditors received about 80 percent of what they were owed and unsecured creditors received just over 10 percent.

Source: The description of the bankruptcy of Eastern Airlines is based on L. A. Weiss and K. H. Wruck, "Information Problems, Conflicts of Interest, and Asset Stripping: Chapter 11's Failure in the Case of Eastern Airlines," *Journal of Financial Economics* 48 (1998), pp. 55–97.

bankruptcy proceedings) have priority over the old creditors and their debt may even be secured by assets that are already mortgaged to existing debtholders. This also gives the pre-petition creditors an incentive to settle quickly, before their claim on assets is diluted by the new debt.

Finally, profitable companies may file for bankruptcy to protect themselves against "burdensome" suits. For example, in 1982, Manville Corporation was threatened by 16,000 damage suits alleging injury from asbestos. Manville filed for bankruptcy under Chapter 11 of the *Bankruptcy Reform Act* in the United States, and the bankruptcy judge agreed to put the damage suits on hold until the company was reorganized. This took six years. Of course, legislators worry that these actions are contrary to the original intent of the bankruptcy acts.

21.7   SUMMARY

1. What are the usual steps in credit management?

The first step in credit management is to set normal **terms of sale**. This means that you must decide the length of the payment period and the size of any cash discounts. In most industries these conditions are standardized.

Your second step is to decide the form of the contract with your customer. Most domestic sales are made on **open account**. In this case the only evidence that the customer owes you money is the entry in your ledger and a receipt signed by the customer. Sometimes, you may require a more formal commitment before you deliver the goods. For example, the supplier may arrange for the customer to provide a trade acceptance.

The third task is to assess each customer's creditworthiness. When you have made an assessment of the customer's credit standing, the fourth step is to establish sensible credit policy. Finally, once the credit policy is set, you need to establish a collection policy to identify and pursue slow payers.

2. How do we measure the implicit interest rate on credit?

The effective interest rate for customers who buy goods on credit rather than taking the discount for quicker payment is

$$\left(\frac{1 + \text{discount}}{\text{discounted price}} \right)^{365/\text{extra days credit}} - 1$$

3. When does it make sense to ask the customer for a formal IOU?

When a customer places a large order, and you want to eliminate the possibility of any subsequent disputes about the existence, amount, and scheduled payment date of the debt, a formal IOU such as a signed commercial draft may be appropriate.

4. How do firms assess the probability that a customer will pay?

Credit analysis is the process of deciding which customers are likely to pay their bills. There are various sources of information: your own experience with the customer, the experience of other creditors, the assessment of a credit agency, a check with the customer's bank, the market value of the customer's securities, and an analysis of the customer's financial statements. Firms that handle a large volume of credit information often use a formal system for combining the various sources into an overall credit score.

5. How do firms decide whether it makes sense to grant credit to a customer?

Credit policy refers to the decision to extend credit to a customer. The job of the credit manager is not to minimize the number of bad debts; it is to maximize profits. This means that you need to weigh the odds that the customer will pay, providing you with a profit, against the odds that the customer will default, resulting in a loss. Remember not to be too shortsighted when reckoning the expected profit. It is often worth accepting the marginal applicant if there is a chance that the applicant may become a regular and reliable customer.

If credit is granted, the next problem is to set a **collection policy**. This requires tact and judgment. You want to be firm with the truly delinquent customer, but you don't want to offend the good one by writing demanding letters just because a cheque has been delayed in the mail. You will find it easier to spot troublesome accounts if you keep a careful **aging schedule** of outstanding accounts.

6. What happens when firms cannot pay their creditors?

A firm that cannot meet obligations may try to arrange a **workout** with its creditors to enable it to settle its debts. If this is unsuccessful, the firm may file for **bankruptcy**, in which case the business may be liquidated or reorganized. **Liquidation** means that the firm's assets are sold and the proceeds used to pay creditors. **Reorganization** means that the firm is maintained as an ongoing concern, and creditors are compensated with securities in the reorganized firm. Ideally, reorganization should be chosen over liquidation when the firm as a going concern is worth more than its liquidation value. However, the conflicting interests of the different parties can result in violations of this principle.

Related Web Links

www.nacm.org Site of the National Association of Credit Management

www.dnb.com Dun & Bradstreet's site; the premier guide to corporate credit decisions

www.osb–bsf.gc.ca Web site of the Office of the Superintendent of Bankruptcy. This site provides a variety of information, including statistics on personal and business bankruptcies, relevant acts and laws, etc.

www.ny.frb.org/404/404/cfm The Federal Reserve Bank of New York's guide to credit management

www.creditworthy.com Useful tips and on-line resources for credit management

http://bankrupt.com Resources for firms that have made some bad decisions

www.tuc.ca TransUnion Canada

www.strategis.gc.ca Web site maintained by Industry Canada, providing a variety of trade, business, and consumer information

www.insolvency.ca The Insolvency Institute of Canada

http://finance.yahoo.com Yahoo's credit analyzer allows you to estimate your personal credit rating

www.myfico.com For information on personal credit ratings

Key Terms

terms of sale	653	collection policy	663	liquidation	664
open account	655	aging schedule	663	reorganization	665
credit analysis	656	bankruptcy	664		
credit policy	658	workout	664		

Questions and Problems

*Answers in Appendix B

BASIC

*1. **Trade Credit Rates.** Company X sells on a 1/20, net 60, basis. Customer Y buys goods with an invoice of $1,000.
   a. How much can Company Y deduct from the bill if it pays on day 20?
   b. How many extra days of credit can Company Y receive if it passes up the cash discount?
   c. What is the effective annual rate of interest if Y pays on the due date rather than day 20?

2. **Terms of Sale.** Complete the following passage by selecting the appropriate terms from the following list (some terms may be used more than once): acceptance, open, commercial, trade, Canada, his or her own, note, draft, account, promissory, bank, banker's, the customer's.

   Most goods are sold on _____ _____. In this case the only evidence of the debt is a record in the seller's books and a signed receipt. When the order is very large, the customer may be asked to sign a(n) _____ _____, which is just a simple IOU. An alternative is for the seller to arrange a(n) _____ _____ ordering payment by the customer. In order to obtain the goods, the customer must acknowledge this order and sign the document. This signed acknowledgment is known as a(n) _____ _____. Sometimes the seller may also ask _____ _____ bank to sign the document. In this case it is known as a(n) _____ _____.

3. **Terms of Sale.** Indicate which firm, of each pair, you would expect to grant shorter or longer credit periods:
   a. One firm sells hardware; the other sells bread.
   b. One firm's customers have an inventory turnover ratio of 10; the other firm's customers have a turnover of 15.
   c. One firm sells mainly to electric utilities; the other to fashion boutiques.

4. **Payment Lag.** The lag between purchase date and the date at which payment is due is known as the *terms lag*. The lag between the due date and the date on which the buyer actually pays is termed the *due lag*, and the lag between the purchase and actual payment dates is the *pay lag*. Thus

   $$\text{Pay lag} = \text{terms lag} + \text{due lag}$$

   State how you would expect the following events to affect each type of lag:
   *a. The company imposes a service charge on late payers.
   b. A recession causes customers to be short of cash.
   *c. The company changes its terms from net 10 to net 20.

5. **Bankruptcy.** True or false?
   a. It makes sense to evaluate the credit manager's performance by looking at the proportion of bad debts.

*b.   When a company becomes bankrupt, it is usually in the interests of the equityholders to seek a liquidation rather than a reorganization.

*c.   A reorganization plan must be presented for approval by each class of creditor.

d.   Canada Revenue Agency has first claim on the company's assets in the event of bankruptcy.

e.   In a reorganization, creditors may be paid off with a mixture of cash and securities.

f.   When a company is liquidated, one of the most valuable assets to be sold is often the tax-loss carry-forward.

EXCEL

6.   **Trade Credit Rates.** A firm currently offers terms of sale of 3/20, net 40. What effect will the following actions have on the implicit interest rate charged to customers that pass up the cash discount? State whether the implicit interest rate will increase or decrease.

a.   The terms are changed to 4/20, net 40.

b.   The terms are changed to 3/30, net 40.

c.   The terms are changed to 3/20, net 30.

PRACTICE

EXCEL

*7.   **Trade Credit and Receivables.** A firm offers terms of 2/15, net 30. Currently, two-thirds of all customers take advantage of the trade discount; the remainder pay bills at the due date.

a.   What will be the firm's typical value for its accounts receivable period? (See Section 19.1 for a review of the accounts receivable period.)

b.   What is the average investment in accounts receivable if annual sales are $20 million?

c.   What would likely happen to the firm's accounts receivable period if it changed its terms to 3/15, net 30?

8.   **Terms of Sale.** Microbiotics currently sells all of its frozen dinners cash on delivery but believes it can increase sales by offering supermarkets one month of free credit. The price per carton is $50 and the cost per carton is $40.

a.   If unit sales will increase from 1,000 cartons to 1,060 per month, should the firm offer the credit? The interest rate is 1 percent per month, and all customers will pay their bills.

b.   What if the interest rate is 1.5 percent per month?

c.   What if the interest rate is 1.5 percent per month, but the firm offers the credit only as a special deal to new customers, while old customers continue to pay cash on delivery?

*9.   **Credit Decision/Repeat Sales.** Locust Software sells computer training packages to its business customers at a price of $101. The cost of production (in present value terms) is $95. Locust sells its packages on terms of net 30 and estimates that about 7 percent of all orders will be uncollectible. An order comes in for 20 units. The interest rate is 1 percent per month.

a.   Should the firm extend credit if this is a one-time order? The sale will not be made unless credit is extended.

b.   What is the break-even probability of collection?

c.   Now suppose that if a customer pays this month's bill, it will place an identical order in each month indefinitely and can be safely assumed to pose no risk of default. Should credit be extended?

d.   What is the break-even probability of collection in the repeat-sales case?

10.   **Bankruptcy.** Explain why equity can sometimes have a positive value even when companies petition for bankruptcy.

11.   **Credit Decision.** Look back at Example 21.3. Cast Iron's costs have increased from $1,000 to $1,050. Assuming there is no possibility of repeat orders, and that the probability of successful collection from the customer is $p = .9$, answer the following:

a.   Should Cast Iron grant or refuse credit?

b.   What is the break-even probability of collection?

12. **Credit Analysis.** Financial ratios were described in Chapter 17. If you were the credit manager, to which financial ratios would you pay most attention?

13. **Credit Decision.** The Branding Iron Company sells its irons for $50 apiece wholesale. Production cost is $40 per iron. There is a 25 percent chance that a prospective customer will go bankrupt within the next half year. The customer orders 1,000 irons and asks for 6 months' credit. Should you accept the order? Assume a 10 percent per year discount rate, no chance of a repeat order, and that the customer will pay either in full or not at all.

14. **Credit Policy.** As treasurer of the Universal Bed Corporation, Aristotle Procrustes is worried about his bad debt ratio, which is currently running at 6 percent. He believes that imposing a more stringent credit policy might reduce sales by 5 percent and reduce the bad debt ratio to 4 percent. If the cost of goods sold is 80 percent of the selling price, should Mr. Procrustes adopt the more stringent policy?

15. **Credit Decision/Repeat Sales.** Surf City sells its network browsing software for $15 per copy to computer software distributors and allows its customers 1 month to pay their bills. The cost of the software is $10 per copy. The industry is very new and unsettled, however, and the probability that a new customer granted credit will go bankrupt within the next month is 25 percent. The firm is considering switching to a cash-on-delivery credit policy to reduce its exposure to defaults on trade credit. The discount rate is 1 percent per month.
    a.   Should the firm switch to a cash-on-delivery policy? If it does so, its sales will fall by 40 percent.
    b.   How would your answer change if a customer that is granted credit pays its bills, and is expected to generate repeat orders with negligible likelihood of default for each of the next six months? Similarly, customers that pay cash also will generate on average six months of repeat sales.

EXCEL

*16. **Credit Policy.** A firm currently makes only cash sales. It estimates that allowing trade credit on terms of net 30 would increase monthly sales from 200 to 220 units per month. The price per unit is $101 and the cost (in present value terms) is $80. The interest rate is 1 percent per month.
    a.   Should the firm change its credit policy?
    b.   Would your answer to part (a) change if 5 percent of all customers fail to pay their bills under the new credit policy?
    c.   What if 5 percent of only the new customers fail to pay their bills? The current customers take advantage of the 30 days of free credit but remain safe credit risks.

CHALLENGE

*17. **Credit Analysis.** Use the data in Example 21.3. Now suppose, however, that 10 percent of Cast Iron's customers are slow payers, and that slow payers have a probability of 30 percent of defaulting on their bills. If it costs $5 to determine whether a customer has been a prompt or slow payer in the past, should Cast Iron undertake such a check? *Hint:* What is the expected savings from the credit check? It will depend on both the probability of uncovering a slow payer and the savings from denying these payers credit.

18. **Credit Analysis.** Look back at the previous problem, but now suppose that if a customer defaults on a payment, you can eventually collect about half the amount owed to you. Will you be more or less tempted to pay for a credit check once you account for the possibility of partial recovery of debts?

*19. **Credit Policy.** Jim Khana, the credit manager of Velcro Saddles, is reappraising the company's credit policy. Velcro sells on terms of net 30. Cost of goods sold is 85 percent of sales. Velcro classifies customers on a scale of 1 to 4. During the past five years, the collection experience was as follows:

Classification	Defaults as Percentage of Sales	Average Collection Period in Days for Non-defaulting Accounts
1	0	45
2	2	42
3	10	50
4	20	80

The average interest rate was 15 percent. What conclusions (if any) can you draw about Velcro's credit policy? Should the firm deny credit to any of its customers? What other factors should be taken into account before changing this policy?

20. **Credit Analysis.** Galenic, Inc., is a wholesaler for a range of pharmaceutical products. Before deducting any losses from bad debts, Galenic operates on a profit margin of 5 percent. For a long time the firm has employed a numerical credit scoring system based on a small number of key ratios. This has resulted in a bad debt ratio of 1 percent.

Galenic has recently commissioned a detailed statistical study of the payment record of its customers over the past eight years and, after considerable experimentation, has identified five variables that could form the basis of a new credit-scoring system. On the evidence of the past eight years, Galenic calculates that for every 10,000 accounts it would have experienced the following default rates:

	Number of Accounts		
Credit Score under Proposed System	Defaulting	Paying	Total
Better than 80	60	9,100	9,160
Worse than 80	40	800	840
Total	100	9,900	10,000

By refusing credit to firms with a poor credit score (less than 80), Galenic calculates that it would reduce its bad debt ratio to 60/9,160 net, or just under .7 percent. While this may not seem like a big deal, Galenic's credit manager reasons that this is equivalent to a decrease of one-third in the bad debt ratio and would result in a significant improvement in the profit margin.

a. What is Galenic's current profit margin allowing for bad debts?

b. Assuming that the firm's estimates of default rates are right, how would the new credit-scoring system affect profits?

c. Why might you suspect that Galenic's estimates of default rates will not be realized in practice?

d. Suppose that one of the variables in the proposed new scoring system is whether the customer has an existing account with Galenic (new customers are more likely to default). How would this affect your assessment of the proposal? Hint: Think about repeat sales.

21. **Internet.** Log in to **www.jaxworks.com/zscore2.htm** and calculate the Z scores for two companies (say, Exxon and American Airlines). You will need to find some financial data for each firm, which you can get from its annual report, available on each company's Web site. Another convenient source is **http://finance.yahoo.com**. At this site, go to the company's profile and then click on the highlights page. Which of your two companies appears more likely to encounter financial distress?

22. **Internet.** Log in to the Web site of the Office of the Superintendent of Bankruptcy Canada at **http://www.osb-bsf.gc.ca**. Has the level of personal bankruptcies been increasing recently? What about business bankruptcies? Do business and personal bankruptcies tend to move in step?

23. **Internet.** When credit managers need a credit check on a small business, they often look up the Dun & Bradstreet report on the company. You can see a sample Comprehensive Report

by logging in to **www.dnb.com** and clicking on "Small Business Owners." On the basis of this report, would you be prepared to extend credit to this company? Why or why not?

24. **Internet.** Credit scoring is widely used to rate applicants for personal loans. You can estimate your own credit rating with Credit Analyzer at **http://finance.yahoo.com** by clicking on "Credit Reports." Try varying some of the inputs and see how your credit rating changes. Would the rating change if in the past you had shopped around to find the best source for a loan? Now log on to **www.myfico.com** and find out how other credit applicants compare and what difference your score makes to the interest rate that you are likely to pay on a loan.

25. **Standard & Poor's.** Go to **www.mcgrawhill.ca/edumarketinsight.Compare** and contrast the accounts receivable turnover and days' sales outstanding for Peets Coffee & Tea, Inc. (PEET), and Harrahs Entertainment, Inc. (HET). Read the business description for information that may explain the level of each company's investment in accounts receivables.

Solutions to Check Points

21.1 To get the cash discount, you have to pay the bill within 10 days, that is, by May 11. With the 2 percent discount, the amount that needs to be paid by May 11 is $20,000 \times .98 = \$19,600$. If you forgo the cash discount, you do not have to pay your bill until May 21, but on that date, the amount due is $20,000.

21.2 The cash discount in this case is 5 percent and customers who choose not to take the discount receive an extra $50 - 10 = 40$ days credit. So the effective annual interest is

$$\text{Effective annual rate} = \left(1 + \frac{\text{discount}}{\text{discounted price}}\right)^{365/\text{extra days credit}} - 1$$

$$= \left(1 + \frac{5}{95}\right)^{365/40} - 1 = .597, \text{ or } 59.7\%$$

In this case the customer who does not take the discount is effectively borrowing money at an annual interest rate of 59.7 percent. This is higher than the rate in Example 21.1 because fewer days of credit are obtained by forfeiting the discount.

21.3 The present value of costs is still $1,000. Present value of revenues is now $1,100. The break-even probability is defined by

$$p \times 100 - (1-p) \times 1,000 = 0$$

which implies that $p = .909$. The break-even probability is higher because the profit margin is now lower. The firm cannot afford as high a bad-debt ratio as before since it is not making as much on its successful sales. We conclude that high-margin goods will be offered with more liberal credit terms.

21.4 The higher the discount rate the less important future sales are. Because the value of repeat sales is lower, the break-even probability on the initial sale is higher. For instance, we saw that the break-even probability was one-third when the discount rate was 10 percent. When the discount rate is 20 percent, the value of a perpetual flow of repeat sales falls to $200/.20 = \$1,000$, and the break-even probability increases to one-half:

$$1/2 \times \$1,000 - 1/2 \times \$1,000 = 0$$

21.5 The customer pays bills 45 days after the invoice date. Because goods are purchased daily, at any time there will be bills outstanding with "ages" ranging from 1 to 45 days. At any time, the customer will have 30 days' worth of purchases, or $10,000, outstanding for a period of up to 1 month, and 15 days' worth of purchases, or $5,000, outstanding for between 1 month and 45 days. The aging schedule will appear as follows:

Age of Account	Amount
< 1 month	$10,000
1–2 months	$ 5,000

MINICASE

George Stamper, a credit analyst with Micro-Encapsulators Corp. (MEC), needed to respond to an urgent e-mail request from the western Canada sales office. The local sales manager reported that she had an opportunity to clinch an order from Surrey Spice (SS) for 50 encapsulators at $10,000 each. She added that she was particularly keen to secure this order since SS was likely to have a continuing need for 50 encapsulators a year and could therefore prove to be a very valuable customer. However, orders of this size for a new customer generally required head office agreement. It was therefore George's responsibility to make a rapid assessment of SS's creditworthiness and to approve or disapprove the sale.

George knew that SS was a medium-sized company with a patchy earnings record. After growing rapidly in the 1980s, SS had encountered strong competition in its principal markets and earnings had fallen sharply. George Stamper was not exactly sure to what extent this was a bad omen. New management had been brought in to cut costs and there were some indications that the worst was over for the company. Investors appeared to agree with this assessment, because the stock price had risen to $5.80 from its low of $4.25 the previous year. George had in front of him SS's latest financial statements, which are summarized in Table 21.3. He rapidly calculated a few key financial ratios and the company's Z score.

George also made a number of other checks on SS. The company had a small issue of bonds outstanding, which were rated BB by Dominion Bond Rating Service. Inquiries through MEC's bank indicated that SS had unused lines of credit totalling $5 million but had entered into discussions with its bank for a renewal of a $15 million bank loan that was due to be repaid at the end of the year. Telephone calls to SS's other suppliers suggested that the company had recently been 30 days late in paying its bills.

George also needed to take into account the profit that the company could make on SS's order. Encapsulators were sold on standard terms of 2/30, net 60. So if SS paid promptly, MEC would receive additional revenues of $50 \times \$9,800 = \$490,000$. However, given SS's cash position, it was more than likely that it would forgo the cash discount and would not pay until sometime after the 60 days. Since interest rates were about 8 percent, any such delays in payment would reduce the present value to MEC of the revenues. George also recognized that there were production and transportation costs in filling SS's order. These worked out at $475,000, or $9,500, a unit. Corporate profits were taxed at 35 percent.

Questions

1. What can you say about Surrey Spice's creditworthiness?
2. What is the break-even probability of default? How is it affected by the delay before SS pays its bills?
3. How should George Stamper's decision be affected by the possibility of repeat orders?

TABLE 21.3
Surrey Spice: summary
financial statements
($ millions)

	2004	2003
Assets		
Current assets		
Cash and marketable securities	5.0	12.2
Accounts receivable	16.2	15.7
Inventories	27.5	32.5
Total current assets	48.7	60.4
Fixed assets		
Property, plant, and equipment	228.5	228.1
Less accumulated depreciation	129.5	127.6
Net fixed assets	99.0	100.5
Total assets	147.7	160.9
Liabilities and shareholders' equity		
Current liabilities		
Debt due for repayment	22.8	28.0
Accounts payable	19.0	16.2
Total current liabilities	41.8	44.2
Long-term debt	40.8	42.3
Shareholders' equity		
Common stock[a]	10.0	10.0
Retained earnings	55.1	64.4
Total shareholders' equity	65.1	74.4
Total liabilities and shareholders' equity	147.7	160.9
Income Statement		
Revenue	149.8	134.4
Cost of goods sold	131.0	124.2
Other expenses	1.7	8.7
Depreciation	8.1	8.6
Earnings before interest and taxes	9.0	− 7.1
Interest expense	5.1	5.6
Income taxes	1.4	− 4.4
Net income	2.5	− 8.3
Allocation of net income		
Addition to retained earnings	1.5	− 9.3
Dividends	1.0	1.0

[a] 10 million shares.

PART EIGHT
Special Topics

LEASING

Most of us occasionally rent a car, bicycle, or boat, and usually these kinds of rentals are short term—we rent them for a day or a week or so. But in corporate finance longer-term rentals are common. A rental agreement that extends for a year or more and involves a series of fixed payments is called a **lease**.[1]

Firms often lease as an alternative to buying capital equipment. Computers are often leased; so are trucks, railroad cars, aircraft, and ships. Just about every kind of asset has been leased some time by somebody including electric and nuclear power plants, handball courts, and even horses.

Every lease involves two parties. The *user* of the asset is called the **lessee**. The lessee makes periodic payments to the *owner* of the asset, who is called the **lessor**. For example, if you sign an agreement to rent an apartment for a year, you are the lessee and the owner is the lessor.

Firms lease assets for a variety of reasons. One reason firms lease is for convenience, if the asset is needed only for a short period of time. Another reason is for the flexibility of cancelling the lease if the asset is no longer needed. However, tax reduction is the main reason for long-term leasing. Companies pay fewer taxes if they acquire the asset by leasing rather than borrowing. The tax savings occur because in a lease arrangement, it is the asset owner not the asset user who can deduct the asset's capital cost allowance (CCA) from its taxable income. By transferring the CCA from a lower-taxed user to a higher-taxed owner, total taxes are lowered and both parties are better off.

After reading this chapter you should be able to
- Understand the different kinds of leases and some of the reasons for their use.
- Assess the net present value of a long-term lease.
- Understand how a long-term lease is an alternative to debt financing.

---

[1] Our discussion of leasing is drawn, in part, from Chapter 25 of R. Brealey and S. Myers, *Principals of Corporate Finance*, 6th ed., (Boston, MA: McGraw-Hill, 2000).

22.1

WHAT IS A LEASE?

lease   Rental agreement for the use of an asset extending for more than one year and involving a series of fixed payments.

lessee   User of the asset in a lease. Responsible for making regular payments to lessor.

lessor   Owner of the asset in a lease. Receives regular payments from lessee.

operating lease   Short-term, cancellable lease.

financial lease   Long-term, non-cancellable lease. It is also known as capital or full-payout lease.

Leases come in many forms, but in all cases the lessee (user) promises to make a series of payments to the lessor (owner). The lease contract specifies the monthly or semi-annual payments; the first payment is usually due as soon as the contract is signed. The payments are usually level, but their time pattern can be tailored to the user's needs. For example, suppose that a manufacturer leases a machine to produce a complex new product. There will be a year's "shakedown" period before volume production starts. In this case, it might be possible to arrange for lower payments during the first year of the lease.

When a lease is terminated, the leased equipment reverts to the lessor. However, the lease agreement often gives the user the option to purchase the equipment or take out a new lease.

Some leases provide for the *temporary* use of an asset. Generally known as **operating leases**, these leases are either short term or cancellable during the contract period at the option of the lessee. On the other hand, a **financial lease** provides for *long-term* use of an asset. With a financial lease, the lessee has the asset for most of its estimated economic life, and the lease cannot be cancelled, or can be cancelled only if the lessor is reimbursed for any losses. This type of lease is also called a *capital* or *full-payout lease*.[2]

Financial leases are a *source of financing*. Signing a financial lease contract is like borrowing money. There is an immediate cash inflow because the lessee is relieved of having to pay for the asset. But the lessee also assumes a binding obligation to make the payments specified in the lease contract. The user could have borrowed the full purchase price of the asset by accepting a binding obligation to make interest and principal payments to the lender. Thus the cash flow consequences of leasing and borrowing are similar. In either case, the firm raises cash now and pays it back later. A large part of this chapter will be devoted to comparing leases and borrowing as financing alternatives.

Leases also differ in the services provided by the lessor. Under a *full-service*, or *rental* lease, the lessor promises to maintain and insure the equipment and to pay any property taxes due on it. In a *net* lease, the lessee agrees to maintain the asset, insure it, and pay any property taxes. Financial leases are usually net leases.

Most financial leases are arranged for brand-new assets. The lessee identifies the equipment, arranges for the leasing company to buy it from the manufacturer, and signs a contract with the leasing company. This is called a *direct lease*. In other cases, the firm sells an asset it already owns and leases it back from the buyer. These *sale and lease-back* arrangements are common in real estate. For example, a company may wish to raise cash by selling its factory, but still retain use of it. It could do this by selling the factory for cash to a leasing company and simultaneously signing a long-term lease for the factory. Legal ownership of the factory passes to the leasing company, but the right to use it stays with the company.

You may also encounter *leveraged* leases. These are financial leases in which the lessor borrows part of the purchase price of the leased asset, using the lease contract as security for the loan. This does not change the lessee's obligations, but it can complicate the lessor's analysis considerably.

The *leasing industry* comprises various types of companies that are in the business of providing leases. Some of the largest lessors are equipment manufacturers. For example, IBM is a large lessor of computers, and Xerox is a large lessor of copiers. By offering leasing, they are able to sell more products.

The other two major groups of lessors are banks and independent leasing companies. In Canada, banks are currently not permitted to engage in consumer car leasing but are active in other types of leasing. Independent leasing companies have grown significantly in number and exist in many different sizes. For example, GE Capital, a large company, operates in many different countries and leases a wide range of assets. Its subsidiary, GE Capital Aviation Services,

---

[2] In the shipping industry, a financial lease is called a *bareboat charter* or a *demise hire*.

owned and leased out about 1,100 commercial aircraft in 2005. A large fraction of the world's airlines rely entirely on leasing to finance their fleet. Some of the independent lessors are small- and medium-sized businesses that specialize in the financing of particular kinds of equipment and vehicles.

Leasing has grown substantially since the 1950s when the first independent leasing companies, completely separate from the manufacturers, were established. Now, leasing provides significant amounts of financing to businesses worldwide. In Canada, it is estimated that 20 to 25 percent of total business investment in machinery and equipment is financed by asset-based financing and leasing. Total value of assets under lease was estimated at $116.7 billion in Canada in 2003.[3]

EXAMPLE 22.1   **OPERATING AND FINANCIAL LESSORS**

GE Capital, with assets of $500 billion (US), is a major global, diversified financial services company. Its businesses include providing operating and financial leases for many different types of assets including cars, trucks and trailers, jets, and commercial equipment. As an operating lessor, GE Capital has a significant number of "off-lease assets"—assets available to be leased but currently not leased. Sometimes off-lease assets are sold, rather than leased again. At **www.GEasset.com**, GE Capital has a long list of off-lease assets for sale. Items for sale include logging equipment, helicopters, and injection molding production lines.

By contrast, lessors specializing in providing financial leases do not end up with off-lease assets. Typically, at the end of the financial lease, the lessee purchases the asset from the lessor. For example, TD Asset Finance primarily offers financial leases and supplies relatively few operating leases; TD does not want to be in the used-equipment business.

22.2   WHY LEASE?

You hear many suggestions about why companies should lease equipment rather than buy it. Let us look at some sensible reasons and then at four more dubious ones.

SENSIBLE REASONS FOR LEASING

Short-Term Leases Are Convenient

Suppose you want the use of a car for a week. You could buy one and sell it seven days later, but that would be silly. Apart from the fact that registering ownership is a nuisance, you would spend some time selecting a car, negotiating its purchase, and arranging insurance. Then at the end of the week you would negotiate resale and cancel the registration and insurance. When you need a car for only a short time, it clearly makes sense to rent it. You save the trouble of registering ownership, and you know the effective cost. In the same way, it pays a company to lease equipment that it needs for only a year or two. This kind of lease is an operating lease.

Sometimes the cost of short-term rentals may seem prohibitively high, or you may find it difficult to rent at any price. This can happen for equipment that is easily damaged by careless use. The owner knows that short-term users are unlikely to take the same care they would with their own equipment. When the danger of abuse becomes too high, short-term rental markets do not survive. Thus, it is easy enough to buy a Lamborghini Diablo, a high-end sports car, provided your pockets are deep enough, but nearly impossible to rent one.

Cancellation Options Are Valuable

Some leases that *appear* expensive really are fairly priced once the option to cancel is recognized.

---

[3] See the Canadian Finance and Leasing Association (CFLA) Web site at **www.cfla-acfl.ca**.

Maintenance Is Provided

Under a full-service lease, the user receives maintenance and other services. Many lessors are well equipped to provide efficient maintenance. However, bear in mind that these benefits will be reflected in higher lease payments.

EXAMPLE 22.2	LEASING A HORSE

Did you know that you can lease a horse? Horse leasing is a good way to find out if you are ready to own a horse without the long-term commitment of purchasing one. It can also make sense for meeting the changing needs of growing teenagers whose horse-riding skills are improving. Rather than buying and selling a succession of horses, it may be cheaper to lease. Leases can include the cost of board, vet, and farrier (someone who puts shoes on the horse) on top of the lease fee. The terms of the lease may include how often the horse can be ridden, what feed it gets, and who pays in the event the horse gets hurt. Like other short-term leases, a horse lease is more expensive than buying the horse itself. If you think you want the horse for many years, you would be better off buying it.

Standardization Leads to Low Administrative and Transaction Costs

Suppose that you operate a leasing company that specializes in financial leases for trucks. You are effectively lending money to a large number of firms (lessees), which may differ considerably in size and risk. But because the underlying asset is, in each case, the same saleable item (a truck), you can safely "lend" the money (lease the truck) without conducting a detailed analysis of each firm's business. You can also use a simple, standard lease contract. This standardization makes it possible to "lend" small sums of money without incurring large investigative, administrative, or legal costs.

For these reasons leasing is often a relatively cheap source of cash for the small company. It offers financing on a flexible, piecemeal basis and has lower transaction costs than a private placement or a public bond or stock issue.

Tax Shields Can Be Used

The lessor owns the leased asset and deducts the asset's capital cost allowance (CCA) from taxable income. If the lessor can make better use of CCA tax shields than an asset's user can, it may make sense for the leasing company to own the equipment and pass on some of the tax benefits to the lessee in the form of lower lease payments.

SOME DUBIOUS REASONS FOR LEASING

Leasing Avoids Capital Expenditure Controls

In many companies lease proposals are scrutinized as carefully as capital expenditure proposals, but in others, leasing may enable an operating manager to avoid the elaborate approval procedures needed to buy an asset. Although this is a dubious reason for leasing, it may be influential, particularly in the public sector. For example, hospitals have sometimes found it politically more convenient to lease their medical equipment than to ask the government to provide funds for purchase.

Leasing Preserves Capital

Leasing companies provide "100 percent financing"; they advance the full cost of the leased asset. Consequently, they often claim that leasing preserves capital, allowing the firm to save its cash for other things.

But the firm can also "preserve capital" by borrowing money. If Greenfield Construction leases a $100,000 backhoe rather than buying it, it conserves $100,000 cash. It could also (1) buy the backhoe for cash, and (2) borrow $100,000, using the backhoe as security. Its bank balance ends up the same whether it leases or buys and borrows. It has the backhoe in either case, and it incurs a $100,000 liability in either case. What's so special about leasing?

Leases May Be Off-Balance-Sheet Financing

The rules for reporting leases in a firm's financial statements vary internationally. In some countries, such as Germany, financial leases are **off-balance-sheet financing**; that is, a firm can acquire an asset, finance it through a financial lease, and show neither the asset nor the lease contract on its balance sheet. All lease payments are recognized as an expense of the lessee and reported as lease income by the lessor. No distinction is made between operating leases, which give temporary use of an asset, and financial leases, which are commitments of the lessee to use and pay for the asset over the bulk of the asset's economic life.

Both the Canadian Accounting Standards Board (AcSB) and the U.S. Financial Accounting Standards Board (FASB) require that leases be accounted for according to who bears the risks and rewards of ownership of the assets. In an operating lease, the lessor bears the risks and rewards of ownership because the lease is short term. At the end of the lease period, the lessor gets the asset back and bears the risk of finding another lessee. The asset stays on the lessor's balance sheet and the lessor reports lease payments as income. Likewise, the lessee is just a temporary user of the asset and the lease payments are another business expense.

With a financial lease, although the lessor is the legal owner of the leased assets, the lessee bears essentially all of the risk and rewards of ownership. As we noted, a financial lease is primarily a means of providing financing so that the lessee can acquire the asset without actually buying it upfront. Canadian and U.S. accounting rules require that the financial statements reflect the true economic consequences of a financial lease. In other words, the leased assets are reported along with the other assets on the balance sheet of the lessee. Likewise, the lease financing shows up as a liability on the lessee's balance sheet. To do this, the lease is *capitalized*.

To capitalize a lease, the present value of the lease payments is calculated and listed along with debt on the right-hand side of the balance sheet. The same amount is shown as an asset on the left-hand side. This leased asset would typically be included with other fixed assets and is amortized over the life of the lease. The amortization is deducted from book income, just as depreciation is deducted for a purchased asset.

According to the *CICA Handbook*, a lease is normally considered to be a financial lease when at least one of the following conditions is present at the start of the lease:[4]

1. There is reasonable assurance that the lessee will obtain ownership of the leased property at the end of the lease term. This would occur if the lease provides for automatic transfer of title to the lessee at the end of the lease, or if the lessee is entitled to purchase the asset at a bargain price (below its expected value) at the end of the lease.
2. The lessee will receive all of the economic benefits expected to be derived through the use of the leased asset. Since assets are most productive in the earlier years of their lives, this condition is presumed to be satisfied if the lease term is at least 75 percent of the asset's economic life.
3. The lessor is assured of recovering the investment in the leased asset plus a return on its investment over the lease term. This condition is presumed to be satisfied if the present value of the lease payments is equal to at least 90 percent of the fair value of the asset at the inception of the lease.

The Canadian criteria are similar to those used in the United States. In Canada and the United States, all other leases are operating leases as far as accountants are concerned.

Many financial managers have tried to take advantage of this arbitrary boundary between operating and financial leases. Suppose that you want to finance a computer-controlled machine tool costing $1 million. The machine tool's life is expected to be 12 years. You could sign a lease contract for 8 years, 11 months (just missing requirement 2) with lease payments having a

---

[4] These criteria are from *CICA Handbook*, para. 3065.06, as summarized in Beechy and Conrod, *Intermediate Accounting, Volume 2*, McGraw-Hill Ryerson (2005), p. 1032. CICA, the Canadian Institute of Chartered Accountants, is the professional association and regulator of Canadian chartered accountants.

present value of $899,000 (just missing requirement 3). You could also make sure the lease contract avoids requirement 1. Result? You have off-balance-sheet financing. This lease would not have to be capitalized, although it is clearly a long-term fixed obligation.

Now we come to the big question: Why should anyone care whether financing is off balance sheet or on balance sheet? Shouldn't the financial manager worry about substance rather than appearance? Indeed, the International Accounting Standards Committee thinks the distinction made between operating and financial leases is arbitrary. In a recent discussion paper, a proposal was made that all leases, both operating and financial, be accounted for in terms of the rights and obligations of lease obligation. This would result in capitalization of operating leases, so that the present value of the minimum lease payments would be reported as a liability of the lessee and no longer treated as off-balance-sheet financing.

When a firm obtains off-balance-sheet financing, the conventional measures of financial leverage, such as the debt-equity ratio, understate the true degree of financial leverage. Some believe that financial analysts do not always notice off-balance-sheet lease obligations (which are still referred to in footnotes) or the greater volatility of earnings that result from the fixed lease payments. They may be right, but we would not expect such an imperfection to be widespread.

When a company borrows money, it must usually consent to certain restrictions on future borrowing. Early bond indentures did not include any restrictions on financial leases. Therefore leasing was seen as a way to circumvent restrictive covenants. Loopholes such as these are easily stopped, and most bond indentures now include limits on leasing.

Long-term lease obligations ought to be regarded as debt whether or not they appear on the balance sheet. Financial analysts may overlook moderate leasing activity, just as they overlook minor debts. But major lease obligations are generally recognized and taken into account.

SEE BOX P. 686 Debt-rating agencies, such as Moody's and Standard and Poor's, do not ignore operating leases when assessing a company's financial leverage. In the nearby Finance in Action box, you can read about Moody's treatment of operating leases. See also Chapter 17 where we examined the financial leverage of Le Château, a retailer that leases most of its retail space. Excluding its operating leases, Le Château's debt ratio was 13.6 percent. Including its extensive leases, the debt ratio jumps to 59.1 percent. No banker would consider lending money to Le Château without first examining its operating lease obligations.

Leasing Affects Book Income

Leasing can make the firm's balance sheet and income statement *look* better by increasing book income or decreasing book asset value, or both.

A lease that qualifies as off-balance-sheet financing affects book income in only one way: The lease payments are an expense. If the firm buys the asset instead and borrows to finance it, both depreciation and interest expense are deducted. Leases are usually set up so that payments in the early years are less than depreciation plus interest under the buy-and-borrow alternative. Consequently, leasing increases book income in the early years of an asset's life. The book rate of return can increase even more dramatically because the book value of assets (the denominator in the book-rate-of-return calculation) is understated if the leased asset never appears on the firm's balance sheet.

Leasing's impact on book income should in itself have no effect on firm value. In efficient capital markets, investors will look through the firm's accounting results to the true value of the asset and the liability incurred to finance it.

22.3   VALUING LEASES

OPERATING LEASES

Leases can be attractive for a variety of reasons. However, the decision to lease requires careful calculation of the cash inflows and outflows from the lease. If you are considering an *operating* lease, decide whether it is cheaper to lease the asset for the time that you need it or to buy it.

Off-Balance-Sheet Leases: Capitalization and Ratings Implications

Out of Sight But Not Out of Mind

Should creditors to a company engaged in off-balance-sheet leases be concerned about the existence of these transactions? The argument is that leases are secured by their own assets and could effectively be ignored for the purpose of analyzing on-balance-sheet debt. However, we beg to differ, and firmly believe that leases represent use of a company's debt capacity and could meaningfully impact the recovery prospects of a balance sheet creditor in a stress scenario.

Debt capacity may be loosely defined as a company's ability to incur *additional* debt. Simply put, a use of debt capacity and a corresponding increase in leverage arises from any transaction that stakes a claim to a company's cash flow.

It is not difficult to see why leases do utilize a company's debt capacity. Lease agreements are contractual obligations, resulting in a claim on cash flow through fixed lease payments over the life of the lease. Failure to comply with the terms of the lease agreement would constitute default. Besides, in the absence of a lease financing option, the company would likely borrow the money and buy the asset.

Our discussion will focus on operating lease transactions. Our objectives are two-fold: to accurately depict a firm's effective leverage and to achieve comparability in analyzing firms employing different financing tools (e.g., lease vs. buy).... The choice of capitalization method is ultimately a judgement call, though we believe the present value approach (or variations thereof) may be the lesser of the evils.... We calculate the net present value of the future minimum lease payments using an appropriate discount rate.

Once an "appropriate" capitalization amount [for the operating leases] is determined we may incorporate it into the analysis and rating of the various debt issues. It is more meaningful to incorporate capitalized lease if the amount is significant and the leased assets are essential to the business.

Source: Moody's Investors Services, Global Credit Research, "Off-Balance Sheet Leases: Capitalization and Rating Implications," (October 1999).

Figure out the *equivalent annual cost*[5] of buying the asset and compare it to the annual lease payment charged by the lessor. In other words, can you "lease" the asset to yourself more cheaply than you can lease it from a lessor? Generally, the longer you need the asset, the more sense it makes to buy it rather than arranging an operating lease.

An attractive feature of an operating lease is the option to cancel the lease, avoiding the risks of obsolescence. The options embedded in an operating lease can be very valuable but are rather tricky to assess and are beyond this book. In general, operating leases make sense when the user needs the equipment for a short time, when the lessor is better able to bear the risks of obsolescence, or when the lessor can offer a good deal on maintenance.

FINANCIAL LEASES

When you are considering a *financial* lease, the decision amounts to "lease versus borrow." Financial leases extend over most of the economic life of the lease equipment. They are not cancellable. The lease payments are fixed obligations equivalent to *debt service*, the sum of interest and principal repayment on the debt.

Financial leases make sense when the company is prepared to take on the business risks of owning and operating the leased asset. Suppose a company is thinking about getting a stretch limousine. If managers aren't sure whether they will use it enough, they will want to consider an operating lease to give them the option of cancelling the lease: They will avoid the risk of owning the limo. If the company signs a financial lease, it is stuck with the limo for a long time. The financial lease is just another way of borrowing to pay for the asset.

Financial leases do offer special advantages to some firms in some circumstances. However, there is no point in discussing this further until you know how to value financial lease contracts.

CASH FLOWS OF A FINANCIAL LEASE

Imagine yourself in the position of Jane Jones, president of Greenfield Construction. Your firm was established by your grandfather, who was quick to capitalize on the growing demand for residential housing in Busy Town. The company has owned all of its construction equipment since

---

[5] Look back to Chapter 7 for a review of equivalent annual cost and an example of the analysis of an operating lease.

the time the company was formed; you are now reconsidering this policy. Your operating manager wants to buy a new backhoe-loader costing $100,000. The backhoe will last seven years before going to the scrapyard. You are convinced that the investment in the additional equipment is worthwhile. A representative of the equipment manufacturer has pointed out that her firm is willing to lease the backhoe to you if you make seven annual payments of $18,500, payable at the start of each year. Greenfield would remain responsible for all maintenance, insurance, and operating expenses.

Table 22.1 shows the direct cash flow consequences of signing the lease contract rather than purchasing the backhoe. (An important indirect effect is considered later.) The consequences are

1. Greenfield does not have to pay for the backhoe. This is equivalent to a cash inflow of $100,000.
2. Greenfield would not own the backhoe, and so it cannot claim any CCA. Therefore it gives up a valuable CCA tax shield. Calculation of the tax shield is shown in Table 22.1. We assume that the backhoe is a Class 38 asset with a 30 percent CCA rate. To simplify the calculations, we assume that Greenfield is able to hold this asset alone in its own asset pool. After seven years of operation, the backhoe is scrapped and a terminal loss equal to the remaining undepreciated capital cost is taken.[6]
3. Greenfield must pay $18,500 per year for 7 years to the lessor. The first payment is due immediately.
4. However, these lease payments are fully tax-deductible. At a 35 percent marginal tax rate, each lease payment generates an annual tax shield of .35 × $18,500, or $6,475. The after-tax lease payment is $18,500 − $6,475, or $12,025.

In Table 22.1, the first CCA deduction occurs at Year 0 because we assume that the backhoe is purchased at the end of Year 0.[7] Table 22.1 also assumes that the backhoe will be worthless when it goes to the scrapyard at the end of Year 7. Otherwise there would be an entry for salvage value lost, and the undepreciated capital cost would have been reduced by the salvage value before we took the terminal loss.

TABLE 22.1

Cash flow consequences to Greenfield Construction by accepting the lease contract rather than purchasing the backhoe-loader (figures in dollars; some columns may not add up due to rounding)

Lease Cash Flows	Year							
	0	1	2	3	4	5	6	7
Saved cost of a new backhoe-loader	+100,000							
Lost CCA tax shield (calculated below)	−5,250	−8,925	−6,248	−4,373	−3,061	−2,143	−1,500	−3,500
Lease payment	−18,500	−18,500	−18,500	−18,500	−18,500	−18,500	−18,500	
Lease payment tax shield	+6,475	+6,475	+6,475	+6,475	+6,475	+6,475	+6,475	
Cash flow of lease	82,725	−20,950	−18,273	−16,398	−15,086	−14,168	−13,525	−3,500
Tax Shield Calculation								
UCC	100,000	85,000	59,500	41,650	29,155	20,409	14,286	10,000
CCA (CCA rate = 30%)	15,000	25,500	17,850	12,495	8,747	6,123	4,286	
CCA tax shield (tax rate = 35%)*	5,250	8,925	6,248	4,373	3,061	2,143	1,500	3,500

Notes:

* At the very end of Year 7 the backhoe is scrapped, generating a terminal loss of $10,000, equal to the undepreciated capital cost. The terminal loss creates a tax savings of .35 × $10,000, or $3,500.

---

[6] This assumption allows us to ignore any tax saving from CCA beyond Year 7. See Example 22.4 for the case where the asset pool is not closed.

[7] In Chapter 7, the first CCA deduction always occurred in Year 1 because we implicitly assumed that the asset was purchased in Year 1. However, it is only an assumption—the asset could have been purchased at the end of Year 0 and the first CCA deduction taken in Year 0. In practice, a company will think about the tax consequences of the timing of significant asset purchases.

Suppose the backhoe-loader cost $85,000, has zero-expected salvage value, and the annual lease payments are $15,000, payable in advance. If the lease is for seven years, what are Greenfield's after-tax cash flows from leasing, rather than buying the backhoe, assuming everything else is unchanged?

WHO REALLY OWNS THE LEASED ASSET?

To a lawyer or a tax accountant, that would be a silly question: The lessor is clearly the legal owner of the leased asset. That is why the lessor is allowed to deduct depreciation from taxable income.

From an *economic* point of view, you might say that the *user* is the real owner, because in a *financial* lease, the user faces the risks and receives the rewards of ownership. Greenfield cannot cancel a financial lease. If the new backhoe turns out be hopelessly expensive and unsuited for Greenfield, that is Greenfield's problem, not the lessor's. If it turns out to be a great success, the profit goes to Greenfield, not the lessor. The success or failure of the firm's business operations does not depend on whether the backhoes are financed by leasing or some other financial instrument.

In many respects, a financial lease is equivalent to a secured loan. The lessee must make a series of fixed payments; if the lessee fails to do so, the lessor can repossess the asset. Thus we can think of a balance sheet like this

Greenfield Construction ($000s)				
Backhoe-loader	100	100	Loan secured by backhoe-loader	
All other assets	1,000	450	Other loans	
		550	Equity	
Total assets	1,100	1,100	Total liabilities	

as being economically equivalent to a balance sheet like this:

Greenfield Construction ($000s)				
Backhoe-loader	100	100	Financial lease	
All other assets	1,000	450	Other loans	
		550	Equity	
Total assets	1,100	1,100	Total liabilities	

Having said this, we must immediately add two qualifications. First, legal ownership can make a big difference when a financial lease expires because the lessor gets the salvage value of the asset. Once a secured loan is paid off, the user owns the asset free and clear.

Second, whether you are a lessor or a secured creditor makes a difference in bankruptcy or reorganization. When a lessee fails to make a lease payment, the lessor is entitled to take back its asset. However, what if the value of that asset is much less than the present value of the future lease payments the lessee had promised to pay? The lessor loses. The lessor can try to recover its loss from the firm but the lessor is only an unsecured creditor.

By contrast, if the firm defaults on a secured lender, the secured lender is entitled to receive the full amount of the principal and unpaid interest, secured by the asset. In default, the lender can sell the asset to recover the full amount owed. If this asset is worth less than the amount the lender is owed, the lender is entitled to make a claim for the full amount of the difference. This claim has priority over the unsecured lenders of the firm.

Of course, neither the lessor nor the secured lender can be sure it will be paid the full amount owed. Our point is that lessors and secured creditors have different rights if the asset user gets into financial trouble.

LEASING AND THE CANADA REVENUE AGENCY (CRA)

We have already noted that the lessee loses the CCA of the leased asset but can deduct the lease payment in full. The *lessor*, as legal owner, uses the CCA tax shield but must report the lease payments as taxable rental income.

However, CRA is suspicious by nature and will not allow the lessee to deduct the entire lease payment unless it is satisfied that the arrangement is a genuine lease and not a disguised instalment purchase or secured loan agreement. Here are examples of lease provisions that will arouse its suspicion:[8]

1. Giving the lessee the option to acquire the asset, say for $1, when the lease expires. Such a provision would effectively give the asset's salvage value to the lessee.
2. The lessee automatically acquires title to the property after payment of a specified amount in lease payments.
3. The lessee is required to buy the asset at the end of lease contract.

FIRST PASS AT VALUING A FINANCIAL LEASE CONTRACT

When we left Jane Jones, president of Greenfield Construction, she was thinking about leasing rather than buying the required new backhoe-loader. She had set down in Table 22.1 the incremental cash flows from leasing the backhoe rather than purchasing it. To recap, by leasing and not purchasing the equipment, Greenfield does not pay upfront for the backhoe. However, in each of the subsequent years, the lease payments must be made and the CCA tax shields are forgone. If leasing is preferred to purchasing, the net present value of these lease cash flows must be positive. In other words, the cash saved upfront must be greater than the present value of the future cash outflows required to service the lease obligation. If the NPV is negative, Greenfield pays out more in future cash flows than the cash saved initially. In this case, shareholders of Greenfield are worse off by leasing than purchasing the backhoe.

What is the appropriate discount rate to use in calculating the NPV of the lease? That depends on the nature of the risks of the cash flows. The lease cash flows are typically assumed to be about as safe as the interest and principal payments on a secured loan issued by the lessee. This assumption is reasonable for the lease payments because the lessor is effectively lending money to the lessee. But the various tax shields might carry enough risk to deserve a higher discount rate. For example, Greenfield might be confident that it could make the lease payments but not confident that it could earn enough taxable income to use these tax shields. In that case the cash flows generated by the tax shields would probably deserve a higher discount rate than the borrowing rate used for the lease payments.

A lessee might, in principle, end up using a separate discount rate for each line of Table 22.1, each rate chosen to fit the risk of that line's cash flow. But established, profitable firms usually find it reasonable to simplify by discounting the types of flows shown in Table 22.1 at a single rate based on the rate of interest the firm would pay if it borrowed rather than leased. We will assume Greenfield's borrowing rate is 10 percent.

We have determined that the risk of the lease cash flows is equal to the risk of its secured debt. However, we must make one further adjustment: The discount rate must be the firm's *after-tax* cost of its secured debt. When a company lends money, it pays tax on the interest it receives. Its net return is the after-tax interest rate. When a company borrows money, it can deduct interest payments from its taxable income. The net cost of borrowing is the after-tax interest rate. Therefore, to value the incremental cash flows stemming from the lease, we need to discount them at the after-tax interest rate.

Since Greenfield can borrow at 10 percent, we should discount the lease cash flows at $r_D(1 - T) = .10(1 - .35) = .065$, or 6.5 percent. This gives

$$\text{NPV lease} = 82{,}725 - \frac{20{,}950}{1.065} - \frac{18{,}273}{(1.065)^2} - \frac{16{,}398}{(1.065)^3} - \frac{15{,}086}{(1.065)^4} - \frac{14{,}168}{(1.065)^5} - \frac{13{,}525}{(1.065)^6} - \frac{3{,}500}{(1.065)^7}$$

$$= -221, \text{ or } -\$221$$

Since the lease has a negative NPV, Greenfield is better off buying the backhoe.

---

[8] This list is based on information contained in CRA Interpretation Bulletin IT 233-R. However, this bulletin was cancelled in June 2001 because it was being misused. CRA stated that whether a contract is a lease or sale, it is based on the legal relationship created by the terms of the agreement.

What is the NPV of the lease in Check Point 22.1? Assume that Greenfield can borrow at 10 percent, before tax.

A positive or negative NPV is not an abstract concept; in this case, Greenfield's shareholders are really $221 poorer if the company leases. Let's now check how this situation comes about.

The lease cash outflows are contractual obligations like the principal and interest payments, or debt service, on secured debt. The cash inflow in Year 0 of the lease is like the amount of money borrowed through the loan. This gives us another way to examine the attractiveness of the lease. Let's compare it to an **equivalent loan**, a loan with identical annual cash outflows as the lease.

Suppose Jane went to the bank and asked, "How much would you lend me today if I promised to make the following after-tax loan payments?" (principal and interest):

equivalent loan Present value of the lease cash outflows, discounted at the after-tax cost of borrowing.

Year	1	2	3	4	5	6	7
Payments	−20,950	−18,273	−16,398	−15,086	−14,168	−13,525	−3,500

Note that Greenfield's loan payments are identical to the lease cash flows shown in years 1 to 7 of Table 22.1. This equivalent loan would carry a 10 percent interest rate, Greenfield's borrowing rate. The bank would be willing to lend Jane an amount equal to the present value of the lease cash outflows, discounted at Greenfield's after-tax borrowing rate:

Equivalent loan = Present value of lease cash outflows in years 1 to 7

$$= \frac{20,950}{1.065} + \frac{18,273}{(1.065)^2} + \frac{16,398}{(1.065)^3} + \frac{15,086}{(1.065)^4} + \frac{14,168}{(1.065)^5} + \frac{13,525}{(1.065)^6} + \frac{3,500}{(1.065)^7}$$

$$= 82,946, \text{ or } \$82,946$$

Table 22.2 shows the details of a loan for $82,946 at 10 percent interest rate with exactly the same annual cash outflows as the lease. At the end of each year, interest on the outstanding loan amount is paid. Also, Greenfield repays part of the loan principal to make that year's total loan payment equal to the lease cash flow the company would have paid had it leased the equipment. For example, at the end of the first year, Greenfield would need to pay interest of .10 × $82,946, or $8,295. Greenfield would receive a tax shield on this interest of .35 × 8,295, or $2,903. In other words, its after-tax interest expense is $8,295 − $2,903, or $5,391. Greenfield could then repay $15,559 of the loan principal, giving a net cash outflow of $5,391 + $15,559 = $20,950, exactly the same as the cash outflow in the first year of the lease. The loan amount outstanding at the start of Year 2 is now the original amount borrowed less the principal repaid in Year 1, $82,946 − $15,559, or $67,387. We repeat the calculation of interest owed and pay down the principal of the loan such that the total cash outflow in Year 2 is $18,273, exactly equal to Year 2's lease cash flow.

Look again at Table 22.2. Explain the calculations for the equivalent loan payments made in Year 2.

The bank receives interest before Greenfield pays tax. Show that the present value of the cash flows received by the bank, discounted at the required 10 percent, equals the equivalent loan of $82,946.

As you walk through the calculations in Table 22.2, you see that it costs exactly the same to service a loan that brings an immediate cash flow of $82,946 as it does to service the lease, which brings in only $82,725. The lease is not as attractive as the loan. The difference between the cash inflow of the lease and cash inflow of an equivalent loan equals the net present value of

TABLE 22.2
Details of equivalent loan offered to Greenfield Construction (figures in dollars; some columns may not add up due to rounding)

	Year							
	0	**1**	**2**	**3**	**4**	**5**	**6**	**7**
Amount borrowed at year-end	82,946	67,388	53,495	40,574	28,125	15,785	3,286	0
Interest paid at 10%		–8,295	–6,739	–5,350	–4,057	–2,813	–1,579	–329
Interest tax shield (35% tax rate)		2,903	2,359	1,872	1,420	984	552	115
Interest paid after tax*		–5,391	–4,380	–3,477	–2,637	–1,828	–1,026	–214
Principal repaid		–15,559	–13,892	–12,921	–12,449	–12,340	–12,499	–3,286
Net cash flow of equivalent loan**	82,946	–20,950	–18,273	–16,398	–15,086	–14,168	–13,525	–3,500

Notes:
* Interest paid after tax = interest paid + interest tax shield
** Net cash flow of equivalent loan = interest paid after tax + principal repaid

the lease: $82,725 – $82,946 = – $221. If Greenfield leases the backhoe rather than raising an equivalent loan,[9] there will be $221 less in Greenfield's bank account.

Our example illustrates two general points about leases and equivalent loans. First, if you can devise a borrowing plan that gives the same cash flow as the lease in every future period but a higher immediate cash flow, then you should not lease. If, however, the equivalent loan provides the same future cash outflows as the lease but a lower immediate inflow, then leasing is the better choice.

Second, our example suggests two ways to value a lease:

1. *Hard way.* Construct a table like Table 22.2 showing the equivalent loan.
2. *Easy way.* Discount the lease cash flows at the after-tax interest rate that the firm would pay on an equivalent loan. Both methods give the same answer—in our case an NPV of –$221.

FINANCIAL LEASE EVALUATION

We concluded that the lease contract offered to Greenfield Construction was not attractive because the lease provided $221 less financing than the equivalent loan. The underlying principle is as follows: A financial lease is superior to buying and borrowing if the financing provided by the lease exceeds the financing generated by the equivalent loan.

The principle implies this formula:

Net value of lease = initial financing provided – value of equivalent loan

Initial financing provided equals the cost of the leased asset minus any immediate lease payment or other cash outflow attributable to the lease.

Notice that the value of the lease is its incremental value relative to borrowing via an equivalent loan. A positive lease value means that *if* you acquire the asset, lease financing is advantageous. It does not prove you should acquire the asset.

However, sometimes favourable lease terms rescue a capital investment project. Suppose that Greenfield had decided *against* buying a new backhoe because the NPV of the $100,000 investment was –$5,000 assuming normal financing. The equipment manufacturer could rescue the deal by offering a lease with a value of, say, +$8,000. By offering such a lease, the manufacturer would in effect cut the price of the backhoe to $92,000, giving the backhoe-lease package a positive value to Greenfield. The total NPV of acquiring the backhoe is the sum of the NPV of the investment in a new backhoe, assuming normal financing, plus the NPV of the lease:

NPV of backhoe investment + lease financing = NPV of project + NPV of lease
= –5,000 + 8,000 = +$3,000

---

[9] When we compare the lease to its equivalent loan, we do not mean to imply that the backhoe alone could support all of the loan. Some part of the loan would be supported by Greenfield's other assets. Some part of the lease would likewise be supported by the other assets.

Notice also that this approach applies to *net* financial leases. Any insurance, maintenance, and other operating costs picked up by the lessor have to be evaluated separately and added to the value of the lease. If the asset has salvage value at the end of the lease, that value should be taken into account also.

| EXAMPLE 22.3 | **LEASE VARIATIONS: A NET FINANCIAL LEASE AND ASSET SALVAGE VALUE** |

The backhoe manufacturer offers to provide routine maintenance that would otherwise cost Greenfield $2,000 per year after tax. However, Ms. Jones reconsiders and decides that the backhoe will probably be worth $10,000 after 7 years, rather than nothing. The value of the lease increases by the present value of the maintenance savings and decreases by the present value of the lost salvage value. In addition, the lost tax savings from giving up the terminal loss (or CCA) will also be lower if the machine has a positive salvage value.

Maintenance and salvage value are harder to predict than the cash flows shown in Table 22.1, and so they normally deserve a higher discount rate. Suppose that Ms. Jones uses 12 percent, the project's (after-tax) discount rate. We assume the maintenance expenses are paid at the start of each year and the salvage value is measured at the end of Year 7. Then the maintenance savings are worth[10]

$2,000 × Annuity due present value factor for 7-year annuity with 12% interest rate

$$= \$2,000 \left[1 + \frac{1}{.12} - \frac{1}{.12(1.12)^6} \right] = \$10,223$$

The lost salvage is worth $10,000/(1.12)^7$, or $4,524. The salvage value would also be subtracted from the asset pool and any balance remaining would be taken as a terminal loss (assuming that the asset pool is closed). From Table 22.1, you see that at the end of Year 7, the backhoe's undepreciated capital cost was $10,000. Once the asset is sold, the asset pool is empty and there is no terminal loss. Originally, when salvage value was assumed to be 0, there was a tax shield from the terminal loss worth $3,500 (.35 × $10,000) and it had a present value of $3,500/(1.065)^7$, or $2,252. By leasing, Greenfield gave up the tax savings from this terminal loss. Now, with the $10,000 salvage value, there is no terminal loss and no lost tax savings.

The original lease was worth –$221. We add the value of the maintenance to be provided by the lessor, $10,223, but subtract the salvage value we give up by not owning the backhoe, $4,524. We also add back the tax savings from the terminal loss originally expected when the salvage value was zero, $2,252. The revised value is therefore –$221 + $10,223 – $4,524 + $2,252 = $7,730. Now the lease looks like a good deal.

| EXAMPLE 22.4 | **ANOTHER VARIATION: ASSET POOL DOES NOT CLOSE** |

Food Express, a grocery chain, needs new electronic cash registers. The cost to purchase them is $150,000. They will last four years and be scrapped with zero value. The allowable CCA is 30 percent and the company has many assets of this type. Thus, if it buys the equipment, the CCA tax savings will continue after four years. The equipment manufacturer is offering to lease the cash registers for $45,000 a year, payable in advance. The tax rate is 35 percent and the company's cost of borrowing is 8 percent. Should it lease or buy the cash registers?

The cash flows of the lease are found in Table 22.3. With the asset pool not closing, CCA would continue to be taken in the 5th year, 6th year, and so on, if the cash registers are purchased. By leasing, Food Express gives up the tax savings from these additional CCA deductions. At the end of the

---

[10] Look in Chapter 4 for the formula for the present value of an annuity due.

TABLE 22.3
Cash flow consequences and lease NPV for Food Express if it leases rather than buys the new cash registers (figures in dollars)

			Year		
	0	**1**	**2**	**3**	**4**
Saved cost of new cash registers	+150,000				
Lost CCA tax shield (calculated below)	–7,875	–13,388	–9,371	–6,560	–13,045
Lease payment	–45,000	–45,000	–45,000	–45,000	
Tax shield of lease payment	+15,750	+15,750	+15,750	+15,750	
Cash flow of lease	112,875	–42,638	–38,621	–35,810	–13,045
NPV of incremental lease cash flows	–3,961				
Tax Shield Calculation					
UCC	150,000	127,500	89,250	62,475	43,732
CCA (CCA rate = 30%)	22,500	38,250	26,775	18,743	
CCA tax shield (tax rate = 35%)	7,875	13,388	9,371	6,560	13,045

4th year, the remaining undepreciated capital cost (UCC) is \$43,732 (\$62,475 – \$18,743). The after-tax discount rate is .08(1–.35), or 5.2 percent. The present value of the tax savings from CCA on the UCC, at the end of Year 4, is[11]

$$PV(\text{tax savings from UCC, at end of Year 4}) = \frac{UCC \times CCA \text{ rate} \times \text{tax rate}}{CCA \text{ rate} + \text{interest rate}}$$

$$= \frac{43,732 \times .3 \times .35}{.3 + .052} = \$13,045$$

Table 22.3 shows that if Fast Food leases rather than buys the cash registers, it will be \$3,961 worse off.

22.4   WHEN DO FINANCIAL LEASES PAY?

We have examined the value of a lease from the viewpoint of the lessee. However, the lessor's criterion is simply the reverse. As long as lessor and lessee are in the same tax bracket, every cash outflow to the lessee is an inflow to the lessor, and vice versa. In our numerical example, the backhoe manufacturer would project cash flows in a table like Table 22.1, but with the signs reversed. The value of the lease to the backhoe manufacturer would be

$$\text{Value of lease to lessor} = -82,725 + \frac{20,950}{1.065} + \frac{18,273}{(1.065)^2} + \frac{16,398}{(1.065)^3} + \frac{15,086}{(1.065)^4}$$

$$+ \frac{14,168}{(1.065)^5} + \frac{13,525}{(1.065)^6} + \frac{3,500}{(1.065)^7}$$

$$= +221, \text{ or } \$221$$

In this case, the values to lessee and lessor offset exactly. The lessor can win only at the lessee's expense.

But both lessee and lessor can win if their tax rates differ. Suppose that Greenfield paid no tax ($T_c = 0$). Then the only cash flows of the equipment lease would be

Year	0	1	2	3	4	5	6
Cost of new backhoe	+100,000						
Lease payment		–18,500	–18,500	–18,500	–18,500	–18,500	–18,500	–18,500

These flows would be discounted at 10 percent, because $r_D(1 - T_C) = r_D$ when $T_C = 0$. The value of the lease is

---

[11] If the cash registers have a salvage value, subtract it from the UCC, reducing the asset value in the pool before calculating the tax savings.

$$\text{Value of lease} = +100,000 - 18,5000 \times \begin{array}{c}\text{annuity due factor for 7-year annuity}\\ \text{with 10\% interest rate}\end{array}$$

$$= +100,000 - 18,500 \left[1 + \frac{1}{.1} - \frac{1}{.1(1.1)^6}\right] = 928, \text{ or } \$928$$

In this case there is a net gain of $221 to the lessor (who has the 35 percent tax rate) *and* a net gain of $928 to the lessee (who pays zero tax). This mutual gain is at the expense of the government. On one hand, the government gains from the lease contract because it can tax the lease payments. On the other hand, the contract allows the lessor to take advantage of CCA and interest tax shields that are of no use to the lessee. However, because the CCA is accelerated and the interest rate is positive, the government suffers a net loss in the present value of its tax receipts as a result of the lease.

Now you should begin to understand the circumstances in which the government incurs a loss on the lease and the other two parties gain. Other things being equal, the potential gains to lessor and lessee are highest when

- The lessor's tax rate is substantially higher than the lessee's.
- The CCA tax shield is received early in the lease period.
- The lease period is long and the lease payments are concentrated toward the end of the period.
- The interest rate, r_D, is high; if it were zero, there would be no advantage in present value terms to postponing tax.

22.5   SUMMARY

1. What is a lease?

A lease is just an extended rental agreement. The owner of the equipment (the **lessor**) allows the user (the **lessee**) to operate the equipment in exchange for regular lease payments.

There is a wide variety of possible arrangements. Short-term, cancellable leases are known as **operating leases**. In these leases the lessor bears the risks of ownership. Long-term, non-cancellable leases are called full-payout, **financial**, or capital leases. In these leases the lessee bears the risks. Financial leases are **sources of financing** for assets the firm wishes to acquire and use for an extended period.

Many vehicle or office equipment leases include insurance and maintenance. They are full-service leases. If the lessee is responsible for insurance and maintenance, the lease is a net lease.

Frequently the lessor acquires the asset directly from the manufacturer. This is a direct lease. Sometimes the lessor acquires the asset from the user and then leases it back to the user. This is a sale and lease-back.

2. How do you value an operating lease?

Operating leases are attractive to equipment users if the lease payment is less than the user's equivalent annual cost of buying the equipment. Operating leases make sense when the user needs the equipment only for a short time, when the lessor is better able to bear the risks of obsolescence, or when the lessor can offer a good deal on maintenance. Remember too that operating leases often have valuable options attached.

3. How do you value a financial lease?

A financial lease extends over most of the economic life of the leased asset and cannot be cancelled by the lessee. Signing a financial lease is like signing a secured loan to finance purchase of the leased asset. With financial leases, the choice is not "lease versus buy" but "lease versus borrow."

Many companies have sound reasons for financing via leases. For example, companies that are not paying taxes can usually strike a favourable deal with a tax-paying lessor. Also, it may be less costly and time consuming to sign a standardized lease contract than to negotiate a long-term secured loan.

When a firm borrows money, it pays the after-tax rate of interest on its debt. Therefore, the opportunity cost of lease financing is the after-tax rate of interest on the firm's bonds. To value a financial lease, we need to discount the incremental cash flows from leasing by the after-tax interest rate.

An equivalent loan is one that commits the firm to exactly the same future cash flow as a financial lease. When we calculate the net present value of the lease, we are measuring the difference between the amount of financing provided by the lease and the financing provided by the equivalent loan:

Net present value of lease = financing provided by lease – value of equivalent loan

We can also analyze leases from the lessor's side of the transaction using the same approaches we developed

for the lessee. If lessee and lessor are in the same tax bracket, they will receive exactly the same cash flows but with signs reversed. Thus, the lessee can gain only at the lessor's expense, and vice versa. However, if the lessee's tax rate is lower than the lessor's, then both can gain at the government's expense.

Related Web Links

www.cfla-acfl.ca The Web site of the Canadian Finance and Leasing Association

www.executivecaliber.ws/sys-tmpl/door Lots of information on leasing, especially accounting issues

www.leasingcanada.com Information on leasing in Canada

www.GEcapitalcanada.com Major Canadian equipment lessor

Key Terms

lease	681	lessor	681	off-balance-sheet	
lessee	681	operating lease	681	financing	684
		financial lease	681	equivalent loan	690

Questions and Problems

*Answers in Appendix B

BASIC

1. **Lease Terms.** The following terms are often used to describe leases:
   i. Direct
   ii. Full-service
   iii. Operating
   iv. Financial
   v. Rental
   vi. Net
   vii. Leveraged
   viii. Sale and lease-back
   ix. Full-payout

   Match one or more of these terms with each of the following statements:
   a. The initial lease period is shorter than the economic life of the asset.
   b. The initial lease period is long enough for the lessor to recover the cost of the asset.
   c. The lessor provides maintenance and insurance.
   d. The lessee provides maintenance and insurance.
   e. The lessor buys the equipment from the manufacturer.
   f. The lessor buys the equipment from the prospective lessee.
   g. The lessor finances the lease contract by issuing debt and equity claims against it.

*2. **Why Lease?** Some of the following reasons for leasing are rational. Others are irrational or assume imperfect or inefficient capital markets. Which of the following reasons are the rational ones?
   a. The lessee's need for the leased asset is only temporary.
   b. Specialized lessors are better able to bear the risk of obsolescence.
   c. Leasing provides 100 percent financing and thus preserves capital.
   d. Leasing allows firms with low tax rates to "sell" CCA tax shields.
   e. Leasing increases earnings per share.
   f. Leasing reduces the transaction cost of obtaining external financing.
   g. Leasing avoids restrictions on capital expenditures.

3. **Reasons to Lease.** True or False? Explain your answers.

   a. It makes sense to enter into an operating lease if you are sure that you want to keep the asset for a long time.

   b. Leasing is advantageous because it provides a company with off-balance-sheet financing, allowing it to hide its financial obligations.

4. **Understanding Leases.** True or false?

   a. Lease payments are usually made at the start of each period. Thus the first payment is usually made as soon as the lease contract is signed.

   b. Financial leases can still provide off-balance-sheet financing.

   c. The cost of capital for a financial lease is the interest rate the company would pay on a bank loan.

   d. An equivalent loan's principal plus after-tax interest payments exactly match the after-tax cash flows of the lease.

   e. A financial lease should not be undertaken unless it provides more financing than the equivalent loan.

   f. It makes sense for firms that pay no taxes to lease from firms that do.

   g. Other things being equal, the net tax advantage of leasing increases as nominal interest rates increase.

*5. **Lease Valuation.** Suppose that National Waferonics has before it a proposal for a four-year financial lease. The firm constructs a table like Table 22.1. The bottom line of its table shows the lease cash flows:

Year	0	1	2	3
Lease cash flow	+62,000	−26,800	−22,200	−17,600

These flows reflect the cost of the machine, CCA tax shields, and the after-tax lease payments. Ignore salvage value. Assume the firm could borrow at 10 percent and faces a 35 percent marginal tax rate.

   a. What is the value of the equivalent loan?

   b. What is the value of the lease?

   c. Suppose the machine's NPV under normal financing is −$5,000. Should National Waferonics invest? Should it sign the lease?

PRACTICE

6. **Lease as Financing.** A lessee does not have to pay to buy the leased asset. Thus it's said that "leases provide 100 percent financing." Explain why this is not a true advantage to the lessee.

*7. **Lease Valuation.** ABC Brickworks proposes to lease a $75,000 forklift. Five annual lease payments of $15,000 are due in advance. ABC's tax rate is 35 percent. If it purchases the forklift, it will be in its own 25 percent CCA class. The half-year rule applies and after six years, the forklift will be worthless. The interest rate is 9 percent.

   a. Using Table 22.1 as a guide, determine the cash flows of leasing rather than purchasing the forklift.

   b. What are the equivalent loan and NPV of the lease?

   c. If the forklift is expected to have a $10,000 salvage value after 6 years and the project's discount rate is 12 percent, what is the NPV of the lease?

EXCEL

8. **Lease Valuation.** Printing World thinks it may need a new colour printing press. The press will cost $500,000 but will substantially reduce annual operating costs by $215,000 a year, before tax. The press has a 30 percent CCA rate and will be in its own asset pool. It will operate for four years and then be worthless. The cost of equity for Printing World is 12 percent, the cost of debt is 8 percent, and the company's target debt-equity ratio is .5. The company's tax rate is 30 percent.

   a. What is the NPV of buying the press?

    b.   The equipment manufacturer is offering to lease the press for $112,000 a year, for 4 years, payable in advance. Should Printing World accept the offer?

9.   **Why Lease?** Why do you think that leasing of trucks, airplanes, and computers is such big business? What efficiencies offset the costs of running these leasing operations?

10.   **Operating Lease.** Financial leases make sense when the lessee faces a lower marginal tax rate than the lessor. Does this tax advantage carry over to operating leases?

The following questions all apply to financial leases.

*11.   **Lease Valuation.** Look again at the backhoe-loader lease described in Table 22.1 Consider each question separately.

    a.   What is the value of the lease if Greenfield's tax rate is 20 percent?

    b.   What would the lease value be if Greenfield's first CCA payment was at the end of Year 1?

    c.   What would the lease value be if Greenfield had many other assets in the equipment asset pool? In this case, the equipment asset pool would not be closed.

*12.   **Setting Lease Payments.** In Section 22.4 we showed that the lease offered to Greenfield Construction had a positive NPV of $928 if Greenfield paid no tax and a +$221 NPV to a lessor paying 35 percent tax.

    a.   What is the minimum lease payment the lessor could accept under these circumstances?

    b.   What is the maximum amount that Greenfield could pay?

13.   **Gains from Leasing.** In Section 22.4 we listed four circumstances in which there are potential gains from leasing. Check them out by conducting a sensitivity analysis on the Greenfield Construction lease, assuming that Greenfield does not pay tax. Try, in turn, (a) a lessor tax rate of 50 percent (rather than 35 percent), (b) a CCA rate of 35 percent rather than 30 percent, (c) a 4-year lease with four annual payments (rather than a 7-year lease), and (d) an interest rate of 20 percent (rather than 10 percent). In each case, find the minimum rental that would satisfy the lessor and calculate the NPV to the lessee.

14.   **Taxes and Leasing.** In Section 22.4 we stated that if the interest rate was zero, there would be no advantage in postponing tax and therefore no advantage in leasing. Value the Greenfield Construction lease with an interest rate of zero. Assume that Greenfield does not pay tax. Can you devise any lease terms that would make both a lessee and a lessor happy?

15.   **Structured Lease.** A lease with varying rental schedule is known as a *structured lease.* Try structuring the Greenfield Construction lease to increase value to the lessee while preserving the value to the lessor. Assume that Greenfield does not pay tax. (*Note:* In practice the tax authorities will allow some structuring of rental payments but might be unhappy with some of the schemes you devise.)

*16.   **Comprehensive.** Nodhead College needs a new computer. It can either buy it for $250,000 or lease it from Compulease. The lease terms require Nodhead to make six annual payments (prepaid) of $55,000. Nodhead pays no tax. Compulease pays tax at 35 percent. Compulease can depreciate the computer for tax purposes at a CCA rate of 30 percent, and will close the asset pool at the end of the 6th year. The computer will have no residual value at the end of Year 5. The interest rate is 8 percent.

    a.   What is the NPV of the lease for Nodhead College?

    b.   What is the NPV for Compulease?

    c.   What is the overall gain from leasing?

EXCEL

17.   **Integrative.** The Safety Razor Company has a large tax-loss carryforward and does not expect to pay taxes for another 10 years. The company is therefore proposing to lease $100,000 of new machinery. The lease terms consist of eight equal lease payments prepaid annually. The lessor will take CCA on the machinery at a 30 percent rate and the pool

will never close. There is no salvage value at the end of the machinery's economic life. The tax rate is 35 percent, and the rate of interest is 10 percent. Wilbur Occam, the president of Safety Razor, wants to know the maximum lease payment that the lessor is likely to accept. Can you help him? Hint: Use the perpetual CCA tax shield formula, Equation (1) on page 255.

18. **Lease Rate of Return.** Many companies calculate the internal rate of return of the incremental after-tax cash flows from financial leases. What problems to you think this may give rise to? To what rate should the IRR be compared?

19. **Why Lease?** Discuss the following two opposite statements. Which do you think makes more sense?
    a. "Leasing is tax avoidance and should be legislated against."
    b. "Leasing ensures that the government's investment incentives work. It does so by allowing companies in non-tax-paying positions to take advantage of CCA deductions."

CHALLENGE

20. **Comprehensive.** Magna Charter has been asked to operate a Beaver bush plane for a mining company exploring in Yukon. Magna will have a one-year contract with the mining company and expects that the contract will be renewed after one year, for the remaining four years of the exploration program. If the mining company renews after one year, it will commit to use the plane for four more years.

Magna Charter has the following choices:

• Buy the plane for $500,000.

• Arrange a 5-year, non-cancellable, net financial lease at a rate of $75,000 per year, paid in advance.

How would you advise Agnes Magna, the charter company's CEO? Assume that the CCA rate is 25 percent and Magna has many other airplanes in its asset pool. The company's tax rate is 35 percent. The weighted-average cost of capital for the bush plane business is 14 percent, but Magna can borrow at 9 percent.

Ms. Magna thinks the plane will be worth $300,000 after 5 years. She also thinks that there is a 20 percent chance that the contract will not be renewed at Year 1. If the contract is not renewed, the plane will have to be sold on short notice for $400,000.

If Magna Charters takes the 5-year financial lease and the mining company cancels at Year 1, Magna can sublet the plane, that is, rent it out to another user.

Make additional assumptions as necessary.

21. **Lease NPV.** Recalculate the value of the lease to Greenfield Construction if the company pays no taxes until Year 3. Calculate the lease cash flows by modifying Table 22.1. Remember that the after-tax borrowing rate for years 1 and 2 differs from the rate for years 3 through 7.

22. **Standard & Poor's.** Go to **www.mcgrawhill.ca/edumarketinsight**. Compare the leverage ratios of two retailers for the past 10 years: Abercrombie & Fitch (ANF) and Wal-Mart (WMT). On the Company page, enter each stock ticker, hit "Go" and then click on "Excel Analytics." The annual ratio reports are found at "Ann. Ratio Rpt." Can you guess which company relies more heavily on operating leases? See if you are right by examining the most recent annual report for each company, found on their Web sites. Look carefully in the notes to the financial statements. Why are operating leases relatively more important to one of the companies?

23. **Internet.** Canadian Capital Leasing's Web site at **www.leasingcanada.com/ leaseguide.htm** has information about leasing in Canada. Click on "Your Guide to Leasing Terms" and identify the terms that deal with the possibility of terminating (or not terminating) a lease. Likewise, identify the various ways the asset can be disposed of at the end of lease.

24. **Internet.** In the same Web site as in problem 23, click on "Leasing for Business," and read the arguments about why businesses should consider leasing. What do you think about the arguments?

25. **Internet.** The "Lease or Buy Calculator" at **http://strategis.ic.gc.ca/epic/internet/ insof-sdf.nsf/en/h_so0333le.html**, the Web site of Industry Canada, shows the cash flows of a lease versus a loan. This calculator assumes that the asset pool is not closed at the end of the lease. A neat feature of this calculator is that it allows you to look up the CCA rate for the asset you are purchasing. Suppose the lease is for a $100,000 Class 38 asset that will have zero salvage value and last for 3 years. The company's tax rate is 40 percent and the cost of debt is 10 percent. If the loan is also three years, can you figure out what the monthly lease payment must be to be indifferent between borrowing and leasing? See if you can figure out the numbers the calculator produces.

Solutions to Check Points

22.1 The lease cash flows are in Table 22.4.

22.2
$$\text{NPV lease} = 70,787 - \frac{17,336}{1.065} - \frac{15,060}{(1.065)^2} - \frac{13,467}{(1.065)^3} - \frac{12,352}{(1.065)^4} - \frac{11,571}{(1.065)^5} - \frac{11,025}{(1.065)^6} - \frac{2,975}{(1.065)^7}$$
$$= \$2,565$$

22.3 Interest paid in Year 2 is 10 percent of the amount borrowed during the year $.1 \times 67,388$ = $6,739. However, Greenfield gets an interest tax shield of 35 percent of the interest paid, $.35 \times \$6,739 = \$2,359$, so the interest paid after tax is $6,739 - $2,359 = $4,380. To match the Year 2 lease cash outflow of $18,273, Greenfield can repay principal equal to $18,273 - $4,380, or $13,893.

22.4 The cash flows received by the bank are the interest paid and the principal repayments. For example, in Year 1 the bank is paid $8,295 + $15,559 = $23,854. The present value of the cash flows received by the bank is

$$= \frac{23,853}{1.1} + \frac{20,631}{(1.1)^2} + \frac{18,271}{(1.1)^3} + \frac{16,506}{(1.1)^4} + \frac{15,152}{(1.1)^5} + \frac{14,078}{(1.1)^6} + \frac{3,615}{(1.1)^7} = \$82,946$$

The bank is willing to lend $82,946 to Greenfield because it receives interest and principal repayment with an equal present value.

TABLE 22.4
Lease cash flows for Check Point 22.1

Lease Cash Flows	Year							
	0	1	2	3	4	5	6	7
Saved cost of a new backhoe-loader	+85,000							
Lost CCA tax shield (calculated below)	−4,463	−7,586	−5,310	−3,717	−2,602	−1,821	−1,275	−2,975
Lease payment	−15,000	−15,000	−15,000	−15,000	−15,000	−15,000	−15,000	
Lease payment tax shield	+5,250	+5,250	+5,250	+5,250	+5,250	+5,250	+5,250	
Cash flow of lease	70,787	−17,336	−15,060	−13,467	−12,352	−11,571	−11,025	−2,975
Tax Shield Calculation								
UCC	85,000	72,250	50,575	35,403	24,782	17,347	12,143	8,500
CCA (CCA rate = 30%)	12,750	21,675	15,173	10,621	7,435	5,204	3,643	
CCA tax shield (tax rate = 35%)	4,463	7,586	5,310	3,717	2,602	1,821	1,275	2,975

MINICASE

Rachel Gold, a newly recruited financial analyst at Halverton Corporation, had just been asked to analyze a proposal to acquire a new dredger.

She reviewed the capital appropriation request. The dredger would cost $3.5 million and was expected to generate cash flows of $470,000 a year for 9 years. After that point, the dredger would almost surely be obsolete and have no significant salvage value. The company's weighted-average cost of capital was 16 percent.

Rachel proposed a standard DCF analysis, but this suggestion was brushed off by Halverton's top management. They seemed to be convinced of the merits of the investment but were unsure of the best ways to finance it. Halverton could raise the money by issuing a secured 8-year note at an interest rate of 12 percent. However, Halverton had large tax-loss carryforwards from a disastrous foray into foreign exchange options. As a result, the company was unlikely to be in a tax-paying position for many years. Halverton's CEO thought it might be better to lease the dredger rather than to buy it.

Rachel's first step was to invite two leasing companies, Mount Zircon Finance and First Cookham Bank, to submit proposals. Both companies were in a tax-paying position and could claim CCA on the dredger. The dredger is a Class 38 asset with a 30 percent CCA rate.

Rachel received the following letters, the first from Mount Zircon Finance:

March 31, 2007

Dear Rachel,

We appreciated the opportunity to meet you the other day and to discuss the possibility of providing lease finance for your proposed new JLT4 dredger. As you know, Mount Zircon has extensive experience in this field, and because of our large volumes and low borrowing costs, we are able to offer very attractive terms.

We would envisage offering a 9-year lease with 10 annual payments of $550,000, with the initial lease payment due on entering into the lease contract. This is equivalent to a borrowing cost of 11.8 percent per annum (i.e., 10 payments of $550,000 paid at the beginning of each year discounted at 11.8 percent amounts to $3,500,000).

We hope that you agree with us that this is an attractive rate. It is well below your company's overall cost of capital. Our leasing proposal will cover the entire $3.5 million cost of the dredger, thereby preserving Halverton's capital for other uses. Leasing will also allow a very attractive return on equity from your company's acquisition of this new equipment.

This proposal is subject to a routine credit check and review of Halverton's financial statements. We expect no difficulties on that score, but you will understand the need for due diligence.

Thank you for contacting Mount Zircon Finance. We look forward to hearing your response.

Sincerely yours,

Henry Attinger
For and on behalf of Mount Zircon Finance

The next letter was from First Cookham.

March 31, 2007

Dear Rachel,

It was an honour to meet you the other day and to discuss how First Cookham Bank can help your company to finance its new dredger. First Cookham has a small specialized leasing operation. This enables us to tailor our proposals to our clients' needs.

We recommend that Halverton consider leasing the dredger on a 7-year term. Subject to documentation and routine review of Halverton's financial statements, we could offer a 7-year lease on the basis of eight payments of $619,400 due at the beginning of each year. This is equivalent to a loan at an interest rate of 11.41 percent.

We expect that this lease payment will be higher than quoted by the large, mass-market leasing companies, but our financial analysts have determined that by offering a shorter lease, we can quote a lower interest rate.

We are confident that this is a highly competitive offer, and we look forward to your response.

Yours sincerely,

George Bucknall
First Cookham Bank

Both proposals appeared to be attractive. However, Rachel realized the need to undertake careful calculations before deciding whether leasing made sense and which firm was offering the better deal. She also wondered whether the terms offered were really as attractive as the two lessors claimed. Perhaps she could persuade them to cut their prices.

MERGERS, ACQUISITIONS, AND CORPORATE CONTROL

In recent years the scale and pace of merger activity have been remarkable. For example, Table 23.1 lists just a few of the important Canadian mergers in the recent past. Many of the largest mergers have involved European as well as American firms. A few Canadian deals are big by world standards.

The mergers listed in Table 23.1 all involved *big* money. During periods of intense merger activity, financial managers spend considerable time either searching for firms to acquire or worrying whether some other firm is about to take over their company.

When one company buys another, it is making an investment, and the basic principles of capital investment decisions apply. You should go ahead with the purchase if it makes a net contribution to shareholders' wealth. But mergers are often awkward transactions to evaluate, and you have to be careful to define benefits and costs properly.

Many mergers are arranged amicably, but in other cases one firm will make a hostile takeover bid for the other. We describe the principal techniques of modern merger warfare, and since the threat of hostile takeovers has stimulated corporate restructurings and leveraged buyouts (LBOs), we describe them too, and attempt to explain why these deals have generated rewards for investors. We close with a look at who gains and who loses from mergers and we discuss whether mergers are beneficial on balance.

TABLE 23.1
Some important recent mergers involving Canadian companies

Year	Buying Company	Selling Company	Value ($ millions)
2003	Manulife Financial Corp.	John Hancock Financial Services Inc.	15,000
2003	Alcan	Pechiney SA	6,252
2004	Toronto-Dominion Bank	Banknorth Group Inc.	4,969
2003	R.R. Donelley & Sons Co.	Moore Wallace Inc.	4,855
2004	Molson Inc. (merger partner)	Adolph Coors Company (merger partner)	4,530
2004	Kohlberg Kravis Roberts & Co.	Masonite International Corp.	3,700
2004	EnCana Corp.	Tom Brown Inc.	3,630
2004	Jean Coutu Group	J.C. Penney Co. (sold Eckerd Drugstores)	3,280
2004	Iamgold Corp.	Wheaton River Minerals Ltd.	2,870
2004	TransCanada Corp	National Energy & Gas Transmission Inc. (sold Gas Transmission NorthWest Corp.)	2,262

Source: Various issues of *Financial Post Crosbie Mergers and Acquisitions in Canada.*

After studying this chapter you should be able to
- Describe ways that companies change their ownership or management.
- Explain why it may make sense for companies to merge.
- Estimate the gains and costs of mergers to the acquiring firm.
- Describe takeover defences.
- Explain some of the motivations for leveraged and management buyouts of the firm.
- Summarize the evidence on whether mergers increase efficiency and how the gains from mergers are distributed between shareholders of the acquired and acquiring firms.

23.1   THE MARKET FOR CORPORATE CONTROL

The shareholders are the owners of the firm. But many shareholders do not feel like the boss, and with good reason. Try buying a share of Royal Bank stock and marching into the boardroom for a chat with your employee, the chief executive officer.

The *ownership* and *management* of large corporations are substantially separated. Shareholders do not directly appoint or supervise the firm's managers. They elect the board of directors, who act as their agents in choosing and monitoring the managers of the firm. Shareholders have a direct say in very few matters. Control of the firm is in the hands of the managers, subject to the general oversight of the board of directors.

The separation of the ownership and management or control of the firm creates potential *agency costs*. Agency costs occur when managers or directors take actions adverse to shareholders' interests.

The temptation to take such actions may be ever present, but there are many forces and constraints working to keep managers' and shareholders' interests in line. As we pointed out in Chapter 1, managers' paycheques in large corporations are almost always tied to the profitability of the firm and the performance of its shares. Boards of directors take their responsibilities seriously—they may face lawsuits if they don't—and therefore are reluctant to rubber-stamp obviously bad financial decisions.

But what ensures that the board has engaged the most talented managers? What happens if managers are inadequate? What if the board of directors is derelict in monitoring the performance of managers? Or what if the firm's managers are fine, but resources of the firm could be used more efficiently by merging with another firm? Can we count on managers to pursue arrangements that would put them out of jobs?

These are all questions about *the market for corporate control*, the mechanisms by which firms are matched up with management teams and owners who can make the most of the firm's resources. You should not take a firm's current ownership and management for granted. If it is possible for the value of the firm to be enhanced by changing management or by reorganizing under new owners, there will be incentives for someone to make a change.

There are four ways to change the management of a firm. These are (1) a successful proxy contest in which a group of shareholders votes in a new group of directors, who then pick a new management team; (2) the purchase of one firm by another in a merger or acquisition; (3) a leveraged buyout of the firm by a private group of investors; and (4) a divestiture, in which a firm either sells part of its operations to another company or spins it off as an independent firm.

We will briefly review each of these methods.

METHOD 1: PROXY CONTESTS

Shareholders elect the board of directors to keep watch on management and replace unsatisfactory managers. If the board is lax, shareholders are free to elect a different board. In theory this ensures that the corporation is run in the best interests of shareholders.

In practice things are not so clear cut. Ownership in large corporations is sometimes widely dispersed and even the largest single shareholder may hold only a small fraction of the shares. Most shareholders have little notion who is on the board or what the members stand for. Management, on the other hand, deals directly with the board and has a personal relationship with its members. In many corporations, management sits on the committee that nominates candidates for the board. It is not surprising that some boards seem less than aggressive in forcing managers to run a lean, efficient operation and act primarily in the interests of shareholders.

proxy contest   Takeover attempt in which outsiders compete with management for shareholders' votes. Also called proxy fight.

When a group of investors believes that the board and its management team should be replaced, they can launch a **proxy contest**. A proxy is the right to vote another shareholder's shares. In a proxy contest, the dissident shareholders attempt to obtain enough proxies to elect their own slate to the board of directors. Once the new board is in control, management can be replaced. A proxy fight is therefore a direct contest for control of the corporation.

EXAMPLE 23.1	**FISHERY PRODUCTS INTERNATIONAL PROXY FIGHT**

In the spring of 2001, a group of dissident shareholders of Fishery Products International (FPI) initiated a proxy fight to change the board and management of the company. Led by John Risley, president and sole shareholder of Clearwater Fine Foods, and largest shareholder of FPI, the dissidents argued that FPI's stock price would benefit from new leadership and modernized plants. The proxy fight was successful, with 82 percent of shareholders voting in favour of the slate of new board members nominated by the dissident shareholders.

In 2004 a group of dissident Creo Inc. shareholders, unhappy with the company's strategy and the stock's poor performance, launched a proxy fight for control of the board of directors. However, just two weeks before the vote at the annual meeting, Creo's board of directors announced their acceptance of a takeover bid by Kodak. The dissidents announced that they would support the takeover and the proxy fight was ended without a vote. Nevertheless, the dissidents claimed victory.

Most proxy contests fail. Dissidents who engage in such fights must use their own money, while management can use the corporation's funds and lines of communication with shareholders to defend itself. Such fights can cost millions of dollars.[1]

Institutional shareholders such as large pension funds have become more aggressive in pressing for managerial accountability. These funds have been able to gain concessions from firms without initiating proxy contests. For example, firms have agreed to split the jobs of chief executive officer

---

[1] J. H. Mulherin and A. B. Poulsen provide an analysis of proxy fights in "Proxy Contests and Corporate Change: Implications for Shareholder Wealth," *Journal of Financial Economics* 47 (1998), pp. 279–313.

and chairperson of the board of directors. This ensures that an outsider is responsible for keeping watch over the company. Also, more firms now bar corporate insiders from serving on the committee that nominates candidates to the board. Perhaps as a result of shareholder pressure, boards also seem to be getting more aggressive. For example, outside directors were widely credited for hastening the replacement of top management at Lucent, Adelphia, and WorldCom.

METHOD 2: MERGERS AND ACQUISITIONS

Proxy contests are rare, and successful ones are rarer still. Poorly performing managers face a greater risk from acquisition. If the management of one firm observes another firm underperforming, it can try to acquire the business and replace the poor managers with its own team. In practice, corporate takeovers are the arenas where contests for corporate control are usually fought.

There are three ways for one firm to acquire another firm: (1) merge with it, (2) purchase a majority of its shares, or (3) purchase its assets.

merger or statutory amalgamation Combination of the assets and liabilities of two firms into one.

In Canada, when people talk about a **merger**, a situation in which the assets and liabilities of two companies are combined into one, they are really referring to a **statutory amalgamation**. The laws governing statutory amalgamations are found in the federal and provincial business corporations acts. For a statutory amalgamation—or merger—to succeed, a large majority of shareholders (typically, two-thirds) must approve it by voting in favour at a special shareholders meeting.

In many mergers there is a clear acquiring company whose management then runs the enlarged firm. In these cases the acquiring company assumes all of the assets and all of the liabilities of the target, and the target company ceases to exist. The former shareholders of the target firm receive cash and/or securities in the acquiring firm. However, sometimes an entirely new company is created through the statutory amalgamation and both original companies disappear. Such is the case when the companies involved are considered equals, with management from both firms having a major say in the running of the new company. For example, the combination of Molson and Adolph Coors in 2004 was a merger of equals.

EXAMPLE 23.2   **THE CREATION OF ALIANT**

In 1999, the four principal telecommunications companies operating in Atlantic Canada—Bruncor Inc., Island Telecom Inc., Maritime Telegraph and Telephone Company, and NewTel Enterprises—determined that by combining their businesses they would create a stronger company. Through a statutory amalgamation they created a new company, Aliant Inc. Shareholders of each of the four selling companies exchanged their old shares for shares in the new company. The number of new shares received was based on the prices of the companies' shares before merging.

A second alternative is for the acquiring firm to buy the target firm's stock in exchange for cash, shares, or other securities. The acquired firm may continue to exist as a separate entity, but it is now owned by the acquirer. The approval and cooperation of the target firm's managers are generally sought, but even if they resist, the acquirer can attempt to purchase a majority of the outstanding shares. By offering to buy shares directly from shareholders, the acquiring firm can bypass the target firm's management and board of directors altogether. The offer to purchase stock is called a **tender offer**. A tender offer is *friendly* if target management and board are in favour of the offer and is *hostile* when target management and the board disapprove. If the tender offer is successful, the buyer obtains control and can, if it chooses, toss out incumbent management.

tender offer Takeover attempt in which outsiders directly offer to buy the stock of the firm's shareholders.

Frequently, a tender offer is the first step toward the final goal of complete acquisition of the publicly traded target company. Consequently, many tender offers are conditional on acquiring two-thirds of the outstanding shares. Why two-thirds, you ask? With two-thirds of the shares, the acquiring firm ensures it will win the subsequent vote to approve statutory amalgamation of the target company with the acquirer.

EXAMPLE 23.3	**THE BATTLE FOR GOLDCORP INC.**

In November 2004, Glamis Gold Corp. made a hostile tender offer to acquire all shares of Goldcorp Inc. Each Goldcorp share tendered would receive 0.89 shares of Glamis shares. Based on stock prices the day before the announcement, the Glamis offer valued Goldcorp at $17.25 a share, or $2.86 billion. The offer was conditional on the tendering of at least two-thirds of Goldcorp's shares. Furthermore, Goldcorp shareholders were required to not approve a previously announced merger proposal of Goldcorp with another company, Wheaton River Mines Ltd. Glamis's offer was ultimately rejected by Goldcorp's shareholders, who voted in favour of the merger with Wheaton.

The third approach for one firm to acquire another is to buy the target firm's assets. In this case ownership of the assets needs to be transferred, and payment is made to the selling firm rather than directly to its shareholders. Usually the target firm sells only some of its assets, but occasionally it sells all of them. In this case, the selling firm continues to exist as an independent entity, but it becomes an empty shell—a corporation engaged in no business activity.

The terminology of mergers and acquisitions (M&A) can be confusing. These phrases are used loosely to refer to any kind of corporate combination or takeover. But strictly speaking, *merger* or *statutory amalgamation* means the combination of all the assets and liabilities of two firms. The purchase of the stock or assets of another firm is an **acquisition**.

acquisition   Takeover of a firm by purchase of that firm's common stock or assets.

METHOD 3: LEVERAGED BUYOUTS

leveraged buyout (LBO) Acquisition of the firm by a private group using substantial borrowed funds.

Sometimes a group of investors takes over a firm by means of a **leveraged buyout**, or **LBO**. The LBO group takes the firm private, so its shares no longer trade in the securities markets. Usually a considerable proportion of LBO financing is borrowed, hence the term *leveraged* buyout.

management buyout (MBO) Acquisition of the firm by its own management in a leveraged buyout.

If the investor group is led by the management of the firm, the takeover is called a **management buyout**, or **MBO**. In this case, the firm's managers actually buy the firm from the shareholders and continue to run it. They become owner-managers. We will discuss LBOs and MBOs later in the chapter.

EXAMPLE 23.4	**ONEX, CANADA'S LEVERAGED BUYOUT LEADER**

Onex, a very profitable Canadian public company with annual sales of $16 billion in 2004, has grown primarily through leveraged buyouts financed largely with debt provided by third-party lenders. This strategy gives the company the potential, with the accompanying risk, to enhance the return on its invested equity and allows the company to pursue larger-scale investment programs. For example, in 2005 two subsidiaries of Laidlaw, American Medical Response and EmCare Holdings, were sold for about $1 billion. Onex, through Onex Partners LP, paid $270 million to acquire 98 percent of the subsidiaries' equity, with the subsidiaries' senior management acquiring the other 2 percent. The remaining $730 million was provided by third-party lenders.

METHOD 4: DIVESTITURES AND SPIN-OFFS

Firms not only acquire businesses, they also sell them. *Divestitures* are part of the market for corporate control. In recent years the number of divestitures has been about half the number of mergers.

Instead of selling a business to another firm, companies may *spin off* the business by separating it from the parent firm and distributing stock in the newly independent company to the shareholders of the parent company. For example, BCE decided to spin off almost all of its holdings of Nortel Networks to BCE shareholders. Although at one time BCE owned all of Nortel, by January 2000, it was a minority shareholder, owning 39 percent of Nortel's stock. These shares accounted for about 78 percent of BCE's value. BCE management and some analysts felt that the non-Nortel assets of BCE were not being fully valued, overshadowed by the Nortel holdings. BCE shareholders received .78 Nortel share for each BCE share. On the announcement of the widely anticipated spin-off, BCE's share price rose about 5 percent. Given the colossal crash of Nortel's stock value in 2001, BCE's management looks pretty smart (or lucky) to have disconnected from Nortel.

EXAMPLE 23.5	CANADIAN PACIFIC STARBURST SPLIT

Another major Canadian spin-off was announced in February 2001 when Canadian Pacific revealed its plans to divide the company into five separate companies, all of which were to be publicly traded. In July 2001, the details of division were finalized. Each common share of Canadian Pacific was to be exchanged for the following: .5 Canadian Pacific Railway common shares, .25 Canadian Pacific Ships common shares, .25 Fairmont Hotel and Resorts common shares, .684 PanCanadian Energy common shares, and .166 Fording common shares. CP stated that the reorganization was designed to maximize value for CP shareholders by unlocking the current value of the businesses and strengthening their ability to pursue further success as independent companies. The stated hope of CP management was that the sum of the value of shares of the new companies would exceed the current market value of the pre-split Canadian Pacific common shares. CP's investors clearly welcomed the split: the stock price jumped nearly 11 percent on the day the plan was announced.

Probably the most frequent motive for divestitures and spin-offs is improved efficiency. Companies sometimes refer to a business as being a "poor fit." By spinning off a poor fit, the management of the parent company can concentrate on its main activity. If each business must stand on its own feet, there is no risk that funds will be siphoned off from one in order to support unprofitable investments in the other. Moreover, if the two parts of the business are independent, it is easy to see the value of each and to reward managers accordingly.

OWNERSHIP STRUCTURE AND THE MARKET FOR CORPORATE CONTROL

The ownership structure, or how shares are distributed among shareholders, affects both the extent of the separation of ownership and control and also the effectiveness of the various corporate control mechanisms. At one extreme are privately owned companies with no publicly traded common shares and only one or a few shareholders. In Canada the largest private companies are owned by other corporations. General Motors of Canada, ranked the largest private Canadian company with 2003 revenues of $37 billion, is owned 100 percent by General Motors Corporation, its American parent. Some private corporations are owned by individuals or families. For example, McCain Foods, the eighth largest private company in Canada, with 2003 revenues of $6.5 billion, is wholly owned by the McCain family.[2]

In a private company, typically shareholders are actively involved in the management of the company, often holding senior management positions, as well as sitting on the board of directors. Thus problems of the separation of ownership from control are much less important than in a publicly owned company. Of course, if the sole shareholder of the company is another company, the shareholders of the parent company are still separated from the control of the various companies they own. A privately held company will never be sold unless the shareholders want it to happen. Proxy contests and hostile tender offers cannot occur.

Some publicly traded companies have a controlling shareholder or shareholder group that owns a significant percentage of the votes. Typically, the controlling shareholders hold at least

---

[2] The corporations' rankings are from the *Report on Business* magazine, July 2004.

40 percent of the votes. These closely held but publicly traded companies use a variety of methods to maintain control while still allowing outsiders to invest in the company's equity. Multiple classes of equity is a commonly used structure. For example, Canadian Tire, as we saw in Chapter 6, has two classes of equity: one with one vote per share and the other with no votes. The Billes family controls about 60 percent of the voting shares. Many Canadian public companies have a controlling shareholder.

A closely held public company has less separation between management and the controlling shareholders. However, minority, non-controlling shareholders have less influence and are unlikely to be able to change management through the market for corporate control mechanisms. If the large shareholder owns more than 50 percent of the votes, any proxy fight or hostile bid is doomed to fail. If the controlling shareholder does not want to sell his shares, control cannot be changed.[3]

Finally, some companies are widely held, where no one shareholder or shareholder group owns a significant number of votes. In these companies, the separation of ownership from control is the most evident. Likewise, the corporate control mechanisms have the greatest chance to succeed.

23.2   SENSIBLE MOTIVES FOR MERGERS

We now look more closely at mergers and acquisitions and consider when they do and do not make sense. Mergers are often categorized as *horizontal, vertical,* or *conglomerate.* A horizontal merger is one that takes place between two firms in the same line of business; the merged firms are former competitors. Most of the mergers around the turn of the 20th century were of this type and mergers of this type are still common today. Recent examples of Canadian horizontal mergers have occurred in transportation (the acquisition of Canadian Airlines by Air Canada) communications (the acquisition of Clearnet by Telus) and oil and gas (Husky Oil's acquisition of Renaissance Energy and Devon Energy's acquisition of Anderson Exploration).

A vertical merger involves companies at different stages of production. The buyer expands back toward the source of raw materials or forward in the direction of the ultimate consumer. Thus, a soft-drink manufacturer might buy a sugar producer (expanding backward) or a fast-food chain as an outlet for its product (expanding forward). A recent example of a vertical merger is Walt Disney's acquisition of the ABC television network. Disney planned to use the network to show its movies to huge audiences.

A conglomerate merger involves companies in unrelated lines of business. For example, before it went belly-up in 1999, the Korean conglomerate, Daewoo, had nearly 400 different subsidiaries and 150,000 employees. It built ships in Korea; manufactured microwaves in France, TVs in Mexico, cars in Poland, and fertilizers in Vietnam; and managed hotels in China and a bank in Hungary. No Canadian or U.S. company is as diversified as Daewoo, but in the 1960s and 1970s it was common in both Canada and the United States for unrelated businesses to merge. However, the number of conglomerate mergers declined in the 1980s. In fact, much of the action in the 1980s came from breaking up the conglomerates that had been formed 10 to 20 years earlier.

Check Point 23.1

Are the following hypothetical mergers horizontal, vertical, or conglomerate?
a. IBM acquires Apple Computer.
b. BCE acquires Stop & Shop (a supermarket chain).
c. Loblaws acquires Fishery Products International (a frozen fish processor).
d. Alcan acquires Canada Bread.

---

[3] To protect non-controlling public shareholders, Canadian securities commissions have implemented special rules governing non–arm's-length transactions by controlling shareholders. For example, if the majority shareholder wants to take the company private by purchasing all the shares held by other shareholders, the company must get an independent valuation of the company and a majority of the minority shareholders must approve the transaction.

We have already seen that one motive for a merger is to replace the existing management team. If this motive is important, one would expect that poorly performing firms would tend to be targets for acquisition; this seems to be the case.[4] However, firms also acquire other firms for reasons that have nothing to do with inadequate management. Many mergers and acquisitions are motivated by possible gains in efficiency from combining operations. These mergers create synergies. By this we mean that the two firms are worth more together than apart.

> A merger adds value only if synergies, better management, or other changes make the two firms worth more together than apart.

It would be convenient if we could say that certain types of mergers are usually successful and other types fail. Unfortunately, there are no such simple generalizations. Many mergers that appear to make sense nevertheless fail because managers cannot handle the complex task of integrating two firms with different production processes, accounting methods, and corporate cultures. Moreover, the value of most businesses depends on *human assets*—managers, skilled workers, scientists, and engineers. If these people are not happy in their new roles in the acquiring firm, many of them will leave. Beware of paying too much for assets that go down in the elevator and out to the parking lot at the close of each business day.

Consider the $36 billion merger between Daimler Benz and Chrysler. Although it was hailed as a model for consolidation in the auto industry, the early years were bedevilled by conflicts between two very different cultures:

> German management-board members had executive assistants who prepared detailed position papers on any number of issues. The Americans didn't have assigned aides and formulated their decisions by talking directly to engineers or other specialists. A German decision worked its way through the bureaucracy for final approval at the top. Then it was set in stone. The Americans allowed midlevel employees to proceed on their own initiative, sometimes without waiting for executive-level approval.
>
> … Cultural integration also was proving to be a slippery commodity. The yawning gap in pay scales fueled an undercurrent of tension. The Americans earned two, three, and, in some cases, four times as much as their German counterparts. But the expenses of U.S. workers were tightly controlled compared with the German system. Daimler-side employees thought nothing of flying to Paris or New York for a half-day meeting, then capping the visit with a fancy dinner and a night in an expensive hotel. The Americans blanched at the extravagance.[5]

These observations illustrate the difficulties in realizing the benefits of merger. There are also occasions when the merger does achieve the intended synergies, but the buyer nevertheless loses because it pays too much. For example, the buyer may overestimate the value of stale inventory or underestimate the costs of renovating old plant and equipment, or it may overlook the warranties on a defective product.

With these caveats in mind, we will now consider some possible sources of synergy.

INCREASED REVENUES

Mergers are frequently justified on the belief that revenues of the combined companies will exceed the sum of the revenues of the two companies if they were to remain separate. However, revenue synergies are difficult to estimate accurately because they are out of the direct control of management. For revenues to increase, customers must buy more than they used to or be willing to pay a higher price and, also, competitors must not lower their prices in response to the acquisition.

Potentially, the most effective way to increase revenues is a horizontal merger. By combining with a competitor in the same business, market share and market power of the companies may be

---

[4] For example, Palepu found that investors in firms that were subsequently acquired earned relatively low rates of return for several years before the merger. See K. Palepu, "Predicting Takeover Targets: A Methodological and Empirical Analysis," *Journal of Accounting and Economics* 8 (March 1986), pp. 3–36.

[5] Bill Vlasic and Bradley A. Stertz, "Taken for a Ride," *BusinessWeek*, June 5, 2000.

increased, allowing the merged company to raise its prices with the expectation of raising revenues. Although this may sound like a great idea to an enterprising capitalist, from society's perspective, mergers that lessen competition to the detriment of customers are not acceptable. In Canada, the *Federal Competition Act*, administered by the Competition Bureau and the Competition Tribunal, prohibits mergers that severely limit competition. However, merger proposals are rarely turned down for anti-competitive reasons in Canada. Instead, the Competition Bureau requests that the companies sell some of their assets to a third company, thereby limiting the reduction in competition. For example, the Competition Bureau requested that Canada Trust and TD Bank sell branches to competitors in particular geographic areas to reduce the anti-competitive impact of the proposed merger of those two companies.

Even mergers expected to create monopolies can be approved, under the federal *Competition Act*. In 1998, Superior Propane and ICG Propane merged to create a company with 70 percent of the Canadian propane market and a 100 percent monopoly in some parts of Canada. The Competition Bureau opposed the merger, citing the likelihood of significant price increases for consumers. However, the Competition Tribunal approved the merger on the strength of Section 96 of the *Competition Act*, which allows mergers where the efficiencies gains—the cost savings realized from joining two companies—exceed the impact of higher prices on consumers. After two failed appeals to the Federal Court to overturn the merger and break up the company, the Competition Bureau gave up in 2003. Although a proposed amendment to the *Competition Act* to disallow mergers of this type has been proposed, as we write this in 2005, the changes are still being debated. One group very interested in the issue is Canadian banks, who might want to use the efficiency argument to justify future bank mergers.

In contrast to the Canadian experience, mergers are frequently disallowed in the United States on anti-competitive grounds.

ECONOMIES OF SCALE

Just as most of us believe that we would be happier if only we were a little richer, so managers always seem to believe their firm would be more competitive if only it were just a little bigger. They hope for *economies of scale,* that is, the opportunity to spread fixed costs across a larger volume of output. The banking industry provides many examples. By the 1970s, it was clear that the United States had too many small, local banks. Some (now very large) banks grew by systematically buying up smaller banks and streamlining their operations. Most of the cost savings came from consolidating "back-office" operations, such as computer systems for processing cheques and credit-card transactions and payments. Similarly, TD Bank management argued it should be permitted to merge with its competitor Canada Trust to increase the scale and scope of its operations, and thereby, better compete with its larger domestic and foreign competitors. In addition to increasing the scale of back-office operations, the merger permitted the companies to reduce the number of branches. The effect is to create increased economies of scale, with higher volume at the remaining branches and lower costs per transaction.

These economies of scale are the natural goal of horizontal mergers. But they have been claimed in conglomerate mergers, too. The architects of these mergers have pointed to the economies that come from sharing central services such as accounting, financial control, and top-level management.

ECONOMIES OF VERTICAL INTEGRATION

Large industrial companies commonly like to gain as much control and coordination as possible over the production process by expanding back toward the output of the raw material and forward to the ultimate consumer. One way to achieve this is to merge with a supplier or a customer. Consider DuPont's purchase of an oil company, Conoco. This was vertical integration because petroleum is the ultimate raw material for much of DuPont's chemical production.

Do not assume that more vertical integration is necessarily better than less. Carried to extremes, it is absurdly inefficient. For example, before the Polish economy was restructured,

LOT, the Polish state airline, found itself raising pigs to make sure that its employees had fresh meat on their tables. (Of course, in a centrally managed economy it may prove necessary to grow your own meat, since you can't be sure you'll be able to buy it.)

Some people mistakenly think that vertical integration is a good idea because if you own your supplier, you will pay less for materials. However, if you pay less, the supplier's profits will fall. No synergy is created if the merger simply moves profits but does not increase total profit. The gains from vertical integration are achieved through improved coordination and control of production.

Vertical integration is now less popular. The advent of just-in-time inventory systems and computerized ordering systems makes it much easier for a company to manage its supply chain without having to own its suppliers. Many companies are finding it more efficient to *outsource* many activities. For example, automobile manufacturers used to manufacture most of the parts used to make cars. Now companies like General Motors and Ford are primarily car assemblers, building vehicles with components purchased from parts manufacturers, such as Magna International. Even DuPont seems to have become less convinced of the benefits of vertical integration: in 1999, it sold off Conoco.

COMBINING COMPLEMENTARY RESOURCES

Many small firms are acquired by large firms that can provide the missing ingredients necessary for the firm's success. The small firm may have a unique product but lack the engineering and sales organization necessary to produce and market it on a large scale. The firm could develop engineering and sales talent from scratch, but it may be quicker and cheaper to merge with a firm that already has ample talent. The two firms have *complementary resources*—each has what the other needs—so it may make sense for them to merge. Also the merger may open up opportunities that neither firm would pursue otherwise. Federal Express's purchase of Caliber System, a trucking company, is an example. Federal Express specializes in shipping packages by air, mostly for overnight delivery. Caliber's subsidiary RMS moves non-express packages by truck. RMS greatly increases Federal Express's capability to move packages on the ground. At the same time, RMS-originated business can move easily on the Federal Express system when rapid or distant delivery is essential. Combining complementary resources may increase total revenues, decrease total costs, or both.

EXAMPLE 23.6	COMPLEMENTARY RESOURCES

Consider the 1989 merger between two electric utilities, Utah Power & Light and PacifiCorp, which serves customers in California. Utah Power's peak demand comes in the summer, for air conditioning. PacifiCorp's peak comes in the winter, for heating. The savings from combining the two firms' generating systems were estimated at $45 million annually.

MERGING TO REDUCE TAXES

The tax implications of a merger or acquisition are often very complicated. However, it may be possible to reduce the total taxes of the combined companies if one of the companies has tax shields it is unable to use. For example, if a company has operating losses, by joining with another company in the same business that has taxable income, the losses may be a valuable tax deduction. However, merging for the sole purpose of using operating losses is not permitted and CRA may disallow the tax deductions.

Unused interest tax shields are another merger motive. As we saw in Chapter 15, the interest on debt generates an interest tax shield. A company with unused debt capacity, perhaps due to poor management, may be an attractive target. The acquirer will increase the target's debt/equity ratio, taking advantage of the interest deduction to reduce taxes and increase target firm value. This is one explanation offered for leveraged buyouts.

MERGERS AS A USE FOR SURPLUS FUNDS

Suppose that your firm is in a mature industry. It is generating a substantial amount of cash but has few profitable investment opportunities. Ideally such a firm should distribute the surplus cash to shareholders by increasing its dividend payment or by repurchasing its shares. Unfortunately, energetic managers are often reluctant to shrink their firm in this way. Furthermore, some shareholders may pay taxes on the dividends and repurchased shares.

If the firm is not willing to purchase its own shares, it can instead purchase someone else's. Thus firms with a surplus of cash and a shortage of good investment opportunities often turn to mergers *financed by cash* as a way of deploying their capital. This also avoids the tax consequences of dividends and share repurchases.

Firms that have excess cash and do not pay it out or redeploy it by acquisition often find themselves targets for takeover by other firms that propose to redeploy the cash for them. During the oil price slump of the early 1980s, many cash-rich oil companies found themselves threatened by takeover. This was not because their cash was a unique asset. The acquirers wanted to capture the companies' cash flow to make sure it was not frittered away on negative-NPV oil exploration projects. We return to this *free-cash-flow* motive for takeovers later in this chapter.

23.3

DUBIOUS REASONS FOR MERGERS

The benefits that we have described so far all make economic sense. Other arguments sometimes given for mergers are more dubious. Here are two.

DIVERSIFICATION

We have suggested that the managers of a cash-rich company may prefer to see that cash used for acquisitions. That is why we often see cash-rich firms in stagnant industries merging their way into fresh woods and new pastures. What about diversification as an end in itself? It is obvious that diversification reduces risk. Isn't that a gain from merging?

The trouble with this argument is that diversification is easier and cheaper for the shareholder than for the corporation. Why should firm A buy firm B to diversify when the shareholders of firm A can buy shares in firm B to diversify their own portfolios? It is far easier and cheaper for individual investors to diversify than it is for firms to combine operations.

THE BOOTSTRAP GAME

During the 1960s some conglomerate companies made acquisitions that offered no evident economic gains. Nevertheless, the conglomerates' aggressive strategy produced several years of rising earnings per share. To see how this can happen, let us look at the acquisition of Muck and Slurry by the well-known conglomerate World Enterprises.

EXAMPLE 23.7 | **THE BOOTSTRAP GAME**

The position before the merger is set out in the first two columns of Table 23.2. Notice that because Muck and Slurry has relatively poor growth prospects, its stock sells at a lower price-earnings ratio than World Enterprises (line 3). The merger, we assume, produces no economic benefits, so the firms should be worth exactly the same together as apart. The value of World Enterprises after the merger is therefore equal to the sum of the separate values of the two firms (line 6).

Since World Enterprises stock is selling for double the price of Muck and Slurry stock (line 2), World Enterprises can acquire the 100,000 Muck and Slurry shares for 50,000 of its own shares. Thus World will have 150,000 shares outstanding after the merger.

World's total earnings double as a result of the acquisition (line 5), but the number of shares increases by only 50 percent. Its earnings *per share* rise from $2 to $2.67. We call this a *bootstrap effect* because there is no real gain created by the merger and no increase in the two firms'

TABLE 23.2
Impact of merger on market value and earnings per share of World Enterprises

	World Enterprises (before merger)	Muck and Slurry	World Enterprises (after acquiring Muck and Slurry)
1. Earnings per share	$2	$2	$2.67
2. Price per share	$40	$20	$40
3. Price-earnings ratio	20	10	15
4. Number of shares	100,000	100,000	150,000
5. Total earnings	$200,000	$200,000	$400,000
6. Total market value	$4,000,000	$2,000,000	$6,000,000
7. Current earnings per dollar invested in stock (line 1 divided by line 2)	$.05	$.10	$.067

Note: When World Enterprises purchases Muck and Slurry, there are no gains. Therefore, total earnings and total market value should be unaffected by the merger. But earnings per share increase. World Enterprises issues only 50,000 of its shares (priced at $40) to acquire the 100,000 Muck and Slurry shares (priced at $20).

combined value. Since World's stock price is unchanged by the acquisition of Muck and Slurry, the price-earnings ratio falls (line 3).

Before the merger, $1 invested in World Enterprises bought 5 cents of current earnings and rapid growth prospects. On the other hand, $1 invested in Muck and Slurry bought 10 cents of current earnings but slower growth prospects. If the *total* market value is not altered by the merger, then $1 invested in the merged firm gives World shareholders 6.7 cents of immediate earnings but slower growth than before the merger. Muck and Slurry shareholders get lower immediate earnings but faster growth. Neither side gains or loses *provided* that everybody understands the deal.

Financial manipulators sometimes try to ensure that the market does not understand the deal. Suppose that investors are fooled by the exuberance of the president of World Enterprises and mistake the 33 percent postmerger increase in earnings per share for *sustainable* growth. If they do, the price of World Enterprises stock rises and the shareholders of both companies receive something for nothing.

You should now see how to play the bootstrap game. Suppose that you manage a company enjoying a high price-earnings ratio. The reason it is high is that investors anticipate rapid growth in future earnings. You achieve this growth not by capital investment, product improvement, or increased operating efficiency, but by purchasing slow-growing firms with low price-earnings ratios. The long-run result will be slower growth and a depressed price-earnings ratio, but in the short run earnings per share can increase dramatically. If this fools investors, you may be able to achieve the higher earnings per share without suffering a decline in your price-earnings ratio. But in order to keep fooling investors, you must continue to expand by merger at the same compound rate. Obviously you cannot do this forever; one day expansion must slow down or stop. Then earnings growth will cease, and your house of cards will fall.

> Buying a firm with a lower P/E ratio can increase earnings per share. But the increase should not result in a higher share price. The short-term increase in earnings should be offset by lower future earnings growth.

Check Point 23.2   Suppose that Muck and Slurry has even worse growth prospects than in our example and its share price is only $10. Recalculate the effects of the merger in this case. You should find that earnings per share increase by a greater amount, since World Enterprises can now buy the same current earnings for fewer shares.

EVALUATING MERGERS

If you are given the responsibility for evaluating a proposed merger, you must think hard about the following two questions:

1. Is there an overall economic gain to the merger? In other words, is the merger value enhancing? Are the two firms worth more together than apart?
2. Do the terms of the merger make my company and its shareholders better off? There is no point in merging if the cost is too high and all the economic gain goes to the other company.

Answering these deceptively simple questions is rarely easy. Some economic gains can be nearly impossible to quantify, and complex merger financing can obscure the true terms of the deal. But the basic principles for evaluating mergers are not too difficult.

MERGERS FINANCED BY CASH

We will concentrate on a simple numerical example. Your company, Cislunar Foods, is considering acquisition of a smaller food company, Targetco. Cislunar is proposing to finance the deal by purchasing all of Targetco's outstanding stock for $19 per share. Some financial information on the two companies is given in the left and centre columns of Table 23.3.

Question 1. Why would Cislunar and Targetco be worth more together than apart? Suppose that operating costs can be reduced by combining the companies' marketing, distribution, and administration. Revenues can also be increased in Targetco's region. The right column of Table 23.3 contains projected revenues, costs, and earnings for the two firms operating together: annual operating costs postmerger will be $2 million less than the sum of the separate companies' costs, and revenues will be $2 million more. Therefore, projected earnings increase by $4 million.[6] We will assume that the increased earnings are the only synergy to be generated by the merger.

The economic gain to the merger is the present value of the extra earnings. If the earnings increase is permanent (a level perpetuity), and the cost of capital is 20 percent,

$$\text{Economic gain} = \text{PV (increased earnings)} = \frac{4}{.20} = \$20 \text{ million}$$

This additional value is the basic motivation for the merger.

Question 2. What are the terms of the merger? What is the cost to Cislunar and its shareholders?

Targetco's management and shareholders will not consent to the merger unless they receive at least the stand-alone value of their shares. They can be paid in cash or by new shares issued by

TABLE 23.3
Cislunar Foods is considering an acquisition of Targetco. The merger would increase the companies' combined earnings by $4 million.

	Cislunar Foods	Targetco	Combined Companies	
Revenues	$ 150	$ 20	$ 172	(+2)
Operating costs	118	16	132	(−2)
Earnings	$ 32	$ 4	$ 40	(+4)
Cash	$ 55	$ 2.5		
Other assets' book value	185	17		
Total assets	$ 240	$ 19.5		
Price per share	$ 48	$ 16		
Number of shares	10	2.5		
Market value	$ 480	$ 40		

Note: Figures in millions except price per share.

---

[6] To keep things simple, the example ignores taxes and assumes that both companies are all-equity financed. We also ignore the interest income that could have been earned by investing the cash used to finance the merger.

Cislunar. In this case we are considering a cash offer of $19 per Targetco share, $3 per share over the prior share price. Targetco has 2.5 million shares outstanding, so Cislunar will have to pay out $47.5 million, a premium of $7.5 million over Targetco's prior market value. On these terms, Targetco shareholders will capture $7.5 million out of the $20 million gain from the merger. That ought to leave $12.5 million for Cislunar.

This is confirmed in the Cash Purchase column of Table 23.4. Start at the *bottom* of the column, where the total market value of the merged firms is $492.5 million. This is derived as follows:

Cislunar market value prior to merger	$480 million
Targetco market value	40
Present value of gain to merger	20
Less cash paid out to Targetco shareholders	−47.5
Postmerger market value	$492.5 million

The postmerger share price for Cislunar will be $49.25, an increase of $1.25 per share. There are 10 million shares now outstanding, so the total increase in the value of Cislunar shares is $12.5 million.

Now let's summarize. The merger makes sense for Cislunar for two reasons. First, the merger adds $20 million of overall value. Second, the terms of the merger give only $7.5 million of the $20 million overall gain to Targetco's shareholders, leaving $12.5 million for Cislunar. You could say that the *cost* of acquiring Targetco is $7.5 million, the difference between the cash payment and the value of Targetco as a separate company.

$$\text{Cost} = \text{cash paid out} - \text{Targetco value} = \$47.5 - 40 = \$7.5 \text{ million}$$

Of course, the Targetco shareholders are ahead by $7.5 million. *Their gain is your cost.* As we've already seen, Cislunar shareholders come out $12.5 million ahead. This is the merger's NPV for Cislunar:

$$\text{NPV} = \text{economic gain} - \text{cost} = \$20 - 7.5 = \$12.5 \text{ million}$$

Writing down the economic gain and cost of a merger in this way separates the motive for the merger (the economic gain, or value added) from the terms of the merger (the *division* of the gain between the two merging companies).

Check Point 23.3

Killer Shark Inc. makes a surprise cash offer of $22 a share for Goldfish Industries. Before the offer, Goldfish was selling for $18 a share. Goldfish has 1 million shares outstanding. What must Killer Shark believe about the present value of the improvement it can bring to Goldfish's operations?

MERGERS FINANCED BY STOCK

What if Cislunar wants to conserve its cash for other investments, and therefore decides to pay for the Targetco acquisition with new Cislunar shares? The deal calls for Targetco shareholders to receive one Cislunar share in exchange for every three Targetco shares.

TABLE 23.4

Financial forecasts after the Cislunar–Targetco merger: The left column assumes a cash purchase at $19 per Targetco share. The right column assumes Targetco shareholders receive one new Cislunar share for every three Targetco shares.

	Cash Purchase	Exchange of Shares
Earnings	$ 40	$ 40
Cash	$ 10	$ 57.5
Other assets' book value	202	202
Total assets	$212	$259.5
Price per share	$ 49.25	$ 49.85
Number of shares	10	10.833
Market value	$492.5	$540

Note: Figures in millions except price per share.

It's the same merger, but the financing is different. The right column of Table 23.4 works out the consequences. Again, start at the *bottom* of the column. Note that the market value of Cislunar's shares after the merger is $540 million, $47.5 million higher than in the cash deal, because that cash is kept rather than paid out to Targetco shareholders. On the other hand, there are more shares outstanding, since 833,333 new shares have to be issued in exchange for the 2.5 million Targetco shares (a 1 to 3 ratio). Therefore, the price per share is 540/10.833 = $49.85, which is 60 cents higher than in the cash offer.

Why do Cislunar shareholders do better from the share exchange? The economic gain from the merger is the same, but the Targetco shareholders capture less of it. They get 833,333 shares at $49.85, or $41.5 million, a premium of only $1.5 million over Targetco's prior market value.

$$\text{Cost} = \text{value of shares issued} - \text{Targetco value}$$
$$= \$41.5 - 40 = \$1.5 \text{ million}$$

The merger's NPV to Cislunar's original shareholders is

$$\text{NPV} = \text{economic gain} - \text{cost} = \$20 - 1.5 = \$18.5 \text{ million}$$

Note that Cislunar stock rises by $1.85 from its pre-merger share price of $48. The total increase in value for Cislunar's original shareholders, who retain 10 million shares, is $18.5 million.

Evaluating the terms of a merger can be tricky when there is an exchange of shares. The target company's shareholders will retain a stake in the merged firms, so you have to figure out what the firm's shares will be worth after the merger is announced and its benefits appreciated by investors. Notice that we started with the total market value of Cislunar and Targetco postmerger, took account of the merger terms (833,333 new shares issued), and worked back to the postmerger share price. Only then could we work out the division of the merger gains between the two companies.

There is a key distinction between cash and stock for financing mergers. If cash is offered, the cost of the merger is not affected by the size of the merger gains. If stock is offered, the cost depends on the gains because the gains show up in the postmerger share price, and these shares are used to pay for the acquired firm. The nearby Finance in Action box illustrates how complex a stock offer can be. When Gillette offered to buy Duracell, giving Duracell shareholders about a 20 percent stake in the merged firm, the attractiveness of the deal depended on the stock market's valuation of *both* firms.

SEE BOX P. 716

Stock financing also mitigates the effects of over- or undervaluation of either firm. Suppose, for example, that A overestimates B's value as a separate entity, perhaps because it has overlooked some hidden liability. Thus A makes too generous an offer. Other things being equal, A's shareholders are better off if it is a stock rather than a cash offer. With a stock offer, the inevitable bad news about B's value will fall partly on B's former shareholders.

Check Point 23.4

Suppose Targetco shareholders demand one Cislunar share for every 2.5 Targetco shares. Otherwise they will not accept the merger. Under these revised terms, is the merger still a good deal for Cislunar?

A WARNING

The cost of a merger is the premium the acquirer pays for the target firm over its value as a separate company. If the target is a public company, you can measure its separate value by multiplying its stock price by the number of outstanding shares. Watch out, though: if investors expect the target to be acquired, its stock price may overstate the company's separate value. The target company's stock price may already have risen in anticipation of a premium to be paid by an acquiring firm.

ANOTHER WARNING

Some companies begin their merger analyses with a forecast of the target firm's future cash flows. Any revenue increases or cost reductions attributable to the merger are included in

Blades, Batteries, and a Fifth of Gillette

Back in 1988, when Kraft Inc. decided to unload its battery subsidiary, Gillette Co. was tempted. But the bidding went up and up and out of Gillette's reach. Kohlberg Kravis Roberts & Co. eventually bought the battery maker—it was Duracell, of course—for a seemingly extravagant $1.8 billion.

After 8 years of due diligence, Gillette has finally agreed to fork over stock valued at more than $7 billion for the very same Duracell International Inc. Just as KKR now looks shrewd, rear-view analysts may snicker at Gillette for buying dear what it could have had then for, let us assume, only $2 billion in stock.

In fact, Gillette shareholders should thank their lucky stars the earlier deal didn't happen. In share-for-share acquisitions, what you are getting is only half the picture; what you are giving up is just as important. The standard analysis values such deals according to the dollar value of the target, but that approach is flawed. The key question isn't whether Duracell is worth $7 billion, because Gillette isn't giving up $7 billion. It is giving up a part—in this case 20%—of itself.

Schematically, Gillette is trading razor blades for batteries (not bucks for batteries), and the results can be very different. Since 1988, for instance, the blade business, at least under Gillette's management, has performed much better than batteries. While Duracell's stock has quadrupled, Gillette's has multiplied eight times. Thus if Gillette had in fact made that "cheap" $2 billion acquisition, it would have acquired a jack rabbit but given up a prize thoroughbred. The passed-over purchase back then would have cost Gillette *more than one-third* of its stock; today, it is buying the same business for only a fifth of its stock.

Clearly, taking a pass was the right move. Duracell was cheap in 1988, but Gillette was cheaper. And shopping with inexpensive currency, meaning issuing undervalued stock, amounts to selling the company (or a piece of it) on the cheap.

Going forward, the same analysis holds. The imputed dollar value of the deal will forever drift with Gillette's share price; the one constant is that each shareholder is trading away one-fifth of his

Gillette's Stock

interest in the old Gillette. Whether Duracell will be worth it, a subject no analyst has addressed, is what matters.

Such deals are manna for investment bankers (and bound to wind up in B-school texts) because you need to size up two businesses instead of one.

On balance, the blade business is more distinct, and better, than batteries. But how much better? Duracell for one-fifth of Gillette works out to this: For each dollar of Gillette earnings that shareholders are giving up, they are getting roughly $1.30 in cash earnings from batteries.

Blades should trade at a premium, but this one is steep. That premium, of course, reflects the current very high price of Gillette's stock, which in turn reflects a view that Gillette will forever keep profit growing twice as fast as its sales. Gillette's managers wouldn't come out and say that 34 times earnings reflects unwarranted optimism, or even a bull-market joie de vivre, but if that is what they thought, trading part of their company at that price for a cheaper one would be a smart move. And that is what they are doing.

Source: Republished with permission of Dow Jones, from "Blades, Batteries, and a Fifth of Gillette," from R. Lowenstein, "Intrinsic Value," *The Wall Street Journal*, September 19, 1996, p. C1; permission conveyed through Copyright Clearance Center.

the forecasts, which are then discounted back to the present and compared with the purchase price:

$$\text{Estimated net gain} = \begin{array}{l} \text{DCF valuation of target including merger benefits} \\ \text{– cash required for acquisition} \end{array}$$

This is a dangerous procedure. Even the brightest and best-trained analyst can make large errors in valuing a business. The estimated net gain may come up positive not because the merger makes sense but simply because the analyst's cash flow forecasts are too optimistic. On the other hand, a good merger may not be pursued if the analyst fails to recognize the target's potential as a stand-alone business.

A better procedure *starts* with the target's current and stand-alone market value and concentrates instead on the *changes* in cash flow that would result from the merger. Always ask why the two firms should be worth more together than apart. Remember, you add value only if you can generate *additional economic benefits*—some competitive edge that other firms can't match and that the target firm's managers can't achieve on their own.

It makes sense to keep an eye on the value that investors place on the gains from merging. If A's stock price falls when the deal is announced, investors are sending a message that the merger benefits are doubtful *or* that A is paying too much for these benefits.

23.5   MERGER MECHANICS

Buying a company is much more complicated than buying a piece of machinery. In addition to properly evaluating the target, managers consider the accounting and tax implications of the possible structures of the transaction. In practice, these issues are often extremely complex, and specialists must be consulted.

MERGER ACCOUNTING

As we saw in Section 23.4, the decision to make an acquisition should be based on the net present value of its cash flows. If the NPV is positive, then shareholders' wealth is increased. In spite of this, managers worry about the deal's accounting implications, especially its impact on the acquirer's earnings per share. Until recently, acquisitions were accounted for using either the purchase method or pooling of interests. Managers preferred to use pooling of interest because of its lesser impact on earnings. Deals would be structured to allow pooling, even though the chosen accounting method had no impact on the acquisition's cash flows. However, in 2001 the U.S. and Canadian accounting standard boards together eliminated pooling of interest accounting, making purchase accounting the required method in both countries.

To illustrate the purchase method, Table 23.5 shows what happens when ACorp buys BCorp for $12 million and forms ABCorp. The two firms' initial balance sheets are at the top of the table and the balance sheet of the merged company, ABCorp, is shown below. We assume that ACorp issues $12 million worth of bonds to fund the acquisition.

ACorp is paying a $3 million premium over BCorp's $9 million book value. Why? There are two possible reasons. First, the market value of BCorp's *tangible* assets on its balance sheet—its working capital, plant, and equipment—may be greater than $9 million. Second, ACorp may be paying for *intangible* assets that are not listed on BCorp's balance sheet. For example, intangible assets could be a promising new technology or product. Or it may be BCorp's share of the expected economic gains from the merger.

With purchase accounting, ACorp first determines the fair value of BCorp's tangible assets and records them on the merged balance sheet. Then, any difference between the purchase price of BCorp's assets and their assessed fair value is put on the merged balance sheet as goodwill. For example, suppose an appraiser determines that BCorp's fixed assets have a fair value of $8 million, rather than their book value of $7 million, and the fair value of the working capital is $2 million. Thus the total tangible asset value of BCorp is $10 million. The remaining $2 million, the difference between the $12 million paid for the assets and the $10 million tangible asset fair value, is recorded as goodwill on ABCorp's balance sheet.[7] The ABCorp balance shows the combined companies' net

TABLE 23.5
Accounting for ACorp's acquisition of BCorp, using the purchase method.

ACorp				BCorp			
Net working capital	4	Debt	5	Net working capital	2	Debt	0
Fixed assets	11	Equity	10	Fixed assets	7	Equity	9
	15		15		9		9

ABCorp			
Net working capital	6	Debt	17
Fixed assets	19	Equity	10
Goodwill	2		27
	27		

---

[7] If part of the $2 million consisted of payment for identifiable intangible assets such as patents, the accountant would place them in their own category. Identifiable intangible assets that have a finite life need to be written off over their life.

working capital of $6 million ($4 million + $2 million), their fixed assets of $19 million ($11 million + $8 million) and goodwill of $2 million, adding up to $27 million.

As long as the goodwill continues to be worth at least $2 million, it stays on the balance sheet and the company's earnings are unaffected. However, each year the company must estimate the fair value of its goodwill. If it falls below $2 million, the amount shown on the balance sheet is lowered and the difference deducted from that year's earnings. The write-off of goodwill has made a nasty dent in some companies' profits. For example, in 2002 Nortel made billions of dollars of writedowns to reflect the lower value of assets it purchased in acquisitions near the peak of the bull market.

Some Tax Issues

An acquisition may be either taxable or tax-free. If the form of payment is cash, the acquisition is regarded as taxable. Why? The selling shareholders are treated as having *sold* their shares, and they must pay tax on any capital gains. On the other hand, if the payment is largely in the form of shares, the acquisition is tax-free. In this case, the shareholders are viewed as having *exchanged* their old shares for new ones; no capital gains or losses are realized. The rules determining the tax-free status of amalgamations, stocks, and assets are complex but the basic message is the same: the selling shareholders must continue to be shareholders or capital gains will be assessed from the share sale.

The tax status of the acquisition also affects the taxation of the company afterward. In a taxable acquisition, the assets of the target are revalued for tax purposes, allowing the acquirer to take more CCA deductions and reduce taxable income. This is called *stepping up the asset pool*. In a tax-free acquisition, the assets are not revalued and no incremental tax savings are generated.

As you can see, the selling shareholders would prefer a tax-free acquisition, while the buyer pays less tax in the future if the acquisition is taxable. If possible, the merger deal will be struck to reduce the total tax consequences of the transaction.

23.6   MERGER TACTICS

In recent years, most mergers have been agreed upon by both parties, but occasionally, an acquirer goes over the heads of the target firm's management and makes a tender offer directly to its shareholders. The management of the target firm may advise shareholders to accept the tender, or it may attempt to fight the bid in the hope that the acquirer will either raise its offer or throw in the towel.

The rules of merger warfare are largely set by the *Ontario Securities Act* and are administered by the Ontario Securities Commission (OSC). Ontario dominates in this area because the Toronto Stock Exchange is located in Ontario. However, the various provincial securities acts tend to be similar, and the provincial securities commissions try to work together. The courts act as referee to see that contests are conducted fairly. We will look at one recent contest that illustrates the tactics and weapons employed.

EXAMPLE 23.8   **A HOSTILE TAKEOVER BID: TRILOGY/INDIGO GOES AFTER CHAPTERS**

In late November 2000, Trilogy Retail Enterprises, a private company owned by Gerald Schwartz, CEO of Onex Corp., and his wife, Heather Reisman, CEO of Indigo Books, offered $63.5 million ($13 cash per share) for 50.1 percent of Chapters, Canada's largest Canadian book retailer at the time. Schwartz and Reisman, majority shareholders of Indigo, the second largest Canadian book retailer, suggested that they would combine Chapters and Indigo and reduce the number of stores. Chapters and Indigo had been engaged in a tough battle for supremacy in the bookselling business and both had expanded aggressively and each was losing money.

The market reacted favourably, increasing Chapters' price to $11.10 from the previous day's price of $9.10. However, the offer was far below Chapters' peak of $35 in mid-1999.

Quickly, Chapters' board of directors advised shareholders to reject the bid. Chapters CEO Larry Stevenson called the offer "completely inadequate."

"Shareholders are much better served by us continuing to run this company the way it should be and doing the things we can to maximize shareholder value," he said in an interview. "Shareholders should hold on to their shares."[8]

In a move viewed by many as defensive, Chapters also announced a $25.5 million plan to buy back the 31 percent of Chapters Online shares it did not own for $3.40 per share. Funds for the buy-back would be raised through additional borrowing by Chapters, which would make the company less attractive to a buyer. Those Chapters Online shares had been sold in an initial public offering in September 1999 at $13.50 per share.

Trilogy continued to purchase Chapters shares on the open market, increasing its stake from 9 percent to 14 percent. In early January, Trilogy raised its bid to $15 per share, for a 50.1 percent stake in Chapters.

Chapters' management felt the bid was too low and disliked the fact that it was a partial bid—offering to purchase only 50.1 percent of the shares. They were concerned that accepting Trilogy's partial bid left shareholders in the dark about the potential value of the shares not taken up in the tender offer.

Chapters' management worked hard to thwart the takeover. On several occasions they asked the OSC to order Reisman to allow Chapters to look at Indigo's financial statements. They wanted to estimate the postmerger price of the remaining Chapters shares. The OSC determined that it was not necessary for Indigo to reveal its financial situation to Chapters.

Trilogy, on the other hand, appealed to the OSC to kill Chapters' **shareholders' rights plan**. The rights plan, or **poison pill**, had been put in place in April 2001 stipulating that anyone who acquired 20 percent or more of the company without meeting the requirements of the Chapters board would find their shareholding diluted through a rights issue. All shareholders other than the raider would be given rights to purchase additional Chapters shares at a low price.

The daily reporting of the very hostile, very public battle for Chapters filled the business press for several months as both sides argued why they were right and the other side was wrong.

On January 18, 2001, Future Shop unexpectedly entered as a **white knight**. Supported by Chapters' board and management, Future Shop bid $200 million for all of Chapters' common shares. The bid was $16 cash or two Future Shop shares for each Chapters share. Had Trilogy been trumped? Would they come back with a higher bid? The business press speculated that Schwartz and Reisman had been beaten.

However, on January 20, 2001, Trilogy raised its bid to $121.5 million, $17 a share for all Chapters shares except the 30 percent locked up in the Future Shop deal. It was revealed that Schwartz and Reisman would be providing half of the money to pay for the purchase, with the other half from bank financing. A condition of the revised bid was the removal of Chapters' poison pill. At an unusual Sunday hearing on January 21, 2001, the OSC ruled that Chapters' shareholders' rights plan had served its purpose and it was in the public interest to end it. Schwartz and Reisman had won this round.

At the same time, Schwartz and Reisman met with the federal Competition Bureau to negotiate a plan to deal with the Bureau's concern about the lessening of competition if the two top book retailers were allowed to merge.

With two bids on the table for Chapters, its board of directors formed a special committee of independent (non-management) directors to examine the bids and inform shareholders which bid was better.

In the end, Chapters' board recommended the Trilogy bid to its shareholders, and Schwartz and Reisman's bid for Chapters was successful. The Competition Bureau gave its approval, conditional on the sale of 13 superstores and 10 mall stores of Chapters and Indigo.

shareholders' rights plan or poison pill   Measures taken by the target firm to avoid acquisition; for example, the right of existing shareholders to buy additional shares at an attractive price if a bidder acquires a significant holding.

white knight   Friendly potential acquirer sought by a target company that is threatened by an unwelcome bidder.

[8] G. Livingston, "Indigo CEO Reisman and Husband Gerry Schwartz Bid for Bookseller Chapters," *Canadian Press Newswire*, November 28, 2000.

The Chapters–Indigo battle illustrates many of the features of Canadian merger warfare. Firms frequently attempt to deter potential bidders by adopting poison pills, which make the company unappealing. In a typical poison pill, or shareholders' rights plan, existing shareholders are given the right to buy additional shares at a low price as soon as the bidder acquires more than 20 percent of the shares. The bidder is not entitled to the discount and finds itself unable to acquire the needed shares.

In Canada, shareholders' rights plans have never been activated, and are typically killed by the OSC at the request of the bidder. Their main value is to extend the bid, giving other bidders time to make an offer.

In addition, bidders and targets ask the securities commissions and the courts to make rulings to prevent or require their opponent to take some action, hoping to help their cause.

The search for a white knight is also typical of many hostile bids. White knights play an important role in raising the bid. Sometimes they successfully acquire the target, sometimes they lose the battle.

Another merger tactic, rare in Canada but used frequently in the United States, is known as **shark repellent**. Managers who are worried about the possibility of a hostile bid will ask shareholders to agree to changes in the corporate charter that make it more difficult for a successful bidder to get control of the board of directors. For example, the charter may be amended to stagger the election of board members, making only one-third of the board up for re-election each year. This means that the bidder cannot obtain majority control of the board immediately after acquiring a majority of the shares. Another example is to require a supermajority of 80 percent of the shares to approve the merger rather than the normal 50 percent. In Canada, most mergers require a two-thirds majority by law.

shark repellent Amendments to a company charter made to forestall takeover attempts.

23.7   LEVERAGED BUYOUTS

Leveraged buyouts, or *LBOs,* differ from ordinary acquisitions in two ways. First, a large fraction of the purchase price is debt financed. Some, perhaps all, of this debt is junk, that is, below investment grade. Second, the shares of the LBO no longer trade on the open market. The remaining equity in the LBO is privately held by a small group of (usually institutional) investors. When this group is led by the company's management, the acquisition is called a *management buyout (MBO).* Many LBOs are in fact MBOs.

In the 1970s and 1980s many management buyouts were arranged for unwanted divisions of large, diversified companies. Smaller divisions outside the companies' main lines of business often lacked top management's interest and commitment, and divisional management chafed under corporate bureaucracy. Many such divisions flowered when spun off as MBOs. Their managers, pushed by the need to generate cash for debt service and encouraged by a substantial personal stake in the business, found ways to cut costs and compete more effectively.

During the 1980s MBO/LBO activity expanded to include buyouts of entire businesses, including large, mature public corporations. The largest, most dramatic, and best-documented LBO of them all was the $25 billion takeover of RJR Nabisco[9] in 1988 by Kohlberg Kravis Roberts (KKR). The players, tactics, and controversies of LBOs are writ large in this case.

Since the 1990s the use of leveraged buyouts to acquire entire companies has become infrequent, although LBOs continue to be used to facilitate the sale of unwanted divisions. For example, in 2000, CIBC World Markets, the investment banking division of the Canadian Imperial Bank of Commerce, along with Deutsche Bank arranged $425 million (US) in loans to help fund a leveraged buyout of Monsanto Co.'s artificial sweetener business by an investment group. The loans were provided by institutional investors and provided almost 75 percent of the $570 million (US) of cash needed to purchase the sweetener business.

---

[9] The story of the RJR Nabisco buyout is reconstructed by B. Burrough and J. Helyar in *Barbarians at the Gate: The Fall of RJR Nabisco* (New York: Harper & Row, 1990) and is the subject of a movie with the same title.

EXAMPLE 23.9	**RJR NABISCO**

On October 28, 1988, the board of directors of RJR Nabisco revealed that Ross Johnson, the company's chief executive officer, had formed a group of investors prepared to buy all the firm's stock for $75 per share in cash and take the company private. Johnson's group was backed up and advised by Shearson Lehman Hutton, the investment bank subsidiary of American Express.

RJR's share price immediately moved to about $75, handing shareholders a 36 percent gain over the previous day's price of $56. At the same time RJR's bonds fell, since it was clear that RJR would be adding a lot more debt.

Johnson's offer lifted RJR onto the auction block. Once the company was in play, its board of directors was obliged to consider other offers. Four days later, a group of investors led by LBO specialists Kohlberg Kravis Roberts (KKR) bid $90 per share, $79 in cash plus preferred stock valued at $11.

The bidding finally closed on November 30, some 32 days after the initial offer was revealed. In the end it was Johnson's group against KKR. KKR offered $109 per share, after adding $1 per share (roughly $230 million) at the last hour. The KKR bid was $81 in cash, convertible subordinated debentures valued at about $10, and preferred shares valued at about $18. Johnson's group bid $112 in cash and securities.

But the RJR board chose KKR. True, Johnson's group had offered $3 per share more, but its security valuations were viewed as "softer" and perhaps overstated. Also, KKR's planned asset sales were less drastic; perhaps their plans for managing the business inspired more confidence. Finally, the Johnson group's proposal contained a management compensation package that seemed extremely generous and had generated an avalanche of bad press.

But where did the merger benefits come from? What could justify offering $109 per share, about $25 billion in all, for a company that only 33 days previously had been selling for $56 per share?

KKR and other bidders were betting on two things. First, they expected to generate billions of additional dollars from interest tax shields, reduced capital expenditures, and sales of assets not strictly necessary to RJR's core businesses. Asset sales alone were projected to generate $5 billion. Second, they expected to make those core businesses significantly more profitable, mainly by cutting back on expenses and bureaucracy. Apparently there was plenty to cut, including the RJR "Air Force," which at one point operated 10 corporate jets.

In the year after KKR took over, new management was installed. This group sold assets and cut back operating expenses and capital spending. There were also layoffs. As expected, high interest charges meant a net loss of $976 million for 1989, but pretax operating income actually increased, despite extensive asset sales, including the sale of RJR's European food operations.

While management was cutting costs and selling assets, prices in the junk bond market were rapidly declining, implying much higher future interest charges for RJR and stricter terms on any refinancing. In mid-1990 KKR made an additional equity investment, and later that year the company announced an offer of cash and new shares in exchange for $753 million of junk bonds. By 1993 the burden of debt had been reduced from $26 billion to $14 billion. For RJR, the world's largest LBO, it seemed that high debt was a temporary, not permanent, virtue.

BARBARIANS AT THE GATE?

The buyout of RJR crystallized views on LBOs, the junk bond market, and the takeover business. For many it exemplified all that was wrong with finance in the 1980s, especially the willingness of "raiders" to carve up established companies, leaving them with enormous debt burdens, basically in order to get rich quick.

There was plenty of confusion, stupidity, and greed in the LBO business. On the other hand, LBOs generated enormous increases in market value, and most of the gains went to selling shareholders, not raiders. For example, the biggest winners in the RJR Nabisco LBO were the company's shareholders.

We should therefore consider briefly where these gains may have come from before we try to pass judgment on LBOs. There are several possibilities.

The Junk Bond Markets

LBOs and debt-financed takeovers may have been driven by artificially cheap funding from the junk bond markets. With hindsight it seems that investors in junk bonds underestimated the risks of default. Default rates climbed painfully between 1989 and 1991. At the same time, the junk bond market became much less liquid after the demise of Drexel Burnham Lambert, the chief market maker. Yields rose dramatically, and new issues dried up. Suddenly junk-financed LBOs seemed to disappear from the scene.[10]

Leverage and Taxes

As we explained in Chapter 15, borrowing money saves taxes. But taxes were not the main driving force behind LBOs. The value of interest tax shields was just not big enough to explain the observed gains in market value.

Of course, if interest tax shields were the main motive for LBOs' high debt, then LBO managers would not be so concerned to pay off debt. We saw that this was one of the first tasks facing RJR Nabisco's new management.

Other Stakeholders

It is possible that the gain to the selling shareholders is just someone else's loss and that no value is generated overall. Therefore, we should look at the total gain to all investors in an LBO, not just the selling shareholders.

Bondholders are the obvious losers. The debt they thought was well secured may turn into junk when the borrower goes through an LBO. We noted how market prices of RJR Nabisco debt fell sharply when Ross Johnson's first LBO offer was announced. But again, the value losses suffered by bondholders in LBOs are not nearly large enough to explain shareholder gains.

Leverage and Incentives

Managers and employees of LBOs work harder and often smarter. They have to generate cash to service the extra debt. Moreover, managers' personal fortunes are riding on the LBO's success. They become owners rather than organization men or women.

It is hard to measure the payoff from better incentives, but there is some evidence of improved operating efficiency in LBOs. Kaplan, who studied 48 management buyouts between 1980 and 1986, found average increases in operating income of 24 percent over the following 3 years. Ratios of operating income and net cash flow to assets and sales increased dramatically. He observed cutbacks in capital expenditures but not in employment. Kaplan suggests that these operating changes "are due to improved incentives rather than layoffs or managerial exploitation of shareholders through inside information."[11]

Free Cash Flow

The free-cash-flow theory of takeovers states that mature firms with a surplus of cash will tend to waste it. This contrasts with standard finance theory, which says that firms with more cash than positive-NPV investment opportunities should give the cash back to investors through higher dividends or share repurchases. But we see firms like RJR Nabisco spending on corporate luxuries and questionable capital investments. One benefit of LBOs is to put such companies on a diet and force them to pay out cash to service debt.

The free-cash-flow theory predicts that mature, "cash cow" companies will be the most likely targets of LBOs. We can find many examples that fit the theory, including RJR Nabisco. The

---

[10] There was a sharp revival of junk bond sales in 1992 and 1993, and 1996 was a banner year. But many of these issues simply replaced existing bonds. It remains to be seen whether junk bonds will make a lasting recovery.

[11] S. Kaplan, "The Effects of Management Buyouts on Operating Performance and Value," *Journal of Financial Economics* 24 (October 1989), pp. 217–254.

theory says that the gains in market value generated by LBOs are just the present values of the future cash flows that would otherwise have been frittered away.[12]

We do not endorse the free-cash-flow theory as the sole explanation for LBOs. We have mentioned several other plausible rationales, and we suspect that most LBOs are driven by a mixture of motives. Nor do we say that all LBOs are beneficial. On the contrary, there are many mistakes, and even soundly motivated LBOs can be dangerous, as the bankruptcies of Campeau, Revco, National Gypsum, and many other highly leveraged companies prove. However, we do take issue with those who portray LBOs simply as Bay Street or Wall Street barbarians breaking up the traditional strengths of corporate North America. In many cases LBOs have generated true gains.

The buyout of RJR Nabisco illustrates how during the merger boom of the 1980s even very large companies were not immune from attack by a rival management team. But by the end of the decade the merger environment had changed. Many of the obvious targets had disappeared and the battle for RJR Nabisco highlighted the increasing cost of victory. Institutions were reluctant to increase their holdings of junk bonds. Moreover, the market for these bonds had depended to a remarkable extent on one individual, Michael Milken, of the investment bank Drexel Burnham Lambert. By the late 1980s Milken and his employer were in trouble. Milken was indicted by a grand jury on 98 counts and was subsequently sentenced to jail. Drexel filed for bankruptcy, but by that time the junk bond market was moribund and the finance for highly leveraged buyouts had largely dried up.[13] Finally, in reaction to the perceived excesses of the merger boom, the state legislatures and the courts began to lean against hostile takeovers.

The decline in merger activity did not last long; by the mid-1990s stock markets and mergers were booming again and the end of the century saw a record volume of mergers. However, LBOs remained out of fashion, and relatively few mergers were intended simply to replace management. Instead, companies began to look once more at the possible benefits from combining two businesses.

23.8   THE BENEFITS AND COSTS OF MERGERS

Merger activity comes in waves and is concentrated in a relatively small number of industries. This urge to merge frequently seems to be prompted by deregulation and by changes in technology or the pattern of demand. Take the merger wave of the 1990s, for example. Deregulation of telecoms and financial services in the United States and Canada earlier in the decade led to a spate of mergers in both industries. In the entertainment industry the prospective advantages from controlling both content and distribution led to mergers between such giants as AOL and Time Warner. Canadian companies followed, including the merger of CTV and *The Globe and Mail* to create Bell Globemedia.

There are undoubtedly good acquisitions and bad acquisitions, but economists find it hard to agree on whether acquisitions are beneficial on balance. In general, shareholders of the target firm make a healthy gain. For example, one study found that following the announcement of the bid, the stock price of the target company jumped by 16 percent on average.[14] On the other hand, it appears that investors expected the acquiring companies to just about break even, for the price of their shares fell by .7 percent. The value of the total package—buyer plus seller—increased by 1.8 percent. Of course, these are averages; selling shareholders, for example, have sometimes obtained much higher returns. When IBM took over Lotus Corporation, it paid a premium of 100 percent, or about $1.7 billion, for Lotus stock.

---

[12] The free-cash-flow theory's chief proponent is Michael Jensen. See M. C. Jensen, "The Eclipse of the Public Corporation," *Harvard Business Review* 67 (September–October 1989), pp. 61–74, and "The Agency Costs of Free Cash Flow, Corporate Finance and Takeovers," *American Economic Review* 76 (May 1986), pp. 323–329.

[13] For a history of the role of Milken in the development of the junk bond market, see C. Bruck, *The Predator's Ball: The Junk Bond Raiders and the Man Who Staked Them* (New York: Simon and Schuster, 1988).

[14] See G. Andrade, M. Mitchell, and E. Stafford, "New Evidence and Perspectives on Mergers," *Journal of Economic Perspectives* 15 (Spring 2001), pp. 103–120.

Since buyers roughly break even and sellers make substantial gains, it seems that there are positive overall benefits from mergers. But not everybody is convinced. Some believe that investors analyzing mergers pay too much attention to short-term earnings gains and don't notice that these gains are at the expense of long-term prospects.

Since we can't observe how companies would have fared in the absence of a merger, it is difficult to measure the effects on profitability. However, several studies of merger activity suggest that mergers do seem to improve real productivity. For example, Healy, Palepu, and Ruback examined 50 large mergers between 1979 and 1983 and found an average increase in the companies' pretax returns of 2.4 percentage points.[15] They argue that this gain came from generating a higher level of sales from the same assets. There was no evidence that the companies were mortgaging their long-term futures by cutting back on long-term investments; expenditures on capital equipment and research and development tracked the industry average.

If you are concerned with public policy toward mergers, you do not want to look only at their impact on the shareholders of the companies concerned. For instance, we have already seen that in the case of RJR Nabisco some part of the shareholders' gain was at the expense of the bondholders and the U.S. government (through the enlarged interest tax shield). The acquirer's shareholders may also gain at the expense of the target firm's employees, who in some cases are laid off or are forced to take pay cuts after takeovers.

Perhaps the most important effect of acquisition is felt by the managers of companies that are not taken over. For example, one effect of LBOs was that the managers of even the largest corporations could not feel safe from challenge. Perhaps the threat of takeover spurs every employee to try harder. Unfortunately, we don't know whether on balance the threat of merger makes for more active days or sleepless nights.

The threat of takeover may be a spur to inefficient management, but it is also costly. It can soak up large amounts of management time and effort. When a company is planning a takeover, it can be difficult to give as much attention as one should to the firm's existing business. In addition, the companies need to pay for the services provided by the investment bankers, lawyers, and accountants. In 2000, merging companies paid in total more than $2 billion for professional assistance.

Even if the gains to the community exceed these costs, one wonders whether the same benefits could not be achieved more cheaply another way. For example, are leveraged buyouts necessary to make managers work harder? Perhaps the problem lies in the way that many corporations reward and penalize their managers. Perhaps many of the gains from takeover could be captured by linking management compensation more closely to performance.

---

[15] See P. Healy, K. Palepu, and R. Ruback, "Does Corporate Performance Improve after Mergers?" *Journal of Financial Economics* 31 (April 1992), pp. 135–175. The study examined the pretax returns of the merged companies relative to industry averages.

23.9   SUMMARY

1. In what ways do companies change the composition of their ownership or management?

If the board of directors fails to replace an inefficient management, there are four ways to effect a change: (1) shareholders may engage in a **proxy contest** to replace the board; (2) the firm may be acquired by another; (3) the firm may be purchased by a private group of investors in a leveraged buyout; or (4) it may sell off part of its operations to another company.

There are three ways for one firm to acquire another: (1) it can **merge** all the assets and liabilities of the target firm into those of its own company through a **statutory amalgamation**; (2) it can buy the stock of the target; or (3) it can buy the individual assets of the target. The offer to buy the stock of the target firm is called a **tender offer**. The purchase of the stock or assets of another firm is called an **acquisition**.

2. Why may it make sense for companies to merge?

A merger may be undertaken in order to replace an inefficient management. But sometimes two business may be
more valuable together than apart. Gains may stem from
increased revenues, economies of scale, economies of vertical integration, the combination of complementary
resources, reduced taxes, or redeployment of surplus
funds. We don't know how frequently these benefits occur,
but they do make economic sense. Sometimes mergers are
undertaken to diversify risks or artificially increase
growth of earnings per share. These motives are dubious.

**3. How should the gains and costs of mergers to the
acquiring firm be measured?**

A merger generates an economic gain if the two firms are
worth more together than apart. The *gain* is the difference
between the value of the merged firm and the value of the
two firms run independently. The *cost* is the premium that
the buyer pays for the selling firm over its value as a separate entity. When payment is in the form of shares, the
value of this payment naturally depends on what those
shares are worth after the merger is complete. You should
go ahead with the merger if the gain exceeds the cost.

4. What are some takeover defences?

Mergers are often amicably negotiated between the management and directors of the two companies, but if the seller is reluctant, the would-be buyer can decide to make a
tender offer for the stock. We sketched some of the offen-
sive and defensive tactics used in takeover battles. These
defenses include **shark repellents** (changes in the company
charter meant to make a takeover more difficult to achieve),
shareholders' rights plans or **poison pills** (measures that

make takeover of the firm more costly), and the search for
white knights (the attempt to find a friendly acquirer before
the unfriendly one takes over the firm).

**5. What are some of the motivations for leveraged and
management buyouts of the firm?**

In a **leveraged buyout** (LBO) or **management buyout**
(MBO), all public shares are repurchased and the company
"goes private." LBOs tend to involve mature businesses
with ample cash flow and modest growth opportunities.
LBOs and other debt-financed takeovers are driven by a
mixture of motives, including (1) the value of interest tax
shields; (2) transfers of value from bondholders, who may
see the value of their bonds fall as the firm piles up more
debt; and (3) the opportunity to create better incentives for
managers and employees, who have a personal stake in the
company. In addition, many LBOs have been designed to
force firms with surplus cash to distribute it to shareholders
rather than plowing it back. Investors feared such companies would otherwise channel free cash flow into negative-
NPV investments.

**6. Do mergers increase efficiency and how are the gains
from mergers distributed between shareholders of the
acquired and acquiring firms?**

We observed that when the target firm is acquired, its
shareholders typically win: target firms' shareholders
earn abnormally large returns. The bidding firm's shareholders roughly break even. This suggests that the typical
merger appears to generate positive net benefits, but competition among bidders and active defence by management of the target firm pushes most of the gains toward
selling shareholders.

Related Web Links

Key Terms

proxy contest	703	acquisition	705	shareholders' rights plan or
merger or statutory		leveraged buyout (LBO)	705	poison pill	719
amalgamation	704	management buyout		white knight	719
tender offer	704	(MBO)	705	shark repellent	720

Questions and Problems

BASIC

1. **Merger Motives.** Which of the following motives for mergers make economic sense?
   a. Merging to achieve economies of scale.
   b. Merging to reduce risk by diversification.
   c. Merging to redeploy cash generated by a firm with ample profits but limited growth opportunities.
   d. Merging to increase earnings per share.

2. **Merger Motives.** Explain why it might make good sense for Northeast Heating and Northeast Air Conditioning to merge into one company.

3. **Empirical Facts.** True or false?
   a. Sellers almost always gain in mergers.
   b. Buyers almost always gain in mergers.
   c. Firms that do unusually well tend to be acquisition targets.
   d. Merger activity in Canada varies dramatically from year to year.
   e. On the average, mergers produce substantial economic gains.
   f. Tender offers require the approval of the selling firm's management.
   g. The cost of a merger is always independent of the economic gain produced by the merger.

4. **Merger Tactics.** Connect each term to its correct definition or description:

   A. LBO
   B. Poison pill
   C. Tender offer
   D. Shark repellent
   E. Proxy contest
   F. White knight

   1. Attempt to gain control of a firm by winning the votes of its shareholders.
   2. Changes in corporate charter designed to deter an unwelcome takeover.
   3. Friendly potential acquirer sought by a threatened target firm.
   4. Shareholders are issued rights to buy shares if a bidder acquires a large stake in the firm.
   5. Offer to buy shares directly from shareholders.
   6. Company or business bought out by private investors, largely debt financed.

5. **Empirical Facts.** True or false?
   a. One of the first tasks of an LBO's financial manager is to pay down debt.
   b. The cost of a merger is affected by the size of the merger gains only when the merger is financed with cash.
   c. Targets for LBOs in the 1980s tended to be profitable companies in mature industries with limited investment opportunities.

PRACTICE

*6. **Merger Gains.** Acquiring Corp. is considering a takeover of Takeover Target Inc. Acquiring has 10 million shares outstanding, which sell for $40 each. Takeover Target has 5 million shares outstanding, which sell for $20 each. If the merger gains are estimated at $20 million, what is the highest price per share that Acquiring should be willing to pay to Takeover Target shareholders? What is Acquiring's NPV if it pays the maximum price?

EXCEL

7. **Mergers and P/E Ratios.** If Acquiring Corp. from the previous problem has a price-earnings ratio of 12, and Takeover Target has a P/E ratio of 8, what should be the P/E ratio of the merged firm? Assume in this case that the merger is financed by an issue of new Acquiring Corp. shares. Takeover Target will get one Acquiring share for every two Takeover Target shares held.

*8. **Merger Gains and Costs.** Velcro Saddles is contemplating the acquisition of Pogo Ski Sticks, Inc. The values of the two companies as separate entities are $20 million and $10 million, respectively. Velcro Saddles estimates that by combining the two companies, it will reduce marketing and administrative costs by $500,000 per year in perpetuity. Velcro Saddles is willing to pay $14 million cash for Pogo. The opportunity cost of capital is 10 percent.

    a.   What is the gain from merger?

    b.   What is the cost of the cash offer?

    c.   What is the NPV of the acquisition under the cash offer?

9.   **Stock versus Cash Offers.** Suppose that instead of making a cash offer as in the previous problem, Velcro Saddles considers offering Pogo shareholders a 50 percent holding in Velcro Saddles.

    a.   What is the value of the stock in the merged company held by the original Pogo shareholders?

    b.   What is the cost of the stock alternative?

    c.   What is its NPV under the stock offer?

10.   **Merger Gains.** Immense Appetite, Inc., believes that it can acquire Sleepy Industries and improve efficiency to the extent that the market value of Sleepy will increase by $5 million. Sleepy currently sells for $20 a share, and there are 1 million shares outstanding.

    a.   Sleepy's management is willing to accept a cash offer of $25 a share. Can the merger be accomplished on a friendly basis?

    b.   What will happen if Sleepy's management holds out for an offer of $28 a share?

EXCEL

11.   **Mergers and P/E Ratios.** Castles in the Sand currently sells at a price-earnings multiple of 10. The firm has 2 million shares outstanding and sells at a price per share of $40. Firm Foundation has a P/E multiple of 8, has 1 million shares outstanding, and sells at a price per share of $20.

    a.   If Castles acquires the other firm by exchanging one of its shares for every two of Firm Foundation's, what will be the earnings per share of the merged firm?

    b.   What should be the P/E of the new firm if the merger has no economic gains? What will happen to Castles' price per share? Show that shareholders of neither Castles nor Firm Foundation realize any change in wealth.

    c.   What will happen to Castles' price per share if the market does not realize that the P/E ratio of the merged firm ought to differ from Castles' pre-merger ratio?

    d.   How are the gains from the merger split between shareholders of the two firms if the market is fooled as in part (c)?

EXCEL

*12.   **Stock versus Cash Offers.** Sweet Cola Corp. (SCC) is bidding to take over Salty Dog Pretzels (SDP). SCC has 3,000 shares outstanding, selling at $50 per share. SDP has 2,000 shares outstanding, selling at $17.50 a share. SCC estimates the economic gain from the merger to be $10,000.

    a.   If SDP can be acquired for $20 a share, what is the NPV of the merger to SCC?

    b.   What will SCC sell for when the market learns that it plans to acquire SDP for $20 a share? What will SDP sell for? What are the percentage gains to the shareholders of each firm? What fraction of the economic gain do SCC's shareholders receive? What fraction goes to SDP's shareholders?

    c.   Now suppose that the merger takes place through an exchange of stock. Based on the pre-merger prices of the firms, SCC issues .40 of its shares for every SDP share. What will be the price of the merged firm?

    d.   What is the NPV of the merger to SCC when it uses an exchange of stock? What fraction of the economic gain do SCC's shareholders receive? Why does your answer differ from parts (a) and (b)? Calculate the share exchange equivalent to the cash offer in part (a).

CHALLENGE

13.   **Internet.** *Mergers and Acquisitions in Canada* reports on current merger activity in Canada. It is available in libraries and parts of it can be found at **www.crosbieco.com/M&A.html**. Select "Press Release" for recent summaries of merger activity in Canada. Read the most current and the oldest press releases and compare them. Is the same industry experiencing the greatest M&A activity? How have the cross-border transactions changed?

14. **Bootstrap Game.** The Muck and Slurry merger has fallen through (see Section 23.3). But World Enterprises is determined to report earnings per share of $2.67. It therefore acquires the Wheelrim and Axle Company.

Once again there are no gains from merging. In exchange for Wheelrim and Axle shares, World Enterprises issues just enough of its own shares to ensure its $2.67 earnings per share objective. Here are the facts you are given:

	World Enterprises	Wheelrim and Axle	Merged Firm
Earnings per share	$2	$2.50	$2.67
Price per share	$40	$25	_____
Price-earnings ratio	20	10	_____
Number of shares	100,000	200,000	_____
Total earnings	$200,000	$500,000	_____
Total market value	$4,000,000	$5,000,000	_____

a. Complete the above table for the merged firm.
b. How many shares of World Enterprises are exchanged for each share of Wheelrim and Axle?
c. What is the cost of the merger to World Enterprises?
d. What is the change in the total market value of those World Enterprises shares that were outstanding before the merger?

EXCEL

15. **Integrative.** As treasurer of Leisure Products, Inc., you are investigating the possible acquisition of Plastitoys. You have the following basic data:

	Leisure Products	Plastitoys
Forecast earnings per share	$5	$1.50
Forecast dividend per share	$3	$.80
Number of shares	1,000,000	600,000
Stock price	$90.00	$20.00

You estimate that investors currently expect a steady growth of about 6 percent in Plastitoys's earnings and dividends. You believe that Leisure Products could increase Plastitoys's growth rate to 8 percent per year, after 1 year, without any additional capital investment required.

a. What is the economic gain from the acquisition?
b. What is the cost of the acquisition if Leisure Products pays $25 in cash for each share of Plastitoys? What is the NPV to Leisure of acquiring Plastitoys?
c. What is the cost of the acquisition if Leisure Products offers 1 share of Leisure Products for every 3.96 shares of Plastitoys? What is the NPV to Leisure of acquiring Plastitoy?
d. Suppose immediately after the completion of the merger, everyone realizes that the expected growth rate will not be improved. Reassess the cost and NPV of the cash and share offers. Explain what you find.

16. **Internet.** The Ontario Teachers Pension Plan Board (Teachers), **www.otpp.com**, and the Ontario Municipal Employees Retirement System (OMERS), **www.omers.com**, manage very large investment portfolios.

a. What are the current sizes of their portfolios?
b. As active shareholders, they closely monitor the activities of the companies they own. Review their corporate governance policies. What issues concern them?
c. Click on the "Proxy Votes" at the Teachers Web site and then look under "Upcoming Meetings" and pick a company. You will see a list of issues to be voted at an upcoming shareholders meeting and how Teachers intends to vote. Click on the little "i" and read the reasons for Teachers' position. Do you agree?
d. At the OMERS Web site, click on "Investments," then "Corporate Governance," and "Proxy Voting Record." What proposals has OMERS voted against?

17. You might be interested in becoming a Chartered Business Valuator, CBV, an expert in business valuation. You can read about this program of study at the Web site of the Canadian Institute of Chartered Business Valulators, **www.cicbv.ca**. The site also provides a list of valuation terms.

Solutions to Check Points

23.1 a. Horizontal merger. IBM is in the same industry as Apple Computer.
b. Conglomerate merger. BCE and Stop & Shop are in different industries.
c. Vertical merger. Loblaws is expanding backward to acquire one of its suppliers, Fishery Products International.
d. Conglomerate merger. Alcan and Canada Bread are in different industries.

23.2 Given current earnings of $2 a share, and a share price of $10, Muck and Slurry would have a market value of $1,000,000 and a price-earnings ratio of only 5. It can be acquired for only half as many shares of World Enterprises, 25,000 shares. Therefore, the merged firm will have 125,000 shares outstanding and earnings of $400,000, resulting in earnings per share of $3.20, higher than the $2.67 value in the third column of Table 23.2.

23.3 The cost of the merger is $4 million: the $4 per share premium offered to Goldfish shareholders × 1 million shares. If the merger has positive NPV to Killer Shark, the gain must be greater than $4 million.

23.4 Yes. Look again at Table 23.4. Total market value is still $540, but Cislunar will have to issue 1 million shares to complete the merger. Total shares in the merged firm will be 11 million. The postmerger share price is $49.09, so Cislunar and its shareholders still come out ahead.

MINICASE

McPhee Food Halls operated a chain of supermarkets in western Scotland. The company had had a lacklustre record and, since the death of its founder in late 2005, it had been regarded as a prime target for a takeover bid. In anticipation of a bid, McPhee's share price moved up from £4.90 in March 2006 to a 12-month high of £5.80 on June 10, despite the fact that the London stock market index as a whole was largely unchanged.

Almost nobody anticipated a bid coming from Fenton, a diversified retail business with a chain of clothing and department stores. Though Fenton operated food halls in several of its department stores, it had relatively little experience in food retailing. Fenton's management, however, had been contemplating a merger with McPhee for some time. They not only felt that they could make use of McPhee's food retailing skills within their department stores, but they believed that better management and inventory control in McPhee's business could result in cost savings worth £10 million.

Fenton's offer of 8 Fenton shares for every 10 McPhee shares was announced after the market close on June 10. Since McPhee had 5 million shares outstanding, the acquisition would add an additional 5 × (8/10) = 4 million shares to the 10 million Fenton shares that were already outstanding. While Fenton's management believed that it would be difficult for McPhee to mount a successful takeover defence, the company and its investment bankers privately agreed that the company could afford to raise the offer if it proved necessary.

Investors were not persuaded of the benefits of combining a supermarket with a department store company, and on June 11, Fenton's shares opened lower and drifted down £.10 to close the day at £7.90. McPhee's shares, however, jumped to £6.32 a share.

Fenton's financial manager was due to attend a meeting with the company's investment bankers that evening, but before doing so, he decided to run the numbers once again. First he reestimated the gain and the cost of the merger. Then he analyzed that day's fall in Fenton's stock price to see whether investors believed there were any gains to be had from merging. Finally, he decided to revisit the issue of whether Fenton could afford to raise its bid at a later stage. If the effect was simply a further fall in the price of Fenton stock, the move could be self-defeating.

INTERNATIONAL FINANCIAL MANAGEMENT

Thus far we have talked principally about doing business at home. But many companies have substantial overseas interests. Of course, the objectives of international financial management are still the same. You want to buy assets that are worth *more* than they cost, and you want to pay for them by issuing liabilities that are worth *less* than the money raised. But when you try to apply these criteria to an international business, you come up against some new wrinkles.

You must, for example, know how to deal with more than one currency. Therefore we open this chapter with a look at foreign exchange markets.

The financial manager must also remember that interest rates differ from country to country. For example, at the end of July 2004 the short-term rate of interest was about .03 percent in Japan, 2.09 percent in Canada, 1.53 percent in the United States, and 2.1 percent in the euro countries. We will discuss the reasons for these differences in interest rates, along with some of the implications for financing overseas operations.

Exchange rate fluctuations can knock companies off course and transform black ink into red. We will therefore discuss how firms can protect themselves against exchange risks.

We will also discuss how international companies decide on capital investments. How do they choose the discount rate? You'll find that the basic principles of capital budgeting are the same as for domestic projects, but there are a few pitfalls to watch for.

After studying this chapter you should be able to
- Understand the difference between spot and forward exchange rates.
- Understand the basic relationships between spot exchange rates, forward exchange rates, interest rates, and inflation rates.
- Formulate simple strategies to protect the firm against exchange rate risk.
- Perform an NPV analysis for projects with cash flows in foreign currencies.

24.1	# FOREIGN EXCHANGE MARKETS

A Canadian company that imports goods from Switzerland may need to exchange its dollars for Swiss francs in order to pay for its purchases. A Canadian company exporting to Switzerland may *receive* Swiss francs, which it sells in exchange for dollars. Both firms must make use of the foreign exchange market, where currencies are traded.

The foreign exchange market has no central marketplace. All business is conducted by computer and telephone. The principal dealers are the large commercial banks, and any corporation that wants to buy or sell currency usually does so through a commercial bank.

Turnover in the foreign exchange markets is huge. In London alone about $640 billion (US) of currency changes hands each day. That is equivalent to an annual turnover of $159 trillion (US) ($159,000,000,000,000). New York and Tokyo together account for a further $500 billion of turnover per day. Compare this to trading volume of the New York Stock Exchange, where no more than $30 billion (US) of stock might change hands on a typical day.

Suppose you ask someone the price of bread. He may tell you that you can buy two loaves for a dollar, or he may say that one loaf costs 50 cents. Similarly, if you ask a foreign exchange dealer to quote you a price for Ruritanian francs, she may tell you that you can buy two francs for a dollar or that one franc costs $.50. The first quote (the number of francs that you can buy for a dollar) is known as an *indirect quote* of the **exchange rate**. The second quote (the number of dollars that it costs to buy one franc) is known as a *direct quote*. Of course, both quotes provide the same information. If you can buy two francs for a dollar, then you can easily calculate that the cost of one franc is 1/2 = $.50.

exchange rate   Amount of one currency needed to purchase one unit of another.

Now look at Table 24.1, which has been adapted from the daily table of exchange rates in *The Globe and Mail*. The table provides exchange rate information for 54 currencies on August 16, 2004.[1] The price of the U.S. dollar is expressed as indirect and direct quotes, while all other currency prices are expressed as direct quotes. Thus you could buy .1148 Canadian dollars with one Mexican peso, or converting to an indirect quote, 8.7108 pesos for one Canadian dollar.[2]

EXAMPLE 24.1	**A YEN FOR TRADE**

How many yen will it cost a Japanese importer to purchase $1,000 worth of potatoes from a P.E.I. farmer? How many dollars will it take for that farmer to buy a Japanese VCR priced in Japan at 30,000 yen (¥)?

The exchange rate is $.011818 per yen. The $1,000 of potatoes will require the Japanese importer to come up with 1,000 ÷ .011818 = ¥84,617. The VCR will require the Canadian importer to come up with 30,000 × .011818 = $354.54.

 Check Point 24.1

Use the exchange rates in Table 24.1. How many euros can you buy for one dollar (an indirect quote)? How many dollars can you buy for one yen (a direct quote)?

spot rate of exchange
Exchange rate for an immediate transaction.

Table 24.1 provides information on spot and forward rates. The **spot rate of exchange** is the price of currency for immediate delivery. For example, the spot rate of exchange for Canadian dollars in terms of Mexican pesos is $.1148/peso. In other words, it costs .1148 dollars to buy one Mexican peso. We could also express the spot rate of exchange for Mexican pesos as 1/.1148 = 8.7108 pesos/$. That is, it will cost 8.7108 pesos to buy one dollar. Notice that the table

---

[1] Notice that 12 countries have adopted a common currency, namely the euro.

[2] In the United States, prices of most currencies are customarily expressed as indirect quotes in terms of the U.S. dollar. However, the price of the euro and the British pound are generally expressed as direct quotes.

TABLE 24.1
Currency exchange rates on August 16, 2004

Mid-market rates in Toronto at noon, Aug. 16, 2004. Prepared by BMO Nesbitt Burns, Capital Markets							
		$1 U.S in Cdn. $ =	$ 1 Cdn. in U.S =	Country	Currency	Cdn $ per unit	U.S $ per unit
U.S/Canada Spot		1.3076	.7648	Denmark	Krone	.2168	.1658
1 month forward		1.3081	.7645	Egypt	Pound	.2106	.1610
2 months forward		1.3086	.7642	Fiji	Dollar	.7524	.5754
3 months forward		1.3091	.7639	Finland	Euro	1.6125	1.2332
6 months forward		1.3104	.7631	France	Euro	1.6125	1.2332
12 months forward		1.3129	.7617	Germany	Euro	1.6125	1.2332
3 years forward		1.3241	.7552	Greece	Euro	1.6125	1.2332
5 years forward		1.3386	.7470	Hong Kong	Dollar	.1677	.1282
7 years forward		1.3511	.7401	Hungary	Forint	.006651	.00498
10 years forward		1.3676	.7312	Iceland	Krona	.01853	.01417
Canadian dollar in	High	1.4003	.7141	India	Rupee	.02824	.02159
2004	Low	1.2683	.7885	Indonesia	Rupiah	.000141	.000108
	Average	1.3348	.7492	Ireland	Euro	1.6125	1.2332
				Israel	N Shekel	.2885	.2207
		Cdn $	U.S $	Italy	Euro	1.6125	1.233175
Country	Currency	per unit	per unit	Jamaica	Dollar	.02139	.01636
Britain	Pound	2.4052	1.8394	Jordan	Dinar	1.8469	1.4124
1 month forward		2.3991	1.8340	Lebanon	Pound	.000864	.000661
2 months forward		2.3941	1.8295	Luxembourg	Euro	1.6125	1.2332
3 months forward		2.3886	1.8246	Malaysia	Ringgit	.3442	.2632
6 months forward		2.3773	1.8111	Mexico	N Peso	.1148	.0878
12 months forward		2.3475	1.7880	Netherlands	Euro	1.6125	1.2332
Europe	Euro	1.6125	1.2332	New Zealand	Dollar	.8702	.6655
1 month forward		1.6123	1.2326	Norway	Krone	.1951	.1492
3 months forward		1.6126	1.2319	Pakistan	Rupee	.02223	.01700
6 months forward		1.6140	1.2317	Panama	Balboa	1.3076	1.0000
12 months forward		1.6185	1.2328	Philippines	Peso	0.2348	.01795
Japan	Yen	.011818	.009038	Poland	Zloty	.3676	.2811
1 month forward		.011840	.009051	Portugal	Euro	1.6125	1.23318
3 months forward		.011884	.009078	Romania	Leu	.000039	.000030
6 months forward		.011960	.009127	Russia	Ruble	.044762	.034233
12 months forward		.012132	.009241	Saudi Arabia	Riyal	.3487	.2667
Algeria	Dinar	.01818	.0139	Singapore	Dollar	.7623	.5830
Antigua, Granada, and St. Lucia	E.C Dollar	.4897	.3745	Slovakia	Koruna	.0403	.0308
				South Africa	Rand	.1993	.1524
Argentina	Peso	.43413	.33201	South Korea	Won	.001128	.000863
Australia	Dollar	.9383	.7176	Spain	Euro	1.6125	1.23318
Austria	Euro	1.6125	1.2332	Sudan	Dinar	.00505	.0039
Bahamas	Dollar	1.3076	1.0000	Sweden	Krona	.1748	.1337
Belgium	Euro	1.6125	1.2332	Switzerland	Franc	1.0515	.8041
Bermuda	Dollar	1.3076	1.0000	Taiwan	Dollar	.03846	.0294
Brazil	Real	.4340	.3319	Thailand	Baht	.03152	.0241
Bulgaria	Lev	.825453	.6313	Trinidad, Tobago	Dollar	.2126	.1626
Chile	Peso	.002049	.001567	Turkey	Lira	.0000009	.0000007
China	Renminbi	.1580	.1208	Venezuela	Bolivar	.000683	.00052
Cyprus	Pound	2.7946	2.1372	Zambia	Kwacha	.000278	.000213
Czech Republic	Koruna	.0513	.0392	Spec. Draw Right	S.D.R	1.9140	1.4637

Source: Reprinted with permission from *The Globe and Mail*. Prepared by BMO Nesbitt Burns.

provides spot and forward rates for a few selected currencies: the U.S. dollar, British pound, euro, and Japanese yen. Only spot rates are available for currencies of 49 other countries.

Many countries allow their currencies to float, so that the exchange rate fluctuates from day to day, and from minute to minute. When the currency increases in value, meaning that you need less of the foreign currency to buy one dollar, the currency is said to *appreciate*. When you need more of the currency to buy one dollar, the currency is said to *depreciate*.

✓ **Check Point 24.2**

Table 24.1 shows the exchange rate for the Swiss franc on August 16, 2004. The next day the spot rate of exchange for the Swiss franc was $1.0489/SFr, or SFr.95338/$. Thus you could buy more Swiss francs for your dollar than one day earlier. Had the Swiss franc appreciated or depreciated?

Some countries try to avoid fluctuations in the value of their currency and seek instead to maintain a fixed exchange rate. But fixed rates seldom last forever. If everybody tries to sell the currency, eventually the country will be forced to allow the currency to depreciate. When this happens, exchange rates can change dramatically. For example, when Indonesia gave up trying to fix its exchange rate in fall 1997, the value of the Indonesian rupiah fell by 80 percent in a few months.

These fluctuations in exchange rates can get companies into hot water. For example, suppose you have agreed to buy a shipment of Japanese VCRs for ¥100 million and to make the payment when you take delivery of the VCRs at the end of 12 months. You could wait until the 12 months have passed and then buy 100 million yen at the spot exchange rate. If the spot rate is unchanged at $.011818/¥, then the VCRs will cost you 100 million × .011818 = $1.1818 million. But you are taking a risk by waiting, for the yen may become more expensive. For example, if the yen appreciates from the existing rate of 1/.011818 = ¥84.62/$ to ¥70/$, then you will have to pay out 100 million/70 = $1.429 million. For much of 2004, the Canadian dollar appreciated against the U.S. dollar. The nearby Finance in Action box describes the impact of this rise on Canadian exporters.

SEE BOX P. 734 ▶

You can avoid exchange rate risk and fix the dollar cost of VCRs by "buying the yen forward," that is, by arranging *now* to buy yen in the future. A foreign exchange *forward contract* is an agreement to exchange at a future date a given amount of currency at an exchange rate agreed to *today*. The **forward exchange rate** is the price of currency for delivery at some time in the future. Table 24.1 shows forward exchange rates for four currencies, namely, the U.S. dollar, British pound, euro, and Japanese yen.[3] For example, the 12-month forward rate for the yen is quoted at .012132 dollars per yen, or 82.43 yen per dollar. If you buy 100 million yen forward, you don't pay anything today; you simply fix today the price that you will pay for your yen in the future. At the end of the year you receive your 100 million yen and hand over 100 million/82.43 = $1.2132 million in payment.

forward exchange rate
Exchange rate for a forward transaction.

Notice that if you buy Japanese yen forward, you get fewer yen for your dollar than if you buy spot. In this case, the yen is said to trade at a forward *premium* relative to the dollar. Expressed as a percentage, the 12-month forward premium is

$$\frac{84.62 - 82.43}{82.43} \times 100 = 2.66\%$$

---

[3] Although forward rates are not quoted for the remaining currencies in Canadian dollars, such rates are available for several currencies in terms of the U.S. dollar, which is recognized as the major international trading currency. For instance, daily spot and forward rate quotes in U.S. dollars are available for Swedish krona; Mexican pesos; and Australian, Hong Kong, and Singapore dollars.

How Does the Soaring Loonie Affect Canadian Exporters?

The potentially punishing impact of a soaring dollar is forcing major players in Canada's hard-hit forest industry to find innovative ways to mitigate the effect on their bottom lines.

In the short term, industry officials say there is only so much they can do to soften the impact of the recent sharp increase in the value of the Canadian dollar against its US counterpart.

But some companies are taking a longer-term view by cutting energy costs, growing their US asset base, and keeping a healthy amount of US-dollar-denominated debt.

"You have to be on the ball," said Marc Jasmin, a spokesman for Cascades Inc., a Montreal-based producer of packaging products, tissues and fine paper.

"Continuous improvements have to be there," he said.

A rising Canadian dollar, which hit a 12-year high of 83.5 cents (US) on Friday, is generally negative for all export-oriented Canadian firms, analysts say.

But companies in the forest sector have traditionally been the hardest hit because they are selling commodities that are priced in US dollars to fund operations that are based mainly in Canada.

The fall in the value of the US dollar means they are getting a lower amount of Canadian dollars as they convert their US-dollar revenue.

Analysts are already preparing investors for the impact by cutting their 2005 earnings forecasts and stock price targets for companies such as Abitibi-Consolidated Inc. and Tembec Inc.

But those that can are fighting back by picking up holdings in the United States in a bid to improve the balance between where their assets are located and where income is being generated.

In the past two years, Cascades has expanded its asset base in the United States by buying fast-food container maker Dopaco Inc. of Exton, PA.

It has also beefed up its tissue paper and corrugated container-making operations south of the border by acquiring conversion plants in Arizona and Lancaster, NY.

"This year, close to 30 per cent of our asset base will be located in the US," Mr. Jasmin said.

Cascades also has operations in Mexico, France, England, Germany and Sweden, which makes it far less sensitive to the impact of fluctuations in US and Canadian-dollar exchange rates

compared with companies such as pulp maker Tembec, which has less than 10 per cent of its assets in the United States.

According to CIBC World Markets analyst Don Roberts, every 1-cent change in the US and Canadian dollar exchange rates adds or subtracts 6 cents from Cascades' share profit.

That compares with 27 cents a share for Tembec Inc., and 26 cents for Vancouver-based lumber producer West Fraser Timber Co. Ltd., according to Mr. Roberts.

In addition to doing more business in the United States, Cascades is also using a combination of US-dollar-denominated debt as well as derivative products to hedge against currency risk.

It is not alone.

Newsprint giant Abitibi-Consolidated reported a third-quarter profit of $182 million or 41 cents a share, which included an after-tax gain of $194 million on the translation of US-dollar-denominated debt. "Hedging is the big thing that we use to mitigate against the impact of fluctuating exchange rates," said Abitibi-Consolidated spokesman Marc Osborne.

There are a number of ways companies can utilize hedging, including entering into an options contract with a bank that allows the company to lock in a specific exchange rate for its US currency in the future.

But they represent only a short-term solution to a rising dollar, especially when the rise has come too quickly.

"Only operational changes are going to protect a company in the long term," said Graham Dallimore, a senior vice-president with Global Futures Corp. in Vancouver.

Cascades is aiming to cut costs by auditing all of its mills in a bid to reduce the amount of oil and natural gas it is using. As part of that effort, it is doing widespread checks on its pipe insulation in order to avoid loss of heat.

Still, analysts say that since a significant proportion of its production comes from Canada, a rising dollar can continue to offset the effect of improvements to Cascades' cost base.

Partly because of the strong loonie, Mark Bishop of RBC Dominion Securities Inc. recently dropped its fourth-quarter profit forecast for Cascades to 16 cents a share from 26 cents. Shares of Cascades closed Friday at $13.75.

Source: Reprinted with permission from *The Globe and Mail*.

You could also say that the dollar was selling at a *forward discount* of about 2.66 percent.[4]

[4] Here is a minor point that sometimes causes confusion. To calculate the forward premium, we divide by the *forward* rate as long as the exchange quotes are *indirect*. If you use *direct* quotes, the correct formula is

$$\text{Forward premium} = \frac{\text{forward rate} - \text{spot rate}}{\text{spot rate}}$$

In our example, the corresponding direct quote for spot yen is $1/84.62 = .011818$, while the direct forward quote is $1/82.63 = .012132$. Substituting these rates in our revised formula gives

$$\text{Forward premium} = \frac{.012132 - .011818}{.011818} = .0266, \text{ or } 2.66\%.$$

The two methods give the same answer.

A forward purchase or sale is a made-to-order transaction between you and the bank. It can be for any currency, any amount, and any delivery day. You could buy, say, 99,999 Sudanese dinar or Slovakian koruna for a year and a day forward as long as you can find a bank ready to deal. From Table 24.1, we see that forward rates are quoted for most currencies for periods ranging from 1 month to a year. However, banks are prepared to buy or sell the U.S. dollar, Canada's major trading currency, for up to 10 years forward.

There is also an organized market for currency for future delivery known as the currency *futures* market. Futures contracts are highly standardized versions of forward contracts—they exist only for the main currencies, they are for specified amounts, and choice of delivery dates is limited. The advantage of this standardization is that there is a very low-cost market in currency futures. Huge numbers of contracts are bought and sold daily on the futures exchanges. In North America, the most important market for foreign currency futures is the International Monetary Market (IMM), a division of the Chicago Mercantile Exchange.

Check Point 24.3

A skiing vacation in Switzerland costs SFr1,500.
a. How many dollars does that represent? Use the exchange rates in Table 24.1.
b. Suppose the dollar depreciates by 10 percent relative to the Swiss franc, so that each dollar buys 10 percent fewer Swiss francs than before. What will be the new value of the (1) direct exchange rate and (2) indirect exchange rate?
c. If the Swiss vacation continues to cost the same number of Swiss francs, what will happen to the cost in dollars?
d. If the tour company that is offering the vacation keeps the price fixed in dollars, what will happen to the number of Swiss francs that it will receive?

24.2

SOME BASIC RELATIONSHIPS

The financial manager of an international business must cope with fluctuations in exchange rates and must be aware of the distinction between spot and forward exchange rates. She must also recognize that two countries may have different interest rates. To develop a consistent international financial policy, the financial manager needs to understand how exchange rates are determined and why one country may have a lower interest rate than another. These are complex issues, but as a first cut we suggest that you think of spot and forward exchange rates, interest rates, and inflation rates as being linked as shown in Figure 24.1. Let's explain.

FIGURE 24.1
Some simple theories linking spot and forward exchange rates, interest rates, and inflation rates

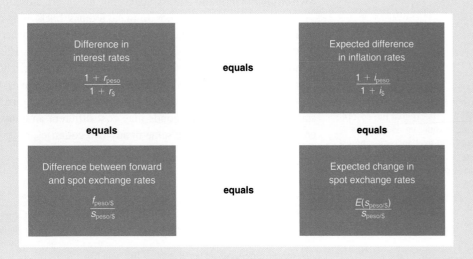

EXCHANGE RATES AND INFLATION

Consider first the relationship between changes in the spot exchange rate and inflation rates (the two boxes on the right of Figure 24.1). The idea here is simple: if country X suffers a higher rate of inflation than country Y, then the value of X's currency will decline relative to Y's. The decline in value shows up in the spot exchange rate for X's currency.

But let's slow down and consider why changes in inflation and spot interest rates are linked. Think first about the prices of the same good or service in two different countries and currencies.

Suppose you notice that gold can be bought in Toronto for $300 an ounce and sold in Mexico City for 4,000 pesos an ounce. If there are no restrictions on the import of gold, you could be on to a good thing. You buy gold for $300 and put it on the first plane to Mexico City, where you sell it for 4,000 pesos. Then (using the exchange rates from Table 24.1) you can exchange your 4,000 pesos for 4,000/8.7108 = $459.20. You have made a gross profit of $159.20 an ounce. Of course, you have to pay transportation and insurance costs out of this, but there should still be something left over for you.

You returned from your trip with a sure-fire profit. But sure-fire profits don't exist—not for long. As others notice the disparity between the price of gold in Mexico and the price in Toronto, the price will be forced down in Mexico and up in Toronto until the profit opportunity disappears. This ensures that the dollar price of gold is about the same in the two countries.[5]

Gold is a standard and easily transportable commodity, but to some degree you might expect that the same forces would be acting to equalize the domestic and foreign prices of other goods. Those goods that can be bought more cheaply abroad will be imported, and that will force down the price of the domestic product. Similarly, those goods that can be bought more cheaply in Canada will be exported, and that will force down the price of the foreign product.

law of one price Theory that prices of goods in all countries should be equal when translated to a common currency.

This conclusion is often called the **law of one price**. Just as the price of goods in Provigo must be roughly the same as the price of goods in Sobey's, so the price of goods in Mexico, when converted into dollars, must be roughly the same as the price in Canada:

$$\text{Dollar price of goods in Canada} = \frac{\text{peso price of goods in Mexico}}{\text{number of pesos per dollar}}$$

$$\$300 = \frac{\text{peso price of gold in Mexico}}{8.7108}$$

Price of gold in Mexico = 300 × 8.7108 = 2,613 pesos

No one who has compared prices in foreign stores with prices at home really believes that the law of one price holds exactly. Look at the first column of Table 24.2, which shows the price of a Big Mac in different countries in 2003. Using the exchange rates at that time (fourth column),[6] we can convert the local price to U.S. dollars (second column). You can see that the price varies considerably across countries. For example, Big Macs were 70 percent more expensive in Switzerland than in the United States, but they were close to half the price in Malaysia.[7]

This suggests a possible way to make a quick buck. Why don't you buy a hamburger to go in Malaysia for $1.33 and take it for resale to Switzerland where the price in dollars is $4.50? The answer, of course, is that the gain would not cover the costs. The law of one price works very well for commodities like gold, where transportation costs are relatively small; it works far less well for Big Macs, and very badly indeed for haircuts and appendectomies, which cannot be transported at all.

purchasing power parity (PPP) Theory that the cost of living in different countries is equal and exchange rates adjust to offset inflation differentials across countries.

A weaker version of the law of one price is known as **purchasing power parity**, or **PPP**. PPP states that although some goods may cost different amounts in different countries, the general cost of living should be the same in any two countries.

---

[5] Activity of this kind is known as *arbitrage*. The arbitrageur makes a riskless profit by noticing discrepancies in prices.

[6] Here, with the exception of the British pound, all other currencies are quoted in terms of 1 unit of the U.S. dollar.

[7] Of course, it could also be that Big Macs come with a bigger smile in Switzerland. If the quality of the hamburgers or the service differs, we are not comparing like with like.

TABLE 24.2
Big Mac Standard

	Price in Local Currency	In US$	Implied PPP[1] of the US$	Actual US$ Exchange Rate April 22, 2003	Under(–)/Over(+) Valuation Against the US$, %
United States	$ 2.71	2.71	—	—	—
Argentina	Peso 4.10	1.40	1.51	2.88	–47
Australia	A $ 3.00	1.80	1.11	1.61	–31
Brazil	Real 4.55	1.44	1.68	3.07	–45
Britain	£ 1.99	3.08	1.36[2]	1.58[2]	+16
Canada	C $ 3.20	2.17	1.18	1.45	–18
Chile	Peso 1,400	1.95	517	716	–28
China	Yuan 9.90	1.20	3.65	8.28	–56
Czech Rep	Koruna 56.57	1.91	20.9	28.9	–28
Denmark	Dkr 27.75	3.99	10.2	6.78	+51
Egypt	Pound 8.00	1.38	2.95	5.92	–50
Euro area	€ 2.71	2.89	1.00[3]	1.10[3]	+10
Hong Kong	HK $ 11.50	1.47	4.24	7.80	–46
Hungary	Forint 490	2.14	181	224	–19
Indonesia	Rupiah 16,100	1.81	5,941	8,740	–32
Japan	¥ 262	2.18	96.7	120	–19
Malaysia	M $ 5.04	1.33	1.86	3.80	–51
Mexico	Peso 23.00	2.14	8.49	10.53	–19
New Zealand	NZ $ 3.95	2.15	1.46	1.78	–18
Peru	New Sol. 7.90	2.28	2.92	3.46	–16
Philippines	Peso 65.00	1.23	24.0	52.5	–54
Poland	Zloty 6.30	1.56	2.32	3.89	–40
Russia	Rouble 41.00	1.31	15.1	31.1	–51
Singapore	S $ 3.30	1.85	1.22	1.78	–31
South Africa	Rand 13.95	1.74	5.15	7.56	–32
South Korea	Won 3,300	2.63	1,218	1,220	nil
Sweden	SK 30.00	3.50	11.1	8.34	+33
Switzerland	SFr 6.30	4.52	2.32	1.37	+69
Taiwan	NT $ 70.00	2.01	25.8	34.8	–26
Thailand	Baht 59.00	1.37	21.8	42.7	–49
Turkey	Lira 3,750,000	2.28	1,383,764	1,600,500	–14
Venezuela	Bolivar 3,700	2.32	1,365	1,598	–15

Source: "McCurrencies," *The Economist*, April 26, 2003, p. 68.
[1] Purchasing power parity: local price divided by price in the United States.
[2] Dollars per pound.
[3] Dollars per euro.

> Purchasing power parity implies that the relative costs of living in two countries will not be affected by differences in their inflation rates. Instead, the different inflation rates in local currencies will be offset by changes in the exchange rate between the two currencies.

For example, between 1995 and 2000, Turkey experienced high inflation. Over those 5 years, the purchasing power of the lira declined by nearly 87 percent compared with other countries' currencies. As prices in Turkey increased, Turkish exporters would have found it impossible to sell their goods if the exchange rate had not also changed. But, of course, the exchange rate did adjust. In fact, by the end of the period the lira bought over 91 percent less foreign currency than before. Thus an 87 percent decline in purchasing power was offset by a 91 percent decline in the value of the Turkish currency.

In Figure 24.2 we have plotted the relative change in purchasing power for a sample of countries against the change in the exchange rate. Turkey is toward the bottom left-hand corner; the United States is closer to the top right. You can see that although the relationship is far from exact, large differences in inflation rates are generally accompanied by an offsetting change in

FIGURE 24.2
A decline in the exchange
rate and a decline in a
country's purchasing power
usually go hand in hand. In
this diagram, each point
represents the experience of a
different country between
1995 and 2000.

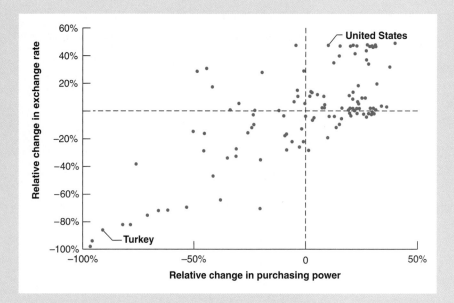

the exchange rate. In fact, if you have to make a long-term forecast of the exchange rate, it is very difficult to do much better than to assume that it will offset the effect of any differences in the inflation rates.

If purchasing power parity holds, then your forecast of the difference in inflation rates is also your best forecast of the change in the spot rate of exchange. Thus the expected difference between inflation rates in Mexico and the United States is given by the right-hand boxes in Figure 24.1:

For example, from Table 24.1, the present spot exchange rate between the U.S. dollar and Mexican peso is U.S.$.0878/peso, or pesos 11.3895/U.S.$. If inflation is 2 percent in the United States and 6 percent in Mexico, then purchasing power parity implies that the expected spot rate for the peso at the end of the year is peso 11.836/U.S.$:

$$\begin{array}{c}\text{Current} \\ \text{spot rate}\end{array} \times \begin{array}{c}\text{expected difference} \\ \text{in inflation rates}\end{array} = \text{expected spot rate}$$

$$11.3895 \times \frac{1.06}{1.02} = 11.836$$

Suppose that gold currently costs $330 an ounce in the United States and £220 an ounce in Great Britain.
a. What must be the pound/dollar exchange rate?
b. Suppose that gold prices rise by 2 percent in the United States and by 5 percent in Great Britain. What will be the price of gold in the two currencies at the end of the year? What must be the exchange rate at the end of the year?
c. Show that at the end of the year each dollar buys about 3 percent more pounds, as predicted by PPP.

INFLATION AND INTEREST RATES

Interest rates in Turkey in 2004 were about 25 percent. So why didn't you (and a few million other investors) put your cash in a Istanbul bank deposit where the return seemed to be so attractive?

The answer lies in the distinction that we made in Chapter 4 between nominal and real rates of interest. Bank deposits usually promise you a fixed nominal rate of interest but they don't promise what that money will buy. If you invested 100 lira for a year at an interest rate of 25 percent, you would have 25 percent more lira at the end of the year than you did at the start. But you wouldn't be 25 percent better off. A good part of the gain would be needed to compensate for inflation.

The nominal rate of interest in 2004 was much lower in Canada, but then so was the inflation rate. The real rates of interest were much closer than the nominal rates.

> There is a general law at work here. Just as water always flows downhill, so capital always flows where returns are greatest. But it is the real returns that concern investors, not the *nominal* returns. Two countries may have different nominal interest rates but the same expected real interest rate.

international Fisher effect
Theory that real interest rates in all countries should be equal, with differences in nominal rates reflecting differences in expected inflation.

Do you remember Irving Fisher's theory from Chapter 4 that changes in the expected inflation rate are reflected in the nominal interest rate? We have just described here the **international Fisher effect**—international variations in the expected inflation rate are reflected in the nominal interest rates:

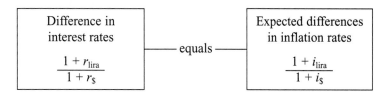

$$\begin{array}{c}\text{Difference in} \\ \text{interest rates} \\[4pt] \dfrac{1 + r_{\text{lira}}}{1 + r_{\$}}\end{array} \quad\text{---- equals ----}\quad \begin{array}{c}\text{Expected differences} \\ \text{in inflation rates} \\[4pt] \dfrac{1 + i_{\text{lira}}}{1 + i_{\$}}\end{array}$$

In other words, capital market equilibrium requires that real interest rates be the same in any two countries.

EXAMPLE 24.2   **INTERNATIONAL FISHER EFFECT**

If the nominal interest rate in Turkey is 25 percent and the expected inflation is 20 percent, then

$$r_{\text{lira}}(\text{real}) = \frac{1 + r_{\text{lira}}}{E(1 + i_{\text{lira}})} - 1 = \frac{1.25}{1.20} - 1 = .042, \text{ or } 4.2\%$$

In Canada, where the nominal interest rate is about 2.5 percent and the expected inflation rate is about 2 percent,

$$r_{\$}(\text{real}) = \frac{1 + r_{\$}}{E(1 + i_{\$})} - 1 = \frac{1.025}{1.02} - 1 = .005, \text{ or } 0.5\%$$

The real interest rate is higher in Turkey than in Canada, but the difference in the real rates is much smaller than the difference in nominal rates.

How similar are real interest rates around the world? It is hard to say, because we cannot directly observe expected inflation. In Figure 24.3 we have plotted the average interest rate in each of 42 countries against the inflation that in fact occurred. You can see that the countries with the highest interest rates generally had the highest inflation rates.

FIGURE 23.3

Countries with the highest interest rates generally have the highest subsequent inflation rates. In this diagram, each point represents a different country.

Check Point 24.5

Canadian investors can invest $1,000 at an interest rate of 3 percent. Alternatively, they can convert those funds to 7,092,199 Rupiah at the current exchange rate and invest at 8 percent in Indonesia. If the expected inflation rate in Canada is 2 percent, what must be investors' forecast of the inflation rate in Indonesia?

INTEREST RATES AND EXCHANGE RATES

You are an investor with $1 million to invest for 1 year. Suppose the interest rate in Canada is 3 percent and in Japan it is .33 percent. Is it better to make a yen loan or a dollar loan?

The answer seems obvious: Isn't it better to earn an interest rate of 3 percent in Canada than .33 percent in Japan? But appearances may be deceptive. If you lend in Japan, you first need to convert your $1 million into yen. When the loan is repaid at the end of the year, you need to convert your yen back into dollars. Of course, you don't know what the exchange rate will be at the end of the year but you can fix the future value of your yen by selling them forward. If the forward rate of exchange is sufficiently high, you may do just as well investing your money in Japan.

Let's use the data from Table 24.1 to check which loan is the better deal:

- *Dollar Loan:* The rate of interest on a dollar loan is 3 percent. Therefore, at the end of the year you get 1,000,000 × 1.03 = $1,030,000.
- *Yen Loan:* The current rate of exchange (from Table 24.1) is $.011818/¥. Therefore, for $1 million, you can buy 1,000,000 ÷ .011818 = 84,616,686 yen. The rate of interest on a 1-year yen loan is .33 percent. So at the end of the year, you get ¥84,616,686 × 1.0033 = ¥84,895,921. Of course, you don't know what the exchange rate will be at the end of the year. But that doesn't matter. You can nail down the price at which you sell your yen. The 12-month forward rate is $.012132¥. Therefore, by selling the ¥84,895,921 forward, you make sure that you will get 84,895,921 × .012132 = $1,029,957.

Thus the two investments offer almost exactly the same rate of return. They have to—they are both risk-free. If the domestic interest rate were different from the "covered" foreign rate, you would have a money machine: you could borrow in the market with the lower rate and lend in the market with the higher rate.

A difference in interest rates must be offset by a difference between spot and forward exchange rates. If the risk-free interest rate in country X is higher than in country Y, then country X's currency will buy less of Y's in a forward transaction than in a spot transaction.

When you make a yen loan, you lose because you get a lower interest rate. But you gain because you sell the yen forward at a higher price than you have to pay for them today. The interest rate differential is

$$\frac{1 + r_¥}{1 + r_\$} = \frac{1.0033}{1.03} = .9741$$

and the differential between the forward and spot exchange rates is virtually identical:[8]

$$\frac{f_{¥/\$}}{s_{¥/\$}} = \frac{82.43}{84.62} = .9741$$

interest rate parity Theory that forward premium equals interest rate differential.

Interest rate parity theory says that the interest rate differential must equal the differential between the forward and spot exchange rates. Thus

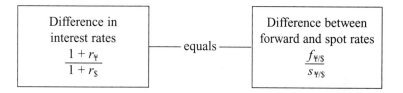

EXAMPLE 24.3   **WHAT HAPPENS IF INTEREST RATE PARITY THEORY DOES NOT HOLD?**

Suppose that the forward rate on the yen is not ¥82.43/$ (or $.012132/¥) but ¥84.00/$ (or $.011905/¥). Here is what you do. Borrow 1 million yen at an interest rate of .33 percent and change these yen into dollars at the spot exchange rate of ¥84.62/$ (or $.011818/¥). This gives you $11,818, which you invest for a year at 3 percent. At the end of the year you will have 11,818 × 1.03 = $12,173. Of course, this is not money to spend because you must repay your yen loan. The amount that you need to repay is 1,000,000 × 1.033 = ¥1,003,300. If you buy these yen forward, you can fix in advance the number of dollars that you will need to lay out. With a forward rate of ¥84.00/$, you need to set aside 1,003,300/84.00 = $11,944. Thus, after paying off your yen loan, you walk away with a risk-free profit of $12,173 – $11,944 = $229. While this amount is small, notice that you would have made a profit of $2,290 had you invested 10 million yen. It is a pity that in practice interest rate parity almost always holds and the opportunities for such easy profits are rare.

Check Point 24.6   Look at the exchange rates in Table 24.1. Does the British pound sell at a forward premium or discount on the dollar? Does this suggest that the interest rate in Britain is higher or lower than in Canada? Use the interest rate parity relationship to estimate the 1-year interest rate in Britain. Assume the Canadian interest rate is 3.55 percent.

THE FORWARD RATE AND THE EXPECTED SPOT RATE

If you buy yen forward, you get fewer yen for your dollar than if you buy them spot. So the yen is selling at a forward premium. Now let us think how this premium is related to expected changes in spot rates of exchange.

---

[8] In our discussion so far, we have used direct quotes from Table 24.1 The indirect quote for the forward rate, $f$yen/$, is 1/.012132 = ¥82.43/$. The indirect spot quote, $s$yen/$ = 1/.011818 = ¥84.62.

The 12-month forward rate for the yen is ¥82.43/$. Would you sell yen at this rate if you expected the yen to rise in value? Probably not. You would be tempted to wait until the end of the year and get a better price for your yen in the spot market. If other traders felt the same way, nobody would sell yen forward and everybody would want to buy. The result would be that the number of yen that you could get for your dollar in the forward market would fall. Similarly, if traders expected the yen to fall sharply in value, they might be reluctant to *buy* forward and, in order to attract buyers, the number of yen that you could buy for a dollar in the forward market would need to rise.[9]

expectations theory of
exchange rates   Theory that
expected spot exchange rate
equals the forward rate.

This is the reasoning behind the **expectations theory of exchange rates**, which predicts that the forward rate equals the expected future spot exchange rate: $f_{¥/\$} = E(s_{¥/\$})$. Equivalently, we can say that the *percentage* difference between the forward rate and today's spot rate is equal to the expected *percentage* change in the spot rate:

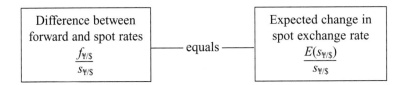

This is the final leg of our quadrilateral in Figure 24.1.

> The expectations theory of forward rates does not imply that managers are perfect forecasters. Sometimes the *actual* future spot rate will turn out to be above the previous forward rate. Sometimes it will fall below. But if the theory is correct, we should find that on *average* the forward rate is equal to the future spot rate.

How well does the expectations theory explain the level of forward rates? Scholars who have studied exchange rates have found that forward rates typically exaggerate the likely change in the spot rate. When the forward rate appears to predict a sharp rise in the spot rate, the forward rate tends to overestimate the rise in the spot rate. Conversely, when the forward rate appears to predict a fall in the currency, it tends to overestimate this fall.[10]

This finding is *not* consistent with the expectations theory. Instead it seems that companies are sometimes prepared to give up return in order to buy forward currency and other times they are prepared to give up return in order to sell forward currency. Almost half the time the forward rate *overstates* the likely future spot rate and half the time it *understates* the likely spot rate. This is important news for the financial manager; it means that a company that always covers its foreign exchange commitments by buying or selling currency in the forward market does not have to pay a premium to avoid exchange rate risk: *on average*, the forward price at which it agrees to exchange currency will equal the eventual spot exchange rate; no better but no worse.

We should, however, warn you that the forward rate does not tell you very much about the future spot rate. For example, when the forward rate appears to suggest that the spot rate is likely to appreciate, you will find that the spot rate is about equally likely to head off in the opposite direction.

SOME IMPLICATIONS

Our four simple relationships ignore many of the complexities of interest rates and exchange rates. But they capture the more important features and emphasize that international capital

---

[9] This reasoning ignores risk. If a forward purchase reduces your risk sufficiently, you *might* be prepared to buy forward even if you expected to pay more as a result. Similarly, if a forward sale reduces risk, you *might* be prepared to sell forward even if you expected to receive less as a result.

[10] Many researchers have even found that, when the forward rate predicts a rise, the spot rate is more likely to fall, and vice versa. For a readable discussion of this puzzling finding, see K. A. Froot and R. H. Thaler, "Anomalies: Foreign Exchange," *Journal of Political Economy* 4 (1990), pp. 179–192.

markets and currency markets function well and offer no free lunches. When managers forget this, it can be costly. For example, in the late 1980s, several Australian banks observed that interest rates in Switzerland were about 8 percentage points lower than those in Australia and advised their clients to borrow Swiss francs. Was this advice correct? According to the international Fisher effect, the lower Swiss interest rate indicated that investors were expecting a lower inflation rate in Switzerland than in Australia and this in turn would result in an appreciation of the Swiss franc relative to the Australian dollar. Thus it was likely that the advantage of the low Swiss interest rate would be offset by the fact that it would cost the borrowers more Australian dollars to repay the loan. As it turned out, the Swiss franc appreciated very rapidly, and the Australian banks found that they had a number of very irate clients and agreed to compensate them for the losses they had incurred. The moral: Don't assume automatically that it is cheaper to borrow in a currency with a low nominal rate of interest.

Check Point 24.7

In October 1998, Stellar Corporation borrowed 100 million Japanese yen at an attractive interest rate of 2 percent, when the exchange rate between the yen and U.S. dollar was ¥123.97/U.S.$. One year later, when Stellar came to repay its loan, the exchange rate was ¥107.52/U.S.$. Calculate in U.S. dollars the amount that Stellar borrowed and the amounts that it paid in interest and principal (assume annual interest payments). What was the effective U.S. dollar interest rate on the loan?

Here is another case where our simple relationships can stop you from falling into a trap. Managers sometimes talk as if you make money simply by buying currencies that go up in value and selling those that go down. But if investors anticipate the change in the exchange rate, then it will be reflected in the interest rate differential; therefore, what you gain on the currency you will lose in terms of interest income. You make money from currency speculation only if you can predict whether the exchange rate will change by more or less than the interest rate differential. In other words, you must be able to predict whether the exchange rate will change by more or less than the forward premium.

EXAMPLE 24.4	**MEASURING CURRENCY GAINS**

The financial manager of Universal Waffle is proud of his acumen. Instead of keeping his cash in U.S. dollars, he for many years invested it in deposits denominated in deutschemarks, which used to be the German currency before the country adopted the euro. He calculates that between the end of 1980 and 1998, the deutschemark increased in value by nearly 47 percent, or about 2.1 percent a year. But did the manager really gain from investing in foreign currency? Let's check.

The compound rate of interest on U.S. dollar deposits during the period was 9.0 percent, while the compound rate of interest on deutschemark deposits was only 6.9 percent. So the 2.1 percent a year appreciation in the value of the deutschemark was almost exactly offset by the lower rate of interest on deutschemark deposits.

The interest rate differential (which by interest rate parity is equal to the forward premium) is a measure of the market's expectation of the change in the value of the currency. The difference between the German and United States interest rates during this period suggests that the market was expecting the deutschemark to appreciate by just over 2 percent a year,[11] and that is almost exactly what happened.

---

[11] If the interest rate is 9 percent on U.S. dollar deposits and 6.9 percent on deutschemark deposits, our simple relationship implies that the expected change in the value of the deutschemark was $(1 + r_{U.S.\$})/(1 + r_{DM}) - 1 = 1.090/1.069 - 1 = .020$, or 2 percent per year.

24.3   HEDGING EXCHANGE RATE RISK

Firms with international operations are subject to exchange rate risk. As exchange rates fluctuate, the dollar value of their revenues or expenses also fluctuates. It helps to distinguish two types of exchange rate risk: *transaction risk* and *economic risk*. Transaction risk arises when the firm agrees to pay or receive a known amount of foreign currency. For example, our VCR importer was committed to pay ¥100 million at the end of 12 months. If the value of the yen appreciates rapidly over this period, those VCRs will cost more dollars than the firm expected.

Economic risk arises because exchange rate fluctuations can affect the competitive position of the firm. For example, during 2000 and 2001 the Japanese yen fell in value relative to the U.S. dollar. As a result Toyota and Nissan were able to compete much more vigorously in the U.S. market. The Big Three U.S. producers claimed that the changed exchange rate gave the Japanese producers an unfair advantage and (unsuccessfully) lobbied President George W. Bush to take up their cause during his visit to Japan. Thus American car producers and their dealers in the United States were exposed to the fall in the value of the yen even though they had no obligation to make any yen payments. Of course, economic risk can cut both ways. In a year or so it may be the dollar that is weak and it will then be the turn of the Japanese producers and their dealers to cry "foul."

✓ **Check Point 24.8**   Interest rate parity theory implies that the cost of buying yen forward is exactly the same as the cost of borrowing dollars, buying yen in the spot market, and leaving them on deposit. Use the exchange rates for U.S. dollars and Japanese yen in Table 24.1 to show that this is the case. Assume a U.S. dollar interest rate of 2 percent and a yen rate of .33 percent.

Exchange rate changes can get companies into big trouble and therefore most companies aim to limit at least their contractual exposure to currency fluctuations. Let us look at an example of how this can be done.

In 1989 a British company, Enterprise Oil, bought some oil properties from Texas Eastern for $440 million (US).[12] Since the payment was delayed a couple of months, Enterprise's plans for financing the purchase could have been thrown out of kilter if the dollar had strengthened during this period.

Enterprise therefore decided to avoid, or *hedge*, this risk. It did so by borrowing pounds, which it converted into U.S. dollars at the current spot rate and invested for two months. In that way Enterprise guaranteed it would have just enough U.S. dollars available to pay for the purchase. Of course, it was possible that the U.S. dollar would *depreciate* over the two months, in which case Enterprise would have regretted that it did not wait and buy the dollars spot. Unfortunately, you cannot have your cake and eat it too. By fixing its dollar cost, Enterprise forfeited the chance of pleasant as well as unpleasant surprises.

Was there any other way that Enterprise could hedge against exchange loss? Of course. It could buy $440 million (US) 2 months forward. No cash would change hands immediately but Enterprise would fix the price at which it buys its U.S. dollars at the end of two months. It would therefore eliminate all exchange risk on the deal. Interest rate parity theory tells us that the difference between buying spot and buying forward is equal to the difference between the rate of interest that you pay at home and the interest that you earn overseas. In other words, the two methods of eliminating risk should be equivalent.

---

[12] See "Enterprise Oil's Mega Forex Option," *Corporate Finance* 53 (April 1989), p. 13.

Let us check this. In March 1989 the 2-month interest rate in the United States was about 9.7 percent and the interest rate in the United Kingdom was 13 percent. The spot exchange rate was U.S.$1.743/£ and the 2-month forward rate was U.S.$1.730/£. Table 24.3 shows that the cash flows from the two methods of hedging the dollar payment for Texas Eastern were almost identical.[13]

What is the cost of such a hedge? You sometimes hear managers say that it is equal to the difference between the forward rate and *today's* spot rate. This is wrong. If Enterprise did not hedge, it would pay the spot rate for U.S. dollars at the time that the payment for Texas Eastern was due. Therefore, the cost of hedging is the difference between the forward rate and the *expected* spot rate when payment is received.

Hedge or speculate? We generally vote for hedging. First, it makes life simpler for the firm and allows it to concentrate on its own business. Second, it does not cost much. (In fact, the cost is zero if the forward rate equals the expected spot rate, as our simple relations imply.) Third, the foreign exchange market seems reasonably efficient, at least for the major currencies. Speculation should be a zero-sum game unless financial managers have superior information to the pros who make the market.

Check Point 24.9   Suppose that the current spot rate for the euro is $1.6215/€ and that the 6-month forward rate is $1.6140/€. What is the cost to a Canadian company of hedging its future need for euros by buying them in the forward market? Assume the expectations theory of exchange rates.

TABLE 24.3
Enterprise Oil could hedge its future U.S. dollar payment either by borrowing sterling and lending U.S. dollars or by buying U.S. dollars forward

	Cash Flow, Millions	
	£	U.S.$
Method 1: Borrow sterling, convert proceeds to U.S. dollars, and invest dollars until needed		
Now:		
Borrow £248.6m at 13%	+248.6	
Convert to U.S.$ at $1.743/£	−248.6	+433.3
Invest U.S.$433.3m for 2 months at 9.7%		−433.3
Net cash flow, Now	0	0
Month 2:		
Repay £ loan with interest	−253.7	
Receive payment on U.S.$ loan		+440
Pay for oil properties		−440
Net cash flow, Month 2	−253.7	0
Method 2: Buy dollars forward		
Now:		
Buy U.S.$440m forward at U.S.$1.73/£	0	0
Month 2:		
Pay for U.S.$	−254.3	+440
Pay for oil properties		−440
Net cash flow, Month 2	−254.3	0

---

[13] We are not sure of Enterprise's borrowing rate but the company is rumoured to have hedged at an effective forward rate of U.S.$1.73/£.

INTERNATIONAL CAPITAL BUDGETING

NET PRESENT VALUE ANALYSIS

KW Corporation is a Canadian firm manufacturing flat-packed kit wardrobes. Its export business has risen to the point that it is considering establishing a small manufacturing operation overseas in Narnia. KW's decision to invest overseas should be based on the same criteria as a decision to invest in Canada—that is, the company needs to forecast the incremental cash flows from the project, discount the cash flows at the opportunity cost of capital, and accept those projects with a positive NPV.

Suppose KW's Narnian facility is expected to generate the following cash flows in *Narnian leos*:

Year	0	1	2	3	4	5
Cash flow (millions of leos)	−7.6	2.0	2.5	3.0	3.5	4.0

The interest rate in Canada is 5 percent. KW's financial manager estimates that the company requires an additional expected return of 10 percent to compensate for the risk of the project, so the opportunity cost of capital for the project is $5 + 10 = 15$ percent.

Notice that KW's opportunity cost of capital is stated in terms of the return on a dollar-denominated investment, but the cash flows are given in leos. A project that offers a 15 percent expected return in leos could fall far short of offering the required return in dollars if the value of the leo is expected to decline. Conversely, a project that offers an expected return of less than 15 percent in leos may be worthwhile if the leo is likely to appreciate.

> You cannot compare the project's return measured in one currency with the return that you require from investing in another currency. If the opportunity cost of capital is measured as a dollar-denominated return, consistency demands that the forecast cash flows should also be stated in dollars.

To translate the leo cash flows into dollars, KW needs a forecast of the leo/dollar exchange rate. Where does this come from? We suggest using the simple parity relationships in Figure 24.1. These tell us that the expected annual change in the spot exchange rate (the bottom right box in Figure 24.1) is equal to the difference between the interest rates in the two countries (the upper left box). For example, suppose that the financial manager looks in the newspaper and finds that the current exchange rate is 2 leos to the dollar ($s_{L/\$} = 2.0$), while the interest rate is 5 percent in Canada ($r_\$ = .05$) and 10 percent in Narnia ($r_L = .10$). Thus the manager sees right away that the leo is likely to depreciate by about 5 percent a year.[14] For example, at the end of 1 year

$$\frac{\text{Expected spot}}{\text{rate in Year 1}} = \frac{\text{spot rate}}{\text{in Year 0}} \times \frac{\text{expected change}}{\text{in spot rate}}$$

$$= 2.0 \times \frac{1.10}{1.05} = L2.095/\$$$

The forecast exchange rates for each year of the project are calculated in a similar way, as follows:

Year	Forecast Exchange Rate		
0	Spot exchange rate	=	L2.0/$
1	$2.0 \times (1.10/1.05)$	=	L2.095/$
2	$2.0 \times (1.10/1.05)^2$	=	L2.195/$
3	$2.0 \times (1.10/1.05)^3$	=	L2.300/$
4	$2.0 \times (1.10/1.05)^4$	=	L2.409/$
5	$2.0 \times (1.10/1.05)^5$	=	L2.524/$

---

[14] The financial manager could use the forward exchange rate ($f_{L/\$}$) equally well to estimate the expected spot rate. In practice, it is usually easier to find interest rates in the financial press than yearly forward rates.

The financial manager can use these projected exchange rates to convert the leo cash flows into dollars:[15]

Year	0	1	2	3	4	5
Cash flow	-7.6	2.0	2.5	3.0	3.5	4.0
($ millions)	2.00	2.095	2.195	2.300	2.409	2.524
	$= -\$3.8$	$= \$.95$	$= \$1.14$	$= \$1.30$	$= \$1.45$	$= \$1.58$

Now the manager discounts these *dollar* cash flows at the 15 percent *dollar* cost of capital:

$$\text{NPV} = -3.8 + \frac{.95}{1.15} + \frac{1.14}{1.15^2} + \frac{1.30}{1.15^3} + \frac{1.45}{1.15^4} + \frac{1.58}{1.15^5}$$
$$= \$.36 \text{ million, or } \$360,000$$

Notice that the manager discounted cash flows at 15 percent, not the Canadian risk-free interest rate of 5 percent. The cash flows are risky, so a risk-adjusted interest rate is appropriate. The positive NPV tells the manager that the project is worth undertaking; it increases shareholder wealth by $360,000.

Check Point 24.10

Suppose that the nominal interest rate in Narnia is 3 percent rather than 10 percent. The spot exchange rate is still L2.0/$ and the forecast leo cash flows on KW's project are also the same as before.

a. What do you deduce about the likely difference in the inflation rates in Narnia and Canada?
b. Would you now forecast that the leo will appreciate or depreciate against the dollar?
c. Do you think that the NPV of KW's project will now be higher or lower than the figure we calculated above? Check your answer by calculating NPV under this new assumption.

THE COST OF CAPITAL FOR FOREIGN INVESTMENT

We did not say how KW arrived at a 15 percent dollar discount rate for its Narnian project. That depends on the risk of overseas investment and the reward that investors require for taking this risk. These are issues on which few economists can agree, but we will tell you where we stand.[16]

Remember that the risk of an investment cannot be considered in isolation; it depends on the securities that the investor holds in his or her portfolio. For example, suppose KW's shareholders invest mainly in companies that do business in Canada. They would find that the value of KW's Narnian venture was relatively unaffected by fluctuations in the value of Canadian shares. So an investment in the Narnian furniture business would appear to be a relatively low-risk project to KW's shareholders. That would not be true of a Narnian company, whose shareholders are already exposed

---

[15] Suppose KW's managers do not go along with what market prices are telling them. For example, perhaps they believe that the leo is likely to appreciate relative to the dollar. Should they plug their own currency forecasts into their present value calculations? We think not. It would be unwise to undertake what might be an unprofitable investment just because management is optimistic about the currency. Given its exchange rate forecast, KW would do better to pass up the investment in wardrobe manufacturing and buy leos instead.

[16] Why don't economists agree? One fundamental reason is that economists have never been able to agree on what makes one country different from another. Is it just that they have different currencies? Or is it that their citizens have different tastes? Or is it that they are subject to different regulations and taxes? The answer affects the relationship between security prices in different countries.

to the fortunes of the Narnian market. To them an investment in the Narnian furniture business might seem a relatively high-risk project. They would therefore demand a higher return (*measured in dollars*) than KW's shareholders.

POLITICAL RISK

When multinational companies invest abroad, their financial managers need to consider the political risks that are involved. By this we mean the threat that governments will change the rules of the game *after* an investment is made. At worst, the government may expropriate the company's assets without compensation. Or it may simply insist that the company keep any profits it makes in the country.

political risk A change in firm value arising from political events.

Political risk refers to any change in the value of a firm arising from political events, which are often unanticipated. Firms operating in domestic as well as international environments can face such risks; businesses in every country are exposed to the risk of unanticipated actions by governments or the courts. But in some parts of the world, foreign companies are particularly vulnerable. Several organizations publish regular rankings of countries in terms of their political risk. For example, the PRS Group places countries on a scale of 1 to 100 based on factors such as regime stability, financial transfer, and turmoil. Table 24.4 presents the 10 least risky and 10 riskiest countries based on these factors. The nearby Finance in Action box describes the recent experiences of the biggest Canadian oil company operating in Russia.

SEE BOX P. 749

AVOIDING FUDGE FACTORS

We certainly don't pretend that we can put a precise figure on the cost of capital for foreign investment. But you can see that we disagree with the frequent practice of *automatically* increasing the domestic cost of capital when foreign investment is considered. We suspect that managers mark up the required return for foreign investment because it is more costly to manage an operation in a foreign country and to cover the risk of expropriation, foreign exchange restrictions, or unfavourable tax changes. A fudge factor is added to the discount factor to cover costs associated with political risk.

We think managers should leave the discount rate alone and reduce expected cash flows instead. For example, suppose that KW is expected to earn L2.5 million in the first year *if no penalties are placed on the operations of foreign firms.* Suppose also that there is a 20 percent chance that KW's cash flow may be expropriated without compensation. The expected cash flow is not L2.5 million but .8 × 2.5 million = L2 million.

The end result may be the same if you pretend that the expected cash flow is L2.5 million but add a fudge factor to the discount rate. Nevertheless, adjusting cash flows brings management's assumptions about "political risk" out in the open for scrutiny and sensitivity analysis.

TABLE 24.4
The top 10 least risky and top 10 most risky countries for investment (March 2004)

10 Least Risky Countries	10 Riskiest Countries
Norway	Zimbabwe
Switzerland	Liberia
Luxembourg	Haiti
Brunei	Somalia
Canada	Iraq
Singapore	Congo, Dem. Republic
Finland	Guinea-Bissau
Sweden	Sierra Leone
Ireland	Korea, D.P.R.
Denmark	Nicaragua
Japan	Serbia & Montenegro
Austria	Malawi

Source: The PRS Group at **www.prsgroup.com**.

Russian Raider Gains Control of Canadian Oil Firm's Accounts

A Russian corporate raider, backed by dozens of armed security guards, has won control of a Canadian oil company's bank accounts, triggering fears that as much as $30 million (US) in assets could be removed from the Canadian firm.

The move is another serious blow for Yugraneft, the biggest Canadian-owned oil firm in Russia, which has been reeling from repeated attacks by its Russian minority shareholder, Tyumen Oil Co.

A local administrator in Siberia yesterday decided to give Yugraneft's corporate seal to Tyumen, allowing it to take control of the company's bank accounts and other assets. "It allows them to go to the bank, take the money, and do anything they want," said Alex Rotzang, president of Calgary-based Norex Petroleum Ltd., which says it owns 98 percent of Yugraneft.

Tyumen, part of the powerful Alfa Group empire of Moscow, deployed about 20 heavily armed men in a military-style operation to seize Yugraneft's headquarters in the Siberian city of Nizhnevartovsk on June 29, citing a court order that the Canadians have disputed. The Russians then dispatched other gunmen to seize Yugraneft's oil field, about 90 kilometres away.

The Canadian embassy in Moscow has sharply protested the takeover, calling it "an illegal confiscation of assets" and "a major negative signal to Canadian and foreign investors."

Norex Petroleum says it rehabilitated the Yugraneft oil field at considerable expense in the early 1990s, and it now produces about 10,000 barrels of oil a day. It has been taking legal action to seek about $50 million from Tyumen to compensate for oil deliveries that it says it was never paid for.

But Tyumen organized a shareholders' meeting last month, without any Norex representatives, and appointed its own managers to take control of Yugraneft. The Canadian embassy says the shareholders' meeting was "fraudulent."

After the takeover, Norex obtained a court order to remove the armed men. It also received a letter from a prosecutor who said the shareholders' meeting was illegal.

Tyumen, however, simply removed one set of security guards and installed a new team. "They have over 1,000 armed men around the city," Mr. Rotzang said. "That's more than the police have."

Yesterday Tyumen won its biggest victory when the local administrator gave it control of the Yugraneft corporate seal, allowing the Russians to gain access to about $30 million in the company's bank accounts.

Mr. Rotzang calls it robbery. "I feel awful about it," he said. "We showed him all the documents, he knows the local prosecutor's opinion, he promised he wouldn't allow it, and then he turned around and did this."

Other asset-stripping moves could follow. The newly installed manager has already tried to sell Yugraneft oil to Tyumen at about one-third of the normal price. The pipeline company refused to send the oil at the below-market price, but after yesterday's move it might have no choice.

The chairman of Tyumen, Sergei Sobyanin, is the powerful governor of the oil-rich Tyumen Region. He enjoys considerable influence over the courts and police forces in his region, including those who acted in the Yugraneft case, Mr. Rotzang noted. "Wouldn't you see a conflict of interest in this situation?"

For its part, Tyumen says it owns 40 percent of Yugraneft, not the 2 percent that Norex says it owns. "We discovered that Yugraneft was being run as if it was completely owned by Norex," Tyumen spokesman Dmitry Ivanov told the English-language *Moscow Times* last week. "We approached Norex. They didn't want to work with us. We took action."

Tyumen has a long history of battles with foreign investors, including Canadians. In 1996, it won control of the oil field licences of Vancouver-based Ivanhoe Energy Inc., which denounced it as an illegal takeover. Ivanhoe eventually accepted about $29 million in compensation but analysts said it had invested about $60 million in the project.

Source: Reprinted with permission from *The Globe and Mail*.

24.5   SUMMARY

1. What is the difference between spot and forward exchange rates?

The exchange rate is the amount of one currency needed to purchase one unit of another currency. The **spot rate of exchange** is the exchange rate for an immediate transaction. The **forward rate** is the exchange rate for a forward transaction, that is, a transaction at a specified future date.

2. What are the basic relationships between spot exchange rates, forward exchange rates, interest rates, and inflation rates?

To produce order out of chaos, the international financial manager needs some model of the relationships between exchange rates, interest rates, and inflation rates. Four very simple theories prove useful:

- In its strictest form, **purchasing power parity** states that $1 must have the same purchasing power in every country. You only need to take a vacation abroad to know that this doesn't square well with the facts. Nevertheless, *on average*, changes in exchange rates match differences in inflation rates, and if you need a long-term forecast of the exchange rate, it is difficult to do much better than to assume that the exchange rate will offset the effect of any differences in the inflation rates.

- In an open world-capital market, *real* rates of interest would have to be the same. Thus differences in *nominal* interest rates result from differences in expected inflation rates. The **international Fisher effect** suggests that firms should not simply borrow where interest rates are lowest. Those countries are also likely to have the lowest inflation rates and the strongest currencies.

- **Interest rate parity theory** states that the interest differential between two countries must be equal to the difference between the forward and spot exchange rates. In the international markets, arbitrage ensures that parity almost always holds.

- The **expectations theory of exchange rates** tells us that the forward rate equals the expected spot rate (though it is very far from being a perfect forecaster of the spot rate).

3. **What are some simple strategies to protect the firm against exchange rate risk?**

Our simple theories about forward rates have two practical implications for the problem of hedging overseas operations. First, the expectations theory suggests that hedging exchange risk is on average cost free. Second, there are two ways to hedge against exchange risk—one is to buy or sell currency forward, the other is to lend or borrow abroad. Interest rate parity tells us that the cost of the two methods should be the same.

4. **How do we perform an NPV analysis for projects with cash flows in foreign currencies?**

Overseas investment decisions are no different in principle from domestic decisions. You need to forecast the project's cash flows and then discount them at the opportunity cost of capital. But it is important to remember that if the opportunity cost of capital is stated in dollars, the cash flows must also be converted to dollars. This requires a forecast of foreign exchange rates. We suggest that you rely on the simple parity relationships and use the interest rate differential to produce these forecasts. In international capital budgeting, the return that shareholders require from foreign investments must be estimated. Adding a premium for the "extra risks," such as political risk, of overseas investment is not a good solution.

Related Web Links

www.stls.frb.org The Federal Reserve Bank of St. Louis Web site, good source of exchange rate data

www.globalfindata.com Good data source for major currencies

www.ny.frb.org Federal Reserve Bank of New York; forward exchange rates for the yen and euro, and other data

www.corporateinformation.com For data on overseas companies and useful links to finance-related sites for each country

www.prsgroup.com For estimates of the political risk of different countries

www.cme.com/trading/prd/about_EC2465.html The Chicago Mercantile Exchange's information centre on managing European foreign exchange risk with euro futures and options contracts

www.bloomberg.com/markets Data on current exchange rates as well as securities

www.global-investor.com Provides financial information and resources including information on international markets

www.emgmkts.com/index.htm Analysis of economic, political, and financial events in emerging markets

www.jpmorgan.com/fm/cs?pagename=chase/Href&uriname=jpmorgan/research/emergingmarkets Information about emerging markets

www.florin.com/v4/valore4.html Issues in currency risk management

www.globeandmail.ca *The Globe and Mail* Web site

http://news.ft.com *Financial Times* Web site

http://cibs.sauder.ubc.ca Foreign exchange data, teaching- and research-related information from the Centre for International Business Studies, Sauder School of Business, University of British Columbia

Key Terms

Questions and Problems

*Answers in Appendix B

BASIC

EXCEL

*1. **Exchange Rates.** Use Table 24.1 to answer these questions:
   a. How many euros can you buy for $100? How many dollars can you buy for 100 euros?
   b. How many Swiss francs can you buy for $100? How many dollars can you buy for 100 Swiss francs?
   c. If the euro depreciates with respect to the dollar, will the direct exchange rate quoted in Table 24.1 increase or decrease? What about the indirect exchange rate?
   d. Is a United States or an Australian dollar worth more?

2. **Exchange Rate Relationships.** Look at Table 24.1.
   a. How many Japanese yen do you get for your dollar?
   b. What is the 12-month forward rate for the yen?
   c. Is the yen at a forward discount or premium on the dollar?
   d. Calculate the annual percentage discount or premium on the yen.
   e. If the interest rate on dollars is 3.5 percent, what do you think is the interest rate on yen?
   f. According to the expectations theory, what is the expected spot rate for the yen in one year's time?
   g. According to purchasing power parity, what is the expected difference in the rate of price inflation in Canada and Japan?

3. **Exchange Rate Relationships.** Define each of the following theories in a sentence or simple equation:
   a. Interest rate parity theory
   *b. Expectations theory of forward rates
   c. Law of one price
   *d. International Fisher effect (relationship between interest rates in different countries)

4. **International Capital Budgeting.** Which of the following items do you need if you do all your capital budgeting calculations in your own currency?
   a. Forecasts of future exchange rates
   b. Forecasts of the foreign inflation rate
   c. Forecasts of the domestic inflation rate
   d. Foreign interest rates
   e. Domestic interest rates

5. **Foreign Currency Management.** Rosetta Stone, the treasurer of International Reprints, Inc., has noticed that the interest rate in Switzerland is below the rates in most other countries. She is therefore suggesting that the company should make an issue of Swiss franc bonds. What considerations should she first take into account?

*6. **Hedging Exchange Rate Risk.** An importer in Canada is due to take delivery of silk scarves from Europe in six months. The price is fixed in euros. Which of the following transactions could eliminate the importer's exchange risk?
   a. Buy euros forward.
   b. Sell euros forward.
   c. Borrow euros, buy dollars at the spot exchange rate.
   d. Sell euros at the spot exchange rate, lend dollars.

7. **Currency Risk.** Sanyo produces audio and video consumer goods and exports a large fraction of its output to the United States under its own name and the Fisher brand name. It prices its products in yen, meaning that it seeks to maintain a fixed price in terms of yen. Suppose the yen moves from ¥110.64/U.S.$ to ¥105/U.S.$. What currency risk does Sanyo face? How can it reduce its exposure?

*8. **Managing Exchange Rate Risk.** A firm in the United States is due to receive payment of 1 million Australian dollars in 8 years' time. It would like to protect itself against a decline in the value of the Australian dollar but finds it difficult to arrange a forward sale for such a long period. Is there any other way that it can protect itself?

9. **Interest Rate Parity.** The following table shows interest rates and exchange rates for the U.S. dollar and Mexican peso. The spot exchange rate is 9.5 pesos per U.S. dollar. Complete the missing entries:

	1 Month	1 Year
U.S. dollar interest rate (annually compounded)	5.5%	7%
Peso interest rate (annually compounded)	20%	—
Forward pesos per U.S. dollar	—	11.2

Hint: When calculating the 1-month forward rate, remember to translate the annual interest rate into a monthly interest rate.

*10. **Exchange Rate Risk.** An American investor buys 100 shares of London Enterprises at a price of £50 when the exchange rate is U.S.$1.60/£. A year later the shares are selling at £52. No dividends have been paid.
a. What is the rate of return to an American investor if the exchange rate is still U.S.$1.60/£?
b. What if the exchange rate is U.S.$1.70/£?
c. What if the exchange rate is U.S.$1.50/£?

*11. **Interest Rate Parity.** Look at Table 24.1. If the 3-month interest rate on dollars is 6 percent (annualized), what do you think is the 3-month sterling (U.K.) interest rate? Explain what would happen if the rate were substantially above your figure. Hint: In your calculations remember to convert the annually compounded interest rate into a rate for three months.

12. **Expectations Theory.** Table 24.1 shows the 12-month forward rate on the U.S. dollar.
a. Is the U.S. dollar at a forward discount or a premium on the Canadian dollar?
b. What is the annualized percentage discount or premium?
c. If you have no other information about the two currencies, what is your best guess about the spot rate in one year?
d. Suppose that you expect to receive 100,000 U.S. dollars in 1 year. How many Canadian dollars is this likely to be worth?

EXCEL

13. **Interest Rate Parity.** Suppose the interest rate on 1-year loans in the United States is 5 percent while in the United Kingdom the interest rate is 6 percent. The spot exchange rate is U.S.$1.55/£ and the forward rate is U.S.$1.54/£. In what country would you choose to borrow? To lend? Can you profit from this situation?

*14. **Purchasing Power Parity.** Suppose that the inflation rate in the United States is 4 percent and in Canada it is 5 percent. What would you expect is happening to the exchange rate between the United States and Canadian dollars?

15. **Cross Rates.** Look at Table 24.1. How many Swiss francs can you buy for $1? How many yen can you buy? What rate do you think a Japanese bank would quote for buying or selling Swiss francs? Explain what would happen if it quoted a rate that was substantially less than your figure.

*16. **International Capital Budgeting.** Suppose that you apply your own views about exchange rates when valuing an overseas investment proposal. Specifically, suppose that you believe that the leo will depreciate by 2 percent per year. Recalculate the NPV of KW's project.

17. **Currency Risk.** You have bid for a possible export order that would provide a cash inflow of €1 million in 6 months. The spot exchange rate is €.687/$ and the 12-month forward rate is €.691/$. There are two sources of uncertainty: (1) the euro could appreciate or depreciate, and (2) you may or may not receive the export order. Illustrate in each case the profits or losses that you would make if you sell €1 million forward by filling in the following table. Assume that the exchange rate in 1 year will be either €.65/$ or €.74/$.

	Profit/Loss	
Spot Rate	**Receive Order**	**Lose Order**
€.65/$	_____	_____
€.74/$	_____	_____

18. **Managing Currency Risk.** General Gadget Corp. (GGC) is a Canada-based multinational firm that makes electrical coconut scrapers. These gadgets are made only in Canada using local inputs. The scrapers are sold mainly to Asian and West Indian countries where coconuts are grown.
    a. If GGC sells scrapers in Trinidad, what is the currency risk faced by the firm?
    b. In what currency should GGC borrow funds to pay for its investment in order to mitigate its foreign exchange exposure?
    c. Suppose that GGC begins manufacturing its products in Trinidad using local (Trinidadian) inputs and labour. How does this affect its exchange rate risk?

19. **Currency Risk.** If investors recognize the impacts of inflation and exchange rate changes on a firm's cash flows, changes in exchange rates should be reflected in stock prices. How would the stock price of each of the following Swiss companies be affected by an unanticipated appreciation in the Swiss franc of 10 percent, only 2 percent of which could be justified by comparing Swiss inflation to that in the rest of the world?
    a. *Swiss Air:* More than two-thirds of its employees are Swiss. Most revenues come from international fares set in U.S. dollars.
    b. *Nestlé:* Fewer than 5 percent of its employees are Swiss. Most revenues are derived from sales of consumer goods in a wide range of countries with competition from local producers.
    c. *Union Bank of Switzerland:* Most employees are Swiss. All non–Swiss franc monetary positions are fully hedged.

20. **Internet.** The *Financial Times* maintains a "special reports" Web site on the euro: **http://specials.ft.com/euro/index.html**. Go to the site and trace the chronology of events that led to the European Monetary Union and the creation of this single currency.

21. **Internet.** The euro has replaced 12 national currencies. Return to the Web site from the previous problem and list these 12 countries. What is the permanent conversion rate of the euro against these eurozone currencies?

22. **Internet.** Go to **http://cibs.sauder.ubc.ca**, the Web site of the Centre for International Business Studies, Sauder School of Business, University of British Columbia. Can you retrieve information on the most recent purchasing-power parity rates for all of the OECD countries?

23. **Internet.** There are plenty of good sites that show current and past spot rates of exchange. For example, for current spot rates look at **www.international.nasdaq.com**. Forward rates are less easy to come by, but the New York Fed Web site **www.ny.frb.org** shows forward rates for the yen and euro. Can you deduce from these whether the interest rate is higher in the United States than in Europe or Japan (warning: look out for the difference

between direct and indirect quotes)? Here is a more tricky problem: can you work out from these rates whether Japan has a higher interest rate than Europe?

24. **Internet.** The Organization for Economic Cooperation and Development (OECD) provides data on nominal and effective (i.e., real) exchange rates. Log in to **www.oecd.org** and then click on "Statistics and On-Line Databases." You need the tables on interest rates and exchange rates. Look at the effective exchange rate for the dollar against other currencies. Has the U.S. dollar been appreciating or declining in real terms? Is this helping or hurting U.S. exporters? Which country has experienced the sharpest fall in the real value of its currency?

25. **Standard & Poor's.** Go to **www.mhhe.com/edumarketinsight**. In August 2004, a Japanese investor bought 2,000 shares of Magna International, Inc. (MG.MV.B), for $80 through his Toronto-based broker. What is the return over the latest calendar year on his investment in Canadian dollar and in Japanese yen? What has been the percentage change in the yen/dollar exchange rate over the 1-year period since he made his investment? (Review the Monthly Valuation Data from Market Insight. To obtain dollar/yen exchange rates, go to **http://www.bank-banque-canada.ca/en/exchange.htm**).

CHALLENGE

26. **International Capital Budgeting.** A Canadian firm is evaluating an investment in Indonesia. The project costs 500 billion Indonesian rupiah and it is expected to produce an income of 250 billion Indonesian rupiah a year in real terms for each of the next 3 years. The expected inflation rate in Indonesia is 12 percent per year and the firm estimates that an appropriate discount rate for the project would be about 8 percent above the risk-free rate of interest. Calculate the net present value of the project in dollars. Exchange rates are given in Table 24.1. The interest rate is about 15 percent in Indonesia and 5 percent in Canada.

27. **Hedging Exchange Rate Risk.** You have decided to purchase a deluxe condominium apartment in a newly built residential complex in South Florida. Your agreement with the real estate developer specifies that construction of the apartment will be completed and its keys will be handed to you three months from today. The purchase price is U.S.$200,000 to be paid at the time of possession. The current spot exchange rate is $1.3076/U.S.$ and the current 3-month forward rate is $1.3091/U.S.$.

You intend to pay for the apartment using your dollar savings from a bank account in Canada. These dollars are earning interest at 5 percent per annum in Canada. Interest rates in the United States are 3 percent per annum.

What options are available to you to pay for the condominium apartment if you want to avoid all foreign exchange risk associated with the transaction? Show which of the choices will work out best for you.

28. **Integrative.** Fleximetals Inc. of Canada is considering a capital investment in Zamboana. The currency of Zamboana is the Zamboa peso (symbol: Zp). Details regarding the project are provided below (all currency amounts are reported in the nearest thousands).

Initial Project Cost (in 2004): $3,500 (Zp7000) for plant and equipment and $250 (Zp500) for working capital.

Sales: 1st year = Zp13,000. It is expected to grow at 10 percent per annum over the next 3 years.

Costs: Variable costs will be 30 percent of sales, and fixed cash costs are Zp1,000 per year.

Working Capital: Gross working capital (i.e., cash, receivables and inventory) = 20 percent of sales. Half financed by local accruals and accounts payable, but other half financed externally.

Depreciation: Straight line over three years. No salvage value.

Taxes: Income taxes are 30 percent in both Zamboana and Canada.

Liquidation Values: (after 3 years) Zp5,000 (free of all Zamboana and Canadian taxes).

Weighted Average Cost of Capital (WACC): The WACC used in Zamboana and Canada for projects of this type is 18 percent.

Exchange Rate in 2004: Zp/$ is 2.0 and is expected to increase by 10 percent in each subsequent year.

Assume that 50 percent of the project's net income after taxes are remitted to the Canadian parent company as dividend.

a. Compute the net present value of the project from the point of view of the affiliate in Zamboana as well as the parent in Canada.

b. Is the project acceptable under both circumstances? If not, briefly comment on factors to be considered in the decision process.

Solutions to Check Points

24.1   Direct quote: $1.6125/€

Indirect quote: 1/1.6125 = €.6202/$

Direct quote: $.011818

Indirect quote: 1/.011818 = ¥84.62/$

24.2   The dollar buys more Swiss francs, so the franc has depreciated with respect to the dollar.

24.3   a. $1,500 × 1.0515 = $1,577.25 using the direct (i.e., $/SFr) quote. Using the indirect quote, we get $1,500/.9510 = $1,577.25.

b. (1) Direct exchange rate: SFr1 = 1.0515/.9 = $1.1683
    (2) Indirect exchange rate: $1 = .9 × .9510 = .8559 francs

c. 1,500 × 1.1683 = $1,752.45

d. 1,577.25/1.1683 = 1,350 francs

24.4   a. £220 = $330. Therefore £1 = 330/220 = $1.50.

b. In the United States, price = $330 × 1.02 = $336.60. In the United Kingdom, price = £220 × 1.05 = £231. The new exchange rate = $336.60/£231 = $1.457/£.

c. Initially $1 buys 1/1.50 = £.667. At the end of the year, $1 buys 1/1.457 = £.686, which is about 3 percent higher than the original value of £.667.

24.5   The real interest rate in Canada is 1.03/1.01 − 1 = .01, or 1%. If the real rate is the same in Indonesia, then expected inflation must be

$$(1 + \text{nominal rate})/(1 + \text{real rate}) − 1 = 1.08/1.01 − 1 = .069, \text{ or } 6.9\%.$$

24.6   The pound is at a forward discount (that is, you get more pounds for $1, or conversely, fewer dollars for £1 in the forward market). This implies that the interest rates in Great Britain are higher than those in Canada.

The interest rate in Canada is 3 percent. Interest rate parity states

$$(1 + r_£)/(1+ r_\$)=f_{£/\$}/s_{£/\$}$$

Therefore, $r_£ = 1.03 × (.4260/.4158) − 1 = .055$, or 5.5%.

24.7   Stellar borrows ¥100 million in 1998. It pays ¥2 million in interest at the end of 1999, when it also repays the loan. Cash flows in U.S. dollars are

1998: $\dfrac{100 \text{ million}}{123.97}$ =   U.S.$806,647

1999:   Interest $=\dfrac{2 \text{ million}}{107.52}$ = $18,601

$$\text{Principal} = \frac{100 \text{ million}}{107.52} = \qquad \$930{,}060$$

$$\text{Total} \qquad = \qquad \text{U.S.}\$948{,}661$$

To find the U.S. dollar interest rate, solve

$$806{,}647 \times (1 + r_{\text{U.S.\$}}) = 948{,}661$$

$$r_{\text{U.S.\$}} = \frac{948{,}661}{806{,}647} - 1 = .176 = 17.6\%$$

24.8 If you buy yen in the forward market, you will exchange ¥108.21 per U.S. dollar in 1 year. Suppose instead that you borrow US $1, convert the dollar to ¥110.64 in the spot market, and invest the funds in Japan. You will have to repay the U.S. dollar loan with 2 percent interest and will earn 0.33 percent interest on your yen investment. Therefore, in 1 year, you will receive ¥110.64 × 1.0033 = ¥110.36, but will have to pay US $1.02. This is effectively an exchange rate of ¥110.36 for US $1.02, corresponding to a forward exchange rate of ¥110.36/US$1.02 = ¥108.2, which except for minor rounding error matches the rate in the forward market.

24.9 According to the expectations theory of exchange rates, the forward rate equals the expected future spot exchange rate. Therefore, the expected cost of the hedge—the difference between the forward rate and expected spot rate is zero!

24.10 a. The lower interest rate in Narnia than in Canada suggests that forecast inflation is lower in Narnia. If real interest rates are the same in the two countries, then the difference in inflation rates is about $5 - 3 = 2$ percent.

b. The lower interest rate (and lower expected inflation rate) in Narnia suggests that investors are expecting the leo to appreciate against the dollar.

c. Since KW can now expect to change its leo cash flows into more dollars than before, the project's NPV is increased. Forecast exchange rates will be as follows:

Year	Forecast Exchange Rate
0	Spot exchange rate = L2.0/$
1	$2.0 \times (1.03/1.05)$ = L1.962/$
2	$2.0 \times (1.03/1.05)^2$ = L1.925/$
3	$2.0 \times (1.03/1.05)^3$ = L1.888/$
4	$2.0 \times (1.03/1.05)^4$ = L1.852/$
5	$2.0 \times (1.03/1.05)^5$ = L1.817/$

The expected dollar cash flows from the project are

Year	0	1	2	3	4	5
Cash flow	−7.6	2.0	2.5	3.0	3.5	4.0
(millions	2.00	1.962	1.925	1.888	1.852	1.817
of dollars)	= −$3.8	= $1.02	= $1.30	= $1.59	= $1.89	= $2.20

Discounting these dollar cash flows at the 15 percent dollar cost of capital gives

$$\text{NPV} = -3.8 + \frac{1.02}{1.15} + \frac{1.30}{1.15^2} + \frac{1.59}{1.15^3} + \frac{1.89}{1.15^4} + \frac{2.20}{1.15^5}$$

$$= \$1.29 \text{ million, or } \$1{,}290{,}000$$

The project is worth more because the reduced interest rate in Narnia suggests that investors expect the leo to appreciate in value. Thus the dollar cash flows from the project are higher than in Section 24.4.

MINICASE

"Jumping jackasses! Not another one!" groaned Mike Luger. This was the third memo he had received that morning from the CEO of VCR Importers. It read as follows:

From: CEO's Office
To: Company Treasurer

Mike,

I have been looking at some of our foreign exchange deals and they don't seem to make sense.

First, we have been buying yen forward to cover the cost of our imports. You have explained that this insures us against the risk that the dollar may depreciate over the next year, but it is incredibly expensive insurance. Each dollar buys only 120.63 yen when we buy forward, compared with the current spot rate of 123.38 yen to the dollar. We could save a fortune by buying yen as and when we need them rather than buying them forward.

Another possibility has occurred to me. If we are worried that the dollar may depreciate (or do I mean "appreciate"?), why don't we buy yen at the low spot rate of ¥123.38 to the dollar and then put them on deposit until we have to pay for the VCRs? That way we can make sure we get a good rate for our yen.

I am also worried that we are missing out on some cheap financing. We are paying about 8 percent to borrow dollars for one year, but Ben Hur was telling me at lunch that we could get a 1-year yen loan for about 1.75 percent. I find that a bit surprising, but if that's the case, why don't we repay our dollar loans and borrow yen instead?

Perhaps we could discuss these ideas at next Wednesday's meeting. I would be interested in your views on the matter.

Jill Edison

OPTIONS

When the Chicago Board Options Exchange (CBOE) was established in 1973, few observers guessed what a success it would be. By creating standardized, listed stock options, the CBOE revolutionized options trading. Today the CBOE is the world's largest options exchange, each year trading options to buy or sell more than 30 billion shares of stock in 1,500 companies. Other exchanges around the world have copied the CBOE model, and in addition to options on individual stocks, options can be traded on stock indexes, bonds, commodities, and foreign exchanges. For example, options on Canadian stocks and bonds are traded on the Bourse de Montréal, home of the Canadian Derivatives Exchange, **www.m-x.ca**.

You will see that options can be valuable tools for managing the risk characteristics of an investment portfolio. But why should the financial manager of an industrial company read further? There are several reasons. First, most capital budgeting projects have options embedded in them that allow the company to expand at a future date or to bail out. These options allow the company to profit if things go well but give downside protection when they don't.

Second, many of the securities that firms issue include an option. For example, companies often issue convertible bonds. The holder has the option to exchange the bond for common stock. Some corporate bonds also contain a call provision, meaning that the issuer has the option to buy back the bond from the investor.

Finally, managers routinely use currency, commodity, and interest rate options to protect the firm against a variety of risks. (We will have more to say about this in Chapter 26.)

In one chapter we can provide you with only a brief introduction to options. Our first goal in this chapter is to explain how options work and how option value is determined. Then we will tell you how to recognize some of the options that crop up in capital investment proposals and in company financing.

After studying this chapter you should be able to
- Calculate the payoff to buyers and sellers of call and put options.
- Understand the determinants of option values.
- Recognize options in capital investment proposals.
- Identify options that are provided in financial securities.

25.1   CALLS AND PUTS

call option Right to buy an asset at a specified exercise price on or before the exercise date.

A **call option** gives its holder the right to buy stock for a fixed *exercise price* (also called the *strike price*) on or before a specified exercise date.[1] For example, if you buy a call option on IBM that has an expiration date in October and an exercise price of $100, you have the right to buy shares of IBM at a price of $100 at any time until October.

You need not exercise a call option; it will be profitable to do so only if the share price exceeds the exercise price. If it does not, the option will be left unexercised and will prove to be valueless. But suppose IBM shares are selling above the $100 exercise price, say at $120, just before the call option expires. You will choose to exercise your option to pay $100 to buy shares worth $120. Your net proceeds upon exercise equal the difference between the $100 paid and the $120 you can realize for the shares. More generally, the proceeds would equal the difference between the stock price and the exercise price.

In summary, the value of the call option at expiration is as follows:

Stock Price at Expiration	Value of Call at Expiration
Greater than exercise price	Stock price – exercise price
Less than exercise price	Zero

Of course, the ultimate value of the option is not all profit: You have to pay for the option. The price of the call is called the option *premium*. Option buyers pay the premium for the right to exercise later. Your profit equals the ultimate payoff to the call option (which may be zero) minus the initial premium.

EXAMPLE 25.1   **CALL OPTIONS ON ATI TECHNOLOGIES**

On January 14, 2005, a call option on ATI Technologies (ATI) common shares with an April 2005 expiration and an exercise price of $22 per share sold for $1.85. If you had purchased the call on this date, you would have had the right to purchase shares of ATI for $22 any time until the option expired in April. On January 14, ATI shares sold for $21.95. Immediate exercise of the call would have resulted in net proceeds of $21.95 – $22 = –$.05. Obviously, anyone who paid $1.85 for the call on January 14 had no intention of exercising it immediately. A buyer of the call was betting on an increase in the stock price, which would make the option turn out to be a profitable investment. For example, if ATI sold in April for $25, the proceeds from exercising the call would have been

$$\text{Proceeds} = \text{stock price} - \text{exercise price} = \$25 - \$22 = \$3.00$$

and the net profit on the call would have been

$$\text{Profits} = \text{proceeds} - \text{original investment} = \$3.00 - \$1.85 = \$1.15$$

In 6 months, you would have earned a return of $1.15/$1.85 = .62, or 62 percent.

---

put option Right to sell an asset at a specified exercise price on or before the exercise date.

Whereas a call option gives you the right to buy a share of stock, a **put option** gives you the right to sell it for the exercise price. If you hold a put on a share of stock and the stock price turns out to be greater than the exercise price, you will not want to exercise your option to sell the shares for the exercise price. The put will be left unexercised and will expire valueless. But if the stock price turns out to be less than the exercise price, it will pay to buy the share at the low price and then exercise your option to sell it for the exercise price. The put would then be worth the difference between the exercise price and the stock price.

---

[1] In some cases, the option can be exercised only on one particular day, which is conventionally known as a *European call;* in other cases, it can be exercised on or before that day, which is called an *American call.*

TABLE 25.1
How the value of an ATI
option on its expiration
date varies with the price
of stock on that data
(exercise price = $22)

Stock Price	$19	$20	$21	$22	$23	$24	$25
Call value	0	0	0	0	$1	$2	$3
Put value	$3	$2	$1	0	0	0	0

EXAMPLE 25.2   **PUT OPTIONS ON ATI TECHNOLOGIES**

On January 14, 2005, it cost $1.65 to buy a put option on ATI common shares with a April 2005 expiration and an exercise price of $22. Suppose ATI is selling for $19 just before the put option expires. Then if you hold a put, you can buy a share of stock for $19 and exercise your right to sell it for $22. The put will be worth $22 – $19 = $3. Because you paid $1.65 for the put originally, your net profit is $1.35. If, however, the stock price is above $22 on the maturity date, you will let the put option expire worthless. Your loss equals the $1.65 you originally spent to purchase the put.

In general, the value of the put option at expiration is as follows:

Stock Price at Expiration	Value of Put Option at Expiration
Greater than exercise price	Zero
Less than exercise price	Exercise price – stock price

Table 25.1 shows how the values of ATI calls and puts are affected by the level of the ATI stock price on the expiration date. You can see that once the stock price is above the exercise price, the call value rises dollar for dollar with the stock price, and once the stock price is below the exercise price, the put value rises a dollar for each dollar *decrease* in the stock price. Figure 25.1 plots the values of each option on the expiration date, for various possible stock prices.

Figure 25.2 is an excerpt of listed stock quotations from *The Globe and Mail* showing options on shares of ATI. The value $21.95, next to the stock name ATI Tech, is the current price of the stock. In the column below the stock name is the expiration month for each option.[2] Next to the expiration month is the exercise price of the option. If the exercise price has the letter "p" next to it, the option is a put; otherwise, the option is a call. The next two numbers in the row are the

FIGURE 25.1
Values of call options and
put options on ATI stock
on option expiration date
(exercise price = $22)

---

[2] For the Bourse de Montréal, the expiry date is the Saturday following the last trading day of the expiration month. The last trading day is the third Friday of the expiration month, providing it is a business day; if not, the first preceding business day. These details vary among the options exchanges.

FIGURE 25.2
Prices of options on shares
of ATI Technologies,
January 14, 2005

| Stock | | Close | | Total Vol | Total O.I. |
Series	Bid	Ask	Last	Vol	Op. Int.
ATI Tech		$21.95		493	9381
Jan05 20.00	2.00	2.15	2.15	95	385
22.00	0.40	0.50	0.50	15	1037
22.00p	0.35	0.40	0.40	100	561
24.00p	1.90	2.00	2.00	34	166
Feb05 20.00p	0.20	0.35	0.35	10	75
22.00	1.00	1.10	1.10	15	211
24.00	0.35	0.40	0.40	46	264
24.00p	2.20	2.30	2.30	24	35
26.00	0.05	0.16	0.15	20	35
Apr05 19.00p	0.45	0.60	0.60	10	80
20.00	2.90	3.05	3.05	3	195
20.00p	0.75	0.85	0.85	2	94
22.00	1.75	1.85	1.85	30	432
22.00p	1.55	1.65	1.65	50	139
24.00	0.95	1.05	1.05	13	548
24.00p	2.70	2.85	2.85	10	44
Jul05 24.00	1.60	1.75	1.75	17	78

Source: Reprinted with permission from *The Globe and Mail.*

bid and ask prices for the option at the market close.[3] The next number is the price of the last trade of the day. The final two numbers on the line are the volume of option contracts traded during the day and open interest.[4] Looking back at the first line of the listing, you will see the total trading volume and open interest for all of the ATI equity options for the day.

You can see from the listings that for any particular maturity calls are worth more when the exercise price is lower, while puts are worth more when the exercise price is higher. This makes sense: You would rather have the right to buy at a low price and the right to sell at high price. Notice also that for any particular exercise price, the longer-dated options are the most valuable. This also makes sense. An option that expires in July 2005 gives you everything that a shorter-dated option offers and more. Naturally, you would be prepared to pay for the chance of keeping your options open for as long as possible.

Check Point 25.1

a. What will be the proceeds and net profits (i.e., net of the option premium) to an investor who purchases the April-maturity ATI call options with exercise price of $24 if the stock price at maturity is $18? What if the stock price at maturity is $30? Use the price of the last trade of the day in Figure 25.2.

b. Now answer part (a) for an investor who purchases a April-maturity ATI put option with exercise price $24.

SELLING CALLS AND PUTS

The traded options that you see quoted in the financial pages are not sold by the companies themselves but by other investors. If one investor buys an option on ATI stock, some other investor must be on the other side of the bargain. We will look now at the position of the investor who sells an option.[5]

---

[3] The bid price is the price at which an options dealer is willing to buy the option; the ask price is the price at which the dealer is willing to sell. The dealer gets the difference between bid and ask prices, the bid-ask spread, as compensation for his willingness to engage in trading of the options. On the other hand, an ordinary investor, thinking of buying an option, pays the ask price when buying and receives the bid price when selling.

[4] Volume is reported as the number of option contracts traded. Each contract is for 100 shares of stock. For example, if a call price is reported as $2, you would pay $200 to buy one contract, which would give you the right to buy 100 shares of stock. You would pay the exercise price for each share. Open interest is the number of option contracts outstanding at the end of the day.

[5] The option seller is known as the *writer*.

We have already seen that the April-maturity ATI calls with exercise price $22 are trading at $1.85. Thus if you *sell* the April call option on ATI stock, the buyer pays you $1.85. However, in return you promise to *sell* ATI shares at a price of $22 if the call buyer decides to exercise his option. The option seller's obligation to sell ATI is just the other side of the coin to the option holder's right to *buy* the stock. The buyer *pays* the option premium for the right to exercise; the seller *receives* the premium but may be required at a later date to deliver the stock for an exercise price that is less than the market price of the stock. If the share price is below the exercise price of $22 when the option expires in April, holders of the call will not exercise their option, and you, the seller, will have no further liability. However, if the price of ATI is greater than $22, it will pay the option holder to exercise, and you must give up your shares for $22 each. You lose the difference between the share price and the $22 that you receive from the buyer.

Suppose that ATI's stock price turns out to be $25. In this case the buyer will exercise the call option and will pay $22 for stock that can be resold for $25. The buyer therefore has a payoff of $3—not bad on an investment of only $1.85. Of course, that positive payoff for the *buyer* means a negative payoff for you, the *seller*, for you are obliged to sell ATI stock worth $25 for only $22.

In general, the seller's loss is the buyer's gain, and vice versa. Figure 25.3a shows the payoffs to the call option seller. Note that Figure 25.3a is just Figure 25.1a drawn upside down.

The position of an investor who sells the ATI put option can be shown in just the same way by standing Figure 25.1b on its head. The put *buyer* has the right to sell a share for $22; so the *seller* of the put has agreed to pay $22 for the share if the put buyer should demand it. Clearly the seller will be safe as long as the share price remains above $22, but will lose money if the share price falls below this figure. The worst thing that can happen to the put seller is for the stock to be worthless. The seller would then be obliged to pay $22 for a worthless stock. The payoff to the seller would be –$22. Note that the advantage always lies with the option buyer, the obligation with the seller. Therefore, the buyer must pay the seller to acquire the option.

> The purchaser of an option has the right to buy or sell an asset at a fixed and possibly advantageous price. The option seller is obliged to sell or buy at this price if the buyer wants to exercise. The option buyer pays the seller to take on this obligation.

Table 25.2 summarizes the rights and obligation of buyers and sellers of calls and puts.

Check Point 25.2

a. What will be the proceeds and net profits to an investor who sells the April-maturity ATI call options with exercise price $24 if the stock price at maturity is $18? What if the stock price at maturity is $30? Use the price of the last trade of the day in Figure 25.2.

b. Now answer part (a) for an investor who sells an April-maturity ATI put option with exercise price $24.

FIGURE 25.3
Payoffs to sellers of call and put options on ATI stock (exercise price = $22)

TABLE 25.2
Rights and obligations of
various options positions

	Buyer	Seller
Call option	Right to buy asset	Obligation to sell asset
Put option	Right to sell asset	Obligation to buy asset

FINANCIAL ALCHEMY WITH OPTIONS

Options can be used to modify the risk characteristics of a portfolio. Suppose, for example, that you are generally optimistic about ATI's prospects, but you understand that a large investment in the stock is a risk and would cause you to have sleepless nights. Here is a strategy that might appeal to you: Buy the stock, but also buy a put option on the stock with exercise price $22. If the stock price rises, your put turns out to be worthless, but you win on the stock investment. If the stock price falls, your losses are limited, since the put gives you the right to sell the stock for the $22 exercise price. Thus the value of your stock-plus-put position cannot be less than $22.

Here is another way to view your overall position. You hold the stock and the put option. The value of each component of the portfolio will be as follows:

	Stock Price < $22	Stock Price ≥ $22
Value of stock	Stock price	Stock price
Value of put option	$22 – stock price	0
Total value	$22	Stock price

No matter how far the stock price falls, the total value of your portfolio cannot fall below the $22 exercise price.

The value of your position when the options expire is graphed in Figure 25.4. You have downside protection at $22 but still share in potential gains on the stock. This strategy is called a *protective put*, because the put option gives protection against losses. Of course, such protection is not free. Look again at Figure 25.2 and you will find the cost of such protection. "Stock price insurance" at a level of $22 between January 2005 and April 2005 cost $1.65 per share; this was the price of the put option with exercise price $22 and April expiration.

EXAMPLE 25.3   **PROFITING FROM VOLATILITY**

Suppose you believe that ATI is going to be subject to considerable volatility over the next few months. Perhaps a new product due to come to the market soon will be either a fabulous success or, if technological bugs cannot be overcome, a dismal failure. How can you bet on the expected volatility of the stock?

FIGURE 25.4
Payoff to protective put
strategy. If the ultimate stock
price exceeds $22, the put is
valueless but you own the
stock. If it is less than $22,
you can sell the stock for the
exercise price.

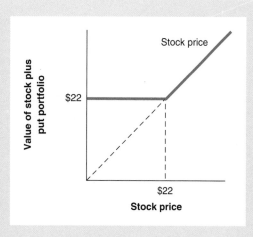

Try buying one call and one put option, both with exercise price $22. This position—holding a call and a put—is called a *straddle*. If the stock price falls, the put will be profitable; if the stock price rises, the call will be profitable. Figure 25.5 illustrates your position. The gold line is the value of the call. The blue line is the value of the put. You hold the call *and* the put, so the total value of your holdings is a V-shaped profile.

Of course, there is no free lunch here. Although the value of the position cannot be negative, remember that you have to pay to establish this position: You pay for both the call and the put. Unless the ultimate payoff exceeds the cost of the two options, you will lose money. Thus the *profit* on this strategy is given by the dashed V-shaped line in Figure 25.5. Unless the stock moves far enough that the profit on either the call or the put covers the initial cost of the two options, your profits will be negative.

Of course, there are many other interesting option strategies that one might envision. These instruments give you considerable leeway to tailor the risk features of a portfolio. Try your skill at financial alchemy with Check Point 25.3.

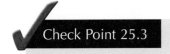

Check Point 25.3   What strategy using call options with different exercise prices can create a payoff that depends on the price of ATI stock in the manner depicted in Figure 25.6? What would it cost for this strategy, using the option price for April maturity options in Figure 25.2. Why might someone establish this position?

25.2   WHAT DETERMINES OPTION VALUES?

Figure 25.2 shows prices of different ATI options. But we have said nothing about how the market values of options are determined. It is time that we did so.

UPPER AND LOWER LIMITS ON OPTION VALUES

We know what an option is worth when it expires. Consider, for example, the option to buy stock at $30. If the stock price is below $30 at the expiration date, the call will be worthless; if the

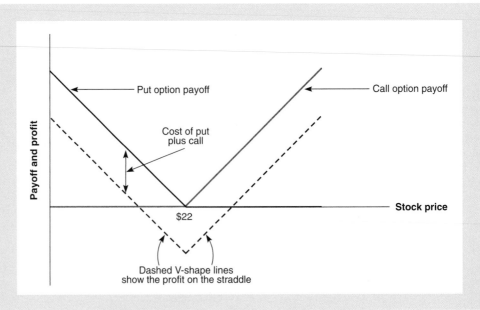

FIGURE 25.5
Payoff and profit on a straddle. Call option is drawn in gold, put option in blue.

FIGURE 25.6
This strategy provides a total payoff of $2 if the stock price is $22, and a payoff of zero if the stock price is either (a) $20 or less, or (b) $24 or more.

stock price is above $30, the call will be worth the value of the stock minus the $30 exercise price. The relationship is depicted by the heavy blue line in Figure 25.7.

Even before expiration, the price of the option can never remain *below* the heavy blue line in Figure 25.7. For example, if our option were priced at $5 and the stock at $40, it would pay any investor to buy the option, exercise it for an additional $30, and then sell the stock for $40. That would give a "money machine" with a profit of $40 − $35 = $5. Money machines can't last; the demand for options from investors using this strategy would quickly force the option price up at least to the heavy blue line in the figure. The heavy blue line is therefore a *lower* limit on the market price of the option. Thus

$$\text{Lower limit on value of call option} = \text{the greater of } zero \text{ or } (stock\ price - exercise\ price)$$

The diagonal gold line in Figure 25.7, which is the plot of the stock price, is the *upper* limit to the option price. Why? Because the stock itself gives a higher final payoff whatever happens. If when the option expires the stock price ends up above the exercise price, the option is worth

FIGURE 25.7
Value of a call before its expiration date (dashed line). The value depends on the stock price. The call is always worth more than its value if exercised now (heavy blue line). It is never worth more than the stock price itself.

the stock price *less* the exercise price. If the stock price ends up below the exercise price, the option is worthless, but the stock's owner still has a valuable security. Thus the extra payoff to holding the stock rather than the option is as follows:

Stock Price at Expiration	Stock Payoff	Option Payoff	Extra Payoff from Holding Stock Rather than Option
Greater than $30	Stock price	Stock price – $30	$30
Less than or equal to $30	Stock price	$0	Stock price

THE DETERMINANTS OF OPTION VALUE

The call option price must lie between the upper and lower limits in Figure 25.7. In fact, the price will lie on a curved, upward-sloping line like the dashed curve shown in the figure. This line begins its travels where the upper and lower bounds meet (at zero). Then it rises, gradually becoming parallel to the lower bound. This line tells us an important fact about option values: Given the exercise price, *the value of a call option increases as the stock price increases.*

That should be no surprise. Owners of call options clearly hope for the stock price to rise and are happy when it does. But let us look more carefully at the shape and location of the dashed line. Three points, *A, B,* and *C,* are marked on the dashed line. As we explain each point, you will see why the option price has to behave as the dashed line predicts.

Point A.   *When the stock is worthless, the option is worthless.* A stock price of zero means that there is no possibility the stock will ever have any future value.[6] If so, the option is sure to expire unexercised and worthless, and it is worthless today.

Point B.   *When the stock price becomes very high, the option price approaches the stock price less the present value of the exercise price.* Notice that the dashed line representing the option price in Figure 25.7 eventually becomes parallel to the ascending heavy blue line representing the lower bound on the option price. The reason is as follows. The higher the stock price, the greater the odds that the option will eventually be exercised. If the stock price is high enough, exercise becomes a virtual certainty; the probability that the stock price will fall below the exercise price before the option expires becomes trivial.

If you own an option that you *know* will be exchanged for a share of stock, you effectively own the stock now. The only difference is that you don't have to pay for the stock (by handing over the exercise price) until later, when formal exercise occurs. In these circumstances, buying the call is equivalent to buying the stock now with deferred payment and delivery. The value of the call is therefore equal to the stock price less the present value of the exercise price.[7]

This brings us to another important point about options. Investors who acquire stock by way of a call option are buying on "instalment credit." They pay the purchase price of the option today, but they do not pay the exercise price until they actually exercise the option. The delay in payment is particularly valuable if interest rates are high and the option has a long maturity. Thus *the value of a call option increases with both the rate of interest and the time to expiration.*

Check Point 25.4

How would the value of a put option be affected by an increase in the stock price? How would the value of a put option be affected by an increase in the exercise price? Explain.

---

[6] If a stock *can* be worth something in the future then investors will pay *something* for it today, although possibly a very small amount.

[7] We assume here that the stock pays no dividends until after the option matures. If dividends were paid, you *would* care about when you get to own the stock because the option holder misses out on any dividends.

Point C.   The option price always exceeds its minimum value (except at maturity or when stock price is zero). We have seen that the dashed and heavy lines in Figure 25.7 coincide when stock price is zero (point A), but elsewhere the lines diverge; that is, the option price must exceed the minimum value given by the heavy blue line. You can see why by examining point C.

At point *C,* the stock price exactly equals the exercise price. The option therefore would be worthless if it expired today. However, suppose that the option will not expire until 3 months hence. Of course, we do not know what the stock price will be at the expiration date. There is roughly a 50 percent chance that it will be higher than the exercise price, and a 50 percent chance that it will be lower. The possible payoffs to the option are therefore:

Outcome	Payoff
Stock price rises	Stock price – exercise price
(50 percent probability)	(option is exercised)
Stock price falls	Zero
(50 percent probability)	(option expires worthless)

If there is some chance of a positive payoff, and if the worst payoff is zero, then the option must be valuable. That means the option price at point *C* exceeds its lower bound, which at point *C* is zero. In general, the option price will exceed the lower bound as long as there is time left before expiration.

One of the most important determinants of the *height* of the dashed curve (that is, of the difference between actual and lower-bound value) is the likelihood of substantial movements in the stock price. An option on a stock whose price is unlikely to change by more than 1 or 2 percent is not worth much; an option on a stock whose price may halve or double is very valuable.

For example, suppose that a call option has an exercise price of $30, and the stock price will be either $25 or $35 when the option expires. The possible payoffs to the option are as follows:

Stock price at expiration	$25	$35
Call value at expiration	0	$ 5

Now suppose that the value of the stock when the option expires can be $20 or $40. The *average* of the possible stock prices is the same as before, but the volatility is greater. In this case the payoffs to the call are

Stock price at expiration	$20	$40
Call value at expiration	0	$10

A comparison of the two cases highlights the valuable asymmetry that options offer. If the stock price turns out to be below the exercise price when the option expires, the option is valueless regardless of whether the shortfall is a cent or a dollar. However, the option holder reaps all the benefits of stock price advances. Thus in our example the option is worth only $5 if the stock price reaches $35, but it is worth $10 if the stock price rises to $40. Therefore, volatility helps the option holder.

The probability of large stock price changes during the remaining life of an option depend on two things: (1) the variability of the stock price *per unit of time,* and (2) the length of time until the option expires. Other things being equal, you would like to hold an option on a volatile stock. Given volatility, you would like to hold an option with a long life ahead of it, since that longer life means that there is more opportunity for the stock price to change.

> The value of an option increases with both the variability of the share price and the time to expiration.

It's hard to keep all these properties straight at first reading. Therefore, we have summed them up in Table 25.3.

Check Point 25.5

Rework our numerical example for a put option with an exercise price of $30. Show that put options also are more valuable when the stock price is more volatile.

TABLE 25.3
What the prices of a call option and a put option depend on

If the following variables *increase*, …	… the value of a call option will	… the value of a put option will
stock price	increase	decrease
exercise price	decrease	increase
interest rate	increase	decrease
time to expiration	increase	increase
volatility of stock price	increase	increase

OPTION-VALUATION MODELS

If you want to value an option, you need to go beyond the qualitative statements of Table 25.3; you need an exact option-valuation model—a formula that you can plug numbers into and come up with a figure for option value.

Valuing complex options is a high-tech business and well beyond the scope of this book. Our aim here is not to instantly make you into option whizzes but to illustrate the basics of option valuation by walking you through an example. The trick to option valuation is to find a combination of borrowing and an investment in the stock that exactly replicates the option. The near-by Finance in Action box illustrates a simple version of one of these option-valuation models.

SEE BOX P. 769

This model achieves simplicity by assuming that the share price can take on only two values at the expiration date of the option. This assumption is clearly unrealistic, but it turns out that this approach can be generalized to allow for a large number of possible future share prices rather than just the two values in our example.

In 1973, Fischer Black, Myron Scholes, and Robert Merton came up with a formula that showed that even when share prices are changing continuously, you can still replicate an option by a series of levered investments in the stock. The Black-Scholes formula is regularly used by option traders, investment bankers, and financial managers to value a wide variety of options. Scholes and Merton shared the 1997 Nobel Prize in economics for their work on the development of this formula.[8] The nearby Excel Spreadsheet box shows you how to set up a Black-Scholes calculator in Excel. In Appendix 25A we present the basics of their remarkable option pricing formula.

SEE BOX P. 770

Today, there are many more sophisticated variants of the Black-Scholes formula that can better capture some aspect of real-life markets. As computer power continues to increase, these models can be made more complex and increasingly accurate.

Check Point 25.6

Use the Finance in Action box on page 769 as a model to help you answer this question. Suppose that the price of Alcan stock is $47 and could either double to $94 or halve to $23.5 over the next 3 months. Show that the following two strategies have exactly the same payoffs regardless of whether the stock price rises or falls: Strategy A—Buy three call options with an exercise price of $47; Strategy B—Buy two shares and borrow the present value of $47. What is your cash outflow today if you follow Strategy B? What does this tell you about the value of three call options? Assume that the interest rate is 1 percent per 3 months.

25.3

SPOTTING THE OPTION

In our discussion so far we may have given you the impression that financial managers are concerned only with traded options to buy or sell shares. But once you have learned to recognize the different kinds of options, you will find that they are everywhere. Unfortunately, they rarely come with a large label attached. Often the trickiest part of the problem is to identify the option.

---

[8] Fischer Black passed away in 1995.

A Simple Option-Valuation Model

It is January 2005 and you are contemplating the purchase of a call option on ATI Technologies stock. The call has a April 2005 exercise date and an exercise price of $24. ATI's stock price is currently $21.95, so the option will be valueless unless the stock price appreciates over the next 3 months. The outlook for ATI stock is uncertain, and we assume that all you know is that at the end of the 3 months it will be either $15 or $30. Finally we assume that the rate of interest on a bank loan is 3 percent a year, or about .74 percent for three months.

The following table depicts the outlook for three alternative investments:

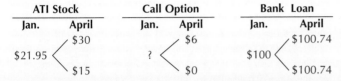

The first investment is ATI stock. Its current price is $21.95 but the price could rise to $30 or fall to $15. The second investment is the call option. When the call expires in April, the option will be valueless if the stock price falls to $15, and it will be worth $30 − $24 = $6 if the stock price rises to $30. We don't know (yet) how much the call is worth today, so for the time being we put a question mark against the January value. Our third investment is a bank loan at an interest rate of .74 percent per 3 months. The payoff on a $100 bank loan is $100.74 no matter what happens to the price of ATI stock.

Consider now two investment strategies. The first (Strategy A) is to buy 10 call options. The second (Strategy B) is to buy four ATI shares and to borrow the present value of $60 from the bank. Table 25.4 shows the possible payoffs from the two strategies. Notice that when you borrow from the bank, you receive a *positive* cash flow now but have a negative flow when the loan is repaid in April.

You can see that *regardless of whether the stock price falls to $15 or rises to $30*, the payoffs from the two strategies are identical. To put it another way, you can exactly *replicate* an investment in call options by a combination of a bank loan and an investment in the stock.[a] If two investments give the same payoffs in all circumstances, then their value must be the same today. In other words, the cost of buying 10 call options must be exactly the same as borrowing $59.56 (= PV($60) = $60/1.0074) from the bank and buying four Ballard shares:

$$\text{Price of 10 calls} = \$87.80 - \$59.56 = \$28.24$$

$$\text{Price of 1 call} = \frac{\$28.24}{10} = \$2.82$$

Presto! You have just valued a call option.

TABLE 25.4

It is possible to replicate the payoffs from ATI call options by borrowing to invest in ATI stock

	Cash Flow in January 2005	Payoff in April 2005 If Stock Price Equals	
		$15	$30
Strategy A			
Buy 10 calls	?	$0	+$60 (= 10 × $6)
Strategy B			
Buy four shares	−$87.80	+$60	+$120
Borrow PV($60)	+$59.56	−60	−60
	−$28.24	$ 0	+$60

Note: PV($60) at an interest rate of .74 percent for 3 months is 60/1.0074 = $59.56.

[a] The only tricky part in valuing the ATI option is to work out the number of shares that are needed to replicate one option. Fortunately, there is a simple formula that says that the number of shares needed is equal to

$$\frac{\text{Spread of possible option prices}}{\text{Spread of possible stock prices}} = \frac{\$6 - \$0}{\$30 - \$15} = .4$$

To replicate a call option, you need to buy .4 of a share of stock. To replicate 10 calls, you need to buy four shares of stock. This ratio is called the hedge ratio or the option delta.

[b] Notice that actual price of the April 2005 ATI call with $24 exercise price was $2.85 (see Figure 25.2), close to our simple estimate of the option's value.

Using the Black-Scholes Formula

	A	B	C	D	E	F	G	H	I	J
1	INPUTS			OUTPUTS			FORMULAS FOR OUTPUT IN COLUMN E			
2	Standard deviation (annual)	0.7		PV(Ex. Price)	23.82330		B6/(1+B4)^B3			
3	Maturity (in years)	0.25		d1	−0.0590		(LN(B5/E2)+(0.5*B2^2)*B3)/(B2*SQRT(B3))			
4	Risk-free rate (effective annual rate)	0.03		d2	−0.4090		E3−B2*SQRT(B3)			
5	Stock price	21.95		N(d1)	0.4765		NORMSDIST(E3)			
6	Exercise price	24		N(d2)	0.3413		NORMSDIST(E4)			
7				B/S call value	2.3285		B5*E5−E2*E6			
8				B/S put value	4.2018		E2*(1−E6)−B5*(1−E5)			

You may like to try your hand at using the Black-Scholes option-pricing formula to value the ATI option. A number of Web sites include a Black Scholes calculator (see, for example, **www.numa.com/derivs/ref/ calculat/option/calc-opa.htm** and **www.schaeffersresearch.com/ streetools/options/calculator.aspx**), but it takes only a few moments to construct your own Excel program to calculate Black-Scholes values. The following spreadsheet shows how you do it. First, type in the formulas shown on the right side of the spreadsheet in cells E2 to E8. Now enter the data for the ATI April 2005 call in cells B2 to B6. Notice that the values for the standard deviation and interest rate are entered as decimals.[9] On past evidence, the standard deviation of Microsoft's annual returns has been about 70 percent, so we enter the standard deviation in cell B2 as .70, not 70. The last two lines of the output column show that the Black-Scholes formula gives a value of $2.33 for the ATI call option, slightly higher than its market price in January 2005. (Don't worry about the other lines of output.)

We will start by looking briefly at options on real assets and then turn to options on financial assets. You should find that you have already encountered many of these options in earlier chapters.

OPTIONS ON REAL ASSETS

In Chapter 9 we pointed out that the capital investment projects that you accept today may affect the opportunities you have tomorrow. Today's capital budgeting decisions need to recognize these future opportunities.

Other things being equal, a capital investment project that generates new opportunities is more valuable than one that doesn't. A flexible project—one that doesn't commit management to a fixed operating strategy—is more valuable than an inflexible one. When a project is flexible or generates new opportunities for the firm, it is said to contain **real options**.

real options Options embedded in real assets.

In Chapter 9 we looked at several ways that companies may build future flexibility into a project. Here is a brief reminder of two types of real options that we introduced in that chapter.

Option to Expand

Many capital investment proposals include an option to expand in the future. For example, some of the world's largest oil reserves are found in the oil sands of northern Alberta. Unfortunately, the cost of extracting oil from the sand is substantially higher than the cost of extracting oil from conventional sources. Even when the market price of oil was substantially below the cost of extracting oil from the sands, oil companies were prepared to pay considerable sums of money for barren tracts of oil sand lands. The reason? Ownership of the oil sands gave the companies an option. At the time, the price of oil was below the cost of extraction and the oil sands remained undeveloped. But the oil companies knew that if the price rose above the extraction cost, the land purchased could be prove to be very valuable. Thus ownership gave them a real option—a call option to extract the oil. Now, more than half of Alberta's oil comes from the oil sands.

---

[9] Chapter 10 described how to calculate standard deviations. Notice also that in cell E2, we compute the present value of the exercise price by treating the interest rate as an effective annual yield. You should be aware, however, that many Black Scholes calculators require that the interest rate be expressed as a continuously compounded rate. See Chapter 4 if you need a review of continuous compounding.

Allegheny Acquires a Real Option

In 2001, Allegheny Energy Corporation acquired open gas-fired power plants in Mississippi and Tennessee. These plants were expected to sit idle most of the year and, when operating, to produce electricity at a cost at least 50 percent higher than the most efficient state-of-the-art facilities. Allegheny's decision to buy these power plants resulted from a sophisticated application of real options analysis.

The firm observed that electricity prices in an increasingly free energy market can be wildly volatile. For example, during some power shortages in the Midwest during hot summer months the cost of 1 megawatt-hour of electricity increased briefly from a typical level of $40 to several thousand dollars. The option to obtain additional energy in these situations obviously would be quite valuable.

Allegheny concluded that it would pay to acquire some cheap power plants, even if they were relatively high-cost electricity producers. Most of the time, the plants will sit idle, with market prices for electricity below the marginal cost of production. But every so often, when electricity prices spike, the plants can be fired up to produce electricity—at a great profit. Even if they operate only a few weeks a year, they can be positive-NPV investments.

These plants are in effect call options on electrical power. The options are currently out of the money, but the possibility that prices will increase makes these calls worth more than their price. The decision to buy them therefore makes the firm more valuable.

The Option to Abandon

Suppose that you need a new plant ready to produce turboencabulators in three years. You have a choice of designs. If design A is chosen, construction must begin immediately. Design B is more expensive but you can wait a year before breaking ground.

If you know with certainty that the plant will be needed, you should opt for design A. But suppose that there is some possibility that demand for turboencabulators will fall off and that in a year's time, you will decide the plant is not required. Then design B may be preferable because it gives you the option to bail out at low cost any time during the next 12 months.

You can think of the option to abandon as a put option. The exercise price of the put is the amount that you could recover if you abandon the project. The abandonment option makes design B more attractive by limiting the downside exposure; the worst outcome is that you receive the project's salvage value. The more uncertain is the need for the new plant, the more valuable is the downside protection offered by the abandonment option.

These are only two examples of options encountered in capital investment decisions. The others could fill (and have filled) entire books. If you look out for real options, you'll find them almost everywhere. The above Finance in Action box describes how a real options perspective was central to Allegheny's analysis of an investment in new power plants.

SEE BOX ABOVE

> Whenever management can decide in the future how best to operate a project—for example, to expand, contract, delay, or abandon it—the project contains a real option.

Check Point 25.7

A real estate developer buys 70 acres of land in a rural area, planning to build a subdivision on the land if and when the population from the city begins to expand into the area. If population growth is less than anticipated, the developer believes that the land can be sold to a country club that would build a golf course on the property.

a. In what way does the possibility of sale to the country club provide a put option to the developer?

b. What is the exercise price of the option? The asset value?

c. How does the golf course option increase the NPV of the land project to the developer?

OPTIONS ON FINANCIAL ASSETS

When companies issue securities, they often include an option in the package. Here are a few examples of the options that are associated with new financing.

Warrants

warrant   Right to buy shares from a company at a stipulated price before a set date.

A **warrant** is a long-term call option on the company's stock. Unlike the ATI option that we considered earlier, a warrant is issued by the company. The company sells the warrant; the investor buys it. For example, Desert Sun Mining sold a package of one common share and one-half of a warrant in October 2004. At the time, Desert Sun's share price was $1.50. Each whole warrant entitled the holder to buy one common share of Desert Sun at a price of $2.50 any time within the next four years. On February 4, 2005, the stock price was $2.46 and only needed to rise by 4 cents before the warrants were "in-the-money." That day, investors were willing to pay $.90 for each warrant, betting that the stock price would rise well above $2.50 before the option expired.

Warrants are often given to underwriters as part of their compensation for managing an issue of securities. At other times they may be issued when a firm becomes bankrupt; the bankruptcy court offers the firm's bondholders warrants in the reorganized company as part of the settlement. When a company issues a bond, it will sometimes add some warrants as a "sweetener." Since these warrants are valuable to investors, they are prepared to pay a higher price for a package of bonds and warrants than for the bond on its own. Managers sometimes look with delight at this higher price, forgetting that in return the company has incurred a liability to sell its shares to the warrant holders at what with hindsight may turn out to be a low price.

Warrants also have become a part of firms' employee compensation packages, especially for upper management. While technically warrants, these are more commonly referred to as stock options.

Convertible Bonds

convertible bond   Bond that the holder may exchange for a specified number of shares.

The **convertible bond** is a close relative of the bond-warrant package. It allows the bondholder to exchange the bond for a given number of shares of common stock. Therefore, it is a package of a straight bond (that is, a bond that is not convertible) with a call option. The exercise price of the call option is the value of the straight bond. If the value of the stock exceeds the value of the straight bond, it will be profitable to convert.

The owner of a convertible bond owns a bond and a call option on the firm's stock. So does the owner of a package of a bond and a warrant. However, there are differences, the most important being that a convertible bond's owner must give up the bond to exercise the option. The owner of a package of bonds and warrants exercises the warrants for cash and keeps the bond.

| **EXAMPLE 25.4** | **CONVERTIBLE BONDS** |

In November 2000 TELUS Corporation issued 10-year convertible bonds with a coupon rate of 6.75 percent. Each bond could be converted at any time before maturity into 25.2 shares of TELUS non-voting stock. In other words, the owner had a 10-year option to return the bond to TELUS and receive 25.2 shares in exchange. The number of shares that are received for each bond is called the bond's *conversion ratio*. The conversion ratio of the TELUS bond was 25.2.

In order to receive 25.2 shares of TELUS stock you had to surrender bonds with a face value of $1,000. Therefore, to receive *one* share, you had to surrender a face amount of 1,000/25.2 = $39.68. This figure is called the *conversion price*. Anybody who bought the bond at $1,000 in order to convert into 25.2 shares paid the equivalent of $39.68 per share.

As we write this in February 2005, TELUS's stock price is $34.50. So, if investors were obliged to convert their bond today, their investment would be worth only 25.2 × $34.50 = $869.40. This figure is called the bond's *conversion value*. Of course, investors do not need to convert immediately. They hope that TELUS's stock price will zoom up and make conversion profitable. If instead the stock price zooms down, investors will choose not to convert and simply hold on to the bond. The value of the bond if it could not be converted is known as its *bond value*.

Since the owner of the convertible always has the option *not* to convert, bond value establishes a lower bound, or *floor,* to the price of a convertible. Of course, this floor is not completely flat. If the firm falls on hard times, the bond may not be worth much. In the extreme case where the firm becomes worthless, the bond is also worthless. In addition, a convertible can never sell for less than its conversion value. If it did, smart investors would buy the convertible, exchange it for stock, and sell the stock. Their profit would be the difference between the conversion value and the price of the convertible.

This means that there are two parts to the lower bound of the price of any convertible: either its bond value or its conversion value. When the firm does well, conversion value exceeds bond value; the investor would choose to convert if forced to make an immediate choice. Bond value exceeds conversion value when the firm does poorly. In these circumstances the investor would hold on to the bonds if forced to choose.

Convertible holders do not have to make a now-or-never choice for or against conversion. They can wait and then, with the benefit of hindsight, take whatever course turns out to give them the highest payoff. Thus a convertible is always worth *more* than both its bond value and its conversion value (except when time runs out at the bond's maturity).

We stated earlier that it is useful to think of a convertible bond as a package of a straight bond and an option to buy the common stock in exchange for the straight bond. The value of this call option is equal to the difference between the convertible's selling price and its bond value.

Check Point 25.8

a. What is the conversion value of the TELUS convertible bond if the stock price is $60? What is its conversion price?

b. Suppose that a straight (non-convertible) bond issued by TELUS had been priced to yield 7 percent. What would be the bond value of the TELUS 6.75 percent convertibles at the time of issue? (Assume annual coupon payments.)

Callable Bonds

callable bond   Bond that may be repurchased by the issuer before maturity at specified call price.

Unlike warrants and convertibles, which give the investor an option, a **callable bond** gives an option to the issuer. A company that issues a callable bond has an option to buy the bond back at the stated exercise or "call" price. Therefore, you can think of a callable bond as a *package* of a straight bond (a bond that is not callable) and a call option held by the issuer.

The option to call the bond is obviously attractive to the issuer. If interest rates decline and bond prices rise, the company has the opportunity to repurchase the bond at a fixed call price. Therefore, the option to call the bond puts a ceiling on the bond price.

Of course, when the company issues a callable bond, investors are aware of this ceiling on the bond price and will pay less for a callable bond than for a straight bond. The difference between the value of a straight bond and a callable bond with the same coupon rate and maturity is the value of the call option that investors have given to the company:

Value of callable bond = value of straight bond – value of the issuer's call option

Check Point 25.9

Extendable or puttable bonds allow the investor to redeem the bond at par or let the bond remain outstanding until maturity. Suppose a 20-year extendable bond is issued with the investor allowed after 5 years to redeem the bond at par.

a. Why are these called puttable bonds? Who holds an implicit put option?

b. On what asset is the option written? (What asset do the option holders have the right to sell?)

c. What is the exercise price of the option?

d. In what circumstances will the option be exercised?

25.4   SUMMARY

1.   What is the payoff to buyers and sellers of call and put options?

There are two basic types of options. A **call option** is the right to buy an asset at a specific exercise price on or before the exercise date. A **put** is the right to sell an asset at a specific exercise price on or before the exercise date. The payoff to a call is the value of the asset minus the exercise price, if the difference is positive, and zero otherwise. The payoff to a put is the exercise price minus the value of the asset if the difference is positive, and zero otherwise. The payoff to the seller of an option is the negative of the payoff to the option buyer.

2.   What are the determinants of option values?

The value of a call option depends on the following considerations:

- To exercise the call option you must pay the exercise price. Other things being equal, the less you are obliged to pay, the better. Therefore, the value of the option is higher when the exercise price is low relative to the stock price.
- Investors who buy the stock by way of a call option are buying on instalment credit. They pay the purchase price of the option today, but they do not pay the exercise price until they exercise the option. The higher the rate of interest and the longer the time to expiration, the more this "free credit" is worth.
- No matter how far the stock price falls, the owner of the call cannot lose more than the price of the call. On the other hand, the more the stock price rises above the exercise price, the greater the profit on the call. Therefore, the option holder does not lose from increased variability if things go wrong, but gains if they go right. The value of the option increases with the variability of stock returns. Of course, the longer the time to the final exercise date, the more opportunity there is for the stock price to vary.

3.   What options may be present in capital investment proposals?

The importance of building flexibility into investment projects (discussed in Chapter 9) can be reformulated in the language of options. For example, many capital investments provide the flexibility to expand capacity in the future if demand turns out to be unusually buoyant. They are in effect providing the firm with a call option on the extra capacity. Firms also think about alternative uses for their assets if things go wrong. The option to abandon a project is a put option; the put's exercise price is the value of the project's assets if shifted to an alternative use. The ability to expand or to abandon are both examples of **real options**.

4.   What options may be provided in financial securities?

Many of the securities that firms issue contain an option. For example, a **warrant** is nothing but a long-term call option issued by the firm. **Convertible bonds** give the investor the option to buy the firm's stock in exchange for the value of the underlying bond. Unlike warrants and convertibles, which give an option to the investor, **callable bonds** give the option to the issuing firm. If interest rates decline and the value of the underlying bond rises, the firm can buy the bonds back at a specified exercise price.

Related Web Links

www.cbot.com The Chicago Board of Trade offers information, simulations, and product descriptions on options and futures

www.cme.com The Chicago Mercantile Exchange is a major centre for options and futures trading

www.cboe.com Chicago Board Options Exchange

www.m-x.ca Bourse de Montréal, Canadian Derivatives Exchange

www.numa.com Information about financial derivatives of all kinds, including options, warrants, and convertible bond calculators

www.real-options.com The real-options approach to valuing projects

Key Terms

Questions and Problems

*Answers in Appendix B

BASIC

EXCEL

1. **Option Payoffs.** Turn back to Figure 25.2, which lists prices of various ATI options. Use the data in the figure to calculate the payoff and the profits for investments in each of the following April 2005 maturity options, assuming that the stock price on the expiration date is $20.
   a. put option with exercise price $19
   *b. call option with exercise price $20
   c. put option with exercise price $20
   d. call option with exercise price $24
   *e. put option with exercise price $24

2. **Option Payoffs.** Redo the preceding problem assuming the stock price on the expiration date is (a) $25 (b) $15.

*3. **Determinants of Option Value.** Look at the data in Figure 25.2.
   a. What is the price of a call option with an exercise price of $22 and expiration in February? What if expiration is in April?
   b. Why do you think the April calls cost more than the February calls?
   c. Is the same true of put options? Why? Find a pair of puts in Figure 25.2 to illustrate.

4. **Option Contracts.** Fill in the blanks by choosing the appropriate terms from the following list: call, exercise, put.

   A(n) _____ option gives its owner the opportunity to buy a stock at a specific price that is generally called the _____ price. A(n) _____ option gives its owner the opportunity to sell stock at a specified _____ price.

*5. **Option Payoffs.** Note Figure 25.8a and 25.8b. Match each figure with one of the following positions and draw the figures for the positions not shown:
   a. call buyer
   b. call seller
   c. put buyer
   d. put seller

6. **Puts versus Calls.** The buyer of a call and the seller of a put both hope that the stock price will rise. Therefore the two positions are identical. Is this true? Illustrate with a simple example and show graphically.

*7. **Hedging with Options.** Suppose that you hold a share of stock and a put option on that share with an exercise price of $100. Show algebraically and graphically the value of your portfolio when the option expires if
   a. the stock price is below $100.
   b. the stock price is above $100.

FIGURE 25.8
See problem 5

8. **Option Portfolios.** Mixing options and securities can often create interesting payoffs. For each of the following combinations show what the payoff would be when the option expires if (1) the stock price is below the exercise price, and (2) the stock price is above the exercise price. Illustrate the payoffs with graphs. Assume that each option has the same exercise price and expiration date.
   a. Buy a call and invest the present value of the exercise price in a bank deposit.
   b. Buy a share and a put option on the share.
   c. Buy a share, buy a put option on the share, and sell a call option on the share.
   d. Buy a call option and a put option on the share.

9. **Option Values.** What is the lower bound to the price of a call option? What is the upper bound?

10. **Option Values.** What is a call option worth if
    a. the stock price is zero?
    b. the stock price is extremely high relative to the exercise price?

11. **Option Valuation.** Figure 25.2 shows call options on ATI stock with the same exercise date in April and with exercise prices $20, $22, and $24. Notice that the price of the middle call option (with exercise price $22) is less than halfway between the prices of the other two calls (with exercise prices $20 and $24). Suppose that this were not the case. For example, suppose that the price of the middle call were the average of the prices of the other two calls. Show that if you sell two of the middle calls and use the proceeds to buy one each of the other calls, your proceeds in April may be positive but cannot be negative despite the fact that your net outlay today is zero. What can you deduce from this example about option pricing?

12. **Put Prices.** How does the price of a *put* option respond to the following changes, other things being equal? Does the put price go up or down? Explain why.
    a. Stock price increases.
    b. Exercise price is increased.
    c. Risk-free interest rate increases.
    d. Expiration date of the option is extended.
    e. Volatility of the stock price falls.
    f. Time passes, so the option's expiration date comes closer.

13. **Internet.** Visit the Canadian Derivatives Exchange at the Bourse de Montréal, **www.m-x.ca**, and look up current prices of call and put options on Canadian equity by clicking on "Stock Options List." Find examples to illustrate the effect on the prices of call and put options from an increase in the exercise price holding constant the other factors. Repeat for an increase in the time to expiration.

14. **Internet.** What other options are traded on the Canadian Derivatives Exchange (**www.m-x.ca**)? Try to explain what these options are.

*15. **Integrative.** As manager of United Bedstead you own substantial executive stock options. These options entitle you to buy the firm's shares during the next 5 years at a price of $100 a share. The plant manager has just outlined two alternative proposals to re-equip the plant. Both proposals have the same net present value but one is substantially riskier than the other. At first you are undecided about which to choose, but then you remember your stock options. How might these influence your choice?

16. **Real and Financial Options.** Are these put or call options? Fill in the blanks:
    a. An oil company acquires mining rights to a silver deposit. It is not obliged to mine the silver, however. The company has effectively acquired a _____ option, where the exercise price is the cost of opening the mine and extracting the silver.
    b. Some preferred shareholders have the right to redeem their shares at par value after a specified date. (If they hand over their shares, the firm sends them a cheque equal to the shares' par value.) These shareholders have a _____ option.

    c.   A firm buys a standard machine with a ready secondhand market. The secondhand market gives the firm a _____ option.

*17. **Real Options.** What is the option in each of the following cases. Is it a call or a put?

    a.   Western Telecom commits to production of digital switching equipment specifically designed for the European market. As a stand-alone venture, the project has a negative NPV, but it is justified by the need for a strong market position in the rapidly growing, and potentially very profitable, market.

    b.   Western Telecom vetoes a fully integrated automated production line for the new digital switches. It will rely on standard, less expensive equipment even though the automated production line would be more efficient overall using the specialized equipment, according to a discounted–cash flow calculation.

18. **Real Options.** Describe each of the following situations in the language of options.

    a.   Mining rights to undeveloped gold mine in Nunavut. Development and production of the gold now is a negative-NPV endeavour. The break-even price is $500 per ounce, versus a spot gold price of $420 per ounce. However, the decision to develop can be put off for up to five years.

    b.   A restaurant producing net cash flows, after all out-of-pocket expenses of $700,000 per year. There is no upward or downward trend in the cash flows, but they fluctuate. The real estate occupied by the restaurant is owned, and it could be sold for $5 million.

*19. **Real Options.** Price support systems for various agricultural products have allowed farmers to sell their crops to the government for a specified "support price." What kind of option has the government given to the farmers? What is the exercise price?

20. **Implicit Options.** Some investment management contracts give the portfolio manager a bonus proportional to the amount by which a portfolio return exceeds a specified threshold.

    a.   In what way is this an implicit call option on the portfolio?

    b.   Can you think of a way in which such contracts can lead to incentive problems? For example, what happens to the value of the prospective bonus if the manager invests in high-volatility stocks?

*21. **Implicit Options.** The Rank and File Company is considering a stock issue to raise $50 million. An underwriter offers to guarantee the success of the issue by buying any unwanted stock at the $25 issue price. The underwriter's fee is $2 million.

    a.   What kind of option does Rank and File acquire if it accepts the underwriter's offer?

    b.   What determines the value of the option?

22. **Implicit Options.**

    a.   Some banks have offered their customers an unusual type of time deposit. The deposit does not pay any interest if the market falls, but instead the depositor receives a proportion of any rise in the Standard & Poor's Index. What implicit option do the investors hold? How should the bank invest the money in order to protect itself against the risk of offering this deposit?

    b.   You can also make a deposit with a bank that does not pay interest if the market index rises but which makes an increasingly large payment as the market index falls. How should the bank protect itself against the risk of offering this deposit?

23. **Loan Guarantees.** The CDIC (Canadian Deposit Insurance Corporation) insures bank deposits. If a bank's assets are insufficient to pay off all depositors, the CDIC will contribute enough money to ensure that all depositors can be paid off in full. (We ignore the $60,000 maximum coverage on each account.) In what way is this guarantee of deposits the provision of a put option by the CDIC? Hint: Write out the funds the CDIC will have to contribute when bank assets are less than deposits owed to depositors. What is the exercise price of the put option?

24. **Real Options.** After dramatic increases in oil prices in the 1970s, the United States government funded several projects to create synthetic oil or natural gas from abundant U.S. supplies of coal and oil shale. Although the cost of producing such synthetic fuels at the time was greater than the price of oil, it was argued that the projects still could be justified for their insurance value, since the cost of synthetic fuel would be essentially fixed while the price of oil was risky. Evaluate the synthetic fuel program as an option on fuel sources. Is it a call or a put option? What is the exercise price? How would uncertainty in the future price of oil affect the amount the United States should have been willing to spend on such projects?

EXCEL

*25. **Arbitrage Opportunities.**
   a. Circular File stock is selling for $25 a share. You see that call options on the stock with exercise price of $20 are selling at $3. What should you do? What will happen to the option price as investors identify this opportunity?
   b. Now you observe that put options on Circular File with exercise price $30 are selling for $4. What should you do?

26. **Implicit Options.** A 10-year maturity convertible bond with a 6 percent coupon on a company with a bond rating of AAA is selling for $1,050. Each bond can be exchanged for 20 shares, and the stock price currently is $50 per share. Other AAA-rated bonds with the same maturity would sell at a yield to maturity of 8 percent. What is the value of the implicit call option on the bond? Why is the bond selling for more than the value of the shares it can be converted into?

27. **Internet.** The application of option pricing models to real options is a rapidly expanding field of finance. Although the details are beyond this textbook in scope, check out the visual discussion of real options at **www.puc-rio.br/marco.ind/faqs.html**. A good list of readings is found at **www.realoptions-software.com/articles.htm**.

CHALLENGE

EXCEL

28. **Option Pricing.** Look again at the ATI call option that we valued on page 769. Suppose that by the end of April the price of ATI stock could rise to $36 or fall to $10. Everything else is unchanged from our example.
   a. What would be the value of the ATI call at the end of April if the stock price is $36? If it is $10?
   b. Show that a strategy of buying 13 calls provides exactly the same payoffs as borrowing the present value of $60 from the bank and buying six shares.
   c. What is the net cash flow in January from the policy of borrowing PV($60) and buying six shares?
   d. What does this tell you about the value of the call option?
   e. Why is the value of the call option different from the value that we calculated on page 769? What does this tell you about the relationship between the value of a call and the volatility of the share price?

29. **Option Pricing.** Look once more at the ATI call option that we valued on page 769. Suppose that the interest rate on bank loans is zero. Recalculate the value of the ATI call option. What does this tell you about the relationship between interest rates and the value of a call?

30. **Standard & Poor's.** Go to **http://www.m-x.ca/cotes_liste_en.php** and get two current call option prices for each of Inco Ltd. (N) and Barrick Gold Corp (ABX). Go to **www.mcgrawhill.ca/edumarketinsight** and download the monthly closing stock prices and monthly rates of return for each company. Using all of the monthly rates of return, calculate the variance of the monthly return, using the Excel function VAR. Multiply your answer by 12 to get the estimated annual variance and then take its square root (SQRT) to get the

estimated annual standard deviation of the stock return. Go to **www.bankofcanada.ca/en/monmrt.htm** and get the one-year treasury bill rate for the risk-free rate. Either using the Excel spreadsheet on page 770 or the option pricing calculator at **www.numa.com**, calculate the prices for your chosen call options. How different are the prices you obtain from the ones from the Canadian Derivatives Exchange? What happens to the calculated price if you change the standard deviation? Why?

Solutions to Check Points

25.1 a. The call with exercise price $24 costs $1.05. If the stock price at maturity is $18, the call expires valueless and the investor loses the entire $1.05. If the stock price is $30, the value of the call is $30 − $24 = $6, and the investor's profit is $6 − $1.05 = $4.95.

   b. The put costs $2.85. If the stock price at maturity is $18, the put value at expiration is $24 − $18 = $6 and the investor's profit is $6 − $2.85 = $3.15. If the stock price is $30, the value of the put is zero, and the investor's loss is the price paid for the put, $2.85.

25.2 a. The call seller receives $1.05 for writing the call. If the stock price at maturity is $18, the call expires valueless, and the investor keeps the entire $1.05 as a profit. If the stock price is $30, the value of the call is $30 − $24 = $6. In other words, the option seller must deliver a stock worth $30 for an exercise price of only $24. The investor's net profit is $1.05 − $6 = −$4.95. The call seller will clear a positive net profit as long as the stock price remains below $25.05 (the exercise price plus option selling price).

   b. The put seller receives $2.85 for writing the put. If the stock price at maturity is $18, the put value at expiration is $24 − $18 = $6. In other words, the put option seller must pay an exercise price of $24 to buy a stock worth only $18. The seller's loss is $6 − $2.85 = $3.15. If the stock price is $30, the final value of the put is zero, and the investor's profit is the price originally received for the put, $2.85.

25.3 This payoff can be achieved by buying one call with an exercise price of $20, selling two calls with an exercise price of $22, and buying one call with an exercise price of $24. The total cost of this position in January 2005 would therefore have been $3.05 − 2 × $1.85 + $1.05 = $0.40.

The following table shows how the payoffs from each of these positions would vary with the stock price. If the stock price is $20 or less, all options expire worthless. If the stock price is $24 or more, the positive payoffs from the two option purchases are exactly canceled out by the negative payoffs from the two options that have been sold. The position provides a net positive payoff only if the stock price lies between $20 and $24. The best that can happen is that the stock price at maturity is $22. In this case the net payoff from your option positions is $2. Thus you are placing a bet that the stock price over the next 4 months will not change by more than $2 up or down from its current level.

| | **Payoffs from Option Positions at Maturity:** | | | |
Stock Price at Maturity	Buy Call; Exercise Price = $20	Sell 2 Calls; Exercise Price = $22	Buy Call; Exercise Price = $24	Total
$20	$0	$0	$0	$0
$22	+$2	$0	$0	+$2
$23	+$3	−$2	$0	+$1
$24	+$4	−$4	+$0	$0
$26	+$6	−$8	+$2	$0

25.4 Given the exercise price, the value of a put option is lower when the stock price is higher. The put gives you the right to sell the stock at the exercise price. The higher the stock price, the less attractive the put. The value of a put option is higher when the exercise price is higher. You would be willing to pay more for the right to sell a stock at a high price than the right to sell it at a low price.

25.5　First consider the payoff to the put holder in the lower volatility scenario:

Stock price	$25	$35
Put value	$ 5	$ 0

In the higher volatility scenario, the value of the stock can be $20 or $40. Now the payoff to the put is

Stock price	$20	$40
Put value	$10	$ 0

The expected value of the payoff of the put doubles.

25.6　The payoffs are as follows:

	Cash Flow Today	Payoff in 3 Months If Stock Price Equals $23.50	$94
Strategy A			
Buy three calls	?	$ 0	+$141 (= 3 × [94 − 47])
Strategy B			
Buy two shares	−$94	+$47	+$188
Borrow PV($47)	+ 46.53	−$47	− $47
	−$47.47	$ 0	+$141

Note: PV($47) at an interest rate of 1 percent for 3 months is 47/1.01 = $46.53.

The initial net cash outflow from strategy B is $47.47. Since the three calls offer the same payoffs in the future, they also cost $47.47. One call is worth 47.47/3 = $15.82.

25.7　a.　The developer has the option to sell the potential housing development to the country club. This abandonment option is like a put that guarantees a minimum payoff from the investment.

　　　b.　The exercise price of the option is the price at which it can be sold to the country club. The asset value is the present value of the project if maintained as a housing development. If this value is less than the value as a golf course, the project will be sold.

　　　c.　The abandonment option increases NPV by placing a lower bound on the possible payoffs from the project.

25.8　a.　Conversion value = 25.2 × $60 = $1,512

　　　　Conversion price = $1,000/25.2 = $39.68 (unchanged)

　　　b.　Bond value = $67.50 × 10-year annuity factor at 7% + $1,000 × 10-year PV factor at 7% = $474.09 + 508.35 = $982.44

25.9　a., b.　In 5 years, the bond will be a 15-year maturity bond. The bondholder can sell the bond back to the firm at par value. The bondholder therefore has a put option to sell a 15-year bond for par value even if interest rates have risen and the bond would otherwise sell below par.

　　　c.　The exercise price is the par value of the bond.

　　　d.　The bondholder will extend the loan if interest rates decrease.

25.5

APPENDIX 25.A: THE BLACK-SCHOLES OPTION VALUATION MODEL[10]

In this appendix you will learn how to price call options with the famous Black-Scholes option pricing formula.

We showed you a simple option-valuation model on page 769. Known as the *binomial model,* it illustrates the general principal of option valuation: Find a combination of borrowing and an investment in the stock that exactly replicates the payoffs from the option. If we can price the stock and the loan, we can also price the option. In general,

$$\text{Value of call option} = [\text{delta} \times \text{current stock price}] - [\text{bank loan}]$$

The delta, or hedge ratio, is the number of shares to purchase. The bank loan is the present value of the amount needed to make the combination of the stock and loan cash flows equal to the option's cash flows at the option's expiry.

In the binomial model, the delta is equal to the ratio of the spread of possible option prices to the spread of possible stock prices at the time of the option's expiry. The bank loan is the present value of the difference between the payoffs from the option and the payoffs from the shares at the option's expiry.

In our ATI example, we determined the price of a 3-month call option with an exercise price of $24. Let's use the formula to price the option.

EXAMPLE 25.A1

The current ATI stock price is $21.95. We assume that the stock price will be either $15 or $30 in 3 months. Thus the call option will be worth either $0, or $30 – $24 = $6 at expiry.

The delta of the leveraged investment in the stock is ($6 – 0)/($30 – 15), or .4. Thus you should buy 40 percent of a share. The cost of the stock purchase is 40 percent of $21.95, or $8.78.

The bank loan is the present value of difference between the possible option payoffs and payoffs from 40 percent of a share at maturity. If the stock price turns out to be $15, the payoff from owning 40 percent of a share is .4 × $15 = $6, and the payoff from the option is zero. The difference in the payoffs is $6 – 0, or $6. Likewise, if the stock price turns out to be $30, the payoff from 40 percent of a share is .4 × $30 = $12, and from the option is $6, also giving a difference of $6. With a .74 percent 3-month interest rate, the bank loan needed is $6/1.0074 = $5.96.

Putting all the pieces together gives the value of 3-month call option:

$$\text{Value of call option} = [\text{delta} \times \text{current stock price}] - [\text{bank loan}] = \$8.78 - \$5.96 = \$2.82$$

The concept of valuing an option by valuing a levered investment that replicates the option's cash flows is completely general. However, the binomial method allows the stock price only two possible changes, giving only two possible future stock prices. This might be reasonable over a very short time but is not sensible over a longer time period.

We could make the problem slightly more realistic by assuming that there are two possible changes in the stock price in each one-month period. That would give a wider range of three-month prices. But why stop at one-month periods? Take shorter and shorter intervals, allowing two price changes per period. Eventually, we would reach a situation in which the stock price was changing continuously and generating a continuum of possible prices at the end of three months.

---

[10] This appendix draws on Chapter 20 of R. Brealey and S. Myers, *Principals of Corporate Finance,* 6th ed. (Boston, MA: McGraw-Hill, 2000).

Calculating the value of this levered investment may sound like a hopelessly tedious business, but Black and Scholes derived a formula that does the trick:

$$\text{Value of call option} = [\text{delta} \times \text{current stock price}, P] - [\text{bank loan}]$$
$$= [N(d_1) \times P] - [N(d_2) \times \text{PV(EX)}]$$

where

d_1 $= \ln \dfrac{[P/\text{PV(EX)}]}{\sigma\sqrt{t}} + \dfrac{\sigma\sqrt{t}}{2}$

d_2 $= d_1 - \sigma\sqrt{t}$

$N(d)$ = cumulative standard normal probability density function[11]

EX   = exercise price of option; PV(EX) is calculated by discounting at the risk-free interest rate, r_f

t = number of periods to expiration date, expressed as a fraction of a year

P = price of stock now

σ = standard deviation per period of (continuously compounded) rate of return on stock, also called volatility

To derive their formula, Black and Scholes assumed that there is a continuum of stock prices, and therefore to replicate an option, investors must continuously adjust their holdings of stocks. Of course, this can't be done in the real world. Despite this, the formula works remarkably well in practice, where stocks trade intermittently and prices jump from one level to another. The Black-Scholes model has also proven very flexible; it can be adapted to value options on a variety of assets with special features, such as foreign currency, bonds, and futures. It is not surprising therefore that it has been extremely influential and become the standard model for valuing options. Every day, dealers on options exchanges use this formula to make huge trades. These dealers are not for the most part trained in the formula's mathematical derivation; they just use a computer or a special programmed calculator to find the value of the option.

Let's apply the Black-Scholes formula to the pricing of a 6-month call option with an exercise price of $85 on a stock with a current price of $85. The standard deviation of the annual stock return is 32 percent. The 6-month interest rate is 2.5 percent.

Price of stock now $= P = \$85$

Exercise price $= \$85$

Standard deviation of continuously compounded annual returns $= \sigma = .32$, or 32 percent

Years to maturity $= t = 6/12 = .5$

Interest rate per 6 month $= r = 2.5$ percent

Step 1: Calculate d_1 and d_2. Just plug the numbers into the formula, noting that "ln" means natural log:

$d_1 = \ln[P/\text{PV(EX)}]/\sigma\sqrt{t} + \sigma\sqrt{t}/2$
    $= \ln[85/(85/1.025)] / (.32 \times \sqrt{.5}) + (.32 \times \sqrt{.5})/2 = .2223$
$d_2 = d_1 - \sigma\sqrt{t} = .2223 - (.32 \times \sqrt{.5}) = -.004$

Step 2: Find $N(d_1)$ and $N(d_2)$. $N(d_1)$ is the probability of observing a standard normal variable of less than d_1. A simple way to find $N(d_1)$ is to use the Excel function NORMSDIST. For example, if you enter NORMSDIST(.2223) into an Excel spreadsheet, you will find that there is a .5879 probability that a standard normal variable will be less than .2223. Likewise, $N(d_2)$ can be found as NORMSDIST(−.004) = .4984.

---

[11] That is, $N(d)$ is the probability that a standardized, normally distributed random variable, z, will be less than or equal to d. $N(d_1)$ in the Black-Scholes formula is the option delta, the number of shares to purchase. Thus the formula tells us that the value of a call is equal to an investment of $N(d_1)$ in the common stock, less borrowing of $N(d_2) \times \text{PV(EX)}$.

Step 3: Plug these numbers into the Black-Scholes formula. You can now calculate the value of the call:

$$= [\text{delta} \times \text{current stock price, } P] - [\text{bank loan}]$$
$$= [N(d_1) \times P] - [N(d_2) \times PV(EX)]$$
$$= [.5879 \times 85] - [.4984 \times 85/1.025] = \$8.64$$

The Black-Scholes call option price is $8.64.

To save yourself from these tedious calculations, use the Excel Black-Scholes program in the Excel Spreadsheet found on page 770. However, you must be sure to use the effective annual equivalent interest rate, $EAR = (1 + r_f)^{1/t} - 1$, not the interest rate for the life of the option, r_f, where t is the maturity of the option, as a fraction of a year. The reason for the change arises from the formula for the present value of the exercise price used in the spreadsheet: $PV(EX) = EX/(1 + EAR)^t$. In Step 1, above, the present value of the exercise price is calculated as $PV(EX) = EX/(1 + r_f)$. Since $(1 + EAR)^t = ((1 + r_f)^{1/t})^t = (1 + r_f)$, the present value of the exercise price is the same, regardless of which formula is used, provided that you use the appropriate interest rate.

Check Point 25.A1   Build the Excel spreadsheet from page 770 and use it to verify the Black-Scholes option value calculated above. Be sure to use the effective annual equivalent interest rate of 2.5 percent per 6 months.

Questions and Problems

BASIC

1. **Binomial Model.** Over the coming year Chance Manufacturing's stock price will halve to $50 from its current level of $100, or it will rise to $200. The 1-year interest rate is 10 percent.
   a. What is the delta of a 1-year call option on Chance stock with an exercise price of $100?
   b. Create a table showing the cash flows from an investment in the stock and borrowing to replicate the option's cash flows. Explain what you have done.
   c. What is the price of the call option?

2. **Black-Scholes Formula.** A call option written on a stock selling for $10 has an exercise price of $12. The call expires in nine months. The stock's standard deviation of return is 30 percent per year and the risk-free interest rate is 1 percent per month.
   a. What is the Black-Scholes price of the call?
   b. What is the price if the call expires in 3 months? Why is it lower than the price you found in part (a)?

PRACTICE

3. **Using the Black-Scholes Formula.** Instead of using the Black-Scholes formula to estimate option values in reference to volatility, it is sometimes useful to turn the question around and back out the volatility implied in option prices. A 3-month call option with a $10 exercise price is trading for $.558, and the current stock price is $9.75. If the risk-free interest rate is 2 percent per 3 months (or $(1.02)^4 - 1 = .0824$ per year), what is the implied volatility of the stock?

4. **Using the Black-Scholes Spreadsheet.** Calculate the Black-Scholes call option value for each case and verify the impact the five factors have on a call price. Summarize in words what you observe.
   a. A call option with a $15 exercise price expires in 6 months. The 6-month interest rate is 3 percent. What is the call price if the stock price is $14? If the stock price is $16? The standard deviation of the stock's annual return is expected to be 40 percent.
   b. A call option with a $10 exercise price expires in 9 months. The 9-month interest rate is 4.5 percent and the stock price is $13. The standard deviation of the stock's annual return is expected to be 70 percent. What is the call price? If the exercise price is $13, what is the call price?

c. A call option with a $25 exercise price expires in 9 months. The 9-month interest rate is 4.5 percent and the stock price is $18. The standard deviation of the stock's annual return is expected to be 55 percent. What is the call price? If the interest rate is 5 percent, what is the call price?

d. A call option with a $20 exercise price expires in 6 months. The effective annual interest rate is 4 percent and the stock price is $23. The standard deviation of the stock's annual return is expected to be 40 percent. What is the call price? If the standard deviation of the stock's annual return is expected to be 70 percent, what is the call price?

e. A call option with a $30 exercise price expires in 3 months. The effective annual interest rate is 4 percent and the stock price is $23. The standard deviation of the stock's annual return is expected to be 50 percent. What is the call price? If the time to expiry is 6 months, what is the call price?

Solution to Check Point

25.A1 The spreadsheet uses the effective annual interest rate. Convert the 6-month interest rate into its annual equivalent rate, noting that time to maturity, t, is .5 of a year. The effective annual interest rate = $(1.025)^{1/.5} - 1 = 0.050625$. The value of the call option calculated is $8.64, as expected.

	A	B	C	D	E
1	**Inputs**		**Outputs**		**Formulas for Output in Column E**
2	Standard deviation (annual)	0.32	PV(Ex. Price)	82.283	B6/(1+B4)^B3
3	Maturity (in years)	0.5	d1	0.2223	(LN(B5/E2)+(0.5*B2^2)*B3)/(B2*SQRT(B3))
4	Risk-free rate (effective annual rate)	0.05063	d2	-0.0040	E3-B2*SQRT(B3)
5	Stock price	85	N(d1)	0.5879	NORMSDIST(E3)
6	Exercise price	85	N(d2)	0.4984	NORMSDIST(E4)
7			B/S call value	8.6446	B5*E5-E2*E6
8			B/S put value	6.5715	E2*(1-E6)-B5*(1-E5)

RISK MANAGEMENT

We often assume that risk is beyond our control. A business is exposed to unpredictable changes in raw material costs, tax rates, technology, and a long list of other variables. There's nothing the manager can do about it.

This is not wholly true. To some extent a manager can *select* the risks of an asset or business. For example, in the last chapter we saw that companies can consciously affect the risk of an investment by building in flexibility. A company that reduces the cost of bailing out of a project by using standardized equipment is taking less risk than a similar firm that uses specialized equipment with no alternative uses. In this case the option to resell the equipment serves as an insurance policy.

Sometimes, rather than building flexibility into the project, companies accept the risk but then use financial instruments to offset it. This practice of taking offsetting risks is known as *hedging*. In this chapter we will explain how hedging works and we will describe some of the specialized financial instruments that have been devised to help manage risk. These instruments include options, futures, forwards, and swaps. Each of these instruments provides a payoff that depends on the price of some underlying commodity or financial asset. Because their payoffs derive from the prices of other assets, they are often known collectively as *derivative instruments* (or derivatives for short).[1]

After reading this chapter you should be able to
- Understand why companies hedge to reduce risk.
- Use options, futures, and forward contracts to devise simple hedging strategies.
- Explain how companies can use swaps to change the risk of securities that they have issued.

---

[1] Derivatives often conjure up an image of wicked speculators. Derivative instruments attract their share of speculators, some of whom may be wicked, but they are also used by sober and prudent businesspeople who simply want to reduce risk.

WHY HEDGE?

In this chapter we will explain *how* companies use derivatives to hedge the risks of their business. But first we should give some of the reasons *why* they do it.

Hedging is seldom free. Most businesses hedge to reduce risk, not to make money. Why then bother to hedge? For one thing, reducing the risk makes financial planning easier and reduces the odds of an embarrassing shortfall. A shortfall might mean only an unexpected trip to the bank, but in extreme cases it could trigger bankruptcy. Why not reduce the odds of these awkward outcomes with a hedge?

We saw in our discussion of debt policy in Chapter 15 that financial distress can result in indirect as well as direct costs to a firm. Costs of financial distress arise from disruption to normal business operations as well as from the effect financial distress has on the firm's investment decisions. The better the risk management policies, the less the risk and lower are the expected costs of financial distress. As a side benefit, better risk management increases the firm's debt capacity.

In some cases hedging also makes it easier to decide whether an operating manager deserves a stern lecture or a pat on the back. Suppose that your export division shows a 50 percent decline in profits when the dollar unexpectedly strengthens against other currencies. How much of that decrease is due to the exchange rate shift and how much to poor management? If the company had protected itself against the effect of exchange rate changes, it's probably bad management. If it wasn't protected, you have to make a judgment with hindsight, probably by asking, "What would profits have been if the firm had hedged against exchange rate movements?"

Finally, hedging extraneous events can help focus the operating manager's attention. We know we shouldn't worry about events outside our control, but most of us do anyway. It's naive to expect the manager of the export division not to worry about exchange rate movements if his bottom line and bonus depend on them. The time spent worrying could be better spent if the company hedged itself against such movements.

A sensible risk strategy must answer the following questions:

- *What are the major risks that the company faces and what are the possible consequences?* Some risks are scarcely worth a thought, but there are others that might bankrupt the company.
- *Is the company being paid for taking these risks?* Managers are not paid to avoid all risks, but if they can reduce their exposure to risks for which there are no compensating rewards, they can afford to place larger bets when the odds are stacked in their favour.
- *Can the company take any measures to reduce the probability of a bad outcome or to limit its impact?* For example, most businesses install alarm and sprinkler systems to prevent damage from fire and invest in backup facilities in case damage does occur.
- *Can the company purchase fairly priced insurance to offset any losses?* Insurance companies have some advantages in bearing risk. In particular, they may be able to spread the risk across a portfolio of different insurers.
- *Can the company use derivatives, such as options or futures, to hedge the risk?* In the remainder of this chapter we explain when and how derivatives may be used.

REDUCING RISK WITH OPTIONS

In the last chapter we introduced you to put and call options. Managers regularly buy options on currencies, interest rates, and commodities to limit their downside risk. Many of these options are traded on options exchanges, but often they are simply private deals between the corporation and a bank.

Petrochemical Parfum, Inc., is concerned about potential increases in the price of heavy crude oil, which is one of its major inputs. To protect itself against such increases, Petrochemical buys 6-month options to purchase 1,000 barrels of crude oil at an exercise price of $70. These options might cost $.50 per barrel.

If the price of crude is above the $70 exercise price when the options expire, Petrochemical will exercise the options and will receive the difference between the oil price and the exercise price. If the oil price falls below the exercise price, the options will expire worthless. The net cost of oil will therefore be

	Oil Price, Dollars per Barrel		
	$68	**$70**	**$72**
Cost of 1,000 barrels	$68,000	$70,000	$72,000
− Payoff on call option	0	0	2,000
Net cost	$68,000	$70,000	$70,000

You can see that by buying options Petrochemical protects itself against increases in the oil price while continuing to benefit from oil price decreases. If prices fall, it can discard its call option and buy its oil at the market price. If oil prices rise, however, it can exercise its call option to purchase oil for $70 a barrel. Therefore, options create an attractive asymmetry. Of course, this asymmetry comes at a price—the $500 cost of the options.

Consider now the problem of Onnex, Inc., which supplies Petrochemical with crude oil. Its problem is the mirror image of Petrochemical's; it loses when oil prices fall and gains when oil prices rise.

Onnex wants to lock in a minimum price of oil but still benefit from rising oil prices. It can do so by purchasing *put* options that give it the right to *sell* oil at an exercise price of $70 per barrel. If oil prices fall, it will exercise the put. If they rise, it will discard the put and sell oil at the market price:

	Oil Price, Dollars per Barrel		
	$68	**$70**	**$72**
Revenue from 1,000 barrels	$68,000	$70,000	$72,000
+ Payoff on put option	2,000	0	0
Net revenues	$70,000	$70,000	$72,000

If oil prices rise, Onnex reaps the benefit. But if oil prices fall below $70 a barrel the payoff of the put option exactly offsets the revenue shortfall. As a result, Onnex realizes net revenues of at least $70 a barrel, which is the exercise price of the put option.

> Once again you don't get something for nothing. The price that Onnex pays for insurance against a fall in the price of oil is the cost of the put option. Similarly, the price that Petrochemical paid for insurance against a rise in the price of oil was the cost of the call option. Options provide protection against adverse price changes for a fee—the option premium.

Notice that both Petrochemical and Onnex use options to insure against an adverse move in oil prices. But the options do not remove all uncertainty. For example, Onnex may be able to sell oil for much more than the exercise price of the option.

Figure 26.1 illustrates the nature of Onnex's hedge. Panel *a* shows the total revenue derived from selling the 1,000 barrels of oil. The firm is currently exposed to oil price risk: as prices fall, so will the firm's revenue. But, as panel *b* illustrates, the payoff on a put option to sell 1,000 barrels rises as oil prices fall below $70 a barrel and, therefore, can offset the firm's exposure. Panel *c* shows the firm's net revenues after it buys the put option. For prices below $70 per barrel, revenues are $70,000. But revenues rise $1,000 for every dollar that oil prices rise above $70. The profile in panel *c* should be familiar to you: think back to the protective put strategy we first saw in Figure 25.4 in Chapter 25. In both cases, the put provides a floor on the value of the overall position.

Check Point 26.1   Draw three graphs like those in Figure 26.1 to illustrate how Petrochemical hedges its costs by purchasing call options on oil.

FIGURE 26.1
Onnex can buy put options to place a floor on its overall revenues.

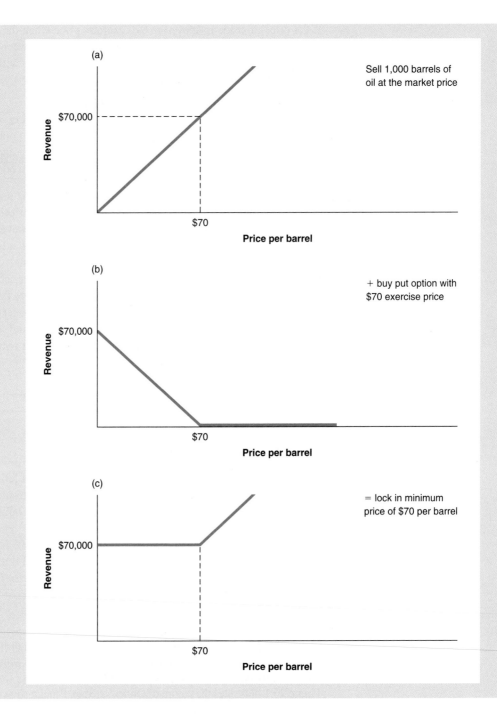

(a)

Revenue

$70,000

$70

Price per barrel

Sell 1,000 barrels of oil at the market price

(b)

Revenue

$70,000

$70

Price per barrel

+ buy put option with $70 exercise price

(c)

Revenue

$70,000

$70

Price per barrel

= lock in minimum price of $70 per barrel

26.3   FUTURES CONTRACTS

Suppose you are a canola farmer.[2] You are optimistic about next year's canola crop, but still you can't sleep. You are worried that when the time comes to sell the canola, prices may have fallen through the floor. The cure for insomnia is to sell canola *futures*. In this case, you agree to deliver so many tonnes of canola in (say) November at a price that is set today. Do not confuse this

---

[2] Canola is a grain used to make canola oil, which is very low in saturated fat and is believed to be healthier than many other oils. Canada produces about 15 percent of the world's output of canola.

futures contract Exchange-traded promise to buy or sell an asset in the future at a prespecified price.

futures contract with an option, where the holder has a choice whether or not to make delivery; your futures contract is a firm promise to deliver canola at a fixed selling price.

A canola oil processor is in the opposite position. She needs to *buy* canola after the harvest. If she would like to fix the price of this canola ahead of time, she can do so by *buying* canola futures. In other words, she agrees to take delivery of canola in the future at a price that is fixed today. The oil processor also does not have an option; if she still holds the futures contract when it matures, she is obliged to take delivery.

Let's suppose the farmer and the oil processor strike a deal. They enter a futures contract. What happens? First, no money changes hands when the contract is initiated.[3] The oil processor agrees to buy canola at the futures price on a stated *future* date (the contract maturity date). The farmer agrees to sell at the same price and date. Second, the futures contract is a binding obligation, not an option. Options give the right to buy or sell if buying or selling turns out to be profitable. The futures contract *requires* the farmer to sell and the oil processor to buy regardless of who profits and who loses.

> No money changes hands when a futures contract is entered into. The contract is a binding obligation to buy or sell at a fixed price at contract maturity.

The profit on the futures contract is the difference between the initial futures price and the ultimate price of the asset when the contract matures. For example, if the futures price is originally $300 per tonne and the market price of canola turns out to be $340, the farmer delivers and the oil processor receives the canola for a price $40 below market value. The farmer loses $40 per tonne and the canola oil processor gains $40 per tonne as a result of the futures transaction. In general, the seller of the contract benefits if the price initially locked in turns out to exceed the price that could have been obtained at contract maturity. Conversely, the buyer of the contract benefits if the ultimate market price of the asset turns out to exceed the initial futures price. Therefore, the profits on the futures contract to each party are

$$\textbf{Profit to seller = initial futures price – ultimate market price} \qquad \textbf{(26.1)}$$

$$\textbf{Profit to buyer = ultimate market price – initial futures price} \qquad \textbf{(26.2)}$$

Now it is easy to see how the farmer and the oil processor can both use the contract to hedge. Consider the farmer's overall cash flows:

	Cash Flow
Sale of canola	Ultimate price of canola
Futures profits	Futures price – ultimate price of canola
Total	Futures price

The profits on the futures contract offset the risk surrounding the sales price of canola and lock in total revenue equal to the futures price. Similarly, the oil processor's all-in cost for the canola is also fixed at the futures price. Any increase in the cost of canola will be offset by a commensurate increase in the profit realized on the futures contract.

Both the farmer and the oil processor have less risk than before. The farmer has hedged (that is, offset) risk by selling canola futures; the oil processor has hedged risk by buying canola futures.[4]

---

[3] Actually, each party will be required to set up a margin account to guarantee performance on the contract. Despite this, the futures contract may still be considered as essentially requiring no money down. First, the amount of margin is small. Second, it may be posted in interest-bearing securities, so that the parties to the trade need not suffer opportunity cost from placing assets in the margin account.

[4] Neither has eliminated all risk. For example, the farmer still has quantity risk. He does not know for sure how many tonnes of canola he will produce.

| EXAMPLE 26.1 | HEDGING WITH FUTURES |

Suppose that the farmer originally sold 50 tonnes of November canola futures at a price of $300 per tonne. In November, when the futures contract matures, the price of canola is only $250 per tonne. The farmer buys back the canola futures at $250 just before maturity, giving him a profit of $50 a tonne on the sale and subsequent repurchase. At the same time he sells his canola at the spot price of $250 a tonne. His total receipts are therefore $300 a tonne:

Profit on sale and repurchase of futures	$50
Sale of canola at the November spot price	$250
Total receipts	$300

You can see that the futures contract has allowed the farmer to lock in total proceeds of $300 a tonne.

Figure 26.2 illustrates how the futures contract enabled the farmer in Example 26.1 to hedge his position. Panel a is the value of 50 tonnes of canola as a function of the spot price of canola. The value rises by $50 for every dollar increase in canola prices. Panel b is the profit on a futures contract to deliver 50 tonnes of canola at a futures price of $300 per tonne. The profit will be zero if the ultimate price of canola equals the original futures price, $300. The profit on the contract to deliver at $300 rises by $50 for every dollar the price of canola *falls* below $300. The exposures to the price of canola depicted in panels a and b obviously cancel out. Panel c shows that the total value of the 50 tonnes plus the futures position is unaffected by the ultimate price of canola, and equals $300 × 50 = $15,000. In other words, the farmer has locked in proceeds per tonne equal to the original futures price.

THE MECHANICS OF FUTURES TRADING

In practice, the farmer and canola oil processor would not sign the futures contract face to face. Instead, each would likely go to the Winnipeg Commodity Exchange, the dominant market for canola futures and options trading.

Table 26.1 shows the price of canola futures at the Winnipeg Commodity Exchange in February 2005, when the price for immediate delivery was about $242 a tonne. Notice that there is a choice of possible delivery dates. If, for example, you were to sell canola for delivery in November, you would get a higher price than by selling September futures.

The oil processor would not be prepared to buy futures contracts if the farmer were free to deliver half-rotten canola to a leaky barn at the end of a cart track. Futures trading is possible only because the contracts are highly standardized. For example, in the case of canola futures, each contract calls for the delivery of 20 tonnes of canola of a specified quality at a warehouse in Saskatchewan.

When you buy or sell a futures contract, the price is fixed today, but payment is not made until later. However, you will be asked to put up some cash or securities as a margin to demonstrate that you are able to honour your side of the bargain.

In addition, futures contracts are *marked to market*. This means that each day any profits or losses on the contract are calculated; you pay the exchange any losses and receive any profits.

TABLE 26.1
The price of canola futures at the Winnipeg Commodity Exchange, on February 7, 2005

Delivery Date	Price per Tonne
May 2005	$246.3
July 2005	250.5
September 2005	252.7
November 2005	257.0
January 2006	263.0

Source: **www.wce.ca**

FIGURE 26.2
The farmer can use canola futures to hedge the value of the crop. See Example 26.1.

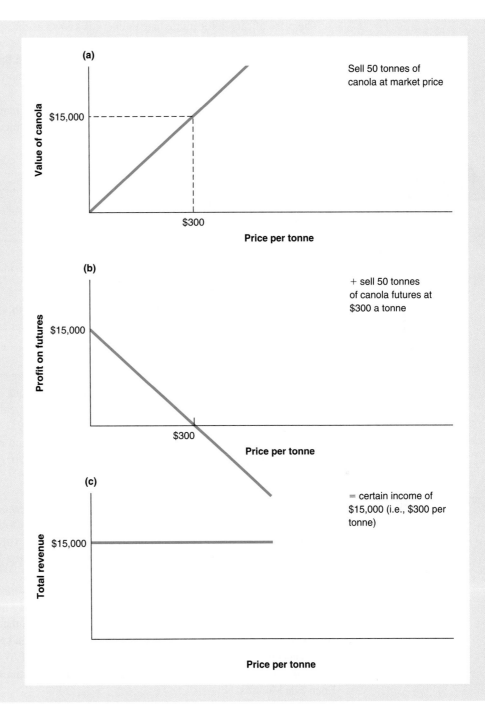

For example, our farmer agreed to deliver 50 tonnes of canola in July at $250 a tonne. Suppose that the next day the price of canola futures increases to $255 a tonne. The farmer now has a loss on his sale of $50 \times \$5 = \$250$ and must pay this sum to the exchange. You can think of the farmer as buying back his futures position each day and then opening up a new position. Thus after the first day the farmer has realized a loss on his trade of $5 a tonne and now has an obligation to deliver canola for $255 per tonne.

Of course, our oil processor is in the opposite position. The rise in the futures price leaves her with a *profit* of $5 a tonne. The exchange will therefore pay her this profit. In effect the oil processor sells her futures position at a profit and opens a new contract to take delivery at $255 per tonne.

The price of canola for immediate delivery is known as the spot price. When the farmer sells canola futures, the price that he agrees to take for his canola may be very different from the spot price. But the future eventually becomes the present. As the date for delivery approaches, the futures contract becomes more and more like a spot contract and the price of the futures contract approaches the spot price.

The farmer may decide to wait until the futures contract matures and then deliver canola to the buyer. But in practice such delivery is rare, for it is more convenient for the farmer to buy back the canola futures just before maturity.[5]

Check Point 26.2

Suppose that 2 days after taking out the futures contracts the price of July canola increases to $270 a tonne. What additional payments will be made by or to the farmer and the oil processor? What will be their remaining obligations at the end of this second day?

COMMODITY AND FINANCIAL FUTURES

We have shown how the farmer and the oil processor can both use canola futures to hedge their risk. It is also possible to trade futures in a wide variety of other commodities, such as sugar, soybean oil, pork bellies, orange juice, crude oil, and copper.

Commodity prices can bounce up and down like a bungee jumper. For example, in early 1999, raw sugar prices fell from 8.8 cents a pound to 4.5 cents before rising to 6.3 cents in August. For a large buyer of sugar, such as Hershey, these price fluctuations could knock the company badly off course. Hershey therefore reduces its exposure to movements in sugar and cocoa prices by hedging with commodity futures.

For many firms, the wide fluctuations in interest rates and exchange rates have become at least as important a source of risk as changes in commodity prices. You can use *financial futures* to hedge against these risks.

Financial futures are similar to commodity futures but, instead of placing an order to buy or sell a commodity at a future date, you place an order to buy or sell a financial asset at a future date. You can use financial futures to protect yourself against fluctuations in short- and long-term interest rates, exchange rates, and the level of share prices.

Financial futures have been a remarkable success. They were invented in 1972; within a few years, trading in financial futures significantly exceeded trading in commodity futures. Table 26.2 lists some of the more popular financial futures contracts and the exchanges where they are traded. The Chicago Board of Trade, where 454 million futures and options contracts were traded in 2004, and Eurex, the European derivatives exchange, where 1.07 billion contracts were traded in 2004, are the largest exchanges. In Canada, all financial futures and options are traded at the Bourse de Montréal.

Check Point 26.3

You plan to issue long-term bonds in nine months but are worried that interest rates may have increased in the meantime. How could you use financial futures to protect yourself against a general rise in interest rates?

---

[5] In the case of some of the financial futures described later, you *cannot* deliver the asset. At maturity the buyer simply receives (or pays) the difference between the spot price and the price at which he or she has agreed to purchase the asset.

TABLE 26.2
Some financial futures contracts and where they are traded

Future	Principal Exchange
Government of Canada Bonds	ME
Standard & Poor's Canada 60 Index	ME
U.S. Treasury notes	CBT
U.S. Treasury bonds	CBT
Eurodollar deposits	IMM
Standard & Poor's Index	IMM
Euro	IMM
Yen	IMM
German government bonds (Bunds)	Eurex

Key to abbreviations:
CBT   Chicago Board of Trade, **www.cbot.com**
IMM   International Monetary Market, at the Chicago Mercantile Exchange, **www.cme.com**
ME   Bourse de Montréal, **www.m-x.ca**
Eurex   European Derivatives Exchange, **www.eurexchange.com**

26.4   FORWARD CONTRACTS

Each day billions of dollars of futures contracts are bought and sold. We have seen that this liquidity is possible only because futures contracts are standardized. Futures contracts mature on a limited number of dates each year (take another look at the canola contracts in Table 26.1), and the contract size is standardized. For example, a contract may call for delivery of 5,000 bushels of wheat, 100 ounces of gold, or 62,500 British pounds. If the terms of a futures contract do not suit your particular needs, you may be able to buy or sell a **forward contract**.

forward contract Agreement to buy or sell an asset in the future at an agreed price.

Forward contracts are custom-tailored futures contracts.[6] You can write a forward contract with any maturity date for delivery of any quantity of goods. For example, suppose that you know that you will need to pay out yen in three months time. You can fix the price today that you will pay for the yen by arranging with your bank to buy yen forward. At the end of the three months, you pay the agreed-upon sum and take delivery of the yen.

EXAMPLE 26.2

A PIZZA FORWARD CONTRACT

Have you ever ordered a pizza by phone? If so, you have entered into a forward contract! Your order specifies the pizza type (cheese, pepperoni, and green olives), size (large), the delivery time and location (to be delivered in 30 minutes to your front door) and the price ($15). You don't pay until the product is delivered but you agree on the price at the time the contract is established. You might even be able to trade your forward contract—that is, if your roommate suddenly arrives home very hungry and is willing to buy your pizza contract from you.

EXAMPLE 26.3

FOREIGN CURRENCY FORWARD CONTRACTS

Computer Parts Inc. has ordered memory chips from its supplier in Japan. The bill for ¥53 million must be paid on July 27. The company can arrange with its bank today to buy this number of yen forward for delivery on July 27 at a forward price of ¥110 per dollar. Therefore, on July 27, Computer Parts pays the bank 53 million/110 = $481,818 and receives ¥53 million, which it can use to pay its

---

[6] One difference between forward and futures contracts is that forward contracts are not marked to market. Thus with a forward contract you settle up any profits or losses when the contract matures.

Japanese supplier. By committing forward to exchange $481,818 for ¥53 million, its dollar costs are locked in. Notice that if the firm had not used the forward contract to hedge and the dollar had depreciated over this period, the firm would have had to pay a greater amount of dollars. For example, if the exchange rate had fallen to ¥100/dollar, the firm would have had to exchange $530,000 for the ¥53 million necessary to pay its bill. The firm could have used a futures contract to hedge its foreign exchange exposure, but standardization of futures would not allow for delivery of precisely ¥53 million on precisely July 27.

The most active trading in forwards is in foreign currencies, but in recent years, companies have increasingly entered into forward rate agreements that allow them to fix the interest rate at which they borrow or lend in advance.

26.5   SWAPS

Suppose Computer Parts from Example 26.3 decides to produce memory chips instead of purchasing them from outside suppliers. It has issued $100 million in floating-rate bonds to help finance the construction of a new plant. (Recall from Chapter 13 that floating-rate bonds make interest payments that go up and down with the general level of interest rates. The coupon payments on the bonds are tied to a specific short-term interest rate.) But the financial manager is concerned that interest rates are becoming more volatile, and she would like to lock in the firm's interest expenses. One approach would be to buy back the floating-rate bonds and replace them with a new issue of fixed-rate debt. But it is costly to issue new debt to the public; in addition, buying back the outstanding bonds in the market will result in considerable trading costs.

A better approach to hedge out its interest rate exposure is for the firm to enter an interest rate **swap**. The firm will pay or "swap" a fixed payment for another payment that is tied to the level of interest rates. Thus, if rates do rise, increasing the firm's interest expense on its floating-rate debt, its cash flow from the swap agreement will rise as well, offsetting its exposure.

Suppose the firm pays the LIBOR rate on its floating-rate bonds. (Recall that LIBOR, or London Interbank Offer Rate, is the interest rate at which banks borrow from each other in the Eurodollar market. It is the most frequently used short-term interest rate in the swap market.) The firm's interest expense each year therefore equals the LIBOR rate times $100 million. It would like to transform this obligation into one that will not fluctuate with interest rates.

Suppose that current rates in the swaps market are LIBOR for 8 percent fixed. This means that Computer Parts can enter into a swap agreement to pay 8 percent on "notional principal" of $100 million to a swap dealer and receive payment of the LIBOR rate on the same amount of notional principal. The firm pays the dealer .08 × $100 million and receives LIBOR × $100 million. The dealer and the firm are called counterparties in the swap. The firm's net cash payment to the dealer is therefore (LIBOR − .08) × $100 million. (If LIBOR exceeds 8 percent, the firm receives money from the dealer; if it is less than 8 percent, the firm pays money to the dealer.) Figure 26.3 illustrates the cash flows paid by Computer Parts and the swap dealer.

swap Arrangement by two counterparties to exchange one stream of cash flows for another.

FIGURE 26.3
Interest rate swap: Computer Parts currently pays the LIBOR rate on its outstanding bonds (the arrow on the left). If the firm enters a swap to pay a fixed rate of 8 percent and receive a floating rate of LIBOR, its exposure to LIBOR will cancel out, and its net cash outflow will be a fixed rate of 8 percent.

TABLE 26.3
An interest rate swap can transform floating-rate bonds into synthetic fixed-rate bonds.

	LIBOR Rate		
	7.5%	8.0%	8.5%
Interest paid on floating-rate bonds (= LIBOR × $100 million)	$7,500,000	$8,000,000	$8,500,000
+ Cash payment on swap [= (.08 − LIBOR) × notional principal of $100 million]	500,000	0	−500,000
Total payment	$8,000,000	$8,000,000	$8,000,000

Table 26.3 shows Computer Parts' net payments for three possible interest rates. The total payment on the bond-with-swap agreement equals $8,000,000 regardless of the interest rate. The swap has transformed the floating-rate bond into synthetic fixed-rate debt with an effective coupon rate of 8 percent. The firm has thus hedged away its interest rate exposure without actually having to replace its floating-rate bonds with fixed-rate bonds. Swaps offer a much cheaper way to "rearrange the balance sheet."[7]

There are many other applications of interest rate swaps. A portfolio manager who is holding a portfolio of long-term bonds but is worried that interest rates might increase, causing a capital loss on the portfolio, can enter a swap to pay a fixed rate and receive a floating rate, thereby converting the holdings into a synthetic floating-rate portfolio (see Check Point 26.4). Or a pension fund manager might identify some money market securities that are paying excellent yields compared to other comparable-risk short-term securities. However, the manager might believe that such short-term assets are inappropriate for the portfolio. The fund can hold these high-yielding securities and enter a swap in which it receives a fixed rate and pays a floating rate. It thus captures the benefit of the advantageous *relative yields* on these securities, but still establishes a portfolio with the fixed-interest-rate risk characteristic of long-term bonds.

Check Point 26.4

Consider the portfolio manager who is holding a $100 million portfolio of long-term bonds and wishes to reduce price risk by transforming the holdings into a synthetic floating-rate portfolio. Assume the portfolio currently pays an 8 percent fixed rate and that swap dealers currently offer terms of 8 percent fixed for LIBOR. What swap would the manager establish? Show the total income on the fund in a table like Table 26.3, and illustrate the cash flows in a diagram like Figure 26.3.

There are many variations on the interest rate swap. For example, currency swaps allow firms to exchange a series of payments in dollars (which may be tied to a fixed or floating rate) for a series of payments in another currency (which also may be tied to a fixed or floating rate). These swaps can therefore be used to manage exposure to exchange rate fluctuations.

EXAMPLE 26.4   **CURRENCY SWAPS**

Suppose that the Moose Company wishes to borrow Swiss francs (SFr) to help finance its European operations. Since Moose is better known in Canada, the financial manager believes that the company can obtain more attractive terms on a dollar loan than on a Swiss franc loan. Therefore, the company borrows $10 million for 5 years at 5 percent in Canada. At the same time Moose arranges with a bank to trade its future dollar liability for Swiss francs. Under this arrangement the bank agrees to pay Moose sufficient dollars to service its dollar loan, and in exchange, Moose agrees to make a series of annual payments in Swiss francs to the bank.

---

[7] You might wonder what's in this arrangement for the swap dealer. The dealer will profit by charging a bid-ask spread. Since the dealer pays LIBOR in return for 8 percent in this swap, it might search for another trader who wishes to receive a fixed rate and pay LIBOR. The dealer will pay a 7.9 percent rate to that trader in return for the LIBOR rate. So the dealer pays a fixed rate and receives floating with one trader but pays floating and receives fixed with the other. Its net cash flow is thus riskless and equal to .1 percent of notional principal.

TABLE 26.4
Cash flows from Moose's
dollar loan and currency
swap ($ millions)

	Year 0		Years 1–4		Year 5	
	$	SFr	$	SFr	$	SFr
1. Issue dollar loan	+10		–.5		–10.5	
2. Arrange currency swap						
a. Moose $ cash flows	–10		+.5		+10.5	
b. Moose SFr cash flows		+20		–1.2		–21.2
3. Net cash flow	0	+20	0	–1.2	0	–21.2

Moose's cash flows are set out in Table 26.4. Line 1 shows that when Moose takes out its dollar loan, it contracts to pay annual interest of $.5 million and repay the $10 million that it has borrowed. Lines 2a and 2b show the cash flows from the swap, assuming that the spot exchange rate for Swiss francs is $1 = SFr2. Moose hands over to the bank the $10 million that it borrowed and receives in exchange 2 × $10 million = SFr20 million. In each of the next 4 years the bank pays Moose $.5 million, which Moose uses to pay the annual interest on its loan. In Year 5 the bank pays Moose $10.5 million, which covers both the final year's interest and the repayment of the loan. In return for these future dollar receipts, Moose agrees to pay the bank SFr1.2 million in each of the next 4 years and SFr21.2 million in Year 5.

The combined effect of Moose's two steps (line 3) is to convert its 5 percent dollar loan into a 6 percent Swiss franc loan. The device that makes this possible is the currency swap.

✓ **Check Point 26.5**   Suppose that the spot exchange rate had been $1 = SFr3 and that Swiss interest rates were 8 percent. Recalculate the Swiss franc cash flows that the bank would agree to (line 2b of Table 26.4) and Moose's net cash flows (line 3).

26.6   INNOVATION IN THE DERIVATIVES MARKET

Almost every day some new derivative contract seems to be invented. At first there may be just a few private deals between a bank and its customers, but, if the contract proves popular, one of the futures exchanges may try to muscle in on the business.

Derivatives dealers try to identify the major risks that face businesses and then design a contract that will allow them to lay off these risks. For example, a major hazard for many financial institutions is the possibility that a large customer will get into difficulties and default on its debts. Credit derivatives offer a way for the lender to insure against such a default. The provider of the insurance promises to pay out if the borrower defaults on its debts and in return charges a premium for taking on the risk. The market for credit derivatives has grown very rapidly in recent years.

Farmers, electric utilities, and soft-drink sellers all worry about the weather. So, wouldn't it be nice if they could stop worrying and hedge themselves against bad weather? Well, now they can do so, either by entering into a private deal with a derivative firm or by dealing in weather futures and options on the Chicago Mercantile Exchange.

It seems to be very difficult to predict which new contracts will succeed and which will bomb. By the time you read this, weather contracts may have been forgotten and everyone will be talking about the new growth market in _____ derivatives. Perhaps you can help fill in the missing word.

26.7   IS "DERIVATIVE" A FOUR-LETTER WORD?

Our earlier examples of the farmer and the oil processor showed how derivatives—futures, options, or swaps, for example—can be used to reduce business risk. However, if you were to copy the farmer and sell canola futures without an offsetting holding of canola, you would not be _reducing_ risk; you would be _speculating_.

Meltdown at Metallgesellschaft

Metallgesellschaft AG was one of Germany's most respected companies with more than 20,000 employees and revenues of some $10 billion. Its 251 subsidiaries were engaged in engineering, mining, financial services, and commodities trading, and its major shareholders included such blue-chip German companies as Deutsche Bank, Daimler-Benz, and Allianz.

However, in 1993, Metallgesellschaft was nearly brought to its knees by losses of $1.4 billion from trading in oil futures. The problem arose in one of its U.S. subsidiaries, MGRM. MGRM offered its customers firm price guarantees for up to 10 years on any oil that they agreed to buy. These guarantees proved very popular, so that by the end of 1993 the company had entered into long-term contracts to supply 160 million barrels of oil worth more than $3 billion.

There was only one problem. MGRM did not own the oil that it had promised to deliver and would therefore have to buy it from the major oil companies. If the price of oil rose above the price that customers had agreed to pay, MGRM would make a loss on every barrel of oil that it had sold. The apparent solution was for MGRM to hedge its exposure by buying oil futures. This would fix the price at which the company could buy oil when it needed to deliver it. The company would have liked to buy oil futures that matured on the same dates as it was obliged to deliver the oil, but, unfortunately, most futures trading takes place in contracts that mature within a year. MGRM's solution was to buy short-term oil futures and to replace them when they matured.

During the second half of 1993 oil prices fell by 25 percent and MGRM's contracts to deliver oil at a predetermined price looked increasingly attractive. However, at the same time, the company started to pile up large losses on its purchases of oil futures. This was not in itself a cause for concern. If MGRM was truly hedged, the profits on the oil contracts should have exactly offset the losses on the futures.

So what went wrong? One view is that management focused on the accumulating losses on the futures positions and failed to recognize the gains on the oil contracts. When the losses became sufficiently large, management's nerve cracked and it sold out of its futures positions at the wrong time. Moreover, because MGRM's futures positions were marked to market, the company had to find the cash each day to cover the losses on these positions. This problem of financing the hedge may have contributed to management's decision to abandon its strategy.

Other commentators are less convinced that all would have come out right if only management had not panicked. They argue that the company's strategy of hedging long-term liabilities with short-term futures was fundamentally flawed. The problem was that MGRM could not predict the price at which it would be able to replace each futures contract when it matured. If the price of the new future was below that of the maturing one, MGRM would make a profit from the trade. But unfortunately for MGRM, the reverse proved to be the case, so that the company incurred a loss each time it replaced the maturing futures contract with a new one.

While financial experts continued to debate the cause of MGRM's losses, the company's bankers struggled to put together a rescue package. A massive $1.9 billion loan from 150 international banks was needed to keep the company from foundering.

A successful futures market needs speculators who are prepared to take on risk and provide the farmer and the canola oil processor with the protection they need. For example, if an excess of farmers wished to sell canola futures, the price of futures would be forced down until enough speculators were tempted to buy in the hope of a profit. If there is a surplus of oil processors wishing to buy canola futures, the reverse will happen. The price will be forced up until speculators are drawn in to sell.

Speculation may be necessary to a thriving derivatives market, but it can get companies into serious trouble. For example, for 10 years a Japanese trading company, Sumitomo Corporation, used the futures market to place huge bets on the price of copper. Its chief trader, known in the business simply as "Mr. Copper," was lauded for his contributions to the firm's profits. However, in June 1996 the copper market was battered by the revelation that the man with the Midas touch had managed to hide losses amounting to about $1 billion.

Sumitomo has plenty of company. In 1995, Baring Brothers, a blue-chip British merchant bank, became insolvent. The reason: Nick Leeson, a trader in its Singapore office, had lost $1.4 billion speculating in futures contracts on the Japanese stock market index. The same year Daiwa Bank reported that a bond trader in its New York office had managed to hide losses over 11 years of $1.1 billion. Procter & Gamble, the blue-chip consumer products company, was painfully embarrassed in 1994 when a bet against rising interest rates lost over $100 million. At least it didn't join the billion-dollar-loss club.

SEE BOX ABOVE ▷ The Finance in Action box above discusses another billion-dollar debacle. In this case, Metallgesellschaft claimed to be using futures markets to hedge but it still managed to lose well over $1 billion. Whether the firm really was hedging, however, is a matter that is still subject to debate.

Do these horror stories mean that firms should ban the use of derivatives? Of course not. But they do illustrate that derivatives need to be used with care. Our view is this:

> Speculation is foolish unless you have reason to believe that the odds are stacked in your favour. If you are not better informed than the highly paid professionals in banks and other institutions, you should use derivatives for hedging, not for speculation.

26.8   SUMMARY

1. **Why do companies hedge to reduce risk?**

   Fluctuations in commodity prices, interest rates, or exchange rates can make planning difficult and can throw companies badly off course. Financial managers therefore look for opportunities to manage these risks, and a number of specialized instruments have been invented to help them. These are collectively known as derivative instruments.

2. **How can options, futures, and forward contracts be used to devise simple hedging strategies?**

   In the last chapter we introduced you to put and call options. Options are often used by firms to limit their downside risk. For example, if you own an asset and have the option to sell it at the current price, then you have effectively insured yourself against loss.

   Futures contracts are agreements made today to buy or sell an asset in the future. The price is fixed today, but the final payment does not occur until the delivery date. Futures contracts are highly standardized and are traded on organized exchanges. Commodity futures allow firms to fix the future price that they pay for a wide range of agricultural commodities, metals, and oil. Financial futures help firms to protect themselves against unforeseen movements in interest rates, exchange rates, and stock prices.

   Forward contracts are equivalent to tailor-made futures contracts. For example, firms often enter into forward agreements with a bank to buy or sell foreign exchange or to fix the interest rate on a loan to be made in the future.

3. **How can companies use swaps to change the risk of securities they have issued?**

   Swaps allow firms to exchange one series of future payments for another. For example, the firm might agree to make a series of regular payments in one currency in return for receiving a series of payments in another currency.

Related Web Links

www.riskmetrics.com/education.html Free online courses in risk management

www.cisco-futures.com Data on a variety of contracts, including simulations and other information

www.home.earthlink.net/~green/whatisan.htm Information about swaps

www.stuart.iit.edu/fmtreview/fmtrev2.htm One company's approach to encouraging managers to manage financial risk

www.appliedderivatives.com, www.erivativesreview.com, www.futuresmag.com, www.risk.net Journals specializing in derivatives

Key Terms

futures contract	789	forward contract	793	swap	794

Questions and Problems

*Answers in Appendix B

BASIC

1. **Risk Management.** Large businesses spend millions of dollars annually on insurance. Why? Should they insure against all risks or does insurance make more sense for some risks than others?

2. **Hedging.**
   a. An investor currently holding $1 million in long-term government bonds becomes concerned about increasing volatility in interest rates. She decides to hedge her risk using government bond futures contracts. Should she buy or sell such contracts?
   b. The treasurer of a corporation that will be issuing bonds in 3 months is also concerned about interest rate volatility and wants to lock in the price at which he could sell 8 percent coupon bonds. How would he use government bond futures contracts to hedge his firm's position?

3. **Commodity Futures.** What commodity futures are traded on futures exchanges? Who do you think could usefully reduce risk by buying each of these contracts? Who do you think might wish to sell each contract?

4. **Hedging.** "The farmer does not avoid risk by selling canola futures. If canola prices stay above $340 per tonne, then he will actually have lost by selling canola futures at $340." Is this a fair comment?

5. **Marking to Market.** Suppose that in the 5 days following a farmer's sale of September wheat futures at a futures price of $3.83 the futures prices are

Day	1	2	3	4	5
Price	$3.83	$3.98	$3.70	$3.50	$3.60

   At the end of day 5 the farmer decides to quit wheat farming and buys back his futures contract. What payments are made between the farmer and the exchange on each day? What is the total payment over the five days? Would the total payment be any different if the contract was not marked to market? The contract size is 5,000 bushels.

*6. **Futures versus Spot Positions.** What do you think are the advantages of holding futures rather than the underlying commodity? What do you think are the disadvantages?

PRACTICE

EXCEL

*7. **Hedging with Futures versus Puts.** A gold mining firm is concerned about short-term volatility in its revenues. Gold currently sells for $300 an ounce, but the price is extremely volatile and could fall as low as $280 or rise as high as $320 in the next month. The company will bring 1,000 ounces to the market next month.
   a. What will be total revenues if the firm remains unhedged for gold prices of $280, $300, and $320 an ounce?
   b. The futures price of gold for 1-month-ahead delivery is $301. What will be the firm's total revenues at each gold price if the firm enters a 1-month futures contract to deliver 1,000 ounces of gold?
   c. What will total revenues be if the firm buys a 1-month put option to sell gold for $300 an ounce? The puts cost $2 per ounce.

8. **Hedging with Calls.** A large dental lab plans to purchase 1,000 ounces of gold in 1 month. Assume again that gold prices can be $280, $300, or $320 an ounce.
   a. What will total expenses be if the firm purchases call options on 1,000 ounces of gold with an exercise price of $300 an ounce? The options cost $3 per ounce.
   b. What will total expenses be if the firm purchases call options on 1,000 ounces of gold with an exercise price of $295 an ounce? These options cost $7 per ounce.

9. **Forward Contract.** Assume that the 1-year interest rate is 6 percent and the 2-year interest rate is 7 percent per year. You approach a bank and ask at what rate the bank will promise to make a 1-year loan in 12 months' time. The bank offers to make a forward commitment to lend to you at 12 percent. Would you accept the offer? Can you think of a simple, cheaper alternative?

10. **Hedging Project Risk.** Your firm has just tendered for a contract in Japan. You won't know for 3 months whether you get the contract but if you do, you will receive a payment of ¥10 million 1 year from now. You are worried that if the yen declines in value, the dollar value of this payment will be less than you expect and the project could even show a loss. Discuss the possible ways that you could protect the firm against a decline in the value of the yen. Illustrate the possible outcomes if you do get the contract and if you don't.

EXCEL

*11. **Hedging with Futures.** Show how Petrochemical Parfum (see Section 26.2) can also use futures contracts to protect itself against a rise in the price of crude oil. Show how the pay-offs would vary if the oil price is $68, $70, or $72 a barrel. What are the advantages and disadvantages for Petrochemical of using futures rather than options to reduce risk? Repeat the exercise for Onnex. Assume the futures price for oil is $70 per barrel.

12. **Futures Contracts.** Look in *The Globe and Mail* or *National Post* at the prices of gold futures quoted on the COMEX futures exchange. What is the date of the most distant contract? Suppose that you buy 100 ounces of gold futures for this date. When do you receive the gold? When do you pay for it? Is the futures price higher or lower than the current spot price? Can you suggest why?

13. **Hedging Currency Risk.** When the deutschemark strengthened in 1991 and 1992, German luxury car manufacturers found it increasingly difficult to compete in the United States market. How could they have hedged themselves against this risk? Would a company that was hedged have been in a better position to compete? Explain why or why not.

14. **Swaps.** What is a currency swap? An interest rate swap? Give one example of how each might be used.

CHALLENGE

15. **Swaps.** Firms A and B face the following borrowing rates for a 5-year fixed-rate debt issue in Canadian dollars or euros:

	Canadian Dollars	Euros
Firm A	10%	7%
Firm B	8%	6%

Suppose that A wishes to borrow Canadian dollars and B wishes to borrow euros. Show how a swap could be used to reduce the borrowing costs of each company. Assume a spot exchange rate of 1 euro to the dollar.

16. **Risk Management.** Discuss each of the following statements:
   a. "The better the risk management policies of a company, the greater a company's debt capacity."
   b. "Managers are not paid to avoid all risk."

17. **Internet.** The International Finance Risk Institute provides three case studies on the sources, types, and control of financial risk at **http://riskinstitute.ch/introduction.htm**. Read the Sumitomo story for insights into the financial trading scandal.

18. **Internet.** Risk management extends beyond using financial instruments to hedge. This Web site offers some ideas on how to manage a business crisis: **http://entrepreneurs.about.com/cs/riskmanagement/**.

19. **Internet.** In Canada, futures are traded on the Bourse de Montréal, **www.m-x.ca**. What futures contracts are offered for trading? Why would an investor be interested in purchasing a bond futures?

20. **Internet.** Algorithmics is a world leader in risk management systems and a Canadian company. Go to **http://www.algorithmics.com/aboutalgo/careers.shtml**. Click on "View/Apply to Current Opportunities" and read a couple of job descriptions. Summarize what skills are needed to be a financial risk management professional, such as a financial engineer.

21. **Standard & Poor's.** Go to **www.mcgrawhill.ca/edumarketinsight**. The Packaged Foods and Meats industry (use Industry link) is made up of companies that buy commodities and package and/or transform them into food for retail customers. Review the list of companies (*Industry Constituents*) in the industry and review the Company Profile of one firm of interest to you. Link to that company's home page, investor relations, and SEC filings. Review the latest 10K filing or annual report for managements' discussion of risk management activities.

1. What areas of risk does the firm manage with derivative contracts?

2. Given the company's products and the commodities they are derived from, what futures and options contracts would make most sense for hedging price risk? Review the list of futures and options contracts traded on exchanges. (See *Currencies, Agricultural, etc.*, links at **http://www.site-by-site.com/usa/optfut.htm**.)

Solutions to Check Points

26.1 See Figure 26.4 on page 802.

26.2 The farmer has a further loss of $15 a tonne ($270 − $255) and will be required to pay 50 × $15, or $750 to the exchange. The oil processor has a further profit of $15 a tonne ($270 − $255) and will receive $750 from the exchange for the 50 tonne contract. The farmer is now committed to delivering canola in July for $270 a tonne and the oil processor is committed to paying $270 a tonne.

26.3 You sell long-term bond futures with a delivery date of nine months. Suppose, for example, that you agree to deliver long-term bonds in 9 months at a price of 100. If interest rates fall, the price of the bond futures will rise to (say) 105. (Remember that when interest rates fall, bond prices rise.) In this case the profit that you make on your bond futures offsets the lower price that the firm is likely to receive on the sale of its own bonds. Conversely, if interest rates fall, the company will make a loss on its futures position but will receive a higher price for its own bonds.

26.4 The manager should enter a swap to pay an 8 percent fixed rate and receive LIBOR on notional principal of $100 million. The cash flows will then rise in tandem with the LIBOR rate:

	LIBOR Rate		
	7.5%	**8.0%**	**8.5%**
Interest received on fixed-rate bonds (= .08 × $100 million)	$8,000,000	$8,000,000	$8,000,000
+ Cash flow on swap [= (LIBOR − .08) × notional principal of $100 million]	−500,000	0	+500,000
Total payment	$7,500,000	$8,000,000	$8,500,000

The diagram describing the cash flows of each party to the swap is as follows:

8% income on bond portfolio → Portfolio manager — 8% → / ← LIBOR — Swap dealer

The manager nets a cash flow proportional to the LIBOR rate.

26.5   The following table shows revised cash flows from Moose's dollar loan and currency swap ($ millions):

	Year 0		Years 1–4		Year 5	
	$	SFr	$	SFr	$	SFr
1. Issue dollar loan	+10		−.5		−10.5	
2. Arrange currency swap						
a. Moose $ cash flows	−10		+.5		+10.5	
b. Moose SFr cash flows		+30		−2.4		−32.4
3. Net cash flow	0	+30	0	−2.4	0	−32.4

Notice that in exchange for $10 million today the bank is now prepared to pay SFr30 million. Since the Swiss interest rate is now 8 percent, the bank will expect to earn .08 × 30 = SFr2.4 million interest on its Swiss franc outlay.

FIGURE 26.4
Diagrams for Check Point 26.1.

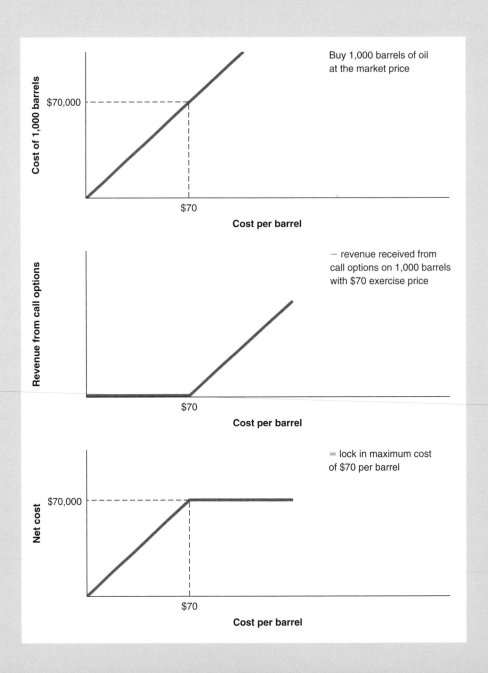

APPENDIX B
Answers to Selected End-of-Chapter Problems

CHAPTER 1

1. real, executive airplanes, brand names, financial, stock, investment, capital budgeting, financing

9. a. financial
   d. real
   f. financial
   g. real

14. The contingency arrangement aligns the interests of the lawyer and the client.

16. Such a plan would burden them with a considerable personal risk tied to the fortunes of the firm.

17. Managers who are more securely entrenched in their positions are more able to pursue their own interests.

CHAPTER 2

3. Options markets, foreign exchange markets, futures markets, commodity markets, money market.

4. Buy shares in a mutual fund.

8. Look up the price of gold in commodity markets, and compare it to $1,500/6 = $250/ounce.

17. a. Find the rate of return available on other riskless investments, e.g., 1-year maturity U.S. Treasury notes.

    b. The opportunity cost is 20%, the same expected rate of return available on other investments of comparable risk.

CHAPTER 3

1.

Assets		Liabilities and Shareholders' Equity	
Cash	$ 10,000	Accounts payable	$ 17,000
Receivables	22,000	Long-term debt	170,000
Inventory	200,000		
Store and property	100,000	Shareholders' equity	145,000
Total assets	$332,000	Liabilities and shareholders' equity	$ 332,000

5. b.

	AB	NF
Total Tax	$17,100	$19,157.17
Average Tax Rate	28.5%	31.93%
Marginal Tax Rate	32%	40.02%

7.

	After-tax	Tax Rate
Interest	$847.50	43.5
Dividends	2,157.38	.281
Capital Gain	1,565	.2175

9. Dividends = $600,000

11. a. Book value = $200,000, Market value = $50,200,000
    b. Price per share = $25.10, Book value per share = $.10

12. a. EBIT = $1,500
    b. NI = $650
    c. Cash flow from operating activities = $1,850
    d. Cash flow from assets = $950

20. a. 2004 Equity = $470
       2005 Equity = $680
    b. Net income = $310
    c. Depreciation = $80
    d. ΔNWC = $80
    e. Debt repaid = $110
    f. Cash flow from operations = $310
       Cash flow from assets = $10
    g. Cash flow to bondholders = $110 − $200
       Cash flow to shareholders = $100

23. Net working capital decreased by 50.
    Noncash net working capital increased by 50.

25. Earnings per share in 2004 = $1.70
    Earnings per share in 2005 = $1.52

31. Price per share = $6,650,000/500,000 = $13.30

CHAPTER 4

1. a. 46.32

2. a. 215.89

4. PV = $548.47

5. 5%, 8%, 0%

7. PV = $812.44

8. a. $t = 23.36$

9. a. 671.01

10. a. 1,448.66

11. 12.68%, 8.24%, 10.25%

12. 9.57%, 6%, 8%

13. $n = 9.01$ years

15. APR = 52%; EAR = 67.77%

22. a. EAR = 6.78%, b. PMT = 573.14

23. a. $r = 11.11\%$, b. $r = 1/(1 − d) − 1 = d/(1 − d)$

28. a. 277.41, b. 247.69

29. PV = $61,796.71

30. Monthly mortgage payment = $1,119.66.
    Balance remaining after 5 years is $157,208.

35. Real rate of interest is zero. Annual consumption = $450,000/30 = $15,000.

41. $n = 44.74$ months

42. The present value of your payments is $671. The present value of your receipts is $579. This is a bad deal.

55. a. The present value of the payoff is $1,228. This is a good deal.
    b. PV is $771. This is a bad deal.

58. $4,126.57

59. a. $408,334.38, b. $3,457.40

63. a. 4%, b. 8.16%, c. 10.24%

65. a. $79.38, b. $91.51, c. 4.854%,
    d. $91.51/(1.04854)^3 = $79.38

69. a. $264,439, b. $16,172

70. 18 years

71. Inflation = 1,099% per year

76. $1.188, $0.8418

CHAPTER 5

1. a. Coupon rate remains unchanged.
   b. Price will fall.
   c. Yield to maturity increases.
   d. Current yield increases.

3. Bond price = $1,066.67

4. Coupon rate = 8.0%, Current yield = 8.42%, Yield to maturity = 9.12%

9. 15%

10. 12%

11. Rate of return on both bonds = 10%

12. a. Price will be $1,000.
    b. Rate of return = 2.86%
    c. Real return = –0.136%

13. b. Price = $939.20

14. c. 7.18%

18. 20 years

20. a. Price = $716.60, b. 12.06%

21. a. YTM today = 8.3%, YTM next year = 7.23%
    b. Rate of return = 15.31%

25. a. 7.5% per year
    b. 7.63% per year
    c. 8.64% per year

26. 8.64 % per year

32. Initial price = $978.12, New price = $959.37

36. a. 3.92%

CHAPTER 6

3. a. $58.33
   b $58.33
   c. Dividend yield = 12%; capital gains yield = 0%; expected return = 12%

6. a. 14%
   b. $P_0 = $20

8. week, semi-strong, strong, fundamental, technical

10. a. $DIV_1 = 1.04, $DIV_2 = 1.0816, $DIV_3 = 1.1249
    b. $P_0 = 13, c. $P_3 = 14.6237
    d. Your payments are:

	Year 1	Year 2	Year 3
DIV	1.04	1.0816	1.1249
Sales price			14.6232
Total cash flow	1.04	1.0816	15.7481
PV of cash flow	0.9286	0.8622	11.2092

Sum of PV = $13.00

12. a. $P_0 = 21, b. $P_0 = 30

14. a. 9.26%, b. 3.74%, c. 12.5%

17. a. In each case, $P_0 = 33.33
    b. (1) Reinvest at 0%: $P_0 = 33.33, PVGO = 0
       (2) Reinvest at 40%: $P_0 = 42.86$, PVGO = $9.53
       (3) Reinvest at 60%: $P_0 = 66.67, PVGO = $33.34
    c. In part (a), the return on reinvested earnings was equal to the discount rate. In part (b), the return on reinvested earnings was greater than the discount rate.

20. a. $P_0 = 18.10, b. $DIV_1/P_0 = 5.52$%

22. a. 6%, b. 23.33, c. 6.66, d. 11.67, e. $P_0 = 16.67, P/E = 8.33, f. High P/E ratios reflect expectations of high PVGO.

24. a. P/E = 33.33/4 = 8.33
    b. P/E increases to 10

26. a. $P_0 = 125
    b. Assets in place = $80, PVGO = $45

29. a. Market-to-book ratio = $400/$100 = 4
    b. Market-to-book ratio = ½

37. Before-tax return is 7.8%, after-tax return is 5.96%.

40. If the price of the shares already reflects this fact, the shares may not be a bargain.

CHAPTER 7

1. Both projects are worth pursuing.

3. $NPV_A = 11.93 and $NPV_B = 12.29. Choose B.

5. No.

7. Project A has a payback period of 2.5 years. Project B has a payback period of 2 years.

13 .2378

16. $IRR_A = 25.7$%
    $IRR_B = 20.7$%
    Project B is best.

17. NPV = –$197.7. Reject.

18. a. $r = 0$ implies NPV = $15,750.
       $r = 50$% implies NPV = $4,250.
       $r = 100$% implies NPV = 0.
    b. IRR = 100%

20. $NPV_{9\%} = $2,139.28$ and $NPV_{14\%} = –$1,444.54$. The IRR is 11.81%.

23. NPV must be negative.

25. a.

Project	Payback	Discounted Payback
A	3	4+
B	2	2.12
C	3	3.30

    b. Project B
    c. Project B

d.

Project	NPV
A	−1,011
B	3,378
C	2,405

e. False

28. a.

Year	Book Rate of Return
1	10%
2	12.5%
3	16.7%
4	25%
5	50%

b. NPV = $1,978

d. NPV unaffected

32. a. If $r = 2\%$, choose A.

b. If $r = 12\%$, choose B.

c. Larger cash flows for project A come later and are more sensitive to discount rate increases.

34. $22,774

36. b. At 5%, NPV = −$.443

c. At 20%, NPV = $.840
At 40%, NPV = −$.634

40. a. The equivalent cost of owning and operating the new machine is $4,590. The old machine costs $5,000 a year to operate. You should replace.

b. If $r = 10\%$, do not replace.

CHAPTER 8

3. $2.2 million

5. Increase in net cash flow = $106 million

8. Cash flow = $3,300

10. Total operating cash flow in thousands (Years 1-6) = $339.45
Net cash flow at time 0 = −$1,000

11. a.

Year	CCA Rate
1	6,000
2	10,200
3	7,140

b. and c.   See Solutions Manual.

16. After-tax cash flow = $17.3 million

18. a. Total incremental operating CF = $6,772 in years 1–6
Net cash flow at time 0 = −$4,000

b. NPV = $403.14

c. NPV = −4,000 + 1,300 × annuity factor (15%, 6 years) = $919.83; IRR = 23.21%

23. NPV = −10,894. Don't buy.

25. Equivalent annual (net-of-tax) capital costs:
Quick and Dirty: $2.12 million
Do-It-Right: $1.84 million
Choose Do-It-Right.

27. NPV = −$372,988

32. NPV = −$0.1817 million

34. c. NPV = $24.92 million
IRR = 31.33%

d. NPV (with CCA) = $9.21 million

CHAPTER 9

1. Variable costs = $.50 per burger
Fixed costs = $1.25 million

5. a. NPV = $5.1 million

b. NPV = $2.5 million

c. NPV = $6.2 million

d. Price = $1.61 per jar

9. a. 4,286 diamonds annually

b. 5,978 diamonds per year

11. Accounting break-even is unaffected. NPV break-even increases.

12. CF break-even is less than zero-profit break-even sales level.

15. a. Accounting break-even increases.

b. NPV break-even falls.

c. The switch to MACRS makes the project more attractive.

17. NPV will be negative.

20. DOL = 1

23. a. Average CF = 0

b. Average CF = $15,000

28. a. Expected NPV = −$681,728. The firm will reject the project.

b. Expected NPV = $69,855. The project is now worth pursuing.

CHAPTER 10

1. Return = 15%, Dividend yield = 5%,
Capital gains yield = 10%

3. a. Rate of return = 0, Real rate = −4.76%

5.

Asset Class	Real Rate
Treasury bills	1.65%
Government bonds	3.3
Common stock	8.16

9. b. Average TSX risk premium = 0.62%; Average long bond risk premium = 5.4%

c. TSX risk premium standard deviation = 17%; Long bond risk premium standard deviation = 5.33%. The riskier TSX has a more variable historic risk premium.

14. Expected return = 23.3%, Standard deviation = 77.63%

17. b. $r_{stock} = 13\%$, Standard deviation = 9.8%
$r_{bonds} = 8.4\%$, Standard deviation = 3.2%

21. a. General Steel,   b. Club Med

25. a., b.

	Average return	Standard deviation
TSX	4.13%	16.8%
Long Bond	8.91	3.51
Treasury Bill	3.51	1.38
Portfolio	5.51	6.01

b. The average standard deviation of the three securities is 7.23%, higher than the portfolio standard deviation of 6.01%, showing the benefit of diversification.

CHAPTER 11

1. a. False
   b. False
   c. False
   d. True
   e. True

7. Required return = 12.75%, Overpriced.

9. a., b. Nike
   c. $\beta = .78$
   d. $\beta = .61$, std. dev. = 12.2%
   e. Exxon: $r = 8.27\%$, Polaroid: $r = 7.71\%$, Nike: $r = 12.4\%$

11. a. $\beta_A = 1.2$, $\beta_D = .75$
    D's return is less sensitive to the return of the overall market.
    b. $r_m = 12\%$, $r_A = 14\%$, $r_D = 9\%$
    c. $r_A = 13.6\%$, $r_D = 10\%$
    d. Stock A

13. NPV = –$21.14

15. $P_1 = \$52.63$

19. $400,000

23. $\beta = .5$

CHAPTER 12

1. 5.50%

3. 9.9%

4. 13.75%

6. No, the risk of the project determines the appropriate discount rate. Use Geothermal's WACC.

8. The cost of equity capital is 10.4%. WACC = 8.78%

10. WACC = 12.4%

14. a. 10.55%

16. WACC = 11.68%

CHAPTER 13

1. a. 80,000 shares
   b.

After new issue:	
Common shares	$110,000
Retained earnings	$ 30,000
Common equity	$140,000
Note:	
Authorized shares	$100,000
Issued shares	$ 30,000

3. a. funded
   b. eurobond
   d. sinking fund
   f. prime rate
   g. floating rate
   h. private placement, public issue

6. a. 90 votes
   b. 900 votes

7. a. 200,001 shares
   b. 80,000 shares

11. Similarity: The firm promises to make specified payments. Advantage of income bonds: interest payments are tax-deductible expenses.

CHAPTER 14

1. a. Subsequent issue
   b. Bond issue
   c. Bond issue

3. a. A large issue
   b. A bond issue
   c. Private placements

4. Less underwriter risk; less signalling effect from debt; easier to value

7. a. 10%
   b. Average return = 3.94%
   c. I have suffered the winner's curse.

10. No.

12. 12% of the value of funds raised.

15. a. $12.5 million
    b. $5.80 per share

17. a. $10
    b. $18.333
    c. $8.333
    d. 200 rights

CHAPTER 15

4. $296 million

11. P/E = 10/1.25 = 8 (no leverage)
    P/E = 10/1.33 = 7.5 (leveraged)

16. $r_{equity} = 18\%$

22. a. 11.27%
    b. Without the tax shield, the value of equity would fall by $296 million. Market-value balance sheet:

Assets	Liabilities and Equity	
2,404	Debt	0
	Equity	2,404

23. a. PV tax shield = $14
    b. Assuming cost of debt = 8% and cost of equity = 15%, WACC = 12.55%.
    c. $150.47

24. Distorted investment decisions, impeded relations with other firms and creditors

34. a. Stockholders gain; bondholders lose.
    b. Bondholders gain; stockholders lose.
    c. Bondholders lose; stockholders gain.
    d. Original stockholders lose; bondholders gain.

CHAPTER 16

1. b. The ex-dividend date, June 7
   c. Dividend yield = 1.1%
   d. Payout ratio = 15.8%
   e. New stock price = $24.55

3. a. Price = $32
   b. Price = $32
   c. Price = $40, unchanged

9. a. No effect on total wealth
   b. Identical to position after the stock repurchase

11. No impact on wealth

12. a. The after-tax dividend, $1.44
    b. No

13. a. 1,250 shares. Value of equity remains at $50,000.
    b. Same effect as the stock dividend

14. a. $50
    b. 26.16%
    c. $48.692

16. a. Price = $19.49
    b. Before-tax return = 12.9%
    c. Price = $20.15
    d. Before-tax return = 14.1%

25. a. $20 per share
    b. If the firm pays a dividend, EPS = $2. If the firm does the repurchase, EPS = $2.105.
    c. If the dividend is paid, the P/E ratio = 9.5. If the stock is repurchased, the P/E ratio = 9.5.

CHAPTER 17

1. a. Long-term debt ratio = .42
   b. Total debt ratio = .65
   c. Times interest earned = 3.75
   d. Cash coverage ratio = 7.42
   e. Current ratio = .74
   f. Quick ratio = .52
   g. Net profit margin = .0994
   h. Inventory turnover = 21.7
   i. Days sales in inventory = 16.8 days
   j. Average collection period = 65.9 days
   k. ROE = .135
   l. ROA = .0473
   m. Payout ratio = .65
   n. Operating profit margin = .151
   o. Operating return on assets = .072
   p. Return on invested capital = .1099

3. Gross investment = $2,576 million

12. The current ratio is unaffected. The quick ratio falls.

14. Days sales in inventory = 2 days

16. a. Times interest earned = 1.25
    b. Cash coverage ratio = 1.5

c. Fixed-charge coverage ratio = 0.923

18. Asset turnover = .73, ROA = 3.65%

20. $\dfrac{\text{Book debt}}{\text{Market equity}} = \dfrac{.5}{2} = .25$

24. a. The shipping company
    b. United Foods
    c. The grocery store
    d. The power company
    e. Fledgling Electronics

CHAPTER 18

4. Sustainable growth rate = 10.5%
   Internal growth rate = 6.3%

7. Possible balancing items: dividends, borrowing or equity issues. With the tendency to keep dividends steady and raise equity in large amounts, borrowing is the most frequently used balancing item.

9. The balancing item is dividends. Dividends must be $200.

11. a. Internal growth rate = 10%
    b. Sustainable growth rate = 15%

15. a. With 20% growth: Addition to retained earnings = $40,000; Increase in net assets = $200,000; Required external financing = $160,000.

    With 5% growth: Add. to r.e. = $34,000; Increase in net assets = $50,000; Required external financing = $16,000. To finance faster growth, more external financing is needed.

    b. **Second-Stage Pro Forma**

Balance Sheet	20% growth
Assets	
Net working capital	240
Fixed assets	960
Net assets	1,200
Liabilities and Shareholders' Equity	
Long-term debt	560
Shareholders' equity	640
Total liabilities and shareholders' equity	1,200

17. a. g = .02564
    b. Issue $1,025.6 in new debt.
    c. g = .0154

21. Payout ratio can be at most 44%.

23. Net profit margin = 8%

25. g = 12%

CHAPTER 19

1.

	Cash	Net Working Capital
a.	$2 million decline	$2 million decline
b.	$2,500 increase	Unchanged
f.	$5 million increase	Unchanged

2. a. long-term financing, total capital requirement, marketable securities
   b. cash, cash, cash balance, marketable securities

5. Lower inventory period and cash conversion cycle; reduce net working capital.

7. a. Cash conversion cycle falls.
   b. Cash conversion cycle increases.
   c. Cash conversion cycle falls.

9. Effective rate = 8.89%. If the compensating balance is 20%, the effective rate is 10%.

11. a. 6.38%
    b. 6.20%

15. The order is .75 times the following quarter's sales forecast:

Quarter	Order
1	270
2	252
3	288
4	288

19.

	Quarter			
	First	**Second**	**Third**	**Fourth**
Cash at start of period	$40	$10	$15	–$14
+ Net cash inflow (from problem 18)	–30	+5	–29	–41
= Cash at end of period	10	15	–14	–55
Minimum operating cash balance	30	30	30	30
Cumulative short-term financing required (minimum cash balance minus cash at end of period)	$20	$15	$44	$85

25. **Sources of Cash**

Sale of marketable securities	2
Increase in bank loans	1
Increase in accounts payable	5
Cash from operations:	
Net income	6
Depreciation	2
Total	16

Uses of Cash

Increase in inventories	6
Increase in accounts receivable	3
Investment in fixed assets	6
Dividend paid	1
Total	16
Change in cash balance	0

27.

	February	**March**	**April**
Sources of cash			
Collections on current sales	$100	$110	$ 90
Collections on accounts receivable	90	100	110
Total sources of cash	$190	$210	$200
Uses of cash			
Payments of accounts payable	$ 30	$ 40	$ 30
Cash purchases	70	80	60
Labour and administrative expenses	30	30	30
Capital expenditures	100	0	0
Taxes, interest, and dividends	10	10	10
Total uses of cash	$240	$160	$130
Net cash inflow (sources – uses)	–$ 50	+$ 50	+$ 70
Cash at start of period	$100	$ 50	$100
+ Net cash inflow	–50	+50	+70
= Cash at end of period	$ 50	$100	$170
Minimum operating cash balance	$100	$100	$100
Cumulative short-term financing required (minimum cash balance minus cash at end of period)	$ 50	$ 0	–$ 70

CHAPTER 20

1. Ledger balance = $215,000
   Net float = $15,000

6. a. $20,000
   b. $4
   c. $120

8. Yes

10. The economic order quantity = 90 gems. The firm should place smaller but more frequent orders.

13. a. Economic order quantity = 600
    b. Total costs = $6,000

15. Economic order quantity falls by a factor of 10.

16. Cash balance = $14,142
    Transfers per month = 7.07

19. a. $1.5 million
    b. $180,000
    c. Yes

20. a. The interest rate, the cost of each transaction, and the variability of each cash flow.
    b. It should restore it to one-third of the distance from the lower to the upper limit.

21. a. Once every 2½ weeks
    b. $204
    c. $102

22. Cash balances fall relative to sales.

CHAPTER 21

1. a. $10
   b. 40 days
   c. 9.6%

4. a. Due lag and pay lag fall.
   c. Terms lag and pay lag increase.

5. b. False
   c. True

7. a. 20 days
   b. $1.096 million
   c. Average days in receivables will fall.

9. a. The expected profit from a sale is –2. Do not extend credit.
   b. $p = .95$
   c. The present value of a sale, net of default, is positive, $458.35
   d. $p = 16\%$

16. a. Yes
    b. Credit should not be advanced.
    c. Net benefit from advancing credit = $100

17. PV (REV) = $1,200
    PV (COST) = $1,000
    Slow payers have a 70% probability of paying their bills. The expected profit of a sale to a slow payer is therefore .70 ($1,200 – $1,000) – .30 ($1,000) = –$160.
    Expected savings = $16. The credit check costs $5, so it is cost effective.

19. Sell only to groups 1, 2, and 3.

CHAPTER 22

2. a, b, d, f

5. a. $59,307i.3
   b. $2,692.7
   c. NPV = –$2,307.3; do not lease.

7. a. Lease cash flows:

	0	1	2	3	4	5	6
Saved cost	75,000						
CCA tax shield	–3,281	–5,742	–4,307	–3,230	–2,422	–1,817	–5,451
Lease payment	–15,000	–15,000	–15,000	–15,000	–15,000	–15,000	
Lease tax shield	5,250	5,250	5,250	5,250	5,250	5,250	0
Lease cash flows	61,969	–15,492	–14,057	–12,980	–12,172	–11,567	–5,451

   b. Equivalent loan = $60,403; NPV = $1,566
   c. NPV = $1,566 – $5,066 = –$3,500

11. a. $188
    b. $1,471
    c. $60

12. a. Minimum lease payment acceptable to lessor = $18,441.5
    b. Maximum lease payment acceptable to lessee = $18,673

16. a. NPV to Nodhead = –$13,493
    b. NPV to Compulease = $9,639
    c. Overall gain = –$13,493 + $9,639 = –$3,855

CHAPTER 23

6. $24 per share, NPV = 0.

8. a. $5 million
   b. $4 million
   c. NPV = $1 million

12. a. NPV = $5,000
    b. SCC will sell for $51.67; SDP will sell for $20; Wealth increase: SCC = 3.3%, SDP = 14.29%; Fraction of economic gain: SCC = 50%, SDP = 50%.
    c. Price = $51.32
    d. NPV = $3,947; SCCs fraction of economic gain = 39.5%. Share offer equivalent to (a): SCC issues .3871 shares for every SDP share.

CHAPTER 24

1. a. 62.02 euros; $161.25
   b. 95.10 Swiss francs; $105.15
   c. Direct exchange rate will decrease and indirect exchange rate will increase.
   d. U.S. dollar is worth more.

3. b. $\dfrac{f_{x/\$}}{s_{x/\$}} = \dfrac{E(s_{x/\$})}{s_{x/\$}}$

   d. $\dfrac{1 + r_x}{1 + r_\$} = \dfrac{E(1 + i_x)}{E(1 + i_\$)}$

6. a

8. Borrow the present value of 1 million Australian dollars, sell them for U.S. dollars in the spot market, and invest the proceeds in an 8-year U.S. dollar loan. In 8 years, it can repay the Australian loan with the anticipated Australian dollar payment.

10. a. 4.0%
    b. 10.5%
    c. –2.5%

11. 8.99%

14. Canadian dollar should be depreciating relative to the U.S. dollar.

16. Net present value = $.72 million

CHAPTER 25

1.

	Payoff	Profit
b. Call option, $X = 20$	0	–3.05
e. Put option, $X = 24$	4	1.15

3. a. The February call costs 1.10. The April call costs $1.85.
   b. Longer time to expiry increases the probability that the stock price will go up, making the call more valuable.
   c. This is true of puts as well.

5. Figure 25.8a represents a call seller; Figure 25.8b represents a call buyer.

7.

	a. $S<100$	b. $S>100$
Value of put	$100 - S$	0
Value of stock	S	S
Total	100	S

15. You will be more tempted to choose the high-risk proposal.

17. a. Call option to pursue a project.
    b. Put option to sell the equipment.

19. Put option with exercise price equal to support price.

21. a. Option to put (sell) the stock to the underwriter.
    b. Volatility of the stock value; the length of the period for which the underwriter guarantees the issue; the interest rate; the price at which the underwriter is obligated to buy the stock; and the market value of the stock.

25. a. Buy a call option for $3. Exercise the call to purchase stock. Pay the $20 exercise price. Sell the share for $25. Riskless profit equals $2.
    b. Buy a share and put option. Exercise the put. Riskless profit equals $1.

CHAPTER 26

6. Advantages: liquidity, no storage costs, no spoilage.
   Disadvantages: no income or benefits that could accrue from holding asset in portfolio.

7.

	Gold Price		
	$280	$300	$320
a. Revenues	$280,000	$300,000	$320,000
Futures contract	21,000	1,000	–19,000
b. Total	$301,000	$301,000	$301,000
c. Revenues	$280,000	$300,000	$320,000
+ Put option payoff	20,000	0	0
– Put option cost	2,000	2,000	2,000
Net revenue	$298,000	$298,000	$318,000

11. Petrochemical will take a long position to hedge its cost of buying oil. Onnex will take a short position to hedge its revenue from selling oil.

	Oil Price ($ per barrel)		
	$68	$70	$72
Cost for Petrochemical:			
Cash flow on purchase of oil	–68,000	–70,000	–72,000
+ Cash flow on long futures position	– 2,000	0	+ 2,000
Total cash flow	–70,000	–70,000	–70,000
Revenue for Onnex:			
Revenue from 1,000 barrels	$68,000	$70,000	$72,000
+ Payoff on short futures position	2,000	0	(2,000)
Net revenue	$70,000	$70,000	$70,000

The benefit of futures is the ability to lock in a riskless position without paying any money. The benefit of the option hedge is that you benefit if prices move in one direction without losing if they move in the other direction. However, this asymmetry comes at a price: the cost of the option.

GLOSSARY

account receivable pledging: A firm assigns its accounts receivable as a security to the lender to obtain a loan. 611

acquisition: Takeover of a firm by purchase of that firm's common stock or assets. 705

additional paid-in capital: Difference between issue price and par value of stock, also called capital surplus. 395

agency problems: Conflict of interest between the firm's owners and managers. 16

aging schedule: Classification of accounts receivable by time outstanding. 16, 663

angel: A wealthy individual investor in early-stage ventures. 429

annual percentage rate (APR): Interest rate that is annualized using simple interest. 112

annuity: Equally spaced and level stream of cash flows. 94

annuity due: Level stream of cash flows starting immediately. 100

annuity factor: Present value of a $1 annuity. 96

asset class: Eligible depreciable assets are grouped into specified asset classes by CRA. Each asset class has a prescribed CCA rate. 251

authorized share capital: Maximum number of shares that the company is permitted to issue as specified in the firm's articles of incorporation. 395

availability float: Cheques already deposited that have not yet been cleared. 628

average tax rate: Total taxes owed divided by total income. 64

balance sheet: Financial statement that shows the value of the firm's assets and liabilities at a particular time. 49, 533

balancing item: Variable that adjusts to maintain the consistency of a financial plan. Also called the plug. 569

banker's acceptance: A firm's time draft that has been accepted by a bank and may be sold to investors as a short-term unsecured note issued by the firm and guaranteed by the bank. 611

bankruptcy: The reorganization or liquidation of a firm that cannot pay its debts. 664

beta: Sensitivity of a stock's return to the return on the market portfolio. 339

bond: Security that obligates the issuer to make specified payments to the bondholder. 131

book rate of return: Accounting income divided by book value. Also called accounting rate of return. 219

book value: Net worth of the firm according to the balance sheet. 51, 168

bought deal: The underwriter buys securities from the issuing company and sells them to investors. 443

break-even analysis: Analysis of the level of sales at which the company breaks even. 281

CAPM: See capital asset pricing model.

CCA tax shield: Tax savings arising from the capital cost allowance charge. 251

CEO: Acronym for chief executive officer.

CFO: Acronym for chief financial officer.

call option: Right to buy an asset at a specified exercise price on or before the exercise date. 759

callable bond: Bond that may be repurchased by the firm before maturity at a specified call price. 405, 773

capital asset pricing model (CAPM): Theory of the relationship between risk and return that states that the expected risk premium on any security equals its beta times the market risk premium. 347

capital budget: List of planned investment projects. 276

capital budgeting decision: Decision as to which real assets the firm should acquire. 6

capital cost allowance (CCA): The amount of write-off on depreciable assets allowed by Canada Revenue Agency (CRA) against taxable income. 251

capital market: Market for long-term financing. 33

capital rationing: Limit set on the amount of funds available for investment. 226

capital structure: A firm's mix of long-term financing. 8, 368, 467

carrying costs: Costs of maintaining current assets, including opportunity cost of capital. 597

cash conversion cycle: Period between firm's payment for materials and collection on its sales. 595

cash dividend: Payment of cash by the firm to its shareholders. 505

cash flow from assets: Cash flow generated by the firm's operations, after investment in working capital and fixed assets. Also called free cash flow. 58

chief financial officer (CFO): Officer who oversees the treasurer and controller and sets overall financial strategy. 9

collection policy: Procedures to collect and monitor receivables. 663

commercial paper: Short-term unsecured notes issued by firms. 610

commitment fee: Fee charged by the lender on the unused portion of a line of credit. 609

common stock: Ownership shares in a publicly held corporation. 165

common-size balance sheet: Balance sheet that presents items as a percentage of total assets. 534

common-size income statement: Income statement that presents items as a percentage of revenues. 532

company cost of capital: Expected rate of return demanded by investors in a company, determined by the average risk of the company's assets and operations. 354

compound interest: Interest earned on interest. 79

concentration banking: System whereby customers make payments to a regional collection centre that transfers funds to a principal bank. 631

constant-growth dividend discount model: Version of the dividend discount model in which dividends grow at a constant rate. 176

controller: Officer responsible for budgeting, accounting, and auditing. 9

convertible bond: Bond that the holder may exchange for a specified amount of another security. 412, 772

corporation: Business owned by shareholders who are not personally liable for the business's liabilities. 3

correlation coefficient: Measure of how closely two variables move together. 323

cost of capital: Minimum acceptable rate of return on capital investment. 41

costs of financial distress: Costs arising from bankruptcy or distorted business decisions before bankruptcy. 479

coupon: The interest payments paid to the bondholder. 131

coupon rate: Annual interest payment as a percentage of face value. 131

credit analysis: Procedure to determine the likelihood a customer will pay its bills. 656

credit policy: Standards set to determine the amount and nature of credit to extend to customers. 658

cumulative voting: Voting system in which all the votes one shareholder is allowed to cast can be cast for one candidate for the board of directors. 397

current yield: Annual coupon payment divided by bond price. 136

debit card: An automated-teller-machine card that allows retail customers to transfer funds directly from their bank accounts to a retailer's account. 635

decision tree: Diagram of sequential decisions and possible outcomes. 289

declining balance depreciation: This is computed by applying the depreciation rate to the asset balance for each year. 252

default premium or credit spread: The additional yield on a bond that investors require for bearing credit risk. 150

default (or credit) risk: The risk that a bond issuer may default on its bonds. 149

degree of operating leverage (DOL): Percentage change in profits given a 1 percent change in sales. 287

depreciation tax shield: Reduction in taxes attributable to the depreciation allowance. 249

discount factor or present value interest factor: Present value of a $1 future payment. 84

discount rate: Interest rate used to compute present values of future cash flows. 83

discounted payback period: The time until discounted cash flows recover the initial investment in the project. 212

diversification: Strategy designed to reduce risk by spreading the portfolio across many investments. 320

dividend: Periodic cash distribution from the firm to its shareholders. 167

dividend clientele effect: Different investor groups prefer different dividend yields. Changing the firm's divided policy may attract a new investor clientele but may not change firm value. 521

dividend discount model: Discounted cash flow model of today's stock price that states that share value equals the present value of all expected future dividends. 172

dividend payout ratio: Percentage of earnings paid out as dividends. 511

dividend reinvestment plan: Enables shareholders to reinvest dividends into additional new shares. 509

Dow Jones Industrial Average: U.S. index of the investment performance of a portfolio of 30 "blue-chip" stocks. 309

DuPont system: A breakdown of ROE and ROA into component ratios. 544

EVA: See economic value added.

economic break-even point: Minimum level of sales needed to cover all costs including the cost of capital. 283

economic order quantity: Order size that minimizes total inventory costs. 638

economic value added or EVA®: Income that is measured after deduction of the cost of capital. 283

effective annual interest rate (EAR): Interest rate that is annualized using compound interest. 111

efficient market: Market in which prices reflect all available information. 187

electronic data interchange (EDI): Direct, electronic information exchange between enterprises, eliminating the mailing and handling of paper invoices. 635

electronic funds transfer: Payments made electronically instead of using paper-based cheques. 634

equivalent annual cost: The cost per period with the same present value as the cost of buying and operating a machine. 222

equivalent loan: Present value of the lease cash outflows, discounted at the after-tax cost of borrowing. 690

eurobond: Bond that is denominated in the currency of one country but issued to investors in other countries. 407

eurodollars: Dollars held on deposit in a bank outside the United States. 406

ex-dividend date: Date that determines whether a stockholder is entitled to a dividend payment; anyone holding stock before this date is entitled to a dividend. 505

ex-rights date: This date is usually four business days before the holder-of-record date. 443

exchange rate: Amount of one currency needed to purchase one unit of another. 731

expectations theory of exchange rates: Theory that expected spot exchange rate equals the forward rate. 742

face value: Payment at the maturity of the bond. Also called par value, maturity value, or principal. 131

factoring: A firm sells its accounts receivable at a discount for the purpose of obtaining short-term financing. 612

financial assets: Claims to the income generated by real assets. Also called securities. 6

financial institution: A bank, insurance company, or similar financial intermediary. 35

financial intermediary: An organization that raises money from investors and provices financing for individuals, corporations, or other organizations. 33

financial lease: Long-term, non-cancellable lease. It is also known as capital or full-payout lease. 681

financial leverage: Debt financing to amplify the effects of changes in operating income on the returns to stakeholders. 472

financial market: Market where securities are issued and traded. 31

financial risk: Risk to shareholders resulting from the use of debt. 472

financial slack: Ready access to cash or debt financing. 488

financing decision: Decision as to how to raise the money to pay for investments in real assets. 7

financing flow: Cash flow to bondholders and shareholders plus increase in cash balances; also equals cash flow to assets. 59

Fisher effect: The nominal interest rate is determined by the real interest rate and the expected rate of inflation. 146

fixed costs: Costs that do not depend on the level of output. 279

fixed-income market: Market for debt securities. 33

floating-rate preferred: Preferred stock paying dividends that vary with short-term interest rates. 403

flotation costs: The costs incurred when a firm issues new securities to the public. 434

foreign bond: Bond issued in the currency of its country but the borrower is from another country. 407

forward contract: Agreement to buy or sell an asset in the future at an agreed price. 793

forward exchange rate: Exchange rate for a forward transaction. 733

free cash flow: Another term for cash flow from assets. 59

fundamental analysts: Investors who attempt to find mispriced securities by analyzing fundamental information, such as accounting data and business prospects. 186

future value (FV): Amount to which an investment will grow after earning interest. 79

future value interest factor: Future value of a current cash flow of $1. 80

futures contract: Exchange-traded promise to buy or sell an asset in the future at a prespecified price. 789

GAAP: See generally accepted accounting principles.

general cash offer: Sale of securities open to all investors by an already-public company. 443

generally accepted accounting principles (GAAP): Procedures for preparing financial statements. 51

growing annuity: A finite stream of cash flows growing at a constant rate. 105

growing perpetuity: An infinite stream of cash flows growing at a constant rate. 104

half-year rule: Only one-half of the purchase cost of the asset is added to the asset class and used to compute CCA in the year of purchase. 253

holder-of-record date: The date on which shareholders appearing on company records are entitled to receive the stock rights. 443

IPO: See initial public offering.

IRR: See internal rate of return.

income statement: Financial statement that shows the revenues, expenses, and net income of a firm over a period of time. 54, 531

inflation: Rate at which prices as a whole are increasing. 106

information content of dividends: Dividend increases send good news about cash flow and earnings. Dividend cuts send bad news. 517

initial public offering (IPO): First offering of stock to the general public. 165, 431

inside information: Relevant information about a company known by its board of directors, management and/or employees and other insiders but not by the public. 186

insider trading: Illegal trading of securities, including stocks, bonds, and options, by insiders or those who are tipped by insiders, on the basis of inside information. 187

insiders: Members of the board of directors, management, employees and others with close relationship to a company, including lawyers, financial advisors, and accountants. 186

interest rate parity: Theory that forward premium equals interest rate differential. 741

interest rate risk: The risk in bond prices due to fluctuations in interest rates. 148

interest tax shield: Tax savings resulting from deductibility of interest payments. 475

internal growth rate: Maximum rate of growth without external financing. 579

internal rate of return (IRR): Discount rate at which project NPV = 0. 215

internally generated funds: Cash reinvested in the firm: depreciation plus earnings not paid out as dividends. 412

international Fisher effect: Theory that real interest rates in all countries should be equal, with differences in nominal rates reflecting differences in expected inflation. 739

investment grade: Bonds rated Baa or above by Moody's, or BBB or above by Standard & Poor's or DBRS. 150

issued shares: Shares that have been issued by the company. 395

junk bond: Bond with a rating below Baa or BBB. 150

just-in-time inventory management: A system of inventory management in which materials are delivered to the firm just when needed. 639

law of one price: Theory that prices of goods in all countries should be equal when translated to a common currency. 736

lease: Long-term rental agreement. 408, 681

lessee: User of the asset in a lease. Responsible for making regular payments to lessor. 681

lessor: Owner of the asset in a lease. Receives regular payments from lessee. 681

leveraged buyout (LBO): Acquisition of the firm by a private group using substantial borrowed funds. 705

levered equity beta: Beta of equity of a firm that has debt, reflecting both the risk arising from the firm's operating business and the risk created by the leverage (debtholders are entitled to be paid principal and interest before shareholders are paid dividends). 382

limited liability: The owners of the corporation are not personally responsible for its obligations. 4

line of credit: Agreement by a bank that a company may borrow at any time up to an established limit. 609

liquidation: Sale of a bankrupt firm's assets. 664

liquidation value: Net proceeds that would be realized by selling the firm's assets and paying off its creditors. 168

liquidity: The ability to sell or exchange an asset for cash on short notice. 39, 537

lock-box system: System whereby customers send payments to a post office box and a local bank collects and processes cheques. 633

long-term debt: Debt with more than one year remaining to maturity. 405

M&A: Abbreviation for mergers and acquisitions.

MM dividend-irrelevance proposition: Under ideal conditions, the value of the firm is unaffected by dividend policy. 514

MM's proposition I (debt irrelevance proposition): The value of a firm is unaffected by its capital structure. 470

MM's proposition II: The required rate of return on equity increases as the firm's debt-equity ratio increases. 473

majority voting: Voting system in which each director is voted on separately. 397

management buyout (MBO): Acquisition of the firm by its own management in a leveraged buyout. 705

marginal tax rate: Additional taxes owed per dollar of additional income. 64

market index: Measure of the investment performance of the overall market. 308

market portfolio: Portfolio of all assets in the economy. In practice, a broad stock market index, such as the S&P/TSX or S&P 500 Composite Index, is used to represent the market. 339

market risk: Economywide (macroeconomic) sources of risk that affect the overall stock market. Also called systematic risk. 326

market risk premium: (check greg's pages) page 344

market value added: The difference between the market value of the firm's equity and its book value. 551

market-value balance sheet: Financial statement that uses the market value of all assets and liabilities. 170

maturity premium: Extra average return from investing in long-term bonds versus short-term Treasury securities. 310

merger or statutory amalgamation: Combination of the assets and liabilities of two firms into one. 704

money market: Market for short-term financing (less than one year). 33, 643

mutual fund: A mutual fund pools the savings of many investors and invests in a portfolio of securities. 33

mutually exclusive projects: Two or more projects that cannot be pursued simultaneously. 220

NPV: See net present value.

net float: Difference between payment float and availability float. 628

net present value (NPV): Present value of cash flows minus initial investment. 205

net working capital: Current assets minus current liabilities. 245, 594

net worth: Book value of common shareholders' equity plus preferred stock. 401

nominal interest rate: Rate at which money invested grows. 108

off-balance-sheet financing: Financing that is not shown as a liability on a company's balance sheet. 684

open account: Agreement whereby sales are made with no formal debt contract. 655

operating lease: Short-term, cancellable lease. 681

operating leverage: Degree to which costs are fixed. 287

operating risk or business risk: Risk in a firm's operating income. 471

opportunity cost: Benefit or cash flow forgone as a result of an action. 244

opportunity cost of capital: Expected rate of return given up by investing in a project. 205

outstanding shares: Shares that have been issued by the company and are held by investors. 395

oversubscription privilege: Given to shareholders in a rights issue, enabling them to purchase any unsold shares at the subscription price. 442

P/E: See price-earnings multiple.

PV: See present value.

par value: Value of security shown on certificate. 395

partnership: Business owned by two or more people who are personally responsible for all its liabilities. 3

payback period: Time until cash flows recover the initial investment of the project. 210

payment float: Cheques written by a company that have not yet cleared. 627

payout ratio: Fraction of earnings paid out as dividends. 180

pecking-order theory: Firms prefer to issue debt rather than equity if internal finance is insufficient. 487

pension fund: Investment plan set up by an employer to provide for employees' retirement. 34

percentage-of-sales models: Planning model in which sales forecasts are the driving variables and most other variables are proportional to sales. 568

perpetuity: Stream of level cash payments that never ends. 94

planning horizon: Time horizon for a financial plan. 565

plowback ratio: Fraction of earnings retained by the firm. Also called retention ratio. 180

political risk: A change in firm value arising from political events. 748

preferred stock: Stock that takes priority over common stock in regards to dividends. 167, 401

present value (PV): Value today of a future cash flow. 83

present value of growth opportunities (PVGO): Net present value of a firm's future investments. 181

price-earnings (P/E) multiple: Ratio of stock price to earnings per share. 167

primary market: Market for the sale of new securities by corporations. 31, 165

prime rate: Benchmark interest rate charged by banks. 404

private equity: Equity capital that is not publicly traded. 35

private placement: Sale of securities to a limited number of investors without a public offering. 407, 445

pro formas: Projected or forecast financial statements. 568

profitability index: Ratio of present value to initial investment. 227

project cost of capital: Minimum acceptable expected rate of return on a project given its risk. 354

prompt offering prospectus (POP) system: Allows qualified firms quicker access to capital markets by enabling them to use a short-form filing process rather than a full prospectus. 444

prospectus: Formal summary that provides information on an issue of securities. 432

protective covenant: Restriction on a firm to protect bondholders. 407

proxy contest: Takeover attempt in which outsiders compete with management for shareholders' votes. 398, 703

purchasing power parity (PPP): Theory that the cost of living in different countries is equal and exchange rates adjust to offset inflation differentials across countries. 736

pure-play approach: Estimating project cost of capital using the cost of capital of another company involved exclusively in the same type of project. 355

put option: Right to sell an asset at a specified exercise price on or before the exercise date. 759

random walk: Security prices change randomly, with no predictable trends or patterns. 184

rate of return: Total income per period per dollar invested. 139

real assets: Assets used to produce goods and services. 6

real interest rate: Rate at which the purchasing power of an investment increases. 108

real options: Options to invest, modify, or dispose of a capital investment project. 291, 770

real return bond: Bond with variable nominal coupon payments, determined by a fixed real coupon payment and the inflation rate. 145

real value of $1: Purchasing power–adjusted value of a dollar. 107

recaptured depreciation: If the sale of an asset causes a negative balance in an asset class, the amount of the negative balance is known as recaptured depreciation and is added to taxable income. 254

refunding: When an old bond issue is replaced with a new one by the firm. Often, this is done when interest rates decline, and the firm can save on the interest cost of the new issue. 405

reorganization: Restructuring of financial claims on a failing firm to allow it to keep operating. 665

residual income (also called economic value added or EVA®): The net profit of a firm or division after deducting the cost of the capital employed. 551

restructuring: Process of changing the firm's capital structure without changing its assets. 468

retained earnings: Earnings not paid out as dividends. 395

reverse split: Issue of new shares in exchange for old shares, which results in the reduction of outstanding shares. 508

rights issue: Issue of securities offered only to current shareholders. 442

risk premium: Expected return in excess of risk-free return as compensation for risk. 310

S&P: Abbreviation for Standard & Poor's stock market indexes.

S&P/TSX Capped Composite Index: Index based on the prices of the TSX stocks, with no stock weighted more than 10 percent. Formerly the TSE 300 Capped Index. 309

S&P/TSX Composite Index: Index of the investment performance of a portfolio of the major stocks listed on the Toronto Stock Exchange. Also called the TSX. Formerly called the TSE 300. 308

scenario analysis: Project analysis given a particular combination of assumptions. 280

seasoned offering: Sale of securities by a firm that is already publicly traded. 442

secondary market: Market in which already issued securities are traded among investors. 32, 165

secured debt: Debt that has first claim on specified collateral in the event of default. 406

security market line: Relationship between expected return and beta. 348

semi-strong form efficiency: Market prices rapidly reflect all publicly available information. 188

sensitivity analysis: Analysis of the effects of changes in sales, costs, and so on, on project profitability. 278

share purchase plan: Allows shareholders to make cash contributions toward the acquisition of new shares. 509

shareholders' rights plan or poison pill: Measures taken by the target firm to avoid acquisition; for example, the right of existing shareholders to buy additional shares at an attractive price if a bidder acquires a significant holding. 719

shark repellent: Amendments to a company charter made to forestall takeover attempts. 720

shelf registration: A procedure followed in the United States that allows firms to file one registration statement for several issues of the same security. 444

shortage costs: Costs incurred from shortages in current assets. 597

simple interest: Interest earned only on the original investment; no interest is earned on interest. 79

simulation analysis: Estimation of the probabilities of different possible outcomes, e.g., from an investment project. 281

sinking fund: Fund established to retire debt before maturity. 405

sole proprietor: Sole owner of a business that has no partners and no shareholders. The proprietor is personally liable for all the firm's obligations. 3

spot rate of exchange: Exchange rate for an immediate transaction. 731

spread: Difference between public offer price and price paid by underwriter. 432

stakeholder: Anyone with a financial interest in the firm. 16

Standard & Poor's Composite Index: U.S. index of the investment performance of a portfolio of 500 large stocks. Also called the S&P 500. 309

standard deviation: Square root of variance. Another measure of volatility. 314

standby underwriting agreement: The underwriter stands ready to purchase any unsold shares. 442

statement of cash flows: Financial statement that shows the firm's cash receipts and cash payments over a period of time. 56

stock dividend: Distribution of additional shares to a firm's shareholders. 507

stock repurchase: Firm buys back stock from its shareholders. 509

stock split: Issue of additional shares to firm's shareholders. 507

straight-line depreciation: Constant depreciation for each year of the asset's accounting life. 252

strong-form efficiency: Market prices rapidly reflect all information that could in principle be used to determine true value. 188

subordinated debt: Debt that may be repaid in bankruptcy only after senior debt is paid. 405

sustainable growth rate: Steady rate at which a firm can grow; return on equity times plowback ratio. 181, 580

swap: Arrangement by two counterparties to exchange one stream of cash flows for another. 794

syndicated loans: Loans provided by a group of banks that combine to provide the loan amount. 609

TRIV: See TSX Total Return Index Value.

TSX: See S&P/TSX Composite Index.

TSX Total Return Index Value (TRIV): Measure of the composite index based on the prices plus dividends paid by the stocks in the S&P/TSX Composite Index. Formerly the TSE 300 Total Return Index. 309

technical analysts: Investors who attempt to identify over- or undervalued stocks by searching for patterns in past stock prices. 183

tender offer: Takeover attempt in which outsiders directly offer to buy the stock of the firm's shareholders. 704

term loans: Loans that last for several years. 609

terminal loss: When an asset class has a positive balance following the disposal of all assets in the class, this balance is called terminal loss. The UCC of the asset class is set to zero after a terminal loss is recognized. 254

terms of sale: Credit, discount, and payment terms offered on a sale. 653

trade-off theory: Debt levels are chosen to balance interest tax shields against the costs of financial distress. 479

treasurer: Manager responsible for financing, cash management, and relationships with financial markets and institutions. 9

undepreciated capital cost (UCC): The balance remaining in an asset class that has not yet been depreciated in that year. 251

underpricing: Issuing securities at an offering price set below the true value of the security. 433

underwriter: Firm that buys an issue of securities from a company and resells it to the public. 431

unique risk: Risk factors affecting only the particular firm. Also called diversifiable risk. 326

unlevered beta: Beta of equity of a debt-free firm, reflecting the risk arising from the firm's operating business. 382

variable costs: Costs that change as the level of output changes. 279

variance: Average value of squared deviations from mean. A measure of volatility. 314

venture capital: Money invested to finance a new firm. 429

WACC: See weighted-average cost of capital.

warrant: Right to buy shares from a company at a stipulated price before a set date. 411, 772

weak-form efficiency: Market prices rapidly reflect all information contained in the history of past prices. 188

weighted-average cost of capital (WACC): Expected rate of return on a portfolio of all the firm's securities, adjusted for tax savings due to interest payments. 372

white knight: Friendly potential acquirer sought by a target company that is threatened by an unwelcome bidder. 719

working capital: See net working capital.

workout: Agreement between a company and its creditors establishing the steps the company must take to avoid bankruptcy. 664

yield curve or term structure of interest rates: Graph of the relationship between time to maturity and yield to maturity, for bonds that differ only in their maturity dates. 144

yield to maturity: Interest rate for which the present value of the bond's payments equals the price. 137

zero-balance account: Regional bank account to which just enough funds are transferred daily to pay each day's bills. 634

INDEX